EUROPE
EUROPA

ATLAS ROUTIER et TOURISTIQUE
TOURIST and MOTORING ATLAS
STRASSEN- und REISEATLAS
TOERISTISCHE WEGENATLAS
ATLANTE STRADALE e TURISTICO
ATLAS DE CARRETERAS y TURÍSTICO
ATLAS RODOVIÁRIO e TURÍSTICO

B Europe / Europa

Sommaire / Contents / Inhaltsübersicht / Inhoud
Sommario / Sumario / Sumário

D - E

Europe des 27 / 27 EU Member States / Europa der 27 / Het Europa van de 27
Europa dei 27 / Europa de los 27 / Europa dos 27

F - G

Informations générales / General information / Allgemeine Informationen
Algemene inlichtingen / Informazioni generali / Informaciones generales
Informações gerais

H

Climat / Climate / Klima / Klimaat / Clima / Climatología / Clima

I - M

Conduire en Europe / Driving in Europe / Autofahren in Europa / Autorijden in Europa
Guidare in Europa / Conducir en Europa / Conduzir na Europa

N - O

Tableau des distances / Distances / Entfernungstabelle / Afstandstabel
Tabella delle distanze / Cuadro de distancias / Quadro de distâncias

1 - 19

Europe 1:3 300 000
Europa 1:3 300 000

20 - 122

Europe 1:1 000 000
Europa 1:1 000 000

123 - 146

Scandinavie 1:1 500 000
Scandinavia 1:1 500 000
Scandinavien 1:1 500 000
Scandinavië 1:1 500 000
Scandinavia 1:1 500 000
Escandinavia 1:1 500 000
Escandinávia 1:1 500 000

147 - 178

Pays Baltes 1:500 000
Baltic Countries 1:500 000
Baltische Länder 1:500 000
Baltische Landen 1:500 000
Paesi Baltici 1:500 000
Países Bálticos 1:500 000

179 - 202

Pologne 1:700 000
Poland 1:700 000
Polen 1:700 000
Polonia 1:700 000
Polónia 1:700 000

203 - 228

Grèce 1:700 000
Greece 1:700 000
Griechenland 1:700 000
Griekenland 1:700 000
Grecia 1:700 000
Grécia 1:700 000

229 - 231

Chypre 1:700 000
Cyprus 1:700 000
Zypern 1:700 000
Cipro 1:700 000
Chipre 1:700 000

232 - 339

Index / Register / Indice completo / Índice

340 - 344

Légende / Key to maps / Zeichenerklärung / Verklaring van de tekens
Legenda / Signos conventionales / Legenda

Plans de ville / Town plans / Stadtpläne / Stadsplattegronden

Piante di città / Planos de ciudades / Plantas de Cidade

233 Amsterdam	250 Budapest	265 Göteborg	288 Madrid	313 Roma
234 Antwerpen	253 Den Haag	268 Hamburg	289 Manchester	314 Rotterdam
235 Athína	254 Dijon	269 Hannover	290 Marseille	317 Salzburg
238 Barcelona	255 Dresden	270 Helsinki	291 Milano	318 Sevilla
239 Basel	256 Dublin	271 Istanbul	292 Monaco-	319 Stockholm
240 Belfast	257 Dubrovnik	272 København	Monte-Carlo	320 Strasbourg
241 Berlin	258 Düsseldorf	273 Köln	294 München	321 Stuttgart
242 Bern	258 Edinburgh	277 Lausanne	296 Nantes	326 Torino
243 Birmingham	259 Essen	278 Leipzig	297 Napoli	327 Toulouse
244 Bologna	260 Firenze	279 Liège	298 Nice	330 València
245 Bonn	261 Frankfurt-	280 Lille	299 Nürnberg	331 Valletta
246 Bordeaux	am-Main	281 Lisboa	302 Oslo	332 Venezia
247 Bratislava	263 Genève	282 Liverpool	303 Palermo	335 Warszawa
248 Bremen	264 Genova	284 London	304 Paris	336 Wien
248 Brugge	264 Gent	283 Luxembourg	309 Porto	337 Zagreb
249 Bruxelles	265 Glasgow	286 Lyon	310 Praha	338 Zürich

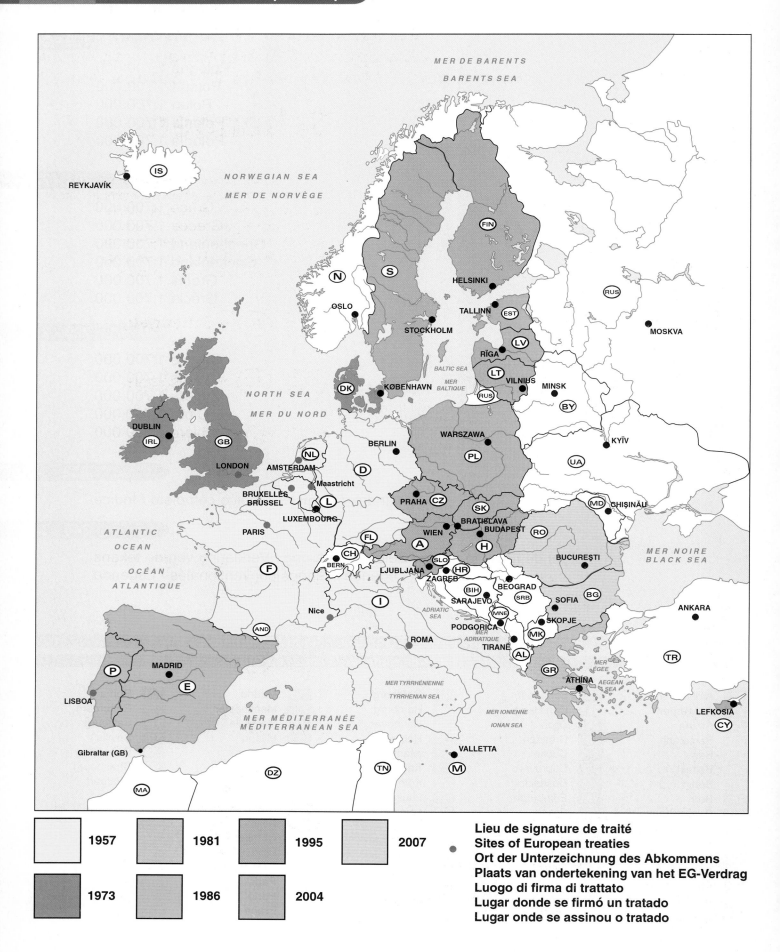

MER DE BARENTS
BARENTS SEA

NORWEGIAN SEA
MER DE NORVÈGE

REYKJAVÍK (IS)

(FIN)

(N) (S) HELSINKI

OSLO TALLINN (EST)
STOCKHOLM (RUS) MOSKVA

RÏGA (LV)
BALTIC SEA (LT)
MER VILNIUS MINSK

NORTH SEA DK KØBENHAVN BALTIQUE (RUS) (BY)

MER DU NORD

DUBLIN WARSZAWA KYÏV

(IRL) (GB) (NL) BERLIN (PL) (UA)

LONDON AMSTERDAM (D)

Maastricht

BRUXELLES PRAHA (CZ) (MD) CHIŞINĂU

BRUSSEL (L) SK

LUXEMBOURG BRATISLAVA

ATLANTIC PARIS (FL) WIEN BUDAPEST (RO)

OCEAN (CH) (A) (H)

OCÉAN (F) BERN SLO BUCUREŞTI MER NOIRE

ATLANTIQUE LJUBLJANA (HR) BLACK SEA

Nice ZAGREB BEOGRAD

(I) (BIH) (SRB) SOFIA (BG)

(AND) SARAJEVO ANKARA

ADRIATIC (MNE) SKOPJE

SEA PODGORICA (MK)

ROMA MER TIRANË (TR)

ADRIATIQUE (AL)

(P) MADRID MER (GR)

ÉGÉE

LISBOA (E) MER TYRRHÉNIENNE ATHÍNA AEGEAN

TYRRHENIAN SEA SEA

LEFKOSIA

MER MÉDITERRANÉE MER IONIENNE (CY)

Gibraltar (GB) MEDITERRANEAN SEA IONIAN SEA

(DZ) VALLETTA

(MA) (TN) (M)

	1957		1981		1995		2007	**Lieu de signature de traité**

Sites of European treaties
Ort der Unterzeichnung des Abkommens
Plaats van ondertekening van het EG-Verdrag

	1973		1986		2004	**Luogo di firma di trattato**

Lugar donde se firmó un tratado
Lugar onde se assinou o tratado

**Europe des 27 / 27 EU Member States
Europa der 27 / Het Europa van de 27
Europa dei 27 / Europa de los 27 / Europa dos 27**

Schengen

Espace de libre circulation des personnes
Area of free movement between member states
Abschaffung der Binnengrenzkontrollen
Ruimte voor vrij verkeer van personen
Area di libera circolazione delle persone
Espacio de libre circulación de personas
Espaço de livre circulação de pessoas

(EU) + **Schengen**

(EU) + **Schengen** ✗

(EU) ✗ + **Schengen**

Euro : €

 (EU) + €

 (EU) + €̸

(EU)
Pays de l'UE
EU states
EU-Staaten
EU-lidstaten
Paesi dell'UE
Países de la UE
Países da UE

🏴	(F)	NOM FRANÇAIS	NOM LOCAL	👪 x 1000	(km²)	(h/km²)	🏛
▬	D	ALLEMAGNE	Deutschland	82 002,3	357 020	230	Berlin
▬	A	AUTRICHE	Österreich	8 355,2	83 859	100	Wien (Vienne)
▮	B	BELGIQUE	België, Belgique	10 754,5	30 518	348	Brussel/Bruxelles
▬	BG	BULGARIE	Balgarija	7 606,5	110 550	69	Sofia
▣	CY	CHYPRE	Kýpros, Kibris	793,9	9 240	86	Lefkosia (Nicosie)
✚	DK	DANEMARK	Danmark	5 511,4	43 094	128	København (Copenhague)
▣	E	ESPAGNE	España	45 828,1	504 790	91	Madrid
▬	EST	ESTONIE	Eesti	1 340,4	43 211	31	Tallin
✚	FIN	FINLANDE	Suomi, Finland	5 326,3	304 529	17	Helsinki/Helsingfors
▮	F	FRANCE	France	64 351,0	543 964	118	Paris
✚	GR	GRÈCE	Ellada	11 257,2	131 625	86	Athína (Athènes)
▬	H	HONGRIE	Magyarország	10 031,2	93 029	108	Budapest
▮	IRL	IRLANDE	Ireland, Éire	4 465,5	70 273	64	Dublin
▮	I	ITALIE	Italia	60 053,4	301 333	199	Roma (Rome)
▬	LV	LETTONIE	Latvija	2 261,2	64 589	35	Riga
▬	LT	LITUANIE	Lietuva	3 349,8	65 300	51	Vilnius
▬	L	LUXEMBOURG	Luxembourg, Lëtzebuerg	493,5	2 586	191	Luxembourg
▣	M	MALTE	Malta	413,6	316	1 309	Valletta (La Valette)
▬	NL	PAYS-BAS	Nederland	16 486,5	37 873	435	Amsterdam
▬	PL	POLOGNE	Polska	38 135,8	312 685	122	Warszawa (Varsovie)
▣	P	PORTUGAL	Portugal	10 627,2	91 906	116	Lisboa (Lisbonne)
▮	R	ROUMANIE	România	21 498,6	238 340	90	Bucuresti (Bucarest)
🇬🇧	GB	ROYAUME-UNI	United Kingdom of Great Britain & Northern Ireland	61 634,5	243 820	253	London (Londres)
▣	SK	SLOVAQUE, République	Slovenská Republika	5 412,2	49 035	110	Bratislava
▬	SLO	SLOVÉNIE	Slovenija	2 032,3	20 273	100	Ljubljana
✚	S	SUÈDE	Sverige	9 256,3	410 934	23	Stockholm
▣	CZ	TCHÈQUE, République	Česká Republika	10 467,5	78 859	133	Praha (Prague)

Sources :
Eurostat 2009

		(1 000 000 000 e)	(en e)	(GMT)	RÉGIME POLITIQUE	FÊTE NATIONALE
25 mars 1957	€	2 390 333,7	29 150	+ 1 (hiver) + 2 (été)	République fédérale	03/10
1 janvier 1995	€	274 286,0	32 828	+ 1 (hiver) + 2 (été)	République fédérale	26/10
25 mars 1957	€	339 721,3	31 589	+ 1 (hiver) + 2 (été)	Monarchie constitutionnelle et parlementaire	21/07
1 janvier 2007	Leva (BGN)	35 219,7	4 630	+ 2 (hiver) + 3 (été)	République	03/03
1 mai 2004	Livre chypriote (CYP)	17 890,2	22 535	+ 2 (hiver) + 3 (été)	République	01/10
1 janvier 1973	Danske Krone (DKK)	228 569,3	41 472	+ 1 (hiver) + 2 (été)	Monarchie parlementaire	16/04
1 janvier 1986	€	1 072 666,4	23 406	+ 1 (hiver) + 2 (été)	Royaume (Monarchie parlementaire)	12/10
1 mai 2004	Eesti Kroon (EEK)	14 411,2	10 751	+ 2 (hiver) + 3 (été)	République	24/02
1 janvier 1995	€	179 184,8	33 642	+ 2 (hiver) + 3 (été)	République	06/12
25 mars 1957	€	1 919 346,4	29 826	+ 1 (hiver) + 2 (été)	République	14/07
1 janvier 1981	€	242 079,6	21 504	+ 2 (hiver) + 3 (été)	République	25/03
1 mai 2004	Forint (HUF)	92 801,9	9 251	+ 1 (hiver) + 2 (été)	République	20/08
1 janvier 1973	€	163 423,7	36 597	GMT (hiver) + 1 (été)	République	17/03
25 mars 1957	€	1 532 521,7	25 519	+ 1 (hiver) + 2 (été)	République	02/06
1 mai 2004	Lats (LVL)	19 645,4	8 688	+ 2 (hiver) + 3 (été)	République	18/11
1 mai 2004	Litas (LTL)	29 326,1	8 755	+ 2 (hiver) + 3 (été)	République	16/02
25 mars 1957	€	38 920,1	78 865	+ 1 (hiver) + 2 (été)	Monarchie constitutionnelle	23/06
1 mai 2004	Maltese Lira (MTL)	5 767,4	13 944	+ 1 (hiver) + 2 (été)	République	21/09
25 mars 1957	€	584 422,4	35 449	+ 1 (hiver) + 2 (été)	Monarchie constitutionnelle et parlementaire	30/04
1 mai 2004	Złoty (PLN)	296 461,2	7 774	+ 1 (hiver) + 2 (été)	République	03/05
1 janvier 1986	€	163 938,9	15 426	+ 1 (hiver) + 2 (été)	République	10/06
1 janvier 2007	Leu (RON)	125 624,7	5 843	+ 2 (hiver) + 3 (été)	République	01/12
1 janvier 1973	Pound Sterling (GBP)	1 599 106,6	25 945	GMT (hiver) + 1 (été)	Monarchie constitutionnelle	13/06
1 mai 2004	Slovenská Koruna (SKK)	67 970,4	12 559	+ 1 (hiver) + 2 (été)	République	01/09
1 mai 2004	€	36 542,8	17 981	+ 1 (hiver) + 2 (été)	République	01/07
1 janvier 1995	Svensk Krona (SEK)	290 760,2	31 412	+ 1 (hiver) + 2 (été)	Monarchie parlementaire	06/06
1 mai 2004	Koruna Česká (CZK)	137 975,4	13 181	+ 1 (hiver) + 2 (été)	République	28/10

Climat / Climate / Klima
Klimaat / Clima / Climatología / Clima

Températures (Moyenne mensuelle)	16 max. quotidien 8 min. quotidien	**Temperature (Medie mensili)**	16 max. giornaliera 8 min. giornaliera
Average daily temperature	16 maximum 8 minimum	**Media mensual de temperaturas**	16 máx.diária 8 mín. diária
Temperaturen (Monatlicher Durchschnitt)	16 maximale Tagestemperatur 8 minimale Tagestemperatur	**Média mensual de temperaturas**	16 máx.diária 8 mín. diária
Temperaturen (Maandgemiddelde)	16 maximum 8 minimum		

Précipitations (Moyenne mensuelle)	0-20mm	**Precipitazioni (Medie mensili)**
Average monthly rainfall	20 - 50mm	**Media mensual de precipitaciones**
Nierderschlagsmengen (Monatlicher Durchschnitt)	50 100mm	**Média mensal de precipitações**
Gemidelde maandelijkse neerslag	+ 100mm	

		1	2	3	4	5	6	7	8	9	10	11	12
Amsterdam	NL	5 / 1	4 / 0	7 / 2	10 / 5	14 / 8	18 / 11	20 / 13	20 / 14	18 / 12	14 / 8	9 / 5	6 / 2
Andorra la Vella	AND	6 / -1	7 / -1	12 / 2	14 / 4	17 / 6	23 / 10	26 / 12	24 / 12	22 / 10	16 / 6	10 / 2	6 / -1
Athína	GR	13 / 6	14 / 7	16 / 8	20 / 11	25 / 16	30 / 20	33 / 23	33 / 23	29 / 19	24 / 15	19 / 12	15 / 8
Beograd	SER	3 / -3	5 / -2	11 / 2	18 / 7	23 / 12	26 / 15	28 / 17	28 / 17	24 / 13	18 / 8	11 / 4	5 / 0
Bergen	N	3 / -1	3 / -1	6 / 0	9 / 3	14 / 7	16 / 10	19 / 12	19 / 12	15 / 10	11 / 6	8 / 3	5 / 1
Berlin	D	2 / -3	3 / -3	8 / 0	13 / 4	19 / 8	22 / 12	24 / 14	23 / 13	20 / 10	13 / 6	7 / 2	3 / -1
Bern	CH	2 / -4	4 / -3	9 / 1	14 / 4	18 / 8	21 / 11	23 / 13	22 / 13	19 / 10	13 / 5	7 / 1	3 / -2
Bordeaux	F	9 / 2	11 / 2	15 / 4	17 / 6	20 / 9	24 / 12	25 / 14	26 / 14	23 / 12	18 / 8	13 / 5	9 / 3
Bratislava	SK	2 / -3	4 / -2	10 / 1	16 / 6	21 / 11	24 / 14	26 / 16	26 / 16	22 / 12	15 / 7	8 / 3	4 / 0
Bremen	D	3 / -2	4 / -2	8 / 0	13 / 4	18 / 7	21 / 11	22 / 13	22 / 12	19 / 10	13 / 6	8 / 3	4 / 0
Brno	CZ	1 / -5	3 / -5	8 / -1	15 / 4	20 / 9	23 / 12	25 / 14	25 / 13	21 / 9	14 / 4	7 / 2	3 / -1
Bruxelles Brussel	B	4 / -1	7 / 0	10 / 2	14 / 5	18 / 8	22 / 11	23 / 12	22 / 12	21 / 11	16 / 7	9 / 3	6 / 0
Bucureşti	RO	1 / -7	4 / -5	10 / -1	18 / 5	23 / 10	27 / 14	30 / 16	30 / 15	25 / 11	18 / 6	10 / 2	4 / -3
Budapest	H	1 / -4	4 / -2	10 / 2	17 / 7	22 / 11	26 / 15	28 / 16	27 / 16	23 / 12	16 / 7	8 / 3	4 / -1
Cagliari	I	14 / 7	15 / 7	17 / 9	19 / 11	23 / 14	27 / 18	30 / 21	30 / 21	27 / 19	23 / 15	19 / 11	16 / 9
Chişinău	MD	-1 / -8	1 / -5	6 / -2	16 / 6	23 / 11	26 / 14	27 / 16	27 / 15	23 / 11	17 / 7	10 / 3	2 / -4
Cork	IRL	9 / 2	9 / 3	11 / 4	13 / 5	16 / 7	19 / 10	20 / 12	20 / 12	18 / 10	14 / 7	11 / 4	9 / 3
Dresden	D	2 / -4	3 / -3	8 / 0	14 / 4	19 / 8	22 / 11	24 / 13	23 / 13	20 / 10	13 / 5	8 / 2	3 / -2
Dublin	IRL	7 / 2	8 / 2	10 / 3	12 / 5	14 / 7	18 / 10	19 / 11	19 / 11	17 / 10	14 / 7	10 / 4	8 / 3
Dubrovnik	HR	12 / 6	13 / 6	14 / 8	17 / 11	21 / 14	25 / 18	29 / 21	28 / 21	25 / 18	21 / 14	17 / 10	14 / 8
Edinburgh	GB	6 / 1	6 / 1	8 / 2	11 / 4	14 / 6	17 / 9	18 / 11	18 / 11	16 / 9	12 / 7	9 / 4	7 / 2
Gibraltar	GB	16 / 9	16 / 9	18 / 11	21 / 11	23 / 14	27 / 17	28 / 19	29 / 20	27 / 19	23 / 15	18 / 12	17 / 9
Göteborg	S	1 / -3	1 / -4	4 / -2	9 / 3	16 / 7	19 / 12	21 / 14	20 / 13	16 / 10	11 / 6	6 / 3	4 / 0
Graz	A	1 / -5	4 / -4	9 / 0	15 / 5	19 / 9	23 / 13	25 / 14	24 / 14	20 / 11	14 / 6	7 / 1	2 / -2
Helsinki	FIN	-3 / -9	-4 / -9	0 / -7	6 / -1	14 / 4	19 / 9	22 / 13	20 / 12	15 / 8	8 / 3	3 / -1	-1 / -5
Iráklio	GR	16 / 9	16 / 9	17 / 10	20 / 12	23 / 15	27 / 19	29 / 22	29 / 22	27 / 19	24 / 17	21 / 14	18 / 11
Istanbul	TR	8 / 3	9 / 2	11 / 3	16 / 7	21 / 12	25 / 16	28 / 18	28 / 19	24 / 16	20 / 13	15 / 9	11 / 5
Kérkira	GR	14 / 6	15 / 6	16 / 8	19 / 10	23 / 13	28 / 17	31 / 19	32 / 19	28 / 17	23 / 14	19 / 11	16 / 8
København	DK	2 / -2	2 / -3	5 / -1	10 / 3	16 / 8	19 / 11	22 / 14	21 / 14	18 / 11	12 / 7	7 / 3	4 / 1
Kyïv	UA	-4 / -10	-2 / -8	3 / -4	14 / 5	21 / 11	24 / 14	25 / 15	24 / 14	20 / 10	13 / 6	6 / 0	-1 / -6
Lisboa	P	14 / 8	15 / 8	17 / 10	20 / 12	21 / 13	25 / 15	27 / 17	28 / 17	24 / 17	23 / 14	17 / 11	15 / 9
Ljubljana	SLO	2 / -4	5 / -4	10 / 0	15 / 4	20 / 9	24 / 12	27 / 14	26 / 14	22 / 11	15 / 6	8 / 2	4 / -1
London	GB	6 / 2	7 / 2	10 / 3	13 / 6	17 / 8	20 / 12	22 / 14	21 / 13	19 / 11	14 / 8	10 / 5	7 / 4
Luxembourg	L	3 / -1	4 / -1	10 / 1	14 / 4	18 / 8	21 / 11	23 / 13	22 / 12	19 / 10	13 / 6	7 / 3	4 / 0
Lyon	F	5 / -1	7 / 0	13 / 3	16 / 6	20 / 9	24 / 13	27 / 15	26 / 14	23 / 12	16 / 7	10 / 4	6 / 0
Madrid	E	9 / 2	11 / 2	15 / 5	18 / 7	21 / 10	27 / 15	31 / 17	30 / 17	25 / 14	19 / 10	13 / 5	9 / 2
Marseille	F	10 / 2	12 / 2	15 / 5	18 / 8	22 / 11	26 / 15	29 / 17	28 / 17	25 / 15	20 / 10	15 / 6	11 / 3
Milano	I	5 / 0	8 / 2	13 / 6	18 / 10	23 / 14	27 / 17	29 / 20	28 / 19	24 / 16	17 / 11	10 / 6	6 / 2
Minsk	BY	-7 / -13	-4 / -11	1 / -7	11 / 2	18 / 8	22 / 11	23 / 12	22 / 12	17 / 8	11 / 4	3 / -1	-3 / -8

		1	2	3	4	5	6	7	8	9	10	11	12
Monaco Monte-Carlo	MC	12 / 8	13 / 8	14 / 10	16 / 12	19 / 15	23 / 19	26 / 22	26 / 22	24 / 20	20 / 16	16 / 12	14 / 10
Moskva	RUS	-9 / -16	-6 / -14	0 / -8	10 / 1	19 / 8	21 / 11	23 / 13	22 / 12	16 / 7	9 / 3	2 / -3	-5 / -10
Napoli	I	12 / 4	13 / 5	15 / 6	18 / 9	22 / 12	26 / 16	29 / 18	29 / 18	26 / 16	22 / 12	17 / 9	14 / 6
Odense	DK	2 / -2	2 / -3	5 / -1	11 / 2	16 / 6	19 / 9	21 / 12	21 / 12	17 / 9	12 / 5	7 / 3	4 / 1
Oslo	N	-2 / -7	-1 / -7	4 / -4	10 / 1	16 / 6	20 / 10	22 / 13	21 / 12	16 / 8	9 / 3	3 / -1	0 / -4
Oulu	FIN	-6 / -13	-6 / -14	-2 / -11	4 / -4	11 / 2	17 / 8	21 / 12	19 / 10	13 / 6	5 / 0	0 / -5	-3 / -9
Palermo	I	16 / 8	16 / 8	17 / 9	20 / 11	24 / 14	27 / 18	30 / 21	30 / 21	28 / 19	25 / 16	21 / 12	18 / 10
Paris	F	6 / 1	7 / 1	12 / 4	16 / 6	20 / 10	23 / 13	25 / 15	24 / 14	21 / 12	16 / 8	10 / 5	7 / 2
Plymouth	GB	8 / 4	8 / 4	10 / 5	12 / 6	15 / 8	18 / 11	19 / 13	19 / 13	18 / 12	15 / 9	11 / 7	9 / 5
Porto	P	13 / 5	14 / 5	16 / 8	18 / 9	20 / 11	23 / 13	25 / 15	25 / 15	24 / 14	21 / 11	17 / 8	14 / 5
Praha	CZ	0 / -5	3 / -4	8 / -1	13 / 2	18 / 7	21 / 10	23 / 12	23 / 12	19 / 9	13 / 4	6 / 0	2 / -3
Rennes	F	8 / 2	9 / 2	13 / 4	15 / 5	18 / 8	22 / 11	23 / 13	23 / 13	21 / 11	16 / 8	11 / 5	8 / 3
Reykjavík	IS	2 / -2	3 / -2	4 / -1	6 / 1	10 / 4	12 / 7	14 / 9	14 / 8	11 / 6	7 / 3	4 / 0	2 / -2
Riga	LV	-4 / -10	-3 / -10	2 / -7	10 / 1	16 / 6	21 / 9	22 / 11	21 / 11	17 / 8	11 / 4	4 / -1	-2 / -7
Roma	I	11 / 5	13 / 5	15 / 7	20 / 10	23 / 13	28 / 17	30 / 20	30 / 19	26 / 17	22 / 13	16 / 9	13 / 6
Salzburg	A	2 / -6	4 / -5	9 / -1	14 / 4	19 / 8	22 / 11	24 / 13	23 / 13	20 / 10	14 / 5	8 / 0	3 / -4
Sarajevo	BIH	3 / -4	5 / -3	10 / 0	15 / 5	20 / 8	24 / 12	26 / 13	27 / 13	23 / 10	16 / 6	10 / 3	6 / -1
Sevilla	E	15 / 6	17 / 7	20 / 9	24 / 11	27 / 13	32 / 17	36 / 20	36 / 20	32 / 18	26 / 14	20 / 10	16 / 7
Skopje	MK	5 / -3	8 / -3	12 / 1	19 / 5	23 / 10	28 / 13	31 / 15	31 / 14	26 / 11	19 / 6	12 / 3	7 / -1
Sofia	BG	2 / -4	4 / -3	10 / 1	16 / 5	21 / 10	24 / 14	27 / 16	26 / 15	22 / 11	17 / 8	9 / 3	4 / -2
Stockholm	S	-1 / -5	-1 / -5	3 / -4	8 / 1	14 / 6	19 / 11	22 / 14	20 / 13	15 / 9	9 / 5	5 / 1	2 / -2
Strasbourg	F	3 / -2	5 / -2	11 / 1	16 / 5	20 / 8	23 / 12	25 / 13	24 / 13	21 / 10	14 / 6	8 / 2	4 / -1
Stuttgart	D	3 / -3	5 / -2	10 / 1	14 / 5	19 / 8	22 / 12	24 / 14	24 / 13	20 / 10	14 / 6	8 / 2	4 / -2
Szczecin	PL	2 / -3	2 / -5	7 / -1	12 / 2	18 / 7	22 / 11	23 / 13	23 / 13	19 / 9	13 / 6	7 / 2	3 / -1
Tallinn	EST	-4 / -10	-4 / -11	0 / -7	8 / 0	14 / 5	19 / 10	20 / 12	20 / 11	15 / 9	10 / 4	3 / -1	-1 / -7
Thessaloníki	GR	9 / 2	12 / 3	14 / 5	20 / 10	25 / 14	29 / 18	32 / 21	32 / 21	28 / 17	22 / 13	16 / 9	11 / 4
Tiranë	AL	12 / 2	12 / 2	15 / 5	18 / 8	23 / 12	28 / 16	31 / 17	31 / 17	27 / 14	23 / 10	17 / 8	14 / 5
Tromsø	N	-2 / -6	-2 / -6	0 / -5	3 / -2	7 / 1	12 / 6	16 / 9	14 / 8	10 / 5	5 / 1	2 / -2	0 / -4
Umeå	S	-4 / -12	-4 / -12	0 / -9	5 / -3	12 / 2	17 / 7	20 / 11	19 / 10	13 / 5	7 / 0	2 / -4	-2 / -8
Vaasa	FIN	-4 / -11	-4 / -11	1 / -10	6 / -3	13 / 2	18 / 8	21 / 11	19 / 10	13 / 5	7 / 1	2 / -3	-1 / -7
València	E	15 / 6	16 / 6	18 / 8	20 / 10	23 / 13	26 / 17	29 / 20	29 / 20	27 / 18	23 / 13	19 / 10	16 / 7
Valladolid	E	8 / 0	10 / 0	14 / 3	17 / 5	20 / 8	26 / 12	29 / 14	29 / 13	25 / 11	19 / 7	12 / 3	8 / 1
Valletta	M	14 / 10	15 / 10	16 / 11	18 / 13	22 / 16	26 / 19	29 / 22	29 / 23	27 / 22	24 / 19	20 / 16	16 / 12
Venezia	I	6 / 1	8 / 2	12 / 5	17 / 10	21 / 14	25 / 17	27 / 19	27 / 18	24 / 16	19 / 11	12 / 7	8 / 3
Vilnius	LT	-5 / -11	-3 / -10	1 / -7	12 / 2	18 / 7	21 / 11	23 / 12	22 / 12	17 / 8	11 / 4	4 / -1	-3 / -7
Warszawa	PL	0 / -6	0 / -6	6 / -2	12 / 3	20 / 9	23 / 12	24 / 15	23 / 14	19 / 10	13 / 5	6 / 1	2 / -3
Wien	A	1 / -4	3 / -3	8 / 1	15 / 6	19 / 10	23 / 14	25 / 15	24 / 15	20 / 11	14 / 7	7 / 3	3 / -1
Zagreb	HR	3 / -2	6 / -1	11 / 3	17 / 8	21 / 12	25 / 15	27 / 17	27 / 16	23 / 13	15 / 8	9 / 4	5 / 0
Zürich	CH	2 / -3	5 / -2	10 / 1	15 / 4	19 / 8	23 / 12	25 / 14	24 / 13	20 / 11	14 / 6	7 / 2	3 / -2

Conduire en Europe

Les tableaux d'information suivants indiquent les principaux règlements routiers communiqués au moment de la rédaction de cet atlas (17.06.09) ; la signification des symboles est indiquée ci-dessous, ainsi que quelques notes supplémentaires.

- Limitations de vitesse en kilomètres/heure s'appliquant aux :

- autoroutes
- routes à une seule chaussée
- routes à chaussées séparées
- agglomérations urbaines
- Péage sur les autoroutes ou toute autre partie du réseau routier
- Jeu d'ampoules de rechange
- Taux maximum d'alcool toléré dans le sang. On ne doit pas considérer ceci comme acceptable ; il n'est JAMAIS raisonnable de boire et de conduire.
- Age minimum du conducteur
- Port de la ceinture de sécurité à l'avant
- Age minimum des enfants admis à l'avant.
- Port de la ceinture de sécurité à l'avant et à l'arrière
- Gilet de sécurité
- Câble de remorquage
- Triangle de présignalisation
- Port du casque pour les motocyclistes et les passagers
- Trousse de premiers secours
- Allumage des codes jour et nuit
- Extincteur
- Pneus cloutés

Documents nécessaires obligatoires à tous les pays :
certificat d'immatriculation du véhicule ou certificat de location, assurance responsabilité civile, plaque d'identification nationale.
Il est vivement conseillé de se renseigner auprès de l'Automobile Club.

Driving in Europe

The information panels which follow give the principal motoring regulations in force when this atlas was prepared for press (17.06.09). An explanation of the symbols is given below, together with some additional notes.

- Speed restrictions in kilometres per hour applying to:

- motorways
- single carriageways
- dual carriageways
- urban areas
- Whether tolls are payable on motorways and/or other parts of the road network.
- Whether a spare bulb set must be carried
- Maximum permitted level of alcohol in the bloodstream. This should not be taken as an acceptable level - it is NEVER sensible to drink and drive.
- Minimum age for drivers
- Minimum age for children to sit in the front passenger seat.
- Whether seatbelts must be worn by the driver and front seat passenger
- Reflective jacket
- Whether seatbelts are compulsory for the driver and all passengers in both front and back seats
- Whether a warning triangle must be carried.
- Tow rope
- Whether a first aid kit must be carried
- Whether crash helmets are compulsory for both motorcyclists and their passengers
- Whether a fire extinguisher must be carried
- Whether headlights must be on at all time
- Studded tyres

Documents required for all countries:
vehicle registration document or vehicle on hire certificate, third party insurance cover, national vehicle indentification plate.
You are strongly advised to contact the national Automobile Club for full details of local regulations.

Autofahren in Europa

Die nachfolgenden Tabellen geben Auskunft über die wichtigsten Verkehrsbestimmungen in den einzelnen Ländern dieses Atlasses (Stand 17.06.09); die Erklärung der Symbole sowie einige ergänzende Anmerkungen finden Sie im Anschluß an diesen Text.

- Geschwindigkeitsbegrenzungen in km/h bezogen auf:

- Autobahnen
- Straßen mit einer Fahrbahn
- Schnellstraßen mit getrennten Fahrbahnen
- geschlossene Ortschaften
- Autobahn-, Straßen- oder Brückenbenutzungsgebühren
- Mitführen eines Satzes von Glühbirnen als Reserve
- Promillegrenze: Es sei darauf hingewiesen, daß auch die kleinste Menge Alkohol am Steuer das Fahrvermögen beeinträchtigt
- Mindestalter für Kfz-Führer
- Anschnallpflicht vorne
- Mindestalter, ab welchem Kinder vorne sitzen dürfen.
- Anschnallpficht vorne und hinten
- Sicherheitsweste
- Abschleppseil
- Mitführen eines Warndreiecks
- Helmpflicht für Motorradfahrer und Beifahrer
- Mitführen eines Verbandkastens
- Abblendlicht vorgeschrieben (Tag und Nacht)
- Mitführen eines Feuerlöschers
- Spikereifen

Notwendige und vorgeschriebene Dokumente in allen Staaten:
Fahrzeugschein oder Mietwagenbescheinigun, Internationale grüne Versicherungskarte, Nationalitätskennzeichen.
Es empfiehlt sich, genauere Informationen bei den jeweiligen Automobilclubs einzuholen.

Autorijden in Europa

In de tabellen hierna staan de voornaamste verkeersregels medegedeeld bij het opstellen van deze Atlas (17.06.09); de betekenis van de symbolen is hieronder beschreven met enkele toelichtingen.

- Snelheidsbeperkingen in km/uur op:

- autosnelwegen
- wegen met één rijbaan
- wegen met gescheiden rijbanen
- binnen de bebouwde kom
- Tol op de autosnelwegen of op een ander gedeelte van het wegennet
- Reservelampen verplicht
- Maximum toegestaan alcoholgehalte in het bloed. Dit dient niet beschouwd te worden als een aanvaardbaar gehalte; het is NOOIT verstandig om te rijden na gebruik van alcohol.
- Minimumleeftijd bestuurder
- Minimum leeftijd voor kinderen voorin het voertuig.
- Autogordel verplicht voor bestuurder en passagier voorin
- Reflecterend vest
- Autogordel, verplicht voor- en achterin
- Gevarendriehoek verplicht
- Sleepkabel
- EHBO-pakket verplicht
- Valhelm verplicht voor motorrijders en passagiers
- Brandblusapparaat
- Dimlichten verplicht zowel 's nachts als overdag
- Spijkerbanden

Vereiste documenten in alle landen:
kentekenbewijs van het voertuig of huurcertificaat, verzekering burgerlijke aansprakelijkheid, plaat land van herkomst.
Het verdient aanbeveling informatie in te winnen bij de automobielclub.

Conduire en Europe

Les tableaux d'information suivants indiquent les principaux règlements routiers communiqués au moment de la rédaction de cet atlas (17.06.09) ; la signification des symboles est indiquée ci-dessous, ainsi que quelques notes supplémentaires.

- 🕐 Limitations de vitesse en kilomètres/heure s'appliquant aux :
- autoroutes
- routes à chaussées séparées
- Péage sur les autoroutes ou toute autre partie du réseau routier
- Taux maximum d'alcool toléré dans le sang. On ne doit pas considérer ceci comme acceptable ; il n'est JAMAIS raisonnable de boire et de conduire.
- Age minimum des enfants admis à l'avant.
- Gilet de sécurité
- Triangle de présignalisation
- Trousse de premiers secours
- Extincteur

- routes à une seule chaussée
- agglomérations urbaines
- Jeu d'ampoules de rechange
- Age minimum du conducteur
- Port de la ceinture de sécurité à l'avant
- Port de la ceinture de sécurité à l'avant et à l'arrière
- Câble de remorquage
- Port du casque pour les motocyclistes et les passagers
- Allumage des codes jour et nuit
- Pneus cloutés

Documents nécessaires obligatoires à tous les pays :
certificat d'immatriculation du véhicule ou certificat de location, assurance responsabilité civile, plaque d'identification nationale.
Il est vivement conseillé de se renseigner auprès de l'Automobile Club.

Guidare in Europa

I riquadri informativi che seguono forniscono le principali norme di circolazione, in vigore al momento della redazione di questo atlante (17.06.09); la spiegazione dei simboli viene data di seguito, insieme ad alcune annotazioni supplementari.

- 🕐 Limiti di velocità in chilometri/ora riferiti a:
- autostrade
- strade a carreggiata doppia
- Pedaggio sulle autostrade o sulle strade
- Tasso massimo di alcol tollerato nel sangue. Tale tasso non dovrebbe essere considerato come accettabile; non è MAI sensato guidare dopo aver bevuto.
- Età minima richiesta, affinché i bambini possano sedere davanti
- Giubbotto di sicurezza
- Triangolo di presegnalazione
- Cassetta di pronto soccorso
- Estintore

- strade a carreggiata unica
- aree urbane
- Assortimento di lampadine di ricambio
- Età minima del guidatore
- Uso delle cinture di sicurezza per i sedili anteriori
- Uso delle cinture di sicurezza per i sedili anteriori e posteriori
- Cavo di traino
- Uso del casco per i motociclisti ed i passeggeri
- Si devono tenere gli anabbaglianti sempre accesi
- Pneumatici chiodati

Documenti obbligatori in tutti i paesi:
carta di circolazione del veicolo oppure certificato di autonoleggio, assicurazione e carta verde, targa d'identificazione nazionale.
E' vivamente consigliato rivolgersi all' Automobile Club.

Conducir en Europa

Los siguientes cuadros informativos recogen las principales reglamentaciones automovilísticas que nos han sido comunicadas en el momento de la redacción de este atlas (17.06.09); el significato de los símbolos, junto con algunas notas complementarias, se indica más abajo.

- 🕐 Límites de velocidad en kilómetros/hora que se aplican en:
- autopistas
- carreteras con calzadas separadas
- Peaje en autopistas o en otro lugar de la red de carreteras
- Máximo permisible de alcohol en sangre. Este máximo no debe considerarse como un nivel aceptable; NUNCA es aconsejable beber si se conduce.
- Edad mínima de los niños para viajar en los asientos delanteros.
- Chaleco reflectante
- Triángulo de señalización de peligro
- Botiquín de primeros auxilios
- Extintor

- carreteras con calzada única
- zona urbanas
- Juego de lámparas de recambio
- Edad mínima del conductor
- Cinturón de seguridad delante
- Cinturón de seguridad delante y detrás
- Cable de remolque
- Casco protector para motociclistas y pasajeros
- Luces encendidas día y noche
- Neumáticos con clavos

Documentación obligatoria en todos países:
certificado de matriculación del vehículo o certificado de aquiler, seguro de responsabilidad civil, placa de identificación del pais.
Recomendamos informarse en el Automóvil Club.

Conduzir na Europa

Os quadros de informação seguintes indicam as principais regras rodoviárias em vigor no momento da redacção deste Atlas (17.06.09); o significado dos símbolos está indicado abaixo assim como algumas notas suplementares.

- 🕐 Limites de velocidade em km/h que se aplicam em:
- auto-estradas
- estradas com faixas de rodagem separadas
- Portagem nas auto-estradas ou outras partes da rede rodoviária
- Taxa máxima de alcoolémia tolerada no sangue. Não é considerada au tável; nunca é razoável beber e conduzir.
- Idade mínima das crianças admitidas à frente
- Colete reflector
- Triângulo de pré-sinalização
- Estojo de primeiros socorros
- Extintor

- estradas com uma única faixa de rodagem
- aglomerações urbanas
- Jogo de lâmpadas sobressalentes
- Idade mínima do condutor
- Uso do cinto de segurança à frente
- Uso do cinto de segurança à frente e atrás
- Cabo de reboque
- Uso do capacete para os motociclistas e acompanhantes
- Acender luzes médias dia e noite
- Uso de pneus com pregos

Documentos obrigatórios em todos os países:
certificado de registo de propriedade ou certificado de aluguer - seguro de responsabilidade civil - Placa de identificação nacional.
Aconselha se pedir informações junto do automóvel clube.

	Motorway	Expressway	Road	Urban	Alcohol	●	●	●	Age	△	+	ext	bulb	vest	Age	2	Period	light	Period	
(A) ÖSTERREICH	130		100	50	0,05	●	●			●	●	○			18	●			1/10-1/5	
(AL) SHQIPËRIA			90	40	0,00					○	○	○				●		●		○
(AND) ANDORRA			90	50	0,05	●			10	●	○	○	●		18	●			1/11-15/5	○
(B) BELGIQUE, BELGIË	120	120	90	50	0,05		●		12	●	●	●			18	●			1/11-31/3	
(BG) BALGARIJA	130		90	50	0,05	●	●		10	●	●	●			18	●	1/11-1/3	●		●
(BIH) BOSNA I HERCEGOVINA	120	100	80	60	0,03		●		12	●	●	○	●	●	18	●		●		●
(BY) BELARUS'			90	60	0,00	●	●		12	●	●	●			18	●				○
(CH) SCHWEIZ, SUISSE, SVIZZERA	120	100	80	50	0,05	●	●			●	○	○			18	●			24/10-30/4	
(CY) KÝPROS, KIBRIS	100		80	50	0,05		●		12	● x 2	○	○			18	●				○
(CZ) CESKÁ REPUBLIKA	130		90	50	0,00		●			●	●	○			18	●		●		●
(D) DEUTSCHLAND			100	50	0,05		●			●	●	○			18	●		●		○
(DK) DANMARK	130		80	50	0,05		●			●	○	○			18	●		●	1/11-15/4	
(E) ESPAÑA	120		90	50	0,05		●			● x 2	○	○	●		18	●				●
(EST) EESTI	110		90	50	0,00		●			●	●	●			18	●	16/10-15/4			○
(F) FRANCE	130	110	90	50	0,05		●		10	●	○	○	○		18	●			15/11-31/3	●
(FIN) SUOMI, FINLAND	120		80	50	0,05		●		3	●	○	○			18	●		●	1/11-5/4	○
(FL) LIECHTENSTEIN			80	50	0,08		●			●	○	○			18	●			1/11-30/4	
(GB) UNITED KINGDOM	112	112	96	48	0,08		●			○	○	○			17	●				○
(GR) ELLÁDA	120		90	50	0,05		●		12	●	●	●			18	●				○
(H) MAGYARORSZÁG	130	110	90	50	0,00	●	●		12	●	●	○	●		17	●		●		○
(HR) HRVATSKA	130	110	90	50	0,00		●		12	●	●	○	●		18	●				○
(I) ITALIA	130		90	50	0,05		●		12	●	○	○			18	●		●	15/11-15/3	●
(IRL) IRELAND	120		80	50	0,08		●			○	○	○			17	●				○
(IS) ÍSLAND			90	50	0,05		●		14	●	○	○			17	●			15/11-15/4	○
(L) LUXEMBOURG	130		90	50	0,05		●		11	●	●	●			18	●			1/12-31/3	●
(LT) LIETUVA	130	110	90	50	0,04		●		12	●	●	●			16	●		●	1/11-1/4	●
(LV) LATVIJA	110		90	50	0,05		●			●	●	●			18	●			1/10-30/4	○
(M) MALTA			80	50	0,08		●		11	○	○	○			18	●				○
(MC) MONACO				50	0,05				10	○	○	○			18	●		●		○
(MD) MOLDOVA			90	60	0,00		●		12	●	●	●			18	●				○
(MK) MAKEDONIJA	130		80	60	0,05		●		12	●	●	○	●	●	18	●		●		
(MNE) CRNA GORA	120		80	50	0,05		●		12	●	○	○				●		●		○
(N) NORGE	90		80	50	0,02		●			●	○	○			18	●			1/11-5/4	○
(NL) NEDERLAND	120	100	80	50	0,05		●		12	●	○	○			18	●		●		○
(P) PORTUGAL	120		90	50	0,05		●			●	○	○			18	●		●		○
(PL) POLSKA	130	110	90	50	0,02		●			●	●	●			18	●				○
(RO) ROMÂNIA	130		90	50	0,00	●	●		12	●	●	●			18	●				○
(RSM) SAN MARINO			70	50	0,08		●		12	○	○	○			18	●			1/1-31/12	○
(RUS) ROSSIJA	110		90	60	0,00		●		12	●	●	●			18	●				○
(S) SVERIGE	110		70	50	0,02		●			●	○	○			18	●			1/10-30/4	○
(SK) SLOVENSKÁ RÉPUBLIKA	130		90	50	0,00	●	●		12	●	●	○	●	●	18	●		●		●
(SLO) SLOVENIJA	130	100	90	50	0,05		●		12	●	●	○			18	●				○
(SRB) SRBIJA	120	100	80	60	0,05		●		12	●	●	●			18	●				○
(TR) TÜRKIYE	120		90	50	0,05		●		10	●	●	○			18	●		●		○
(UA) UKRAÏNA	130		90	60	0,00	●		●	12	●	●	●			18	●	22/12-20/3		1/11-31/12	○

Obligatoire ● Obbligatorio Recommandé ○ Raccomandato Interdit ● Vietato Période d'autorisation 1/11-30/4 Periodo d'autorizzazione Renseignement non communiqué ❋ Informazione non disponibile
Compulsory Obligatorio Recommended Recomendado Prohibited Prohibido Periode of regulation enforcement Periodo de autorización No information currently available Información no comunicada
Vorgeschrieben Obrigatório Empfohlen Recomendado Verboten Proibido Genehmigungsdauer Período de autorização Keine Auskunft erhalten Informação não comunicada
Verplicht Aanbevolen Verboden Toegelaten periode Informatie niet meegedeeld

Österreich

ÖAMTC
Schubertring 1-3, 1010 WIEN
☎ : +43 (0) 1 711 990
Fax : +43 (0) 1 711 99 13 20
http:// www.oeamtc.at
e-mail : office@oeamtc.at

ARBÖ
Mariahilfer Straße 180, 1150 WIEN
☎ : +43 1 891 217
Fax : +43 1 891 21 236
http:// www.arboe.or.at
e-mail : id@arboe.or.at

Andorra

Automòbil Club d'Andorra (ACA)
Carrer Babot Camp 13,
ANDORRA la VELLA
☎ : +376 803 400
Fax : +376 822 560
http:// www.aca.ad

Belgique, België

R.A.C.B
Rue d'Arlon 53 bte 3 /
Aarlenstraat 53 bus 3
1040 BRUXELLES / BRUSSEL
☎ : +32 2 287 09 11
Fax : +32 2 230 75 84
http://www.racb.com
e-mail : autoclub@racb.com

Touring Club Belgium (TCB)
Rue de la Loi 44 / Wetstraat 44,
1040 BRUXELLES / BRUSSEL
☎ : +32 2 233 22 02
Fax : +32 2 286 33 23
http://www.touring.be
e-mail :presid@touring.be

Balgarija

Union des Automobilistes Bulgares (UAB)
Place Pozitano 3,
1090 SOFIA
☎ : +359 2 935 79 35
Fax : +359 2 981 61 51
http://www.sab.bg
e-mail :sba@uab.org

Bosna Hercegovina

BIHAMK
Skenderija 23,
71000 SARAJEVO
☎ : +387 33 212 772
Fax : +387 33 213 668
 http:// www.bihamk.ba
e-mail : info@bihamk.ba

Belarus'

Belorusskij Klub Avtomototurizma (BKA)
ul. Zaharova, 55,
220088 MINSK
☎ : +375 17 222 06 66
Fax : +375 17 233 90 45
http://www.bka.by
e-mail : info@bka.by

Schweiz, Suisse, Svizzera

Touring Club Suisse / Schweiz / Svizzero (TCS)
Case postale 820, 1214 VERNIER
☎ : +41 22 417 27 27
Fax : +41 22 417 20 20
http://www.tcs.ch
e-mail : irtge@tcs.ch

Automobil Club der Schweiz Automobile Club de Suisse (ACS)
Wasserwerkgasse 39
3000 BERN 9
☎ : +41 31 328 31 11
Fax : +41 31 311 03 10
http://www.acs.ch
e-mail : acszv@acs.ch

Kýpros, Kibris

Cyprus Automobile Association (CAA)
PO Box 22279
1519 LEFKOSIA
☎ : +357 22 313 233
Fax : +357 22 313 482
http://www.caa.com.cy
e-mail : info@caa.com.cy

Ceská Republika

Ústrední automotoklub Ceské republiky (UAMK)
Na Strzi 9,
14002 PRAHA 4
☎ : +420 2 611 04 242
Fax : +420 2 611 04 235
http://www.uamk-cr.cz
e-mail : sekretar@uamk-cr.cz

Autoklub Ceské republiky (ACCR)
Opletalova 29,
11000 PRAHA 1
☎ : +420 224 210 266
Fax : +420 222 246 275
http://www.autoklub.cz
e-mail : inet@autoklub.cz

Deutschland

ADAC
Am Westpark 8,
81373 MÜNCHEN
☎ : +49 89 76 76 0
Fax : +49 89 76 76 25 00
http://www.adac.de
e-mail : adac@adac.de

Automobilclub von Deutschland (AVD)
Lyoner Str. 16
60528 FRANKFURT am MAIN
☎ : +49 69 660 60
Fax : +49 69 660 67 89
http://www.avd.de
e-mail : avd@avd.de

Danmark

Forenede Danske Motorejere (FDM)
Postboks 500
2800 KGS. LYNGBY
☎ : +45 45 27 07 07
Fax : +45 45 27 09 93
http://www.fdm.dk
e-mail : fdm@fdm.dk

España

Real Automóvil Club de España (RACE)
c/ Isaac Newton, 4
28760 - Tres Cantos MADRID
☎ : +34 91 594 72 75
Fax : +34 91 594 75 36
http://www.race.es
e-mail : presidencia@race.es

Real Federación Española de Automovilismo (RFE de A)
c/ Escultor Peresejo, 68bis
28023 MADRID
☎ : +34 91 729 94 30
Fax : +34 91 357 02 03
http://www.rfeda.es
e-mail : rfeda@rfeda.es

Eesti

Eesti Autoklubi (EAK)
Laki 11
12915 TALLINN
☎ : +372 6979 188
Fax : +372 6979 110
http://www.autoclub.ee
e-mail : eak@autoclub.ee

Eesti Autosporti Liit (EAL)
Vabaduse pst 13,
11214 TALLINN
☎ : +372 6398 666
Fax : +372 6398 553
http://www.autosport.ee
e-mail : eal@sport.ee

France

Automobile Club de France
6, Place de la Concorde
75008 PARIS
☎ : +33 1 43 12 43 12
Fax : +33 1 43 12 43 43

Fédération Française des Automobiles Clubs et Usagers de la Route
76 Avenue Marceau
75008 PARIS
☎ : +33 1 56 89 20 70
Fax : +33 1 47 20 37 23
http://www.automobileclub.org
e-mail : ffac.presse1@wanadoo.fr

Suomi, Finlande

Autoliitto (AL)
Hämeentie 105 A
00550 HELSINKI
☎ : +358 9 72 58 44 00
Fax : +358 9 72 58 44 60
http://www.autoliitto.fi
e-mail : autoliitto@autoliitto.fi

Liechtenstein

Automobilclub des Fürstentums Liechtenstein (ACFL)
Pflugstrasse 20, Post Fach 934,
9490 VADUZ
☎ : +423 237 67 67
Fax : +423 233 30 50

United Kingdom

Automobile Association (AA)
Basing View
RG21 4DA - BASINGSTOKE
☎ : +44 870 600 0371
Fax : +44 191 235 5111
http:// www.theaa.com
e-mail : customer.services@theaa.com

Green Flag Motoring Assistance
Cote Lane, Pudsey
LS28 5GF - LEEDS
☎ : +44 (0)141 221 38 50
Fax : + 44 (0)845 246 15 57
http://www.greenflag.com
e-mail :
member-queries@greenflag.com

Elláda

Automobile and Touring Club of Greece (ELPA)
L. Messogion 395
153 43 - ATHINA
☎ : +30 210 606 8800
Fax : +30 210 606 8981
http://www.elpa.gr
e-mail : info@elpa.gr

Magyarország

Magyar Autóklub (MAK)
Rómer Flóris u. 4/a
1024 BUDAPEST
☎ : +36 1 345 1 800
Fax : +36 1 345 1 801
http://www.autoklub.hu
e-mail : info@ autoklub.hu

Hrvatska

Hrvatski Autoklub (HAK)
Avenija Dubrovnik 44,
10020 ZAGREB
☎ : +385 1 66 11 999
Fax : +385 1 66 23 111
http://www.hak.hr
e-mail : borse@hak.hr

Italia

Automobile Club d'Italia (ACI)
B.P 2839,
00185 ROMA
☎ : +39 6 499 81
Fax : +39 6 499 827 23
http://www.aci.it
e-mail : info@aci.it

Touring Club Italiano (TCI)
Corso Italia 10,
20122 MILANO
☎ : +39 2 85 261
Fax : +39 2 852 63 20
http://www.touringclub.it
e-mail :
ufficio.comunicazione@touringclub.it

Ireland

Royal Irish Automobile Club (RIAC)
34, Dawson Street,
DUBLIN 2
☎ : +353 1 677 51 41
Fax : +353 1 671 55 51
http://www.riac.ie
e-mail : info@riac.ie

The Automobile Association Ireland Limited
56, Dury Street,
DUBLIN 2
☎ : +353 1 617 99 99
Fax : +353 1 617 99 00
http://www.aaireland.ie
e-mail : aa@aaireland.ie

Ísland

Félag Islenskra Bifreidaeigenda (FIB)
Borgartúni 33, 105 REYKJAVIK
☎ : +354 414 99 99
Fax : +354 414 99 98
http://www.fib.is
e-mail : fib@fib.is

Icelandic Motorsport Association (LIA)
Engjavegur 6, 130 REYKJAVIK
☎ : +354 58 89 100
Fax : +354 58 89 102
http://www.centrum.is/zystua
e-mail : lia@centrum.is

 Luxembourg

Automobile Club du Grand Duché de Luxembourg (ACL)
54 Route de Longwy,
8007 BERTRANGE
☎ : +352 45 00 45
Fax : +352 45 04 55
http://www.acl.lu
e-mail : acl@acl.lu

 Lietuvia

Lietuvos Automobilininku Sajunga (LAS)
Trinpoliog.9B
08337 VILNIUS
☎ : +370 5 210 44 33
Fax : +370 5 270 95 92
http://www.las.lt
e-mail : info@las.lt

Lietuvos Automobiliu Sporto Federacija (LASF)
Draugystes 19-344, - 51230 KAUNAS
☎ : +370 37 350 106
Fax : +370 37 350 106
http://www.lasf.lt
e-mail : lasf@lasf.lt

 Latvija

Latvijas Automoto Biedriba (LAMB)
Raunas 16b,
1039 RIGA
☎ : +37 1 6756 6222
Fax : +37 1 6751 3678
http://www.lamb.lv
e-mail : lamb@lamb.lv

Latvijas Automobilu Federacija (LAF)
Brivibas Gatve 266-107,
1006 RIGA
☎ : +37 1 701 22 09
Fax : +37 1 755 14 65
http://www.laf.lv
e-mail : laf@latnet.lv

 Malte

Touring Club (TCM)
P.O. Box 16
MSD 01 – MSIDA
☎ : +356 7900 0116
Fax : +356 2123 8226

 Monaco

Automobile Club de Monaco (ACM)
23 Boulevard Albert 1er, BP 464

98012 MONACO
☎ : +377 93 15 26 00
Fax : +377 93 25 80 08
http://www.acm.mc
e-mail : info@acm.mc

 Moldava

Automobil Club din Moldova (ACM)
str. Armeneasca 33/1
2012 CHISINAU
☎ : +373 22 29 27 03
Fax : +373 22 20 22 24
http://www.acm.md
e-mail : office@acm.md

 Makedonija

Avto Moto Sojuz na Makedonija
Ivo Ribar Lola br. 51- 1000 SKOPJE
☎ : +389 2 318 11 81
Fax : +389 2 318 11 19
http://www.amsm.com.mk
e-mail : amsm@amsm.com.mk

 Crna Gora

Auto Moto Savez Crne Gore (AMS)
Cetinjski put b.b.
81000 PODGORICA
☎ : +381 81 234 467
Fax : +381 81 234 467
http://www.amscg.org

 Norge

Kongelig Norsk Automobilklub (KNA)
Postboks 2425 Solli
0201 OSLO
☎ : +47 21 60 49 00
Fax : +47 21 60 49 01
http://www.kna.no
e-mail : kna@kna.no

Norges Automobil-Forbund (NAF)
Postboks 6682 Etterstad
0609 OSLO
☎ : +47 22 34 14 00
Fax : +47 22 33 13 72
http://www.naf.no
e-mail : medlemsservice@naf.no

 Nederland

Koninklijke Nederlandse Toeristenbond (ANWB)
Wassenaarseweg 220
2509 BA - DEN HAAG
☎ : +31 70 314 71 47
Fax : +31 70 314 69 69
http://www.anwb.nl
e-mail : info@anwb.nl

Koninklijke Nederlandse Automobiel Club (KNAC)
Postbus 93114
2509 AC - DEN HAAG
☎ : +31 70 383 16 12
Fax : +31 70 383 19 06
http://www.knac.nl
e-mail : ledenservice@knac.nl

 Portugal

Automóvel Club de Portugal (ACP)
Rua Rosa Araújo 24-26,

1250-195 LISBOA
☎ : +351 21 318 02 02
Fax : +351 21 318 02 27
http://www.acp.pt
e-mail : info@acp.pt

 Polska

Polski Zwiazek Motorowy (PZM)
Ul. Kazimierzowska 66
02-518 WARSZAWA
☎ : +48 22 849 93 61
Fax : +48 22 848 19 51
http://www.pzm.pl
e-mail : office@pzm.pl

Polskie Towarzystwo Turystyczno-Krajoznawcze (PTTK)
ul. Senatorska 11
00-075 WARSZAWA
☎ : +48 22 826 57 35
Fax : +48 22 826 25 05
http://www.pttk.pl
e-mail : poczta@pttk.pl

 România

Automobil Clubul Român (ACR)
Strada Tache Ionescu 27, Sector 1
010353 BUCURESTI
☎ : +40 21 222 22 22
Fax : +40 21 222 15 52
http://www.acr.ro
e-mail : acr@acr.ro

 **Rossija**

Russian Automobile Society (VOA)
Leotjevskij per., 23
125009 MOSKVA
☎ : +7 495 747 66 66
http://www.voa.ru
e-mail : voa@voa.ru

Avtoclub assistance Rus (ACAR)
Krasnogo Mayaka 26
117570 - MOSKVA
☎ : +7 095 105 50 00
Fax : +7 095 105 50 96
e-mail : acar@acarus.ru

 San Marino

Automobile Club San Marino (ACS)
Via A. Giangi, 66
47891 DOGANA
☎ : +378 549 90 88 60
Fax : +378 549 97 29 26
http:// www.automobileclub.sm
e-mail : info@automobileclub.sm

 Srbija

Auto-Moto Savez Srbije (AMSS)
Kneginje Zorke 58
11000 BEOGRAD
☎ : +381 11 333 11 00
http://www.amss.org.rs
e-mail : info@amss.org.rs

 Sverige

Kungl Automobil Klubben
Södra Blasieholmshamnen 6
11148 STOCKHOLM
☎ : +46 8 678 00 55
Fax : +46 8 678 00 68

http://www.kak.se
e-mail : info@kak.se

Motormännens Riksförbund (M)
Box 49163
100 29 STOCKHOLM
☎ : +46 8 690 38 00
Fax : +46 8 690 38 24
http://www.motormannen.se
e-mail : service@motormannen.se

 Slovenská Republika

Autoklub Slovenskej Republiky (AKSR)
na Holícskej 30
851 01 BRATISLAVA
☎ : +421 2 638 346 78
Fax : +421 2 638 345 67
http://www.aksr.sk
e-mail : autoklub@autoklubsr.sk

Slovensky Autoturist Klub (SATC)
Bosákova 3
851 04 BRATISLAVA
☎ : +421 2 682 492 11
http://www.satc.sk
e-mail : satc@satc.sk

 Slovenija

Avto-Moto Zveza Slovenije (AMZS)
Dunajska 128a
1000 LJUBLJANA
☎ : +386 1 530 53 00
Fax : +386 1 530 54 10
http://www.amzs.si
e-mail : info.center@amzs.si

 Türkiye

Türkiye Otomobil Sporlari Federasyonu (TOSFED)
Göksuevleri Kartopu Cad. B168/A
Anadoluhisari - Beykoz
ISTANBUL
☎ : +90 216 465 11 55
Fax : +90 216 465 11 57
http://www.tosfed.org.tr
e-mail : ik@tosfed.org.tr

Turkiye Turing ve Otomobil Kurumu (TTOK)
1. Otosanayi Sitesi yani - 4. Levent
ISTANBUL
☎ : +90 212 282 81 40
Fax : +90 212 282 80 42
http://www.turing.org.tr
e-mail : turing@turing.org.tr

Ukraïna

Fédération Automobile d'Ukraine (FAU)
PO Box 10697,
01019 KYIV
☎ : +380 44 404 21 74
Fax : +380 44 404 21 74
e-mail : fau-kiev@ukr.net

112UA
bul. Ak. Pidstrigacha, 6
79060 LVIV
☎ : +380 32 29 70 112
Fax : +380 32 29 71 112
http://www.112ua.com
e-mail : office@112ua.com

Amsterdam
Athína
Barcelona
Basel
Beograd
Bergen
Berlin
Bilbao
Bordeaux
Bratislava
Bruxelles/Brussel
București
Budapest
Calais
Cherbourg
Clermont-Ferrand
Dublin
Dubrovnik
Firenze
Frankfurt-am-Main
Genève
Genova
Göteborg
Hamburg
Helsinki
İstanbul
København
Köln
Kraków
Kyïv
Lille
Lisboa
Ljubljana
London
Luxembourg

```
2179
1536 1576
 743  995 1038
1727  891 1985 1352
1383 2667 2716 1740 2469
 666 1591 1870  871 1255 1202
1399 1915  617 1230 2327 2699 1950
1069 1654  567  898 2037 2369 1621  340
1242 1229 1870  916  573 1883  687 2139 1808
 210 1560 1339  544 1677 1504  768 1204  875 1192
2224 1620 2714 1898  677 2898 1703 3052 2764 1021 2175
1406 1258 1899 1080  375 2080  885 2237 1972  203 1357  824
 365 1752 1322  735 1878 1669  932 1183  854 1393  201 2376 1558
 793 1865 1285  877 2162 2094 1346 1029  682 1687  599 2671 1852  468
 924 1264  621  532 1647 2191 1344  700  371 1431  727 2376 1560  708  720
 639 2335 1906 1319 2462  642 1516 1763 1434 1977  785 2960 2142  589  532 1296
1919  544 2052 1420  524 2786 1663 2391 2103 1005 1871  813 2071 2290 1713 2655
1384  549 1080  639 1009 2310 1234 1419 1223  892 1206 1738  922 1395 1495  883 1980 1076
 447 1329 1338  339 1291 1413  546 1468 1139  805  399 1789  970  599  939  814 1183 1483  972
 922  973  788  250 1333 1984 1114 1049  718 1108  723 2062 1273  757  902  328 1341 1400  604  584
1222  744  855  478 1157 2175 1182 1194  998 1040 1050 1885 1070 1192 1269  658 1776 1223  238  812  380
 978 2088 2311 1431 1793  800  544 2294 1965 1226 1101 2242 1423 1263 1690 1789  909 2159 1732 1105 1676 1862
 474 1746 1818  819 1548  921  296 1789 1460  981  596 1997 1178  759 1186 1294 1091 1864 1390  493 1063 1251  516
1680 2893 3024 2025 2073 1277 1138 2996 2667 1671 1803 2110 1708 1965 2392 2501 2297 2668 2556 1699 2270 2457  732 1220
2696 1861 2955 2322  975 3419 2223 3293 3005 1541 2647  702 1344 2847 3122 2616 3431 1292 1977 2264 2303 2118 2761 2517 2846
 779 1936 2124 1124 1640 1111  391 2095 1766 1074  902 2090 1271 1064 1491 1600 1396 2007 1580  798 1369 1556  319  319  914 2609
 270 1488 1355  498 1474 1338  580 1387 1058  989  217 1972 1153  417  784  833 1001 1666 1132  195  742  966  934  429 1637 2443  735
1224 1651 2253 1253  761 1792  596 2428 2094  430 1295 1134  395 1490 1862 1729 2074 1197 1314  969 1498 1455 1135  885 1308 1730  982 1083
2004 2422 3063 2154 1531 2567 1376 3328 2995 1311 2107 1116 1129 2270 2684 2630 2854 1967 2085 1870 2399 2226 1909 1660 1425 1854 1757 1917  901
 286 1655 1252  638 1790 1587  851 1117  788 1305  113 2288 1470  111  513  642  696 1982 1299  511  684 1122 1183  678 1886 2759  984  328 1405 2189
2233 2748 1256 2064 3161 3533 2784  866 1174 2973 2038 3889 3074 2016 1863 1535 2596 3227 2253 2303 1879 2028 3128 2623 3831 4129 2929 2222 3260 4161 1951
1241  814 1455  801  537 2109  999 1794 1506  434 1182 1265  447 1382 1615 1116 1966  728  477  811  803  622 1499 1188 2094 1505 1346  986  858 1611 1284 2627
 213 1863 1434  846 1990  659 1044 1291  962 1504  312 2488 1669  116  128  823  463 2181 1507  710  865 1303 1376  870 2078 2958 1177  527 1603 2381  224 2124 1501
 411 1324 1150  334 1480 1536  765 1256  928 1027  218 2011 1192  412  727  629  995 1671  968  232  512  803 1132  626 1840 2448  933  192 1187 2087  305 2090  941  523
 926 1082  636  407 1465 2080 1234  898  567 1265  727 2194 1378  760  822  178 1344 1531  702  704  158  477 1676 1183 2391 2433 1489  720 1616 2517  693 1732  938  871  518
1764 2177  629 1639 2590 3064 2316  398  705 2473 1569 3318 2502 1548 1395 1066 2128 2656 1681 1834 1385 1455 2660 2154 3362 3558 2461 1753 2792 3666 1483  630 2063 1654 1622
2305 2566 1001 2028 2979 3605 2860  939 1246 2862 2110 3707 2891 2089 1936 1612 2669 3045 2070 2330 1774 1845 3201 2695 3904 3947 3002 2294 3243 4055 2024  612 2452 2195 2141
1238 1120  504  668 1533 2392 1549  843  647 1416 1044 2261 1445 1072 1132  476 1655 1599  624 1018  419  400 1988 1497 2711 2501 1804 1031 1839 2609 1004 1677 1005 1183  829
1082  659  980  338 1026 2035 1042 1319 1021  909  904 1754  938 1094 1208  632 1678 1092  303  672  319  142 1728 1115 2323 1994 1421  826 1332 2102  997 2152  499 1205  668
1756 2430 2960 1961 1514 2022 1129 3040 2711 1208 1859 1362 1148 2022 2437 2436 2606 1950 2092 1638 2205 2234 1230 1412  800 2099 1509 1669  822  549 1942 3874 1631 2133 1859
2462 3135 3666 2667 2220 2399 1834 3746 3417 1914 2565 1992 1854 2728 3142 3142 3312 2656 2798 2343 2911 2940 1854 2118 1125 2729 2215 2375 1528  861 2648 4579 2337 2839 2564
 832 1001 1378  397  948 1701  590 1621 1289  492  782 1476  657  982 1215  914 1566 1140  645  402  590  632 1090  780 1685 1916  938  577  973 1821  884 2454  409 1093  535
 883 1784  956  858 2118 2183 1435  663  334 1700  687 2683 1865  598  341  537  709 2185 1404  953  753 1179 1779 1273 2487 3087 1580  872 1911 2812  601 1496 1591  705  741
1859  592 1555 1114 1483 2785 1709 1893 1697 1366 1680 2212 1396 1870 1969 1358 2454  786  476 1448 1079  712 2208 1864 3026 2452 2056 1602 1790 2560 1773 2727  956 1981 1443
1110 2379 2443 1466 2083  502  834 2426 2097 1516 1233 2532 1714 1395 1822 1921  525 2450 2023 1141 1711 1899  300  648  775 3052  610 1066 1424 2198 1316 3259 1787 1506 1253
2554  886 2250 1809 2179 3480 2404 2589 2393 2062 2375 2907 2092 2565 2665 2053 3149 1507 1172 2143 1775 1408 2904 2560 3721 3147 2752 2297 2486 3256 2469 3422 1652 2676 2139
 508 1507 1035  518 1799 1808 1060  900  571 1325  312 2308 1490  294  357  425  877 1934 1139  578  542  914 1404  899 2112 2768 1205  497 1536 2437  226 1734 1261  405  367
2080 2596 1183 1911 3009 3380 2632  714 1022 2821 1885 3737 2921 1864 1711 1382 2444 3075 2100 2150 1727 1876 2976 2471 3679 3977 2777 2069 3108 4009 1799  318 2482 1971 1938
 898 1392 1741  741  895 1558  362 1913 1582  328  925 1344  526 1125 1418 1217 1710 1230 1036  542  986 1016  900  656 1637 1864  748  717  546 1447 1037 2747  658 1236  759
1750 2574 2954 1955 1754 1037 1122 3034 2705 1352 1853 1791 1389 2016 2430 2430 2600 2349 2237 1631 2199 2263  485 1406  320 2528  976 1663  991 1122 1936 3867 1776 2127 1852
1661  763 1358  917 1286 2588 1512 1696 1500 1169 1483 2015 1199 1673 1772 1161 2257  671  279 1251  882  515 2011 1667 2829 2255 1859 1404 1593 2363 1576 2530  759 1784 1246
  74 1706 1481  690 1736 1412  695 1346 1017 1251  158 2234 1415  313  742  871  593 1928 1350  457  866 1185 1008  503 1711 2705  809  272 1254 2033  234 2179 1251  164  357
 977 1016 1517  536  823 1843  733 1759 1428  383  916 1366  548 1116 1053 1700 1015  663  545  729  700 1323  923 2042 1791 1081  720  807 1712 1019 2593  284 1227  669
1775  627 2033 1400  308 2641 1462 2372 2084  780 1726  999  583 1926 2200 1694 2510  275 1055 1342 1381 1197 2017 1720 2279 1181 1865 1518  971 1739 1837 3205  556 2037 1520
2226 2609 1045 2059 3022 3527 2779  861 1169 2905 2032 3751 2935 2011 1858 1529 2591 3089 2114 2297 1817 1886 3123 2618 3826 3991 2924 2216 3255 4099 1946  463 2495 2118 2086
2151 1089 2409 1776  430 2873 1678 2748 2460  996 2102  629  799 2302 2576 2070 2886  498 1431 1718 1757 1573 2216 1971 2495  802 2063 1894 1186 1753 2213 3581  961 2413 1896
2107 1271 2365 1733  386 2830 1634 2704 2416  952 2058  398  755 2258 2533 2027 2842  689 1388 1675 1713 1529 2172 1927 2514  587 2020 1850 1143 1522 2170 3538  917 2369 1852
2334 3078 3538 2539 2258 1671 1707 3618 3289 1857 2438 2326 1893 2600 3015 3015 3184 2853 2741 2216 2784 2847 1126 1614  397 3064 1308 2248 1496 1204 2520 4452 2280 2711 2437
1427 2429 2771 1771 2133 1030  884 2742 2413 1566 1549 1669 1764 1712 2139 2247 2044 2500 2073 1446 2016 2204  478  966  261 3102  660 1382 1474 1206 1632 3576 1836 1823 1569
 613 1135 1130  145 1320 1627  756 1303  971  896  431 1880 1061  621  850  606 1205 1511  779  228  390  613 1320  707 1915 2288 1013  355 1139 2040  524 2136  781  731  221
 665 2884 3281 2282 2065 1288 1450 3361 3032 1663  788 2101 1700  950 2758 2758 1282 2660 2547 1959 2527 2590  743  205   14 2839  925 1991 1302 1416  871 4195 2086 1061 2180
2350  516 2610 1977  630 3074 1878 2948 2660 1196 2302  713  999 2502 2777 2271 3086  725 1632 1919 1958 1772 2417 2172 2695  886 2264 2094 1387 1837 2414 3782 1162 2613 2096
1179 1476  325  937 1888 2480 1715  445  247 1771  985 2617 1801  966  898  376 1550 1955  980 1185  683  757 2076 1570 2778 2857 1877 1169 2098 2965  899 1279 1361 1077  999
3053 4055 4398 3398 3760 1894 2511 4369 4040 3193 3176 3465 3390 3338 3765 3874 3670 4126 3699 3072 3643 3830 2105 2593 1362 4203 2287 3008 2666 2780 3258 5202 3463 3449 3195
1879 1922  357 1383 2334 3059 2216  655  854 2217 1685 3063 2247 1666 1543  968 2250 2401 1426 1686 1129 1200 2655 2165 3373 3303 2471 1698 2598 3411 1599  981 1807 1777 1496
1279  591 1232  599  775 2167 1091 1571 1283  658 1172 1503  688 1355 1469  893 1939  841  254  866  580  396 1590 1246 2317 1743 1438 1022 1081 1852 1258 2404  248 1466  929
1689 2316 2843 1844 1491 1839 1012 2923 2594 1094 1793 1554 1126 1955 2370 2320 2539 2091 1978 1521 2089 2120 1047 1345  617 2291  915 1553  733  733 1875 3757 1517 2066 1742
1224 1884 2428 1429 1121 1775  597 2508 2179  662 1328 1262  750 1490 1905 1905 2074 1659 1547 1106 1674 1737 1118  881  989 2000  978 1138  301  799 1410 3342 1086 1601 1327
1154 1180 1820  827  616 1854  658 2051 1720   81 1105 1065  246 1305 1598 1345 1889  955  842  722 1021  984 1196  951 1708 1584 1044  897  472 1410 1217 2885  381 1416  939
1332  496 1590  957  404 2198 1075 1929 1641  418 1283 1133  358 1483 1757 1251 2067  603  612  899  938  754 1574 1277 2077 1373 1422 1075  754 1522 1394 2762  142 1594 1077
 824  947 1067   85 1261 1803  849 1309  977  837  624 1820 1002  841  957  602 1425 1371  591  420  279  425 1495  882 2090 2229 1189  565 1232 2133  717 2142  722  952  415
```

Distances / Distances / Entfernungen
Afstandstabel /Distanze / Distancias / Distâncias

Les distances sont comptées à partir du centre-ville et par la route la plus pratique, c'est à dire celle qui offre les meilleures conditions de roulage, mais qui n'est pas nécessairement la plus courte.

Distances are calculated from town-centres and using the best roads from a motoring point of view - not necessarily the shortest.

Die Entfernungen gelten ab Stadtmitte unter Berücksichtigung der günstigsten (nicht immer kürzesten) Strecke.

De afstanden zijn in km berekend van centrum tot centrum langs de geschickste, dus niet noodzakelijkerwijze de kortste route.

Le distanze sono calcolate a partire dal centro delle città e seguendo la strada che, pur non essendo necessariamente la più breve, offre le migliori condizioni di viaggio.

El kilometraje está calculado desde el centro de la ciudad y por la carretera más práctica para el automovilista, que no tiene porqué ser la más corta.

As distâncias entre as principais cidades são contadas a partir do centro da cidade e pela estrada mais pratica, ou seja, a que oferece melhores condições de acesso, mas que não é necessáriamente a mais curta.

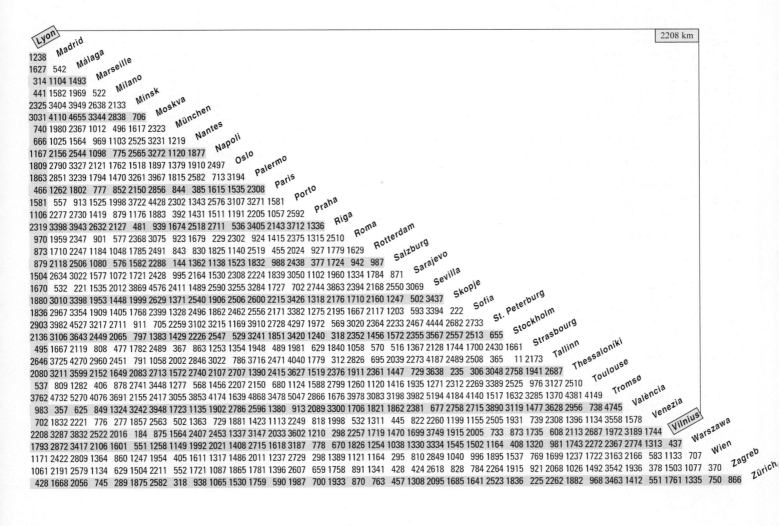

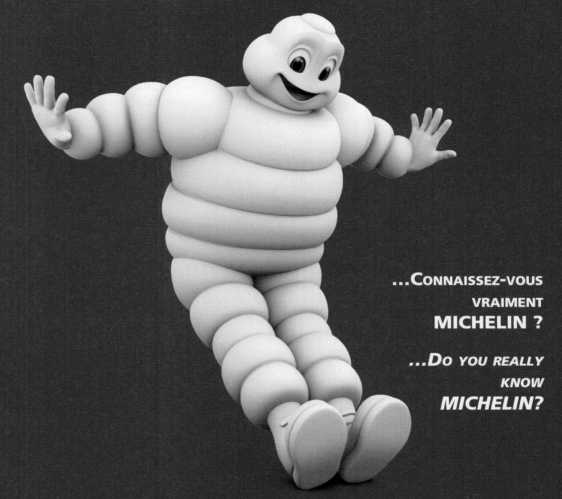

Vous CONNAISSEZ
les atlas MICHELIN

You KNOW
MICHELIN atlases

...CONNAISSEZ-VOUS
VRAIMENT
MICHELIN ?

...DO YOU REALLY
KNOW
MICHELIN?

Une meilleure façon d'avancer

N°1 mondial des pneumatiques avec 17,1 % du marché

Une présence commerciale
dans plus de **170 pays**

Une implantation industrielle
au cœur des marchés

68 sites industriels dans **19** pays ont produit en 2008 :

- **177** millions de pneus
- **16** millions de cartes et guides

Des équipes très internationales

Plus de **117 500** employés* de toutes cultures sur tous les continents dont **6 000** personnes employées dans les centres de R&D en Europe, aux Etats-Unis, en Asie.

*110 252 en équivalent temps plein

The world No.1 in tires with 17.1% of the market

A business presence
*in over **170 countries***

A manufacturing footprint
at the heart of markets

In 2008, **68** industrial sites in **19** countries produced:

- **177** million tires
- **16** million maps and guides

Highly international teams

Over **117,500** employees* from all cultures on all continents including **6,000** people employed in R&D centers in Europe, the US and Asia.

*110,252 full-time equivalent staff

Le groupe Michelin en un coup d'œil
The Michelin Group at a glance

Michelin présent en compétition

A fin 2008

24h du Mans
11 années de victoires consécutives

Endurance 2008
- 5 victoires sur 5 épreuves en Le Mans Series
- 10 victoires sur 10 épreuves en American Le Mans Series

Paris-Dakar
Depuis le début de l'épreuve, le groupe Michelin remporte toutes les catégories

Moto GP
26 titres de champion du monde des pilotes en catégorie reine

Trial
Tous les titres de champion du monde depuis 1981 (sauf 1992)

Michelin competes

At the end of 2008

Le Mans 24-hour race
11 consecutive years of victories

Endurance 2008
- 5 victories on 5 stages in Le Mans Series
- 10 victories on 10 stages in American Le Mans Series

Paris-Dakar
Since the beginning of the event, the Michelin group has won in all categories

Moto GP
26 Drivers' World Champion titles in the premier category

Trial
Every World Champion title since 1981 (except 1992)

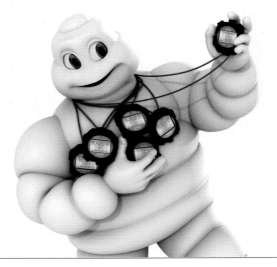

• Données au 31/12/2008 / *Data 31/12/2008*

- **Un centre de Technologies réparti sur 3 continents**
  - Amérique du Nord
  - Asie
  - Europe

- **2 plantations d'hévéa**
  - Brésil

- **68 sites de production dans 19 pays**
  - Algérie
  - Allemagne
  - Brésil
  - Canada
  - Chine
  - Colombie
  - Espagne
  - Etats-Unis
  - France
  - Hongrie
  - Italie
  - Japon
  - Mexique
  - Pologne
  - Roumanie
  - Royaume-Uni
  - Russie
  - Serbie
  - Thaïlande

Michelin, implanté près de ses clients

Michelin, established close to its customers

- **A Technologies Center spread over 3 continents**
  - Asia
  - Europe
  - North America

- **2 natural rubber plantations**
  - Brazil

- **68 plants in 19 countries**
  - Algeria
  - Brazil
  - Canada
  - China
  - Colombia
  - France
  - Germany
  - Hungary
  - Italy
  - Japan
  - Mexico
  - Poland
  - Romania
  - Russia
  - Serbia
  - Spain
  - Thailand
  - UK
  - USA

Notre mission

Contribuer, de manière durable, au progrès de la mobilité des personnes et des biens en facilitant la liberté, la sécurité, l'efficacité et aussi le plaisir de se déplacer.

Our mission

To make a sustainable contribution to progress in the mobility of goods and people by enhancing freedom of movement, safety, efficiency and pleasure when on the move.

Michelin s'engage pour l'environnement

Michelin, 1er producteur mondial de pneus à basse résistance au roulement, contribue à la diminution de la consommation de carburant et des émissions de gaz par les véhicules.

Michelin développe, pour ses produits, les technologies les plus avancées afin de :

- diminuer la consommation de carburant, tout en améliorant les autres performances du pneumatique ;
- allonger la durée de vie pour réduire le nombre de pneus à traiter en fin de vie ;
- privilégier les matières premières à faible impact sur l'environnement.

Par ailleurs, à fin 2008, 99,5 % de la production de pneumatiques en tonnage est réalisé dans des usines certifiées ISO 14001*.

Michelin est engagé dans la mise en œuvre de filières de valorisation des pneus en fin de vie.

*certification environnementale

Michelin committed to environmental-friendliness

Michelin, world leader in low rolling resistance tires, actively reduces fuel consumption and vehicle gas emission.

For its products, Michelin develops state-of-the-art technologies in order to:

- Reduce fuel consumption, while improving overall tire performance.
- Increase life cycle to reduce the number of tires to be processed at the end of their useful lives;
- Use raw materials which have a low impact on the environment.

Furthermore, at the end of 2008, 99.5% of tire production in volume was carried out in ISO 14001* certified plants.

Michelin is committed to implementing recycling channels for end-of-life tires.

*environmental certification

Tourisme camionnette
Passenger Car Light Truck

Poids lourd
Truck

Michelin au service de la mobilité
Michelin a key mobility enabler

Génie civil
Earthmover

Avion
Aircraft

Agricole
Agricultural

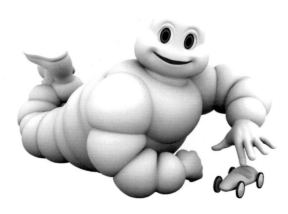

Deux roues
Two-wheel

Distribution

Partenaire des constructeurs, à l'écoute des utilisateurs, présent en compétition et dans tous les circuits de distribution, Michelin ne cesse d'innover pour servir la mobilité d'aujourd'hui et inventer celle de demain.

Partnered with vehicle manufacturers, in tune with users, active in competition and in all the distribution channels, Michelin is continually innovating to promote mobility today and to invent that of tomorrow.

Cartes et Guides
Maps and Guides

ViaMichelin,
des services d'aide au voyage /
travel assistance services

Michelin Lifestyle,
des accessoires pour vos déplacements /
for your travel accessories

MICHELIN
joue l'équilibre des performances / *plays on balanced performance*

- **Longévité des pneumatiques**
- **Economies de carburant**
- ○ **Sécurité sur la route**

... les pneus MICHELIN vous offrent les meilleures performances, sans en sacrifier aucune.

- **Long tire life**
- **Fuel savings**
- ○ **Safety on the road**

... MICHELIN tires provide you with the best performance, without making a single sacrifice.

Le pneu MICHELIN, un concentré de technologie
The MICHELIN tire, pure technology

❶ Bande de roulement
Une épaisse couche de gomme assure le contact avec le sol. Elle doit évacuer l'eau et durer très longtemps.

Tread
A thick layer of rubber provides contact with the ground. It has to channel water away and last as long as possible.

❷ Armature de sommet
Cette double ou triple ceinture armée est à la fois souple verticalement et très rigide transversalement. Elle procure la puissance de guidage.

Crown plies
This double or triple reinforced belt has both vertical flexibility and high lateral rigidity. It provides the steering capacity.

❸ Flancs
Ils recouvrent et protègent la carcasse textile dont le rôle est de relier la bande de roulement du pneu à la jante.

Sidewalls
These cover and protect the textile casing whose role is to attach the tire tread to the wheel rim.

❹ Talons d'accrochage à la jante
Grâce aux tringles internes, ils serrent solidement le pneu à la jante pour les rendre solidaires.

Bead area for attachment to the rim
Its internal bead wire clamps the tire firmly against the wheel rim.

❺ Gomme intérieure d'étanchéité
Elle procure au pneu l'étanchéité qui maintient le gonflage à la bonne pression.

Inner liner
This makes the tire almost totally impermeable and maintains the correct inflation pressure.

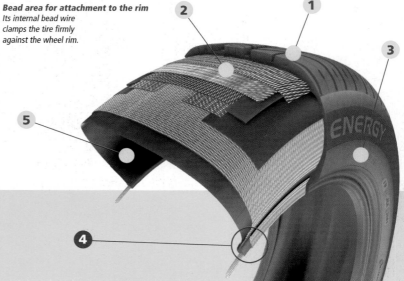

Suivez les conseils du bonhomme MICHELIN
Heed the MICHELIN Man's advice

Pour gagner en sécurité :
- Je roule avec une pression adaptée
- Je vérifie ma pression tous les mois
- Je fais contrôler régulièrement mon véhicule
- Je contrôle régulièrement l'aspect de mes pneus (usure, déformations)
- J'adopte une conduite souple
- J'adapte mes pneus à la saison

To improve safety:
- I drive with the correct tire pressure
- I check the tire pressure every month
- I have my car regularly serviced
- I regularly check the appearance of my tires (wear, deformation)
- I am responsive behind the wheel
- change my tires according to the season

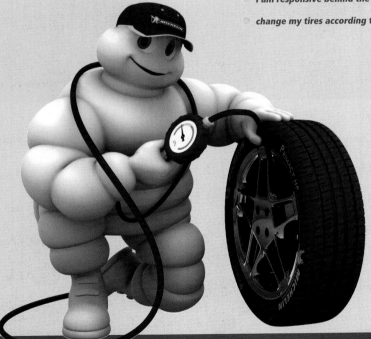

www.michelin.com
www.michelin. (votre extension pays - ex : fr pour France / *your country extension – e.g. : fr for France*)

S. Sauvignier/MICHELIN

D. Chapuis/MICHELIN

C. Eymenier/MICHELIN

(A)	Österreich	(DK)	Danmark	(IS)	Ísland	(PL)	Polska
(AL)	Shqipëria	(E)	España	(L)	Luxembourg	(RO)	România
(AND)	Andorra	(EST)	Eesti	(LT)	Lietuva	(RSM)	San Marino
(B)	Belgique, België	(F)	France	(LV)	Latvija	(RUS)	Rossija
(BG)	Bălgarija	(FIN)	Suomi, Finland	(M)	Malta	(S)	Sverige
(BIH)	Bosna i Hercegovina	(FL)	Liechtenstein	(MC)	Monaco	(SK)	Slovenská Republika
(BY)	Belarus'	(GB)	United Kingdom	(MD)	Moldova	(SLO)	Slovenija
(CH)	Schweiz, Suisse, Svizzera	(GR)	Elláda	(MK)	Makedonija	(SRB)	Srbija
(CY)	Kýpros, Kibris	(H)	Magyarország	(MNE)	Crna Gora	(TR)	Türkiye
(CZ)	Česká Republika	(HR)	Hrvatska	(N)	Norge	(UA)	Ukraïna
(D)	Deutschland	(I)	Italia	(NL)	Nederland	(V)	Vaticano
		(IRL)	Ireland	(P)	Portugal		

EUROPE
1/3 300 000

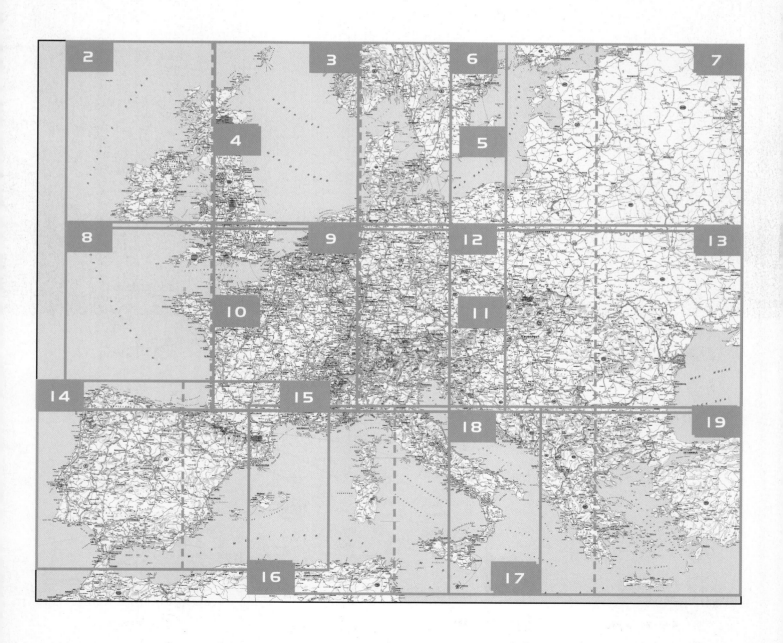

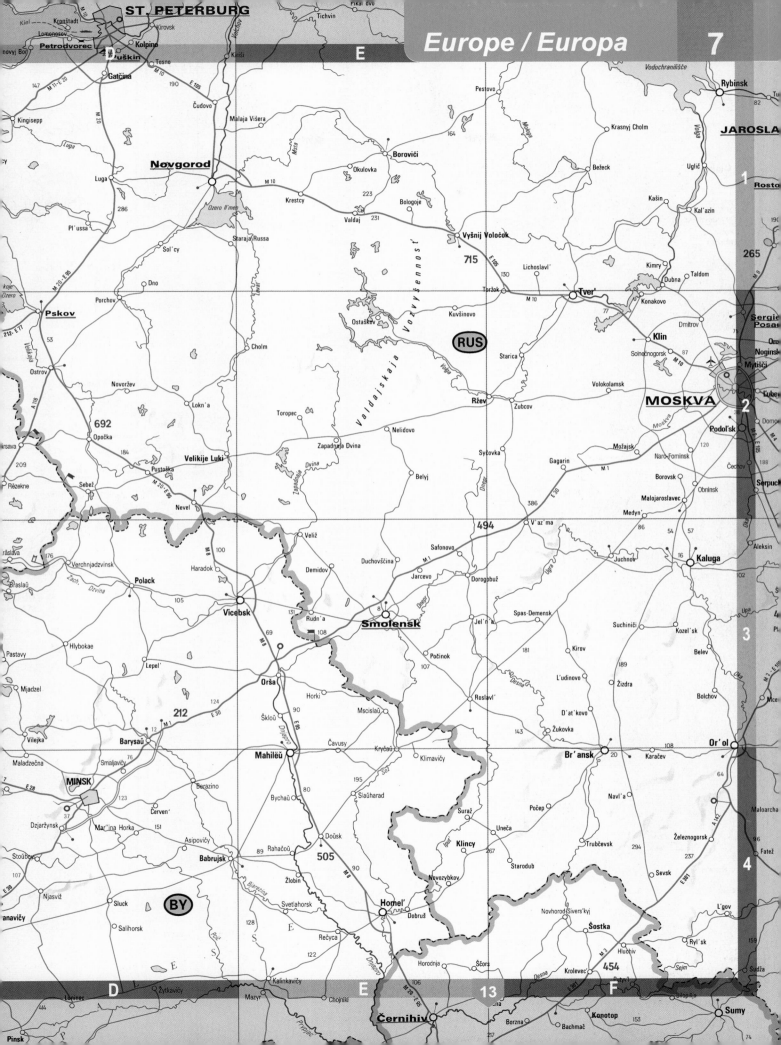

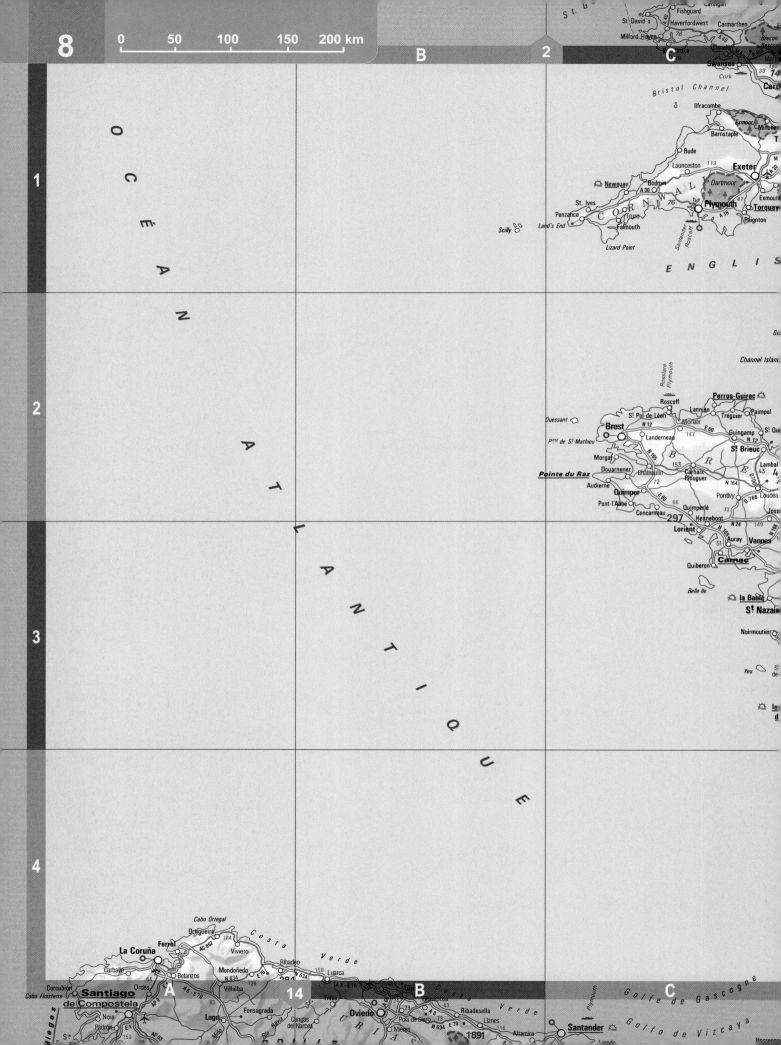

0   50   100   150   200 km

A   **B**   **2**   **C**

1

O
C
É
A
N

St. G

Fishguard · Cardigan
St David's · Haverfordwest · Carmarthen
Milford Haven · 76 · Brecon Beacon
· · · A 48 · Lanelli · Meri
Swansea · Cork · 14 · 33
Bristol Channel · 14

· Ilfracombe
Minehea
Barnstaple · Exmoor · T
· · M
· Bude · A 30
Launceston · 113 · **Exeter**
C O R N W A L Dartmoor · A 30
· Newquay · Bodmin · 41 · Exmout
St. Ives · A 30 · 76 · Exmouth
Penzance · Truro · **Plymouth** · **Torquay**
· Falmouth · A 38 · Paignton
Scilly · Land's End · Santander · Roscoff
· Lizard Point · Roscoff

E N G L I S

2

A
T
L
A
N
T
I
Q
U
E

Channel Island

Gui

Rosslare
Plymouth

· Roscoff · Perros-Guirec
· Lannion · Paimpol
Ouessant · St Pol-de-Léon · Tréguier
Brest · N 12 · Morlaix · E 50 · Guingamp · St Qu
· Landerneau · 147 · N 12
P^te de St Mathieu · Morgat · B · St Brieuc
· Douarnenez · R · Lamball
Pointe du Raz · Châteaulin · 153 · Carhaix · 43 · 4
· · 72 · Plouguer · N 164
Audierne · · Pontivy · Loudéa
Quimper · E 60 · 66 · D 768
Pont-l'Abbé · Quimperlé · 73 · Joss
Concarneau · 297 · Hennebont · N 165
Lorient · N 24 · 149
· 51 · Auray · **Vannes**
Quiberon · **Carnac**

Belle Ile

· la Baule
St Nazai

3

Noirmoutier

Yeu

le
d

4

Cabo Ortegal
Ortigueira
· 184
La Coruña · **Ferrol** · Viveiro · Costa
· AC 862 · · Verde
La Coruña · Betanzos · Mondoñedo · Ribadeo
Carballo · N 634 · 158
· 64 · Santiago · N 634 · Luarca
Corcubión · Ordes · Villalba · A 8 · E 70 · 284 · B · Costa Verde
Cabo Finisterre · **Santiago** · A 6 · E 70 · · Golfe de Gascogne
· **de Compostela** · 14 · A 8 · E 70 · Plymouth
Muros · Noia · Fonsagrada · ASTURIAS · Ribadesella · **Santander**
· Padrón · AP 53 · 83 · Tineo · Villaviciosa · 43
· **Lugo** · Cangas · **Oviedo** · Pola de Siero · Llanes · Golfe de Vizcaya
· 153 · del Narcea · N 634 · A 8 · Altamira · Larede · Hossegor
· AP 9 · Mieres · 116 · 1891

A   **14**   **B**   **C**

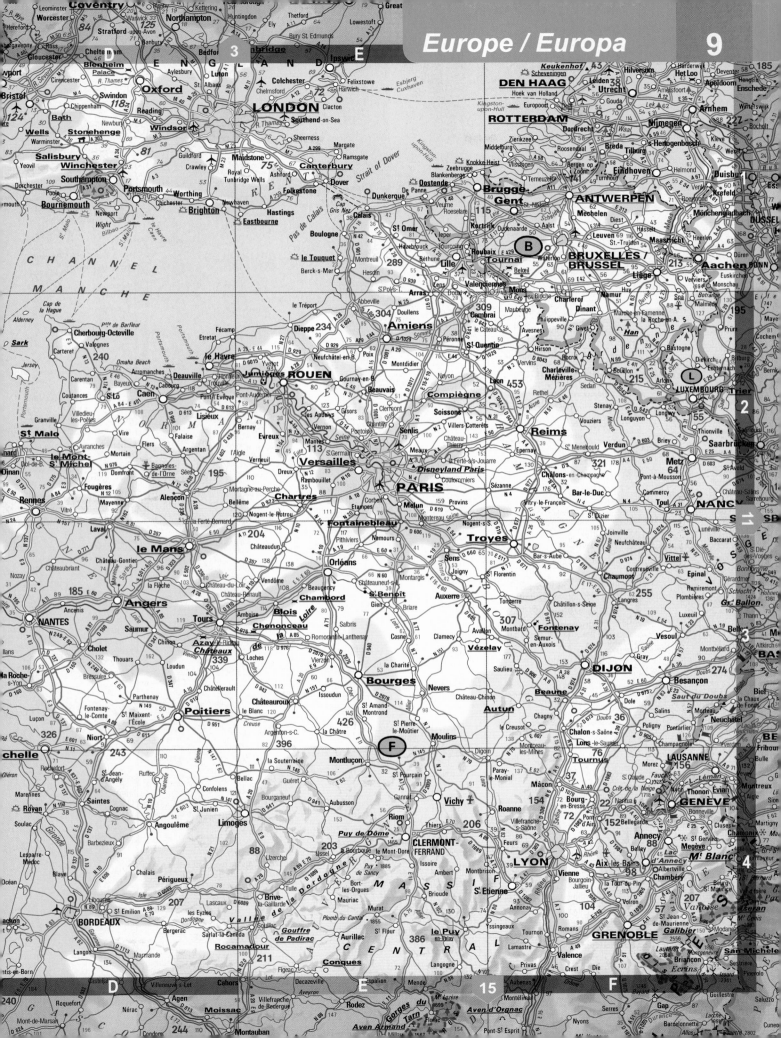

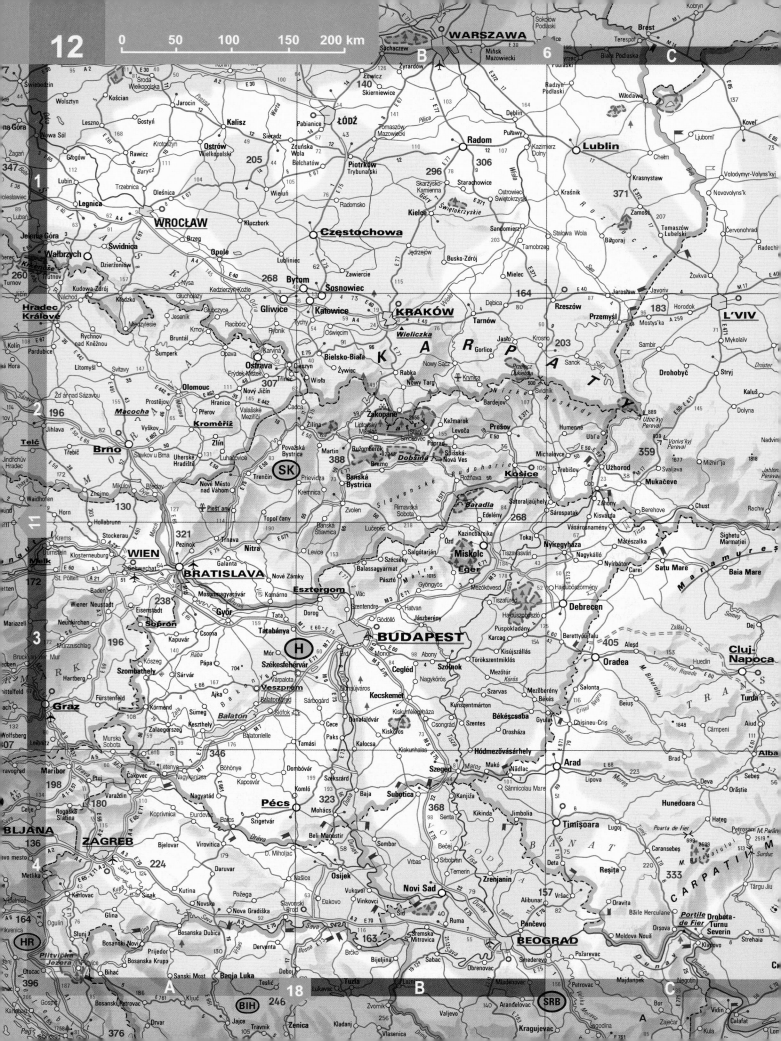

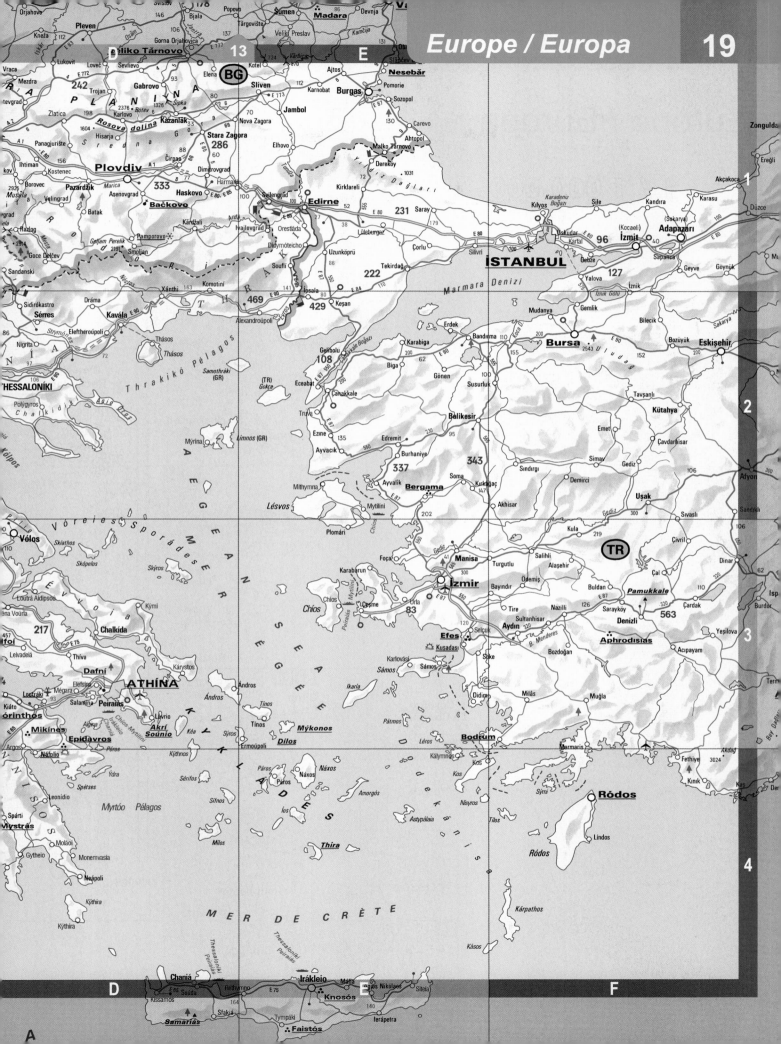

Europe / Europa

1 / 1 000 000

0 10 20 30 40 50 km

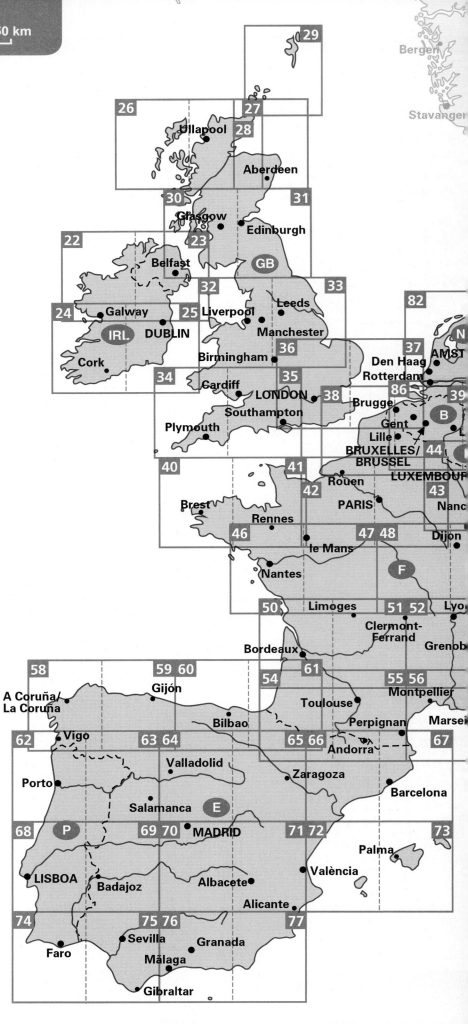

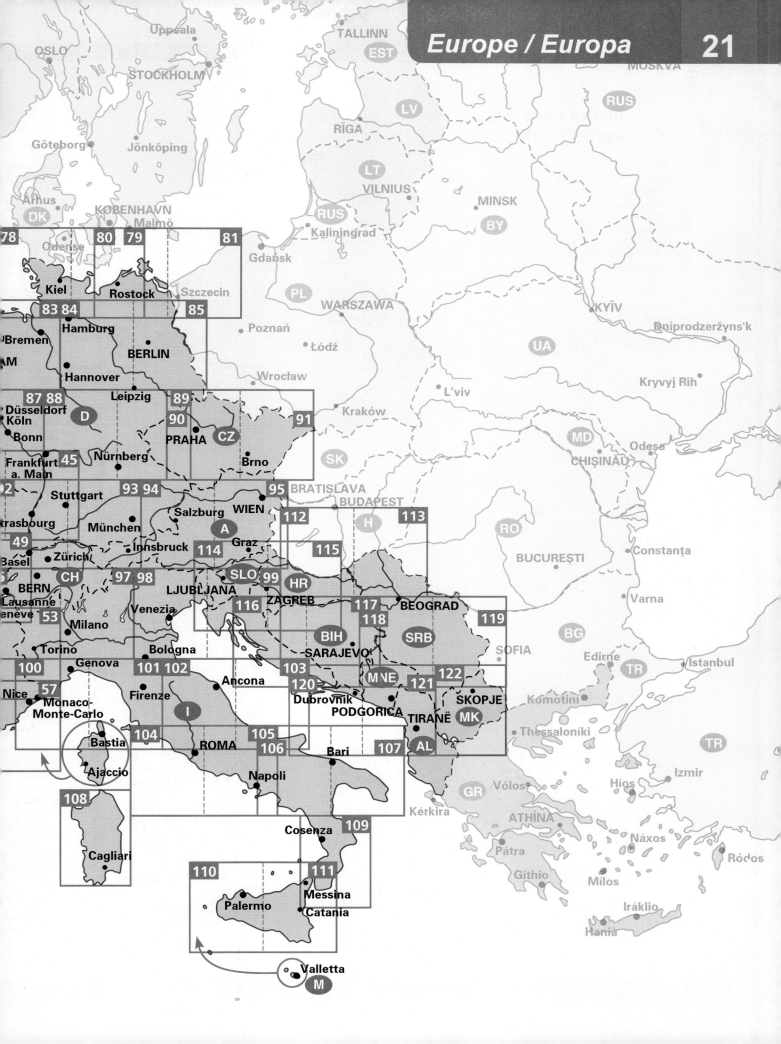

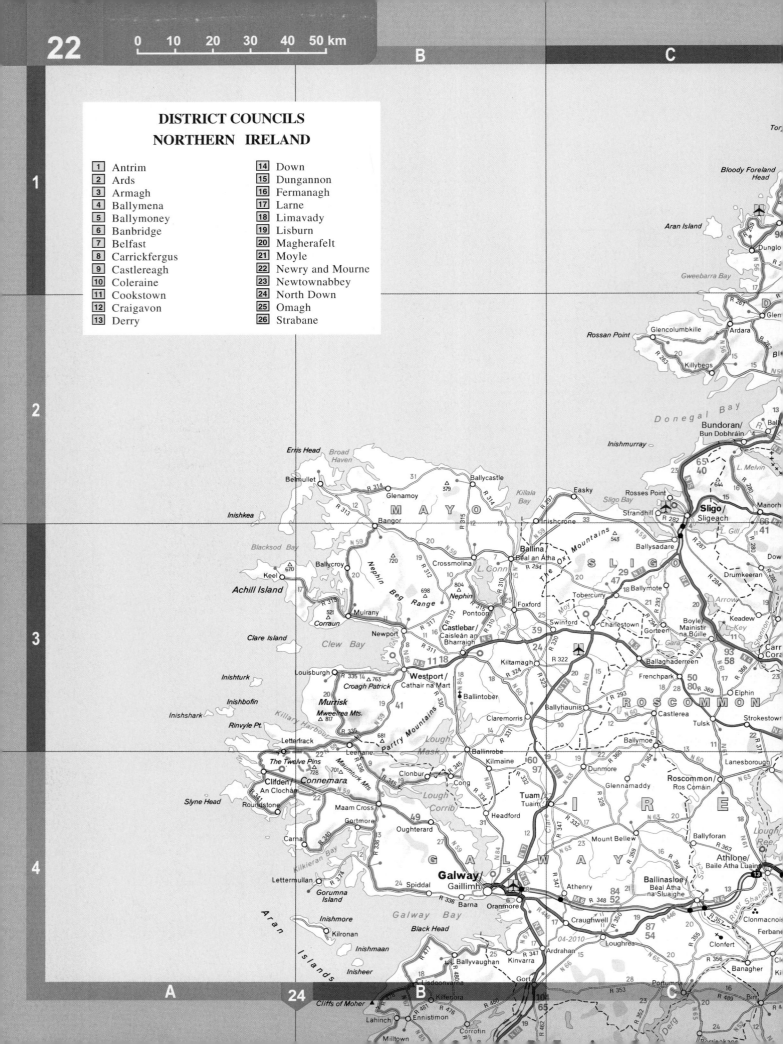

0 10 20 30 40 50 km

A   B   C

DISTRICT COUNCILS
NORTHERN IRELAND

1	Antrim	14	Down
2	Ards	15	Dungannon
3	Armagh	16	Fermanagh
4	Ballymena	17	Larne
5	Ballymoney	18	Limavady
6	Banbridge	19	Lisburn
7	Belfast	20	Magherafelt
8	Carrickfergus	21	Moyle
9	Castlereagh	22	Newry and Mourne
10	Coleraine	23	Newtownabbey
11	Cookstown	24	North Down
12	Craigavon	25	Omagh
13	Derry	26	Strabane

Longford / An Longfort
Granard
Virginia
Oldcastle
Lanesborough
Edgeworthstown Meath as Troim
Ballymahon
R 392
Ballymore
Kells
Navan / An Uaimh
Slane
Newgrange
Drogheda / Droichead Átha
Duleek
Naul
Balbriggan
Skerries
Rush
Athlone
le Átha Luain
Moate
Kilbeggan
Mullingar / An Muileann gCearr
Delvin
Athboy
Trim
Dunshaughlin
Ashbourne
Swords
Lusk
Malahide
Portmarnock
Howth
Clonmacnoise
Ferbane
Clara
Tullamore / Tulach Mhór
Edenderry
Kilcock
Maynooth
Lucan
DUBLIN / BAILE ÁTHA CLIATH
Douglas (I. of Man)
Liverp
Cloghan
Kilcormac
Banagher
Portarlington
Newbridge (An Droichead Nua)
Kildare
Clondalkin
S. DUBLIN
Dún Laoghaire
Dalkey
Birr
Kinnitty
Monasterevin
Naas
Russborough
Kippure
Enniskerry
Bray
Mountmellick
Kilcullen
Powerscourt
Greystones
Portlaoise
Hollywood
Poulaphouca Resr.
WICKLOW
Mountrath
Roscrea
Athy
Baltinglass
Glendalough
Laragh
Rathnew
Wicklow / Cill Mhantáin
Wicklow Head
Rathdowney
Durrow
Castlecomer
Carlow Ceatharlach
Tullow
Rathdrum
Aughrim
LAOIS
Thurles / Durlas
Freshford
KILKENNY
Tinahely
Arklow / An tInbhear Mór
Urlingford
CARLOW
Kilkenny (Cill Chainnigh)
Bagenalstown (Muine Bheag)
Cárnew
Killenaule
Ballingarry
Gorey
Callan
Borris
Kiltealy
Bunclody
Courtown
Fethard
Thomastown
Graiguenamanagh
Slievenamon
Jerpoint
WEXFORD
Enniscorthy / Inis Córthaidh
Cahore Point
Cahir
Carrick-on-Suir Carraig na Siúire
New Ross
Blackwater
Clonmel / Cluain Meala
Comeragh Mts.
Waterford / Port Láirge
Wexford / Loch Garman
Rosslare
Cappoquin
Wellington Bridge
Rosslare Harbour / Calafort Ros Láir
Dungarvan / Dún Garbhán
Bunmahon
Tramore
Dunmore East
Kilmore Quay
Carnsore Point
Ardmore
Dungarvan Harbour
Helvick Head
Hook Head
Saltee Islands
ughal / chaill
Youghal Bay
Pembroke
Roscoff
Cherbourg-Octeville
ST. GEORGE'S CHANNEL
Strumble Head
Newport
Pembrokeshire Coast National Park
Fishguard Abergwaun
St. David's Head
St. David's
PEMBROKESHI
St. Bride's Bay
Haverfordwest / Hwlffordd
Milford Haven / Aberdaugleddau
Neyland
Narberth
Pembroke Dock / Doc Penfro
Pembroke
Rosslare
St. Govan's Head

0 10 20 30 40 50 km

UNITARY AUTHORITIES
SCOTLAND

1	Aberdeen City	17	Inverclyde
2	Aberdeenshire	18	Midlothian
3	Angus	19	Moray
4	Argyll and Bute	20	North Ayrshire
5	Clackmannanshire	21	North Lanarkshire
6	City of Edinburgh	22	Orkney Islands
7	City of Glasgow	23	Perthshire and Kinross
8	Dumfries and Galloway	24	Renfrewshire
9	Dundee City	25	Scottish Borders
10	East Ayrshire	26	Shetland Islands
11	East Dunbartonshire	27	South Ayrshire
12	East Lothian	28	South Lanarkshire
13	East Renfrewshire	29	Stirling
14	Falkirk	30	West Dunbartonshire
15	Fife	31	West Lothian
16	Highland	32	Western Isles

A   B   C

1

Flannan I.

O   U   T   E   R   H   E   B   R   I   D   E   S

LEWIS

Butt of

Barvas

Carloway

A 858   292   12

34   Stornoway

Garynahine   A 858   A 857

A 859   A 859

574

36   A 859

W

Hushinish

B 887   Clisham   572   Keb

West Loch Tarbert   799

2

St. Kilda

Toe Head   24   Harris

A 859

Leverburgh   Sound of Harris

Rodel

Renish Point

I S

North Uist

Otternish

Tigharry   A 865   Lochmaddy   Waternish Point

25   A 865   A 867   Loch Snizort   Uig   A 855

Sound of Monach   13   347   The Sto

Balivanich   The Little Minch   Dunvegan Head

Benbecula   A 865   A 850   22   16   A 87

Creagorry   Dunvegan   Portree

3

South Uist   22   Bracadale   A 863   21   52

A 865   620   SEA OF   Idrigill Point   84

Daliburgh   THE HEBRIDES   Loch Bracadale   Sligachan   SKYE

Lochboisdale   The Cuillins   993

Cuillin Sound

Sound of Barra   Canna

Barra   A 888   Bayhirivagh   Rhum   812

Castlebay   583   Sound of Rhum

Eigg

Mingulay

Barra Head   Muck

4

Kilchoan

T   I   C

Coll   Arinagour

Tiree   Tobermory

Dervaig   B 8073

Scarinish   Salen

Ulva   L. Tuath   na Keal

Staffa   B 8035

A   B   C

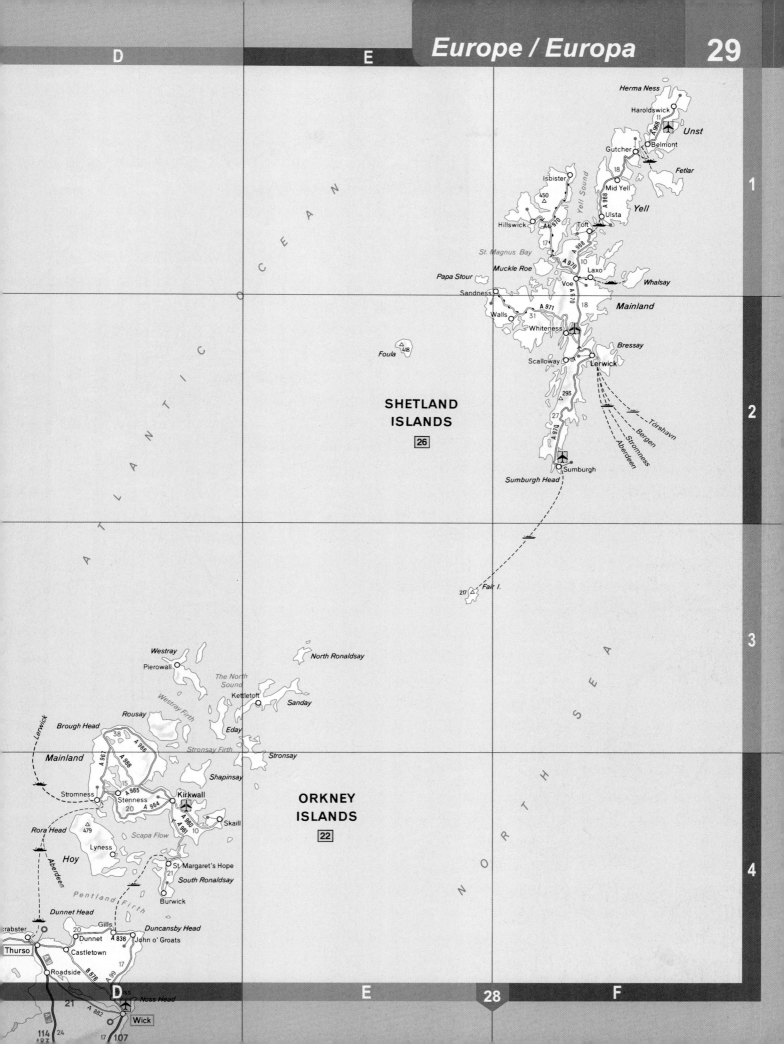

D E F

ATLANTIC OCEAN

Herma Ness

Haroldswick
A 968
Belmont
Gutcher
Unst
Fetlar
18
Isbister
Mid Yell
450 △
Yell
Hillswick
A 970
Toft
Ulsta
17
A 968
10
St. Magnus Bay
A 970
Laxo
Muckle Roe
Voe
Whalsay
Papa Stour
Sandness
A 970
Mainland
Walls
31
A 971
18
Whiteness
Bressay
Foula △ 418
Scalloway
Lerwick

**SHETLAND
ISLANDS**

[26]

△ 293
27
A 970
Tórshavn
Bergen
Stromness
Aberdeen

Sumburgh
Sumburgh Head

217 △ *Fair I.*

Westray
Pierowall
*The North
Sound*
North Ronaldsay
Westray Firth
Rousay
Kettletoft
Brough Head
38
A 961
A 986
Sanday
Lerwick
Mainland
A 986
Eday
A 961
Stronsay Firth
Stronsay
15
Shapinsay
Stromness
A 965
Stenness Kirkwall

**ORKNEY
ISLANDS**

[22]

20
A 964
479 △
A 960
Skaill
Rora Head
A 961
10
Scapa Flow
Lyness
Hoy
St. Margaret's Hope
21
South Ronaldsay
Pentland Firth
Burwick

NORTH SEA

Aberdeen
Dunnet Head
Gills
20
Duncansby Head
rabster
Dunnet
A 836
John o' Groats
Thurso
Castletown
17
Roadside
B 876
A 99
Noss Head
21
A 882
Wick
114
24
17
107

1

2

3

4

28

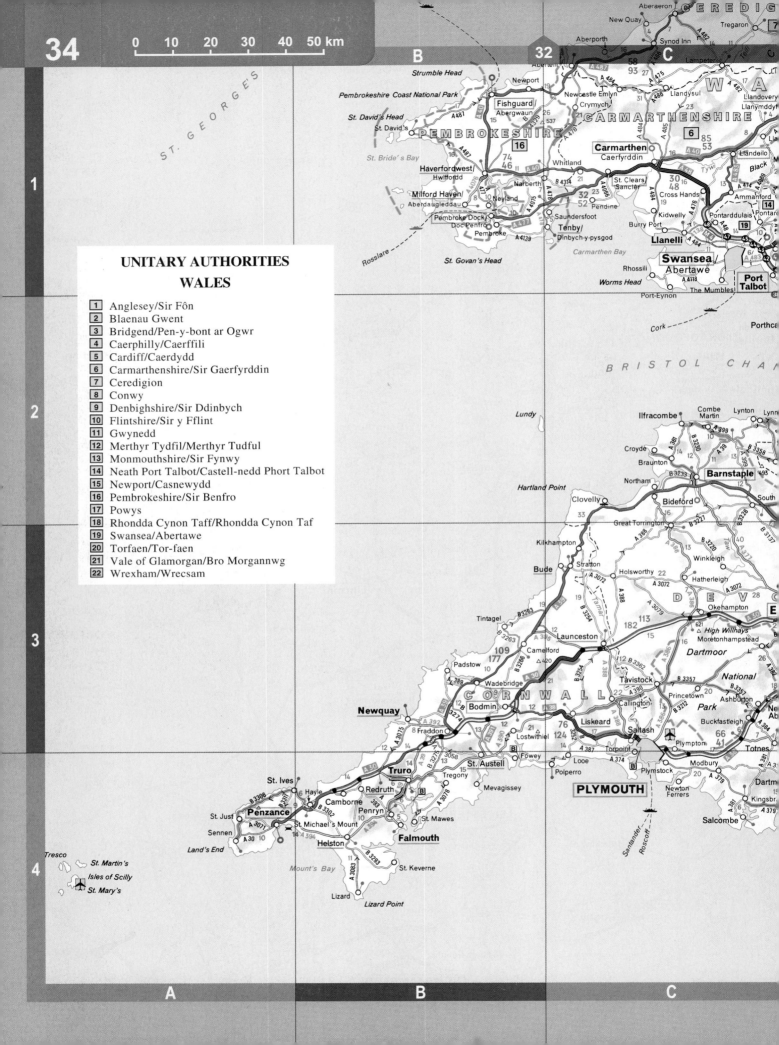

0 10 20 30 40 50 km

UNITARY AUTHORITIES
WALES

1 Anglesey/Sir Fôn
2 Blaenau Gwent
3 Bridgend/Pen-y-bont ar Ogwr
4 Caerphilly/Caerffili
5 Cardiff/Caerdydd
6 Carmarthenshire/Sir Gaerfyrddin
7 Ceredigion
8 Conwy
9 Denbighshire/Sir Ddinbych
10 Flintshire/Sir y Fflint
11 Gwynedd
12 Merthyr Tydfil/Merthyr Tudful
13 Monmouthshire/Sir Fynwy
14 Neath Port Talbot/Castell-nedd Phort Talbot
15 Newport/Casnewydd
16 Pembrokeshire/Sir Benfro
17 Powys
18 Rhondda Cynon Taff/Rhondda Cynon Taf
19 Swansea/Abertawe
20 Torfaen/Tor-faen
21 Vale of Glamorgan/Bro Morgannwg
22 Wrexham/Wrecsam

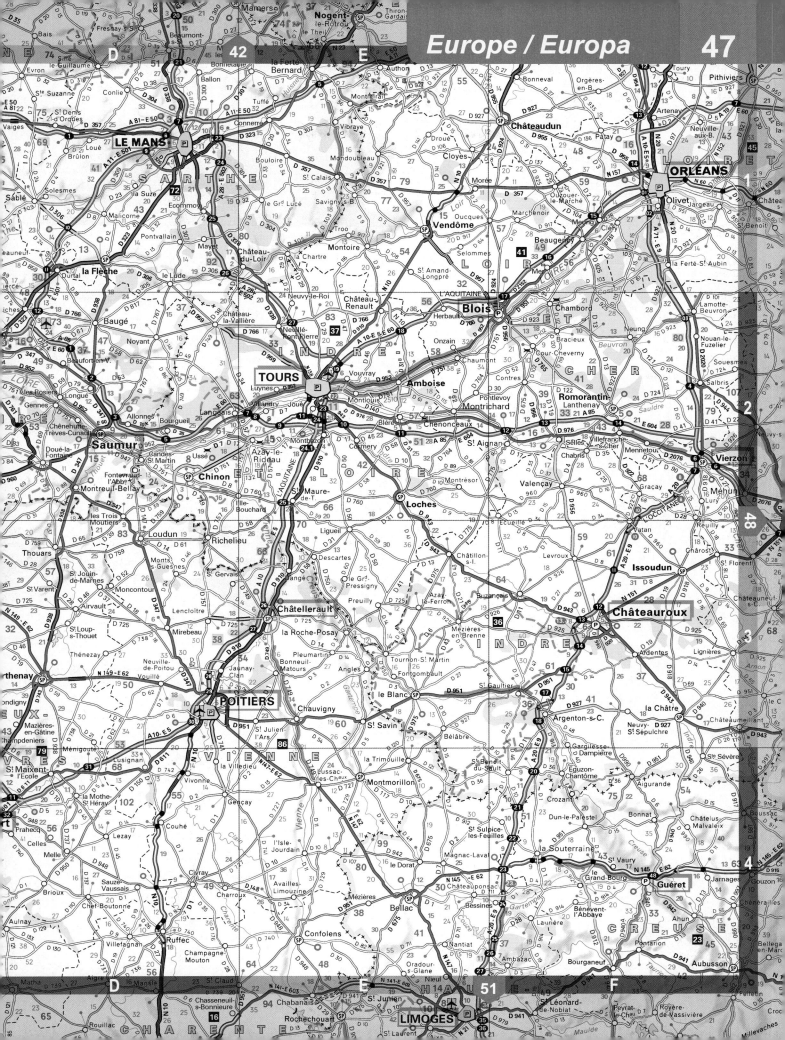

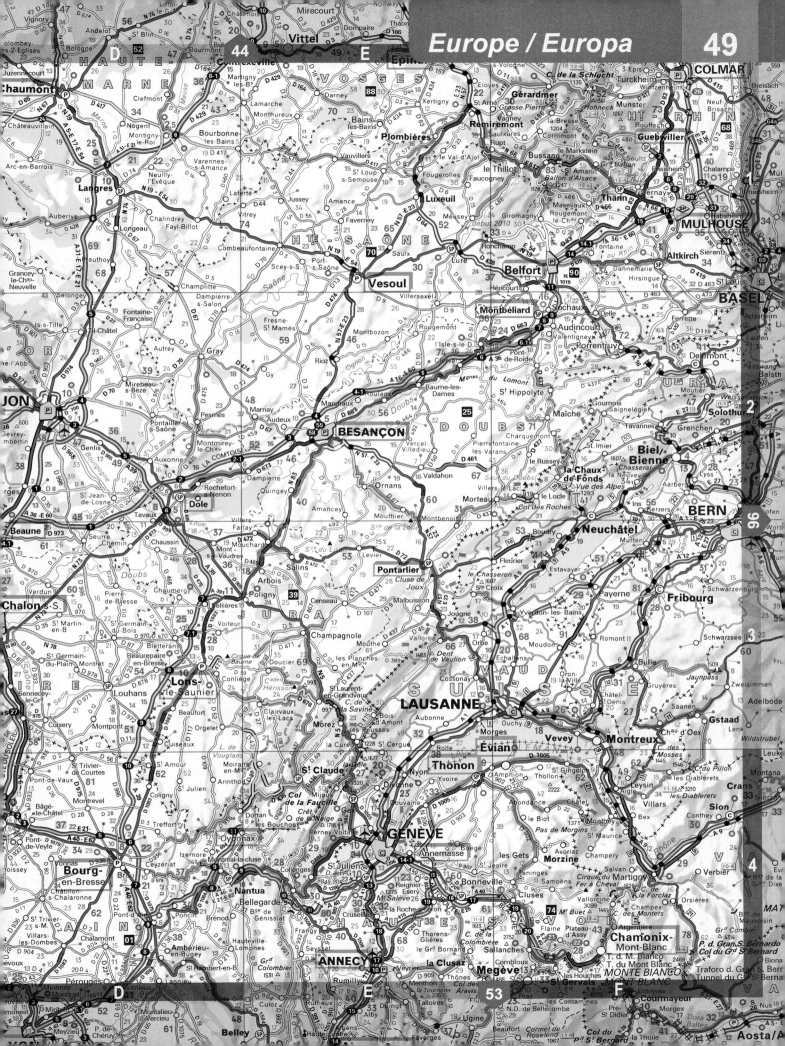

0 10 20 30 40 50 km

A   B   C

1

Cabo Ortegal   Estaca de Bares

Cariño   Porto do Barqueiro

Cedeira   Ortigueira   **115**

Cabo Prior   Atios   Campo del Hospital   LU 862

Gándara   Xubia   S. Sadurniño   Viveiro   Cervo   Bu

17   13   AC 862

Ferrol   34F   Ourol   Ferreira   S. Martín de Mondoñedo

Eda   31F   AG 64   **45**   As Pontes de García Rodríguez

Fene   27F   Xistral   Mondoñedo

Ares

Pontedeume   Río Eume   Cabreiros   Puerto da Xesta   545

2

A CORUÑA   Sada   E. del Eume   13

Malpica   Caión   Arteixo   Oleiros   **53**   **17**   572   N 634-E 70   Villalba

Cambre   Carrió   **40**   Betanzos   Irixoa   E 70   Parajes   Mei

Laxe   Ponte-Ceso   A Laracha   583   **46**   540

Cabo Vilán   Baio   **12**   **Carballo**   Carral   565   Guitiriz   Baamonde   **140**

Camariñas   Vimianzo   San Roque   Anxeriz (Cerceda)   567   Sobrado dos Monxes   510   **22**   Castro   N 640

Muxía   **64**   Mesón do Vento   Curtis   Teixeiro   Outerio de Rei   Castroverde

Cabo Touriñán   Dumbría   Sta Comba   Ordes   **56**   **83**   Corredoiras   Rábade   500   497

Corcubión   E. de Fervenza   Portomouro   Friol   **Lugo**   493   488

Fisterra   Negreira   Lavacolla   Melide   Nadela   Corgo

Cabo Fisterra/ Cabo Finisterre   Bertamiráns   67   Arzúa   A 54   Guntín de Pallares   Baralla   Becerrea

Carnota   Serra de Outes   **60**   **75**   72   **SANTIAGO** DE COMPOSTELA   Palas de Rei   **103**   Monterroso   Portomarín   Sarriá   Samos

3

Muros   Noia   Ramallosa   Padrón   Oca   Vila de Cruces   **93**

Porto do Son   93   **38**   Catoira   A Estrada   Silleda   **49**   Agolada   Taboada

Boiro   Rianxo   Cuntis   **56**   41   Lalín   Rodeiro   Embalse de Belesar

A Pobra do Caramiñal   Vilagarcía de Arousa   110   Forcarei   Chantada   Escairón   Bóveda

Sta Eugenia   Vilanova de A   Caldas de Reis   Cachafeiro   Soutelo   Sta María la Real de Oseira   La Barrela   E. de los Peares

Cambados   Mosteiro   Cerdedo   **88**   Cea   Pico Piapaxa   1607

O Grove   119   N 541   Beariz   Carballiño   **37**   Monforte de Lemos   **147**   Quiroga

I. de Sálvora   Sanxenxo   Combarro   **Pontevedra**   Brués   S. Amaro   Luintra   Gargantas del Sil

Isla de Ons   Portonovo   Marín   132   Ponte-Caldelas   Carballiño   Nogueira de Ramuín   Castro Caldelas

Mirador de Coto Redondo   Rial   **46**   Avión   Leiro   **241**   **Ourense**   Alto del Couso

Bueu   146   **76**   252   240   16   233   A Pobra de Trives

Islas Cíes   Cangas   Moaña   Redondela   Mondariz   Ribadavia   224   Maceda   Alto del Rodicio   Manzaneda

4

Cabo Silleiro   **VIGO**   Ponteareas   A Cañiza   Outomuro   A Merca   Xunqueira de Ambía   Seixo   1707

Baiona   57   305   Porriño   Salvaterra de Miño   Cortegada   Celanova   Allariz   Vilar de Barrio   Embalse de Bao

A Ramallosa   166   160   As Neves   São Gregório   **63**

Arrabal   Tui   Monção   Melgaço   Bande   Xinzo de Limia   188   Laza   Peña Nofre   A Gudiña

Tomiño   Valença do Minho   Castro Laboreiro   E. de Las Portas

A Guarda   Sto Pedro da   **65**   Parque peneda   **106**   Cualedro   Alto do Cañizo

Citania de Sta Tegra   Vila Nova de Cerveira   Baltar   Alto de Estivadas   Alto de Fumaces

Oledo do Minho   Caminha   Parada de Coura   **62**   Fondevila   Muguimes   Verín   A 52

Vila Praia de Âncora   Arcos de Valdevez   Ponte da Barca   Lindoso   Larouco   Montalegre

GALICIA

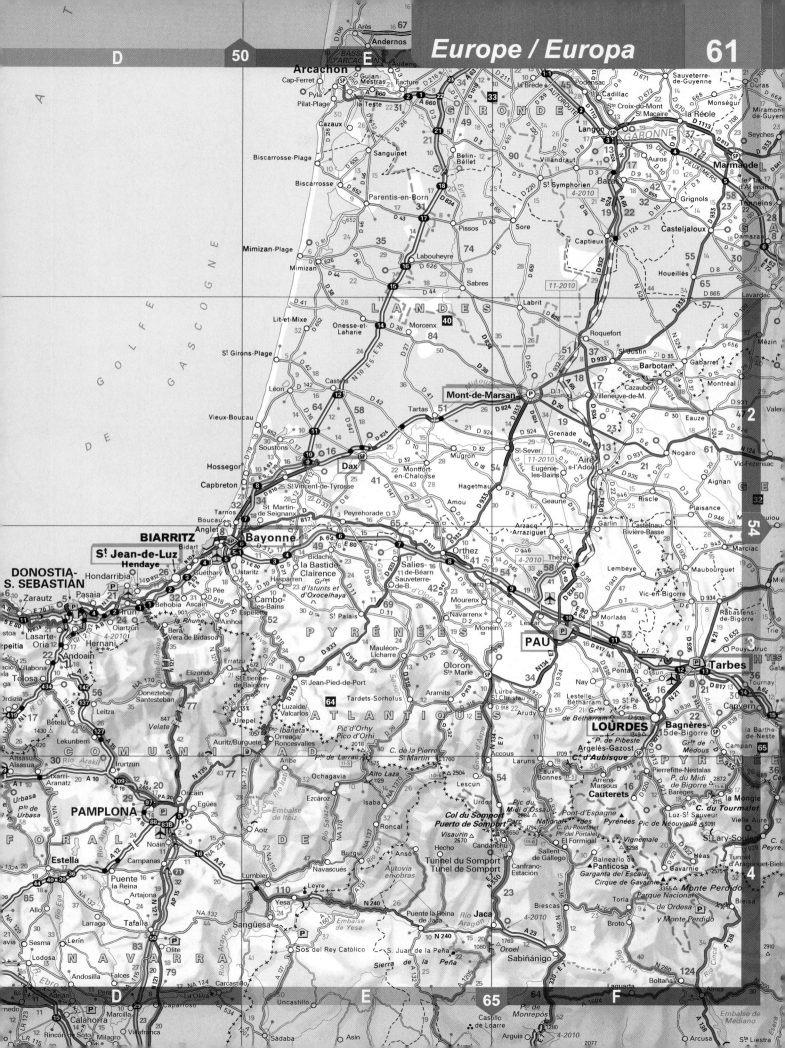

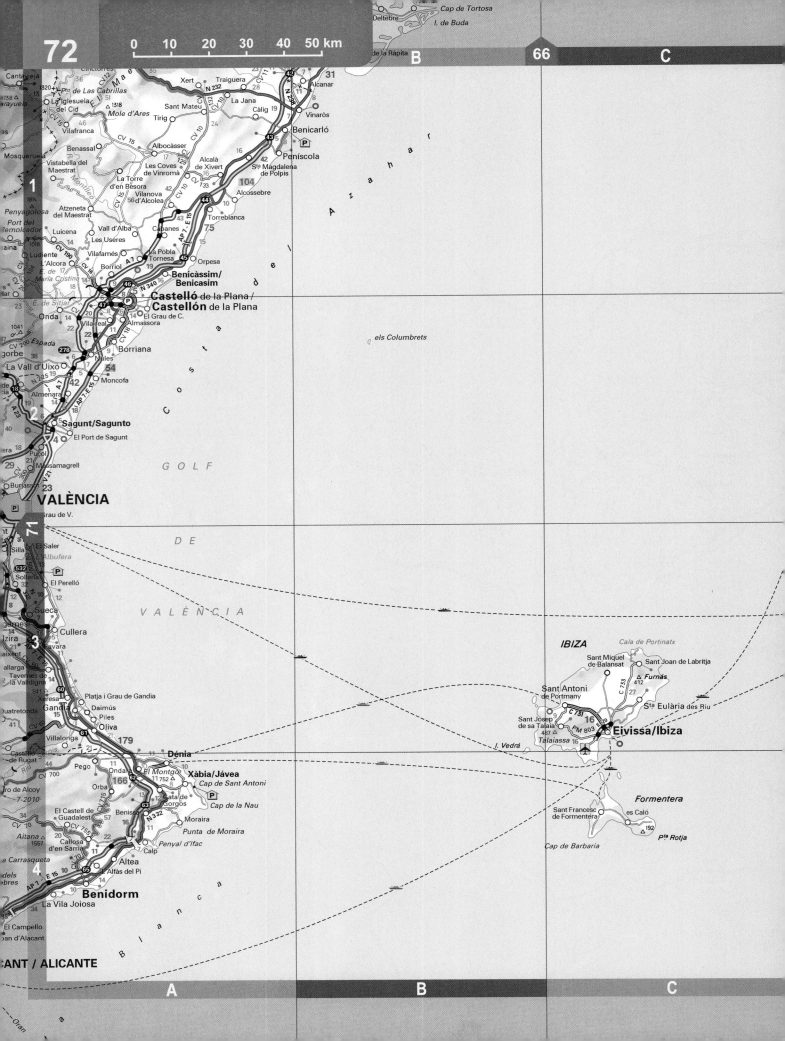

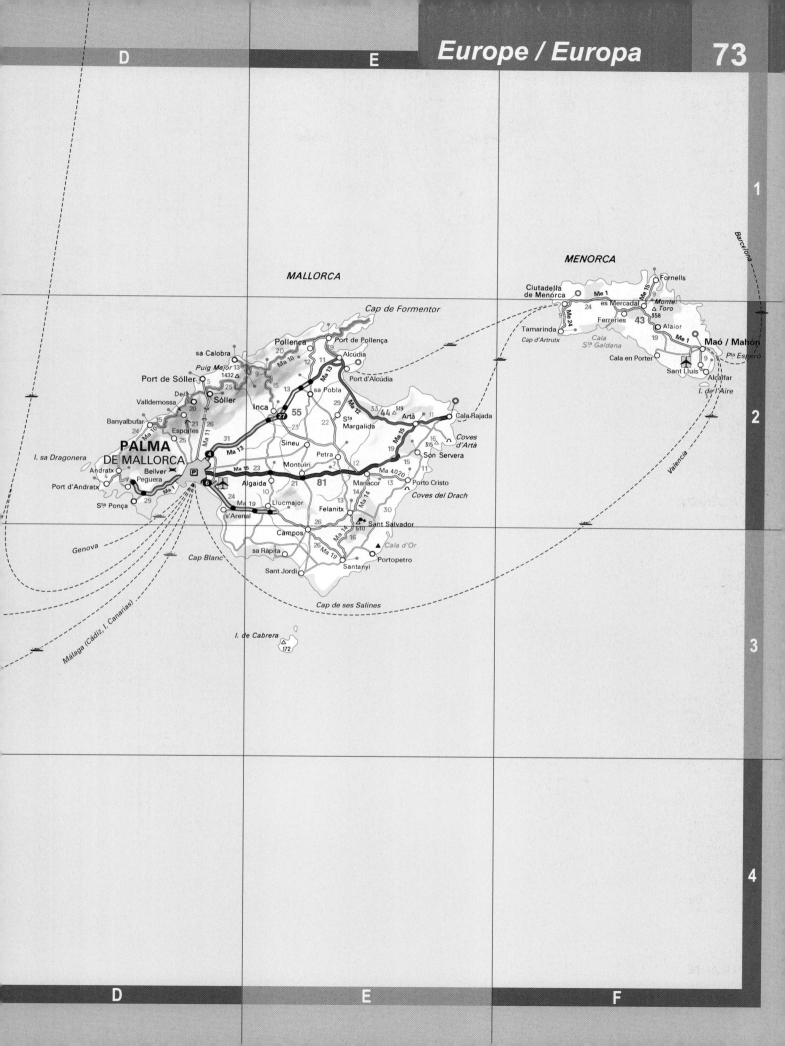

MALLORCA

MENORCA

Cap de Formentor

Ciutadella
de Menorca   Me 1   Fornells
24   es Mercadal   Monte
△ Toro
Pollença   Port de Pollença   Tamarinda   Ferreries   **43**   358
sa Calobra   20   Alcúdia   *Cap d'Artrutx*   Cala   Alaior
Ma 10   12   11   Sᵗᵃ Galdana   19   Me 1   **Maó / Mahón**
Puig Major 13   9   Port d'Alcúdia   Cala en Porter
1432 △   15   13   sa Pobla   Sant Lluís   Alcalfar
Port de Sóller   5   25   29   Ma 12   33   519   *I. de l'Aire*
Deià   Sóller   Inca   **55**   **44**   Artà
Valldemossa   20   **27**   Sᵗᵃ   11   Cala Rajada
Banyalbufar   15   21   26   23   Margalida   *Coves*
24   Ma 10   Esporles   22   Ma 15   *d'Artà*
25   Sineu   16   315 △
PALMA   31   Petra   Son Servera
DE MALLORCA   Ma 13   Montuïri   12   15
I. sa Dragonera   Bellver   Ma 15   23   7   Ma 40 20   11
Andratx   Peguera   **6**   Algaida   21   **81**   7   Manacor   13   Porto Cristo
Port d'Andratx   Ma 1   10   14   *Coves del Drach*
29   24   Ma 19   Llucmajor   13   Ma 14   30
Sᵗᵃ Ponça   s'Arenal   Felanitx   Sant Salvador
Genova   26   Ma 14   510
Cap Blanc   Campos   16   ▲ *Cala d'Or*
sa Ràpita   26 Ma 19   Portopetro
Sant Jordi   Santanyí
Málaga (Cádiz, I. Canarias)   *Cap de ses Salines*

I. de Cabrera   △ 172

Barcelona

Valencia

145

BORNHOLM
(DK)

Christiansø

Hammershus
Allinge-Sandvig
Hasle
Gudhjem
Svaneke
23 159
158
9
Rønné
38 Åkirkeby
30
Nekso
Pedersker

MORZE BAŁTYCKIE

LTIQUE)

MORZE

Słowiński Park Narodowy
Łeba 1
Jezioro Łebsko
Kluki
Główczyce
Gardno
Gardna Wlk
Rowy 51
Ustka Objazda 6 50
Jarosławiec J. Wicko 21
Słupsk 19
J. Kopań 37 27 24 211
Darłowo Dębnica Kaszubska
Sławno 203 Czarna Dąbrów
70 6 33 209 Suchorze 55 2
Malechowo 43 Kępice 75 Bytów
Łazy 37 203 30 26 35
Mielno Sianów 45
Sarbinowo 37 206 Polanów 61
Ustronie Morskie Koszalin Mostowo 25 Miastko
11 Kołobrzeg 41 28 39 16 181
Mrzeżyno 12 Parsęta 25 Biały Bór
Dźwirzyno 29 163 Radew 32 Bobolice 18 57 45
Niechorze 10 30 102 Karlino 30 69 J. Wierzchowo Przechlewo
Rewal 18 28 6 Białogard J. Wielimie 30 21 29 25 Brda
Pobierowo 12 Trzebiatów 162 15 Tychowo 34 Czarne 41 Człuchów
Dziwnów 24 102 6 Słupsk
Kołczewo 102 Cerkwica 18 Sławoborze 103 163 Szczecinek 47
Wolin Kamień Pomorski Świerzno 31 Rymań 25 Połczyn-Zdrój Barwice 172 40
Międzyzdroje Gryfice 119 162 25 152 Silnowo 42 Okonek Lędyczek
Woliński Park Narodowy 12 109 Resko 152 38 Świdwin Kluczewo J. Pile
Warszów 13 Płoty 151 Rega 21 J. Drawsko 36 20 Czaplinek
Wolin 107 19 Łobez 17 Jastrowie
Stettiner Haff Przybiernów Złocieniec Machliny 28 Złotów
Zalew Szczeciński Nowogard 20 Drawsko Pomorskie 163 Krajenka
Nowe Warpno Dobra 111 Węgorzyno 13 27 33 Piła
Trzebież Stepnica 94 31 J. Woświn 19 J. Lubie 211 Racza
Dobieszczyn Goleniów 144 133 Mirosławiec J. Bytyń Wałcz 10 28
Police 21 Maszewo Chociwel Insko 29 Tuczno 178
SZCZECIN Ina Dobrzany Kalisz Pomorski 106 33 Ujście
Löcknitz Lubieszyn 15 Dąbie Morzyczyn 24 Stargard Szcz. Recz Drawno 13 Piła
Pomellen 31 12 9 20 Kołbacz Suchan Drawno Człopa Trzcianka
Penkun 37 34 Kołbaskowo Str. Czarnowo 144 56 40 Choszczno Drawieński Park Narodowy Czarnków
Mescherin Gartz Gryfino 58 Pyrzyce J. Płoń 107 Chodzież
Banie 155 Pełczyce Dobiegniew 85 Czarnów
Hohen-Landin Vierraden Lipiany Barlinek Wieleń
Schwedt Krajnik Dln Myślibórz Strzelce Krajeńskie Drezdenko Piłka

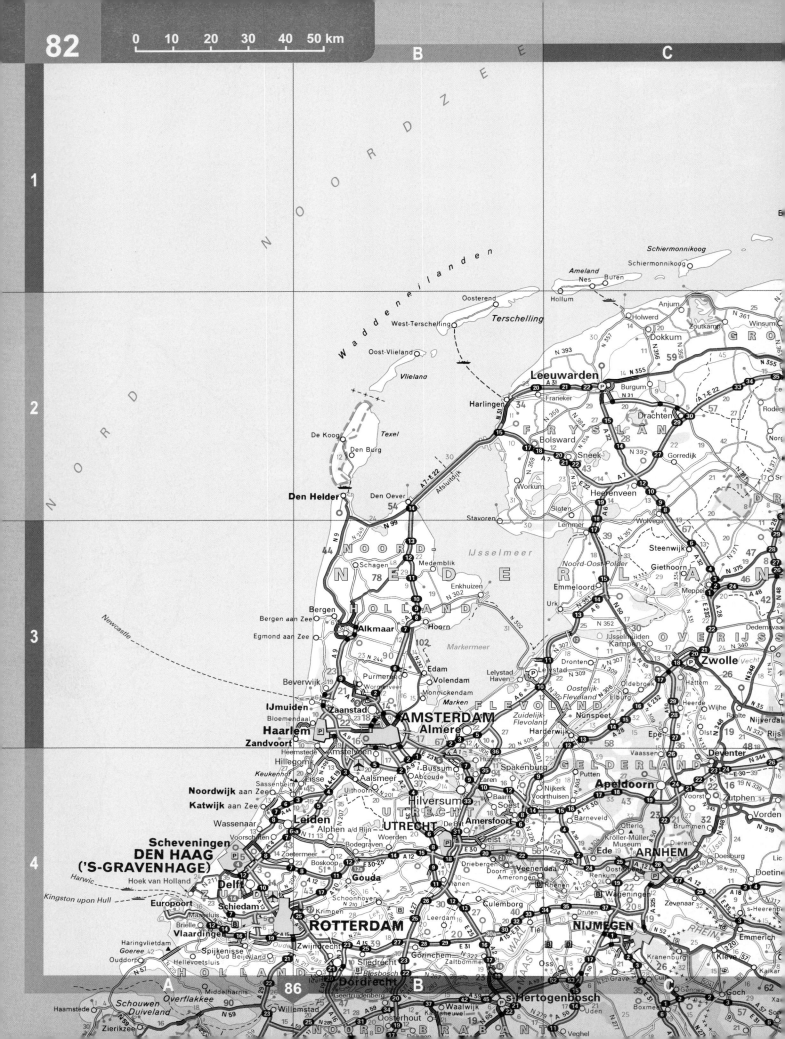

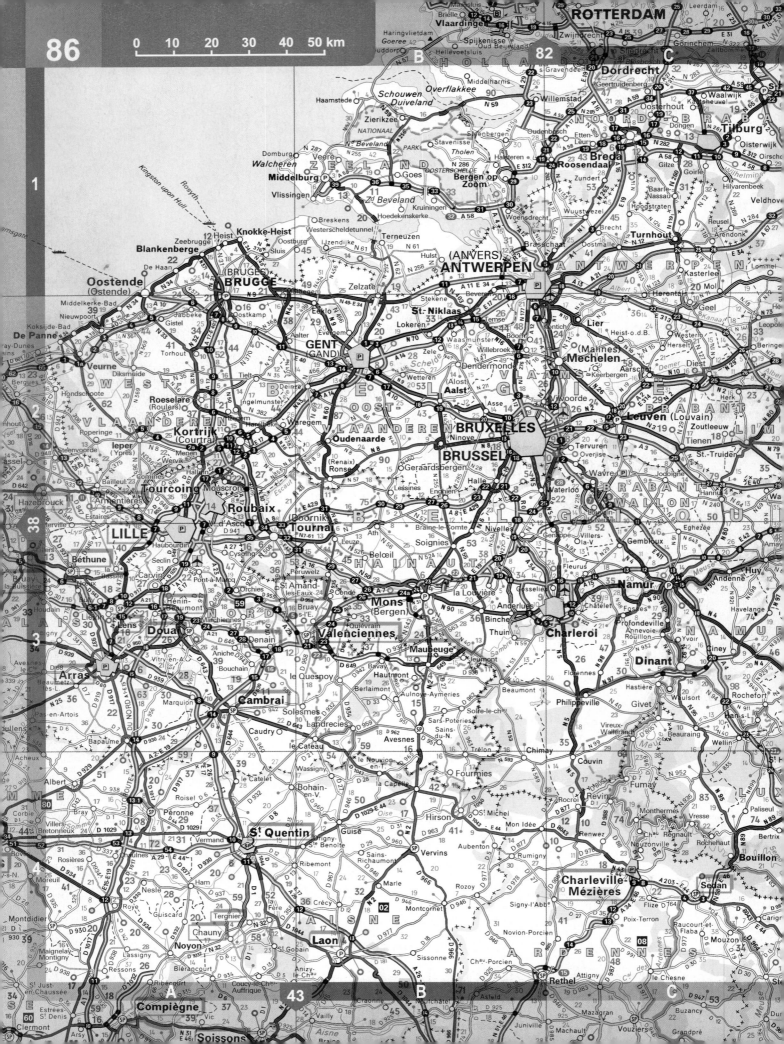

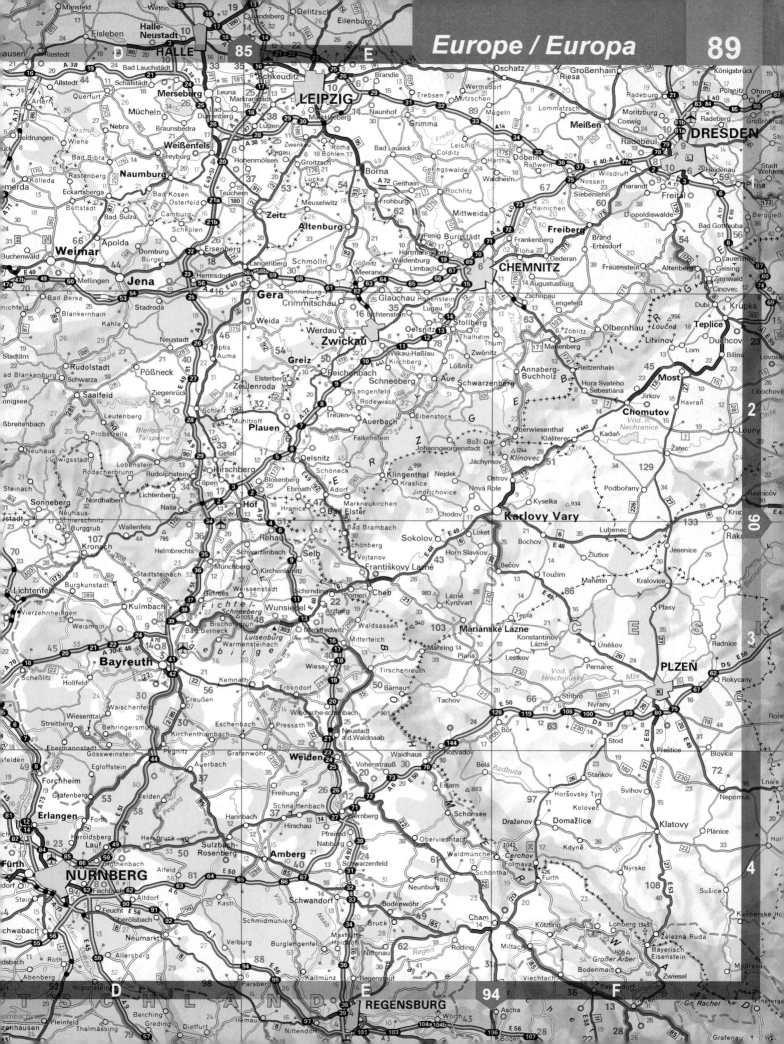

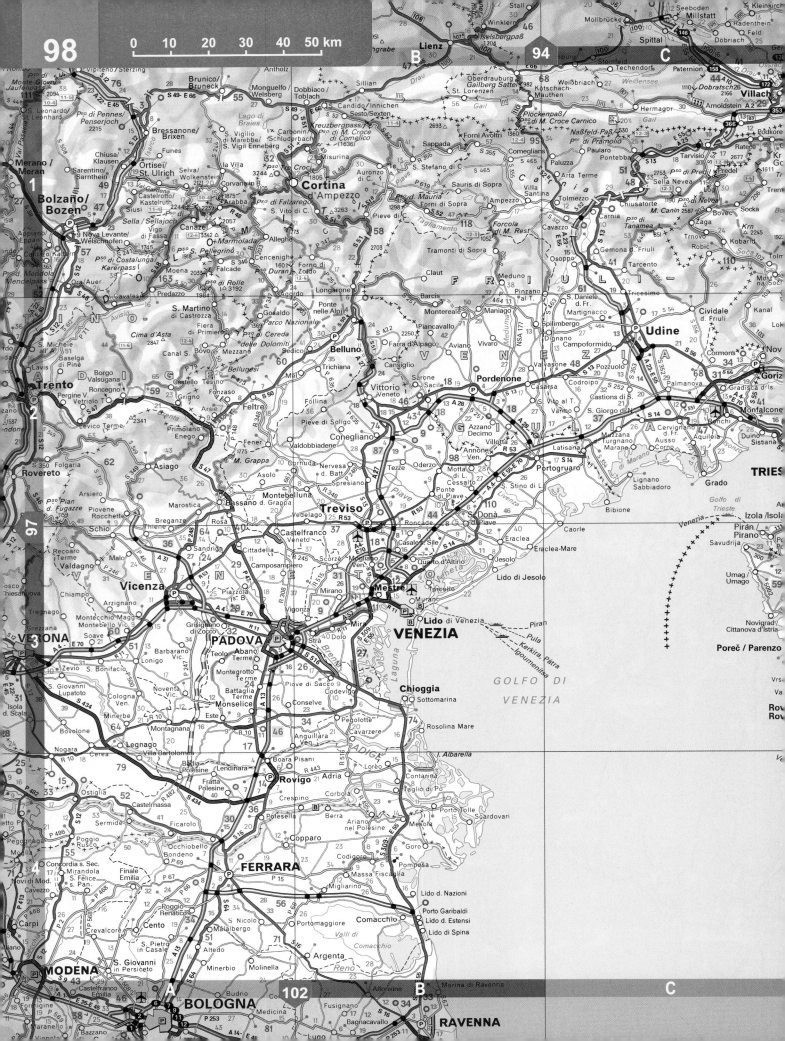

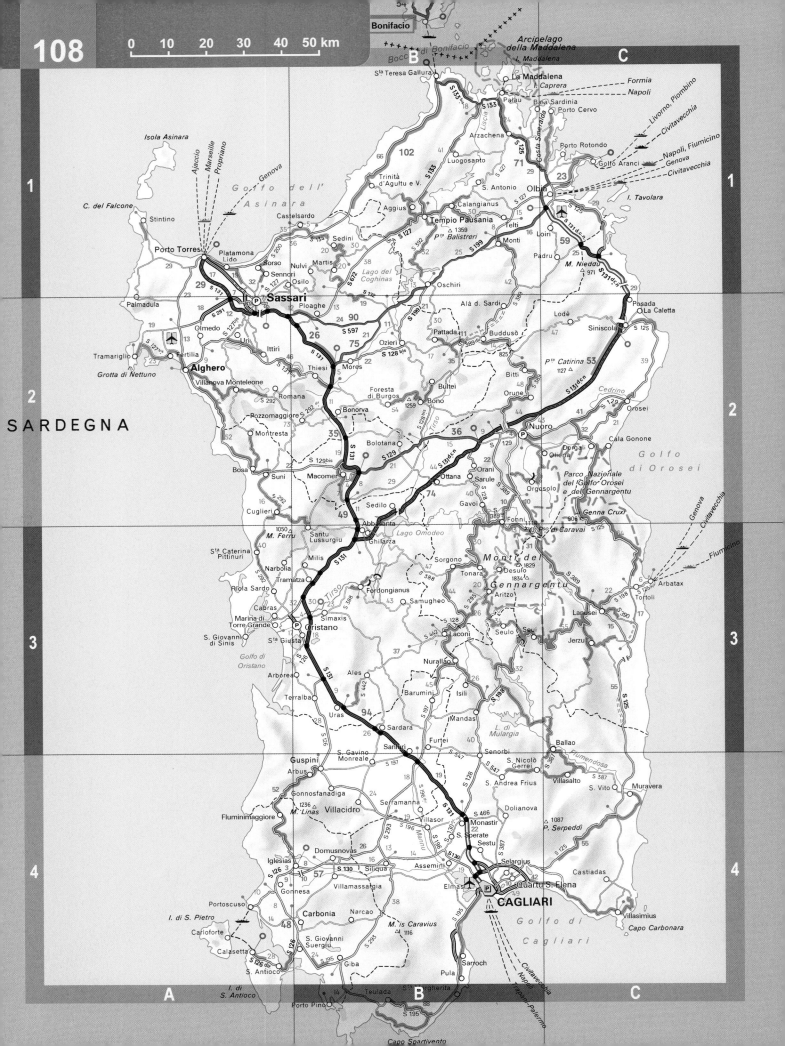

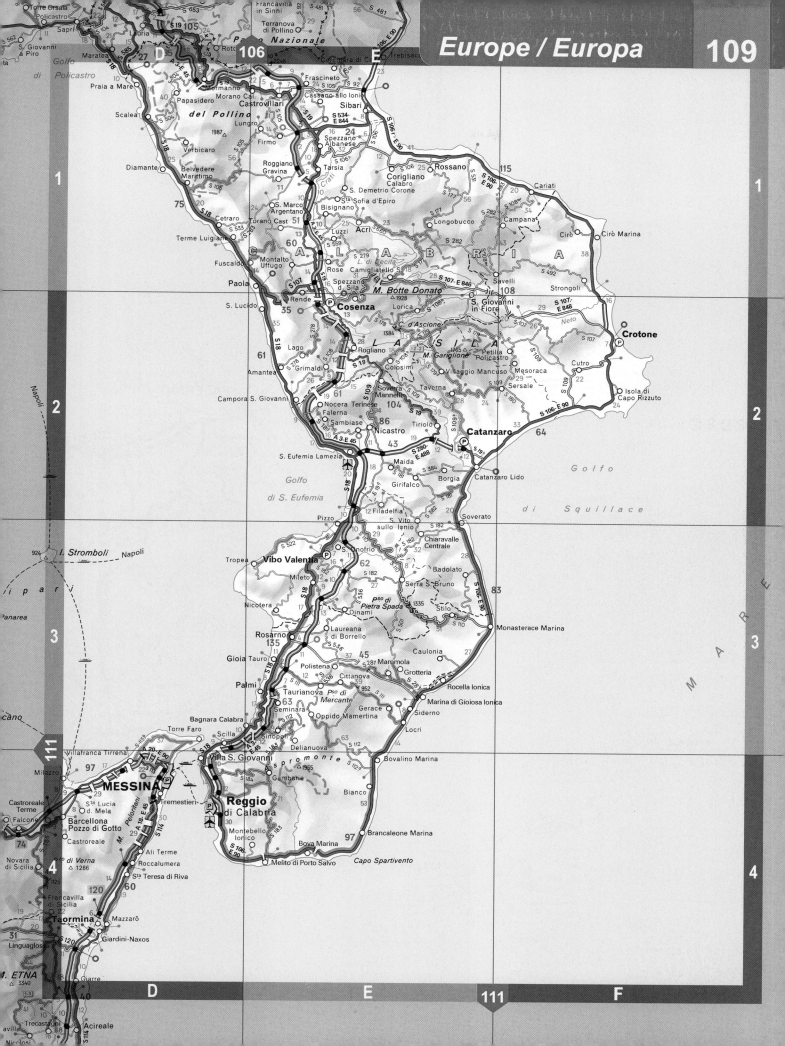

0   10   20   30   40   50 km

A | B | C

1

I. di Ustica

MARE   TIRRE

SICILIA

Livorno
Tunis
Genova
Cagliari
Civitavecchia
Napoli
Salerno

Capo Gallo
Sferracavallo
Mondello
M. Pellegrino
Punta Raisi 6 30
PALERMO
S. Vito lo Capo
Torre d. Impiso
Carini
Capaci
Soluto
Golfo di Castellammare
Cinisi 17 44
Bagheria
Casteldaccia
Cefalù
2
Castellammare d. Golfo 26 16
Monreale 63
44
Misilmeri
Altavilla
S 113 54 Termini Imerese
A 20 · 28
Collesano
Cagliari
Erice 34
Partinico 29 31
Piana d. Albanesi
Trabia 47
Buonfornello
Trapani S 113 32
Alcamo S 113 15
Marineo
Caccamo
Montemaggiore Belsito
Isole Egadi
I. Levanzo
Paceco 14 20
Fulgatore 12
Segesta
S 119 16
S. Cipirello
S 118 34
Villafrati
Caltavuturo
I-Maréttimo
I. Favignana
Birgi
42 9
Calatafimi
Rca Busambra
△ 1613
Roccapalumba S 205
Alia 38
66
36 **50**
S 115
11 S 188
41 **57**
155
Corleone
44 624
28
Prizzi
18
S 121 23 Resuttano
Lercara Friddi 27
126
I. di Pantelleria
Salemi 38
S 119
45
126
Marsala S 188
Sta Ninfa
S 188
Chiusa Sclafani
S 188
3
Partanna
Sta Margherita di Belice 31
Alessandria d. Rocca
S. Stefano Quisquina
Mussomeli
Caltaniss
S. Cato
Castelvetrano
Sambuca di Sicilia
Casteltermini 62
Serradifalco
22 A 29 · E 90 **21**
S 115 · E 931
Caltabellotta
S. Biagio Platani 83
Montedoro
Mazara d. Vallo
Campobello di Mazara
Menfi 44
20
94 16
Ribera
Platani
Aragona
Raffadali
58 Delia
Selinunte
Marinella
Sciacca
S 640
Canicatti
S 115 41 E 931
Agrigento
Naro S 123
Favara
Campobello di Licata

Gozo
Marsalforn
Ras San Dimitri
Ta'Pinu
Ramla Bay
San Blas Bay
Xaghra
Nadur
118
Porto Empedocle
72
Palma di Montechiaro
Gharb
Victoria (Rabat)
Xewkija 7 **Mgarr**
Qala
Ras ti-Qala
Dwejra Bay
Xlendi
North Comino Channel
Comino (Kemmuna)
Armier Bay
MARE
Pozzallo
Catania
Marfa Ridge
Mellieha Bay
Ras Il-Qammich 10
Mellieha
St Paul's Bay
Bugibba
Anchor Bay
25 15
St Julian's
Golden Bay
Zebbiegh
Naxxar
Sliema
MEDITERR
Mgarr
Mosta 7
Gzira
VALLETTA
Balzan
4
Ghajn Tuffieha Bay
Mdina
Sta Vennera
Vittoriosa
Marsaskala
Rabat
Zebbug
Cospicua
Zabbar
St Thomas bay
Verdala Palace
Siggiewi
Zejtun
Dinali
253 △
Zurrieg 5
Marsaxlokk
Dingli Cliffs
Hagar Qim
Birzebugga
Marsaxlokk Bay
MALTA
Blue Grotto
Filfla
1/500 000
0   5   10 km
0   5 miles

A | B | C

Isole Eolie o Lipari

Napoli

I. Filicudi
I. Alicudi

I. Panarea
I. Salina
962
I. Lipari
Lipari
I. Vulcano

I. Stromboli
924

NO

Villafranca Tirrena
Milazzo 97 17
A 20·E 90
MESSINA
29

Capo d'Orlando
Brolo 42
Tyndaris
Castroreale Terme
Falcone
Sta Lucia d. Mela
Torre Faro
Scilla
Villa S. Giovanni
1955

Patti S 113
7 13 36
Naso
Barcellona Pozzo di Gotto
Castroreale
74
Ali Terme
Tremestieri
Reggio di Calabria

Nicotera
Mileto S 182
Serra S. Bruno
Badolato
Pso di Pietra Spada 1335
Stilo
S 106·E 90

Rosarno 135
Laureana di Borrello
S 536
S 18

Gioia Tauro
Palmi
Polistena
Cittanova
S 281 Mammola
45
Grotteria
Caulonia
Rocella Ionica

Taurianova Pso di Mercante
63
Seminara
Oppido Mamertina
Gerace
Siderno
Marina di Gioiosa Ic

Bagnara Calabra
Sinopoli
Delianuova S 112
Locri
14

Gambarie
Bianco
Montebello Ionico
Bova Marina
Brancaleone Marina 97

Melito di Porto Salvo
Capo Spartivento

S. Stefano di Camastra S 113
98 27
S. Agata di Militello
S. Fratello
Naso
Tortorici
66
Novara di Sicilia
Pzo di Verna 1286
Roccalumera
Sta Teresa di Riva
120 60

Mistretta
M. Soro 1847
Randazzo
1264
Francavilla di Sicilia
Taormina
Mazzarò
Giardini-Naxos

Castelbuono
Portella Femmina Morta Miraglia
Cesarò
31 S 284
Linguaglossa
S 120

C. del Contrasto 1107
68
M. ETNA 3340
Giarre
40

Gangi
Troina
Bronte
I·3
41

Nicosia
Adrano
Regalbuto
Biancavilla
Trecastagni
Acireale
S 114

Leonforte
Agira
Centuripe
Nicolosi
Aci Trezza

95
Catenanuova
Paternò
Misterbianco
Aci Castello
Napoli

Enna 22 33
Valguarnera
S 192
Motta S. A.
CATANIA
Valletta (Malta)

15
Pietraperzia
Aidone
Ramacca
Golfo di Catania
Simeto

Piazza Armerina 64
Palagonia
S 114·E 45

Barrafranca
Mirabella Imbaccari
Militello in Val di C.
Scordia
Lentini
Augusta

Mazzarino
Caltagirone
Grammichele
Francofonte
Melilli
31

Riesi
73 57
33
Vizzini
Buccheri
986
Sortino
Floridia
6 Siracusa

Butera
36
Niscemi
Chiaramonte Gulfi
Palazzolo Acreide
Canicattini Bagni
77

Gela 52
Comiso
Ragusa
Noto
Avola 87

Vittoria
Modica
94 S 115
Rosolini

Marina di Ragusa
Scicli
Ispica
Pozzallo
Pachino
Capo Passero

Trapani
Pantelleria
Tracino
836
I. di Pantelleria

I. di Linosa
Porto Empedocle

Isole Pelagie

I. di Lampedusa
Lampedusa

ANEO

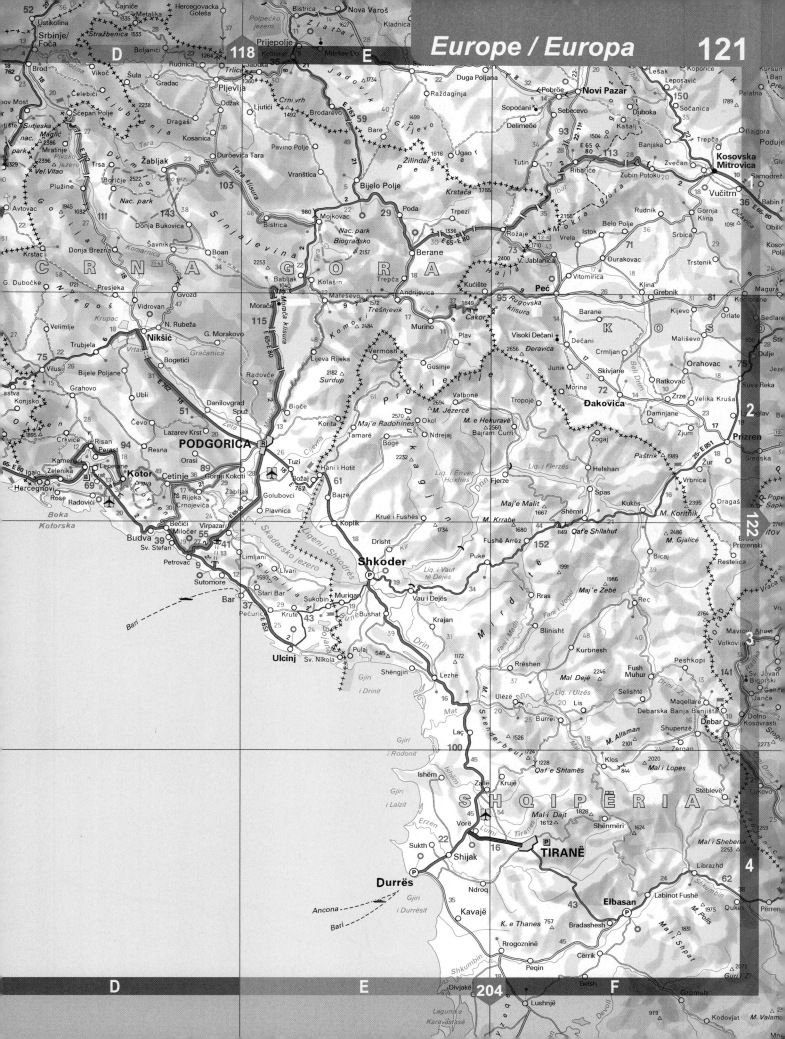

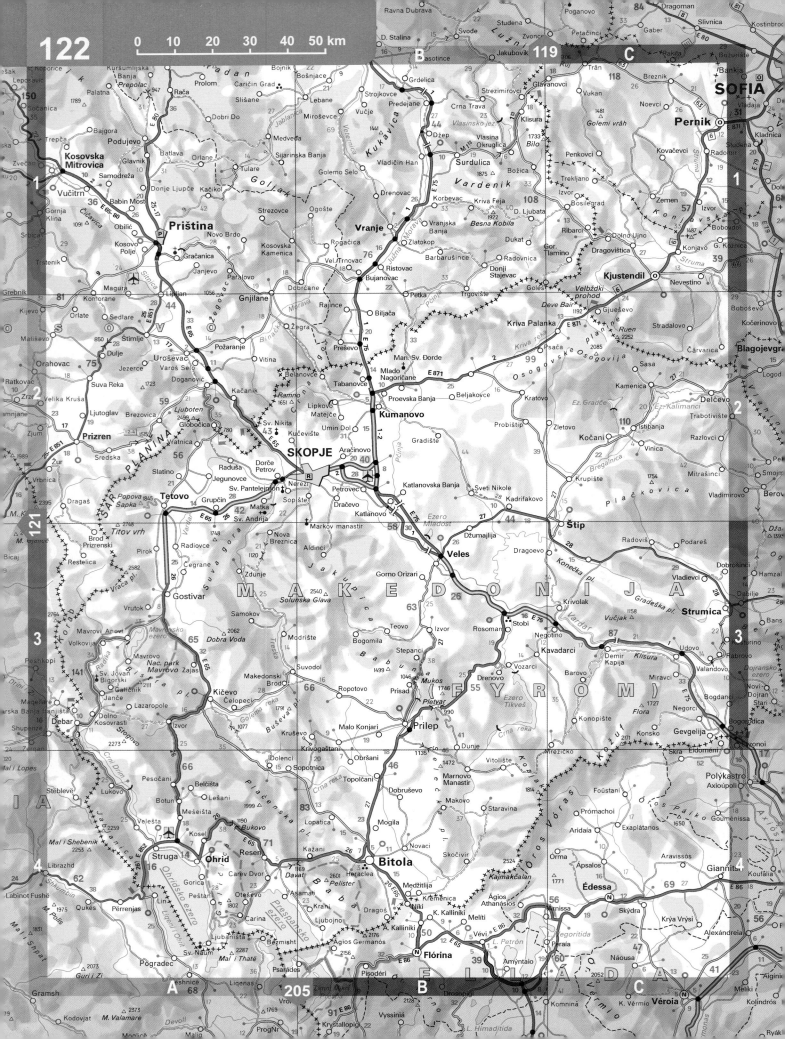

Scandinavie / Scandinavia
Skandinavien / Scandinavië
Escandinavia / Escandinávia

1 / 1 500 000

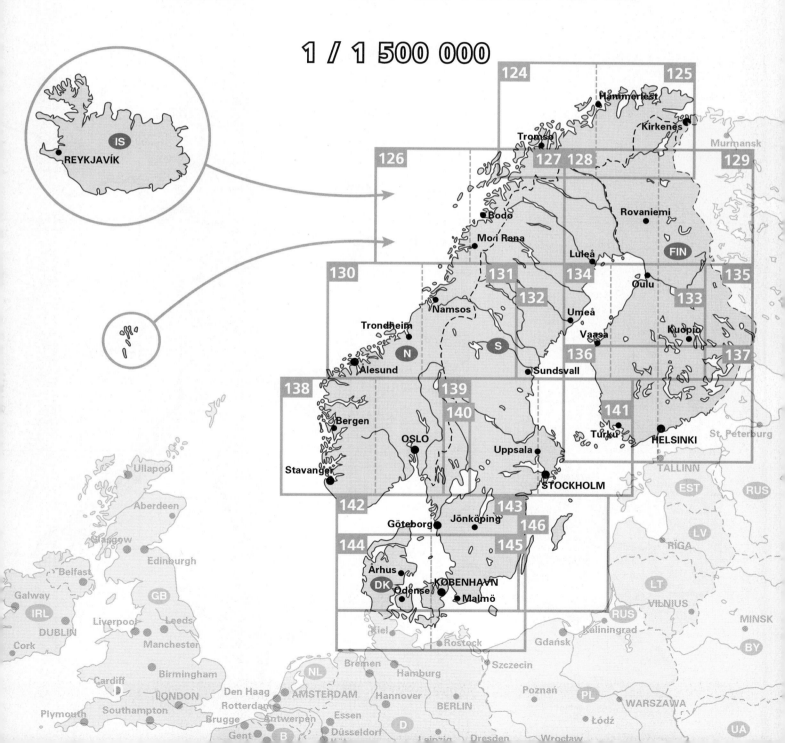

D E

Knivskjelodden
NORDKAPP
Gjesvær
Skarsvåg
Magerøya
Hjelmsøya
Havøysund
Honningsvåg
Kåfjord
Måsøy
Rolvsøya
Repvåg
Hurtigruten
Kjøllefjord
Kiljord
Gamvik
Mehamn
Sandfjellet 486
Bérlevåg
Store Molvik
Kongsfjord
Båtsfjord
Syltefjord
Hamningberg

E 69
105
E 69
Porsangerhalvøya
Veidnesklubben
Kalak
Lebesby
Ifjord
Vestertana
Nordkinnhalvøya
Duolbbadasgai'sa 668
Langfjorden

Hammerfest
Rypefjord
Kvaløya
Kvalsund
Skaidi
Komagfjord
Nyvoll
Leirbotn
Alta
Russenes
Børselv
Børselva
Stabbursdalen
Lakselv
Skuov'gilraš'sa
Vuorji 1024
1144
Seiland
Seilandsjøkelen 985
Revsbotn

Falkefjellet 548
Vardø
Kiberg
E 75
76
Rustefjelbma
Varangerbotn
Vestre Jakobselv
Nesseby
E 6
Bugøynes
Skogerøya
Vadsø
Varangerfjorden
Hurtigruten
Tana
Skipagurra
17
124
890
891
890

Nuorgam
Polmak
Korgåsen 400
Villavaara 344
Sevettijärvi
177
Kirkenes
Neiden
Hesseng
Bjørnevatn
Boris Gleb
Svanvik
Nikel
E 105
10
E 6
35

Sirma
E 6 · E 75
Utsjoki
Kevo
Kuorboaivi 443
Petsamontunturit

Børselvfjellet
Rastegai'sa 1067
Ul'ugai'sa 604
Levajok 970
Nuvvos-Ailigas 535
Valjok
Teno Paistunturit 619
Kuivi
Kevo
Ruohtir 552
970
113
74
101

FINNMARK
Bæskades 620
Karasjok
Karigasniemi
Nuhppir 516
Is'kuras 642
Masi
Karašjåkka
Partakko
Nyrud
Øvre Pasvik
Pasvikelva
18 92
93 92
92
72
Muotkatunturit 520
Kaamanen
Koarvikodds 590
Koavikodds
Sikovuono
INARIJÄRVI
Nellim
Veskoniemi
969
34
26
971
27

Vuoskuvarri 529
Kautokeinoelva
Øvre Anarjokka
Angeli
Otsamo 418
Inari
Ukonselkä
Akku
Akujärvi
Sarmitunturi 411
Lavvuoai'vi
Noarvaš 536
Maarestatunturit 575
Menesjärvi
Lemmenjoki
Ivalo
Törmänen
91
Lotta
39
955
64

Tupalaki 400
Viipustunturit 599
Repojoki
Kuttura
Kakslauttanen
Saariselkä
Raja-Jooseppi
Jonn Njuhtshoaiv 715
Øvre Anarjokka
Lappalaisten-Kesätuvat
Naltijärvi
Lemmenjoki
Lutto
110
194
71
9694
40
E 75-4

Leppäjärvi
Nunnanen
Pokka
Vuotso
Kekkosen kansallispuisto
Sompio
Nattaset 544
Talkkunapää 483
Korvatunturi 552
Saariselkä
Sokosti 718
633
956
37
Enontekiö
Pelkovuoma
144
160
32

Pallastunturi
Pallastunturi 807
Raattama
Lompolo
Tepasto
Pomokaira
Pomovaara 424
Porttipahdan tekojärvi
Lokan tekojärvi
Vintilänkaira
Varriotunturit
E 8-21
47
189
985

Kätkäsuvanto
Yli-Muonio
Muonio
Muodoslompolo
Halju 555
Kangosjärvi
Sirkka 531
Levi
Kumpuntunturi 581
Kiistala
Kaukonen
Petkula
Tulppio
128
82
79
38

1
2
3
4

0   20   40   60   80 km

A   B   C

Cercle polaire arctique

Norðurheimskautsbaugur

ISLAND

FØROYAR FÆRØERNE
(DK)

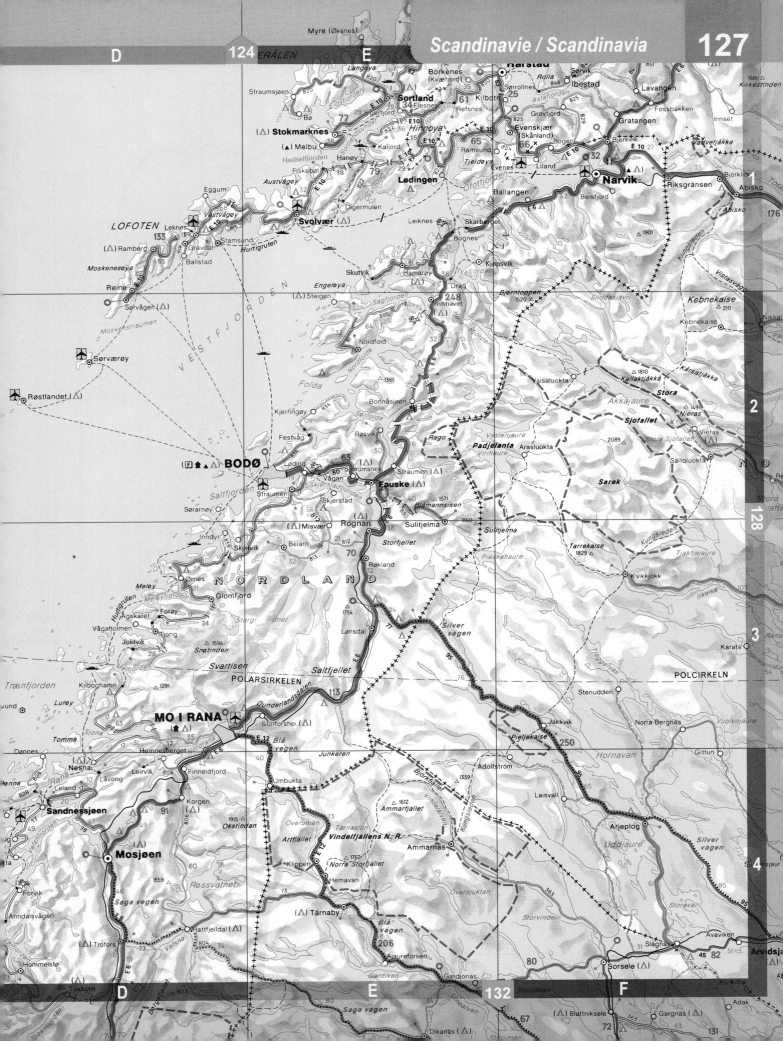

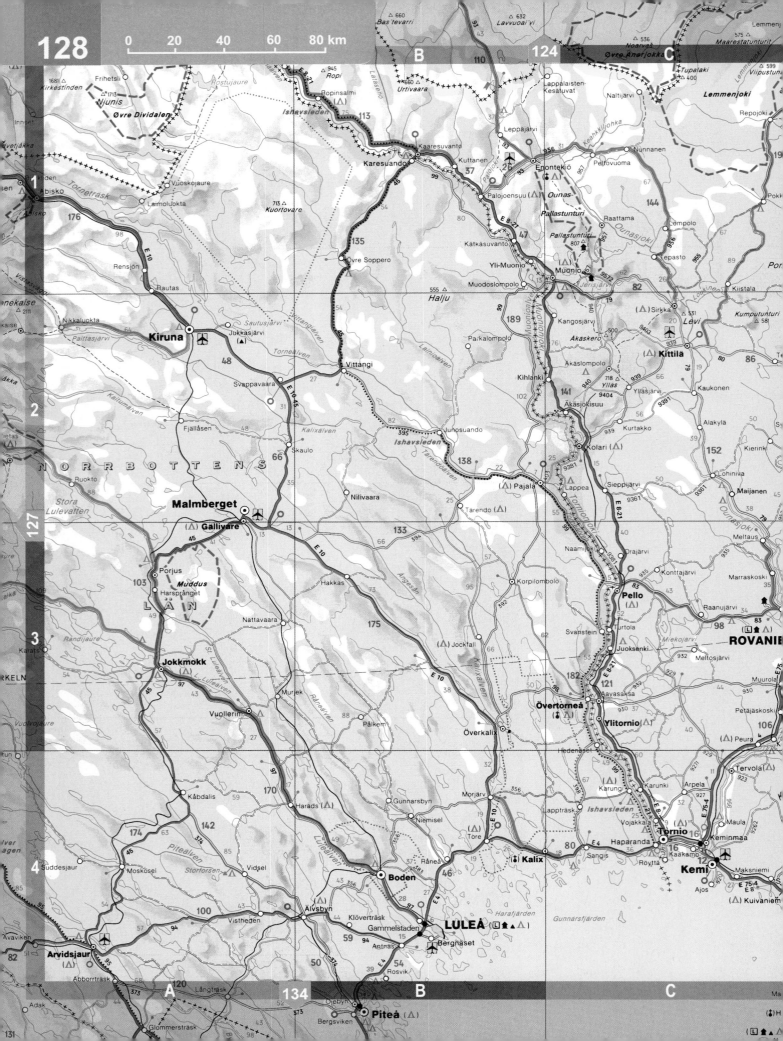

Njurundabommen

Norrfjärden D **132** E

Gnarp (△)

Harmånger (△)

Strömsbruk

Maista (▣)

udiksvall (△)

er (♦)

Enhammarsfjärden

derhamn

andarne (△)

sne

rrsundet

Gävle (L △)

Skutskär

Älvkarleby (△) *Lovstabukten*

Gävlebukten *Oregrunds-*
grepen

Skarplinge

108 Tierp **193** Östhammar (△)

rfors **191** Österbybruk 13 Gimo

/102 Vendel 292

58 Viksta *Singöl*

△ Tensta **190** Salsta 288

Björklinge 290

Bälinge **188** Rasbo 49

72 **187** Gävsta 273

186 27 *Singöl*

UPPSALA
(L △) **102**

Skokloster **184** 21 Rimbo **191**

Knivsta **181** ARLANDA

g **147** Märsta **189** 94

68 Sigtuna Norrsunda

Baista **148** Upplands- **188** Vallentuna
Väsby **176** **187**

Sollentuna 265 **185** Åkersberga
Täby E18

LÄN

Drottningholm

fred Sturehov Boo
Gripsholm Turinge **146** 222
140 **144** Tyresö *Namndöfi*

141 **STOCKHOLM**

kvarn **Södertälje** Jordbro 227

Järna **141** 39 257 57 Väster-Haninge

44 235 73
138 Sorunda Ösmo
harg△ Trullgarn

Trosa (△) *Galöf* *Mysingen*

Nynäshamn(△)

ing (L ✈)

(△) D **146** E **132**

BOTTENHAVET

BOTTNISKA VIKEN PO

(GOLFE DE BOTN

SELKÄMERI

ÅLANDS

LÄN

Åland
Ahvenanmaa

Geta

Hammarland Finström Saltvik
Storby Godby Sund
Eckerö 33 Kastelholm Vårdö (♦)

Lumparn Jomala
Lemland Lumparland

Mariehamn
(L △) *Kokarsfjärden*

Kökar

BOTTNISKA VIKEN (GOLFE DE BOTN

Ängsö

Norrtälje
(△)

Grisslehamn

Hallstavik

Väddö

Edsbro 283

280

23 76

Kapellskär

(MER BALTIQUE)

ITÄMERI

Tallinn
Helsinki

Klaipeda

Sideby 660 Honkajoki
108 270 Korvaluoma
Siikainen 2703 40
(△)Merikarvia 270 Ala-Honkajoki **Kankaanpää**
24 Leväsjoki 51 Vihteljärvi Niinisalo Hameer
Ahlainen 268 23 Pomarkku 30 Lavia Kyrösko
(△)Reposaari Noormarkku (▲) 34 88 Suodenniemi **1**
Mäntyluoto Pihlava Harjunpää Küllaa **109**
♦ ▲ △ **PORI**
(BJÖRNEBORG) Ulvila 11 Kiikoinen (△)Vammala
Luvia **49** Nakkila Kiikka
Kuivalahti Harjavalta Äetsä
62 Kokemäki Vampula
Eurajoki Kiukainen 33 **Huittiner**
12 209 Eura **65** Ala
(♦ △)**Rauma** Lappi 12 Köyliö
Kodiksami Kauttua Sakylä
Kodisjoki Pyhäjoki 213
Pyhäranta *Pyhäjärvi* Loima
196 2021 Yläne Oripää
Kalanti **Laitila** **92** *Vaskijärvi* **89** **85**
Juva *Pöytyä*
(▲ △)**Uusikaupunki** Vehmaa 194 **Mynämäki** Aura
Lokalahti Mietoinen Nousiainen **2**
Kustavi Taivassalo Masku Lieto
Velkua Askainen Raisio 51 E 18
Iniö **Naantali** **TURKU** Pargas
Brändö Rymättylä **ÅBO** Paraïnen
Kumlinge Mossala Airisto
Houtskär Nagu E 18
Houtskäri Nauvo
Delet Teili Korpo Kimito
Berghamn fjärden Korppoo Kemio
Sottunga Dragsfjärd 183
Berghamn fjärden **136**
Skärgårdshavet Dalsbro
Saaristomeri
Föglö *Gullkrona fjärd* **3**
Jurmofjärden Hango vastra

BALTIQUE)

4

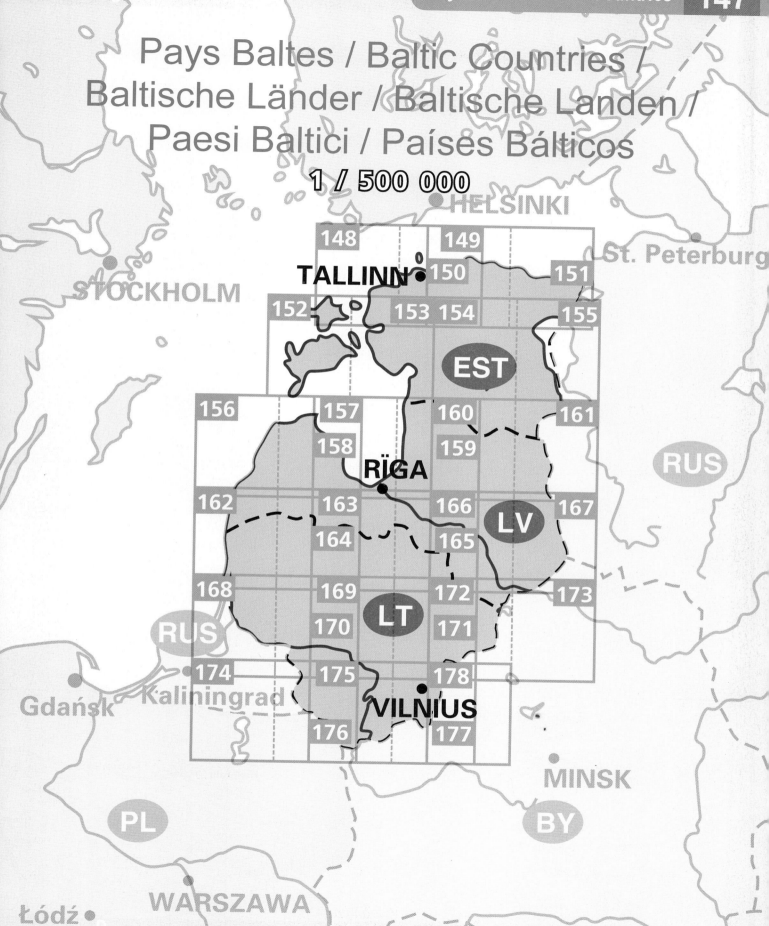

Pays Baltes / Baltic Countries /
Baltische Länder / Baltische Landen /
Paesi Baltici / Países Bálticos
1 / 500 000

HELSINKI

148 149

St. Peterburg

STOCKHOLM

TALLINN

150

151

152 153 154 155

EST

156 157 160 161

158 159

RÏGA

RUS

162 163 166 167

LV

164 165

168 169 172 173

LT

RUS 170 171

174 175 178

Gdańsk Kaliningrad VILNIUS

176 177

MINSK

Łódź PL BY

WARSZAWA

S O O M E   L A H T

Naissaar

Aegna

Prangli

Purekkari neem

Pärispea
Viinistu
Hara Laht
Tapurla
Suurpea
Käsmu
Kiiu
Aabla
Loksa
Eru Laht
Vihasoo

Tallinna Laht
Rohuneeme
Püünsi
Leppneeme
Tammneeme
Kolga Laht
Uuri
Kolga
Kolgaküla
Kõnnu
Laukasoo

Ninamaa neem
Pringi
Lubja
Randvere
Uusküla
Pedassaar
Kahala
Viti
Haabneeme
Miiduranna
Viimsi
Metsakasti
Kallavere
Neeme
Ihasalu
Valkla
Kiiu
Uuri
Kõnnu
43
Väana-Jõesuu
Muraste
Rannamõisa
Tiskre
TALLINN
Lasnamäe
Iru
Muuga
Maardu
Jägala-Joa
Kostivere
Kiiu
Kuusalu
E20
11
Türisalu
Tabasalu
Harküjärve
Laabi
Hüüru
Harku
Peetri
Loo
Saha
16
Jõelähtme
Jägala
26
Lohusalu
Keila-Joa
Väana
Lagedi
Rae
Haljava
Aruaru
Anija
Soodla veehoidla
Põhja-Kõrvemaa maastikukaitseala
57

H A R J U M A A

Kloogaranna
Karjaküla
Kila
Alliku
Laagri
Järveküla
Assaku
Lehmja
Pajupea
Järsi
Arukula
Raasiku
Lilli
13
Klooga
Vanamõisa
Männiku
Luige
Jüri
Vaskjala
Peningi
Ülejõe
Lehtmetsa
Keila
Vanamõisa
Jälgimäe
Saku
Kiili
Patika
Vaida
Kalesi
Perila
Kehra
Pikva
35
Lehola
Valingu
Lokuti
Nabala
Vaidasoo
Härma
33
Aegviidu
Ohtu
Jõgisoo
Tuula
Paekna
Piissoo
Aruvalla
25
Kose
Uuemõisa
Palvere
Alavere
Voose
Kakerdaja Raba
Kõrvemaa maastikukaitseala
Lehtse
Ämari
Kiisa
Tõdva
19
Tagadi
42
Saula
Oru
Viskla
Ravila
12
Mustjõgi
Jõgisoo
Rummu
Vasalemma
Maidla
Kurtna
Prillimäe
Pahkla
Kuivajõe
Kose
Vardja
Paunküla
Albu
Aravete
Roo
Kasepere
Laitse
Tagametsa
Äasmäe
Sütlema
Kohatu
Kohila
Hageri
Salutaguse
Lohu
Karla
Ojasoo
Paunküla veehoidla
Järva-Madise
Käravete
nalaskme
Kaasiku
Haiba
Rabivere
Pirgu
Järlepa
Habaja
Ardu
Tartussaare Raba
Kaalepi
Ahula
49
40
Riisipere
45
Purila
Roosna-Alliku
Valasti
Järva-Jaar
Turba
Varbola
Kodila
Hagudi
Juuru
37
Kuimetsa
46
Anna
Kaaruka
Kuksema
Kar
Lehetu
Alu
Uusküla
Pae
Ingliste
Toomja
14
Vahastu
Lõõla
Eivere
Viisu
40
Müüsleri
Rangu
36
Orjita
Rapla
Iira
Kuusiku
Valtu
Kaiu
Vana-Kaiu
Tarbja
Öötla
Peetri
J Ä R V A M A A
Sipa
26
23
Raikküla
Kumma
Keava
Keava Soo
Kehtna
Röa
Mäo
Särgvere
23
29
Märjamaa
3
Tamme
Lipa
Kaerepere
Hertu
Kalbu
Lelle
Väätsa
18
Paide
25
Haimre
Mõisamaa
Purku
Velise
Reopalu
Kirna
Kasti
Valgu
54
50
Käru
Lokuta
 Änari
Türi-Alliku
Koigi
Teenuse
Vigala
Lelle
Kolu
Türi
Särevere
Laupa
Taikse
Oisu
Vigala
Päärdu
Järvakandi
Eidapere
Ellamaa Raba
Ojaäärse
Kivi-Vigala
Laupa
Alamaa
Painurme
Kasukonna

D   E   F

1   2   3   4

D
E
F

1

Väike-Tütarsaar

Suur-Tütarsaar

NARVA LAHT

2

Letipea neem

Kunda Laht

Kunda
Mahu

Ojaküla
Narva-Jõesuu

15
13
Vasta
Aseri

20
Viru-Nigula
Rannu
23
Saka
Toila
Voka
Sillamäe
12
14

Kohala
62
Purtse
Aa
Pühajõe
Konju
18

Ubja
Uhtna
Erra
Varja
21
Kohtla-Järve
Kukruse
Jõhvi
Voka
22
Vaivara
Soldina

Näpi
18
E20
Lüganuse
96
Kohtla-Nõmme
Edise
Sötke
10

Sõmeru
Viru-Kabala
Sonda
Kohtla
Sompa
Sinimäe

Ussimäe
Vaeküla
Püssi
Kose

Vetiku
Ulvi
Maidla
Savala
Tammiku
33

Pajusti
Soonurme
Uniküla
Kiikla
Vasavere

Vinni
89
88
Oandu
IDA - VIRUMAA
Kurtna
Kuremäe

Viru-Jaagupi
66
Anguse
59
Tarumaa
Pagari
Illuka
52

Küti
Muraka Raba
Maetaguse
33
32

Aruküla
91
68
Roela
Tudu
Jõuga
Kuningaküla
Загривье
Сланцы (Slancy)

49
54
Oonurme
Iisaku
Jaama

Muuga
50
17
18
Vasknarva
46

Rahkla
Paasvere
35
51

Moora
17

Laekvere
21
7
Tudulinna
Alajõe
Губин Перевоз

Simuna
Venevere
Rannapungerja
Лядины

Avinurme
7

Käru
Kõveriku
Lohusuu
Kaменный Конец
Добруци

19
Adraku
22

Ulvi
16

Leedi
126
Võtikvere
Подолесе

Sädala
3

Kantküla
Vaiatu
37
Mustvee
Peipsi

34
Raja

Laiusevaldai
Torma
Könnu
Kükita

Tõikvere
Tiheda
155

Laiuse
Metsaküla
Kasepää

Võduvere
Omedu

Peipsi

0 5 10 15 20 25 km

B

C

LÄÄNEMERI

Tankuna nina

Hari
Kurk

1

28 80

Ⓜ **Kärdla**

Kõrgessaare

Lauka

Lõpe Palade

Ristna neem

H I I U M A A

Pihla
Raba

19

20

Hellamaa

Luidja 55

81

38

25

Vohilaid

Suuremõisa

5

Mardihansu
Laht

27

Männamaa

Putkaste

12 36

Heltermaa

84

83

Käina

Jausa

19

Kassari

Kassari

Kõinastu
Laid

2

Sõru

5 Emmaste

Kassari Laht

Soela Väin

Tinuri nina

Metsküla

Triigi

Panga

Leisi

Orissaare

Võhma

Suur-Rahula

Karja

Pärsama

Tagalaht

Koikla

76

Kärne

Mustjala

S A A R E M A A

Tagavere

10

Tornimäe

Käo

3

Vilsandi

86

47

55

39

Eikla

79

Laimjala

V I L S A N D I

Sauvere

Äste Haamse

Kõljala

Loonalaid

Kihelkonna

Aste

Sakla

r a h v u s p a r k

45

Kärla

78

Pähkla

Arandi

Upa

Pihtla

Püha

Sandla

Lümanda

Kõrkküla

Mullutu
Laht

76

Jõgela

Kudjape

Koimla

Nasva

Ⓜ **Kuressaare**

Sutu Laht

44

Suur

Väike-
Tulpe

Katel

Salme

4

Läätsa

Abruka

77

51

Jämaja

A

Vesiku

B

C

Iide

157

6

LIIVI I AHT

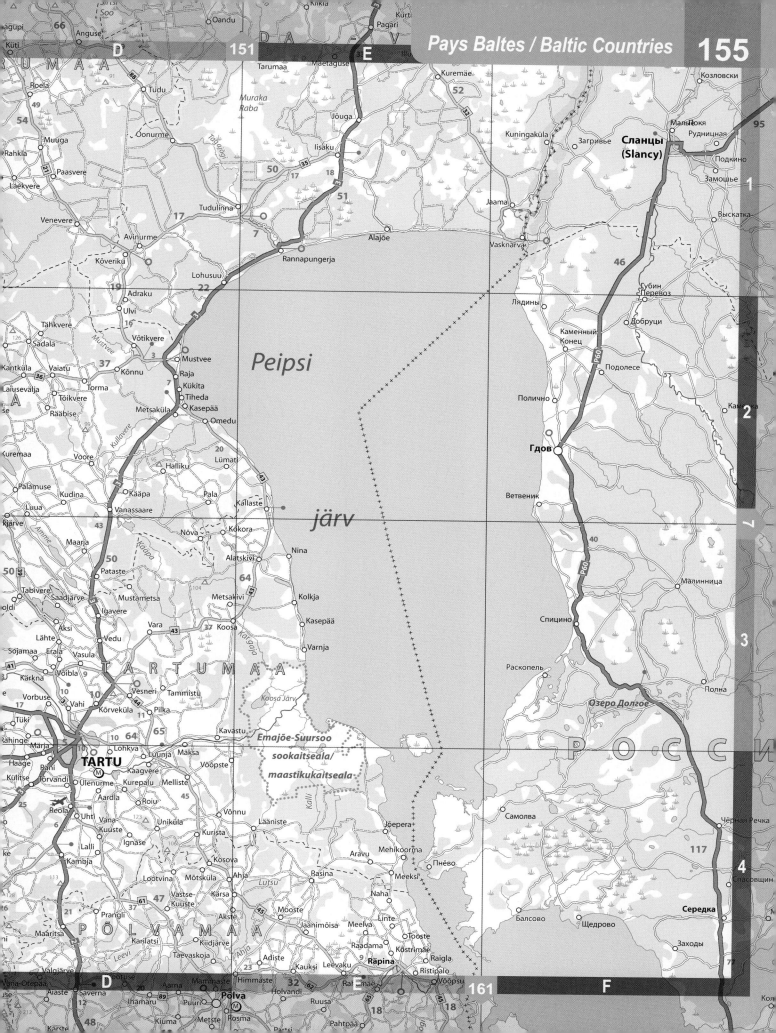

DA V E

151

E V

161

F

Peipsi

järv

Emajõe-Suursoo
sookaitseala/
maastikukaitseala

TARTU

P O C C И

Сланцы
(Slancy)

Гдов

Озеро Долгое

Середка

66
D'

Küti
Muuga
Rahkla
54
49
Roela
Anguse
Мägüpi
Sli Ha
Soo
Oandu
Kiikla
Pagari
Kurti
21
Laekvere
Paasvere
Venevere
Oonurme
Tarumaa
Maetaguse
Kuremäe
52
32
Козловски
Рудничная
Мальково
Подкино
Замошье
95
1
Muraka
Raba
Jõuga
Kuningaküla
Загривье
Выскатка
Tudu
91
88
Iisaku
50
35
17
18
Tudulinna
51
Avinurme
17
7
Köveriku
Alajõe
Jaama
Vasknarva
46
Губин
Перевоз
Добруци
Rannapungerja
Lohusuu
22
Лядины
19
Adraku
Каменный
Конец
Ulvi
16
Подолесе
Tähkvere
Võtikvere
Sadala
126
Поличино
Kantküla
Vaiatu
37
Kõnnu
3
Mustvee
36
Raja
7
Torma
Tõikvere
Kükita
Tiheda
Rääbise
Metsaküla
Kasepää
Ветвеник
Omedu
Kuremaa
Voore
20
Lümati
Palamuse
Halliku
Kudina
Pala
Käapa
43
40
Luua
Vanassaare
Kõllaste
kjärve
Amme
Nõva
Kokora
Malinnица
Малинница
50
39
Tabivere
Saadjärve
Mustametsa
Alatskivi
Nina
Патаste
Pataste
64
104
43
Igavere
Metsakivi
Lähte
Vara
Kolkja
Спицино
Спицино
Aksi
Vedu
43
37
Koosa
Kasepää
Sojamaa
Erala
Vasula
41
Võibla
9
Tammistu
Varnja
Раскопель
Раскопель
Kärkna
10
Vesneri
Pilka
10
Vorbuse
Vahi
Körveküla
11
Полна
Vähi
17
Tüki
5
10
64
65
Kavastu
Märja
Rahinge
M
10
Lohkva
Luunja
Mäksa
Самолва
Самолва
Häage
Räni
Jõepera
Küliste
Torvandi
Kaagvere
Võõpste
Mehikoorma
Пнёво
Ülenurme
Kurepalu
Melliste
25
Aardla
Roiu
45
Vana-
Kuuste
Meeksi
Reola
Uhti
Unikula
Kurista
Kosova
Aravu
Балсово
Щедрово
6
Lalli
Võnnu
Самолва
Заходы
Kambja
Lootvina
Mõtsküla
Ahja
Lääniste
Rasina
Наha
117
Спасовщина
113
128
Prangli
Karilatsi
Vastse-
Kuuste
Akste
Mooste
Meelva
Linte
Чёрная Речка
26
21
37
61
47
45
Jaanimõisa
Tooste
77
Maaritsa
Leevi
Kiidjärve
Taevaskoja
Raadama
Kostrimäe
Raigla
Vana-Otepää
48
Aiaste
Saverna
20
89
Mammaste
Aarna
Adiste
Kauksi
Leevaku
9
Räpina
Ristipalo
ke
12
Ihamaru
Puuri
Metste
Polva
32
62
Rahkmae
Võõpsu
18
45
18
Vana-Otepää
Kärste
Kiuma
Rosma
Holvandi
Pahtpää
Partsi
Koja

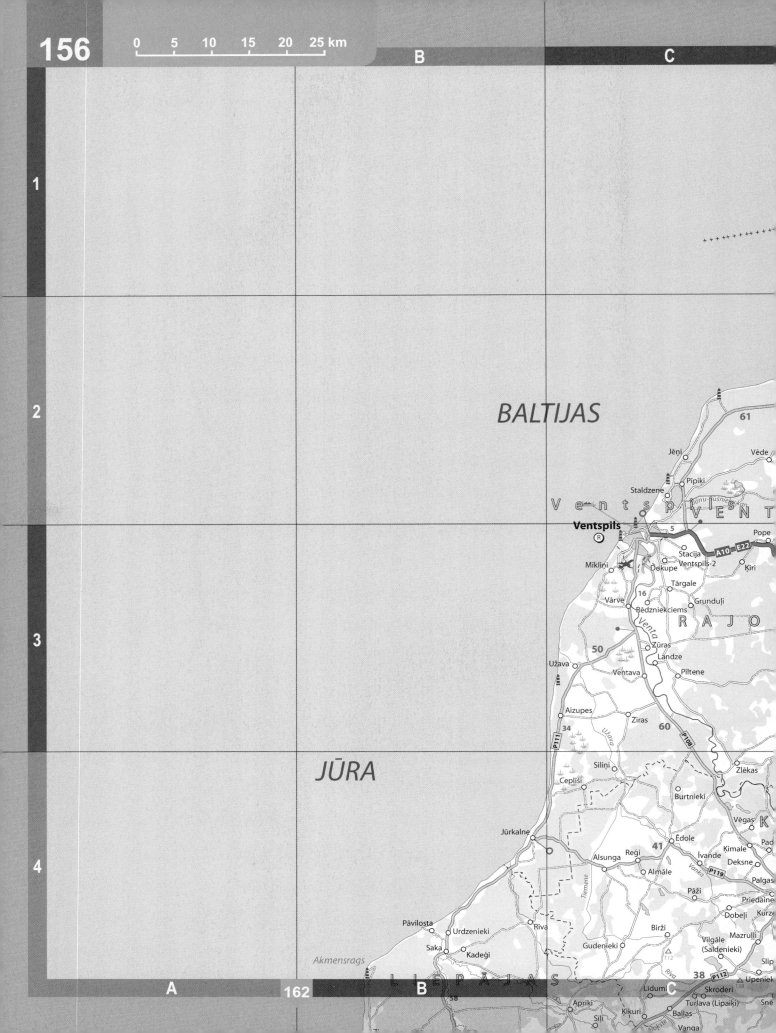

0 5 10 15 20 25 km

B

C

A10 E22 P112

BALTIJAS

61

Jēņi

Vēde

Pīpiķi

Staldzene

V e n t s p i l s V E N T

Ventspils

5

Pope

R

Stacija

Mīkliņi

Dokupe Ventspils-2

Ķiri

Tārgale

16

Vārve

Grunduļi

Rēdzniekciems

R A J O

Venta

50

Zūras

Lāndze

Užava

Ventava

Piltene

Aizupes

Ziras

60

34

P111

P108

JŪRA

Siliņi

Zlēkas

Cepliši

Burtnieki

Vēgas

K

Jūrkalne

Ēdole

41

Ķimale

Pad

Reģi

Ivande

Alsunga

Deksne

Almāle

P119

Palgas

Pāži

Priedaine

Dobeļi

Kurze

Pāvilosta

Urdzenieki

Rīva

Birži

Vilgāle

Mazruļi

Saka

Kadeģi

Gudenieki

(Sāldenieki)

Slip

Akmensrags

112

38

P112

Upeniek

L I E P Ā J A S

B

C

Līdum

Skroderi

58

Aprīki

Kikuri

Baļļas

Sne

Sīļi

Turlava (Lipaiķi)

Vanga

D 152 E

LIIVI

1

ura Kurk

Irbes Jūras Šaurums

Kolkasrags

Ruhnu

Ruhņu

Kolka

Pitrags   Slīteres
Mazirbe   Bāžu Purvs
Sīkrags   20
           nacionālais   53
P124   parks
Ziemeļnieki   Mellsils
                           (Melnsils)

Vīdale

2

Neveja   33
Nevejas Skola   TALSU
Tirumi   Gipka
Ance   Jauntīļi   Kaļķi
Jorņiņi Jaundundaga   P131
         Pāce Dundaga   Roja
              Kārļmuiža
                        Rude
57
         Tiņģere   Kaltene
Kurzemnieki P125 38 P126 Mārkciems 18
         Dūmciems Anuži   Valgalciems
51   Lubezēre
Amele   31   Jaunciems
Blāzma   Uguņciems   JŪRAS
Puzes   Nogale   Upesgrīva
Ezers   Stikļi Cīruļi Valdemārpils   9
Puze   Pūņas   Smilktini   35
                        Vandzenes Upītes   Mērsrags
Ugāle   Vidusskola
        74   Valdgale P127 Vandzene
A10 E22   Mežklabji Roceži Lādzere
Lakšezers   R 6 Laidze   Engures
Usma   Talsi Paugurciems Laukmaļi Ezers
Gaiļi   Spāre   Ratnieki   Lauciene Pļavas Bērzciems
        38   Pastende 4 Ieleja RAJONS 29
Usmas   Mundigciems Lauciene
                Aizupes Pansionāts
Dārziņi Ezers (Mazgavilnieki) Dižstende Dursupe 43 Bazāni
        Līči Lībagi Balgale P128
15   Stende Lēdas   Engure
        Jaunpagasts 22 Zentene Pines
51   Strazde   Dzirciems Kesterciems
P120   Veģi Varoņi Cēre Lamiņi Airītes Plieņciems
LDĪGAS Renda Valgale 64 Priedes Bebrupe Apšuciems
36   Salmiņi Sabile Rūmene Viljete Kaivē Sēme 16 Lāčupīte
        Kārkli   5 Kandava   Klapkalnciems 22 P128 35
Veldze (Rumbenieki) 23 P130 Pūre Dumbrāji Induļi Ezerkauki Rauda Ragaciems
Mežvalde   19 Valdeķi Gobas 23 Milzkalne Lapmežciems
Venta Abele Cīruļi Matkule Kukšas Lubas Pārupe Bērzāji
57 P121 Kabile TUKUMA 14 Abavnieki 5 Tukums Smārde
Sātiņi Airītes Vālodzes Vāne Zemīte Kīši Tume Garauši 21
Bauņi Dzelmes Lāčkalni Kinguti Grenči P121 Sāti Vienība 24
Rogas Ēdas Kārkliņi Zante Varieba Irlava Slampe Avoti

158

3

4

J JŪR

Slokas Ezers Kūdra

A10 E22

Kēmeru nacionalais parks 1.5

163 F

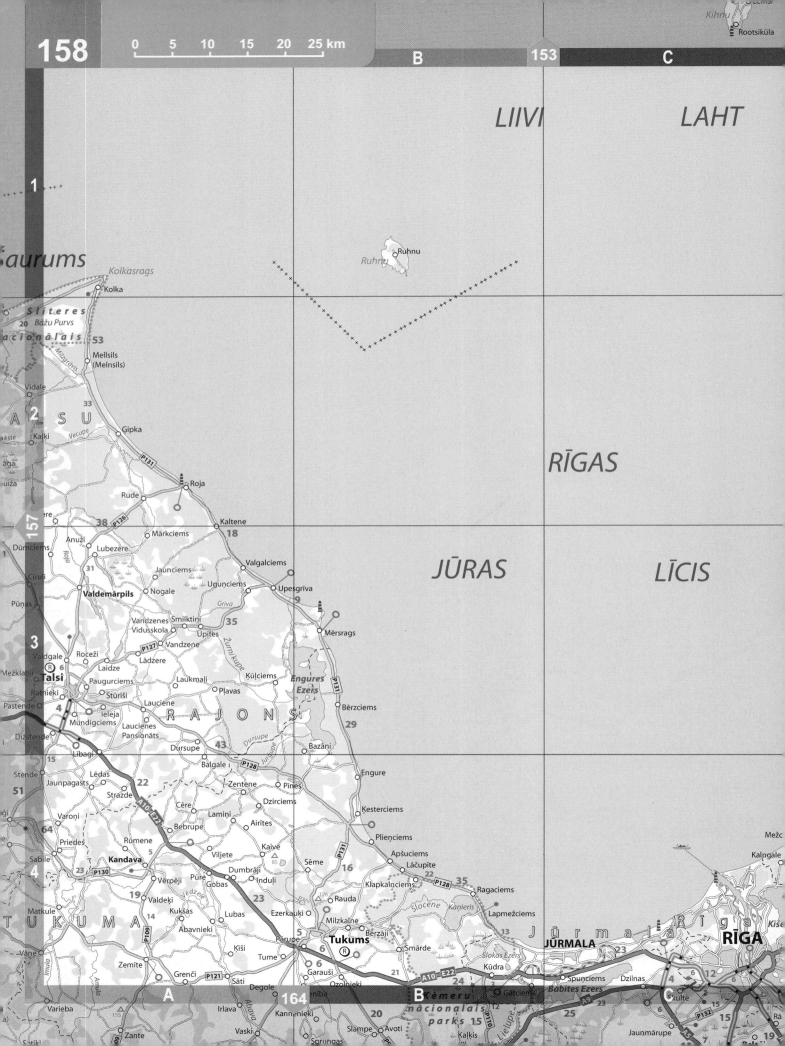

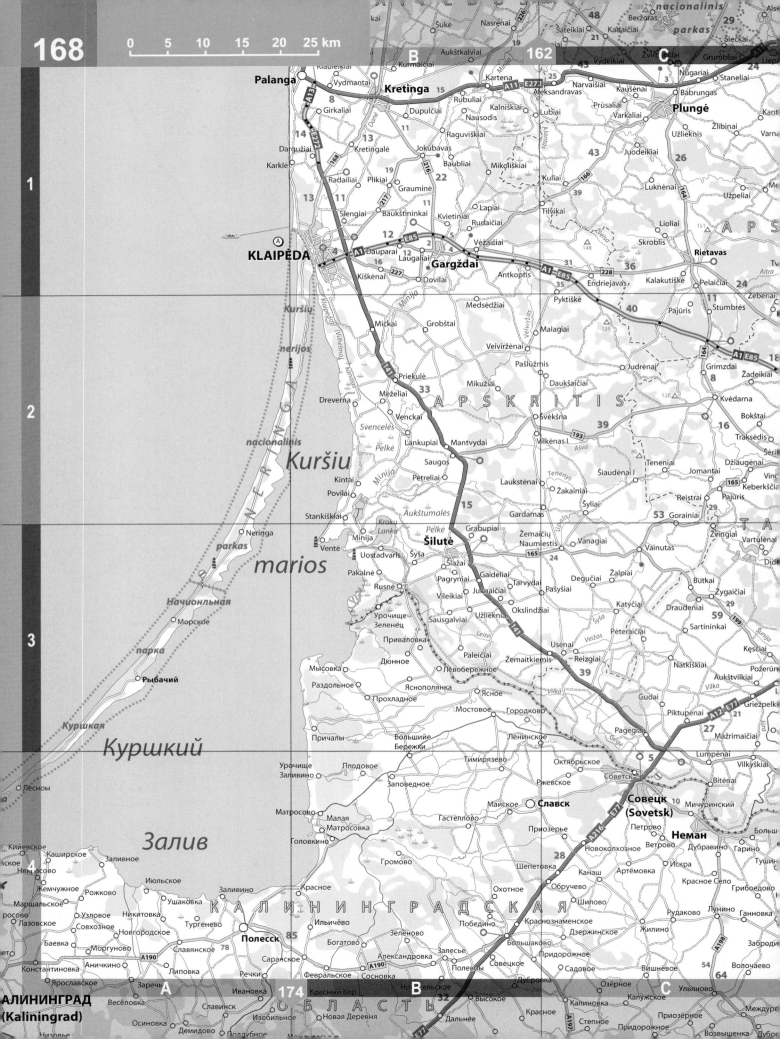

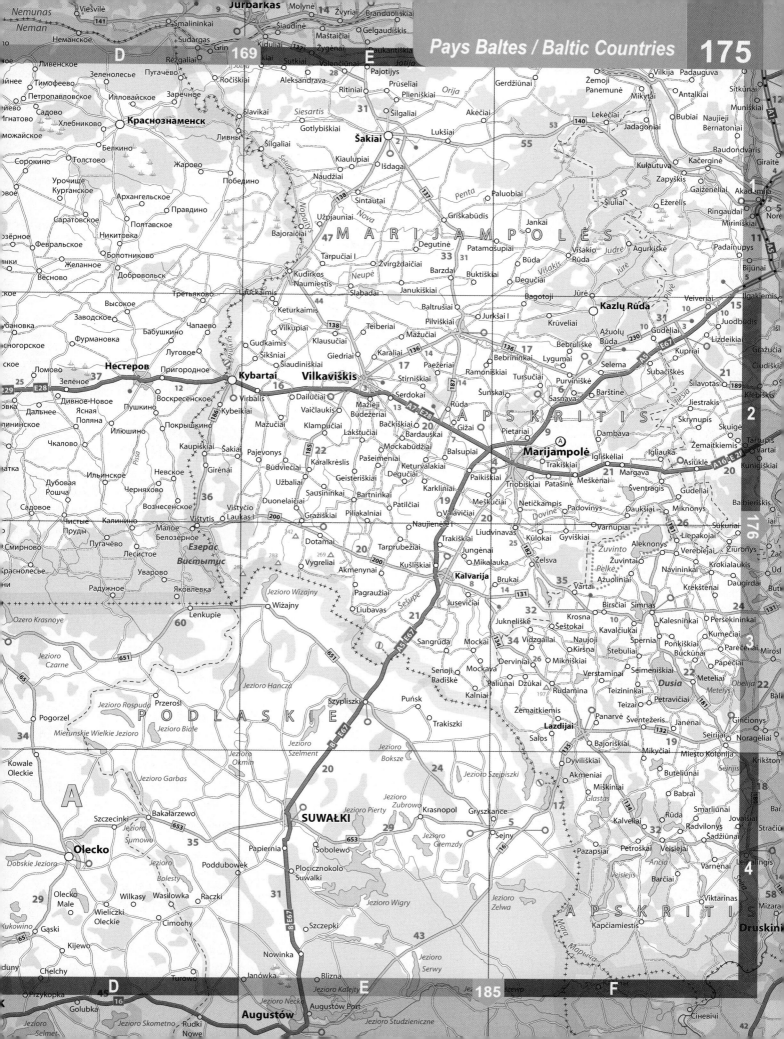

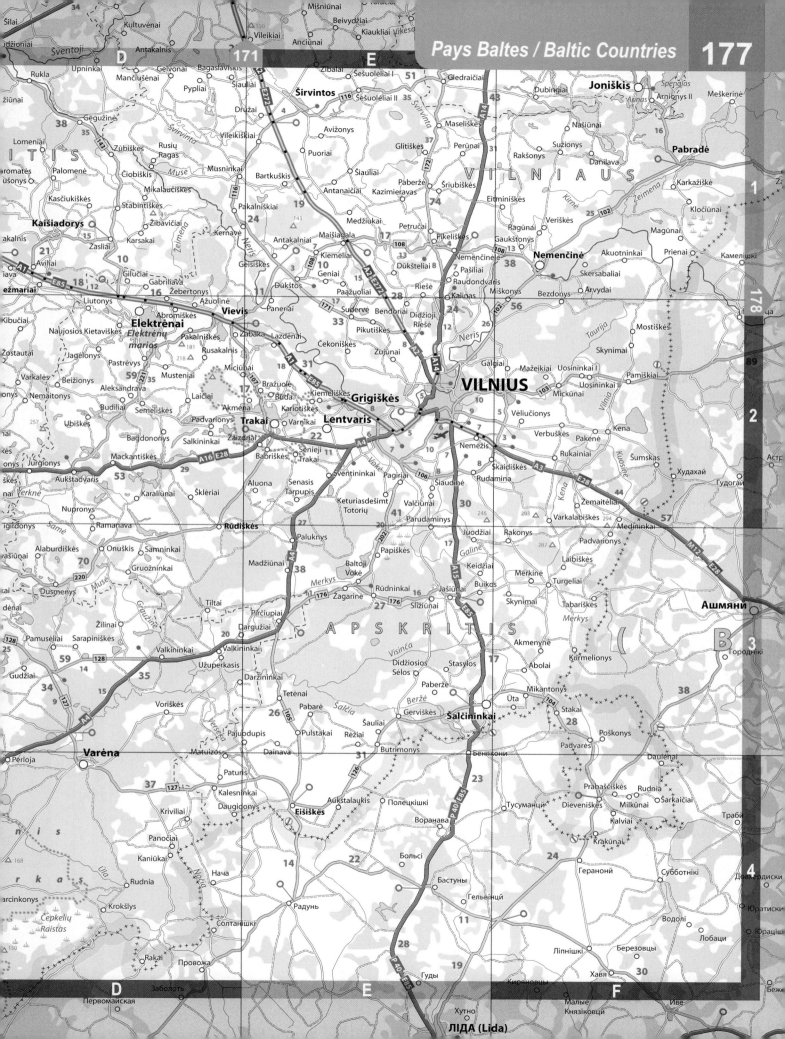

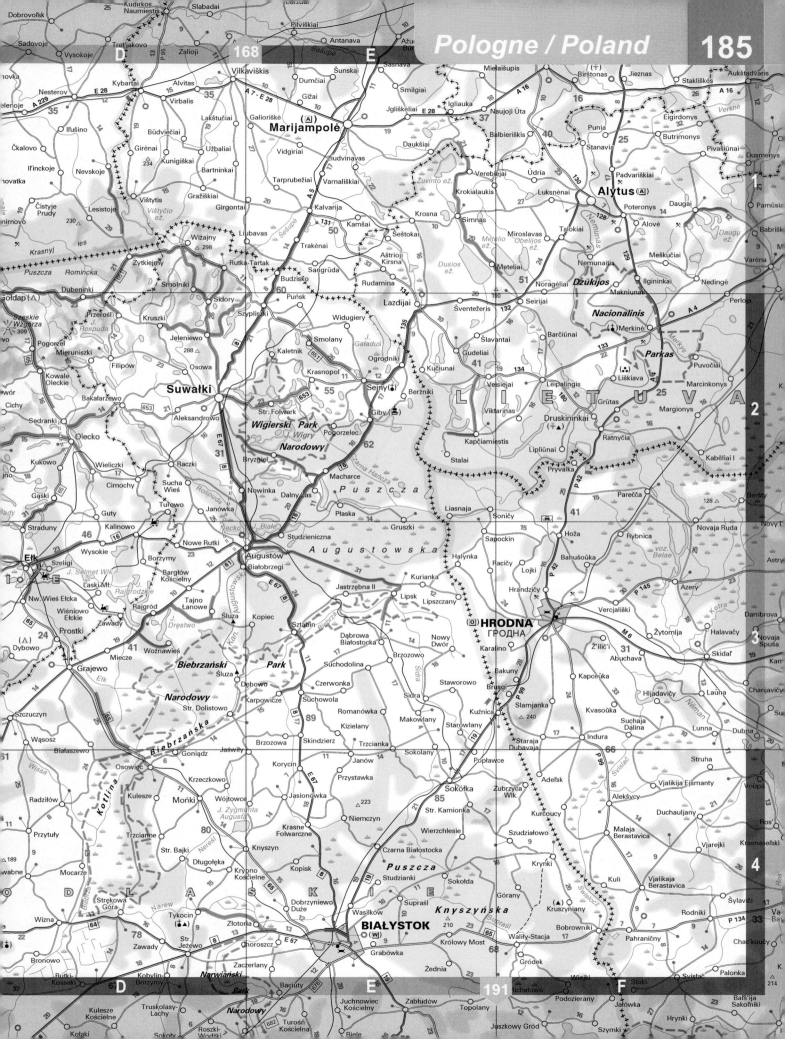

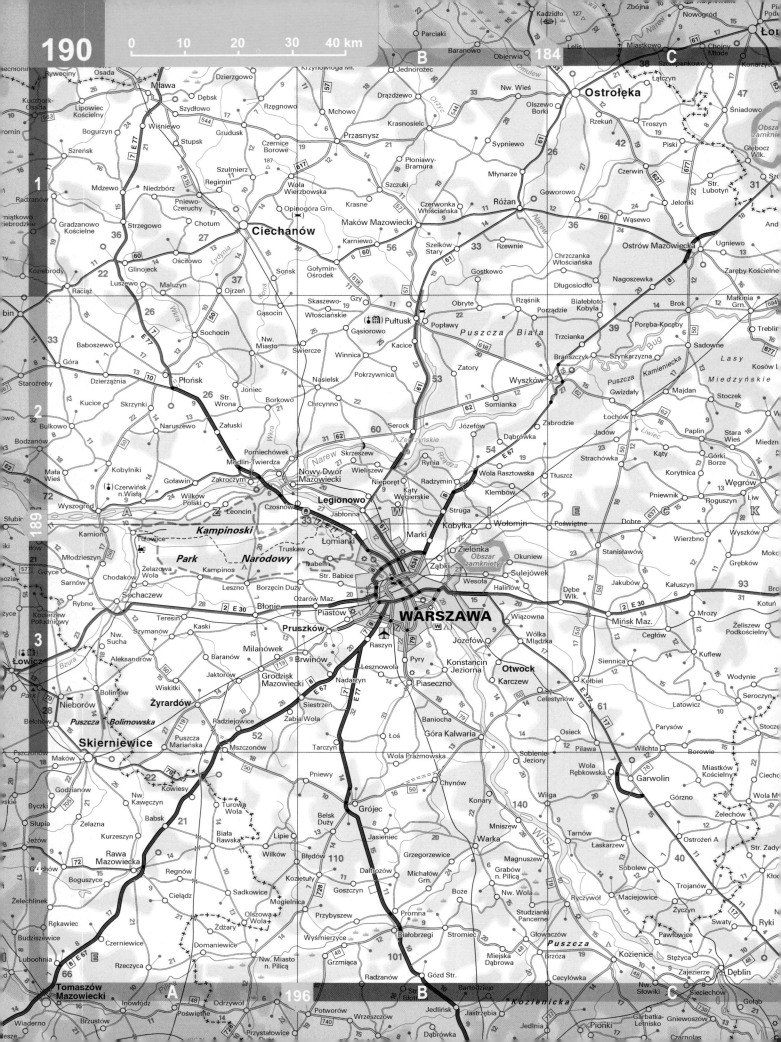

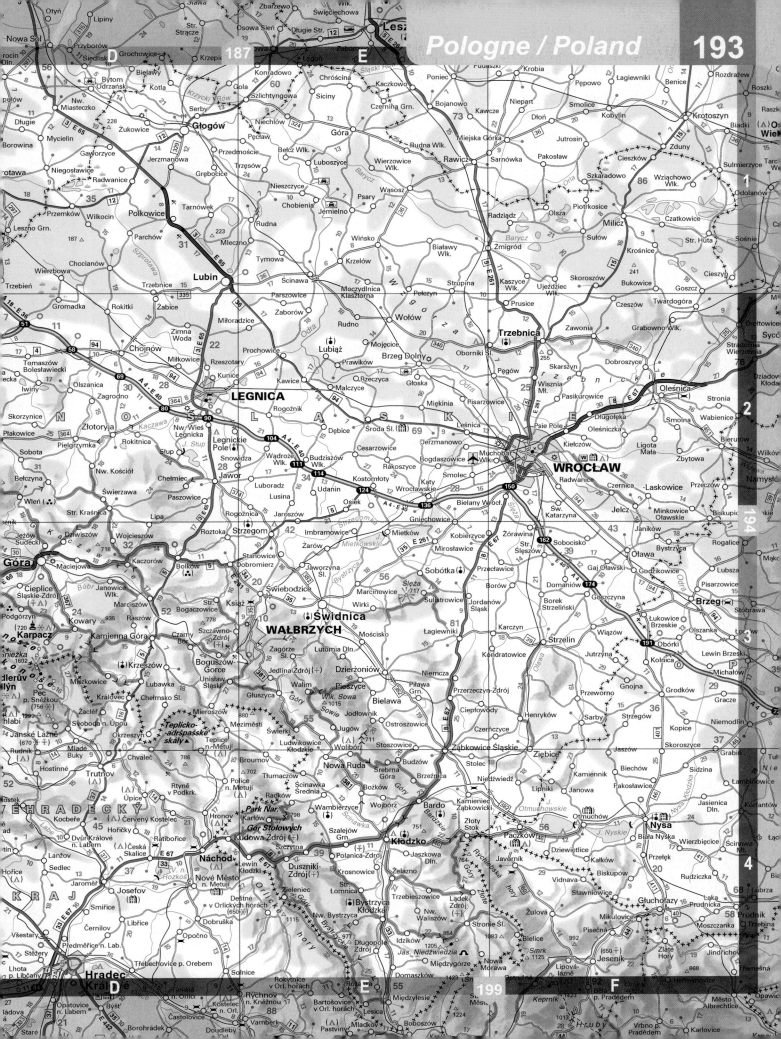

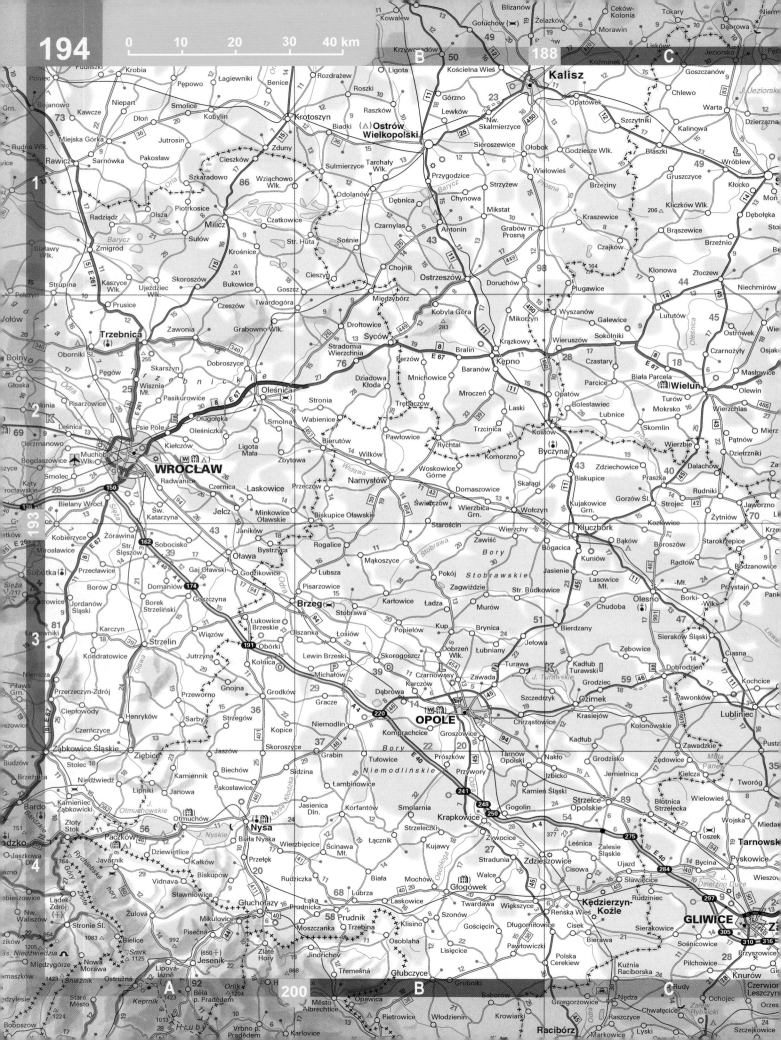

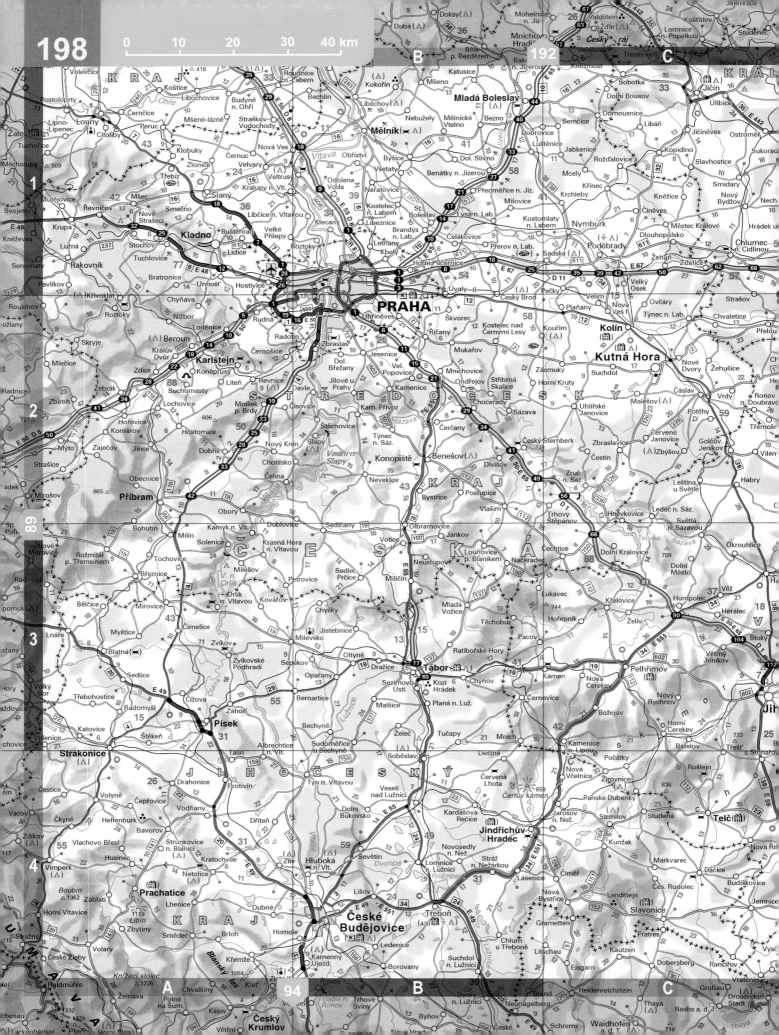

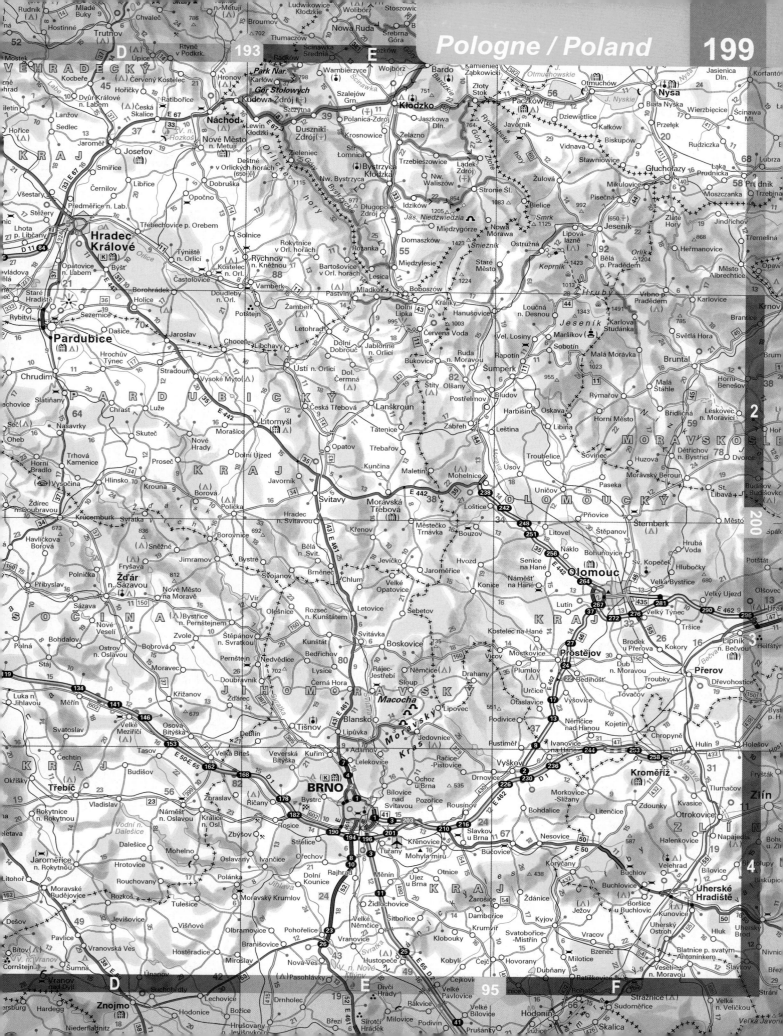

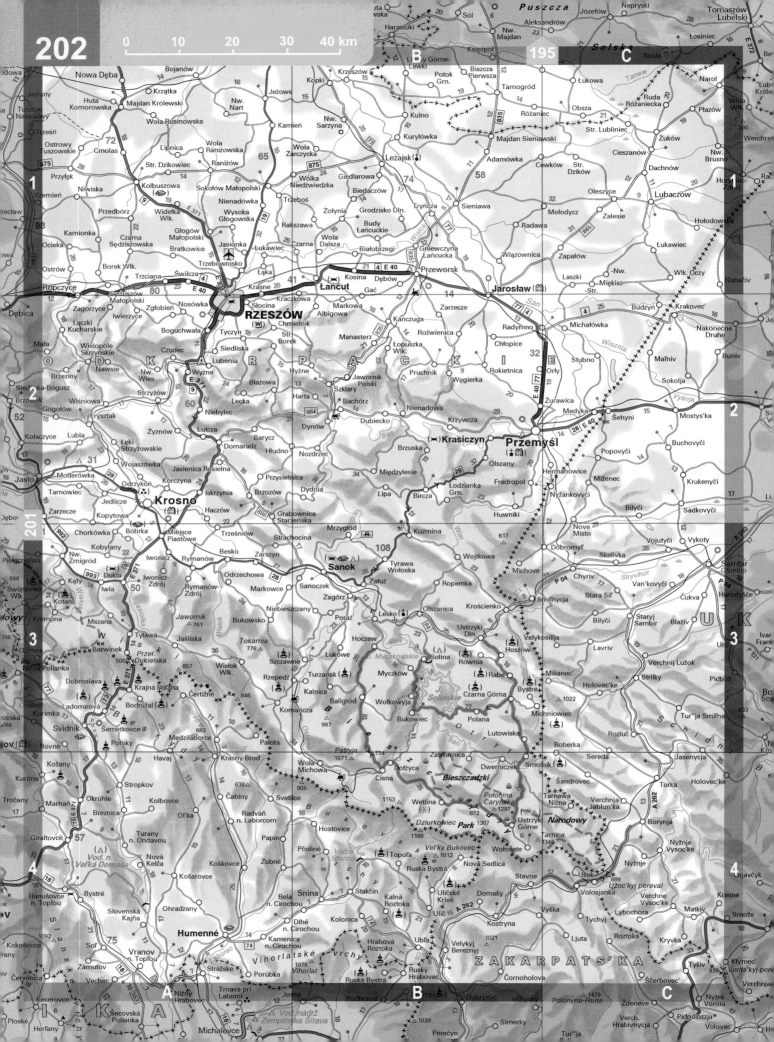

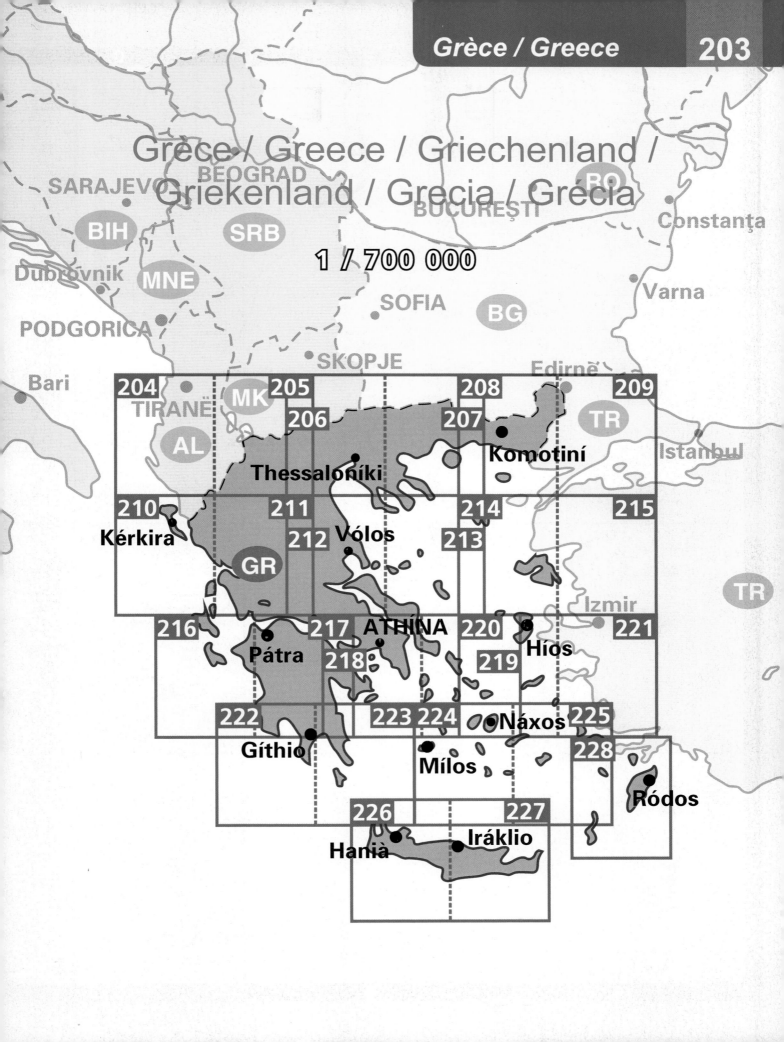

Grèce / Greece / Griechenland / Griekenland / Grecia / Grécia

1 / 700 000

SARAJEVO

BEOGRAD

BUCUREŞTI

Constanţa

BIH

SRB

RO

Dubrovnik

MNE

PODGORICA

SOFIA

Varna

BG

Bari

SKOPJE

Edirne

204

TIRANË

MK

205

208

209

206

207

TR

Istanbul

AL

Komotiní

Thessaloníki

210

211

214

215

Kérkira

212

213

Vólos

GR

Izmir

TR

216

217

ATHÍNA

220

221

Pátra

218

219

Híos

222

223

224

225

Náxos

Gíthio

228

Mílos

Ródos

226

227

Haniá

Iráklio

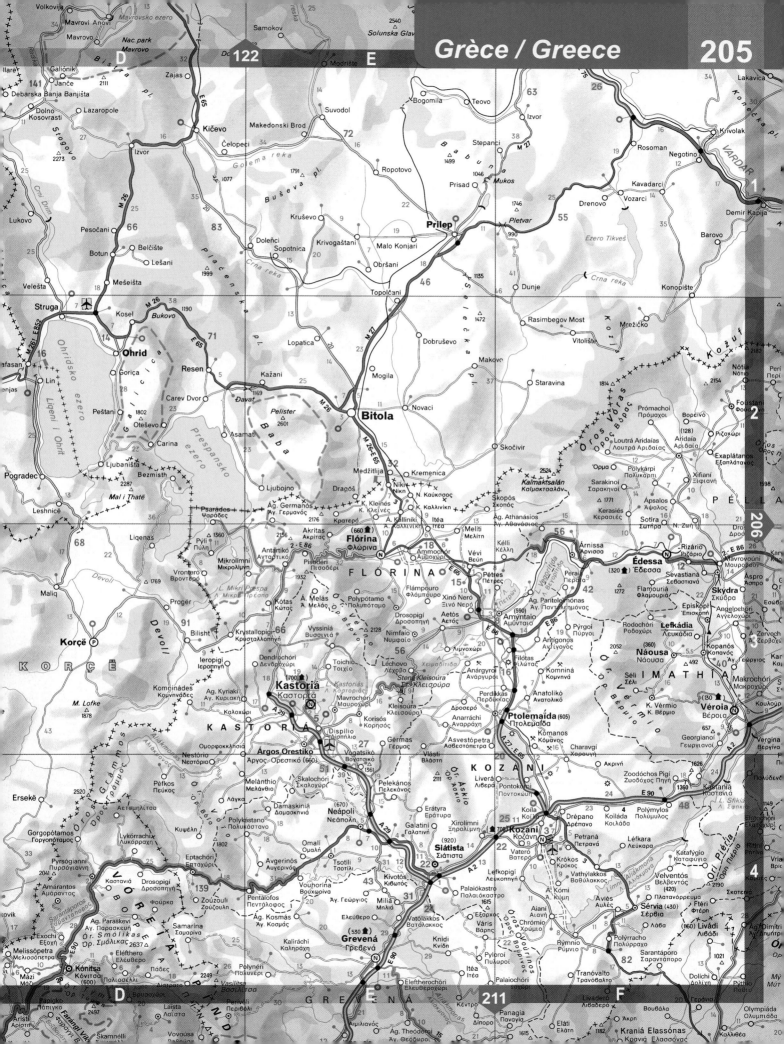

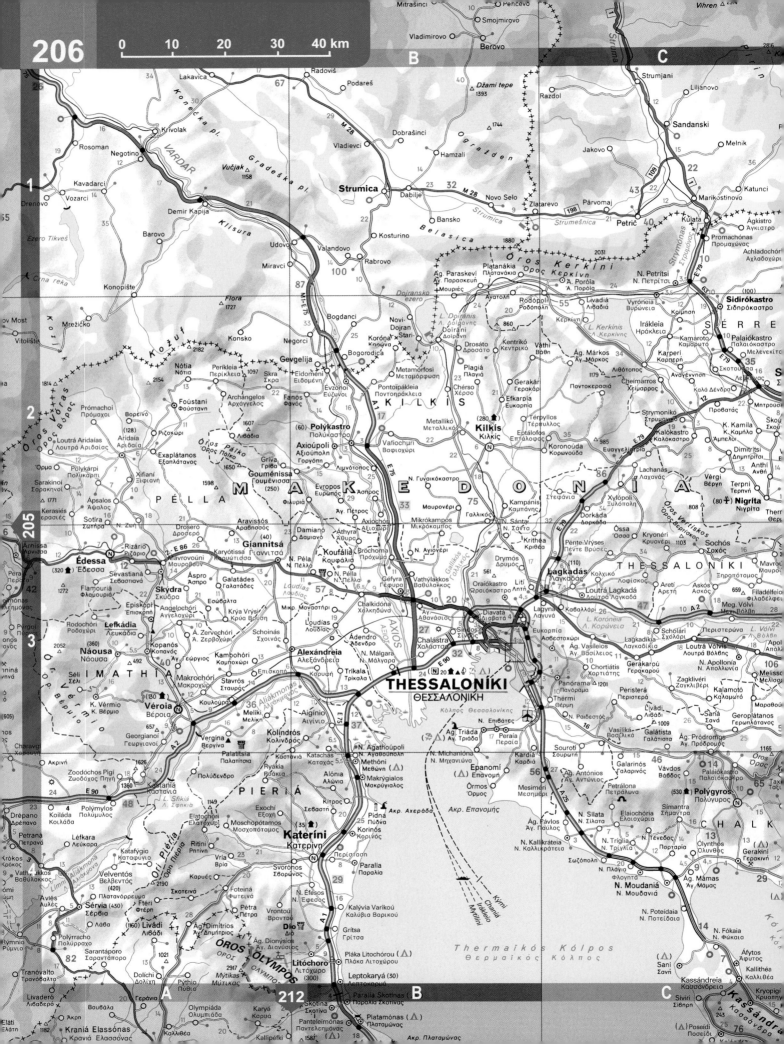

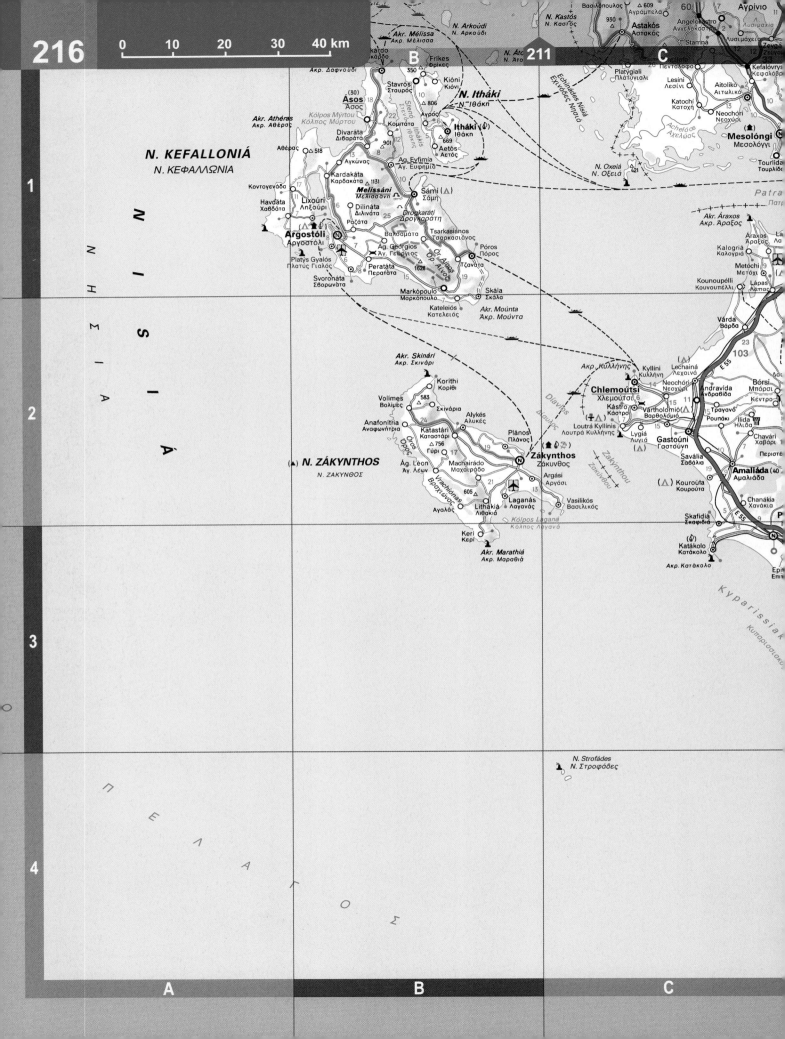

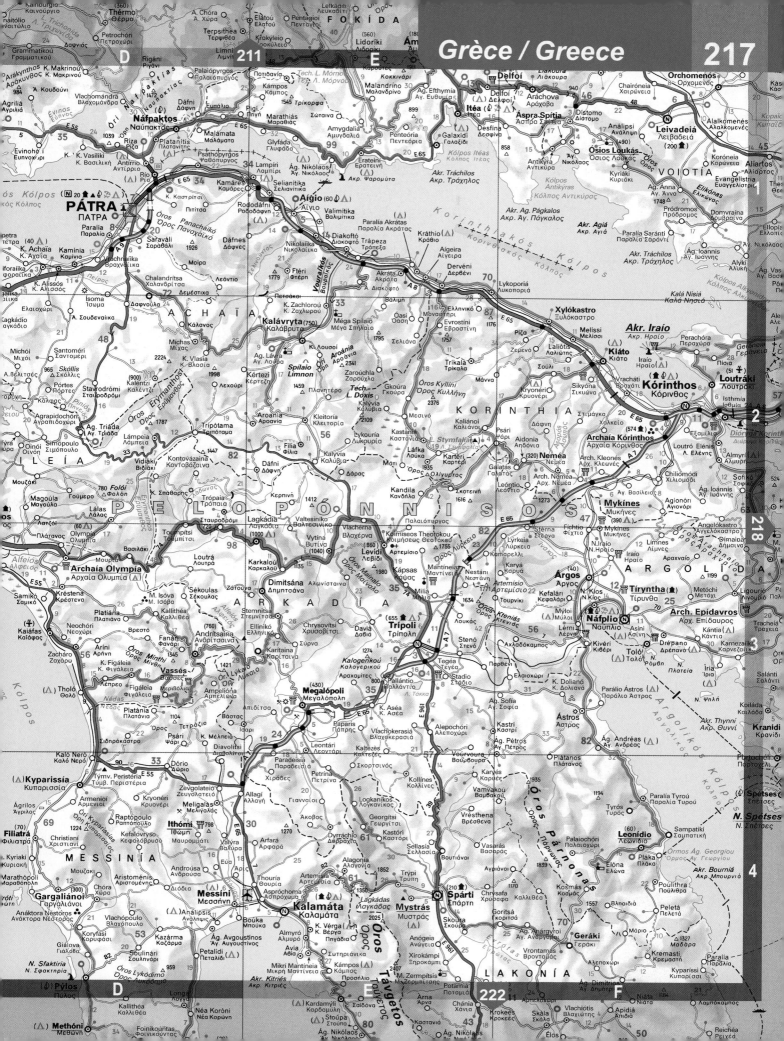

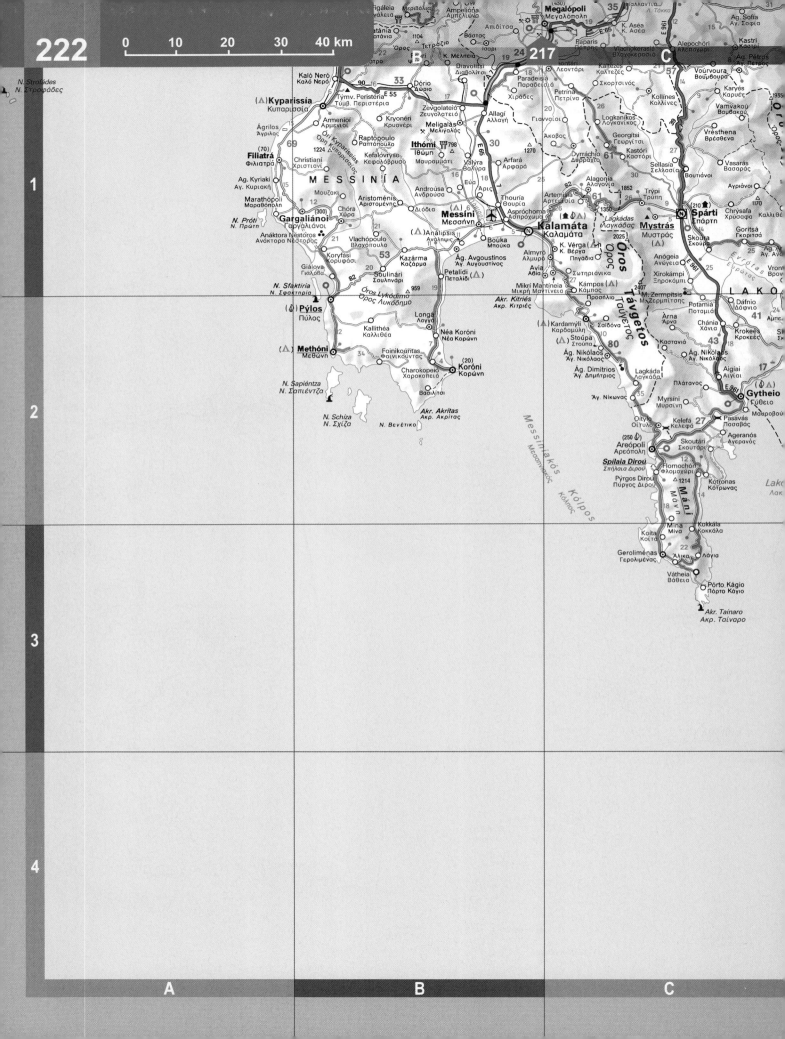

0 10 20 30 40 km

N. Strofádes
Ν. Στροφάδες

A

B

C

1

2

3

4

Kaló Neró
Καλό Νερό

(Δ)Kyparissía
Κυπαρισσία

Filiatrá
Φιλιατρά

Ag. Kyriaki
Αγ. Κυριακή

Marathópoli
Μαραθόπολη

Gargaliánoi
Γαργαλιάνοι

N. Próti
Ν. Πρώτη

Anáktora Néstoros
Ανάκτορα Νέστορος

Gialova
Γιάλοβα

N. Sfaktiría
Ν. Σφακτηρία

(Δ) Pylos
Πύλος

(Δ) Methóni
Μεθώνη

N. Sapiéntza
Ν. Σαπιέντζα

N. Schíza
Ν. Σχίζα

N. Βενέτικο

Ágrilos
Άγριλος

Armenioí
Αρμενιοί

Raptópoulo
Ραπτόπουλο

Christiani
Χριστιάνη

Kefalóvryso
Κεφαλόβρυσο

Mouzaki
Μουζάκι

Aristoménis
Αριστομένης

Chóra
Χώρα

Koryfási
Κορυφάσι

Vlachópoulo
Βλαχόπουλο

Kazárma
Καζάρμα

Soulinári
Σουλινάρι

Óros Lykódimo
Όρος Λυκόδημο

Kallithéa
Καλλιθέα

Longá
Λογγά

Foinikoúntas
Φοινικούντας

Charokopeió
Χαροκοπειό

Vasilítai
Βασιλίται

Akr. Akrítas
Ακρ. Ακρίτας

Néa Koróni
Νέα Κορώνη

Koróni
Κορώνη

MESSINÍA

Óri Kyparissías
Όρη Κυπαρισσίας

Kryonéri
Κρυονέρι

Meligalás
Μελιγαλάς

Ithómi
Ιθώμη

Mavromáti
Μαυρομάτι

Androúsa
Ανδρούσα

Diódia
Διόδια

Messíni
Μεσσήνη

Análipsis
Ανάληψις

Boúka
Μπούκα

Ág. Avgoustínos
Άγ. Αυγουστίνος

Petalidi
Πεταλίδι

Dório
Δώρι

Zevgolateió
Ζευγολατειό

Allagí
Αλλαγή

Vályra
Βαλύρα

Arfará
Αρφαρά

Eúa
Εύα

Thouría
Θουρία

Aspróchoma
Ασπρόχωμα

Kalamáta
Καλαμάτα

K. Vérga
Κ. Βέργα

Almyró
Αλμυρό

Avia
Αβία

Sotirianika
Σωτηριάνικα

Mikrí Mantíneia
Μικρή Μαντίνεια

Kámpos
Κάμπος

Akr. Kitriés
Ακρ. Κιτριές

Kardamyli
Καρδαμύλη

Stoúpa
Στούπα

Áq. Nikólaos
Άγ. Νικόλαος

Áq. Dimítrios
Άγ. Δημήτριος

Lagkáda
Λαγκάδα

Myrsíni
Μυρσίνη

Oítylo
Οίτυλο

Areópoli
Αρεόπολη

Spílaia Diroú
Σπήλαια Διρού

Pýrgos Diroú
Πύργος Διρού

Mina
Μίνα

Koita
Κοίτα

Gerolimémas
Γερολιμένας

Vátheia
Βάθεια

Akr. Taínaro
Ακρ. Ταίναρο

Pórto Kágio
Πόρτο Κάγιο

Kokkála
Κοκκάλα

Láqia
Λάγια

Álika
Άλικα

Máni
Μάνη

Kótronas
Κότρωνας

Skoutári
Σκουτάρι

Kelefá
Κελεφά

Pasavás
Πασαβάς

Ageranós
Αγερανός

Gytheio
Γύθειο

Aigíai
Αίγιαι

Plátanos
Πλάτανος

Krokeés
Κροκεές

Chánia
Χάνια

Potamiá
Ποταμιά

Dáfnio
Δάφνιο

Kokkála
Κοκκάλα

Megalópoli
Μεγαλόπολη

Paradeisiá
Παραδεισιά

Diavolítsi
Διαβολίτσι

Leontári
Λεοντάρι

Skortsinós
Σκορτσινός

Petrina
Πετρίνα

Logkanikós
Λογκανικός

Dyrráchio
Δυρράχιο

Alagonía
Αλαγονία

Artemisía
Αρτεμισία

Lagkádas
Λαγκάδας

Mystrás
Μυστράς

Anógeia
Ανώγεια

Xirokámpi
Ξηροκάμπι

M. Zerrmpitsis
Μ.Ζερμπίτσης

Proσήλιο
Προσήλιο

Árna
Άρνα

Kastaniá
Καστανιά

Lagkáda
Λαγκάδα

Áq. Níkonas
Άγ. Νίκωνας

Georgítsi
Γεωργίτσι

Kastóri
Καστόρι

Sellasia
Σελλασία

Voutiánoi
Βουτιάνοι

Trýpi
Τρύπη

Sparti
Σπάρτη

Chrýsafa
Χρύσαφα

Αg. Αν

Goritsá
Γκοριτσά

Evrótas
Ευρώτας

Oros Tävgetos
Όρος Ταΰγετος

LAKO

Vourvoura
Βούρβουρα

Karyés
Καρυές

Vamvakoú
Βαμβακού

Vrésthena
Βρέσθενα

Vasarás
Βασαράς

Agriánoi
Αγριάνοι

Kastri
Κάστρι

Ag. Sofía
Αγ. Σοφία

Ag. Pétros
Αγ. Πέτρος

Vlachokerasiá
Βλαχοκερασιά

Kaltezés
Καλτεζές

Kollínes
Κολλίνες

K. Ásea
Κ. Άσέα

K. Méleia
Κ. Μέλεια

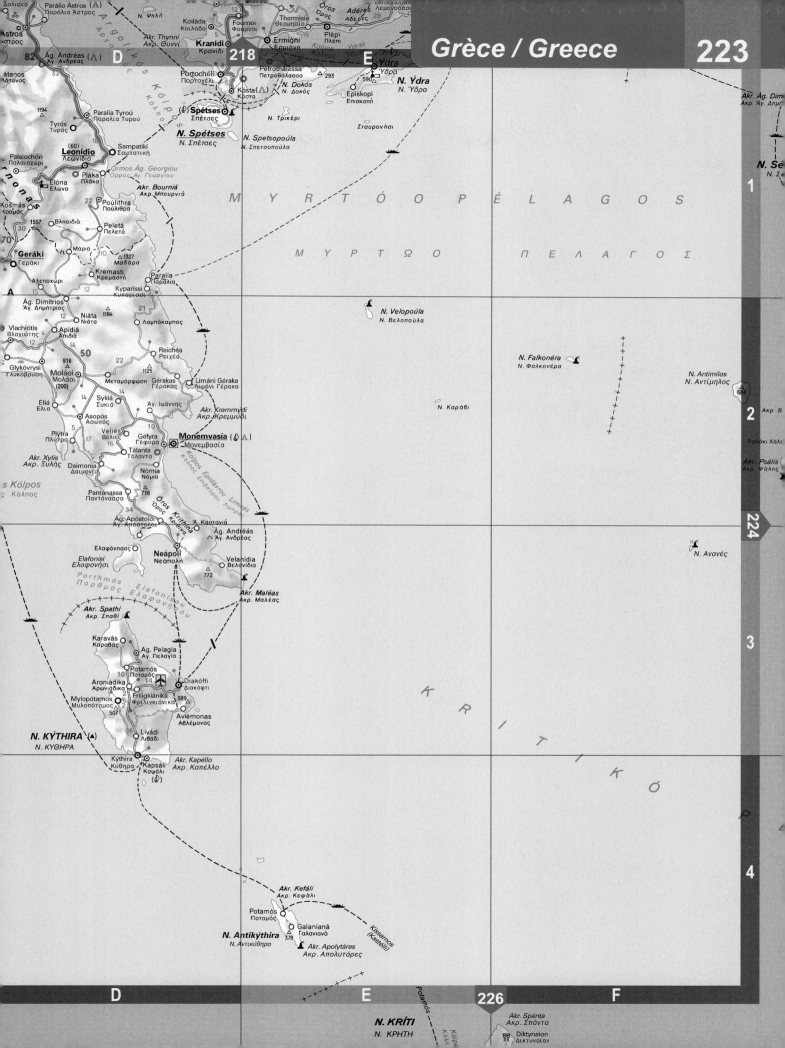

Paralío Astros
Paράλιο Άστρος
N. Ψηλή
Koiláda
Κοιλάδα
Fournoi
Φούρνοι
Thermisia
Θερμισία
Óros
Óρoς
Adéres
Adέρες
N. Sé

Akr. Thynni
Akρ. Θυννί
Kranídi
Κρανίδι
218
Ermióni
Ερμιόνη
Plépi
Πλέπι
Ydra
Ύδρα
E
Akr. Ag. Dim
Akρ. Αγ. Δημπ

Ág. Andréas (△)
Αγ. Ανδρέας
82
D
Petrothalassa
Πετροθάλασσα
Ydras
293
N. Ydra
N. Ύδρα
Akr. Ág. Dim
Akρ. Αγ. Δημπ

Portochéli
Πορτοχέλι
N. Sé
N. Σ

Astros
Άστρος
Kósta (△)
Κόστα
N. Dokós
N. Δοκός
590
Episkopí
Επισκοπή
N. Ydra
N. Ύδρα

1194
Paralía Tyroú
Παραλία Τυρού
Spétses
Σπέτσες
N. Trikéri
N. Τρικέρι
Stavronísi
Σταυρονήσι

Tyrós
Τυρός
18
N. Spétses
N. Σπέτσες
N. Spetsopoúla
N. Σπετσοπούλα

Palaiochóri
Παλαιοχώρι
(60)
Sampatikí
Σαμπατική

Leonídio
Λεωνίδιο
Plaka
Πλάκα
16
Ormos Ag. Georgiou
Όρμος Αγ. Γεωργίου
MYRTÓ O PÉLAGOS

Elóna
Ελώνα
Poúlithra
Πούλιθρα
Akr. Bourniá
Akρ. Μπουρνιά
1

Kosmás
Κοσμάς
22
ΜΥΡΤΩΟ ΠΕΛΑΓΟΣ

1557
Vloidiá
Βλοιδιά
Peletá
Πελετά

30
70
Mário
Μάριο
Paralía
Παραλία

Geráki
Γεράκι
Kremasti
Κρεμαστή
1327
Μαδάρα
N. Velopoúla
N. Βελοπούλα

A
Alepochóri
Αλεποχώρι
Kyparíssi
Κυπαρίσσι

Ág. Dimítrios
Αγ. Δημήτριος
Niáta
Νιάτα
1184
Lampókampos
Λαμπόκαμπος
N. Falkonéra
N. Φαλκονέρα
N. Antímilos
N. Αντίμηλος

Vlachiótis
Βλαχιώτης
Apidiá
Απιδιά
Reichéa
Ρειχέα
N. Καράβι
684

Glykóvrysi
Γλυκόβρυση
916
Molái
Μολάοι
1125
Gérakas
Γέρακας
Limáni Géraka
Λιμάνι Γέρακα
2
Akr. B

Eliá
Ελιά
(200)
Sykiá
Συκιά
Ág. Ioánnis
Αγ. Ιωάννης
Akr. Kremmýdi
Akρ. Κρεμμύδι
Akr. Psális
Akρ. Ψάλης

Plýtra
Πλύτρα
Asopós
Ασωπός
5

Akr. Xylís
Akρ. Ξυλής
Veliés
Βελιές
Géfyra
Γέφυρα
Monemvasía
Μονεμβασία

Daimonia
Δαιμονιά
Tálanta
Τάλαντα
Kólpos Epidávrou Limirás
Κόλπος Επιδαύρου Λιμηράς

s Kólpos
Nómia
Νόμια
716

Pantánassa
Παντάνασσα
Óros Kríthina
Όρος Κρίθινα

Ág. Apóstoloi
Αγ. Απόστολοι
Á. Kastaniá
Ά. Καστανιά

224
Ág. Andréas
Αγ. Ανδρέας

Elafónisos
Ελαφόνησος
Neápoli
Νεάπολη
N. Ananés
N. Ανανές

Elafonísi
Ελαφονήσι
772

Porthmós Elafonísou
Πορθμός Ελαφονήσου
Velanídia
Βελανίδια

3
Akr. Maléas
Akρ. Μαλέας

Akr. Spathí
Akρ. Σπαθί
KRITIKÓ

Karavás
Καραβάς
Ag. Pelagía
Αγ. Πελαγία

Potamós
Ποταμός

Aroniádika
Αρωνιάδικα
14
Diakófti
Διακόφτι

Mylopótamos
Μυλοπόταμος
Friligkiánika
Φριλιγκιάνικα
389

507
Avlémonas
Αβλέμονας

N. KÝTHIRA (▲)
N. ΚΥΘΗΡΑ
Livádi
Λιβάδι

Kýthira
Κύθηρα
Akr. Kapéllo
Akρ. Καπέλλο
4

Kapsáli
Καψάλι

Akr. Kefáli
Akρ. Κεφάλι

Potamós
Ποταμός

Galanianá
Γαλανιανά
Kíssamos (Kastélli)
Κίσσαμος (Καστέλλι)

N. Antikýthira
N. Αντικύθηρα
378
Akr. Apolytáres
Akρ. Απολυτάρες

D
E
226
F

N. KRÍTI
N. ΚΡΗΤΗ
Akr. Spánta
Akρ. Σπάντα
Diktynaion
Δικτυναίον

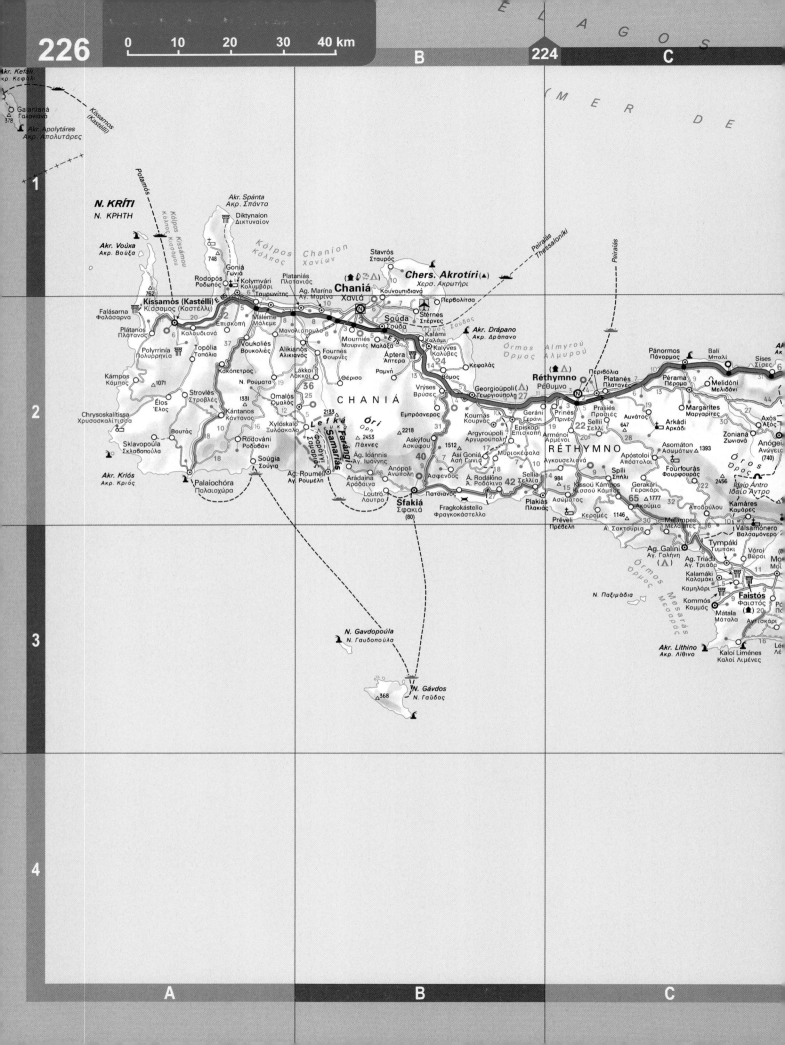

ΚΡΗΤΙΚΟ ΠΕΛΑΓΟΣ

RÈTE)

N. Chamilí
N. Χαμηλή

Nº Divoùnia
Nºι Διβούνια

N. KRÍTI
Ν. ΚΡΗΤΗ

Αυγό

Thessaloníki
Peiraiás

N. Día
Ν. Δία

263

Kárpathos
Ródos
Lemessós (Kípros)
Haïfa

Thira
Sífnos

Ag. Pelagía
Αγ. Πελαγία

Peiraiás

Thira
Anáfi
Kárpathos

N. Paximáda
Ν. Παξιμάδα

N. Dragonáda
Ν. Δραγονάδα

(N) 33

IRÁKLEIO
ΗΡΑΚΛΕΙΟ

N. Alikarnassós
Ν. Αλικαρνασσός

Goúrnes
Γούρνες

Limáni Chersonísou
Λιμάνι Χερσονήσου

(200)
Vrouchás
Βρουχάς

Akr. Ág. Ioánnis
Ακρ. Αγ. Ιωάννης

N. Gianusáda
Ν. Γιανυσάδα

Akr. Síderos
Ακρ. Σίδερος

Ροδιά

E 75

Karterós
Καρτερός

Goùves
Γούβες

Stalida
Σταλίδα

Sísi
Σίσι

Milatos
Μίλατος

Skiniás
Σκινιάς

760

Spinalónga
Σπιναλόγκα

Itanós
Ιτανός

Βάϊ
Vái

Ammoudára
Αμμουδάρα

11

4

17

16,5

5

12

11,5

18

71

Foúrni
Φούρνι

16

10

Chers. Spinalónga
Χερσ. Σπιναλόγκα

N. Elása
Ν. Ελάσα

Toploú
Τοπλού

Tylisos
Τύλισος

23

Knosós
Κνωσός

14

Episkopí
Επισκοπή

Potamiés
Ποταμιές

9

Mochós
Μοχός

Mália
Μάλια

(280)

Neápoli
Νεάπολη

15

Eloúnta
Ελούντα

Siteía
Σητεία

Palaíkastro
Παλαίκαστρο

Gioúchtas
Γιούχτας

(400)

811

Ag. Mýronas
Αγ. Μύρωνας

Archánes
Αρχάνες

Kastélli
Καστέλλι

1559

Tzermiádo
Τζερμιάδο

19

10

Móchlos
Μόχλος

Skopí
Σκοπή

428

Piskokéfalo
Πισκοκέφαλο

539

Mitáto
Μητάτο

(35)

Síva
Σίβα

22

50

Ag. Paraskiés
Αγ. Παρασκιές

(840)
Psychró
Ψυχρό

Lasíthi
Λασίθι

12

Ag. Geórgios
Αγ. Γεώργιος

Lató
Λατώ

Ag. Nikólaos
Αγ. Νικόλαος

N. Psíra
Ν. Ψείρα

49

30

11

63

Zákros
Ζάκρος

(260)

K. Zákros
Κ. Ζάκρος

Vathýpetro
Βαθύπετρο

777

107

Arkalochóri
Αρκαλοχώρι

26

Diktaío Antro
Δικταίο Άντρο

Katharó
Καθαρό

Kritsá
Κριτσά

20

Sfáka
Σφάκα

LASÍTHI

Karydi
Καρύδι

14

Chandrás
Χανδράς

16

Zíros
Ζίρος

819

11

Ag. Thomás
Αγ. Θωμάς

2148

1485

Kaló Chorió
Καλό Χωριό

Gournià
Γουρνιά

Kavoúsi
Καβούσι

19

Sfáka
Σφάκα

Kaló Chorió
Καλό Χωριό

Ziros
Ζίρος

Xerókampos
Ξερόκαμπος

IRÁKLEIO

498

Garípa
Γαρίπα

Panagía
Παναγία

16

Óros Díkti
Όρος Δίκτη

1783

Máles
Μάλες

Meseléroi
Μεσελέροι

14

Or-0770
Ορεινό

1476

Pefkoi
Πεύκοι

Lithines
Λιθίνες

Gkagkáles
Γκαγκάλες

Tefeli
Τεφέλι

Ligórtynos
Λιγόρτυνος

118

Skiniás
Σκινιάς

9

Kalamáfka
Καλαμάφκα

Episkopí
Επισκοπή

Koutsourás
Κουτσουράς

26

Stavrochóri
Σταυροχώρι

Kaló Chorió
Καλό Χωριό

Gortys
Γόρτυς

Ag. Déka
Αγ. Δέκα

Stóloi
Στόλοι

Pýrgos
Πύργος

13

K. Kastelianá
Κ. Καστελιανά

785

Anatolí
Ανατολή

Ag. Fotiá
Αγ. Φωτιά

Makrygialós
Μακρυγιαλός

Goúdouras
Γούδουρας

16

Stóloi
Στόλοι

10

Cháras
Χάρακας

6

Mesochóri
Μεσοχώρι

Oríi
Ορή

Arvi
Άρβη

24

Péfkos
Πεύκος

Myrtos
Μύρτος

Ammoudára
Αμμουδάρα

Ierápetra
Ιεράπετρα

Koufonísi
Κουφονήσι

Vagioniá
Βαγιονιά

Kapetanianá
Καπετανιανά

1231

Achentriás
Αχεντριάς

Tsoútsouros
Τσούτσουρος

Keratókampos
Κερατόκαμπος

Árvi
Άρβη

Myrtos
Μύρτος

N. Chrysí
Ν. Χρυσή

Krótos
Κρότος

Trypití
Τρυπητή

Treis Ekklisíes
Τρεις Εκκλησίες

Loutrá
Λουτρά

M. Koudoumá
Μ. Κουδουμά

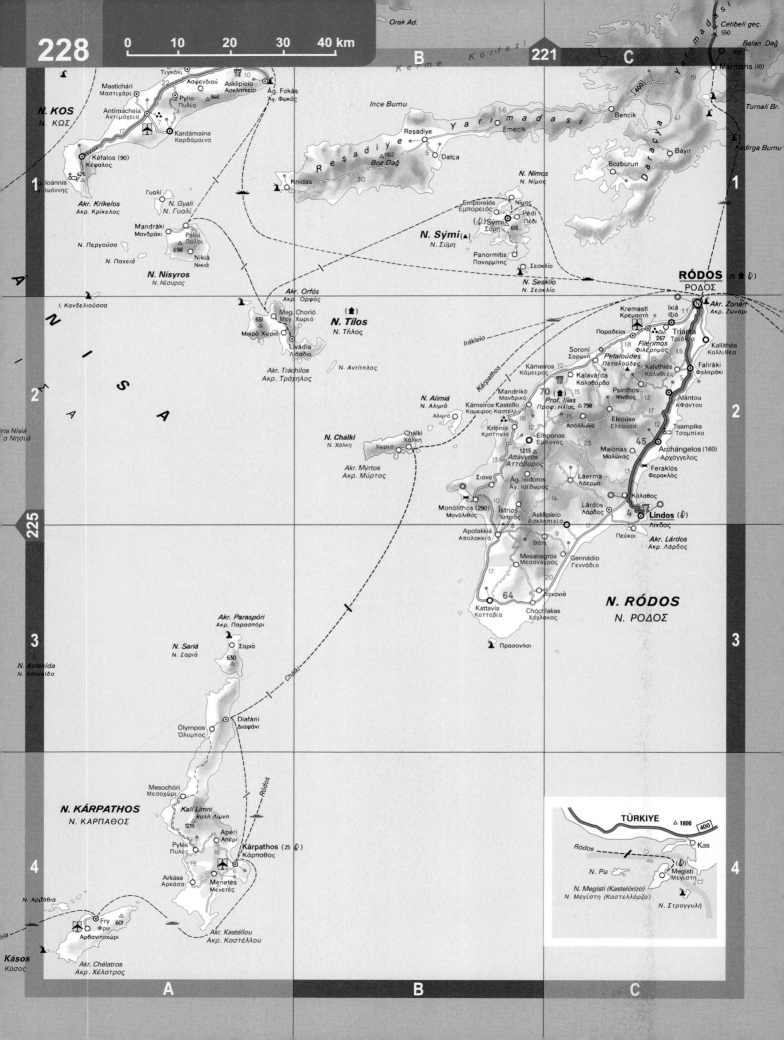

Chypre / Cyprus / Zypern / Cipro / Chipre

1 / 700 000

Lefkoşa/
Lefkosia

CY

KÝPROS / KIBRIS

Scale: 0 10 20 30 40 km

Cape Kormakitis

Livera
Kormakitis
Vasiléia
122
Diorios
Myrtou
Syrianochori
MORFOU BAY
Kyra
Morfou
Argaki
Fyllia
Prastio
Kato Zodeia
Katokopia
Pachyammos
Kato Pyrgos
Pentageia
Nikitas
Pano Zodeia
Pomos
Galini
Soloi
Karavostasi
20
Astromeritis
Peristerona
Akaki
Ampelikou
Kalo Chorio
Lefka
Petra
19
Cape Arnaoutis
(Akamas)
590
CHRYSOCHOU BAY
E 704
22
Gialia
Orounta
375
Argaka
600
Panagia Forviotissa
(Asinou)
67
Baths of Aphrodite
428
9
Polis
Neo Chorio
Kampos
Agia
Marina
Mitsero
1212
Evrychou
Korakou
683
53
Lysos
Peristerona
1407
Kalopanagiotis
Galata
Kakopetria
1158
E 907
Klirou
Drouseia
Kritou
668
Ineia
Tera
923
Kykkos
Meutoullas
Pedoulas
Agios Nikolaos
tis Stegis
Prodromos
1512
773
Fikardou
Pano Arodes
Giolou
Pano Panagia
Lemithou
Chandria
Platanistasa
Gourri
Kaminaria
Kyperounta
Agros
Alona
Kathikas
Stroumpi
33
Polemi
Statos-Agios
Fotios
Óros Ólimbos
(1951)
1554
Palaichori
1423
Cape Drepano
38
E 709
Troodítissa
Pano Platres
Pelendri
1234
Pano Lefkara
Pegeia
Tala
Agios
Neofytos
Letymvou
Salamiou
Arsos
Foini
1112
Agios
Ioannis
Agios
Theodoros
Coral Bay
Kallepeia
Amargeti
Mandria
Omodos
Kalo Chorio
Choirokoitia
Kissonerga
Tsada
Kalokedara
771
Malia
Vasa
Vouni
1001
Asgata
Tochni
Mesogi
485
Dora
Agios
Therapon
692
Kalavasos
Chlorakas
Empa
Agios Georgios
Pachna
466
Pafos
410
Epiksop
Pano
Archimandrita
Germasogeia
Dam
Parekklisia
Pyrgos
Pentakomo
Geroskipou
A 6
B 6
15
Anarita
Asprokremmos
Dam
Anogyra
Kouris Dam
Agios
Athanasios
39
Zygi
13
Timi
Agios Georgios
Alamanos
Kouklia
61
Avdimou
A 6
Souni-
Zanakia
E 601
**Kato
Polemidia**
Germasogeia
Pafos International Airport
Mandria
37
Sanctuary of
Apollon Ylatis
B 6
Episkopi
Ypsonas
12
**Mesa
Géitonia**
Amathous
Pissouri
44
Kourion
Kolossi
**LEMESOS
(LIMASSOL)**
276
Petra tou Romiou
(Aphrodite's birthplace)
Cape Aspro
Akrotiri
Sovereign Base Area
Salt Lake
EPISKOPI BAY
AKROTIRI BAY
Akrotiri
Cape Zevgari
Cape Gata

D E F

1

Cape Apostolos Andreas

△ 136

Apostolos
Andreas

191 △

Rizokarpaso

△ 241

Aigialousa

KARPASIA

Agios
Andronikos

Leonarisso

Vothylakas

2

Eptakomi 166 △

Koma
toú Gialou

330 △

Davlos

Komi

64

724 △

Akanthou

Patriki

Agios Theodoros

Cape Elaia

Agios
Amvrosios

740 △

819 △

Kalograia

Charkeia

30 △ 740

91
△ 540

Trikomo

Kastros

AMMOCHOSTOS BAY

Kythrea

Neo Chorio

Trachoni

Marathovounos

Lefkonoiko

Gypsou

Lapathos

Milia

Exo
Metochi

Peristèrona

Gerokolympos

Limnia

Palaikythro

Genagra

Agios Sergios

Angastina

61

Prastio

Stylloi

Salamis

Pediaios

47

Afanteia

Apostolos
Varnavas

Egkomi

Tymvou

Askeia

Vatili

△ 186

140 △

Lysi

Acheritou

AMMOCHOSTOS / GAZIMAĞUSA
(FAMAGUSTA)

Tremetousia

Kontea

Kalopsida

45

Arsos

Makrasyka

E 903

Giallas

Potamia

Achna

28

Deryneia

Athienou

Troulloi

Avgorou

Frenaros

20

350 △

Dhekelia
Base

Pyla

Sovereign
Area

Liopetri

Sotira

Paralimni

Lympia

Xylotymvou

174 △

32

Voroklini

17

Ormideia

25

Tremithos

A 2

A 3

Xylofagou

Aradippou

B 2

19

B 3

Agia Napa

Cape Gkreko

48

Kalo Chorio

6

Livadia

LARNAKA BAY

Cape Pyla

3

72

Hala Sultan
Tekkesi

B 5

Salt Lake

LARNAKA

A 5

33

Dromolaxia

△

Larnaka International Airport

32

B 5

Anglisides

Kiti

Anafotida

Perivolia

Mazotos

Cape Kiti

M E D I T E R R A N E A N   S E A

▬▬▬	Ligne de démarcation - Green Line
⬤	Passage contrôlé - Check point

0 ————————— 20 km

4

D E F

Numéro de page / Page number / Seitenzahl / Paginanummer
Numero di pagina / Número de página / Número da página

Localité / Place / Ort / Plaatsen
Località / Localidad / Localidade ⟶ Aarau *(CH)* 92   B 4 ⟵

Coordonnées de carroyage / Grid coordinates
Koordinatenangabe / Verwijstekens ruitsysteem
Coordinate riferite alla quadrettatura /
Coordenadas en los mapas / Referência da
quadrícula

Pays / Country / Land / Paesi / País

A	Österreich	**FIN**	Suomi, Finland	**MK**	Makedonija
AL	Shqipëria	**FL**	Liechtenstein	**MNE**	Crna Gora
AND	Andorra	**GB**	United Kingdom	**N**	Norge
B	Belgique, België	**GR**	Elláda	**NL**	Nederland
BG	Balgarija	**H**	Magyarország	**P**	Portugal
BIH	Bosna i Hercegovina	**HR**	Hrvatska	**PL**	Polska
BY	Belarus'	**I**	Italia	**RO**	România
CH	Schweiz, Suisse, Svizzera	**IRL**	Ireland, Éire	**RSM**	San Marino
CY	Kýpros, Kibris	**IS**	Island	**RUS**	Rossija
CZ	Česká Republika	**L**	Luxembourg, Lëtzebuerg	**S**	Sverige
D	Deutschland	**LT**	Lietuva	**SK**	Slovenská Republika
DK	Danmark	**LV**	Latvija	**SLO**	Slovenija
E	España	**M**	Malta	**SRB**	Srbija
EST	Eesti	**MC**	Monaco	**TR**	Türkiye
F	France	**MD**	Moldova	**UA**	Ukraïna

A

A Baiuca *(E)*	58	B 2	
A Cañiza *(E)*	58	B 4	
A Coruña *(E)*	58	B 2	
A Estrada *(E)*	58	B 3	
A Fonsagrada *(E)*	59	D 3	
A Guarda *(E)*	58	A 4	
A Gudiña *(E)*	63	D 1	
Á. Kómi *(GR)*	205	F 4	
A Laracha *(E)*	58	B 2	
Á. Melás *(GR)*	205	E 3	
Á. Merá *(E)*	219	F 3	
A Merca *(E)*	58	B 4	
A Mezquita *(E)*	63	D 1	
A Pobra do Caramiñal *(E)*	58	A 3	
A Pontenova *(E)*	59	D 2	
A. Poróia *(GR)*	206	C 1	
A Ramallosa *(E)*	58	A 4	
Á. Rodákino *(GR)*	226	B 2	
A Rúa *(E)*	58	C 4	
A Veiga *(E)*	59	D 4	
Aa *(EST)*	151	E 3	
Aachen *(D)*	87	D 2	
Aakre *(EST)*	154	C 4	
Aalen *(D)*	93	D 1	
Aalsmeer *(NL)*	82	B 4	
Aalst *(B)*	39	E 2	
Aalten *(NL)*	83	D 4	
Aalter *(B)*	37	F 4	
Äänekoski *(FIN)*	133	F 4	
Aapajärvi *(FIN)*	129	D 2	
Aarau *(CH)*	92	B 4	
Aarberg *(CH)*	49	F 2	
Aarburg *(CH)*	92	B 4	
Aardla *(EST)*	155	D 4	
Aarna *(EST)*	161	D 1	
Aarschot *(B)*	39	F 2	
Ääsmäe *(EST)*	149	D 3	
Aaspere *(EST)*	150	B 4	
Aavasaksa *(FIN)*	128	C 3	
Aavere *(EST)*	150	C 4	
Abades *(E)*	64	C 3	
Abadiño *(E)*	60	C 3	
Abanilla *(E)*	77	F 1	
Abano Terme *(I)*	98	A 3	
Abavnieki *(LV)*	157	E 4	
Abbadia San Salvatore *(I)*	102	A 4	
Abbasanta *(I)*	108	B 3	
Abbeville *(F)*	38	C 3	
Abbey Town *(GB)*	31	D 4	
Abbeyfeale *(IRL)*	24	B 2	

Abbeyleix / Mainistir Laoise *(IRL)*	25	D 2	
Abbiategrasso *(I)*	97	D 3	
Abborrträsk *(S)*	132	B 1	
Abbots Bromley *(GB)*	33	D 3	
Abbotsbury *(GB)*	35	E 3	
Abcoude *(NL)*	82	B 4	
Abejar *(E)*	65	D 2	
Abejuela *(E)*	71	F 2	
Abela *(P)*	68	B 4	
Ābele *(LV)*	157	D 4	
Ābeles *(LV)*	163	F 2	
Ābelīte *(LV)*	159	D 3	
Abenberg *(D)*	89	D 4	
Abenójar *(E)*	70	A 3	
Åbenrå *(DK)*	142	B 4	
Abensberg *(D)*	93	F 1	
Aberaeron *(GB)*	32	A 4	
Aberdare / Aberdâr *(GB)*	35	D 1	
Aberdaron *(GB)*	32	A 3	
Aberdeen *(GB)*	28	C 4	
Aberdovey / Aberdyfi *(GB)*	32	B 4	
Aberfeldy *(GB)*	31	D 1	
Aberfoyle *(GB)*	30	C 1	
Abergavenny / Y-Fenni *(GB)*	35	D 1	
Abergele *(GB)*	32	B 3	
Aberlady *(GB)*	31	D 2	
Abermaw / Barmouth *(GB)*	32	B 3	
Aberporth *(GB)*	32	A 4	
Abersoch *(GB)*	32	A 3	
Abertillery *(GB)*	35	D 1	
Aberystwyth *(GB)*	32	B 4	
Abetone *(I)*	101	E 1	
Abiego *(E)*	54	C 4	
Abingdon *(GB)*	35	F 1	
Abington *(GB)*	31	D 3	
Abisko *(S)*	124	B 4	
Abja-Paluoja *(EST)*	154	A 4	
Abja-Vanamõisa *(EST)*	154	A 4	
Abla *(E)*	76	C 2	
Ablis *(F)*	42	C 3	
Abolai *(LT)*	177	F 3	
Āboliņi *(LV)*	159	F 3	
Abondance *(F)*	49	F 4	
Abony *(H)*	113	D 1	
Aboyne *(GB)*	28	B 4	
Abrantes *(P)*	68	B 2	
Abreschviller *(F)*	45	D 3	
Abriès *(F)*	53	E 3	
Abromiškės *(LT)*	177	D 2	

Abtenau *(A)*	94	B 3	
Åby *(S)*	143	F 1	
Åbybro *(DK)*	142	B 2	
Acceglio *(I)*	53	E 3	
Accettura *(I)*	106	C 4	
Acciaroli *(I)*	106	B 4	
Accous *(F)*	54	B 2	
Accrington *(GB)*	32	C 2	
Acebo *(E)*	69	D 1	
Acedo *(E)*	60	D 1	
Acehúche *(E)*	69	D 1	
Acerno *(I)*	106	B 3	
Acerra *(I)*	105	E 3	
Aceuchal *(E)*	69	D 3	
Acharnés *(GR)*	218	C 2	
Achenkirch *(A)*	94	A 3	
Achentriás *(GR)*	227	D 3	
Acheritou *(CY)*	231	E 3	
Achern *(D)*	45	E 3	
Acheux-en-Amiénois *(F)*	38	C 3	
Achílleio Kérkyra *(GR)*	210	B 2	
Achílleio Lárisa *(GR)*	212	F 2	
Achinós *(GR)*	207	D 2	
Achladerí *(GR)*	219	D 1	
Achladochóri *(GR)*	207	D 1	
Achna *(CY)*	231	E 3	
Achnacroish *(GB)*	30	B 1	
Achnasheen *(GB)*	27	D 3	
Aci Castello *(I)*	111	E 3	
Aci Trezza *(I)*	111	E 3	
Acireale *(I)*	111	E 3	
Acle *(GB)*	37	D 1	
Acokavai *(LT)*	169	F 2	
Acone *(I)*	165	D 1	
Acqualagna *(I)*	102	A 4	
Acquapendente *(I)*	102	A 4	
Acquasanta Terme *(I)*	102	C 3	
Acquasparta *(I)*	102	A 4	
Acquaviva delle Fonti *(I)*	107	D 3	
Acqui Terme *(I)*	100	C 1	
Acri *(I)*	109	E 4	
Ada *(SRB)*	113	E 3	
Adak *(S)*	132	B 1	
Adakavas I *(LT)*	169	F 4	
Adámantas *(GR)*	224	A 2	
Adamclisi *(RO)*	13	E 4	
Ādami *(LV)*	163	C 4	
Adamova (Odumova) *(LV)*	167	E 2	
Adamów Lubelskie *(PL)*	197	E 3	

Adamówka *(PL)*	197	E 4	
Adamuz *(E)*	76	A 1	
Adanero *(E)*	64	A 4	
Adapazarı *(TR)*	19	F 1	
Adare *(IRL)*	24	C 2	
Adaševci *(SRB)*	117	F 1	
Adavere *(EST)*	154	B 2	
Ādaži *(LV)*	159	D 4	
Adelboden *(CH)*	96	B 2	
Adelfia *(I)*	107	D 2	
Adelsheim *(D)*	45	F 2	
Ademuz *(E)*	71	E 1	
Adenau *(D)*	87	E 3	
Ádendro *(GR)*	206	B 3	
Adíste *(EST)*	155	E 4	
Adjud *(RO)*	13	E 3	
Admont *(A)*	95	D 3	
Adolfsström *(S)*	127	F 1	
Adorf *(D)*	89	E 2	
Adra *(E)*	76	C 3	
Adradas *(E)*	65	D 3	
Adraku *(EST)*	151	D 4	
Adrall *(E)*	55	D 4	
Adrano *(I)*	111	E 3	
Adria *(I)*	98	B 4	
Aduliena *(LV)*	160	C 4	
Adutiškis *(LT)*	173	D 4	
Ādžūni *(LV)*	164	C 3	
Aegviidu *(EST)*	149	F 3	
Ænes *(N)*	138	C 2	
Aerinó *(GR)*	212	B 2	
Ærøskøbing *(DK)*	144	B 3	
Aetós Etolia-Akarnanía *(GR)*	211	D 4	
Aetós Flórina *(GR)*	205	E 3	
Aetós Kefalonniá *(GR)*	216	B 1	
Äetsä *(FIN)*	136	B 3	
Afáia *(GR)*	218	B 2	
Afanteia *(CY)*	231	D 3	
Afántou *(GR)*	228	C 2	
Afiónas *(GR)*	210	B 1	
Afjord *(N)*	131	D 2	
Aflenz Kurort *(A)*	95	E 3	
Afráti *(GR)*	218	C 1	
Áfyssos *(GR)*	212	C 3	
Áfytos *(GR)*	206	C 4	
Ag. Andréas *(GR)*	217	F 3	
Ág. Avgoustínos *(GR)*	217	D 4	
Ág. Déka *(GR)*	227	D 3	

Ag. Dimítrios Atikí-Peireiás *(GR)*	218	C 1	
Ág. Dimítrios Etolía-Akarnanía *(GR)*	211	F 4	
Ág. Dimítrios Éwoia *(GR)*	219	D 2	
Ág. Dimítrios Lakonía *(GR)*	222	C 2	
Ág. Dimítrios Pieriá *(GR)*	206	A 4	
Ág. Fokás *(GR)*	225	F 2	
Ág. Fotiá *(GR)*	227	E 3	
Ág. Galíni *(GR)*	226	C 3	
Ág. Geórgios Éwoia *(GR)*	212	B 4	
Ág. Geórgios Fthiótida *(GR)*	211	F 3	
Ág. Geórgios Kefalonniá *(GR)*	216	B 1	
Ág. Geórgios Lasithi *(GR)*	227	E 2	
Ág. Germanós *(GR)*	205	E 2	
Ág. Górdis *(GR)*	210	B 2	
Ág. Kosmás Grevená *(GR)*	205	E 4	
Ág. Kosmás Kavála *(GR)*	207	F 2	
Ág. Léon *(GR)*	216	B 2	
Ág. Loukás *(GR)*	218	C 1	
Ág. Mámas *(GR)*	206	C 4	
Ag. Marína Aígina *(GR)*	218	B 2	
Ag. Marína Atikí-Peireiás *(GR)*	218	C 1	
Ag. Marína Chánia *(GR)*	226	B 3	
Ag. Marína Dodekánissa *(GR)*	221	E 4	
Ag. Marína Fthiótida *(GR)*	212	B 4	
Ág. Márkos *(GR)*	206	C 2	
Ág. Nikítas *(GR)*	210	C 4	
Ag. Nikólaos Atikí-Peireiás *(GR)*	218	B 3	
Ag. Nikólaos Etolía-Akarnanía *(GR)*	211	D 4	
Ag. Nikólaos Fokída *(GR)*	217	E 1	
Ag. Nikólaos Fthiótida *(GR)*	212	B 4	
Ág. Nikólaos Halkidikí *(GR)*	207	D 4	
Ág. Nikólaos Lakonía *(GR)*	222	C 2	
Ag. Nikólaos Lasíthi *(GR)*	227	E 2	
Ag. Nikólaos Messinía *(GR)*	222	C 1	
Ag. Nikólaos Thesprotía *(GR)*	210	C 1	
Ag. Paraskeví Dráma *(GR)*	207	E 2	
Ag. Paraskeví Ioánnina *(GR)*	205	D 4	
Ág. Paraskeví Kilkis *(GR)*	206	B 1	
Ag. Paraskeví Lésvos *(GR)*	214	C 3	

Ag. Paraskiés *(GR)*	227	D 2	
Ág. Pávlos *(GR)*	206	B 3	
Ág. Pelagía Atikí-Peireiás *(GR)*	223	D 3	
Ag. Pelagía Irákleio *(GR)*	227	D 2	
Ág. Pétros *(GR)*	217	F 3	
Ag. Pnévma *(GR)*	207	D 2	
Ág. Pródromos *(GR)*	206	C 4	
Ag. Rouméli *(GR)*	226	B 2	
Ag. Sofia Arkadía *(GR)*	217	F 3	
Ag. Sofia Éwoia *(GR)*	213	D 4	
Ag. Sóstis *(GR)*	211	F 4	
Ag. Sotíra *(GR)*	218	B 2	
Ag. Stéfanos Atikí-Peireiás *(GR)*	218	C 1	
Ag. Stéfanos Kikládes *(GR)*	219	F 3	
Ag. Thomás Irákleio *(GR)*	227	D 2	
Ag. Thomás Viotía *(GR)*	218	B 1	
Ag. Triáda *(GR)*	218	C 1	
Ag. Triáda Ilía *(GR)*	217	D 2	
Ag. Triáda Thessaloníki *(GR)*	206	B 3	
Ag. Varvára *(GR)*	227	D 2	
Ag. Vissários *(GR)*	211	F 3	
Agathonísi *(GR)*	221	E 3	
Agay *(F)*	57	E 2	
Agazzano *(I)*	97	E 4	
Agde *(F)*	56	A 2	
Agen *(F)*	51	D 4	
Ageniškis *(LT)*	165	E 4	
Àger *(E)*	66	B 2	
Ageranós *(GR)*	222	C 2	
Agerbæk *(DK)*	142	A 4	
Aggius *(I)*	108	B 1	
Aggsbach *(A)*	95	E 1	
Agiá *(GR)*	212	B 1	
Agía Ánna Éwoia *(GR)*	212	C 4	
Agía Ánna Viotía *(GR)*	217	F 1	
Agía Efthymía *(GR)*	217	E 1	
Agía Evfimía *(GR)*	216	B 1	
Agía Kyriakí Kastoriá *(GR)*	205	E 3	
Agía Kyriakí Messinía *(GR)*	217	D 4	
Agía Kyriakí Sámos *(GR)*	221	D 3	
Agía Lávra *(GR)*	217	E 2	
Agia Marina *(CY)*	231	C 3	
Agia Napa *(CY)*	231	E 3	
Agia Varvara *(CY)*	231	C 3	
Agíasma *(GR)*	207	F 2	
Agiásmata *(GR)*	214	C 4	
Agiásos *(GR)*	214	C 3	

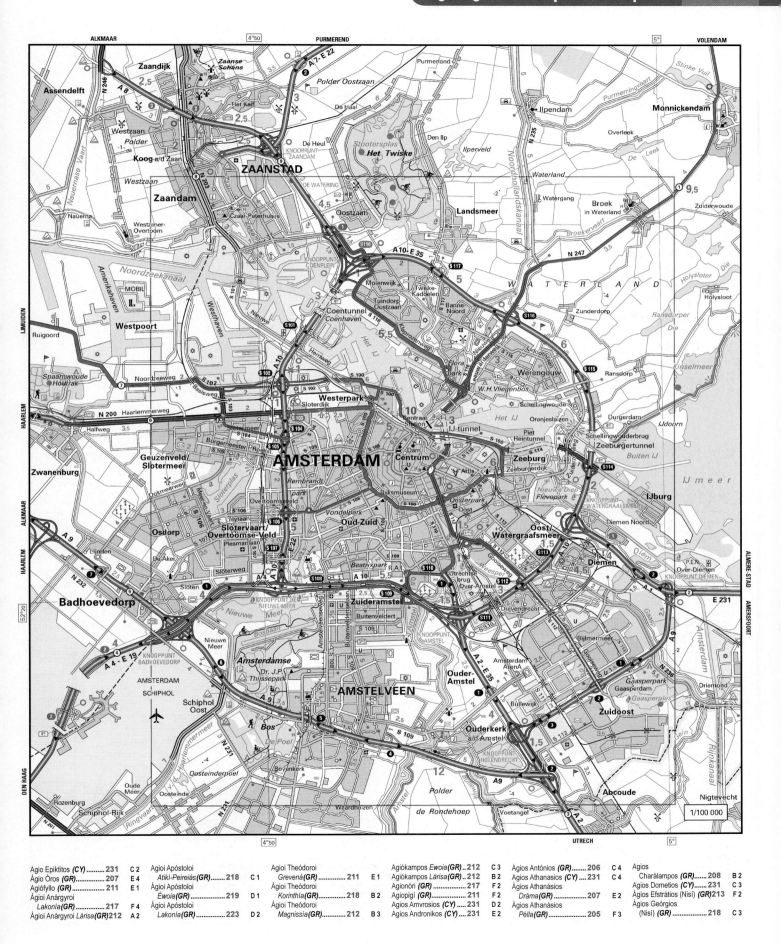

Agio Epíktitos (CY) .... 231 C 2
Ágio Óros (GR) .... 207 E 4
Agiófyllo (GR) .... 211 E 1
Ágioi Anárgyroi
  Lakonía (GR) .... 217 F 4
Ágioi Anárgyroi Lárisa (GR) 212 A 2

Agioi Apóstoloi
  Atikí-Peireiás (GR) .... 218 C 1
Ágioi Apóstoloi
  Évoia (GR) .... 219 D 1
Ágioi Apóstoloi
  Lakonía (GR) .... 223 D 2

Agioi Theódoroi
  Grevená (GR) .... 211 E 1
Ágioi Theódoroi
  Korinthía (GR) .... 218 B 2
Ágioi Theódoroi
  Magnissía (GR) .... 212 B 3

Agiókampos Evoia (GR) .. 212 C 3
Agiókampos Lárisa (GR) .. 212 B 2
Agionóri (GR) .... 217 F 2
Agiopigí (GR) .... 211 F 2
Agios Amvrosios (CY) ..... 231 D 2
Agios Andronikos (CY) .... 231 E 2

Ágios Antónios (GR) .... 206 C 4
Ágios Athanásios (CY) .... 231 C 4
Ágios Athanásios
  Dráma (GR) .... 207 E 2
Ágios Athanásios
  Péla (GR) .... 205 F 3

Ágios
  Charálampos (GR) ...... 208 B 2
Agios Dometios (CY) .... 231 C 3
Ágios Efstrátios (Nisí) (GR) 213 F 2
Ágios Geórgios
  (Nisí) (GR) .... 218 C 3

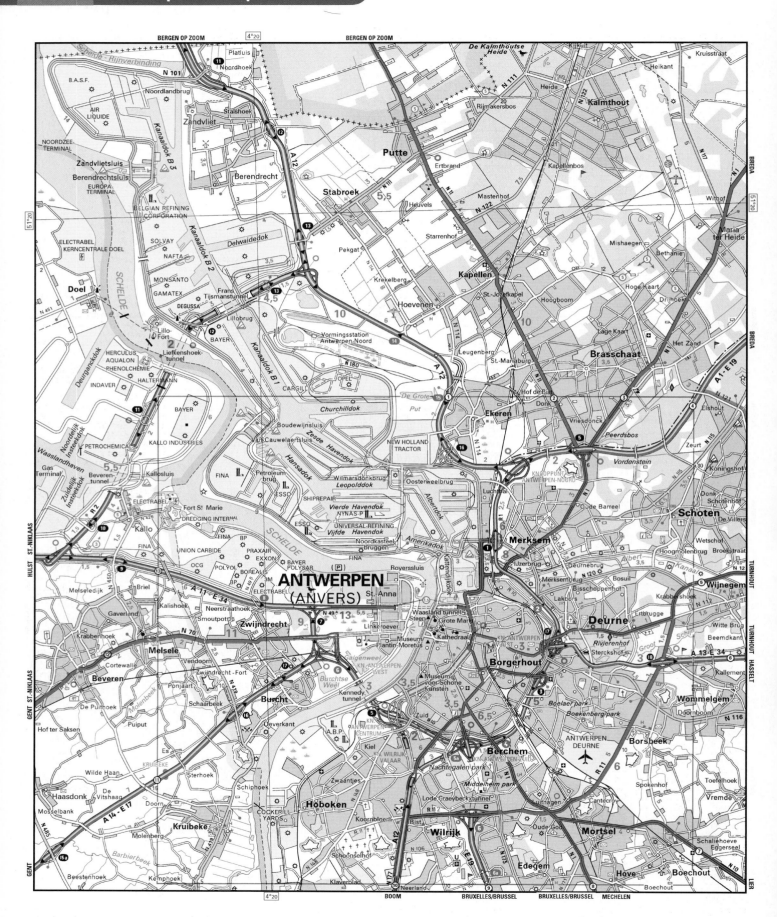

Agios Georgios
(Keryneia) *(CY)*............231 C 2
Agios Georgios
(Pafos) *(CY)*...............230 B 4
Agios Georgios Alamanos *(CY)*
231...........................C 4
Agios Ilerion *(CY)*...........231 C 2
Ágios Ioánnis *Almyrós(GR)*212 B 3
Ágios Ioánnis
Korinthia(GR)..........217 F 2
Ágios Ioánnis *Kríti(GR)*....226 B 2
Ágios Ioánnis *Viotía(GR)*.217 F 1
Ágios Ioánnis *Vólos(GR)*.212 C 2
Agios Ioannis
Lefkoşa *(CY)*...........231 C 3
Agios Ioannis
(Óros Ólimbos) *(CY)*....231 C 3
Ágios Isídoros *(GR)*.........228 B 2
Ágios Kírykos *(GR)*.........220 C 3
Agios Konstantínos
Fthiótida(GR)...........212 B 4
Ágios Konstantínos
Lárisa(GR).............212 B 2
Ágios Matthaíos *(GR)*.....210 B 2
Ágios Myronas *(GR)*.......227 D 2
Agios Neofytos *(CY)*........230 A 3
Agios Nikolaos
tis Stegis *(CY)*.........230 B 3
Ágios
Panteleïmónas *(GR)*...205 F 3
Agios Sergios *(CY)*.........231 E 2
Agios Theodoros
(Karpasia) *(CY)*........231 E 2
Agios Theodoros
(Larnaka) *(CY)*.........231 C 4
Agios Theodoros
(Óros Ólimbos) *(CY)*....231 C 3
Agios Therapon *(CY)*.......230 B 4
Ágios Vasíleios *(CY)*.......231 C 2
Ágios Vasíleios
Thessaloníki(GR).......206 C 3
Ágios Vasíleios
Viotía(GR).............218 B 1
Agira *(I)*....................111 D 3
Agkáli *(GR)*.................212 C 4
Agkístri *(GR)*...............218 B 3
Agkístri (Nisí) *(GR)*.......218 B 3
Ágkistro *(GR)*...............206 C 1
Aglangia (Aglantzia) *(CY)*231 C 3
Aglona *(LV)*.................167 D 4
Aglonas Stacija *(LV)*.......167 D 4
Ágnanta *(GR)*...............211 D 2
Agnanteró *(GR)*.............211 F 2
Ágnanti *(GR)*...............212 B 4
Agnone *(I)*..................105 F 2
Agnóntas *(GR)*.............213 D 3
Agolada *(E)*.................58 B 3
Agon-Coutainville *(F)*.....41 E 2
Agorá *(GR)*.................207 E 2
Agordo *(I)*..................98 A 1
Agost *(E)*...................71 F 4
Agra *(LV)*...................159 E 3
Agramunt *(E)*...............66 E 2
Agrate Brianza *(I)*.........97 E 3
Ágreda *(E)*..................65 E 2
Agreliá *(GR)*................211 F 1
Agriá *(GR)*..................212 C 2
Agrigento *(I)*...............110 C 3
Agriliá *(GR)*................217 D 1
Agrínio *(GR)*...............211 E 4
Agriovótano *(GR)*..........212 C 3
Agro *(LV)*...................164 B 2
Agropoli *(I)*.................106 B 4
Agros *(CY)*..................231 C 3
Ágskaret *(N)*...............127 C 3
Aguadulce *(E)*..............76 C 3
Aguadulce *(E)*..............75 F 2
Aguaviva *(E)*...............66 A 4
Agudo *(E)*..................70 A 3
Águeda *(P)*.................62 B 4
Aguiar *(P)*..................68 B 3
Aguiar da Beira *(P)*........62 C 3
Aguilafuente *(E)*...........64 B 3
Aguilar de Campóo *(E)*....65 E 2
Aguilar de la Frontera *(E)*.76 A 1
Aguilar del Alfambra *(E)*..65 F 4
Águilas *(E)*.................77 E 2
Agurkiškė *(LT)*.............175 F 1
Ahaste *(EST)*...............153 B 3
Ahaus *(D)*..................83 D 4
Åheim *(N)*..................130 A 4
Ahigal *(E)*..................69 E 1
Ahja *(EST)*.................155 D 4
Ahjärvi *(FIN)*...............137 F 2
Ahlainen *(FIN)*.............136 B 2
Ahlbeck *(D)*................81 D 3
Ahlen *(D)*...................83 E 4

Ahlhorn *(D)*................83 E 2
Ahrensbök *(D)*.............79 D 3
Ahrensburg *(D)*............79 D 4
Ahrweiler *(D)*..............87 E 3
Ähtäri *(FIN)*................133 E 2
Ahtopol *(BG)*...............19 E 1
Ahula *(EST)*................149 F 3
Ahun *(F)*....................47 F 1
Åhus *(S)*...................143 E 4
Ahvenselkä *(FIN)*..........129 E 2
Äiamaa *(EST)*..............154 B 2
Aianí *(GR)*..................205 F 4
Aiánteio *(GR)*..............218 B 2
Aiaste *(EST)*...............161 D 1
Aichach *(D)*................93 F 2
Aidenbach *(D)*.............94 B 1
Aidipsós *(GR)*.............212 C 4
Aidone *(I)*..................111 D 3
Aidonia *(GR)*..............217 F 2
Aidu *Jõgeva(EST)*.........154 C 2
Aidu *Viljandi(EST)*.........154 B 4
Aígeira *(GR)*...............217 E 1
Aigiái *(GR)*.................222 C 2
Aigiáli *(GR)*................225 D 3
Aígina *(GR)*................218 B 2
Aígina (Nisí) *(GR)*.........218 B 3
Aigínio *(GR)*...............206 B 3
Aígio *(GR)*.................217 E 1
Aigle *(CH)*..................49 E 1
Aignan *(F)*.................54 C 2
Aignay-le-Duc *(F)*.........48 C 1
Aigósthena *(GR)*..........218 B 1
Aigre *(F)*...................50 C 1
Aigrefeuille-d'Aunis *(F)*...46 C 4
Aigrefeuille-sur-Maine *(F)*.46 B 4
Aigua Blava *(E)*............67 E 2
Aiguebelette-le-Lac *(F)*...53 D 2
Aiguebelle *(F)*..............53 D 2
Aigueperse *(F)*.............48 B 4
Aigues-Mortes *(F)*.........56 B 2
Aiguilles *(F)*................53 E 3
Aiguillon *(F)*................50 C 4
Aigurande *(F)*..............47 F 4
Ailefroide *(F)*...............53 D 3
Aillant-sur-Tholon *(F)*.....43 E 4
Ailly-le-Haut-Clocher *(F)*...38 C 3
Ailly-sur-Noye *(F)*..........38 C 3
Aimargues *(F)*..............56 B 2
Aime *(F)*....................53 E 2
Ainas *(LV)*..................161 D 2
Ainaži *(LV)*.................159 D 1
Ainhoa *(F)*..................54 A 2
Ainsa *(E)*...................54 C 4
Ainsdale *(GB)*..............32 C 2
Ainzón *(E)*..................65 E 2
Airaines *(F)*.................38 C 4
Airasca *(I)*..................53 F 3
Airdrie *(GB)*................30 C 2
Aire-sur-la-Lys *(F)*.........38 C 2
Aire-sur-l'Adour *(F)*........54 B 2
Airîtes *Kuldïgas(LV)*......157 D 3
Airîtes *Saldus(LV)*.........163 D 2
Airîtes *Tukuma(LV)*.......157 F 4
Airolo *(CH)*.................97 D 1
Airvault *(F)*.................47 D 3
Aistere *(LV)*................162 B 2
Aisými *(GR)*................208 F 2
Aiterhofen *(D)*.............94 A 1
Aitoliko *(GR)*...............216 C 1
Aitrach *(D)*.................93 E 3
Aiud *(RO)*..................12 C 3
Aiviekste *(LV)*..............166 B 2
Aix-en-Othe *(F)*............43 E 3
Aix-en-Provence *(F)*.......56 C 2
Aix-les-Bains *(F)*...........53 D 1
Aixe-sur-Vienne *(F)*........51 D 1
Aizdârzi *(LV)*...............161 E 4
Aizenay *(F)*.................46 B 3
Aizgârša *(LV)*..............161 E 3
Aizkalne (Jāsmuiža) *(LV)*167 D 4
Aizkraukle *(LV)*............165 E 2
Aizpûre (Lïdumnieki) *(LV)*167 F 2
Aizpuri *(LV)*................159 E 3
Aizpurve *(LV)*..............160 C 4
Aizpute *(LV)*...............162 C 1
Aizupe *(LV)*................172 C 1
Aizupes *(LV)*...............156 C 3
Aizupes
(Mazgavilnieki) *(LV)*..157 E 3
Aizvïki *(LV)*................162 C 3
Ajaccio *(F)*.................57 E 4
Ajaureforsen *(S)*...........127 E 4
Ajdanovac *(SRB)*..........119 D 3

Ajdovščina *(SLO)*..........99 D 2
Ajka *(H)*....................112 A 2
Ajo *(E)*......................60 B 2
Ajos *(FIN)*..................128 C 4
Ajtos *(BG)*..................19 E 1
Akácijas *(LV)*...............163 F 2
Akademija *Kaunas(LT)*....176 B 1
Akademija *Kédainiai(LT)*.170 C 3
Akaki *(CY)*..................231 C 3
Akaki *(CY)*..................231 C 3
Akanthou *(CY)*.............231 D 2
Äkäsjokisuu *(FIN)*..........128 C 2
Äkäslompolo *(FIN)*.........128 C 2
Akéčiai *(LT)*................169 F 4
Aken *(D)*....................84 C 4
Åkers styckebruk *(S)*.......140 C 4
Åkersberga *(S)*.............141 D 4
Akhisar *(TR)*................19 F 2
Åkirkeby *(DK)*..............145 E 3
Akkerhaugen *(N)*...........139 D 3
Akmena *(LT)*...............177 E 2
Akmenãja *(LV)*.............167 E 3
Akmené *(LT)*...............163 E 3
Akmené Iii *(LT)*............163 E 3
Akmeniai *Alytaus(LT)*.....175 F 4
Akmeniai *Panevėžio(LT)*.171 D 1
Akmenynai *(LT)*...........175 E 3
Akmenynė *(LT)*............177 E 3
Akníste *(LV)*...............165 F 4
Aknyščiai *(LT)*.............171 E 2
Akraífnio *(GR)*.............218 B 1
Akranes *(IS)*...............126 A 2
Akráta *(GR)*................217 E 1
Åkrehamn *(N)*.............138 B 3
Akrestrømmen *(N)*........139 F 1
Akritas *(GR)*...............205 E 2
Akrogiáli *(GR)*.............207 D 3
Akropótamos *(GR)*........207 D 3
Akrotíri *(CY)*...............230 B 4
Akrotíri *Kikládes(GR)*.....224 C 3
Akrotíri
(Chersónisos) *(GR)*.....224 C 3
Akrotíri Bay *(CY)*..........231 C 4
Akrovoúni *(GR)*............207 E 2
Äksi *(EST)*..................155 D 3
Akste *(EST)*................155 E 3
Akstinai *Kauno(LT)*........169 F 2
Akstinai *Tauragés(LT)*....169 D 3
Akujärvi *(FIN)*.............125 F 3
Akuotninkai *(LT)*..........177 F 1
Akureyri *(IS)*...............126 B 1
Ål *(N)*......................139 D 3
Ala *(EST)*...................159 F 1
Åla *(I)*......................97 F 3
Alà dei Sardi *(I)*............108 B 2
Ala di Stura *(I)*.............53 E 2
Ala-Honkajoki *(FIN)*.......136 B 2
Ala-Vuokki *(FIN)*...........135 E 1
Alaburdiškės *(LT)*..........177 D 3
Alacant / Alicante *(E)*......71 F 4
Alaejos *(E)*.................63 F 3
Alagna Valsesia *(I)*.........53 F 1
Alagón *(E)*..................65 F 2
Alagoniá *(GR)*.............217 F 2
Alahärmä *(FIN)*............133 D 3
Alaior *(E)*...................73 F 2
Alajõe *(EST)*...............151 F 4
Alakylä *(FIN)*...............128 C 2
Alalkomenés *(GR)*.........217 F 1
Alameda *(E)*................76 A 2
Alamillo *(E)*................70 A 3
Alaminos *(CY)*.............231 C 4
Alampra *(CY)*..............231 C 3
Alanäs *(S)*..................132 A 2
Ålande *(LV)*................162 B 2
Alandroal *(P)*...............68 E 3
Alange *(E)*..................69 E 3
Alanís *(E)*..................69 E 4
Alanta *(LT)*.................171 E 3
Alantês *(LT)*................171 D 2
Alar del Rey *(E)*...........60 A 4
Alaraz *(E)*..................63 F 4
Alarcón *(E)*................71 D 2
Alaşehir *(TR)*...............19 F 2
Alassio *(I)*..................100 B 2
Alastaro *(FIN)*.............136 C 3
Alatoz *(E)*..................71 E 3
Alatri *(I)*....................105 D 2
Alatskivi *(EST)*.............155 D 3
Alavere *(EST)*..............149 F 3
Alavieska *(FIN)*............133 E 2
Alavus / Alavo *(FIN)*.......133 D 3
Alba *(I)*.....................53 F 3
Alba Adriatica *(I)*...........103 D 3
Alba de Tormes *(E)*........63 F 4
Alba Iulia *(RO)*............12 C 4

Albacete *(E)*...............71 D 3
Albacken *(S)*...............132 A 4
Álbæk *(DK)*................142 C 2
Albaida *(E)*.................71 F 4
Albaladejo *(E)*.............70 C 4
Albalate de Cinca *(E)*......66 A 3
Albalate
de las Nogueras *(E)*....71 D 1
Albalate del Arzobispo *(E)*.65 F 4
Alban *(F)*...................55 F 1
Albánchez *(E)*.............77 D 2
Albano di Lucania *(I)*.......106 C 3
Albano Laziale *(I)*..........105 D 2
Albarca *(E)*.................66 B 3
Albares de la Ribera *(E)*....59 D 4
Albarracín *(E)*..............71 E 1
Albatana *(E)*...............71 E 4
Albatera *(E)*................77 F 1
Albena *(BG)*...............19 E 1
Albenga *(I)*.................100 B 2
Albens *(F)*..................53 D 1
Alberga *(S)*.................140 C 4
Albergaria-a-Velha *(P)*.....62 B 3
Alberic *(E)*..................71 F 3
Albernoa *(P)*...............68 B 4
Alberobello *(I)*.............107 D 3
Albersdorf *(D)*.............78 C 3
Albert *(F)*...................38 C 3
Albertville *(F)*..............53 D 1
Albestroff *(F)*...............45 D 3
Albi *(F)*.....................55 E 1
Albiano d'Ivrea *(I)*..........53 F 2
Albinia *(I)*...................101 F 2
Albino *(I)*...................97 E 3
Albissola Marina *(I)*........100 C 1
Albocàsser *(E)*.............72 A 1
Alboloduy *(E)*..............76 C 3
Albolote *(E)*................76 B 2
Alborea *(E)*.................71 E 3
Ålborg *(DK)*................142 B 2
Albox *(E)*...................77 D 2
Albstadt *(D)*................45 F 4
Albu *(EST)*.................149 F 3
Albufeira *(P)*...............74 A 4
Albujón *(E)*................77 E 1
Albuñol *(E)*.................76 B 3
Alburquerque *(E)*..........69 D 2
Alby *(S)*.....................131 F 4

Alby-sur-Chéran *(F)*........53 D 1
Alcácer do Sal *(P)*.........68 B 3
Alcáçovas *(P)*..............68 B 3
Alcadozo *(E)*...............71 D 4
Alcafozes *(P)*..............69 D 1
Alcains *(P)*.................68 C 1
Alcalá de Guadaíra *(E)*....75 E 1
Alcalá de Henares *(E)*.....64 C 4
Alcalá de la Selva *(E)*......71 F 1
Alcalá de los Gazules *(E)*..75 E 3
Alcalá de Xivert *(E)*........72 A 1
Alcalá del Júcar *(E)*........71 E 3
Alcalá del Río *(E)*..........75 E 1
Alcalá la Real *(E)*..........76 B 2
Alcalfar *(E)*.................73 F 2
Alcamo *(I)*..................110 B 3
Alcampel *(E)*...............66 A 3
Alcanar *(E)*.................72 B 1
Alcanede *(P)*...............68 A 2
Alcanena *(P)*...............68 A 2
Alcanhões *(P)*.............68 B 2
Alcañices *(E)*...............63 E 2
Alcañiz *(E)*..................66 A 4
Alcántara *(E)*...............69 D 1
Alcantarilha *(P)*............74 A 4
Alcantarilla *(E)*.............77 E 1
Alcaracejos *(E)*............69 F 4
Alcaraz *(E)*.................71 D 4
Alcaria Ruiva *(P)*...........74 A 4
Alcarràs *(E)*................66 B 3
Alcaudete *(E)*..............76 A 1
Alcaudete de la Jara *(E)*...70 A 1
Alcázar de San Juan *(E)*...70 C 2
Alceda *(E)*..................60 A 3
Alcester *(GB)*..............36 A 2
Alcoba de los Montes *(E)*..70 A 2
Alcobaça *(P)*...............68 A 2
Alcobendas *(E)*............64 B 4
Alcocer *(E)*.................71 D 1
Alcochete *(P)*..............68 B 2
Alcoi / Alcoy *(E)*...........71 F 4
Alcolea *(E)*.................76 A 1
Alcolea de Cinca *(E)*.......66 A 3
Alcolea del Pinar *(E)*.......65 D 4
Alcolea del Río *(E)*........75 E 1
Alconchel *(E)*..............69 D 3
Alcorisa *(E)*................65 F 4
Alcossebre *(E)*.............72 A 1

Alcoutim *(P)*...............74 C 1
Alcover *(E)*.................66 B 3
Alcoy / Alcoi *(E)*...........71 F 4
Alcubierre *(E)*..............65 F 2
Alcubilla de Avellaneda *(E)*64 C 2
Alcublas *(E)*................71 F 2
Alcúdia *(E)*.................73 E 2
Alcudia de Guadix *(E)*.....76 C 2
Alcuéscar *(E)*...............69 E 2
Aldea del Cano *(E)*........69 E 2
Aldea del Fresno *(E)*.......70 B 1
Aldea del Rey *(E)*..........70 B 3
Aldea Quintana *(E)*........75 F 1
Aldeacentenera *(E)*........69 F 2
Aldeanueva de Ebro *(E)*...65 E 2
Aldeanueva de la Vera *(E)*.69 F 1
Aldeanueva del Camino *(E)*69 E 1
Aldeburgh *(GB)*............37 D 2
Aldeia da Ponte *(P)*........63 D 4
Aldeia Gavinha *(P)*........68 A 2
Alderi *(LV)*..................159 D 4
Aldershot *(GB)*.............36 B 4
Aldinci *(MK)*...............122 B 3
Aledo *(E)*...................77 E 1
Aleknonys *(LT)*............175 F 3
Aleknos *(LT)*...............165 F 4
Aleksa Šantić *(SRB)*.......113 D 3
Aleksandrava
Marijampolés(LT).....169 E 4
Aleksandrava *Vilniaus(LT)*177 F 4
Aleksandravas *(LT)*........162 C 4
Aleksandravélé *(LT)*.......172 B 1
Aleksandrov *(RUS)*........7 F 2
Aleksandrovac
Kruševac(SRB)........119 D 3
Aleksandrovac
Požarevac(SRB)........118 C 1
Aleksandrów Łodzkie *(PL)*195 E 2
Aleksandrów Lubelskie *(PL)*197 E 4
Aleksandrów
Kujawski(PL)..........188 C 1
Aleksandrów Łódzki *(PL)*189 D 4
Aleksin *(RUS)*.............7 F 3
Aleksinac *(SRB)*...........119 D 3
Alektora *(CY)*..............230 B 4
Alençon *(F)*................42 A 3
Alenquer *(P)*...............68 A 2
Alepochóri *Arkadía(GR)*..217 E 3

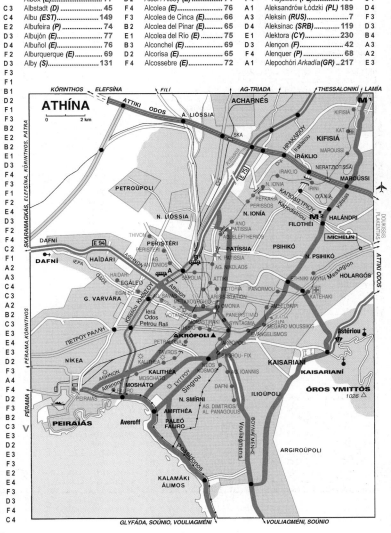

Alepochóri
  Atikí-Peireiás (GR)....218 B2
Aléria (F)....57 F3
Alès (F)....52 B4
Ales (I)....108 B3
Aleşd (RO)....12 C3
Alessandria (I)....97 D4
Alessandria
  della Rocca (I)....110 C3
Ålestrup (DK)....142 B3
Ålesund (N)....130 B3
Alexándreia (GR)....206 A3
Alexandria (GB)....30 C2
Alexandria (RO)....13 D4
Alexandroúpoli (GR)....208 B3
Alf (D)....45 D1
Alfajarín (E)....65 F3
Alfambra (E)....71 F1
Alfambra (P)....74 A1
Alfândega da Fé (P)....63 D2
Alfaro (E)....54 A4
Alfarràs (E)....66 B2
Alfedena (I)....105 E2
Alfeiós (GR)....217 B3
Alfeizerão (P)....68 A1
Alfeld (D)....89 D4
Alfeld (D)....84 A4
Alfonsine (I)....102 A1
Alford (GB)....28 B4
Alfreton (GB)....33 F3
Alfta (S)....140 C1
Algaida (E)....73 E2
Algar (E)....75 E3
Algar de Palància (E)....71 F2
Ålgård (N)....138 B4
Algarinejo (E)....76 A2
Algarrobo (E)....76 A3
Algatocín (E)....75 F3
Algeciras (E)....75 E4
Algemesí (E)....71 F3
Alghero (I)....108 A2
Alginet (E)....71 F3
Algodonales (E)....75 F3
Algora (E)....65 D4
Algorta (E)....60 C3
Algoz (P)....74 B2
Alhama de Almería (E)....76 C3
Alhama de Aragón (E)....65 E3
Alhama de Granada (E)....76 A2
Alhama de Murcia (E)....77 E1
Alhambra (E)....70 C3
Alhaurín el Grande (E)....75 F3
Alhóndiga (E)....64 C4
Ali Terme (I)....111 F2
Alía (E)....69 F2
Alia (I)....110 C3
Aliaga (E)....65 F4
Aliaguilla (E)....71 E2
Aliartos (GR)....218 B1
Alibunar (SRB)....113 F4
Alicante / Alacant (E)....71 F4
Alicún de Ortega (E)....76 C1
Alieši (LV)....160 C2
Alife (I)....105 F2
Alijó (P)....63 D3
Alikianós (GR)....226 A2
Alimiá (Nisí) (GR)....228 B2
Alingsås (S)....143 D1
Alinyà (E)....55 D4
Alise-Ste-Reine (F)....48 C2
Aliseda (E)....69 D2
Alistráti (GR)....207 D2
Alivéri (GR)....218 C1
Alizava (LT)....165 E4
Aljezur (P)....74 A1
Aljucén (E)....69 E3
Aljustrel (P)....68 B4
Alkión (GR)....208 B2
Alkiškiai (LT)....163 E3
Alkmaar (NL)....82 B3
Alksnénai (LT)....170 C2
Alksniši (LV)....167 D3
Alksniupiai (LT)....170 C2
Allagí (GR)....217 E4
Allaire (F)....41 D4
Allanche (F)....51 F2
Alland (A)....95 E2
Allariz (E)....58 C4
Allaži (LV)....159 E4
Allažmuiža (Ausmas) (LV)159 E4
Alleen (N)....142 A1
Alleghe (I)....98 A1
Allègre (F)....52 A2
Allensbach (D)....93 D3
Allentsteig (A)....95 D1
Allepuz (E)....71 F1
Allersberg (D)....89 D4

Allershausen (D)....93 F2
Alleuze (F)....52 A3
Allevard (F)....53 D2
Alliku (EST)....149 D3
Allinge Sandvig (DK)....143 E4
Allo (E)....61 D4
Alloa (GB)....31 D2
Allonnes (F)....47 D2
Alloza (E)....65 F4
Allstedt (D)....89 D1
Almacelles (E)....66 B3
Almáchar (E)....76 A3
Almada (P)....68 A3
Almadén (E)....70 A3
Almadén de la Plata (E)....75 E1
Almadenejos (E)....70 A3
Almagro (E)....70 B3
Almajano (E)....65 D2
Almále (LV)....156 C4
Almancil (P)....74 B2
Almansa (E)....71 E3
Almanza (E)....59 F4
Almaraz (E)....69 F1
Almargen (E)....75 F2
Almarza (E)....65 D2
Almassora (E)....72 A2
Almazán (E)....65 D3
Almedinilla (E)....76 A2
Almeida (E)....63 D3
Almeida (P)....63 D4
Almeirim (P)....68 B2
Almelo (NL)....83 D3
Almenar (E)....66 B2
Almenar de Soria (E)....65 D2
Almenara (E)....72 A2
Almendral (E)....69 D3
Almendralejo (E)....69 D3
Almere-Stad (NL)....82 B3
Almería (E)....76 C3
Almerimar (E)....76 C3
Almese (I)....53 F2
Ålmhult (S)....143 E3
Almodóvar (P)....74 B1
Almodóvar del Campo (E)....70 A3
Almodóvar del Pinar (E)....71 E2
Almodóvar del Río (E)....75 F2
Almogía (E)....76 A3
Almoguera (E)....70 C1
Almohárin (E)....69 E3
Almonacid de la Sierra (E)65 E3
Almonacid de Toledo (E)....70 C2
Almonacid de Zorita (E)....70 C1
Almonaster la Real (E)....75 D1
Almonte (E)....75 D2
Almoradí (E)....77 F1
Almorox (E)....70 A1
Almudévar (E)....65 F2
Almuñécar (E)....76 A3
Almuradiel (E)....70 B4
Almyrí (GR)....217 F2
Almyró (GR)....217 E2
Almyrós (GR)....212 B3
Alness (GB)....27 E3
Alnö (S)....132 A4
Alnwick (GB)....31 E3
Aloja (LV)....159 E3
Alona (CY)....231 C3
Alónia (P)....206 D3
Alónnisos (GR)....213 D3
Alónnisos (Nisí) (GR)....213 D3
Álora (E)....75 F3
Alosno (E)....74 C1
Aloupos (CY)....230 B2
Alové (LT)....176 C3
Alozaina (E)....75 F3
Alp (E)....55 E4
Alpalhão (P)....68 C2
Alpedrinha (P)....68 C1
Alpera (E)....71 E3
Alphen aan den Rijn (NL)..82 B4
Alpiarça (P)....68 B2
Alpignano (I)....53 F2
Alpirsbach (D)....45 E4
Alpua (FIN)....133 E2
Alqueva (P)....68 C4
Als (DK)....142 C3
Alsdorf (D)....87 D2
Alsédžiai (LT)....163 D2
Alsen (S)....131 F3
Alsfeld (D)....88 B2
Alši (LV)....163 D2
Alsíninkai (LT)....176 C3
Alsleben (D)....84 C4

Alstahaug (N)....127 D4
Alston (GB)....31 E4
Alsunga (LV)....156 C4
Alsviķi (LV)....161 D2
Alt Ruppin (D)....85 D2
Alta (N)....125 D2
Altamura (I)....106 C3
Altastenberg (D)....88 A1
Altaussee (A)....94 C3
Altavilla Milicia (I)....110 C2
Altdöbern (D)....85 E4
Altdorf (CH)....97 D1
Altdorf b. Nürnberg (D)....89 D4
Altea (E)....72 A4
Altedo (I)....98 A4
Altena (D)....87 F1
Altenahr (D)....87 E3
Altenau (D)....84 A4
Altenberg (D)....89 F1
Altenberge (D)....83 E3
Altenburg (D)....89 E1
Altenholz (D)....79 D3
Altenhundem (D)....87 F1
Altenkirchen (D)....80 C2
Altenkirchen
  i. Westerwald (D)....87 F2
Altenmarkt (A)....94 C3
Altenmarkt a. d. Alz (D)....94 A2
Altenmarkt
  bei Sankt Gallen (A)....95 D3
Altenstadt (D)....93 E2
Altensteig (D)....45 F3
Altentreptow (D)....80 C4
Altenwalde (D)....78 C2
Alter do Chão (P)....68 C2
Altglashütten (D)....45 A2
Altheim (A)....94 B2
Althofen (A)....95 D4
Altkirch (F)....49 F1
Altlandsberg (D)....85 E2
Altlengbach (A)....95 E2
Altmünster (A)....94 C2
Altnaharra (GB)....27 E2
Alton (GB)....35 F2
Altopascio (I)....101 D4
Altorricón (E)....66 B2
Altötting (D)....94 B2
Altrincham (GB)....32 C2
Altsasu / Alsasua (E)....61 D4
Altshausen (D)....93 D3
Altstätten (CH)....93 D4
Altura (E)....71 F2
Altweilnau (D)....88 A3
Altzola (E)....60 C3
Alu (EST)....149 E4
Alūksne (LV)....161 D3
Aluona (LT)....177 F2
Alustante (E)....65 E4
Aluste (EST)....154 A3
Alva (GB)....31 B1
Alvaiázere (P)....68 B1
Alvalade (P)....68 B4
Alvdal (N)....131 D2
Älvdalen (S)....140 B1
Alverca do Ribatejo (P)....68 A2
Alvesta (S)....143 E2
Alvignac (F)....51 E3
Ålvik (N)....138 C2
Alvito (P)....68 B4
Älvkarleby (S)....141 D2
Alvor (P)....74 A2
Älvros (S)....140 B1
Älvsbyn (S)....128 B4
Alwernia (PL)....201 A2
Alykés (CY)....230 C3
Alýki (GR)....219 E4
Alyth (GB)....31 D1
Alytus (LT)....176 C3
Alzenau (D)....88 B3
Alzey (D)....45 E1
Alzira (E)....71 F3
Alzon (F)....52 A4
Alzonne (F)....51 E3
Ama (EST)....150 A3
Amadora (P)....68 A3
Åmål (S)....139 F4
Amalfi (I)....105 F4
Amaliáda (GR)....216 C2
Amaliápoli (GR)....212 B3
Amáló (P)....220 D2
Amance (F)....49 E1
Amancey (F)....49 E2
Amandola (I)....102 E2
Amantea (I)....109 C2
Amarante (P)....62 C2
Amárantos Ioánnina (GR)205 D4
Amárantos Kardítsa (GR)..211 F3

Amareleja (P)....68 C4
Amares (P)....62 C2
Amargeti (CY)....230 A3
Amári (EST)....149 D3
Amári (LV)....163 F2
Amárynthos (GR)....218 C1
Amatrice (I)....159 F4
Amatas Skola (LV)....159 F4
Amathous (CY)....231 C4
Amatnieki (LV)....166 C2
Amatrice (I)....102 C4
Amay (B)....39 F2
Ambarès-et-Lagrave (F)....50 B3
Ambasaguas (E)....59 F4
Ambazac (F)....47 D4
Ambeļi (LV)....167 D4
Amberg (D)....89 E4
Ambérieu-en-Bugey (F)....49 D3
Ambert (F)....52 A2
Ambès (F)....50 B3
Ambierle (F)....48 B3
Ambla (EST)....149 E3
Amble (GB)....31 F3
Ambleside (GB)....32 C1
Amboise (F)....47 E2
Ambra (I)....102 A3
Ambrières-les-Vallées (F)...41 F3
Ameixial (P)....74 B1
Amele (LV)....157 D3
Amelia (I)....102 B2
Amélie-les-Bains-
  Palalda (F)....55 F4
Amelinghausen (D)....84 A3
Amer (E)....67 D2
Amerongen (NL)....82 B4
Amersfoort (NL)....82 B3
Amersham (GB)....36 B3
Amesbury (GB)....35 F2
Amfiaraeío (GR)....218 C1
Amfikleia (GR)....212 B4
Amfilochía (GR)....211 E4
Amfípoli (GR)....207 D3
Ámfissa (GR)....212 A4
Amiens (F)....38 C4
Amilly (F)....43 D4
Åmli (N)....139 D4
Amlwch (GB) /
  Ammanford (GB)....32 A2
Ammanford /
  Rhydaman (GB)....34 C1
Ämmänsaari (FIN)....135 E1
Ammarnäs (S)....127 E4
Ammochóri (GR)....205 F2
Ammochostos /
  Gazimağusa (CY)....231 E3
Ammochostos Bay (CY)..231 E2
Ammótopos (GR)....211 D3
Ammoudára Irákleio (GR)..227 D2
Ammoudára Lasíthi (GR)..227 E3
Amolianí (GR)....207 E2
Amolianí (Nisí) (GR)....207 E2
Amorbach (D)....45 F1
Amorebieta (E)....60 C3
Amorgós (GR)....225 D2
Amorgós (Nisí) (GR)....225 D2
Amório (GR)....208 A2
Åmot (N)....139 E3
Åmot (S)....138 C3
Åmot (S)....140 C2
Åmotfors (S)....139 F3
Amou (F)....54 B2
Ampelákia Évros (GR)....208 A3
Ampelákia Lárisa (GR)....212 B2
Ampeleía (GR)....212 B2
Ampelikó (GR)....214 C3
Ampelikou (CY)....230 B3
Ampelióna (GR)....217 E4
Ampelónas (GR)....212 A1
Ampelóchori (GR)....206 B1
Amphion-les-Bains (F)....49 F4
Amplepuis (F)....48 C4
Amposta (E)....66 B4
Ampthill (GB)....36 B2
Ampudia (E)....60 A4
Ampuero (E)....60 C3
Amriswil (CH)....93 D4
Amsele (S)....132 B2
Amstelveen (NL)....82 B3
Amsterdam (NL)....82 B3
Amstetten (A)....95 D2
Amurrio (E)....60 C3
Amusco (E)....60 B4
Amvrosía (GR)....207 F2
Amygdaleónas (GR)....207 E2
Amygdaliá (GR)....217 E2
Amýntaio (GR)....205 F2
Åna Sira (N)....138 B4

Anadia (P)....62 C2
Anáfi (GR)....224 C3
Anáfi (Nisí) (GR)....224 C3
Anafonítria (GR)....216 B2
Anafotida (CY)....231 D3
Anagni (I)....105 C1
Análipsi Dodekánissa (GR)225 F4
Análipsi Viotía (GR)....217 F1
Análipsis (GR)....217 D4
Anan'ïv (UA)....13 E2
Anárgyroi (GR)....205 E3
Änari (EST)....149 F4
Anarita (CY)....230 A4
Anarráchi (GR)....205 F4
Anascaul (IRL)....24 A3
Änäset (S)....132 D4
Anatolí Lárisa (GR)....212 B1
Anatolí Lasíthi (GR)....227 E3
Anatolikó (GR)....205 F3
Anávatos (GR)....220 C1
Anávra Kardítsa (GR)....211 F3
Anávyssos (GR)....218 C2
Ance (LV)....157 D2
Ancene (LV)....166 B4
Ancenis (F)....46 E2
Ancerville (F)....44 B3
Anchuras (E)....70 A2
Ančiškiai (LT)....165 D4
Anciškis (LT)....170 C3
Anciūnai (LT)....171 E4
Ancona (I)....102 C4
Ancy-le-Franc (F)....43 F4
Anda (N)....130 A4
Andalo (I)....97 D2
Åndalsnes (N)....130 B4
Andebu (N)....139 E4
Andelot (F)....44 B3
Andenes (N)....124 A3
Andenne (B)....39 F2
Anderlues (B)....39 E4
Andermatt (CH)....96 C1
Andernach (D)....87 D3
Andernos-les-Bains (F)....50 B3
Anderstorp (S)....143 E2
Andoain (E)....61 D3
Andorno Micca (I)....53 F4
Andorra (E)....65 F4
Andosilla (E)....61 E1
Andover (GB)....35 F2
Andratx (E)....73 D1
Andravída (GR)....216 C2
Andrespol (PL)....189 C3
Andretta (I)....106 B3
Andrézieux-Bouthéon (F)...52 B2
Andria (I)....106 C2
Andrijevica (MNE)....121 E2
Andrioniškis (LT)....171 E3
Andritsaina (GR)....217 D2
Ándros (GR)....219 E2
Ándros (Nisí) (GR)....219 E2
Androúsa (GR)....217 D4
Andrupene
  (Ondrupine) (LV)....167 E3
Andrychów (PL)....200 F2
Andselv (N)....124 B3
Andújar (E)....76 A1
Anduze (F)....52 A4
Andzeļi (LV)....167 E4
Åne (LV)....164 C2
Aneby (S)....143 E1
Anet (F)....42 C1
Angastina (CY)....231 D2
Ånge (S)....131 F4
Ånge (S)....131 F4
Angeja (P)....62 B2
Ängelholm (S)....143 D3
Angeli (FIN)....125 E3
Angelókastro
  Etolía-Akarnanía (GR)..211 E4
Angelókastro
  Korinthía (GR)....217 F2
Anger (A)....95 E3
Angermünde (D)....85 E2
Angern a. d. March (A)....95 F1
Angers (F)....46 C2
Angerville (F)....42 C2
Anghiari (I)....102 A3
Ängi (EST)....154 B3
Angítis (GR)....207 D2
Anglès (E)....67 D2
Anglesola (E)....66 B3
Angles-sur-l'Anglin (F)....47 E3
Anglet (F)....54 A2
Anglisides (CY)....231 D3

Anglure (F)....43 F3
Angoulême (F)....50 C1
Angri (I)....105 F3
Angüés (E)....54 C4
Anguiano (E)....65 D1
Anguillara Veneta (I)....98 B3
Anguse (EST)....151 E2
Aniane (F)....56 A2
Aniche (F)....39 D3
Anija (EST)....149 E3
Anikatsi (EST)....154 B4
Anizy-le-Château (F)....39 D4
Anjalankoski (FIN)....137 E3
Anjum (NL)....82 C2
Ankaran (SLO)....99 D2
Ankarsrum (S)....143 F1
Anklam (D)....80 C3
Ankum (D)....83 E3
Ánmēmele
  Jaunmēmele) (LV)....165 D3
Ånn (S)....131 E3
Anna (EST)....149 F4
Anna (LV)....161 D3
Annaberg-Buchholz (D)....89 F2
Annaberg im Lammertal (A)95 D4
Annaburg (D)....85 D4
Anndalsvågen (N)....127 D4
Annecy (F)....49 E4
Annemasse (F)....49 E4
Annenieki (LV)....163 F2
Annevoie-Rouillon (B)....39 F3
Annikoru (EST)....154 C4
Annikvere (EST)....150 C2
Annonay (F)....52 B2
Annone Veneto (I)....98 C3
Annopol (PL)....196 C3
Annot (F)....53 E4
Annweiler (F)....45 E2
Áno Chóra (GR)....211 F4
Áno Kalentíni (GR)....211 E3
Áno Kalliníki (GR)....205 E2
Áno Lefkímmi (GR)....210 B2
Áno Polydéndri (GR)....212 B2
Áno Sagkrí (GR)....219 F4
Áno Sýros (GR)....219 E3
Áno Viánnos (GR)....227 D3
Áno Vrontoú (GR)....207 D1
Áno Zervochóri (GR)....206 A3
Anógeia Lakonía (GR)....217 E4
Anógeia Réthymno (GR)..226 C2
Anogyra (CY)....230 B4
Ánoixi (GR)....211 E1
Anópoli (GR)....226 B2
Añover de Tajo (E)....70 B1
Ansbach (D)....88 C4
Ansedonia (I)....104 B1
Ansião (P)....68 B1
Ansnes (N)....130 C2
Ansó (E)....54 B3
Anstruther (GB)....31 E1
Antakalniai (LT)....177 E1
Antakalnis
  Kaišiadorys (LT)....176 C1
Antakalnis Prienai (LT)....176 C2
Antalgė (LT)....171 F3
Antaliepté (LT)....171 F2
Antalkiai (LT)....169 F4
Antalksné (LT)....172 B3
Antanaičiai (LT)....171 E4
Antanašė (LT)....171 F1
Antartikó (GR)....205 E3
Antas (E)....77 D2
Antášava (LT)....171 D1
Antazavė (LT)....172 B1
Antegnate (I)....97 E3
Antemil (E)....58 B2
Antequera (E)....76 A2
Anterselva di Mezzo /
  Antholz Mittertal (I)....98 A1
Ántheia (GR)....208 C2
Anthí (GR)....206 C2
Anthíli (GR)....212 B4
Anthótopos (GR)....212 B3
Antibes (F)....57 E2
Antígonos (GR)....205 F3
Antikýra (GR)....217 F1
Antikýthira (Nisí) (GR)....223 E4
Antimácheia (GR)....225 E2
Antímilos (Nisí) (GR)....224 A2
Antíparos (GR)....219 E4
Antípaxoi (Nisí) (GR)....210 C3
Antipsara (Nisí) (GR)....214 B4
Antírrio (GR)....217 D1
Ántissa (GR)....214 C3

Antkalniškiai (LT) 169 F4
Antkoptis (LT) 168 C1
Antnäs (S) 128 B4
Antonin (PL) 194 B1
Antraigues-sur-Volane (F). 52 B3
Antrain (F) 41 E3
Antrim (GB) 23 E2
Antrodoco (I) 102 C4
Antsla (EST) 161 D2
Anttola (FIN) 137 B2
Antuži (LV) 166 B2
Antwerpen (B) 39 E1
Anuži (LV) 157 F2
Anykščiai (LT) 171 E2
Anzano di Puglia (I) 106 B3
Anzio (I) 105 D3
Anzola d'Ossola (I) 96 C2
Anzy-le-Duc (F) 48 C4
Aoiz / Agoitz (E) 54 A3
Aosta / Aoste (I) 53 E1
Apaļi (LV) 167 F4
Apaščia (LT) 165 C4
Apatin (SRB) 113 D4
Apatovac (HR) 112 A4
Ape (LV) 161 D2
Apecchio (I) 102 B2
Apeiranthos (GR) 219 F4
Apeldoorn (NL) 82 C4
Apen (D) 83 E2
Aperāni (LV) 165 F3
Apéri (GR) 228 A4
Apgulde (LV) 163 F2
Aphrodisias (TR) 19 F3
Apidiá (GR) 223 D2
Apoíkia (GR) 219 E2
Apolakkiá (GR) 228 B3
Apolda (D) 89 D1
Apollon Ylatis
  (Sanctuary of) (CY) 230 B4
Apóllonas (GR) 219 F4
Apollonía Kikládes(GR).. 219 E4
Apollonía
  Thessaloníki(GR) 206 C3
Apóstoloi (GR) 226 C2
Apostolos Andreas
  (Cape) (CY) 231 F1
Apostolos Andreas
  (Karpasia) (CY) 231 F1
Apostolos Varnavas (CY) 231 E3
Apostolove (UA) 13 F2
Äppelbo (S) 140 B2
Appenweier (D) 45 E3
Appenzell (CH) 93 D4
Appiano
  s. str. d. vino / Eppan (I). 98 A1
Appingedam (NL) 83 D2
Appleby (GB) 31 E4
Aprica (I) 97 E2
Apricena (I) 106 B1
Apriķi (LV) 162 C1
Aprilia (I) 105 F2
Ápsalos (GR) 205 F2
Apšeni (LV) 165 F1
Apses (LV) 172 C1
Apšuciems (LV) 157 F4
Apt (F) 56 C1
Apta (N) 142 A1
Áptera (GR) 226 B2
Aptiekas (LV) 163 E2
Aquileia (I) 98 C2
Arabba (I) 98 A1
Aracena (E) 75 D1
Aráchova
  Etolía-Akarnanía(GR).. 211 F4
Aráchova Viotía(GR) 217 F1
Aračinovo (MK) 122 B2
Arad (RO) 113 F2
Arádaina (GR) 226 B2
Aradippou (CY) 231 D3
Aragona (I) 110 C3
Aramits (F) 54 B3
Aranda de Duero (E) 64 C3
Aranđelovac (SRB) 118 C2
Arandi (EST) 152 B3
Aranjuez (E) 70 B1
Arantzazu (E) 60 C3
Aras de los Olmos (E) 71 F2
Arasluokta (S) 127 F2
Arasvika (N) 130 C3
Áratos (GR) 208 B2
Aravaca (E) 64 B4
Aravete (EST) 149 F3
Aravissós (GR) 206 A3
Aravu (EST) 155 E4
Áraxos (GR) 216 C1
Arazede (P) 62 B4
Arbatax (I) 108 C3

Arbeca (E) 66 B3
Arbesbach (A) 95 D1
Arboga (S) 140 C4
Arbois (F) 49 E3
Arbon (CH) 93 D4
Arborea (Località) (I) 108 A3
Arborio (I) 96 C3
Arbrå (S) 140 C1
Arbroath (GB) 31 E1
Arbúcies (E) 67 D2
Arbus (I) 108 A4
Arc-en-Barrois (F) 49 D1
Arcachon (F) 50 B3
Arce (I) 105 E2
Arcen (NL) 87 D1
Arcevia (I) 102 B2
Archaía Epídavros (GR). 218 A3
Archaía Kórinthos (GR).. 217 F2
Archaía Neméa (GR) 217 F2
Archaía Olympía (GR) 217 D3
Archaía Thíra (GR) 224 C3
Archaíes Kleonés (GR).. 217 F2
Archánes (GR) 227 D2
Archángelos
  Dodekánissa(GR) 228 C2
Archángelos Pélla(GR) 206 A2
Archena (E) 77 E1
Archiac (F) 50 C2
Archidona (E) 76 A2
Arcidosso (I) 102 A3
Arcis-sur-Aube (F) 43 F3
Arco (I) 97 F3
Arco de Baulhe (P) 62 C2
Arcos (E) 64 B1
Arcos de Jalón (E) 65 D3
Arcos de la Frontera (E).. 75 E3
Arcos de Valdevez (P) 62 C1
Arcusa (E) 54 C4
Arczy (UA) 13 E3
Ardales (E) 75 F3
Årdalstangen (N) 139 D1
Ardánio (GR) 208 C2
Ardara (IRL) 22 C2
Ārdava (LV) 167 D4
Ardberg (GB) 30 A2
Ardee /
  Baile Átha Fhirdhia (IRL)23 E3
Ardentes (F) 47 F3
Ardentinny (GB) 30 F2
Ardes (F) 52 A2
Ardez (CH) 97 E1
Ardglass (GB) 23 F3
Ardisa (E) 54 B2
Ardlussa (GB) 30 B2
Ardmore / Aird Mhór (IRL). 25 D3
Ardrahan (IRL) 22 B4
Ardres (F) 43 E4
Ardrishaig (GB) 30 B3
Ardrossan (GB) 30 C2
Ardu (EST) 149 F4
Arduaine (GB) 30 B1
Ardvasar (GB) 27 D4
Åre (S) 131 E3
Areeta (E) 60 C1
Arenas de Cabrales (E).. 59 F3
Arenas de Iguña (E) 60 A3
Arenas de San Juan (E).. 70 B3
Arenas de San Pedro (E). 69 F1
Arendal (N) 139 D4
Arendole (Randauka) (LV)167 D4
Arendonk (B) 39 F1
Arendsee (D) 84 B2
Arenys de Mar (E) 67 D3
Arenzano (I) 100 C1
Areópoli (GR) 222 B2
Ares (E) 58 B2
Arês (F) 50 B3
Ares (S) 138 B2
Aréthousa (GR) 207 D3
Areti (GR) 206 C3
Arévalo (E) 64 A3
Arez (P) 68 C2
Arezzo (I) 102 A2
Arfará (GR) 217 D1
Argaka (CY) 230 A3
Árgaki (CY) 231 C2
Argalastí (GR) 212 C2
Argamasilla de Alba (E).. 70 C3
Argamasilla
  de Calatrava (E) 70 B3
Arganda del Rey (E) 70 C1
Arganil (P) 62 C2
Árnés (E) 58 A3
Argelès-Gazost (F) 54 C1
Argelès-sur-Mer (F) 55 F4
Argent-sur-Sauldre (F) 48 A2

Argenta (I) 98 B4
Argentan (F) 42 A2
Argentat (F) 51 E3
Argente (E) 65 F4
Argentière (F) 49 E3
Argenton-Château (F) 47 D3
Argenton-sur-Creuse (F).. 47 F3
Argentona (E) 67 D2
Arginónta (GR) 221 E1
Argithéa (GR) 211 E2
Árgos (GR) 217 F3
Árgos Orestikó (GR) 205 E3
Arpela (FIN) 128 C2
Argostóli (GR) 216 B1
Arguedas (E) 54 A4
Argueil (F) 38 B4
Arguellite (E) 71 D4
Arguis (E) 54 B4
Argyrádes (GR) 210 B2
Argyró (GR) 219 D1
Argyropoúleio (GR) 212 A1
Argyroúpoli (GR) 226 B2
Árhus (DK) 142 B2
Arianá (GR) 208 B2
Ariano Irpino (I) 106 A3
Ariano nel Polesine (I) 98 B2
Aribe (E) 54 A3
Aridaía (GR) 205 F2
Arija (E) 60 A3
Árikula (EST) 159 F1
Arild (S) 143 D3
Arilje (SRB) 118 C2
Arinagour (GB) 26 C4
Aríni (GR) 217 D3
Ariño (E) 65 F3
Arinthod (F) 49 D4
Ariogala (LT) 169 F3
Arísti (GR) 211 D1
Aristoménis (GR) 217 D1
Arísvi (GR) 208 B2
Aritzo (I) 108 B3
Ariza (E) 65 D3
Árjäng (S) 139 F4
Arjeplog (S) 127 F2
Arjona (E) 76 A1
Arkádi (GR) 226 C2
Arkadia (PL) 189 F3
Arkalochóri (GR) 227 D2
Arkása (GR) 228 A4
Arkesíni (GR) 225 C2
Arkítsa (GR) 212 C4
Arklow /
  An tInbhear Mór (IRL) 25 E2
Arkma (EST) 154 B3
Arkna (EST) 151 D3
Arkoí (Nisí) (GR) 221 D3
Arkoúdi (Nisí) (GR) 211 D4
Arlanc (F) 52 A2
Arlanda (S) 141 D3
Arlanzón (E) 60 B4
Arlaviškés (LT) 176 C1
Arlempdes (F) 52 A3
Arles (F) 56 B2
Arles-sur-Tech (F) 55 F4
Arlesheim (CH) 92 B4
Arlon (B) 44 B1
Arma di Taggia (I) 53 F4
Armação de Pêra (P) 74 B2
Armadale (GB) 31 D2
Armagh (GB) 23 E3
Armamar (P) 62 C3
Armenioi (GR) 217 D4
Armenístis (GR) 220 B2
Arménoi (GR) 226 C2
Armentières (F) 39 D2
Armilla (E) 76 B2
Armólia (GR) 220 C1
Árna (GR) 222 C2
Arnac-Pompadour (F) 51 E2
Arnaía (GR) 207 D3
Arnaoutis (Cape) (CY) 230 A3
Árnay-le-Duc (F) 48 C2
Arneburg (D) 84 C2
Arnedillo (E) 65 D2
Arnedo (E) 65 D2
Arnés (F) 66 A4
Árnes (S) 139 F3
Árni (GR) 101 E2
Árņi (LV) 159 D3
Arnionys II (LT) 171 F4
Árnissa (GR) 205 F3
Arnoldstein (A) 98 C1
Arnsberg (D) 87 F1
Arnstadt (D) 88 C2

Arnstein (D) 88 C3
Aroánia (GR) 217 E2
Aroche (E) 69 D4
Arogí (GR) 207 F2
Arona (I) 97 D3
Aroniádika (GR) 223 D3
Aronkylä (FIN) 133 D4
Áros (N) 139 E3
Arosa (CH) 97 E1
Arouca (P) 62 C2
Árøysund (N) 139 E4
Arpajon (F) 43 F3
Arpela (FIN) 128 C2
Arquata del Tronto (I) 102 C3
Arques (F) 38 C2
Arques-la-Bataille (F) 38 A4
Arquillos (E) 70 B4
Arrabal (E) 58 A4
Arracourt (F) 44 C2
Arraiolos (P) 68 B3
Arras (F) 39 D3
Arrasate / Mondragón (E).. 60 C3
Arreau (F) 54 C3
Arredondo (E) 60 B3
Arrens-Marsous (F) 54 B3
Arrifana (P) 63 D4
Arrigorriaga (E) 60 C3
Arriondas (E) 59 F2
Arroba de los Montes (E). 70 A3
Arrochar (GB) 30 C1
Arromanches-les-Bains (F) 41 F1
Arronches (P) 68 C2
Arroyo de la Luz (E) 69 D2
Arroyo de San Serván (E). 69 D3
Arroyo del Ojanco (E) 70 C4
Arroyomolinos de Léon (E) 69 D4
Arroyomolinos
  de Montánchez (E) 69 E2
Arruda dos Vinhos (P) 68 A2
Ārs (DK) 142 B2
Ars-en-Ré (F) 46 B4
Ars-sur-Moselle (F) 44 C2
Arsié (I) 98 A2
Arsiero (I) 98 A2
Arskógssandur (IS) 126 B2
Arsos (Lemesos) (CY) 230 B3
Arsos (Lysi) (CY) 231 D3
Ársunda (S) 140 C2
Arsy (F) 43 D1
Artà (E) 73 E2
Árta (GR) 211 D2
Arta Terme (I) 98 C1
Artajona (E) 54 A4
Artea (E) 60 C3
Artemísia (GR) 216 B2
Artemísio (GR) 212 C3
Artemónas (GR) 219 E4
Artena (I) 105 D2
Artenay (F) 42 C4
Artern (D) 89 D1
Artés (E) 66 C2
Artesa de Segre (E) 66 B2
Artesianó (GR) 211 F2
Arth (CH) 96 C1
Arth (D) 94 A2
Arthurstown (IRL) 25 D3
Arties (E) 55 D3
Artjärvi (FIN) 137 D3
Artotína (GR) 211 F4
Artziniega (E) 60 C3
Aruaru (EST) 149 E2
Arúküla Harju(EST) 149 E3
Arúküla Lääne-Viru(EST) 151 D3
Arumetsa (EST) 159 D1
Arundel (GB) 36 B4
Aruvalla (EST) 149 E3
Árvi (GR) 227 D2
Arvidsjaur (S) 128 A4
Árvik (N) 130 A4
Arvika (S) 139 F3
Árviksand (N) 124 A3
Arvydai (LT) 177 F1
Arzachena (I) 108 B1
Arzacq-Arraziguet (F) 54 B2
Arzano (F) 40 C4
Arzberg (D) 89 E1
Arzignano (I) 98 A3
Árzos (GR) 208 C1
Arzúa (E) 58 B3

Ascain (F) 54 A2
Ascha (D) 94 A1
Aschach an der Donau (A) 94 C2
Aschaffenburg (D) 45 F1
Aschau i. Chiemgau (D).. 94 A3
Aschbach-Markt (A) 95 D2
Ascheberg (D) 83 E4
Ascheberg (D) 79 D3
Aschendorf (Ems) (D) 83 D2
Aschersleben (D) 84 C4
Asciano (I) 102 A3
Ascó (E) 66 B3
Asco (F) 57 F3
Ascoli Piceno (I) 102 C3
Ascoli Satriano (I) 106 B2
Ascona (CH) 97 D2
Åse (N) 124 B2
Åseda (S) 143 F2
Åsele (S) 132 A2
Åsen (N) 131 D3
Asenovgrad (BG) 19 D3
Åseral (N) 138 C4
Aseri (EST) 151 E3
Asfáka (GR) 211 D1
Asfeld (F) 39 E4
Åsgårdstrand (N) 139 E4
Asgata (CY) 231 C4
Ashbourne (GB) 33 D3
Ashbourne (IRL) 23 C1
Ashburton (GB) 34 C3
Ashby de la Zouch (GB).. 33 D4
Ashford (GB) 36 C3
Ashington (GB) 31 D2
Ashton-under-Lyne (GB).. 33 D2
Asiago (I) 98 A3
Asikkala (FIN) 137 D3
Asín (E) 54 A4
Asíni (GR) 217 E3
Asinou (CY) 230 B3
Asipovičy (BY) 7 D4
Asiūklė (LT) 176 B3
Ask (N) 139 E3
Askainen (FIN) 136 B3
Askeaton (IRL) 24 B1
Askeia (CY) 231 D3
Askersund (S) 140 B4
Askim (N) 139 E3
Asklipieío Kos(GR) 225 F2
Asklipieío Ródos(GR) 228 C3
Askola (FIN) 137 E2
Askós (GR) 206 C3
Askvoll (N) 138 B1
Askýfou (GR) 226 B2
Ašmínta (LT) 176 C2
Asmunti (FIN) 129 D3
Asola (I) 97 F4
Asolo (I) 98 A2
Asomatos (CY) 231 C4
Asopía (GR) 218 B1
Asopós (GR) 223 D2
Ásos Kefalloniá(GR) 216 B1
Ásos Préveza(GR) 211 D2
Aspang Markt (A) 95 D3
Aspatria (GB) 31 D3
Aspe (E) 71 F4
Asperg (D) 45 F3
Aspet (F) 55 D3
Áspra Spítia (GR) 217 F1
Áspro (GR) 206 A3
Aspro (Cape) (CY) 230 B4
Aspróchoma (GR) 217 E4
Asprokremmos Dam (CY)230 A4
Asprópyrgos (GR) 218 B2
Asproválta (GR) 207 D3
Assaku (EST) 149 E3
Assamalla (EST) 150 C3
Asse (B) 39 E2
Assemini (I) 108 B4
Assen (NL) 83 D2
Assergi (I) 102 C4
Assens (DK) 142 B4
Assisi (I) 102 C3
Assmannshausen (D) 45 E1
Astaffort (F) 51 D4
Astakída (Nisí) (GR) 225 F4
Astakós (GR) 211 D4
Astášova (LV) 167 F3
Aste (EST) 152 A3
Aste Haamse (EST) 152 A3
Astere (LV) 159 D3
Asten (NL) 87 D2
Asti (I) 96 C4
Astipálea (GR) 225 D2
Astorga (E) 59 E3
Astorp (S) 143 D3
Ástros (GR) 217 E4
Astromeritis (CY) 231 C3

Astudillo (E) 64 B1
Astypálaia (GR) 225 E2
Astypálaia (Nisí) (GR) 225 E2
Asūne (LV) 167 F4
Ašvénai (LT) 163 A3
Asvestádes (GR) 208 C1
Asvestochóri (GR) 211 E4
Asvestópetra (GR) 205 F3
Atalánti (GR) 212 B4
Ataquines (E) 64 A3
Atarfe (E) 76 B2
Atašiene (LV) 166 C2
Ateca (E) 65 D3
Atella (I) 106 B3
Atessa (I) 103 D4
Ath (B) 39 E2
Athamánio (GR) 211 E2
Athánio (GR) 210 C4
Athboy (IRL) 23 D4
Athenry /
  Baile Átha an Rí (IRL) 22 C4
Atherstone (GB) 33 D4
Athienou (CY) 231 D3
Athína (GR) 218 C2
Athlone /
  Baile Átha Luain (IRL) 22 C4
Áthos (GR) 207 E4
Athy / Baile Átha Í (IRL) 25 D2
Áthyra (GR) 206 B3
Atienza (E) 64 C3
Atina (I) 105 E2
Atios (E) 58 B2
Atkočiai (LT) 171 D3
Atkočiškés (LT) 171 F2
Átokos (Nisí) (GR) 211 D4
Atouguia da Baleia (P) 68 A2
Atpūta Daugavpils(LV) 172 C1
Atpūta Jelgavas(LV) 164 B2
Ātran (S) 143 D2
Atri (I) 103 D3
Atsikí (GR) 214 A1
Atsítsa (GR) 213 E4
Atspuka (LV) 167 D2
Áttali (GR) 213 D4
Attendorn (D) 87 F1
Attersee (A) 94 C2
Attigliano (I) 102 B4
Attigny (F) 39 F4
Attleborough (GB) 37 D1
Attnang-Puchheim (A) 94 C2
Åtvidaberg (S) 143 F1
Atzeneta del Maestrat (E).. 72 A1
Au (D) 93 F2
Aub (D) 88 C4
Aubagne (F) 57 D2
Aubange (B) 44 B2
Aubenas (F) 52 B2
Aubenton (F) 39 E4
Aubergenville (F) 42 C2
Auberive (F) 49 D1
Aubeterre-sur-Dronne (F).. 50 C2
Aubigny-sur-Nère (F) 48 A2
Aubin (F) 51 F3
Aubonne (CH) 49 E3
Aubrac (F) 51 F3
Aubusson (F) 51 E1
Auce (LV) 163 E3
Auch (F) 55 D2
Auchencairn (GB) 30 C3
Auchterarder (GB) 31 D1
Auchtermuchty (GB) 31 D1
Auciems (LV) 159 A3
Audenge (F) 50 B3
Audeux (F) 49 E2
Audierne (F) 40 A3
Audincourt (F) 49 F2
Audlem (GB) 32 C3
Audriņi (LV) 167 E3
Audru (EST) 153 D3
Audruicq (F) 37 E4
Audun-le-Roman (F) 44 C2
Audun-le-Tiche (F) 44 C2
Aue (D) 89 E2
Auerbach (D) 89 E2
Auerbach
  i. d. Oberpfalz (D) 89 D4
Auffach (A) 94 A4
Aughnacloy (GB) 23 E2
Aughrim (IRL) 25 E2
Augménai (LT) 170 B2
Augsburg (D) 93 F2
Augstāsala (LV) 161 E4
Augstkalne Dobeles(LV).. 163 F3
Augstkalne Krāslavas(LV)173 E1
Augusta (I) 111 E3
Augustavas (LT) 172 C4
Auguste (LV) 162 C2

Augustenborg (DK) 144 B3
Augustow (PL) 185 E3
Augustowska (Puszcza) (PL) 185 E2
Augustusburg (D) 89 F1
Aukan (N) 130 C3
Aukra (N) 130 B3
Aukštadvaris (LT) 177 D2
Aukštalaukis (LT) 177 E4
Aukštdvaris (LT) 169 F4
Aukštelkai (LT) 170 B1
Aukštkalviai (LT) 162 B4
Aukštpamedžiai (LT) 169 E2
Aukštvilkiai (LT) 169 D3
Auleja (LV) 167 E4
Auletta (I) 106 B4
Aulla (I) 101 E1
Aullène (F) 57 F4
Aulnay (F) 47 D4
Aulnoye-Aymeries (F) 39 E3
Ault (F) 38 B3
Aulus-les-Bains (F) 55 D3
Auma (D) 89 D2
Aumale (F) 38 B4
Aumetz (F) 44 C2
Aumont-Aubrac (F) 52 A3
Aunay-sur-Odon (F) 41 F2
Auneau (F) 42 C3
Auneuil (F) 43 D1
Auning (DK) 142 C3

Aups (F) 57 D2
Aura (FIN) 136 B3
Auray (F) 40 C4
Aurdal (N) 139 D2
Aure (N) 130 D2
Aurec-sur-Loire (F) 52 B2
Auri (LV) 163 F2
Aurich (D) 83 D1
Aurignac (F) 55 D3
Aurillac (F) 51 F2
Auritz / Burguete (E) 54 A3
Aurland (N) 138 C1
Auros (F) 50 C4
Auronzo di Cadore (I) 98 B1
Auschwitz = Oświęcim (PL) 200 F2
Aušgiriai (LT) 169 D4
Ausonia (I) 105 E2
Aušra (LT) 170 A2
Aussa-Corno (I) 98 C2
Außernbrünst (D) 94 B1
Austbygd (N) 139 D2
Austrumi (LV) 163 D2
Auterive (F) 55 E2
Authon-du-Perche (F) 42 A2
Autol (E) 65 E2
Autrans (F) 52 C2
Autrey-lès-Gray (F) 49 D3
Autti (FIN) 129 D3

Auttoinen (FIN) 137 D2
Autun (F) 48 C3
Auvillar (F) 51 D4
Auxerre (F) 43 E4
Auxi-le-Château (F) 38 C3
Auxonne (F) 49 D2
Auzances (F) 48 A4
Auzeņi (LV) 167 E3
Auziņas (LV) 159 F1
Auzon (F) 52 A2
Availles-Limouzine (F) 47 C2
Avaldsnes (N) 138 B3
Avallon (F) 48 B2
Avanduse (EST) 151 D4
Avántas (GR) 208 B2
Avaviken (S) 127 A4? — Avaviken (S) 127
Avdimou (CY) 230 B4
Ávdira (GR) 207 F2
Avebury (GB) 35 E2
Aveiras de Cima (P) 68 A2
Aveiro (P) 62 B3
Avellino (I) 105 F3
Aversa (I) 105 F3
Avesnes-le-Comte (F) 38 C3
Avesnes-sur-Helpe (F) 39 E3
Avesta (S) 140 C3
Avetrana (I) 107 E2
Avezzano (I) 105 E4
Avgerinós (GR) 205 E4
Avgorou (CY) 231 D3

Avía (GR) 217 E4
Aviano (I) 98 B2
Aviemore (GB) 27 F4
Avigliana (I) 53 F2
Avigliano (I) 106 B3
Avignon (F) 52 C4
Ávila (E) 64 A4
Avilčiai (LT) 171 E3
Avilés (E) 59 E2
Aviliai (LT) 177 D1
Aviliai II (LT) 172 C2
Avintes (P) 62 B3
Avinurme (EST) 151 D4
Avión (E) 58 B4
Avioth (F) 39 F4
Avis (P) 68 C2
Avize (F) 43 F2
Avižonys (LT) 171 E4
Avlákia (GR) 221 D2
Avlémonas (GR) 223 D3
Avlés (GR) 205 F4
Avlíotes (GR) 210 B1
Avlóna (CY) 231 C1
Avlóna (GR) 218 C1
Avlum (DK) 142 B3
Avola (I) 111 E4
Avonmouth (GB) 35 E2
Avord (F) 48 A3

Avoriaz (F) 49 F4
Avoti (LV) 163 F1
Avotiņi Cēsu(LV) 159 F4
Avotiņi Jelgavas(LV) 163 F2
Ávra (GR) 208 B2
Avranches (F) 41 E2
Avtovac (BIH) 117 A4
Ax-les-Thermes (F) 55 E3
Axams (A) 93 F3
Axat (F) 55 F3
Axiochóri (GR) 206 B2
Axioúpoli (GR) 206 B3
Axminster (GB) 35 D3
Axós (GR) 226 C2
Ay (F) 43 F4
Ayamonte (E) 74 C2
Aydın (TR) 19 F3
Ayerbe (E) 54 B2
Aylesbury (GB) 36 B3
Ayllón (E) 64 C3
Aylsham (GB) 37 D1
Ayna (E) 71 D4
Ayora (E) 71 F3
Ayvacık (TR) 19 E2
Ayvalık (TR) 19 E2
Aywaille (B) 87 D3
Azaila (E) 65 F3
Azambuja (P) 68 A2
Azanja (SRB) 118 C1

Azaruja (P) 68 C3
Azay-le-Ferron (F) 47 E3
Azay-le-Rideau (F) 47 E2
Azinheira dos Barros (P) 68 B4
Azkoitia (E) 60 C3
Aznalcázar (E) 75 D3
Aznalcóllar (E) 75 E1
Azpeitia (E) 60 C3
Azuaga (E) 69 E4
Azuara (E) 65 F3
Azuel (E) 70 A4
Ažuolaičiai (LT) 170 C3
Ažuolija (LT) 171 F3
Ažuoliné (LT) 177 D2
Ažuoliniai (LT) 175 F3
Ažuolų Būda (LT) 175 F2
Ažuolytė (LT) 170 C2
Azuqueca de Henares (E) 64 C4

B

Baad (A) 93 E4
Baal (D) 87 D2
Baamonde (E) 58 C2
Baarle-Nassau (NL) 39 E2
Baarn (NL) 82 B4
Babadag (RO) 13 E4
Babelsberg (D) 85 D3
Babenhausen (D) 93 E2
Babenhausen (D) 45 F1

BARCELONA

Arnau d'Oms ... CS 4
Berlin ... BT 12
Bisbe Català ... AT 13
Bonanova (Pas. de la) ... BT 16
Borbó (Av. de) ... BT 17
Carles III (Gran Via de) ... BT 38
Constitució ... BT 50
Creu Coberta ... BT 53
Dalt (Travessera de) ... CS 56
Doctor Pi i Molist ... CS 65
Entença ... BT 71
Estadi (Av. de l') ... BCT 75
Fabra i Puig (Pas. de) ... CS 77
Gavà ... BT 84
Gran de Sant Andreu ... CS 88
Guinardó (Ronda del) ... CS 90
Josep Tarradellas (Av. de) ... BT 102
Madrid (Av. de) ... BT 110
Manuel Girona (Pas. de) ... BT 112
Mare de Déu de Montserrat (Av. de la) ... CS 113
Marina ... CT 114
Marquès de Comillas (Av. del) ... BT 115
Miramar (Av. de) ... CT 119
Numància ... BT 129
Piferrer ... CS 136
Pi i Margall ... CS 138
Poblenou (Rambla del) ... DT 141
Príncep d'Astúries ... BT 144
Pujades (Pas. de) ... CT 145
Ramiro de Maeztu ... CS 146
Ramon Albó ... CS 147
Reina Elisenda de Montcada (Pas. de) ... BT 151
Reina Maria Cristina (Av. de la) ... BT 152
Ribes (Carret.) ... CS 154
Rio de Janeiro (Av. de) ... CS 156
Santa Coloma (Pas. de) ... CS 186
Sant Antoni Maria Claret ... CS 162
Sant Antoni (Ronda de) ... CT 160
Sant Gervasi (Pas. de) ... BS 164
Sant Pau (Ronda de) ... CT 174
Sardenya ... CT 191
Tarragona ... CT 194
Tibidabo (Av. del) ... BS 196
Universitat (Pl. de la) ... CT 198
Verdum (Pas. de) ... CS 200

Legend

E — POBLE ESPANYOL
M4 — MUSEU D'ART DE CATALUNYA
M5 — MUSEU ARQUEOLÒGIC
P1 — PALAU SANT JORDI
T1 — TEATRE GREC
W — FUNDACIÓ JOAN MIRÓ
Z — PAVELLÓ MIES VAN DER ROHE

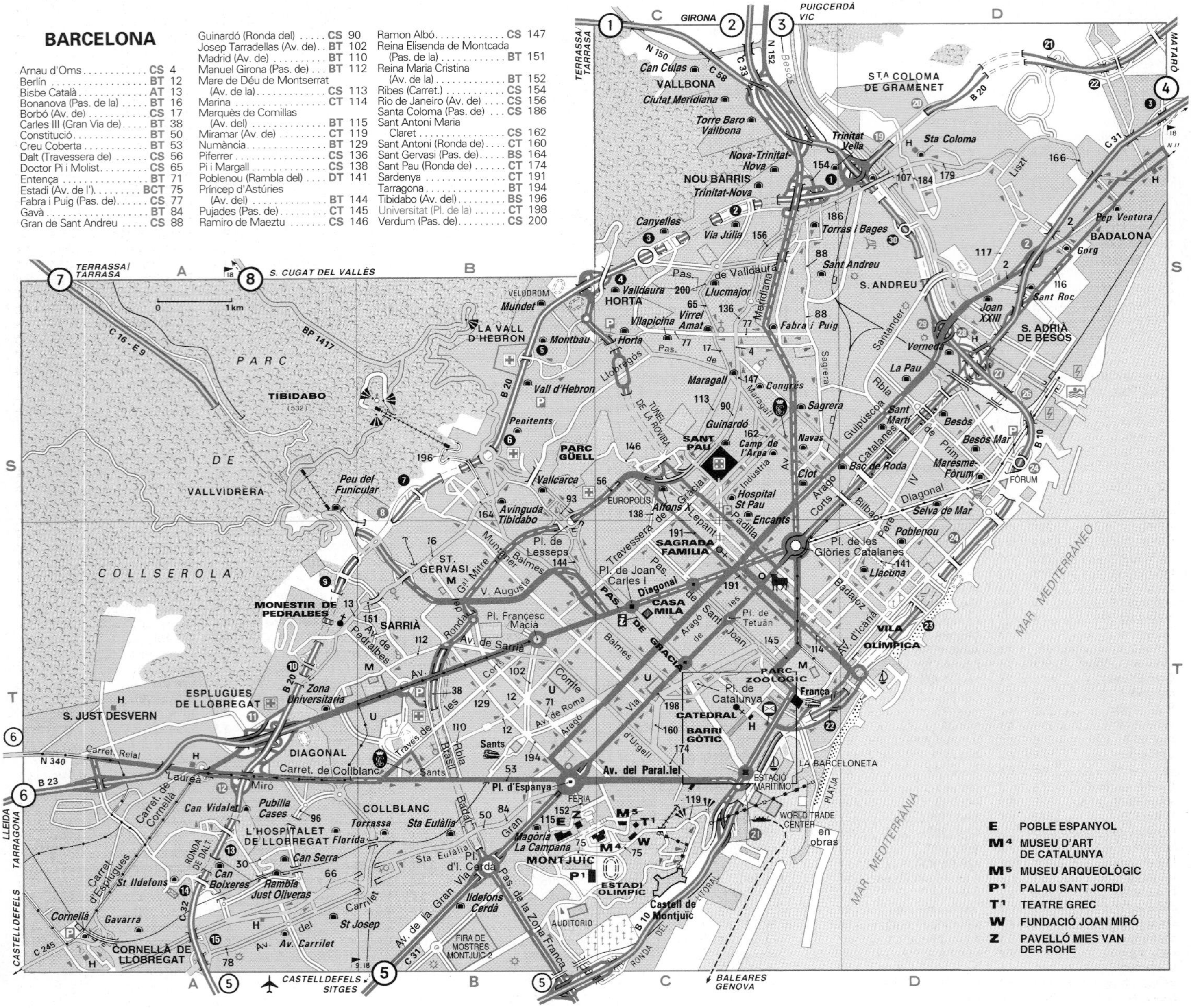

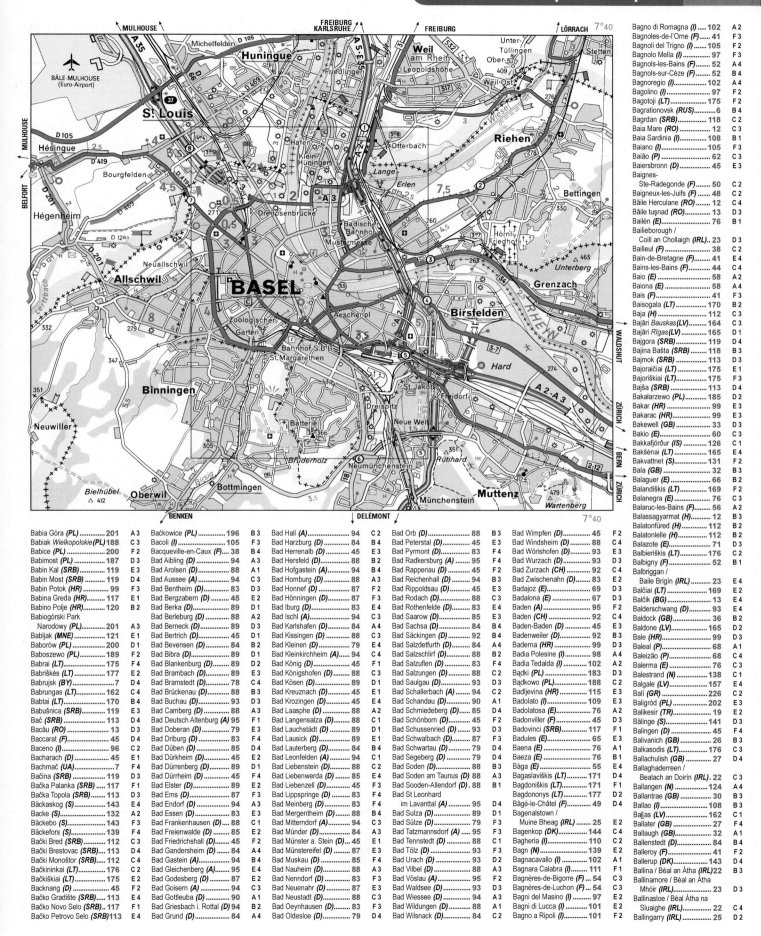

Bagno di Romagna (I) ...... 102 A 2
Bagnoles-de-l'Orne (F) ..... 41 F 3
Bagnoli del Trigno (I) .... 105 F 2
Bagnoli Mella (I) .... 97 F 3
Bagnols-les-Bains (F) ...... 52 A 4
Bagnols-sur-Cèze (F) .... 52 B 4
Bagnoregio (I) .... 102 A 4
Bagolino (I) .... 97 F 2
Bagotoji (LT) .... 175 F 2
Bagrationovsk (RUS) .... 6 B 4
Bagrdan (SRB) .... 118 C 2
Baia Mare (RO) .... 12 C 3
Baia Sardinia (I) .... 108 B 1
Baiano (I) .... 105 F 2
Baião (P) .... 62 C 3
Baiersbronn (D) .... 45 E 3
Baignes-
  Ste-Radegonde (F) .... 50 C 2
Baigneux-les-Juifs (F) ..... 48 C 2
Bäile Herculane (RO) .... 12 C 4
Bäile tuşnad (RO) .... 13 D 3
Bailén (E) .... 76 B 1
Bailieborough /
  Coill an Chollaigh (IRL).. 23 D 3
Bailleul (F) .... 38 C 2
Bain-de-Bretagne (F) .... 41 E 4
Bains-les-Bains (F) .... 44 C 4
Baio (E) .... 58 A 2
Baiona (E) .... 58 A 4
Bais (F) .... 41 F 3
Baisogala (LT) .... 170 E 2
Baja (H) .... 112 C 3
Bajàri Bauskas(LV) .... 164 C 3
Bajàri Rïgas(LV) .... 165 D 1
Bajgora (SRB) .... 119 D 4
Bajina Bašta (SRB) .... 118 B 3
Bajmok (SRB) .... 113 D 3
Bajoraičiai (LT) .... 175 E 1
Bajoriškiai (LT) .... 175 F 3
Bajša (SRB) .... 113 D 4
Bakalarzewo (PL) .... 185 D 2
Bakar (HR) .... 99 E 3
Bakarac (HR) .... 99 E 3
Bakewell (GB) .... 33 D 3
Bakio (E) .... 60 C 3
Bakkafjörður (IS) .... 126 C 1
Bakšénai (LT) .... 165 E 4
Bakvattnet (S) .... 131 F 2
Bala (GB) .... 32 B 3
Balaguer (E) .... 66 C 3
Balandiškis (LT) .... 169 F 2
Balanegra (E) .... 76 C 3
Balaruc-les-Bains (F) ...... 56 A 2
Balassagyarmat (H) .... 12 B 3
Balatonfüred (H) .... 112 B 2
Balatonlelle (H) .... 112 B 2
Balazote (E) .... 71 D 3
Balbieriškis (LT) .... 176 D 3
Balbigny (F) .... 52 B 1
Balbriggan /
  Baile Brigín (IRL) ...... 23 E 4
Balčiai (LT) .... 169 E 2
Balčik (BG) .... 13 E 4
Balderschwang (D) .... 93 E 4
Baldock (GB) .... 36 B 2
Baldone (LV) .... 165 D 2
Bale (HR) .... 98 D 3
Baleal (P) .... 68 A 1
Baleizão (P) .... 68 C 4
Balerma (E) .... 76 C 3
Balestrand (N) .... 138 C 1
Balgale (LV) .... 157 E 2
Balí (GR) .... 226 E 4
Baligród (PL) .... 202 E 3
Balikesir (TR) .... 19 E 2
Bälinge (S) 141
Balingen (D) .... 45 F 4
Balivanich (GB) .... 26 B 3
Balkasodis (LT) .... 176 D 3
Ballachulish (GB) .... 27 D 4
Ballaghaderreen /
  Bealach an Doirín (IRL). 22 C 3
Ballangen (N) .... 124 A 4
Ballantrae (GB) .... 30 B 3
Ballao (I) .... 108 B 3
Baļļas (LV) .... 162 C 1
Ballater (GB) .... 27 F 4
Ballaugh (GB) .... 32 A 1
Ballenstedt (D) .... 84 B 4
Balleroy (F) .... 41 F 2
Ballerup (DK) .... 143 D 2
Ballina / Béal an Átha (IRL)22 B 3
Ballinamore / Béal an Átha
  Mhóir (IRL) .... 23 D 3
Ballinasloe / Béal Átha na
  Sluaighe (IRL) .... 22 C 4
Ballingarry (IRL) .... 25 D 2

Babia Góra (PL) .... 201 A 3
Babiak Wielkopolskie(PL)188 C 3
Babice (PL) .... 200 F 2
Babimost (PL) .... 187 D 3
Babin Kal (SRB) .... 119 E 3
Babin Most (SRB) .... 119 D 4
Babin Potok (HR) .... 99 F 3
Babina Greda (HR) .... 117 E 1
Babino Polje (HR) .... 120 B 2
Babiogórski Park
  Narodowy (PL) .... 201 A 3
Babljak (MNE) .... 121 E 1
Baborów (PL) .... 200 D 1
Baboszewo (PL) .... 189 F 2
Babrai (LT) .... 175 F 4
Babriškès (LT) .... 177 E 2
Babrujsk (BY) .... 7 F 4
Babrungas (LT) .... 162 C 4
Babtai (LT) .... 170 B 4
Babušnica (SRB) .... 119 E 3
Bač (SRB) .... 113 D 4
Bacău (RO) .... 13 D 3
Baccarat (F) .... 45 D 4
Baceno (I) .... 96 C 2
Bacharach (D) .... 45 E 1
Bachmač (UA) .... 7 F 4
Bačina (SRB) .... 119 D 3
Bačka Palanka (SRB) ...... 117 F 1
Bačka Topola (SRB) .... 113 D 4
Bäckaskog (S) .... 143 E 4
Backe (S) .... 132 A 2
Bäckebo (S) .... 143 F 3
Bäckefors (S) .... 139 F 4
Bački Bred (SRB) .... 112 C 3
Bački Brestovac (SRB) ..... 113 D 4
Bački Monoštor (SRB) ...... 112 C 4
Bačkininkai (LT) .... 176 C 2
Bačkiškiai (LT) .... 175 C 2
Backnang (D) .... 45 F 2
Bačko Gradište (SRB) ...... 113 E 4
Bačko Novo Selo (SRB).. 117 F 1
Bačko Petrovo Selo (SRB)113 E 4

Baćkowice (PL) .... 196 B 3
Bacoli (I) .... 105 F 3
Bacqueville-en-Caux (F). 38 B 4
Bad Aibling (D) .... 94 A 3
Bad Arolsen (D) .... 88 A 1
Bad Aussee (A) .... 94 C 3
Bad Bentheim (D) .... 83 D 3
Bad Bergzabern (D) .... 45 E 2
Bad Berka (D) .... 89 D 1
Bad Berleburg (D) .... 88 A 2
Bad Berneck (D) .... 89 D 3
Bad Bertrich (D) .... 45 D 1
Bad Bevensen (D) .... 84 A 1
Bad Bibra (D) .... 89 D 1
Bad Blankenburg (D) .... 89 D 2
Bad Brambach (D) .... 89 E 3
Bad Bramstedt (D) .... 78 C 4
Bad Brückenau (D) .... 88 B 3
Bad Buchau (D) .... 93 D 3
Bad Camberg (D) .... 88 A 2
Bad Deutsch Altenburg (A) 95 F 1
Bad Doberan (D) .... 79 E 3
Bad Driburg (D) .... 83 F 4
Bad Düben (D) .... 85 D 4
Bad Dürkheim (D) .... 45 E 2
Bad Dürrenberg (D) .... 89 D 1
Bad Dürrheim (D) .... 45 F 4
Bad Elster (D) .... 89 E 3
Bad Ems (D) .... 45 E 1
Bad Endorf (D) .... 94 A 3
Bad Essen (D) .... 83 E 3
Bad Frankenhausen (D) ..... 88 C 1
Bad Freienwalde (D) .... 80 C 1
Bad Friedrichshall (D) .... 45 F 2
Bad Gandersheim (D) .... 84 A 4
Bad Gastein (A) .... 94 B 4
Bad Gleichenberg (A) ...... 95 E 4
Bad Godesberg (D) .... 87 C 2
Bad Goisern (A) .... 94 C 3
Bad Gottleuba (D) .... 90 A 1
Bad Griesbach i. Rottal (D) 94 B 2
Bad Grund (D) .... 84 A 4

Bad Hall (A) .... 94 C 2
Bad Harzburg (D) .... 84 B 4
Bad Herrenalb (D) .... 45 E 3
Bad Hersfeld (D) .... 88 B 2
Bad Hofgastein (A) .... 94 B 4
Bad Homburg (D) .... 88 A 3
Bad Honnef (D) .... 87 F 2
Bad Hönningen (D) .... 87 F 3
Bad Iburg (D) .... 83 E 3
Bad Ischl (A) .... 94 C 3
Bad Karlshafen (D) .... 84 A 4
Bad Kissingen (D) .... 88 C 3
Bad Kleinen (D) .... 79 E 4
Bad Kleinkirchheim (A) .... 94 C 1
Bad König (D) .... 45 F 1
Bad Königshofen (D) .... 88 C 3
Bad Kösen (D) .... 89 D 1
Bad Kreuznach (D) .... 45 E 2
Bad Krozingen (D) .... 45 E 4
Bad Laasphe (D) .... 88 A 2
Bad Langensalza (D) .... 88 C 1
Bad Lauchstädt (D) .... 89 D 1
Bad Lausick (D) .... 89 E 1
Bad Lauterberg (D) .... 84 B 4
Bad Leonfelden (A) .... 94 C 1
Bad Liebenstein (D) .... 88 C 2
Bad Liebenwerda (D) .... 85 F 4
Bad Liebenzell (D) .... 45 F 3
Bad Lippspringe (D) .... 83 F 3
Bad Meinberg (D) .... 83 F 4
Bad Mergentheim (D) .... 88 B 4
Bad Mitterndorf (A) .... 94 C 3
Bad Münder (D) .... 84 A 3
Bad Münster a. Stein (D).. 45 E 1
Bad Münstereifel (D) ...... 87 E 3
Bad Muskau (D) .... 85 F 4
Bad Nauheim (D) .... 88 A 3
Bad Nenndorf (D) .... 83 F 2
Bad Neuenahr (D) .... 87 E 3
Bad Neustadt (D) .... 88 C 3
Bad Oeynhausen (D) .... 83 F 2
Bad Oldesloe (D) .... 79 D 4

Bad Orb (D) .... 88 B 3
Bad Peterstal (D) .... 45 E 3
Bad Pyrmont (D) .... 83 F 4
Bad Radkersburg (A) .... 95 F 4
Bad Rappenau (D) .... 45 F 2
Bad Reichenhall (D) .... 94 B 3
Bad Rippoldsau (D) .... 45 E 3
Bad Rodach (D) .... 88 C 2
Bad Rothenfelde (D) .... 83 E 4
Bad Saarow (D) .... 85 E 3
Bad Sachsa (D) .... 84 B 4
Bad Säckingen (D) .... 92 B 4
Bad Salzdetfurth (D) ...... 84 A 4
Bad Salzschlirf (D) .... 88 B 2
Bad Salzuflen (D) .... 83 F 4
Bad Salzungen (D) .... 88 C 2
Bad Schallerbach (D) ...... 94 C 2
Bad Schandau (D) .... 90 A 1
Bad Schmiedeberg (D) ...... 85 D 4
Bad Schönborn (D) .... 45 F 2
Bad Schussenried (D) ...... 93 D 3
Bad Schwalbach (D) .... 87 F 4
Bad Schwartau (D) .... 79 D 4
Bad Segeberg (D) .... 79 D 4
Bad Soden (D) .... 88 B 3
Bad Soden am Taunus (D) 88 A 3
Bad Sooden-Allendorf (D). 88 B 1
Bad St Leonhard
  im Lavanttal (A) .... 95 D 4
Bad Sulza (D) .... 89 D 1
Bad Sülze (D) .... 79 F 3
Bad Tatzmannsdorf (A) ..... 95 F 3
Bad Tennstedt (D) .... 88 C 1
Bad Tölz (D) .... 93 F 3
Bad Urach (D) .... 93 D 2
Bad Vilbel (D) .... 88 A 3
Bad Vöslau (A) .... 95 F 3
Bad Waldsee (D) .... 93 D 3
Bad Wiessee (D) .... 94 A 3
Bad Wildungen (D) .... 88 A 1
Bad Wilsnack (D) .... 84 C 2

Bad Wimpfen (D) .... 45 F 2
Bad Windsheim (D) .... 88 C 4
Bad Wörishofen (D) .... 93 E 3
Bad Wurzach (D) .... 93 D 3
Bad Zurzach (CH) .... 92 C 4
Bad Zwischenahn (D) .... 83 E 2
Badajoz (E) .... 69 D 3
Badalona (E) .... 67 D 3
Baden (A) .... 95 F 2
Baden (CH) .... 92 C 4
Baden-Baden (D) .... 45 E 3
Badenweiler (D) .... 92 B 4
Baderna (HR) .... 99 D 3
Badia Polesine (I) .... 98 A 4
Badia Tedalda (I) .... 102 A 2
Bądki (PL) .... 183 D 3
Bądkowo (PL) .... 188 C 2
Badljevina (HR) .... 115 F 2
Badolato (I) .... 109 E 3
Badolatosa (E) .... 76 A 2
Badonviller (F) .... 45 D 3
Badovinci (SRB) .... 117 F 1
Badules (E) .... 65 E 3
Baena (E) .... 76 A 1
Baeza (E) .... 76 B 1
Båga (S) .... 55 E 4
Bagaslaviškis (LT) .... 171 D 4
Bagdoniškis (LT) .... 171 F 1
Bagdononys (LT) .... 177 D 2
Bâgé-le-Châtel (F) .... 49 D 2
Bagenalstown /
  Muine Bheag (IRL) .... 25 E 2
Bagenkop (DK) .... 144 C 4
Bagheria (I) .... 110 C 2
Bagn (N) .... 139 E 2
Bagnacavallo (I) .... 102 A 1
Bagnara Calabra (I) ...... 111 F 1
Bagnères-de-Bigorre (F) ... 54 C 3
Bagnères-de-Luchon (F) .... 54 C 3
Bagni del Masino (I) ...... 97 E 3
Bagni di Lucca (I) .... 101 E 2
Bagno a Ripoli (I) .... 101 F 2

LONDONDERRY
6°
LARNE
CARRICKFERGUS
BELFAST AIRPORT
BANGOR
NEWTOWNARDS
COMBER
LISBURG
CRAIGAVON
ENNISKILLEN, DUBLIN
DOWNPATRICK, NEWCASTLE
54°40
Millbank
Ballymartin Water
Mossley
Monkstown
Greenisland
Carnmoney
Mallusk
Jordanstown
Whiteabbey
NEWTOWNABBEY
Hyde Park
Glengormley
Rathcoole
Boghil
Whitehouse
Belfast Zoological Gardens
Greencastle
BELFAST LOUGH
Liverpool
Stranraer
Douglas (Isle of Man)
Heysham
Ulster Way
Transport Museum
Craigavad
Cultra
The Ulster Folk Museum
ANTRIM
Cave Hill
368
Squires Hill
374
Flush
Back Burn
Belfast Castle
BELFAST
Holywood
NORTH-DOWN
Fortwilliam
Ballysillan
Legoniel
Skegoneill
Forth
Clady Water
Oldpark
Cliftonville
Ardoyne
Ballygomartin
BELFAST CITY AIRPORT
Redburn
Crons Hill
199
Craigantlet
Knocknagoney
Divis
478
390
Blackmountain
Whiterock
Woodvale
Shankill
Falls
Victoria Park
Sydenham
Parliament House
Stormont
Dundonald
Belmont
City Hall
Ballymacarrett
Ballyhackmore
Tullycarnet
Hannahstown
Black Hill
360
Bloomfield
Orangefield
Ormeau
Willowfield
Shandon
Gilnahirk
Enler
Queen's University
Botanic Gardens
Ulster Museum
Milltown
Castlereagh
Andersontown
Windsor
Cregagh
Braniel
176
Suffolk
Colin
Ballynafeigh
Ladybrook
Malone
Rosetta
CASTLEREAGH
Poleglass
Balmoral
Stranmillis
LISBURN
Finaghy
Taughmonagh
Crossnacreevy
Belvoir Park Forest
Newtownbreda
Gransha
Lisleen
Ballystokart
Twinbrook
Dunmurry
Belvoir
Derryaghy
Upper Malone
Lagan
Giants Ring
Purdysburn
Lagan Valley Regional Park
Moneyreagh
Lambeg
Drumbeg
Ballylesson
0 1 2 km
0 1 mile

Ballinrobe /
Baile an Róba *(IRL)* 22 B 3
Ballintubber *(IRL)* 22 B 3
Ballobar *(E)* 66 A 3
Ballon *(F)* 42 B 3
Ballstad *(N)* 127 D 1
Ballybay *(IRL)* 23 E 3
Ballybofey /
Bealach Féich *(IRL)* 23 D 2
Ballybunnion *(IRL)* 24 B 2
Ballycastle *(GB)* 23 E 1
Ballycastle *(IRL)* 22 B 2
Ballyclare *(GB)* 23 F 2
Ballyconnell *(IRL)* 23 D 3
Ballycotton *(IRL)* 24 C 4
Ballycroy *(IRL)* 22 B 3
Ballyduff *(IRL)* 24 B 2
Ballyforan *(IRL)* 22 C 4
Ballygawley *(GB)* 23 E 2
Ballyhaunis /
Béal Átha hAmhnais *(IRL)* 22 C 3
Ballyheige *(IRL)* 24 B 2
Ballyjamesduff *(IRL)* 23 D 3
Ballymahon /
Baile Uí Mhatháin *(IRL)* 23 D 4
Ballymena *(GB)* 23 E 2
Ballymoe *(IRL)* 22 C 3
Ballymoney *(GB)* 23 E 1
Ballymore *(IRL)* 23 D 4
Ballymote /
Baile an Mhóta *(IRL)* 22 C 3
Ballynahinch *(GB)* 23 F 3
Ballysadare *(IRL)* 22 C 3
Ballyshannon /
Béal Átha Seanaidh *(IRL)* 22 C 2
Ballyvaughan *(IRL)* 22 B 4
Balmaseda *(E)* 60 B 3
Balme *(I)* 53 E 2
Balneario de Panticosa *(E)* 54 B 3
Balninkai *Alytaus* *(LT)* 176 C 3
Balninkai *Utenos* *(LT)* 171 E 3
Baloži *Liepājas* *(LV)* 162 C 3
Baloži *Rīgas* *(LV)* 164 C 1
Balsareny *(E)* 66 C 2
Balsiai *(LT)* 169 D 2
Balsicas *(E)* 77 F 1
Balsorano *(I)* 105 E 2
Bålsta *(S)* 141 D 4
Balsthal *(CH)* 92 B 4
Balsupiai *(LT)* 175 F 2
Balta *(UA)* 13 E 2
Baltaiskrogs *(LV)* 163 D 2
Baltanás *(E)* 64 B 2
Baltar *(E)* 62 C 1
Baltezers *(LV)* 159 D 4
Bălți *(MD)* 13 E 2
Baltijsk *(RUS)* 6 B 4
Baltinava (Baļtinova) *(LV)* 167 F 1
Baltinglass /
Bealach Conglais *(IRL)*. 25 E 2
Baltmuiža *(LV)* 166 C 4
Baltoji Vokė *(LT)* 177 E 3
Bałtów *(PL)* 196 C 2
Baltrimai *(LT)* 162 C 3
Baltrum *(D)* 78 A 4
Baltrušaičiai *(LT)* 169 D 3
Baltrušiai *(LT)* 175 F 2
Balvi *(LV)* 161 E 4
Balvu Stacija *(LV)* 161 E 4
Bamberg *(D)* 89 D 3
Bamburgh Castle *(GB)* 31 E 3
Bampalió *(GR)* 211 E 4
Bampíni *(GR)* 211 D 4
Bampton *(GB)* 35 D 3
Banagher *(IRL)* 22 C 4
Banatska Palanka *(SRB)* 118 C 1
Banatska Topola *(SRB)* 113 E 4
Banatski
Brestovac *(SRB)* 118 C 1
Banatski Dvor *(SRB)* 113 E 4
Banatski Karlovac *(SRB)*. 113 F 4
Banatsko
Aranđelovo *(SRB)* 113 E 3
Banatsko
Karađorđevo *(SRB)* 113 E 4
Banatsko
Novo Selo *(SRB)* 118 C 1
Banbridge *(GB)* 23 E 3
Banbury *(GB)* 35 F 1
Banchory *(GB)* 28 B 4
Bande *(E)* 58 B 4
Bandenieki *(LV)* 163 F 3
Bandırma *(TR)* 19 E 2
Bandol *(F)* 57 D 3
Bandon / Droichead
na Bandan *(IRL)* 24 C 4
Bandoriai *(LT)* 163 F 3
Banff *(GB)* 28 B 3
Bangor *(IRL)* 22 B 2
Bangor *Gwynedd* *(GB)* 32 B 3
Bangor *North-Down* *(GB)* 23 F 2
Bangsund *(N)* 131 D 2
Banie *(PL)* 186 B 1
Banie Mazurskie *(PL)* 184 C 2
Banja *Kragujevac* *(SRB)* 118 C 2
Banja *Užice* *(SRB)* 118 B 3
Banja Koviljača *(SRB)* 117 F 2
Banja Luka *(BIH)* 115 E 4
Banjani *(SRB)* 118 B 2
Banjska *(SRB)* 118 C 4
Bankeryd *(S)* 143 E 1
Bannalec *(F)* 40 C 4
Bañón *(E)* 65 F 4
Banon *(F)* 53 D 4
Baños de Cerrato *(E)* 64 A 2
Baños de la Encina *(E)* 70 B 4
Baños de la Fuensanta *(E)* 77 D 1
Baños de Molgas *(E)* 58 C 4
Baños de Montemayor *(E)* 63 F 4
Banova Jaruga *(HR)* 115 E 3
Banovići *(BIH)* 117 E 2
Bansin *(D)* 80 C 3
Banská Bystrica *(SK)* 12 B 2
Banská Štiavnica *(SK)* 12 B 2
Bansko *(MK)* 122 C 3
Bantry / Beanntrai *(IRL)* 24 B 4
Banyalbufar *(E)* 73 D 2
Banyeres de Mariola *(E)* 71 F 4
Banyoles *(E)* 67 D 2
Banyuls-sur-Mer *(F)* 56 A 4
Bapaume *(F)* 39 D 3
Baqueira *(E)* 55 D 3
Bar *(MNE)* 121 E 3
Bar *(UA)* 13 D 2
Bar-le-Duc *(F)* 44 B 3
Bar-sur-Aube *(F)* 44 A 4
Bar-sur-Seine *(F)* 43 F 4
Baraći *(BIH)* 117 D 3
Barahona *(E)* 65 D 3
Barajas *(E)* 64 B 4
Barajas de Melo *(E)* 70 C 1
Barajevo *(SRB)* 118 B 1
Barakaldo *(E)* 60 C 3
Baralla *(E)* 58 C 3
Baranavičy *(BY)* 7 D 4
Barane *(SRB)* 121 F 2
Baranów *Wielkopolskie* *(PL)* 194 B 2
Baranów
Sandomierski *(PL)* 196 C 4
Baranowo
Wielkopolskie *(PL)* 187 E 2
Baraque-de-Fraiture *(B)* 87 D 3
Baraque-Michel *(B)* 87 D 3
Baraqueville *(F)* 51 F 4
Barbadillo del Mercado *(E)* 64 C 2
Barban *(HR)* 99 D 3
Barbarano Vicentino *(I)* 98 A 3
Barbarušince *(SRB)* 122 B 1
Barbastro *(E)* 66 A 2
Barbat *(HR)* 99 E 4
Barbate *(E)* 75 E 4
Barbazan *(F)* 55 D 3
Bārbele *(LV)* 165 D 3
Barberino di Mugello *(I)* 101 F 2
Barbezieux *(F)* 50 C 2
Barbizon *(F)* 43 D 3
Barbotan-les-Thermes *(F)*. 50 C 4
Barby *(D)* 84 C 4
Barca de Alva *(P)* 63 D 3
Barcarrota *(E)* 69 D 3
Barcellona
Pozzo di Gotto *(I)* 111 E 2
Barcelona *(E)* 67 D 3
Barcelonnette *(F)* 53 E 4
Barcelos *(P)* 62 B 2
Barchfeld *(D)* 88 C 2
Barčiai *(LT)* 175 F 4
Barciany *(PL)* 184 B 2
Barcin *(PL)* 188 B 1
Barcis *(I)* 98 B 2
Barcones *(E)* 64 C 3
Barcs *(H)* 112 B 4
Barczewo *(PL)* 183 F 3
Bardal *(N)* 131 D 2
Bardauskai *(LT)* 175 E 2
Bardejov *(SK)* 12 B 2
Bardi *(I)* 101 D 1
Bardineto *(I)* 100 B 2
Bardo *(PL)* 193 E 4
Bardolino *(I)* 97 F 3
Bardonecchia *(I)* 53 E 2
Bardufoss *(N)* 124 B 3
Bare *(SRB)* 118 B 4
Barèges *(F)* 54 C 3
Barentin *(F)* 38 B 4
Barenton *(F)* 41 F 3
Barfleur *(F)* 41 E 1
Bargas *(E)* 70 B 1
Bargłów Kościelny *(PL)* 185 D 3
Bargoed *(GB)* 35 D 1
Bargteheide *(D)* 79 D 4
Bari *(I)* 107 D 2
Barić Draga *(HR)* 99 F 4
Barisciano *(I)* 102 C 4
Bariūnai *(LT)* 164 B 3
Barjac *(F)* 52 B 4
Barjols *(F)* 57 D 2
Barkava *(LV)* 167 D 2
Barkiškis *(LT)* 165 F 4
Barklainiai *(LT)* 165 D 4
Barklainiai I *(LT)* 171 D 2
Barkūniškis *(LT)* 170 B 3
Bârlad *(RO)* 13 E 3
Barlby *(GB)* 33 E 2
Barletta *(I)* 106 C 2
Barlinek *(PL)* 186 C 1
Barmouth / Abermaw *(GB)* 32 B 3
Barmstedt *(D)* 78 C 3
Barna / Bearna *(IRL)* 22 B 4
Barnard Castle *(GB)* 31 E 4
Bärnau *(D)* 89 E 3
Barneveld *(NL)* 82 C 4
Barneville-Carteret *(F)* 41 E 1
Barnsley *(GB)* 33 D 2
Barnstaple *(GB)* 34 C 2
Barnstorf *(D)* 83 F 3
Barntrup *(D)* 83 F 4
Barovo *(MK)* 122 C 3
Barqueiro *(P)* 68 B 1
Barr *(F)* 45 D 4
Barracas *(E)* 71 F 1
Barrachina *(E)* 65 F 4

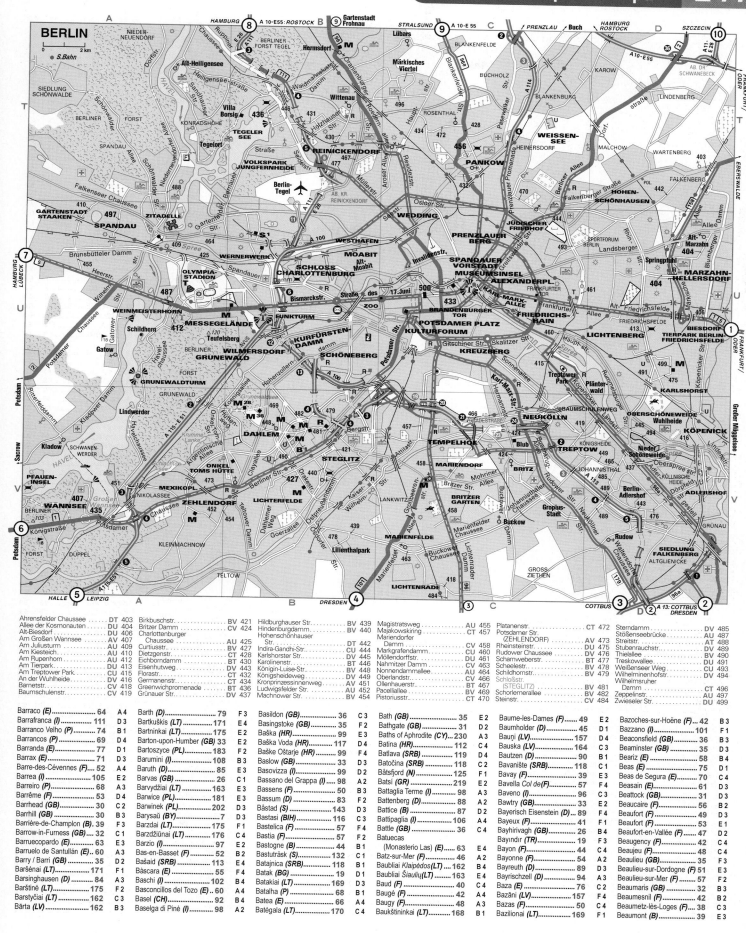

BERLIN

Ahrensfelder Chaussee . . . . . DT 403	Birkbuschstr. . . . . BV 421	Hildburghauser Str. . . . . BV 439
Allee der Kosmonauten . . . . . DU 404	Britzer Damm . . . . CV 424	Hindenburgdamm . . . . BV 440
Alt-Biesdorf . . . . DU 406	Charlottenburger	Hohenschönhauser
Am Großen Wannsee . . . . . . AV 407	Chaussee . . . . DT 442	Str. . . . . DT 442
Am Juliusturm . . . . AU 409	Curtiusstr. . . . . BV 425	Indira-Gandhi-Str. . . . . CU 444
Am Kiesteich . . . . AU 410	Dietzgenstr. . . . . CT 428	Karlshorster Str. . . . . DV 445
Am Rupenhorn . . . . AU 412	Eichborndamm . . . . BT 430	Karolinenstr. . . . . BT 446
Am Tierpark . . . . DU 413	Eisenhutweg . . . . DV 443	Königin-Luise-Str. . . . . BV 448
Am Treptower Park . . . . CU 415	Florastr. . . . . CT 432	Königsheideweg . . . . DV 449
An der Wuhlheide . . . . DV 416	Germanenstr. . . . . CT 434	Kronprinzessinnenweg . . . . . . AV 451
Barnetstr. . . . . CV 418	Greenwichpromenade . . . . . . BT 436	Ludwigsfelder Str. . . . . AU 452
Baumschulenstr. . . . . CV 419	Grünauer Str. . . . . CT 437	Machnower Str. . . . . BV 454

Magistratsweg . . . . AU 455	Platanenstr. . . . . CT 472	Sterndamm . . . . DV 485
Majakowskiring . . . . CT 457	Potsdamer Str.	Stößenseebrücke . . . . AU 487
Mariendorfer	(ZEHLENDORF) . . . . AV 473	Streitstr. . . . . AT 488
Damm . . . . CV 458	Rheinsteinstr. . . . . DU 475	Stubenrauchstr. . . . . DV 489
Markgrafendamm . . . . CU 460	Rudower Chaussee . . . . DV 476	Thielallee . . . . BV 490
Möllendorffstr. . . . . DU 461	Scharnweberstr. . . . . BT 477	Treskowallee . . . . DU 491
Nahmitzer Damm . . . . CV 463	Scheelestr. . . . . BV 478	Weißenseer Weg . . . . CU 493
Nonnendammallee . . . . CV 464	Schildhornstr. . . . . BV 479	Wilhelminenhofstr. . . . . CV 494
Oberlandstr. . . . . CV 466	Schloßstr.	Wilhelmsruher
Ollenhauerstr. . . . . BT 467	(STEGLITZ) . . . . BV 481	Damm . . . . CT 496
Paccelliallee . . . . BV 469	Schorlemerallee . . . . BV 482	Zeppelinstr. . . . . CT 497
Pistoriusstr. . . . . CT 470	Steinstr. . . . . CV 484	Zwieseler Str. . . . . DU 499

Barraco (E) 64	A 4	Barth (D) 79	F 3	Basildon (GB) 36	C 4
Barrafranca (I) 111	D 3	Bartkuškis (LT) 171	E 4	Basingstoke (GB) 35	F 2
Barranco Velho (P) 74	B 1	Bartninkai (LT) 175	E 2	Baška (HR) 99	E 3
Barrancos (P) 69	D 4	Barton-upon-Humber (GB) 33	E 2	Baška Voda (HR) 117	D 4
Barranda (E) 77	D 3	Bartoszyce (PL) 183	F 2	Baške Oštarije (HR) 99	F 4
Barrax (E) 71	D 3	Barumini (I) 108	B 3	Baslow (GB) 33	D 3
Barre-des-Cévennes (F) 52	A 4	Baruth (D) 85	E 3	Basovizza (I) 99	D 2
Barrea (I) 105	A 2	Barvas (GB) 26	C 1	Bassano del Grappa (I) 98	A 2
Barreiro (P) 68	A 3	Barvydžiai (LT) 163	E 3	Bassens (F) 50	B 3
Barrême (F) 53	F 2	Barwice (PL) 181	E 3	Bassum (D) 83	F 2
Barrhead (GB) 30	C 2	Barwinek (PL) 202	D 3	Båstad (S) 143	D 3
Barrhill (GB) 30	B 3	Barysaŭ (BY) 7	D 3	Bastasi (BIH) 116	C 3
Barrière-de-Champlon (B) . 39	F 3	Barzdai (LT) 175	F 1	Bastelica (F) 57	F 4
Barrow-in-Furness (GB) 32	B 3	Barzdžiūnai (LT) 176	C 4	Bastia (F) 57	F 4
Barruecopardo (E) 63	E 3	Barzio (I) 97	E 2	Bastia (I) 97	A 2
Barruelo de Santullán (E) 60	A 3	Bas-en-Basset (F) 52	B 1	Bastogne (B) 44	B 1
Barry / Barri (GB) 35	D 2	Bašaid (SRB) 113	E 4	Bastuträsk (S) 132	C 1
Baršėnai (LT) 171	F 1	Bàscara (E) 55	F 4	Batajnica (SRB) 118	A 3
Barsinghausen (D) 84	A 3	Baschi (I) 102	A 2	Batak (BG) 19	D 1
Barštinė (LT) 175	F 3	Basconcillos del Tozo (E) . . 60	A 4	Batakiai (LT) 169	D 3
Barstyčiai (LT) 162	C 3	Basel (CH) 92	B 4	Batalha (P) 68	B 3
Bārta (LV) 162	B 3	Baselga di Pinè (I) 98	A 2	Batégala (LT) 170	C 4

Bath (GB) 35	E 2	Baume-les-Dames (F) 49	E 2	Bazoches-sur-Hoëne (F) . . 42	B 3
Bathgate (GB) 31	D 2	Baumholder (D) 45	D 1	Bazzano (I) 101	F 1
Baths of Aphrodite (CY) . 230	A 3	Bauņi (LV) 157	D 1	Beaconsfield (GB) 36	B 3
Batina (HR) 112	C 4	Bauska (LV) 164	C 3	Beaminster (GB) 35	D 3
Batlava (SRB) 119	D 4	Bautzen (D) 90	B 1	Beariz (E) 58	B 4
Batočina (SRB) 118	C 2	Bavanište (SRB) 118	A 3	Beas (E) 75	D 1
Båtsfjord (N) 125	F 1	Bavay (F) 39	E 3	Beas de Segura (E) 70	C 4
Batsí (GR) 219	E 2	Bavella Col de (F) 57	F 4	Beasain (E) 61	D 3
Battaglia Terme (I) 98	A 3	Baveno (I) 96	C 3	Beattock (GB) 31	D 3
Battenberg (D) 88	A 2	Bawtry (GB) 33	E 2	Beaucaire (F) 56	B 2
Battice (D) 87	D 2	Bayerisch Eisenstein (D) . . 89	F 1	Beaufort (F) 49	D 3
Battipaglia (I) 106	A 4	Bayeux (F) 41	F 1	Beaufort (F) 53	E 1
Battle (GB) 36	C 4	Bayhirivagh (GB) 26	B 4	Beaufort-en-Vallée (F) 47	D 2
Batuecas		Bayındır (TR) 19	F 3	Beaugency (F) 42	C 4
(Monasterio Las) (E) 63	E 4	Bayon (F) 44	C 4	Beaujeu (F) 48	C 4
Batz-sur-Mer (F) 46	A 2	Bayonne (F) 54	A 2	Beaulieu (GB) 35	F 3
Baubliai Klaipėdos (LT) . . 162	B 4	Bayreuth (D) 89	D 3	Beaulieu-sur-Dordogne (F) 51	D 2
Baubliai Šiauliu (LT) 163	E 4	Bayrischzell (D) 94	A 3	Beaulieu-sur-Mer (F) 57	F 2
Baud (F) 40	C 4	Baza (E) 76	C 2	Beaumaris (GB) 32	B 3
Baugé (F) 47	D 2	Bazāni (LV) 157	F 4	Beaumesnil (F) 42	B 2
Baugy (F) 48	A 3	Bazas (F) 50	B 3	Beaumetz-lès-Loges (F) . . 38	C 3
Baukštininkai (LT) 168	B 1	Bazilionai (LT) 169	F 1	Beaumont (B) 39	E 3

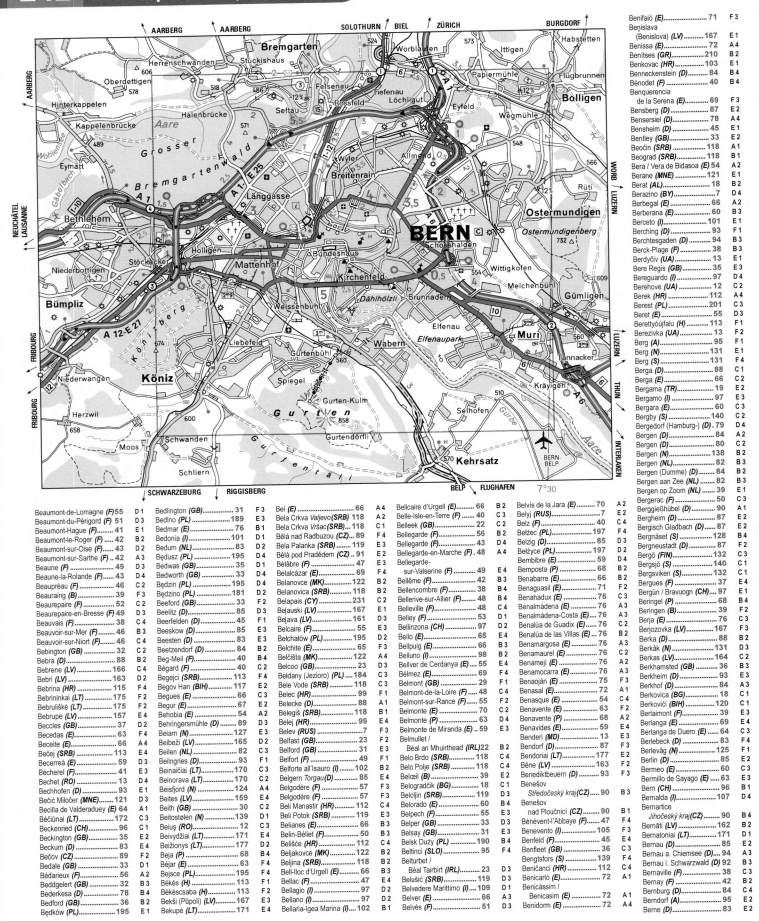

Benifaió (E)............... 71 F 3
Benislava
(Benislova) (LV)........167 E 1
Benissa (E)............... 72 A 4
Benitses (GR)............210 B 2
Benkovac (HR)...........103 E 1
Benneckenstein (D)......84 B 4
Bénodet (F)............... 40 B 4
Benquerencia
de la Serena (E)...... 69 F 3
Bensberg (D)............. 87 E 2
Bensersiel (D)........... 78 A 4
Bensheim (D)............. 45 E 1
Bentley (GB)............. 33 E 2
Beoćin (SRB)............118 A 1
Beograd (SRB).........118 B 1
Bera / Vera de Bidasoa (E) 54 A 2
Berane (MNE)...........121 E 1
Berat (AL)............... 18 B 2
Berazino (BY)............ 7 D 4
Berbegal (E)............. 66 A 2
Berberana (E)........... 60 B 3
Berceto (I)................101 E 1
Berching (D).............. 93 F 1
Berchtesgaden (D)...... 94 B 3
Berck-Plage (F).......... 38 B 3
Berdýčiv (UA)............ 13 E 1
Bere Regis (GB)........ 35 E 3
Bereguardo (I)........... 97 D 4
Berehove (UA)........... 12 C 2
Berek (HR)...............112 A 4
Berest (PL)...............201 C 3
Beret (E)................. 55 D 3
Berettyóújfalu (H)........113 F 1
Berezivka (UA)........... 13 F 2
Berg (A)................. 95 F 1
Berg (N)..................131 E 1
Berg (S)..................131 F 4
Berga (F)................. 88 C 1
Berga (E)................. 66 C 2
Bergama (TR)............ 19 E 2
Bergamo (I).............. 97 E 3
Bergara (S).............. 60 C 3
Bergby (S)...............140 C 1
Bergedorf (Hamburg-) (D). 79 D 4
Bergen (D)............... 84 A 2
Bergen (D)............... 80 C 2
Bergen (N)...............138 B 2
Bergen (NL).............. 82 B 3
Bergen (Dumme) (D)..... 84 B 2
Bergen aan Zee (NL).... 82 B 3
Bergen op Zoom (NL)... 39 E 1
Bergerac (F)............. 50 C 3
Berggießhübel (D)....... 90 A 1
Bergheim (D)............. 87 E 2
Bergisch Gladbach (D)... 87 E 2
Bergnäset (S)...........128 B 4
Bergneustadt (D)........ 87 F 2
Bergö (FIN).............132 C 3
Bergsjö (S)..............140 C 1
Bergsviken (S)..........132 C 1
Bergün / Bravuogn (CH)... 97 E 1
Beringel (P).............. 68 B 4
Beringen (B)............. 39 F 2
Berja (E)................. 76 C 3
Berjozovka (LV).........167 E 3
Berka (D)................. 88 B 2
Berkåk (N)...............131 D 3
Berkas (LV)..............164 C 2
Berkhamsted (GB)....... 36 B 3
Berkheim (D)............. 93 E 3
Berkhof (D)............... 84 A 3
Berkovica (BG)........... 18 C 1
Berković (BIH)...........120 C 1
Berlaimont (F)........... 39 E 3
Berlanga (E)............. 69 E 4
Berlanga de Duero (E) ...64 C 3
Berlebeck (D)............ 83 F 4
Berlevåg (N).............125 F 1
Berlin (D)................. 85 E 2
Bermeo (E)............... 60 C 3
Bermillo de Sayago (E)... 63 D 4
Bern (CH)................ 96 B 1
Bernalda (I).............107 D 4
Bernartice
Jihočeský kraj (CZ)..... 90 B 4
Bernāti (LV)..............162 B 3
Bernatonai (LT)..........171 D 1
Bernau (D)............... 85 E 2
Bernau a. Chiemsee (D)..94 A 3
Bernau i. Schwarzwald (D) 92 C 3
Bernaville (F)............. 38 C 3
Bernay (F)............... 42 B 2
Bernburg (D)............. 84 C 4
Berndorf (A)............. 95 E 2
Berne (D)................. 83 E 2

Beaumont-de-Lomagne (F)55 D 1
Beaumont-du-Périgord (F) 51 D 3
Beaumont-Hague (F)..... 41 E 1
Beaumont-le-Roger (F)... 42 B 2
Beaumont-sur-Oise (F)... 43 D 2
Beaumont-sur-Sarthe (F) .. 42 A 3
Beaune (F)............... 49 D 3
Beaune-la-Rolande (F)... 43 D 4
Beaupréau (F)........... 46 C 2
Beauraing (B)............ 39 F 3
Beaurepaire (F).......... 52 C 2
Beaurepaire-en-Bresse (F) 49 D 3
Beauvais (F)............. 38 C 4
Beauvoir-sur-Mer (F).... 46 B 3
Beauvoir-sur-Niort (F)... 46 C 4
Bebington (GB).......... 32 C 2
Bebra (D)................. 88 B 2
Bebrene (LV).............166 C 4
Bebri (LV)................163 D 2
Bebrina (HR).............115 F 4
Bebrininkai (LT).........175 F 2
Bebruliškė (LT)..........175 F 2
Bebrupe (LV)............157 E 4
Beccles (GB)............. 37 D 2
Becedas (E).............. 63 F 4
Beceite (E)............... 66 A 4
Bečej (SRB).............113 E 2
Becerreá (E)............. 59 D 3
Bécherel (F)............. 41 E 3
Bechet (RO).............. 13 D 4
Bechhofen (D)........... 93 E 1
Bečić Miločer (MNE)....121 D 3
Becilla de Valderaduey (E) 64 A 1
Bečiūnai (LT)............172 C 3
Beckenried (CH)......... 96 C 1
Beckington (GB)......... 35 E 4
Beckum (D)............... 83 E 4
Bečov (CZ)............... 89 F 2
Bedale (GB).............. 33 E 4
Bédarieux (F)............ 56 A 2
Beddgelert (GB)......... 32 B 3
Bederkesa (D)........... 78 B 2
Bedford (GB)............. 36 B 2
Będków (PL).............195 E 1

Bedlington (GB)......... 31 F 3
Bedlno (PL)..............189 E 3
Bedmar (E)............... 76 B 1
Bedonia (I)...............101 E 4
Będusz (PL).............195 D 4
Bedwas (GB)............. 35 D 1
Bedworth (GB).......... 33 D 4
Będzin (PL)..............195 D 2
Będzino (PL)............181 D 2
Beeford (GB)............ 33 F 2
Beelitz (D)............... 85 D 2
Beerfelden (D).......... 45 F 1
Beeskow (D)............. 85 E 3
Beesten (D).............. 83 E 4
Beetzendorf (D)......... 84 B 2
Beg-Meil (F)............. 40 B 4
Bégard (F)............... 40 C 2
Begejci (SRB)...........113 F 4
Begov Han (BIH)........117 E 2
Begues (E)............... 66 C 3
Begur (E)................. 67 E 2
Behobia (E).............. 54 A 2
Behringersmühle (D).... 89 D 3
Beiarn (N)................127 E 3
Beibeži (LV).............165 D 2
Beilen (NL)............... 82 C 3
Beilngries (D)............ 93 F 1
Beinaičiai (LT)...........170 C 3
Beinorava (LT)..........170 C 2
Beisfjord (N).............124 A 4
Beitostølen (N)..........139 D 1
Beites (LV)...............159 E 4
Beith (GB)............... 30 C 2
Beitostølen (N)..........139 D 1
Beiuș (RO)............... 12 C 3
Beivydžiai (LT)..........171 E 4
Beižionys (LT)...........177 D 2
Beja (P).................. 68 B 4
Béjar (E)................. 63 F 4
Bejsce (PL)..............195 F 4
Békés (H)................113 F 1
Békéscsaba (H).........113 F 2
Bekši (Pūpoli) (LV).....167 E 3
Bekupė (LT)..............171 E 4

Bel (E)................... 66 A 4
Bela Crkva Valjevo (SRB) 118 C 3
Bela Crkva Vršac (SRB)...118 C 1
Bělá nad Radbuzou (CZ).. 89 F 4
Bela Palanka (SRB).....119 D 2
Bělá pod Pradědem (CZ)... 91 E 2
Bélâbre (F)............... 47 E 3
Balalcázar (E)........... 69 F 4
Belanovce (MK).........122 B 2
Belanovica (SRB).......118 B 2
Belapais (CY)............231 C 2
Belauski (LV)............167 E 1
Belava (LV)..............161 D 3
Belcaire (F).............. 55 E 3
Bełchatów (PL)..........195 D 2
Belchite (E).............. 65 F 3
Belčišta (MK)............122 A 4
Belcoo (GB).............. 23 D 3
Beldany (Jezioro) (PL)...184 C 3
Bele Vode (SRB)........118 C 3
Belec (HR)............... 99 F 1
Belecke (D).............. 88 A 1
Belegiš (SRB)...........118 B 1
Belej (HR)...............99 D 3
Belev (RUS).............. 7 F 3
Belfast (GB)............. 23 F 2
Belford (GB)............. 31 E 3
Belfort (F)............... 49 F 1
Belforte all'Isauro (I)....102 C 3
Belgern Torgau (D)..... 85 E 4
Belgodère (F)........... 57 F 3
Belgodère (F)........... 57 F 3
Beli Manastir (HR)......112 C 4
Beli Potok (SRB)........119 E 3
Belianes (E)............. 66 B 3
Belin-Béliet (F).......... 50 B 3
Belišće (HR).............112 C 4
Beljakovce (MK)........122 B 2
Beljina (SRB)...........118 B 2
Bell-lloc d'Urgell (E).... 66 B 3
Bellac (F)................. 47 E 2
Bellagio (I)............... 97 D 2
Bellano (I)............... 97 D 2
Bellaria-Igea Marina (I)...102 B 1

Bellcaire d'Urgell (E)..... 66 B 2
Belle-Isle-en-Terre (F)..... 40 C 3
Belleek (GB)............. 22 C 4
Bellegarde (F)........... 56 B 2
Bellegarde (F)........... 51 D 4
Bellegarde-en-Marche (F) . 48 A 2
Bellegarde-
sur-Valserine (F)...... 49 E 4
Bellême (F)............... 42 B 3
Bellencombre (F)........ 38 B 4
Bellerive-sur-Allier (F).... 48 A 4
Belleville (F)............. 48 C 4
Belley (F)................. 53 D 1
Bellinzona (CH)......... 97 D 2
Bello (E)................. 65 E 4
Bellpuig (E).............. 66 B 3
Belluno (I)............... 98 B 1
Bellver de Cerdanya (E)... 55 E 4
Bélmez (E)............... 69 F 4
Belmont (GB)............ 29 F 1
Belmont-de-la-Loire (F)... 48 C 4
Belmont-sur-Rance (F)... 55 F 2
Belmonte (E)............. 65 D 2
Belmonte (P)............. 63 D 4
Belmonte de Miranda (E) .. 59 E 3
Belmullet /
Béal an Mhuirthead (IRL)22 B 2
Belo Brdo (SRB)........118 C 4
Belo Polje (SRB)........118 C 4
Belœil (B)............... 39 E 2
Belogradčik (BG)....... 18 C 1
Beloljin (SRB)...........119 D 3
Belorado (E)............. 60 B 4
Belpech (F)............... 55 E 3
Belper (GB).............. 33 E 2
Belsay (GB).............. 31 E 3
Belsk Duży (PL).........190 B 4
Beltinci (SLO)........... 95 F 4
Belturbet /
Béal Tairbirt (IRL)..... 23 D 3
Belušić (SRB)...........119 D 3
Belvedere Marittimo (I)...109 D 1
Belver (E)................. 66 A 3
Belvès (F)................ 51 D 3

Belvís de la Jara (E)..... 70 A 2
Belyj (RUS).............. 7 E 2
Belz (F)................... 40 C 4
Bełżec (PL)..............197 F 4
Belz (D)................. 85 D 1
Bełżyce (PL)............197 D 2
Bembibre (E)............. 59 D 3
Bemposta (P)............ 68 B 2
Benabarre (E)........... 66 B 2
Benaguasil (E)........... 71 F 2
Benahadux (E).......... 76 C 3
Benalmádena (E)........ 76 A 3
Benalmádena-Costa (E)... 76 A 3
Benalúa de Guadix (E)... 76 B 2
Benalúa de las Villas (E)... 76 B 2
Benamargosa (E)........ 76 A 3
Benamaurel (E)......... 76 C 2
Benameji (E)............ 76 A 2
Benamocarra (E)........ 76 A 3
Benaoján (E)............ 75 F 3
Benasal (E)............... 72 A 1
Benasque (E)............ 54 C 4
Benavente (E)........... 63 F 2
Benavente (P)........... 68 A 2
Benavides (E)........... 59 E 4
Benderi (MD)............ 13 E 1
Bendorf (D).............. 87 F 2
Bendoriai (LT)..........177 F 2
Bène (LV)...............163 F 2
Benediktbeuern (D)..... 93 F 3
Benešov
Středočeský kraj (CZ)... 90 B 3
Benešov
nad Ploučnicí (CZ).... 90 B 1
Bénévent-l'Abbaye (F)... 47 F 2
Benevento (I)............105 F 3
Benfeld (F)............... 45 E 4
Benfleet (GB)............ 36 C 3
Bengtsfors (S)...........139 F 4
Benicàrló (E)............. 72 A 1
Benicàssim /
Benicasim (E)......... 72 A 1
Benidorm (E)............ 72 A 4

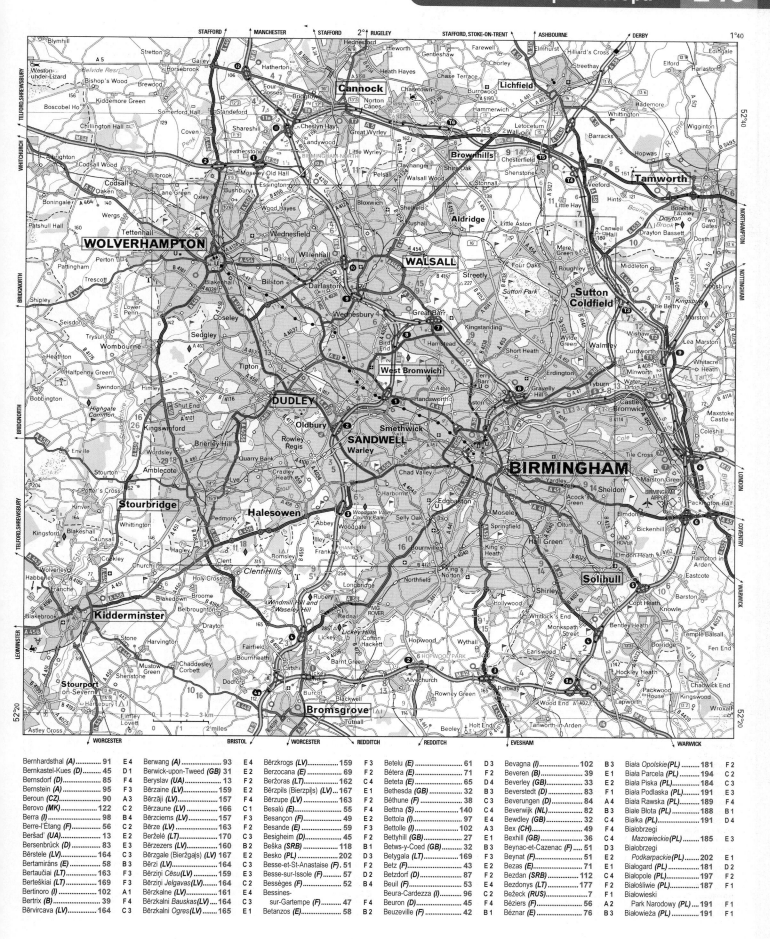

BOLOGNA

Amaseo (V. R.) .... GU 6
Arno (V.) .... HV 9
Artigiano (V. d.) .... GU 10
Bandiera (V. I.) .... FV 12
Barbieri (V. F.) .... GU 13
Barca (V. d.) .... FV 15

Battaglia (V. d.) .... HU 16
Bentivogli (V. G.) .... GV 19
Beverara (V. della) .... FU 20
Cadriano (V. d.) .... GHU 21
Castiglione (V.) .... HU 25
Cavazzoni (V. F.) .... HV 27
Codivilla (V.) .... GV 31
Colombo (V. C.) .... FU 34
Coubertin (V. de) .... FV 36

Dagnini (V. G.) .... GV 39
Firenze (V.) .... HV 42
Foscherara (V. d.) .... GV 43
Gagarin (V. Y.) .... FU 45
Gandhi (Viale M. K.) .... FU 49
Marconi (V.) .... EV 61
Marco Polo
Mario (V. A.) .... GV 63

Martelli (V. T.) .... HV 66
Matteotti (V.) .... GU 67
Mazzini (V.) .... GV 69
Mezzofanti (V. G.) .... GV 70
Montefiorino
(V.) .... FV 73
Ospedaletto (V. d.) .... EU 79
Palagi (V. P.) .... GV 81
Panigale (V.) .... EU 82

Persicetana Vecchia
(V.) .... EU 85
Persicetana (V.) .... EU 84
Pietra (V. d.) .... EU 88
Pirandello (V. L.) .... HU 90
Porrettana (V. d.) .... FVE 91
Putti (V. V.) .... GV 96
Sabbioni (V. d.) .... GV 100
Sabotino (V.) .... FUV 102

Saffi (V. A.) .... FU 103
Sigonio (V. C.) .... GV 111
Sturzo (V. Don L.) .... FV 112
S. Barbara (V.) .... GV 105
S. Mamolo
(V.) .... FV 108
Timavo (V.) .... FU 115
Tolmino (V.) .... FV 117
Tosarelli (V. B.) .... HU 118

Biały Bór (PL) .... 181 F 3
Biały Dunajec (PL) .... 201 A 3
Białystok (PL) .... 185 E 4
Biancavilla (I) .... 111 F 4
Bianco (I) .... 111 F 1
Biandrate (I) .... 96 C 3
Biar (E) .... 71 F 4
Biasteri (E) .... 60 C 4
Bibbiena (I) .... 102 A 2
Biberach an der Riß (D) .... 93 D 3
Biberach i. Kinzigtal (D) .... 45 E 4
Bibinje (HR) .... 103 E 1
Bibione (I) .... 98 C 2
Bibury (GB) .... 35 F 1
Bicaz (RO) .... 13 D 3
Bicester (GB) .... 35 F 1
Bichl (D) .... 93 F 3
Bidache (F) .... 54 A 2
Bidart (F) .... 54 A 2
Biddenden (GB) .... 36 C 4
Bideford (GB) .... 34 C 4
Biebelried (D) .... 88 C 4
Biebrza (PL) .... 185 E 4
Biebrzanska (Kotlina) (PL) 185 D 3
Biebrzański Park
  Narodowy (PL) .... 185 D 3
Biecz (PL) .... 201 C 2
Biedenkopf (D) .... 88 A 2
Biedrusko (PL) .... 187 F 2
Biel / Bienne (CH) .... 49 F 2
Bielany-Żyłaki (PL) .... 191 D 2
Bielawa (PL) .... 193 E 3
Bielawy Łodzkie (PL) .... 189 E 3
Bielefeld (D) .... 83 F 4
Bielice
  Zachodniopomorskie (PL) 180 B 4
Bieliny Kapitulne (PL) .... 196 B 3
Biella (I) .... 53 F 1
Bielsa (E) .... 54 C 4
Bielsk (PL) .... 189 E 2

Bielsk Podlaski (PL) .... 191 E 1
Bielsko-Biała (PL) .... 200 F 2
Bieniów (PL) .... 186 C 4
Bienne / Biel (CH) .... 49 F 2
Bientina (I) .... 101 E 2
Bienvenida (E) .... 69 E 4
Bierawa (PL) .... 194 F 4
Bierné (F) .... 41 F 4
Bieruń (PL) .... 200 F 2
Bierutów (PL) .... 193 F 2
Bierzwnik (PL) .... 187 D 1
Biescas (E) .... 54 B 4
Biesenthal (D) .... 85 D 2
Biesiekierz (PL) .... 181 D 2
Bieszczady (PL) .... 202 E 3
Bieszczadzki Park
  Narodowy (PL) .... 202 E 4
Bietigheim (D) .... 45 F 2
Bieżuń (PL) .... 189 E 1
Biga (TR) .... 19 E 2
Biggar (GB) .... 31 D 2
Biggleswade (GB) .... 36 B 2
Bignasco (CH) .... 97 D 2
Bihać (BIH) .... 167 D 2
Bijele Poljane (MNE) .... 121 C 1
Bijeljani (BIH) .... 120 C 1
Bijeljina (BIH) .... 117 F 1
Bijelo Brdo (HR) .... 113 D 4
Bijelo Polje (MNE) .... 118 B 4
Bijotai (LT) .... 176 B 1
Bijūnai (LT) .... 176 B 1
Bijutiškis (LT) .... 171 F 4
Bikernieki (Bikernīki) (LV) 169 D 4
Bikoniai (LT) .... 171 E 4
Biksēre (LV) .... 166 C 1
Biksti (LT) .... 163 F 2
Bila Cerkva (UA) .... 13 E 1
Bilbao (E) .... 60 C 3
Bildudalur (IS) .... 126 A 1
Bile (HR) .... 112 C 4
Bileća (BIH) .... 120 C 2

Bilecik (TR) .... 19 F 2
Bilgoraj (PL) .... 197 E 3
Bilhorod-Dnistrovs'kyj (UA) 13 F 3
Biliakiemis (LT) .... 171 F 3
Biliūnai (LT) .... 171 E 1
Bilina (CZ) .... 89 D 4
Biljača (SRB) .... 122 B 2
Biljanovac (SRB) .... 118 B 4
Bille (LV) .... 159 E 4
Billerbeck (D) .... 83 D 4
Billericay (GB) .... 36 C 3
Billingham (GB) .... 31 F 4
Billingshurst (GB) .... 36 B 4
Billom (F) .... 52 A 1
Billund (DK) .... 142 B 4
Bilopillja (UA) .... 7 F 4
Bílovec (CZ) .... 91 F 2
Bilska (LV) .... 160 C 3
Bilto (N) .... 124 C 3
Bilzen (B) .... 39 E 2
Binaced (E) .... 66 A 2
Binarowa (PL) .... 201 C 2
Binasco (I) .... 97 D 3
Binche (B) .... 39 E 3
Bindari (LV) .... 167 D 3
Binéfar (E) .... 66 A 2
Binēnai (LT) .... 164 C 4
Bingen (D) .... 45 E 1
Bingham (GB) .... 33 F 4
Bingley (GB) .... 33 D 2
Bingsjö (S) .... 140 C 2
Binic (F) .... 41 E 2
Binz (D) .... 80 C 2
Bioče (MNE) .... 121 C 2
Biograd na moru (HR) .... 103 E 1
Bionaz (I) .... 53 F 1
Birchington (GB) .... 37 D 3
Bircza (PL) .... 202 E 1
Biri (N) .... 139 E 2
Birkeland (N) .... 142 B 1

Birkeneļi (LV) .... 172 C 1
Birkenfeld (D) .... 45 D 1
Birkenhead (GB) .... 32 C 2
Birkenwerder (D) .... 85 D 2
Birkerød (DK) .... 143 D 4
Birkfeld (A) .... 95 E 3
Birmingham (GB) .... 33 D 4
Birnau (D) .... 93 D 3
Birr / Biorra (IRL) .... 25 D 1
Birsči (LV) .... 175 F 3
Biršiūnai (LT) .... 172 C 2
Birštonas (LT) .... 176 C 2
Biržai (LT) .... 165 D 4
Birzebugga (M) .... 110 A 4
Birzes (LV) .... 165 D 2
Birzgale (LV) .... 165 C 4
Birži Jēkabpils (LV) .... 165 F 3
Birži Kuldīgas (LV) .... 156 C 4
Birztalas (LV) .... 159 F 2
Biržūnai (LT) .... 172 C 4
Biržuvėnai (LT) .... 163 D 4
Biržų Laukas (LT) .... 169 D 2
Bisaccia (I) .... 106 A 4
Biscarrosse (F) .... 50 A 4
Biscarrosse-Plage (F) .... 50 A 4
Bisceglie (I) .... 106 C 2
Bischofsgrün (D) .... 89 D 3
Bischofsheim an der Rhön
  Kreis Rhön-Grabfeld (D) 88 B 3
Bischofshofen (A) .... 94 B 3
Bischofswerda (D) .... 90 A 1
Bischofswiesen (D) .... 94 B 3
Bischofszell (CH) .... 93 D 4
Bischwiller (F) .... 45 E 3
Bisenti (I) .... 103 B 2
Biševo (HR) .... 103 F 2
Bishop Auckland (GB) .... 31 E 4
Bishop's Castle (GB) .... 32 C 4
Bishop's Stortford (GB) .... 36 C 3
Bisignano (I) .... 109 E 1
Bisko (HR) .... 117 B 3
Biskupiec
  Kujawsko-Pomorskie (PL) 183 D 4

Biskupiec Warmińsko-
  Mazurskie (PL) .... 184 B 3
Biskupin (PL) .... 188 B 2
Biskupin (PL) .... 84 C 2
Bismo (N) .... 130 C 4
Bispgården (S) .... 132 A 3
Bispingen (D) .... 84 A 2
Bistrica Prijepolje (SRB) 118 B 4
Bistrica Žabljak (MNE) .... 118 B 4
Bistrica ob. S. (SLO) .... 99 F 1
Bistriţa (RO) .... 13 D 3
Bisztynek (PL) .... 183 F 2
Bitburg (D) .... 44 C 1
Bitche (F) .... 45 D 2
Bitėnai (LT) .... 168 C 4
Bitetto (I) .... 107 D 2
Bitola (MK) .... 122 B 4
Bitonto (I) .... 106 C 2
Bitterfeld (D) .... 85 D 4
Bitti (I) .... 108 B 2
Bizau (A) .... 93 E 4
Bizovac (HR) .... 112 C 4
Bjala (BG) .... 19 D 1
Bjaroza (BY) .... 6 C 4
Bjästa (S) .... 132 B 3
Bjelovar (HR) .... 112 A 4
Bjerkreim (N) .... 138 B 4
Bjerkvik (N) .... 124 A 4
Bjerringbro (DK) .... 142 B 3
Bjørkelangen (N) .... 139 F 3
Björketorp (S) .... 143 F 3
Björkliden (S) .... 124 B 4
Björklinge (S) .... 141 D 3
Björköby (FIN) .... 132 C 3
Björksele (S) .... 132 B 1
Björna (N) .... 130 C 4
Bjørnevatn (N) .... 125 F 2
Björsäter (S) .... 143 F 1
Bjurholm (S) .... 132 B 2
Bjursås (S) .... 140 C 2
Bjuv (S) .... 143 D 4

Blace (SRB) .... 119 D 3
Blachownia (PL) .... 195 D 3
Blackburn (GB) .... 32 C 2
Blackpool (GB) .... 32 C 2
Blackwater (IRL) .... 25 E 3
Blackwaterfoot (GB) .... 23 F 1
Blaenau Ffestiniog (GB) 32 B 3
Blaenavon (GB) .... 35 D 1
Blagaj (BIH) .... 117 E 4
Blagnac (F) .... 55 D 2
Blagoevgrad (BG) .... 18 C 1
Blåhammaren (S) .... 131 E 3
Blain (F) .... 46 A 1
Blainville-sur-l'Eau (F) .... 44 C 3
Blair Atholl (GB) .... 27 F 4
Blairgowrie (GB) .... 31 E 1
Blakeney (GB) .... 37 D 1
Blakstad (N) .... 139 D 4
Blâmont (F) .... 45 D 3
Blanca (E) .... 77 E 1
Blandford Forum (GB) .... 35 E 3
Blandžiai (LT) .... 169 F 3
Blanes (E) .... 67 E 3
Blangy-le-Château (F) .... 42 B 2
Blangy-sur-Bresle (F) .... 38 B 4
Blankenberge (B) .... 37 F 4
Blankenburg (D) .... 84 B 4
Blankenfelde
  (Saulīte) (LV) .... 164 B 3
Blankenhain (D) .... 89 D 2
Blankenheim (D) .... 87 E 3
Blanquefort (F) .... 50 B 3
Blansko (CZ) .... 91 D 3
Blanzac (F) .... 50 C 2
Blanzy (F) .... 48 C 3
Blarney (IRL) .... 24 C 3
Błaszki (PL) .... 188 C 4
Blatná (CZ) .... 90 A 4
Blatnica (BIH) .... 117 E 2
Blato (HR) .... 117 D 4
Blattnikselе (S) .... 132 A 1
Blaubeuren (D) .... 93 D 2

BONN

An der Josefshöhe AV 5
Augustusring AV 6
Friedrich-Breuer-Str. AV 13
Friedrich-Ebert-Allee AX 14
Hausdorffstr. AX 17
Heinrich-Böll-Ring AV 21
Hermann-Wandersleb-Ring AX 18
Kaiser-Karl-Ring AV 19
Meckenheimer Allee AX 25
Poppelsdorfer Allee AX 32
Provinzialstr. AX 35
St. Augustiner Str. AV 42

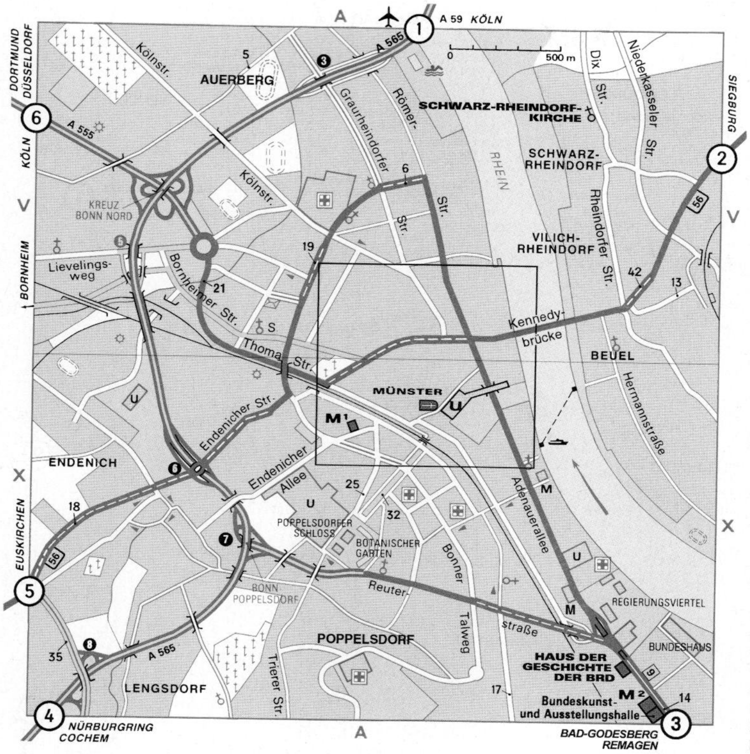
A 59 KÖLN
DORTMUND DÜSSELDORF
AUERBERG
SCHWARZ-RHEINDORF-KIRCHE
SCHWARZ-RHEINDORF
VILICH-RHEINDORF
SIEGBURG
KÖLN
BORNHEIM
Kennedybrücke
BEUEL
MÜNSTER
ENDENICH
EUSKIRCHEN
POPPELSDORFER SCHLOSS
BOTANISCHER GARTEN
REGIERUNGSVIERTEL
POPPELSDORF
BUNDESHAUS
HAUS DER GESCHICHTE DER BRD
Bundeskunst- und Ausstellungshalle
LENGSDORF
NÜRBURGRING COCHEM
BAD-GODESBERG REMAGEN

Blaufelden (D) 88 C 4
Blaustein (D) 93 D 2
Blaye (F) 50 B 2
Blaževo (SRB) 119 D 4
Blāzma (LV) 157 D 3
Błażowa (PL) 202 E 2
Bleckede (D) 84 B 1
Bled (SLO) 99 D 1
Błędów Śląskie (PL) 195 E 4
Bledzew (PL) 186 C 2
Bleiburg (A) 114 B 2
Bleicherode (D) 88 C 1
Bleik (N) 124 A 3
Bléneau (F) 43 E 4
Blénod-lès-Pont-à-Mousson (F) 44 C 3
Blérancourt (F) 39 D 4
Bléré (F) 47 E 2
Blesle (F) 52 A 2
Bletchley (GB) 36 B 2
Bletterans (F) 49 D 3
Blexen (D) 78 B 4
Blīdene (LV) 163 E 2
Blieskastel (D) 45 D 2
Bligny-sur-Ouche (F) 48 C 2
Blinja (HR) 115 D 3
Bliūdžiai *Biržai* (LT) 165 E 3
Bliūdžiai *Kauno* (LT) 169 E 3
Bliūdžiai *Panevėžys* (LT) 171 D 1
Blizanów (PL) 188 B 4
Bliżyn (PL) 195 F 2
Bloemendaal (NL) 82 B 3
Blois (F) 42 C 4
Blokhus (DK) 142 B 2
Blomberg (D) 83 F 4
Blome (LV) 159 F 3
Blomi (LV) 159 D 4
Blönduós (IS) 126 B 1
Błonie *Mazowieckie* (PL) 189 F 3
Blonti (LV) 167 F 2
Blonville-sur-Mer (F) 42 A 1
Blosenberg (D) 89 E 2
Bloška polica (SLO) 99 D 2
Blovice (CZ) 89 F 3
Bludenz (A) 93 D 4
Blukas (LV) 164 C 2
Blumberg (D) 45 F 4
Blumberg (D) 85 E 2
Blyth (GB) 31 F 3
Bnin (PL) 187 F 3
Bø (N) 139 D 3
Bo' Ness (GB) 31 D 2
Boal (E) 59 D 2
Boan (MNE) 121 D 1
Boara Pisani (I) 98 A 4
Bobbio (I) 97 E 4
Bobbio Pellice (I) 53 E 3
Bobigny (F) 43 D 2
Bobingen (D) 93 E 2
Böblingen (D) 45 F 3
Boblitz (D) 85 E 3
Bobolice (PL) 181 E 3
Boboszów (PL) 199 B 1
Bobowa (PL) 201 C 2
Bóbr (PL) 193 D 3
Bóbrka (PL) 202 D 3
Bobrovycja (UA) 13 E 1
Bobrowice (PL) 186 C 4
Bobrowniki *Podkarpackie* (PL) 185 F 4
Bobrynec' (UA) 13 F 2
Bočac (BIH) 117 D 2
Bocairent (E) 71 F 4
Boceguillas (E) 64 B 3
Bochnia (PL) 201 B 2
Bocholt (D) 83 D 4
Bochov (CZ) 89 F 3
Bochum (D) 87 E 1
Bockenem (D) 84 A 4
Boćki (PL) 191 E 2
Böckstein (A) 94 B 4
Bockum-Hövel (D) 83 E 4
Bocognano (F) 57 F 4
Boda (S) 140 B 2
Böda (S) 146 A 2
Bodafors (S) 143 E 2
Bođani (SRB) 113 D 4
Bodegraven (NL) 82 B 4
Boden (S) 128 B 4
Bodenmais (D) 89 F 4
Bodenteich (D) 84 B 2
Bodenwerder (D) 84 A 4
Bodenwöhr (D) 89 E 4
Bodman (D) 45 F 4
Bodmin (GB) 34 B 3
Bodø (N) 127 E 2
Bodzentyn (PL) 196 B 3
Boecillo (E) 64 A 2
Boëge (F) 49 E 4
Boën (F) 52 B 1
Boeza (E) 59 E 4
Boffalora sopra Ticino (I) 97 D 3
Bogarra (E) 71 D 4
Bogatić (SRB) 117 F 1
Bogatynia (PL) 192 C 3
Bogdanci (MK) 122 C 3
Bogdaniec (PL) 186 C 2
Bogen (D) 94 A 1
Bogen (N) 124 A 4
Bogense (DK) 142 B 4
Bogetići (MNE) 121 D 2
Bognanco (I) 96 C 2
Bognes (N) 124 A 4
Bognor Regis (GB) 36 B 4
Bogodol (BIH) 117 E 4
Bogojevo (SRB) 113 D 4
Bogomila (MK) 122 B 3
Bogomolje (HR) 120 B 2
Bogoria (PL) 196 B 3
Bogorodica (MK) 122 C 3
Bogovina (SRB) 119 D 2
Boguchwała (PL) 202 D 2
Bogušiškiai (LT) 169 F 2
Boguslavas (LT) 163 D 3
Boguszów Gorce (PL) 193 D 3
Bogutovac (SRB) 118 C 3
Boguty-Pianki (PL) 191 D 1
Bohain-en-Vermandois (F) 39 D 3
Boherboy (IRL) 24 B 3
Bohinjska Bistrica (SLO) 99 D 1
Böhlen (D) 89 E 1
Böhmenkirch (D) 93 D 2
Bohmte (D) 83 E 3
Böhönye (H) 112 B 3
Bohumín (CZ) 91 F 2
Bohuslav (UA) 13 E 1
Boiro (E) 58 A 3
Bois-d'Amont (F) 49 E 3
Boitzenburg (D) 80 C 4
Boíxols (E) 55 D 4
Boizenburg (D) 84 B 1
Bojadła (PL) 187 D 4
Bojano (I) 105 F 2
Bojanów (PL) 197 D 4
Bojanowo (PL) 187 E 4
Bojas (LV) 162 C 1
Bøjden (DK) 142 B 4
Bojkovice (CZ) 91 F 4
Bojnik (SRB) 119 E 4
Bojszowy (PL) 200 F 2
Bokštai (LT) 169 D 2
Bol (HR) 120 A 1
Bolaños de Calatrava (E) 70 B 3
Bolbec (F) 38 A 4
Bolchov (RUS) 7 F 3
Bolesław *Małopolskie* (PL) 195 E 4
Bolesławiec *Dolnośląskie* (PL) 192 C 2
Bolesławiec *Łodzkie* (PL) 194 C 2
Boleszkowice (PL) 186 B 2
Bolhrad (UA) 13 E 3
Boliden (S) 132 C 1
Bolimów (PL) 189 F 3
Bolimowska (Puszcza) (PL) 189 F 3
Boliqueime (P) 74 B 2
Boljanići (MNE) 118 A 4
Boljevac (SRB) 119 E 2
Boljevci (SRB) 118 B 1
Boljkovci (SRB) 118 B 2
Boljuni (BIH) 120 C 2
Bolkesjø (N) 139 D 3
Bolków (PL) 193 D 3
Bollebygd (S) 143 D 2
Bollène (F) 52 C 4
Bollnäs (S) 140 C 1
Bollstabruk (S) 132 B 3
Bollullos de la Mitación (E) 75 E 2
Bollullos Par del Condado (E) 75 D 2
Bologna (I) 101 F 1
Bologne (F) 44 B 4
Bologoje (RUS) 7 E 1
Bolotana (I) 108 B 2
Bolsena (I) 102 A 4
Bolsward (NL) 82 B 2
Boltaña (E) 54 C 4
Boltenhagen (D) 79 E 3
Boltmuiža (Indrāne) (LV) 166 B 4
Bolton (GB) 32 C 2
Bolungarvik (IS) 126 A 1
Bolzano / Bozen (I) 98 A 1
Bom Jesus do Monte (P) 62 C 2
Bombarral (P) 68 A 2
Bömenzien (D) 84 C 2
Boñar (E) 59 F 3
Bonar Bridge (GB) 27 E 2
Bonares (E) 75 D 2
Bonassola (I) 101 D 1
Bondeno (I) 98 A 4
Bonefro (I) 105 F 2
Bonete (E) 71 E 3
Bonifacio (F) 57 F 4
Boniškiai (LT) 170 C 4
Bonn (D) 87 E 2
Bonnåsjøen (N) 127 E 2
Bonnat (F) 47 F 4
Bonndorf *Kreis Waldshut* (D) 92 C 3
Bonnétable (F) 42 B 3
Bonneuil-Matours (F) 47 E 3
Bonneval (F) 42 C 3
Bonneville (F) 49 E 4
Bonnières-sur-Seine (F) 42 C 2
Bonnieux (F) 56 C 1
Bono (I) 108 B 2
Bonorva (I) 108 B 2
Boo (S) 141 D 4
Boom (B) 39 E 2
Boos (F) 42 C 1
Bootle (GB) 32 C 2
Bopfingen (D) 93 E 1
Boppard (D) 87 F 3
Bor (CZ) 89 F 3
Bor (SRB) 119 E 2
Borås (S) 143 D 2
Borba (P) 68 C 3
Borbona (I) 102 C 4
Borča (SRB) 118 B 1
Borci (BIH) 117 E 4
Bordeaux (F) 50 B 3
Bordères-Louron (F) 54 C 3
Bordesholm (D) 78 C 3
Bordighera (I) 57 F 1
Bore (I) 97 E 4
Borek Wielkopolski (PL) 187 F 4
Borello (I) 102 A 1
Borensberg (S) 143 F 1
Borgafjäll (S) 131 F 1
Borgarfjörður (IS) 126 C 1
Borgarnes (IS) 126 A 2
Börger (D) 83 E 2
Borger (NL) 83 D 2
Borghetto (I) 102 B 4
Borghetto Santo Spirito (I) 100 C 2
Borgholm (S) 143 F 3
Borgholzhausen (D) 83 E 4
Borghorst (D) 83 D 4
Borgia (I) 109 E 2
Borgo San Dalmazzo (I) 53 F 4
Borgo San Lorenzo (I) 101 F 2
Borgo Tufico (I) 102 B 2
Borgo Val di Taro (I) 101 D 1
Borgo Valsugana (I) 98 A 2
Borgomanero (I) 96 C 3
Borgone Susa (I) 53 E 2
Borgonovo Val Tidone (I) 97 E 4
Borgorose (I) 102 C 4
Borgosesia (I) 96 C 3
Borgsjö (S) 132 A 4
Borgvattnet (S) 132 A 3
Boričie (MNE) 117 F 4
Borisova (LV) 161 F 4
Borja (E) 65 E 2
Borken (D) 83 D 4
Borkenes / Kvæfjord (N) 124 A 4
Borki *Lubelskie* (PL) 191 D 4
Børkop (DK) 142 B 4
Borkowice (PL) 195 F 2
Borkum (D) 83 D 1
Borlänge (S) 140 C 2
Bormaņi (LV) 165 F 2
Bormes-les-Mimosas (F) 57 D 3
Bormio (I) 97 F 1
Born am Darß *Kreis Nordvorpommern* (D) 79 F 3
Borna *Kreis Leipziger Land* (D) 89 E 1
Borne Sulinowo (PL) 181 E 3
Bornes (P) 63 D 2
Bornhöved (D) 79 D 3
Börnicke *Kreis Havelland* (D) 85 D 2
Bornos (E) 75 E 3
Boroughbridge (GB) 33 D 1
Borovec (BG) 19 D 1
Boroviči (RUS) 7 E 1
Borovka (Barauka) (LV) 173 D 1
Borovnica (SLO) 99 D 2
Borovo (HR) 113 D 4
Borovsk (RUS) 7 F 2
Borów *Dolnośląskie* (PL) 193 F 3
Borowa (PL) 196 C 4
Borowie (PL) 190 C 3
Borre (N) 139 E 3
Borriana / Burriana (E) 72 A 2
Borriol (E) 72 A 1
Borris (IRL) 25 E 2
Borrisokane / Buiríos Uí Chéin (IRL) 25 D 2
Borşa (RO) 13 D 3
Børselv (N) 125 E 2
Bórsi (GR) 216 C 2
Bort-les-Orgues (F) 51 F 2
Börtnan (S) 131 F 4
Boryspil' (UA) 13 E 1
Borzechowo (PL) 182 C 3
Borzęcin (PL) 201 B 2
Borzna (UA) 7 F 4
Borzonasca (I) 101 D 1
Borzytuchom (PL) 181 F 2
Bosa (I) 108 A 2
Bosanci (HR) 99 E 2
Bosanska Dubica / Kosarska Dubica (BIH) 115 E 4
Bosanska Gradiska (BIH) 115 E 4
Bosanska Gradiška / Gradiška (BIH) 115 E 4
Bosanska Kostajnica / Srpska Kostajnica (BIH) 115 D 4
Bosanska Krupa (BIH) 115 D 4
Bosanska Rača / Rača (BIH) 117 F 1
Bosanski Brod / Srpski Brod (BIH) 115 F 3
Bosanski Kobaš / Kobaš (BIH) 115 F 4
Bosanski Novi / Novi Grad (BIH) 115 D 4
Bosanski Petrovac (BIH) 116 C 2
Bosanski Šamac / Šamac (BIH) 117 E 1
Bosansko Grahovo (BIH) 116 C 3
Bosansko Petrovo Selo / Petrovo (BIH) 117 E 2
Bosco (I) 102 B 3
Bosco Chiesanuova (I) 97 F 3
Boscoreale (I) 105 F 3
Bosilegrad (SRB) 119 F 4
Bosiljevo (HR) 99 E 2
Bosjökloster (S) 143 D 4
Boskoop (NL) 82 B 4
Boskovice (CZ) 91 E 3
Bošnjace (SRB) 119 E 4
Bošnjaci (HR) 117 F 1
Bossolasco (I) 53 F 3
Bossòst (E) 55 D 3
Boštanj (SLO) 99 E 1
Boston (GB) 33 F 3
Botevgrad (BG) 19 D 1
Bothel (GB) 31 D 4
Boticas (P) 63 D 2
Botley (GB) 35 F 3
Botngård (N) 131 D 2
Botoš (SRB) 113 F 4
Botoşani (RO) 13 D 2
Botsmark (S) 132 C 2
Bottrop (D) 87 E 1
Botun (MK) 122 A 4
Bouaye (F) 46 B 2
Boucau (F) 54 A 2
Bouchain (F) 39 D 3
Boudry (CH) 49 F 3
Bouillon (B) 39 F 4
Bouilly (F) 43 F 3
Boúka (GR) 217 E 4
Boulay-Moselle (F) 44 C 2
Boulogne-sur-Gesse (F) 55 D 2
Boulogne-sur-Mer (F) 38 B 2
Bouloire (F) 42 B 4
Bourbon-Lancy (F) 48 B 3
Bourbon-l'Archambault (F) 48 A 3
Bourbonne-les-Bains (F) 44 B 4
Bourbourg (F) 37 E 4
Bourbriac (F) 40 C 3
Bourdeaux (F) 52 C 3
Bourdeilles (F) 51 D 2
Bourg (F) 50 B 3
Bourg-Achard (F) 42 B 1
Bourg-Argental (F) 52 B 2
Bourg-de-Péage (F) 52 C 3
Bourg-de-Visa (F) 51 D 4
Bourg-en-Bresse (F) 49 D 4
Bourg-Lastic (F) 51 F 2
Bourg-Madame (F) 55 E 4
Bourg-St-Andéol (F) 52 B 4
Bourg-St-Maurice (F) 53 E 1
Bourganeuf (F) 51 E 1
Bourges (F) 48 A 3
Bourgneuf-en-Retz (F) 46 B 2
Bourgoin-Jallieu (F) 52 C 2
Bourgtheroulde-Infreville (F) 42 B 1
Bourgueil (F) 47 D 2
Bourmont (F) 44 B 4
Bourne (GB) 33 E 4
Bournemouth (GB) 35 E 3
Bouro (P) 62 C 2
Boussac (F) 48 A 4
Boussens (F) 55 D 3
Bouxwiller (F) 45 D 3
Bouzonville (F) 44 C 2
Bova Marina (I) 111 F 2
Bovalino Marina (I) 111 F 1
Bovan (SRB) 119 D 3
Bovec (SLO) 98 C 1
Bóveda *Lugo* (E) 58 C 3
Bøverdal (N) 139 D 1
Boves (F) 38 C 4
Boves (I) 53 F 4
Bovey Tracey (GB) 34 C 3
Bovolone (I) 98 A 3
Bowes (GB) 31 E 4
Bowness (GB) 32 C 1
Bowness-on-Solway (GB) 31 D 4
Boxholm (S) 143 F 1
Boxmeer (NL) 87 D 1
Boxtel (NL) 39 F 1
Boyle / Mainistir na Búille (IRL) 22 C 3
Božaj (MNE) 121 E 2
Božavar (HR) 103 D 1
Bozdoğan (TR) 19 F 3
Bozel (F) 53 E 2
Bozen / Bolzano (I) 98 A 1
Boží Dar (CZ) 89 F 2
Božica (SRB) 119 F 4
Bozouls (F) 51 F 4
Bozova (LV) 167 F 1
Bozüyük (TR) 19 F 2
Bozzolo (I) 97 F 4
Bra (I) 53 F 3
Brač (Otok) (HR) 120 A 1
Bracadale (GB) 26 C 3
Bracciano (I) 104 C 1
Bračevci (HR) 112 C 4
Bracieux (F) 47 F 2
Bräcke (S) 131 F 4
Brackenheim (D) 45 F 2
Brackley (GB) 35 F 1
Bracknell (GB) 36 B 3
Brackwede (D) 83 F 4
Brad (RO) 12 C 4
Bradford (GB) 33 D 2

BÈGLES

Buisson (R. F.) . . . . BV 28
Capelle (Av. A.) . . . . BV 31
Chevalier-de-la-Barre (R. du) BV 42
Guesde (Av. J.) . . . . BV 76

BORDEAUX

Aliénor-d'Aquitaine
(Bd) . . . . BT 3
Arnozan (Crs Xavier) . . . . . BU 5
Arsenal (R. de l') . . . . BU 6
Bacalan (Quai de) . . . . . . BT 9
Barthou (Av. L.) . . . . AU 12
Boutaut (Allée de) . . . . . . BT 22
Brandenburg (BD) . . . . . . BT 24

Brazza (Quai de) . . . . BT 25
Brienne (Quai de) . . . . BU 27
Chartrons (Quai des) . . . . BTU 39
Croix-de-Seguey
(R.) . . . . BU 45
Dassault (Av. M.) . . . . BT 46
Domergue (Bd G.) . . . . . . BT 51
Duché (R. des Gén.) . . . . . BT 55
Galin (R.) . . . . BU 66
Gautier (Bd A.) . . . . AU 72
Georges-V (Bd) . . . . BU 73
Johnston (R. D.) . . . . BU 81
Joliot-Curie (Bd) . . . . BU 84
Leclerc (Av. Gén.) . . . . . . AU 90
Leclerc (Bd Mar.) . . . . . . BU 93
Lombard (R.) . . . . BT 96
Mérignac (Av. de) . . . . . . AU 101

Pierre-1er (Bd) . . . . BT 115
Président-Wilson
(Bd) . . . . AU 119
République (Av. de la) . . . AU 121
Roosevelt (Bd Franklin) . . . BU 123
Thiers (Av.) . . . . BU 134
Tourville (Av. de). . . . . . . BT 136

BRUGES

Gaulle (Av. Gén.-de) . . . . . AT 70
Quatre-Ponts (R. des) . . . . AT 120

CENON

Carnot (Av.) . . . . BT 32
Entre-Deux-Mers (Bd de l') BU 61

EYSINES

Libération (Av. de la) . . . . . AT 94

FLOIRAC

Gambetta (Crs) . . . . BU 67
Guesde (R. J.) . . . . BU 78

LE BOUSCAT

Libération (Av. de la) . . . . . AT 95
Louis-Blanc
(Cours) . . . . BT 97
Tivoli (Av. de) . . . . BT 135

Jean-Jaurès (Av.) . . . . BU 79

LORMONT

Paris (Rte de) . . . . BT 108

MÉRIGNAC

Barbusse (Av. H.) . . . . . . AT 10
Beaudésert (Av. de) . . . . . AU 13
Belfort (Av. de) . . . . AU 15
Bon-Air (Av.) . . . . AU 18
Cassin (Av. R.) . . . . AU 34
Garros (Av. Rolland) . . . . AU 69
Gouraud (Pl. du Gén.) . . . AU 74
Kaolack (Av. de) . . . . . . AU 87
Leclerc (Av. M.) . . . . AU 91

Zola (R. Émile) . . . . AT 145

PESSAC

Dr-Nancel-Pénard
(Av.) . . . . AV 47
Eiffel (Av. Gustave) . . . . . AV 60
Madran (R. de) . . . . AV 99
Montagne (R. P.) . . . . . . AV 103
Pont-d'Orient (Av. du) . . . AV 117
Transvaal (Av. du). . . . . . AV 137

TALENCE

Lamartine (R.) . . . . BV 88
Roul (Av.) . . . . BV 124
Université (Av. de l') . . . . AV 138

Souvenir (Av. du). . . . . AU 131

Bradford-on-Avon (GB) 35	E 2	Bramberge (LV) 164	B 2	Braniewo (PL) 183	E 1	Braunau (A) 94	B 2	Brechin (GB) 31	E 1	Breitungen (D) 88	C 2
Bradina (BIH) 117	E 3	Bramming (DK) 142	A 4	Brankas (LV) 164	C 2	Braunfels (D) 88	A 2	Brecht (B) 39	F 1	Breivikbotn (N) 124	C 2
Brading (GB) 35	F 3	Brampton (GB) 31	D 4	Branne (F) 50	C 3	Braunlage (D) 84	B 4	Břeclav (CZ) 91	E 4	Breivikeidet (N) 124	B 3
Bradwell-on-Sea (GB) 36	C 3	Bramsche (D) 83	E 3	Brañosera (E) 60	A 3	Braunsbedra (D) 89	D 1	Brecon / Aberhonddu (GB) 35	D 1	Brekke (N) 138	B 1
Braemar (GB) 27	F 4	Brancaleone Marina (I) ... 111	F 2	Brańsk (PL) 191	E 1	Braunschweig (D) 84	B 3	Breda (E) 67	D 3	Brekken (N) 131	E 4
Braga (P) 62	C 2	Brancion (F) 49	D 4	Br'ansk (RUS) 7	F 3	Braunton (GB) 34	C 2	Breda (NL) 39	E 1	Brekkvassely (N) 131	E 1
Bragança (P) 63	E 2	Brand (A) 93	D 4	Brantôme (F) 51	D 2	Bravães (P) 62	C 2	Bredbyn (S) 132	B 3	Brekstad (N) 131	D 2
Brăila (RO) 13	E 4	Brand-Erbisdorf (D) 89	F 1	Braskereidfoss (N) 139	E 4	Bray / Bré (IRL) 25	F 1	Bredelar (D) 88	A 1	Bremen Kreis Bremen (D) .. 83	F 2
Braine (F) 43	E 1	Brandbu (N) 139	E 2	Braslaŭ (BY) 7	D 3	Bray-Dunes (F) 37	E 4	Bredstedt (D) 78	A 2	Bremerhaven (D) 78	B 4
Braine-le-Comte (B) 39	E 2	Brande (DK) 142	B 3	Brasli (LV) 162	C 2	Bray-sur-Seine (F) 43	E 3	Bree (B) 87	D 2	Bremervörde (D) 78	C 4
Braintree (GB) 36	C 3	Brande-Hörnerkirchen (D). 78	A 4	Braşov (RO) 13	D 4	Bray-sur-Somme (F) 38	C 4	Breganze (I) 98	A 3	Bremsnes (N) 130	B 3
Brake (Unterweser)		Brandenburg (D) 85	D 3	Brassac (F) 55	F 2	Brazatortas (E) 70	A 4	Bregenz (A) 93	D 4	Brenci (LV) 161	E 3
Kreis Wesermarsch (D) .. 83	E 2	Brandis Muldentalkreis (D). 89	E 1	Brassac-les-Mines (F) 52	A 2	Bražuolė (LT) 177	E 2	Bréhal (F) 41	E 2	Brenes (E) 85	F 1
Brakel (D) 83	F 4	Brändö (FIN) 136	B 4	Brasschaat (B) 39	E 1	Brbinj (HR) 103	E 1	Brehna (D) 85	D 1	Brenguļi (LV) 159	F 2
Bräkne-Hoby (S) 143	E 3	Brandon (GB) 33	C 4	Bratislava (SK) 12	A 3	Brčko (BIH) 117	F 1	Breiðdalsvik (IS) 126	C 2	Brenna (PL) 200	F 2
Bralin (PL) 194	B 2	Branduoliškiai (LT) 169	E 4	Brattvåg (N) 130	B 3	Brđani (SRB) 118	C 2	Breil-sur-Roya (F) 53	F 4	Brennilis (F) 40	B 3
Brallo di Pregola (I) 101	D 1	Branice (PL) 200	D 2	Bratunac (BIH) 117	F 2	Brea (E) 65	C 2	Breisach (D) 45	E 3	Breno (I) 97	F 2
Brálos (GR) 212	A 4	Braničevo (SRB) 119	D 1	Braubach (D) 87	F 3	Brécey (F) 41	E 2	Breitengüßbach (D) 88	C 3	Brénod (F) 49	D 4

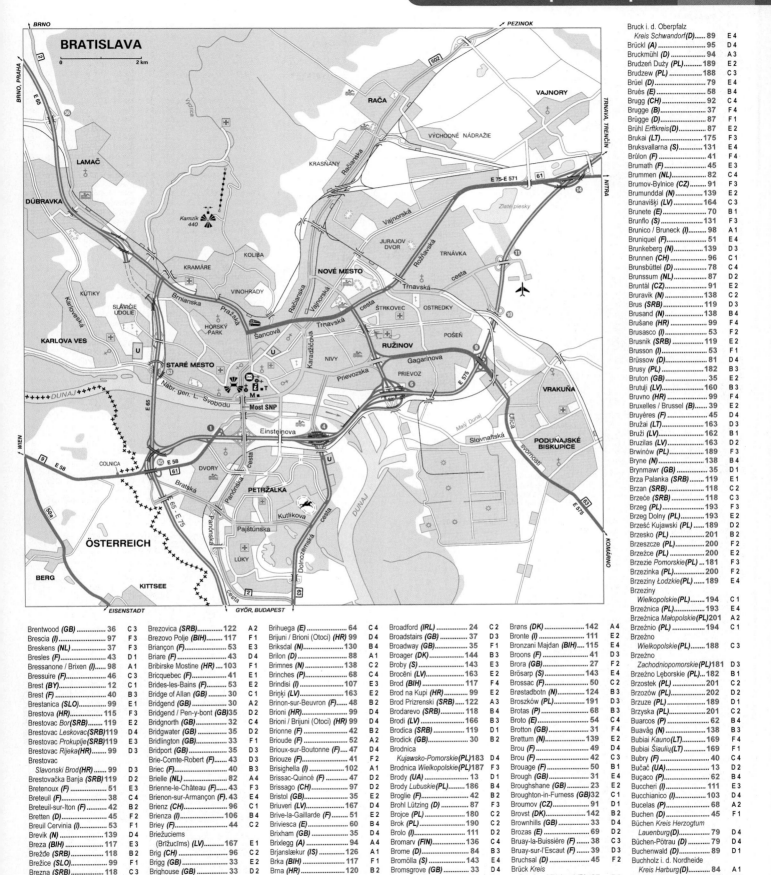

BRATISLAVA

Bruck i. d. Oberpfalz
  Kreis Schwandorf(D) ...... 89 E 4
Brückl (A) ...... 95 D 4
Bruckmühl (D) ...... 94 A 3
Brudzeń Duży (PL) ...... 189 E 2
Brudzew (PL) ...... 188 C 3
Brüel (D) ...... 79 E 4
Bruès (E) ...... 58 B 4
Brugg (CH) ...... 92 C 4
Brugge (B) ...... 37 F 2
Brügge (D) ...... 87 F 1
Brühl *Erftkreis(D)* ...... 87 E 2
Brukai (LT) ...... 175 F 3
Bruksvallarna (S) ...... 131 F 3
Brûlon (F) ...... 41 F 4
Brumath (F) ...... 45 E 3
Brummen (NL) ...... 82 C 4
Brumov-Bylnice (CZ) ...... 91 F 3
Brumunddal (N) ...... 139 E 2
Brunaviški (LV) ...... 164 C 3
Brunete (E) ...... 70 B 1
Brunflo (S) ...... 131 F 2
Brunico / Bruneck (I) ...... 98 A 1
Bruniquel (F) ...... 51 E 4
Brunkeberg (N) ...... 139 E 2
Brunnen (CH) ...... 96 C 1
Brunsbüttel (D) ...... 78 C 4
Brunssum (NL) ...... 87 E 2
Bruntál (CZ) ...... 91 E 2
Bruravik (N) ...... 138 C 2
Brus (SRB) ...... 119 D 3
Brusand (N) ...... 138 B 4
Brušane (HR) ...... 99 F 4
Brusasco (I) ...... 53 F 2
Brusnik (SRB) ...... 119 E 2
Brusson (F) ...... 53 F 1
Brüssow (D) ...... 81 D 4
Brusy (PL) ...... 182 B 3
Bruton (GB) ...... 35 E 2
Brutuļi (LV) ...... 160 B 3
Bruvno (HR) ...... 99 F 4
Bruxelles / Brussel (B) ...... 39 E 2
Bruyères (F) ...... 45 D 4
Bružai (LT) ...... 163 D 3
Bruži (LV) ...... 162 B 1
Bruzilas (LV) ...... 163 D 2
Brwinów (PL) ...... 189 F 3
Bryne (N) ...... 138 B 4
Brynmawr (GB) ...... 35 D 1
Brza Palanka (SRB) ...... 119 E 1
Brzan (SRB) ...... 118 C 2
Brzeće (SRB) ...... 118 C 3
Brzeg (PL) ...... 193 F 3
Brzeg Dolny (PL) ...... 193 E 2
Brześć Kujawski (PL) ...... 189 D 2
Brzesko (PL) ...... 201 B 2
Brzeszcze (PL) ...... 200 E 2
Brzeźce (PL) ...... 200 E 2
Brzezie Pomorskie(PL) ...... 181 F 3
Brzezinka (PL) ...... 200 E 2
Brzeziny Łódzkie(PL) ...... 189 E 4
Brzeziny
  Wielkopolskie(PL) ...... 194 C 1
Brzeźnica (PL) ...... 193 E 4
Brzeźnica Małopolskie(PL)201 A 2
Brzeźnio (PL) ...... 194 C 1
Brzeźno
  Wielkopolskie(PL) ...... 188 C 3
Brzeźno
  *Zachodniopomorskie(PL)*181 D 3
Brzeźno Lęborskie (PL) ...... 182 B 1
Brzostek (PL) ...... 201 C 2
Brzozów (PL) ...... 202 D 2
Brzuze (PL) ...... 189 D 1
Brzyska (PL) ...... 201 C 2
Buarcos (P) ...... 62 B 4
Buavåg (N) ...... 138 B 3
Bubiai *Kauno(LT)* ...... 169 F 2
Bubiai *Šiaulių(LT)* ...... 169 F 1
Bubry (F) ...... 40 C 4
Bučač (UA) ...... 13 D 2
Buçaco (P) ...... 62 B 4
Buccheri (I) ...... 111 E 3
Bucchianico (I) ...... 103 D 4
Bucelas (P) ...... 68 A 2
Buchen (D) ...... 45 F 1
Büchen *Kreis Herzogtum
  Lauenburg (D)* ...... 79 D 4
Büchen-Pötrau (D) ...... 79 D 1
Buchenwald (D) ...... 89 D 1
Buchholz i. d. Nordheide
  Kreis Harburg(D) ...... 84 A 1
Buchloe (D) ...... 93 E 3
Buchlovice (CZ) ...... 91 D 4
Buchs (CH) ...... 93 D 4
Buchy (F) ...... 38 B 4
Bucine (I) ...... 102 A 2

Brentwood (GB) ...... 36 C 3
Brescia (I) ...... 97 F 3
Breskens (NL) ...... 37 F 3
Bresles (F) ...... 43 D 1
Bressanone / Brixen (I) ... 98 A 1
Bressuire (F) ...... 46 C 3
Brest (BY) ...... 12 C 1
Brest (F) ...... 40 B 3
Brestanica (SLO) ...... 99 E 1
Brestova (HR) ...... 115 F 3
Brestovac Bor(SRB) ...... 119 E 2
Brestovac Leskovac(SRB)119 D 4
Brestovac Prokuplje(SRB)119 D 2
Brestovac Rijeka(HR) ...... 99 D 3
Brestovac
  Slavonski Brod(HR) ...... 99 D 3
Brestovačka Banja (SRB)119 D 2
Bretenoux (F) ...... 51 E 3
Breteuil (F) ...... 38 C 4
Breteuil-sur-Iton (F) ...... 42 B 2
Breuil Cervinia (I) ...... 53 F 1
Brevik (N) ...... 139 D 4
Breza (BIH) ...... 117 E 3
Brežđe (SRB) ...... 118 B 2
Brežice (SLO) ...... 99 F 1
Brezna (SRB) ...... 118 C 3
Breznica (HR) ...... 99 F 1
Breznica Đakovačka (HR)115 F 3
Březnice (CZ) ...... 90 A 3
Brezno (SK) ...... 12 B 2
Brézolles (F) ...... 42 C 3

Brezovica (SRB) ...... 122 A 2
Brezovo Polje (BIH) ...... 117 F 1
Briançon (F) ...... 53 E 3
Briare (F) ...... 43 D 4
Bribirske Mostine (HR) ... 103 A 1
Bricquebec (F) ...... 41 E 1
Brides-les-Bains (F) ...... 53 E 2
Bridge of Allan (GB) ...... 30 C 1
Bridgend (GB) ...... 30 A 2
Bridgend / Pen-y-bont (GB)35 D 2
Bridgnorth (GB) ...... 32 C 4
Bridgwater (GB) ...... 35 D 2
Bridlington (GB) ...... 33 F 1
Bridport (GB) ...... 35 D 2
Brie-Comte-Robert (F) ...... 43 D 3
Briec (F) ...... 40 B 3
Brielle (NL) ...... 82 A 3
Brienne-le-Château (F) ...... 43 F 3
Brienon-sur-Armançon (F). 43 D 2
Brienz (CH) ...... 96 C 1
Brienza (I) ...... 106 B 4
Briey (F) ...... 44 C 2
Briežuciems
  (Brižučīms)(LV) ...... 167 E 1
Brig (CH) ...... 96 C 2
Brigg (GB) ...... 33 F 2
Brighouse (GB) ...... 33 D 2
Brightlingsea (GB) ...... 37 D 3
Brighton (GB) ...... 36 C 4
Brigi (LV) ...... 167 F 3
Brignogan-Plages (F) ...... 40 B 2
Brignoles (F) ...... 57 D 2

Brihuega (E) ...... 64 C 4
Brijuni / Brioni (Otoci)(HR) 99 D 4
Briksdal (N) ...... 130 B 4
Brilon (D) ...... 88 A 1
Brimnes (N) ...... 138 C 2
Brinches (P) ...... 68 C 4
Brindisi (I) ...... 107 E 3
Briņķi (LV) ...... 163 E 2
Brinon-sur-Beuvron (F) ...... 48 B 2
Brinje (HR) ...... 99 B 1
Brioni / Brijuni (Otoci)(HR) 99 D 4
Brionne (F) ...... 42 B 2
Brioude (F) ...... 52 A 2
Brioux-sur-Boutonne (F) ...47 D 4
Briouze (F) ...... 41 F 2
Brisighella (I) ...... 102 A 1
Brissac-Quincé (F) ...... 47 D 2
Brissago (CH) ...... 97 D 2
Bristol (GB) ...... 35 E 2
Briuveri (LV) ...... 167 D 4
Brive-la-Gaillarde (F) ...... 51 E 2
Briviesca (E) ...... 60 C 2
Brixham (GB) ...... 35 D 4
Brixlegg (A) ...... 94 A 4
Brjanslækur (IS) ...... 126 A 1
Brka (BIH) ...... 117 B 2
Brna (HR) ...... 120 B 2
Brnaze (HR) ...... 116 D 4
Brno (CZ) ...... 91 D 4
Bro (S) ...... 146 B 2
Bro (S) ...... 141 D 4
Broadford (GB) ...... 27 D 3

Broadford (IRL) ...... 24 C 2
Broadstairs (GB) ...... 37 D 3
Broadway (GB) ...... 35 F 1
Broager (DK) ...... 144 B 3
Broby (S) ...... 143 E 3
Bročeni (LV) ...... 163 E 2
Brod (BIH) ...... 117 F 4
Brod na Kupi (HR) ...... 99 E 1
Brod Prizrenski (SRB) ...... 122 A 3
Brodarevo (SRB) ...... 118 B 4
Brodi (LV) ...... 166 B 3
Brodica (SRB) ...... 119 D 1
Brodick (GB) ...... 30 B 2
Brodnica
  *Kujawsko-Pomorskie(PL)*183 D 4
Brodnica Wielkopolskie(PL)187 A 1
Brody (UA) ...... 13 D 1
Brody Lubuskie(PL) ...... 186 B 4
Broglie (F) ...... 42 B 2
Brohl Lützing (D) ...... 87 F 3
Brojce (PL) ...... 180 C 2
Brok (PL) ...... 190 C 2
Brolo (I) ...... 111 D 2
Bromarv (FIN) ...... 136 C 3
Brome (D) ...... 84 B 3
Bromölla (S) ...... 143 E 4
Bromsgrove (GB) ...... 33 D 4
Bromyard (GB) ...... 32 C 4
Bronchales (E) ...... 71 E 1
Brønderslev (DK) ...... 142 B 2
Broni (I) ...... 97 D 4
Brønnøysund (N) ...... 126 C 4

Brøns (DK) ...... 142 A 4
Bronte (I) ...... 111 E 2
Bronzani Majdan (BIH) ...... 115 E 4
Broons (F) ...... 41 B 3
Brora (GB) ...... 27 F 2
Brösarp (S) ...... 143 E 4
Brössac (F) ...... 50 C 2
Brøstadbotn (N) ...... 124 B 3
Broszków (PL) ...... 191 D 3
Brotas (P) ...... 68 B 3
Broto (E) ...... 54 C 4
Brotton (GB) ...... 31 F 4
Brøttum (N) ...... 139 D 2
Brou (F) ...... 49 D 4
Brou (F) ...... 42 C 3
Brouage (F) ...... 50 B 1
Brough (GB) 31
Broughshane (GB) 23
Broughton-in-Furness (GB)32
Broumov (CZ) ...... 91 D 1
Brovst (DK) ...... 142 B 2
Brownhills (GB) ...... 33 D 4
Brozas (E) ...... 69 D 2
Bruay-la-Buissière (F) ...... 38 C 3
Bruay-sur-l'Escaut (F) ...... 39 D 3
Bruchsal (D) ...... 45 F 2
Brück *Kreis
  Potsdam-Mittelmark(D)* ... 85 D 3
Bruck an der
  Großglocknerstraße (A). 94 B 4
Bruck an der Leitha (A) ...... 95 D 2
Bruck an der Mur (A) ...... 95 E 3

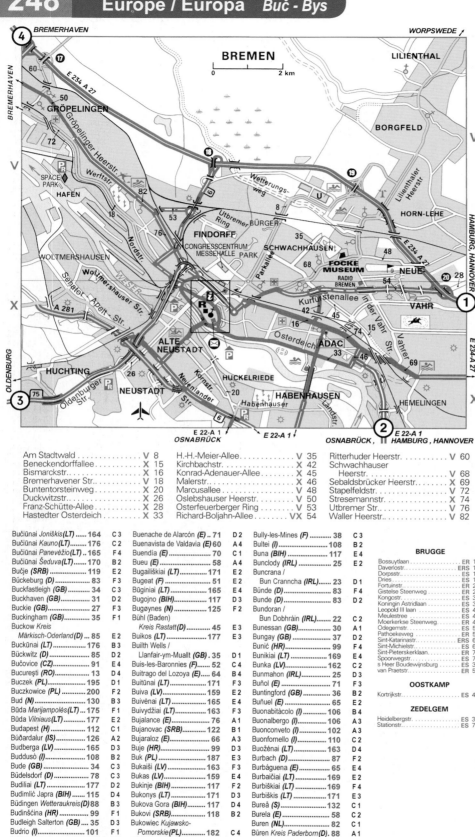

Burgdorf (CH)	96	B 1	Busseto (I)	97	E 4
Burgdorf (D)	84	A 3	Bussière-Badil (F)	51	D 1
Bürgel Saale-			Bussolengo (I)	97	F 3
Holzland-Kreis(D)	89	D 1	Bussum (NL)	82	B 4
Burgess Hill (GB)	36	B 4	Busto Arsizio (I)	97	D 3
Burggrub (D)	89	D 3	Busto de Bureba (E)	60	B 4
Burghasungen (D)	88	B 1	Büsum (D)	78	B 3
Burghausen			Buteliūnai (LT)	175	F 4
Kreis Altötting (D)	94	B 2	Butėnai (LT)	170	C 2
Burgjoß (D)	88	B 3	Butera (I)	111	D 4
Burgkunstadt (D)	89	D 3	Butkai (LT)	168	C 3
Burglengenfeld (D)	89	E 4	Butkaičiai (LT)	169	E 3
Burgohondo (E)	64	A 4	Butkiškė (LT)	169	E 2
Burgos (E)	60	B 4	Būtnāri (Kurzeme) (LV)	163	E 2
Burgsinn (D)	88	B 3	Butniūnai Panevėžio(LT)	165	D 4
Burgstädt			Butniūnai Šiauliu(LT)	164	C 4
Kreis Mittweida (D)	89	E 1	Butrimiškiai (LT)	176	C 3
Burgsvik (S)	146	B 2	Butrimonys Alytaus (LT)	176	C 3
Burgui/Burgi (E)	54	A 3	Butrimonys Vilniaus (LT)	177	E 4
Burguillos del Cerro (E)	69	D 4	Buttermere (GB)	31	D 4
Burgum (NL)	82	C 2	Buttevant (IRL)	24	C 3
Burgwedel (D)	84	A 3	Buttstädt (D)	89	D 1
Burhaniye (TR)	19	E 2	Butzbach (D)	88	A 3
Burhave (D)	78	A 4	Bützow Kreis Güstrow(D)	79	E 4
Burie (F)	50	B 1	Buxtehude (D)	78	C 4
Burjassot (E)	71	F 2	Buxton (GB)	33	D 3
Burkau (D)	90	A 1	Buxy (F)	48	C 3
Burnham-on-Crouch (GB)	36	C 3	Buzançais (F)	47	F 3
Burnham-on-Sea (GB)	35	D 2	Buzancy (F)	39	F 4
Burnley (GB)	33	D 2	Buzău (RO)	13	D 4
Burntisland (GB)	31	D 2	Buzet (HR)	96	C 3
Buronzo (I)	96	C 3	Bužim (BIH)	99	F 3
Burrel (AL)	121	F 3	Buxy (F)		
Burry Port /			Bychaŭ (BY)	7	E 4
Porth Tywyn (GB)	34	C 1	Bychawa (BY)	197	D 2
Bursa (TR)	19	E 2	Byčiai (LT)	171	E 1
Burscheid (D)	87	E 2	Byczyna Opolskie(PL)	194	C 2
Bürstadt (D)	45	E 1	Byczyna Śląskie(PL)	200	F 1
Burtnieki Kuldīgas(LV)	156	C 3	Bydgoski (Kanał) (PL)	188	B 1
Burtnieki Valmieras(LV)	159	F 2	Bydgoszcz (PL)	188	B 1
Burton-upon-Trent (GB)	33	D 4	Bygdeå (S)	132	C 2
Burträsk (S)	132	C 2	Bygdin (N)	139	D 1
Burveliai (LT)	170	C 2	Bygdsiljum (S)	132	C 2
Burwick (GB)	28	B 1	Bygland (N)	138	C 4
Bury (GB)	32	C 2	Byglandsfjord (N)	138	C 4
Bury St Edmunds (GB)	36	C 2	Bykle (N)	138	C 3
Burzenin (PL)	195	D 1	Bylderup-Bov (DK)	144	B 3
Busalla (I)	100	C 1	Byrkjelo (N)	130	B 4
Busca (I)	53	F 3	Byske (S)	132	C 1
Buševac (HR)	99	F 2	Bystra (PL)	201	A 3
Bushmills (GB)	23	E 1	Bystre (PL)	202	F 3
Busko-Zdrój (PL)	196	B 4	Bystřice		
Busovača (BIH)	117	E 3	nad Pernštejnem (CZ)	91	D 3
Bussang (F)	49	F 1	Bystřice		
			pod Hostýnem (CZ)	91	F 3

BREMEN

Am Stadtwald	V 8	H.-H.-Meier-Allee	V 35	Ritterhuder Heerstr.	V 60
Beneckendorffallee	X 15	Kirchbachstr.	X 42	Schwachhauser	
Bismarckstr.	X 16	Konrad-Adenauer-Allee	V 45	Heerstr.	V 68
Bremerhavener Str.	V 18	Malerstr.	X 46	Sebaldsbrücker Heerstr.	X 69
Buntentorsteinweg	X 20	Marcusallee	V 48	Stapelfeldstr.	V 72
Duckwitzstr.	X 26	Oslebshauser Heerstr.	V 50	Stresemannstr.	X 74
Franz-Schütte-Allee	X 28	Osterfeuerberger Ring	V 53	Utbremer Str.	V 76
Hastedter Osterdeich	X 33	Richard-Boljahn-Allee	VX 54	Waller Heerstr.	V 82

Bučiūnai Joniškis(LT)	164	C 3	Buenache de Alarcón (E)	71	D 2
Bučiūnai Kauno (LT)	176	C 2	Buenavista de Valdavia (E)	60	C 1
Bučiūnai Panevėžio(LT)	165	F 4	Buendía (E)	70	C 1
Bučiūnai Šeduva(LT)	170	B 2	Bueu (E)	58	A 4
Bučje (SRB)	119	E 2	Bugailiškiai (LT)	171	E 2
Bückeburg (D)	83	F 2	Bugeat (F)	51	E 2
Buckfastleigh (GB)	34	C 3	Būginiai (LT)	165	E 4
Buckhaven (GB)	31	D 2	Bugojno (BIH)	117	D 3
Buckie (GB)	27	F 1	Bunde (D)	83	D 2
Buckingham (GB)	35	F 1	Bühl (Baden)		
Buckow Kreis			Kreis Rastatt(D)	45	E 3
Märkisch-Oderland(D)	85	E 2	Buikos (LT)	177	E 3
Buckūnai (LT)	176	B 3	Builth Wells /		
Bückwitz (D)	85	D 2	Llanfair-ym-Muallt (GB)	35	D 1
Bučovice (CZ)	91	D 3	Buis-les-Baronnies (F)	52	C 4
București (RO)	13	D 4	Buitrago del Lozoya (E)	64	B 4
Buczek (PL)	195	D 1	Buitūnai (LT)	171	F 3
Buczkowice (PL)	200	A 3	Buiva (LV)	159	E 2
Bud (N)	130	B 3	Buivėnai (LT)	165	E 4
Būda Marijampolės (LT)	175	D 3	Buivydžiai (LT)	163	F 3
Būda Vilniaus (LT)	177	E 2	Bujalance (E)	76	A 1
Budapest (H)	112	C 1	Bujanovac (SRB)	122	B 1
Búðardalur (IS)	126	A 2	Bujaraloz (E)	66	A 3
Budberga (LV)	165	D 3	Buje (HR)	99	D 3
Buddusò (I)	108	B 2	Buk (PL)	187	E 3
Bude (GB)	34	C 3	Bukaiši (LV)	163	F 3
Büdelsdorf (D)	78	C 4	Bukas (LV)	159	E 4
Budiliai (LT)	177	D 2	Bukinje (BIH)	117	F 2
Budimlić Japra (BIH)	115	D 4	Bukonys (LT)	169	F 4
Büdingen Wetteraukreis(D)	88	B 3	Bukova Gora (BIH)	117	D 4
Budinščina (HR)	99	F 1	Bukovi (SRB)	118	B 2
Budleigh Salterton (GB)	35	D 2	Bukowiec Kujawsko-		
Budrio (I)	101	F 1	Pomorskie(PL)	182	C 4
Budry (PL)	184	C 2	Bukowina Tatrzańska (PL)	201	A 3
Budva (MNE)	121	D 3	Bukowno (PL)	195	E 4
Būdviečiai (LT)	175	D 3	Bukowsko (PL)	202	E 3
Budy Łancuckie (PL)	202	E 1	Buktiškiai (LT)	175	F 1
Budyně nad Ohří (CZ)	90	A 2	Bülach (CH)	92	A 1
Budzisko (PL)	185	E 1	Buldan (TR)	19	F 3
Budziszewice (PL)	189	E 4	Bulgnéville (F)	44	C 4
Budziszów Wielki (PL)	193	C 2	Bullas (E)	77	E 1
Budzów Dolnośląskie(PL)	193	E 4	Bulle (CH)	49	F 3
Budzów Małopolskie(PL)	201	A 2	Büllingen (B)	87	D 3

Bully-les-Mines (F)	38	C 3			
Bultei (I)	108	B 2			
Buna (BIH)	117	E 4			
Bunclody (IRL)	25	E 2			
Buncrana /			**BRUGGE**		
Bun Cranncha (IRL)	23	D 1	Bossuytlaan	ER	10
Bünde (D)	83	F 4	Daverlostr.	ERS	15
Bunde (D)	83	D 2	Dorpsstr.	ES	18
Bundoran /			Dries	ES	18
Bun Dobhráin (IRL)	22	C 2	Fortuinstr.	ER	21
Bunessan (GB)	30	A 1	Gistelse Steenweg	ER	24
Bungay (GB)	37	D 2	Kongostr.	ES	34
Bunić (HR)	99	F 4	Koningin Astridlaan	ES	36
Bunikiai (LT)	169	E 4	Leopold III laan	ES	42
Bunka (LV)	162	C 2	Meulestree	ES	46
Bunmahon (IRL)	25	D 3	Moerkerkse Steenweg	ER	47
Buñol (E)	71	F 3	Odegemstr.	ER	52
Buntingford (GB)	36	B 2	Pathoekeweg	ER	55
Buñuel (E)	65	E 2	Sint-Katarinastr.	ERS	67
Buonabitácolo (I)	106	B 4	Sint-Michielstr.	ES	69
Buonalbergo (I)	106	A 3	Sint-Pieterskerklaan	ER	70
Buonconvento (I)	102	A 3	Spoorwegstr.	ES	72
Buonfornello (I)	110	C 2	s Heer Boudewijnsburg	ES	30
Buožėnai (LT)	163	D 4	van Praetstr.	ER	58
Burbach (D)	87	F 2			
Burbáguena (E)	65	E 4	**OOSTKAMP**		
Burbaičiai (LT)	169	E 2	Kortrijkstr.	ES	40
Burbiškiai (LT)	169	F 4			
Burbiškis (LT)	171	E 3	**ZEDELGEM**		
Bureå (S)	132	C 1	Heidelbergstr.	ES	31
Burela (E)	58	C 2	Stationstr.	ES	75
Buren (NL)	82	C 1			
Büren Kreis Paderborn(D)	88	A 1			
Burfjord (N)	124	C 2			
Burford (GB)	35	F 1			
Burg auf Fehmarn					
Kreis Ostholstein(D)	79	E 3			
Burg b. Magdeburg (D)	84	C 3			
Burg Stargard Kreis					
Mecklenburg-Strelitz(D)	80	C 4			
Burgas (BG)	13	E 4			
Burgau Kreis Günzburg(D)	93	E 2			
Burgbernheim (D)	88	C 4			

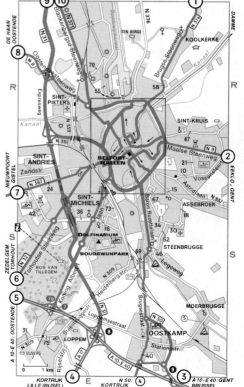

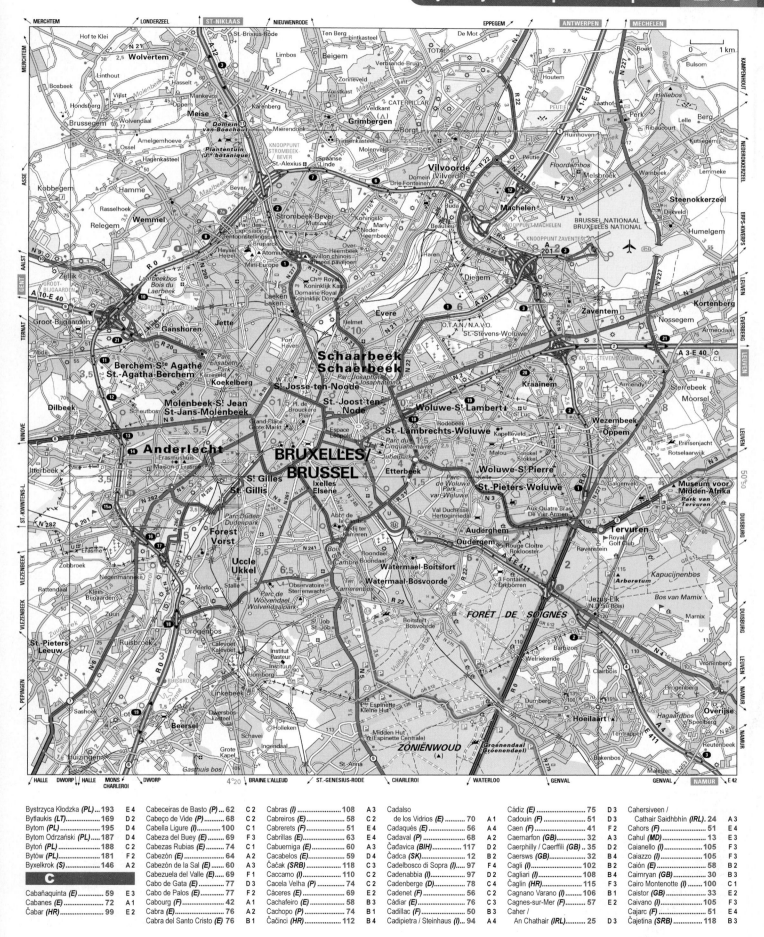

Bystrzyca Kłodzka (PL)...193	E 4	Cabeceiras de Basto (P)...62	C 2	Cabras (I)...108	A 3	Cadalso		Cádiz (E)...75	D 3	Cahersiveen /
Bytlaukis (LT)...169	D 2	Cabeço de Vide (P)...68	C 2	Cabreiros (E)...58	C 2	de los Vidrios (E)...70	A 1	Cadouin (F)...51	D 3	Cathair Saidhbhín (IRL)...24	A 3
Bytom (PL)...195	D 4	Cabella Ligure (I)...100	C 1	Cabrerets (F)...51	E 4	Cadaqués (E)...56	A 4	Caen (F)...41	F 2	Cahors (F)...51	E 4
Bytom Odrzański (PL)...187	D 4	Cabeza del Buey (E)...69	F 3	Cabrillas (E)...63	E 4	Cadaval (P)...68	A 2	Caerbarfon (GB)...32	A 3	Cahul (MD)...13	E 3
Bytoń (PL)...188	C 2	Cabezas Rubias (E)...74	C 1	Cabuerniga (E)...60	A 3	Cadavica (BIH)...117	D 2	Caerphilly / Caerffili (GB)...35	A 3	Caianello (I)...105	F 3
Bytów (PL)...181	F 2	Cabezón (E)...64	A 2	Cacabelos (E)...59	D 4	Čadca (SK)...12	B 2	Caersws (GB)...32	B 4	Caiazzo (I)...105	F 3
Byxelkrok (S)...146	A 2	Cabezón de la Sal (E)...60	A 3	Čačak (SRB)...118	C 3	Cadelbosco di Sopra (I)...97	D 1	Caión (E)...58	B 2
		Cabezuela del Valle (E)...69	F 1	Caccamo (I)...110	C 2	Cadenabbia (I)...97	D 2	Cagli (I)...102	B 2	Cairnryan (GB)...30	B 3
		Cabo de Gata (E)...77	D 3	Cacela Velha (P)...74	C 2	Cadenberge (D)...78	C 4	Cagliari (I)...108	A 3	Cairo Montenotte (I)...100	C 1
C		Cabo de Palos (E)...77	F 2	Cáceres (E)...69	E 2	Cadenet (F)...56	C 2	Čaglin (HR)...115	F 3	Caistor (GB)...33	E 2
Cabañaquinta (E)...59	E 3	Cabourg (F)...42	A 1	Cachafeiro (E)...58	B 3	Cagnano Varano (I)...106	B 1	Caivano (I)...105	F 3
Cabanes (E)...72	A 1	Cabra (E)...76	A 2	Cachopo (P)...74	B 1	Cádiar (E)...76	C 3	Cagnes-sur-Mer (F)...57	E 2	Cajarc (F)...51	E 4
Čabar (HR)...99	E 2	Cabra del Santo Cristo (E)...76	B 1	Čačinci (HR)...112	B 4	Cadillac (F)...50	B 3	Caher /		Čajetina (SRB)...118	B 3
						Cadipietra / Steinhaus (I)...94	A 4	An Chathair (IRL)...25	D 3	

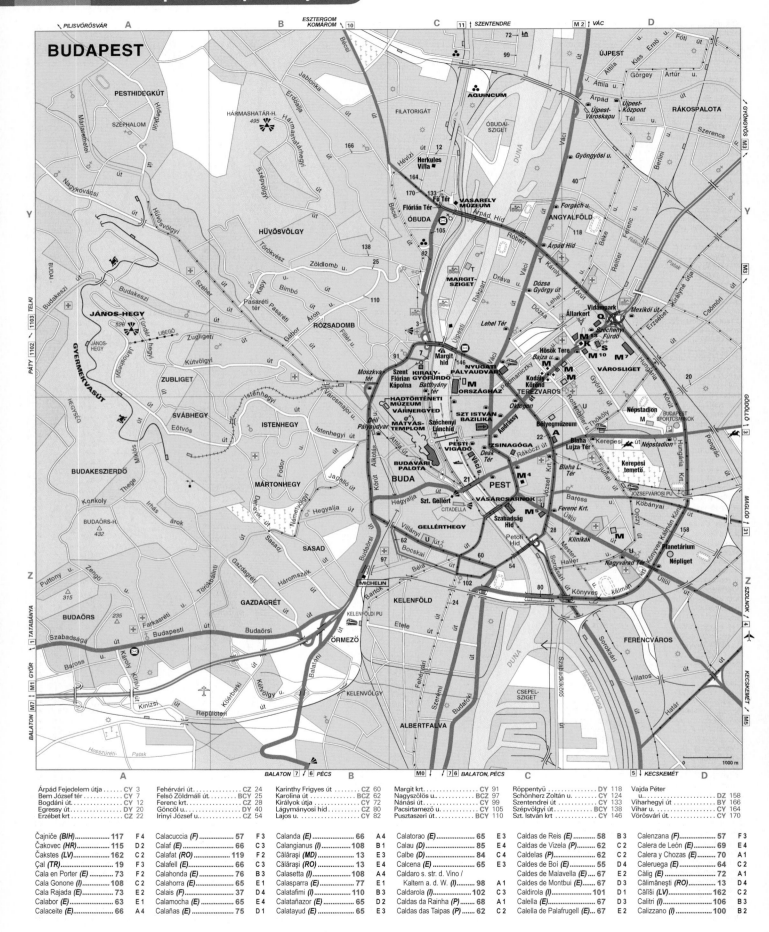

BUDAPEST

Árpád Fejedelem útja	CY 3	Fehérvári út	CZ 24	Karinthy Frigyes út	CZ 60	Margit krt.	CY 91	Röppentyű	DY 118	Vajda Péter	
Bem József tér	CY 7	Felső Zöldmáli út	BCY 25	Karolina út	BCZ 62	Nagyszőlős u.	BCZ 97	Schönherz Zoltán u.	CY 124	u.	DZ 158
Bogdáni út	CY 12	Ferenc krt.	CZ 28	Királyok útja	CY 72	Nánási út	CY 99	Szentendrei út	CY 133	Viharhegyi út	BY 166
Egressy u.	DY 20	Göncöl u.	DY 40	Lágymányosi híd	CZ 80	Pacsirtamező u.	CY 105	Szépvölgyi út	BCY 138	Vihar u.	CY 164
Erzsébet krt.	CZ 22	Irinyi József u.	CZ 54	Lajos u.	CY 82	Pusztaszeri út	BCY 110	Szt. István krt.	CY 146	Vörösvári út	CY 170

Čajniče (BIH)	117	F 4	Calacuccia (F)	57	F 3	Calanda (E)	66	A 4	Calatorao (E)	65	E 3	Caldas de Reis (E)	58	B 3	Calenzana (F)	57	F 3
Čakovec (HR)	115	D 2	Calaf (E)	66	C 3	Calangianus (I)	108	B 1	Calau (D)	85	E 4	Caldas de Vizela (P)	62	C 2	Calera de León (E)	69	E 4
Čakstes (LV)	162	C 2	Calafat (RO)	119	F 2	Călăraşi (MD)	13	E 3	Calbe (D)	84	C 4	Caldelas (P)	62	C 2	Calera y Chozas (E)	70	A 1
Çal (TR)	19	F 3	Calafell (E)	66	C 3	Călăraşi (RO)	13	E 3	Calcena (E)	65	E 3	Caldes de Boí (E)	55	D 4	Caleruega (E)	64	C 2
Cala en Porter (E)	73	F 2	Calahonda (E)	76	B 3	Calasetta (I)	108	A 4	Caldaro s. str. d. Vino /			Caldes de Malavella (E)	67	D 3	Càlig (E)	72	A 1
Cala Gonone (I)	108	C 2	Calahorra (E)	65	E 1	Calasparra (E)	77	E 1	Kaltern a. d. W. (I)	98	A 1	Caldes de Montbui (E)	67	D 3	Călimăneşti (RO)	13	D 4
Cala Rajada (E)	73	F 2	Calais (F)	37	D 4	Calatafimi (I)	110	B 3	Caldarola (I)	102	D 1	Caldirola (I)	101	D 1	Călliši (LV)	162	C 2
Calabor (E)	63	E 1	Calamocha (E)	65	E 4	Calatañazor (E)	65	D 2	Caldas da Rainha (P)	68	A 1	Calella (E)	67	D 3	Calitri (I)	106	B 3
Calaceite (E)	66	A 4	Calañas (E)	75	D 1	Calatayud (E)	65	E 3	Caldas das Taipas (P)	62	C 2	Calella de Palafrugell (E)	67	E 2	Calizzano (I)	100	B 2

Callac (F) .... 40 — C 3
Callan / Callainn (IRL) .. 25 — D 2
Callander (GB) .... 30 — C 1
Callas (I) .... 57 — E 2
Callington (GB) .... 34 — C 3
Callosa de Segura (E) .. 77 — F 1
Callosa d'en Sarrià (E) .. 72 — A 4
Calmazzo (I) .... 102 — B 2
Calmbach (D) .... 45 — F 3
Calne (GB) .... 35 — C 2
Calolziocorte (I) .... 97 — E 3
Calonge (E) .... 67 — E 2
Calp / Calpe (E) .... 72 — A 4
Caltabellotta (I) .... 110 — B 3
Caltagirone (I) .... 111 — D 3
Caltanissetta (I) .... 111 — D 3
Caltavuturo (I) .... 110 — C 2
Caluso (I) .... 53 — F 2
Calvi (F) .... 57 — E 3
Calvörde (D) .... 84 — B 3
Calw (D) .... 45 — F 3
Calzada de Calatrava (E). 70 — B 4
Calzada de Valduncel (E). 63 — F 3
Camaiore (I) .... 101 — E 2
Camaldoli (Convento) (I). 102 — A 2
Camaleño (E) .... 60 — A 3
Camarasa (E) .... 66 — B 2
Camarena (E) .... 70 — B 1
Camarès (F) .... 55 — F 2
Camaret-sur-Mer (F) ..... 40 — B 3
Camarillas (E) .... 65 — E 4
Camariñas (E) .... 58 — A 2
Camarzana de Tera (E). 63 — F 1
Camas (E) .... 75 — A 3
Cambados (E) .... 58 — A 3
Cambas (E) .... 68 — C 1
Camberley (GB) .... 36 — B 3
Cambil (E) .... 76 — B 1
Cambo-les-Bains (F) ..... 54 — A 2
Camborne (GB) .... 34 — B 4
Cambrai (F) .... 39 — D 3
Cambre (E) .... 58 — B 2
Cambremer (F) .... 42 — A 2
Cambridge (GB) .... 36 — C 2
Cambrils (E) .... 66 — B 4
Camburg (D) .... 89 — D 1
Camelford (GB) .... 34 — B 3
Camerino (I) .... 102 — A 3
Camigliatello Silano (I) . 109 — E 1
Caminha (P) .... 62 — B 1
Caminomorisco (E) ...... 63 — E 4
Caminreal (E) .... 65 — E 4
Camogli (I) .... 101 — D 1
Campagna (I) .... 106 — A 3
Campagne-lès-Hesdin (F). 38 — C 3
Campan (F) .... 54 — C 3
Campana (I) .... 109 — F 1
Campanario (E) .... 69 — F 3
Campanas (E) .... 54 — A 3
Campaspero (E) .... 64 — B 3
Campbeltown (GB) .... 23 — F 1
Campi Bisenzio (I) .... 101 — F 2
Campi Salentina (I) ...... 107 — F 3
Campiglia Marittima (I) . 101 — F 3
Campillo de Altobuey (E). 71 — E 2
Campillo de Aragón (E) . 65 — E 3
Campillo de Arenas (E) . 76 — B 2
Campillo de Llerena (E) . 69 — E 4
Campillos (E) .... 75 — E 3
Campitello Matese (I) ... 105 — F 2
Campli (I) .... 102 — C 3
Campo (E) .... 54 — C 4
Campo de Besteiros (P). 62 — C 4
Campo de Caso (E) ...... 59 — F 3
Campo de Criptana (E) . 70 — C 4
Campo del Hospital (E) . 58 — C 2
Campo di Giove (I) ...... 105 — E 1
Campo Ligure (I) .... 100 — C 1
Campo Maior (P) .... 69 — D 3
Campo Tures /
   Sand in Taufers (I) .... 94 — A 4
Campobasso (I) .... 105 — F 2
Campobello di Licata (I) .. 110 — C 3
Campobello di Mazara (I) 110 — B 3
Campodonico (I) .... 102 — B 3
Campoformido (I) .... 98 — C 2
Campogalliano (I) .... 97 — F 4
Campomanes (E) .... 59 — E 3
Campomarino (I) .... 103 — E 4
Campóo (Alto) (E) .... 60 — A 3
Campora San Giovanni (I)109 — E 2
Camporrobles (E) .... 71 — E 2
Campos (E) .... 73 — E 3
Camposampiero (I) .... 98 — A 3
Camprodon (E) .... 55 — F 4
Camucia (I) .... 102 — A 3
Camuñas (E) .... 70 — B 2

Cañada de Benatanduz (E)65 — F 4
Çanakkale (TR) .... 19 — E 2
Canal San Bovo (I) .... 98 — A 2
Canales (E) .... 64 — C 2
Canals (E) .... 71 — F 3
Cañamero (E) .... 69 — F 2
Canas de Senhorim (P). 62 — C 4
Cañaveral (E) .... 69 — E 1
Cañaveral de Léon (E) .. 69 — D 4
Cañaveras (E) .... 71 — D 1
Canazei (I) .... 98 — A 1
Cancale (F) .... 41 — E 2
Cancarix (E) .... 71 — E 4
Cancon (F) .... 51 — D 3
Candanchú (E) .... 54 — A 3
Candás (E) .... 59 — E 2
Candasnos (E) .... 66 — A 3
Candela (I) .... 106 — B 3
Candelario (E) .... 63 — F 4
Candeleda (E) .... 69 — F 1
Candes-St-Martin (F) ..... 47 — D 2
Canelli (I) .... 100 — B 1
Canet de Mar (E) .... 67 — D 3
Canet-Plage (F) .... 55 — F 4
Cañete (E) .... 71 — E 1
Cañete de las Torres (E) . 76 — A 1
Cañete la Real (E) .... 75 — F 2
Canfranc-Estación (E) .... 54 — B 3
Cangas (E) .... 58 — A 4
Cangas de Onís (E) .... 59 — F 3
Cangas del Narcea (E) .. 59 — D 3
Canha (P) .... 68 — B 3
Canicattì (I) .... 110 — C 3
Canicattini Bagni (I) .... 111 — E 4
Caniles (E) .... 76 — C 2
Canino (I) .... 102 — A 4
Canisy (F) .... 41 — E 1
Cañizal (E) .... 63 — F 3
Cannero Riviera (I) .... 97 — D 2
Cannes (F) .... 57 — E 2
Canneto (I) .... 101 — F 3
Cannich (GB) .... 27 — E 3
Cannobio (I) .... 97 — D 2
Cannock (GB) .... 33 — D 4
Canonbie (GB) .... 31 — D 3
Canosa di Puglia (I) ..... 106 — C 2
Cansano (I) .... 105 — E 1
Cantalapiedra (E) .... 63 — F 3
Cantalejo (E) .... 64 — B 3
Cantalpino (E) .... 63 — F 3
Cantanhede (P) .... 62 — B 4
Cantavieja (E) .... 71 — F 1
Čantavir (SRB) .... 113 — F 3
Canterbury (GB) .... 37 — D 4
Cantillana (E) .... 75 — E 1
Cantoira (I) .... 53 — F 2
Cantoral (E) .... 60 — A 4
Cantoria (E) .... 77 — D 2
Cantù (I) .... 97 — D 3
Canvey Island (GB) .... 36 — C 3
Cany-Barville (F) .... 38 — A 4
Caorle (I) .... 98 — C 3
Caorso (I) .... 97 — E 4
Cap-Ferret (F) .... 50 — A 3
Capaccio (I) .... 106 — B 4
Capaci (I) .... 110 — B 2
Caparde (BIH) .... 117 — E 4
Caparroso (E) .... 54 — A 4
Capbreton (F) .... 54 — A 2
Capdenac-Gare (F) .... 51 — E 3
Capel Curig (GB) .... 32 — B 3
Capellades (E) .... 66 — C 3
Capendu (F) .... 55 — F 3
Capestang (F) .... 55 — F 2
Capestrano (I) .... 103 — D 4
Capileira (E) .... 76 — B 3
Capistrello (I) .... 105 — D 2
Čapljina (BIH) .... 120 — C 1
Capmany (E) .... 55 — F 4
Capo d'Orlando (I) ...... 111 — D 2
Cappelle sul Tavo (I) ... 103 — D 4
Cappoquin /
   Ceapach Choinn (IRL)... 25 — D 3
Capracotta (I) .... 105 — F 1
Capri (I) .... 105 — F 4
Capriati a Volturno (I) . 105 — F 2
Captieux (F) .... 50 — C 2
Capua (I) .... 105 — F 3
Capurso (I) .... 107 — D 2
Capvern (F) .... 54 — C 3
Caracal (RO) .... 13 — D 4
Caracuel de Calatrava (E). 70 — B 3
Caraman (F) .... 55 — E 2

Caramanico Terme (I) ... 103 — D 4
Caramulo (P) .... 62 — C 4
Caransebeş (RO) .... 12 — C 4
Carantec (F) .... 40 — B 2
Caravaca de la Cruz (E). 77 — D 1
Carbajales de Alba (E) .. 63 — F 2
Carballiño (E) .... 58 — B 4
Carballo (E) .... 58 — B 2
Carbon-Blanc (F) .... 50 — B 3
Carboneras (E) .... 77 — D 3
Carboneras
   de Guadazaón (E) ...... 71 — E 2
Carbonero el Mayor (E) .. 64 — B 3
Carbonia (I) .... 108 — A 4
Carbonin / Schluderbach (I)98 — B 1
Carbonne (F) .... 55 — D 2
Carcaboso (E) .... 69 — E 1
Carcabuey (E) .... 76 — A 2
Carcaixent (E) .... 71 — F 3
Carcans (F) .... 50 — B 2
Carcans-Plage (F) .... 50 — A 2
Carcare (I) .... 100 — C 1
Carcassonne (F) .... 55 — F 3
Carcastillo (E) .... 54 — A 4
Carcès (F) .... 57 — D 2
Čardak (BIH) .... 117 — E 2
Çardak (TR) .... 19 — F 3
Cardedeu (E) .... 67 — D 3
Cardeña (E) .... 70 — A 4
Cardenete (E) .... 71 — E 2
Cardiff / Caerdydd (GB) . 35 — D 2
Cardigan / Aberteifi (GB). 34 — C 1
Cardona (E) .... 66 — C 2
Carei (RO) .... 12 — C 3
Carentan (F) .... 41 — E 1
Carev Dvor (MK) .... 122 — A 4
Carevdar (HR) .... 112 — A 4
Carevo (BG) .... 19 — E 1
Cargèse (F) .... 57 — E 3
Caria (P) .... 63 — D 4
Cariati (I) .... 109 — F 1
Carignan (F) .... 39 — F 4
Carignano (I) .... 53 — F 3
Carina (MK) .... 122 — A 4
Cariñena (E) .... 65 — E 3
Carini (I) .... 110 — B 2
Cariño (E) .... 58 — C 1
Carinola (I) .... 105 — F 3
Carisio (I) .... 96 — C 3
Carlet (I) .... 71 — F 3
Carling (F) .... 44 — D 2
Carlingford (IRL) .... 23 — E 3
Carlisle (GB) .... 31 — D 4
Carloforte (I) .... 108 — A 4
Carlow / Ceatharlach (IRL)25 — E 2
Carloway (GB) .... 26 — C 1
Carluke (GB) .... 30 — C 1
Carmagnola (I) .... 53 — F 3
Carmarthen /
   Caerfyrddin (GB) .... 34 — C 1
Carmaux (F) .... 51 — E 4
Carmona (E) .... 75 — E 1
Carna (IRL) .... 22 — A 4
Carnac (F) .... 40 — C 4
Carndonagh /
   Carn Domhnach (IRL) . 23 — D 1
Carnew (IRL) .... 25 — E 2
Carnforth (GB) .... 32 — C 1
Carnia (I) .... 98 — C 1
Carnikava (LV) .... 159 — D 4
Carnlough (GB) .... 23 — F 1
Carnon-Plage (F) .... 56 — B 2
Carnota (E) .... 58 — A 3
Carnoustie (GB) .... 31 — E 1
Carnwath (GB) .... 31 — D 2
Carolles (F) .... 41 — E 2
Carovigno (I) .... 107 — E 3
Carpaneto Piacentino (I). 97 — E 4
Carpegna (I) .... 102 — A 2
Carpenedolo (I) .... 97 — F 3
Carpentras (F) .... 52 — C 4
Carpi (I) .... 97 — F 4
Carpignano Sesia (I) ...... 96 — C 3
Carpineti (I) .... 101 — E 1
Carpineto Romano (I) .. 105 — D 2
Carpinone (I) .... 105 — F 2
Carquefou (F) .... 46 — B 2
Carqueiranne (F) .... 57 — D 3
Carracedelo (E) .... 59 — D 4
Carradale (GB) .... 30 — B 2
Carral (E) .... 58 — B 2
Carrapateira (P) .... 74 — A 1
Carrara (I) .... 101 — E 2
Carrascosa
   del Campo (E) .... 70 — C 1
Carrazeda de Ansiães (P). 63 — D 3

Carrazedo
   de Montenegro (P) .... 63 — D 2
Carrbridge (GB) .... 27 — F 3
Carregado (P) .... 68 — A 2
Carregal do Sal (P) .... 62 — C 4
Carreña (E) .... 59 — F 3
Carrenza (E) .... 60 — B 3
Carrick-on-Shannon-
   Cora Droma Rùisc (IRL) 22 — C 3
Carrick-on-Suir / Carraig na
   Siúire (IRL) .... 25 — D 3
Carrickfergus (GB) .... 23 — F 2
Carrickmacross / Carraig
   Mhachaire Rois (IRL).. 23 — E 3
Carrigart / Carraig Airt (IRL)23 — D 1
Carrió (E) .... 58 — B 2
Carrión de Calatrava (E). 70 — B 3
Carrión de los Condes (E). 64 — A 1
Carrizo de la Ribera (E). 59 — E 4
Carro (F) .... 56 — C 2
Carrouges (F) .... 42 — A 3
Carrù (I) .... 53 — F 3
Carry-le-Rouet (F) .... 56 — C 2
Carsoli (I) .... 105 — D 1
Cartagena (E) .... 77 — F 2
Cártama (E) .... 76 — A 3
Cartaxo (P) .... 68 — B 2
Cartaya (E) .... 74 — C 2
Carteret (F) .... 41 — E 1
Carviçais (P) .... 63 — D 3
Carvin (F) .... 39 — D 3
Carvoeiro (P) .... 74 — A 2
Casa Branca (P) .... 68 — A 4
Casa Branca (P) .... 68 — C 3
Casabermeja (E) .... 76 — A 3
Casacalenda (I) .... 105 — F 2
Casaio (E) .... 59 — D 4
Casal di Principe (I) ..... 105 — F 3
Casalbordino (I) .... 103 — E 4
Casalbuttano ed Uniti (I). 97 — E 4
Casale Monferrato (I) .... 97 — D 3
Casale sul Sile (I) .... 98 — B 3
Casalecchio di Reno (I). 101 — F 1
Casalmaggiore (I) .... 97 — F 4
Casalpusterlengo (I) ...... 97 — E 4
Casamari (Abbazia di) (I) 105 — E 2
Casamassima (I) .... 107 — D 3
Casamicciola Terme (I) . 105 — F 4
Casar de Cáceres (E) .... 69 — E 2
Casarabonela (E) .... 75 — F 3
Casarano (I) .... 107 — F 4
Casares (E) .... 75 — F 3
Casares de las Hurdes (E) 63 — E 4
Casariche (E) .... 75 — F 2
Casarsa della Delizia (I). 98 — B 2
Casas de Don Pedro (E) . 69 — F 3
Casas de
   Fernando Alonso (E) ... 71 — D 3
Casas de Juan Núñez (E). 71 — E 3
Casas de Luján (E) .... 70 — C 2
Casas de Miravete (E) .. 69 — F 1
Casas del Puerto (E) ..... 71 — E 4
Casas Ibáñez (E) .... 71 — E 3
Casas Nuevas (E) .... 77 — E 1
Casasimarro (E) .... 71 — D 2
Casatejada (E) .... 69 — F 1
Casavieja (E) .... 70 — A 1
Cascais (P) .... 68 — A 3
Cascante (E) .... 65 — E 2
Cascia (I) .... 102 — C 4
Casciana Terme (I) ...... 101 — E 2
Cascina (I) .... 101 — E 2
Casei Gerola (I) .... 97 — D 4
Caselle in Pittari (I) ..... 106 — B 4
Caselle Torinese (I) .... 53 — F 2
Caserta (I) .... 105 — F 3
Casetas Vecchia (I) ..... 105 — F 3
Casetas (E) .... 65 — F 2
Cashel / Caiseal (IRL) ... 25 — D 2
Casicas del Río Segura (E)76 — C 1
Casillas de Coria (E) ..... 69 — D 1
Casina (I) .... 101 — E 1
Casinos (E) .... 71 — F 2
Čáslav (CZ) .... 90 — C 3
Casltepollard (IRL) .... 23 — D 4
Casola in Lunigiana (I) . 101 — E 1
Casoli (I) .... 103 — D 4
Casoria (I) .... 105 — F 3
Caspe (E) .... 66 — A 3
Cassà de la Selva (E) .... 67 — E 2
Cassagnes-Bégonhès (F) . 51 — F 4
Cassano allo Ionio (I) .. 109 — E 1
Cassano delle Murge (I).. 107 — D 3
Cassel (F) .... 38 — C 2
Cassino (I) .... 105 — F 2
Cassis (F) .... 57 — D 3

Castalla (E) .... 71 — F 4
Castanet-Tolosan (F) ..... 55 — E 2
Castanheira de Pêra (P). 68 — B 1
Castasegna (CH) .... 97 — E 2
Casteggio (I) .... 97 — D 4
Castejón (E) .... 54 — A 4
Castejón de Monegros (E) 66 — A 3
Castejón de Sos (E) ...... 54 — C 4
Castejón de Valdejasa (E). 65 — F 2
Castel del Monte (I) .... 102 — C 4
Castel del Monte (I) .... 106 — C 2
Castel del Río (I) .... 101 — F 1
Castel di Sangro (I) ..... 105 — F 2
Castel Gandolfo (I) ...... 105 — D 2
Castel Madama (I) .... 105 — D 2
Castel San Giovanni (I) . 97 — E 4
Castel San Lorenzo (I) . 106 — B 4
Castel San Pietro
   Terme (I) .... 101 — F 1
Castel Volturno (I) ...... 105 — E 3
Castelbuono (I) .... 111 — D 2
Casteldaccia (I) .... 110 — C 2
Casteldelfino (I) .... 53 — E 3
Castelfidardo (I) .... 102 — C 2
Castelfiorentino (I) ...... 101 — F 2
Castelfranco Emilia (I) . 101 — F 1
Castelfranco
   in Miscano (I) .... 106 — A 2
Castelfranco Veneto (I) . 98 — A 3
Casteljaloux (F) .... 50 — C 4
Castell de Ferro (E) ...... 76 — B 3
Castellabate (I) .... 106 — B 4
Castellammare
   del Golfo (I) .... 110 — B 2
Castellammare
   di Stabia (I) .... 105 — F 4
Castellamonte (I) .... 53 — F 2
Castellana Grotte (I) ... 107 — D 3
Castellane (F) .... 57 — E 1
Castellaneta (I) .... 107 — D 3
Castellar de la Muela (E). 65 — E 4
Castellar del Vallès (E) . 67 — D 3
Castell'Arquato (I) .... 97 — E 4
Castellar
   de Santisteban (E) .... 70 — C 4
Castelldans (E) .... 66 — B 3
Castelldefels (E) .... 66 — C 3
Castelleone (I) .... 97 — E 3
Castellfollit de la Roca (E). 55 — F 4
Castellina in Chianti (I) . 101 — F 2
Castelló de la Plana /
   Castellón de la Plana (E)72 — A 2
Castello de Rugat (E) ... 71 — F 4
Castelló d'Empúries (E). 55 — F 4
Castello di Lago (I) ..... 106 — A 3
Castello Tesino (I) .... 98 — A 2
Castelloli (I) .... 66 — C 3
Castellón de la Plana /
   Castelló de la Plana (E). 72 — A 2
Castellote (E) .... 66 — A 4
Castellterçol (E) .... 67 — D 3
Castelluccio (I) .... 102 — C 3
Castelmassa (I) .... 98 — A 4
Castelmauro (I) .... 105 — F 1
Castelmoron-sur-Lot (F) . 50 — C 4
Castelnau-de-Médoc (F) . 50 — B 3
Castelnau-de-Montmiral (F)51 — E 4
Castelnau-Magnoac (F) . 54 — C 2
Castelnau-Montratier (F). 51 — D 4
Castelnau-
   Rivière-Basse (F) .... 54 — C 2
Castelnaudary (F) .... 55 — E 2
Castelnovo ne' Monti (I)..101 — E 1
Castelnuovo
   Berardenga (I) .... 102 — A 3
Castelnuovo
   Bocca d'Adda (I) .... 97 — E 4
Castelnuovo
   della Daunia (I) .... 106 — A 2
Castelnuovo
   di Garfagnana (I) ...... 101 — E 1
Castelnuovo di Porto (I).104 — C 1
Castelnuovo Scrivia (I) .. 97 — D 4
Castelo Branco (P) .... 68 — C 1
Castelo de Paiva (P) ..... 62 — C 3
Castelo de Vide (P) .... 68 — C 2
Castelraimondo (I) ...... 102 — B 3
Castelrotto / Kastelruth (I). 98 — A 1
Castelsardo (I) .... 108 — A 1
Castelsarrasin (F) .... 51 — D 4
Castelserás (E) .... 66 — A 4
Casteltermini (I) .... 110 — C 3
Castelvecchio Subequo (I)103 — D 4
Castelvetrano (I) .... 110 — B 3
Castets (F) .... 54 — A 1
Castiadas (I) .... 108 — C 4

Castiglion Fiorentino (I) .. 102 — A 3
Castiglioncello (I) .... 101 — E 3
Castiglion d'Adda (I) ..... 97 — E 4
Castiglione dei Pepoli (I). 101 — F 1
Castiglione del Lago (I) . 102 — A 3
Castiglione
   della Pescaia (I) ...... 101 — F 4
Castiglione delle Stiviere (I)97 — F 3
Castiglione in Teverina (I)102 — B 4
Castiglione
   Messer Marino (I) .... 105 — F 1
Castiglione Olona (I) ..... 97 — D 3
Castilblanco (E) .... 69 — F 2
Castilblanco
   de los Arroyos (E) ..... 75 — E 1
Castilleja del Campo (E). 75 — D 2
Castilléjar (E) .... 76 — C 1
Castillejo
   de Martín Viejo (E) ... 63 — E 4
Castillo de Locubín (E) .. 76 — B 2
Castillon-en-Couserans (F)55 — D 3
Castillon-la-Bataille (F) . 50 — C 3
Castillonnès (F) .... 51 — D 3
Castilruiz (E) .... 65 — E 2
Castions di Strada (I) .... 98 — C 2
Castle Douglas (GB) ...... 30 — C 4
Castlebar / Caisleán
   an Bharraigh (IRL) .... 22 — B 3
Castlebay (GB) .... 26 — B 4
Castlebellingham (IRL)... 23 — E 3
Castleblayney / Baile na
   Lorgan (IRL) .... 23 — E 3
Castlecomer / Caisleán an
   Chomair (IRL) .... 25 — D 2
Castledawson (GB) .... 23 — E 2
Castlederg (GB) .... 23 — D 2
Castledermot (IRL) .... 25 — E 2
Castleford (GB) .... 33 — D 2
Castleisland /
   Oileán Ciarraí (IRL) ... 24 — B 3
Castlemaine (IRL) .... 24 — B 3
Castlerea / An Caisleán Riab-
   hach (IRL) .... 22 — C 3
Castlerock (GB) .... 23 — E 1
Castleton (GB) .... 33 — D 3
Castletown (GB) .... 27 — F 1
Castletown
   Isle of Man(GB) .... 32 — A 1
Castletownbere (IRL) ..... 24 — A 4
Castlewellan (GB) .... 23 — F 3
Castrejón (E) .... 64 — A 3
Castres (F) .... 55 — F 2
Castries (F) .... 56 — B 2
Castril (E) .... 76 — C 1
Castrillo de la Reina (E). 64 — C 2
Castrillo de Villavega (E). 60 — A 4
Castro (E) .... 58 — C 3
Castro Caldelas (E) .... 58 — C 4
Castro Daire (P) .... 62 — C 3
Castro del Río (E) .... 76 — A 1
Castro Laboreiro (P) ..... 58 — B 4
Castro Marim (P) .... 74 — C 2
Castro-Urdiales (E) .... 60 — B 3
Castro Verde (P) .... 74 — B 1
Castrocalbón (E) .... 59 — E 4
Castrocaro Terme (I) ... 102 — A 1
Castrocontrigo (E) .... 59 — E 4
Castrojeriz (E) .... 60 — A 4
Castromonte (E) .... 64 — A 2
Castronuevo (E) .... 63 — F 3
Castronuño (E) .... 63 — F 3
Castrop-Rauxel (D) .... 87 — E 1
Castropol (E) .... 59 — D 2
Castroreale (I) .... 111 — E 2
Castroreale Terme (I) ... 111 — E 2
Castrotierra (E) .... 59 — F 4
Castroverde (E) .... 58 — C 3
Castroverde de Campos (E)63 — F 2
Castrovillari (I) .... 109 — E 1
Castuera (E) .... 69 — F 3
Catania (I) .... 111 — E 3
Catanzaro (I) .... 109 — E 2
Catanzaro Lido (I) .... 109 — E 2
Catarroja (E) .... 71 — F 3
Catenanuova (I) .... 111 — D 3
Čatež ob Savi (SLO) ...... 99 — F 2
Čatići (BIH) .... 117 — D 4
Catignano (I) .... 103 — D 4
Catoira (E) .... 58 — B 3
Catral (E) .... 77 — F 1
Cattenom (F) .... 44 — C 2
Cattolica (I) .... 102 — B 1
Catus (F) .... 51 — D 3
Caudebec-en-Caux (F).... 38 — A 4
Caudete (E) .... 71 — F 4
Caudiel (E) .... 71 — F 2
Caudry (F) .... 39 — D 3

Caulnes (F) 41 D3
Caulonia (I) 111 F1
Caumont-l'Éventé (F) 41 F2
Caunes-Minervois (F) 55 F2
Căuşani (MD) 13 E3
Caussade (F) 51 E4
Cauterets (F) 54 C3
Cava de' Tirreni (I) 105 F3
Cavaglià (I) 53 F2
Cavaillon (F) 56 C1
Cavalaire-sur-Mer (F) 57 E3
Cavalese (I) 98 A2
Cavalière (F) 57 E3
Cavan / An Cabhán (IRL) .. 23 D3
Cavarzere (I) 98 B3
Cavazzo Carnico (I) 98 C1
Çavdarhisar (TR) 19 F2
Cavezzo (I) 98 A4
Cavo (I) 101 E4
Cavour (I) 53 F3
Cavtat (HR) 120 C2
Čavusy (RUS) 7 E3
Cayeux-sur-Mer (F) 38 B3
Caylus (F) 51 E4
Cayres (F) 52 A3
Cazalla de la Sierra (E) 75 E1
Cazals (F) 51 D3
Cazaubon (F) 54 C1
Cazaux (F) 50 A3
Cazères (F) 55 D3
Cazin (BIH) 99 F3
Čazma (HR) 112 A4
Cazorla (E) 76 C1
Cea (E) 58 B4
Ceadîr-Lunga (MD) 13 E3
Ceanannus Mór (Kells) /
   Ceanannas (IRL) 23 E4
Cebolla (E) 70 A1
Cebreros (E) 64 A4
Ceccano (I) 105 D2
Cece (H) 112 C2
Čechov (RUS) 7 F2
Čechtice (CZ) 90 C3
Cecina (I) 101 E3
Ceclavín (E) 69 D1
Čedasai (LT) 165 F4
Cedeira (E) 58 C2
Cedillo (E) 68 C1
Cedrillas (E) 71 F4
Cedynia (PL) 186 B1
Cegléd (H) 113 D1
Ceglie Messapia (I) 107 E3
Čegrane (MK) 122 A3
Čehegín (E) 77 D1
Ceikiniai (LT) 172 C3
Čejč (CZ) 91 E4
Cekcyn (PL) 182 B4
Čekiškė (LT) 169 F4
Ceknica (SLO) 99 D2
Čekoniškes (LT) 177 E2
Čekonys (LT) 171 E2
Ceków-Kolonia (PL) 188 C3
Cekule (LV) 165 D1
Čelákovice (CZ) 90 B2
Celano (I) 105 D2
Celanova (E) 58 B4
Celarevo (SRB) 113 D4
Čelebić (BIH) 117 D4
Čelebići (BIH) 117 F4
Čelić (BIH) 117 F2
Čelinac (BIH) 115 E4
Celje (SLO) 99 E1
Cella (E) 71 E1
Celle (D) 84 A3
Celle Ligure (I) 100 C1
Celles-sur-Belle (F) 47 D4
Cejmalas (LV) 161 F4
Celmiņi (LV) 164 C2
Čelopeci (MK) 122 A3
Celorico da Beira (P) 63 D1
Celorico de Basto (P) 62 C2
Čemerno (BIH) 117 F4
Cempi (LV) 159 F2
Cena (LV) 164 C2
Cencenighe Agordino (I) 98 A1
Cenicero (E) 60 C2
Čenta (SRB) 113 E4
Centelles (E) 67 D2
Cento (I) 98 A4
Centuripe (I) 111 D3
Cepagatti (I) 103 D4
Čepin (F) 112 C4
Čepinski Martinci (HR) 112 C4
Cepļi (LV) 162 C2
Ceplis (LV) 164 C3
Cepļīši Ogres(LV) 165 D1

Cepļīši Ventspils(LV) 156 C4
Ceppo di Rocca
   Santa Maria (I) 102 C4
Ceprano (I) 105 E2
Ceptuve (LV) 167 D1
Čepukai (LT) 173 D2
Čeralije (HR) 112 B4
Ceranów (PL) 191 D3
Cerauskste (LV) 165 D3
Cerbère (F) 56 A4
Cercal (P) 68 A4
Cercal (P) 68 A2
Cercedilla (E) 64 B4
Cerchiara di Calabria (I) .. 109 E1
Cerdedo (E) 58 B3
Cerdeira (P) 63 D4
Cère (LV) 157 F2
Cerea (I) 98 A4
Ceres (I) 53 F2
Ceresole Reale (I) 53 F4
Céret (F) 55 F4
Cerezo de Abajo (E) 64 C3
Cerezo de Riotirón (E) 60 B3
Cergy (F) 43 D2
Cerignola (I) 106 B2
Cérilly (F) 48 A3
Cerisiers (F) 43 E3
Cerisy-la-Salle (F) 41 E2
Cerizay (F) 46 C3
Čerkasy (UA) 13 F1
Cerkno (SLO) 99 D1
Cerler (I) 54 C4
Cerna (HR) 117 C1
Černá v Pošumaví (CZ) 94 C1
Cernache de Bonjardim (P)68 B1
Čern'achovsk (RUS) 6
Cernavodă (RO) 13 E4
Cernay (F) 49 F1
Černihiv (UA) 7 E4
Černivci (UA) 13 D2
Cernobbio (I) 97 D3
Cerreto Sannita (I) 105 F2
Cerrigydrudion (GB) 32 B3
Cèrrik (AL) 121 F4
Certaldo (I) 101 F2
Cervatos (E) 60 A3
Cervatos de la Cueza (E).. 59 F4
Červen' (BY) 7 D4
Červená Voda (CZ) 91 D2
Červený Kostelec (CZ) 90 C1
Cervera (E) 66 C3
Cervera de la Cañada (E). 65 E3
Cervera de Pisuerga (E) 60 A3
Cervera del Río Alhama (E)65 E2
Cerveteri (I) 104 C2
Cervia (I) 102 A1
Cervignano del Friuli (I) 98 C2
Cervinara (I) 105 F3
Cervione (F) 57 F3
Cervo (E) 58 C2
Červonka (LV) 173 D1
Červonohrad (UA) 12 C1
Cesana Torinese (I) 53 E3
Cesaria (HR) 99 E4
Cesarò (I) 111 D3
Cesarzowice (PL) 193 E2
Cesena (I) 102 A1
Cesenatico (I) 102 A1
Cēsis (LV) 161 F3
Česká Kamenice (CZ) 90 B1
Česká Lípa (CZ) 90 B1
Česká Skalice (CZ) 90 C2
Česká Třebová (CZ) 91 D2
České Budějovice (CZ) 90 B4
České Velenice (CZ) 95 D1
Český Brod (CZ) 90 B2
Český Krumlov (CZ) 94 C1
Český Těšín (CZ) 91 F2
Çeşme (TR) 19 E3
Cespedosa (E) 63 F4
Cessalto (I) 98 B2
Cesvaine (LV) 160 C4
Cetina (E) 65 E3
Cetinje (MNE) 121 D2
Cetraro (I) 109 D1
Ceuta (E) 75 D2
Ceutí (E) 77 E1
Ceva (I) 53 F4
Cevico de la Torre (E) 64 B2
Cevo (MNE) 121 D2
Cewice (PL) 182 B1
Ceyrat (F) 51 F2
Ceyzériat (F) 49 D4
Chabanais (F) 51 D1

Chabeuil (F) 52 C3
Chablis (F) 43 F4
Chabówka (PL) 201 A3
Chabris (F) 47 F3
Chagny (F) 48 C3
Chailland (F) 41 F3
Chaillé-les-Marais (F) 46 E3
Chalabre (F) 55 E3
Chalais (F) 50 C2
Chalamont (F) 49 D4
Chalampé (F) 92 B3
Chalandrítsa (GR) 217 D1
Chalchida (GR) 206 B3
Chalindrey (F) 49 D1
Chalkeió (GR) 220 C1
Chalkeró (GR) 207 E2
Chálki Dodekánissa(GR) 228 B2
Chálki Lárisa(GR) 212 B2
Chálki Náxos(GR) 219 E4
Chálki (Nisí) (GR) 228 B2
Chalkiádes (GR) 212 A2
Chalkidóna (GR) 206 B3
Challans (F) 46 B3
Challes-les-Eaux (F) 53 D2
Chalon-sur-Saône (F) 49 D3
Chalonnes-sur-Loire (F) 46 C2
Châlons-
   en-Champagne (F) 43 F2
Chalupki (PL) 200 E2
Chalupy (PL) 182 C1
Chálus (F) 51 D2
Cham (D) 89 F4
Chambéry (F) 53 D2
Chambley-Bussières (F) 44 C3
Chambly (F) 43 D2
Chambon-sur-Lac (F) 51 F2
Chambon-sur-Voueize (F). 48 A4
Chambord (F) 42 D4
Chamili (Nisí) (GR) 225 D4
Chamonix-Mont-Blanc (F). 49 F4
Champagnac-de-Belair (F) 51 D2
Champagne-Mouton (F) 47 D4
Champagnole (F) 49 E3
Champdeniers-
   Saint-Denis (F) 47 D4
Champeaux (F) 41 E3
Champeix (F) 52 A2
Champéry (CH) 49 F4
Champex (CH) 49 F4
Champlitte-et-le-Prélot (F). 49 D4
Champoluc (I) 53 F1
Champorcher (I) 53 F1
Champs-sur-Tarentaine (F)51 F1
Champtoceaux (F) 46 C2
Chamrousse (F) 53 D2
Chamusca (P) 68 A4
Chanac (F) 52 A2
Chanákia (GR) 216 C2
Chanas (F) 52 C2
Chandrás (GR) 227 F3
Chandria (CY) 230 B3
Chánia Kríti(GR) 226 B2
Chánia Lakonía(GR) 222 C2
Chaniótis (GR) 213 D1
Chantada (E) 58 C3
Chantelle (F) 48 B4
Chantemerle (F) 53 E3
Chantilly (F) 43 D2
Chantonnay (F) 46 C3
Chaource (F) 43 F3
Chapel-en-le-Frith (GB) 33 D3
Chapinería (E) 70 B1
Chapotami (CY) 230 B4
Charavgí (GR) 205 F4
Charbonnières-
   les-Bains (F) 52 B1
Charbowo (PL) 187 F2
Chard (GB) 35 D3
Charenton-du-Cher (F) 48 A3
Chári (GR) 216 B2
Charitoméni (GR) 207 B2
Charkeia (CY) 230 B2
Charleroi (B) 39 D2
Charlestown (IRL) 22 C3
Charleville-Mézières (F) 39 F4
Charlieu (F) 48 C4
Charlottenberg (S) 139 D2
Charly-sur-Marne (F) 43 E2
Charmes (F) 44 C4
Charny (F) 43 F4
Charny-sur-Meuse (F) 44 B2
Charokopeió (GR) 222 B2
Charolles (F) 48 C4
Chârost (F) 47 F3
Charquemont (F) 49 F2
Charroux (F) 47 D4

Chartleville / An Ràth (IRL) 24 C3
Chartres (F) 42 C3
Charzykowy (PL) 182 B3
Chasseneuil-
   sur-Bonnieure (F) 50 C1
Château-Arnoux-
   St-Auban (F) 53 D4
Château-Chinon (F) 48 B3
Château-d'Oex (CH) 49 F3
Château-du-Loir (F) 42 B4
Château-Gontier (F) 41 F1
Château-la-Vallière (F) 47 D2
Château-Landon (F) 43 D3
Château-Porcien (F) 39 C1
Château-Queyras (F) 53 E3
Château-Regnault (F) 39 F4
Château-Renard (F) 43 B4
Château-Renault (F) 42 B2
Château-Salins (F) 44 C3
Château-Thierry (F) 43 E2
Châteaubourg (F) 41 A2
Châteaubriant (F) 41 E4
Châteaudun (F) 42 E4
Châteaugiron (F) 41 E4
Châteaulin (F) 40 B3
Châteaumeillant (F) 48 A3
Châteauneuf-
   de-Randon (F) 52 A3
Châteauneuf-
   d'Ille-et-Vilaine (F) 41 E2
Châteauneuf-du-Faou (F). 40 B3
Châteauneuf-du-Pape (F). 52 C4
Châteauneuf-
   en-Thymerais (F) 42 C3
Châteauneuf-la-Forêt (F). 51 E1
Châteauneuf-les-Bains (F) 48 A4
Châteauneuf-
   sur-Charente (F) 50 C2
Châteauneuf-sur-Cher (F). 48 A3
Châteauneuf-sur-Loire (F). 43 D4
Châteauneuf-sur-Sarthe (F)41 F4
Châteauponsac (F) 48 E4
Châteaurenard (F) 56 C1
Châteauroux (F) 47 F3
Châteauvillain (F) 44 B4
Châtel (F) 49 F4
Châtel-Guyon (F) 51 F1
Châtel-Montagne (F) 48 B4
Châtel-St Denis (CH) 49 F3
Châtel-sur-Moselle (F) 44 C4
Châtelaillon-Plage (F) 46 C4
Châtelaudren (F) 40 C3
Châteldon (F) 48 B4
Châtelet (B) 39 E3
Châtellerault (F) 47 E3
Châtelus-Malvaleix (F) 47 F4
Châtenois (F) 44 C4
Chatham (GB) 36 C3
Châtillon (I) 53 F1
Châtillon-Coligny (F) 43 D4
Châtillon-en-Bazois (F) 48 B3
Châtillon-en-Diois (F) 52 C3
Châtillon-
   sur-Chalaronne (F) 49 D4
Châtillon-sur-Indre (F) 47 E3
Châtillon-sur-Loire (F) 43 D4
Châtillon-sur-Marne (F) 43 E2
Châtillon-sur-Seine (F) 43 F4
Chatteris (GB) 33 F3
Chaudes-Aigues (F) 51 F3
Chauffailles (F) 48 C4
Chaufour-lès-Bonnières (F)42 C2
Chaulnes (F) 39 D4
Chaumergy (F) 49 D3
Chaumont (F) 44 B4
Chaumont-en-Vexin (F) 42 C2
Chaumont-sur-Loire (F) 47 E2
Chauny (F) 39 B1
Chaussin (F) 49 D3
Chauvigny (F) 47 E3
Chavári (GR) 216 C2
Chavdáta (GR) 216 B1
Chaves (P) 63 D2
Chazelles-sur-Lyon (F) 52 B2
Cheb (CZ) 89 E3
Chęciny (PL) 195 F3
Chef-Boutonne (F) 47 D4
Cheímarros (GR) 206 C2
Cheles (E) 68 C2
Chełm (PL) 197 F2
Chełmek (PL) 200 F2
Chełmiec Małopolskie(PL)201 B3
Chełmno (PL) 182 C4
Chelmsford (GB) 36 C3
Chełmża (PL) 188 C1
Cheltenham (GB) 35 E1
Chelva (E) 71 D4

Chemillé (F) 46 C2
Chemin (F) 49 D3
Chemnitz Kreis
   Chemnitz Stadt(D) 89 E1
Chénérailles (F) 51 E1
Chenonceaux (F) 47 E2
Chepstow /
   Cas-Gwent (GB) 35 E1
Chera (E) 71 F2
Cherbourg-Octeville (F) 41 E1
Cheróneia (GR) 217 F1
Chéroy (F) 43 E3
Chérso (GR) 206 F3
Cherson (UA) 13 F3
Cheshunt (GB) 36 B3
Cheste (E) 71 F4
Chester (GB) 32 C3
Chester-le-Street (GB) 31 F4
Chesterfield (GB) 33 C3
Chevagnes (F) 48 B3
Chevillon (F) 44 B3
Chevreuse (F) 43 D2
Chiampo (I) 98 A3
Chianciano Terme (I) 102 A3
Chiaramonte Gulfi (I) 111 E4
Chiaravalle (I) 102 C2
Chiaravalle Centrale (I) 109 E3
Chiari (I) 97 E3
Chiasso (CH) 97 D3
Chiavari (I) 101 D1
Chiavenna (I) 97 D2
Chichester (GB) 36 B4
Chiclana de la Frontera (E)75 D3
Chieming (D) 94 A3
Chieri (I) 53 F2
Chiesa in Valmalenco (I) 97 E2
Chiesina Uzzanese (I) 101 F2
Chieti (I) 103 D4
Chiliomódi (GR) 217 F2
Chimay (B) 39 E3
Chinchilla
   de Monte Aragón (E) 71 E3
Chinchón (E) 70 C1
Chinon (F) 47 D2
Chioggia (I) 98 B3
Chíos (GR) 220 C1
Chíos (Nisí) (GR) 220 C1
Chipiona (E) 75 D3
Chippenham (GB) 35 E2
Chipping Campden (GB) 35 F1
Chipping Norton (GB) 35 F1
Chipping Sodbury (GB) 35 E2
Chirivel (E) 77 D2
Chișinău (MD) 13 E3
Chișineu-Criș (RO) 113 F2
Chiusa / Klausen (I) 98 A1
Chiusa di Pesio (I) 53 F4
Chiusa Sclafani (I) 110 C3
Chiusaforte (I) 98 C1
Chiusi (I) 102 A3
Chiva (E) 71 F2
Chivasso (I) 53 F2
Chlemoútsi (GR) 216 C2
Chlewiska (PL) 196 B2
Chlorakas (GR) 230 A4
Chlum u Třeboně (CZ) 90 C4
Chlumec nad Cidlinou (CZ)90 C2
Chmel'nyc'kyj (UA) 13 D2
Chmielnik (PL) 202 B2
Chmielnik (PL) 196 B3
Chmielno Pomorskie(PL) 182 B2
Chmil'nyk (UA) 13 D2
Chobienice (PL) 187 D3
Choceň (CZ) 91 D2
Chóchlakas (GR) 228 B3
Chocholów (PL) 201 B3
Chocianów (PL) 193 D1
Chociwel (PL) 180 C4
Chocz (PL) 188 B4
Choczewo (PL) 182 B1
Chodaków (PL) 189 F3
Chodecz (PL) 189 D2
Chodel (PL) 197 D2
Chodov Sokolov(CZ) 89 E3
Chodów (PL) 191 D3
Chodzież (PL) 187 D2
Choirokoitia (CY) 231 D4
Chojna (PL) 186 B1
Chojnice (PL) 182 B3
Chojnik zamek(PL) 193 D2
Chojniki (BY) 7 E1
Chojnów (PL) 193 D1
Cholet (F) 46 C3
Chollerford (GB) 31 E3
Cholm (RUS) 7 F2
Chomutov (CZ) 89 F2

Chomutov (CZ) 89 F2
Chónikas (GR) 217 F3
Chóra Messinía(GR) 217 D4
Chóra Sámos(GR) 221 E3
Choreftó (GR) 212 C2
Chorges (F) 53 D3
Chorkówka (PL) 202 D3
Chorley (GB) 32 C2
Chorol (UA) 13 F1
Choroszcz (PL) 185 E4
Chortiátis (GR) 206 C3
Chorzele (PL) 184 B4
Chorzów (PL) 195 D4
Choszczno (PL) 180 C4
Chotěboř (CZ) 90 B3
Chotyn (UA) 13 D2
Choumnikó (GR) 207 D2
Choúni (GR) 211 E4
Chouto (P) 68 B2
Chozoviótissa (GR) 225 D2
Chrast (CZ) 90 C3
Chrastava (CZ) 90 B1
Christchurch (GB) 35 E3
Christianí (GR) 217 D4
Christianí (Nisí) (GR) 224 B3
Christiansfeld (DK) 142 B4
Christós (GR) 220 C3
Chrómio (GR) 205 F4
Chrostkowo (PL) 189 D1
Chrudim (CZ) 90 C2
Chrýsafa (GR) 217 F4
Chrysí Akti (GR) 207 F3
Chrysí Ammoudiá (GR) 207 F3
Chrysó (GR) 207 D2
Chrysochou Bay (CY) 230 A3
Chrysoúpoli (GR) 207 F2
Chrysovítsi (GR) 217 E3
Chryssí (Nisí) (GR) 227 E3
Chrzanów
   Małopolskie(PL) 200 F1
Chrząstowice (PL) 194 B3
Chrzypsko Wielkie (PL) 187 F2
Chuchelná (CZ) 91 F2
Chur (CH) 97 E1
Church Stretton (GB) 32 C4
Chust (UA) 12 C2
Chwałęcice (PL) 200 E1
Chwarszczany (PL) 186 E4
Chwaszczyno (PL) 182 C1
Chybie (PL) 200 E2
Chynów Lubuskie(PL) 187 D4
Chynów Mazowieckie(PL)190 B4
Chyżne (PL) 201 A3
Ciasna (PL) 194 C3
Cibla (LV) 167 F2
Cicciano (I) 105 F3
Čičevac (SRB) 119 D3
Čičevo (BIH) 120 C2
Čičinai (LT) 170 C4
Cidones (E) 65 D2
Ciechanów (PL) 189 F1
Ciechanowiec (PL) 191 D2
Ciechocinek (PL) 188 C1
Cieladz (PL) 189 F4
Ciempozuelos (E) 70 B1
Ciemupe (LV) 165 C2
Ciepielów (PL) 196 C2
Cieplice (PL) 193 D3
Ciepłowody (PL) 193 E4
Cieszanów (PL) 197 E4
Cieszyn Pomorskie(PL) 187 E4
Cieszyn Śląskie(PL) 200 E2
Cieza (E) 77 E1
Ciężkowice
   Małopolskie(PL) 201 C2
Ciężkowice Śląskie(PL).. 195 D4
Cifuentes (E) 65 D4
Cigliano (I) 53 F2
Cilavegna (I) 97 D4
Cildi (LV) 162 C1
Cillas (E) 65 E4
Cilleros (E) 69 D1
Cilleruelo de Bezana (E).. 60 B3
Cimdenieki (LV) 162 B2
Cimişlia (MD) 13 E3
Cîmpeni (RO) 12 C3
Cîmpulung (RO) 13 D4
Cîmpulung
   Moldovenesc (RO) 13 D3
Cinctorres (E) 66 A4
Ciney (B) 39 F3
Cinfães (P) 62 C3
Cingoli (I) 102 C2
Cinigiano (I) 101 F3
Cinisi (I) 110 B2

Cínovec *(CZ)*	89	F 1	Cividale del Friuli *(I)*	98	C 2	Clisson *(F)*	46	C 2	Codogno *(I)*	97	E 4	Collioure *(F)*	56	A 4	Commercy *(F)*	44	B 3
Cintegabelle *(F)*	55	E 2	Civita Castellana *(I)*	102	B 4	Clitheroe *(GB)*	32	C 2	Codos *(E)*	65	E 3	Collobrières *(F)*	57	D 2	Como *(I)*	97	D 3
Cintruénigo *(E)*	65	E 2	Civitanova Marche *(I)*	102	C 2	Clogh Mills *(GB)*	23	E 1	Codroipo *(I)*	98	C 2	Collodi *(I)*	101	E 2	Cómpeta *(E)*	76	A 3
Čiobiškis *(LT)*	171	D 4	Civitavecchia *(I)*	104	B 2	Cloghan *(IRL)*	22	C 4	Coesfeld *(D)*	83	D 4	Collonges *(F)*	49	E 4	Compiègne *(F)*	44	D 4
Čiovo (Otok) *(HR)*	103	F 2	Civitella del Tronto *(I)*	102	C 3	Clogheen *(IRL)*	24	C 3	Coevorden *(NL)*	83	F 3	Colonges-la-Rouge *(F)*	51	D 4	Comporta *(P)*	68	A 3
Cirava *(LV)*	162	C 1	Civitella Roveto *(I)*	105	C 3	Clogherhead *(IRL)*	23	E 4	Cofrentes *(E)*	71	F 3	Colmar *(F)*	45	D 4	Comps-sur-Artuby *(F)*	57	E 2
Cirencester *(GB)*	35	E 1	Civray *(F)*	47	D 4	Clonakilty /			Cognac *(F)*	50	C 1	Colmars *(F)*	53	E 4	Comrat *(MD)*	13	E 3
Cirey-sur-Vezouze *(F)*	45	D 3	Čivril *(TR)*	19	F 3	Cloich na Coillte *(IRL)*	24	B 4	Cogne *(I)*	53	F 1	Colmenar *(E)*	76	A 3	Comunanza *(I)*	102	C 3
Ciria *(E)*	65	E 3	Cjurupyns'k *(UA)*	13	F 3	Clonbur / An Fhairche *(IRL)*	22	B 4	Cogolin *(F)*	57	E 2	Colmenar de Oreja *(E)*	70	C 1	Concarneau *(F)*	40	B 4
Cirié *(I)*	53	F 1	Clacton-on-Sea *(GB)*	37	D 3	Clondalkin *(IRL)*	23	E 4	Cogolludo *(E)*	64	C 4	Colmenar Viejo *(E)*	64	B 2	Conches-en-Ouche *(F)*	42	B 2
Cirklíškis *(LT)*	172	C 4	Clairvaux-les-Lacs *(F)*	49	E 3	Clones / Cluain Eois *(IRL)*	23	D 3	Coimbra *(P)*	62	B 4	Colnabaichin *(GB)*	27	F 4	Concordia sulla Secchia *(I)*	98	A 4
Cirò *(I)*	109	F 1	Clamecy *(F)*	48	B 2	Clonmel /			Coín *(E)*	75	F 3	Colne *(GB)*	33	D 2	Condat *(F)*	51	F 2
Cirò Marina *(I)*	109	F 1	Clanaig *(GB)*	30	B 2	Cluain Meala *(IRL)*	25	D 3	Coina *(P)*	68	A 3	Colobraro *(I)*	106	C 4	Condé-en-Brie *(F)*	43	E 2
Čírpan *(BG)*	19	D 1	Clapham *(GB)*	32	C 1	Cloppenburg *(D)*	83	E 2	Čoka *(SRB)*	113	D 1	Cologna Veneta *(I)*	98	A 3	Condé-sur-l'Escaut *(F)*	39	D 3
Círuļi *Kuldīgas (LV)*	157	D 4	Clara / Clóirtheach *(IRL)*	23	D 4	Clovelly *(GB)*	34	C 2	Col *(SLO)*	99	D 2	Cologne *(F)*	55	D 2	Condé-sur-Noireau *(F)*	41	D 4
Círuļi *Talsu (LV)*	157	C 4	Clare *(I)*	36	C 2	Cloyes-sur-le-Loir *(F)*	42	C 4	Colares *(E)*	68	A 2	Colombey-les-Belles *(F)*	44	C 3	Condeixa-a-Nova *(P)*	62	B 4
Círuļi (Druvas) *(LV)*	165	F 4	Claremorris / Clár Chlainne			Cluj-Napoca *(RO)*	12	C 3	Cölbe *(D)*	88	A 2	Colombey-			Condom *(F)*	50	C 4
Cirulīši *Daugavpils (LV)*	173	D 1	Mhuiris *(IRL)*	22	B 4	Clun *(GB)*	32	C 4	Colchester *(GB)*	36	C 2	les-Deux-Églises *(F)*	44	A 4	Condrieu *(F)*	52	B 2
Cirulīši *Rīgas (LV)*	164	C 1	Claudy *(GB)*	23	D 2	Cluny *(F)*	48	C 4	Coldbackie *(GB)*	27	E 1	Colombres *(E)*	60	A 3	Conegliano *(I)*	98	B 2
Cisek *(PL)*	194	C 4	Clausthal-Zellerfeld *(D)*	84	B 4	Cluses *(F)*	49	F 4	Colditz *(D)*	89	F 1	Colomera *(E)*	76	B 2	Conflans-en-Jarnisy *(F)*	44	C 2
Ciskods *(LV)*	167	E 3	Claut *(I)*	98	B 1	Clusone *(I)*	97	E 2	Coldstream *(GB)*	31	E 2	Colorno *(I)*	97	F 4	Confolens *(F)*	47	E 4
Cisna *(PL)*	202	E 4	Clavière *(I)*	53	E 3	Clydebank *(GB)*	30	C 2	Coleford *(GB)*	35	E 1	Colosimi *(I)*	109	E 2	Cong / Conga *(IRL)*	22	B 4
Cisneros *(E)*	64	A 1	Clay Cross *(GB)*	33	D 3	Čmielów *(PL)*	196	C 3	Coleraine *(GB)*	23	E 1	Colunga *(E)*	59	F 2	Conga / Cong *(IRL)*	22	B 4
Cisowa *(PL)*	194	C 4	Claye-Souilly *(F)*	43	D 2	Cmolas *(PL)*	196	C 4	Colfiorito *(I)*	102	B 3	Colwyn Bay /			Congleton *(GB)*	33	D 3
Čista Mala *(HR)*	103	F 1	Clécy *(F)*	41	F 2	Coachford *(IRL)*	24	C 3	Colico *(I)*	97	D 2	Bae Colwyn *(GB)*	32	B 3	Congosto de Valdavia *(E)*	60	A 4
Cista Provo *(HR)*	117	D 4	Cleethorpes *(GB)*	33	F 2	Coalisland *(GB)*	23	E 2	Coligny *(F)*	49	D 3	Coma-ruga *(E)*	66	C 4	Congresbury *(GB)*	35	D 2
Cisterna di Latina *(I)*	105	D 2	Clefmont *(F)*	44	B 4	Coalville *(GB)*	33	D 4	Colinas *(E)*	75	E 2	Comacchio *(I)*	98	B 4	Conil de la Frontera *(E)*	75	E 4
Cisternino *(I)*	107	E 2	Cléguérec *(F)*	40	C 3	Coaña *(E)*	59	D 2	Colindres *(E)*	60	B 3	Comănești *(RO)*	13	D 3	Conisbrough *(GB)*	33	E 2
Cisterna *(E)*	59	F 3	Clelles *(F)*	53	D 3	Coatbridge *(GB)*	30	C 2	Colintraive *(GB)*	30	B 2	Combarro *(E)*	58	B 4	Coniston *(GB)*	32	C 1
Čitluk *(BIH)*	117	E 4	Clères *(F)*	38	B 4	Cobeña *(E)*	64	C 4	Coll de Nargó *(E)*	55	D 4	Combe Martin *(GB)*	34	C 2	Conlie *(F)*	42	A 3
Città della Pieve *(I)*	102	A 3	Clermont *(F)*	43	D 1	Cobh / An Cóbh *(IRL)*	24	C 3	Colle di Val d'Elsa *(I)*	101	F 3	Combeaufontaine *(F)*	49	E 1	Conliège *(F)*	49	D 3
Città di Castello *(I)*	102	A 2	Clermont-en-Argonne *(F)*	44	B 2	Coburg *(D)*	89	D 3	Colle Isarco /			Comber *(GB)*	23	F 2	Connel *(GB)*	30	B 1
Città Sant'Angelo *(I)*	103	D 4	Clermont-Ferrand *(F)*	52	A 1	Coca *(E)*	64	A 3	Gossensaß *(I)*	93	F 4	Combloux *(F)*	49	F 4	Connerré *(F)*	42	B 4
Cittadella *(I)*	98	A 3	Clermont-l'Hérault *(F)*	56	A 2	Cocconato *(I)*	53	F 2	Colle Sannita *(I)*	105	D 2	Combourg *(F)*	41	D 2	Čonoplja *(SRB)*	113	D 1
Cittaducale *(I)*	102	C 4	Clerval *(F)*	49	E 2	Cocentaina *(E)*	71	F 4	Collecchio *(I)*	97	F 4	Combronde *(F)*	48	B 4	Conques *(F)*	51	F 3
Cittanova *(I)*	111	F 4	Clervaux *(L)*	44	C 1	Cochem *(D)*	45	D 1	Colleferro *(I)*	105	D 2	Comeglians *(I)*	98	B 1	Conquista *(E)*	70	A 4
Cittareale *(I)*	102	C 4	Cléry-St-André *(F)*	42	C 4	Cockburnspath *(GB)*	31	E 2	Collesalvetti *(I)*	101	E 4	Comillas *(E)*	60	A 3	Conselice *(I)*	102	A 1
Ciudad Real *(E)*	70	B 3	Cles *(I)*	97	F 1	Cockermouth *(GB)*	31	D 4	Collesano *(I)*	110	C 2	Comines *(B)*	36	F 4	Conselve *(I)*	98	A 3
Ciudad Rodrigo *(E)*	63	D 3	Clevedon *(GB)*	35	D 2	Code *(LV)*	164	C 2	Colli a Volturno *(I)*	105	D 2	Comines *(F)*	37	F 4	Consett *(GB)*	31	E 4
Čiudiškiai *(LT)*	176	C 2	Cleveleys *(GB)*	32	C 2	Codevigo *(I)*	98	B 3	Collinée *(F)*	41	D 3	Comiso *(I)*	111	D 4	Constância *(P)*	68	B 2
Ciutadella de Menorca *(E)*	73	F 2	Clifden / An Clochán *(IRL)*	22	A 4	Codigoro *(I)*	98	B 4	Collio *(I)*	97	F 3	Commentry *(F)*	48	A 4	Constanța *(RO)*	13	E 3

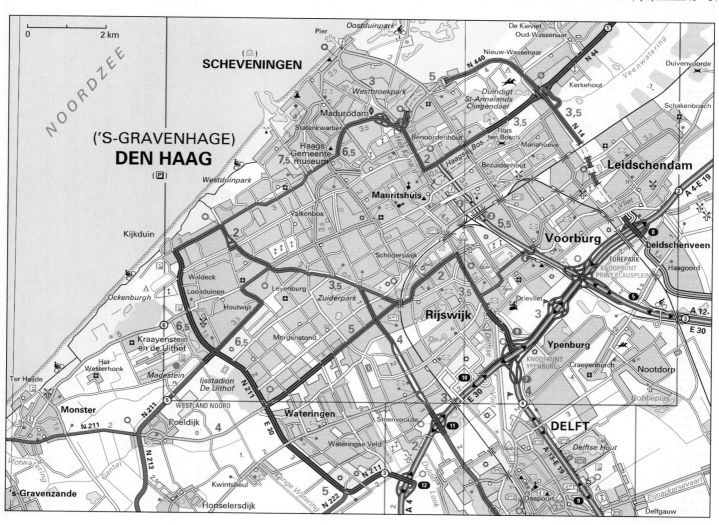

Constantina (E) 75	E 1	
Consuegra (E) 70	B 2	
Consuma (I) 102	A 2	
Contarina (I) 98	B 4	
Conthey (CH) 49	F 4	
Contigliano (I) 102	A 2	
Contin (GB) 27	E 3	
Contres (F) 47	F 2	
Contrexéville (F) 44	C 4	
Contursi Terme (I) 106	B 3	
Conty (F) 38	C 4	
Conversano (I) 107	D 2	
Conwy (GB) 32	B 3	
Cookstown (GB) 23	E 2	
Cootehill / Muinchille (IRL) 23	D 3	
Čop (UA) 12	C 2	
Cope (E) 77	E 2	
Copertino (I) 107	E 3	
Copparo (I) 98	A 4	
Corabia (RO) 13	D 4	
Coral Bay (CY) 230	A 3	
Corato (I) 106	C 2	
Coray (F) 40	B 3	
Corbeil-Essonnes (F) 43	D 3	
Corbie (F) 38	C 4	
Corbigny (F) 48	B 2	
Corbola (I) 98	B 4	
Corbridge (GB) 31	E 4	
Corby (GB) 37	E 4	
Corcieux (F) 45	D 4	
Corconte (E) 60	A 3	
Corcubión (E) 58	A 3	
Cordes-sur-Ciel (F) 51	E 4	
Córdoba (E) 76	A 1	
Cordobilla de Lácara (E) 69	E 2	
Corduente (E) 65	E 4	
Corella (E) 65	E 2	
Coreses (E) 63	F 2	
Corfe Castle (GB) 35	E 3	
Corgo (E) 58	C 3	
Cori (I) 105	D 2	
Coria (E) 69	E 1	
Coria del Río (E) 75	D 4	
Corias (E) 59	D 3	
Corigliano Calabro (I) 109	E 1	
Corinaldo (I) 102	B 2	
Coripe (E) 75	F 2	
Cork / Corcaigh (IRL) 24	C 3	
Corlay (F) 40	C 3	
Corleone (I) 110	C 3	
Corleto Perticara (I) 106	C 4	
Çorlu (TR) 19	E 1	
Cormatin (F) 48	C 3	
Cormeilles (F) 42	B 2	
Cormery (F) 47	F 3	
Cormòns (I) 98	C 2	
Cornago (E) 65	E 2	
Čornaja (LV) 167	E 3	
Cornellana (E) 59	E 2	
Corniglio (I) 101	E 1	
Cornimont (F) 45	D 4	
Čornobyl' (UA) 13	E 1	
Čornomors'ke (UA) 13	F 3	
Cornuda (I) 98	B 2	
Cornus (F) 56	A 1	
Corps (F) 53	D 3	
Corral de Almaguer (E) 70	C 2	
Corrales del Vino (E) 63	F 3	
Corran (GB) 27	D 4	
Corredoiras (E) 58	B 3	
Correggio (I) 97	F 4	
Corrèze (F) 51	E 2	
Corridonia (I) 102	C 3	
Corrofin (IRL) 24	C 2	
Corsham (GB) 35	E 2	
Čortanovci (SRB) 118	B 1	
Corte (F) 57	F 3	
Corte de Peleas (E) 69	D 3	
Cortegada (E) 58	B 4	
Cortegana (E) 75	D 1	
Cortemaggiore (I) 97	E 4	
Cortemilia (I) 100	B 1	
Corteolona (I) 97	E 4	
Cortes (E) 65	E 2	
Cortes de Aragón (E) 65	F 4	
Cortes de Baza (E) 76	C 1	
Cortes de la Frontera (E) 75	F 3	
Cortijos Nuevos (E) 70	C 4	
Cortina d'Ampezzo (I) 98	B 1	
Čortkiv (UA) 13	D 1	
Cortona (I) 102	A 3	
Coruche (P) 68	B 2	
Corvara in Badia (I) 98	A 1	
Corvera (E) 77	E 1	
Corvera de Toranzo (E) 60	A 3	
Corwen (GB) 32	B 3	
Cosenza (I) 109	E 2	

Cosham (GB) 35	F 3	
Cosne-d'Allier (F) 48	A 4	
Cosne-sur-Loire (F) 48	A 2	
Cossato (I) 53	F 1	
Cossé-le-Vivien (F) 41	F 4	
Cossonay (CH) 49	E 3	
Costa de Caparica (F) 68	A 3	
Costa de Santo André (P) 68	A 3	
Costigliole d'Asti (I) 100	B 1	
Coswig (D) 85	D 3	
Coswig (D) 89	F 1	
Cotignac (F) 57	D 2	
Cottbus (D) 85	F 4	
Couches (F) 48	C 3	
Couço (P) 68	B 2	
Coucy-le-Château-		
Auffrique (F) 39	D 4	
Couhé (F) 47	D 4	
Couilly-		
Pont-aux-Dames (F) 43	D 2	
Couiza (F) 55	F 3	
Coulanges-la-Vineuse (F) 43	E 4	
Coulanges-sur-Yonne (F) .. 48	B 3	
Coulommiers (F) 43	E 2	
Coulon (F) 46	C 4	
Coulonges-sur-l'Autize (F) . 46	C 4	
Coupar Angus (GB) 31	D 1	
Couptrain (F) 41	F 3	
Cour-Cheverny (F) 47	F 3	
Courçon (F) 46	C 4	
Courmayeur (I) 53	E 1	
Cournon-d'Auvergne (F) 52	A 1	
Courpière (F) 52	A 1	
Cours (F) 48	C 4	
Coursan (F) 55	F 3	
Coursegoules (F) 57	E 1	
Courseulles-sur-Mer (F) 41	F 1	
Courson-les-Carrières (F) . 43	E 4	
Courtenay (F) 43	E 4	
Courthézon (F) 52	C 4	
Courtomer (F) 42	B 3	
Courtown (IRL) 25	E 4	
Courville-sur-Eure (F) 42	C 3	
Coussey (F) 44	B 4	
Coutances (F) 41	E 2	
Coutras (F) 50	C 3	
Couvin (B) 39	E 3	
Cova da Iria (P) 68	B 1	
Covadonga (E) 59	F 3	
Covarrubias (E) 64	C 2	
Coventry (GB) 33	D 4	
Covilhã (P) 62	C 4	
Cowbridge /		
Bont-faen (GB) 35	D 2	
Cowdenbeath (GB) 31	D 2	
Cowes Isle of Wight (GB) .. 35	F 3	
Cowfold (GB) 36	B 4	
Cozes (F) 50	B 2	
Craco (I) 106	C 4	
Craigavon (GB) 23	E 2	
Craigellachie (GB) 27	F 3	
Craighouse (GB) 30	A 2	
Craignure (GB) 30	B 1	
Crail (GB) 31	E 1	
Crailsheim (D) 93	D 1	
Craiova (RO) 119	F 1	
Cranborne (GB) 35	E 3	
Crans-sur-Sierre (CH) 96	B 2	
Craon (F) 41	F 4	
Craonne (F) 39	E 4	
Craponne-sur-Arzon (F) 52	A 2	
Crato (P) 68	C 2	
Craughwell (IRL) 22	C 4	
Craven Arms (GB) 32	C 4	
Crawinkel (D) 88	C 2	
Crawley (GB) 36	B 4	
Creagorry (GB) 26	B 3	
Crécy-en-Ponthieu (F) 38	C 3	
Crécy-la-Chapelle (F) 43	E 2	
Crécy-sur-Serre (F) 39	D 4	
Crediton (GB) 34	C 3	
Creegh (IRL) 24	B 2	
Creeslough (IRL) 23	D 1	
Creglingen (D) 88	C 4	
Creil (F) 43	D 2	
Crema (I) 97	E 3	
Crémieu (F) 52	C 1	
Cremona (I) 97	E 4	
Créon (F) 50	B 3	
Crepaja (SRB) 118	B 1	
Crépy-en-Valois (F) 43	E 2	
Cres (HR) 99	E 3	
Cres (HR) 99	E 4	
Crescentino (I) 53	F 2	
Crespino (I) 98	B 4	
Crest (F) 52	C 3	
Cresta (CH) 97	E 1	

Créteil (F) 43	D 2	
Creully (F) 41	F 1	
Creußen (D) 89	D 3	
Creutzwald (F) 44	C 2	
Creuzburg (D) 88	C 1	
Crevacuore (I) 96	C 3	
Crevalcore (I) 98	A 4	
Crèvecœur-le-Grand (F) 38	C 4	
Crevillent (E) 77	F 1	
Crewe (GB) 32	C 3	
Crewkerne (GB) 35	D 3	
Crianlarich (GB) 30	C 1	
Criccieth (GB) 32	A 3	
Crickhowell (GB) 35	D 1	
Cricklade (GB) 35	E 2	
Crieff (GB) 31	D 1	
Criel-sur-Mer (F) 38	B 3	
Crikvenica (HR) 99	E 3	
Crimmitschau (D) 89	E 1	
Crinan (GB) 30	B 1	

Criquetot-l'Esneval (F) 38	A 4	
Crissolo (I) 53	E 3	
Crivitz (D) 79	E 4	
Crkvice (MNE) 121	D 2	
Crmljan (SRB) 121	D 2	
Črmošnjice (SLO) 99	E 2	
Crna Bara (SRB) 117	F 1	
Črna na K. (SLO) 99	D 1	
Crna Trava (SRB) 119	E 4	
Crnac (HR) 112	A 4	
Crni Guber (BIH) 118	A 3	
Crni Lug (BIH) 116	C 3	
Crni Lug (HR) 99	D 3	
Čmi Vrh (SLO) 99	D 1	
Crnjelovo Donje (BIH) 117	F 1	
Črmkovci (HR) 112	A 4	
Črnomelj (SLO) 99	E 2	
Crocq (F) 51	F 1	
Crolly / Croithli (IRL) 22	C 1	
Crumlin (GB) 23	E 2	
Cromarty (GB) 27	E 3	

Cromer (GB) 37	D 1	
Crook (GB) 31	E 4	
Croom (IRL) 24	C 2	
Cross Hands (GB) 35	C 1	
Crosshaven (IRL) 24	C 4	
Crossmaglen (GB) 23	E 3	
Crossmolina /		
Crois Mhaoiliona (IRL) 22	B 3	
Crotone (I) 109	F 2	
Crowborough (GB) 36	C 4	
Crowland (GB) 33	F 4	
Crowle (GB) 33	E 3	
Croyde (GB) 34	C 2	
Croydon (GB) 36	B 3	
Crozant (F) 47	E 4	
Crozon (F) 40	B 3	
Cruden Bay (GB) 28	C 3	
Crudgington (GB) 32	C 4	
Cruis (GB) 23	E 2	
Cruseilles (F) 49	E 4	

Cruz da Légua (P) 68	B 1	
Cruzamento de Pegões (P) 68	B 3	
Crveni Grm (BIH) 120	B 1	
Crvenka (SRB) 113	D 4	
Csongrád (H) 113	C 2	
Csorna (H) 112	A 1	
Cuacos de Yuste (E) 69	F 1	
Cualedro (E) 63	D 1	
Cuba (P) 68	B 4	
Cubel (E) 65	E 4	
Cuckfield (GB) 36	B 4	
Čude (D) 117	F 3	
Cudillero (E) 59	E 2	
Čudovo (RUS) 7	D 1	
Cuéllar (E) 64	B 3	
Cuenca Cuenca (E) 71	D 1	
Cuers (F) 57	D 2	
Cuerva (E) 70	B 2	
Cuevas		
de San Clemente (E) 64	C 2	

DIJON

Aiguillottes (Bd des)	A	2
Allobroges (Bd des)	A	3
Bachelard (Bd Gaston)	A	4
Bellevue (R. de)	A	5
Bertin (Av. J.B.)	B	6
Briand (Av. A.)	B	8
Camus (Av. Albert)	B	12
Castel (Bd du)	A	13
Champollion (Av.)	B	15
Chanoine-Bardy (Imp.)	B	16
Chanoine-Kir (Bd)	A	17
Chateaubriand (R. de)	B	19
Chèvre-Morte (Bd de)	A	20
Churchill (Bd W.)	B	24
Clomiers (Bd des)	A	26

Concorde (Av. de la)	B	28
Einstein (Av. Albert)	A	36
Europe (Bd de l')	B	38
Europe (Rd-Pt de l')	B	40
Fauconnet (R. Gén.)	AB	42
Fontaine-des-Suisses (Bd)	A	44
Fontaine-lès-Dijon (R.)	A	43
France-Libre (Pl. de la)	AB	45
Gabriel (Bd)	B	46
Gallieni (Bd Mar.)	AB	48
Gaulle (Crs Gén.-de)	B	50
Gorgets (Bd des)	A	52
Jeanne-d'Arc (Bd)	B	55
Kennedy (Bd J.)	A	56
Magenta (R.)	B	58
Maillard (Bd)	B	60
Mansard (Bd)	B	62
Mont-Blanc (Av. du)	B	65

Moulin (R. Jean)	B	63
Nation (Rd-Pt de la)	B	66
Orfèvres (R. des)	A	68
Ouest (Bd de l')	A	69
Parc (Cours du)	B	70
Poincaré (Av. R.)	B	71
Pompidou (Rd-Pt Georges)	B	72
Pompon (Bd F.)	B	73
Prat (Av. du Colonel)	B	75
Rembrandt (Bd)	B	78
Rolin (Q. Nicolas)	A	79
Roosevelt (Av. F. D.)	B	80
Saint-Exupéry (Pl.)	B	85
Schuman (Bd Robert)	B	88
Strasbourg (Bd de)	B	90
Trimolet (Bd)	B	91
8-Mai-1945 (Rd-Pt du)	B	96
26e-Dragons (R. du)	B	98

Cuevas de San Marcos (E) 76 A 2
Cuevas del Almanzora (E). 77 D 2
Cuevas del Becerro (E).... 75 F 3
Cuevas del Campo (E)..... 76 C 2
Cuevas del Valle (E)....... 70 A 1
Cuglieri (I)................ 108 A 2
Cuijk (NL)................. 87 D 1
Cuiseaux (F).............. 49 D 3
Cuisery (F)................ 49 D 3
Cukurciems (LV)......... 164 C 1
Culan (F)................. 48 A 3
Culdaff (IRL)............. 23 E 1
Culemborg (NL).......... 82 B 4
Cúllar Baza (E).......... 76 C 2
Cullen (GB)............... 28 B 3
Cullera (E)................ 72 C 4
Cullompton (GB)......... 35 D 3
Culoz (F)................. 53 D 1
Culross (GB)............. 31 C 2
Cumbernauld (GB)....... 30 C 2
Cumbres Mayores (E)... 69 D 4
Cumiana (I)............... 53 F 3
Čumić (SRB)............. 118 C 2
Cumnock (GB)........... 30 C 3
Cunault (F)............... 47 D 2
Cuneo (I)................. 53 F 4
Cunlhat (F)............... 52 A 2
Čunski (HR).............. 99 E 4
Cuntis (E)................ 58 B 3
Cuorgnè (I)............... 53 F 2
Cupar (GB)............... 31 D 1
Cupello (I)............... 103 E 4
Cupramontana (I)....... 102 B 2
Čuprija (SRB)........... 119 C 3
Cureggio (I).............. 96 C 3
Curia (P)................. 62 B 4
Curtea de Argeş (RO)... 13 D 1
Curtis (E)................ 58 B 2
Čurug (SRB)............. 113 E 4
Cusano Mutri (I)....... 105 E 4
Cushendall (GB)......... 23 F 1
Cushendun (GB)......... 23 F 1
Cusset (F)................ 48 A 3
Cutro (I)................. 109 F 2
Cuxhaven (D)............ 78 B 4
Cvikov (CZ).............. 90 B 1
Čvrstec (HR)............. 112 A 4
Cwmbrân (GB)........... 35 D 1
Cybinka (PL)............ 186 B 3
Cyców (PL).............. 197 E 1
Čypénai (LT)............. 165 E 4
Cysoing (F).............. 39 D 2
Czacz (PL)............... 187 E 3
Czaplinek (PL).......... 181 F 2
Czarna Podkarpackie(PL)202 E 1
Czarna Białostocka (PL).185 E 4
Czarna Dąbrówka (PL)....182 E 3
Czarna Góra (PL)....... 202 E 3
Czarne (PL).............. 181 F 3
Czarnków (PL).......... 187 E 3
Czarnocin Łodzkie(PL)..195 E 1
Czarnożyły (PL)......... 194 C 2
Czarny Bór (PL)......... 193 E 2
Czarny Dunajec (PL)....201 A 3
Czastary (PL)........... 194 C 2
Czchów (PL)............. 201 B 2
Czechowice-
  Dziedzice (PL)......... 200 F 2
Czechy (PL).............. 181 E 3
Czempiń (PL)............ 187 E 3
Czeremcha (PL)......... 191 E 2
Czermin
  Wielkopolskie(PL)...... 188 B 4
Czerniawa-Zdrój (PL)... 192 C 3
Czernica (PL)............ 193 E 2
Czernice Borowe (PL)... 189 F 1
Czerniejewo (PL)....... 187 F 2
Czerniewice (PL)....... 189 F 1
Czerników (PL).......... 186 B 1
Czernikowo (PL)........ 189 D 1
Czersk (PL).............. 182 E 3
Czerwieńsk (PL)........ 186 C 3
Czerwin (PL)............ 190 C 1
Czerwińsk nad Wisłą (PL)189 F 2
Czerwionka-
  Leszczyny (PL)........ 200 E 1
Czerwonak (PL)......... 187 F 2
Częstochowa (PL)...... 195 D 3
Człopa (PL).............. 187 D 1
Człuchów (PL).......... 181 F 2
Czosnów (PL)........... 189 F 2
Czudec (PL)............. 202 D 2
Czyżew-Osada (PL)..... 191 E 2

D

D. Brela (HR)............. 117 D 4
D. Kazanci (BIH)......... 116 C 3

D. Ljubata (SRB)........ 119 F 4
D. Lukavac (BIH)........ 117 F 4
D. Malovan (BIH)........ 117 D 3
D. Rujani (BIH).......... 116 C 4
D. Seget (HR)............ 103 F 1
D. Stalina (SRB)......... 119 A 2
D. Zemunik (HR)........ 103 E 1
Dabar (HR)............... 99 F 3
Dąbie Lubuskie(PL)..... 186 C 3
Dąbie Wielkopolskie(PL).189 D 3
Dąbie
  Zachodniopomorskie(PL)180 B 2
Dąbie (Jezioro) (PL)..... 180 B 4
Dabilje (MK)............. 122 C 3
Dabo (F)................. 45 D 3
Dabromani (BIH)........ 120 C 2
Dąbroszyn (PL).......... 186 B 2
Dąbrowa Kujawsko-
  Pomorskie(PL).......... 188 B 2
Dąbrowa Opolskie(PL)..194 B 3
Dąbrowa
  Wielkopolskie(PL)...... 188 C 4
Dąbrowa Białostocka (PL)185 E 3
Dąbrowa Biskupia (PL)..188 C 2
Dąbrowa Chełmińska (PL)188 C 1
Dąbrowa Górnicza (PL)..195 D 4
Dąbrowa Tarnowska (PL)196 D 4
Dąbrowa Zielona (PL)... 195 E 3
Dąbrówno (PL).......... 183 E 4
Dachau (D).............. 93 D 2
Dačice (CZ)............. 90 C 4
Dadià (GR).............. 208 C 2
Dáfnes (GR)............. 217 E 1
Dafní (GR)............... 218 C 2
Dáfni Ágio Óros(GR).... 207 E 4
Dáfni Ahaïa(GR)........ 217 D 1
Dáfni Etolía-
  Akarnanía(GR)......... 217 E 2
Dáfni Lésvos(GR)....... 214 A 1
Dáfnio (GR)............. 217 F 4
Dafnónas Fokída(GR)... 211 F 4
Dafnónas Xánthi(GR)... 207 E 2
Dafnotí (GR)............. 211 D 2
Dagali (N)............... 139 D 2
Dagda (LV).............. 167 E 4
Dagebüll (D)............. 78 B 2
Dagenham (GB)......... 36 C 3
Dagiai (LT).............. 165 D 3
Dahlen (D)............... 85 D 4
Dahlenburg (D).......... 84 B 2
Dahme
  Kreis Ostholstein(D)... 79 E 3
Dahme
  Kreis Teltow-Fläming(D) 85 E 4
Dahn (D)................. 45 E 2
Dailiūnai (LT)........... 171 E 1
Dailučiai (LT)........... 175 E 2
Daimiel (E).............. 70 B 3
Daimonía (GR).......... 223 E 2
Daimús (E).............. 72 A 3
Dainava (LT)............ 177 E 3
Dainiai li (LT)........... 169 E 2
Đakovica (SRB)......... 121 F 2
Đakovo (HR)............. 117 E 1
Daksti (LV).............. 159 F 2
Dal (N).................. 139 E 2
Đala (SRB).............. 113 E 3
Dalbe (LV).............. 164 C 2
Dalbeattie (GB)......... 30 C 4
Dalby (S)................ 143 D 4
Dale (N)................. 138 B 1
Dale (N)................. 138 B 2
Dalen (N)................ 138 C 3
Daleszyce (PL).......... 196 B 3
Dalhem (S).............. 146 D 2
Dali (CY)................ 231 C 3
Dalías (E)............... 76 C 3
Daliburgh (GB).......... 26 B 3
Dalików (PL)............ 189 D 4
Dalj (HR)................ 113 D 1
Dalkeith (GB)........... 31 D 2
Dalkey (IRL)............ 25 F 1
Dalmally (GB)........... 30 B 1
Dalmellington (GB)..... 30 C 3
Dalmine (I).............. 97 E 3
Dalry (GB)............... 30 C 2
Dals Långed (S)........ 139 F 4
Dalsbruk (FIN).......... 136 B 4
Dalsjöfors (S).......... 143 D 2
Dalton in Furness (GB). 32 C 1
Dalvík (IS)............. 126 B 1
Dalwhinnie (GB)........ 27 E 4
Dáma (LV)............... 162 A 3
Damási (GR)............ 211 F 1
Damaskiniá (GR)....... 205 E 4
Damasławek (PL)....... 187 F 1
Damazan (F)............. 50 C 4

Dambava (LT)........... 175 F 2
Dambenieki (LV)........ 161 D 4
Damelevières (F)....... 44 C 3
Dameliai (LT)........... 163 F 3
Damgan (F)............. 41 D 4
Damianó (GR).......... 206 B 3
Dammartin-en-Goële (F). 43 D 2
Damme Kreis Vechta(D).. 83 E 3
Damnjane (SRB)........ 121 F 2
Dampierre (F)........... 49 E 2
Dampierre-sur-Salon (F). 49 D 2
Damville (F)............. 42 C 2
Damvillers (F).......... 44 B 2
Dangé-St-Romain (F)... 47 E 3
Danilava (LT)........... 171 F 4
Danilovgrad (MNE)..... 121 D 2
Dannemarie (F)......... 49 F 1
Dannenberg (Elbe) Kreis
  Lüchow-Dannenberg(D) 84 B 2
Daoulas (F)............. 40 B 3
Dapkūniškiai (LT)....... 171 E 3
Darbénai (LT)........... 162 B 4
Darda (HR).............. 112 C 4
Dardedzes (LV)......... 165 F 3
Dardesheim (D)......... 84 B 4
Darfo-Boario Terme (I).. 97 E 2
Dargiai (LT)............. 163 D 3
Dargin (Jezioro) (PL)... 184 C 2
Darginiai (LT)........... 164 C 3
Dargun (D).............. 79 F 3
Dargužiai Alytaus(LT)... 177 E 3
Dargužiai Klaipėdos(LT). 162 B 4
Dargužiai Šiaulių(LT).... 164 D 2
Darlington (GB)......... 31 F 4
Darłówko (PL)........... 181 E 1
Darłowo (PL)............ 181 E 1
Darmstadt (D).......... 45 E 1
Darney (F).............. 44 C 4
Daroca (E).............. 65 E 4
Darque (P).............. 62 B 2
Darsūniškis (LT)........ 176 C 2

Dartford (GB)........... 36 C 3
Dartmouth (GB)........ 35 D 4
Daruvar (HR)........... 112 B 4
Darwen (GB)............ 32 C 2
Darželiai (LT)........... 176 C 2
Dārziņi (LV)............. 157 D 4
Daržininkai (LT)........ 177 D 3
Dasburg (D)............. 44 C 1
Dasing (D).............. 93 F 2
Dasochóri (GR)......... 207 F 2
Dassel (D).............. 84 A 4
Dassow (D)............. 79 D 4
Dasze (PL).............. 191 B 2
Daszyna (PL)........... 189 D 3
D'ať kovo (RUS).......... 7 F 1
Datteln (D).............. 87 F 1
Daubiškiai (LT)......... 163 E 4
Dauburaičiai (LT)....... 170 C 2
Daudzese (LV).......... 165 E 3
Daudzeva (LV).......... 165 D 2
Dauggai (LT)........... 176 C 3
Daugailiai (LT)......... 171 F 4
Daugava (LV)........... 172 C 1
Daugavpils (LV)........ 172 C 1
Daugėlaičiai (LT)....... 169 F 2
Daugeliškiai (LT)....... 169 F 4
Daugidonys (LT)....... 177 D 4
Daugirdai (LT)......... 176 B 3
Dauglaukis (LT)........ 169 D 3
Daugmale (LV)......... 165 D 1
Dauguļi (LV)............ 159 E 2
Daujėnai (LT)........... 165 D 2
Daujočiai (LT).......... 171 F 2
Daukantiškiai (LT)..... 169 E 4
Daukniūnai (LT)........ 170 C 1
Daukšaičiai (LT)....... 168 C 2
Daukšiai Klaipėdos(LT).. 162 C 3
Daukšiai Marijampolės(LT)175 D 4
Daukšiai Vilniaus(LT)... 172 C 2
Daukstes (LV).......... 161 D 4

Daulénai (LT)........... 177 F 4
Daumanti (Volfärte) (LV)..164 C 3
Dauménai (LT).......... 165 D 4
Daumilai (LT)........... 172 C 4
Daun (D)................ 87 E 3
Daunoriai (LT)......... 165 E 4
Dauparai (LT).......... 168 B 1
Daužnagiai (LT)........ 169 F 2
Dava (GB)............... 27 E 3
Daviá (GR).............. 217 E 3
Dávleia (GR)............ 217 F 1
Davlos (CY)............. 231 E 2
Davor (HR)............. 115 E 1
Davos (CH)............. 97 E 1
Dawlish (GB)........... 35 D 3
Dax (F)................. 54 B 2
De Bilt (NL)............ 82 B 4
De Haan (B)............ 37 F 4
De Koog (NL)........... 82 B 2
De Panne (B)........... 37 E 4
Deal (GB)............... 37 D 4
Deauville (F)............ 42 A 1
Deba (E)................ 60 C 3
Debar (MK)............. 122 A 3
Debarska Banja
  Banjišta (MK)......... 122 A 3
Dębe Wielkie (PL)...... 190 C 3
Debeikiai (LT).......... 171 E 2
Debeli Lug (SRB)....... 119 D 1
Debeljača (SRB)........ 113 F 4
Dębica (PL)............. 165 E 2
Dęblin (PL)............. 190 C 4
Dębnica Kaszubska (PL).181 F 1
Dębno Nowy Targ (PL)..201 B 2
Dębno Tarnów (PL)..... 201 B 2
Dębno
  Zachodniopomorskie(PL)186 B 2
Dębołęka (PL).......... 194 C 1
Dębów (PL)............. 202 E 1

Dębowa Kłoda (PL)..... 191 E 4
Dębowa Łąka (PL)...... 183 D 4
Dębowiec (PL).......... 202 D 2
Dębowiec Śląskie(PL)... 200 E 2
Dębowo (PL)............ 190 C 1
Debrc (SRB)............ 118 B 1
Debrecen (H)............ 12 C 3
Debrzno (PL)........... 181 F 4
Dečani (SRB)........... 121 F 2
Decazeville (F)......... 51 F 3
Děčín (CZ).............. 90 A 1
Decize (F).............. 48 B 3
Dedemsvaart (NL)...... 82 C 3
Degaičiai (LT).......... 163 D 4
Degaňa (E)............. 59 D 3
Degerfors (S).......... 140 B 4
Degerndorf a. Inn (D)... 94 A 3
Degėsiai (LT)........... 164 C 4
Deggendorf (D)......... 94 B 1
Deglénai (LT)........... 164 C 4
Deglova (LV)............ 167 F 2
Dego (I)................. 100 C 1
Degole (LV)............. 163 F 1
Degracias (P)........... 68 B 1
Degučiai Būda(LT)...... 175 F 1
Degučiai Karkliniai(LT).. 175 E 2
Degučiai Šiaulių(LT).... 164 C 3
Degučiai Šiaulių(LT).... 164 B 4
Degumniai (LV)........ 167 D 1
Degutinė (LT).......... 175 E 1
Dehesa de Montejo (E). 60 A 4
Deidesheim (D)......... 45 E 2
Deinze (B).............. 37 F 4
Deiva Marina (I)........ 101 D 1
Dej (RO)................ 12 C 3
Deje (S)................ 140 A 3
Deksne (LV)............ 157 D 4
Dekteri (LV)............ 167 E 2
Delčevo (MK)........... 122 C 2
Delden (NL)............. 83 D 4
Deleitosa (E)........... 69 F 2

DRESDEN

Alttolkewitz . . . . V 57
Borsbergstr. . . . . V 58
Emerich-Ambros-Ufer . . . . U 60
Flügelwegbrücke . . . . UV 61
Fritz-Löffler-Str. . . . . V 62
Gerhart-Hauptmann-Str. . . . . . . V 63
Hamburger Str. . . . . U 64
Innsbrucker Straße . . . . V 84
Lommatzscher Str. . . . . U 69
Moritzburger Landstr. . . . . U 74
Moritzburger Weg . . . . U 75
Naumannstr. . . . . V 78
Nossener Brücke . . . . V 71
Nürnberger
  Str. U 72
Washingtonstr. . . . . U 79
Wehlener Str. . . . . V 81
Zellescher Weg . . . . V 83

DUBLIN / BAILE ÁTHA CLIATH

Place	Pg	Grid
Delémont (CH)	49	F2
Deléria (GR)	212	A1
Delfoi (GR)	217	E1
Delft (NL)	82	A4
Delfzijl (NL)	83	D2
Delia (I)	110	C3
Delianuova (I)	111	F1
Deliblato (SRB)	118	C1
Deliceto (I)	106	B2
Delimeđe (SRB)	118	C4
Delitzsch (D)	85	D2
Delle (F)	49	F2
Delme (F)	44	C3
Delmenhorst (D)	83	D2
Delnice (HR)	99	E3
Delsbo (S)	140	C1
Deltebre (E)	66	B4
Deltuva (LT)	171	D3
Delvin (IRL)	23	D4
Delvináki (GR)	210	C1
Demene (LV)	173	D2
Demidov (RUS)	7	E3
Demir Kapija (MK)	122	A2
Demirci (TR)	19	F2
Demmin (D)	80	B3
Den Burg (NL)	82	B2
Den Haag = 's-Gravenhage (NL)	82	A4
Den Helder (NL)	82	B2
Den Oever (NL)	82	B2
Denain (F)	39	D3
Denbigh / Dinbych (GB)	32	A4
Dendermonde (B)	39	E2
Dendrochóri (GR)	205	E3
Denekamp (NL)	83	D3
Dénia (E)	72	A4
Denizli (TR)	19	F3
Denkendorf (D)	93	F1
Dennington (GB)	37	D2
Denny (GB)	30	C2
Derby (GB)	33	D3
Dereköy (TR)	19	E1
Derenburg (D)	84	B4
Dermbach Wartburgkreis (D)	88	C2
Derneburg (D)	84	A4
Deruta (I)	102	B3
Dervaig (GB)	26	C4
Derval (F)	41	E4
Derveliai (LT)	170	B1
Dervéni (GR)	217	E1
Derventa (BIH)	115	F4
Derviniai (LT)	175	F3
Dervíziana (GR)	211	D2
Deryneia (CY)	231	E3
Desborough (GB)	33	E4
Descartes (F)	47	D2
Desenzano del Garda (I)	97	F3
Desfina (GR)	217	F1
Desimirovac (SRB)	118	C2
Desio (I)	97	D3
Deskáti (GR)	211	F1
Despotikó (Nisí) (GR)	219	E4
Despotovac (SRB)	119	D2
Despotovo (SRB)	113	D4
Dessau Kreis Dessau Stadt (D)	85	D4
Deštné v Orlických horach (CZ)	91	D2
Destriana (E)	59	E4
Desulo (I)	108	B3
Desvres (F)	38	C2
Deszczno (PL)	186	C2
Deta (RO)	113	F4
Detmold (D)	83	F4
Dettelbach (D)	88	C4
Deurne (NL)	87	D1
Deutsch Wagram (A)	95	F1
Deutschkreutz (A)	95	F2
Deutschlandsberg (A)	95	E4
Deva (RO)	12	C1
Deveikiškiai (LT)	170	B3
Deventer (NL)	82	C4
Devil's Bridge / Pontarfynach (GB)	32	A3
Devizes (GB)	35	E2
Devnja (BG)	19	E1
Devynduoniai (LT)	170	C2
Dewsbury (GB)	33	D3
Deyá (E)	73	D2
Deza (E)	65	E3
Dezzo (I)	97	E2
Dhekelia Sovereign Base (CY)	231	D3
Día (Nisí) (GR)	227	D4
Diafáni (GR)	225	F4
Diakófti (GR)	223	D3
Diakoftó (GR)	217	E1
Diamante (I)	109	D1
Diano Marina (I)	100	B2
Diápora Nissiá (GR)	218	B2
Diarizos (CY)	230	B3
Diavatá (GR)	206	B3
Diavolítsi (GR)	217	D2
Dibbersen Kreis Harburg (D)	84	A1
Dicmo (HR)	116	C4
Dicomano (I)	101	F2
Dílotos (GR)	208	C1
Dílos (Nisí) (GR)	219	F3
Dímaina (GR)	218	A3
Dímitra (GR)	212	B2
Dimitriškès (LT)	172	B2
Dimítritsi (GR)	206	C2
Dimitrovgrad (BG)	19	D1
Dimitrovgrad (SRB)	119	E3
Dimitsána (GR)	217	E3
Dimzukalns (LV)	165	D2
Dinali (M)	110	A4
Dinami (I)	111	F1
Dinan (F)	41	D3
Dinant (B)	39	F3
Dinar (TR)	19	F3
Dinard (F)	41	D3
Dingelstädt (D)	88	C1
Dingle (S)	143	D1
Dingle / An Daingean (IRL)	24	A1
Dingolfing (D)	94	A1
Dingwall (GB)	27	E3
Dinjiška (HR)	99	F4
Dinkelsbühl (D)	93	E1
Dinklage (D)	83	E3
Dinsdurbe (LV)	162	C1
Dinslaken (D)	87	E1
Dio (GR)	206	B4
Diónysos (GR)	218	C2
Diorios (CY)	231	C2
Dipótama (GR)	207	E1
Dippoldiswalde (D)	89	F1
Dirdal (N)	138	B4
Diroú (Spílaia) (GR)	222	C2
Dirvonénai Šiauliu (LT)	163	E4
Dirvonénai Telšiu (LT)	163	E4
Diržiai (LT)	164	C3
Dobrodzień (PL)	194	C3
Dobromierz (PL)	193	D3
Dolnośląskie (PL)	193	D3
Dobroń (PL)	189	D4
Dobrošinci (MK)	122	B2
Dobroszyce (PL)	193	F2
Dobrovnik (SLO)	95	F4
Dobrun (BIH)	118	A3
Dobruš (BY)	7	F1
Dobruševo (MK)	122	B4
Dobruška (CZ)	91	D2
Dobryszyce (PL)	195	D3
Dobrzany (PL)	181	D4
Dobrzeń Wielki (PL)	194	B3
Dobrzyń nad Wisłą (PL)	189	D2
Docksta (S)	132	B3
Dodóni (GR)	211	D2
Doesburg (NL)	82	C4
Doetinchem (NL)	82	C4
Doganović (SRB)	122	A2
Dogliani (I)	53	F3
Doïráni (GR)	206	B2
Dokanj (BIH)	117	F2
Dokka (N)	139	E2
Dokkum (NL)	82	C2
Dokós (Nisí) (GR)	218	B4
Doksy (CZ)	90	B4
Dokupe (LV)	156	C3
Dol-de-Bretagne (F)	41	D3
Dole (F)	49	E3
Dølemo (N)	139	D2
Dolenci (MK)	122	A4
Dolenjavas (SLO)	99	F1
Dolenjske Toplice (SLO)	99	E2
Dolgas Vas (SLO)	95	D3
Dolgellau (GB)	32	B4
Donawitz (A)	95	D3
Doncaster (GB)	33	E2
Donegal / Dún na nGall (IRL)	23	D2
Doneztebe / Santesteban (E)	54	A3
Dongen (NL)	39	F1
Donges (F)	46	B2
Donington (GB)	33	F3
Donja Brezna (MNE)	121	D1
Donja Bukovica (MNE)	118	C4
Donja Šatornja (SRB)	118	C2
Donje Crniljevo (SRB)	118	B2
Donje Dragovlje (SRB)	119	E3
Donje Ljupče (SRB)	119	D4
Donji Andrijevci (HR)	115	F3
Donji Barbeš (SRB)	119	E3
Donji Kneginec (HR)	99	F1
Donji Lapac (HR)	99	F4
Donji Miholjac (HR)	112	C4
Donji Milanovac (SRB)	119	D1
Donji Stajevac (SRB)	122	B1
Donji Vakuf (BIH)	117	D3
Donji Vijačani (BIH)	115	F4
Donnemarie-Dontilly (F)	43	E3
Donnersbachwald (A)	94	C3
Dønnes (N)	127	C3
Donostia- San Sebastián (E)	61	D3
Donoúsa (Nisí) (GR)	220	C4
Donzac (F)	51	E2
Donzère (F)	52	B2
Donzy (F)	48	B2
Doorn (NL)	82	B4
Dora (CY)	230	B4
Đorče Petrov (MK)	122	A2

Bana Josipa Jelačića . **BYZ** 4
Čingrije (Pera) . . . . **BZ** 10
Dr. Ante Starčevića. . **BCZ** 12
Dr. Ante Sercera . . . . . **AYZ** 13
Dr. Roka Mišetića . . . . . **AZ** 15
Kranjčevića
  (Silvija Strahimira) . . **BY** 31
Nazora (Vladimira) . . **BCZ** 43
Od Svetog Mihajla . . . . **BY** 50
Od Tabakarije. . . . . **CZ** 52
Petra Krešimira
  IV. . . . . **CZ** 56

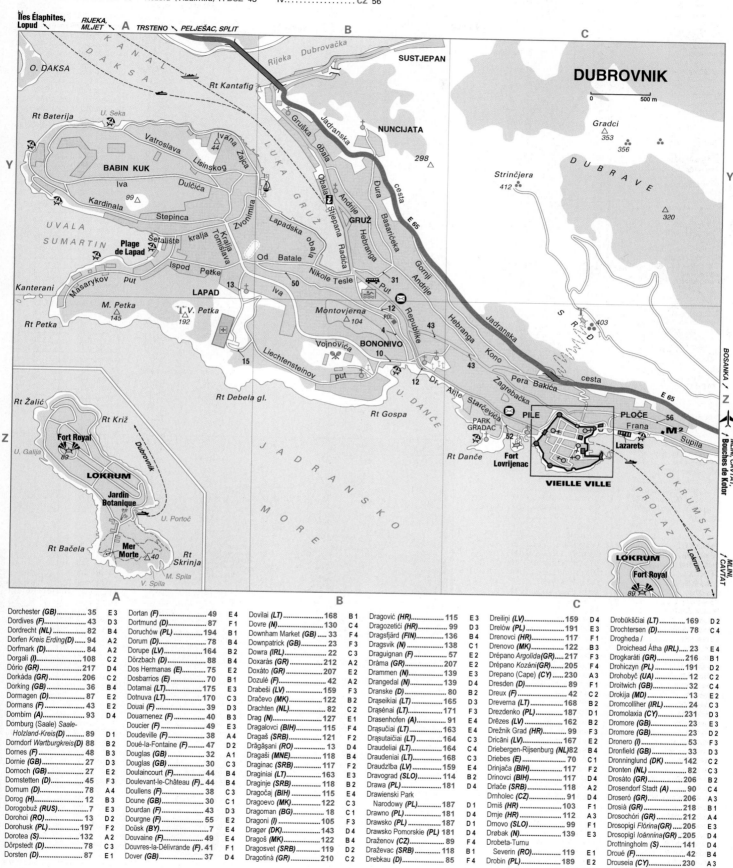

Dorchester (GB) 35	E 3	Dortan (F) 49	E 4	Dovilai (LT) 168	B 1
Dordives (F) 43	D 3	Dortmund (D) 87	F 1	Dovre (N) 130	C 4
Dordrecht (NL) 82	B 4	Doruchów (PL) 194	B 1	Downham Market (GB) 33	F 4
Dorfen Kreis Erding(D) 94	A 2	Dorum (D) 78	B 4	Downpatrick (GB) 23	F 3
Dorfmark (D) 84	A 2	Dorupe (LV) 164	B 2	Dowra (IRL) 22	C 3
Dorgali (I) 108	C 2	Dörzbach (D) 88	B 4	Doxarás (GR) 212	A 2
Dório (GR) 217	D 4	Dos Hermanas (E)........... 75	E 2	Doxáto (GR) 207	E 2
Dorkáda (GR) 206	C 2	Dosbarrios (E) 70	B 1	Dozulé (F) 42	A 2
Dorking (GB) 36	B 4	Dotamai (LT) 175	E 3	Drabeši (LV) 159	F 3
Dormagen (D) 87	E 2	Dotnuva (LT) 170	C 3	Dračevo (MK) 122	B 2
Dormans (F) 43	D 3	Douai (F) 39	D 3	Drachten (NL) 82	C 2
Dornbirn (A) 93	D 4	Douarnenez (F) 40	B 3	Drag (N) 127	E 1
Dornburg (Saale) Saale-		Doucier (F) 49	E 3	Dragalovci (BIH) 115	F 4
Holzland-Kreis(D) 89	D 1	Doudeville (F) 38	A 4	Dragaš (SRB) 121	F 2
Dorndorf Wartburgkreis(D) 88	B 2	Doué-la-Fontaine (F) 47	D 2	Drăgăşani (RO) 13	D 1
Dornes (F) 48	B 3	Douglas (GB) 32	A 1	Dragaši (MNE) 118	B 4
Dornie (GB) 27	D 3	Douglas (GB) 30	C 3	Draginac (SRB) 117	F 2
Dornoch (GB) 27	E 2	Doulaincourt (F) 44	B 4	Draginiai (LT) 163	E 3
Dornstetten (D) 45	F 3	Doulevant-le-Château (F).. 44	B 4	Draginje (SRB) 118	B 2
Dornum (D) 78	A 4	Doullens (F) 38	C 3	Dragočaj (BIH) 115	E 4
Dorog (H) 12	B 3	Doune (GB) 30	C 1	Dragoevo (MK) 122	C 3
Dorogobuž (RUS)............. 7		Dourdan (F) 43	D 3	Dragoman (BG) 18	C 1
Dorohoi (RO) 13	D 2	Dourgne (F) 55	E 2	Dragoni (I) 105	F 3
Dorohusk (PL) 197	F 2	Doúsk (BY) 7	E 4	Dragør (DK) 143	D 3
Dorotea (S) 132	A 2	Douvaine (F) 49	E 4	Dragoš (MK) 122	B 4
Dörpstedt (D) 78	C 3	Douvres-la-Délivrande (F). 41	F 1	Dragosvet (SRB) 119	D 4
Dorsten (D) 87	E 1	Dover (GB) 37	D 4	Dragotiná (GR) 210	C 2

Dragović (HR) 115	E 3	Dreiliņi (LV) 159	D 4	Drobūkščiai (LT) 169	D 2
Dragozetići (HR)............. 99	D 3	Drelów (PL) 191	E 3	Drochtersen (D)............. 78	C 4
Dragsfjärd (FIN) 136	C 4	Drenovci (HR)................ 117	F 1	Drogheda /
Dragsvik (N) 138	C 1	Drenovo (MK) 122	B 3	Droichead Átha (IRL).. 23	E 4
Draguignan (F) 57	F 2	Drépano Argolida(GR).... 217	F 3	Drogkaráti (GR) 216	B 1
Dráma (GR) 207	E 2	Drépano Kozáni(GR)....... 205	F 4	Drohiczyn (PL) 191	D 2
Drammen (N) 139	E 3	Drepano (Cape) (CY) 230	A 3	Drohobyč (UA) 12	C 2
Drangedal (N) 139	D 4	Dresden (D) 89	F 1	Droitwich (GB) 32	C 4
Dranske (D) 80		Dreux (F) 42	C 2	Drokija (MD) 13	E 2
Drąseikiai (LT) 165	D 3	Dreverna (LT) 168	B 2	Dromcolliher (IRL) 24	C 3
Drasenhofen (A) 91	F 4	Drezdenko (PL) 187	D 1	Dromore (GB)................ 23	E 3
Drašćiai (LT) 163	E 4	Drēzes (LV) 162	B 2	Dromore (GB)................ 23	D 2
Drąsutaičiai (LT) 164	C 3	Drežnik Grad (HR).......... 99	F 3	Dronero (I) 53	F 3
Draudeliai (LT) 164	C 4	Dricāni (LV) 167	E 2	Dronfield (GB) 33	D 3
Draudeniai (LT) 168	C 3	Driebergen-Rijsenburg (NL)82	B 4	Dronninglund (DK) 142	C 2
Dravograd (SLO) 114	B 2	Driebes (D) 70	C 1	Dronten (NL) 82	C 3
Drawa (PL) 181	D 4	Drinjača (BIH) 117	F 2	Drosáto (GR) 206	B 2
Drawienski Park		Drinovci (BIH) 117	D 4	Drlače (SRB) 118	A 2
Narodowy (PL) 187	D 1	Drnholec (CZ) 91		Drosendorf Stadt (A) 90	C 4
Drawno (PL) 181	D 4	Drniš (HR) 103	F 1	Droseró (GR) 206	A 3
Drawsko (PL) 187	D 4	Drnje (HR) 112	A 3	Drosiá (GR) 218	B 1
Drawsko Pomorskie (PL) 181	D 4	Drnovo (SLO) 99	F 1	Drosochóri (GR) 212	A 4
Draženov (CZ) 89	F 4	Drøbak (N) 139	E 3	Drosopigí Flórina(GR).... 205	E 3
Draževac (SRB) 118	B 1	Drobeta-Turnu		Drosopigí Ioánnina(GR) ..205	D 2
Drebkau (D) 85	F 4	Severin (RO) 119	E 1	Drottningholm (S) 141	D 4
		Drobin (PL) 189	E 2	Droué (F) 42	B 4
				Drouseia (CY) 230	A 3

Am Schönenkamp	T	2
Arnulfstr.	T	3
Benderstr.	T	4
Bernburger Str.	T	5
Brehmstr.	S	10
Corneliusstr.	T	14
Danziger Str.	S	16
Deutzer Str.	T	17
Düsseldorfer Str.	ST	18
Eckenerstr.	S	20
Fahneburgstr.	S	26
Grafenberger Allee	T	35
Graf-Adolf-Str.	T	34
Graf-Recke-Str.	S	36
Hamborner Str.	T	37
Heerdter Landstr.	T	40
Heidelberger Str.	T	41
Heinrich-Ehrhardt-Str.	T	42
In den Kötten	T	48
Kaiserswerther Str.	S	54
Kalkumer Str.	S	56
Klein-Eller	T	57
Königsberger Str.	T	58
Krefelder Str.	T	61
Lindemannstr.	T	63
Ludenberger Str.	S	65
Luegallee	T	66
Lütticher Str.	T	67
Merowingerstr.	T	71
Münchener Str.	T	72
Münsterstr.	T	73
Niederlöricker Str.	S	75
Niederrheinstr.	S	76
Oberkasseler Brücke	T	82
Oberlöricker Str.	S	83
Oberrather Str.	S	84
Pariser Str.	T	85
Pöhlenweg	T	86
Rather Broich	S	87
Reichswaldallee	S	89
Reisholzer Str.	S	90
Rennbahnstr.	S	91
Rheinkniebrücke	T	116
Sandträgerweg	T	92
Südlicher Zubringer	T	99
Ulmenstr.	S	102
Unterrather Str.	S	103
Vennhauser Allee	T	106
Werdener Str.	T	109
Werstener Str.	S	110
Westfalenstr.	S	112

Dumbarton (GB)	30	C 2
Dumbrǎji (LV)	157	F 4
Dumbría (E)	58	A 3
Dumbriai (LT)	163	E 3
Dūmciems (LV)	157	E 3
Dumfries (GB)	31	D 3
Dun Laoghaire (IRL)	23	E 4
Dun-le-Palestel (F)	47	F 4
Dun-sur-Auron (F)	48	A 3
Dunaföldvár (H)	112	C 2
Dunaïvci (UA)	13	D 2
Dunajec (PL)	201	D 2
Dunalka (LV)	162	B 1
Dunaújváros (H)	112	C 2
Dunava (Dunova) (LV)	166	C 4
Dunbar (GB)	31	E 2
Dunblane (GB)	30	C 1
Dundaga (LV)	157	E 2
Dundalk / Dún Dealgan (IRL)	23	E 3
Dundee (GB)	31	D 1
Dundonnell (GB)	27	D 2
Dunfanaghy (IRL)	23	D 1
Dunfermline (GB)	31	D 2
Dungannon (GB)	23	E 2
Dungarvan / Dún Garbhán (IRL)	25	D 3
Dungiven (GB)	23	E 2
Dunglow / An Clochán Liath (IRL)	22	C 1
Dunika (LV)	162	B 3
Dunje (MK)	122	B 3
Dunkeld (GB)	31	D 1
Dunkerque (F)	37	E 4
Dunmanway / Dún Mánmhai (IRL)	24	B 4
Dunmore / Dún Mór (IRL)	22	C 4
Dunmore East (IRL)	25	D 3
Dunnamanagh (GB)	23	D 2
Dunnet (GB)	27	F 1
Dunoon (GB)	30	B 2
Duns (GB)	31	E 2
Dunshaughlin (IRL)	23	E 4
Dunski (LV)	173	D 1
Dunstable (GB)	36	D 2
Dunster (GB)	35	D 2
Dunte (LV)	159	D 3
Dunvegan (GB)	26	C 3

Drozdowo (PL)	181	E 1
Drugovci (BIH)	117	E 3
Drūlėnai (LT)	171	E 1
Drulingen (F)	45	D 3
Drumkeeran (IRL)	22	C 3
Drummore (GB)	30	B 4
Drumnadrochit (GB)	27	E 3
Drumshanbo (IRL)	22	C 3
Drusenheim (F)	45	E 3
Druskininkai (LT)	176	C 4
Druskininkai miestas(LT)	176	C 4
Drusti (LV)	160	B 4
Druten (NL)	82	C 4
Druva (LV)	163	E 2
Druvāni (LV)	165	F 3
Druviena (LV)	160	C 4
Druviņas (LV)	165	D 2
Družai (LT)	171	E 4
Družbice (PL)	195	D 1
Drvar (BIH)	116	C 3
Drvenik (HR)	120	B 1
Drvenik (Otok) (HR)	103	F 2
Drwęca (PL)	183	E 3
Drwęckie (Jezioro) (PL)	183	E 3
Drwinia (PL)	201	E 2
Dryburgh Abbey (GB)	31	E 3
Drymaía (GR)	212	B 4
Drymen (GB)	30	C 2
Drymós (GR)	206	B 3
Dryopída (GR)	219	D 3
Dryós (GR)	219	E 4
Drzewica (PL)	195	F 1
Drzycim (PL)	182	C 4
Dubǎsari (MD)	13	E 3
Duben (D)	85	E 3
Dubeņi (LV)	162	B 2
Dubeņi-1 (LV)	162	B 2
Dubeninki (PL)	185	D 2
Dubí (CZ)	89	F 2
Dubicze Cerkiewne (PL)	191	F 2
Dubiecko (PL)	202	E 2
Dubienka (PL)	197	F 2
Dubingiai (LT)	171	F 4
Dublin / Baile Átha Cliath (IRL)	23	E 4
Dubna (LV)	167	D 2
Dubna (RUS)	7	F 1
Dubňany (CZ)	91	E 4
Dubno (UA)	13	D 1
Duboka (SRB)	118	C 4

Dubona (SRB)	118	C 1
Duboštica (BIH)	117	E 3
Dubovac (SRB)	118	C 1
Dubovsko (BIH)	99	F 3
Dubów (PL)	191	E 3
Dubrava Pelješac Otok (HR)	120	B 2
Dubrava Zagreb (HR)	112	A 4
Dubrava Stara (BIH)	115	F 4
Dubrave Brčko(BIH)	117	F 2
Dubrave Tuzla(BIH)	117	E 1
Dubravica (SRB)	118	C 1
Dubrovnik (HR)	120	C 2
Dubuļi (LV)	167	F 3
Dubulti (LV)	165	F 3
Ducey (F)	41	E 3
Duchcov (CZ)	89	F 2
Ducherow (D)	80	C 3
Duchovščina (RUS)	7	F 2
Duclair (F)	38	A 4
Dudelange (L)	44	C 2
Duderstadt (D)	88	C 1
Dudley (GB)	33	D 4
Dudweiler (D)	45	D 2
Dueñas (E)	64	A 2
Duesund (N)	138	B 1
Dufftown (GB)	27	F 3
Duga Poljana (SRB)	118	C 2
Duga Reka (HR)	99	F 2
Dugi Otok (Otok) (HR)	103	E 1
Dugi Rat (HR)	117	D 4
Dugi Selo (HR)	99	F 2
Duingt (F)	53	D 1
Duino-Aurisina (I)	98	C 2
Duisburg (D)	87	E 1
Dukat (SRB)	119	F 4
Dukielska (Przełęcz) (PL)	202	D 3
Dukla (PL)	202	D 3
Dūkštas (LT)	172	C 2
Dūkšteliai (LT)	177	E 1
Dūkštos (LT)	177	E 1
Dukstyna (LT)	171	D 3
Dukurnonys (LT)	176	C 2
Duleek (IRL)	23	E 4
Dulje (SRB)	122	A 2
Dülken (D)	87	E 1
Dülmen (D)	83	D 4
Dulnain Bridge (GB)	27	F 3
Đulovac (HR)	112	B 4
Dulovo (BG)	13	E 3

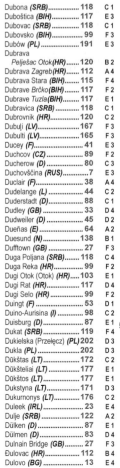

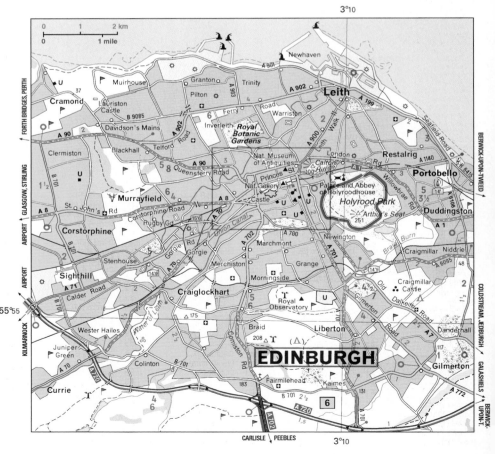

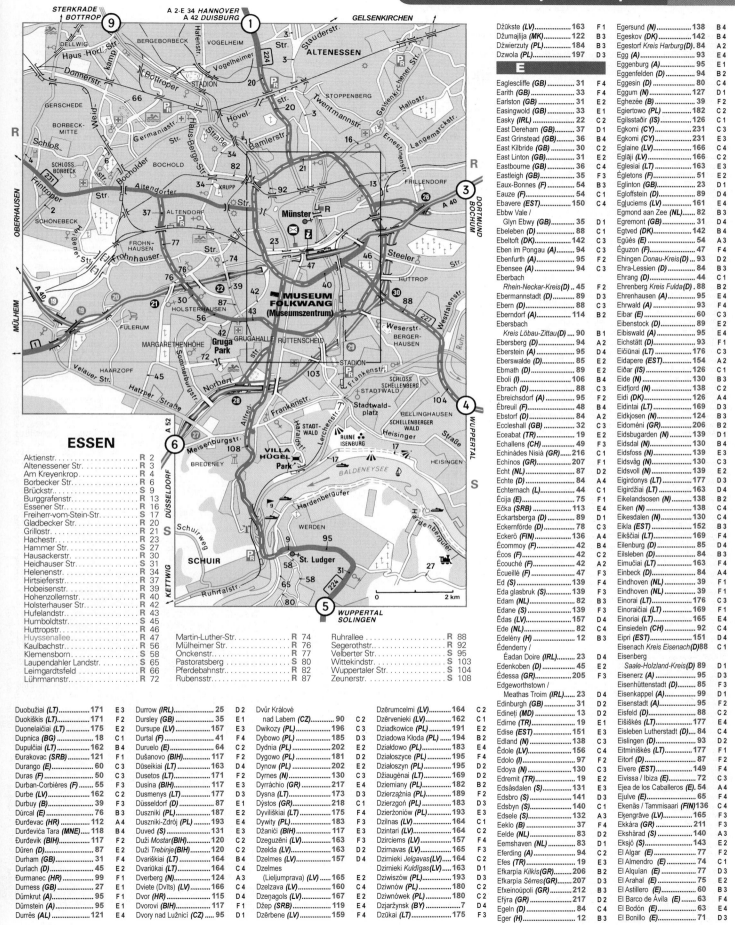

ESSEN

Street	Ref
Aktienstr.	R 2
Altenessener Str.	R 3
Am Kreyenkrop	R 4
Borbecker Str.	R 6
Brückstr.	S 9
Burggrafenstr.	R 13
Essener Str.	R 16
Freiherr-vom-Stein-Str.	R 17
Gladbecker Str.	R 20
Grillostr.	R 21
Hachestr.	R 23
Hammer Str.	R 27
Hausackerstr.	R 30
Heidhauser Str.	S 31
Helenenstr.	R 34
Hirtsieferstr.	R 37
Hobeisenstr.	R 39
Hohenzollernstr.	R 40
Holsterhauser Str.	R 42
Hufelandstr.	R 43
Humboldtstr.	S 45
Huttropstr.	R 46
Huyssenallee	R 47
Kaulbachstr.	R 56
Klemensstr.	S 58
Laupendahler Landstr.	S 65
Leimgardtsfeld	R 66
Lührmannstr.	R 72
Martin-Luther-Str.	R 74
Mülheimer Str.	R 76
Onckenstr.	R 77
Pastoratsberg	S 80
Pferdebahnstr.	R 82
Rubensstr.	R 87
Ruhrallee	R 88
Segerothstr.	R 92
Velberter Str.	S 95
Wittekindstr.	S 103
Wuppertaler Str.	S 104
Zeunerstr.	S 108

Name	Page	Grid
Džūkste (LV)	163	F 1
Džumajlija (MK)	122	B 3
Dźwierzuty (PL)	184	B 3
Dzwola (PL)	197	D 3

E

Name	Page	Grid
Eaglescliffe (GB)	31	F 4
Earith (GB)	33	F 4
Earlston (GB)	31	E 2
Easingwold (GB)	33	E 1
Easky (IRL)	22	C 2
East Dereham (GB)	37	D 1
East Grinstead (GB)	36	B 4
East Kilbride (GB)	30	C 4
East Linton (GB)	31	E 2
Eastbourne (GB)	36	C 4
Eastleigh (GB)	35	F 3
Eaux-Bonnes (F)	54	B 3
Eauze (F)	54	C 1
Ebavere (EST)	150	C 4
Ebbw Vale / Glyn Ebwy (GB)	35	D 1
Ebeleben (D)	88	C 4
Ebeltoft (DK)	142	C 3
Eben im Pongau (A)	94	C 3
Ebenfurth (A)	95	F 2
Ebensee (A)	94	C 3
Eberbach Rhein-Neckar-Kreis(D)	45	F 2
Ebermannstadt (D)	89	D 3
Ebern (D)	88	C 2
Eberndorf (A)	114	C 2
Ebersbach Kreis Löbau-Zittau(D)	90	B 1
Ebersberg (D)	94	A 2
Eberstein (A)	95	D 4
Eberswalde (D)	85	E 2
Ebmath (D)	89	D 2
Eboli (I)	106	B 4
Ebrach (D)	88	C 3
Ebreichsdorf (A)	95	F 2
Ébreuil (F)	48	B 4
Ebstorf (D)	84	A 2
Eccleshall (GB)	32	C 3
Eceabat (TR)	19	E 2
Echallens (CH)	49	F 3
Echinádes Nisiá (GR)	216	C 1
Echínos (GR)	207	F 1
Echt (NL)	87	D 2
Echte (D)	84	A 4
Echternach (L)	44	C 1
Écija (E)	75	F 1
Ečka (SRB)	113	E 4
Eckartsberga (D)	89	D 1
Eckernförde (D)	78	C 3
Eckerö (FIN)	136	A 4
Écommoy (F)	42	B 4
Écos (F)	42	C 2
Écouché (F)	42	A 2
Écueillé (F)	47	F 3
Ed (S)	139	F 4
Eda glasbruk (S)	139	F 3
Edam (NL)	82	B 3
Edane (S)	139	F 3
Êdas (LV)	157	D 4
Ede (NL)	82	C 4
Edelény (H)	12	B 3
Édenderry / Éadan Doire (IRL)	23	D 4
Edenkoben (D)	45	E 2
Édessa (GR)	205	F 3
Edgeworthstown / Meathas Troim (IRL)	23	D 4
Edinburgh (GB)	31	D 2
Edineţ (MD)	13	D 2
Edirne (TR)	19	E 1
Edise (EST)	151	E 3
Edland (N)	138	C 3
Édole (LV)	156	C 2
Edolo (I)	97	F 2
Edoya (N)	130	C 3
Edremit (TR)	19	E 3
Edsåsdalen (S)	131	E 3
Edsbro (S)	141	D 3
Edsbyn (S)	140	C 2
Edsele (S)	132	A 3
Eeklo (B)	37	F 4
Eelde (NL)	83	D 1
Eemshaven (NL)	83	D 1
Eferding (A)	94	C 2
Efes (TR)	19	E 3
Efkarpía Kilkís(GR)	206	B 2
Efkarpía Sérres(GR)	207	D 3
Efxeinoúpoli (GR)	212	B 3
Efýra (GR)	217	D 2
Egeln (D)	84	C 4
Eger (H)	12	B 3
Egersund (N)	138	B 4
Egeskov (DK)	142	B 4
Egestorf Kreis Harburg(D)	84	A 2
Egg (A)	93	E 4
Eggenburg (A)	95	E 1
Eggenfelden (D)	94	B 2
Eggesin (D)	80	C 4
Eggum (N)	127	D 1
Eghezée (B)	39	F 2
Egiertowo (PL)	182	C 2
Egilsstaðir (IS)	126	C 1
Egkomi (CY)	231	C 3
Egkomi (CY)	231	E 3
Eglaine (LV)	166	C 4
Egläji (LV)	166	C 2
Eglesiai (LT)	163	E 3
Égletons (F)	51	E 2
Eglinton (GB)	23	D 1
Egloffstein (D)	89	D 4
Egluciems (LV)	161	E 4
Egmond aan Zee (NL)	82	B 3
Egremont (GB)	31	D 4
Egtved (DK)	142	B 4
Egüés (E)	54	A 3
Éguzon (F)	47	F 4
Ehingen Donau-Kreis(D)	93	D 2
Ehra-Lessien (D)	84	B 3
Ehrang (D)	44	C 1
Ehrenberg Kreis Fulda(D)	88	B 2
Ehrenhausen (A)	95	E 4
Ehrwald (A)	93	F 4
Eibar (E)	60	C 3
Eibenstock (D)	89	E 2
Eibiswald (A)	95	E 4
Eichstätt (D)	93	F 1
Eičiūnai (LT)	176	C 3
Eidapere (EST)	154	A 2
Eiðar (IS)	126	C 1
Eide (N)	130	B 3
Eidfjord (N)	138	C 2
Eidi (DK)	126	A 4
Eidkjosen (N)	124	B 1
Eidoméni (GR)	206	B 2
Eidsbugarden (N)	139	D 1
Eidsdal (N)	130	B 4
Eidsfoss (N)	139	E 3
Eidsvåg (N)	130	C 3
Eidsvoll (N)	139	D 2
Eigirdonys (LT)	177	D 3
Eigirdžiai (LT)	176	C 3
Eikelandsosen (N)	138	B 2
Eiken (N)	138	C 4
Eikesdalen (N)	130	C 4
Eikla (EST)	152	B 3
Eikščiai (LT)	169	F 4
Eilenburg (D)	85	D 4
Eilsleben (D)	84	B 3
Eimučiai (LT)	163	F 4
Einbeck (D)	84	A 4
Eindhoven (NL)	39	F 1
Eindhoven (NL)	39	F 1
Einorai (LT)	176	C 3
Einoraičiai (LT)	169	F 4
Einoriai (LT)	165	E 4
Einsiedeln (CH)	92	C 4
Eipri (EST)	151	E 2
Eisenach Kreis Eisenach(D)	88	C 1
Eisenberg Saale-Holzland-Kreis(D)	89	D 1
Eisenerz (A)	95	D 3
Eisenhüttenstadt (D)	85	F 3
Eisenkappel (A)	99	D 1
Eisenstadt (A)	95	F 2
Eisfeld (D)	88	C 2
Eišiškės (LT)	177	E 4
Eisleben Lutherstadt (D)	84	C 4
Eislingen (D)	93	D 2
Eitminiškės (LT)	177	F 1
Eitorf (D)	87	F 2
Eivere (EST)	149	F 4
Eivissa / Ibiza (E)	72	C 3
Ejulve (E)	65	F 4
Ejea de los Caballeros (E)	54	A 4
Ekenäs / Tammisaari (FIN)	136	F 3
Eķengrāve (LV)	165	F 3
Ekkára (GR)	211	F 3
Ekshärad (S)	140	A 3
Eksjö (S)	143	E 2
El Algar (E)	77	F 2
El Almendro (E)	74	C 1
El Alquián (E)	77	D 3
El Arahal (E)	75	E 2
El Astillero (E)	60	B 3
El Barco de Ávila (E)	63	F 4
El Bodón (E)	63	E 4
El Bonillo (E)	71	D 3

Name	Page	Grid
Duobužiai (LT)	171	E 3
Duokiškis (LT)	171	F 2
Duonelaičiai (LT)	175	C 2
Dupnica (BG)	18	C 1
Dupulčiai (LT)	162	B 4
Đurakovac (SRB)	121	F 1
Durango (E)	60	C 3
Duras (F)	50	C 3
Durban-Corbières (F)	55	F 3
Durbe (LV)	162	C 2
Durbuy (B)	39	F 3
Dúrcal (E)	76	B 3
Đurđevac (HR)	112	A 4
Đurđevića Tara (MNE)	118	B 4
Đurđevik (BIH)	117	F 2
Düren (D)	87	E 2
Durham (GB)	31	F 4
Durlach (D)	45	E 2
Đurmanec (HR)	99	F 1
Durness (GB)	27	E 1
Dürnkrut (A)	95	F 1
Dürnstein (A)	95	E 1
Durrës (AL)	121	E 4
Durrow (IRL)	25	D 2
Dursley (GB)	35	E 1
Dursupe (LV)	157	E 2
Durtal (F)	41	F 4
Duruelo (E)	64	C 2
Dušanovo (BIH)	117	F 2
Düseikiai (LT)	163	D 4
Dusetos (LT)	171	F 2
Dusina (BIH)	117	E 3
Dusmenys (LT)	177	D 3
Düsseldorf (D)	87	E 1
Duszniki (PL)	187	E 2
Duszniki-Zdrój (PL)	193	E 4
Duved (S)	131	E 3
Duži Mostar (BIH)	120	C 2
Duži Trebinje(BIH)	120	C 2
Dvariškiai (LT)	164	B 4
Dvariškiai (LT)	164	C 4
Dverberg (N)	124	A 3
Dviete (Dvīts) (LV)	166	C 4
Dvor (HR)	115	D 4
Dvorovi (BIH)	117	F 1
Dvory nad Lužnicí (CZ)	95	D 1
Dvůr Králové nad Labem (CZ)	90	C 2
Dwikozy (PL)	196	C 3
Dybowo (PL)	185	D 3
Dydnia (PL)	202	E 2
Dygowo (PL)	181	D 2
Dynów (PL)	202	E 2
Dyrnes (N)	130	C 3
Dyrráchio (GR)	217	E 4
Dysna (LT)	173	D 2
Dýstos (GR)	218	C 1
Dyviliškiai (LT)	175	F 4
Dywity (PL)	183	F 2
Džaniči (BIH)	117	E 3
Dzeguzēni (LV)	163	F 3
Dzelda (LV)	163	D 2
Dzelmes (LV)	157	D 4
Dzelmes (Lieljumprava) (LV)	165	E 2
Dzelzava (LV)	160	C 4
Dzęnagols (LV)	167	E 2
Dzērumcelmi (LV)	164	C 2
Džérvenieki (LV)	162	C 1
Dziadkowice (PL)	191	D 2
Dziadowa Kłoda (PL)	194	B 2
Działdowo (PL)	183	E 4
Działoszyce (PL)	195	D 4
Działoszyn (PL)	195	D 2
Džiaugénai (LT)	169	D 2
Dziemiany (PL)	182	B 2
Dzierzążnia (PL)	189	F 2
Dzierzgoń (PL)	183	D 3
Dzierżoniów (PL)	193	E 3
Dzilnas (LV)	164	C 1
Dzintari (LV)	164	C 2
Dzirciems (LV)	157	F 4
Dzirnavas (LV)	165	F 3
Dzirnieki Jelgavas(LV)	164	C 2
Dzirnieki Kuldīgas(LV)	163	D 2
Dziwiszów (PL)	193	D 2
Dziwnów (PL)	180	C 2
Dzjaržynsk (BY)	7	D 4
Dzūkai (LT)	175	F 3

El Bosque *(E)* 75	E 3
El Burgo *(E)* 75	F 3
El Burgo de Osma *(E)* 64	C 3
El Burgo Ranero *(E)* 59	E 4
El Cabaco *(E)* 63	E 4
El Campello *(E)* 71	F 4
El Campo de Peñaranda *(E)* 63	F 3
El Cañigral *(E)* 71	E 1
El Carpio *(E)* 76	A 1
El Carpio de Tajo *(E)* 70	A 1
El Casar *(E)* 64	C 4
El Castell de Guadalest *(E)*72	A 4
El Castillo de las Guardas *(E)*.. 75	D 1
El Centenillo *(E)* 70	B 4
El Cerro de Andévalo *(E)*.. 75	D 1
El Coronil *(E)* 75	E 2
El Cubillo *(E)* 71	E 1
El Cubo de Don Sancho *(E)* 63	E 3
El Cubo de Tierra del Vino *(E)*.. 63	F 3
El Cuervo *(E)* 75	E 3
El Ejido *(E)* 76	C 3
El Escorial *(E)* 64	B 4
El Espinar *(E)* 64	B 4
El Figaró *(E)* 67	D 3
El fondó de les Neus *(E)*.. 71	F 4
El Formigal *(E)* 54	B 3
El Grado *(E)* 54	C 4
El Grau de València *(E)*... 71	F 2
El Hoyo de Pinares *(E)* 64	A 4
El Madroño *(E)* 75	D 1
El Masnou *(E)* 67	D 3
El Molar *(E)* 64	B 4
El Molinillo *(E)* 70	A 2
El Moral *(E)* 77	D 1
El Pardo *(E)* 64	B 4
El Paular *(E)* 64	B 4
El Pedernoso *(E)* 70	C 2
El Pedroso *(E)* 75	E 1
El Perelló *(E)* 66	B 4
El Perelló *(E)* 72	A 3
El Picazo *(E)* 71	D 2
El Pinell de Brai *(E)* 66	B 4
El Pobo de Dueñas *(E)*.... 65	E 4
El Pont d'Armentera *(E)*.. 66	C 3
El Port de la Selva *(E)* 56	A 4
El Port de Llançà *(E)* 56	A 4
El Port de Sagunt *(E)* 72	A 2
El Portal *(E)* 75	E 3
El Portet de Morella *(E)*... 72	A 4
El Prat de Llobregat *(E)*... 67	D 3
El Provencio *(E)* 71	D 2
El Puente *(E)* 60	B 3
El Puente del Arzobispo *(E)*69	F 1
El Puerto de Santa María *(E)* .. 75	D 3
El Real de la Jara *(E)* 75	E 1
El Real de San Vicente *(E)*70	A 1
El Robledo *(E)* 70	A 3
El Rocío *(E)* 75	D 2
El Romeral *(E)* 70	C 2
El Rompido *(E)* 74	C 2
El Ronquillo *(E)* 75	E 1
El Royo *(E)* 65	D 2
El Rubio *(E)* 75	F 2
El Saler *(E)* 71	F 3
El Salobral *(E)* 71	D 3
El Saucejo *(E)* 75	F 2
El Tiemblo *(E)* 64	A 4
El Toboso *(E)* 70	C 2
El Vendrell *(E)* 66	C 3
El Villar de Arnedo *(E)*.... 65	E 1
El Viso *(E)* 69	F 4
El Viso del Alcor *(E)* 75	E 2
Elafochóri *(GR)*.............208	C 1
Elafonísi *(GR)* 223	D 3
Élafos *(GR)* 211	D 2
Elaía *(CY)* 230	B 3
Elaía (Cape) *(CY)* 231	E 2
Elaiochóri *(GR)* 207	E 3
Elaiochória *(GR)* 206	C 4
Elaiófyto *(GR)* 211	E 4
Elaiónas *(GR)* 212	A 4
Elassóna *(GR)* 211	F 1
Eláteia *(GR)* 212	B 4
Eláti *(GR)* 211	E 2
Elatochóri *(GR)* 206	A 4
Elatoú *(GR)* 211	F 4
Elatóvrysi *(GR)* 211	F 4
Elbasan *(AL)* 121	F 4
Elbeuf *(F)* 42	B 1
Elbigenalp *(A)* 93	E 4
Elbingerode (Harz) *(D)* 84	B 1
Elbląg *(PL)*.............183	D 2

Elbląski (Kanal) *(PL)* 183	E 2
Elburg *(NL)* 82	C 3
Elche / Elx *(E)*.............. 77	F 1
Elche de la Sierra *(E)* 71	D 4
Elda *(E)* 71	F 4
Eldena *Kreis Ludwigslust(D)*84	B 1
Elefsína *(GR)*.............218	B 2
Eleftherés *Atikí-Peireiás(GR)*.218	B 1
Eleftherés *Kavála(GR)* 207	E 3
Eleftherés *Lárisa(GR)*.....212	A 2
Eléfthero *(GR)* 205	D 4
Eleftherochóri *(GR)* 211	E 1
Eleftheroúpoli *(GR)*.......207	E 2
Eleja *(LV)* 164	B 3
Elektrėnai *(LT)* 177	D 2
Elemir *(SRB)* 113	E 4
Elena *(BG)* 19	D 1
Eleoúsa *(GR)*.............228	C 2
Elgå *(N)* 131	E 4
Elganowo *(PL)*.............182	C 3
Elgin *(GB)* 27	F 3
Elgoibar *(E)* 60	C 3
Elgol *(GB)* 26	C 4
Elhovo *(BG)* 19	E 1
Eliá *(GR)*.............223	D 2
Elie *(GB)* 31	D 1
Elimäki *(FIN)*.............137	D 3
Elizondo *(E)* 54	A 3
Elk *(PL)* 185	D 2
Elkšņi (Dzeņiši) *(LV)*.....165	F 3
Ellamaa *(EST)* 149	D 4
Ellesmere *(GB)*.............. 32	C 3
Ellesmere Port *(GB)*.......... 32	C 3
Ellingen *Kreis Weißenburg-Gunzenhausen(D)* 93	E 1
Ellinikó *(GR)*.............217	E 3
Ellinochóri *(GR)*.............208	C 1
Ellon *(GB)* 28	C 3
Ellopía *(GR)*.............218	B 1
Ellös *(S)* 142	C 1
Ellrich *(D)*.............. 84	B 4
Ellwangen *Ostalbkreis(D)*.. 93	E 1
Elmas *(I)* 108	B 4
Elmininkai I *(LT)* 171	E 2
Elmshorn *(D)* 78	C 4
Elne *(F)* 55	F 4
Elnesvågen *(N)* 130	B 3
Elóna *(GR)* 217	D 4
Elorrio *(E)* 60	C 3
Élos *Chánia(GR)*.............226	A 2
Élos *Lakonía(GR)*.............223	D 2
Eloúnta *(GR)*.............227	E 2
Éloyes *(F)*.............. 44	C 4
Elphin *(IRL)* 22	C 4
Elsdorf *Erftkreis(D)* 87	E 2
Elsendorf *Kreis Kelheim(D)*93	F 1
Elsfleth *(D)* 83	E 2
Elsterberg *(D)* 89	E 2
Elsterwerda *(D)* 85	E 4
Eltisley *(GB)* 36	B 2
Elva *(EST)* 154	C 4
Elvanfoot *(GB)*.............. 31	D 3
Elvas *(P)*.............. 69	D 3
Elvekrok *(N)*.............130	B 4
Elven *(F)* 41	D 4

Elverum *(N)* 139	F 2
Elx / Elche *(E)*.............. 77	F 1
Ely *(GB)* 33	F 4
Elzach *Kreis Emmendingen(D)*.............. 45	E 4
Elze *Kreis Hildesheim(D)* .. 84	A 4
Embid *(E)* 65	E 4
Embid de Ariza *(E)* 65	E 3
Embrun *(F)*.............. 53	E 3
Emburga *(LV)* 164	C 2
Embûte *(LV)* 162	C 2
Emden *Kreis Emden(D)* 83	D 2
Emet *(TR)*.............. 19	F 3
Emlíl *(FIN)* 159	F 3
Emlichheim *(D)*.............. 83	D 3
Emmaboda *(S)* 143	F 1
Emmanouil Pappás *(GR)*207	D 2
Emmaste *(EST)*.............152	B 2
Emmeloord *(NL)*.............. 82	C 3
Emmen *(NL)*.............. 83	D 3
Emmendingen *(D)* 45	E 4
Emmerich *(D)*.............. 82	C 4
Empa *(CY)*.............230	A 4
Empesós *(GR)* 211	E 3
Empoli *(I)*.............101	F 2
Émponas *(GR)* 228	B 2
Emporeíos *Chíos(GR)*.....220	C 1
Emporeíos *Kálymnos(GR)*221	E 4
Emporeíos *Sými(GR)* 228	B 1
Emsdetten *(D)* 83	D 4
Emskirchen *(D)* 88	C 4
Enafors *(S)* 131	E 3
Enäjärvi *(FIN)* 137	E 3

Encausse-les-Thermes *(F)* 55	D 3
Encinas de Abajo *(E)* 63	F 3
Encinasola *(E)* 69	D 4
Encinedo *(E)*.............. 59	D 4
Endriejavas *(LT)* 168	C 1
Endrinal *(E)* 63	F 1
Endzele *(LV)* 159	F 1
Enego *(I)* 98	A 2
Energ̀ētiķis *(LV)* 165	D 1
Enfesta *(E)* 58	B 3
Eng *(A)* 93	F 4
Engarés *(GR)* 219	F 4
Enge *(EST)*.............153	C 2
Engelberg *(CH)* 96	C 1
Engelhartszell *(A)*.............. 94	C 1
Engelsdorf *(D)* 87	F 2
Engelskirchen *(D)* 87	F 2
Engen *(D)*.............. 45	F 4
Enger *(D)* 83	F 4
Engerdal *(N)* 139	F 1
Enghien *(B)* 39	E 2
Engstingen *(D)* 45	F 3
Enguera *(E)* 71	F 3
Enguídanos *(E)* 71	E 2
Engure *(LV)* 157	F 4
Enkhuizen *(NL)* 82	B 3
Enköping *(S)* 140	C 3
Enna *(I)* 111	F 4
Ennepetal *(D)* 87	F 1
Ennezat *(F)* 52	A 1
Ennis / Inis *(IRL)* 24	C 2
Enniscorthy / Inis Córthaidh *(IRL)* 25	E 3

Enniskerry *(IRL)* 25	F 1
Enniskillen *(GB)* 23	D 2
Ennistimon / Inis Díomáin *(IRL)* 24	B 1
Enns *(A)* 95	D 2
Eno *(FIN)* 135	F 3
Enonkoski *(FIN)* 135	E 4
Enontekiö *(FIN)* 125	D 4
Enschede *(NL)* 83	D 4
Ensisheim *(F)* 49	F 1
Entlebuch *(CH)* 96	C 1
Entraygues-sur-Truyère *(F)*51	F 3
Entre-os-Rios *(P)* 62	C 2
Entrevaux *(F)* 53	E 4
Entrèves *(I)* 53	E 1
Entroncamento *(P)* 68	B 2
Envermeu *(F)* 38	B 4
Enviken *(S)* 140	C 2
Enzklösterle *(D)* 45	E 3
Epanomí *(GR)* 206	B 4
Epe *(NL)* 82	C 3
Épernay *(F)* 43	C 3
Épernon *(F)* 42	C 3
Épila *(E)* 65	E 3
Épinac *(F)* 48	C 3
Épinal *(F)* 44	C 4
Episkopí *(GR)* 226	B 2
Episkopí *Atikí-Peireiás(GR)*.218	B 4
Episkopí *Imathía(GR)* 205	F 3
Episkopí *Irákleio(GR)* 227	E 4
Episkopí Bay *(CY)* 230	B 4
Episkopi (Lemesos) *(CY)* 230	B 4

FIRENZE

Agnelli (V. Giovanni)	BS	4
Alberti (Pza L. B.)	BS	6
Aretina (V.)	BS	13
Chiantigiana (V.)	BS	36
Colombo (Lungarno C.)	BS	37
D'Annunzio (V. G.)	BS	41
De Amicis (Viale E.)	BS	45
Europa (Viale)	BS	49
Giannotti (Viale D.)	BS	58
Guidoni (Viale A.)	AR	67
Mariti (V. G. F.)	BR	81
Novoli (V. di)	AR	91
Panche (V. delle)	BR	100
Paoli (V.)	AS	103
Paoli (Viale Pasquale)	AS	105
Pietro Leopoldo (Pza)	BR	114
Poggio Imperiale (Viale del) .	BS	118
Pollaiuolo (V. A. del)	AS	121
Salviati (V.)	BR	144
S. Domenico (V.)	BR	147
Villamagna (V. di)	BS	196

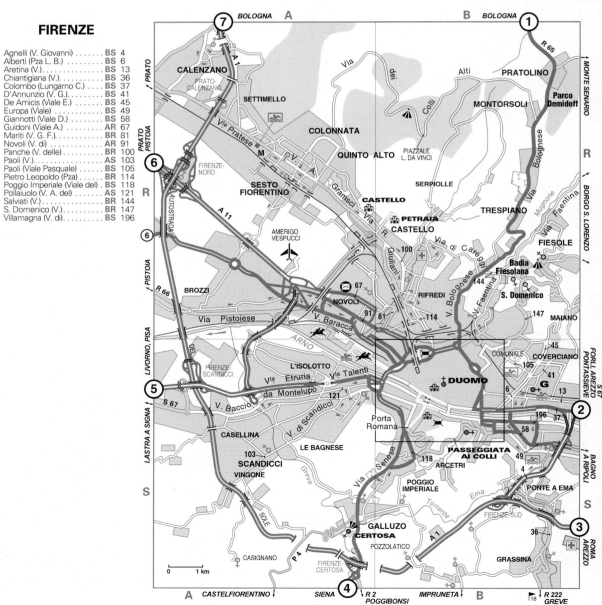

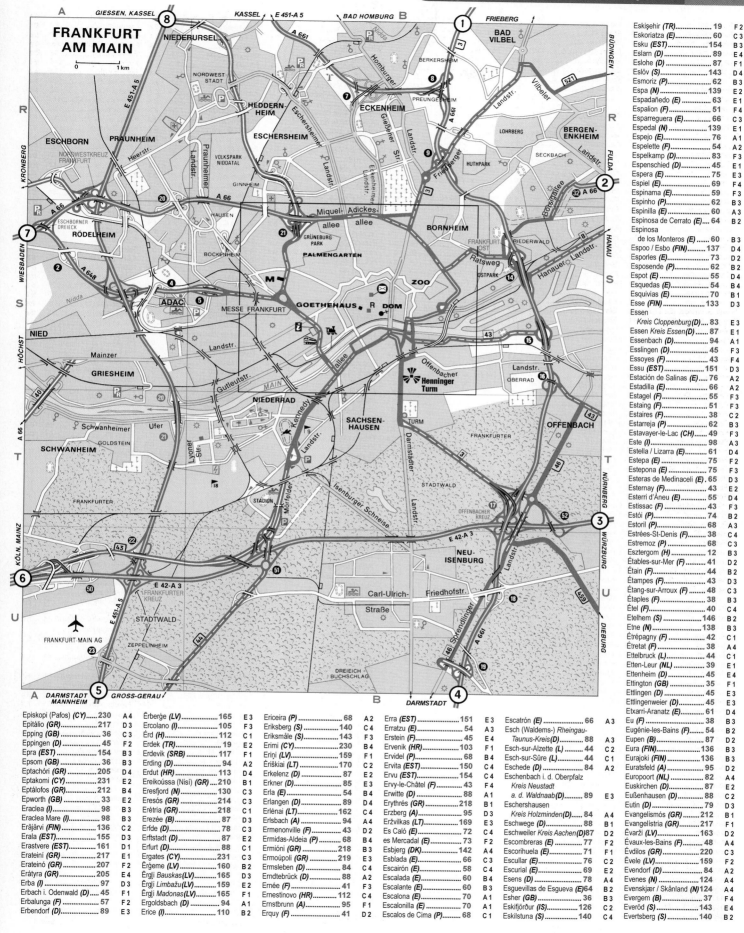

FRANKFURT AM MAIN

Eskişehir (TR) .... 19 F 2
Eskoriatza (E) .... 60 C 3
Esku (EST) .... 154 B 3
Eslarn (D) .... 89 E 4
Eslohe (D) .... 87 F 1
Eslöv (S) .... 143 D 4
Esmoriz (P) .... 62 B 3
Espa (N) .... 139 E 2
Espadañedo (E) .... 63 E 1
Espalion (F) .... 51 F 4
Esparreguera (E) .... 66 C 3
Espedal (N) .... 139 E 1
Espejo (E) .... 76 A 1
Espelette (F) .... 54 A 2
Espelkamp (D) .... 83 F 3
Espenschied (D) .... 45 E 1
Espera (E) .... 75 D 4
Espiel (E) .... 69 F 4
Espinama (E) .... 59 F 3
Espinho (P) .... 62 B 3
Espinilla (E) .... 60 A 3
Espinosa de Cerrato (E) .... 64 B 2
Espinosa
  de los Monteros (E) .... 60 A 3
Espoo / Esbo (FIN) .... 137 D 4
Esporles (E) .... 73 D 2
Esposende (P) .... 62 B 3
Espot (E) .... 55 D 4
Esquedas (E) .... 54 B 4
Esquivias (E) .... 70 B 1
Esse (FIN) .... 133 D 3
Essen
  Kreis Cloppenburg (D) .... 83 E 3
Essen Kreis Essen (D) .... 87 E 1
Essenbach (D) .... 94 A 1
Esslingen (D) .... 45 F 3
Essoyes (F) .... 43 F 4
Essu (EST) .... 151 D 3
Estación de Salinas (E) .... 76 A 2
Estadilla (E) .... 66 A 2
Estagel (F) .... 55 F 3
Estaing (F) .... 51 F 3
Estaires (F) .... 38 C 2
Estarreja (P) .... 62 B 3
Estavayer-le-Lac (CH) .... 49 F 3
Este (I) .... 98 A 3
Estella / Lizarra (E) .... 61 D 4
Estepa (E) .... 75 F 2
Estepona (E) .... 75 F 3
Esteras de Medinaceli (E) ..... 65 D 3
Esternay (F) .... 43 E 2
Esterri d'Àneu (E) .... 55 D 4
Estissac (F) .... 43 F 3
Estói (P) .... 74 B 2
Estoril (P) .... 68 A 3
Estrées-St-Denis (F) .... 38 C 4
Estremoz (P) .... 68 C 3
Esztergom (H) .... 12 B 3
Étables-sur-Mer (F) .... 41 D 2
Étain (F) .... 44 B 2
Étampes (F) .... 43 D 3
Étang-sur-Arroux (F) .... 48 C 3
Étaples (F) .... 38 B 3
Étel (F) .... 40 C 4
Etelhem (S) .... 146 B 2
Etne (N) .... 138 B 3
Étrépagny (F) .... 42 C 1
Étretat (F) .... 38 A 4
Ettelbruck (L) .... 44 C 1
Etten-Leur (NL) .... 39 E 1
Ettenheim (D) .... 45 E 4
Ettington (GB) .... 35 F 1
Ettlingen (D) .... 45 E 3
Ettlingenweier (D) .... 45 E 3
Etxarri-Aranatz (E) .... 61 D 4
Eu (F) .... 38 B 3
Eugénie-les-Bains (F) .... 54 B 2
Eupen (B) .... 87 D 2
Eura (FIN) .... 136 B 3
Eurajoki (FIN) .... 136 B 3
Euratsfeld (A) .... 95 D 2
Europoort (NL) .... 82 A 4
Euskirchen (D) .... 87 E 2
Eußenhausen (D) .... 88 C 2
Eutin (D) .... 79 D 3
Evangelismós (GR) .... 212 B 1
Evangelistria (GR) .... 217 F 1
Évarži (LV) .... 163 D 2
Évaux-les-Bains (F) .... 48 A 4
Évdilos (GR) .... 220 C 3
Évele (LV) .... 159 F 2
Evendorf (D) .... 84 A 2
Evenes (N) .... 124 A 4
Evenskjær / Skånland (N) ...... 124 A 4
Evergem (B) .... 37 F 4
Everöd (S) .... 143 E 4
Evertsberg (S) .... 140 B 2

Episkopi (Pafos) (CY) ...... 230 A 4
Epitálio (GR) .... 217 D 3
Epping (GB) .... 36 C 3
Eppingen (D) .... 45 F 2
Epra (EST) .... 154 B 3
Epsom (GB) .... 36 B 3
Eptachóri (GR) .... 205 D 4
Eptakomi (CY) .... 231 E 2
Eptálofos (GR) .... 212 B 4
Epworth (GB) .... 33 F 1
Eraclea (I) .... 98 B 3
Eraclea Mare (I) .... 98 B 3
Eräjärvi (FIN) .... 136 C 2
Erala (EST) .... 155 D 3
Erastvere (EST) .... 161 D 1
Erateiní (GR) .... 217 E 1
Erateinó (GR) .... 207 F 2
Erátyra (GR) .... 205 E 4
Erba (I) .... 97 D 3
Erbach i. Odenwald (D) ..... 45 F 1
Erbalunga (F) .... 57 F 2
Erbendorf (D) .... 89 E 3

Érberģe (LV) .... 165 E 3
Ercolano (I) .... 105 F 3
Érd (H) .... 112 C 1
Erdek (TR) .... 19 E 2
Erdevik (SRB) .... 117 F 1
Erding (D) .... 94 A 2
Erdut (HR) .... 113 D 4
Ereikoússa (Nisí) (GR) ..... 210 B 1
Eresfjord (N) .... 130 C 3
Eresós (GR) .... 214 C 3
Erétria (GR) .... 218 C 1
Erezée (B) .... 87 D 3
Erfde (D) .... 78 C 3
Erftstadt (D) .... 87 E 2
Erfurt (D) .... 88 B 1
Ergates (CY) .... 231 C 3
Érgeme (LV) .... 160 B 3
Érgļi Bauskas (LV) .... 165 D 3
Érgļi Limbažu (LV) .... 159 E 2
Érgļi Madonas (LV) .... 165 E 3
Ergoldsbach (D) .... 94 A 1
Erice (I) .... 110 B 2

Ericeira (P) .... 68 A 2
Eriksberg (S) .... 140 C 4
Eriksmåle (S) .... 143 F 3
Erimi (CY) .... 230 B 4
Eriņi (LV) .... 159 F 1
Ériškiai (LT) .... 170 C 2
Erkelenz (D) .... 87 E 2
Erkner (D) .... 85 E 3
Erla (E) .... 54 B 4
Erlangen (D) .... 89 D 4
Erlėnai (LT) .... 162 C 4
Erlsbach (A) .... 94 A 4
Ermenonville (F) .... 43 D 2
Ermidas-Aldeia (P) .... 68 B 4
Ermióni (GR) .... 218 B 3
Ermoúpoli (GR) .... 219 E 3
Ernée (F) .... 41 F 3
Ernestinovo (HR) .... 112 C 4
Ernstbrunn (A) .... 95 F 1
Erquy (F) .... 41 D 2

Erra (EST) .... 151 E 3
Erratzu (E) .... 54 A 3
Erstein (F) .... 45 E 4
Ervenik (HR) .... 103 F 1
Ervidel (P) .... 68 B 4
Ervita (EST) .... 150 C 4
Ervu (EST) .... 154 C 4
Erwitte (D) .... 88 A 1
Erythrés (GR) .... 218 B 1
Erzberg (A) .... 95 D 3
Erzvilkas (LT) .... 169 E 3
Es Caló (E) .... 72 C 4
es Mercadal (E) .... 73 F 2
Esbjerg (DK) .... 142 A 4
Esblada (E) .... 66 C 3
Escairón (E) .... 58 C 4
Escalada (E) .... 60 A 3
Escalante (E) .... 60 A 3
Escalona (E) .... 70 A 1
Escalonilla (E) .... 70 A 2
Escalos de Cima (P) .... 68 C 1

Escatrón (E) .... 66 A 3
Esch (Waldems-) Rheingau-
  Taunus-Kreis (D) .... 88 A 3
Esch-sur-Alzette (L) .... 44 C 2
Esch-sur-Sûre (L) .... 44 C 1
Eschede (D) .... 84 A 2
Eschenbach i. d. Oberpfalz
  Kreis Neustadt
  a. d. Waldnaab (D) .... 89 E 3
Eschershausen
  Kreis Holzminden (D) ..... 84 A 4
Eschwege (D) .... 88 B 1
Eschweiler Kreis Aachen (D) 87 D 2
Escombreras (E) .... 77 F 2
Escorihuela (E) .... 71 F 1
Escucha (E) .... 66 C 3
Escullar (E) .... 76 C 2
Escurial (E) .... 69 E 2
Esens (D) .... 78 A 4
Esguevillas de Esgueva (E) 64 B 2
Esher (GB) .... 36 B 3
Eskifjörður (IS) .... 126 C 2
Eskilstuna (S) .... 140 C 4

Evesham *(GB)*............ 35 E 1
Évian-les-Bains *(F)*..... 49 F 4
Evijärvi *(FIN)*........... 133 D 3
Evinochóri *(GR)*........ 217 D 1
Évisa *(F)*................. 57 F 3
Evje *(N)*................. 138 C 4
Évlalo *(GR)*............. 207 F 2
Evolène *(CH)*........... 96 B 2
Évora *(P)*................ 68 C 3
Évoramonte *(P)*........ 68 C 3
Évran *(F)*................ 41 E 3
Évrecy *(F)*............... 41 F 2
Évreux *(F)*.............. 42 C 2
Évron *(F)*................ 41 F 3
Evropós *(GR)*........... 206 B 2
Evrostina *(GR)*......... 217 D 3
Évry *(F)*................. 43 D 3
Evrychou *(CY)*......... 230 B 3
Évvoia (Nísí) *(GR)*..... 213 E 4
Évzonoi *(GR)*........... 206 B 2
Exaplátanos *(GR)*...... 205 F 2
Éxarchos *(GR)*.......... 212 B 4
Excideuil *(F)*............ 51 D 2
Exeter *(GB)*............. 35 D 3
Exmes *(F)*............... 42 F 2
Exmouth *(GB)*.......... 35 D 3
Exo Metochi *(CY)*...... 230 B 2
Exochí *Dráma(GR)*..... 207 D 1
Exochí *Ioánnina(GR)*.. 205 D 4
Exochí *Pieriá(GR)*...... 206 A 4
Exochí *Xánthi(GR)*..... 207 F 2
Exómvourgo *(GR)*...... 219 E 3
Exter *(D)*................ 83 F 4
Eydehavn *(N)*........... 139 D 4
Eye *(GB)*................ 33 F 4
Eyemouth *(GB)*......... 31 E 2
Eyguières *(F)*........... 56 C 2
Eygurande *(F)*.......... 51 F 2
Eymet *(F)*............... 50 C 3
Eymoutiers *(F)*......... 51 E 1
Ezcaray *(E)*............. 64 C 1
Eczároz/Ezkaroze *(E)*.. 54 A 3
Èze *(F)*.................. 57 F 2
Ezere *(LV)*.............. 163 D 3
Ežerėlis *(LT)*............ 175 F 1
Ezeriņi *(LV)*............ 172 C 1
Ezerkauķi *(LV)*......... 157 F 4
Ezernieki (Bukmuiža) *(LV)*167 F 4
Ezersala (Azarsola) *(LV)*.167 F 2
Ezine *(TR)*.............. 19 E 2
Ezousa *(CY)*............ 230 A 3

F

Faak *(A)*................. 99 D 1
Fabara *(E)*.............. 66 A 3
Fåberg *(N)*............. 139 E 1
Fabero *(E)*.............. 59 D 3
Fåborg *(DK)*........... 142 B 4
Fabriano *(I)*............ 102 D 4
Fábricas de Riópar *(E)*.. 71 E 4
Fabro *(I)*............... 102 A 3
Facinas *(E)*............. 75 D 4
Facture *(F)*............. 50 B 3
Faenza *(I)*.............. 102 A 1
Faeto *(I)*............... 106 B 2
Fafe *(P)*................ 62 C 2
Fǎgǎraş *(RO)*.......... 13 D 4
Fågelfors *(S)*........... 143 F 2
Fagernes *(N)*........... 124 B 3
Fagernes *(N)*........... 139 D 2
Fagersta *(S)*............ 140 C 3
Fagurhólsmýri *(IS)*..... 126 C 2
Fairford *(GB)*........... 35 F 1
Faistós *(GR)*............ 226 B 2
Fajsławice *(PL)*......... 197 E 2
Fakenham *(GB)*......... 36 C 1
Fakovići *(BIH)*.......... 118 A 3
Fakse *(DK)*............. 143 D 4
Fakse Ladeplads *(DK)*.. 143 D 4
Falaise *(F)*.............. 42 A 2
Falakró *(GR)*............ 207 D 1
Falásarna *(GR)*......... 226 A 1
Falcade *(I)*............. 98 A 3
Falces *(E)*.............. 65 E 1
Falconara Marittima *(I)*. 102 C 2
Falcone *(I)*............. 111 E 2
Falerna *(I)*............. 109 E 2
Faliráki *(GR)*........... 228 C 2
Falkenberg *(S)*......... 143 D 2
Falkenberg
  Kreis Elbe-Elster(D).. 85 E 4
Falkensee *(D)*.......... 85 D 2
Falkenstein
  Vogtlandkreis(D).... 89 E 2
Falkirk *(GB)*............ 31 E 1
Falkland *(GB)*.......... 31 D 1
Falkonéra (Nísí) *(GR)*.. 223 F 2

Falköping *(S)*.......... 143 E 1
Falków *(PL)*............ 195 F 2
Fallersleben *(D)*........ 84 B 3
Fällfors *(S)*............. 132 C 1
Fallingbostel *(D)*....... 84 A 2
Falmouth *(GB)*......... 34 B 4
Falset *(E)*............... 66 B 4
Fălticeni *(RO)*.......... 13 D 3
Faļtopi *(LV)*............ 173 D 1
Falun *(S)*............... 140 C 2
Famagusta *(CY)*........ 231 E 3
Famjin *(DK)*............ 126 A 4
Fanári Atikí-Peireiás *(GR)* 218 B 3
Fanári *Ilía(GR)*......... 217 D 3
Fanári *Karditsa(GR)*... 211 F 2
Fanári *Rodópi(GR)*..... 207 F 2
Fanefjord *(DK)*......... 144 C 4
Fanjeaux *(F)*........... 55 E 3
Fano *(I)*................ 102 B 2
Fanós *(GR)*............. 206 B 2
Fara Novarese *(I)*...... 96 A 3
Farángi Víkou *(GR)*.... 211 D 1
Fårbo *(S)*............... 143 F 2
Fareham *(GB)*.......... 35 F 3
Fårevejle *(DK)*......... 142 C 4
Färgelanda *(S)*......... 143 D 1
Färila *(S)*............... 140 C 1
Farindola *(I)*........... 103 E 3
Faringdon *(GB)*........ 35 F 1
Färjestaden *(S)*........ 143 F 2
Farkadóna *(GR)*....... 211 F 2
Farkaždin *(SRB)*....... 113 E 4
Farlete *(E)*............. 65 E 4
Farmakonísi *(GR)*...... 221 E 4
Farnborough *(GB)*..... 36 B 3
Farnese *(I)*............. 102 A 4
Farnham *(GB)*.......... 36 B 4
Faro *(P)*................ 74 B 2
Fårösund *(S)*........... 146 B 1
Farra d'Alpago *(I)*..... 98 B 2
Fársala *(GR)*........... 212 A 3
Farsø *(DK)*............. 142 B 2
Farsund *(N)*............ 142 A 1
Farum *(DK)*............ 143 D 4
Fasano *(I)*.............. 107 C 2
Fáskrúðsfjörður *(IS)*.... 126 C 2
Fastiv *(UA)*............. 13 E 1
Fastez *(RUS)*........... 7 F 4
Fátima *(P)*.............. 68 B 1
Fatmomakke *(S)*....... 131 E 1
Faucogney-et-la-Mer *(F)*. 49 E 1
Faulquemont *(F)*........ 44 C 2
Fauquembergues *(F)*.... 38 E 2
Fauske *(N)*............. 127 E 2
Fauville-en-Caux *(F)*.... 38 A 4
Fåvang *(N)*............. 139 E 1
Favara *(I)*.............. 72 A 3
Favara *(E)*............. 110 C 3
Faverges *(F)*........... 53 D 3
Faverney *(F)*........... 49 E 1
Faversham *(GB)*....... 36 C 4
Fawley *(GB)*........... 35 F 3
Fay-sur-Lignon *(F)*..... 52 B 3
Fayence *(F)*............ 57 E 2
Fayl-Billot *(F)*.......... 49 D 1
Fayón *(E)*.............. 66 A 3
Fažana *(HR)*........... 99 D 4
Fécamp *(F)*............ 38 A 4
Feces de Abaixo *(E)*.... 63 D 2
Feda *(N)*............... 138 C 4
Fehmarn (Insel)
  Kreis Ostholstein(D).. 79 E 3
Fehrbellin *(D)*.......... 85 D 2
Fehring *(A)*............. 95 E 2
Feimaņi *(LV)*........... 167 D 3
Feketić *(SRB)*.......... 113 D 4
Felanitx *(E)*............ 73 D 4
Feldafing *(D)*........... 93 D 3
Feldbach *(A)*........... 95 E 2
Feldberg *Kreis Breisgau-Hochs-*
  chwarzwald(D)..... 45 D 4
Feldberg *Kreis Mecklenburg-*
  Strelitz(D).......... 80 C 4
Feldkirch *(A)*........... 93 D 3
Feldkirchen in Kärnten *(A)* 94 C 4
Felgueiras *(P)*.......... 62 C 2
Felgueras *(E)*........... 59 E 3
Felicianova *(LV)*........ 167 F 2
Felixstowe *(GB)*........ 37 D 2
Fellabær *(IS)*........... 126 C 1
Fellbach *(D)*............ 45 F 3
Felletin *(F)*............. 51 E 1
Fellingsbro *(S)*......... 140 C 3
Felton *(GB)*............ 31 E 3
Feltre *(I)*............... 98 A 2

Fene *(E)*................ 58 B 2
Fener *(I)*................ 98 A 2
Fenestrelle *(I)*........... 53 E 2
Fénétrange *(F)*......... 45 D 3
Feolin Ferry *(GB)*....... 30 A 2
Feraklós *(GR)*.......... 228 C 2
Ferbane *(IRL)*.......... 22 C 4
Ferdinandovac *(HR)*.... 112 A 4
Ferdinandshof *(D)*...... 80 C 4
Fère-Champenoise *(F)*.. 43 F 2
Fère-en-Tardenois *(F)*.. 43 E 2
Ferentino *(I)*............ 105 D 2
Féres *(GR)*............. 208 C 2
Feria *(E)*................ 69 D 4
Feričanci *(HR)*.......... 112 B 4
Ferlach *(A)*............. 99 D 1
Fermo *(I)*............... 102 C 3
Fermoselle *(E)*......... 63 E 3
Fermoy /
  Mainistir Fhear Mai *(IRL)* 24 C 3
Fernán Caballero *(E)*... 70 A 1
Fernán Núñez *(E)*...... 76 A 1
Ferney-Voltaire *(F)*..... 49 E 4
Ferrandina *(I)*.......... 106 C 3
Ferrara *(I)*.............. 98 A 4
Ferreira *(E)*............. 58 C 2
Ferreira do Alentejo *(P)*. 68 B 4
Ferreira do Zêzere *(P)*.. 68 B 1
Ferreiras *(P)*........... 74 B 2
Ferreras de Abajo *(E)*.. 63 F 2
Ferreries *(E)*............ 73 F 2
Ferreruela de Huerva *(E)* 65 E 4
Ferrette *(F)*............ 49 F 2
Ferriere *(I)*............. 101 D 1
Ferrières-en-Gâtinais *(F)*. 43 D 4
Ferrol *(E)*.............. 58 B 2
Fertilia *(I)*............. 108 A 2
Festvåg *(N)*............ 127 E 2
Fethard / Fíodh Ard *(IRL)* 25 D 3
Fetsund *(N)*............ 139 E 3
Feucht *(D)*............. 89 D 4
Feuchtwangen *(D)*..... 93 E 1
Feurs *(F)*............... 52 B 1
Feyzin *(F)*.............. 52 C 1
Ffestiniog *(GB)*......... 32 B 3
Fiamignano *(I)*......... 102 C 4
Fiano Romano *(I)*...... 104 C 1
Fiastra *(I)*.............. 102 C 3
Ficarolo *(I)*............ 98 A 4
Fichtio *(GR)*........... 217 F 1
Fidenza *(I)*............. 97 E 4
Fieberbrunn *(A)*........ 94 B 3
Fier *(AL)*............... 18 A 2
Fiera di Primiero *(I)*.... 98 A 2
Fiesole *(I)*.............. 101 F 2
Figeac *(F)*.............. 51 E 2
Figline Valdarno *(I)*..... 101 F 2
Figueira da Foz *(P)*..... 62 B 4
Figueira
  de Castelo Rodrigo *(P)*. 63 D 3
Figueiró dos Vinhos *(P)*. 68 B 1
Figueres *(E)*............ 55 C 4
Figueruela de Arriba *(E)*. 63 E 2
Fikardou *(CY)*.......... 231 C 3
Filadélfeio *(GR)*........ 206 C 3
Filadelfia *(I)*............ 109 E 2
Filérimos *(GR)*......... 228 C 2
Filey *(GB)*.............. 33 E 1
Filia *Achaïa(GR)*........ 217 C 3
Filia *Lésvos(GR)*........ 214 C 3
Filiátes *(GR)*............ 210 C 2
Filiatrá *(GR)*............ 217 D 4
Filipów *(PL)*............ 185 D 2
Filippiáda *(GR)*......... 211 D 2
Filippoi *(GR)*........... 207 E 2
Filipstad *(S)*............ 140 C 3
Fillan *(N)*............... 130 C 2
Filótas *(GR)*............ 205 F 3
Filottrano *(I)*........... 102 C 2
Finale Emilia *(I)*........ 98 A 4
Finale Ligure *(I)*........ 100 C 2
Fiñana *(E)*.............. 76 C 2
Finchingfield *(GB)*...... 36 C 2
Finja *(S)*................ 143 E 3
Finneidfjord *(N)*........ 127 D 4
Finnentrop *(D)*......... 87 F 1
Finnsnes / Lenvik *(N)*... 124 B 3
Finow *Kreis Barnim(D)*. 85 E 3
Finowfurt *Kreis Barnim(D)*. 85 E 2
Finspång *(S)*........... 140 C 4
Finsterau *(D)*........... 94 B 2
Finsterwalde *(D)*....... 85 E 3
Finström *(FIN)*......... 136 A 4
Fintona *(GB)*........... 23 D 2
Fintown /
  Baile na Finne *(IRL)*.. 23 D 1

Fionnphort *(GB)*....... 30 A 1
Fiorenzuola d'Arda *(I)*.. 97 E 4
Firenze *(I)*.............. 101 F 2
Firenzuola *(I)*.......... 101 F 1
Firlej *(PL)*.............. 191 D 4
Firminy *(F)*............. 52 B 2
Firmo *(I)*............... 109 E 1
Fischamend Markt *(A)*.. 95 F 2
Fischbach *Kreis Nürnberger*
  Land(D)............ 89 D 4
Fischbeck *Kreis Stendal(D)*84 C 3
Fischen i. Allgäu *(D)*... 93 F 3
Fishbourne *(GB)*....... 35 F 3
Fishguard /
  Abergwaun *(GB)*.... 34 B 1
Fisini *(GR)*............. 214 B 1
Fiskárdo *(GR)*.......... 216 B 1
Fiskari *(FIN)*............ 136 C 4
Fiskebøl *(N)*............ 127 E 1
Fismes *(F)*.............. 43 E 1
Fisterra *(E)*............. 58 A 3
Fitero *(E)*............... 65 E 2
Fitjar *(N)*............... 138 B 2
Fiuggi *(I)*............... 105 D 2
Fiumicino *(I)*........... 104 C 2
Fivemiletown *(GB)*..... 23 D 2
Fivizzano *(I)*........... 101 E 1
Fjærland *(N)*........... 138 C 1
Fjällåsen *(S)*............ 128 A 2
Fjällbacka *(S)*.......... 139 E 4
Fjällnäs *(S)*............. 131 E 4
Fjärdhundra *(S)*........ 140 C 3
Fjätervålen *(S)*......... 139 F 1
Fjelie *(S)*............... 143 D 4
Fjellerup *(DK)*.......... 142 C 3
Fjerritslev *(DK)*......... 142 B 2
Flå *(N)*................. 139 D 2
Fladungen *(D)*.......... 88 C 2
Flaine *(F)*............... 49 F 4
Flakk *(N)*............... 131 D 3
Flåm *(N)*............... 138 C 1
Flamouriá *(GR)*........ 205 F 3
Flampourári *(GR)*...... 211 D 1
Flámpouro *Flórina(GR)*. 205 E 3
Flámpouro *Sérres(GR)*. 207 D 2
Flattnitz *(A)*............ 94 C 4
Flatval *(N)*............. 130 C 2
Fleetwood *(GB)*........ 32 C 1
Flekkefjord *(N)*........ 138 B 4
Flen *(S)*................ 140 C 4
Flensburg *(D)*.......... 78 C 2
Flers *(F)*................ 41 F 2
Flesberg *(N)*........... 139 D 3
Flesnes *(N)*............ 124 A 4
Fleurance *(F)*........... 55 F 2
Fleurier *(CH)*........... 96 B 1
Fleurus *(B)*............. 39 E 3
Fleury-en-Bière *(F)*..... 43 D 4
Fleury-sur-Andelle *(F)*.. 42 C 1
Fléves (Nísí) *(GR)*...... 218 C 2
Flims-Waldhaus *(CH)*... 97 D 1
Flint / Fflint *(GB)*...... 32 C 3
Flintsbach *(D)*.......... 94 A 3
Flisa *(N)*............... 139 F 2
Flix *(E)*................. 66 B 3
Flixecourt *(F)*.......... 38 C 3
Flize *(F)*................ 39 F 4
Floda *(S)*............... 140 B 2
Flogny-la-Chapelle *(F)*.. 43 F 4
Flöha *(D)*............... 89 F 1
Flomochóri *(GR)*....... 222 C 2
Flor da Rosa *(P)*....... 68 C 2
Florac *(F)*.............. 52 A 4
Florennes *(B)*.......... 39 E 3
Florensac *(F)*.......... 56 A 2
Florenville *(B)*.......... 39 F 4
Floreşti *(MD)*........... 13 D 1
Floriáda *(GR)*.......... 211 E 3
Floridia *(I)*............. 111 E 3
Floridon *(GR)*.......... 205 F 3
Flörsheim-Dalsheim *(D)*. 45 E 1
Flötningen *(S)*.......... 139 F 1
Fluðir *(IS)*.............. 126 B 2
Flüelen *(CH)*........... 96 C 1
Flühli *(CH)*............. 96 C 1
Flumet *(F)*............. 53 D 1
Fluminimaggiore *(I)*.... 108 A 4
Flums *(CH)*............ 93 D 3
Foça *(TR)*.............. 19 E 3
Foça / Srbinje *(BIH)*... 117 F 4
Foce Verde *(I)*......... 105 D 2
Fochabers *(GB)*........ 27 F 3
Fockbek *(D)*............ 78 C 3
Focşani *(RO)*........... 13 D 2
Fódele *(GR)*............ 227 D 2
Foggia *(I)*.............. 106 B 2
Föglö *(FIN)*............. 136 A 4

Fohnsdorf *(A)*.......... 95 D 4
Foiano della Chiana *(I)*. 102 A 3
Foini *(CY)*.............. 230 B 3
Foinikas *(GR)*.......... 219 E 3
Foinikoúntas *(GR)*..... 222 B 2
Foix *(F)*................ 55 E 3
Fojnica *Mostar(BIH)*... 117 F 4
Fojnica *Zenica(BIH)*.... 117 E 3
Foldereid *(N)*........... 131 E 1
Foléa *(GR)*............. 207 E 3
Folégandros *(GR)*...... 224 B 2
Folégandros (Nísí) *(GR)*. 224 B 2
Folgaria *(I)*............. 98 A 2
Folgoso de la Ribera *(E)*. 59 D 4
Foligno *(I)*.............. 102 B 3
Folkestad *(N)*.......... 130 A 4
Folkestone *(GB)*........ 37 D 4
Follafoss *(N)*........... 131 D 2
Folldal *(N)*.............. 130 C 4
Follebu *(N)*............. 139 E 1
Follina *(I)*.............. 98 B 2
Föllinge *(S)*............. 131 F 3
Follonica *(I)*............ 101 F 4
Folmava *(CZ)*.......... 89 F 4
Fombellida *(E)*.......... 64 B 2
Fondevila *(E)*........... 62 C 1
Fondi *(I)*................ 105 E 3
Fondo *(I)*............... 97 F 1
Fonfría *(E)*.............. 65 E 2
Fonn *(N)*............... 138 C 1
Fonni *(I)*................ 108 B 2
Fonollosa *(E)*........... 56 C 3
Font-Romeu-Odeillo-Via *(F)*55 E 4
Fontaine *(F)*............ 49 F 1
Fontaine-de-Vaucluse *(F)*. 56 C 1
Fontaine-Française *(F)*.. 49 D 2
Fontaine-le-Dun *(F)*.... 38 A 4
Fontainebleau *(F)*...... 43 D 2
Fontanigorda *(I)*........ 101 D 1
Fontenay-le-Comte *(F)*. 46 C 4
Fontevraud-l'Abbaye *(F)*. 47 D 2
Fontgombault *(F)*....... 47 E 3
Fontibre *(E)*............ 60 B 3
Fontiveros *(E)*.......... 64 A 3
Fontoy *(F)*............. 44 C 2
Fontvieille *(F)*.......... 56 B 2
Fonz *(E)*............... 66 A 2
Fonzaso *(I)*............ 98 A 2
Foppolo *(I)*............ 97 E 2
Forbach *(F)*............ 45 D 2
Forcall *(E)*............. 66 A 4
Forcalquier *(F)*......... 53 B 3
Forcarei *(E)*............ 58 B 3
Forchheim
  Kreis Forchheim(D).. 89 D 4
Førde *(N)*.............. 138 B 1
Førde *(N)*.............. 138 C 1
Förderstedt *(D)*........ 84 C 1
Fordingbridge *(GB)*..... 35 E 3
Fordon *(PL)*............ 188 C 2
Fordongianus *(I)*....... 108 B 3
Forenza *(I)*............. 106 C 3
Foresta di Burgos *(I)*... 108 B 2
Føresvik *(N)*............ 138 B 3
Forfar *(GB)*............. 31 D 1
Forges-les-Eaux *(F)*.... 38 B 4
Forio *(I)*................ 105 E 3
Forlì *(I)*................. 102 A 1
Forli del Sannio *(I)*..... 105 E 2
Forlimpopoli *(I)*........ 102 A 1
Formazza *(I)*............ 96 C 2
Formby Point *(GB)*..... 32 C 2
Formentor (Cap de) *(E)*. 73 E 2
Formerie *(F)*............ 38 B 4
Formia *(I)*.............. 105 E 3
Formigine *(I)*........... 101 F 1
Fornaci di Barga *(I)*.... 101 E 2
Fornells *(E)*............ 73 F 1
Forni Avoltri *(I)*........ 98 B 1
Forni di Sopra *(I)*...... 98 B 1
Forno di Zoldo *(I)*...... 98 B 1
Fornos de Algodres *(P)*. 62 C 4
Fornovo di Taro *(I)*..... 97 E 4
Forøy *(N)*.............. 127 D 3
Forres *(GB)*............ 27 F 3
Forserum *(S)*........... 143 E 2
Forshaga *(S)*........... 140 C 3
Forsnes *(N)*............ 130 C 2
Forssa *(FIN)*............ 136 C 3
Forst *Kreis Spree-Neiße(D)*85 F 3
Fort Augustus *(GB)*.... 27 E 3
Fort-Mahon-Plage *(F)*.. 38 B 3
Fort William *(GB)*...... 27 D 4
Forte dei Marmi *(I)*.... 101 E 2
Forth *(D)*............... 89 D 4

Fortrose *(GB)*.......... 27 E 3
Fortuna *(E)*............ 77 E 3
Forvik *(N)*.............. 127 D 4
Fos *(F)*................. 55 D 3
Fos-sur-Mer *(F)*........ 56 C 2
Foslandsosen *(N)*...... 131 E 1
Fosnavåg *(N)*........... 130 A 4
Fossacesia *(I)*........... 103 D 4
Fossano *(I)*............. 53 F 3
Fossanova (Abbazia di) *(I)*105 D 2
Fossbakken *(N)*......... 124 B 4
Fosses-la-Ville *(B)*...... 39 E 3
Fossombrone *(I)*....... 102 B 2
Foteiná *(GR)*........... 206 A 4
Fotolívos *(GR)*......... 207 D 2
Fouesnant *(F)*.......... 40 B 4
Foug *(F)*............... 44 B 3
Fougères *(F)*........... 41 E 3
Fougerolles *(F)*......... 49 E 1
Fouras *(F)*.............. 46 C 4
Fourchambault *(F)*..... 48 B 3
Fourfourás *(GR)*....... 226 C 2
Fourmies *(F)*........... 39 E 3
Fourná *(GR)*........... 211 F 3
Fournels *(F)*............ 52 A 3
Fournés *(GR)*........... 226 B 2
Fourní *(GR)*............ 227 E 2
Foúrnoi *Argolída(GR)*.. 218 B 3
Foúrnoi *Sámos(GR)*.... 221 D 3
Foúrnoi (Nísí) *(GR)*.... 221 D 3
Fours *(F)*............... 48 B 3
Foústani *(GR)*.......... 205 F 2
Fowey *(GB)*............ 34 B 4
Foxford *(IRL)*.......... 22 B 3
Foyers *(GB)*............ 27 E 3
Foz *(E)*................. 59 D 2
Foz do Arelho *(P)*...... 68 A 1
Foz Giraldo *(P)*........ 68 C 1
Frabosa Soprana *(I)*.... 53 F 4
Fraddon *(GB)*.......... 34 B 3
Fraga *(E)*............... 66 A 3
Fragkádes *(GR)*........ 211 D 1
Fragkísta *(GR)*......... 211 E 3
Fragkokástello *(GR)*.... 226 B 2
Frailes *(E)*.............. 76 B 2
Fraize *(F)*.............. 45 D 4
Fram *(SLO)*............ 99 F 1
Frammersbach *(D)*..... 88 B 3
Frampol *(PL)*........... 197 E 3
Francavilla al Mare *(I)*.. 103 D 4
Francavilla di Sicilia *(I)*. 111 E 2
Francavilla Fontana *(I)*. 107 C 3
Francavilla in Sinni *(I)*.. 106 C 4
Francofonte *(I)*........ 111 E 3
Francorchamps *(B)*.... 87 D 3
Frändefors *(S)*.......... 143 D 1
Franeker *(NL)*.......... 82 B 2
Frangy *(F)*............. 49 E 3
Frankenberg
  Kreis Mittweida(D).. 89 F 1
Frankenberg *Kreis*
  *Waldeck-Frankenberg(D)*88 A 1
Frankenburg *(A)*....... 94 B 2
Frankenmarkt *(A)*...... 94 B 2
Frankenstein *Kreis*
  Kaiserslautern Land(D).. 45 E 2
Frankenthal *Kreis*
  Frankenthal Pfalz(D).. 45 E 1
Frankfurt a. Main *Kreis*
  Frankfurt am Main(D).. 88 A 3
Frankfurt an der Oder
  Kreis Frankfurt Oder(D). 85 F 3
Františkovy Lázně *(CZ)*. 89 E 3
Franz Josephs-Höhe *(A)*. 94 B 4
Franzburg *(D)*.......... 79 F 3
Frascati *(I)*............. 105 D 2
Frascineto *(I)*........... 109 E 1
Fraserburgh *(GB)*...... 28 C 3
Fratel *(P)*.............. 68 C 1
Fratta Polesine *(I)*...... 98 A 4
Frauenfeld *(CH)*........ 92 C 4
Frauenkirchen *(A)*...... 95 F 2
Frauenstein
  Kreis Freiberg(D).... 89 F 1
Frechen *(D)*............ 87 E 2
Frechilla *(E)*............ 64 A 1
Freckenhorst *(D)*....... 83 E 4
Fredensborg *(DK)*...... 143 D 4
Fredericia *(DK)*......... 142 B 4
Frederikshavn *(DK)*.... 142 C 2
Frederikssund *(DK)*.... 143 D 4
Frederiksværk *(DK)*.... 143 D 4
Fredrika *(S)*............ 132 B 2
Fredrikstad *(N)*......... 139 E 4
Fredropol *(PL)*......... 202 F 2
Fregenal de la Sierra *(E)*. 69 D 4

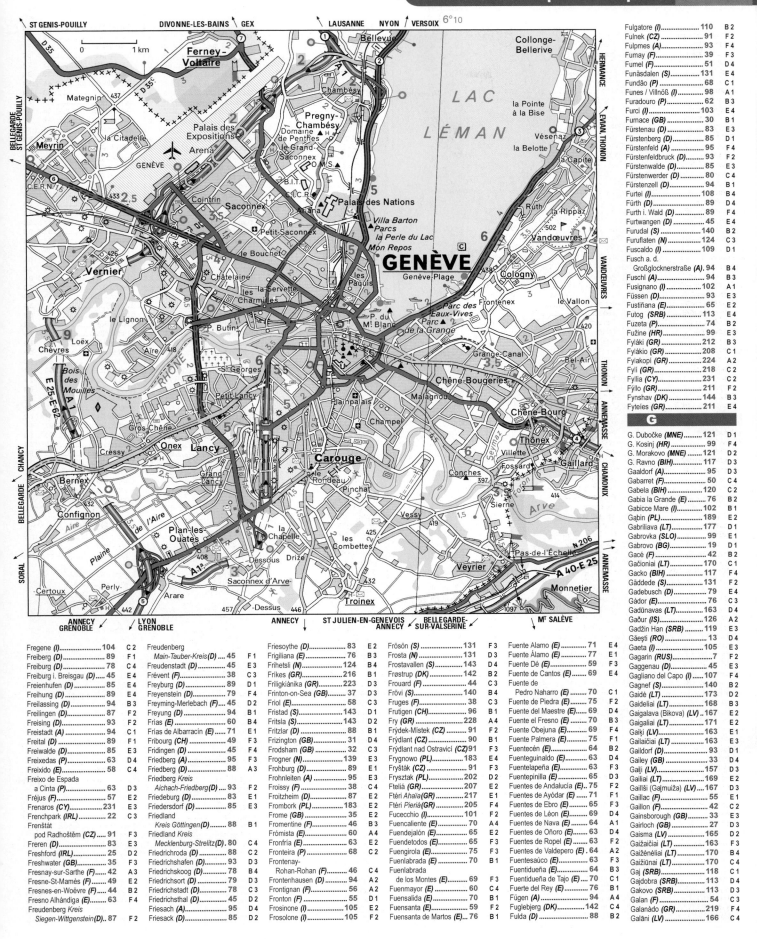

Fulgatore (I) .... 110 B 2
Fulnek (CZ) .... 91 F 2
Fulpmes (A) .... 93 F 4
Fumay (F) .... 39 F 4
Fumel (F) .... 51 D 4
Funäsdalen (S) .... 131 E 4
Fundão (P) .... 68 C 1
Funes / Villnöß (I) .... 98 A 1
Furadouro (P) .... 62 B 3
Furci (I) .... 103 E 4
Furnace (GB) .... 30 B 1
Fürstenau (D) .... 83 E 3
Fürstenberg (D) .... 85 D 1
Fürstenfeld (A) .... 95 F 4
Fürstenfeldbruck (D) .... 93 F 2
Fürstenwalde (D) .... 85 E 3
Fürstenwerder (D) .... 80 C 4
Fürstenzell (D) .... 94 B 1
Furtei (I) .... 108 B 4
Fürth (D) .... 89 D 4
Furth i. Wald (D) .... 89 F 4
Furtwangen (D) .... 45 E 4
Furudal (S) .... 140 B 2
Furuflaten (N) .... 124 C 3
Fuscaldo (I) .... 109 D 1
Fusch a. d.
    Großglocknerstraße (A). 94 B 4
Fuschl (A) .... 94 B 3
Fusignano (I) .... 102 A 1
Füssen (D) .... 93 E 3
Fustiñana (E) .... 65 E 2
Futog (SRB) .... 113 E 4
Fuzeta (P) .... 74 B 2
Fužine (HR) .... 99 E 3
Fyláki (GR) .... 212 B 3
Fylákio (GR) .... 208 C 1
Fylakopi (GR) .... 224 A 2
Fyli (GR) .... 218 C 2
Fyllia (CY) .... 231 C 2
Fýllo (GR) .... 211 F 2
Fynshav (DK) .... 144 B 3
Fyteíes (GR) .... 211 E 4

G

G. Dubočke (MNE) .... 121 D 1
G. Kosinj (HR) .... 99 F 4
G. Morakovo (MNE) .... 121 D 2
G. Ravno (BIH) .... 117 D 3
Gaaldorf (A) .... 95 D 3
Gabarret (F) .... 50 C 4
Gabela (BIH) .... 120 C 2
Gabia la Grande (E) .... 76 B 2
Gabicce Mare (I) .... 102 B 1
Gąbin (PL) .... 189 E 2
Gabriliava (LT) .... 177 D 1
Gabrovka (SLO) .... 99 E 1
Gabrovo (BG) .... 19 D 1
Gacé (F) .... 42 B 2
Gačioniai (LT) .... 170 C 1
Gacko (BIH) .... 117 D 4
Gäddede (S) .... 131 F 2
Gadebusch (D) .... 79 E 4
Gádor (E) .... 76 C 3
Gadūnavas (LT) .... 163 D 4
Gaðdur (IS) .... 126 A 2
Gadžin Han (SRB) .... 119 E 3
Găeşti (RO) .... 13 D 4
Gaeta (I) .... 105 E 3
Gagarin (RUS) .... 7 F 2
Gaggenau (D) .... 45 E 3
Gagliano del Capo (I) .... 107 F 4
Gagnef (S) .... 140 B 2
Gaidė (LT) .... 173 D 2
Gadeliai (LT) .... 168 B 3
Gaigalava (Bikova) (LV) . 167 E 2
Gaigaliai (LT) .... 171 E 2
Gaikį (LV) .... 163 E 1
Gailaičiai (LT) .... 163 E 3
Gaildorf (D) .... 93 D 1
Gailey (GB) .... 33 D 4
Gaiļi (LV) .... 157 D 3
Gailiai (LT) .... 169 E 2
Gailiši (Gaļmuiža) (LV) . 167 E 2
Gaillac (F) .... 55 E 1
Gaillon (F) .... 42 C 2
Gainsborough (GB) .... 33 E 3
Gairloch (GB) .... 27 D 3
Gaisma (LV) .... 165 D 2
Gaižaičiai (LT) .... 163 E 3
Gaiženėliai (LT) .... 170 B 4
Gaižiūnai (LT) .... 170 C 4
Gaj (SRB) .... 118 C 1
Gajdobra (SRB) .... 113 D 3
Gakovo (SRB) .... 113 D 3
Galan (F) .... 54 C 3
Galanádo (GR) .... 219 F 4
Galáni (LV) .... 166 C 4

Fregene (I) .... 104 C 2
Freiberg (D) .... 89 F 1
Freiburg (D) .... 78 C 4
Freiburg i. Breisgau (D) .. 45 E 4
Freienhufen (D) .... 85 E 4
Freihung (D) .... 89 E 4
Freilassing (D) .... 94 B 3
Freilingen (D) .... 87 F 2
Freising (D) .... 93 F 2
Freistadt (A) .... 94 C 1
Freital (D) .... 89 F 1
Freiwalde (D) .... 85 E 3
Freixedas (P) .... 63 D 4
Freixido (E) .... 58 C 4
Freixo de Espada
    a Cinta (P) .... 63 D 3
Fréjus (F) .... 57 F 2
Frenaros (CY) .... 231 E 3
Frenchpark (IRL) .... 22 C 3
Frenštát
    pod Radhoštěm (CZ) .... 91 F 3
Freren (D) .... 83 E 3
Freshford (IRL) .... 25 D 2
Freshwater (GB) .... 35 F 3
Fresnay-sur-Sarthe (F) ... 42 A 3
Fresne-St-Mamès (F) .... 49 E 4
Fresnes-en-Woëvre (F) ... 44 B 2
Fresno Alhándiga (E) .... 63 F 4
Freudenberg Kreis
    Siegen-Wittgenstein (D).. 87 F 2

Freudenberg
    Main-Tauber-Kreis (D) .... 45 F 1
Freudenstadt (D) .... 45 E 3
Frévent (F) .... 38 C 3
Freyburg (D) .... 89 D 4
Freyenstein (D) .... 79 F 4
Freyming-Merlebach (F)... 45 D 2
Freyung (D) .... 94 B 1
Frías (E) .... 60 B 4
Frías de Albarracín (E) .. 71 E 1
Fribourg (CH) .... 49 F 3
Fridingen (D) .... 45 F 4
Friedberg (A) .... 95 F 3
Friedberg (D) .... 88 A 3
Friedberg Kreis
    Aichach-Friedberg (D) .. 93 F 2
Friedeburg (D) .... 83 E 2
Friedersdorf (D) .... 85 E 3
Friedland
    Kreis Göttingen (D) .... 88 B 1
Friedland Kreis
    Mecklenburg-Strelitz (D). 80 C 4
Friedrichroda (D) .... 88 C 2
Friedrichshafen (D) .... 93 D 3
Friedrichskoog (D) .... 78 B 4
Friedrichsort (D) .... 79 D 3
Friedrichstadt (D) .... 78 C 3
Friedrichsthal (D) .... 45 D 2
Friesach (A) .... 95 D 4
Friesack (D) .... 85 D 3

Friesoythe (D) .... 83 E 2
Frigiliana (E) .... 76 B 3
Frihetsli (N) .... 124 B 4
Frikes (GR) .... 216 B 1
Friligkiánika (GR) .... 223 D 3
Frinton-on-Sea (GB)........ 37 D 3
Friol (I) .... 58 C 3
Fristad (S) .... 143 D 1
Fritsla (S) .... 143 D 2
Fritzlar (D) .... 88 B 1
Frizington (GB) .... 31 D 4
Frodsham (GB) .... 32 C 3
Frogner (N) .... 139 E 3
Frohburg (D) .... 89 E 1
Frohnleiten (A) .... 95 E 3
Froissy (F) .... 38 C 4
Froitzheim (D) .... 87 E 2
Frombork (PL) .... 183 E 2
Frome (GB) .... 35 E 2
Fromentine (F) .... 46 B 3
Frómista (E) .... 60 A 4
Fronfría (E) .... 63 E 2
Fronteira (P) .... 68 C 2
Frontenay-
    Rohan-Rohan (F)........ 46 C 4
Frontenhausen (D) .... 94 A 2
Frontignan (F) .... 56 A 2
Fronton (F) .... 55 D 1
Frosinone (I) .... 105 E 2
Frosolone (I) .... 105 F 2

Fröson (S) .... 131 F 3
Frosta (N) .... 131 D 3
Frostavallen (S) .... 143 D 4
Frøstrup (DK) .... 142 B 2
Frouard (F) .... 44 C 3
Frövi (S) .... 140 B 4
Fruges (F) .... 38 C 3
Frutigen (CH) .... 96 B 1
Fry (GR) .... 228 A 4
Frýdek-Místek (CZ) .... 91 F 2
Frýdlant (CZ) .... 90 B 1
Frýdlant nad Ostravicí (CZ)91 F 3
Frygnowo (PL) .... 183 F 3
Fryšták (CZ) .... 91 E 3
Frysztak (PL) .... 202 D 2
Fteliá (GR) .... 207 E 2
Ftéri Aḥaïa(GR) .... 217 E 1
Ftéri Pieriá(GR) .... 205 F 4
Fucecchio (I) .... 101 F 2
Fuencaliente (E) .... 70 A 4
Fuendejalón (E) .... 65 E 2
Fuendetodos (E) .... 65 F 3
Fuengirola (E) .... 75 D 2
Fuenlabrada (E) .... 70 B 1
Fuenlabrada
    de los Montes (E) .... 69 F 3
Fuenmayor (E) .... 60 C 4
Fuensalida (E) .... 70 B 1
Fuensanta (E) .... 59 F 2
Fuensanta de Martos (E)..76 B 1

Fuente Alamo (E) .... 71 E 4
Fuente Álamo (E) .... 77 E 1
Fuente Dé (E) .... 59 F 3
Fuente de Cantos (E) .... 69 E 4
Fuente de
    Pedro Naharro (E) .... 70 C 1
Fuente de Piedra (E) .... 75 F 2
Fuente del Maestre (E) .. 69 F 4
Fuente el Fresno (E) .... 70 B 3
Fuente Obejuna (E) .... 69 F 4
Fuente Palmera (E) .... 75 F 1
Fuentecén (E) .... 64 B 2
Fuenteguinaldo (E) .... 63 D 4
Fuentelapeña (E) .... 63 F 3
Fuentepinilla (E) .... 65 D 3
Fuentes de Andalucía (E).. 75 F 1
Fuentes de Ayódar (E) .. 71 F 1
Fuentes de Ebro (E) .... 65 F 3
Fuentes de León (E) .... 69 D 4
Fuentes de Nava (E) .... 64 A 1
Fuentes de Oñoro (E) .... 63 D 4
Fuentes de Ropel (E) .... 63 F 3
Fuentes de Valdepero (E) . 64 A 2
Fuentesaúco (E) .... 63 F 3
Fuentidueña (E) .... 64 B 3
Fuentidueña de Tajo (E) .. 70 C 1
Fuerte del Rey (E) .... 76 B 1
Fügen (A) .... 94 A 4
Fuglebjerg (DK) .... 142 C 4
Fulda (D) .... 88 B 2

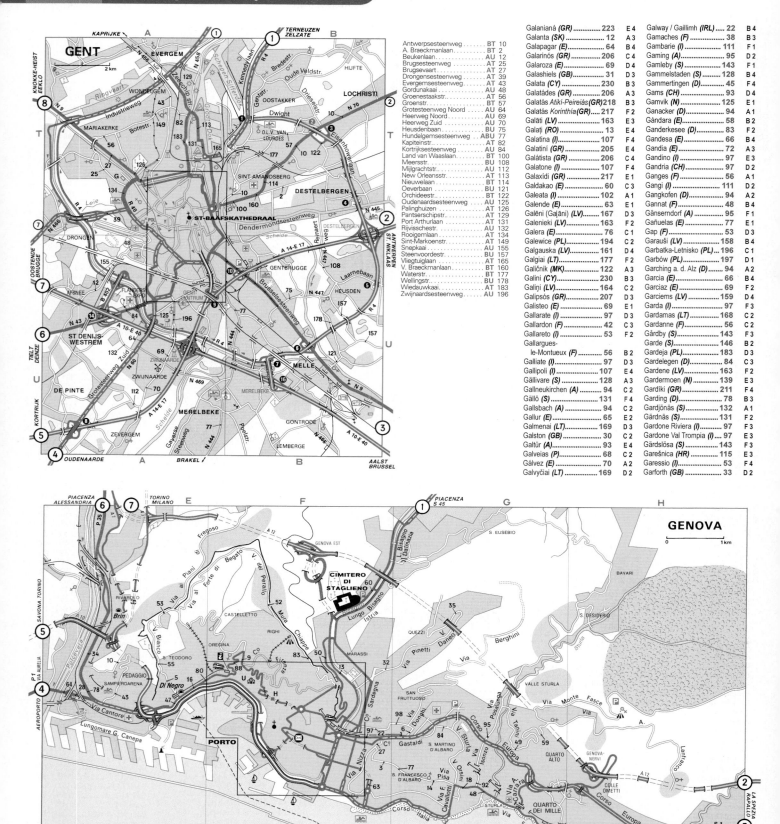

Antwerpsesteenweg	BT 10	Galanianá *(GR)*	223 E 4
A. Braeckmanlaan	BT 2	Galanta *(SK)*	12 A 3
Beukenlaan	AU 12	Galapagar *(E)*	64 B 4
Brugsesteenweg	AT 25	Galarinós *(GR)*	206 C 4
Brugsevaart	AT 27	Galaroza *(E)*	69 D 4
Drongensesteenweg	AT 39	Galashiels *(GB)*	31 D 3
Evergemsesteenweg	AT 43	Galata *(CY)*	230 B 3
Gordunakaai	AU 48	Galátades *(GR)*	206 A 3
Groenestaakstr.	AT 56	Galatás *Atikí-Peireiás* *(GR)*	218 B 3
Groenstr.	AT 57	Galatás *Korinthía* *(GR)*	217 F 2
Grotesteenweg Noord	AU 64	Galáti *(LV)*	163 E 3
Heerweg Noord	AU 69	Galáti *(RO)*	13 E 4
Heerweg Zuid	AU 70	Galatina *(I)*	107 F 4
Heusdenbaan	BU 75	Galatiní *(GR)*	205 E 4
Hundelgemsesteenweg	ABU 77	Galátista *(GR)*	206 C 4
Kapiteinstr.	AT 82	Galatone *(I)*	107 F 4
Kortrijksesteenweg	AU 84	Galaxídi *(GR)*	217 E 1
Land van Waaslaan	BT 100	Galdakao *(E)*	60 C 3
Meersstr.	BU 108	Galeata *(I)*	102 A 1
Mijlgrachtstr.	AU 112	Galende *(E)*	63 E 1
New Orleansstr.	AT 113	Galēni (Galáni) *(LV)*	167 D 3
Nieuwelaan	BT 114	Galenieki *(LV)*	163 F 2
Oeverbaan	BU 121	Galera *(E)*	76 C 1
Orchideestr.	BT 122	Galewice *(PL)*	194 C 2
Oudenaardsesteenweg	AT 125	Galgauska *(LV)*	161 F 2
Palinghuizen	AT 126	Galgiai *(LT)*	177 F 2
Pantserschipstr.	AT 129	Galičnik *(MK)*	122 A 3
Port Arthurlaan	AT 131	Galini *(CY)*	230 B 3
Rijvisschestr.	AU 132	Galiņi *(LV)*	164 C 2
Rooigemlaan	AT 134	Galipsós *(GR)*	207 D 2
Sint-Markoenstr.	AU 149	Galisteo *(E)*	69 E 1
Snepkaai	AU 155	Gallarate *(I)*	97 D 3
Steenvoordestr.	BU 157	Gallardon *(F)*	42 C 3
Vliegtuiglaan	AT 165	Gallareto *(I)*	53 F 2
V. Braeckmanlaan	BT 160	Gallargues-	
Waterstr.	BT 177	le-Montueux *(F)*	56 B 2
Wellingstr.	BU 178	Galliate *(I)*	97 D 3
Wiedauwkaai	AT 183	Gallipoli *(I)*	107 E 4
Zwijnaardsesteenweg	AU 196	Gällivare *(S)*	128 A 3
		Gallneukirchen *(A)*	94 C 2
		Gällö *(S)*	131 F 4
		Gallsbach *(A)*	94 C 2
		Gallur *(E)*	65 E 2
		Galmenai *(LT)*	169 D 3
		Galston *(GB)*	30 C 2
		Galtür *(A)*	93 E 4
		Galveias *(P)*	68 C 2
		Gálvez *(E)*	70 A 2
		Galvyčiai *(LT)*	169 D 2

Galway / Gaillimh *(IRL)*	22 B 4
Gamaches *(F)*	38 B 3
Gambarie *(I)*	111 F 1
Gaming *(A)*	95 D 2
Gamleby *(S)*	143 F 1
Gammelstaden *(S)*	128 B 4
Gammertingen *(D)*	45 D 4
Gams *(CH)*	93 D 4
Gamvik *(N)*	125 E 1
Ganacker *(D)*	94 A 1
Gándara *(E)*	58 B 2
Ganderkesee *(D)*	83 B 2
Gandesa *(E)*	66 B 4
Gandia *(E)*	72 A 3
Gandino *(I)*	97 E 3
Gandria *(CH)*	97 D 2
Ganges *(F)*	56 A 1
Gangi *(I)*	111 D 2
Gangkofen *(D)*	94 A 2
Gannat *(F)*	48 B 4
Gänserndorf *(A)*	95 F 1
Gañuelas *(E)*	77 E 1
Gap *(F)*	53 D 3
Garauši *(LV)*	158 B 4
Garbatka-Letnisko *(PL)*	196 C 1
Garbów *(PL)*	197 D 1
Garching a. d. Alz *(D)*	94 A 2
Garcia *(E)*	66 B 4
Garciaz *(E)*	69 F 2
Garciems *(LV)*	159 D 4
Garda *(I)*	97 F 3
Gardamas *(LT)*	168 C 2
Gardanne *(F)*	56 C 2
Gårdby *(S)*	143 F 3
Garde *(S)*	146 B 2
Gardeja *(PL)*	183 D 3
Gardelegen *(D)*	84 C 3
Gardene *(LV)*	163 F 2
Gardermoen *(N)*	139 E 3
Gardíki *(GR)*	211 F 4
Garding *(D)*	78 B 3
Gardjönäs *(S)*	132 A 1
Gårdnäs *(S)*	131 F 2
Gardone Riviera *(I)*	97 F 3
Gardone Val Trompia *(I)*	97 F 3
Gårdslösa *(S)*	143 F 3
Garešnica *(HR)*	115 E 3
Garessio *(I)*	53 F 4
Garforth *(GB)*	33 D 2

Albaro (V.)	F 3
Angeli (Salita degli)	E 5
Barrili (V.)	G 6
Bassi (Cso U.)	F 9
Belvedere (Cso)	E 10
Bobbio (V.)	F 13
Boselli (V.)	G 14
Buozzi (V.)	E 16
Caprera (V.)	F 18
Casoni (V.)	F 22
Dassori (V. F.)	F 27
Degola (V.)	E 28
Fereggiano (V.)	F 32
Fillak (V. W.)	E 34
Fontanarossa (V. S.)	G 35
Gianelli (V. A.)	H 41
Martinetti (Corso L. A.)	E 43
Milano (V.)	E 47
Mille (V. dei)	G 48
Monaco Simone (V.)	G 49
Montaldo (V. L.)	F 50
Mura del Castellaccio (V.)	F 52
Mura di Granorolo (V.)	E 53
Mura di Porta Murata (V. delle)	E 55
Murcarolo (V.)	H 56
Olivieri (V.)	G 59
Piacenza (V.)	F 60
Piave (V.)	F 63
Pieragostini (V. R.)	E 64
Ricci (V.)	F 77
Rolando (V. C.)	E 78
S. Benedetto (V.)	EF 80
S. Erasmo (Mura)	F 83
S. Martino (V.)	G 84
S. Ugo (V.)	F 88
Timavo (V.)	G 95
Tolemaide (V.)	F 97
Torti (V. G.)	G 98
Sturla (V.)	G 92

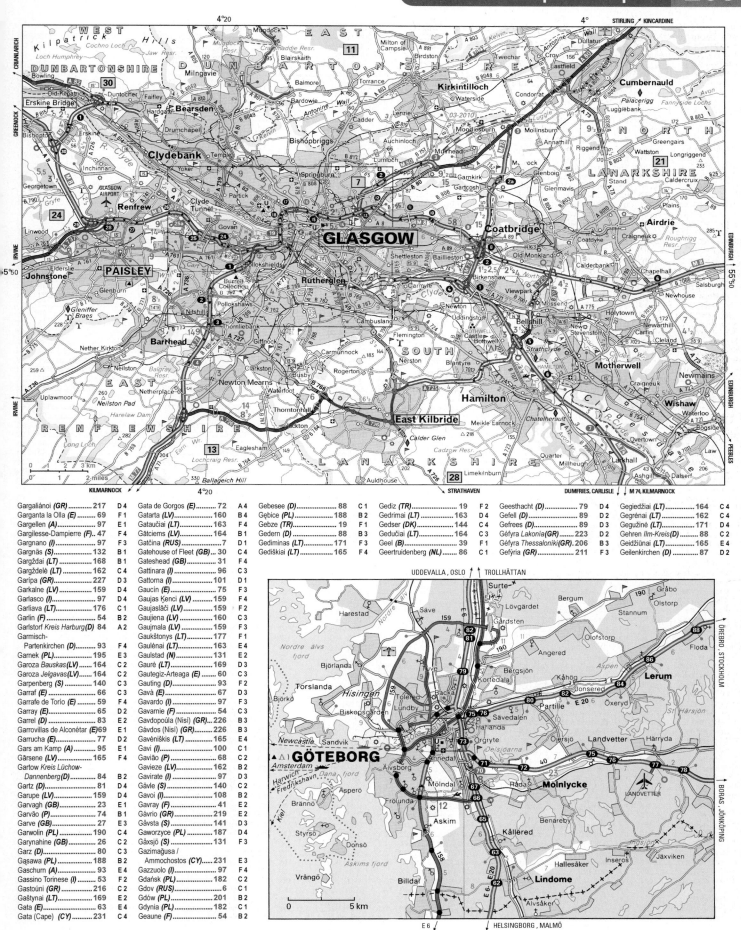

Gargaliánoi (GR) 217   D 4
Garganta la Olla (E) 69   F 1
Gargellen (A) 97   E 1
Gargilesse-Dampierre (F).. 47   F 3
Gargnano (I) 97   E 1
Gargnäs (S) 132   B 1
Gargždai (LT) 168   B 1
Gargždelė (LT) 162   C 4
Garípa (GR) 227   D 3
Garkalne (LV) 159   D 4
Garlasco (I) 97   D 4
Garliava (LT) 176   C 1
Garlin (F) 54   F 2
Garlstorf Kreis Harburg (D) 84   A 2
Garmisch-
   Partenkirchen (D) 93   F 4
Garnek (PL) 195   E 3
Garoza Bauskas (LV) 164   C 2
Garoza Jelgavas (LV) 164   C 2
Garpenberg (S) 140   C 3
Garraf (E) 66   C 3
Garrafe de Torío (E) 59   F 4
Garray (E) 65   D 2
Garrel (D) 83   E 2
Garrovillas de Alconétar (E) 69 E 1
Garrucha (E) 77   E 2
Gars am Kamp (A) 95   E 2
Gärsene (LV) 165   F 4
Gartow Kreis Lüchow-
   Dannenberg (D) 84   B 2
Gartz (D) 81   D 4
Garupe (LV) 159   E 4
Garvagh (GB) 23   E 1
Garvão (P) 74   B 1
Garve (GB) 27   E 4
Garwolin (PL) 190   C 4
Garynahine (GB) 26   E 4
Garz (D) 80   C 3
Gąsawa (PL) 188   B 2
Gaschurn (A) 93   E 4
Gassino Torinese (I) 53   F 2
Gastoúni (GR) 216   C 2
Gaštynai (LT) 169   E 4
Gata (E) 63   E 4
Gata (Cape) (CY) 231   C 4

Gata de Gorgos (E) 72   A 4
Gatarta (LV) 160   B 4
Gataučiai (LT) 163   F 4
Gâtciems (LV) 164   B 1
Gatčina (RUS) 7   D 1
Gatehouse of Fleet (GB) .. 30   C 4
Gateshead (GB) 31   F 4
Gattinara (I) 96   C 3
Gattorna (I) 101   D 1
Gaucín (E) 75   F 3
Gaujas Kenci (LV) 159   F 4
Gaujaslāči (LV) 159   F 2
Gaujiena (LV) 160   C 3
Gaujmala (LV) 159   F 3
Gaukštonys (LT) 177   F 1
Gaulénai (LT) 163   E 4
Gaulstad (N) 131   E 2
Gauré (LT) 169   D 3
Gautegiz-Arteaga (E) 60   C 3
Gauting (D) 93   F 2
Gavà (E) 67   D 3
Gavardo (I) 97   F 3
Gavarnie (F) 54   C 3
Gavdopoúla (Nisí) (GR).. 226   B 3
Gávdos (Nisí) (GR) 226   B 3
Gavėniškis (LT) 165   E 4
Gavi (I) 100   C 1
Gavião (P) 68   C 2
Gavieze (LV) 162   B 2
Gavirate (I) 97   D 3
Gävle (S) 140   C 2
Gavoi (I) 108   B 2
Gavray (F) 41   E 2
Gávrio (GR) 219   G 2
Gâvsta (S) 141   D 3
Gaworzyce (PL) 187   D 4
Gazimağusa /
   Ammochostos (CY) 231   E 3
Gazzuolo (I) 97   F 4
Gdańsk (PL) 182   C 2
Gdov (RUS) 6   C 1
Gdów (PL) 201   B 2
Gdynia (PL) 182   C 1
Geaune (F) 54   B 2

Gebesee (D) 88   C 1
Gębice (PL) 188   B 2
Gebze (TR) 19   F 1
Gedern (D) 88   B 3
Gediminas (LT) 171   E 4
Gediškiai (LT) 165   F 4

Gediz (TR) 19   F 2
Gedrimai (LT) 163   D 4
Gedser (DK) 144   C 4
Gedučiai (LT) 164   C 3
Geel (B) 39   F 1
Geertruidenberg (NL) 86   C 1
Géfyra Lakonía (GR) 223   D 2
Géfyra Thessaloníki (GR) 206 B 3
Gefýria (GR) 211   F 3

Geesthacht (D) 79   D 4
Gefell (D) 89   D 2
Gefrees (D) 89   D 3
Gehren Ilm-Kreis (D) 88   C 2
Geidžiūnai (LT) 165   E 4
Geilenkirchen (D) 87   D 2

Gegiedžiai (LT) 164   C 4
Gegrėnai (LT) 162   C 4
Gegužinė (LT) 171   D 4
Gehren Ilm-Kreis (D) 88   C 2
Geidžiūnai (LT) 165   E 4
Geilenkirchen (D) 87   D 2

Geilo (N) ... 139 D 2
Geiranger (N) ... 130 B 4
Geisa (D) ... 88 B 2
Geiselhöring (D) ... 94 A 1
Geisenfeld (D) ... 93 F 1
Geisenhausen (D) ... 94 A 2
Geising (D) ... 89 F 1
Geisingen
 Kreis Tuttlingen (D) ... 45 F 4
Geisiškės (LT) ... 177 D 2
Geislingen a. d. Steige (D) 93 D 2
Geismar Kreis Eichsfeld (D)88 B 1
Geisnes (N) ... 131 E 2
Geisteriškiai (LT) ... 175 E 2
Geithain (D) ... 89 E 1
Gela (I) ... 111 D 4
Geldern (D) ... 87 D 1
Geldrop (NL) ... 39 F 1
Geleen (NL) ... 87 D 2
Geležiai (LT) ... 171 D 4
Gelgaudiškis (LT) ... 169 E 4
Gelibolu (TR) ... 19 E 4
Gelnhausen (D) ... 88 B 3
Gelsa (E) ... 65 F 3
Gelsdorf (D) ... 87 E 2
Gelsenkirchen (D) ... 87 E 1
Gelting (D) ... 78 C 2
Gėluva (LT) ... 169 F 3
Gelvonai (LT) ... 171 D 4
Gembloux (B) ... 39 F 2
Gemeaux (F) ... 49 D 2
Gémenos (F) ... 57 D 2
Gemert (NL) ... 87 D 1
Gemlik (TR) ... 19 E 2
Gemona del Friuli (I) ... 98 C 1
Gémozac (F) ... 50 B 2
Gemünd (Eifel) (D) ... 87 E 3
Gemünden (D) ... 45 D 1
Gemünden (Wohra) (D) ... 88 A 2
Gemünden a. Main (D) ... 88 B 3
Genagra (CY) ... 230 B 2
Genaralski Stol (HR) ... 99 F 3
Gençay (F) ... 47 C 3
General-Toševo (BG) ... 13 E 4
Genève (F) ... 49 E 4
Geniai Alytus(LT) ... 176 C 3
Geniai Merkinė(LT) ... 176 C 4
Geniai Vilniaus(LT) ... 177 E 1
Geniséa (GR) ... 207 F 2
Genk (B) ... 39 F 2
Genlis (F) ... 49 D 2
Gennádio (GR) ... 228 C 3
Gennep (NL) ... 87 D 1
Gennes (F) ... 47 D 2
Génolhac (F) ... 52 B 4
Genova (I) ... 100 C 1
Gent (B) ... 37 F 4
Genthin (D) ... 84 C 3
Gentioux (F) ... 51 E 1
Genzano di Lucania (I) ... 106 D 2
Genzano di Roma (I) ... 105 D 2
Georgianoí (GR) ... 205 F 3
Georgioúpoli (GR) ... 226 B 2
Georgitsi (GR) ... 217 E 4
Georgsmarienhütte (D) ... 83 E 4
Gera (D) ... 89 E 1
Geraardsbergen (B) ... 39 E 2
Gerabronn (D) ... 93 D 1
Gerace (I) ... 111 E 3
Gerakári Kilkis(GR) ... 206 B 2
Gerakári Réthymno(GR) . 226 C 2
Gerakaroú (GR) ... 206 C 2
Gérakas (GR) ... 223 D 2
Geráki (GR) ... 217 F 4
Gerakiní (GR) ... 206 C 4
Geráni (GR) ... 226 B 2
Gérardmer (F) ... 45 D 4
Geras (A) ... 91 D 4
Gerbéviller (F) ... 44 C 3
Gerbini (I) ... 111 E 3
Gerbstedt (D) ... 84 C 4
Gerdžiūnai (LT) ... 169 F 4
Gerena (E) ... 75 E 1
Gerês (P) ... 62 C 2
Geretsried (D) ... 93 F 3
Gérgal (E) ... 76 C 2
Gergždeliai (LT) ... 163 F 4
Geri (CY) ... 231 C 3
Geringswalde (D) ... 89 E 1
Gerlos (A) ... 165 A 3
Germaniškis (LT) ... 165 D 3
Gérmas (GR) ... 205 E 3
Germasogeia (CY) ... 231 C 4
Germasogeia (CY) ... 231 C 4
Germasogeia Dam (CY). 231 C 4
Germering (D) ... 93 F 2
Germersheim (D) ... 45 E 2

Gernika-Lumo (E) ... 60 C 3
Gernrode Kreis
 Quedlinburg(D) ... 84 B 4
Gernsheim (D) ... 45 E 1
Gerokolympos (CY) ... 230 B 2
Gerola Alta (I) ... 97 E 2
Gerolakkos (CY) ... 231 C 2
Geroliménas (GR) ... 222 C 3
Gerolstein (D) ... 87 E 3
Gerolzhofen (D) ... 88 C 3
Geroplátanos (GR) ... 206 C 3
Gerovo (HR) ... 99 E 2
Gerri de la Sal (E) ... 55 D 4
Gersfeld (D) ... 88 B 2
Gerstetten (D) ... 93 D 2
Gersthofen (D) ... 93 E 2
Gerswalde (D) ... 80 C 4
Gerūčiai (LT) ... 170 C 3
Gervénai (LT) ... 176 C 3
Gerviškės (LT) ... 177 E 3
Gėsalai (LT) ... 162 C 3
Gescher (D) ... 83 D 4
Geseke (D) ... 83 F 4
Gesualdo (I) ... 106 A 3
Geta (FIN) ... 136 A 4
Getafe (E) ... 70 B 1
Getlinji (LV) ... 165 D 1
Gettorf (D) ... 78 C 3
Getxo (E) ... 60 C 3
Gevelsberg (D) ... 87 F 1
Gevgelija (MK) ... 122 C 3
Gevrey-Chambertin (F) ... 49 D 2
Gex (F) ... 49 E 4
Geyve (TR) ... 19 F 1
Göfhl (A) ... 95 E 1
Ghedi (I) ... 97 F 3
Gheorgheni (RO) ... 13 D 3
Ghilarza (I) ... 108 B 3
Ghisonaccia (F) ... 57 F 4
Ghisoni (F) ... 57 F 3
Gialia (CY) ... 230 A 3
Gialias (CY) ... 231 D 3
Giálova (GR) ... 217 D 4
Giáltra (GR) ... 212 B 4
Giannádes (GR) ... 210 B 2
Giannitsá (GR) ... 206 A 3
Giannítsi (GR) ... 219 D 1
Giannoúli (GR) ... 208 C 2
Giardini-Naxos (I) ... 111 E 2
Giarratana (I) ... 111 E 4
Giarre (I) ... 111 E 2
Giat (F) ... 51 F 1
Giaveno (I) ... 53 F 2
Giba (I) ... 108 B 4
Gibostad (N) ... 124 B 3
Gibraleón (E) ... 75 D 1
Gibraltar (GB) ... 75 F 4
Giby (PL) ... 185 E 2
Gideå (S) ... 132 B 3
Gidle (PL) ... 195 E 3
Gieboldehausen (D) ... 84 A 4
Giedraičiai Šiauliu(LT) ... 169 F 2
Giedraičiai Utenos(LT) ... 171 E 4
Giedriai (LT) ... 175 E 2
Gielczew (PL) ... 197 E 2
Gielniów (PL) ... 195 F 1
Gien (F) ... 43 D 4
Giengen a. d. Brenz (D) ... 93 D 1
Giens (F) ... 57 D 3
Giethoorn (NL) ... 82 C 3
Gietrzwałd (PL) ... 183 F 3
Gifhorn (D) ... 84 A 2
Giglio Porto (I) ... 101 F 4
Gignac (F) ... 56 A 2
Gijón (E) ... 59 E 3
Ğikşi (LV) ... 159 F 4
Gilching (D) ... 93 F 2
Gilford (GB) ... 23 E 1
Gilleleje (DK) ... 143 D 3
Gillhov (S) ... 131 F 4
Gillingham (GB) ... 35 C 2
Gillingham (GB) ... 36 C 3
Gilučiai (LT) ... 177 D 1
Gilūtos (LT) ... 173 D 3
Gilužiai (LT) ... 171 D 3
Gilvyčiai (LT) ... 163 D 4
Gilze (NL) ... 39 F 1
Gimenells (E) ... 66 A 3
Gimo (S) ... 141 D 3
Gimont (F) ... 55 D 2
Ğinarti (LV) ... 164 C 3
Ginčionys (LT) ... 176 B 3

Gineikiai (LT) ... 164 C 3
Gingst (D) ... 80 C 2
Ginosa (I) ... 107 D 3
Gintalai (LT) ... 169 D 1
Gintališkė (LT) ... 162 F 2
Ginučiai (LT) ... 172 B 3
Ginzling (A) ... 94 A 4
Gioia del Colle (I) ... 107 D 3
Gioia Tauro (I) ... 111 F 1
Giolou (CY) ... 230 E 2
Gioúra (Nisí) (GR) ... 213 E 2
Giovinazzo (I) ... 106 C 2
Ğipka (LV) ... 157 C 4
Giraitė (LT) ... 170 C 4
Girdiškė (LT) ... 169 D 2
Girėnai (LT) ... 175 E 2
Girifalco (I) ... 109 E 2
Girininkai (LT) ... 176 C 2
Girionys (LT) ... 176 C 1
Girkaliai (LT) ... 162 B 4
Girkalnis (LT) ... 169 F 3
Girne / Keryneia (CY) ... 231 C 2
Girnikai (LT) ... 169 E 1
Giromagny (F) ... 49 F 1
Girona (E) ... 67 C 2
Gironella (E) ... 66 C 2
Girsteitiškis (LT) ... 171 E 3
Girsūdai (LT) ... 165 D 4
Girvan (GB) ... 30 B 3
Gisburn (GB) ... 33 D 1
Gislaved (S) ... 143 F 3
Gisors (F) ... 42 C 1
Gissi (I) ... 106 B 1
Gistel (B) ... 37 F 4
Gittun (S) ... 127 D 1
Giugliano in Campania (I) 105 F 3
Giulianova Lido (I) ... 103 D 3
Giurgiu (RO) ... 13 E 2
Give (DK) ... 142 B 4
Givet (F) ... 39 F 3
Givors (F) ... 52 B 2
Givry (F) ... 48 C 3
Givry-en-Argonne (F) ... 44 C 1
Gižai (LT) ... 175 F 2
Gizałki (PL) ... 188 B 3
Gizéla (GR) ... 207 F 2
Giżycko (PL) ... 184 C 2
Gjendesheim (N) ... 139 D 1
Gjermundshavn (N) ... 138 D 2
Gjesvær (N) ... 125 D 1
Gjirokastër (AL) ... 18 B 2
Gjøra (N) ... 130 C 2
Gjov (DK) ... 126 A 4
Gjøvik (N) ... 139 E 2
Gkagkáles (GR) ... 227 F 2
Gkoritsá (GR) ... 217 F 4
Gkoúra (GR) ... 217 E 2
Gkreko (Cape) (CY) ... 231 D 3
Gla (GR) ... 218 B 1
Gladbeck (D) ... 87 E 1
Gladenbach (D) ... 88 A 2
Gladstad (N) ... 126 C 4
Glamis (GB) ... 31 D 1
Glamoč (BIH) ... 117 D 3
Glamsbjerg (DK) ... 142 B 4
Glan-Münchweiler (D) ... 45 D 2
Glandorf (D) ... 83 E 4
Glanshammar (S) ... 140 B 4
Glarus (CH) ... 93 D 4
Glasgow (GB) ... 30 C 2
Glastonbury (GB) ... 35 E 2
Glauchau (D) ... 89 E 1
Glava (S) ... 139 E 4
Glavatičevo (BIH) ... 117 E 4
Glavice (BIH) ... 117 D 3
Glavičice (BIH) ... 117 F 2
Glavnik (SRB) ... 119 D 4
Glâznieki (LV) ... 165 E 1
Glâžšķūnis (LV) ... 165 E 1
Gledić (SRB) ... 118 C 3
Ğķisdorf (A) ... 95 E 3
Glenamoy / Gleann na
 Muaidhe (IRL) ... 22 B 2
Glenariff or Waterfoot (GB) 23 F 1
Glenarm (GB) ... 23 F 1
Glenbeigh (IRL) ... 24 A 3
Glencolumbkille / Gleann Cholm
 Cille (IRL) ... 22 B 2
Glendalough (IRL) ... 25 E 2
Glenelg (GB) ... 27 D 3
Glenfinnan (GB) ... 27 D 4
Glengarriff /
 An Gleann Garbh (IRL).. 24 A 3
Glenluce (GB) ... 30 B 4
Glennamaddy (IRL) ... 22 C 4
Glenrothes (GB) ... 31 D 1
Glenties (IRL) ... 22 C 2

Glina (HR) ... 99 F 2
Glinojeck (PL) ... 189 F 1
Glitiškės (LT) ... 171 E 4
Golßen (D) ... 85 E 3
Gliwice (PL) ... 194 C 4
Głodowa (PL) ... 181 D 1
Gloggnitz (A) ... 95 E 2
Głogów (PL) ... 187 D 4
Głogów Małopolski (PL) .197 D 4
Głogówek (PL) ... 194 B 4
Glomfjord (N) ... 127 D 3
Glommersträsk (S) ... 132 B 1
Glossop (GB) ... 33 D 2
Gloucester (GB) ... 35 E 2
Głowaczów (PL) ... 190 B 4
Głowno (PL) ... 189 E 4
Głubczyce (PL) ... 200 C 1
Głuchołazy (PL) ... 193 F 4
Głuchów (PL) ... 189 E 4
Glücksburg (D) ... 78 C 2
Glückstadt (D) ... 78 C 4
Glūdas (LV) ... 163 D 2
Glumsø (DK) ... 142 C 4
Glušci (SRB) ... 117 F 1
Głusk (PL) ... 197 D 2
Głuszyca (PL) ... 193 E 3
Glyfá (GR) ... 212 B 3
Glyfáda Atiki-Peireiás(GR)218 C 2
Glyfáda Fokída(GR) ... 217 E 1
Glyki (GR) ... 210 D 2
Glykóvrysi (GR) ... 223 D 2
Gmünd (A) ... 94 C 4
Gmünd (A) ... 95 D 1
Gmund (D) ... 94 A 3
Gmunden (A) ... 94 C 2
Gnarp (S) ... 141 D 1
Gnesta (S) ... 141 D 4
Gniew (PL) ... 183 D 3
Gniewczyna
 Łańcucka (PL) ... 202 B 1
Gniewkowo (PL) ... 188 C 1
Gniewoszów (PL) ... 196 C 1
Gniezno (PL) ... 188 B 2
Gnjilane (SRB) ... 122 A 1
Gnoien (D) ... 79 F 3
Gnojno (PL) ... 196 B 3
Gnosjö (S) ... 143 E 2
Gobas (LV) ... 157 F 4
Goce Delčev (BG) ... 19 D 3
Goch (D) ... 87 D 1
Goczałkowice-Zdrój (PL). 200 F 2
Goczałkowickie
 (Jezioro) (PL) ... 200 F 2
Godalming (GB) ... 36 B 4
Godby (FIN) ... 136 A 4
Godelheim (D) ... 84 A 4
Goderville (F) ... 38 A 4
Godkowo (PL) ... 183 F 2
Godmanchester (GB) ... 33 F 4
Gödöllő (H) ... 12 B 3
Godovič (SLO) ... 99 D 2
Godów (PL) ... 200 E 2
Godzieszów Wielkie (PL)..188 C 4
Godziszewo (PL) ... 182 C 2
Goes (NL) ... 39 E 1
Göggingen
 Kreis Augsburg Stadt(D) 93 E 2
Gogolin (PL) ... 194 B 4
Göhren Kreis Rügen(D).. 80 C 2
Goirle (NL) ... 39 F 1
Góis (P) ... 62 C 4
Goito (I) ... 97 F 3
Gójsk (PL) ... 189 D 1
Gökçanica (SRB) ... 118 C 3
Gol (N) ... 139 D 2
Gola (HR) ... 112 A 3
Gołąb (PL) ... 196 C 1
Gołańcz (PL) ... 187 F 1
Golčův Jeníkov (CZ) ... 90 C 3
Gołcza (PL) ... 195 E 4
Golczewo (PL) ... 180 C 3
Gołdap (PL) ... 185 D 2
Goldbach Kreis
 Aschaffenburg(D) ... 45 F 1
Goldberg Kreis Parchim(D)79 D 4
Goldenstedt (D) ... 83 E 2
Golegã (P) ... 68 B 2
Golemo Selo (SRB) ... 119 E 4
Goleniów (PL) ... 180 C 2
Golešów (PL) ... 200 E 2
Golfe-Juan (F) ... 57 E 2
Golfo Aranci (I) ... 108 C 1
Goli (Otok) (HR) ... 99 E 4
Golina Wielkopolskie (PL) 188 B 2
Gološeva (Aizgârša) (LV) .167 C 2
Golling (A) ... 94 B 2
Golnik (SLO) ... 99 D 1

Golpejas (E) ... 63 F 3
Golspie (GB) ... 27 F 2
Golßen (D) ... 85 E 3
Golub-Dobrzyń (PL) ... 189 D 1
Golubac (SRB) ... 119 E 2
Golubinje (SRB) ... 119 E 1
Golubovci (MNE) ... 121 D 4
Golubovec (HR) ... 99 F 1
Gołuchów (PL) ... 188 B 4
Gołymin-Ośrodek (PL) ... 190 B 1
Golzow Kreis Potsdam-
 Mittelmark(D) ... 85 D 3
Gómara (E) ... 65 D 3
Gomáti (GR) ... 207 D 2
Gombrèn (E) ... 55 E 4
Gomecello (E) ... 63 F 3
Gómfoi (GR) ... 211 D 2
Gommern (D) ... 84 C 3
Gomunice (PL) ... 195 E 2
Goncelin (F) ... 53 D 2
Gondomar (E) ... 58 A 4
Gondomar (P) ... 62 D 2
Gondrecourt-le-Château (F)44 C 2
Gönen (TR) ... 19 E 2
Goniá (GR) ... 226 A 1
Goniądz (PL) ... 185 D 4
Goniés (GR) ... 226 C 2
Gonnesa (I) ... 108 A 4
Gónnoi (GR) ... 212 D 1
Gonnosfanadiga (I) ... 108 B 4
Goole (GB) ... 33 E 2
Goor (NL) ... 83 D 1
Goppenstein (CH) ... 96 C 2
Göppingen (D) ... 93 D 2
Gór Stołowych
 (Park Narodowy) (PL)..187 D 1
Gor. Tlamino (SRB) ... 122 C 2
Gor. Vratno (HR) ... 99 F 1
Gora (PL) ... 189 F 2
Góra Dolnośląskie (PL) ... 187 E 4
Góra Mazowieckie (PL) ... 189 E 2
Góra Kalwaria (PL) ... 190 B 3
Góra Świętej
 Małgorzaty (PL) ... 189 D 3
Gorainiai (LT) ... 168 C 3
Goraj (PL) ... 197 E 2
Górale (PL) ... 183 D 4
Goražde (BIH) ... 117 F 3
Gorczański Park
 Narodowy (PL) ... 201 B 3
Gördalen (S) ... 139 F 1
Gordes (F) ... 56 C 1
Gorenja Vas (SLO) ... 99 D 1
Gorey / Guaire (IRL) ... 25 E 2
Gorgonzola (I) ... 97 E 2
Gorgopótamos (GR) ... 205 D 2
Gorica (BIH) ... 117 D 4
Gorica (MK) ... 122 C 3
Goričan (HR) ... 112 A 3
Gorinchem (NL) ... 82 B 4
Gorizia (I) ... 98 C 2
Gorlice (PL) ... 201 C 3
Görlitz (D) ... 85 D 1
Gorna Orjahovica (BG) ... 19 D 3
Gorni Kokoti (MNE) ... 121 E 2
Gornica (LV) ... 167 E 3
Gornja Grabovica (BIH)...117 E 3
Gornja Kamenica (SRB).. 119 E 3
Gornja Klina (SRB) ... 119 D 4
Gornja Ljubovida (SRB) .. 118 A 2
Gornja Ploča (HR) ... 99 F 4
Gornja Radgona (SLO) ... 95 F 4
Gornja Sabanta (SRB) ... 118 C 3
Gornja Slatina (BIH) ... 117 E 1
Gornja Toponica (SRB) ... 119 E 3
Gornja Tuzla (BIH) ... 117 C 1
Gornje Jelenje (HR) ... 99 E 3
Gornje Ratkovo (BIH) ... 117 C 2
Gornje Selo (MNE) ... 103 E 3
Gornji Grad (SLO) ... 99 E 1
Gornji Kneginec (HR) ... 99 F 1
Gornji Lapac (HR) ... 116 B 2
Gornji Milanovac (SRB).. 118 C 2
Gornji Petrovci (SLO) ... 95 F 4
Gornji Podgradci (BIH) ...115 B 2
Gornji Rajić (HR) ... 115 B 2
Gornji Vakuf (BIH) ... 117 D 4
Górno (PL) ... 196 B 3
Gorno Orizari (MK) ... 122 B 3
Goro (I) ... 98 B 4
Górowo Iławeckie (PL) ... 183 F 2
Gorredijk (NL) ... 82 C 1
Gorron (F) ... 42 B 3
Gorsleston-on-Sea (GB) .. 37 D 1
Gort / An Gort (IRL) ... 24 C 3
Gorteen (GB) ... 22 B 1
Gortin (GB) ... 23 D 2

Gortmore /
 An Gort Mór (IRL) ... 22 B 4
Górtys (GR) ... 227 D 3
Goryń (PL) ... 183 D 3
Görzke (D) ... 85 D 3
Gorzków-Osada (PL) ... 197 E 2
Gorzkowice (PL) ... 195 E 2
Górzno Kujawsko-
 Pomorskie(PL) ... 183 E 4
Górzno Mazowieckie(PL) 190 C 4
Gorzów Śląski (PL) ... 194 C 2
Gorzów Wielkopolski (PL)186 C 2
Górzyca Lubuskie(PL) ... 186 B 2
Górzyca
 Zachodniopomorskie(PL)180 C 2
Gorzyce Podkarpackie(PL)196 F 2
Gorzyce Śląskie(PL) ... 200 E 2
Gosaldo (I) ... 98 A 2
Gosau (A) ... 94 C 3
Göschenen (CH) ... 96 C 1
Gościeradów
 Ukazowy (PL) ... 197 D 3
Gościno (PL) ... 181 D 2
Gosforth (GB) ... 32 B 1
Goslar (D) ... 84 B 4
Gościce (PL) ... 189 E 2
Gospić (HR) ... 99 F 4
Gospodinci (SRB) ... 113 A 4
Gosport (GB) ... 35 F 3
Gossau (CH) ... 93 D 4
Gosselies (B) ... 39 E 3
Gößnitz (D) ... 89 E 1
Gößweinstein (D) ... 89 D 3
Gostivar (MK) ... 122 A 3
Göstling (A) ... 95 D 2
Gostycyn (PL) ... 182 B 4
Gostyń Śląskie(PL) ... 200 F 2
Gostyń Wielkopolskie(PL)187 F 4
Gostynin (PL) ... 189 D 2
Goszczanów (PL) ... 188 C 4
Göteborg (S) ... 143 D 2
Götene (S) ... 143 E 1
Gotha (D) ... 88 C 1
Gothem (S) ... 146 B 2
Gotlybiškiai (LT) ... 169 E 4
Göttingen (D) ... 88 B 1
Götzis (A) ... 93 D 4
Gouarec (F) ... 40 C 3
Gouda (NL) ... 82 B 4
Gouménissa (GR) ... 206 B 2
Goumois (F) ... 49 F 2
Gourdon (F) ... 51 E 3
Gourin (F) ... 40 C 3
Gournay-en-Bray (F) ... 38 B 4
Goúrnes (GR) ... 227 D 2
Gourniá (GR) ... 227 E 3
Gourock (GB) ... 30 C 2
Gourri (CY) ... 231 C 3
Gouveia (P) ... 62 C 4
Gouviá (GR) ... 210 B 1
Gouzon (F) ... 48 A 4
Govedari (I) ... 120 B 2
Gowarczów (PL) ... 195 F 2
Gowidlino (PL) ... 182 B 2
Göynük (TR) ... 19 F 2
Gózd (PL) ... 196 C 1
Gozdnica (PL) ... 192 C 1
Gozdowo (PL) ... 189 E 2
Gozzano (I) ... 96 C 3
Graal-Müritz (D) ... 79 F 3
Graben-Neudorf (D) ... 45 E 2
Grabenstätt (D) ... 94 A 3
Grabica (PL) ... 195 E 1
Grabiny-Zameczek (PL)..182 C 2
Grabovac (HR) ... 117 D 4
Grabovci (SRB) ... 118 B 3
Grabów (PL) ... 189 D 3
Grabow
 Kreis Ludwigslust(D)... 84 C 1
Grabów nad Pilicą (PL) ...190 B 4
Grabów nad Prosna (PL) 194 C 1
Grabowiec Lubelskie(PL) 197 E 2
Grabupiai (LT) ... 168 B 3
Gračac (HR) ... 99 F 4
Gračanica (BIH) ... 117 E 2
Gračanica Priština(SRB).122 A 1
Gračanica Valjevo(SRB)..118 A 2
Graçay (F) ... 47 F 2
Grächen (CH) ... 96 C 2
Gradac (HR) ... 120 B 2
Gradac (MNE) ... 118 A 4
Gradac (SRB) ... 118 C 3
Gradačac (BIH) ... 117 E 1
Gradara (I) ... 102 B 1
Gradec (HR) ... 112 A 4

Gradefes (E) 59 F4
Gradina (HR) 112 B4
Gradina (SRB) 119 F3
Gradisca d'Isonzo (I) 98 C2
Gradište (HR) 115 F3
Gradište (MK) 122 B2
Grado (E) 59 E2
Grado (I) 98 C2
Gradsko (MK) 122 B3
Gradskovo (SRB) 119 E2
Gräfelfing (D) 93 F2
Grafenau Kreis
  Freyung-Grafenau(D) 94 B1
Gräfenberg
  Kreis Forchheim(D) 89 D4
Gräfenhainichen (D) 85 D4
Grafenwöhr (D) 89 E3
Grafing (D) 94 A2
Gragnano (I) 105 F4
Grahovo (MNE) 121 D2
Grahovo (SLO) 99 D1
Graiguenamanagh / Graig na
  Manach (IRL) 25 E3
Grain (GB) 36 C3
Grainau (D) 93 F4
Grajewo (PL) 185 D3
Grajvoron (RUS) 7 F4
Gram (DK) 142 B4
Gramat (F) 51 E3
Grametten (A) 90 C4
Grammatikó (GR) 211 E4
Grammatikoú (GR) 211 E4
Gramméni (GR) 207 D2
Gramméno (GR) 211 E2
Grammichele (I) 111 D3
Gramzda (LV) 162 C3
Gramzow
  Kreis Uckermark(D) 81 D4
Gran (N) 139 E2
Granada (E) 76 E2
Gránard / Granard (IRL) 23 D3
Grancey-le-Château (F) 49 D1
Grand-Champ (F) 41 D4
Grand-Couronne (F) 42 B1
Grand-Fougeray (F) 41 E4
Grandas de Salime (E) 59 D3
Grandcamp-Maisy (F) 41 F1
Grândola (P) 68 A4
Grandpré (F) 44 A2
Grandrieu (F) 52 A3
Grandvilliers (F) 38 C4
Grañén (E) 66 A2
Grängärde (S) 140 B3
Grange-over-Sands (GB) .. 32 C1
Grangemouth (GB) 31 D2
Granges-sur-Vologne (F) ... 45 D4
Grängesberg (S) 140 B3
Granítis (GR) 207 D1
Granítsa (GR) 211 E3
Granja (P) 68 C4
Granja
  de Torrehermosa (E) 69 F4
Gränna (S) 143 E1
Granollers (E) 67 D3
Granön (S) 132 B2
Granowo (PL) 187 D3
Gransee (D) 85 D2
Grantham (GB) 33 E3
Grantown-on-Spey (GB) 27 E2
Granville (F) 41 E2
Granvin (N) 138 C2
Grasleben (D) 84 B3
Grasmere (GB) 31 D4
Grassano (I) 106 C3
Grasse (F) 57 E2
Gråsten (DK) 144 B3
Gråstorp (S) 143 D1
Gratangen (N) 124 C2
Gratiní (GR) 208 B2
Gratkorn (A) 95 E4
Grau de Castelló (E) 72 C4
Graulhet (F) 55 E2
Grauminė (LT) 168 B1
Graus (E) 54 C4
Grávalos (E) 65 E2
Gravas (LV) 159 D3
Gravdal (N) 127 D1
Grave (NL) 82 C4
Gravedona (I) 97 D2
Gravelines (F) 37 E1
Gravellona Toce (I) 96 C3
Gräveri (LV) 167 E3
Gravesend (GB) 36 C3
Graviá (GR) 212 A4
Gravina in Puglia (I) 106 C3
Gravouna (GR) 207 F2
Gray (F) 49 D2

Grays Thurrock (GB) 36 C3
Graz (A) 95 E4
Grazalema (E) 75 F3
Grążawy (PL) 183 E3
Gražiškiai (LT) 175 E3
Gražučiai (LT) 176 C2
Grazzanise (I) 105 F3
Grčak (SRB) 118 C3
Grdelica (SRB) 119 E4
Great Driffield (GB) 33 E1
Great Dunmow (GB) 36 C3
Great Malvern (GB) 35 E1
Great Torrington (GB) 34 C3
Great Yarmouth (GB) 37 D1
Grebbestad (S) 139 E4
Grębków (PL) 190 B3
Grebnik (SRB) 121 F1
Grębów (PL) 196 C3
Greccio (I) 102 B4
Greding (D) 93 F1
Greenhead (GB) 31 E4
Greenlaw (GB) 31 E2
Greenock (GB) 30 C2
Greenodd (GB) 32 C1
Greggio (I) 96 C3
Greifenburg (A) 98 C1
Greiffenberg (D) 85 E2
Greifswald (D) 80 C3
Greikonys (LT) 176 C2
Grein (A) 95 D2
Greiškāni (LV) 167 E2
Greiveri (LV) 159 F4
Greiz (D) 89 E2
Grenå (DK) 142 C3
Grenade (F) 55 D2
Grenade-sur-l'Adour (F) 54 B2
Grenchen (CH) 49 F2
Grenči (LV) 163 E1
Grenctāle (LV) 165 D3
Grenoble (F) 53 D2
Gréoux-les-Bains (F) 57 D2
Gresse-en-Vercors (F) 52 C3
Gressoney-la Trinité (I) 53 F1
Gressoney-St Jean (I) 53 E1
Gresten (A) 95 D2
Grésy-sur-Isère (F) 53 D1
Greußen (D) 88 C1
Greve in Chianti (I) 101 F2
Greve Strand (DK) 143 A3
Greven (D) 83 E4
Grevená (GR) 205 E4
Grevenbroich (D) 87 D3
Grevenbrück (D) 87 F1
Grevenítio (GR) 211 D1
Grevenmacher (L) 44 C4
Grevesmühlen (D) 79 E4
Greviškiai (LT) 171 F1
Greyabbey (GB) 23 F2
Greystones /
  Na Clocha Liatha (IRL) .. 25 F2
Grez-en-Bouère (F) 41 E4
Grezzana (I) 97 F3
Grgur (Otok) (HR) 99 E3
Gribuļi (LV) 173 E1
Gricaičiai (LT) 163 D3
Griciai (LT) 169 F3
Griebenow (D) 80 C3
Gries am Brenner (A) 93 F4
Gries im Sellrain (A) 93 F4
Grieskirchen (A) 94 C2
Grieze
  (Marijas Skola) (LV) 163 D2
Griežpelkiai I (LT) 169 E3
Griffen (A) 95 D4
Grigiškēs (LT) 177 E2
Grignan (F) 52 C4
Grigno (I) 98 A2
Grignols (F) 50 C4
Griķi (LV) 159 D4
Grimaldi (I) 109 E2
Grimaud (F) 57 E2
Grimma (D) 89 E1
Grimmen (D) 79 F3
Grimsbu (N) 131 D4
Grimsby (GB) 33 F2
Grimstad (N) 142 B1
Grimzdai (LT) 168 C2
Griniačiai (LT) 169 E4
Grindaheim (N) 139 D1
Grindavík (IS) 126 A2
Grindelwald (CH) 96 A1
Grindsted (DK) 142 B4
Grinkiškis (LT) 170 B2
Gripiškēs (LT) 176 C2
Gripsholm (S) 141 D4

Grisignano di Zocco (I) 98 A3
Griškabūdis (LT) 175 F1
Grisolles (F) 55 D2
Grisslehamn (S) 141 D3
Gritsa (GR) 206 B4
Griva (GR) 206 A4
Grizáno (GR) 211 F2
Grk (BIH) 115 F4
Grljan (SRB) 119 E2
Grnča (SRB) 117 F2
Grøa (N) 130 C3
Grobiņa (LV) 162 B2
Gröbming (A) 94 C3
Grobštai (LT) 168 B2
Grocholice (PL) 195 D2
Grocka (SRB) 118 C1
Gródek
  nad Dunajcem (PL) 201 B2
Gröditz (D) 85 E4
Gródki (PL) 197 E3
Gródków (PL) 193 F3
Grodziczno (PL) 183 E4
Grodziec
  Wielkopolskie(PL) 188 B3
Grodzisk (PL) 191 D2
Grodzisk Mazowiecki (PL) 189 F3
Grodzisk
  Wielkopolski (PL) 187 E3
Groenlo (NL) 83 D4
Groitzsch (D) 89 E1
Groix (F) 40 C4
Grójec (PL) 190 B4
Grömitz (D) 79 D3
Gromnik (PL) 201 C2
Gronau (Westfalen) (D) 83 D4
Grönenbach (D) 93 E3
Grong (N) 131 E2
Grönhögen (S) 143 F3
Gröningen (D) 84 B4
Groningen (NL) 82 D2
Gronowo (PL) 183 D2
Gronowo (PL) 183 E1
Grönskåra (S) 143 F2
Gropello Cairoli (I) 97 D4
Groscavallo (I) 53 E2
Grosio (I) 97 E2
Groß-Gerau (D) 45 E1
Groß Gerungs (A) 95 D1
Groß Schönebeck (D) 85 E2
Groß-Siegharts (A) 95 D1
Groß-Umstadt (D) 45 F1
Großbreitenbach (D) 89 D2
Großenbrode (D) 79 D3
Großenhain (D) 85 A1
Großenkneten (D) 83 E2
Großenzersdorf (A) 95 F1
Grosseto (I) 101 F4
Großhabersdorf (D) 88 C4
Großheubach (D) 45 F1
Großpetersdorf (A) 95 F3
Großraming (A) 95 D2
Großraschen (D) 85 E4
Großreken (D) 83 D4
Großröhrsdorf (D) 90 A1
Großschönau (D) 90 B1
Großweil (D) 93 F3
Großwitzeetze (D) 84 B2
Grostenquin (F) 45 D3
Grosuplje (SLO) 99 E2
Groszowice (PL) 194 B3
Grötlingbo (S) 146 B2
Grottaglie (I) 107 E3
Grottaminarda (I) 106 A3
Grottammare (I) 102 C3
Grotteria (I) 111 F1
Grövelsjön (S) 131 E4
Grovfjord (N) 124 A4
Grubišno Polje (HR) 112 A4
Gruda (HR) 121 D2
Grude (BIH) 117 D4
Grudusk (PL) 189 F1
Grudziądz (PL) 182 C4
Gruissan (F) 56 A3
Grumbliai (LT) 163 E3
Grums (S) 139 F4
Grünau im Almtal (A) 94 C3
Grünberg (D) 88 A2
Grundarfjörður (IS) 126 A2
Grundforsen (S) 139 F1
Grundlsee (A) 94 C3
Grundsund (S) 142 C1
Grundtjärn (S) 132 A3
Grunduļi (LV) 156 C3
Grundzāle (LV) 160 C3
Grünstadt (D) 45 E1
Grünwald (D) 93 F2
Gruožninkai (LT) 177 D3

Grupčin (MK) 122 A2
Grūšlaukė (LT) 162 B4
Gruta (PL) 183 D4
Grūtas (LT) 176 C4
Gruyères (CH) 49 F3
Gruž (SRB) 118 C2
Gruzdžiai (LT) 163 F4
Grūžiai (LT) 164 C3
Grybénai (LT) 172 C3
Grybów (PL) 201 C3
Grycksbo (S) 140 C3
Gryfice (PL) 180 C3
Gryfino (PL) 180 B4
Gryfów Śląski (PL) 192 C2
Gryllefjord / Torsken (N) .. 124 A3
Grythyttan (S) 140 B3
Grza (SRB) 119 D2
Grzebienisko (PL) 187 E2
Grzegorzew (PL) 188 C3
Grzmiąca
  Zachodniopomorskie(PL)181 E3
Grzybno (PL) 183 D2
Gstaad (CH) 49 F3
Gstadt (D) 94 A3
Guadahortuna (E) 76 B4
Guadalajara (E) 64 C4
Guadalaviar (E) 71 E1
Guadalcanal (E) 69 E4
Guadalupe (E) 69 F2
Guadarrama (E) 64 B4
Guadassuar (E) 71 D4
Guadiaro (E) 75 F4
Guadix (E) 76 C2
Gualdo Tadino (I) 102 B4
Guarda (P) 63 D2
Guardamar del Segura (E) 77 F1
Guardia Sanframondi (I) .. 105 F3
Guardiagrele (I) 103 D4
Guareña (E) 69 E3
Guarromán (E) 70 B4
Guastalla (I) 97 F4
Gubbio (I) 102 B4
Guben (D) 85 F3
Guberevac (SRB) 118 C3
Gubin (PL) 186 B4
Guča (SRB) 118 B3
Guča Gora (BIH) 117 E3
Gudai (LT) 168 C3
Gudakiemis (LT) 176 C4
Gudavac (BIH) 115 D4
Gudeliai Kazlų Rūda(LT).175 F2
Gudeliai Šventragis(LT)...175 F2
Gudenieki (LT) 156 C4
Gudhjem (DK) 145 E3
Gudikaimis (LT) 175 E3
Gudow (D) 79 D4
Gudvangen (N) 138 C1
Gudžiai (LT) 177 D3
Gudžioniai (LT) 170 C2
Gudžiūnai (LT) 170 B2
Guebwiller (F) 45 D4
Guémené-Penfao (F) 41 E4
Guémené-sur-Scorff (F) 40 C3
Güenes (E) 60 B3
Guer (F) 41 D4
Guérande (F) 46 A2
Guéret (F) 47 F2
Guérigny (F) 48 B2
Guéthary (F) 54 A2
Gueugnon (F) 48 C3
Güglingen (D) 45 F1
Guglionesi (I) 105 F1
Guichen (F) 41 E4
Guidonia (I) 105 D2
Guignes (F) 43 D2
Guijo de Granadilla (E) 69 E1
Guijuelo (E) 63 F2
Guildford (GB) 36 B4
Guillaumes (F) 53 E4
Guillena (E) 75 E1
Guillestre (F) 53 E3
Guillon (F) 48 C2
Guilvinec (F) 40 B4
Guimarães (P) 62 C2
Guimiliau (F) 40 B3
Guînes (F) 37 E1
Guingamp (F) 40 C3
Guipavas (F) 40 B3
Guisborough (GB) 31 E4
Guiscard (F) 39 D4
Guise (F) 39 D4
Guissona (E) 66 C2
Guist (GB) 37 D1
Guitiriz (E) 58 C2
Guîtres (F) 50 C3
Gujan-Mestras (F) 50 B3

Gulbene (LV) 161 D4
Gulbinai (LT) 169 F2
Gulbinėnai (LT) 165 D4
Gulbiši (LV) 159 F2
Gulbju Ciems (LV) 164 B1
Gullspång (S) 140 B4
Gumiel de Hizán (E) 64 B2
Gummersbach (D) 87 F2
Gundegas (LV) 159 E3
Gundelfingen
  a.d. Donau (D) 93 E2
Gundelsheim (D) 45 F2
Gunnarn (S) 132 B1
Gunnarsbyn (S) 128 B4
Gunnarskog (S) 139 F3
Gunten (CH) 96 B1
Günterode (D) 88 B1
Güntín de Pallares (E) 58 C3
Günzburg (D) 93 E2
Gunzenhausen (D) 93 E1
Guptilčiai (LT) 170 B3
Gurk (A) 95 D4
Gurrea de Gállego (E) 65 F2
Gusev (RUS) 6
Gusinje (MNE) 121 E2
Guspini (I) 108 A4
Güssing (A) 95 F3
Güssten (D) 84 C4
Güstrow (D) 79 F4
Gutcher (GB) 29 F1
Gutenstein (A) 95 E2
Gütersloh (D) 83 F4
Gützkow (D) 80 C3
Guyhirn (GB) 33 F4
Gūžas (LV) 162 B2
Guzet-Neige (F) 55 D3
Gvardejsk (RUS) 6
Gvarv (N) 139 D3
Gvozd (MNE) 121 D1
Gvozdmost (HR) 99 F2
Gwda Mała (PL) 181 F3
Gwda Wielka (PL) 181 E3
Gwizdały (PL) 190 C2
Gy (F) 49 E2
Gyali (Nisí) (GR) 225 F2
Gyáros (Nisí) (GR) 219 E3
Gymnó (GR) 218 C1
Gyöngyös (H) 12 B3
Györ (H) 112 A1
Gypsou (CY) 230 B2
Gysinge (S) 140 C3
Gýtheio (GR) 222 C2
Gyula (H) 113 F2
Gyviškiai (LT) 175 F3
Gyvoliai (LT) 163 E3

H
H. E. Đerdap (SRB) 119 E1
Haabneeme (EST) 149 E1
Häädemeeste (EST) 159 D1
Haag (A) 95 D2
Haag am Hausruck (A) 94 C2
Haag i. Oberbayern (D) 94 A2
Haage (EST) 155 D4
Haaksbergen (NL) 83 D4
Haamstede (NL) 37 E3
Haanja (EST) 161 D2
Haapajärvi (FIN) 133 E2
Haapakoski (FIN) 133 F4
Haapamäki (FIN) 133 E3
Haapamäki (FIN) 133 F3
Haapavesi (FIN) 133 E2
Haapsalu (EST) 148 B4
Haar (D) 93 F2
Haaren (D) 88 A1
Haarlem (NL) 82 B3
Habaja (EST) 149 E3
Habartice (CZ) 90 B1
Habay-la-Neuve (B) 44 B1
Habo (S) 143 E1
Habsheim (F) 45 E1
Håbu (N) 139 E4
Hachenburg (D) 87 F2
Hachmühlen (D) 84 A4
Hackås (S) 131 F3
Hadamar (D) 87 F3
Haddington (GB) 31 D2
Hadersdorf am Kamp (A) .. 95 E1
Haderslev (DK) 142 B4
Hadjač (UA) 13 F1
Hadleigh (GB) 37 D2
Hadmersleben (D) 84 C4
Hadsten (DK) 142 B3
Hadsund (DK) 142 B3
Hadžići (BIH) 117 E4
Hægebostad (N) 138 C4
Haganj (HR) 112 A4

Hagen (D) 87 F1
Hagen i. Bremischen (D) .. 83 F1
Hagenow (D) 79 E4
Hageri (EST) 149 D3
Hagetmau (F) 54 B2
Hagfors (S) 140 B3
Häggdånger (S) 132 B4
Haggenäs (S) 131 F3
Hagondange (F) 44 C2
Hagudi (EST) 149 E4
Haguenau (F) 45 E3
Hahnbach (D) 89 E4
Haiba (EST) 149 D3
Haidaku (EST) 161 D1
Haigerloch (D) 45 F4
Hailsham (GB) 36 C4
Hailuoto (FIN) 133 E1
Haimre (EST) 149 D4
Hainburg a. d. Donau (A) .. 95 F1
Hainfeld (A) 95 E2
Hainichen (D) 89 F1
Hajdúböszörmény (H) 12 C3
Hajdučica (SRB) 113 F4
Hajdúszoboszló (H) 12 B3
Hajnówka (PL) 191 F1
Hajsyn (UA) 13 E2
Hajvoron (UA) 13 E2
Hakarp (S) 143 E2
Hakkas (S) 128 B3
Häkkilä (FIN) 133 F3
Hala Sultan Tekkesi (CY) 231 D3
Halbe (D) 85 E3
Halberstadt (D) 84 B4
Halden (N) 139 E4
Haldensleben (D) 84 C3
Halesowen (GB) 35 D4
Halesworth (GB) 37 D2
Halhjem (N) 138 B2
Halifax (GB) 33 D2
Halikko (FIN) 136 C4
Halinga (EST) 153 C3
Halinów (PL) 190 B3
Haljala (EST) 150 C3
Haljava (EST) 149 E2
Hall in Tirol (A) 93 F4
Halle (B) 39 E2
Halle (D) 83 E4
Halle (D) 84 C4
Halle-Neustadt (D) 84 C4
Hällefors (S) 140 B3
Hälleforsnäs (S) 140 C4
Hallein (A) 94 B3
Hällekis (S) 143 E1
Hallenberg (D) 88 A1
Hallencourt (F) 38 C3
Hällesjö (S) 132 A4
Hällevadsholm (S) 139 E4
Halliku (EST) 155 D2
Halliste (EST) 154 B4
Hällnäs (S) 132 B2
Hallörmsstaður (IS) 126 C2
Hallsberg (S) 140 B4
Hallstadt (D) 88 C3
Hallstahammar (S) 140 C4
Hallstatt (A) 94 C3
Hallstavik (S) 141 D3
Halluin (F) 37 F4
Halmstad (S) 143 D3
Hals (DK) 142 C2
Halsa (N) 130 C3
Hälsingtuna (S) 140 C1
Halsskov (DK) 142 C4
Halstead (GB) 36 C2
Halsteren (NL) 39 E1
Halsua (FIN) 133 E3
Haltdålen (N) 131 D3
Haltern Kreis
  Recklinghausen(D) 83 D4
Halver (D) 87 F1
Ham (F) 39 D4
Hamar (N) 139 E2
Hamaröy (N) 127 E2
Hamburg (D) 79 D4
Hamdorf Kreis Rendsburg-
  Eckernsförde(D) 78 C3
Hämeenkyrö (FIN) 136 C3
Hämelerwald (D) 84 A3
Hameln (D) 83 F4
Hamersleben (D) 84 B4
Hamilton (GB) 30 C2
Hamina (FIN) 137 F3
Hamm (Westfalen) (D) 83 E4
Hammarland (FIN) 136 A4
Hammarstrand (S) 132 A3
Hammaslahti (FIN) 135 F3
Hammel (DK) 142 B3

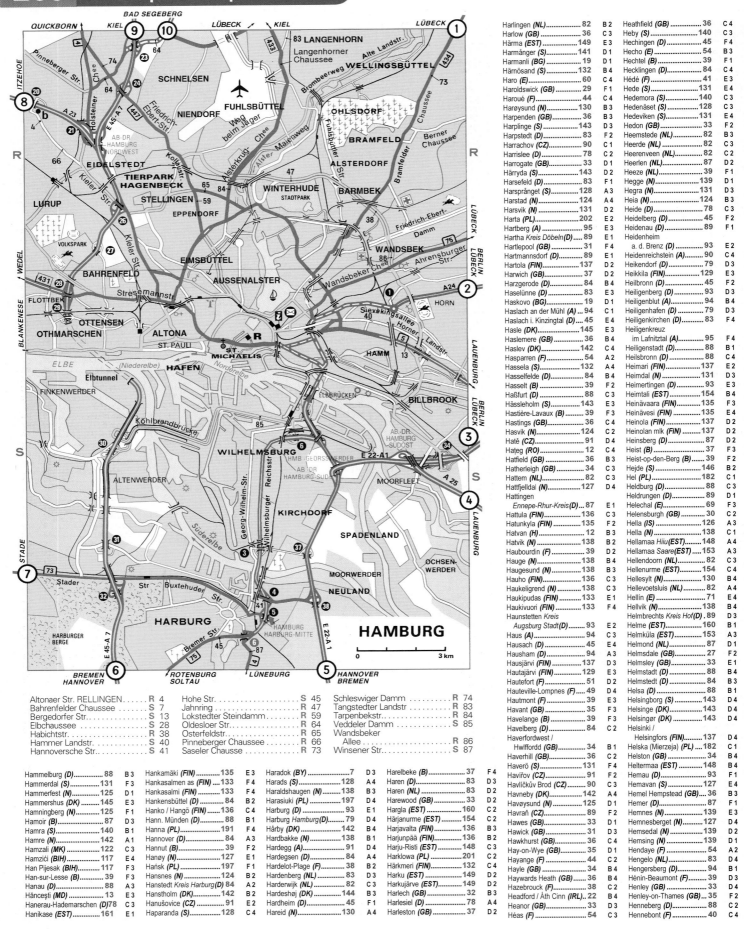

Harlingen (NL)	82	B 2	
Harlow (GB)	36	C 3	
Härma (EST)	149	E 3	
Harmånger (S)	141	D 1	
Harmanli (BG)	19	D 1	
Härnösand (S)	132	B 4	
Haro (E)	60	C 4	
Haroldswick (GB)	29	F 1	
Haroué (F)	44	C 4	
Harøysund (N)	130	B 3	
Harpenden (GB)	36	B 3	
Harplinge (S)	143	D 3	
Harpstedt (D)	83	F 2	
Harrachov (CZ)	90	C 1	
Harrislee (D)	78	C 2	
Harrogate (GB)	33	D 1	
Härryda (S)	143	D 2	
Harsefeld (D)	83	F 1	
Harsprånget (S)	128	A 3	
Harstad (N)	124	A 4	
Harsvik (N)	131	E 1	
Harta (PL)	202	E 2	
Hartberg (A)	95	E 3	
Hartha Kreis Döbeln (D)	89	F 3	
Hartlepool (GB)	31	F 4	
Hartmannsdorf (D)	89	E 1	
Hartola (FIN)	137	D 2	
Harwich (GB)	37	D 2	
Harzgerode (D)	84	B 4	
Haselünne (D)	83	E 3	
Haskovo (BG)	19	D 1	
Haslach an der Mühl (A)	94	C 1	
Haslach i. Kinzingtal (D)	45	E 4	
Hasle (DK)	145	E 3	
Haslemere (GB)	36	B 4	
Haslev (DK)	142	F 4	
Hasparren (F)	54	A 2	
Hassela (S)	132	A 4	
Hasselfelde (D)	84	B 4	
Hasselt (B)	39	F 2	
Haßfurt (D)	88	C 3	
Hässleholm (S)	143	E 3	
Hastière-Lavaux (B)	39	F 3	
Hastings (GB)	36	C 4	
Hasvik (N)	124	C 2	
Hatě (CZ)	91	D 4	
Hațeg (RO)	12	C 4	
Hatfield (GB)	36	B 3	
Hatherleigh (GB)	34	C 3	
Hattem (NL)	82	C 3	
Hattfjelldal (N)	127	D 4	
Hattingen Ennepe-Ruhr-Kreis (D)	87	E 1	
Hattula (FIN)	136	F 2	
Hatunkyla (FIN)	135	F 2	
Hatvan (H)	12	B 3	
Hatvik (N)	138	B 2	
Haubourdin (F)	39	D 2	
Hauge (N)	138	B 4	
Haugesund (N)	138	C 3	
Hauho (FIN)	136	C 3	
Haukeligrend (N)	138	C 3	
Haukipudas (FIN)	133	E 1	
Haukivuori (FIN)	133	F 4	
Haunstetten Kreis Augsburg Stadt (D)	93	E 2	
Haus (A)	94	C 3	
Hausach (D)	45	E 4	
Hausham (D)	94	C 3	
Hausjärvi (FIN)	137	D 3	
Hautajärvi (FIN)	129	E 3	
Hautefort (F)	51	D 4	
Hauteville-Lompnes (F)	49	D 4	
Hautmont (F)	39	E 3	
Havant (GB)	35	F 3	
Havelange (B)	39	F 3	
Havelberg (D)	84	C 2	
Haverfordwest / Hwlffordd (GB)	34	B 1	
Haverhill (GB)	36	C 2	
Haverö (S)	131	F 4	
Havířov (CZ)	91	F 2	
Havlíčkův Brod (CZ)	90	C 3	
Havneby (DK)	142	A 4	
Havøysund (N)	125	D 1	
Havraň (CZ)	89	F 2	
Hawes (GB)	33	D 1	
Hawick (GB)	31	D 3	
Hawkhurst (GB)	36	C 4	
Hay-on-Wye (GB)	35	D 1	
Hayange (F)	44	C 3	
Hayle (GB)	34	B 4	
Haywards Heath (GB)	36	B 4	
Hazebrouck (F)	38	C 2	
Headford / Áth Cinn (IRL)	22	B 4	
Heanor (GB)	33	D 3	
Héas (F)	54	C 3	

Heathfield (GB)	36	C 4	
Heby (S)	140	C 3	
Hechingen (D)	45	F 4	
Hecho (E)	54	B 3	
Hechtel (B)	39	F 1	
Hecklingen (D)	84	C 4	
Hédé (F)	41	E 3	
Hede (S)	131	E 4	
Hedemora (S)	140	C 3	
Hedenäset (S)	128	C 3	
Hedeviken (S)	131	E 4	
Hedon (GB)	33	F 2	
Heemstede (NL)	82	B 3	
Heerde (NL)	82	C 3	
Heerenveen (NL)	82	C 2	
Heerlen (NL)	87	D 2	
Heeze (NL)	39	F 1	
Hegge (N)	139	D 1	
Hegra (N)	131	D 3	
Heia (N)	124	B 3	
Heide (D)	78	C 3	
Heidelberg (D)	45	F 2	
Heidenau (D)	89	F 1	
Heidenheim a. d. Brenz (D)	93	E 2	
Heidenreichstein (A)	90	C 4	
Heikendorf (D)	79	D 3	
Heikkila (FIN)	129	E 3	
Heilbronn (D)	45	F 2	
Heiligenberg (D)	93	D 3	
Heiligenblut (A)	94	B 4	
Heiligenhafen (D)	79	D 3	
Heiligenkirchen (D)	83	F 4	
Heiligenkreuz im Lafnitztal (A)	95	F 4	
Heiligenstadt (D)	88	B 1	
Heilsbronn (D)	88	C 4	
Heimari (FIN)	137	E 2	
Heimdal (N)	131	D 3	
Heimertingen (D)	93	E 3	
Heimtali (EST)	154	B 4	
Heinävaara (FIN)	135	F 2	
Heinävesi (FIN)	135	E 4	
Heinola (FIN)	137	D 2	
Heinolan mlk (FIN)	137	D 2	
Heinsberg (D)	87	D 2	
Heist (B)	37	F 3	
Heist-op-den-Berg (B)	39	F 1	
Hejde (S)	146	B 2	
Hel (PL)	182	C 1	
Heldburg (D)	88	C 3	
Heldrungen (D)	89	D 1	
Helechal (E)	69	F 3	
Helensburgh (GB)	30	C 2	
Hella (IS)	126	A 3	
Hellamaa Hiiu (EST)	148	A 4	
Hellamaa Saare (EST)	153	A 3	
Hellendoorn (NL)	82	C 3	
Hellenurme (EST)	154	C 4	
Hellesylt (N)	130	B 4	
Hellevoetsluis (NL)	82	A 4	
Hellin (E)	71	E 4	
Hellvik (N)	138	B 4	
Helmbrechts Kreis Hof (D)	89	D 2	
Helme (EST)	160	B 1	
Helmküla (EST)	153	A 3	
Helmond (NL)	87	D 1	
Helmsdale (GB)	27	F 1	
Helmsley (GB)	33	E 1	
Helmstadt (D)	88	B 4	
Helmstedt (D)	84	B 3	
Helsa (D)	88	B 1	
Helsingborg (S)	143	D 3	
Helsinge (DK)	143	D 4	
Helsingør (DK)	143	D 4	
Helsinki / Helsingfors (FIN)	137	D 4	
Helska (Mierzeja) (PL)	182	C 1	
Heltermaa (EST)	148	B 4	
Hemau (D)	93	F 1	
Hemavan (S)	127	C 4	
Hemel Hempstead (GB)	36	B 3	
Hemer (D)	87	F 1	
Hemnes (N)	139	E 3	
Hemnesberget (N)	127	D 3	
Hemsedal (N)	139	D 2	
Hemsing (N)	139	D 1	
Hendaye (F)	54	A 2	
Hengelo (NL)	83	D 4	
Hengersberg (D)	94	B 1	
Hénin-Beaumont (F)	39	D 3	
Henley (GB)	33	D 4	
Henley-on-Thames (GB)	36	B 3	
Henneberg (D)	88	C 2	
Hennebont (F)	40	C 4	

Altonaer Str. RELLINGEN	R 4		
Bahrenfelder Chaussee	S 7		
Bergedorfer Str.	S 13		
Elbchaussee	S 28		
Habichtstr.	R 38		
Hammer Landstr.	S 40		
Hannoversche Str.	S 41		
Hohe Str.	S 45		
Jahnring	R 47		
Lokstedter Steindamm	R 59		
Oldesloer Str.	R 64		
Osterfeldstr.	R 65		
Pinneberger Chaussee	R 66		
Saseler Chausse	R 73		
Schleswiger Damm	R 74		
Tangstedter Landstr	R 83		
Tarpenbekstr.	R 84		
Veddeler Damm	S 85		
Wandsbeker Allee	S 86		
Winsener Str.	S 87		

Hammelburg (D)	88	B 3	Hankamäki (FIN)	135	E 3	Haradok (BY)	7	D 3	Harelbeke (B)	37	F 4
Hammerdal (S)	131	F 3	Hankasalmen as (FIN)	133	F 4	Harads (S)	128	A 4	Haren (D)	83	D 1
Hammerfest (N)	125	D 1	Hankasalmi (FIN)	133	F 4	Haraldshaugen (N)	138	B 3	Haren (NL)	83	D 2
Hammershus (DK)	145	E 3	Hanko / Hangö (FIN)	136	C 4	Harasiuki (PL)	197	D 4	Harewood (GB)	33	D 2
Hamningberg (N)	125	F 1	Hann. Münden (D)	88	B 1	Harburg (D)	93	E 1	Hargla (EST)	160	C 2
Hamoir (B)	87	D 3	Hann. Münden (D)	88	B 1	Harburg Hamburg (D)	79	D 2	Härjanurme (EST)	154	C 2
Hamra (S)	140	B 1	Hanna (PL)	191	F 4	Hardbakke (N)	138	B 1	Härjavalta (FIN)	136	B 3
Hamre (N)	141	A 1	Hannover (D)	84	A 3	Hardegg (A)	91	D 4	Harjunpää (FIN)	136	B 2
Hamzali (MK)	122	C 3	Hannut (B)	39	F 2	Hardegsen (D)	84	A 4	Harju-Risti (EST)	148	C 3
Hamziči (BIH)	117	E 4	Hanøy (N)	127	E 1	Hardelot-Plage (F)	38	B 2	Harklowa (PL)	201	C 2
Han Pijesak (BIH)	117	F 3	Hańsk (PL)	197	F 1	Hardenberg (NL)	83	D 3	Härkmeri (FIN)	132	C 2
Han-sur-Lesse (B)	39	F 3	Hansnes (N)	124	B 3	Harderwijk (NL)	82	C 3	Harku (EST)	149	D 3
Hanau (D)	88	A 3	Hanstedt Kreis Harburg (D)	84	A 2	Hardeshøj (DK)	144	B 3	Harkujärve (EST)	149	D 2
Hânceşti (MD)	13		Hanstholm (DK)	142	A 2	Hardheim (D)	45	F 1	Harlech (GB)	32	B 3
Hanerau-Hademarschen (D)	78	C 3	Hanušovice (CZ)	91	D 4	Hardt (N)	130	A 4	Harlesiel (D)	78	A 4
Hanikase (EST)	161	E 1	Haparanda (S)	128	C 4	Hareid (N)	130	A 4	Harleston (GB)	37	D 2

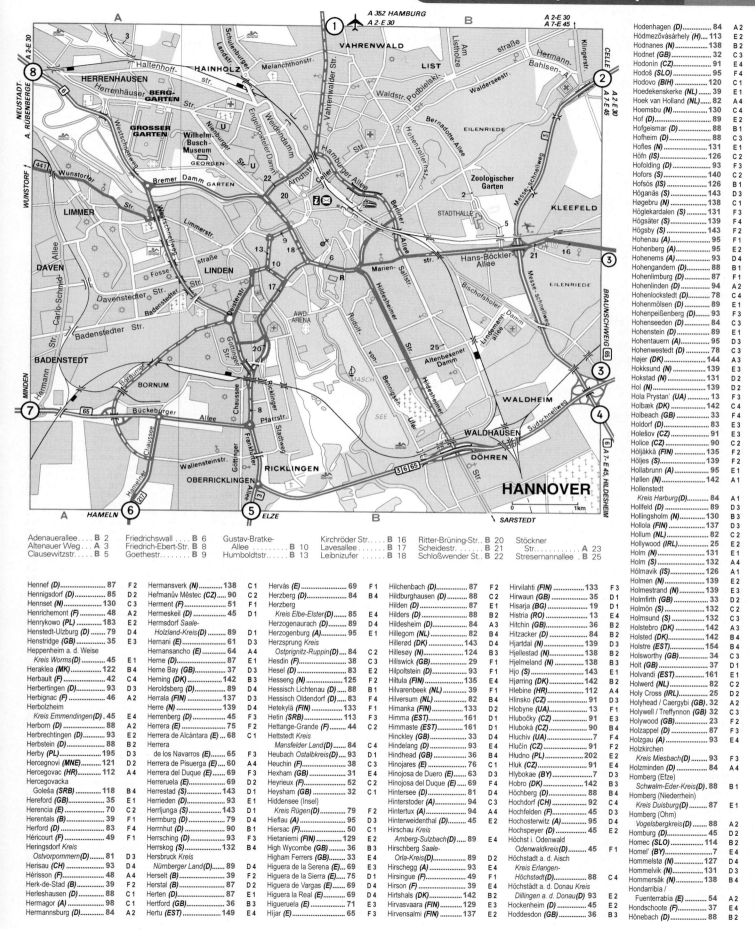

HANNOVER

Adenauerallee.... B 2
Altenauer Weg... A 3
Clausewitzstr.... B 5
Friedrichswall.... B 6
Friedrich-Ebert-Str. B 8
Goethestr........ B 9
Gustav-Bratke-Allee...... B 10
Humboldtstr..... B 13
Kirchröder Str.... B 16
Lavesallee...... B 17
Leibnizufer..... B 18
Ritter-Brüning-Str. B 20
Scheidestr...... B 21
Schloßwender St.. B 22
Stöckner Str........... A 23
Stresemannallee . B 25

Hennef (D)............. 87 F 2
Hennigsdorf (D)....... 85 D 2
Hennset (N)........... 130 C 3
Henrichemont (F)...... 48 A 2
Henrykowo (PL)........ 183 E 2
Henstedt-Ulzburg (D).. 79 D 4
Henstridge (GB)....... 35 E 3
Heppenheim a. d. Weise
  Kreis Worms(D)....... 45 E 1
Heraklea (MK)......... 122 B 4
Herbault (F).......... 42 C 4
Herbertingen (D)...... 93 D 3
Herbignac (F)......... 46 A 2
Herbolzheim
  Kreis Emmendingen(D). 45 E 4
Herborn (D)........... 88 A 1
Herbrechtingen (D).... 93 E 2
Herbstein (D)......... 88 B 2
Herby (D)............. 195 D 3
Hercegnovi (MNE)...... 121 D 4
Hercegovac (HR)....... 112 A 4
Hercegovacka
  Goleša (SRB)........ 118 B 4
Hereford (GB)......... 35 E 1
Herencia (E).......... 70 C 2
Herentals (B)......... 39 F 1
Herford (D)........... 83 F 4
Héricourt (F)......... 49 F 1
Heringsdorf Kreis
  Ostvorpommern(D).... 81 D 3
Herisau (CH).......... 93 D 4
Hérisson (F).......... 48 A 4
Herk-de-Stad (B)...... 39 F 2
Herleshausen (D)...... 88 C 1
Hermagor (A).......... 98 C 1
Hermannsburg (D)...... 84 A 2

Hermansverk (N)....... 138 C 1
Heřmanův Městec (CZ).. 90 C 2
Herment (F)........... 51 F 1
Hermeskeil (D)........ 45 D 1
Hermsdorf Saale-
  Holzland-Kreis(D)... 89 D 1
Hernani (E)........... 61 D 3
Hernansancho (E)...... 64 C 1
Herne (D)............. 87 E 1
Herne Bay (GB)........ 37 D 3
Herrala (FIN)......... 137 D 3
Herre (N)............. 139 D 4
Herrenberg (D)........ 45 F 3
Herrera (E)........... 75 F 2
Herrera de Alcántara (E) . 68 C 1
Herrera
  de los Navarros (E). 65 F 2
Herrera de Pisuerga (E) . 60 A 4
Herrera del Duque (E). 69 F 3
Herreruela (E)........ 69 D 2
Herrestad (S)......... 143 D 1
Herrieden (D)......... 93 E 1
Herrljunga (S)........ 143 D 1
Herrnburg (D)......... 79 D 4
Herrnhut (D).......... 90 B 1
Herrsching (D)........ 93 F 3
Herrskog (S).......... 132 C 2
Hersbruck Kreis
  Nürnberger Land(D).. 89 D 2
Herselt (B)........... 39 F 2
Herstal (B)........... 87 D 2
Herten (D)............ 87 E 1
Hertford (GB)......... 36 B 3
Hertu (EST)........... 149 E 4

Hervás (E)............ 69 F 1
Herzberg (D).......... 84 B 4
Herzberg
  Kreis Elbe-Elster(D). 85 E 4
Herzogenaurach (D).... 89 D 4
Herzogenburg (A)...... 95 E 1
Herzsprung Kreis
  Ostprignitz-Ruppin(D). 84 C 2
Hesdin (F)............ 38 C 3
Hesel (D)............. 83 E 2
Hesseng (N)........... 125 F 2
Hessisch Lichtenau (D)... 88 B 1
Hessisch Oldendorf (D)... 83 F 4
Hetekylä (FIN)........ 133 F 1
Hetin (SRB)........... 113 F 3
Hettange-Grande (F)... 44 C 2
Hettstedt Kreis
  Mansfelder Land(D)... 84 C 4
Heubach Ostalbkreis(D)... 93 D 3
Heuchin (F)........... 38 C 3
Hexham (GB)........... 31 E 4
Heyrieux (F).......... 52 C 2
Heysham (GB).......... 32 C 1
Hiddensee (Insel)
  Kreis Rügen(D)...... 79 F 2
Hieflau (A)........... 95 D 3
Hiersac (F)........... 50 C 1
Hietaniemi (FIN)...... 129 F 3
High Wycombe (GB)..... 36 B 3
Higham Ferrers (GB)... 33 E 4
Higuera de la Serena (E). 69 F 2
Higuera de la Sierra (E). 75 D 1
Higuera de Vargas (E). 69 D 4
Higuera la Real (E)... 69 D 4
Higueruela (E)........ 71 E 3
Híjar (E)............. 65 F 3

Hilchenbach (D)....... 87 F 2
Hildburghausen (D).... 88 C 2
Hilden (D)............ 87 E 1
Hilders (D)........... 88 B 2
Hildesheim (D)........ 84 A 3
Hillegom (NL)......... 82 B 4
Hillerød (DK)......... 143 D 4
Hillesøy (N).......... 124 B 3
Hillswick (GB)........ 29 F 1
Hilpoltstein (D)...... 93 F 1
Hiltula (FIN)......... 135 E 4
Hilvarenbeek (NL)..... 39 F 1
Hilversum (NL)........ 82 B 4
Himanka (FIN)......... 133 D 2
Himma (EST)........... 161 D 1
Himmaste (EST)........ 161 D 1
Hinckley (GB)......... 33 D 4
Hindelang (D)......... 93 E 4
Hindhead (GB)......... 36 B 4
Hinojares (E)......... 76 C 1
Hinojosa de Duero (E). 63 D 3
Hinojosa del Duque (E). 69 F 4
Hintersee (D)......... 81 D 4
Hinterstoder (A)...... 94 C 3
Hintertux (A)......... 94 A 4
Hinterweidenthal (D).. 45 E 2
Hirschau Kreis
  Amberg-Sulzbach(D)... 89 D 4
Hirschberg Saale-
  Orla-Kreis(D)....... 89 D 2
Hirschegg (A)......... 93 E 4
Hirsingue (F)......... 49 F 1
Hirson (F)............ 39 E 4
Hirtshals (DK)........ 142 B 2
Hirvasvaara (FIN)..... 129 E 3
Hirvensalmi (FIN)..... 137

Hirvilahti (FIN)...... 133 F 3
Hirwaun (GB).......... 35 D 1
Hisarja (BG).......... 19 D 1
Histria (RO).......... 13 E 4
Hitchin (GB).......... 36 B 2
Hitzacker (D)......... 84 B 2
Hjartdal (N).......... 139 D 3
Hjellestad (N)........ 138 B 3
Hjelmeland (N)........ 138 B 3
Hjo (S)............... 143 E 1
Hjørring (DK)......... 142 B 2
Hlebine (HR).......... 112 A 4
Hlinsko (CZ).......... 91 D 3
Hlobyne (UA).......... 13 F 1
Hlubočky (CZ)......... 91 E 3
Hluboká (CZ).......... 90 B 4
Hluchiv (UA).......... 7 F 1
Hlučín (CZ)........... 91 F 2
Hludno (PL)........... 202 E 2
Hluk (CZ)............. 91 E 4
Hlybokae (BY)......... 7 D 3
Hobro (DK)............ 142 B 3
Höchberg (D).......... 88 B 4
Hochdorf (CH)......... 92 C 4
Hochfelden (F)........ 45 D 4
Hochosterwitz (A)..... 95 D 4
Hochspeyer (D)........ 45 E 2
Höchst i. Odenwald
  Odenwaldkreis(D).... 45 F 1
Höchstadt a. d. Aisch
  Kreis Erlangen-
  Höchstadt(D)........ 88 C 4
Höchstädt a. d. Donau Kreis
  Dillingen a. d. Donau(D) 93 E 2
Hockenheim (D)........ 45 E 2
Hoddesdon (GB)........ 36 B 3

Hodenhagen (D)........ 84 A 2
Hódmezővásárhely (H).. 113 E 2
Hodnanes (N).......... 138 B 2
Hodnet (GB)........... 32 C 3
Hodonín (CZ).......... 91 E 4
Hodoš (SLO)........... 95 F 4
Hodovo (BIH).......... 120 C 1
Hoedekenskerke (NL)... 39 E 1
Hoek van Holland (NL). 82 A 4
Hoemsbu (N)........... 130 C 4
Hof (D)............... 89 E 2
Hofgeismar (D)........ 88 B 1
Hofheim (D)........... 88 C 3
Hofles (N)............ 131 E 1
Höfn (IS)............. 126 C 2
Hofolding (D)......... 93 F 3
Hofors (S)............ 140 C 2
Hofsós (IS)........... 126 B 1
Höganäs (S)........... 143 D 3
Høgebru (N)........... 138 C 1
Höglekardalen (S)..... 131 F 3
Högsäter (S).......... 139 F 4
Högsby (S)............ 143 F 2
Hohenau (A)........... 95 F 1
Hohenberg (A)......... 95 E 2
Hohenems (A).......... 93 D 4
Hohengandern (D)...... 88 B 1
Hohenlimburg (D)...... 87 F 1
Hohenlinden (D)....... 94 A 2
Hohenlockstedt (D).... 78 C 4
Hohenmölsen (D)....... 89 E 1
Hohenpeißenberg (D)... 93 E 4
Hohenseeden (D)....... 84 C 3
Hohenstein (D)........ 89 E 1
Hohentauern (A)....... 95 D 3
Hohenwestedt (D)...... 78 C 3
Højer (DK)............ 144 A 3
Hokksund (N).......... 139 E 3
Hokstad (N)........... 131 D 2
Hol (N)............... 139 D 2
Hola Prystan' (UA).... 13 F 3
Holbæk (DK)........... 142 C 4
Holbeach (GB)......... 33 E 3
Holdorf (D)........... 83 E 3
Holešov (CZ).......... 91 E 4
Holice (CZ)........... 90 C 2
Höljäkkä (FIN)........ 135 F 2
Höljes (S)............ 139 F 2
Hollabrunn (A)........ 95 E 1
Høllen (N)............ 142 A 1
Hollenstedt
  Kreis Harburg(D).... 84 A 1
Hollfeld (D).......... 89 D 3
Hollingsholm (N)...... 130 C 4
Hollola (FIN)......... 137 D 3
Hollum (NL)........... 82 C 2
Hollywood (IRL)....... 25 C 2
Holm (N).............. 131 E 1
Holm (S).............. 132 A 4
Hólmavík (IS)......... 126 A 1
Holmen (N)............ 139 E 2
Holmestrand (N)....... 139 E 3
Holmfirth (GB)........ 33 D 2
Holmön (S)............ 132 C 2
Holmsund (S).......... 132 C 3
Holstebro (DK)........ 142 A 3
Holsted (DK).......... 142 B 4
Holstre (EST)......... 154 B 4
Holsworthy (GB)....... 34 C 3
Holt (N).............. 37 D 1
Holvandi (EST)........ 161 E 1
Holwerd (NL).......... 82 C 2
Holy Cross (IRL)...... 25 D 2
Holyhead / Caergybi (GB). 32 A 2
Holywell / Treffynnon (GB) 32 C 3
Holywood (GB)......... 23 D 4
Holzappel (D)......... 87 F 3
Holzgau (A)........... 93 E 4
Holzkirchen
  Kreis Miesbach(D)... 93 F 3
Holzminden (D)........ 84 A 4
Homberg (Efze)
  Schwalm-Eder-Kreis(D). 88 B 1
Homberg (Niederrhein)
  Kreis Duisburg(D)... 87 E 1
Homberg (Ohm)
  Vogelsbergkreis(D).. 88 A 2
Homburg (D)........... 45 D 2
Homec (SLO)........... 114 B 2
Homel' (BY)........... 7 D 4
Hommelstø (N)......... 127 D 4
Hommelvik (N)......... 131 D 3
Hommersåk (N)......... 138 B 4
Hondarribia /
  Fuenterrabía (E).... 54 A 2
Hondschoote (F)....... 37 E 4
Hönebach (D).......... 88 B 2

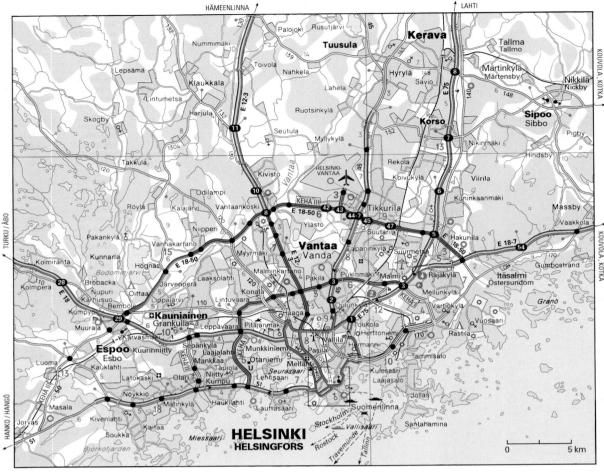

I

Iaşi (RO)	13	E 3
Íasmos (GR)	207	F 2
Ibbenbüren (D)	83	E 3
Ibestad (N)	124	A 4
Ibi (E)	71	F 4
Ibiza / Eivissa (E)	72	C 3
Ibutoniai (LT)	170	C 2
Ičnja (UA)	13	F 1
Idanha-a-Nova (P)	69	D 1
Idar-Oberstein (D)	45	D 1
Idoš (SRB)	113	E 3
Idre (S)	139	F 1
Idrija (SLO)	99	D 2
Idro (I)	97	F 3
Idstein (D)	88	A 3
Idzików (PL)	193	E 4
Iecava (LV)	164	C 2
Iegrīvas (LV)	165	F 2
Ieleja (LV)	157	E 3
Ieper (B)	37	F 4
Ierápetra (GR)	227	E 3
Ieriķi (LV)	159	E 4
Ierissós (GR)	207	D 4
Ieropigí (GR)	205	D 3
Ifaistía (GR)	214	A 1
Ifjord (N)	125	E 1
Ifta (D)	88	C 1
Ig (SLO)	99	D 2
Iga vas (SLO)	99	D 2
Igalo (MNE)	121	D 2
Igavere (EST)	155	D 3
Iggesund (S)	140	C 1
Iglesias (I)	108	A 4
Igliauka (LT)	175	F 2
Igliškéliai (LT)	175	F 2
Igls (A)	93	F 4
Ignacava (LT)	176	C 2
Ignalina (LT)	172	C 3
Ignase (EST)	155	D 4
Ignāti (LV)	162	B 2
Igoumenítsa (GR)	210	C 2
Igrane (HR)	120	B 1
Igualada (E)	66	C 3
Ihamaru (EST)	161	D 1
Ihasalu (EST)	149	E 2
Ihtiman (BG)	19	D 1
Ii (FIN)	129	D 4
Iide (EST)	157	D 1
Iira (EST)	149	E 4
Iisaku (EST)	151	E 4
Iisalmi (FIN)	133	F 2
Iisvesi (FIN)	133	F 3
IJmuiden (NL)	82	B 3
IJsselmuiden (NL)	82	C 3
IJzendijke (NL)	37	F 4
Ikaalinen (FIN)	136	C 2
Ikaría (Nisí) (GR)	220	C 1
Ikast (DK)	142	B 3
Ikla (EST)	159	D 1
Ikškile (LV)	165	D 1
Ilandža (SRB)	113	F 4
Ilanz (CH)	97	D 1
Iława (PL)	183	E 3
Ilche (E)	66	A 2
Ilchester (GB)	35	E 3
Ilčiukai (LT)	171	F 2
Île (LV)	163	F 2
Îles Sanatorija (LV)	163	F 2
Ilfracombe (GB)	34	C 2
Ilgai (LT)	176	C 3
Ilgakiemis (LT)	176	C 2
Ilgi (LV)	162	C 2
Ilgininkai (LT)	176	C 3
Ilguva (LT)	169	F 4
Ílhavo (P)	62	B 3
Ilia (GR)	212	C 2
Ilída (GR)	216	C 2
Ilidža (BIH)	117	E 3
Ilijas (BIH)	117	E 3
Iliókastro (GR)	218	B 3
Ilirska Bistrica (SLO)	99	D 2
Ilkeston (GB)	33	D 2
Ilkley (GB)	33	D 2
Illana (E)	70	C 1
Illano (E)	59	D 2
Illar (E)	76	C 3
Ille-sur-Têt (F)	55	F 2
Illertissen (D)	93	E 2
Illescas (E)	70	B 1
Illhaeusern (F)	45	D 4
Illi (EST)	154	C 4
Illičivs'k (UA)	13	F 3
Illiers-Combray (F)	42	C 3
Illingen (D)	45	D 2
Illmitz (A)	95	F 2

Hønefoss (N)	139	E 3
Honfleur (F)	38	A 4
Høng (DK)	142	C 4
Honiton (GB)	35	D 3
Honkajoki (FIN)	136	B 2
Honningsvåg (N)	125	E 1
Honrubia (E)	71	D 2
Honrubia de la Cuesta (E)	64	B 3
Hontalbilla (E)	64	B 3
Hontoria del Pinar (E)	64	C 2
Hoogeveen (NL)	82	C 3
Hoogezand Sappemeer (NL)	83	D 2
Hoogstraten (B)	39	F 1
Höör (S)	143	D 4
Hoorn (NL)	82	B 3
Hopfgarten (A)	94	A 4
Hora Svatého Šebestiána (CZ)	89	F 2
Horažďovice (CZ)	90	A 4
Horb (D)	45	F 3
Hörby (S)	143	E 4
Horcajo de los Montes (E)	70	A 2
Horcajo de Santiago (E)	70	C 2
Horcajo Medianero (E)	63	F 4
Horche (E)	64	C 4
Horden (GB)	31	F 4
Hořejší Kunčice (CZ)	91	E 2
Horezu (RO)	13	E 2
Horgen (CH)	92	C 4
Horgoš (SRB)	113	E 3
Hořice (CZ)	90	C 2
Horki (BY)	7	E 3
Horley (GB)	36	B 4
Horn (A)	95	E 1
Horn (D)	92	C 3
Horn (D)	83	F 4
Horn (N)	127	D 4
Hornachos (E)	69	D 4
Hornachuelos (E)	75	F 1
Hornberg (D)	45	E 3
Hornburg Kreis Wolfenbüttel (D)	84	B 4
Horncastle (GB)	33	F 3
Horndal (S)	140	C 3
Horneburg (D)	78	C 4
Hörnefors (S)	132	C 3
Horní Benešov (CZ)	91	E 2
Horní Lideč (CZ)	91	F 3
Horní Počernice (CZ)	90	B 2
Horní Slavkov (CZ)	89	F 3
Horníndal (N)	130	B 3
Hørning (DK)	142	B 3
Hornos (E)	70	C 4
Hornoy (F)	38	C 4
Höxter (D)	84	A 4
Hoya (D)	83	F 2
Høyanger (N)	138	C 1
Hoyerswerda (D)	85	F 4
Hoylake (GB)	32	C 2
Høylandet (N)	131	E 1
Hoym (D)	84	C 4
Hoyos (E)	69	D 1
Hradec Králové (CZ)	90	C 2
Hrádek Znojmo (CZ)	91	D 4
Hrádek nad Nisou (CZ)	90	B 1
Hrafnagil (IS)	126	B 1
Hranice (CZ)	91	F 3
Hranice Karlovarský kraj (CZ)	89	E 2
Hrasnica (BIH)	117	E 3
Hrastnik (SLO)	99	D 2
Hrastovlje (SLO)	99	D 3
Hrebenne (PL)	197	F 4
Hřensko (CZ)	90	A 1
Hrissí Amoúdia (F)	55	F 2
Hrodna (BY)	6	C 4
Hronov (CZ)	91	D 1
Hrtkovci (SRB)	118	B 1
Hrubieszów (PL)	197	F 3
Hrušovany nad Jevišovkou (CZ)	91	D 4
Hrvatska Dubica (HR)	115	E 4
Hrvatska Kostajnica (HR)	115	D 4
Hückeswagen (D)	87	F 1
Hucknall (GB)	33	E 3
Hucqueliers (F)	38	C 2
Huddersfield (GB)	33	D 2
Hude (D)	83	D 1
Hudiksvall (S)	140	C 1
Houtskär / Houtskari (FIN)	136	B 4
Hov (DK)	142	B 3
Hovden (N)	138	C 3
Hove (GB)	36	B 4
Hovet (N)	139	D 2
Hovmantorp (S)	143	E 3
Høvringen (N)	130	C 4
Howden (GB)	33	E 2
Howth / Binn Éadair (IRL)	23	E 4
Hoya (D)	83	F 2
Höxter (D)	84	A 4
Hradec Hov		
Huedin (RO)	12	C 3
Huélago (E)	76	B 2
Huélamo (E)	71	E 1
Huelgas (Real Monasterio de las) (E)	60	B 4
Huelgoat (F)	40	C 3
Huelma (E)	76	B 1
Huelva (E)	75	D 2
Huércal Overa (E)	77	D 2
Huérguina (E)	71	E 1
Huerta de Valdecarábanos (E)	70	B 2
Huerta del Rey (E)	64	C 2
Huertahernando (E)	65	D 4
Huerto (E)	66	A 2
Huesa (E)	76	C 1
Huesca (E)	54	B 4
Huéscar (E)	76	C 1
Huete (E)	71	D 1
Huétor Santillán (E)	76	B 2
Huétor Tájar (E)	76	A 2
Hüfingen (D)	45	F 4
Huftarøy (N)	138	B 2
Huittinen (FIN)	136	B 3
Huizen (NL)	82	B 4
Hulín (CZ)	91	E 3
Hulja (EST)	150	C 3
Hullo (EST)	148	B 4
Hulst (NL)	39	E 1
Hultsfred (S)	143	F 2
Humac (BIH)	120	B 1
Humada (E)	60	A 4
Humanes (E)	64	C 4
Humenné (SK)	12	C 2
Hummeln (EST)	160	B 1
Humpolec (CZ)	90	C 3
Humppila (FIN)	136	C 3
Hundested (DK)	142	C 4
Hundorp (N)	139	E 1
Hunedoara (RO)	12	C 4
Hünfeld (D)	88	B 2
Hungerford (GB)	35	F 2
Hunnebostrand (S)	142	C 1
Hunspach (F)	45	E 3
Hunstanton (GB)	33	F 4
Huntingdon (GB)	33	F 4
Huntly (GB)	28	B 3
Hurdal (N)	139	E 2
Huriel (F)	48	A 1
Hurskaala (FIN)	135	E 4
Hürth (D)	87	E 2
Hurup (DK)	142	A 2
Húsafell (IS)	126	A 2
Husavík (N)	138	B 2
Husbands Bosworth (GB)	33	E 4
Hushinish (GB)	26	C 2
Huşi (RO)	13	E 2
Huskvarna (S)	143	E 2
Husnes (N)	138	B 3
Hustopeče (CZ)	91	E 4
Husum (D)	132	B 3
Husum Kreis Nordfriesland (D)	78	A 3
Hutovo (BIH)	120	C 2
Hüttenberg (A)	95	D 4
Hüttschlag (A)	94	B 4
Huttula (FIN)	133	E 4
Huttwil (CH)	92	B 4
Hüüru (EST)	149	D 2
Huy (B)	39	F 2
Hvalba (DK)	126	A 4
Hvalpsund (DK)	142	B 3
Hvalvik (DK)	126	A 4
Hvammstangi (IS)	126	A 1
Hvar (HR)	120	A 2
Hvar (Otok) (HR)	120	A 2
Hveragerdi (IS)	126	A 2
Hvidbjerg (DK)	142	A 3
Hvide Sande (DK)	142	A 3
Hvittarøy (N)	139	E 3
Hvittråsk (FIN)	136	C 4
Hvolsvöllur (IS)	126	A 2
Hyaler (N)	139	E 4
Hyde (GB)	33	D 2
Hyen (N)	130	B 4
Hyères (F)	57	D 3
Hyltebruk (S)	143	D 2
Hyrynsalmi (FIN)	135	E 3
Hythe (GB)	37	D 4
Hyvinkää (FIN)	137	D 3
Hyypiö (FIN)	129	D 3
Hyžne (PL)	202	E 2

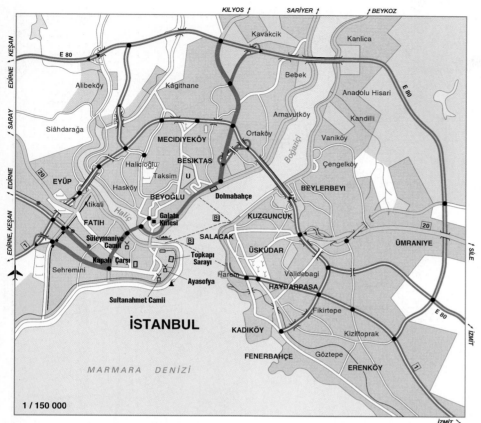

İSTANBUL
1 / 150 000

Ivančice (CZ)....91 D 4
Ivančići (BIH)....117 F 3
Ivančna gorica (SLO)....99 E 2
Ïvande (LV)....156 C 2
Ivanec (HR)....99 F 1
Ivanić Grad (HR)....112 A 4
Ivanjica (SRB)....118 C 3
Ivanjska (BIH)....115 F 3
Ivano-Frankivs'k (UA)....12 C 2
Ivanska (HR)....112 A 4
Ïvira (GR)....207 D 2
Ivrea (I)....53 F 2
Ivry-la-Bataille (F)....42 C 2
Iwaniska (PL)....196 B 3
Iwanowice
  Włościański (PL)....195 E 4
Iwierzyce (PL)....202 D 2
Iwonicz-Zdrój (PL)....202 D 3
Ixiá (GR)....228 C 2
Ixworth (GB)....36 C 2
Izbica Lubelskie(PL)....197 E 2
Izbica Kujawska (PL)....188 C 2
Izbicko (PL)....194 C 4
Izeda (P)....63 E 2
Izernore (F)....49 D 4
Izlake (SLO)....99 E 1
Izmaïl (UA)....13 E 4
İzmir (TR)....19 C 3
İzmit (Kocaeli) (TR)....19 F 1
Iznájar (E)....76 A 2
Iznalloz (E)....76 A 2
İznik (TR)....19 F 1
Izola (SLO)....99 D 3
Izvalta (Izvolts) (LV)....167 F 3
Izvor Jagodina(SRB)....119 D 2
Izvor Kičevo(MK)....122 A 3
Izvor Veles(MK)....122 B 3
Izvor Vranje(SRB)....118 C 2

J

Jaagupi (EST)....159 D 1
Jaala (FIN)....137 D 3
Jaama (EST)....151 F 4
Jaamaküla (EST)....153 C 4
Jaanimõisa (EST)....155 E 4
Jabbeke (B)....37 F 4
Jablan Do (BIH)....121 D 2
Jablanac (HR)....99 E 4
Jablanica (BIH)....117 E 4
Jabłoń Lubelskie(PL)....191 E 4
Jablonec nad Nisou (CZ)....90 B 1
Jabłonna
  Mazowieckie(PL)....190 B 2
Jabłonna Lacka (PL)....191 D 2
Jabłonna Pierwsza (PL)....197 D 2
Jablonné v Podještědí (CZ)90 B 1
Jabłonowo
  Pomorskie (PL)....183 D 2
Jabłowo (PL)....182 C 3
Jablunkov (CZ)....91 F 2
Jabugo (E)....75 D 1
Jabuka (BIH)....117 E 4
Jabuka Beograd(SRB)....118 B 1
Jabuka Prijepolje(SRB)....118 B 2
Jabuka (Otok) (HR)....103 E 2
Jabukovac (HR)....115 D 4
Jabukovac (SRB)....119 E 1
Jaca (E)....54 B 4
Jáchymov (CZ)....89 F 2
Jadagoniai (LT)....169 F 2
Jäder (S)....140 C 4
Jaderberg (D)....83 E 2
Jadów (PL)....190 C 2
Jadranska Lešnica (SRB)117 F 2
Jadraque (E)....64 C 4
Jaén (E)....76 B 1
Jägala (EST)....149 E 2
Jägala-Joa (EST)....149 E 2
Jagėlonys (LT)....177 E 2
Jagodina (SRB)....119 D 2
Jagodnjak (HR)....112 C 4
Jagsthausen (D)....45 F 2
Jahotyn (UA)....13 F 1
Jajce (BIH)....117 D 3
Jakeliai (LT)....173 D 4
Jäkkvik (S)....127 F 3
Jakobstad /
  Pietersaari (FIN)....133 D 3
Jakšiai (LT)....170 B 3
Jakšić (HR)....115 F 3
Jaksonek (PL)....195 D 3
Jakštai (LT)....169 D 3
Jaktorów (PL)....189 F 3
Jakubovik (SRB)....119 E 4
Jakuszyce (PL)....192 C 3

Jakutiškiai (LT)....171 D 3
Jalasjärvi (FIN)....133 D 4
Jälgimäe (EST)....149 D 3
Jaligny-sur-Besbre (F)....48 B 4
Jalovik Izvor (SRB)....119 E 3
Jämaja (EST)....157 D 1
Jambol (BG)....19 E 1
Jämejala (EST)....154 B 3
Jamena (SRB)....117 F 1
Jämijärvi (FIN)....136 B 3
Jäminkipohja (FIN)....136 C 2
Jämjö (S)....143 F 3
Jamnička Kiselica (HR)....99 F 2
Jämsä (FIN)....137 D 2
Jämsänkoski (FIN)....133 E 4
Janakkala (FIN)....136 C 3
Janapolė (LT)....169 D 1
Janaučiai (LT)....169 E 2
Jančė (MK)....122 A 3
Jäneda (EST)....149 F 3
Janeikas (LV)....165 D 3
Janėnai (LT)....175 F 3
Janikowo (PL)....188 B 2
Janionys (LT)....172 C 3
Janja (BIH)....117 F 2
Janjevo (SRB)....122 A 1
Janjina (HR)....120 B 2
Jankai (LT)....175 F 1
Jankūnai (LT)....163 E 3
Jāņmuiža (LV)....159 F 3
Janopole (LV)....167 E 3
Janów Podlaskie(PL)....185 E 4
Janów Śląskie(PL)....195 E 3
Janów Lubelski (PL)....197 E 3
Janów Podlaski (PL)....191 E 3
Janowiec (PL)....196 C 2
Janowiec
  Wielkopolski (PL)....187 F 2
Janowskie (Lasy) (PL)....197 D 3
Jāņuciems
  (Janovka) (LV)....173 D 2
Jāņukalns (LV)....166 B 2
Janukiškiai (LT)....175 E 1
Jāņupe (LV)....164 C 2
Janušava (LT)....171 E 3
Janville (F)....42 C 3
Janzé (F)....41 E 4
Jäppilä (FIN)....135 E 4
Jaraba (E)....65 E 3
Jaraczewo (PL)....187 F 4
Jarafuel (E)....71 F 3
Jaraicejo (E)....69 E 2
Jaraiz de la Vera (E)....69 F 1
Jarak (SRB)....118 A 1
Jarandilla de la Vera (E)....69 F 1
Järbo (S)....140 C 2
Jarcevo (RUS)....7 E 3
Jard-sur-Mer (F)....46 B 3
Jaren (N)....139 E 2
Jargeau (F)....43 D 4
Jarkovac (SRB)....113 F 4
Järlepa (EST)....149 E 3
Jarmen (D)....80 C 3
Jarmenovci (SRB)....118 C 2
Järna (S)....140 B 4
Järna (S)....141 D 4
Jarnac (F)....50 C 1
Jarnages (F)....47 F 4
Jarny (F)....44 C 2
Jarocin Wielkopolskie(PL)187 F 4
Jaroměř (CZ)....90 C 2
Jaroměřice
  nad Rokytnou (CZ)....91 D 4
Jaroslavl' (RUS)....7 F 1
Jarosław (PL)....202 E 2
Järpen (S)....131 E 3
Jarrow (GB)....31 F 4
Järsi (EST)....149 E 3
Järtsaare (EST)....154 B 3
Järva-Jaani (EST)....150 C 4
Järvakandi (EST)....153 C 2
Järve (EST)....151 E 3
Järva-Madise (EST)....149 F 3
Järveküla (EST)....149 E 3
Järvelä (FIN)....137 D 3
Järvenpää (FIN)....137 D 3
Järvere (EST)....161 D 1
Järvsö (S)....140 C 1
Jaša Tomić (SRB)....113 F 4
Jasenak (HR)....99 E 3
Jasenica (BIH)....115 D 4
Jasenovac (HR)....115 E 4
Jasenovo Užice(SRB)....118 B 3
Jasenovo Vršac(SRB)....118 C 1
Jasień Lubuskie(PL)....186 C 4
Jasień Pomorskie(PL)....182 B 2
Jasienica Śląskie(PL)....200 F 2

Illora (E)....76 B 2
Illueca (E)....65 E 3
Illuka (EST)....151 F 3
Ilmajoki (FIN)....133 D 4
Ilmatsalu (EST)....155 D 3
Ilmenau (D)....88 C 2
Ilminster (GB)....35 D 3
Ilok (HR)....117 F 1
Ilomantsi (FIN)....135 F 3
Ilovik (Otok) (HR)....99 E 4
Iłów (PL)....189 E 3
Iłowa (PL)....192 C 1
Iłowo-Osada (PL)....184 A 4
Ilsenburg (D)....84 B 4
Ilsfeld (D)....45 F 2
Ilūkste (LV)....166 C 4
Ilvese (EST)....153 C 4
Iłża (PL)....196 B 2
Ilze (LV)....166 C 4
Ilzenieki (LV)....166 C 3
Ilzeskalns (Ilžukolns) (LV)167 E 2
Imastu (EST)....150 C 3
Imatra (FIN)....137 F 3
Imavere (EST)....154 B 2
Imbarė (LT)....162 C 4
Imbradas (LT)....172 C 2
Ímeros (GR)....208 A 2
Imielin (PL)....200 F 1
Imielno (PL)....195 F 3
Immenstaad (D)....93 D 3
Immenstadt (D)....93 E 3
Immingham (GB)....33 F 2
Immingham Dock (GB)....33 F 2
Imola (I)....102 A 1
Imotski (HR)....117 D 4
Imperia (I)....57 F 1
Imphy (F)....48 B 3
Impruneta (I)....101 F 2
Imst (A)....93 E 4
Inari (FIN)....125 E 3
Inca (E)....73 E 2
Inchnadamph (GB)....27 E 1
Inchree (GB)....27 D 4
Inciems (LV)....159 E 3
Incisa in Val d'Arno (I)....101 F 2
Indal (S)....132 A 4
Indija (SRB)....118 B 1
Indra (LV)....173 E 1
Induļi (LV)....157 F 1
Ineia (CY)....230 A 3

Ineši (LV)....160 B 4
Infiesto (E)....59 F 3
Ingå / Inkoo (FIN)....136 C 4
Ingelmunster (B)....37 F 4
Ingleton (GB)....32 C 1
Ingliste (EST)....149 E 4
Ingolstadt (D)....93 F 1
Ingrandes (F)....46 C 2
Ingwiller (F)....45 D 3
Iniö (FIN)....136 B 4
Iniesta (E)....71 E 1
Iniö (FIN)....136 B 4
Inishcrone (IRL)....22 B 2
Inju (EST)....151 D 3
Inkee (FIN)....129 E 4
Innbygda (N)....139 F 1
Innellan (GB)....30 B 2
Innerleithen (GB)....31 D 2
Innfield (IRL)....23 E 2
Innhavet (N)....127 E 2
Inning a. Ammersee (D)....93 F 2
Innsbruck (A)....93 F 4
Innsbruck (A)....93 F 4
Inset (N)....124 B 4
Innvik (N)....130 B 4
Inowłódz (PL)....195 F 1
Inowrocław (PL)....188 C 1
Ins (CH)....49 E 4
Ińsko (PL)....181 D 4
Interlaken (CH)....96 C 1
Internätskola (S)....163 F 2
Întorsura Buzăului (RO)....13 D 4
Intsu (EST)....154 B 4
Inturkė (LT)....171 F 4
Inveraray (GB)....30 B 1
Inverbervie (GB)....28 B 4
Invergarry (GB)....27 E 3
Invergordon (GB)....27 E 3
Inverkeithing (GB)....31 D 2
Invermoriston (GB)....27 E 3
Inverness (GB)....27 E 3
Inverurie (GB)....28 B 3
Inzell (D)....94 B 3
Ioánnina (GR)....211 D 2
Ioannion (Límni) (GR)....211 D 2
Íos (GR)....224 C 2
Íos (Nisí) (GR)....224 C 2
Iphofen (D)....88 C 4
Ipiķi (LV)....159 E 1

Ipswich (GB)....37 D 2
Iraío Argolída(GR)....217 F 3
Iraío Sámos(GR)....221 E 3
Iraío (Akrotírio) (GR)....217 F 2
Irákleia Fthiótida(GR)....212 A 4
Irákleia Sérres(GR)....206 C 2
Irákleia (Nisí) (GR)....224 C 2
Irákleio (GR)....227 D 2
Irdning (A)....94 C 3
Íria (GR)....217 F 3
Irig (SRB)....118 B 1
Irixoa (E)....58 C 2
Irlava (LV)....163 F 1
Ironbridge (GB)....32 C 4
Irschenberg (D)....94 A 3
Irši (LV)....165 F 1
Irsina (I)....106 C 3
Iru (EST)....149 E 2
Irún (E)....54 A 2
Irurtzun (E)....61 D 4
Irvine (GB)....30 C 2
Irvinestown (GB)....23 D 2
Irxleben (D)....84 C 3
Is-sur-Tille (F)....49 D 2
Isaba/Izaba (E)....54 B 3
Isaccea (RO)....13 E 4
İsafjörður (IS)....126 A 1
Isane (N)....130 A 4
Isbister (GB)....29 F 1
Iscar (E)....64 A 3
Ischgl (A)....93 E 4
Ischia (I)....105 E 4
Išdagai (LT)....169 E 4
Ise (N)....139 E 4
Iselle (I)....96 C 2
Iselsberg (A)....94 B 4
Iseo (I)....97 E 3
Iserlohn (D)....87 F 1
Isernia (I)....105 F 2
Isfjorden (N)....130 B 3
Isili (E)....108 B 3
Isla (E)....60 B 2
Isla Cristina (E)....74 C 2
Išlauzas (LT)....176 C 2
Isle of Whithorn (GB)....30 C 4
Isleornsay (GB)....27 D 3
Ïslīce (Rītausma) (LV)....164 C 2
Išmanai (LT)....176 C 2
Ismaning (D)....93 F 2
Isnäs (FIN)....137 D 3
Isny (D)....93 E 3

Iso-Evo (FIN)....137 D 3
Isojoki (FIN)....133 D 4
Isokylä (FIN)....129 D 3
Isokyrö (FIN)....133 D 3
Isola 2000 (F)....53 E 4
Isola del Gran
  Sasso d'Italia (I)....102 C 4
Isola del Liri (I)....105 E 2
Isola della Scala (I)....97 F 3
Isola di Capo Rizzuto (I)..109 F 2
Ísoma (GR)....217 D 2
Isona (E)....66 B 2
Isorella (I)....97 F 3
Isóva (Moní) (GR)....217 D 3
Ispica (I)....111 E 4
Issigeac (F)....51 D 3
Issoire (F)....52 A 2
Issoudun (F)....47 F 3
Issy-l'Évêque (F)....48 C 3
Ist (Otok) (HR)....116 A 3
Istalsna (LV)....167 F 3
Istán (E)....75 F 3
İstanbul (TR)....19 F 1
Istarske Toplice (HR)....99 D 3
Istebna (PL)....200 F 3
Istérnia (GR)....219 E 3
Istha (D)....88 B 1
Isthmía (GR)....217 F 2
Istiaía (GR)....212 C 3
Istibanja (MK)....122 C 2
Istok (SRB)....118 C 4
Istra (LV)....167 F 3
Istres (F)....56 C 2
Ístrios (GR)....228 B 2
Itä-Aure (FIN)....133 E 4
Itäsalmi /
  Östersundom (FIN)....137 D 4
Itéa Flórina(GR)....205 E 3
Itéa Fokída(GR)....217 E 1
Itéa Grevená(GR)....205 E 4
Itéa Karditsa(GR)....211 F 2
Itháki (GR)....216 B 1
Itháki (Nisí) (GR)....216 B 1
Ithómi (GR)....217 D 4
Itri (I)....105 E 3
Itti (FIN)....137 D 3
Ittiri (I)....108 A 2
Itzehoe (D)....78 C 4
Ivacevičy (BY)....6 C 4
Ivajlovgrad (BG)....19 E 1
Ivalo (FIN)....125 F 4

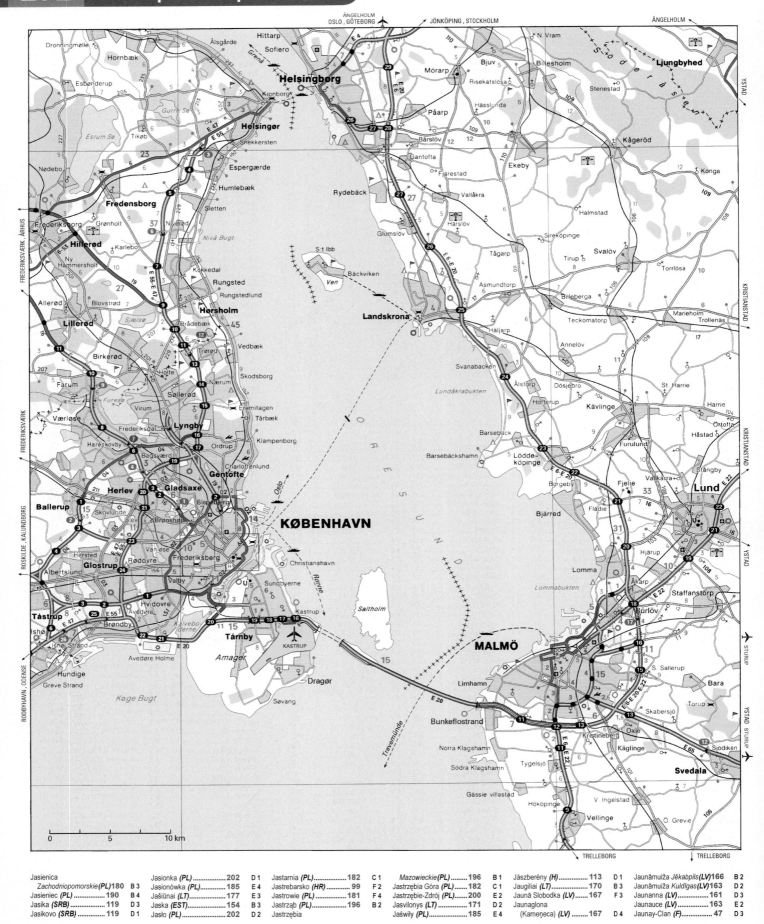

Jaunbērze *(LV)* .... 163 F 1
Jaunciems *(LV)* .... 157 E 3
Jauncode *(LV)* .... 164 C 3
Jaundaņumārki *(LV)* .... 161 D 3
Jaundundaga *(LV)* .... 157 E 2
Jaungulbene *(LV)* .... 161 D 2
Jauniške *(LT)* .... 169 E 2
Jaunjelgava *(LV)* .... 165 E 2
Jaunkaģi *(LV)* .... 159 D 4
Jaunkalsnava *(LV)* ...... 166 B 2
Jaunkārkli *(LV)* .... 165 E 2
Jaunklidzis *(LV)* .... 159 F 2
Jaunlaicene *(LV)* .... 161 D 3
Jaunlazdona *(LV)* .... 166 C 1
Jaunlutriņi
 (Jaunmuiža) *(LV)* ..... 163 E 1
Jaunmārupe *(LV)* .... 164 C 1
Jaunmazsāvas *(LV)* ..... 160 C 4
Jaunmeķeļi *(LV)* .... 159 F 4
Jaunodava *(LT)* .... 169 D 1
Jaunolaine *(LV)* .... 164 C 1
Jaunpagasts *(LV)* .... 157 E 4
Jaunpēternieki *(LV)* ..... 164 C 2
Jaunpiebalga *(LV)* .... 160 C 4
Jaunpils *(LV)* .... 163 F 1
Jaunplamši *(LV)* .... 163 F 2
Jaunsaule *(LV)* .... 165 D 3
Jaunsilavas *(LV)* .... 166 C 3
Jaunsvirlauka *(LV)* ...... 164 C 2
Jauntīļi *(LV)* .... 157 D 2
Jaunvijāni *(LV)* .... 167 D 2
Jaunzemi *Alūksnes(LV)* . 161 D 3
Jaunzemi *Daugavpils(LV)* 173 D 2
Jausa *(EST)* .... 148 A 4
Jausiers *(F)* .... 53 E 4
Jàvea : Xàbia *(E)* .... 72 A 4
Jävenitz *(D)* .... 84 C 3
Javoriv *(UA)* .... 12 C 1
Javorník
 Olomoucký kraj(CZ) .. 91 D 1
Jävre *(S)* .... 132 C 1
Javron *(F)* .... 41 F 3
Jawor *(PL)* .... 193 D 2
Jaworki *(PL)* .... 201 B 3
Jaworzno Śląskie(PL) ... 200 F 1
Jaworzyna *(PL)* .... 201 C 3
Jaworzyna Śląska *(PL)* . 193 E 3
Ječi *(LV)* .... 162 B 3
Jedburgh *(GB)* .... 31 E 3
Jedlicze *(PL)* .... 202 D 2
Jedlina-Zdrój *(PL)* .... 193 E 3
Jedlińsk *(PL)* .... 196 B 1
Jednia-Letnisko *(PL)* .... 196 B 1
Jędrychowo *(PL)* .... 183 D 3
Jędrzejów *(PL)* .... 195 F 3
Jędrzychów *(PL)* .... 186 C 4
Jedwabne *(PL)* .... 183 D 4
Jedwabno *(PL)* .... 183 F 4
Jeesiö *(FIN)* .... 129 D 2
Jegun *(F)* .... 54 C 2
Jegunovce *(MK)* .... 122 A 2
Jēkabnieki *(LV)* .... 164 B 2
Jēkabpils *(LV)* .... 166 B 3
Jektevik *(N)* .... 138 B 2
Jektvik *(N)* .... 127 D 3
Jelah *(BIH)* .... 115 F 4
Jelašca *(BIH)* .... 117 F 4
Jelcz-Laskowice *(PL)* ... 193 F 2
Jeleń *(PL)* .... 200 F 1
Jelenia Góra *(PL)* .... 193 D 3
Jeleniewo *(PL)* .... 185 D 2
Jeleśnia *(PL)* .... 200 F 3
Jelgava *(LV)* .... 164 C 2
Jelgavkrasti *(LV)* .... 159 D 1
Jelling *(DK)* .... 142 B 4
Jel'n'a *(RUS)* .... 7 E 3
Jelsa *(HR)* .... 120 A 2
Jelsa *(N)* .... 138 B 3
Jelsi *(I)* .... 105 F 2
Jemielnica *(PL)* .... 194 C 4
Jemielno *(PL)* .... 193 E 1
Jemnice *(CZ)* .... 90 C 4
Jena *(D)* .... 89 D 1
Jenbach *(A)* .... 94 A 4
Jenči *(LV)* .... 165 D 2
Jēņi *(LV)* .... 156 C 2
Jennersdorf *(A)* .... 95 F 4
Jeppo *(FIN)* .... 133 E 2
Jērcēni *(LV)* .... 159 F 2
Jerez de la Frontera *(E)* . 75 F 3
Jerez de los Caballeros *(E)* 69 E 2
Jeri *(LV)* .... 159 F 1
Jérica *(E)* .... 71 F 2
Jerichow *(D)* .... 84 C 3
Jersika *(LV)* .... 166 C 3
Jerte *(E)* .... 69 F 1

Jerxheim *(D)* .... 84 B 3
Jerzmanowa *(PL)* .... 187 D 4
Jerzu *(I)* .... 108 C 3
Jesenice *(SLO)* .... 99 D 1
Jesenice *Rakovník(CZ)* .. 89 F 3
Jeseník *(CZ)* .... 91 E 2
Jesi *(I)* .... 102 C 2
Jesolo *(I)* .... 98 B 3
Jessen *(D)* .... 85 D 4
Jessheim *(N)* .... 139 E 3
Jeßnitz *(D)* .... 85 D 4
Jeti *(EST)* .... 160 B 1
Jetzelsdorf *(A)* .... 95 E 1
Jeumont *(F)* .... 39 E 3
Jevenstedt *(D)* .... 78 C 3
Jever *(D)* .... 78 A 4
Jevíčko *(CZ)* .... 91 D 3
Jevišovice *(CZ)* .... 91 D 4
Jevnaker *(N)* .... 139 E 2
Jevpatorija *(UA)* .... 13 C 1
Jezerane *(HR)* .... 99 E 3
Jezerce *(SRB)* .... 122 A 2
Jezero *(BIH)* .... 117 D 3
Ježevica *(SRB)* .... 118 B 3
Jeżewo *(PL)* .... 182 C 4
Jeziorany *(PL)* .... 183 F 2
Jeziorsko *(PL)* .... 188 C 4
Jeziorzany *(PL)* .... 191 D 4
Jeżów *(PL)* .... 189 E 4
Jeżów Sudecki *(PL)* ..... 193 D 3
Jeżowe *(PL)* .... 197 D 4
Jičín *(CZ)* .... 90 C 2
Jiestrakis *(LT)* .... 176 B 2
Jieznas *(LT)* .... 176 C 2
Jiezno Kolonijos *(LT)* .... 176 C 2
Jihlava *(CZ)* .... 90 C 3
Jihlava Sídla(CZ) .... 90 C 3
Jilemnice *(CZ)* .... 90 C 1
Jílové u Prahy *(CZ)* ...... 90 B 3
Jimbolia *(RO)* .... 113 F 3
Jimena *(E)* .... 76 B 1
Jimena de la Frontera *(E)*. 75 E 3
Jindřichovice *(CZ)* .... 89 E 2
Jindřichův Hradec *(CZ)* .. 90 C 4
Jirkov *(CZ)* .... 89 D 2
Joachimsthal *(D)* .... 85 E 2
Jockfall *(S)* .... 128 B 3
Jódar *(E)* .... 76 B 1
Jodłowa *(PL)* .... 201 C 2
Jodoigne *(B)* .... 39 F 2
Jöelähtme *(EST)* .... 149 E 2
Joensuu *(FIN)* .... 135 F 3
Jõepera *(EST)* .... 155 E 4
Jõesuu *(EST)* .... 153 C 3
Jõgela *(EST)* .... 152 A 3
Jõgeva *(EST)* .... 154 C 2
Jõgeveste *(EST)* .... 160 C 1
Jõgisoo *Harju(EST)* ...... 149 D 3
Jõgisoo *Järva(EST)* ..... 150 C 3
Johanngeorgenstadt *(D)*. 89 E 2
John o' Groats *(GB)* ..... 27 F 1
Johnstone *(GB)* .... 30 C 2
Johovac *(BIH)* .... 115 F 4
Joigny *(F)* .... 43 E 4
Joinville *(F)* .... 44 B 4
Jokela *(FIN)* .... 137 D 3
Jokijärvi *(FIN)* .... 129 E 2
Jokikylä *(FIN)* .... 135 E 1
Jokioinen *(FIN)* .... 136 C 3
Jokkmokk *(S)* .... 128 A 3
Jokūbavas *(LT)* .... 162 B 4
Joloskylä *(FIN)* .... 133 F 1
Jomala *(FIN)* .... 136 A 4
Jomantai *(LT)* .... 168 C 2
Jönåker *(S)* .... 140 C 4
Jonava *(LT)* .... 170 C 4
Joniec *(PL)* .... 189 F 2
Joniškėlis *(LT)* .... 164 C 4
Joniškis *Šiaulių(LT)* ..... 164 B 3
Joniškis *Utenos(LT)* ..... 171 F 4
Jönköping *(S)* .... 143 G 2
Jonzac *(F)* .... 50 B 2
Joosu *(EST)* .... 161 D 1
Jootme *(EST)* .... 150 C 3
Jordanów *(PL)* .... 201 A 3
Jordbro *(S)* .... 141 D 4
Jormlien *(S)* .... 131 F 1
Jörn *(S)* .... 132 C 1
Jorniņi *(LV)* .... 157 D 2
Joroinen *(FIN)* .... 135 E 4
Jørpeland *(N)* .... 138 B 2
Jørstadmoen *(N)* .... 139 E 1
Jošanica *(SRB)* .... 119 D 2
Jošanička Banja *(SRB)* .. 118 C 3

Jošavka *(BIH)* .... 115 F 4
Josipdol *(HR)* .... 99 E 3
Josipovac *(HR)* .... 112 C 4
Josselin *(F)* .... 41 C 4
Josvainiai *(LT)* .... 170 C 3
Jouarre *(F)* .... 43 E 2
Joué-lès-Tours *(F)* .... 47 C 2
Jõuga *(EST)* .... 151 E 4
Jougne *(F)* .... 49 E 3
Joukokylä *(FIN)* .... 133 F 1
Joutsa *(FIN)* .... 137 D 2
Joutseno *(FIN)* .... 137 E 4
Joutsijärvi *(FIN)* .... 129 E 3
Jovaišai *(LT)* .... 176 B 4
Joyeuse *(F)* .... 52 B 4
Józefów *Lublin(PL)* ...... 196 C 2
Józefów *Mazowieckie(PL)*190 B 3
Józefów *Zamość(PL)* .... 197 C 2
Juan-les-Pins *(F)* .... 57 E 2
Juankoski *(FIN)* .... 135 E 3
Jucaičiai *(LT)* .... 169 D 2
Jüchen *(D)* .... 87 E 2
Juchnajcie *(PL)* .... 184 C 2
Juchnov *(RUS)* .... 7 F 3
Judaberg *(N)* .... 138 B 3
Jūdaži *(LV)* .... 159 E 4
Judenau *(A)* .... 95 E 1
Judenburg *(A)* .... 95 D 4
Judrėnai *Klaipėdos(LT)* .. 168 C 2
Judrėnai *Telšių(LT)* ...... 163 D 4
Jūdzkalni *(LV)* .... 161 D 4
Juelsminde *(DK)* .... 142 B 4
Jugla *(LV)* .... 165 E 1
Jugon-les-Lacs *(F)* ...... 41 D 3
Jugorje *(SLO)* .... 99 E 2
Juillac *(F)* .... 51 D 2
Juist *(D)* .... 78 A 4
Jukkasjärvi *(S)* .... 128 A 2
Juknaičiai *Klaipėdos(LT)* .168 C 2
Juknaičiai *Šiaulių(LT)* ... 164 B 4
Jukneliškė *(LT)* .... 175 F 3
Jülich *(D)* .... 87 E 2
Jullouville *(F)* .... 41 E 2
Jumaliskylä *(FIN)* .... 135 E 1
Jumeaux *(F)* .... 52 A 2
Jumièges *(F)* .... 38 A 4
Jumilhac-le-Grand *(F)* .. 51 D 2
Jumilla *(E)* .... 71 E 2
Juminen *(FIN)* .... 135 E 2
Jumisko *(FIN)* .... 129 E 2
Jumprava *(LV)* .... 165 E 2
Jumurda *(LV)* .... 165 F 1
Jundžionys *(LT)* .... 176 C 3
Juneda *(E)* .... 66 B 3
Juneļi *(LV)* .... 172 C 1
Jungėnai *(LT)* .... 175 F 3
Junik *(SRB)* .... 121 F 2
Juniville *(F)* .... 39 E 4
Junosuando *(S)* .... 128 B 2
Junsele *(S)* .... 132 A 3
Juntusranta *(FIN)* .... 129 F 4
Juodaičiai *(LT)* .... 169 F 3
Juodbūdis *(LT)* .... 176 B 2
Juodeikiai *Klaipėdos(LT)* .162 B 3
Juodeikiai *Telšių(LT)* .... 162 C 4
Juodupė *(LT)* .... 165 F 4
Juodupėnai *(LT)* .... 162 C 4
Juodžiai *(LT)* .... 177 E 3
Juoksenki *(FIN)* .... 128 C 3
Juorkuna *(FIN)* .... 133 F 1
Juostaviečiai *(LT)* .... 165 D 3
Juostininkai *(LT)* .... 171 D 2
Juozapavas *(LT)* .... 163 D 4
Juozapavičiai *(LT)* .... 176 C 3
Jupatovka *(LV)* .... 167 E 2
Jurata *(PL)* .... 182 C 1
Jurbarkas *(LT)* .... 169 E 4
Jurdaičiai *(LT)* .... 163 F 3
Jūrė *(LT)* .... 175 F 2
Jurgi *(LV)* .... 163 E 1
Jurgionys *(LT)* .... 177 D 2
Jūri *(EST)* .... 149 E 2
Jūrkalne *(LV)* .... 156 C 4
Jurkšai I *(LT)* .... 175 F 2
Jūrmala *(LV)* .... 158 C 4
Jūrmalciems *(LV)* .... 162 B 3
Jurmu *(FIN)* .... 129 E 4
Juromenha *(P)* .... 68 C 3
Jurva *(FIN)* .... 133 D 4
Jusevičiai *(LT)* .... 175 F 3
Juškonys *(LT)* .... 170 C 2
Jussey *(F)* .... 49 E 1
Justel *(E)* .... 59 D 4
Jüterbog *(D)* .... 85 D 3
Jutkonys *(LT)* .... 171 E 1
Jutrosin *(PL)* .... 187 F 4
Juuka *(FIN)* .... 135 F 3

Juuma *(FIN)* .... 129 E 3
Juupajoki *(FIN)* .... 136 C 2
Juuru *(EST)* .... 149 E 4
Juva *(FIN)* .... 136 B 3
Juva *(FIN)* .... 135 E 4
Juvigny-le-Tertre *(F)* .... 41 F 2
Juvigny-sous-Andaine *(F)*. 41 F 3
Juvola *(FIN)* .... 135 E 4
Juvola *(EST)* .... 170 B 4
Jūžintai *(LT)* .... 171 F 2
Jyderup *(DK)* .... 142 C 4
Jyrkkä *(FIN)* .... 135 E 2
Jyväskylä *(FIN)* .... 133 F 4

K

K. Alissós *(GR)* .... 217 D 1
K. Doliána *(GR)* .... 217 F 3
K. Kamíla *(GR)* .... 206 C 2
K. Makrinoú *(GR)* .... 217 D 1
K. Meriá *(GR)* .... 219 D 3
K. Nevrokópi *(GR)* .... 207 D 1
K. Tithoréa *(GR)* .... 212 B 4
K. Vérga *(GR)* .... 217 E 4
K. Vérmio *(GR)* .... 205 F 3
Kaagjärve *(EST)* .... 160 C 2
Kaagvere *(EST)* .... 155 D 4
Kaakamo *(FIN)* .... 128 C 4
Kaalepi *(EST)* .... 149 F 4
Kaamanen *(FIN)* .... 125 E 3
Kaansoo *(EST)* .... 154 A 3
Kääpa *Jõgeva(EST)* ...... 155 D 2
Kääpa *Võru(EST)* .... 161 E 1
Käärdi *(EST)* .... 154 C 4
Kaarepere *(EST)* .... 154 C 3
Kaaresuvanto *(FIN)* ...... 125 D 4
Kaarina *(FIN)* .... 136 B 4
Kaarli *(EST)* .... 154 B 4
Kaarlijärve *(EST)* .... 154 C 4
Kaaruka *(EST)* .... 149 F 4
Kaasiku *(EST)* .... 149 D 3
Kaatsheuvel *(NL)* .... 86 C 1
Kaavere *(EST)* .... 154 C 3
Kaavi *(FIN)* .... 135 E 3
Kabala *(EST)* .... 154 B 2
Kâbdalis *(S)* .... 128 A 4

Kabeliai *Alytaus(LT)* .... 176 C 4
Kabeliai *Panevėžio(LT)* ... 171 E 2
Kabile *(LT)* .... 157 E 2
Kabli *(EST)* .... 159 D 1
Kabriste *(EST)* .... 153 B 4
Kać *(SRB)* .... 113 C 4
Kačanik *(SRB)* .... 122 A 2
Kačarevo *(SRB)* .... 118 C 1
Kačerginė *(LT)* .... 170 B 4
Kachovka *(UA)* .... 13 F 2
Kačikol *(SRB)* .... 119 D 4
Kačkāres *(LV)* .... 166 C 1
Kaczorów *(PL)* .... 193 D 3
Kadaga *(LV)* .... 159 D 4
Kadaiciai *(LT)* .... 162 C 4
Kadaň *(CZ)* .... 89 F 2
Kadeģi *(LV)* .... 156 B 4
Kadila *(EST)* .... 151 D 3
Kadjaste *(EST)* .... 154 A 2
Kadrifakovo *(MK)* .... 122 B 2
Kadrina *(EST)* .... 150 C 3
Kadziadlo *(PL)* .... 184 B 4
Kaera *(EST)* .... 154 C 2
Kåfjord *(N)* .... 125 E 1
Kåge *(S)* .... 132 C 1
Kagkádio *(GR)* .... 217 D 2
Kahala *Harju(EST)* .... 149 F 2
Kahala *Järva(EST)* .... 154 B 3
Kahla *Jena(D)* .... 89 D 1
Kähri *(EST)* .... 161 D 1
Kaiáfas *(GR)* .... 217 D 3
Kaibala *(LV)* .... 165 E 2
Kaiguciems *(LV)* .... 164 B 1
Kaija *(LV)* .... 172 C 1
Kailbach *(D)* .... 45 F 1
Kaimiņi *(LV)* .... 155 F 3
Käina *(EST)* .... 148 A 4
Kaindorf *(A)* .... 95 E 3
Kainourgio *(GR)* .... 211 D 4
Kaipola *(FIN)* .... 137 D 2
Kairala *(FIN)* .... 129 D 2
Kairėnai *(LT)* .... 170 B 2

Kaisariáni *(GR)* .... 218 C 2
Kaiserslautern *(D)* .... 45 E 2
Kaisheim *(D)* .... 93 E 1
Kaišiadorys *(LT)* .... 177 D 1
Kaisma *(EST)* .... 153 C 3
Kaiu *(EST)* .... 149 E 4
Kaive *Cēsu(LV)* .... 159 F 4
Kaive *Tukuma(LV)* .... 157 F 4
Kajaani *(FIN)* .... 133 F 2
Kakan (Otok) *(HR)* ...... 103 E 1
Kakanj *(BIH)* .... 117 E 3
Kakavía *(GR)* .... 210 C 1
Kakciems *(LV)* .... 165 D 1
Kaķenieki *(LV)* .... 163 F 2
Kakí Thálassa *(GR)* ...... 218 C 2
Kakí Vígla *(GR)* .... 218 C 3
Kāķišķe *(LV)* .... 162 B 3
Kąkolewnica
 Wschodnia *(PL)* ...... 191 D 4
Kakopetria *(CY)* .... 230 B 3
Kakslauttanen *(FIN)* ..... 125 F 4
Kalá Nerá *(GR)* .... 212 C 2
Kalá Nisiá *(GR)* .... 217 F 2
Kalajoki *(FIN)* .... 133 E 2
Kalak *(N)* .... 125 E 1
Kalakutiške *(LT)* .... 168 C 1
Kalamáki *(GR)* .... 226 C 3
Kalamáki *Lárisa(GR)* .... 212 B 2
Kalamáki *Magnissía(GR)* 212 C 2
Kalámata *(GR)* .... 217 E 4
Kalámi *Chánia(GR)* ...... 226 B 2
Kalámi *Sámos(GR)* ...... 221 E 2
Kalamítsi *Halkidikí(GR)* . 213 D 1
Kalamítsi *Lefkáda(GR)* .. 210 C 4
Kálamos (Nisí) *(GR)* ..... 211 D 4
Kalamotó *(GR)* .... 206 C 3
Kalamoullis *(CY)* .... 231 D 2
Kalampáki *(GR)* .... 211 E 1
Kalampáki *(GR)* .... 207 E 2
Kalana *(EST)* .... 154 C 2
Kalándra *(GR)* .... 212 C 1
Kalanti *(FIN)* .... 136 B 3
Kalapódi *(GR)* .... 212 B 4
Kälarne *(S)* .... 132 A 3

KÖLN

Agrippina-Ufer .... S 2
An der Schanz .... S 12
Bergischer Ring .... S 23
Bergisch-Gladbacher-Str. .. R 24
Berliner Str. .... R 25
Boltensternstr. .... S 29
Bremerhavener Str. .... R 30
Buchheimer Ring .... R 33
Butzweiler Str. .... S 34
Clevischer Ring .... S 35
Ehrenfeldgürtel .... S 40

Gustav-Heinemann-Ufer ... T 56
Industriestr. .... R 59
Innere Kanalstr. .... S 60
Kalker Hauptstr. .... S 63
Kapellenstr. .... S 64
Klettenberggürtel .... T 70
Mauenheimer Gürtel .... R 75
Mercatorstr. .... S 81
Mülheimer Brücke .... S 85
Niederländer Ufer .... S 87
Niehler Damm .... R 88

Opladener Str. .... S 91
Ostheimer Str. .... S 92
Parkgürtel .... S 93
Pfälzischer
 Ring .... S 97
Rösrather Str. .... S 103
Stadtaubahn .... S 109
Stadtwaldgürtel .... S 110
Universitätsstr. .... S 113
Zoobrücke .... S 123
Zülpicher Str. .... S 124

Kalavárda (GR) 228 C 2
Kalavasos (CY) 231 C 4
Kalávryta (GR) 217 E 2
Kaława (PL) 187 D 3
Kal'azin (RUS) 7 F 1
Kalbe (D) 84 B 2
Kalbu (EST) 149 E 4
Kalce (SLO) 99 D 2
Kaldabruņa (LV) 166 C 4
Kalēji (LV) 167 D 4
Kaléntzi Ahaïa(GR) 217 D 2
Kaléntzi Ioánnina(GR) 211 D 2
Kalérgo (GR) 219 D 1
Kalesi (EST) 149 E 3
Kalesija (BIH) 117 F 2
Kalesninkai Alytaus(LT) 175 F 3
Kalesninkai Vilniaus(LT) 177 D 4
Kalēti (LV) 162 C 3
Kaletnik (PL) 185 E 2
Kalety (PL) 195 D 4
Kalevai (LT) 164 C 4
Kali (HR) 103 E 1
Kaliánoi (GR) 217 E 2
Kaliekiai (LT) 171 F 2
Kalinas (LT) 177 E 2
Kaliningrad (RUS) 6 B 4
Kalinkavičy (BY) 7 E 4
Kalinovnik (BIH) 117 F 4
Kalinowo (PL) 185 D 3
Kalirráchi (GR) 205 E 4
Kalisz (PL) 188 B 4
Kalisz Pomorski (PL) 181 D 4
Kalita (EST) 153 C 4
Kalix (S) 128 B 4
Kaljord (N) 124 A 4
Kalkar (D) 82 C 4
Kaļķi (LV) 157 E 2
Kaļķis (Plostmuiža) (LV) 164 B 1
Kalkkinen (FIN) 137 D 2
Kall (S) 131 E 3
Kallaste (EST) 155 E 3
Kallavere (EST) 149 E 2
Kållby (FIN) 133 D 3
Källby (S) 143 E 1
Kallepeia (CY) 230 A 3
Kalli (EST) 153 B 3
Kallífytos (GR) 207 E 2
Kallimasiá (GR) 220 C 1
Kallinge (S) 143 F 3
Kallio (FIN) 134 C 4
Kalliojoki (FIN) 135 F 1
Kallipéfki (GR) 212 B 1
Kallislahti (FIN) 135 E 4
Kallithéa Dodekánissa(GR) 228 C 2
Kallithéa Dráma(GR) 207 D 2
Kallithéa Etolía-Akarnanía(GR) 211 E 4
Kallithéa Halkidikí(GR) 212 C 1
Kallithéa Ilía(GR) 217 D 3
Kallithéa Messinía(GR) 222 B 2
Kallíthiro (GR) 211 F 3
Kallmünz (D) 89 E 4
Kalloní Atikí-Peireiás(GR) 218 B 3
Kalloní Lésvos(GR) 214 C 3
Kalmar (S) 143 F 3
Kalme Jõgeva(EST) 154 B 2
Kalme Tartu(EST) 154 C 4
Kalme Valga(EST) 160 C 1
Kalna (SRB) 119 E 3
Kalnaberžė (LT) 170 C 3
Kalnadruvas (LV) 161 E 3
Kalnagaliai (LT) 165 E 4
Kalnāji (LV) 161 D 3
Kalnas (LT) 165 D 4
Kalncempji (LV) 161 D 3
Kalnciems Alūksnes(LV) 161 D 3
Kalnciems Jelgavas(LV) 164 B 1
Kalnēji (LV) 157 D 4
Kalnelis (LT) 164 B 3
Kalneliškiai (LT) 164 C 4
Kalnėnai (LT) 170 C 4
Kalnenieki (LV) 162 C 2
Kalngale (LV) 158 C 4
Kalni (LV) 163 D 2
Kalniai (LT) 175 F 3
Kalnieši (LV) 173 E 1
Kalnik (HR) 112 A 4
Kalniņi Jelgavas(LV) 164 B 2
Kalniņi Rīgas(LV) 165 D 1
Kalniškiai Klaipėdos(LT) 162 C 4
Kalniškiai Ramučiai(LT) 169 E 1
Kalniškiai Venta(LT) 163 E 3
Kalnrozes (LV) 164 B 3
Kalnujai (LT) 169 E 3
Kalnzaķi (LV) 159 D 2
Kaló Chorió (GR) 227 E 3
Kalo Chorio (Kapouti) (CY) 231 C 2
Kalo Chorio (Larnaka) (CY) 231 D 3
Kalo Chorio (Lefka) (CY) 230 B 3
Kalo Chorio (Lemesos) (CY) 231 C 3
Kaló Neró (GR) 217 D 4
Kalochóri (GR) 211 F 1
Kalocsa (H) 112 C 2
Kalograia (CY) 230 B 2
Kalogriá (GR) 216 C 1
Kaloí Liménes (GR) 226 C 3
Kalókastro (GR) 206 C 2
Kalokedara (CY) 230 B 4
Kalopanagiotis (CY) 230 B 3
Kalopsida (CY) 231 D 3
Kaloskopí (GR) 212 A 4
Kalpáki (GR) 211 D 1
Kals (A) 94 B 4
Kalsdorf (A) 95 E 4
Kaltanėnai (LT) 172 B 3
Kaltbrunn (CH) 93 D 4
Kaltene (LV) 157 E 3
Kaltenkirchen (D) 78 C 4
Kaltennordheim (D) 88 C 2
Kaltezés (GR) 217 E 3
Kaltinėnai (LT) 169 D 2
Kaluđerovo (SRB) 119 D 1
Kaluga (RUS) 7 F 3
Kalundborg (DK) 142 C 4
Kalupe (Kolups) (LV) 167 D 4
Kaluš (UA) 12 C 2
Kałuszyn (PL) 190 C 3
Kalvåg (N) 130 A 4
Kalvarija (LT) 175 F 3
Kalvehave (DK) 145 D 3
Kalveliai (LT) 175 F 4
Kalvene (LV) 162 C 2
Kälviä (FIN) 133 D 2
Kalviai Kauno(LT) 176 C 2
Kalviai Vilniaus(LT) 177 F 4
Kalviškiai (LT) 163 E 4
Kalvola (FIN) 136 C 3
Kalvträsk (S) 132 C 1
Kalwaria Zebrzydowska (PL) 201 A 2
Kálymnos (GR) 221 E 4
Kálymnos (Nisí) (GR) 221 E 4
Kalythiés (GR) 228 C 2
Kalyvári (GR) 219 E 2
Kalýves (GR) 226 B 2
Kalývia Ahaïa(GR) 217 E 2
Kalývia Atikí-Peireiás(GR) 218 C 2
Kalývia Etolía-Akarnanía(GR) 211 E 3
Kalývia Korinthía(GR) 217 E 2
Kalývia Varikoú (GR) 206 B 4
Kam»janec'-Podil's'kyj (UA) 13 D 2
Kam»janka (UA) 13 F 1
Kamajai (LT) 171 F 1
Kamaldiņa (LV) 160 B 3
Kamara (EST) 154 A 4
Kamáres Ahaïa(GR) 217 E 1
Kamáres Irákleio(GR) 226 C 2
Kamáres Páros(GR) 219 F 4
Kamáres Sífnos(GR) 219 E 4
Kamari (EST) 154 C 3
Kamári (GR) 224 C 3
Kamariótissa (GR) 208 B 3
Kambja (EST) 155 D 4
Kámeiros (GR) 228 C 2
Kámeiros Kastéllo (GR) 228 B 2
Kamen (D) 87 F 1
Kaména Voúrla (GR) 212 B 4
Kamenari (MNE) 121 D 1
Kaméni (Nisí) (GR) 224 C 3
Kamenica (MK) 122 C 2
Kamenica (SRB) 118 B 2
Kamenice nad Lipou (CZ) 90 C 4
Kamensko Daruvar(HR) 115 E 3
Kamensko Split(HR) 117 D 4
Kamenz (D) 85 F 4
Kamień Chełm(PL) 197 F 2
Kamień Lublin(PL) 197 D 4
Kamień Podkarpackie(PL) 197 D 4
Kamień Warmińsko-Mazurskie(PL) 184 C 3
Kamień Krajeński (PL) 182 B 4
Kamień Pomorski (PL) 180 C 2
Kamienica (PL) 201 B 3
Kamieniec Warmińsko-Mazurskie(PL) 183 D 3
Kamieniec Wielkopolskie(PL) 187 E 3
Kamieniec Ząbkowicki (PL) 193 E 4
Kamienna Góra (PL) 193 D 3
Kamiennik (PL) 193 F 4
Kamieńsk (PL) 195 E 2
Kamieński (Zalew) (PL) 180 C 2
Kaminaria (CY) 230 B 3
Kaminiá (GR) 211 D 1
Kamínia Ahaïa(GR) 217 D 1
Kamínia Lésvos(GR) 214 A 1
Kamionek Wielki (PL) 184 C 2
Kamionka Wielka (PL) 201 C 3
Kamnik (SLO) 99 D 1
Kamp Bornhofen (D) 87 F 3
Kamp-Lintfort (D) 87 E 1
Kampai II (LT) 170 B 3
Kampánis (GR) 206 B 2
Kampen (NL) 82 C 3
Kampen (Sylt) (D) 78 B 2
Kampiá (GR) 214 C 4
Kampinos (PL) 189 F 3
Kampinoski Park Narodowy (PL) 189 F 3
Kampochóri (GR) 206 A 3
Kampos (CY) 230 B 3
Kámpos Chánia(GR) 226 A 2
Kámpos Fokída(GR) 217 E 1
Kámpos Messinía(GR) 217 E 4
Kanaküla (EST) 154 A 4
Kanal (SLO) 98 C 2
Kanála (GR) 219 D 3
Kanália Kardítsa(GR) 211 F 2
Kanália Magnissía(GR) 212 B 2
Kanalláki (GR) 210 C 3
Kanatádika (GR) 212 C 3
Kánava (GR) 224 A 2
Kančiškiai (LT) 171 D 3
Kańczuga (PL) 202 E 2
Kandava (LV) 157 E 4
Kandel (D) 45 E 2
Kandern (D) 92 B 3
Kandersteg (CH) 96 B 2
Kandíla Arkadía(GR) 217 E 2
Kandíla Etolía-Akarnanía(GR) 211 D 4
Kandıra (TR) 19 F 1
Kandrėnai (LT) 171 E 1
Kandrše (SLO) 99 E 1
Kaneišiai (LT) 172 C 3
Kanepi (EST) 161 D 1
Kanestraum (N) 130 C 3
Kanfanar (HR) 99 D 3
Kangasala (FIN) 136 C 2
Kangaslampi (FIN) 135 E 4
Kangasniemi (FIN) 133 F 4
Kangosjärvi (FIN) 128 C 2
Kangsti (EST) 161 D 2
Kaniūkai Alytus(LT) 176 C 3
Kaniūkai Panočiai(LT) 177 D 4
Kaniūkai Skudutiškis(LT) 171 F 3
Kaniūkai Užpaliai(LT) 171 F 2
Kaniv (UA) 13 F 1
Kaniwola (PL) 197 E 1
Kanjiža (SRB) 113 E 3
Kankaanpää (FIN) 136 B 2
Kannenieki (LV) 163 F 1
Kannonkoski (FIN) 133 E 3
Kannus (FIN) 133 D 2
Kannusjärvi (FIN) 137 E 3
Kántanos (GR) 226 A 2
Kantaučiai (LT) 163 D 4
Kanteniai (LT) 163 D 3
Kántia (GR) 217 F 3
Kantküla (EST) 155 D 2
Kanturk / Ceann Toirc (IRL) 24 C 3
Käo (EST) 152 C 3
Kaona (SRB) 118 C 3
Kaonik (BIH) 117 E 3
Kaonik (SRB) 119 D 3
Kąp (PL) 184 C 2
Kapandriti (GR) 218 C 1
Kaparélli (GR) 218 B 1
Kapčiamiestis (LT) 175 F 4
Kapellskär (S) 141 E 3
Kapėnai (LT) 163 E 3
Kapfenberg (A) 95 E 3
Kaplava (LV) 173 D 1
Kaplice (CZ) 94 C 1
Kaposvár (H) 112 B 3
Kapp (N) 139 E 2
Kappariá (GR) 219 E 2
Kappel (D) 45 D 1
Kappeln (D) 78 C 2
Kaprije (Otok) (HR) 103 F 1
Kaprun (A) 94 B 4
Kapsáli (GR) 223 D 4
Kápsas (GR) 217 E 3
Kapsēde (LV) 162 B 2
Kapsoúri (GR) 219 D 2
Kapūne (LV) 167 E 1
Kapuvár (H) 112 A 1
Karabiga (TR) 19 E 2
Karaburun (TR) 19 E 3
Karačev (RUS) 7 F 3
Karaliai (LT) 175 E 2
Karaliūnai (LT) 177 D 2
Karalkrēslis (LT) 175 E 2
Karan (SRB) 118 B 3
Karasjok (N) 125 E 3
Karasu (TR) 19 F 1
Karats (S) 127 F 3
Karavas (CY) 231 C 2
Karavás (GR) 223 D 3
Karávete (EST) 149 F 3
Karavómylos (GR) 212 B 4
Karavónisia (Nisiá) (GR) 225 E 4
Karavostasi (CY) 230 B 3
Karavostásis (GR) 224 B 2
Kårböle (S) 140 C 1
Karcag (H) 113 E 1
Karčiomka (LT) 172 C 1
Karczew (PL) 190 B 3
Karczmiska (PL) 197 D 2
Karczmy (PL) 195 D 1
Kardakáta (GR) 216 B 1
Kardámaina (GR) 225 F 2
Kardámyla (GR) 214 C 4
Kardamýli (GR) 222 C 2
Kärde (EST) 154 C 2
Kardiá (GR) 206 C 4
Kardítsa (GR) 211 F 2
Kärdla (EST) 148 A 4
Kărdžali (BG) 19 D 1
Kareļi (LV) 163 D 2
Karesuando (S) 125 D 4
Kärevere Järva(EST) 154 B 2
Kärevere Tartu(EST) 154 C 3
Karfás (GR) 220 C 1
Kargowa (PL) 187 D 3
Karhukangas (FIN) 133 E 2
Karhula (FIN) 137 E 3
Kariani (GR) 207 D 3
Karigasniemi (FIN) 125 E 3
Karijoki (FIN) 133 D 4
Karilatsi (EST) 155 D 4
Karinainen (FIN) 136 B 3
Karinu (EST) 150 C 4
Kariotiškės (LT) 177 E 2
Karis / Karjaa (FIN) 136 C 4
Karítaina (GR) 217 E 3
Karitsa (EST) 151 D 3
Karja (EST) 152 C 3
Karjaküla (EST) 149 D 3
Karjalohja (FIN) 136 C 4
Karjatnurme (EST) 159 F 1
Karkaloú (GR) 217 E 3
Karkažiškė (LT) 171 F 4
Kārķi (LV) 159 F 1
Karkinágri (GR) 220 C 3
Karkkila (FIN) 136 C 3
Karkku (FIN) 136 C 2
Karklė (LT) 162 B 4
Karklėnai (LT) 169 E 2
Kārkli (LV) 157 D 4
Kārkliņi (LV) 157 D 4
Karkliniai (LT) 175 E 2
Kārklumuiža (LV) 163 F 3
Kärkna (EST) 155 D 3
Kärkölä (FIN) 137 D 3
Karkonosze (PL) 193 D 3
Karksi (EST) 159 F 1
Karksi-Nuia (EST) 154 B 4
Karla (EST) 149 E 3
Kárlas (L.) (GR) 212 B 2
Karlevi (S) 143 F 3
Kārļi (LV) 159 E 3
Karlino (PL) 181 D 2
Karlivka (UA) 13 F 1
Kārļmuiža (LV) 157 E 2
Karlobag (HR) 99 E 4
Karlova Studánka (CZ) 91 E 2
Karlovac (HR) 99 F 2
Karlovási (GR) 221 D 2
Karlovo (BG) 19 D 1
Karlovy Vary (CZ) 89 F 2
Karłów (PL) 193 E 4
Karlsborg (S) 143 E 1
Karlsburg (D) 80 C 3
Karlsfeld (D) 93 F 2
Karlshamn (S) 143 E 3
Karlshuld (D) 93 F 1
Karlskoga (S) 140 B 4
Karlskrona (S) 143 F 3
Karlsruhe (D) 45 E 2
Karlstad (S) 140 A 4
Karlstadt (D) 88 B 3
Karlštejn (CZ) 90 B 3
Karlstift (A) 95 D 1
Karmėlava (LT) 170 C 4
Karmi (CY) 231 C 2
Kärneri (EST) 152 C 3
Karnezaíika (GR) 218 A 3
Karnice (PL) 180 C 2
Karniewo (PL) 190 B 1
Karnobat (BG) 19 E 1
Karolinka (CZ) 91 F 3
Karow Kreis Parchim(D) 79 F 4
Karpacz (PL) 193 D 3
Kärpänkylä (FIN) 129 F 3
Kárpathos (GR) 228 A 4
Kárpathos (Nisí) (GR) 228 A 4
Karpenísi (GR) 211 F 3
Karperí (GR) 206 C 2
Karperó (GR) 211 E 1
Karpicko (PL) 187 D 3
Kärsa (EST) 155 D 4
Karsakai (LT) 177 D 1
Karsakiškis (LT) 171 D 1
Kärsämäki (FIN) 133 E 2
Kärsava (LV) 167 F 2
Karšinauka (LT) 171 D 2
Karsko (PL) 186 C 1
Karstädt Kreis Prignitz(D) 84 C 1
Karste (EST) 161 D 1
Karšteniai (LT) 169 D 1
Kärstna (EST) 154 B 4
Karstula (FIN) 133 E 3
Kartal (TR) 19 F 1
Kartena (LT) 162 C 4
Kartéri Korinthía(GR) 217 E 2
Kartéri Thesprotía(GR) 210 C 2
Karterós (GR) 227 D 2
Kartonfabrika (LV) 160 C 4
Karttula (FIN) 133 E 3
Kartupiai (LT) 169 E 3
Kartuzy (PL) 182 C 2
Käru Lääne-Viru(EST) 151 D 4
Käru Rapla(EST) 149 E 4
Karula Valga(EST) 160 C 2
Karula Viljandi(EST) 154 B 3
Karungi (S) 128 C 4
Karunki (FIN) 128 C 4
Karup (DK) 142 B 3
Karva (LV) 161 D 3
Karvala (FIN) 133 D 3
Kärväskylä (FIN) 133 F 3
Karvia (FIN) 133 D 4
Karviná (CZ) 91 F 2
Karvoskylä (FIN) 133 E 2
Karvounári (GR) 210 C 2
Karwia (PL) 182 C 1
Karyá Argolída(GR) 217 F 3
Karyá Fthiótida(GR) 212 B 4
Karyá Lárisa(GR) 212 A 1
Karyá Lefkáda(GR) 211 D 4
Karyés Ágio Óros(GR) 207 E 4
Karyés Fthiótida(GR) 212 A 3
Karyés Lakonía(GR) 217 E 4
Karyótissa (GR) 206 A 3
Kárystos (GR) 219 D 2
Kašalj (SRB) 118 C 4
Kasčiukiškės (LT) 177 D 1
Kasepere (EST) 149 D 3
Kasepää Jõgeva(EST) 155 D 2
Kasepää Tartu(EST) 155 E 3
Kašin (RUS) 7 F 1
Kašina (HR) 99 F 1
Kaskinen / Kaskö (FIN) 132 C 4
Käsmu (EST) 150 C 2
Kašonys (LT) 176 C 2
Kásos (Nisí) (GR) 228 A 4
Kaspakas (GR) 213 F 1
Kašperské Hory (CZ) 90 A 4
Kasprowy Wierch (PL) 201 A 4
Kassándra (GR) 212 C 1
Kassándreia (GR) 212 C 1
Kassari (EST) 148 A 4
Kassel (D) 88 B 1
Kassinurme (EST) 154 C 2
Kassiópi (GR) 210 B 1
Kassópi (GR) 211 D 3
Kastaniá Imathía(GR) 205 F 4
Kastaniá Kardítsa(GR) 211 F 3
Kastaniá Korinthía(GR) 217 E 2
Kastaniá Tríkala(GR) 211 E 1
Kastaniés (GR) 208 C 1
Kastaniótissa (GR) 212 C 4
Kaštel Stari (HR) 103 F 1
Kaštel Žegarski (HR) 99 F 4
Kastelholm (FIN) 136 A 4
Kastélla (GR) 213 D 4
Kastellaun (D) 45 D 1
Kastélli (GR) 227 D 2
Kasterlee (B) 39 F 1
Kasti (EST) 149 D 4
Kastīre (LV) 167 D 4
Kastl Kreis Amberg-Sulzbach(D) 89 D 4
Kastorf Kreis Herzogtum Lauenburg(D) 79 D 4
Kastóri (GR) 217 E 4
Kastoriá (GR) 205 E 3
Kastós (Nisí) (GR) 211 D 4
Kastráki Etolía-Akarnanía(GR) 211 E 4
Kastráki Kikládes(GR) 219 F 4
Kastráki Tríkala(GR) 211 E 1
Kastrāne (Upespils) (LV) 165 E 1
Kastrí Arkadía(GR) 217 F 3
Kastrí Fthiótida(GR) 211 F 3
Kastrí Lárisa(GR) 212 B 2
Kástro Ilía(GR) 216 C 2
Kástro Magnissía(GR) 212 C 3
Kástro Viotía(GR) 219 E 4
Kastros (CY) 231 E 2
Kastrosykiá (GR) 211 D 3
Käsukonna (EST) 154 B 2
Kaszyce Wielkie (PL) 193 F 1
Katachás (GR) 206 B 4
Katáfourko (GR) 211 D 3
Katafýgio (GR) 205 F 4
Katáfyto (GR) 207 D 1
Katákolo (GR) 216 C 3
Katálakko (GR) 213 F 1
Katápola (GR) 225 D 2
Katastári (GR) 216 B 2
Kateleiós (GR) 216 B 2
Katerini (GR) 206 B 4
Katharó (GR) 227 E 2
Kathenoí (GR) 213 D 4
Kathikas (CY) 230 A 3
Katići (SRB) 118 B 3
Kätkäsuvanto (FIN) 125 D 4
Katlanovo (MK) 122 B 2
Katlanovska Banja (MK) 122 B 2
Katlenburg-Lindau (D) 84 A 4
Katlėriai (LT) 171 E 3
Káto Achaïa (GR) 217 D 1
Káto Aséa (GR) 217 E 3
Kato Deftera (CY) 231 C 3
Kato Dikomo (CY) 231 C 2
Káto Drosiní (GR) 208 B 2
Káto Figáleia (GR) 217 D 3
Káto Gatzéa (GR) 212 C 3
Káto Kleinés (GR) 205 E 2
Kato Lakatameia (CY) 231 C 3
Káto Mousounítsa (GR) 211 F 4
Kato Polemidia (CY) 230 B 4
Kato Pyrgos (CY) 230 B 3
Káto Vasilikí (GR) 217 D 1
Káto Vlasía (GR) 217 D 2
Káto Zachlorou (GR) 217 E 2
Káto Zákros (GR) 227 F 3
Kato Zodeia (CY) 230 B 3
Katochí (GR) 216 C 1
Katokopia (CY) 231 C 3
Katoúna Etolía-Akarnanía(GR) 211 D 4
Katoúna Lefkáda(GR) 211 D 4
Katowice (PL) 195 D 4
Katrineholm (S) 140 C 4
Kattavía (GR) 228 B 3
Katwijk aan Zee (NL) 82 A 4
Katy Rybackie (PL) 183 D 2
Katyčiai (LT) 168 C 3
Kaub (D) 45 E 1
Kaufbeuren (D) 93 E 3
Kauguri (LV) 159 F 3
Kauhajärvi (FIN) 133 D 3
Kauhajoki (FIN) 133 D 4
Kauhava (FIN) 133 D 3
Kaukonen (FIN) 128 C 2
Kauksi (EST) 161 E 1
Kauksnujai (LT) 164 B 4
Kaulakiai (LT) 169 F 3
Kaunas (LT) 176 C 1
Kaunata (LV) 167 E 3
Kaunatava (LT) 163 E 4
Kaupanger (N) 138 C 1
Kaupiškiai (LT) 175 E 2
Kaušai (LT) 169 D 2
Kaušėnai (LT) 162 C 4
Kaustinen (FIN) 133 E 3
Kautokeino (N) 125 D 3
Kauttua (FIN) 136 B 3
Kavadarci (MK) 122 C 3
Kavajë (AL) 121 E 4
Kavála (GR) 207 E 2
Kavalčiukai (LT) 175 F 3
Kavarna (BG) 13 E 4

- Kavarskas *(LT)* 171 E 3
- Kavastu *(EST)* 155 D 4
- Kaveírio-Chlói *(GR)* 214 B 1
- Kävlinge *(S)* 143 D 4
- Kavoliai *(LT)* 171 F 2
- Kávos *(GR)* 210 C 2
- Kavoúsi *(GR)* 227 E 4
- Kavýli *(GR)* 209 D 1
- Kawęczyn *(PL)* 188 C 4
- Käylä *(FIN)* 129 F 3
- Kaysersberg *(F)* 45 D 4
- Kazafáni *(CY)* 231 C 2
- Kažani *(MK)* 122 B 4
- Kazanlăk *(BG)* 19 D 1
- Kazanów *(PL)* 196 C 2
- Kazárma *(GR)* 217 D 4
- Kazas *(LV)* 161 E 4
- Kazdanga *(LT)* 162 C 1
- Kazimieravas *(LT)* 177 E 1
- Kazimierz Biskupi *(PL)* 188 C 3
- Kazimierz Dolny *(PL)* 196 C 2
- Kazimierza Wielka *(PL)* 195 F 4
- Kazincbarcika *(H)* 12 B 3
- Kazitiškis *(LT)* 172 C 3
- Kazliškėlis *(LT)* 165 F 4
- Kazlų Rūda *(LT)* 175 F 2
- Kaźmierz *(PL)* 187 E 2
- Kažoki *(LV)* 165 D 2
- Kcynia *(PL)* 187 F 1
- Kdyně *(CZ)* 89 F 4
- Kéa *(GR)* 219 D 3
- Kéa (Nisí) *(GR)* 219 D 3
- Keadew *(IRL)* 22 C 3
- Keady *(GB)* 23 E 3
- Keava *(EST)* 149 E 4
- Keberkščiai *(LT)* 169 D 2
- Keblonys *(LT)* 171 F 2
- Kebnekaise *(S)* 127 F 2
- Kechrókampos *(GR)* 207 C 2
- Kéchros *(GR)* 208 B 2
- Kecskemét *(H)* 113 D 2
- Kėdainiai *(LT)* 170 C 3
- Kedonys *(LT)* 176 C 2
- Kédros *(GR)* 211 F 3
- Kędzierzyn-Koźle *(PL)* 194 C 4
- Keel *(IRL)* 22 A 3
- Keeni *(EST)* 160 C 1
- Keerbergen *(B)* 39 F 2
- Kefalári *(GR)* 217 E 2
- Kefaloniá (Nisí) *(GR)* 216 B 1
- Kéfalos *(GR)* 225 F 2
- Kefalóvryso *Etolia-Akarnanía(GR)* 216 C 1
- Kefalóvryso *Ioánnina(GR)* 210 F 1
- Kefalóvryso *Lárisa(GR)* 211 F 1
- Kefalóvryso *Messinía(GR)* 217 D 4
- Keflavík *(IS)* 126 A 2
- Kegai *(LT)* 169 D 1
- Ķegums *(LV)* 165 C 2
- Kehl *(D)* 45 E 3
- Kehra *(EST)* 149 F 3
- Kehtna *(EST)* 149 E 4
- Keidžiai *(LT)* 177 E 3
- Keighley *(GB)* 33 D 2
- Keila *(EST)* 149 D 3
- Keila-Joa *(EST)* 149 E 4
- Keipene *(LV)* 165 E 1
- Ķeiši *(LV)* 167 D 4
- Keitele *(FIN)* 133 E 3
- Keith *(GB)* 27 E 3
- Ķekava *(LV)* 165 D 1
- Kelankylä *(FIN)* 129 D 4
- Kelberg *(D)* 87 E 3
- Kelbra *(D)* 88 C 1
- Këlcyrë *(AL)* 18 B 2
- Kelefá *(GR)* 222 C 2
- Kellinghusen *(D)* 78 C 4
- Kellokoski *(FIN)* 137 D 3
- Kelmė *(LT)* 169 E 4
- Kelso *(GB)* 31 E 3
- Kelujärvi *(FIN)* 129 D 2
- Kemberg *(D)* 85 D 4
- Kembs *(F)* 92 B 4
- Kemi *(FIN)* 128 C 3
- Kemijärvi *(FIN)* 129 D 3
- Keminmaa *(FIN)* 128 C 4
- Kemnath *(D)* 89 D 3
- Kempele *(FIN)* 133 E 1
- Kempen *Kreis Viersen(D)* 87 C 4
- Kempenich *(D)* 87 E 3
- Ķempji *(LV)* 159 E 4
- Kempten *(D)* 93 E 3
- Kemsiai *(LT)* 163 F 2
- Kena *(LT)* 177 F 2
- Kendal *(GB)* 32 C 1
- Kenilworth *(GB)* 33 D 4
- Ķeniņkalns *(LV)* 161 E 3
- Kenmare / Neidín *(IRL)* 24 B 3
- Kennacraig *(GB)* 30 B 2
- Kentallen *(D)* 27 C 4
- Kentraičiai *(LT)* 163 E 4
- Kentrikó *(GR)* 206 B 2
- Kenzingen *(D)* 45 E 4
- Kepaliai *(LT)* 164 B 3
- Ķepenes *(LV)* 163 F 3
- Kepi i Gjuhezës *(AL)* 18 B 2
- Kępice *(PL)* 181 F 2
- Kępno *(PL)* 194 B 2
- Kerameía *(GR)* 215 D 3
- Keramídi *(GR)* 212 B 2
- Keramítsa *(GR)* 210 C 1
- Kéramos *(GR)* 214 C 4
- Keramotí *(GR)* 207 F 3
- Kerasiá *Évoia(GR)* 212 C 4
- Kerasiá *Magnisía(GR)* 212 B 2
- Kerasiés *(GR)* 205 F 2
- Kerasochóri *(GR)* 211 E 3
- Kerasóna *(GR)* 211 D 2
- Keratéa *(GR)* 218 C 2
- Kerava *(FIN)* 137 D 3
- Kergu *(EST)* 153 C 2
- Keri *(GR)* 216 B 3
- Kerimäki *(FIN)* 135 F 4
- Kerken *(D)* 87 E 1
- Kerkonkoski *(FIN)* 133 F 3
- Kerkrade *(NL)* 87 D 2
- Kérkyra *(GR)* 210 B 2
- Kérkyra (Nisí) *(GR)* 210 B 2
- Kernai *(LT)* 162 C 3
- Kernascléden *(F)* 40 C 4
- Kernavé *(LT)* 177 D 1
- Kéros (Nisí) *(GR)* 224 C 2
- Kerpen *Erftkreis(D)* 87 E 2
- Kerteminde *(DK)* 142 C 4
- Kértezi *(GR)* 217 E 2
- Keryneia / Girne *(CY)* 231 C 2
- Kerzers *(CH)* 49 F 3
- Kesälahti *(FIN)* 135 F 4
- Keşan *(TR)* 19 E 1
- Kesh *(GB)* 23 D 2
- Kęsowo *(PL)* 182 B 4
- Kesterciems *(LV)* 157 F 4
- Kestilä *(FIN)* 133 F 2
- Keswick *(GB)* 31 D 4
- Keszthely *(H)* 112 A 2
- Kętrzyn *(PL)* 184 B 2
- Kettering *(GB)* 33 E 4
- Kettletoft *(GB)* 29 E 3
- Kettwig *(D)* 87 E 1
- Ketūnai *(LT)* 163 D 3
- Keturiasdešimt Totorių *(LT)* 177 E 2
- Keturkaimis *(LT)* 175 E 2
- Keturvalakiai *(LT)* 175 E 2
- Kęty *(PL)* 200 F 2
- Ketzin *(D)* 85 D 3
- Keuruu *(FIN)* 133 E 4
- Kevelaer *(D)* 87 D 1
- Ķevele *(LV)* 163 E 2
- Kevo *(FIN)* 125 E 2
- Keynsham *(GB)* 35 E 2
- Kežmarok *(SK)* 12 B 2
- Ķęsai *(LT)* 169 D 2
- Kęsčiai *(LT)* 169 D 3
- Kiáto *(GR)* 217 E 2
- Kiaukliai *(LT)* 171 E 4
- Kiauleikiai *(LT)* 162 B 4
- Kiaulupiai *(LT)* 169 E 4
- Kiaunoriai *(LT)* 169 F 2
- Kibučiai *(LT)* 177 D 2
- Kičevo *(MK)* 122 A 3
- Kidderminster *(GB)* 32 C 4
- Kidlington *(GB)* 35 F 1
- Kidsgrove *(GB)* 32 C 3
- Kiduliai *(LT)* 169 E 4
- Kidwelly / Cydweli *(GB)* 34 C 1
- Kiefersfelden *(D)* 94 A 3
- Ķieģeļceplis *(LV)* 163 E 2
- Ķieģeļnieki *(LV)* 163 D 1
- Kiekinkoski *(FIN)* 135 F 2
- Kiel *(D)* 79 C 4
- Kielce *(PL)* 195 F 3
- Kiełczygłów *(PL)* 195 D 2
- Kielno *(PL)* 182 C 1
- Kiemeliai *(LT)* 177 E 1
- Kiemeliškés *(LT)* 177 E 2
- Kiental *(CH)* 96 B 1
- Kierinki *(FIN)* 128 C 2
- Kiernozia *(PL)* 189 E 3
- Kietrz *(PL)* 200 F 2
- Kietz *(D)* 85 F 2
- Kifisiá *(GR)* 218 C 2
- Kifjord *(N)* 125 E 1
- Kihelkonna *(EST)* 152 A 3
- Kihlanki *(FIN)* 128 C 2
- Kihlepa *(EST)* 153 D 1
- Kihlevere *(EST)* 150 C 3
- Kihniö *(FIN)* 133 D 4
- Kiia *(EST)* 149 E 3
- Kiidjärve *(EST)* 155 D 4
- Kiihtelysvaara *(FIN)* 135 F 3
- Kiikala *(FIN)* 136 C 3
- Kiikka *(FIN)* 136 B 3
- Kiikla *(EST)* 151 E 3
- Kiikoinen *(FIN)* 136 B 3
- Kiili *(EST)* 149 E 3
- Kiiminki *(FIN)* 133 E 1
- Kiisa *(EST)* 149 E 3
- Kiiskilä *(FIN)* 133 E 2
- Kiistala *(FIN)* 128 C 1
- Kiiu *(EST)* 149 F 2
- Kiiu-Aabla *(EST)* 149 F 2
- Kije *(PL)* 195 F 3
- Kijevo *(HR)* 103 F 1
- Kijevo *(SRB)* 121 F 2
- Kikinda *(SRB)* 113 D 1
- Kikół *(PL)* 189 D 1
- Kikuri *(LV)* 162 C 1
- Kil *(S)* 139 F 3
- Kilafors *(S)* 140 C 2
- Kilbaha *(IRL)* 24 B 2
- Kilbeggan *(IRL)* 23 D 2
- Kilbirnie *(GB)* 30 C 2
- Kilboghamn *(N)* 127 D 3
- Kilbotn *(N)* 124 A 4
- Kilchoan *(GB)* 26 C 4
- Kilcock *(IRL)* 23 E 4
- Kilcormac *(IRL)* 23 D 2
- Kilcreggan *(GB)* 30 C 2
- Kildare / Cill Dara *(IRL)* 25 E 1
- Kildorrery *(IRL)* 24 C 3
- Kildu *(EST)* 154 B 3
- Kilelér *(GR)* 212 B 2
- Kilfenora *(IRL)* 24 B 1
- Kilgarvan *(IRL)* 24 B 3
- Kilija *(UA)* 13 F 1
- Kilingi-Nõmme *(EST)* 154 A 4
- Kilkee / Cill Chaoi *(IRL)* 24 B 2
- Kilkeel *(GB)* 23 E 4
- Kilkenny / Cill Chainnigh *(IRL)* 25 D 2
- Kilkhampton *(GB)* 34 C 4
- Kilkís *(GR)* 206 B 2
- Kilksama *(EST)* 153 C 3
- Killadysert *(IRL)* 24 C 2
- Killaloe / Cill Dalua *(IRL)* 24 C 2
- Killarney / Cill Airne *(IRL)* 24 B 3
- Killashandra *(IRL)* 23 D 2
- Killenaule *(IRL)* 25 D 2
- Killimer *(IRL)* 24 B 2
- Killin *(GB)* 30 C 1
- Killinkoski *(FIN)* 133 E 4
- Killorglin / Cill Orglan *(IRL)* 24 B 3
- Killybegs / Na Cealla Beaga *(IRL)* 22 C 2
- Killyleagh *(GB)* 32 E 2
- Kilmaine *(IRL)* 22 B 4
- Kilmallock / Cill Mocheallóg *(IRL)* 24 C 2
- Kilmarnock *(GB)* 30 C 2
- Kilmartin *(GB)* 30 B 1
- Kilmore Quay *(IRL)* 25 E 3
- Kilmurry *(IRL)* 24 C 2
- Kilninver *(GB)* 30 B 1
- Kilnsea *(GB)* 33 F 2
- Kilpisjärvi *(FIN)* 124 C 1
- Kilrea *(GB)* 23 E 2
- Kilronan / Cill Rónáin *(IRL)* 22 B 4
- Kilrush / Cill Rois *(IRL)* 24 B 2
- Kilsyth *(GB)* 30 C 2
- Kiltealy *(IRL)* 25 E 3
- Kiltimagh *(IRL)* 22 B 3
- Kiltsi *(EST)* 150 A 3
- Kilwinning *(GB)* 30 C 2
- Kilyos *(TR)* 19 F 1
- Kímale *(LT)* 157 D 4
- Kimbartiškė *(LT)* 172 C 3
- Kimito / Kemiö *(FIN)* 136 B 4
- Kimméria *(GR)* 207 F 2
- Kímolos *(GR)* 224 A 2
- Kímolos (Nisí) *(GR)* 224 A 2
- Kimry *(RUS)* 7 F 1
- Kimstad *(S)* 143 F 1
- Kínaros (Nisí) *(GR)* 220 C 4
- Kinbrace *(GB)* 27 D 2
- Kincardine *(GB)* 31 D 2
- Kindberg *(A)* 95 E 3
- Kindelbrück *(D)* 88 C 1
- Kinderai *(LT)* 171 E 1
- Kinéta *(GR)* 218 B 2
- Kingisepp *(RUS)* 7 D 1
- King's Lynn *(GB)* 33 F 4
- Kingsbridge *(GB)* 34 D 4
- Kingscourt *(IRL)* 23 E 3
- Kingston-upon-Hull *(GB)* 33 E 2
- Kingston-upon-Thames *(GB)* 36 B 3
- Kingswear *(GB)* 35 D 4
- Kington *(GB)* 32 C 4
- Kingussie *(GB)* 27 C 4
- Kinguti *(LV)* 157 D 4
- Kinloch Rannoch *(GB)* 27 C 4
- Kinlochbervie *(GB)* 27 E 1
- Kinlochewe *(GB)* 27 D 3
- Kinna *(S)* 143 F 2
- Kinnasniemi *(FIN)* 135 F 3
- Kinnegad *(IRL)* 23 F 2
- Kinnitty *(IRL)* 25 D 1
- Kinnula *(FIN)* 133 E 3
- Kinross *(GB)* 31 D 1
- Kinsale / Cionn tSáile *(IRL)* 24 C 2
- Kinsarvik *(N)* 138 C 2
- Kintai *(LT)* 168 B 2
- Kintaus *(FIN)* 133 D 4
- Kintore *(GB)* 28 B 4
- Kinvarra *(IRL)* 22 B 4
- Kióni *(GR)* 216 B 1
- Kipinä *(FIN)* 129 D 4
- Kípoi *Évros(GR)* 208 C 2
- Kípoi *Ioánnina(GR)* 211 D 1
- Kipoureío *(GR)* 211 E 1
- Kirbla *(EST)* 153 C 2
- Kirchbach in Steiemark *(A)* 95 E 4
- Kirchberg *(A)* 94 A 3
- Kirchberg *Kreis Zwickauer Land(D)* 89 E 2
- Kirchberg (Hunsrück) *Rhein-Hunsrück-Kreis(D)* 45 D 1
- Kirchberg am Wagram *(A)* 95 E 1
- Kirchberg an der Pielach *(A)* 95 F 3
- Kirchdorf an der Krems *(A)* 94 C 2
- Kirchenlamitz *(D)* 89 E 3
- Kirchenthumbach *(D)* 89 D 3
- Kirchhain *(D)* 88 A 2
- Kirchheim *Kreis Hersfeld-Rotenburg(D)* 88 D 2
- Kirchheim a. Neckar *(D)* 45 F 2
- Kirchheimbolanden *(D)* 45 E 1
- Kirchhundem *(D)* 87 F 4
- Kirchlengern *(D)* 83 F 4
- Kirchmöser *(D)* 85 D 3
- Kirchschlag in der Bucklingen Welt *(A)* 95 F 3
- Kirdeikiai *(LT)* 172 B 3
- Kirepi *(EST)* 154 C 4
- Kiri *(LV)* 157 D 3
- Kirikuküla *(EST)* 160 B 1
- Kirimäe *(EST)* 148 D 1
- Kiriši *(RUS)* 7 E 2
- Kirkağaç *(TR)* 19 E 2
- Kirkby Lonsdale *(GB)* 32 C 1
- Kirkby Stephen *(GB)* 33 D 1
- Kirkcaldy *(GB)* 31 D 2
- Kirkcolm *(GB)* 30 C 4
- Kirkcudbright *(GB)* 30 C 4
- Kirkenær *(N)* 139 F 2
- Kirkenes *(N)* 125 C 2
- Kirkham *(GB)* 32 C 2
- Kirki *(GR)* 208 B 2
- Kirkintilloch *(GB)* 30 C 2
- Kirkjubæjarklaustur *(IS)* 126 B 3
- Kirkjubøur *(DK)* 126 A 4
- Kirkonummi / Kyrkslätt *(FIN)* 136 C 4
- Kırklareli *(TR)* 19 E 1
- Kirkliai *(LT)* 163 E 1
- Kirkwall *(GB)* 29 D 4
- Kirmėliai *(LT)* 171 D 2
- Kirn *(D)* 45 D 1
- Kirna *Järva(EST)* 149 F 4
- Kirna *Lääne(EST)* 148 C 4
- Kirov *(RUS)* 7 F 2
- Kirovohrad *(UA)* 13 F 2
- Kirovsk *(RUS)* 7 D 1
- Ķirpēni *(LV)* 163 F 2
- Kirriemuir *(GB)* 31 D 1
- Kirtorf *(D)* 88 A 2
- Kirumpää *(EST)* 161 A 2
- Kiruna *(S)* 128 A 2
- Kisa *(S)* 143 F 1
- Kisajno (Jezioro) *(PL)* 184 C 2
- Kiseljak *Sarajevo(BIH)* 117 F 2
- Kiseljak *Tuzla(BIH)* 117 E 2
- Ķīši *(LV)* 157 F 4
- Kisielice *(PL)* 183 D 3
- Kisieliškés *(LT)* 176 C 2
- Kiškėnai *(LT)* 168 B 1
- Kisko *(FIN)* 136 C 4
- Kiskőrös *(H)* 113 D 2
- Kiskunfélegyháza *(H)* 113 D 2
- Kiskunhalas *(H)* 113 E 2
- Kíssamos (Kastéli) *(GR)* 226 C 4
- Kißlegg *(D)* 93 D 3
- Kissonerga *(CY)* 230 A 3
- Kissoú Kámpos *(GR)* 226 C 2
- Kistanje *(HR)* 103 F 1
- Kisújszállás *(H)* 113 E 1
- Kisvárda *(H)* 12 B 3
- Kiszkowo *(PL)* 187 F 2
- Kitee *(FIN)* 135 F 4
- Kíti *(GR)* 231 D 3
- Kíti (Cape) *(CY)* 231 D 3
- Kitka *(FIN)* 129 E 3
- Kittilä *(FIN)* 128 C 2
- Kitzbühel *(A)* 94 A 3
- Kitzingen *(D)* 88 C 4
- Kiudalova *(LV)* 167 F 3
- Kiukainen *(FIN)* 136 B 3
- Kiuma *(EST)* 161 D 1
- Kiuruvesi *(FIN)* 133 F 2
- Kivéri *(GR)* 217 F 3
- Kivijärvi *(FIN)* 133 E 3
- Kivilahti *(FIN)* 135 F 3
- Kivitaipale *(FIN)* 129 D 3
- Kivi-Vigala *(EST)* 153 C 2
- Kiviõli *(EST)* 151 E 3
- Kivotós *(GR)* 205 E 4
- Kiwity *(PL)* 183 F 2
- Kizári *(GR)* 208 B 2
- Kjellerup *(DK)* 142 B 3
- Kjerringøy *(N)* 127 E 2
- Kjerringvåg *(N)* 130 C 2
- Kjøllefjord *(N)* 125 E 1
- Kjøpsvik *(N)* 127 E 1
- Kjustendil *(BG)* 18 C 1
- Kladanj *(BIH)* 117 F 2
- Kladnica *(SRB)* 119 E 1
- Kladnice *(HR)* 103 F 1
- Kladno *(CZ)* 90 A 2
- Kladovo *(SRB)* 119 E 1
- Klæbu *(N)* 131 D 3
- Klagenfurt *(A)* 114 A 2
- Klaipėda *(LT)* 168 B 1
- Klaksvik *(DK)* 126 A 4
- Klampučiai *(LT)* 175 E 2
- Klana *(HR)* 99 D 3
- Klanac *(HR)* 99 F 4
- Klangiai *(LT)* 169 F 4
- Klanxbüll *(D)* 78 B 2
- Klapkalnciems *(LV)* 157 F 4
- Klašnice *(BIH)* 115 E 4
- Klässbol *(S)* 139 F 3
- Kláśterec nad Ohří *(CZ)* 89 F 2
- Klatovy *(CZ)* 89 F 4
- Klaukkala *(FIN)* 137 D 4
- Klausučiai *(LT)* 175 E 2
- Ķlavas *(LV)* 159 D 4
- Klazienaveen *(NL)* 83 D 3
- Klebiškis *(LT)* 176 B 2
- Klecko *(PL)* 187 F 2
- Kleczew *(PL)* 188 C 3
- Kleinhaugsdorf *(A)* 91 D 4
- Kleisoúra *(GR)* 205 E 3
- Kleitoría *(GR)* 217 E 2
- Klembów *(PL)* 190 C 3
- Klenovica *(HR)* 99 E 3
- Kleppe *(N)* 138 B 4
- Kleppestø *(N)* 138 B 2
- Kleszczele *(PL)* 191 E 2
- Kleszczewo *(PL)* 187 F 3
- Kleszczów *(PL)* 195 D 2
- Kleve *(D)* 82 C 4
- Klewki *(PL)* 183 F 3
- Kličevac *(SRB)* 118 C 1
- Klimavičy *(BY)* 7 E 4
- Klimontów *Świętokrzyskie(PL)* 196 C 3
- Klimpfjäll *(S)* 131 F 1
- Klin *(RUS)* 7 F 2
- Klina *(SRB)* 121 F 1
- Klinča Selo *(HR)* 99 F 2
- Klincy *(RUS)* 7 E 3
- Klingenbach *(A)* 95 F 2
- Klingenthal *(D)* 89 E 2
- Klintehamn *(S)* 146 B 2
- Klintnieki *(LV)* 163 D 1
- Klippan *(S)* 143 E 2
- Klippen *(S)* 127 F 4
- Klirou *(CY)* 231 C 2
- Klis *(HR)* 116 C 4
- Klisura *(SRB)* 119 E 4
- Klitten *(D)* 85 F 4
- Klixbüll *(D)* 78 B 2
- Kljajićevo *(SRB)* 113 D 4
- Ključ *(BIH)* 116 C 2
- Kłobuck *(PL)* 195 D 3
- Kločiūnai *(LT)* 171 F 4
- Kłocko *(PL)* 194 C 1
- Kłodawa *Lubuskie(PL)* 186 C 1
- Kłodawa *Wielkopolskie(PL)* 189 D 3
- Kłodzko *(PL)* 193 E 4
- Kløfta *(N)* 139 E 3
- Klokkarvik *(N)* 138 B 2
- Klokočevac *(SRB)* 119 E 1
- Kłomnice *(PL)* 195 D 3
- Kloniniai Mijaugonys *(LT)* 177 D 2
- Klonowa *(PL)* 194 C 1
- Klooga *(EST)* 149 D 3
- Kloogaranna *(EST)* 149 D 3
- Kloštar Ivanić *(HR)* 112 A 4
- Kloštar Podravski *(HR)* 112 A 4
- Klösterle *(A)* 93 E 4
- Klosterneuburg *(A)* 95 F 1
- Klosters *(CH)* 97 E 1
- Kloten *(CH)* 92 C 4
- Kłótno Baruchowo *(PL)* 189 D 2
- Klötze *(D)* 84 B 3
- Klovainiai *(LT)* 164 C 4
- Klöverträsk *(S)* 128 B 4
- Klövsjö *(S)* 131 F 4
- Kluczbork *(PL)* 194 C 3
- Klucze *(PL)* 195 E 3
- Kluczewsko *(PL)* 195 D 3
- Kluki *Łódzkie(PL)* 195 D 2
- Kluki *Pomorskie(PL)* 181 F 1
- Klukowa Huta *(PL)* 182 B 2
- Klukowo *(PL)* 191 E 2
- Klūnas *(LV)* 163 F 2
- Klupe *(BIH)* 115 F 4
- Klütz *(D)* 79 E 3
- Klwów *(PL)* 195 F 1
- Klykoliai *(LT)* 163 E 3
- Knäred *(S)* 143 D 3
- Knaresborough *(GB)* 33 D 1
- Knarvik *(N)* 138 B 2
- Knivsta *(S)* 141 D 3
- Knjaževac *(SRB)* 119 E 4
- Knokke-Heist *(B)* 37 F 3
- Knurów *(PL)* 194 C 4
- Knutsford *(GB)* 32 C 3
- Knyszyn *(PL)* 185 E 4
- Knyszyńska (Puszcza) *(PL)* 185 E 4
- Kobarid *(SLO)* 98 C 2
- Kobaš / Bosanski Kobaš *(BIH)* 115 F 4
- Kobela *(EST)* 160 C 1
- Kobeljaky *(UA)* 13 F 1
- København *(DK)* 143 D 4
- Kobern-Gondorf *(D)* 87 F 3
- Kobierzyce *(PL)* 193 F 3
- Kobiór *(PL)* 200 F 2
- Kobišnica *(SRB)* 119 E 1
- Koblenz *(D)* 87 F 3
- Kobruvere *(EST)* 154 B 3
- Kobryn *(BY)* 6 C 4
- Kobyla Góra *(PL)* 194 C 2
- Kobylanka *(PL)* 180 C 4
- Kobylin-Borzymy *(PL)* 191 D 1
- Kobyłka *(PL)* 190 B 3
- Kobylnica *Pomorskie(PL)* 181 F 1
- Kočani *(MK)* 122 B 2
- Koceljevo *(SRB)* 118 B 2
- Kočēni *(LV)* 159 F 2
- Kočerin *(BIH)* 117 E 4
- Kočevje *(SLO)* 99 E 2
- Kochanowice *(PL)* 194 C 3
- Kochel a. See *(D)* 93 F 3

Kochłowice (PL) 195 D4
Kock (PL) 191 D4
Koczała (PL) 181 F3
Kodeń (PL) 191 F3
Kodiksami (FIN) 136 B3
Kodila (EST) 149 D4
Kodisjoki (FIN) 136 B3
Kodrąb (PL) 195 E2
Kõduküla (EST) 154 C4
Koeru (EST) 150 C4
Kofinou (CY) 231 C3
Köflach (A) 95 E4
Køge (DK) 143 D4
Kohala (EST) 151 D3
Kohatu (EST) 149 D3
Kohila (EST) 149 E3
Kohtla (EST) 151 E3
Kohtla-Järve (EST) 151 E3
Kohtla-Nõmme (EST) 151 E3
Kõidama (EST) 154 B3
Koidu (EST) 154 B4
Koigi (EST) 149 F4
Koikkala (FIN) 135 E4
Koikküla (EST) 160 C2
Koikla (EST) 152 C2
Koila (GR) 205 F4
Koiláda Argolída (GR) 218 B3
Koiláda Kozáni (GR) 205 F4
Koilani (CY) 230 B3
Kõima (EST) 153 B3
Koimíseos Theotókou (GR) 217 E3
Koímla (EST) 152 A4
Koínyra (GR) 207 F3
Koíta (GR) 222 C3
Koivu (FIN) 128 C3
Kojetín Olomoucký kraj(CZ) 91 E3
Kökar (S) 136 A4
Kokari (LV) 167 D2
Kokemäki (FIN) 136 B3
Kokin Brod (SRB) 118 B3
Kokkála (GR) 222 C3
Kokkári (GR) 221 E2
Kókkino Neró (GR) 212 B1
Kokkinotrimithia (CY) 231 C3
Kokkola / Karleby (FIN) 133 C2
Kokkotoí (GR) 212 B3
Koknese (LV) 165 F2
Kokora (EST) 155 D3
Koksijde-Bad (B) 37 E4
Koksvere (EST) 154 B3
Kola (EST) 115 E4
Kołaczkowo (PL) 188 B3
Kołaczyce (PL) 201 C2
Kołaki Kościelne (PL) 191 D1
Kolari (LV) 128 C3
Kolari (SRB) 118 C1
Kolåsen (S) 131 E2
Kolašin (MNE) 121 E1
Kolbäck (S) 140 C4
Kolbacz (PL) 180 C2
Kolberġis (LV) 161 E3
Kolbermoor (D) 94 A3
Kölbi (EST) 160 C1
Kolbiel (PL) 190 C3
Kolbudy (PL) 182 C2
Kolbuszowa (PL) 196 C4
Kolby Kås (DK) 142 C4
Kołczygłowy (PL) 181 F2
Kolding (DK) 142 B4
Kolga (EST) 149 F2
Kolga-Jaani (EST) 154 C3
Kolgaküla (EST) 149 F2
Kolho (FIN) 133 E4
Koli (FIN) 135 F3
Kolin (CZ) 90 C2
Kolín (CZ) 90 C2
Kolindrós (GR) 206 B3
Kõljala (EST) 152 C3
Kolka (LV) 157 E2
Kolkanlahti (FIN) 133 E4
Kolkja (EST) 155 E2
Kölleda (D) 89 D1
Kollínes (GR) 217 E4
Kollino (EST) 161 D1
Köln (D) 87 E2
Kolnica (PL) 193 F3
Kolno Podlaskie(PL) 184 C4
Koło (PL) 188 B3
Kołobrzeg (PL) 181 D2
Koločep (Otok) (HR) 120 B2
Kołodzieje (PL) 183 D3
Kolomyja (UA) 13 D2
Kolonowskie (PL) 194 B3
Kolossi (CY) 230 B3

Koloveč (CZ) 89 F4
Kolovrat (SRB) 118 B4
Kolpino (RUS) 7 D1
Kolsko (PL) 187 D4
Kolsva (S) 140 C3
Kolu (EST) 154 A2
Koluszki (PL) 189 E4
Koluvere (EST) 148 C4
Kolvereid (N) 131 E1
Kolymvári (GR) 226 A1
Koma tou Gialou (CY) 231 C3
Komagfjord (N) 125 D2
Komańcza (PL) 202 E3
Kómanos (GR) 205 F4
Kómara (GR) 208 C1
Komárno (SK) 12 A3
Komarów-Osada (PL) 197 F3
Komarówka Podlaska (PL) 191 E4
Kombuļi (LV) 167 E4
Komi (CY) 231 E2
Kómi Chíos (GR) 220 C1
Kómi Kikládes(GR) 219 C4
Komílio (GR) 210 C4
Komin (HR) 99 F1
Kómito (GR) 219 D2
Komiža (HR) 103 F2
Kömlő (H) 112 C3
Komméno (GR) 211 D3
Komniná Kozáni(GR) 205 F3
Komniná Xánthi(GR) 207 F2
Komninádes (GR) 205 D3
Komorane (SRB) 122 A2
Komornik (PL) 187 E3
Komorowo Żuławskie (PL) 183 D2
Komotiní (GR) 208 B2
Kompóti (GR) 211 D3
Komprachcice (PL) 194 B3
Kömsi (EST) 153 A4
Konak (SRB) 113 F4
Konakovo (RUS) 7 F2
Konarzyce (PL) 184 C4
Konarzyny Pomorskie(PL) 181 F3
Končanica (HR) 112 B4
Kondratowice (PL) 193 F3
Kondrić (HR) 115 F3
Koneck (PL) 188 C2
Køng (DK) 144 C3
Köngernheim (D) 45 E1
Konginkangas (FIN) 133 E3
Kongsberg (N) 139 D3
Kongsfjord (N) 125 F1
Kongsvinger (N) 139 E3
Konguta (EST) 154 C4
Konice (CZ) 91 E3
Koniecpol (PL) 195 E3
Königs Wusterhausen (D) 85 E3
Königsbrück (D) 90 A1
Königsbrunn (D) 93 E2
Königsee (D) 89 D2
Königsfeld i. Schwarzwald (D) 45 E4
Königslutter (D) 84 B3
Königssee (D) 94 B3
Königstein (D) 88 A3
Königstein (D) 90 A1
Königswiesen (A) 95 D1
Königswinter (D) 87 D2
Konin (PL) 188 C3
Koniskós (GR) 211 F1
Konístres (GR) 213 D4
Kónitsa (GR) 205 D4
Konjevrate (HR) 103 F1
Konjic (BIH) 117 E4
Konjsko (BIH) 121 D2
Konju (EST) 151 F3
Könnern (D) 84 C2
Konnevesi (FIN) 133 F4
Konopiska (PL) 195 D3
Konopište (MK) 122 C4
Konopki Wielkie (PL) 184 C3
Konopnica (PL) 195 D2
Konotop (UA) 7 F3
Konotop Lubuskie(PL) 187 D4
Końskie (PL) 195 E2
Konsko (MK) 122 C4
Końskowola (PL) 197 D1
Konsmo (N) 138 C4
Konstancin-Jeziorna (PL) 190 C2
Konstantinova (LV) 167 E4
Konstantinovy Lázně (CZ) 89 F3
Konstantynów (PL) 191 E3

Konstantynów Łódzki (PL) 189 D4
Konstanz (D) 93 D3
Kontea (CY) 231 D3
Kontemenos (CY) 231 C2
Korsør (DK) 142 C4
Kontiàs (GR) 213 F1
Kontich (B) 39 E1
Kontiolahti (FIN) 135 F3
Kontiomäki (FIN) 135 E1
Kontopoúli (GR) 214 A1
Kontovázaina (GR) 217 D2
Konttajärvi (FIN) 128 C3
Konz (D) 44 C1
Kooperators Daugavpils(LV) 172 C1
Kooperators Ogres(LV) 165 D1
Kooraste (EST) 161 D1
Koosa (EST) 155 D3
Kopań (Jezioro) (PL) 181 E1
Kopáni (GR) 211 D2
Kopanós (GR) 205 F3
Koparnes (N) 130 A4
Kópasker (IS) 126 C1
Köpenick (D) 85 E2
Koper (SLO) 99 D2
Kopervik (N) 138 B3
Kopidlno (CZ) 90 C2
Köping (S) 140 C4
Köpingsvik (S) 143 F3
Köpmanholmen (S) 132 B3
Koporiće (SRB) 118 C4
Koppang (N) 139 E1
Kopparberg (S) 140 C3
Kopperby (D) 78 C2
Koprivna (BIH) 115 E4
Koprivnica (HR) 112 A4
Koprivnica (SRB) 119 E2
Koprzywnica (PL) 196 C3
Kõpu (EST) 154 A4
Korakou (CY) 230 B3
Korbach (D) 88 A1
Korbevac (SRB) 119 C4
Korbielów (PL) 200 F3
Korbovo (SRB) 119 E1
Korçë (AL) 18 C2
Korčula (HR) 120 B2
Korčula (Otok) (HR) 120 B2
Korczew (PL) 191 D2
Korczyna (PL) 202 D2
Korenica (HR) 99 F3
Korfantów (PL) 194 B4
Kórfos (GR) 218 B2
Korgen (N) 127 D1
Korgene (LV) 159 D2
Körgessaare (EST) 148 A4
Koria (FIN) 137 D3
Korinós (GR) 206 B4
Kórinthos (GR) 217 F2
Korínthou (Dióriga) (GR) 217 F2
Korissía (GR) 219 D3
Korita (BIH) 121 D2
Korita (HR) 120 C2
Korita (MNE) 121 E2
Korithi (GR) 216 B3
Koritnik (SRB) 118 C3
Korkeakangas (FIN) 135 F3
Kõrkküla (EST) 152 A3
Körkvere (EST) 153 A3
Kormakitis (CY) 231 C2
Kormakitis (Cape) (CY) 230 F1
Körmend (H) 95 F3
Kornat (Otok) (HR) 103 E1
Korneti (LV) 161 D2
Korneuburg (A) 95 F3
Kórnik (PL) 187 F3
Kornofoléa (GR) 208 C3
Kornos (CY) 231 C3
Kornwac (PL) 200 E2
Kornwestheim (D) 45 F2
Koromáčno (HR) 99 D3
Koróna (GR) 206 B2
Koróneia (GR) 217 E1
Koróni (GR) 222 B2
Koronída (GR) 219 F4
Koronisia (GR) 211 D3
Kóronos (GR) 219 F4
Koronoúda (GR) 206 C2
Koronowo (PL) 182 B2
Koropí (GR) 218 C2
Korosten' (UA) 13 E1
Korostyšiv (UA) 13 D1
Korpilahti (FIN) 133 F4
Korpilombolo (S) 128 B3
Korpo / Korppoo (FIN) 136 B4
Korsberga (S) 143 F2

Korsholm / Mustasaari (FIN) 133 D3
Korsnäs (FIN) 132 C4
Korsze (PL) 184 B2
Kortesjärvi (FIN) 133 D3
Kórthio (GR) 219 E2
Kortrijk (B) 37 D2
Kortteenperä (FIN) 129 D3
Koruste (EST) 154 C4
Korvala (FIN) 129 D3
Korvaluoma (FIN) 136 B2
Kõrveküla (EST) 155 D3
Korycin (PL) 185 E4
Koryfási (GR) 217 D4
Korýkeio Ántro (GR) 212 B4
Korytków Duży (PL) 197 E3
Kos (GR) 225 F2
Kos (Nisí) (GR) 225 F2
Kosančić (SRB) 119 E4
Kosanica (MNE) 118 B4
Kosarska Dubica / Bosanska Dubica (BIH) 115 E4
Kościan (PL) 187 E3
Kościelec (PL) 188 C3
Kościerzyna (PL) 182 B2
Kose Harju(EST) 149 E3
Kose Ida-Viru(EST) 151 F3
Kose Võru(EST) 161 D2
Kosel (PL) 194 C4
Koserow (D) 80 C3
Kose-Uuemõisa (EST) 149 E3
Košetice (CZ) 90 B3
Koši Iai (LT) 169 D2
Košice (SK) 12 B2
Köylio (FIN) 136 B3
Kožáni (GR) 205 F4
Koška (HR) 112 C4
Koškele (LT) 159 E2
Koskenkorva (FIN) 133 D4
Koskenpää (FIN) 133 E4
Koski (FIN) 137 D3
Koski (FIN) 136 C3
Kóskina (GR) 219 D1
Koskue (FIN) 133 D4
Kosmás (GR) 217 F4
Kósmio (GR) 208 B2
Kosova (SRB) 155 D4
Kosovo Polje (SRB) 122 A1
Kosovska Kamenica (SRB) 119 C4
Kosovska Mitrovica (SRB) 119 D4
Kosów Lacki (PL) 191 D2
Kössen (A) 94 A3
Kósta (GR) 218 B4
Kostanjevac (HR) 99 F2
Kostanjevica na K. (SLO) 98 C2
Kostelec nad Černými Lesy (CZ) 90 B3
Kostelec nad Orlicí (CZ) 91 D2
Kostenec (BG) 19 E1
Koster (S) 139 E4
Kostivere (EST) 149 E2
Kostolac (SRB) 118 C1
Kostopil' (UA) 13 E1
Kóstos (GR) 219 F4
Kostrimäe (EST) 161 E1
Kostrzyn Lubuskie(PL) 186 B2
Kostrzyń Wielkopolskie(PL) 187 F3
Kosturino (MK) 122 C3
Kosula (FIN) 135 E3
Koszalin (PL) 181 E2
Koszęcin (PL) 195 D3
Köszeg (H) 95 F3
Koszyce (PL) 201 B1
Kotala (FIN) 129 E4
Kotala (FIN) 133 E4
Kotan (PL) 202 D3
Kótas (GR) 205 F3
Kotel (BG) 19 E1
Koterka (PL) 191 E4
Köthen (D) 84 C2
Kotka (FIN) 137 D3
Kotlin (PL) 188 B4
Kotor (MNE) 121 D2
Kotor Varoš (BIH) 117 E4
Kotoriba (HR) 99 F1
Kotorsko (BIH) 115 F4
Kotovs'k (UA) 13 D2
Kotraža (SRB) 118 C3
Kótronas (GR) 222 C3

Kotroniá (GR) 208 C2
Köttsjön (S) 132 A3
Kotuń (PL) 191 D3
Kötzting (D) 89 F4
Koufália (GR) 206 B3
Koufonísi (GR) 227 F3
Koufós (GR) 213 C1
Kouklia (CY) 230 A4
Kouklioí (GR) 210 C1
Koukounariés (GR) 212 C3
Koumaíika (GR) 221 D4
Koúndouros (GR) 219 D3
Kounoupélli (GR) 216 C2
Koura (GR) 133 D4
Koúrenta (GR) 211 D2
Kourion (CY) 230 B4
Kouris (CY) 230 B4
Kouris Dam (CY) 230 B4
Kourkouloí (GR) 212 C4
Kournás (GR) 226 B2
Kouroúta (GR) 216 C2
Koutselió (GR) 211 D2
Koutsó (GR) 207 F2
Koutsóchero (GR) 212 A2
Kouvola (FIN) 137 D3
Kovačica (SRB) 113 F4
Kovel' (UA) 12 C1
Kõveriku (EST) 151 E4
Kovero (FIN) 135 F3
Kovil (SRB) 113 E4
Kovin (SRB) 118 C1
Kowal (PL) 189 D2
Kowala-Stępocina (PL) 196 B2
Kowale Oleckie (PL) 185 D2
Kowalewo Pomorskie (PL) 189 D1
Kowary (PL) 193 D3
Kowiesy (PL) 189 F4
Köylio (FIN) 136 B3
Kozáni (GR) 205 F4
Kozarac (BIH) 115 E4
Kozarac (HR) 112 C4
Kozel'sk (RUS) 7 F3
Kozica (HR) 120 B1
Kozięgłowy (PL) 195 D3
Kozienice (PL) 190 C4
Kozienicka (Puszcza) (PL) 190 C4
Kozina (SLO) 99 D2
Kozjatyn (UA) 13 E1
Kozłówka (PL) 197 D1
Kozłowo (PL) 183 D3
Kozluk (BIH) 117 F2
Kozmin (PL) 187 F4
Koźminek (PL) 188 C3
Kozubszczyzna (PL) 197 D2
Kożuchów (PL) 187 D4
Kozy Śląskie(PL) 200 F3
Kraavi (EST) 161 D1
Krabi (EST) 161 D2
Krag (PL) 181 E2
Kragenæs (DK) 144 C3
Kragerø (N) 139 D4
Kragujevac (SRB) 118 C2
Krajenka (PL) 181 F2
Krajišnik (SRB) 113 F4
Krajkovac (SRB) 119 D3
Krajnik Dolny (PL) 186 B1
Krakés (LT) 170 B2
Krakhella (N) 138 B1
Krakow (D) 79 E4
Kraków (PL) 201 A2
Krakūnai (LT) 177 F4
Kraljevica (HR) 99 E3
Kraljevo (SRB) 118 C2
Kralovec (CZ) 90 C1
Kralovice (CZ) 90 A2
Kralupy nad Vltavou (CZ) 90 B3
Kramarzyny (PL) 181 F2
Kramfors (S) 132 B4
Kramsk (PL) 188 C3
Kranenburg (D) 82 D4
Krani (MK) 122 B4
Kranía Grevená(GR) 211 E1
Kranía Trikala(GR) 211 F1
Kranía Elassónas (GR) 211 F1
Kranichfeld (D) 89 D2
Kranidi (GR) 218 B3
Kranj (SLO) 99 D1
Kranjska Gora (SLO) 98 C1
Krapa (GR) 161 D4
Krape (Lobe) (LV) 165 D2
Krapina (HR) 99 E1
Krapinske Toplice (HR) 99 E1
Krapkowice (PL) 194 B4
Krašić (HR) 99 E2

Kräslava (LV) 173 E1
Kräslavas Stacija (LV) 173 E1
Kraslice (CZ) 89 B1
Krásná Lípa (CZ) 90 B1
Krasne Podkarpackie(PL) 202 D1
Kraśniczyn (PL) 197 F3
Kraśnik (PL) 197 D3
Krasno Polje (HR) 99 E3
Krasnobród (PL) 197 E3
Krasnopol (PL) 185 E2
Krasnosielc (PL) 190 B1
Krasnyj Cholm (RUS) 7 F1
Krasnystaw (PL) 197 F3
Krasocin (PL) 195 F3
Kraštai (LT) 165 D4
Kraszewice (PL) 194 C1
Kráthio (GR) 217 E1
Krátigos (GR) 215 D3
Kratiškiai (LT) 165 D4
Kratovo (MK) 122 B2
Kratovska Stena (SRB) 118 B3
Krauchenwies (D) 45 F2
Krauja (Hoftenberga) (LV) 173 D1
Kraujas (LV) 165 C4
Kraukļi (LV) 160 C4
Krautheim (D) 88 B4
Kravaře Moravskoslezský kraj(CZ) 91 F2
Kravarsko (HR) 99 F2
Kražiai (LT) 169 C2
Krążkowy (PL) 194 B2
Krefeld (D) 87 E1
Krekenava (LV) 170 C2
Krekštėnai (LT) 176 B3
Kremastí Dodekánissa(GR) 228 C2
Kremastí Lakonia(GR) 217 F4
Kremastón (Teh. L.) (GR) 211 E4
Kremenčuk (UA) 13 F1
Kremenec' (UA) 13 D1
Kremenica (MK) 122 B4
Kremmen (D) 85 D2
Kremna (SRB) 118 B3
Kremnica (SK) 12 B2
Krems a. d. Donau (A) 95 E1
Kremsmünster (A) 94 C2
Krepoljin (SRB) 119 D2
Krepštai (LT) 163 D4
Kreševo (BIH) 117 E3
Krėslynai (LT) 170 C4
Krestcy (RUS) 7 E1
Kréstena (GR) 217 D3
Kretinga (LT) 162 B4
Kretingalė (LT) 162 B4
Kretowiny (PL) 183 E3
Kreuth (D) 94 A3
Kreuzlingen (CH) 93 D3
Kreuztal (D) 87 F2
Kriaušiškiai (LT) 164 C4
Krieglach (A) 95 E3
Kriens (CH) 96 C1
Krievgaļi (LV) 164 C3
Krievupe (LV) 159 D4
Krikello (GR) 211 F4
Krikellos (GR) 211 E3
Krikliniai (LT) 171 D1
Krikštonys (LT) 176 C4
Krimml (A) 94 A4
Krimpen aan den IJssel (NL) 82 B4
Krimūnas (LV) 163 F2
Krinčinas (LT) 165 D4
Krinídes (GR) 207 E2
Kriokiškiai (LT) 169 D3
Krišjāņi (Krišani) (LV) 167 E1
Krišķalni (LV) 165 F2
Kristdala (S) 143 F2
Kristiansand (N) 142 A1
Kristianstad (S) 143 E4
Kristiansund (N) 130 B3
Kristineberg (S) 132 B1
Kristinehamn (S) 140 C4
Kristinehov (S) 143 E4
Kristinestad / Kristiinankaupunki(FIN) 132 C4

Krivogaštani *(MK)* .... 122 B 3
Krivolak *(MK)* .... 122 C 3
Křižanov *(CZ)* .... 91 D 3
Križevci *(HR)* .... 112 A 4
Krk *(HR)* .... 99 E 3
Krk (Otok) *(HR)* .... 99 E 3
Krnjača *(SRB)* .... 118 B 1
Krnjak *(HR)* .... 99 F 2
Krnjeuša *(BIH)* .... 116 C 2
Krnjevo *(SRB)* .... 118 C 1
Krnov *(CZ)* .... 91 E 2
Krobia *(PL)* .... 187 F 4
Krobica *(PL)* .... 192 C 3
Kroczyce *(PL)* .... 195 E 4
Krokeés *(GR)* .... 222 C 2
Krokeíde *(N)* .... 138 B 2
Krokek *(S)* .... 143 F 1
Krokialaukis *(LT)* .... 176 B 3
Krokom *(S)* .... 131 F 3
Krókos *(GR)* .... 205 F 4
Krokowa *(PL)* .... 182 C 1
Kroksjö *(S)* .... 132 B 2
Krokšlys *(LT)* .... 177 D 4
Krokýleio *(GR)* .... 211 F 4
Krolevec' *(UA)* .... 7 D 1
Królikowo *(PL)* .... 188 B 1
Kroměříž *(CZ)* .... 91 E 2
Kromołów *(PL)* .... 195 E 4
Kronach *(D)* .... 89 D 3
Kronauce *(LV)* .... 163 F 2
Kronoby /
  Kruunupyy *(FIN)* .... 133 D 2
Kronshagen *(D)* .... 79 D 1
Kronštadt *(RUS)* .... 7 D 1
Krootuse *(EST)* .... 161 D 1
Kröpelin *(D)* .... 79 D 1
Kropp *(D)* .... 78 C 3
Kroppenstedt *(D)* .... 84 C 4
Krościenko
  nad Dunajcem *(PL)* .. 201 B 3
Krosna *(LT)* .... 175 F 3
Krośnice *(PL)* .... 193 F 1
Krośniewice *(PL)* .... 189 D 3
Krosno *(PL)* .... 202 D 2
Krosno Odrzańskie *(PL)* .. 186 D 2
Krote *(LV)* .... 162 C 2
Krotoszyn *(PL)* .... 187 F 4
Krousónas *(GR)* .... 227 F 2
Krška vas *(SLO)* .... 99 E 2
Krško *(SLO)* .... 99 F 1
Krstac *(MNE)* .... 121 D 1
Krstinja *(HR)* .... 99 F 3
Kruiningen *(NL)* .... 39 E 1
Krujë *(AL)* .... 121 F 4
Kruki *(LV)* .... 167 D 3
Kruklanki *(PL)* .... 184 C 2
Krumbach (Schwaben) *(D)* 93 E 2
Krūmēni *(LV)* .... 160 B 4
Krummhörn *(D)* .... 83 D 1
Krumpendorf *(A)* .... 99 D 1
Krün *(D)* .... 93 F 3
Krundikūla *(EST)* .... 159 D 1
Kruonis *(LT)* .... 176 C 2
Kruopiai *(LT)* .... 163 F 3
Krupá *(CZ)* .... 89 F 2
Krupa na Vrbasu *(BIH)* .. 117 D 2
Krupac *(BIH)* .... 117 E 3
Krupac *(SRB)* .... 119 E 4
Krupaja *(SRB)* .... 119 D 2
Krupanj *(SRB)* .... 117 F 2
Krupe *(PL)* .... 197 D 2
Krupi *(LV)* .... 167 E 2
Krupište *(MK)* .... 122 C 2
Krupka *(CZ)* .... 90 A 2
Kruså *(DK)* .... 144 B 3
Kruščica *(BIH)* .... 117 E 3
Kruševdol *(SRB)* .... 118 B 1
Kruševac *(SRB)* .... 119 D 4
Kruševica *(SRB)* .... 118 B 2
Kruševo *(MK)* .... 122 B 3
Krūškalne *(LV)* .... 163 F 2
Krustceles *(LV)* .... 161 F 4
Krustiņi *(LV)* .... 159 D 4
Krustkalni *(LV)* .... 159 F 4
Kruszwica *(PL)* .... 188 C 2
Kruszyna *(PL)* .... 195 E 4
Kruszyniany *(PL)* .... 185 F 4
Krūte *(LV)* .... 162 C 2
Krute *(MNE)* .... 121 E 4
Krūveliai *(LT)* .... 175 F 2
Kružiūnai *(LT)* .... 176 C 3
Krýa Vrýsi Éwoia *(GR)* .. 212 C 1
Krýa Vrýsi Pélla *(GR)* .... 206 A 3
Kryčaŭ *(BY)* .... 7 E 3
Krynica Małopolskie *(PL)* . 201 B 3
Krynica Morska *(PL)* ...... 183 D 1
Krynice *(PL)* .... 197 F 3

Krynki Podlaskie *(PL)* ...... 185 F 4
Kryonéri Etolía-
  Akarnanía *(GR)* .... 217 D 1
Kryonéri Korinthía *(GR)* .. 217 F 2
Kryonéri Messinía *(GR)* .. 217 D 4
Kryonéri
  Thessaloníki *(GR)* .... 206 C 3
Kryopigí *(GR)* .... 212 C 1
Kryos *(CY)* .... 230 E 4
Krypno Kościelne *(PL)* ... 185 E 4
Krystallopigí *(GR)* .... 205 D 3
Kryvyj Rih *(UA)* .... 13 E 2
Krywosądów *(PL)* .... 188 B 4
Krzęcin *(PL)* .... 187 D 1
Krzelów *(PL)* .... 193 E 1
Krzemieniewo
  Wielkopolskie *(PL)* .. 187 E 4
Krzepice *(PL)* .... 194 C 3
Krzeszów
  Dolnośląskie *(PL)* .... 193 D 3
Krzeszów
  Podkarpackie *(PL)* ... 197 D 4
Krzeszowice *(PL)* .... 201 A 1
Krzeszyce *(PL)* .... 186 C 2
Krzykosy *(PL)* .... 187 F 3
Krzynowłoga Mała *(PL)* .. 189 F 1
Krzywa Góra *(PL)* .... 189 D 2
Krzywcza *(PL)* .... 202 E 2
Krzywiń *(PL)* .... 187 E 4
Krzywin *(PL)* .... 186 B 1
Krzyż Wielkopolskie *(PL)* . 187 D 1
Krzyżanowice *(PL)* .... 200 D 2
Krzyżtopór (Zamek) *(PL)* . 196 C 3
Książ *(PL)* .... 193 E 3
Książ Wielki *(PL)* .... 195 F 4
Książ Wielkopolski *(PL)* .. 187 F 3
Ktismata *(GR)* .... 210 C 1
Kubiliūnai Panevėžio *(LT)* 165 D 3
Kubiliūnai Šiauliu *(LT)* .... 170 B 2
Küblis *(CH)* .... 97 E 1
Kubuli *(LV)* .... 161 E 4
Kučevo *(SRB)* .... 119 D 1
Kučgalys *(LT)* .... 165 E 4
Kuchl *(A)* .... 94 B 3
Kuciny *(PL)* .... 189 D 4
Kućište *(HR)* .... 120 B 2
Kućište *(SRB)* .... 119 F 1
Kuczbork-Osada *(PL)* ... 189 E 1
Kudina *(EST)* .... 155 D 2
Kudirkos Naumiestis *(LT)* 175 E 1
Kudjape *(EST)* .... 152 B 4
Kudowa-Zdrój *(PL)* .... 193 D 4
Kūdra Bauskas *(LV)* ..... 165 D 3
Kūdra Liepājas *(LV)* ...... 162 C 2
Kūdra Rīgas *(LV)* .... 158 B 4
Kūdums *(LV)* .... 159 E 3
Kufstein *(A)* .... 94 A 3
Kühlungsborn *(D)* .... 79 E 3
Kuhmalahti *(FIN)* .... 136 C 2
Kuhmo *(FIN)* .... 135 C 2
Kuhmoinen *(FIN)* .... 137 D 2
Kuigatsi *(EST)* .... 160 C 1
Kuimetsa *(EST)* .... 149 E 4
Kuivajärvi *(FIN)* .... 135 F 1
Kuivajõe *(EST)* .... 149 E 3
Kuivalahti *(FIN)* .... 136 B 3
Kuivaniemi *(FIN)* .... 128 C 4
Kuivastu *(EST)* .... 153 A 3
Kūkas *(LV)* .... 166 C 2
Kukës *(AL)* .... 121 F 2
Kukiškė *(LT)* .... 172 C 4
Kukita *(EST)* .... 155 D 2
Kukko *(FIN)* .... 133 E 4
Kukšas *(LT)* .... 157 C 4
Kuksema *(EST)* .... 150 C 4
Kuktiškės *(LT)* .... 171 F 3
Kukujevci *(SRB)* .... 117 F 1
Kukulje *(BIH)* .... 115 E 4
Kula *(BG)* .... 12 C 1
Kula *(SRB)* .... 113 D 4
Kula *(TR)* .... 19 F 3
Kūlaoru *(EST)* .... 161 E 2
Kulautuva *(LT)* .... 169 F 4
Kūlciems *(LV)* .... 157 F 3
Kuldīga *(LV)* .... 157 D 4
Kuldre *(EST)* .... 160 C 1
Kulen Vakuf *(BIH)* .... 116 C 3
Kulennoinen *(FIN)* .... 135 E 4
Kulesze Kościelne *(PL)* .. 191 D 1
Kuliai *(LT)* .... 168 C 1
Kulina *(SRB)* .... 119 D 3
Kulionys *(LT)* .... 171 F 3
Külitse *(EST)* .... 155 D 2
Kulju *(FIN)* .... 136 C 2

Kulkjica *(HR)* .... 103 E 1
Kulla *(EST)* .... 154 B 4
Kullaa *(FIN)* .... 136 B 2
Kullamaa *(EST)* .... 148 C 4
Kulli *(EST)* .... 153 B 3
Kulm *(CH)* .... 92 B 4
Kulmbach *(D)* .... 89 D 3
Kuloharju *(FIN)* .... 129 E 4
Kūlokai *(LT)* .... 175 F 3
Kulšėnai *(LT)* .... 163 D 3
Kultakero *(FIN)* .... 129 D 2
Kultuvėnai *(LT)* .... 171 D 4
Kuluse *(EST)* .... 148 C 1
Kumane *(SRB)* .... 113 E 4
Kumanovo *(MK)* .... 122 B 3
Kumbuļi *(LV)* .... 173 D 2
Kumečiai *(LT)* .... 176 B 3
Kumla *(S)* .... 140 B 3
Kumlinge *(FIN)* .... 136 A 4
Kumma *(EST)* .... 149 E 4
Kummavuopio *(S)* .... 124 C 2
Kumpji *(LV)* .... 162 C 2
Kumrovec *(HR)* .... 99 F 1
Kunda *(EST)* .... 151 D 2
Kundrėnai *(LT)* .... 170 D 2
Kundzini *(LV)* .... 163 E 2
Kungälv *(S)* .... 143 D 2
Kungsbacka *(S)* .... 143 D 2
Kungshamn *(S)* .... 142 C 1
Kungsör *(S)* .... 140 C 2
Kunice *(PL)* .... 193 E 2
Kunigiškiai Kauno *(LT)* .. 176 B 2
Kunigiškiai Šiaulėnai *(LT)* 169 D 3
Kunigiškiai Tauragės *(LT)* 169 D 3
Kunigiškiai Užventis *(LT)* . 169 E 1
Kuningaküla *(EST)* .... 151 E 4
Kunioniai *(LT)* .... 170 C 3
Kunów *(PL)* .... 196 B 2
Kunowo *(PL)* .... 187 F 4
Kunrau *(D)* .... 84 B 3
Kunszentmárton *(H)* ...... 113 E 2
Kunzelsau *(D)* .... 93 D 1
Kuolio *(FIN)* .... 129 E 4
Kuopio *(FIN)* .... 135 C 2
Kuorevesi *(FIN)* .... 136 C 2
Kuortane *(FIN)* .... 133 D 4
Kuortti *(FIN)* .... 137 D 2
Kupa *(HR)* .... 99 E 2
Kupferzell *(D)* .... 93 D 1
Kupinovo *(SRB)* .... 118 B 1
Kupiškis *(LT)* .... 171 E 4
Kuprava *(LV)* .... 161 E 4
Kupreliškis *(LT)* .... 165 E 4
Kupres *(BIH)* .... 117 D 3
Kupriai Kauno *(LT)* .... 175 F 2
Kupriai Šiauliu *(LT)* ...... 163 F 2
Kureküla *(EST)* .... 154 C 4

Kuremaa *(EST)* .... 155 D 2
Kuremäe *(EST)* .... 151 F 3
Kurėnai *(LT)* .... 171 D 3
Kurenurme *(EST)* .... 161 D 1
Kurepalu *(EST)* .... 155 D 4
Kurikka *(FIN)* .... 133 D 4
Kuřim *(CZ)* .... 91 D 3
Kurista Jõgeva *(EST)* .... 154 C 2
Kurista Tartu *(EST)* .... 155 D 3
Kurklaičiai II *(LT)* .... 165 E 4
Kurkliai Šiauliu *(LT)* ...... 170 B 1
Kurkliai Utenos *(LT)* ...... 171 E 3
Kurkliai II *(LT)* .... 171 E 3
Kurmaičiai *(LT)* .... 162 B 4
Kurmelionys *(LT)* .... 177 D 2
Kurmene *(LV)* .... 165 E 3
Kurna *(LV)* .... 161 E 4
Kurów Lubelskie *(PL)* .... 197 D 1
Kurpiowskie *(PL)* .... 184 C 4
Kurplowska
  (Puszcza) *(PL)* .... 184 B 4
Kuršėnai *(LT)* .... 163 E 4
Kuršiai *(LT)* .... 169 F 2
Kursīši Limbažu *(LV)* ..... 159 D 3
Kursīši Saldus *(LV)* ...... 163 E 3
Kursk *(RUS)* .... 7 F 4
Kursu *(FIN)* .... 129 E 3
Kuršumlija *(SRB)* .... 119 D 4
Kuršumlijska Banja *(SRB)* 119 E 4
Kurtakko *(FIN)* .... 128 C 2
Kurtna Harju *(EST)* .... 149 E 3
Kurtna Ida-Viru *(EST)* ... 151 F 3
Kurtuvėnai *(LT)* .... 169 E 1
Kuru *(FIN)* .... 136 C 2
Kurylówka *(PL)* .... 197 D 4
Kurzeme *(LV)* .... 157 D 4
Kurzemīte *(LV)* .... 157 D 3
Kurzemnieki *(LV)* .... 157 D 3
Kurzętnik *(PL)* .... 183 E 4
Kusa *(LV)* .... 166 C 1
Kusadak *(SRB)* .... 118 C 2
Kušaiņi *(LV)* .... 163 D 2
Kusel *(D)* .... 45 D 2
Kušliškiai *(LT)* .... 175 F 3
Küsnacht *(CH)* .... 92 C 4
Kušneri *(LV)* .... 167 E 3
Küssnacht *(CH)* .... 92 C 4
Kustavi *(FIN)* .... 136 B 3
Kütahya *(TR)* .... 19 F 3
Küti *(EST)* .... 151 D 3
Kutina *(HR)* .... 115 E 3
Kutjevo *(HR)* .... 115 F 3
Kutná Hora *(CZ)* .... 90 C 3
Kutno *(PL)* .... 189 D 3
Kuttanen *(FIN)* .... 125 D 4
Kuttura *(FIN)* .... 125 E 4
Kuusalu *(EST)* .... 149 E 2

Kuusamo *(FIN)* .... 129 E 3
Kuusankoski *(FIN)* .... 137 E 3
Kuusiku *(EST)* .... 149 E 4
Kuusjärvi *(FIN)* .... 135 C 3
Kuusjoki *(FIN)* .... 136 C 3
Kuutsi *(EST)* .... 160 C 2
Kuvšinovo *(RUS)* .... 7 F 4
Kužiai *(LT)* .... 163 F 4
Kuzma *(SLO)* .... 95 F 4
Kuzmin *(SRB)* .... 117 F 1
Kuźnia
  Raciborska *(PL)* .... 200 E 1
Kuźnica *(PL)* .... 185 F 3
Kvænangsbotn *(N)* .... 124 C 3
Kværndrup *(DK)* .... 142 B 4
Kvalsund *(N)* .... 125 D 2
Kvam *(N)* .... 139 E 1
Kvanndal *(N)* .... 138 C 2
Kvanne *(N)* .... 130 C 3
Kvédarna *(LT)* .... 168 C 2
Kvernes *(N)* .... 130 B 3
Kvevlax *(FIN)* .... 133 D 3
Kvietiniai *(LT)* .... 168 B 1
Kvikkjokk *(S)* .... 127 F 3
Kvikne *(N)* .... 131 D 4
Kvinesdal *(N)* .... 138 C 4
Kviteseid *(N)* .... 139 D 3
Kwidzyn *(PL)* .... 183 D 3
Kwilcz *(PL)* .... 187 D 1
Kyani *(GR)* .... 208 C 1
Kybartai *(LT)* .... 175 E 2
Kybeikiai *(LT)* .... 175 D 3
Kybučiai *(LT)* .... 169 F 2
Kyburiai *(LT)* .... 164 C 3
Kyïv *(UA)* .... 13 E 1
Kyjov *(CZ)* .... 91 E 4
Kykkos *(CY)* .... 230 B 3
Kylänlahti *(FIN)* .... 135 C 3
Kylänpää *(FIN)* .... 133 D 3
Kyle of Lochalsh *(GB)* ... 27 D 3
Kyleakin *(GB)* .... 27 D 3
Kylerhea *(GB)* .... 27 D 3
Kylestrome *(GB)* .... 27 E 2
Kyllburg *(D)* .... 44 C 1
Kyllíni *(GR)* .... 216 C 2
Kylmäkoski *(FIN)* .... 136 C 3
Kylmälä *(FIN)* .... 133 F 1
Kymási *(GR)* .... 212 C 2
Kými *(GR)* .... 213 D 2
Kypárissi *(GR)* .... 217 F 4
Kyparissía *(GR)* .... 217 D 4
Kypárissos *(GR)* .... 212 A 2
Kyperounta *(CY)* .... 230 B 3
Kyra *(GR)* .... 231 C 2
Kyrá Panagiá (Nisí) *(GR)* 213 C 2
Kyriaki *(GR)* .... 208 C 1
Kyriáki *(GR)* .... 217 F 1
Kyritz *(D)* .... 84 B 2

Kyrksæterøra /
  Hemme *(N)* .... 130 C 3
Kyröskoski *(FIN)* .... 136 C 2
Kyselka *(CZ)* .... 89 F 2
Kythira *(GR)* .... 223 D 3
Kýthira (Nisí) *(GR)* .... 223 D 3
Kýthnos *(GR)* .... 219 D 3
Kýthnos (Nisí) *(GR)* ...... 219 D 3
Kythrea *(CY)* .... 230 B 2
Kytróni *(GR)* .... 212 C 4
Kyyjärvi *(FIN)* .... 133 E 3

L

La Adrada *(E)* .... 70 A 1
La Alberca *(E)* .... 63 E 4
La Alberca de Záncara *(E)* 71 D 2
La Alberguería
  de Argañán *(E)* .... 63 D 4
La Albuera *(E)* .... 69 D 3
La Algaba *(E)* .... 75 E 1
La Almarcha *(E)* .... 71 D 2
La Almunia
  de Doña Godina *(E)* .. 65 E 3
La Antilla *(E)* .... 74 C 2
La Azohía *(E)* .... 77 E 2
La Bañeza *(E)* .... 59 E 4
La Barca de la Florida *(E)* 75 E 3
La Barrela *(E)* .... 58 C 4
La Barthe-de-Neste *(F)* .. 54 A 2
La Bassée *(F)* .... 39 D 3
La Bastide-Clairence *(F)* 54 A 2
La Bastide-de-Sérou *(F)* . 55 E 3
La Bâtie-Neuve *(F)* .... 53 D 3
La Baule *(F)* .... 46 A 2
La Bégude-de-Mazenc *(F)* 52 C 3
La Bérarde *(F)* .... 53 D 3
La Bisbal de Falset *(E)* .. 66 B 3
La Bisbal d'Empordà *(E)* . 67 E 2
La Bonneville-sur-Iton *(F)*. 42 B 2
La Bourboule *(F)* .... 51 F 2
La Bóveda de Toro *(E)* .. 63 F 3
La Brède *(F)* .... 50 B 3
La Bresse *(F)* .... 45 D 4
La Cabrera *(E)* .... 64 B 4
La Calahorra *(E)* .... 76 C 2
La Caletta *(I)* .... 108 C 2
La Calzada
  de Oropesa *(E)* .... 69 F 1
La Campana *(E)* .... 75 F 1
La Canourgue *(F)* .... 52 A 4
La Capelle *(F)* .... 39 E 3
La Carlota *(E)* .... 75 F 1
La Carolina *(E)* .... 70 B 4
La Cava *(E)* .... 66 B 4
La Cavalerie *(F)* .... 52 A 4
La Chaise-Dieu *(F)* .... 52 A 2
La Chambre *(F)* .... 53 D 2
La Chapelle-d'Angillon *(F)*. 48 A 2

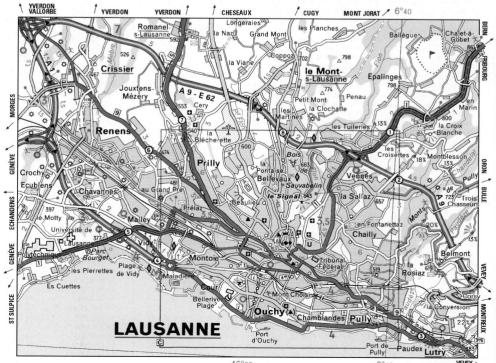

LAUSANNE

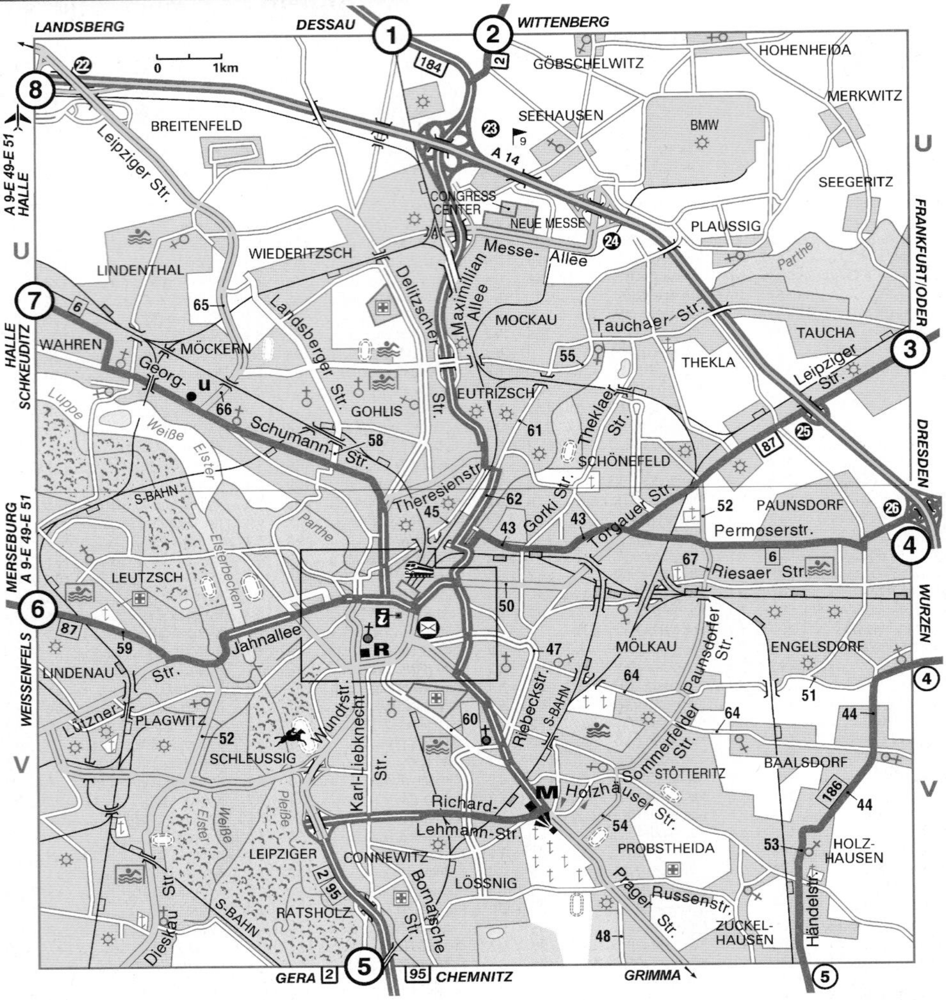

LEIPZIG

Map labels:

LANDSBERG — DESSAU — ① — ② — WITTENBERG
GÖBSCHELWITZ · HOHENHEIDA · MERKWITZ
BREITENFELD · SEEHAUSEN · BMW
A 14 · CONGRESS CENTER · NEUE MESSE · PLAUSSIG · SEEGERITZ
WIEDERITZSCH · Messe-Allee · MOCKAU · Tauchaer Str. · TAUCHA
LINDENTHAL · Maximilian Allee · EUTRITZSCH · THEKLA · Leipziger Str.
WAHREN · MÖCKERN · GOHLIS · SCHÖNEFELD
Georg-Schumann-Str. · Theresienstr. · PAUNSDORF · Permoserstr.
LEUTZSCH · Gorki Str. · Torgauer Str. · Riesaer Str.
LINDENAU · Jahnallee · MÖLKAU · ENGELSDORF
PLAGWITZ · Lützner Str. · Wundstr. · BAALSDORF
SCHLEUSSIG · Karl-Liebknecht-Str. · STÖTTERITZ · HOLZHAUSEN
LEIPZIGER · CONNEWITZ · Richard-Lehmann-Str. · PROBSTHEIDA
RATSHOLZ · LÖSSNIG · Prager Str. · Russenstr. · ZÜCKELHAUSEN
GERA — ⑤ — CHEMNITZ — GRIMMA — ⑤

Street index:

Adenauerallee ..... V 43
Baalsdorfer Str. .... V 44
Berliner Str. ...... V 45
Breite Str. .... V 47
Chemnitzer Str. .... V 48
Eisenbahnstr. ..... V 50
Hauptstr. .... V 53
Hohentichelnstr. .... V 52
Kieler Str. .... U 55
Kommandant-Prendel-Allee .... V 54
Lindenthaler Str. .... U 58
Louise-Otto-Peters-Allee .... U 65
Merseburger Str. ... V 59
Mockauer Str. ..... U 61
Philipp-Rosenthal-Str. .... V 60
Rackwitzer Str. ..... V 62

La Chapelle-de-Guinchay (F)48 C 4
La Chapelle-en-Valgaudémar (F) .. 53 D 3
La Chapelle-en-Vercors (F)52 C 3
La Charité-sur-Loire (F) .. 48 A 2
La Chartre-sur-le-Loir (F) .. 42 B 4
La Châtaigneraie (F) ...... 46 C 3
La Châtre (F) .... 47 F 3
La Chaux-de-Fonds (CH) .. 49 F 2
La Chèze (F) .... 41 D 3
La Ciotat (F) .... 57 D 3
La Clayette (F) .... 48 C 4
La Clusaz (F) .... 49 E 4
La Codosera (E) .... 69 D 2
La Coronada (E) .... 69 D 3
La Côte-St-André (F) .... 52 C 2
La Couronne (F) .... 50 C 2
La Courtine (F) .... 51 F 1
La Couvertoirade (F) .... 56 A 1
La Crau (F) .... 57 D 3
La Croix-Valmer (F) ..... 57 E 2
La Cumbre (E) .... 69 E 2
La Cure (F) .... 49 E 3
La Espina (E) .... 59 E 2
La Féclaz (F) .... 53 D 1
La Fère (F) .... 39 D 4
La Ferté-Alais (F) ...... 43 D 3
La Ferté-Bernard (F) .... 42 B 3
La Ferté-Frênel (F) ..... 42 B 2
La Ferté-Gaucher (F) .... 43 E 2
La Ferté-Macé (F) ...... 41 F 3
La Ferté-Milon (F) ...... 43 E 2
La Ferté-sous-Jouarre (F). 43 E 2
La Ferté-St-Aubin (F) .... 42 C 4
La Ferté-Vidame (F) ..... 42 B 3
La Flèche (F) .... 42 A 4
La Font de la Figuera (E). 71 F 4
La Franca (E) .... 60 A 3
La Fregeneda (E) ...... 63 D 3
La Frontera (E) .... 71 D 1
La Fuente de San Esteban (E). 63 D 4
La Gacilly (F) .... 41 E 4
La Garde-Freinet (F) .... 57 E 2

La Garriga (E) .... 67 D 3
La Gineta (E) .... 71 D 3
La Granadella (E) .... 66 B 3
La Grand-Combe (F) .... 52 B 4
La Grand-Croix (F) ..... 52 B 2
La Grande-Motte (F) .... 56 B 2
La Granjuela (E) .... 69 F 4
La Grave (F) .... 53 D 2
La Guardia (E) .... 70 B 2
La Guardia de Jaén (E) .. 76 B 1
La Guerche-de-Bretagne (F) .. 41 E 4
La Guerche-sur-l'Aubois (F) .. 48 A 3
La Haye-du-Puits (F) .... 41 E 1
La Haye-Pesnel (F) ..... 41 E 1
La Hermida (E) .... 60 A 3
La Herradura (E) .... 76 B 3
La Horcajada (E) ...... 63 F 4
La Horra (E) .... 64 B 2
La Iglesuela del Cid (E) .. 72 A 1
La Jana (E) .... 72 A 1
La Javie (E) .... 53 D 4
La Jonquera (E) .... 67 F 4
La Lantejuela (E) ...... 75 F 2
La Léchère (F) .... 53 D 2
La Línea de la Concepción (E).. 75 F 4
La Losa (E) .... 76 C 1
La Loupe (F) .... 42 B 3
La Louvière (B) .... 39 E 3
La Luisiana (E) .... 75 F 1
La Machine (F) .... 48 B 3
La Maddalena (I) ...... 108 B 1
La Magdalena (E) ...... 59 E 3
La Malène (F) .... 52 A 4
La Manga del Mar Menor (E)... 77 F 2
La Mesa Roldán (E) .... 77 D 3
La Molina (E) .... 55 D 1
La Mothe-Achard (F) .... 46 B 3
La Mothe-St-Héray (F) .. 47 D 4
La Motte-Chalancon (F) .. 52 C 3
La Motte-du-Caire (F) ... 53 D 4

La Mudurra (E) .... 64 A 2
La Muela (E) .... 65 F 3
La Mure (F) .... 53 D 3
La Napoule (F) .... 57 E 2
La Nava de Ricomalillo (E)69 F 2
La Nava de Santiago (E).. 69 D 3
La Neuve-Lyre (F) ...... 42 B 2
La Neuveville (CH) ..... 49 F 2
La Nuez de Arriba (E) ... 60 B 1
La Paca (E) .... 77 D 1
La Pacaudière (F) ...... 48 B 4
La Pallice (F) .... 46 D 1
La Palma del Condado (E)75 D 1
La Petite-Pierre (F) ..... 45 D 3
La Pinilla (E) .... 64 C 3
La Plagne (F) .... 53 E 2
La Plaza (E) .... 59 E 3
La Pobla de Benifassà (E) 66 A 4
La Pobla de Lillet (E) .... 55 E 4
La Pobla de Massaluca (E)66 A 3
La Pobla de Segur (E) ... 66 B 2
La Pobla de Vallbona (E). 71 F 2
La Pobla Llarga (E) ..... 71 F 3
La Pobla Tornesa (E) .... 72 A 1
La Pola de Gordón (E) ... 59 E 1
La Porta (F) .... 57 F 3
La Preste (F) .... 55 F 4
La Primaube (F) .... 51 F 4
La Puebla de Almoradiel (E) ... 70 C 2
La Puebla de Cazalla (E) . 75 F 2
La Puebla de Híjar (E) ... 65 F 3
La Puebla de los Infantes (E) ... 75 F 1
La Puebla de Montalbán (E) ... 70 A 1
La Puebla de Valverde (E)71 F 1
La Puebla del Río (E) .... 75 E 2
La Pueblanueva (E) ..... 70 A 1
La Puerta de Segura (E) . 70 C 4
La Rábita (E) .... 76 B 3
La Rambla (E) .... 75 F 1
La Réole (F) .... 50 C 3
La Rinconada (E) ...... 75 E 1

La Rivière-Thibouville (F). . 42 B 2
La Robla (E) .... 59 E 3
La Roca de la Sierra (E). 69 D 3
La Roca del Vallès (E) ... 67 D 3
La Roche-Bernard (F) ... 41 D 4
La Roche-Canillac (F) ... 51 E 2
La Roche-Chalais (F) .... 50 C 2
La Roche-Derrien (F) .... 40 C 2
La Roche-en-Ardenne (B) 44 B 1
La Roche-Guyon (F) ..... 42 C 2
La Roche-Posay (F) ..... 47 E 3
La Roche-sur-Foron (F) .. 49 E 4
La Roche-sur-Yon (F) ... 46 B 3
La Rochefoucauld (F) .... 50 C 1
La Rochelle (F) .... 46 C 4
La Rochepot (F) .... 48 C 3
La Rochette (F) .... 53 D 2
La Roda (E) .... 71 D 3
La Roda de Andalucía (E) 75 F 2
La Roque-Gageac (F) ... 51 D 3
La Roquebrussanne (F) .. 57 D 2
La Rosière-1850 (F) ..... 53 E 1
La Salceda (E) .... 64 B 3
La Salvetat-Peyralès (F).. 51 F 4
La Salvetat-sur-Agout (F).. 55 F 4
La Seca (E) .... 64 A 3
La Selva del Camp (E) ... 66 B 3
La Sénia (E) .... 66 A 4
La Seu d'Urgell / Seo de Urgel (E)...... 55 E 4
La Seyne-sur-Mer (F) .... 57 D 3
La Solana (E) .... 70 C 3
La Souterraine (F) ...... 47 F 4
La Spezia (I) .... 101 D 2
La Sterza (I) .... 101 F 3
La Suze-sur-Sarthe (F)... 42 A 4
La Teste-de-Buch (F) .... 50 A 3
La Thuile (I) .... 53 E 1
La Torre del Valle (E) .... 63 F 1
La Torre d'en Besora (E).. 72 A 1
La Tour-d'Auvergne (F) .. 51 F 2
La Tour-du-Pin (F) ...... 52 C 2
La Tour-Fondue (F) ..... 57 D 3
La Toussuire (F) .... 53 D 2

La Tranche-sur-Mer (F) ... 46 B 4
La Tremblade (F) .... 50 B 1
La Trimouille (F) .... 47 E 4
La Trinité-Porhoët (F) .... 41 D 3
La Trinité-sur-Mer (F) .... 40 C 4
La Turballe (F) .... 46 A 1
La Turbie (F) .... 57 F 2
La Unión (E) .... 77 F 2
La Vall d'Uixó (E) ...... 72 A 2
La Vecilla (E) .... 59 F 3
La Vellés (E) .... 63 F 3
La Verna (F) .... 102 A 2
La Verpillière (F) .... 52 C 1
La Vila Joiosa / Villajoyosa (E) .... 72 A 4
La Villa / Stern (I) ...... 98 A 1
La Villedieu-du-Clain (F).. 47 D 4
La Virgen del Camino (E). 59 E 4
La Voulte-sur-Rhône (F).. 52 C 3
La Wantzenau (F) ...... 45 E 3
La Yesa (E) .... 71 F 2
Laa an der Thaya (A) .... 91 F 2
Laabi (EST) .... 149 D 2
Laadi (EST) .... 153 C 4
Laage (D) .... 79 F 3
Laagri (EST) .... 149 D 3
Laanemetsa (EST) ..... 160 C 2
Lääniste (EST) .... 155 A 4
Laasme (EST) .... 154 C 3
Laatre (EST) .... 155 E 4
Laatre (EST) .... 160 C 1
Labacolla (E) .... 58 B 3
Labajos (E) .... 64 A 4
Labanoras (LT) .... 171 D 2
Labasheeda (IRL) ..... 24 B 2
Labastida (E) .... 60 C 4
Labastide-Murat (F) .... 51 E 3
Labastide-Rouairoux (F).. 55 F 2
Labeikiai (LT) .... 171 D 2
L'Aber-Wrac'h (F) ..... 40 B 2
Labin (HR) .... 99 D 3
Labiszyn (PL) .... 188 B 1
Laboe (D) .... 79 D 2
Laborai (LT) .... 164 C 4

Labouheyre (F)........ 50 B 4
Łabowa (PL).......... 201 C 3
Labrit (F)............ 50 B 4
Labruguière (F)........ 55 F 2
Labudnjaca (SRB)...... 113 D 4
Labūnava Kauno(LT).... 170 C 3
Labūnava Šiauliu(LT).... 169 E 2
Łabunie (PL).......... 197 F 3
Lacanau (F).......... 50 B 3
Lacanau-Océan (F)..... 50 A 3
Lacapelle-Marival (F).... 51 E 3
Laćarak (SRB)........ 117 F 1
Lacaune (F).......... 55 F 2
Lacco Ameno (I)....... 105 E 4
Lacedonia (I)......... 106 B 3
Lachanás (GR)........ 206 C 2
Łąck (PL)............ 189 E 2
Lačkalni (LV)......... 157 D 4
Łącko (PL)........... 201 B 3
Läckö (S)............ 139 F 4
Laconi (I)............ 108 B 3
Lačplēši (LV)......... 162 B 2
Lacq (F)............. 54 B 2
Lačupīte (LV)......... 157 F 4
Ląd (PL)............. 188 B 3
Ladbergen (D)........ 83 E 4
Lāde (LV)........... 159 D 3
Lądek (PL).......... 188 B 3
Lądek-Zdrój (PL)...... 193 E 4
Lādezers (LV)........ 159 D 3
Ládi (GR)........... 208 C 1
Ladispoli (I).......... 104 C 2
Ladoeiro (P)......... 69 D 1
Lādzere (LV)......... 157 E 3
Ładzice (PL)......... 195 D 2
Laekvere (EST)....... 151 D 4
Lærdalsøyri (N)....... 138 C 1
Láerma (GR)......... 228 C 2
Laeva (EST)......... 154 C 3
Laferté-sur-Amance (F).. 49 D 1
Laffrey (F).......... 53 D 3
Láfka (GR).......... 217 E 2
Láfkos (GR)......... 212 C 3
Lafrançaise (F)....... 51 D 4
Lagan (S)........... 143 E 3
Laganás (GR)........ 216 B 2
Lagartera (E)........ 69 F 1
Lage Kreis Lippe(D).... 83 F 4
Lagedi (EST)........ 149 E 2
Laggan (GB)........ 27 E 4
Łagiewniki Dolnośląskie(PL). 193 E 3
Lagkáda Chíos(GR).... 220 C 1
Lagkáda Messinía(GR). 222 C 2
Lagkadás (GR)....... 206 C 3
Lagkádia (GR)....... 217 E 3
Lagkadíkia (GR)...... 206 C 3
Lagnieu (F)......... 52 C 1
Lagny-sur-Marne (F)... 43 D 2
Lago (I)............ 109 E 2
Lagoa (P).......... 74 A 2
Lagoaça (P)........ 63 E 3
Lagonegro (I)....... 106 C 4
Lagonísi (GR)....... 218 C 2
Lágos (GR)......... 207 F 2
Lagos (P).......... 74 A 2
Lagoudera (CY)..... 230 B 3
Łagów Lubuskie(PL)... 186 C 3
Łagów Świętokrzyskie(PL)196 B 3
Lagrasse (F)........ 55 F 3
Laguarres (E)....... 54 C 4
Laguarta (E)........ 54 C 4
Laguépie (F)........ 51 E 4
Laguiole (F)........ 51 F 3
Laguna de Duero (E).. 64 A 2
Lagyná Évros(GR).... 208 C 2
Lagyná Thessaloníki(GR)206 C 2
Lahavere (EST)...... 154 C 2
Lahe (EST)......... 161 D 1
Lahiguera (E)....... 76 B 1
Lahinch / An Leacht (IRL). 24 B 1
Lahnstein (D)....... 87 F 3
Laholm (S)......... 143 D 3
Lahr Ortenaukreis(D).. 45 E 4
Lähte (EST)........ 155 D 3
Lahti (FIN)......... 137 D 3
Laibiškės (LT)...... 177 F 3
Laibiškiai (LT)...... 171 D 3
Laichingen (D)...... 93 D 2
Laičiai Panevėžio(LT). 171 E 1
Laičiai Utenos(LT)... 171 E 3
Laičiai Vilniaus(LT)... 177 D 2
Laide (GB)......... 27 D 2
Laidi (LV)......... 163 D 1
Laidze (LV)........ 157 E 3
L'Aigle (F)......... 42 B 2
Laignes (F)........ 43 F 4

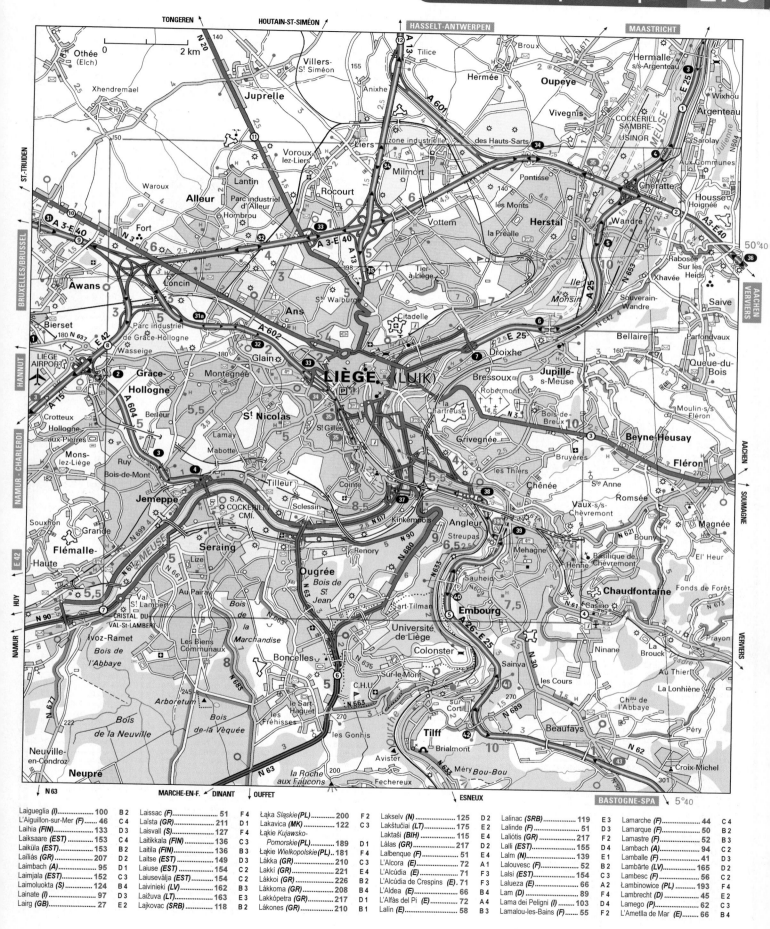

Laigueglia *(I)* 100	B 2	Laissac *(F)* 51	F 4	Łąka Śląskie *(PL)* 200	F 2	Lakselv *(N)* 125	D 2	Lalinac *(SRB)* 119	E 3	Lamarche *(F)* 44 C 4
L'Aiguillon-sur-Mer *(F)* 46	C 4	Laïsta *(GR)* 211	D 1	Lakavica *(MK)* 122	C 3	Lakštučiai *(LT)* 175	E 2	Lalinde *(F)* 51	D 3	Lamarque *(F)* 50 B 2
Laihia *(FIN)* 133	D 3	Laisvall *(S)* 127	F 4	Łąkie Kujawsko-		Laktaši *(BIH)* 115	E 4	Laliótis *(GR)* 217	F 2	Lamastre *(F)* 52 B 3
Laiksaare *(EST)* 153	C 3	Laitikkala *(FIN)* 136	C 3	Pomorskie *(PL)* 189	D 1	Lálas *(GR)* 217	D 2	Lalli *(EST)* 155	D 4	Lambach *(A)* 94 C 2
Laiküla *(EST)* 153	B 2	Laitila *(FIN)* 136	B 3	Łąkie Wielkopolskie *(PL)* 181	F 4	Lalbenque *(F)* 51	E 4	Lalm *(N)* 139	E 1	Lamballe *(F)* 41 D 3
Laïliás *(GR)* 207	D 2	Laitse *(EST)* 149	D 3	Lákka *(GR)* 210	C 3	L'Alcora *(E)* 72	A 1	Lalouvesc *(F)* 52	B 2	Lambärte *(LV)* 165 D 2
Laimbach *(A)* 95	C 2	Laiuse *(EST)* 154	C 2	Lakkí *(GR)* 221	E 4	L'Alcúdia *(E)* 71	F 3	Lalsi *(EST)* 154	C 3	Lambesc *(F)* 56 C 2
Laimjala *(EST)* 152	C 3	Laiusevälja *(EST)* 154	C 2	Lákkoi *(GR)* 226	B 2	L'Alcúdia de Crespins *(E)* 71	F 3	Lalueza *(E)* 66	A 2	Łambinowice *(PL)* 193 F 4
Laimoluokta *(S)* 124	B 4	Laivinieki *(LV)* 162	B 3	Lákkoma *(GR)* 208	B 4	L'Aldea *(E)* 66	B 4	Lam *(D)* 89	F 4	Lambrecht *(D)* 45 E 2
Lainate *(I)* 97	D 3	Laižuva *(LT)* 163	E 3	Lakkópetra *(GR)* 217	D 1	L'Alfàs del Pi *(E)* 72	A 4	Lama dei Peligni *(I)* 103	D 4	Lamego *(P)* 62 C 3
Lairg *(GB)* 27	E 2	Lajkovac *(SRB)* 118	B 2	Lákones *(GR)* 210	B 1	Lalín *(E)* 58	B 3	Lamalou-les-Bains *(F)* 55	F 2	L'Ametlla de Mar *(E)* 66 B 4

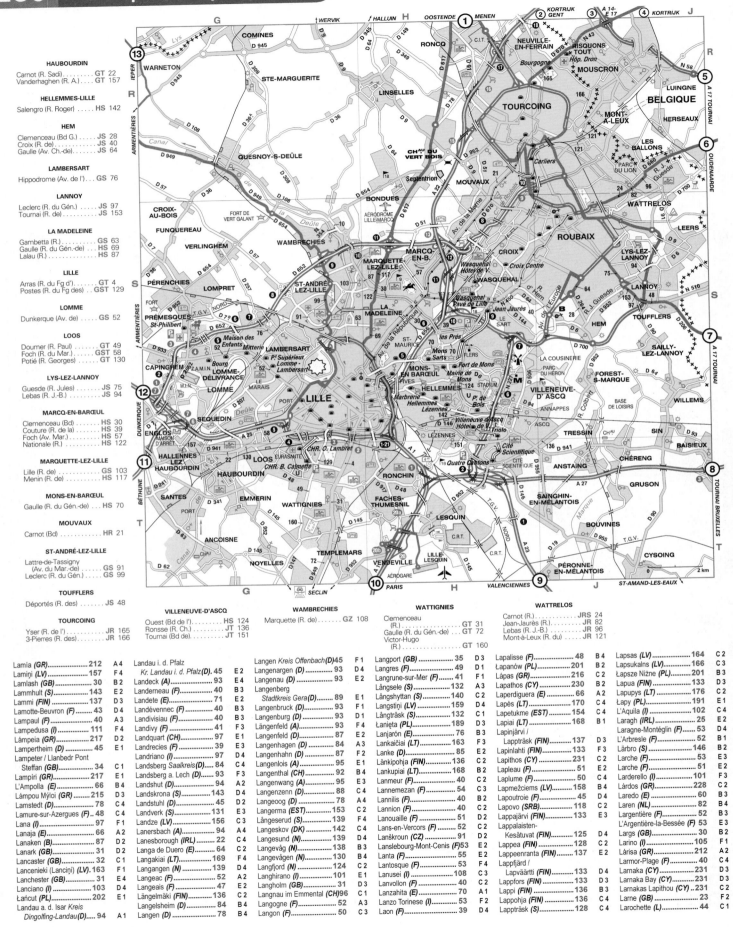

HAUBOURDIN
Carnot (R. Sadi)........ GT 22
Vanderhaghen (R. A.).. GT 157

HELLEMMES-LILLE
Salengro (R. Roger) ..... HS 142

HEM
Clemenceau (Bd G.) .... JS 28
Croix (R. de) .... JS 40
Gaulle (Av. Ch.-de).... JS 64

LAMBERSART
Hippodrome (Av. de l')... GS 76

LANNOY
Leclerc (R. du Gén.) .... JS 97
Tournai (R. de) .... JS 153

LA MADELEINE
Gambetta (R.)........... GS 63
Gaulle (R. du Gén.-de) .. HS 69
Lalau (R.) .... HS 87

LILLE
Arras (R. du Fg d')...... GT 4
Postes (R. du Fg des) .. GST 129

LOMME
Dunkerque (Av. de) ..... GS 52

LOOS
Doumer (R. Paul) ...... GT 49
Foch (R. du Mar.)...... GST 58
Potié (R. Georges) ..... GT 130

LYS-LEZ-LANNOY
Guesde (R. Jules) ...... JS 75
Lebas (R. J.-B.) .... JS 94

MARCQ-EN-BARŒUL
Clemenceau (Bd)....... HS 30
Couture (R. de la) ...... HS 39
Foch (Av. Mar.)....... HS 57
Nationale (R.) .... HS 122

MARQUETTE-LEZ-LILLE
Lille (R. de) .... GS 103
Menin (R. de) .... HS 117

MONS-EN-BARŒUL
Gaulle (R. du Gén.-de) ... HS 70

MOUVAUX
Carnot (Bd) .... HR 21

ST-ANDRÉ-LEZ-LILLE
Lattre-de-Tassigny
(Av. du Mar.-de) ..... GS 91
Leclerc (R. du Gén.) ... GS 99

TOUFFLERS
Déportés (R. des) .... JS 48

TOURCOING
Yser (R. de l') .... JR 165
3-Pierres (R. des)...... JR 166

VILLENEUVE-D'ASCQ
Ouest (Bd de l')......... HS 124
Ronsse (R. Ch.) .... JT 136
Tournai (Bd du) .... JT 151

WAMBRECHIES
Marquette (R. de)....... GZ 108

WATTIGNIES
Clemenceau
(R.) .... GT 31
Gaulle (R. du Gén.-de) .. GT 72
Victor-Hugo
(R.) .... GT 160

WATTRELOS
Carnot (R.).......... JRS 24
Jean-Jaurès (R.)....... JR 82
Lebas (R. J.-B.) ...... JR 96
Mont-à-Leux (R. du) .... JR 121

Lamía (GR).............212 A 4
Lamiņi (GR)...........157 F 4
Lamlash (GB)...........30 B 2
Lammhult (S)..........143 E 2
Lammi (FIN)...........137 D 3
Lamotte-Beuvron (F)....43 D 4
Lampaul (F)............40 A 3
Lampedusa (I).........111 F 4
Lámpeia (GR).........217 D 2
Lampertheim (D)........45 E 1
Lampeter / Llanbedr Pont
  Steffan (GB)..........34 C 1
Lampíri (GR).........217 E 1
L'Ampolla (E)..........66 B 4
Lámpou Mýloi (GR)...215 D 3
Lamstedt (D)...........78 C 4
Lamure-sur-Azergues (F)..48 C 4
Lana (I)...............97 F 1
Lanaja (E).............66 A 2
Lanaken (B)............87 D 2
Lanark (GB)............31 D 2
Lancaster (GB).........32 C 1
Lancenieki (Lancinį) (LV).163 E 4
Lanchester (GB)........31 E 4
Lanciano (I)..........103 D 4
Łańcut (PL)...........202 E 1
Landau a. d. Isar Kreis
  Dingolfing-Landau (D)..94 A 1

Landau i. d. Pfalz
  Kr. Landau i. d. Pfalz (D). 45 E 2
Landeck (A)............93 E 4
Landerneau (F).........40 B 3
Landete (E)............71 E 2
Landévennec (F).......40 B 3
Landivisiau (F).......40 B 3
Landivy (F)............41 F 3
Landquart (CH)........97 E 1
Landrecies (F).........39 E 3
Landriano (I).........97 D 4
Landsberg Saalkreis (D)..84 C 4
Landsberg a. Lech (D)...93 F 3
Landshut (D)...........94 A 2
Landskrona (S)........143 D 4
Landstuhl (D).........45 D 2
Landverk (S).........131 E 3
Landze (LV)..........156 F 3
Lanersbach (A)........94 A 4
Lanesborough (IRL)....22 C 4
Langa de Duero (E)....64 C 2
Langakiai (LT).......169 F 4
Langangen (N).......139 D 4
Langeac (F)............52 E 2
Langeais (F)...........47 E 2
Längelmäki (FIN).....136 C 2
Langelsheim (D).......84 B 4
Langen (D).............78 B 4

Langen Kreis Offenbach (D)45 F 1
Langenargen (D).......93 D 4
Langenau (D)...........93 E 2
Langenberg
  Stadtkreis Gera (D)...89 E 1
Langenbruck (D).......93 F 1
Langenburg (D)........93 D 3
Langenfeld (A)........93 F 4
Langenfeld (D)........87 E 2
Langenhagen (D)......84 B 3
Langenhahn (D).......87 F 2
Langenlois (A)........95 E 1
Langenthal (CH)......92 B 4
Langenwang (A)......95 E 3
Langenzenn (D)......88 C 4
Langeoog (D)..........78 A 4
Langerma (EST)......153 C 2
Långeserud (S).......139 F 4
Langeskov (DK)......142 A 4
Langesund (N).......139 D 4
Langevåg (N).........138 B 3
Langevågen (N)......130 B 4
Langhirano (I).......101 E 1
Langholm (GB)........31 C 1
Langnau im Emmental (CH)96 C 1
Langogne (F)..........52 A 3
Langon (F)............50 C 3

Langport (GB) ....35 D 3
Langres (F)............49 D 1
Langrune-sur-Mer (F)..41 F 1
Langsele (S).........132 A 3
Långshyttan (S)......140 C 2
Langstiņi (LV).......159 D 4
Långträsk (S)........132 C 1
Łanięta (PL).........189 D 3
Lanjarón (E).........76 B 3
Lankaičiai (LT)......163 F 3
Lanke (D)............85 E 2
Lankupiai (LT)......168 B 2
Lanmeur (F)..........40 C 2
Lannilis (F).........40 B 2
Lannion (F)..........40 C 2
Lanouaille (F).......51 D 2
Lans-en-Vercors (F)..52 C 2
Lanškroun (CZ)......91 D 2
Lanta (F)............55 E 2
Lantosque (F).......53 F 4
Lanusei (I).........108 C 3
Lanvollon (F)........40 C 2
Lanzahita (E).......70 A 1
Lanzo Torinese (I)...53 F 2
Laon (F)............39 D 4

Lapalisse (F).........48 B 4
Łapanów (PL)........201 B 2
Lápas (GR).........216 C 2
Lapathos (CY).......230 C 2
Lapeš (LT).........170 C 4
Lapetukme (EST)....154 C 1
Lapiai (LT)........168 B 1
Lapinjärvi /
  Lappträsk (FIN)...137 D 3
Lapinlahti (FIN)....133 F 3
Lapithos (CY)......231 C 2
Laplume (F)........51 E 2
Lapmežciems (LV)...158 B 4
Lappajärvi (FIN)....133 E 3
Lappalaisten-
  Kesäutuvat (FIN)..125 D 4
Lappea (FIN).......128 C 2
Lappeenranta (FIN)..137 E 2
Lappfjärd /
  Lapväärtti (FIN)..133 D 4
Lappi (FIN)........136 B 3
Lappohja (FIN).....136 C 2
Lappträsk (S)......128 C 4

Lapsas (LV).........164 C 2
Lapsukalns (LV)....166 C 3
Łapsze Niżne (PL)..201 B 3
Lapua (FIN)........133 D 3
Lapupys (LT).......176 C 2
Łapy (PL).........191 E 1
L'Aquila (I).......102 C 4
Laragh (IRL)........25 E 2
Laragne-Montéglin (F).53 D 2
L'Arbresle (F)......52 B 1
Lärbro (S).........146 B 2
Larche (F).........53 E 3
Larche (F).........51 E 2
Larderello (I).....101 F 3
Lárdos (GR).......228 C 2
Laredo (E).........60 B 3
Laren (NL).........82 B 4
Largentière (F)....53 E 3
L'Argentière-la-Bessée (F) 53 E 3
Largs (GB).........30 B 2
Larino (I)........105 F 2
Lárisa (GR).......212 A 2
Larmor-Plage (F)...40 C 4
Larnaka (CY)......231 D 3
Larnaka Bay (CY)..231 D 3
Larnakas Lapithou (CY)..231 C 2
Larne (GB).........23 F 1
Larochette (L).....44 C 1

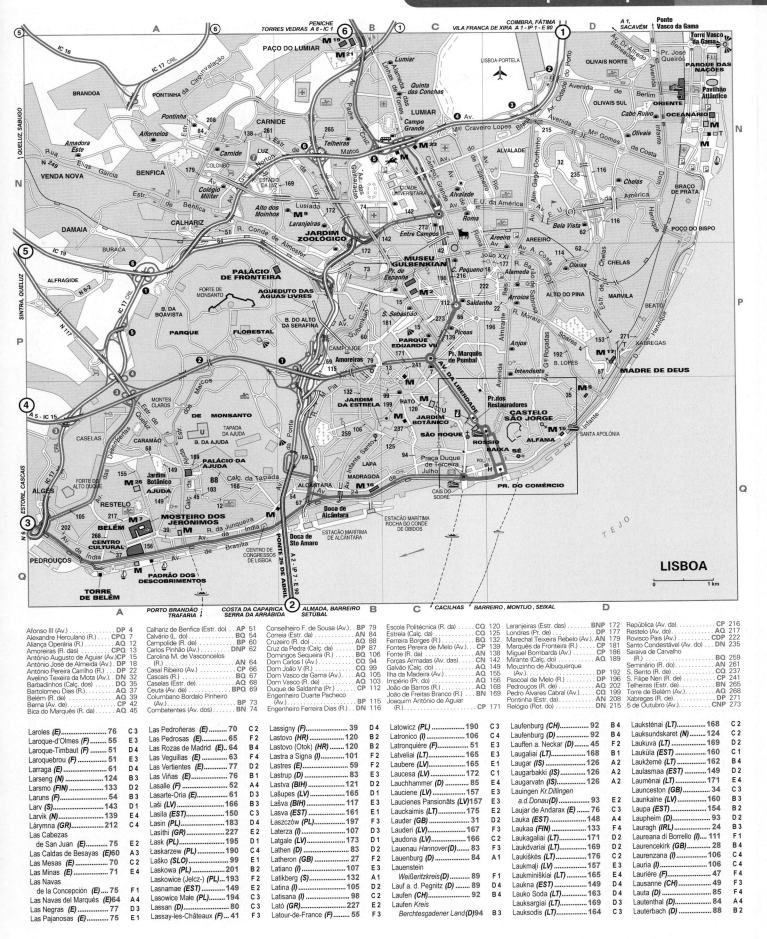

LISBOA

Afonso III (Av.) . . . . DP 4	Calhariz de Benfica (Estr. do) . . . . AP 51	Conselheiro F. de Sousa (Av.) . . . BP 79
Alexandre Herculano (R.) . . . . CPQ 7	Calvário (L. do) . . . . BQ 54	Correia (Estr. da) . . . . AN 84
Aliança Operária (R.) . . . . AQ 12	Campolide (R. de) . . . . BP 60	Cruzeiro (R. do) . . . . AQ 88
Amoreiras (R. das) . . . . CPQ 15	Carlos Pinhão (Av.) . . . . DNP 62	Cruz da Pedra (Calç. da) . . . . . . CP 87
António Augusto de Aguiar (Av.)CP 15	Carolina M. de Vasconcelos	Domingos Sequeira (R.) . . . . . . BQ 106
António José de Almeida (R.) . DP 18	(R.) . . . . AN 64	Dom Carlos I (Av.) . . . . CQ 94
António Pereira Carrilho (R.) . . DP 22	Casal Ribeiro (Av.) . . . . CP 66	Dom João V (R.) . . . . CQ 99
Avelino Teixeira da Mota (Av.). DN 32	Cascais (R.) . . . . BQ 67	Dom Vasco da Gama (Av.) . . . . AQ 103
Barbadinhos (Calç. dos) . . . . . DQ 35	Caselas (Estr. de) . . . . AQ 68	Dom Vasco (R.) . . . . AQ 103
Bartolomeu Dias (R.) . . . . AQ 37	Ceuta (Av. de) . . . . BPQ 69	Duque de Saldanha (Pr.) . . . . . . CP 112
Belém (R. de) . . . . AQ 39	Columbano Bordalo Pinheiro	Engenheiro Duarte Pacheco
Berna (Av. de) . . . . CP 42	(Av.) . . . . BP 73	(Av.) . . . . BP 115
Bica do Marquês (R. da) . . . . . . AQ 45	Combatentes (Av. dos) . . . . BN 74	Engenheiro Ferreira Dias (R.) . . . DN 116

Escola Politécnica (R. da) . . . . . CQ 120	Laranjeiras (Estr. das) . . . . BNP 172	República (Av. da). . . . . CP 216
Estrela (Calç. da) . . . . CQ 125	Londres (Pr. de) . . . . DP 177	Restelo (Av. do) . . . . AQ 217
Ferreira Borges (R.) . . . . BQ 132	Marechal Teixeira Rebelo (Av.) . AN 179	Rovisco Pais (Av.) . . . . CDP 222
Fontes Pereira de Melo (Av.) . . CP 139	Marquês da Fronteira (R.) . . . . . CP 181	Santo Condestável (Av. do) . . . DN 235
Fonte (R. da) . . . . AN 138	Miguel Bombarda (Av.) . . . . CP 186	Saraiva de Carvalho
Forças Armadas (Av. das) . . . . CN 142	Mirante (Calç. do) . . . . AQ 189	(R.) . . . . BQ 259
Galvão (Calç. do) . . . . AQ 149	Mouzinho de Albuquerque	Seminário (R. do) . . . . AN 261
Ilha da Madeira (Av.) . . . . AQ 155	(R.) . . . . DP 192	S. Bento (R. de) . . . . CQ 237
Império (Pr. do) . . . . AQ 156	Pascoal de Melo (R.) . . . . CP 196	S. Filipe Neri (R. de) . . . . CP 241
João de Barros (R.) . . . . AQ 168	Pedrouços (R. de) . . . . AQ 202	Telheiras (Estr. de) . . . . BN 265
João de Freitas Branco (R.) . . . BN 169	Pedro Alvares Cabral (R.) . . . . CQ 199	Torre de Belém (Av.) . . . . AQ 268
Joaquim António de Aguiar	Pontinha (Estr. da) . . . . AN 208	Xabregas (R.) . . . . DP 271
. . . . CP 171	Relógio (Rot. do) . . . . DN 215	5 de Outubro (Av.) . . . . CNP 273

Laroles (E) **76**	C 3	Las Pedroñeras (E) **70**	C 2	Lassigny (F) **39**	D 4	Latowicz (PL) **190**	C 3	Laufenburg (CH) **92**	B 4	Laukstėnai (LT) **168**	C 2
Laroque-d'Olmes (F) . . . **55**	E 3	Las Pedrosas (E) **65**	F 2	Lastovo (HR) **120**	B 2	Latronico (I) **106**	C 4	Laufenburg (D) **92**	B 4	Lauksundskaret (N) **124**	C 2
Laroque-Timbaut (F) . . . **51**	D 4	Las Rozas de Madrid (E). **64**	B 4	Lastovo (Otok) (HR) **120**	B 2	Latronquière (F) **51**	E 3	Lauffen a. Neckar (D) . . . **45**	C 2	Laukuva (LT) **169**	D 2
Laroquebrou (F) **51**	E 3	Las Veguillas (E) **63**	F 4	Lastra a Signa (I) **101**	F 2	Latveliai (LT) **165**	E 3	Laugaliai (LT) **168**	B 1	Laukūla (EST) **120**	C 1
Larra (E) **61**	D 4	Las Vertientes (E) **77**	D 2	Lastres (I) **59**	F 2	Laubere (LV) **165**	E 1	Laugar (IS) **126**	A 2	Laukžemė (LT) **162**	B 4
Larseng (N) **124**	B 3	Las Viñas (E) **76**	B 1	Lastrup (D) **83**	E 3	Laucesa (LV) **172**	C 1	Laugarbakki (IS) **126**	A 2	Laulasmaa (EST) **149**	D 1
Larsmo (FIN) **133**	D 2	Lasalle (F) **52**	A 4	Lastva (BIH) **121**	D 2	Lauchhammer (D) **85**	E 4	Laugarvatn (IS) **126**	A 2	Lauménai (LT) **171**	E 4
Laruns (F) **54**	B 3	Lasarte-Oria (E) **61**	D 3	Lašupes (LV) **165**	D 1	Lauciene (LV) **157**	E 3	Lauingen Kr.Dillingen		Launceston (GB) **34**	C 3
Larv (S) **143**	D 1	Laši (LV) **166**	B 3	Lašva (BIH) **117**	E 1	Lauckaimis (LT) **175**	E 2	a.d.Donau (D) **93**	E 2	Launkalne (LV) **160**	B 3
Larvik (N) **139**	A 4	Lasila (EST) **150**	C 3	Lasva (EST) **161**	F 3	Lauder (GB) **31**	D 2	Laujar de Andarax (E) . . **76**	C 2	Laupa (EST) **154**	B 2
Lárymna (GR) **212**	C 4	Łasin (PL) **183**	D 2	Łaszczów (PL) **197**	F 3	Lauderi (LV) **167**	E 1	Lauka (EST) **148**	A 4	Laupheim (D) **93**	D 2
Las Cabezas		Lasíthi (GR) **227**	E 2	Laterza (I) **107**	D 3	Łaudona (LV) **166**	C 2	Laukaa (FIN) **133**	F 4	Lauragh (IRL) **24**	B 3
de San Juan (E) **75**	E 2	Łask (PL) **195**	D 1	Latgale (LV) **173**	D 1	Laukagaliai (LT) **171**	D 2	Laureana di Borrello (I) . . **111**	F 3
Las Caldas de Besayas (E)60	A 3	Łaskarzew (PL) **190**	C 4	Latheron (GB) **27**	F 2	Laukdvariai (LT) **169**	D 2	Laurencekirk (GB) **28**	B 4
Las Mesas (E) **70**	C 2	Laško (SLO) **99**	E 1	Latiano (I) **107**	D 3	Laukiškės (LT) **176**	C 2	Laurenzana (I) **106**	C 4
Las Minas (E) **71**	E 4	Laskowa (PL) **201**	B 2	Latina (I) **105**	D 2	Laukmaļi (LV) **157**	E 3	Lauria (I) **106**	C 4
Las Navas		Laskowice (Jelcz-) (PL) . **193**	F 2	Latikberg (S) **132**	A 1	Laukna (EST) **149**	D 4	Laurière (F) **47**	F 4
de la Concepción (E) . . **75**	F 1	Lasnamäe (EST) **149**	E 4	Lauf a. d. Pegnitz (D) . . . **89**	D 2	Laukņa (LV) **157**	E 3	Lausanne (CH) **49**	F 3
Las Navas del Marqués (E)64	F 1	Lasowice Małe (PL) **194**	C 3	Latisana (I) **98**	D 2	Lauko Soda (LT) **163**	D 4	Lauta (D) **85**	F 3
Las Negras (E) **77**	D 3	Lassan (D) **80**	C 3	Lató (GR) **227**	E 2	Lauksargiai (LT) **169**	D 3	Lautenthal (D) **84**	A 4
Las Pajanosas (E) **75**	E 1	Lassay-les-Châteaux (F) . **41**	F 3	Latour-de-France (F) **55**	F 3	Lauksodis (LT) **164**	C 3	Lauterbach (D) **88**	B 2

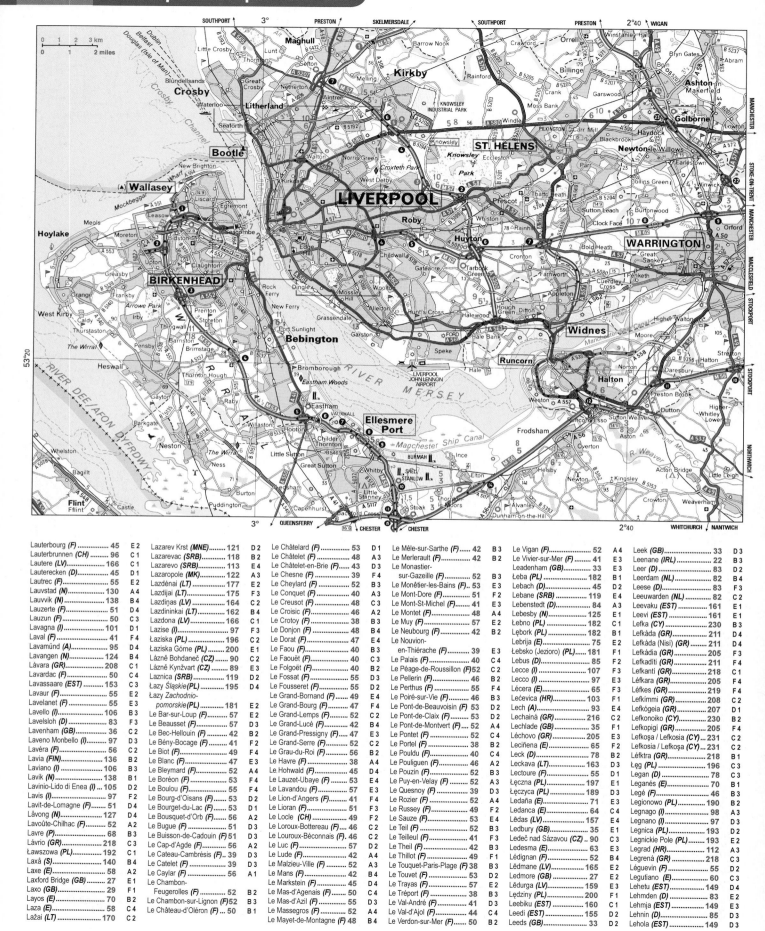

Lauterbourg *(F)* 45	E 2	Lazarev Krst *(MNE)* .. 121	D 2
Lauterbrunnen *(CH)* 96	C 1	Lazarevac *(SRB)* 118	B 2
Lautere *(LV)* 166	C 1	Lazarevo *(SRB)* 113	E 4
Lauterecken *(D)* 45	D 1	Lazaropole *(MK)* 122	A 3
Lautrec *(F)* 55	E 2	Lazdėnai *(LT)* 177	E 2
Lauvstad *(N)* 130	A 4	Lazdijai *(LT)* 175	D 4
Lauvvik *(N)* 138	B 4	Lazdiņas *(LV)* 164	C 2
Lauzerte *(F)* 51	D 4	Lazdininkai *(LT)* 162	B 4
Lauzun *(F)* 50	C 3	Lazdona *(LV)* 166	C 3
Lavagna *(I)* 101	D 1	Lazise *(I)* 97	F 3
Laval *(F)* 41	F 4	Le Châtelard *(F)* 53	D 1
Lavamünd *(A)* 95	D 4	Le Châtelet *(F)* 48	A 3
Lavangen *(N)* 124	B 4	Le Châtelet-en-Brie *(F)* .. 43	D 3
Lávara *(GR)* 208	C 1	Le Chesne *(F)* 39	F 4
Lavardac *(F)* 50	C 4	Le Cheylard *(F)* 52	E 3
Lavassaare *(EST)* 153	C 3	Le Conquet *(F)* 40	A 3
Lavaur *(F)* 55	E 2	Le Creusot *(F)* 48	C 3
Lavelanet *(F)* 55	E 3	Le Croisic *(F)* 46	A 4
Lavello *(I)* 106	B 3	Le Crotoy *(F)* 38	B 3
Lavelsloh *(D)* 83	F 3	Le Donjon *(F)* 48	B 4
Lavenham *(GB)* 36	C 2	Le Dorat *(F)* 47	E 4
Laveno Monbello *(I)* 97	E 3	Le Faou *(F)* 40	B 3
Lavéra *(F)* 56	C 2	Le Faouët *(F)* 40	C 3
Lavia *(FIN)* 136	B 2	Le Folgoët *(F)* 40	B 3
Laviano *(I)* 106	B 3	Le Fossat *(F)* 55	D 3
Lavik *(N)* 138	B 1	Le Perthus *(F)* 55	F 4
Lavinio-Lido di Enea *(I)* . 105	C 2	Le Fousseret *(F)* 55	D 2
Lavis *(I)* 97	F 2	Le Grand-Bornand *(F)* 49	E 4
Lavit-de-Lomagne *(F)* 51	D 4	Le Grand-Bourg *(F)* 47	F 4
Låvong *(N)* 127	D 4	Le Grand-Lemps *(F)* 52	C 2
Lavoûte-Chilhac *(F)* 52	A 2	Le Grand-Lucé *(F)* 42	B 4
Lavre *(P)* 68	B 3	Le Grand-Pressigny *(F)* .. 47	E 3
Lávrio *(GR)* 218	C 3	Le Grand-Serre *(F)* 52	C 2
Ławszowa *(PL)* 192	C 1	Le Grau-du-Roi *(F)* 56	B 2
Laxå *(S)* 140	B 4	Le Havre *(F)* 38	A 4
Laxe *(E)* 58	A 4	Le Hohwald *(F)* 45	D 4
Laxford Bridge *(GB)* 27	E 1	Le Lauzet-Ubaye *(F)* 53	E 3
Laxo *(GB)* 29	F 1	Le Lavandou *(F)* 57	F 4
Layos *(E)* 70	C 3	Le Lion-d'Angers *(F)* 41	F 4
Laza *(E)* 58	C 4	Le Lioran *(F)* 51	F 4
Lažai *(LT)* 170	C 2	Le Locle *(CH)* 49	F 2
		Le Loroux-Bottereau *(F)* .. 46	C 2
		Le Louroux-Béconnais *(F)* . 46	C 2
		Le Luc *(F)* 57	D 2
		Le Lude *(F)* 42	A 4
		Le Malzieu-Ville *(F)* 52	A 3
		Le Mans *(F)* 42	B 4
		Le Markstein *(F)* 45	D 4
		Le Mas-d'Agenais *(F)* 50	C 4
		Le Mas-d'Azil *(F)* 55	D 3
		Le Massegros *(F)* 52	A 4
		Le Mayet-de-Montagne *(F)* . 48	B 4

Le Mêle-sur-Sarthe *(F)* ... 42	B 3
Le Merlerault *(F)* 42	B 2
Le Monastier-	
sur-Gazeille *(F)* 52	B 3
Le Monêtier-les-Bains *(F)*.. 53	E 3
Le Mont-Dore *(F)* 51	F 2
Le Mont-St-Michel *(F)* 41	E 3
Le Montet *(F)* 48	A 4
Le Muy *(F)* 57	E 2
Le Neubourg *(F)* 42	B 2
Le Nouvion-	
en-Thiérache *(F)* 39	E 3
Le Palais *(F)* 40	C 3
Le Péage-de-Roussillon *(F)*52	C 2
Le Pellerin *(F)* 46	B 2
Le Poiré-sur-Vie *(F)* 46	B 3
Le Pont-de-Beauvoisin *(F)* 53	D 2
Le Pont-de-Claix *(F)* 53	D 2
Le Pont-de-Montvert *(F)* .. 52	A 4
Le Pontet *(F)* 52	C 4
Le Portel *(F)* 38	C 4
Le Pouldu *(F)* 40	C 4
Le Pouliguen *(F)* 46	A 2
Le Pouzin *(F)* 52	B 3
Le Puy-en-Velay *(F)* 52	A 3
Le Quesnoy *(F)* 39	D 3
Le Rozier *(F)* 52	A 4
Le Russey *(F)* 49	F 2
Le Sauze *(F)* 53	E 4
Le Teil *(F)* 52	B 3
Le Teilleul *(F)* 41	F 3
Le Theil *(F)* 42	B 3
Le Thillot *(F)* 49	F 1
Le Touquet-Paris-Plage *(F)* 38	B 3
Le Touvet *(F)* 53	D 2
Le Trayas *(F)* 57	E 2
Le Tréport *(F)* 38	B 3
Le Val-André *(F)* 41	D 3
Le Val-d'Ajol *(F)* 44	C 4
Le Verdon-sur-Mer *(F)* 50	B 2

Le Vigan *(F)* 52	A 4
Le Vivier-sur-Mer *(F)* 41	E 3
Leadenham *(GB)* 33	E 3
Leba *(PL)* 182	B 1
Lebach *(D)* 45	D 2
Lebane *(SRB)* 119	E 4
Lebenstedt *(D)* 84	A 3
Lebesby *(N)* 125	E 1
Lebork *(PL)* 182	B 1
Lebrija *(E)* 75	E 2
Łebsko (Jezioro) *(PL)*.... 181	F 1
Lebus *(D)* 85	F 2
Lecce *(I)* 107	F 3
Lecco *(I)* 97	E 3
Lécera *(E)* 65	F 3
Lećevica *(HR)* 103	F 1
Lech *(A)* 93	E 4
Lechainá *(GR)* 216	C 2
Lechlade *(GB)* 35	F 1
Leciñena *(E)* 65	F 2
Leck *(D)* 78	B 2
Leckava *(LT)* 163	D 3
Lectoure *(F)* 55	D 1
Łęczna *(PL)* 197	E 1
Łęczyca *(PL)* 189	D 3
Ledaña *(E)* 71	E 3
Ledanca *(E)* 64	C 4
Lēdas *(LV)* 157	E 4
Ledbury *(GB)* 35	E 1
Ledeč nad Sázavou *(CZ)* .. 90	C 3
Ledesma *(E)* 63	D 4
Lédignan *(F)* 52	B 4
Ledmore *(GB)* 27	E 2
Lēdmane *(LV)* 165	E 2
Lēdurga *(LV)* 159	E 2
Lędziny *(PL)* 200	F 1
Leebiku *(EST)* 160	C 1
Leedi *(EST)* 155	D 2
Leeds *(GB)* 33	E 3

Leek *(GB)* 33	D 3
Leenane *(IRL)* 22	B 3
Leer *(D)* 83	D 2
Leerdam *(NL)* 82	B 4
Leese *(D)* 83	F 3
Leeuwarden *(NL)* 82	C 2
Leevaku *(EST)* 161	E 1
Leevi *(EST)* 161	E 1
Lefka *(CY)* 230	B 3
Lefkáda *(GR)* 211	D 4
Lefkáda (Nisí) *(GR)* 211	F 3
Lefkádia *(GR)* 205	F 3
Lefkadíti *(GR)* 211	E 4
Lefkantí *(GR)* 218	C 1
Lefkára *(GR)* 205	F 4
Lefkes *(GR)* 219	F 4
Lefkímmi *(GR)* 208	C 2
Lefkógeia *(GR)* 207	D 1
Lefkonoiko *(CY)* 230	B 2
Lefkopigi *(GR)* 205	F 4
Léchovo *(GR)* 205	E 3
Lefkosía / Lefkosa *(CY)* .. 231	C 2
Lefkosía / Lefkoşa *(CY)* .. 231	C 2
Léfktra *(GR)* 218	B 1
Łęg *(PL)* 196	C 3
Legan *(E)* 78	C 3
Leganés *(E)* 70	B 1
Legé *(F)* 46	B 3
Legionowo *(PL)* 190	B 2
Legnago *(I)* 98	A 3
Legnano *(I)* 97	D 3
Legnica *(PL)* 193	C 2
Legnickie Pole *(PL)* 193	D 2
Legrad *(HR)* 112	A 3
Legrená *(GR)* 218	C 3
Léguevin *(F)* 55	D 2
Legutiano *(E)* 60	C 3
Lehtu *(EST)* 149	D 4
Lehmden *(D)* 83	E 3
Lehmja *(EST)* 149	E 3
Lehnin *(D)* 85	D 3
Lehola *(EST)* 149	D 3

LUXEMBOURG

Auguste-Charles (R.)	**BX**	10
Carrefours (R. des)	**AV**	18
Cents (R.)	**BV**	19
Cimetière (R. du)	**BX**	25
Eich (R. d')	**ABV**	36
Guillaume (Av.)	**AV**	55
Hespérange (R. d')	**BX**	61
Merl (R. de)	**AX**	76
Mulhenbach (R. de)	**AV**	79
Patton (Bd du Général)	**BV**	86
Rollingergrund (R. de)	**AV**	102
Strassen (R. de)	**AV**	112
10-Septembre (Av. du)	**AV**	127

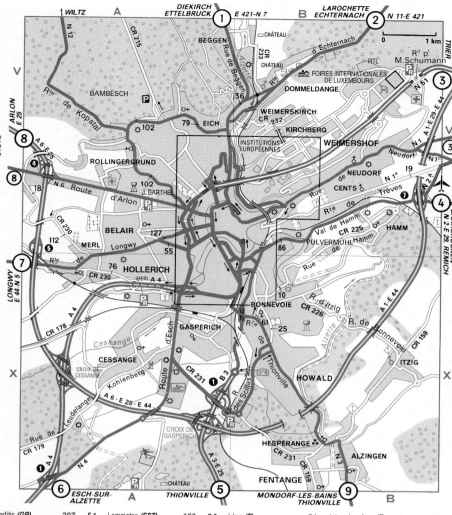

Lešani (MK)	122	A 4
Lešć (HR)	99	F 2
L'Escala / La Escala (E)	67	E 2
Lescar (F)	54	B 2
L'Escarène (F)	57	F 1
Lesce (SLO)	99	D 1
Lescun (F)	54	B 3
Lesina (I)	106	B 1
Lesini (GR)	216	C 1
Lesja (N)	130	C 4
Lesjöfors (S)	140	B 3
Lesko (PL)	202	E 3
Leskovac (SRB)	119	E 4
Lesna (N)	192	C 2
Lesneven (F)	40	B 2
Lešnica (BIH)	117	F 2
Leśnica Dolnośląskie (PL)	193	E 2
Leśnica Opolskie (PL)	194	C 4
Leśniowice (PL)	197	F 2
Lesparre-Médoc (F)	50	B 2
L'Espluga de Francolí (E)	66	B 3
L'Espunyola (E)	66	C 2
Lessay (F)	41	E 1
Lessebo (S)	143	F 3
Lessines (B)	39	E 2
L'Estartit (E)	67	E 2
Lestelle-Bétharram (F)	54	C 3
Lestene (LV)	163	F 1
Lestijärvi (FIN)	133	E 3
Lestkov (CZ)	89	F 3
Lésvos (Nisí) (GR)	214	C 3
Leszno Mazowieckie (PL)	189	F 3
Leszno Wielkopolskie (PL)	187	E 4
Lesznowola (PL)	190	B 3
Letchworth (GB)	36	B 2
Léteniai (LT)	163	D 3
Letenye (H)	112	A 3
Letes (LV)	161	D 3
Letino (I)	105	F 2
Letmathe (D)	87	F 1
Letterfrack (IRL)	22	A 3
Letterkenny / Leitir Ceanainn (IRL)	23	D 1
Lettermullan / Leitir Mealláin (IRL)	22	B 4
Letur (E)	71	D 4
Letuš (SLO)	99	E 1
Letymvou (CY)	230	A 3
Letzlingen (D)	84	C 3
Leuchars (GB)	31	D 1
Leukerbad (CH)	96	B 2
Leuna (D)	89	D 1
Leutenberg (D)	89	D 2
Leutershausen (D)	88	C 4
Leutkirch (D)	93	E 3
Leutschach (A)	95	E 4
Leuven (B)	39	F 2
Leuze-en-Hainaut (B)	39	D 2
Levajok (N)	125	E 2
Levala (EST)	150	C 3
Levanger (N)	131	D 2
Levaniškiai (LT)	171	D 2
Levanjska Varoš (HR)	115	F 3
Levanto (I)	101	F 3
Levåsjoki (FIN)	136	B 2
Leven (B)	31	D 1
Leven (GB)	33	E 2
Levene (S)	143	D 1
Levens (F)	53	F 4
Leverano (I)	107	E 3
Leverburgh (GB)	26	C 2
Leverkusen (D)	87	E 2
Leveste (LV)	163	F 1
Levet (F)	48	A 3
Levice (SK)	12	B 3
Levico Terme (I)	98	A 2
Levidi (GR)	217	E 3
Levie (F)	57	F 4
Levier (F)	49	E 3
Levitha (Nisí) (GR)	221	D 4
Levroux (F)	47	F 3
Lewes (GB)	36	B 4
Lewin Brzeski (PL)	194	B 3
Lewin Kłodzki (PL)	193	E 4
Leyburn (GB)	33	D 1
Leyland (GB)	32	C 2
Leysdown-on-Sea (GB)	36	B 4
Leysin (CH)	49	F 4
Leżajsk (PL)	197	D 2
Lézardrieux (F)	40	C 2
Lézat-sur-Lèze (F)	55	D 2
Lezay (F)	47	D 4
Lezhë (AL)	121	D 2
Lézignan-Corbières (F)	55	F 3
Ležimir (SRB)	117	F 1
Lezoux (F)	52	A 1

Lehrberg (D)	88	C 4
Lehre (D)	84	B 3
Lehrte (D)	84	A 3
Lehtimäki (FIN)	133	E 4
Lehtmetsa (EST)	149	F 3
Lehtovaara (FIN)	129	D 2
Lehtse (EST)	149	F 3
Leianokládi (GR)	212	A 3
Leibnitz (A)	95	E 4
Leicester (GB)	33	E 4
Leiden (NL)	82	A 4
Leie (E)	154	C 3
Leighton Buzzard (GB)	36	B 2
Leikanger (N)	138	C 1
Leimaņi (LV)	166	B 3
Leinefelde (D)	88	C 1
Leini (I)	53	F 2
Leipalingis (LT)	176	B 4
Leipheim (D)	93	E 2
Leipsoí (GR)	221	D 4
Leipsoí (Nisí) (GR)	221	D 4
Leipste (EST)	154	A 4
Leipzig (D)	89	E 1
Leira (N)	139	D 3
Leira (N)	130	C 3
Leirbotn (N)	125	D 2
Leiria (P)	68	B 1
Leiro (E)	58	B 4
Leirpollskogen (N)	125	F 1
Leirvåg (N)	138	B 3
Leirvik (DK)	126	A 4
Leirvik (N)	127	D 4
Leirvik (N)	138	B 1
Leirvik (N)	138	B 1
Leisi (EST)	152	C 3
Leisnig (D)	89	E 1
Leiston (GB)	37	D 2
Leith (GB)	31	D 2
Leitza (E)	61	D 2
Leitzkau (D)	84	C 3
Leivadeiá (GR)	206	C 2
Leivadi (CY)	230	A 3

Leivadítis (GR)	207	F 1
Leivonmäki (FIN)	133	F 4
Lejas Strazdi (LV)	162	B 1
Lejasciems (LV)	161	D 3
Lejaskauguri (LV)	159	D 2
Lejasozoli (LV)	159	D 3
Lejasstrazdi (LV)	163	F 2
Lēļēji (LV)	162	C 2
Léka (GR)	221	D 2
Leka (N)	131	E 1
Lekáni (GR)	207	E 2
Łękawa (PL)	195	D 2
Łękawica (PL)	200	F 2
Lekeitio (E)	60	C 3
Lekenik (HR)	99	F 2
Leknes (N)	130	B 4
Leknes (N)	127	B 1
Łęknica Lubuskie (PL)	192	B 1
Leksand (S)	140	B 2
Leksvik (N)	131	D 2
Lekunberri (E)	61	D 3
Leland (N)	127	D 4
Leliūnai Antalgė (LT)	171	F 2
Leliūnai Klaipėdos (LT)	162	C 4
Leliūnai Mičkūnai (LT)	171	E 2
Lelkowo (PL)	183	E 2
Lelle (EST)	149	E 4
Lelów (PL)	195	E 3
Lelystad (NL)	82	B 3
Lelystad Haven (NL)	82	B 3
Lembach (F)	45	E 2
Lembeye (F)	54	C 2
Lemesos (CY)	231	C 4
Lemešova (LV)	167	F 2
Lemförde (D)	83	E 3
Lemgo (D)	83	F 4
Lemi (FIN)	137	E 3
Lemithou (CY)	230	B 3
Lemland (FIN)	136	A 4
Lemmenjoki (FIN)	125	E 3
Lemmer (NL)	82	C 3

Lemmetsa (EST)	153	C 3
Lemonodásos (GR)	218	B 3
Lempäälä (FIN)	136	C 2
Lempdes-sur-Allagnon (F)	52	A 2
Lemsi (EST)	153	C 3
Lemvig (DK)	142	A 3
Lenart-v-Slov.-gor (SLO)	95	E 4
Lēnas (LT)	171	F 2
Lēnas (LV)	163	D 2
Lencloître (F)	47	D 3
Lendava (SLO)	95	F 4
Lendinara (I)	98	A 4
Lendži (LV)	167	E 2
Lengefeld Mittlerer Erzgebirgkreis (D)	89	F 2
Lengenfeld (D)	89	E 2
Lengerich (D)	83	E 4
Lenggries (D)	93	F 3
L'Épine (F)	43	F 4
Lepna (EST)	150	C 3
Lepoglava (HR)	99	F 1
Leposavić (SRB)	118	C 4
Lépoura (GR)	218	C 1
Leppäjärvi (FIN)	125	D 4
Leppävirta (FIN)	135	E 4
Leppneeme (EST)	149	E 2
Leptokaryá Évros (GR)	208	B 2
Leptokaryá Pieriá (GR)	212	B 1
Lercara Friddi (I)	110	C 3
Léré (F)	48	A 2
Lerici (I)	101	F 3
Lerín (E)	61	D 4
Lerma (E)	64	B 2
Lérni (GR)	217	F 3
Léros (Nisí) (GR)	221	D 4
Lerum (S)	143	D 1
Lerwick (GB)	29	F 1
Les (E)	55	D 3
Les Abrets (F)	52	C 2
Les Aix-d'Angillon (F)	48	A 2
León (E)	59	E 4

Léon (F)	54	A 1
Leonarisso (CY)	231	E 2
Leonberg (D)	45	F 3
Léoncel (F)	52	C 3
Leonessa (I)	102	B 4
Leonforte (I)	111	D 3
Leonídio (GR)	217	F 4
Leontári Arkadía (GR)	217	E 3
Leontári Kardítsa (GR)	211	F 3
Leóntio (GR)	217	F 2
Leopoldsburg (B)	39	F 1
Leopoldsdorf im Marchfelde (A)	95	F 1
Leova (MD)	13	E 3
Lepe (E)	74	C 2
Lepel' (BY)	7	F 2
Lepenoú (GR)	211	E 4
Lepetane (MNE)	121	D 2
Les Arcs (F)	53	E 1
Les Arcs (F)	57	E 2
Les Baux-de-Provence (F)	56	C 2
Les Bézards (F)	43	D 4
Les Borges Blanques (E)	66	B 3
Les Bouchoux (F)	49	E 4
Les Cabannes (F)	55	E 3
Les Contamines-Montjoie (F)	53	E 1
Les Coves de Vonromà (E)	72	A 1
Les Deux-Alpes (F)	53	D 3
Les Diablerets (CH)	49	F 4
Les Écharmeaux (F)	48	C 4
Les Échelles (F)	53	D 2
Les Essarts (F)	46	C 3
Les Eyzies-de-Tayac (F)	51	D 3
Les Gets (F)	49	F 4
Les Herbiers (F)	46	C 3
Les Houches (F)	49	F 4
Les Issambres (F)	57	E 2
Les Lecques (F)	57	D 3
Les Llosses (E)	55	E 4
Les Matelles (F)	56	A 2
Les Mées (F)	53	D 4
Les Menuires (F)	53	E 2
Les Olllières-sur-Eyrieux (F)	52	B 3
Les Pieux (F)	41	E 1
Les Planches-en-Montagne (F)	49	E 3
Les Ponts-de-Cé (F)	46	C 2
Les Quatre Chemins (F)	46	C 4
Les Riceys (F)	43	F 4
Les Rosiers-sur-Loire (F)	47	D 2
Les Rousses (F)	49	E 4
Les Sables-d'Olonne (F)	46	B 3
Les Settons (F)	48	C 2
Les Trois-Épis (F)	45	D 1
Les Trois-Moutiers (F)	47	D 3
Les Useres (E)	72	A 1
Les Vans (F)	52	B 4
Les Vignes (F)	52	A 2
Lešak (SRB)	118	C 4

Map labels: WILTZ, DIEKIRCH ETTELBRUCK, E 421-N 7, LAROCHETTE ECHTERNACH, N 11-E 421, TRIER, BEGGEN, CHÂTEAU, d'Echternach, 0 1 km, R⁴ pᵗ M.Schumann, RTL, FOIRES INTERNATIONALES DE LUXEMBOURG, DOMMELDANGE, BAMBËSCH, WEIMERSKIRCH, KIRCHBERG, WEIMERSHOF, EICH, INSTITUTIONS EUROPÉENNES, NEUDORF, CENTS, Trèves, ROLLINGERGRUND, J. BARTHEL, BELAIR, MERL, Longwy, HAMM, PULVERMÜHL, Hamm, HOLLERICH, BONNEVOIE, GASPERICH, Cessange, CESSANGE, Kohlenberg, HOWALD, ITZIG, CROIX DE GASPERICH, HESPÉRANGE, ALZINGEN, FENTANGE, ESCH-SUR-ALZETTE, THIONVILLE, MONDORF-LES-BAINS THIONVILLE

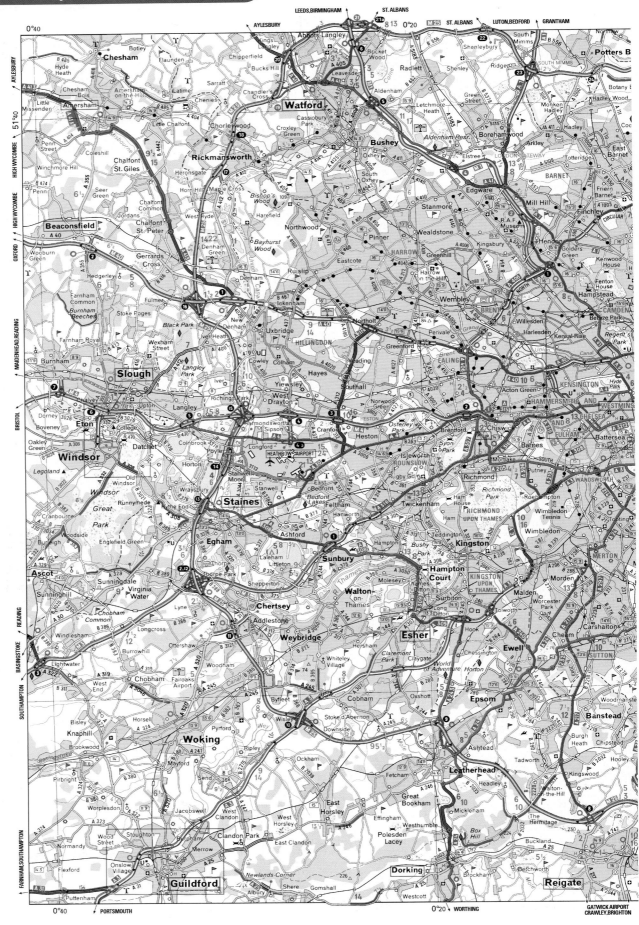

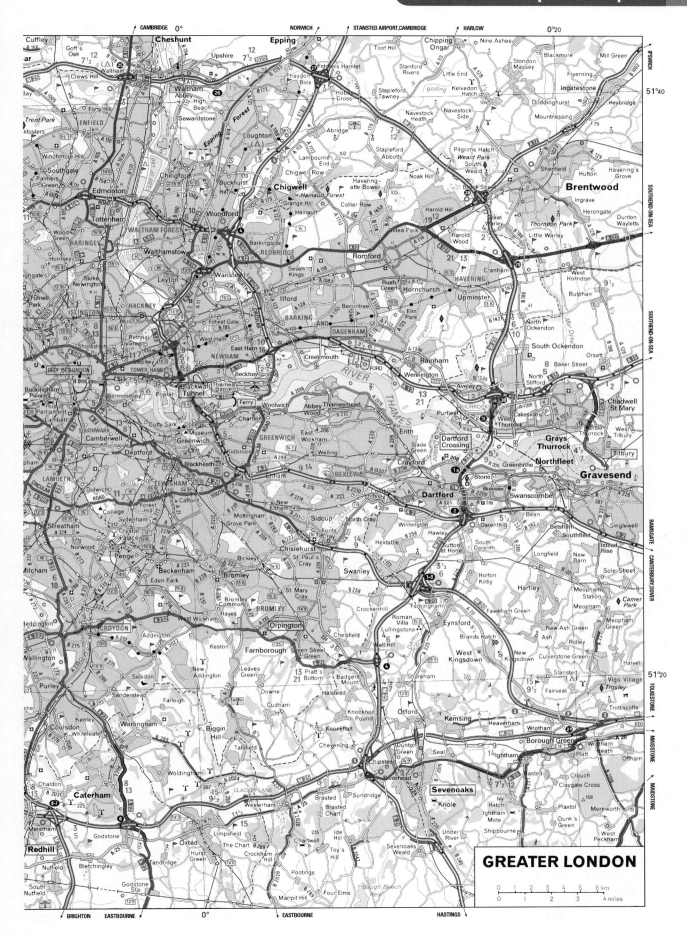

GREATER LONDON

0 1 2 3 4 5 6 km
0 1 2 3 4 miles

BRON
Mendès-France (Av. P.) . . . **DR** 103
Roosevelt (Av. F.) . . . . . . **DQR** 143
8 Mai 1945 (R. du) . . . . . . **DQ** 188

ÉCULLY
Champagne
(Rte de) . . . . **AP** 25
Dr-Terver (Av. du) . . . . . . **AP** 38
Marietton (R.) . . . . **AP** 99
Roosevelt (Av. F.) . . . . . . **AP** 142

LA MULATIÈRE
Mulatière (Pont de la) . . . **BQ** 111

LYON
Bourgogne (R. de) . . . . **BP** 14
Chambaud-de-la-Bruyère
(Bd) . . . . **BR** 23
Mulatière (Pont de la) . . . **BQ** 111
Pasteur (Pt) . . . . **BQ** 115
Rockefeller (Av.) . . . . **CQ** 138
St-Simon (R.) . . . . **APB** 153

OULLINS
Perron (R. du) . . . . **BR** 119

PIERRE-BÉNITE
Europe (Bd de l') . . . . **BR** 43

STE-FOY-LÈS-LYON
Fonts (Ch. des) . . . . **AQ** 55

Thomas (Crs A.) . . . . **CQ** 168

ST-FONS
Jean-Jaurès
(Av.) . . . . **CR** 79
Semard (Bd P.) . . . . **BR** 159
Sembat (R. M.) . . . . **BR** 161

ST-PRIEST
Herriot (Bd E.) . . . . **DR** 77
Maréchal (R. H.) . . . . **DR** 97

Franche-Comté (R. de) . . . **BQ** 59

TASSIN-LA-DEMI-LUNE
Foch (Av. Mar.) . . . . **AQ** 53
République (Av.) . . . . **AQ** 134
Victor-Hugo
(Av.) . . . . **APQ** 175

VAULX-EN-VELIN
Allende
(Av. S.) . . . . **DP** 3

Rostand (R. E.) . . . . **DR** 145

VÉNISSIEUX
Cachin (Av. M.) . . . . **CR** 18
Frères L. et É.
Bertrand (R. des
) . . . . **CR** 61

Gaulle (Av. Ch.-de) . . . . . . **DP** 67

VILLEURBANNE
Chirat (R. F.) . . . . **CQ** 29
Jean-Jaurès (R.) . . . . **CQ** 80

Lezuza (E) 71	D 3	Lich (D) 88	A 2	Lidhult (S) 143	D 3	Lidzbark Warmiński (PL) . 183	F 2	Lienz (A) 94	B 4	Lieto (FIN) 136	B 3
Lgota Wielka (PL) 195	D 2	Licháda (GR) 212	B 4	Lidingö (S) 141	D 4	Liebenwalde (D) 85	D 2	Liepa (LV) 159	F 3	Liétor (E) 71	D 4
L'gov (RUS) 7	F 4	Lichfield (GB) 33	D 4	Lidköping (S) 143	D 1	Lieberose (D) 85	F 3	Liepāja (LV) 162	B 2	Lieurey (F) 42	B 2
L'Hermenault (F) 46	C 3	Lichoslavl' (RUS) 7	F 1	Lido degli Estensi (I) 98	B 4	Liechtenstein (FL) 93	D 4	Liepakojai (LT) 175	F 3	Lievestuore (FIN) 133	F 4
L'Hospitalet de l'Infant (E) 66	B 4	Lichtenberg (D) 89	D 2	Lido delle Nazioni (I) 98	B 4	Liège (B) 87	D 2	Liepas (Mežauiža) (LV) 166	C 3	Liévin (F) 39	D 3
Liabygda (N) 130	B 4	Lichtenfels (D) 89	D 3	Lido di Camaiore (I) 101	E 2	Lieģi (LV) 162	B 2	Liepiai (LT) 170	C 4	Liezen (A) 94	C 3
Liaušiai (LT) 171	E 3	Lichtenstein (D) 89	E 2	Lido di Classe (I) 102	A 1	Lieksa (FIN) 135	F 2	Liepiškiai (LT) 169	F 2	Liezēre (LV) 160	C 4
Lībagi (LV) 157	E 4	Lichtenvoorde (NL) 83	D 3	Lido di Jesolo (I) 98	B 3	Lielauce (LV) 163	E 2	Liepkalne (LV) 165	F 1	Liffol-le-Grand (F) 44	B 3
Libáň (CZ) 90	C 2	Līči Preiļu (LV) 167	D 3	Lido di Metaponto (I) . . . 107	D 2	Lielie Anspoki (LV) 167	D 4	Lieplaukė (LV) 163	D 3	Lifford (IRL) 23	D 2
Libatse (EST) 153	C 2	Līči Rīgas (LV) 159	D 4	Lido di Ostia (I) 104	C 2	Lielie Mukoni (LV) 166	C 4	Liepna (LV) 161	E 3	Liffré (F) 41	E 3
Liberec (CZ) 90	B 1	Līči Talsu (LV) 157	E 3	Lido di Savio (I) 102	A 1	Lielionys (LT) 176	C 2	Lieporai (LV) 164	C 3	Līgatne (LV) 159	E 4
Liberec (CZ) 90	B 1	Līči Valmieras (LV) 159	D 4	Lido di Spina (I) 98	B 4	Liellauki (LV) 165	E 3	Liepudruvas (LV) 167	D 3	Līgatne (Augšlīgatne) (LV)159	E 4
Liberiškis (LT) 170	C 2	Ličiūnai (LT) 165	D 4	Lido di Torre Mileto (I) . . 103	F 4	Lielmēmele (LV) 165	E 3	Liepupe (LV) 159	D 3	Lignano Pineta (I) 98	C 2
Libiąż (PL) 200	F 2	Lička Jesenica (HR) 99	F 3	Lido di Venezia (I) 98	B 3	Lielplatone (LV) 164	C 3	Liepziedi (LV) 163	F 2	Lignano Sabbiadoro (I) . . 98	C 2
Libochovice (CZ) 90	A 2	Lički Osik (HR) 99	F 3	Lido Silvana (I) 107	E 3	Lielplatones		Lier (B) 39	E 1	Lignières (F) 47	E 3
Libourne (F) 50	C 3	Ličko Lešće (HR) 99	F 3	Lidoríki (GR) 211	F 4	Internātskola (LV) . . . 164	B 3	Liérganes (E) 60	B 3	Ligny-en-Barrois (F) 44	B 3
Librilla (E) 77	E 1	Līčupe (LV) 165	F 1	Līdumi Alūksnes (LV) . . . 161	C 1	Lielšļukas (LV) 165	C 1	Liernais (F) 48	C 1	Ligny-le-Châtel (F) 43	F 4
Licata (I) 111	D 4	Lida (BY) 6	C 4	Līdumi Kuldīgas (LV) . . . 162	C 1	Lielvārde (LV) 165	E 2	Liestal (CH) 92	B 4	Līgo (LV) 161	D 4
Licciana Nardi (I) 101	E 3	Liden (S) 132	A 4	Lidzbark (PL) 183	E 4	Lielvircava (LV) 164	C 2	Liesumi (LV) 159	F 1	Ligourió (GR) 218	A 3

Ligowo (PL) 189   D 1
Ligueil (F) 47   E 3
Līguti (LV) 162   C 2
Lihula (EST) 153   B 2
Liigvalla (EST) 150   C 4
Liikasenvaara (FIN) ... 129   E 3
Liiva (EST) 153   A 3
Liivi (EST) 148   C 4
Lijeva Rijeka (MNE) .. 121   E 2
Lijevi Dubravčak (HR) 115   D 3
Likenäs (S) 139   F 2
Līksna (Leiksna) (LV) 166   C 4
Līkupēni (LV) 163   E 2
Līlaia (GR) 212   B 4
Liland (N) 124   A 4
Lilaste (LV) 159   D 4
L'Ile-Bouchard (F) 47   E 2
L'Ile-Rousse (F) 57   F 3
Lilienfeld (A) 95   E 2
Liljendal (FIN) 137   D 3
Lilla Edet (S) 143   D 1
Lillby (FIN) 133   D 3
Lille (F) 39   D 2
Lillebonne (F) 38   A 4
Lillehammer (N) 139   E 1
Lillerød (DK) 143   D 4
Lillers (F) 38   C 2
Lillesand (N) 142   B 1
Lillestrøm (N) 139   E 3
Lillhärdal (S) 140   B 1
Lillholmsjön (S) 131   F 3
Lilli Harju(EST) 149   F 3
Lilli Viljandi(EST) 159   F 1
Lillo (E) 70   C 2
Lillögda (S) 132   B 2
Lima (N) 140   A 2
Limáni Chersonísou 227 D 2
Limáni Géraka (GR) .. 223   D 2
Limanowa (PL) 201   B 2
Limassol (CY) 231   C 4
Limavady (GB) 23   E 1
Limbach (D) 88   F 3
Limbaži (LV) 159   E 3
Limburg a. d. Lahn (D) . 87   F 3
Limenária (GR) 207   E 3
Limerick / Luimneach (IRL) 24 C 2
Limingen (N) 131   F 1
Liminka (FIN) 133   E 1
Liminpuro (FIN) 133   F 1
Limljani (MNE) 121   E 3
Limnatis (CY) 230   B 4
Límnes (GR) 217   F 3
Límni (GR) 212   C 4
Limnia (CY) 230   D 2
Limniá (GR) 207   E 2
Limnitis (CY) 230   B 3
Limnítsa (GR) 211   F 4
Límnos (GR) 214   A 1
Limoges (F) 51   D 1
Limogne-en-Quercy (F) . 51   E 2
Limone Piemonte (I) 53   F 4
Limonest (F) 52   B 1
Limours-en-Hurepoix (F) 43 D 3
Limoux (F) 55   E 3
Linaküla (EST) 153   B 4
Linares (E) 76   B 3
Linares de Mora (E) 71   F 1
Linares de Riofrío (E) ... 63   E 4
Linariá (GR) 213   C 4
Lincoln (GB) 33   E 3
Lindås (N) 138   B 1
Lindau i. Bodensee Kreis
    LindauBodensee(D) .. 93   D 4
Linden (D) 88   C 3
Lindenberg i. Allgäu
    Kr.LindauBodensee(D) .. 93 D 3
Lindern (D) 83   E 2
Lindesberg (S) 140   B 4
Lindesnes (N) 142   A 1
Lindi (EST) 153   B 4
Lindö (S) 143   F 1
Líndos (GR) 228   C 2
Lindoso (P) 62   C 1
Lindow (D) 85   D 2
Lindsdal (S) 143   F 3
Lingbo (S) 140   C 2
Linge (N) 130   B 4
Lingen (D) 83   D 3
Linghem (S) 143   F 1
Linguaglossa (I) 111   A 3
Linkaičiai (LT) 163   F 3
Linken (D) 81   D 4
Linkmenys (LT) 172   B 3
Linköping (S) 143   F 1
Linkuva (LT) 164   C 4
Linlithgow (GB) 31   D 2
Linna (EST) 160   B 1

Linnamäe (EST) 148   C 4
Linsell (S) 131   F 4
Linslade (GB) 36   B 2
Linte (EST) 155   E 4
Linthal (CH) 97   D 1
Linyola (E) 66   B 3
Linz (A) 94   C 2
Linz a. Rhein (D) 87   F 3
Lioliai Šiaulių(LT) 169   E 2
Lioliai Telšiu(LT) 168   C 1
Lion-sur-Mer (F) 41   F 1
Lioni (I) 106   B 3
Liopetri (CY) 231   E 3
Liópraso (GR) 211   F 2
Lipa (EST) 149   E 4
Lipa Dolnośląskie(PL) 193 D 3
Lipar (SRB) 113   D 4
Liperi (FIN) 135   F 3
Lipiany (PL) 186   C 1
Lipica (SLO) 99   D 2
Lipie Śląskie(PL) 195   D 2
Lipiniški (LV) 167   D 4
Lipinki (PL) 201   C 3
Lipinki Łużyckie (PL) . 186   C 4
Lipka (PL) 181   F 4
Lipkovo (MK) 122   B 2
Lipljan (SRB) 122   A 2
Lipnica Kujawsko-
    Pomorskie(PL) 183   D 4
Lipnica Pomorskie(PL) 181 F 2
Lipnica Wielkopolskie(PL)187 E 2
Lipnica Murowana (PL) 201 B 2
Lipnica Wielka (PL) ... 201   A 3
Lipnik (PL) 196   C 3
Lipník nad Bečvou (CZ) . 91 E 3
Lipno Kujawsko-
    Pomorskie(PL) 189   D 1
Lipno Wielkopolskie (PL). 187 D 1
Lipno nad Vltavou (CZ) .. 94 C 1
Lipová-lázně (CZ) 91   E 2
Lipovac (HR) 117   F 1
Lipowa (PL) 200   F 3
Lipowiec Kościelny (PL).189 E 1
Lipowo (PL) 183   D 1
Lippstadt (D) 83   F 4
Lipsk (PL) 185   E 3
Lipsko Mazowieckie(PL) 196 C 2
Liptovský Mikuláš (SK) 12 D 2
Lipuški (LV) 167   E 3
Lisac (BIH) 117   E 3
Lisboa (P) 68   A 3
Lisburn (GB) 23   E 2
Lisdoonvarna / Lios Dúin
    Bhearna (IRL) 24   B 1
Lisewo Kujawsko-
    Pomorskie(PL) 182   C 1
Lisia Góra (PL) 201   B 2
Lisieux (F) 42   B 2
Liskeard (GB) 34   C 3
Liškiava (LT) 176   C 2
Lisków (PL) 188   C 4
L'Isle-Adam (F) 43   D 2
L'Isle-d'Abeau (F) 52   C 2
L'Isle-de-Noé (F) 54   C 2
L'Isle-en-Dodon (F) 55   D 2
L'Isle-Jourdain (F) 55   D 1
L'Isle-Jourdain (F) 47   E 4
L'Isle-sur-la-Sorgue (F) .. 56 C 1
L'Isle-sur-le-Doubs (F) .. 49 E 2
L'Isle-sur-Serein (F) 43   F 4
Lisle-sur-Tarn (F) 55   E 1
Lismore / Lios Mór (IRL) 25 D 3
Lisnaskea (GB) 23   D 3
Lišnja (BIH) 115   F 4
Lisova (LV) 167   F 3
Lisovići (BIH) 117   E 2
Lisse (NL) 84   B 4
List (D) 78   B 2
Listowel /
    Lios Tuathail (IRL) 24   B 1
Liszki (PL) 201   A 2
Liszna (PL) 191   F 4
Lit (S) 131   F 3
Lit-et-Mixe (F) 50   A 2
Litene (LV) 161   D 4
Lithakiá (GR) 216   B 2
Lithínes (GR) 227   F 3
Lithío (GR) 220   C 1
Liti (GR) 206   B 3
Litija (SLO) 99   E 1
Litóchoro (GR) 206   B 4
Litoměřice (CZ) 90   A 2
Litomyšl (CZ) 91   D 3
Litovel (CZ) 91   E 3
Litschau (A) 90   C 4
Littlehampton (GB) 36   B 4

Littleport (GB) 33   F 4
Litvínov (CZ) 89   F 2
Liu (EST) 153   B 4
Liubavas (LT) 175   C 3
Liučiūnai (LT) 169   F 4
Liudvinavas (LT) 175   F 3
Liutkiškiai (LT) 169   F 1
Liutonys (LT) 177   D 2
Liuža (LV) 167   E 2
Livade (HR) 99   D 3
Livaderó Dráma(GR) . 207   E 1
Livaderó Kozáni(GR) . 211   F 1
Liváđi Atikí-Peireiás(GR).223 E 3
Liváđi Kikládes(GR) .. 219   D 4
Liváđi Lárisa(GR) 205   F 2
Liváđi Thessaloníki(GR)..206 C 3
Livadia (CY) 231   D 3
Livádia (GR) 217   F 1
Livadochóri (GR) 214   A 1
Livanátes (GR) 212   C 4
Līvāni (LV) 166   C 3
Livari (MNE) 121   E 3
Livarot (F) 42   A 2
Līvbērze (LV) 164   B 2
Livera (CY) 230   B 2
Liverá (GR) 205   F 4
Liverdun (F) 44   C 3
Livernon (F) 51   E 2
Liverpool (GB) 32   C 2
Līvi (LV) 159   E 3
Livigno (I) 97   E 3
Livingston (GB) 31   D 2
Livno (BIH) 117   D 4
Livo (FIN) 129   D 4
Livold (SLO) 99   E 2
Livorno (I) 101   E 2
Livorno Ferraris (I) 53   F 2
Livron-sur-Drôme (F) ... 52   C 3
Liw (PL) 190   C 2
Lixoúri (GR) 216   B 1
Lizard (GB) 34   B 4
Lizdeikiai (LT) 176   B 2
Lizdēni (LV) 159   F 2
Līzespasts (LV) 161   D 3
Lizums (LV) 160   C 4
Lizy-sur-Ourcq (F) 43   D 2
Lizzano in Belvedere (I)..101 F 1
Ljeskove Vode (BIH) .. 115   F 4
Ljig (SRB) 118   B 2
Ljubaništa (MK) 122   A 4
Ljubašivka (UA) 13   C 2
Ljubija (BIH) 115   E 4
Ljubinje (BIH) 120   C 2
Ljubiš (SRB) 118   B 3
Ljubljana (SLO) 99   D 1
Ljubno (SLO) 99   E 1
Ljubojno (MK) 122   A 4
Ljuboml' (UA) 12   C 1
Ljubovija (SRB) 118   A 2
Ljubuški (BIH) 120   C 1
Ljugarn (S) 146   B 2
Ljungby (S) 143   E 3
Ljungbyhed (S) 143   D 4
Ljungdalen (S) 131   E 3
Ljungsbro (S) 143   F 1
Ljungskile (S) 143   D 1
Ljusdal (S) 140   C 1
Ljusne (S) 140   C 2
Ljuta (BIH) 117   E 4
Ljutići (MNE) 118   B 4
Ljutoglav (SRB) 122   A 2
Ljutomer (SLO) 95   F 4
Llagostera (E) 67   C 2
Llanberis (GB) 32   B 3
Llançà (E) 56   A 4
Llandeilo (GB) 34   C 1
Llandovery /
    Llanymddyfri (GB) 35   D 1
Llandrindod Wells (GB) . 32 B 4
Llandudno (GB) 32   B 2
Llandysul (GB) 34   C 1
Llanelli (GB) 34   C 1
Llanerchymedd (GB) ... 32   A 2
Llanes (E) 59   F 2
Llanfairfechan (GB) 32   B 3
Llanfyllin (GB) 32   B 3
Llangadog (GB) 34   C 1
Llangefni (GB) 32   A 3
Llangollen (GB) 32   C 3
Llangurig (GB) 32   B 4
Llanidloes (GB) 32   B 4
Llanrhystud (GB) 32   A 4
Llanrwst (GB) 32   B 3
Llanwrtyd Wells (GB) ... 35   D 1
Llavorsí (E) 55   D 4
Lleida (E) 66   B 3
Llera (E) 69   E 4

Llerena (E) 69   E 4
Lles de Cerdanya (E) ... 55   E 4
Llessui (E) 55   D 4
Llíria (E) 71   F 2
Llodio / Laudio (E) 60   C 3
Lloret de Mar (E) 67   E 3
Llucena (E) 72   A 1
Llucmajor (E) 73   D 2
Llynclys (GB) 32   C 3
Lnáře (CZ) 90   A 4
Lniano (PL) 182   C 4
Loanhead (GB) 31   D 2
Loano (I) 100   C 2
Löbau (D) 90   B 1
Löbejün (D) 84   C 4
Lobenstein (D) 89   D 2
Loberģi (LV) 160   C 2
Łobez (PL) 181   D 3
Löbnitz (D) 79   F 3
Lobón (E) 69   D 3
Loburg (D) 84   C 3
Łobżenica (PL) 181   F 4
Locana (I) 53   F 2
Ločarica (HR) 112   B 4
Locarno (CH) 97   D 2
Lochaline (GB) 30   B 1
Lochcarron (GB) 27   D 3
Lochearnhead (GB) 30   C 1
Lochem (NL) 82   C 4
Loches (F) 47   E 2
Lochgelly (GB) 31   D 2
Lochgilphead (GB) 30   B 2
Lochinver (GB) 27   D 2
Lochmaben (GB) 31   D 3
Lochmaddy (GB) 26   C 3
Łochów (PL) 190   C 2
Łochowice (GB) 186   C 3
Lochranza (GB) 30   B 2
Lochvycja (UA) 13   F 1
Lociki (Loči) (LV) 173   D 1
Lociši (LV) 167   F 3
Lockenhaus (A) 95   F 3
Lockerbie (GB) 31   D 3
Löcknitz (D) 81   D 4
Locmariaquer (F) 40   C 4
Locminé (F) 41   D 4
Locorotondo (I) 107   D 3
Locquirec (F) 40   C 2
Locri (I) 111   F 1
Locronan (F) 40   B 3
Loctudy (F) 40   B 4
Lodè (I) 108   C 2
Lode Limbažu(LV) 159   E 3
Lode Valmieras(LV) ... 159   F 1
Lodève (F) 56   A 2
Lodi (I) 97   D 3
Løding (N) 127   E 2
Lødingen (N) 124   A 4
Lodiņi (LV) 164   C 3
Łodja (EST) 153   C 4
Lodosa (E) 61   D 4
Łodygowice (PL) 200   F 2
Łódź (PL) 189   E 4
Loeches (E) 70   C 1
Loen (N) 130   B 4
Løfallstrand (N) 138   B 2
Lofário (P) 208   B 2
Lofer (A) 94   B 3
Löffingen (D) 45   E 4
Lofsdalen (S) 131   E 4
Lofthus (N) 138   B 2
Loftus (GB) 31   F 4
Log (SLO) 98   C 1
Logarska dolina (SLO) . 99 D 1
Logatec (SLO) 99   D 2
Logkanikos (GR) 217   E 4
Logroño (E) 60   C 4
Logrosán (E) 69   F 2
Løgstør (DK) 142   B 2
Løgten (DK) 142   B 3
Løgumkloster (DK) 142   A 4
Lohals (DK) 142   C 4
Lõhavere (EST) 154   B 3
Lohberg (D) 89   F 4
Lohilahti (FIN) 137   F 2
Lohiniva (FIN) 128   C 2
Lohja / Lojo (FIN) 136   C 4
Lohkva (EST) 155   D 4
Löhne (D) 83   F 4
Lohne (Oldenburg) (D) . 83   E 3
Lohr a. Main (D) 88   B 4
Lohtaja (FIN) 133   D 2
Lohu (EST) 149   D 2
Lohusalu (EST) 149   D 2
Lohusuu (EST) 151   E 4
Loiano (I) 101   F 1
Loimaa (FIN) 136   C 3

Loimaan kunta (FIN) . 136   C 3
Loiri (I) 108   B 1
Loiron (F) 41   F 4
Loitz (D) 80   B 3
Loja (E) 76   A 2
Loja (LV) 159   D 4
Lojsta (S) 146   B 2
Lokalahti (FIN) 136   B 3
Løken (N) 139   E 3
Lokeren (B) 39   E 1
Loket (CZ) 89   E 3
Lokka (FIN) 125   E 3
Løkken (DK) 142   B 2
Løkken (N) 130   C 3
Lokn'a (RUS) 7   D 2
Lokrum (Otok) (HR) ... 120   C 2
Loksa (EST) 149   F 2
Lokuta Järva(EST) 149   F 4
Lokuta Rapla(EST) ... 154   A 2
Lokuti (EST) 149   E 3
Lokve (HR) 99   E 3
Lokve (SLO) 99   D 2
Lokve (SRB) 113   F 4
L'Olleria (E) 71   F 3
Lom (BG) 12   C 4
Lom (N) 130   C 4
Lom Ústecký kraj(CZ) . 89 F 2
Łomazy (PL) 191   D 3
Lomazzo (I) 97   D 3
Lombez (F) 55   D 2
Lomello (I) 97   D 3
Lomen (N) 139   D 1
Lomeniai (LT) 171   D 4
Lomiai (LT) 169   D 3
Łomianki (PL) 190   B 3
Lomi-Bortnīki (LV) 167   D 3
Lomma (S) 143   D 4
Lommatzsch (D) 89   F 1
Lommel (B) 39   F 1
Lomnice
    nad Popelkou (CZ) ... 90   C 2
Lomonosov (RUS) 7   D 1
Lompolo (FIN) 125   E 4
Łomża (PL) 184   C 3
Lonato (I) 97   F 3
Lončari (BIH) 117   E 1
Londinières (F) 38   B 4
London (GB) 36   B 3
Londonderry (GB) 23   D 3
Lone (LV) 165   D 1
Long Eaton (GB) 33   D 3
Long Preston (GB) 33   D 1
Long Sutton (GB) 33   F 4
Longá (GR) 222   B 2
Longádes (GR) 211   D 2
Longares (E) 65   F 3
Longarone (I) 98   B 1
Longeau (F) 49   D 1
Longford /
    An Longfort (IRL) 23   D 4
Longny-au-Perche (F) .. 42   B 3
Longobucco (I) 109   E 1
Longós (GR) 210   C 3
Longtown (GB) 31   D 3
Longué (F) 47   D 2
Longueville-sur-Scie (F). 38 B 4
Longuyon (F) 44   B 2
Longwy (F) 44   B 2
Lonigo (I) 98   A 3
Löningen (D) 83   E 3
Łoniów (PL) 196   C 3
Lonja (HR) 115   E 3
Lons-le-Saunier (F) 49   D 2
Lönsboda (S) 143   E 4
Lønstrup (DK) 142   B 1
Loo (EST) 149   E 2
Loodi (EST) 154   B 4
Lõõla (EST) 149   F 4
Loosdorf (A) 95   E 2
Loosu (EST) 161   D 1
Lootvina (EST) 155   D 4
Lopar (HR) 99   E 4
Lopare (BIH) 117   F 2
Lopatica (MK) 122   B 4
Lopcombe Corner (GB) . 35 D 1
Lõpe Hiiu(EST) 148   A 4
Lõpe Pärnu(EST) 153   B 4
Lopera (E) 76   A 1
Łopiennik Górny (PL) . 197   D 2
Loppa (N) 124   C 2
Loppi (FIN) 136   C 3
Lopud (HR) 120   C 2
Lopud (Otok) (HR) 120   C 2
Łopuszna (PL) 201   A 3
Łopuszno (PL) 195   F 3
Lora (N) 130   C 4
Lora del Río (E) 75   D 1

Lorca (E) 77   E 2
Lorcé (B) 87   D 3
Lorch (D) 93   D 1
Lorch (D) 45   E 1
Loreo (I) 98   B 4
Loreto (I) 102   C 2
Loreto Aprutino (I) 103   D 4
Lorgues (F) 57   D 2
Lorica (I) 109   E 2
Lorient (F) 40   C 4
Loriga (P) 62   C 4
Loriol-sur-Drôme (F) ... 52   C 3
Lormes (F) 48   B 2
Loro Ciuffenna (I) 102   A 2
Lorquin (F) 45   D 3
Lörrach (D) 92   B 4
Lorrez-le-Bocage (F) ... 43   E 3
Lorris (F) 43   E 4
Los (S) 140   B 1
Los Alcázares (E) 77   F 1
Los Arcos (E) 61   D 4
Los Baños
    de Guardias Viejas (E).. 76 C 3
Los Barrios (E) 75   E 4
Los Corrales de Buelna (E)60 A 3
Los Cortijos de Abajo (E). 70 B 2
Los Dolores (E) 77   F 2
Los Gallardos (E) 77   D 2
Los Hinojosos (E) 70   C 2
Los Lobos (E) 77   D 2
Los Navalmorales (E) .. 70   A 2
Los Navalucillos (E) 70   A 2
Los Palacios
    y Villafranca (E) 75   E 2
Los Santos (E) 63   F 4
Los Santos
    de Maimona (E) 69   E 4
Los Villares (E) 76   B 1
Los Yébenes (E) 70   B 2
Losar de la Vera (E) 69   F 1
Losenstein (A) 95   D 2
Losheim (D) 44   C 2
Łosice (PL) 191   D 3
Lošinj (HR) 99   E 4
Łososina Dolna (PL) .. 201   B 2
Loßburg (D) 45   E 3
Lossiemouth (GB) 27   F 3
Lossküla (EST) 160   C 1
Lossimäe (EST) 154   C 4
Lößnitz (D) 89   E 2
Lostwithiel (GB) 34   B 3
Lote (N) 130   A 4
Løten (N) 139   F 2
Löttorp (S) 146   A 2
Loudéac (F) 41   D 3
Loudes (F) 52   A 3
Loudías (GR) 206   B 3
Loudun (F) 47   D 3
Loué (F) 42   A 4
Loughborough (GB) 33   E 4
Loughrea /
    Baile Locha Riach (IRL) 22 C 4
Louhans (F) 49   D 3
Louhisaari (FIN) 136   B 3
Louisburgh (IRL) 22   B 3
Loukísia (GR) 218   C 4
Loulay (F) 46   C 4
Loulé (P) 74   B 2
Louny (CZ) 90   A 2
Lourdes (F) 54   C 3
Loures (P) 68   A 2
Louriçal (P) 68   B 1
Lourinhã (P) 68   A 2
Loúros (GR) 211   D 3
Lousã (P) 62   B 4
Lousada (P) 62   B 2
Louth (GB) 33   F 3
Loutrá Arkadía(GR) ... 217   D 3
Loutrá Halkidikí(GR) . 213   D 1
Loutrá Irákleio(GR) ... 217   F 2
Loutrá Kikládes(GR) .. 219   D 3
Loutrá Lésvos(GR) 215   D 3
Loutrá Aidipsoú (GR) . 212   C 4
Loutrá Aridaías (GR) .. 205   F 4
Loutrá Elefterón (GR) . 207   E 3
Loutrá Kaïtsas (GR) ... 211   F 3
Loutrá Kyllínis (GR) ... 216   C 2
Loutrá Lagkadá (GR) .. 206   C 3
Loutrá Smokóvou (GR) 211 F 3
Loutrá Vólvis (GR) 206   C 3
Loutrá Ypátis (GR) 212   A 4
Loutrá Etolía-
    Akarnanía (GR) 211   D 4
Loutráki Korinthía(GR) 217 F 2
Loutráki Magnissía(GR) 213 D 3
Loutró (GR) 226   B 2

Loutropigí *(GR)*	211	F 3	Luarca *(E)*	59	D 2	Lubin *Dolnośląskie(PL)*	193	D 1	Lucan *(IRL)*	23	E 4	Lug *(BIH)*	117	E 4	Lukovo *(SRB)*	119	D 2
Loutrópyrgos *(GR)*	218	B 2	Lubaczów *(PL)*	197	E 4	Lubja *(EST)*	149	E 2	Lučani *(SRB)*	118	B 3	Luga *(RUS)*	7	D 1	Lukovo Šugarje *(HR)*	99	F 4
Loutrós *(GR)*	208	C 2	Lubań *(PL)*	192	C 2	Lublin *(PL)*	197	D 2	Lucca *(I)*	101	E 2	Lugagnano Val d'Arda *(I)*	97	E 4	Łuków *(PL)*	191	D 3
Loútsa *Atikí-Peireiás(GR)*	218	C 2	Lubāna *(LV)*	167	D 1	Lubliniec *(PL)*	194	C 3	Luče *(SLO)*	99	E 1	Lugano *(CH)*	97	D 2	Łukowa *(PL)*	197	E 3
Loútsa *Préveza(GR)*	210	C 3	Lubars *(D)*	84	A 2	Lubmin *(D)*	80	C 3	Lucena *(E)*	76	A 2	Lügánuse *(EST)*	151	D 2	Łukowica *(PL)*	201	B 3
Louvain-la-Neuve *(B)*	39	F 2	Lubartów *(PL)*	197	D 1	Łubniany *(PL)*	194	B 3	Lucenay-l'Évêque *(F)*	48	C 2	Lugau *(D)*	89	E 2	Lukšiai *(LT)*	169	F 4
Louviers *(F)*	42	C 1	Lubas *(LV)*	157	F 4	Łubnice *Łódzkie(PL)*	194	C 2	Lučenec *(SK)*	12	B 3	Lugaži *(LV)*	160	E 2	Luksnénai *(LT)*	176	C 3
Louvigné-du-Désert *(F)*	41	E 3	Łubasz *(PL)*	187	E 4	Łubnice			Luceni *(E)*	65	F 4	Lügde *(D)*	83	F 4	Lukštai *(LT)*	165	F 4
Lövånger *(S)*	132	C 2	Lubawa *(PL)*	183	E 4	*Świętokrzyskie(PL)*	196	B 4	Lucera *(I)*	106	B 2	Lugnano in Teverina *(I)*	102	B 4	Lukstkalni *(LV)*	159	E 4
Löyberga *(S)*	132	A 2	Łubawka *(PL)*	193	D 3	Lubniewice *(PL)*	186	C 2	Lüchow *(D)*	84	B 2	Lugo *(E)*	58	C 3	Łukta *(PL)*	183	E 3
Loveč *(BG)*	19	D 1	Lübbecke *(D)*	83	F 4	Lubny *(UA)*	13	F 1	Luciana *(E)*	70	A 3	Lugo *(I)*	102	A 1	Ļūļākas *(LV)*	166	C 2
Lovere *(I)*	97	E 3	Lübben *(D)*	85	E 3	Lubochnia *(PL)*	189	E 4	Lucito *(I)*	105	F 2	Lugoj *(RO)*	12	C 4	Luleå *(S)*	128	B 4
Loviisa / Lovisa *(FIN)*	137	D 3	Lübbenau *(D)*	85	E 3	Lubomia *(PL)*	200	E 2	Luc'k *(UA)*	13	D 1	Lugones *(E)*	59	E 2	Lüleburgaz *(TR)*	19	E 1
Loviste *(HR)*	120	B 2	Lübbow *(D)*	84	B 2	Lubomierz			Lucka *(D)*	89	E 1	Luhačovice *(CZ)*	91	F 4	Ļuļiški *(LV)*	167	D 4
Lovosice *(CZ)*	90	A 2	Lubczyna *(PL)*	180	B 4	*Dolnośląskie(PL)*	192	C 2	Luckau *(D)*	85	E 4	Luhalahti *(FIN)*	136	C 2	Lüllemäe *(EST)*	160	C 2
Lovran *(HR)*	99	D 3	Lübeck *(D)*	79	D 4	Lubomino *(PL)*	183	E 4	Luckenwalde *(D)*	85	D 3	Luhanka *(FIN)*	137	D 2	Lümanda *(EST)*	152	A 3
Lövstabruk *(S)*	141	D 3	Lubenec *(CZ)*	89	F 3	Luboń *(PL)*	187	F 3	Luçon *(F)*	46	A 2	Luhtapohja *(FIN)*	135	F 3	Lümati *(EST)*	155	D 2
Lovund *(N)*	127	D 3	L'ubercy *(RUS)*	7	F 2	Lubowidz *(PL)*	189	E 1	Ludbreg *(HR)*	112	A 3	Luige *(EST)*	149	E 3	Lumbarda *(HR)*	120	B 2
Low Street *(GB)*	37	D 1	Lubersac *(F)*	51	E 2	Lubowidz *(PL)*	189	D 2	Ludiente *(E)*	71	F 3	Luino *(I)*	97	D 2	Lumbier *(E)*	54	A 3
Löwenberg *(D)*	85	D 2	Lubezere *(LV)*	157	E 3	Lubrin *(E)*	77		Lüdenscheid *(D)*	87	F 1	Luka *(BIH)*	117	E 4	Lumbrales *(E)*	63	E 3
Lowestoft *(GB)*	37	D 1	Lubiaň *(LT)*	162	C 4	Lubrza *Lubuskie(PL)*	186	C 2	Lüdinghausen *(D)*	83	E 4	Luka *(HR)*	103	E 1	Lumbres *(F)*	38	C 2
Łowicz *(PL)*	189	E 3	Łubianka *Kujawsko-*			Lubrza *Opolskie(PL)*	194	B 4	Ludinovo *(RUS)*	7	F 3	Luka *(SRB)*	119	E 2	Lumezzane *(I)*	97	F 3
Łowyń *(PL)*	187	D 2	*Pomorskie(PL)*	188	C 1	Lubsko *(PL)*	186	C 4	Ludlow *(GB)*	32	C 4	Lukavac *(BIH)*	117	E 2	Lumijoki *(FIN)*	133	E 1
Lož *(SLO)*	99	D 2	Lubiąż *(PL)*	193	C 3	Lubsza *(PL)*	193	F 3	Ludvika *(S)*	140	B 3	Lukavica *(BIH)*	115	F 4	Lumparland *(FIN)*	136	A 4
Lozna *(SRB)*	118	C 3	Lubichowo *(PL)*	182	C 2	Lübtheen *(D)*	84	B 1	Ludwigsfelde *(D)*	85	D 3	Luke *(EST)*	155	D 2	Lumpénai *(LT)*	168	C 2
Loznica *(SRB)*	117	F 2	Lubicz Dolny *(PL)*	188	C 1	Lubycza Królewska *(PL)*	197	F 4	Ludwigshafen *(D)*	45	E 2	Luknénai *(LT)*	168	C 1	Lumsås *(DK)*	142	C 4
Lozovac *(HR)*	103	F 1	Lubień *Małopolskie(PL)*	201	A 2	Lübz *(D)*	79	D 2	Ludwigshafen *(D)*	45	F 4	Lukovica-p-K. *(SLO)*	99	E 1	Lumsheden *(S)*	140	C 2
Lozovik *(SRB)*	118	C 1	Lubień Kujawski *(PL)*	189	D 2	Luc-en-Diois *(F)*	52	C 3	Ludwigslust *(D)*	84	B 1	Lukovit *(BG)*	19	D 1	Luna *(E)*	54	B 4
Lozoyuela *(E)*	64	B 4	Lubieszyn *(PL)*	180	B 4	Luc-sur-Mer *(F)*	41	F 1	Ludwigsstadt *(D)*	89	D 2	Lukovo *(MK)*	122	A 4	Lunas *(F)*	56	A 2
Luanco *(E)*	59	E 2	Lubiewo *(PL)*	182	B 4	Lucainena de las Torres *(E)*	77	D 3	Ludza *(LV)*	167	F 2	Lukovo *(SRB)*	119	D 4	Lund *(S)*	143	D 4

MADRID

Andalucía (Av. de) .... BM 12
Andes (Av. de los) .... CL 13
Atocha (R. de) .... BM 22
Ciudad de Barcelona
  (Av. de la) .... BM 46
Complutense (Av.) .... AL 51
Delicias (Pas. de las) .... BM 66
Estación de Hortaleza
  (Carret. a la) .... CL 89
Florida (Pas. de la) .... BL 100
General Ricardos .... BM 110
Ginzo de Limia .... BL 113
Infanta Isabel (Pas. de la) .... BM 119
Isla de Oza .... BL 120
Manzanares (Av. del) .... BM 142
Mar de Cristal (Glta del) .... CL 144
Miraflores (Av. de) .... AL 161
Monforte de Lemos (Av. de) .... BL 165
Raimundo Fernández
  Villaverde .... BT 195
Reina Cristina (Pas. de la) .... BM 198
Reina Victoria (Pas. de la) .... BL 200
Reyes Católicos (Av. de los) .... BL 204
Ribera del Sena .... CL 205
Santa María de la Cabeza
  (Pas. de) .... BM 209
San Francisco de Sales
  (Pas. de) .... BL 216
San Luis (Av. de) .... CL 223
Toledo (Ronda de) .... BM 235
Valdetorres de Jarama .... CL 241
Valladolid (Av. de) .... AL 244
Veinticinco de Septiembre
  (Av. del) .... CL 247

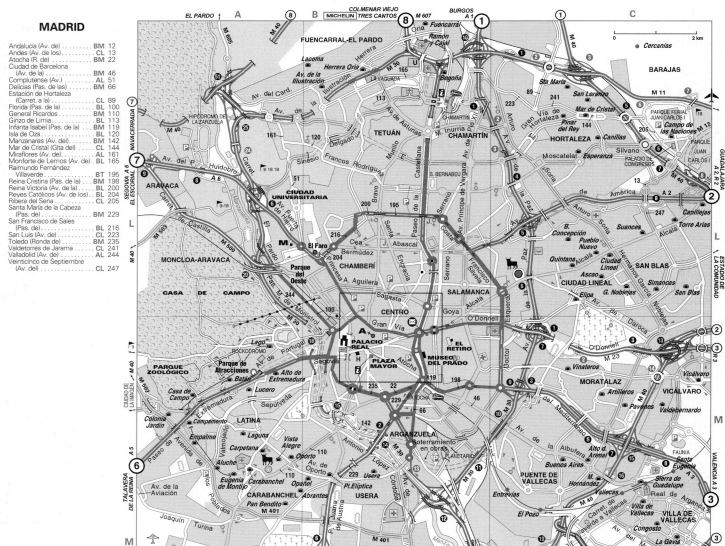

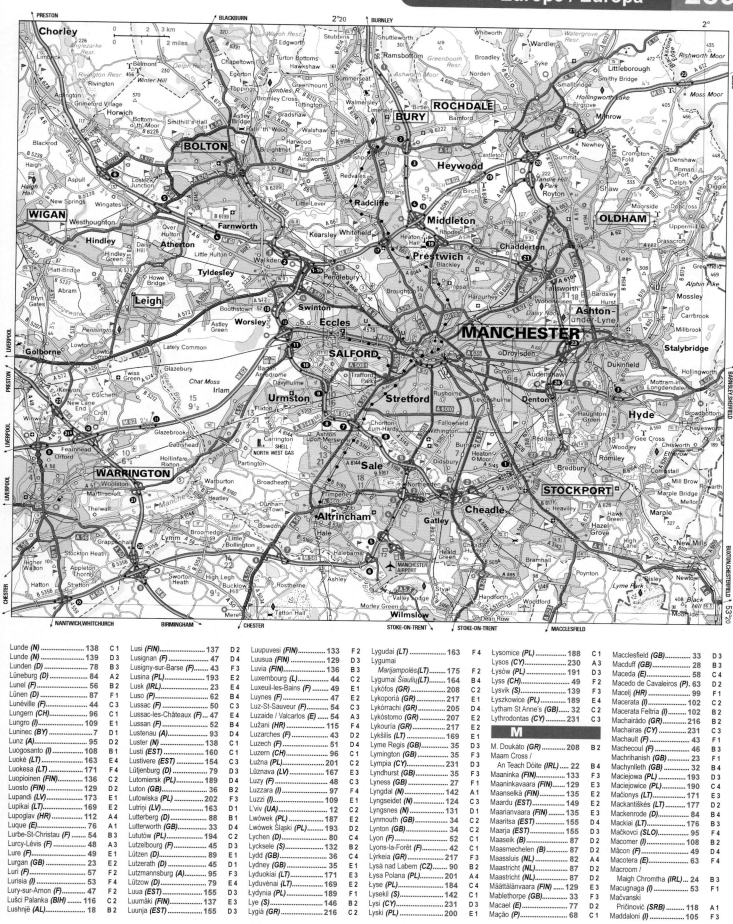

Lunde *(N)* 138	C 1	Lusi *(FIN)* 137	D 2	Luupuvesi *(FIN)* ... 133	F 2
Lunde *(N)* 139	D 3	Lusignan *(F)* 47	D 4	Luusua *(FIN)* 129	D 3
Lunden *(D)* 78	B 3	Lusigny-sur-Barse *(F)* ... 43	F 3	Luvia *(FIN)* 136	B 3
Lüneburg *(D)* 84	A 2	Lusina *(PL)* 193	E 2	Luxembourg *(L)* 44	C 2
Lunel *(F)* 56	F 2	Lusk *(IRL)* 23	E 4	Luxeuil-les-Bains *(F)* ... 49	E 1
Lünen *(D)* 87	F 1	Luso *(P)* 62	B 4	Luynes *(F)* 47	C 3
Lunéville *(F)* 44	C 1	Lussac *(F)* 50	C 3	Luz-St-Sauveur *(F)* ... 54	C 3
Lungern *(CH)* 96	C 3	Lussac-les-Châteaux *(F)* ... 47	C 3	Luzaide / Valcarlos *(E)* ... 54	A 3
Lungro *(I)* 109	E 1	Lussan *(F)* 52	B 4	Lužani *(HR)* 115	F 4
Luninec *(BY)* 7	D 1	Lustenau *(A)* 93	D 4	Luzarches *(F)* 43	D 2
Lunz *(A)* 95	C 1	Luster *(N)* 138	C 1	Luzech *(F)* 51	D 4
Luogosanto *(I)* 108	B 1	Lusti *(EST)* 160	C 1	Luzern *(CH)* 96	C 3
Luoké *(LT)* 163	E 2	Lustivere *(EST)* 154	C 3	Łużna *(PL)* 201	C 2
Luokesa *(LT)* 171	F 4	Lütjenburg *(D)* 79	D 3	Lûznava *(LV)* 167	E 3
Luopioinen *(FIN)* 136	C 2	Lutomiersk *(PL)* 189	D 4	Luzy *(F)* 48	C 3
Luosto *(FIN)* 129	D 2	Luton *(GB)* 36	B 2	Luzzara *(I)* 97	F 4
Lupandi *(LV)* 173	E 1	Lutowiska *(PL)* 202	F 3	Luzzi *(I)* 109	E 1
Lupikai *(LT)* 169	E 2	Lutriņi *(LV)* 163	D 1	L'viv *(UA)* 12	C 1
Lupoglav *(HR)* 112	A 4	Lutterberg *(D)* 88	B 1	Lwówek *(PL)* 187	E 2
Luque *(E)* 76	C 2	Lutterworth *(GB)* 33	D 4	Lwówek Śląski *(PL)* ... 193	C 4
Lurbe-St-Christau *(F)* ... 54	B 3	Lututów *(PL)* 194	C 2	Lychen *(D)* 80	C 4
Lurcy-Lévis *(F)* 48	A 3	Lutzelbourg *(F)* 45	D 1	Lyckeby *(S)* 132	B 2
Lure *(F)* 49	E 1	Lützen *(D)* 89	E 1	Lydd *(GB)* 36	C 4
Lurgan *(GB)* 23	E 2	Lutzerath *(D)* 45	D 1	Lydney *(GB)* 35	E 1
Luri *(F)* 57	F 2	Lutzmannsburg *(A)* ... 95	F 3	Lyduokiai *(LT)* 171	E 2
Lurisia *(I)* 53	F 4	Lützow *(D)* 79	E 4	Lydvénai *(LT)* 169	E 2
Lury-sur-Arnon *(F)* ... 47	C 2	Luua *(EST)* 155	D 3	Łydynia *(PL)* 189	F 4
Lušci Palanka *(BIH)* 116	C 2	Luumäki *(FIN)* 137	E 3	Łyse *(PL)* 184	C 1
Lushnjë *(AL)* 18	B 2	Luunja *(EST)* 155	D 3	Lygiá *(GR)* 216	C 2

Lygudai *(LT)* 163	F 4	Łysomice *(PL)* 188	C 1	Macclesfield *(GB)* ... 33	D 3
Lygumai		Lysós *(CY)* 230	A 3	Macduff *(GB)* 28	B 3
Marijampolés *(LT)* ... 175	F 2	Łysów *(PL)* 191	D 3	Maceda *(E)* 58	C 4
Lygumai Šiaulių *(LT)* 164	B 4	Lyss *(CH)* 49	F 2	Macedo de Cavaleiros *(P)*. 63	D 2
Lykófos *(GR)* 208	C 2	Lysvik *(S)* 139	F 3	Macelj *(HR)* 99	F 1
Lykóporiá *(GR)* 217	E 1	Łyszkowice *(PL)* 189	E 4	Macerata *(I)* 102	C 2
Lykórrachi *(GR)* 205	D 4	Lytham St Anne's *(GB)*. 32	C 2	Macerata Feltria *(I)* ... 102	B 2
Lykóstomo *(GR)* 207	E 2	Lythrodontas *(CY)* ... 231	C 3	Machairádo *(GR)* 216	B 2
Lykouría *(GR)* 217	E 2			Machairas *(CY)* 231	C 3
Lyksilis *(LT)* 169	E 1	**M**		Machault *(F)* 43	E 2
Lyme Regis *(GB)* 35	F 3	M. Doukáto *(GR)* 208	B 2	Machecoul *(F)* 46	B 3
Lymington *(GB)* 35	F 3	Maam Cross /		Machrihanish *(GB)* ... 23	F 1
Lympia *(CY)* 231	D 3	An Teach Dóite *(IRL)* 22	B 4	Machynlleth *(GB)* 32	B 4
Lyndhurst *(GB)* 35	F 3	Maaninka *(FIN)* 133	F 3	Maciejowa *(PL)* 193	D 3
Lyness *(GB)* 27	F 1	Maaninkavaara *(FIN)* 129	E 3	Maciejowice *(PL)* 190	C 4
Lyngdal *(N)* 142	A 1	Maanselkä *(FIN)* 135	E 2	Mačionys *(LT)* 171	E 3
Lyngseidet *(N)* 124	C 3	Maardu *(EST)* 149	E 2	Mackantiškės *(LT)* ... 177	D 2
Lyngsnes *(N)* 131	D 1	Maarianvaara *(FIN)* 135	E 3	Mackenrode *(D)* 84	B 4
Lynmouth *(GB)* 34	C 2	Maaritsa *(EST)* 155	D 4	Mackiai *(LT)* 176	B 3
Lynton *(GB)* 34	C 2	Maarja *(EST)* 155	D 3	Mačkovci *(SLO)* 95	F 4
Lyon *(F)* 52	C 1	Maaseik *(B)* 87	D 2	Macomer *(I)* 108	B 2
Lyons-la-Forêt *(F)* 42	C 1	Maasmechelen *(B)* ... 87	D 2	Mâcon *(F)* 49	D 4
Lýrkeia *(GR)* 217	E 2	Maassluis *(NL)* 82	A 4	Macotera *(E)* 63	F 4
Lysá nad Labem *(CZ)* 90	B 2	Maastricht *(NL)* 87	D 2	Macroom /	
Łysa Polana *(PL)* 201	A 4	Maastricht *(NL)* 87	D 2	Maigh Chromtha *(IRL)* 24	B 3
Lysekil *(S)* 142	C 1	Määttälänvaara *(FIN)* 129	E 3	Macugnaga *(I)* 53	F 1
Lysi *(CY)* 231	D 3	Mablethorpe *(GB)* 33	F 3	Mačvanski	
Lyski *(PL)* 200	E 1	Macael *(E)* 77	D 2	Pričinović *(SRB)* ... 118	A 1
		Mação *(P)* 68	C 1	Maddaloni *(I)* 105	F 3

MARSEILLE

Aix (R. d')	BY	
Briançon (Bd de)	BX	13
Canebière (La)	BY	
Catalans (R. des)	CY	17
Chartreux (Av. des)	BY	35
Guesde (Pl. Jules)	BX	36
Guigou (Bd)	AX	40
Lesseps (Bd Ferdinand de)	CY	47
Moulin (Bd Jean)	BYZ	
Paradis (R.)	BYZ	
Pologne (Pl. de)	CY	51
Pompidou (Prom. Georges)	BZ	52
Sartre (Av. Jean-Paul)	CX	59
Strasbourg (Bd)	BX	61
Verdun (R. de)	CY	70

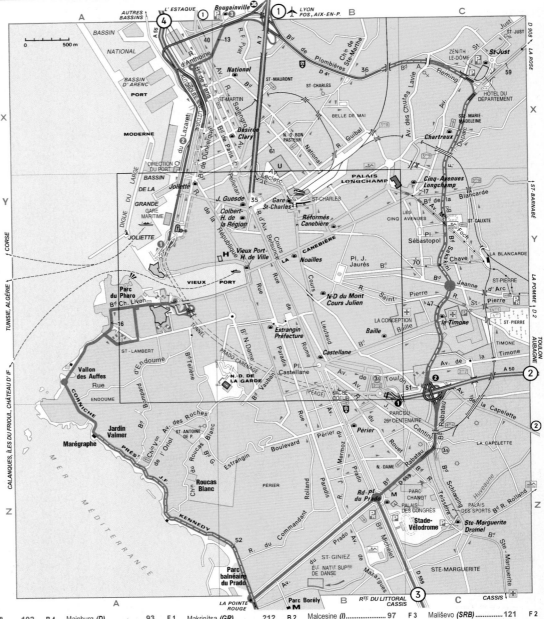

Maderuelo (E)	64	C 3	Magliano Sabina (I)	102	B 4	Mainburg (D)	93	F 1	Makrinítsa (GR)	212	B 2
Madesimo (I)	97	D 2	Maglič (SRB)	118	C 3	Maintenon (F)	42	C 3	Makrochóri (GR)	206	A 3
Madliena (LV)	165	E 1	Maglie (I)	107	F 4	Mainz (D)	45	F 4	Makronísi (Nisí) (GR)	218	C 3
Madona (LV)	166	C 1	Magnac-Laval (F)	47	A 4	Maiori (I)	105	F 4	Makryámmos (GR)	207	F 3
Madlno (E)	70	B 1	Magnor (N)	139	F 3	Mairena del Alcor (E)	75	E 2	Makrychóri Kaválas (GR)	207	E 2
Madridejos (E)	70	B 2	Magnuszew (PL)	190	C 4	Maironiai (LT)	169	E 2	Makrychóri Lárisa (GR)	212	B 1
Madrigal de la Vera (E)	69	F 1	Magny-en-Vexin (F)	42	F 2	Maisach (D)	93	F 2	Makrygialós (GR)	227	F 3
Madrigal			Magoúla (GR)	217	D 2	Maišiagala (LT)	177	E 1	Makrygialos (GR)	206	B 4
de las Altas Torres (E)	64	A 3	Magūnai (LT)	177	F 1	Maison-Neuve (F)	43	F 3	Makryplágio (GR)	207	E 2
Madrigalejo (E)	69	F 3	Magura (SRB)	122	A 2	Maissau (A)	95	E 1	Makryrráchi (GR)	211	F 3
Madrona (E)	64	B 4	Mahiľ(u (BY)	7	E 4	Maizières-lès-Metz (F)	44	C 2	Mäksa (EST)	155	D 4
Madroñera (E)	69	F 2	Mahlu (FIN)	133	E 4	Maja (HR)	99	F 2	Maksniemi (FIN)	128	C 4
Madžiūnai (LT)	177	E 3	Mahora (E)	71	E 3	Majdan Królewski (PL)	196	C 4	Malá (I)	132	B 1
Maël-Carhaix (F)	40	C 3	Mahovo (HR)	115	D 3	Majdanek (PL)	197	D 2	Mala Bosna (SRB)	113	D 3
Maella (E)	66	A 4	Mähring (D)	89	E 3	Majdanpek (SRB)	119	D 1	Mala Krsna (SRB)	118	C 1
Mäeltküla (EST)	154	B 4	Mahu (EST)	151	F 2	Majšperk (SLO)	99	F 2	Mala Subotica (HR)	112	A 3
Mære (N)	131	D 2	Maia (I)	62	B 2	Makarska (HR)	117	D 4	Mala Vyska (UA)	13	F 2
Maesteg (GB)	35	D 1	Maials (E)	66	B 3	Makce (SRB)	119	D 1	Maladzečna (BY)	7	D 4
Mäetaguse (EST)	151	E 3	Maîche (F)	49	F 2	Makedonski Brod (MK)	122	B 3	Málaga (E)	76	A 3
Mafra (P)	68	A 2	Maida (I)	109	F 3	Makniūnai (LT)	176	C 3	Malagai (LT)	168	C 2
Magacela (E)	69	E 3	Maidenhead (GB)	36	B 3	Makó (H)	113	E 2	Malagón (E)	70	B 3
Magallón (E)	65	E 2	Maidla Harju(EST)	149	E 3	Mäkoni (LV)	166	C 4	Malahide /		
Magaña (E)	65	D 2	Maidla Ida-Viru(EST)	151	E 3	Makounta (CY)	230	A 3	Mullach Íde (IRL)	23	E 4
Magaz (E)	64	B 2	Maidla Rapla(EST)	149	E 4	Maków Łódzkie(PL)	189	E 4	Malaja Višera (RUS)	7	A 4
Magdeburg (D)	84	C 3	Maidla Rapla(EST)	149	D 4	Maków Mazowiecki (PL)	190	B 2	Malalbergo (I)	98	A 4
Magenta (I)	97	D 3	Maidstone (GB)	36	C 4	Maków Mazowiecki (PL)	196	B 2	Malámata (GR)	217	D 1
Maghera (GB)	23	E 2	Maienfeld (CH)	97	E 1	Maków Podhalański (PL)	201	A 2	Malandríno (GR)	217	E 1
Magherafelt (GB)	23	E 2	Maignelay-Montigny (F)	38	C 3	Makowlany (PL)	185	E 3	Malanów (PL)	188	C 4
Maglaj (BIH)	115	F 4	Maijanen (FIN)	128	C 2	Makrachómi (GR)	211	F 3	Malaucène (F)	52	C 4
Magliano de' Marsi (I)	105	D 1	Mailly-le-Camp (F)	43	F 3	Makrasyka (CY)	231	B 3	Malax / Maalahti (FIN)	132	C 1
Magliano in Toscana (I)	101	F 4	Mainar (E)	65	E 2	Mákri (GR)	208	B 3	Malbork (PL)	183	D 2
									Malbuisson (F)	49	E 3
Makrinítsa (GR)	212	B 2	Malcesine (I)	97	F 3	Mališevo (SRB)	121	F 2			
			Malchin (D)	79	F 4	Maliskylä (FIN)	133	E 2			
			Malchow (D)	79	F 4	Małkinia Górna (PL)	190	C 2			
			Malczyce (PL)	193	E 2	Malko Tirnovo (BG)	19	E 1			
			Malda (EST)	153	B 3	Mallaig (GB)	27	D 4			
			Maldegem (B)	37	F 4	Mallén (E)	65	E 2			
			Maldeniai (LT)	163	F 3	Mallersdorf (D)	94	A 1			
			Maldon (GB)	36	C 3	Malles Venosta / Mals (I)	97	F 1			
			Maldyty (PL)	183	E 2	Mällikvere (EST)	154	C 3			
			Malďžiūnai (LT)	170	C 1	Mallnitz (A)	94	B 4			
			Malé (I)	97	F 1	Mallow / Mala (IRL)	24	C 3			
			Małe Gacno (PL)	182	B 3	Mallwyd (GB)	32	B 4			
			Małe Pijace (SRB)	113	E 2	Malm (N)	131	D 2			
			Malechowo (PL)	181	E 2	Malmberget (S)	128	A 2			
			Máleme (GR)	226	A 2	Malmédy (B)	87	D 3			
			Malente (D)	79	D 3	Malmesbury (GB)	35	E 2			
			Máles (GR)	227	E 3	Malmköping (S)	140	C 4			
			Malesherbes (F)	43	D 3	Malmö (S)	143	D 4			
			Malesína (GR)	212	C 4	Malmö-Sturup		
			Malestroit (F)	41	D 4	(Flygplats) (S)	143	D 4			
			Malgrat de Mar (E)	67	D 2	Malmslätt (S)	143	F 1			
			Mali Iđoš (SRB)	113	D 4	Malnava (Malnova) (LV)	167	F 2			
			Mali Lošinj (HR)	99	E 4	Malo (I)	98	A 3			
			Mali Požarevac (SRB)	118	C 1	Malo Konjari (MK)	122	B 3			
			Mali Zvornik (SRB)	117	E 4	Malo-les-Bains (F)	37	F 4			
			Malia (CY)	230	B 4	Maloarchangel'sk (RUS)	7	F 4			
			Málinec (PL)	188	C 4	Małogoszcz (PL)	195	F 3			
			Maliniec (PL)	188	C 4	Maloja (CH)	97	E 2			
			Malinska (HR)	99	E 3	Malojaroslavec (RUS)	7	E 1			
						Małomice (PL)	192	C 1			
						Malónas (GR)	228	C 2			
						Måløy (N)	130	A 4			

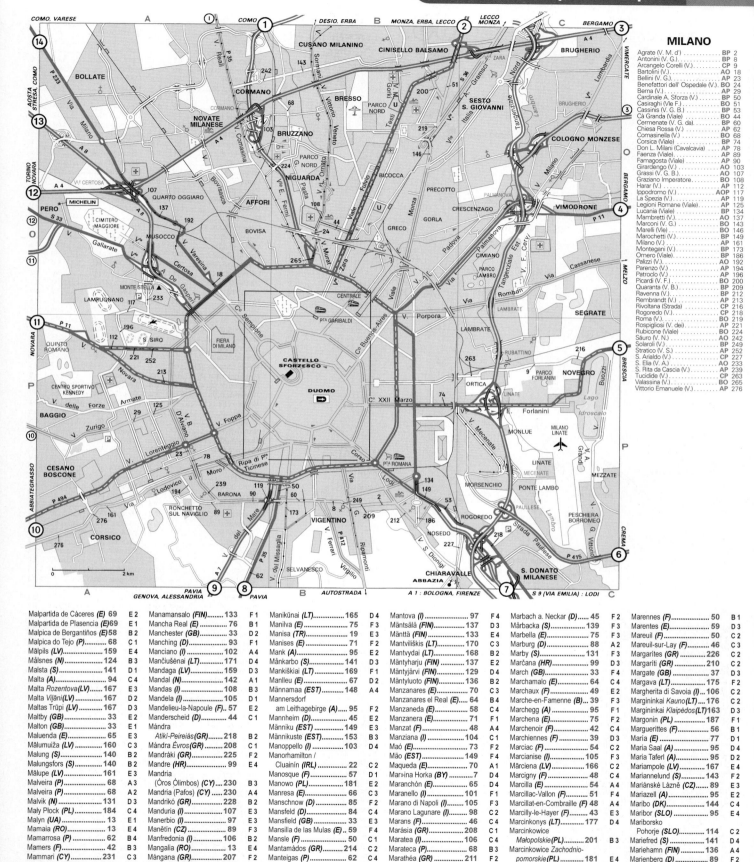

MILANO

Agrate (V. M. d') .... BP 2
Antonini (V. G.) .... BP 8
Arcangelo Corelli (V.) .... CP 9
Bartolini (V.) .... AO 18
Bellini (V. G.) .... AP 23
Benefattori dell' Ospedale (V.) . BO 24
Berna (V.) .... AP 29
Cardinale A. Sforza (V.) ...... BP 50
Casiraghi (Vle F.) .... BO 51
Cassinis (V. G. B.) .... BP 53
Cà Granda (Viale) .... BO 44
Cernenate (V. G. da) .... BP 60
Chiesa Rossa (V.) .... AP 62
Comasinella (V.) .... BO 68
Corsica (Viale) .... BP 74
Don L. Milani (Cavalcavia) .... AP 78
Faenza (Viale) .... AP 89
Famagosta (Viale) .... AP 90
Girardengo (V.) .... AO 103
Grassi (V. G. B.) .... AO 107
Graziano Imperatore .... BO 108
Harar (V.) .... AP 112
Ippodromo (V.) .... AOP 117
La Spezia (V.) .... AP 119
Legioni Romane (Viale) ...... AP 125
Lucania (Viale) .... BP 134
Mambretti (V.) .... AO 137
Marconi (V. G.) .... BO 143
Marelli (Vle) .... BO 146
Marochetti (V.) .... AP 149
Milano (V.) .... AP 161
Montegani (V.) .... AP 173
Ornero (Viale) .... BP 186
Palizzi (V.) .... AO 192
Parenzo (V.) .... AP 194
Patrocio (V.) .... AP 196
Picardi (V. F.) .... BP 200
Quaranta (V. B.) .... BP 209
Ravenna (V.) .... AP 212
Rembrandt (V.) .... AP 213
Rivoltana (Strada) .... CP 216
Rogoredo (V.) .... CP 218
Roma (V.) .... BO 219
Rospigliosi (V. dei) .... AP 221
Rubicone (Viale) .... BO 224
Sàuro (V. N.) .... AO 242
Solaroli (V.) .... BP 249
Stratico (V. S.) .... AP 252
S. Arialdo (V.) .... CP 227
S. Elia (V. A.) .... AO 233
S. Rita da Cascia (V.) .... AP 239
Tucidide (V.) .... CP 263
Valassina (V.) .... BO 265
Vittorio Emanuele (V.) .... AP 276

Malpartida de Cáceres (E) 69	E 2	Manamansalo (FIN) 133	F 1	Manikūnai (LT) 165	D 4	Mantova (I) 97	F 4	Marbach a. Neckar (D) 45	F 2	Marennes (F) 50	B 1
Malpartida de Plasencia (E)69	E 1	Mancha Real (E) 76	B 1	Manilva (E) 75	F 3	Mäntsälä (FIN) 137	D 3	Mårbacka (S) 139	F 3	Marentes (E) 59	D 3
Malpica de Bergantiños (E)58	B 2	Manching (D) 93	F 1	Manisa (TR) 19	E 3	Mänttä (FIN) 133	E 4	Marbella (E) 75	F 3	Mareuil (F) 50	C 2
Malpica do Tejo (P) 68	C 1	Manciano (I) 102	A 4	Manises (F) 71	F 2	Mantviliškis (LT) 170	C 3	Marburg (D) 88	A 2	Mareuil-sur-Lay (F) 46	C 3
Mâlpils (LV) 159	E 4	Mancor (I) 95	A 1	Mank (A) 95	C 4	Mantvydai (LT) 168	B 2	Marby (S) 131	F 3	Margarites (GR) 226	C 2
Mâlsnes (N) 124	B 3	Mančiušėnai (LT) 171	D 4	Mânkarbo (S) 141	D 3	Mäntyharju (FIN) 137	E 2	Marčana (HR) 99	D 3	Margariti (GR) 210	C 2
Malsta (S) 141	D 1	Mandaga (LV) 159	D 3	Mankiškiai (LT) 169	F 1	Mäntyjärvi (FIN) 129	B 3	March (A) 33	F 4	Margate (GB) 37	D 3
Malta (A) 94	C 4	Mandal (N) 142	A 1	Manlleu (E) 67	D 2	Mäntyluoto (FIN) 136	B 2	Marchamalo (E) 64	C 4	Margava (LT) 175	D 4
Malta Rozentova(LV) 167	E 3	Mandas (I) 108	B 3	Mânnamaa (EST) 148	A 4	Manzanares (E) 70	C 3	Marchaux (F) 49	E 2	Margherita di Savoia (I) 106	C 2
Malta Viļāni (LV) 167	D 2	Mandela (I) 105	D 3	Mannersdorf		Manzanares el Real (E)... 64	B 4	Marche-en-Famenne (B) .. 39	E 2	Margininkai Kauno(LT) . 176	C 2
Maltas Trūpi (LV) 167	D 3	Mandelieu-la-Napoule (F).. 57	E 2	am Leithagebirge (A)..... 95	F 2	Manzaneda (E) 58	C 4	Marchegg (I) 95	F 1	Margininkai Klaipėdos(LT)163	D 3
Maltby (GB) 33	E 2	Manderscheid (D) 44	C 1	Männiku (EST) 149	A 4	Manzanera (E) 71	F 1	Marchena (E) 75	F 3	Margonin (PL) 187	F 1
Malton (GB) 33	E 1	Mändra		Männiku (EST) 149	B 3	Manzat (F) 48	A 4	Marchenoir (F) 42	C 4	Marguerittes (F) 56	B 1
Maluenda (E) 65	E 3	Atikí-Peireiás(GR)...218	B 2	Männikuste (EST) 153	B 3	Manziana (I) 104	C 4	Marchiennes (F) 39	D 3	María (E) 77	D 1
Mālumuiža (LV) 160	C 3	Mándra Évros(GR) 208	C 1	Manoppello (I) 103	D 4	Maó (E) 73	F 2	Marciac (F) 54	C 2	Maria Saal (A) 95	D 4
Malung (S) 140	B 2	Mandráki (GR) 225	C 2	Manorhamilton /		Mão (EST) 149	F 4	Marcianise (I) 105	F 3	Maria Taferl (A) 95	D 2
Malungsfors (S) 140	B 2	Mandre (HR) 99	E 4	Cluainín (IRL) 22	C 2	Maqueda (E) 70	A 1	Marciana (LV) 166	C 2	Mariampole (LV) 167	E 4
Malveira (P) 68	A 3	Mandria		Manosque (F) 57	D 1	Mar»ina Horka (BY) 7	D 4	Marcigny (F) 48	C 4	Mariannelund (S) 143	F 2
Malveira (E) 68	A 2	(Óros Ólimbos)(CY) .230	B 3	Manowo (PL) 181	E 2	Maranchón (E) 65	D 4	Marcilla (E) 64	A 4	Mariánské Lázně (CZ) .. 89	E 3
Malvik (N) 131	D 3	Mandria (Pafos) (CY) .230	A 4	Manresa (E) 66	D 2	Maranello (I) 101	F 1	Marcillac-Vallon (F) ... 51	F 4	Mariazell (A) 95	C 2
Mały Płock (PL) 184	E 1	Mandriko (GR) 228	B 2	Manschnow (D) 85	F 2	Marano di Napoli (I) .. 105	F 3	Marcillac-en-Combraille (F) 48	A 4	Maribo (DK) 144	C 4
Małyn (UA) 13	E 1	Manduria (I) 107	E 3	Mansfeld (D) 84	C 4	Marano Lagunare (I) .. 98	C 2	Marcilly-le-Hayer (F) .. 43	E 3	Maribor (SLO) 95	E 4
Mamaia (RO) 13	E 4	Manětín (CZ) 89	F 3	Mansfield (GB) 33	E 1	Marans (F) 46	C 2	Marcinkonys (LT) ... 177	D 4	Mariborsko	
Mamarrosa (P) 62	B 4	Manfredonia (I) 106	B 2	Mansilla de las Mulas (E).. 59	F 4	Marásia (GR) 208	C 1	Marcinkowice		Pohorje (SLO) 114	C 2
Mamers (F) 42	B 3	Mangalia (RO) 13	E 4	Mantamádos (GR) 214	C 1	Maratea (I) 106	C 4	Małopolskie(PL) 201	B 3	Mariefred (S) 141	D 4
Mammari (CY) 231	C 3	Mángana (GR) 207	F 2	Manteigas (P) 62	C 4	Marateca (P) 68	B 3	Marcinkowice Zachodnio-		Mariehamn (FIN) 136	A 4
Mammaste (EST) 161	D 1	Manganári (GR) 224	C 2	Mantes-la-Jolie (F) .. 42	C 3	Marathéa (GR) 211	F 2	pomorskie(PL) 181	E 4	Marienberg (D) 89	F 2
Mammola (I) 111	F 2	Manger (N) 138	B 2	Mantiel (E) 65	D 4	Marathiás (GR) 217	E 1	Marcinowice (PL) ... 193	D 3	Marienberg (D) 84	B 3
Mamonovo (RUS) 6	B 4	Mangualde (P) 62	C 4	Mantíneia (GR) 217	E 3	Marathókampos (GR) 221	F 2	Marcisów (PL) 193	D 3	Marienstedt (D) 79	B 3
Mamry (Jezioro) (PL) . 184	E 1	Máni Évros(GR)...... 208	C 1	Mantorp (S) 143	F 1	Marathónas (GR) ... 218	C 1	Marckolsheim (F) ... 45	D 4	Mariental (LV) 167	E 2
Manacor (I) 73	E 2	Máni Lakonía(GR) 222	C 2	Mantoúdi (GR) 212	B 3	Marathópoli (GR) ... 217	D 4	Marco de Canaveses (P).. 62	C 3	Mariestad (S) 140	B 4
Manacore (I) 103	F 4	Maniago (I) 98	B 2	Mantoúdi (GR) 212	C 4	Màrathos (GR) 212	B 3	Marcoule (F) 52	B 4	Marignane (F) 56	C 2
						Marathovoúnos (CY) 230	B 2	Marene (I) 53	F 3	Marigny (F) 41	E 2

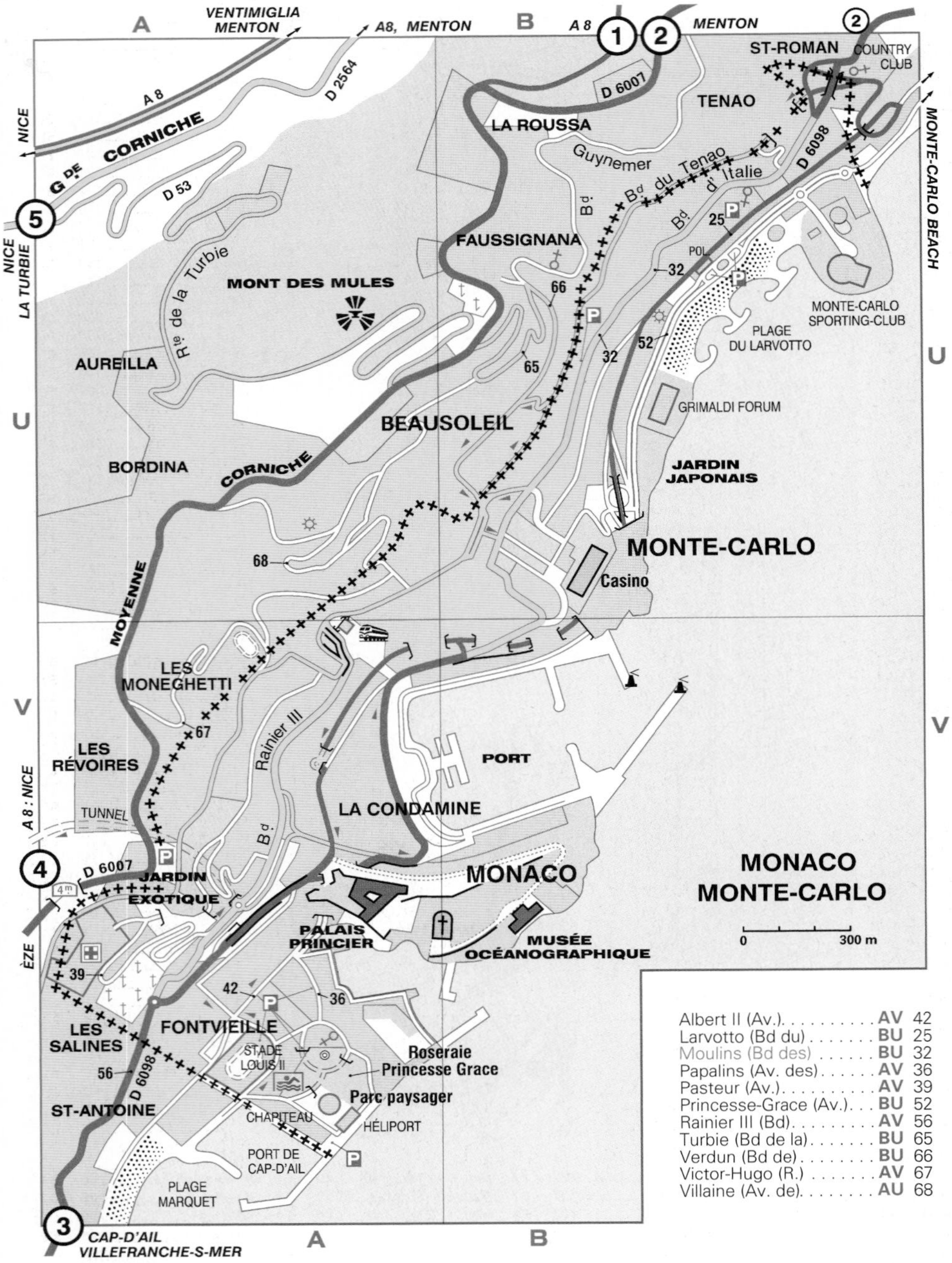
VENTIMIGLIA MENTON
A8, MENTON
A 8
MENTON
A
B
NICE
A8
D 2564
G^{DE} CORNICHE
D 53
D 6007
LA ROUSSA
ST-ROMAN
COUNTRY CLUB
TENAO
Guynemer
Bd du Tenao
Bd d'Italie
D 6098
MONTE-CARLO BEACH
NICE LA TURBIE
FAUSSIGNANA
MONT DES MULES
Rte de la Turbie
POL
MONTE-CARLO SPORTING-CLUB
PLAGE DU LARVOTTO
AUREILLA
GRIMALDI FORUM
BEAUSOLEIL
JARDIN JAPONAIS
BORDINA
CORNICHE
MOYENNE
MONTE-CARLO
Casino
LES MONEGHETTI
Rainier III
LES RÉVOIRES
PORT
A 8 : NICE
TUNNEL
LA CONDAMINE
D 6007
JARDIN EXOTIQUE
MONACO
MONACO MONTE-CARLO
PALAIS PRINCIER
MUSÉE OCÉANOGRAPHIQUE
0 300 m
ÈZE
FONTVIEILLE
LES SALINES
STADE LOUIS II
Roseraie Princesse Grace
Parc paysager
D 6098
ST-ANTOINE
CHAPITEAU
HÉLIPORT
PORT DE CAP-D'AIL
PLAGE MARQUET
CAP-D'AIL VILLEFRANCHE-S-MER
U
V
Albert II (Av.) . . . . AV 42
Larvotto (Bd du) . . . . BU 25
Moulins (Bd des) . . . . . . BU 32
Papalins (Av. des) . . . . . . AV 36
Pasteur (Av.) . . . . AV 39
Princesse-Grace (Av.) . . . BU 52
Rainier III (Bd) . . . . AV 56
Turbie (Bd de la) . . . . BU 65
Verdun (Bd de) . . . . BU 66
Victor-Hugo (R.) . . . . AV 67
Villaine (Av. de) . . . . AU 68

Međeđa (BIH) 117 F 3
Medeikiai (LT) 165 E 3
Medelim (P) 69 D 1
Medellín (E) 69 E 3
Medemblik (NL) 82 B 3
Mediaş (RO) 13 D 3
Medicina (I) 101 F 1
Medikoniai (LT) 170 C 1
Medina Azahara (E) 75 F 1
Medina de Pomar (E) 60 B 3
Medina de Rioseco (E) 64 A 2
Medina del Campo (E) 64 A 3
Medina-Sidonia (E) 75 E 3
Medinaceli (E) 65 D 3
Medingėnai (LT) 169 D 1
Medininkai Kauno(LT) 170 B 3
Medininkai Vilniaus(LT) 177 F 2
Mediniškiai (LT) 170 C 1
Medjugorje (BIH) 120 B 1
Medne (LV) 163 F 2
Medņi (LV) 166 C 2
Médousa (GR) 207 F 1
Medsėdžiai (LT) 168 C 2
Medulin (HR) 99 D 4
Međumajdam (HR) 115 D 4
Medumi (LV) 172 C 2
Meduno (I) 98 B 1
Međurečje (SRB) 118 C 3
Medveđa (SRB) 119 D 4
Medveja (HR) 99 D 3
Medviđa (HR) 103 F 1
Medvode (SLO) 99 D 1
Medyka (PL) 202 F 2
Medyn' (RUS) 7 F 2
Medžionys (LT) 176 C 2
Medžitlija (MK) 122 B 4
Medžiukai (LT) 177 E 1
Meegomäe (EST) 161 D 2
Meeksi (EST) 155 E 4
Meelva (EST) 155 E 4
Meerane (D) 89 E 1
Meeri (EST) 154 C 4
Meersburg (D) 93 D 3
Mefjordbotn (N) 124 B 3
Mefjordvær (N) 124 A 3
Meg. Livádi (GR) 219 D 4
Meg. Monastíri (GR) 212 B 2
Meg. Panagía (GR) 207 D 4
Meg. Vólvi (GR) 206 C 3
Méga Déreio (GR) 208 C 2
Méga Spílaio (GR) 217 E 2
Megálo Chorió
Dodekánissa(GR) 221 E 3
Megálo Chorió
Evritanía(GR) 211 F 4
Megálo Chorió Tílos(GR) 228 A 2
Megalochóri (GR) 211 F 2
Megalópoli (GR) 217 E 3
Meganísi (GR) 211 D 4
Megaplátanos (GR) 212 B 4
Mégara (GR) 218 B 2
Megárchi (GR) 211 E 2
Megève (F) 53 E 1
Megísti (GR) 228 C 4
Megísti (Kastelórizo)
(Nisí) (GR) 228 C 4
Megučioniai (LT) 164 C 4
Mehamn (N) 125 E 1
Mehedeby (S) 141 D 2
Mehikoorma (EST) 155 E 4
Mehun-sur-Yèvre (F) 48 A 2
Meigle (GB) 31 D 1
Meijel (NL) 87 D 1
Meikštai (LT) 172 C 3
Meilen (CH) 92 C 4
Meillant (F) 48 A 3
Meilūnai Panevėžio(LT) 165 E 4
Meilūnai Vilniaus(LT) 171 D 3
Meimoa (P) 63 D 4
Meina (I) 97 D 3
Meinerzhagen (D) 87 F 2
Meiningen (D) 88 C 2
Meira (E) 58 C 2
Meirāni (LV) 167 D 1
Meiringen (CH) 96 C 1
Meironiškiai (LT) 170 B 3
Meironys (LT) 172 C 3
Meisenheim (D) 45 D 1
Meißen (D) 89 F 1
Meitingen (D) 93 E 2
Mekiai (LT) 163 F 4
Mel (I) 98 B 2
Melalahti (FIN) 133 F 1
Mélampes (GR) 226 C 3
Melaniós (GR) 214 C 4
Melánthio (GR) 205 E 4
Melátes (GR) 211 D 3
Melbārži (LV) 160 B 4
Melbeck (D) 84 A 2
Melbu (N) 127 E 1
Meldal (N) 130 C 3
Meldola (I) 102 A 1
Meldorf (D) 78 C 3
Meldzere (LV) 163 D 2
Melegnano (I) 97 E 3
Melenci (SRB) 113 E 4
Melendugno (I) 107 F 3
Meleski (EST) 154 C 3
Melfi (I) 106 B 3
Melgaço (P) 58 B 4
Melgar de Abajo (E) 59 F 4
Melgar de Fernamental (E) 60 A 4
Melhus (N) 131 D 3
Melía (GR) 212 B 2
Melide (E) 58 B 3
Melides (P) 68 A 4
Melidóni (GR) 226 C 2
Meligalás (GR) 217 D 4
Melíki (GR) 206 A 3
Melilli (I) 111 E 3
Melisey (F) 49 E 1
Mélissa (GR) 207 F 2
Melissáni (GR) 216 B 1
Melíssi (GR) 217 F 2
Melissochóri (GR) 218 B 1
Melissópetra (GR) 205 D 4
Melissourgós (GR) 206 C 3
Melíti (GR) 205 E 3
Melito Porto Salvo (I) 111 F 2
Melívoia Lárisa(GR) 212 B 1
Melívoia Xánthi(GR) 207 F 1
Melk (A) 95 D 2
Melksham (GB) 35 E 2
Mellansel (S) 132 B 3
Melle (D) 83 E 4
Melle (F) 47 D 4
Mellendorf (D) 84 A 3
Mellerud (S) 139 F 4
Mellieħa (M) 110 A 4
Mellilä (FIN) 136 C 3
Mellin (D) 84 B 2
Mellingen (D) 89 D 1
Melliste (EST) 155 D 4
Mellrichstadt (D) 88 C 2
Mellsils (Melnsils) (LV) 157 E 2
Melniai (LT) 164 C 3
Melnica (SRB) 119 D 1
Melnice (HR) 99 E 3
Mělník (CZ) 90 B 4
Meļņiki (LV) 167 F 3
Melpers (D) 88 C 2
Melrose (GB) 31 E 3
Melsungen (D) 88 B 1
Meltaus (FIN) 128 C 3
Melton Mowbray (GB) 33 E 4
Meltosjärvi (FIN) 128 C 3
Melun (F) 43 D 3
Melvich (GB) 27 F 1
Membrilla (E) 70 C 3
Membrío (E) 69 D 2
Memmingen (D) 93 E 3
Mena (UA) 7 F 4
Menaggio (I) 97 D 2
Menai Bridge /
Porthaethwy (GB) 32 B 3
Mėnaičiai (LT) 169 F 2
Menasalbas (E) 70 A 2
Menat (F) 48 A 4
Mendavia (E) 60 C 4
Mende (F) 52 A 4
Menden (Sauerland) (D) 87 F 1
Mendenítsa (GR) 212 B 4
Mendig (D) 87 F 3
Mendrisio (CH) 97 D 3
Menen (B) 37 F 4
Menesjärvi (FIN) 125 E 3
Menetés (GR) 228 A 4
Ménez-Hom (F) 40 B 3
Menfi (I) 110 B 3
Mengamuñoz (E) 64 A 4
Mengara (I) 102 B 3
Meņģele (LV) 165 F 1
Mengen (D) 45 F 4
Mengeš (SLO) 99 D 1
Mengíbar (E) 76 B 1
Menidi (GR) 211 D 3
Ménigoute (F) 47 D 4
Meniko (CY) 231 C 3
Mennetou-sur-Cher (F) 47 F 2
Mens (F) 53 D 3
Mentana (I) 105 D 2
Menthon-St-Bernard (F) 53 D 1
Menton (F) 57 F 1
Méntrida (E) 70 B 1
Meppel (NL) 82 C 3
Meppen (D) 83 D 3
Mequinenza (E) 66 A 3
Mer (F) 42 C 4
Merag (HR) 99 E 3
Meråker (N) 131 E 3
Meran / Merano (I) 97 F 1
Merano / Meran (I) 97 F 1
Merate (I) 97 E 3
Mercatale (I) 102 B 2
Mercatale (I) 102 A 3
Mercatino Conca (I) 102 B 2
Mercato San Severino (I) 105 F 3
Mercato Saraceno (I) 102 A 1
Mercendarbe (LV) 165 D 1
Merćez (SRB) 119 D 3
Mercœur (F) 51 E 3
Merdrignac (F) 41 D 3
Mērdzene (LV) 167 F 2
Mere (GB) 35 E 2
Meremäe (EST) 161 E 2
Méréville (F) 43 D 3
Mergozzo (I) 96 C 2
Mēri (LV) 160 C 3
Méribel (F) 53 E 2
Mérichas (GR) 219 D 3
Mérida (E) 69 E 3
Mérignac (F) 50 B 3
Merijärvi (FIN) 133 E 2
Merikarvia (FIN) 136 B 2
Mering (D) 93 F 2
Merkendorf (D) 93 E 1
Merkinė Alytaus(LT) 176 C 4
Merkinė Vilniaus(LT) 177 F 3
Merklingen (D) 93 D 2
Merošina (SRB) 119 D 3
Mers-les-Bains (F) 38 B 3
Mersch (L) 44 C 1
Merseburg (D) 89 D 1
Mērsrags (LV) 157 F 3
Merthyr Tydfil (GB) 35 D 1
Mértola (P) 74 C 1
Méru (F) 43 D 2
Merville (F) 38 C 2
Merville-
Franceville-Plage (F) 42 A 1
Méry-sur-Seine (F) 43 F 3
Merzig (D) 44 C 2
Mesa Geitonia (CY) 231 C 4
Mesagne (I) 107 E 3
Mesanagrós (GR) 228 B 3
Mesão Frio (P) 62 C 3
Mesariá (GR) 219 E 2
Meschede (D) 88 A 1
Mescherin (D) 81 D 4
Meschers-sur-Gironde (F) 50 B 2
Mešeišta (MK) 122 A 4
Mési (GR) 208 A 2
Mesići (BIH) 117 F 3
Mesihovina (BIH) 117 D 4
Mesiméri (GR) 206 C 4
Mesimvría (GR) 208 B 2
Meškėnai (LT) 175 F 2
Meškerinė (LT) 171 F 4
Meškučiai Alytaus(LT) 176 C 3
Meškučiai
Marijampolės(LT) 175 F 2
Meškučiai Mekiai(LT) 163 F 4
Meškučiai
Pabutkalnis(LT) 169 E 2
Meslay-du-Maine (F) 41 F 4
Mesocco (CH) 97 D 2
Mesochóra (GR) 211 E 2
Mesochóri
Dodekánissa(GR) 228 A 4
Mesochóri Lárisa(GR) 211 F 1
Mesogi (CY) 230 A 4
Mesola (I) 98 B 4
Mesológi (GR) 216 C 1
Mesón do Vento (E) 58 B 2
Mesongí (GR) 210 B 2
Mesopótamo (GR) 210 C 3
Mesoraca (I) 109 F 2
Mesótopos (GR) 214 C 3
Mespelbrunn (D) 45 F 1
Meßdorf (D) 84 C 2
Messei (F) 41 F 2
Messina (I) 111 E 1
Messíni (GR) 217 E 4
Meßkirch (D) 45 F 4
Messlingen (S) 131 E 4
Meßstetten (D) 45 F 4
Mestá (GR) 220 C 1
Mestanza (E) 70 B 4
Mésti (GR) 208 B 2
Mestlin (D) 79 E 4
Město Albrechtice (CZ) 91 E 2
Mestre (I) 98 B 3
Mesvres (F) 48 C 3
Metagkítsi (GR) 207 D 4
Metajna (HR) 99 E 4
Metaljka (BIH) 117 F 4
Metalleío (GR) 212 A 3
Metallikó (GR) 206 B 2
Metamórfosi Halkidikí(GR) 207 D 4
Metamórfosi Kilkís(GR) 206 B 2
Metaxádes (GR) 208 C 1
Meteliai (LT) 176 B 3
Metéora (GR) 211 E 1
Méthana (GR) 218 B 3
Methil (GB) 31 D 1
Methóni Messinía(GR) 222 B 2
Methóni Piería(GR) 206 B 4
Metković (HR) 120 C 2
Metlika (SLO) 99 E 2
Metnitz (A) 95 D 4
Metóchi Ahaïa(GR) 216 C 1
Metóchi Argolída(GR) 217 F 3
Metóchi Évoia(GR) 213 D 4
Metóchi Magnissía(GR) 212 C 3
Mētriena (LV) 166 C 2
Metsakasti (EST) 149 E 2
Metsakivi (EST) 155 D 3
Metsaküla (EST) 155 D 2
Metsäkyla (FIN) 129 E 4
Metsäkylä (FIN) 137 E 3
Metsalaane (EST) 154 C 4
Metsämaa (FIN) 136 C 3
Metsapoole (EST) 159 D 1
Metsküla Saare(EST) 152 B 2
Metsküla Viljandi(EST) 154 B 3
Métsovo (GR) 211 E 1
Metste (EST) 161 D 1
Mettingen (D) 83 E 3
Mettlach (D) 44 C 2
Mettmann (D) 87 E 1
Metz (F) 44 C 2
Metzervisse (F) 44 C 2
Metzingen (D) 45 F 3
Meulan (F) 42 C 2
Meung-sur-Loire (F) 42 C 4
Meursault (F) 48 C 3
Meuselwitz (D) 89 E 1
Mevagissey (GB) 34 B 4
Meximieux (F) 52 C 1
Meyenburg (D) 79 F 4
Meymac (F) 51 E 2
Meyrueis (F) 52 A 4
Meyzieu (F) 52 C 1
Mežāre (LV) 166 C 2
Mežciems Jelgavas(LV) 164 C 2
Mežciems Rīgas(LV) 159 D 4
Meždārzi (LV) 165 F 2
Mezdra (BG) 19 D 1
Mèze (F) 56 A 2
Mézel (F) 53 D 4
Mėželiai (LT) 168 B 2
Mežgale (LV) 166 B 3
Mežica (SLO) 99 E 1
Mézidon (F) 42 A 2
Mézières-en-Brenne (F) 47 E 3
Mézières-sur-Issoire (F) 47 E 4
Mézin (F) 50 C 4
Mėžionėliai (LT) 172 B 4
Mežklabji (LV) 157 E 3
Mežmala (LV) 165 D 1
Mežmalieši (LV) 163 F 2
Mezőberény (H) 113 E 1
Mezőkövesd (H) 12 B 3
Mežotne (LV) 164 C 3
Mezőtúr (H) 113 E 1
Mezquita de Jarque (E) 65 F 4
Mežrozītes (LV) 161 D 3
Mežsargi (LV) 159 E 3
Mežvalde (LV) 157 D 4
Mežvidi Baldone(LV) 165 D 2
Mežvidi Liepājas(LV) 162 B 2
Mežvidi Ogres(LV) 165 D 1
Mežvidi Saldus(LV) 163 E 2
Mežvidi Saulkrasti(LV) 159 D 3
Mežvidi Valmieras(LV) 159 F 2
Mežvidi (Mežavidi) (LV) 167 E 2
Mežvidu Muiža (LV) 167 E 2
Mezzano (I) 98 A 2
Mezzolombardo (I) 97 F 2
Mgarr (M) 110 A 4
Mia Milia (CY) 231 C 2
Miączyn (PL) 197 F 3
Miajadas (E) 69 E 2
Miałkówek (PL) 189 D 2
Miasteczko
Krajeńskie (PL) 187 F 1
Miasteczko Śląskie (PL) 195 D 4
Miastko (PL) 181 F 2
Miastkowo (PL) 184 C 4
Michałkowo (PL) 184 B 2
Michalovce (SK) 12 C 2
Michałów
Świętokrzyskie(PL) 195 F 4
Michałowice (PL) 201 A 1
Michałowo (PL) 191 F 1
Míchas (GR) 217 D 2
Micheldorf (A) 94 C 2
Michelin (PL) 189 D 2
Michelstadt (D) 45 F 1
Michendorf (D) 85 D 3
Michói (GR) 217 D 2
Michorzewo (PL) 187 E 3
Michów (PL) 197 D 1
Miciūnai (LT) 177 D 2
Mickai (LT) 168 B 2
Mickiemė (LT) 170 C 2
Mickūnai Utenos(LT) 171 E 2
Mickūnai Vilniaus(LT) 177 F 2
Mičurinietis (LV) 172 C 1
Mid Yell (GB) 29 F 1
Middelburg (NL) 37 F 3
Middelfart (DK) 142 B 4
Middelharnis (NL) 86 B 1
Middelkerke-Bad (B) 37 E 4
Middlesbrough (GB) 31 F 4
Middleton-
in-Teesdale (GB) 31 E 4
Middlewich (GB) 32 C 3
Midhurst (GB) 36 B 4
Midleton / Mainistir
na Corann (IRL) 24 C 3
Midsund (N) 130 B 3
Miechocin (PL) 196 C 3
Miechów (PL) 195 E 4
Miedes (E) 65 E 3
Miedwie (Jezioro) (PL) 180 C 4
Miedziana Góra (PL) 195 F 3
Miedzichowo (PL) 187 D 3
Miedzna (PL) 190 C 2
Miedźno (PL) 195 D 3
Międzybórz (PL) 194 B 2
Międzybrodzie
Bialskie (PL) 200 F 2
Międzychód (PL) 187 D 2
Międzygórze (PL) 193 E 4
Międzylesie
Dolnośląskie(PL) 199 B 1
Międzyrzec Podlaski (PL) 191 E 3
Międzyrzecz (PL) 187 D 2
Międzyrzecze Górne (PL) 200 F 2
Międzyzdroje (PL) 180 B 3
Miegėnai (LT) 170 C 2
Miegonys (LT) 165 F 4
Miegupīte (LV) 159 F 3
Miehikkälä (FIN) 137 E 3
Miejsce Piastowe (PL) 202 D 3
Miejska Górka (PL) 187 F 4
Miękinia (PL) 193 E 2
Mielagėnai (LT) 172 C 3
Miélan (F) 54 C 2
Mielec (PL) 196 C 4
Mielęcin (PL) 186 C 1
Mieleszyn (PL) 187 F 2
Mieliūnai Bugailiškiai(LT) 171 E 1
Mieliūnai Mockūnai(LT) 165 D 4
Mielno (PL) 181 D 2
Mieluskylä (FIN) 133 E 2
Miercurea-Ciuc (RO) 13 D 3
Mieres (E) 59 E 3
Mierkalns (LV) 160 C 2
Mieroszów (PL) 193 D 3
Mierzęcice (PL) 195 D 4
Miesbach (D) 94 A 3
Mieścisko (PL) 187 F 2
Miestalis (LT) 169 D 1
Miesto Kolonija (LT) 176 B 4
Mieszków (PL) 187 F 3
Mieszkowice (PL) 186 B 1
Mietków (PL) 193 E 3
Mietoinen (FIN) 136 B 3
Miettila (FIN) 137 F 2
Mieziškiai (LT) 171 D 2
Migennes (F) 43 E 4
Migliarino (I) 98 B 4
Miglionico (I) 106 C 3
Migonys (LT) 176 C 2
Miguel Esteban (E) 70 C 2
Miguelturra (E) 70 B 3
Mihajlovac Negotin(SRB) 118 C 1
Mihajlovac
Smederevo(SRB) 119 E 1
Miiduranna (EST) 149 E 2
Mijas (E) 75 F 3
Mijoux (F) 49 E 4
Mikalaučiškės (LT) 177 D 1
Mikalauka (LT) 175 F 3
Mikalavas (LT) 172 C 3
Mikantonys (LT) 177 F 3
Miķelēni (LV) 165 E 1
Mikėnai (LT) 171 D 3
Mikitamäe (EST) 161 E 1
Mikkelbostad (N) 124 A 3
Mikkeli (FIN) 137 E 2
Mikkelvik (N) 124 B 2
Mikleuš (HR) 112 B 4
Mīkliņi (LV) 156 C 3
Miklusėnai (LT) 176 C 3
Mikniškiai (LT) 175 F 3
Mikniūnai (LT) 164 C 4
Miknonys (LT) 175 F 2
Mikolaičiai (LT) 163 F 4
Mikołajki (PL) 184 C 3
Mikołajki Pomorskie (PL) 183 D 3
Mikoliškiai (LT) 168 C 1
Mikoliškis (LT) 164 C 3
Mikołów (PL) 200 F 1
Mikrí Mantíneia (GR) 217 E 4
Mikrí Préspa (GR) 205 D 3
Mikró Chorió (GR) 211 F 4
Mikró Déreio (GR) 208 C 1
Mikró Eleftherochóri (GR) 211 F 1
Mikrókampos (GR) 206 B 3
Mikrokleisoúra (GR) 207 D 1
Mikrolímni (GR) 205 E 3
Mikromiliá (GR) 207 E 1
Mikrópoli (GR) 207 D 2
Mikstat (PL) 194 B 1
Mikulčiai (LT) 162 C 3
Mikulov (CZ) 91 E 4
Mikulovice
Olomoucký kraj(CZ) 91 E 2
Mikuszewo (PL) 188 B 3
Mikužiai (LT) 168 C 2
Mikyčiai (LT) 175 F 4
Mikytai (LT) 169 F 4
Milagro (E) 54 A 4
Miłakowo (PL) 183 E 2
Milano (I) 97 D 3
Milano Marittima (I) 102 A 1
Milanówek (PL) 189 F 3
Mílatos (GR) 227 E 2
Milazzo (I) 111 E 1
Milejczyce (PL) 191 E 2
Milejewo (PL) 183 E 2
Milejów (PL) 197 E 2
Milešev Dol (SRB) 118 B 4
Mileševo (SRB) 113 E 4
Milestone (IRL) 24 C 2
Miletići (HR) 99 F 4
Mileto (I) 111 F 1
Milevsko (CZ) 90 B 4
Milford (GB) 36 B 4
Milford Haven /
Aberdaugleddau (GB) 25 F 4
Milhão (P) 63 E 2
Milia (CY) 230 B 2
Miliá Arkadía(GR) 217 E 3
Miliá Évros(GR) 208 C 1
Miliá Grevená(GR) 205 E 4
Milići (BIH) 117 F 2
Milicz (PL) 193 F 1
Miliés (GR) 212 C 2
Milín (CZ) 90 B 3
Milína (GR) 212 C 3
Milis (I) 108 A 3
Militello in Val
di Catania (I) 111 E 3
Miliūnai (LT) 171 D 1
Miljevina (BIH) 117 F 4
Miłki (PL) 184 C 2
Miłkowice (PL) 193 D 2
Milkūnai (LT) 177 F 4
Milkuškos (LT) 172 C 4
Millares (E) 71 F 3
Millas (F) 55 F 4
Millau (F) 52 A 4
Millesimo (I) 100 B 1
Millford (IRL) 23 D 1
Millom (GB) 32 C 1
Millport (GB) 30 B 2
Millstatt (A) 94 C 4
Millstreet (IRL) 24 B 3
Milltown Malbay / Sráid na
Cathrach (IRL) 24 B 2
Milly-la-Forêt (F) 43 D 3
Milmarcos (E) 65 E 4
Milmersdorf (D) 85 E 1
Milna (HR) 120 A 1
Milohnići (HR) 99 E 3
Miłomłyn (PL) 183 E 3
Milos (GR) 224 A 2
Milos (Nisí) (GR) 224 A 2

Albert-Roßhaupter-Str.	BT	2
Aschheimer Str.	DS	9
Berg-am-Laim-Str.	DS	23
Brudermühlstr.	CT	29
Candidstr.	CT	31
Englschalkinger Str.	DS	47
Georg-Brauchle-Ring	BCR	57
Hanauer Str.	CR	66
Handsastr.	CS	68
Heckenstallerstr.	BT	70
Johanneskirchner Str.	DS	80
Leuchtenbergring	DS	104
Melchiorstr.	BT	131
Meyerbeerstr.	AS	136
Münchner Str.	DR	142
Murnauer Str.	BT	145
Neubiberger Str.	DT	146
Offenbachstr.	AS	153
Ottobrunner Str.	DT	158
Plinganserstr.	CT	166
Schäftlarnstr.	CT	187
Siemensallee	BT	197
Südl.		
Auffahrtsallee	BS	205
Tierparkstr.	CT	209
Triebstr.	CR	212
Tübinger Str.	BCS	217
Waldfriedhofstr.	BT	226
Wendl-Dietrich-		
	BS	229

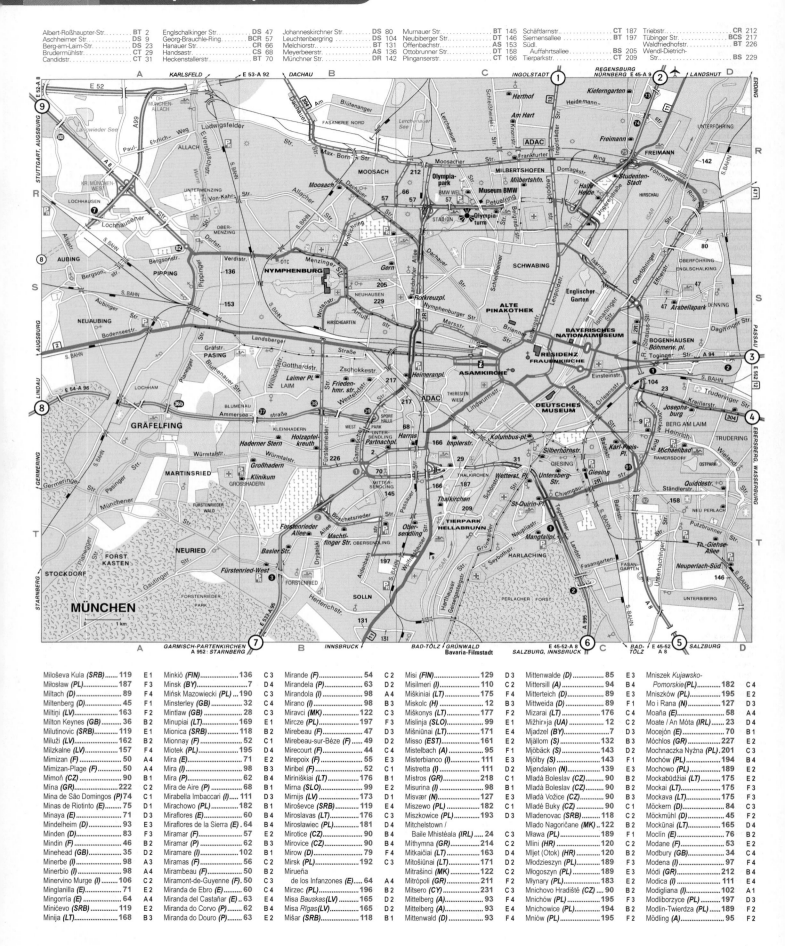

Miloševa Kula (SRB)	119	E 1	Minkiö (FIN)	136	C 3	Mirande (F)	54	C 2	Misi (FIN)	129	D 3	Mittenwalde (D)	85	E 3	Mniszek Kujawsko-		
Miłosław (PL)	187	F 3	Minsk (BY)	7	D 4	Mirandela (P)	63	D 2	Misilmeri (I)	110	C 2	Mittersill (A)	94	B 4	Pomorskie(PL)	182	C 4
Miltach (D)	89	F 4	Mińsk Mazowiecki (PL)	190	C 3	Mirandola (I)	98	A 4	Miškiniai (LT)	175	F 4	Mitterteich (D)	89	E 3	Mniszków (PL)	195	E 2
Miltenberg (D)	45	F 1	Minsterley (GB)	32	C 4	Mirano (I)	98	B 3	Miskolc (H)	12	B 3	Mittweida (D)	89	F 1	Mo i Rana (N)	127	D 3
Miltiņi (LV)	163	F 2	Mintlaw (GB)	28	C 3	Miravci (MK)	122	C 2	Miškonys (LT)	177	F 2	Mizarai (I)	98	A 4	Moaña (E)	58	A 4
Milton Keynes (GB)	36	B 2	Minupiai (LT)	169	E 1	Mircze (PL)	197	F 3	Mislinja (SLO)	99	E 1	Mjadzel (BY)	7	D 3	Moate / An Móta (IRL)	23	C 2
Milutinovic (SRB)	119	E 1	Mionica (SRB)	118	B 2	Mirebeau (F)	47	D 3	Mišiūnai (LT)	171	E 4	Mjällom (S)	132	B 3	Móchlos (GR)	227	C 2
Miluži (LV)	162	F 4	Mionnay (F)	52	C 1	Mirebeau-sur-Bèze (F)	49	D 2	Misso (EST)	161	F 2	Mjöbäck (S)	143	C 1	Mochnaczka Nyżna (PL)	201	C 3
Milzkalne (LV)	157	F 4	Miotek (PL)	195	D 4	Mirecourt (F)	44	E 2	Mistelbach (A)	95	F 1	Mjölby (S)	143	F 1	Mochów (PL)	194	B 4
Mimizan (F)	50	A 4	Mira (E)	71	E 2	Mirepoix (F)	55	E 3	Misterbianco (I)	111	E 3	Mjøndalen (N)	139	E 3	Mochowo (PL)	189	E 2
Mimizan-Plage (F)	50	A 4	Mira (I)	98	B 3	Miribel (F)	52	C 1	Mistretta (I)	111	D 2	Mladá Boleslav (CZ)	90	B 1	Mockabüdžiai (LT)	175	E 2
Mimoň (CZ)	90	B 1	Mira (P)	62	B 4	Miriniškiai (LT)	176	B 1	Mistros (GR)	218	C 1	Mladá Boleslav (CZ)	90	B 1	Mockai (LT)	175	F 3
Mína (GR)	222	C 2	Mira de Aire (P)	68	B 1	Mirna (SLO)	99	E 2	Misurina (I)	98	B 1	Mladá Vožice (CZ)	90	B 3	Mockava (LT)	175	F 3
Mina de São Domingos (P)	74	D 1	Mirabella Imbaccari (I)	111	D 3	Mirnijs (LT)	173	D 1	Misvær (N)	127	C 1	Mladé Buky (CZ)	90	C 1	Möckern (D)	84	C 3
Minas de Riotinto (E)	75	D 1	Mirachowo (PL)	182	B 3	Miroševce (SRB)	119	E 2	Miszewo (PL)	182	C 1	Mladenovac (SRB)	118	C 2	Möckmühl (D)	45	F 2
Minaya (E)	71	D 3	Miraflores (E)	60	B 4	Miroslavas (LT)	176	C 3	Miszkowice (PL)	193	D 3	Mládkūnai (LT)	165	D 4	
Mindelheim (D)	93	F 3	Miraflores de la Sierra (E)	64	B 4	Mirosławiec (PL)	181	D 4	Mitchelstown /			Mława (PL)	189	F 1	Moclín (E)	76	B 2
Minden (D)	83	F 3	Miramar (F)	57	E 2	Mirotice (CZ)	90	B 4	Baile Mhistéala (IRL)	24		Mini (HR)	120	C 4	Modane (F)	53	E 2
Mindin (F)	46	B 2	Miramar (P)	62	B 4	Mirovice (CZ)	90	B 4	Míthymna (GR)	214	C 2	Mljet (Otok) (HR)	120	B 2	Modbury (GB)	34	C 4
Minehead (GB)	35	E 2	Miramare (I)	102	B 1	Mirow (F)	79	F 4	Mitkaičiai (LT)	163	D 4	Mitošiūnai (LT)	171	E 4	Modena (I)	97	E 2
Minerbe (I)	98	A 3	Miramas (F)	56	C 2	Mirsk (PL)	192	C 3	Mitošiūnai (LT)	171	E 4	Młodzieszyn (PL)	189	E 2	Módi (GR)	212	B 4
Minerbio (I)	98	A 4	Mirambeau (F)	50	B 2				Mitrašinci (MK)	122	C 2	Młogoszyn (PL)	189	E 3	Modica (I)	111	E 4
Minervino Murge (I)	106	C 3	Miramont-de-Guyenne (F)	50	C 3	Mirueña			Mitrópoli (GR)	211	D 2	Mlynary (PL)	183	E 2	Modigliana (I)	102	A 1
Minglanilla (E)	71	E 2	Miranda de Ebro (E)	60	C 4	de los Infanzones (E)	64	A 4	Mitsero (CY)	231	C 3	Mnichovo Hradiště (CZ)	90	B 1	Modliborzyce (PL)	197	D 3
Mingorría (E)	64	A 4	Miranda del Castañar (E)	63	E 2	Mirzec (PL)	196	C 4	Mittelberg (A)	93	F 4	Mnichów (PL)	195	F 3	Modlin-Twierdza (PL)	189	F 2
Miničevo (SRB)	119	E 2	Miranda do Corvo (P)	62	B 4	Misa Bauskas(LV)	165	D 2	Mittelberg (A)	93	E 4	Mnichowice (PL)	194	B 2	Mödling (A)	95	F 2
Minija (LT)	168	B 3	Miranda do Douro (P)	63	E 2	Misa Rīgas(LV)	165	D 2	Mittenwald (D)	93	F 4	Mišar (SRB)	118	B 1	Mniów (PL)	195	F 2

Modran (BIH) 115 F 4
Modrava (CZ) 90 A 4
Modrica (BIH) 117 E 1
Modrište (MK) 122 B 3
Modugno (I) 107 D 2
Moe (EST) 150 C 3
Moëlan-sur-Mer (F) 40 C 4
Moelv (N) 139 E 2
Moen / Målselv (N) 124 B 3
Moena (I) 98 A 1
Moers (D) 87 E 1
Moffat (GB) 31 D 3
Mogadouro (P) 63 E 3
Mogielnica (PL) 189 F 4
Mogila (MK) 122 B 4
Mogilany (PL) 201 A 2
Mogilno (PL) 188 B 2
Moglia (I) 97 F 4
Mogliano Veneto (I) 98 B 3
Mogón (E) 76 C 1
Moguer (E) 75 D 2
Mohács (H) 112 C 3
Mohelnice (CZ) 91 E 3
Mohill / Maothail (IRL) 23 D 3
Mõhküla (EST) 154 C 3
Moholm (S) 143 E 1
Mohyliv-Podil's'kyj (UA) 13 E 2
Moi (N) 138 B 4
Moià (E) 67 D 2
Moie (I) 102 B 2
Moimenta (P) 63 D 1
Moimenta da Beira (P) 62 C 3
Moirans (F) 52 C 2
Moirans-en-Montagne (F) 49 E 4
Moíres (GR) 226 C 3
Mõisaküla *Pärnu*(EST) 153 C 3
Mõisaküla *Viljandi*(EST) 154 A 4
Mõisamaa (EST) 149 D 4
Mõisanurme (EST) 154 C 4
Moisdon-la-Rivière (F) 41 E 4
Moisiovaara (FIN) 135 E 1
Moisling (D) 79 D 4
Moissac (F) 51 D 4
Moita (P) 68 A 3
Moixent (E) 71 F 3
Mojácar (E) 77 D 3
Mojados (E) 64 A 3
Mojkovac (MNE) 118 B 4
Mojstrana (SLO) 99 D 1
Mokobody (PL) 191 D 3
Mokolai (LT) 175 F 2
Mokra Gora (SRB) 118 B 3
Mokre (PL) 182 C 4
Mokrin (SRB) 113 E 3
Mokro Polje (HR) 103 F 1
Mokronog (SLO) 99 E 2
Mokrsko (PL) 194 C 2
Mokrzesz (PL) 195 D 3
Mol (B) 39 F 1
Mol (SRB) 113 E 3
Mola di Bari (I) 107 D 2
Moláoi (GR) 223 D 2
Molat (HR) 103 D 1
Molat (Otok) (HR) 103 D 1
Mold / Yr Wyddgrug (GB) 32 C 3
Molde (N) 130 B 3
Moldova Nouă (RO) 119 D 1
Møldrup (DK) 142 B 3
Moledo do Minho (P) 62 B 1
Molėtai (LT) 171 F 3
Molfetta (I) 106 C 2
Molières (F) 51 D 4
Molina de Aragón (E) 65 E 4
Molina de Segura (E) 77 E 1
Molinella (I) 98 A 4
Molinicos (E) 71 D 4
Molinos (E) 66 F 4
Molins de Rei (E) 67 D 3
Moliterno (I) 106 C 4
Molitg-les-Bains (F) 55 F 4
Moliūnai (LT) 165 D 4
Molkom (S) 140 B 3
Möllbrücke (A) 94 C 4
Mollerussa (E) 66 B 3
Molliens-Dreuil (F) 38 C 4
Mollina (E) 76 A 2
Mölln (D) 79 D 4
Mollösund (S) 142 C 1
Mólos *Fthiótida*(GR) 212 B 4
Molpe (FIN) 132 C 4
Molsheim (F) 45 D 3
Molve (HR) 112 A 4
Molveno (I) 97 F 2
Molynė (LT) 169 E 4
Mombeltrán (E) 70 A 1
Mombuey (E) 63 E 1
Mommark (DK) 144 B 3
Momo (I) 97 D 3
Mon Idée (F) 39 E 4
Monaco *Principauté de*(MC) 57 F 1
Monaghan /
Muineachán (IRL) 23 E 3
Monasterace Marina (I) 109 E 3
Monasterevin (IRL) 25 E 1
Monasterio de Rodilla (E) 60 B 4
Monastir (I) 108 B 4
Monastiráki
Etolía-Akarnanía(GR) 211 D 4
Monastiráki *Évros*(GR) 208 C 2
Monbazillac (F) 50 C 3
Moncalieri (I) 53 F 2
Moncalvo (I) 96 C 4
Monção (P) 58 B 4
Moncarapacho (P) 74 B 2
Mönchdorf (A) 95 D 1
Mönchengladbach (D) 87 E 1
Monchique (P) 74 A 1
Monclar-de-Quercy (F) 51 E 4
Moncofa (E) 72 A 2
Moncontour (F) 41 D 3
Moncontour (F) 47 D 3
Moncoutant (F) 46 C 3
Monda (E) 75 F 3
Mondariz (E) 58 B 4
Mondavio (I) 102 B 2
Mondéjar (E) 70 C 1
Mondello (I) 110 B 2
Mondim de Basto (P) 62 C 2
Mondolfo (I) 102 B 2
Mondoñedo (E) 58 C 2
Mondorf-les-Bains (L) 44 C 2
Mondoubleau (F) 42 B 4
Mondovì (I) 53 F 4
Mondragon (F) 52 B 4
Mondragone (I) 105 E 3
Mondsee (A) 94 B 3
Monein (F) 54 B 2
Monemvasía (GR) 223 D 2
Mónesi di Triora (I) 53 F 4
Monesterio (E) 69 E 4
Monestier-de-Clermont (F) 53 D 3
Monestiés (F) 51 E 4
Moneygall (IRL) 25 D 2
Moneymore (GB) 23 E 2
Monfalcone (I) 98 C 2
Monflanquin (F) 51 D 3
Monforte (P) 68 C 2
Monforte de Lemos (E) 58 C 4
Monfortinho (P) 69 D 1
Monguelfo / Welsberg (I) 98 A 1
Monheim (D) 93 E 1
Moní (Nisí) (GR) 218 B 3
Monice (PL) 194 C 1
Mönichkirchen (A) 95 E 3
Monifieth (GB) 31 E 1
Mõniste (EST) 161 D 2
Monistrol-d'Allier (F) 52 A 3
Monistrol de Montserrat (E) 66 C 3
Monistrol-sur-Loire (F) 52 B 2
Mönkebude (D) 80 C 3
Mońki (PL) 185 D 4
Monmouth /
Trefynwy (GB) 35 E 1
Mõnnaste (EST) 154 B 4
Monnickendam (NL) 82 B 3
Monodéndri (GR) 211 D 1
Monódryo (GR) 213 D 4
Monólithos (GR) 228 B 2
Monopoli (I) 107 D 2
Monor (H) 113 D 1
Monòver (E) 71 E 4
Monpazier (F) 51 D 3
Monreal (D) 87 E 3
Monreal del Campo (E) 65 E 4
Monreale (I) 110 B 2
Monroy (E) 69 E 2
Monroyo (E) 66 A 4
Mons (B) 39 E 3
Monsagrati (I) 101 E 2
Monsanto (P) 69 D 1
Monsaraz (P) 68 C 4
Monschau (D) 87 D 3
Monségur (F) 50 C 3
Monselice (I) 98 A 3
Monsols (F) 48 C 4
Mönsterås (S) 143 F 2
Monsummano Terme (I) 101 F 2
Mont-de-Marsan (F) 54 B 1
Mont-Louis (F) 55 E 4
Mont-roig del Camp (E) 66 B 4
Mont-sous-Vaudrey (F) 49 D 3
Mont-St-Vincent (F) 48 C 3
Montabaur (D) 87 F 3
Montagnac (F) 56 A 2
Montagnana (I) 98 A 3
Montagrier (F) 50 C 2
Montaigu (F) 46 C 3
Montaigu-de-Quercy (F) 51 D 4
Montaigut (F) 48 A 4
Montaione (I) 101 F 2
Montalbán (E) 65 F 4
Montalbo (E) 71 D 2
Montalcino (I) 102 A 3
Montalegre (P) 62 C 2
Montalieu-Vercieu (F) 52 C 1
Montalivet-les-Bains (F) 50 B 2
Montalto di Castro (I) 102 A 4
Montalto di Marche (I) 102 C 3
Montalto Uffugo (I) 109 E 1
Montalvão (P) 68 C 1
Montamarta (E) 63 F 2
Montana (BG) 18 C 1
Montana (CH) 96 B 2
Montañana (E) 65 F 3
Montánchez (E) 69 E 2
Montanejos (E) 71 F 1
Montargil (P) 68 B 2
Montargis (F) 43 D 4
Montastruc-
la-Conseillère (F) 55 E 2
Montauban (F) 51 D 4
Montauban-
de-Bretagne (F) 41 D 3
Montbard (F) 43 F 4
Montbazens (F) 51 F 4
Montbazon (F) 47 E 2
Montbéliard (F) 49 F 2
Montbenoît (F) 49 E 3
Montblanc (E) 66 B 3
Montbozon (F) 49 E 2
Montbrió del Camp (E) 66 B 4
Montbrison (F) 52 B 2
Montbron (F) 51 D 1
Montceau-les-Mines (F) 48 C 3
Montcenis (F) 48 C 3
Montchanin (F) 48 C 3
Montcornet (F) 39 E 4
Montcuq (F) 51 D 4
Montdidier (F) 38 C 4
Monte da Pedra (P) 68 C 2
Monte Real (P) 68 B 1
Monte Redondo (P) 68 B 1
Monte San Savino (I) 102 A 3
Monte Sant'Angelo (I) 106 B 1
Monteagudo
de las Vicarías (E) 65 D 3
Montealegre (E) 64 A 2
Montealegre
del Castillo (E) 71 E 4
Montebello Ionico (I) 111 F 2
Montebello Vicentino (I) 98 A 3
Montebelluna (I) 98 B 2
Montebourg (F) 41 E 1
Montecarotto (I) 102 B 2
Montecassino
(Abbazia di) (I) 105 E 2
Montecatini Terme (I) 101 F 2
Montecchio (I) 102 B 2
Montecchio Maggiore (I) 98 A 3
Montech (F) 55 D 1
Montecorvino Rovella (I) 106 A 3
Montedoro (I) 110 C 3
Montefalco (I) 102 B 3
Montefalcone
di Val Fortore (I) 106 A 2
Montefalcone
nel Sannio (I) 105 F 1
Montefiascone (I) 102 A 4
Montefiore dell'Aso (I) 102 C 3
Montefiorino (I) 101 E 1
Montefrío (E) 76 A 2
Montegallo (I) 102 C 3
Montegiorgio (I) 102 C 3
Montegranaro (I) 102 C 3
Montegrotto Terme (I) 98 A 3
Montehermoso (E) 69 E 1
Montejícar (E) 76 B 2
Montejo de Tiermes (E) 64 C 3
Monteleone di Spoleto (I) 102 B 4
Montélimar (F) 52 B 3
Montella (I) 106 A 3
Montellano (E) 75 E 2
Montelupo Fiorentino (I) 101 F 2
Montemaggiore
Belsito (I) 110 C 2
Montemagno (I) 96 C 4
Montemayor (E) 76 A 1
Montemayor de Pililla (E) 64 A 3
Montemor-o-Novo (P) 68 B 3
Montemor-o-Velho (P) 62 B 4
Montendre (F) 50 B 2
Montenegro
de Cameros (E) 65 D 2
Montenero di Bisaccia (I) 105 F 1
Montenero Sabino (I) 102 B 4
Montepulciano (I) 102 A 3
Montereale (I) 102 C 4
Montereale Valcellina (I) 98 B 2
Montereau-Fault-Yonne (F) 43 E 3
Monterenzio (I) 101 F 1
Monteriggioni (I) 101 F 3
Monteroni di Lecce (I) 107 F 3
Monterosso al Mare (I) 101 D 2
Monterotondo (I) 104 C 1
Monterotondo Marittimo (I) 101 F 3
Monterroso (E) 58 C 3
Monterrubio
de la Serena (E) 69 F 4
Monterubbiano (I) 102 C 3
Montesano
sulla Marcellana (I) 106 B 4
Montesarchio (I) 105 F 3
Montescaglioso (I) 107 D 3
Montesilvano Marina (I) 103 D 4
Montesquieu-Volvestre (F) 55 D 3
Montesquiou (F) 54 C 2
Montevarchi (I) 102 A 2
Montfaucon-d'Argonne (F) 44 B 2
Montfaucon-en-Velay (F) 52 B 2
Montfaucon-Montigné (F) 46 C 2
Montfort-en-Chalosse (F) 54 B 2
Montfort-l'Amaury (F) 42 C 2
Montfort-sur-Meu (F) 41 E 3
Montfort-sur-Risle (F) 42 B 1
Montgaillard (F) 55 E 3
Montgenèvre (F) 53 E 3
Montgiscard (F) 55 E 2
Montgomery /
Trefaldwyn (GB) 32 B 4
Montguyon (F) 50 C 2
Monthermé (F) 39 F 4
Monthey (CH) 49 F 4
Monthois (F) 44 A 2
Monthureux-sur-Saône (F) 44 C 4
Monti (I) 108 B 1
Montichiari (I) 97 F 3
Monticiano (I) 101 F 3
Montiel (E) 70 C 4
Montier-en-Der (F) 44 A 4
Montignac (F) 51 D 3
Montigny-le-Roi (F) 44 B 4
Montigny-sur-Aube (F) 48 C 1
Montijo (E) 69 D 3
Montijo (P) 68 A 3
Montilla (E) 76 A 1
Montioni (I) 101 F 3
Montivilliers (F) 38 A 4
Montjean-sur-Loire (F) 46 C 2
Montlhéry (F) 43 D 3
Montlieu-la-Garde (F) 50 C 2
Montlouis-sur-Loire (F) 47 E 2
Montluçon (F) 48 A 4
Montluel (F) 52 C 1
Montmarault (F) 48 A 4
Montmartin-sur-Mer (F) 41 E 2
Montmédy (F) 39 F 4
Montmélian (F) 53 D 2
Montmirail (F) 43 E 2
Montmirail (F) 42 B 4
Montmirey-le-Château (F) 49 D 2
Montmoreau-St-Cybard (F) 50 C 2
Montmorillon (F) 47 E 4
Montmort (F) 43 F 2
Montoggio (I) 100 C 1
Montoire-sur-le-Loir (F) 42 B 4
Montoito (P) 68 C 3
Montorio al Vomano (I) 102 C 4
Montoro (E) 76 A 1
Montpellier (F) 56 A 2
Montpezat-de-Quercy (F) 51 E 4
Montpezat-
sous-Bauzon (F) 52 B 3
Montpon-Ménestérol (F) 50 C 3
Montpont-en-Bresse (F) 49 D 3
Montréal (F) 55 E 3
Montréal (F) 50 C 4
Montréal-la-Cluse (F) 49 D 4
Montredon-Labessonnié (F) 55 F 2
Montréjeau (F) 54 C 3
Montrésor (F) 47 E 3
Montresta (I) 108 A 2
Montret (F) 49 D 3
Montreuil (F) 38 B 3
Montreuil-Bellay (F) 47 D 2
Montreux (CH) 49 F 3
Montrevault (F) 46 C 2
Montrevel-en-Bresse (F) 49 D 4
Montrichard (F) 47 E 2
Montrond-les-Bains (F) 52 B 2
Montrose (GB) 31 E 1
Monts-sur-Guesnes (F) 47 D 3
Montsalvy (F) 51 F 3
Montsauche-les-Settons (F) 48 C 2
Montseny (E) 67 D 2
Montserrat (E) 71 F 3
Montserrat (Monestir) (E) 66 C 3
Montsûrs (F) 41 F 3
Montuenga (E) 64 A 3
Montuïri (E) 73 E 2
Monza (I) 97 D 3
Monzón (E) 66 A 2
Monzón de Campos (E) 64 A 1
Moora (EST) 151 D 4
Moordorf (D) 83 D 1
Moosburg a. d. Isar (D) 94 A 2
Mooste (EST) 155 E 4
Mór (H) 112 B 1
Mora (E) 70 B 2
Mora (P) 68 B 2
Mora (S) 140 B 2
Mora de Rubielos (E) 71 F 1
Móra d'Ebre (E) 66 B 4
Móra la Nova (E) 66 B 4
Morąg (PL) 183 E 3
Morais (P) 63 E 2
Moraítika (GR) 210 B 2
Moral de Calatrava (E) 70 B 3
Moraleda de Zafayona (E) 76 A 2
Moraleja (E) 69 D 1
Moraleja de Sayago (E) 63 E 3
Moraleja del Vino (E) 63 F 2
Morales de Rey (E) 63 F 1
Morales de Toro (E) 63 F 2
Morano Calabro (I) 109 E 1
Mörarp (S) 143 D 4
Morasverdes (E) 63 E 4
Morata de Jalón (E) 65 E 3
Morata de Tajuña (E) 70 C 1
Moratalla (E) 77 D 1
Moravče (SLO) 99 E 1
Moravci-v-Slov.-gor (SLO) 95 F 4
Moravice (HR) 99 E 2
Morávka (CZ) 91 F 2
Moravská Třebová (CZ) 91 D 3
Moravské Budějovice (CZ) 91 D 4
Moravske Toplice (SLO) 95 F 4
Moravský Beroun (CZ) 91 E 2
Moravský Krumlov (CZ) 91 D 4
Morawica (PL) 195 F 3
Morbach (D) 45 D 1
Morbegno (I) 97 E 2
Mörbisch (A) 95 F 2
Mörbylånga (S) 143 F 3
Morcenx (F) 50 B 4
Morciano di Romagna (I) 102 B 1
Morcone (I) 105 F 2
Morcote (CH) 97 D 2
Mordelles (F) 41 E 3
Mordy (PL) 191 D 3
More (LV) 159 E 4
Morecambe (GB) 32 C 1
Moreda (E) 76 B 2
Morée (F) 42 C 4
Morella (E) 66 A 4
Mores (I) 108 B 2
Morestel (F) 52 C 1
Moret-sur-Loing (F) 43 D 3
Moreton-in-Marsh (GB) 35 F 1
Moretonhampstead (GB) 34 C 3
Moreuil (F) 38 C 4
Morez (F) 49 E 3
Morfasso (I) 97 E 4
Mórfio (GR) 210 C 2
Morfou (CY) 230 B 2
Morfou Bay (CY) 230 B 2
Morgat (F) 40 B 3
Morges (CH) 49 E 3
Morgex (I) 53 E 1
Morhange (F) 44 C 3
Mori (I) 97 F 2
Morina (SRB) 121 F 2
Moritzburg (D) 89 F 1
Morjärv (S) 128 B 4
Morlaàs (F) 54 B 2
Morlaix (F) 40 C 2
Mormanno (I) 109 D 1
Mormant (F) 43 E 3
Mormoiron (F) 52 C 4
Mornant (F) 52 B 2
Morón de Almazán (E) 65 D 3
Morón de la Frontera (E) 75 F 2
Morosaglia (F) 57 F 3
Morović (SRB) 117 F 1
Morpeth (GB) 31 E 3
Mörrum (S) 143 E 3
Morsbach (D) 87 F 2
Mörsil (S) 131 F 3
Morsleben (D) 84 B 3
Mortagne-au-Perche (F) 42 B 3
Mortagne-sur-Gironde (F) 50 B 2
Mortagne-sur-Sèvre (F) 46 C 3
Mortain (F) 41 F 3
Mortara (I) 97 D 4
Morteau (F) 49 F 2
Mortrée (F) 42 A 3
Moryń (PL) 186 B 1
Morzeszczyn (PL) 182 C 3
Morzewo (PL) 183 E 3
Morzine (F) 49 F 4
Mosbach (D) 45 F 2
Mosby (N) 142 A 1
Mošćenice (HR) 99 D 3
Mošćenička Draga (HR) 99 D 3
Moschendorf (A) 95 F 3
Moschokaryá (GR) 212 A 3
Moschopótamos (GR) 206 A 4
Mosėdis (LT) 162 C 3
Mosina (PL) 187 E 3
Mosjøen (N) 127 D 4
Mosko (BIH) 121 D 2
Moskorzew (PL) 195 E 3
Moskosel (S) 128 A 4
Moskva (RUS) 7 F 2
Moslavina (HR) 112 B 4
Mosonmagyaróvár (H) 112 A 1
Mosqueruela (E) 71 F 1
Moss (N) 139 E 3
Mossala (FIN) 136 B 4
Mossat (GB) 27 F 4
Mössingen (D) 45 F 3
Most (CZ) 89 F 2
Most na Soči (SLO) 98 C 1
Mosta (M) 110 A 4
Mostar (BIH) 117 E 4
Mosteiro (E) 58 B 3
Mosterhamn (N) 138 B 3
Mostiškės (LT) 177 F 2
Móstoles (E) 70 B 1
Mostys'ka (UA) 12 C 2
Mosvik (N) 131 D 2
Moszczenica
Łodzkie(PL) 195 E 1
Moszczenica
Małopolskie(PL) 201 C 2
Mota del Cuervo (E) 70 C 2
Mota del Marqués (E) 64 A 2
Motala (S) 143 F 1
Motherwell (GB) 30 C 2
Motilla del Palancar (E) 71 D 2
Motovun (HR) 99 D 3
Motril (E) 76 B 3
Mõtsküla (EST) 155 D 4
Motta di Livenza (I) 98 B 2
Motta Sant'Anastasia (I) 111 E 3
Motta Visconti (I) 97 D 4
Mottola (I) 107 E 3
Mouchard (F) 49 E 3
Moudon (CH) 49 F 3
Moúdros (GR) 214 A 1
Mougins (F) 57 E 1
Mouhijärvi (FIN) 136 C 2
Mouilleron-en-Pareds (F) 46 C 3
Moulins (F) 48 B 3
Moulins-Engilbert (F) 48 B 3
Moulins-la-Marche (F) 42 B 3
Moult (F) 42 A 2
Mount Bellew /
An Creagán (IRL) 22 C 4
Mountain Ash /
Aberpennar (GB) 35 D 1
Mountmellick /
Móinteach Mílic (IRL) 25 D 1
Mountrath (IRL) 25 D 2
Moura (P) 68 C 4
Mourão (P) 68 C 4
Mourenx (F) 54 B 2
Mouriki (GR) 218 B 1
Mourmelon-le-Grand (F) 43 F 2
Mourniés (GR) 226 B 2
Mourujärvi (FIN) 129 E 3
Mouscron (B) 39 D 2
Moustiers-Ste-Marie (F) 57 D 1
Mouthe (F) 49 E 3
Mouthier-Haute-Pierre (F) 49 E 2
Mouthoumet (F) 55 F 3
Moutier (CH) 49 F 2
Moûtiers (F) 53 E 2
Moutiers-les-Mauxfaits (F) 46 B 3
Moutoullas (CY) 230 B 3
Moutsoúna (GR) 219 F 4
Mouy (F) 43 D 1
Mouzakaíoi (GR) 211 D 2

NANTES

Aiguillon (Q. d') . . . . **BX** 2
Anglais (Bd des) . . . . **BV** 4
Beaujoire (Bd de la) . . . . . . **CV** 12
Belges (Bd des) . . . . **CV** 14
Bocquerel (Bd H.) . . . . **BV** 22
Bouley Paty (Bd) . . . . **BV** 34
Cassin (Bd R.) . . . . **BV** 39
Chapelle-sur-Erdre (Rte) . . . **BV** 39
Cholet (Bd Bâtonnier) . . . . . **BX** 42

Churchill (Bd W.) . . . . **BX** 43
Clemenceau (Pont G.) . . . . . **CX** 45
Coty (Bd R.) . . . . **BX** 55
Courbet (Bd Amiral) . . . . . . **CV** 58
Dalby (Bd E.) . . . . **CV** 61
Dos-d'Âne (R.) . . . . **CX** 68
Doulon (Bd de) . . . . **CV** 70
Dreyfus
(R. Commandant A.) . . . . . **CV** 71
Einstein (Bd A.) . . . . **BV** 75
Fraternité (Bd de la) . . . . . . **BX** 84

Gabory (Bd E.) . . . . **CX** 85
Gaulle (Bd Gén.-de) . . . . . . **CX** 87
Jean XXIII (Bd) . . . . **BV** 100
Jouhaux (Bd L.) . . . . **BX** 102
Juin (Bd Mar.) . . . . **BX** 103
Koenig (Bd Gén.) . . . . **BX** 107
Landreau (R. du) . . . . **CV** 108
Le Lasseur
(R. Commandant A.) . . . . . **CV** 112
Lauriol (Bd G.) . . . . **BV** 110
Liberté (Bd de la) . . . . **BX** 115

Luther-King (Bd M.) . . . . . . **CV** 118
Michelet (Bd) . . . . **CV** 127
Mollet (Bd G.) . . . . **CV** 128
Monod (Bd du Prof.-J.) . . . . **CV** 130
Orieux (Bd) . . . . **CV** 133
Petite Baratte
(R.) . . . . **CV** 141
Pirmil (Pont de) . . . . **CX** 145
Poilus (Bd des) . . . . **CX** 147
Roch (Bd Gustave) . . . . **CX** 160
Romanet (Bd) . . . . **BX** 163

St-Jacques (R.) . . . . **CX** 169
St-Joseph (Rte de) . . . . **CV** 171
St-Sébastien
(Côte) . . . . **CX** 184
Sarrebrück (Bd de) . . . . **CX** 184
Say (R. L.) . . . . **BV** 186
Stalingrad (Bd de) . . . . **BV** 190
Tertre (Bd du) . . . . **BX** 193
Tortière (Pont de la) . . . . . . **CV** 196
Victor-Hugo (Bd) . . . . **CX** 201
Viviani (R. René) . . . . **CX** 204

ORVAULT

Ferrière (Av. de la) . . . . **BV** 80
Goupil (Av. A.) . . . . **BV** 88
Mendès-France
Rennes (Rte de) . . . . **BV** 124
. . . . **BV** 156

REZÉ

Gaulle (Bd Gén.-de) . . . . . . **CX** 87

NANTES map with scale 0 — 1 km

NAPOLI

Augusto (Viale) . . . . **AU** 10
Capodichino (Calata) . . . . **CT** 16
Caravaggio
　(V. Michelangelo Da) . . . . . . **AU** 19
Casoria (Str. Prov.) . . . . **CT** 21
Cilea (V. Francesco) . . . . **BU** 26
Claudio (V.) . . . . **AU** 28
De Amicis (V. Tommaso) . . . . . **BT** 41
De Pinedo (V.) . . . . **CT** 44
Di Vittorio (Pza) . . . . **CT** 45
Domiziana (V.) . . . . **AU** 46
Don Bosco (V.) . . . . **CT** 47
Europa (Cso) . . . . **BU** 52
Ferraris (V. Galileo) . . . . **CTU** 54
Garibaldi (Cso G.) . . . . **DU** 62
Gianturco (V. E.) . . . . **CTU** 64
Giulio Cesare (V.) . . . . **AU** 66
Imparato (V. F.) . . . . **CTU** 68
Jannelli (V. Gabriele) . . . . **BT** 69
Kennedy (Viale J. F.) . . . . **AU** 70
Maddalena (Viale U.) . . . . **CT** 71
Miraglia (V. Nicola) . . . . **CT** 79
Napoli Capodimonte (V.) . . . . **BT** 92
Nicolini (V. Nicola) . . . . **CT** 95
Orazio (V.) . . . . **BU** 103
Piave (V.) . . . . **AU** 112
Pietravalle (V. M.) . . . . **BT** 114
Pigna (V.) . . . . **BU** 116
Ponti Rossi (V.) . . . . **BT** 122
Reggia di Portici (V.) . . . . . . **CU** 128
Riposo (V. del) . . . . **CT** 132
S. Giovanni a Teduccio
　(Cso) . . . . **CU** 141
Taddeo da Sessa (V.) . . . . . . **CT** 157
Tasso (V. Torquato) . . . . **BU** 158
Tecchio (Piazzale V.) . . . . . . **AU** 160
Traccia a Poggioreale (V.) . . . **CT** 164
Volta (V. A.) . . . . **CU** 173

Palazzo e Galleria di Capodimonte . . . . **BT** **M¹**

PIANTA D'INSIEME

0　　2 km

Murnau (D) . . . . 93 　F 3
Mürnieki (LV) . . . . 164 　C 1
Muro (F) . . . . 57 　F 3
Muro de Alcoy (E) . . . . 71 　F 4
Muro Lucano (I) . . . . . 106 　B 3
Murol (F) . . . . 51 　F 2
Murole (FIN) . . . . 136 　C 2
Muros (E) . . . . 58 　A 3
Murowana Goślina (PL) .187 　F 2
Mürren (CH) . . . . 96 　C 1
Murrhardt (D) . . . . 93 　D 1
Murska Sobota (SLO) . . 95 　F 4
Mursko Središče (HR) . . 95 　F 4
Murten (CH) . . . . 49 　F 3
Murter (HR) . . . . 103 　E 1
Murter (Otok) (HR) . . . 103 　E 1
Murtosa (P) . . . . 62 　B 3
Murtovaara (FIN) . . . . 129 　E 4
Murvica (HR) . . . . 103 　E 1
Murviel-lès-Béziers (F) . . 56 　A 2

Mürzsteg (A) . . . . 95 　E 3
Mürzzuschlag (A) . . . . . 95 　E 3
Müsa (LV) . . . . 165 　D 3
Musninkai (LT) . . . . . . 171 　D 4
Musselburgh (GB) . . . . . 31 　D 2
Mussidan (F) . . . . 50 　C 3
Mussomeli (I) . . . . 110 　C 3
Mussy-sur-Seine (F) . . . . 43 　F 4
Mustahamba (EST) . . . . 161 　D 2
Müstair (CH) . . . . 97 　F 1
Mustametsa (EST) . . . . 155 　D 3
Musteniai (LT) . . . . . . 177 　C 2
Mustion as (FIN) . . . . . 136 　C 4
Mustivere (EST) . . . . . . 154 　B 3
Mustjala (EST) . . . . 152 　B 3
Mustkalni (LV) . . . . . . 159 　D 3
Mustla (EST) . . . . 154 　B 4
Mustvee (EST) . . . . 155 　C 3
Muszyna (PL) . . . . 201 　C 3

Muszynka (PL) . . . . . . 201 　C 3
Muta (SLO) . . . . 95 　E 4
Mutala (FIN) . . . . 136 　C 2
Mutterstadt (D) . . . . . . 45 　D 4
Mutzschen (D) . . . . 89 　E 1
Muuga Harju (EST) . . . 149 　E 2
Muuga Lääne-Viru (EST) .151 　D 4
Muurame (FIN) . . . . . . 133 　F 4
Muurasjärvi (FIN) . . . . 133 　E 3
Muurla (FIN) . . . . 136 　C 4
Muurola (FIN) . . . . . . 128 　C 3
Muuruvesi (FIN) . . . . . 135 　E 3
Müüsleri (EST) . . . . . . 150 　C 4
Muxia (E) . . . . 58 　A 2
Muxía (E) . . . . 58 　A 2
Muzillac (F) . . . . 41 　D 4
Muzzana del Turgnano (I) . 98 　C 3
Myckelgensjö (S) . . . . . 132 　A 3
Myczkowskie
　(Jezioro) (PL) . . . . . 202 　E 3
Mykanów (PL) . . . . . . 195 　D 3

Mýki (GR) . . . . 207 　F 2
Mykines (DK) . . . . 126 　A 4
Mykolaïv (UA) . . . . 12 　C 2
Mykolaïv (UA) . . . . 13 　E 3
Mýkonos (GR) . . . . . . 219 　F 3
Mýkonos (Nisí) (GR) . . 219 　F 3
Myllykoski (FIN) . . . . . 137 　E 3
Myllykylä (FIN) . . . . . 133 　D 4
Myllymäki (FIN) . . . . . 133 　E 4
Mýloi (GR) . . . . 217 　F 3
Mylopótamos (GR) . . . 223 　D 3
Mynämäki (FIN) . . . . . 136 　B 3
Myre / Øksnes (N) . . . 124 　A 3
Myrhorod (UA) . . . . 13 　F 1
Mýrina (GR) . . . . 213 　F 1
Myronivka (UA) . . . . . . 13 　E 1
Myrsíni (GR) . . . . 222 　C 2
Myrskylä /
　Mörskom (FIN) . . . . 137 　D 3
Myrtiés (GR) . . . . 221 　E 4

Mýrtos (GR) . . . . 227 　E 3
Myrtou (CY) . . . . 231 　C 2
Myrviken (S) . . . . 131 　F 3
Mysen (N) . . . . 139 　E 3
Myślenice (PL) . . . . . . 201 　A 2
Myślibórz (PL) . . . . . . 186 　C 1
Mysłowice (PL) . . . . . . 195 　D 4
Myszków (PL) . . . . . . 195 　D 4
Myszyniec (PL) . . . . . . 184 　B 4
Mýtikas (GR) . . . . 211 　D 4
Mytilíni (GR) . . . . 215 　D 3
Mytilinioí (GR) . . . . . . 221 　E 2
Mytíšči (RUS) . . . . 7 　F 2

N

N. Agathoúpoli (GR) . . 206 　B 4
N. Alikarnassós (GR) . . 227 　D 2
N. Artáki (GR) . . . . . . 218 　C 1
N. Erásmio (GR) . . . . . 207 　F 2
N. Iraklitsa (GR) . . . . . 207 　F 2

N. Karváli (GR) . . . . . . 207 　E 2
N. Korito (SRB) . . . . . . 119 　E 2
N. Mákri (GR) . . . . . . 218 　C 2
N. Málgara (GR) . . . . . 206 　D 3
N. Marmarás (GR) . . . . 207 　D 4
N. Monastíri (GR) . . . . 212 　A 3
N. Moudaniá (GR) . . . . 206 　C 4
N. Péramos
　Atikí-Peireiás (GR) . . 218 　B 2
N. Péramos Kavála (GR) . 207 　E 3
N. Perivóli (GR) . . . . . 212 　B 2
N. Petrítsi (GR) . . . . . . 206 　C 1
N. Róda (GR) . . . . 207 　D 4
N. Rubeži (MNE) . . . . . 121 　D 2
N. Senkovac (HR) . . . . 112 　B 4
N. Síata (GR) . . . . 206 　C 4
N. Skióni (GR) . . . . . . 212 　C 1
N. Skopós (GR) . . . . . . 207 　D 2
N. Tríglia (GR) . . . . . . 206 　C 4
N. Zoí (GR) . . . . 205 　F 3

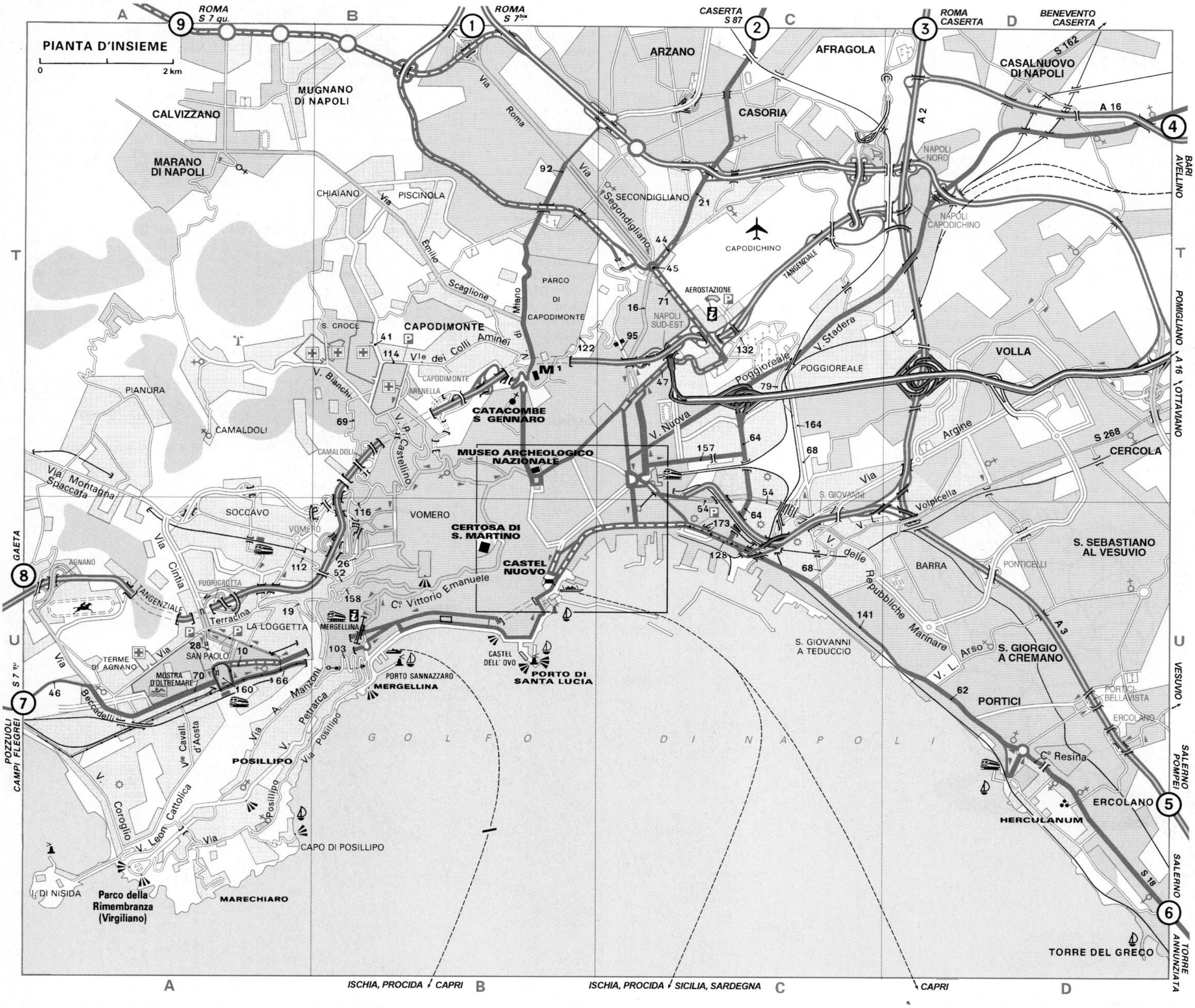

Naamijoki (FIN)	128	C 3
Naantali (FIN)	136	B 4
Naarajärvi (FIN)	133	F 4
Naarva (FIN)	135	F 3
Naas / An Nás (IRL)	25	E 1
Nabala (EST)	149	E 3
Nabburg (D)	89	E 4
Nabe (LV)	159	D 3
Načeradec (CZ)	90	B 3
Náchod (CZ)	91	D 2
Nadarzyn (PL)	190	B 3
Naddvik (N)	139	D 1
Nadela (N)	58	C 3
Nădlac (RO)	113	E 3
Nadróż (PL)	189	D 1
Nadur (M)	110	A 4
Nadvirna (UA)	12	C 2
Nærbø (N)	138	B 4
Nærøy (N)	131	D 2
Næstved (DK)	142	C 4
Näfels (CH)	93	D 4
Náfpaktos (GR)	217	E 4
Náfplio (GR)	217	F 3
Naggen (S)	132	A 4
Nagli (LV)	167	D 2
Nagłowice (PL)	195	F 3
Nagold (D)	45	F 3
Nagu / Nauvo (FIN)	136	B 4
Nagyatád (H)	112	B 3
Nagykálló (H)	12	C 3
Nagykanizsa (H)	112	A 3
Nagykőrös (H)	113	D 1
Naha (EST)	155	E 4
Nahe (D)	79	D 4
Nahodka (LV)	167	D 4
Naila (D)	89	D 2
Nailloux (F)	55	E 2
Nailsworth (GB)	35	E 1
Nairai (LT)	164	C 3
Nairn (GB)	27	F 3
Naisiai (LT)	163	F 4
Naiviai (LT)	171	E 1
Najac (F)	51	
Nájera (E)	60	C 4
Nakkila (FIN)	136	B 2
Nakło Opolskie (PL)	194	C 4
Nakło nad Notecią (PL)	188	B 1
Nákotne (LV)	163	F 2
Nakovo (SRB)	113	B 4
Nakskov (DK)	144	C 4
Nałęczów (PL)	197	D 2
Náljänkä (FIN)	129	C 4
Naltijärvi (FIN)	125	D 2
Namdalseid (N)	131	D 2
Namiki (LV)	163	D 1
Namišiai (LT)	165	D 3
Namsos (N)	131	E 1
Namsskogan (N)	131	E 1
Namur / Namen (B)	39	F 3
Namysłów (PL)	194	C 3
Nancy (F)	44	C 3
Nangis (F)	43	E 3
Nannestad (N)	139	E 3
Nant (F)	52	A 4
Nanterre (F)	43	D 2
Nantes (F)	46	B 2
Nanteuil-le-Haudouin (F)	43	D 2
Nantiat (F)	47	E 4
Nantua (F)	49	D 4
Nantwich (GB)	32	C 3
Náousa Imathía (GR)	205	F 3
Náousa Kikládes (GR)	219	F 4
Nápi (EST)	151	D 2
Napoli (I)	105	F 3
Naravere (EST)	153	C 2
Narberth / Arberth (GB)	34	B 1
Narbolia (I)	108	A 3
Narbonne (F)	55	F 3
Narbonne-Plage (F)	56	A 3
Narcao (I)	108	B 4
Nardo (I)	107	E 4
Narewka (PL)	191	F 1
Narila (FIN)	135	E 3
Narkaus (FIN)	129	D 3
Narni (I)	102	A 4
Naro (I)	110	C 3
Naro-Fominsk (RUS)	7	F 2
Narol (PL)	197	E 4
Närpes (FIN)	132	C 4
Narta (HR)	112	A 4
Nartháki (GR)	212	A 4
Naruszewo (PL)	189	F 2
Narva (EST)	151	F 3
Narvaišiai (LT)	162	C 4
Narva-Jõesuu (EST)	151	F 3
Narvik (N)	124	A 4
Narwiański Park Narodowy (PL)	191	E 1
Nås (S)	140	B 2
Näsåker (S)	132	A 3
Năsăud (RO)	13	D 3
Nasbinals (F)	51	F 3
Našice (HR)	112	C 4
Nasielsk (PL)	189	F 2
Našiūnai (LT)	171	F 4
Naso (I)	111	D 2
Nasrėnai (LT)	162	C 4
Nassau (D)	87	F 3
Nassereith (A)	93	F 4
Nässjo (S)	143	E 2
Nastola (FIN)	137	D 3
Nasva (EST)	152	B 4
Natalinci (SRB)	118	C 2
Natiškiai (LT)	165	D 4
Natkiškiai (LT)	168	C 3
Nattavaara (S)	128	A 3
Nättraby (S)	143	F 3
Naucelle (F)	51	F 4
Naudaskalns (LV)	161	E 4
Nauders (A)	97	F 1
Naudīte (LV)	163	F 2
Naudvaris Kauno (LT)	169	E 2
Naudvaris Šiaulių (LT)	169	E 2
Naudžiai (LT)	169	E 4
Naudžiūnai (LT)	176	D 2
Nauen (D)	85	D 2
Naujamiestis (LT)	170	C 2
Naujas Strūnaitis (LT)	172	C 4
Naujasis Daugėliškis (LT)	172	C 3
Naujasodis Kauno (LT)	170	C 4
Naujasodis Šiaulių (LT)	170	C 1
Naujasodis Utenos (LT)	171	E 3
Naujieji Bernatoniai (LT)	170	B 4
Naujienėlė I (LT)	175	F 3
Naujikai (LT)	171	D 1
Naujoji Akmenė (LT)	163	F 2
Naujoji Įpiltis (LT)	162	B 3
Naujoji Kirsna (LT)	175	F 3
Naujosios Kietaviškės (LT)	177	D 2
Naukšēni (LV)	159	F 1
Naul (IRL)	23	E 4
Nauļāni (LV)	167	F 2
Naumburg (D)	89	D 1
Naunhof (D)	89	E 1
Nausēdžiai (LT)	165	C 3
Nausėdė (LT)	170	C 2
Nausodis (LT)	162	B 4
Naustdal (N)	138	C 1
Nava (E)	59	F 2
Nava de la Asunción (E)	64	A 3
Nava del Rey (E)	64	A 3
Navacepeda de Tormes (E)	63	F 4
Navacerrada (E)	64	B 4
Navaconcejo (E)	69	F 1
Navahermosa (E)	70	A 2
Navahrudak (BY)	6	C 2
Navalcán (E)	69	F 1
Navalcarnero (E)	70	B 1
Navaleno (E)	64	C 2
Navalmanzano (E)	64	B 3
Navalmoral de la Mata (E)	69	F 1
Navalperal de Pinares (E)	64	A 4
Navaluenga (E)	64	A 4
Navalvillar de Pela (E)	69	F 3
Navamorcuende (E)	70	A 1
Navan / An Uaimh (IRL)	23	D 2
Navarredonda de Gredos (E)	63	F 4
Navarrenx (F)	54	B 2
Navarrés (E)	71	F 3
Navarrete (E)	60	C 4
Navàs (E)	66	C 2
Navas de Oro (E)	64	A 3
Navas de San Juan (E)	70	A 4
Navas del Madroño (E)	69	D 2
Navascués (E)	54	A 3
Navasfrias (E)	63	D 4
Navatalgordo (E)	64	A 4
Nave (I)	97	F 3
Nave Redonda (P)	74	B 2
Nävekvarn (S)	146	A 1
Navelli (I)	103	D 4
Naveros (E)	75	C 3
Navesti (EST)	154	B 3
Navi (EST)	161	D 1
Navia (E)	59	D 2
Navia de Suarna (E)	59	D 3
Navininkai (LT)	176	B 3

NICE

Map street index:

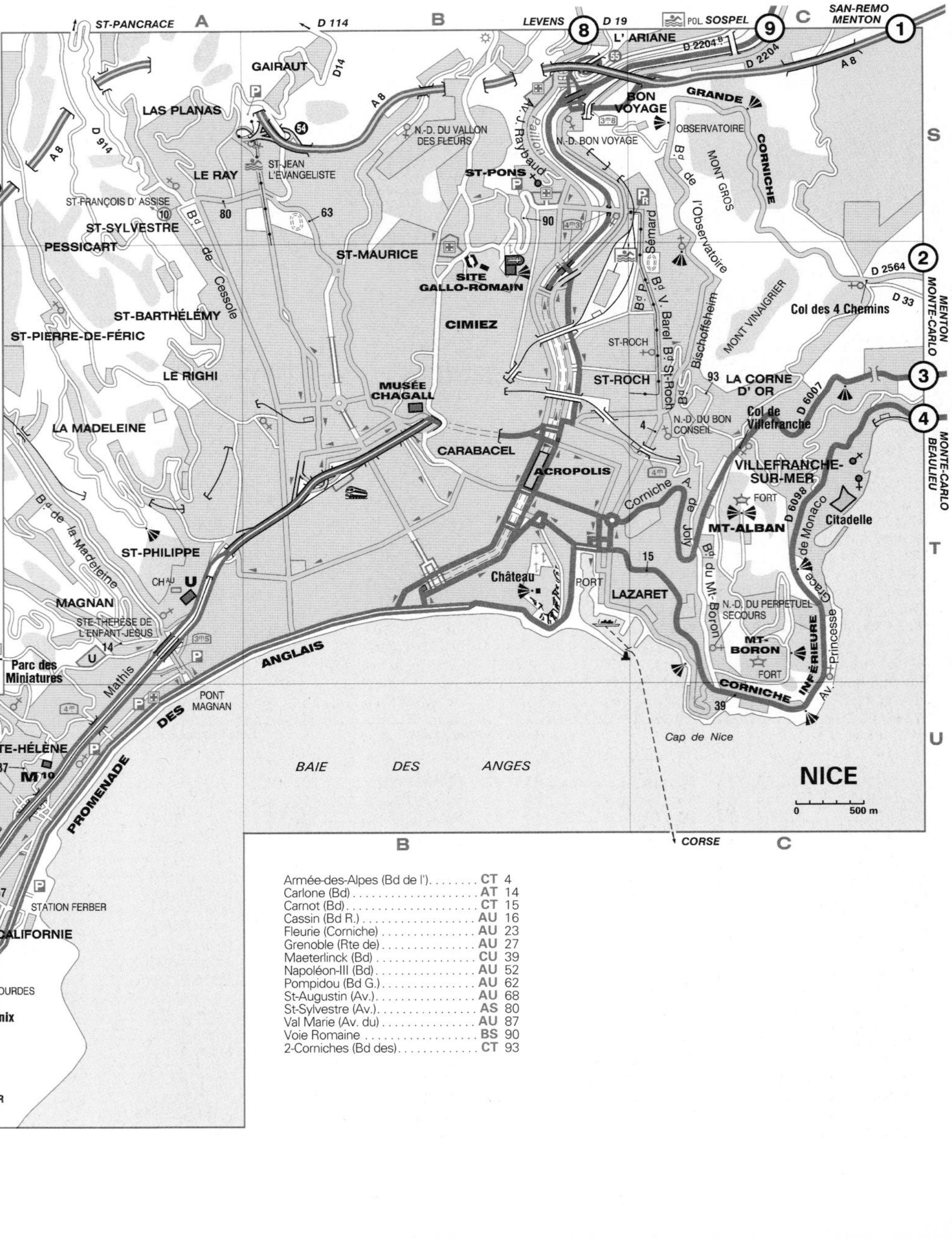

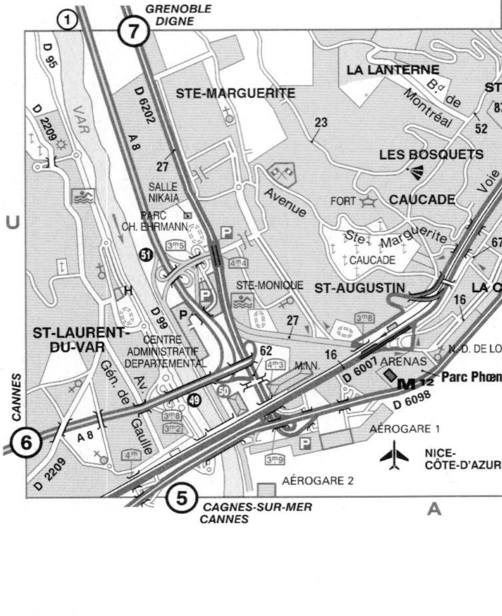

Armée-des-Alpes (Bd de l')	CT	4
Carlone (Bd)	AT	14
Carnot (Bd)	CT	15
Cassin (Bd R.)	AU	16
Fleurie (Rte de)	AU	23
Grenoble (Rte de)	CU	27
Maeterlinck (Bd)	CU	39
Napoléon-III (Bd)	AU	52
Pompidou (Bd G.)	AU	62
St-Augustin (Av.)	AU	68
St-Sylvestre (Av.)	AS	80
Val Marie (Av. du)	AU	87
Voie Romaine	BS	90
2-Corniches (Bd des)	CT	93

Map labels: ST-PANCRACE · D 114 · LEVENS · D 19 · SOSPEL · SAN-REMO MENTON · GAIRAUT · L'ARIANE · D 2204 · BON VOYAGE · GRANDE CORNICHE · LAS PLANAS · N.-D. DU VALLON DES FLEURS · OBSERVATOIRE · MONT GROS · LE RAY · ST-JEAN L'EVANGELISTE · ST-PONS · N.-D. BON VOYAGE · ST-FRANÇOIS D'ASSISE · ST-SYLVESTRE · ST-MAURICE · PESSICART · SITE GALLO-ROMAIN · Col des 4 Chemins · D 2564 · CIMIEZ · ST-ROCH · MONT VINAIGRIER · ST-BARTHÉLÉMY · ST-PIERRE-DE-FÉRIC · LA CORNE D'OR · LE RIGHI · MUSÉE CHAGALL · N.-D. DU BON CONSEIL · Col de Villefranche · LA MADELEINE · CARABACEL · VILLEFRANCHE-SUR-MER · MONTE-CARLO BEAULIEU · ACROPOLIS · MT-ALBAN · Citadelle · FORT · ST-PHILIPPE · Château · PORT · LAZARET · N.-D. DU PERPÉTUEL SECOURS · MAGNAN · STE-THÉRÈSE DE L'ENFANT-JÉSUS · MT-BORON · Parc des Miniatures · PROMENADE DES ANGLAIS · INFÉRIEURE CORNICHE · Cap de Nice · PONT MAGNAN · BAIE DES ANGES · CORSE · MENTON MONTE-CARLO · 0 — 500 m

Lower map: GRENOBLE DIGNE · STE-MARGUERITE · LA LANTERNE · STE-HÉLÈNE · VAR · LES BOSQUETS · CAUCADE · FORT · STATION FERBER · ST-LAURENT-DU-VAR · CENTRE ADMINISTRATIF DEPARTEMENTAL · STE-MONIQUE · ST-AUGUSTIN · LA CALIFORNIE · CANNES · N.-D. DE LOURDES · ARENAS · Parc Phœnix · AÉROGARE 1 · NICE-CÔTE-D'AZUR · AÉROGARE 2 · CAGNES-SUR-MER CANNES · SALLE NIKAIA · PARC CH. EHRMANN

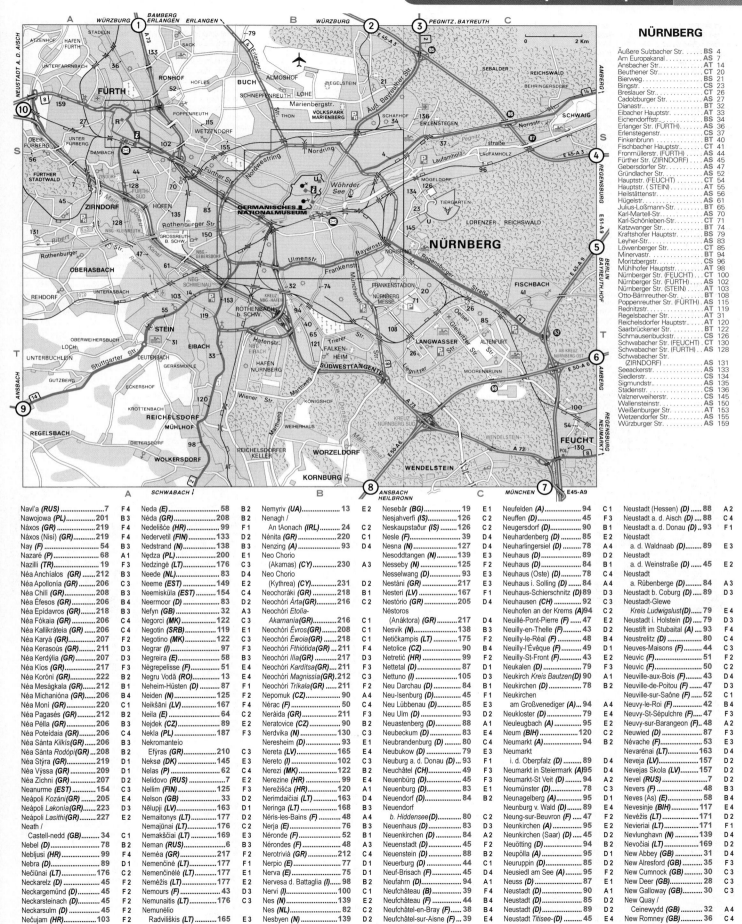

NÜRNBERG

Street	Grid	No.
Äußere Sulzbacher Str.	BS	4
Am Europakanal	AS	7
Ansbacher Str.	AT	14
Beuthener Str.	CT	20
Bierweg	BS	21
Bingstr.	CS	23
Breslauer Str.	CT	26
Cadolzburger Str.	AS	27
Dianastr.	BT	32
Eibacher Hauptstr.	AT	33
Eichendorffstr.	BS	34
Erlanger Str. (FÜRTH)	AS	36
Erlenstegenstr.	CS	37
Finkenbrunn	BT	40
Fischbacher Hauptstr.	CT	41
Fronmüllerstr. (FÜRTH)	AS	44
Fürther Str. (ZIRNDORF)	AS	45
Gebersdorfer Str.	AS	47
Gründlacher Str.	AS	52
Hauptstr. (FEUCHT)	CT	54
Hauptstr. (STEIN)	AT	55
Heilstättenstr.	AS	56
Hügelstr.	AS	61
Julius-Loßmann-Str.	BT	65
Karl-Martell-Str.	AT	70
Karl-Schönleben-Str.	CT	71
Katzwanger Str.	BT	74
Kraftshofer Hauptstr.	BS	79
Leyher-Str.	AS	83
Löwenberger Str.	CT	85
Minervastr.	BT	94
Moritzbergstr.	CS	96
Mühlhofer Hauptstr.	AT	98
Nürnberger Str. (FEUCHT)	CT	100
Nürnberger Str. (FÜRTH)	AS	102
Nürnberger Str. (STEIN)	AT	103
Otto-Bärnreuther-Str.	BT	108
Poppenreuther Str. (FÜRTH)	AS	115
Rednitzstr.	AT	119
Regelsbacher Str.	AT	31
Reichelsdorfer Hauptstr.	AT	120
Saarbrückener Str.	BT	122
Schmausenbuckstr.	CS	126
Schwabacher Str. (FEUCHT)	CT	130
Schwabacher Str. (FÜRTH)	AS	128
Schwabacher Str. (ZIRNDORF)	AS	131
Seeackerstr.	CS	133
Siedlerstr.	CS	134
Sigmundstr.	CS	135
Stadenstr.	CS	136
Valznerweiherstr.	CS	145
Wallensteinstr.	AS	150
Weißenburger Str.	AT	153
Wetzendorfer Str.	AS	155
Würzburger Str.	AS	159

Navl'a (RUS) 7 F4
Nawojowa (PL) 201 B3
Náxos (GR) 219 F4
Náxos (Nisí) (GR) 219 F4
Nay (F) 54 B3
Nazaré (P) 68 A4
Nazilli (TR) 19 F3
Néa Anchíalos (GR) 212 B3
Néa Apollonía (GR) 206 C3
Néa Chilí (GR) 208 B3
Néa Éfesos (GR) 206 B4
Néa Epídavros (GR) 218 B3
Néa Fókaia (GR) 206 C4
Néa Kallikráteia (GR) 206 C4
Néa Karyá (GR) 207 F2
Néa Kerasoús (GR) 211 F3
Néa Kerdília (GR) 207 D3
Néa Kíos (GR) 217 F3
Néa Koróni (GR) 222 B2
Néa Meságkala (GR) 212 B1
Néa Michanióna (GR) 206 B4
Néa Moní (GR) 220 C1
Néa Pagasés (GR) 212 B2
Néa Pélla (GR) 206 B3
Néa Poteídaia (GR) 206 C4
Néa Sánta Kilkís (GR) 206 B3
Néa Sánta Rodópi (GR) 208 C3
Néa Stýra (GR) 219 D1
Néa Výssa (GR) 209 D1
Néa Zíchni (GR) 207 D2
Neanurme (EST) 154 C3
Neápoli Kozáni (GR) 205 E4
Neápoli Lakonía (GR) 223 E2
Neápoli Lasíthi (GR) 227 E2
Neath / Castell-nedd (GB) 34 C1
Nebel (D) 78 B2
Nebljusi (HR) 99 F4
Nebra (D) 89 C2
Nečiūnai (LT) 176 D1
Neckarelz (D) 45 F2
Neckargemünd (D) 45 F2
Neckarsteinach (D) 45 F2
Neckarsulm (D) 45 F2
Nečujam (HR) 103 F2

Neda (E) 58 B2
Néda (GR) 208 B2
Nedelišće (HR) 99 F1
Nedervetil (FIN) 133 D2
Nedstrand (N) 138 B3
Nędza (PL) 200 E1
Nedzingė (LT) 176 D2
Neede (NL) 83 D4
Neeme (EST) 149 E2
Neemisküla (EST) 154 C4
Neermoor (D) 83 D2
Nefyn (GB) 32 A3
Negorci (MK) 122 C3
Negotin (SRB) 119 E1
Negotino (MK) 122 C3
Negrar (I) 97 F3
Negreira (E) 58 B3
Nègrepelisse (F) 51 E4
Negru Vodă (RO) 13 E4
Neheim-Hüsten (D) 87 F1
Neiden (N) 125 F2
Neikšäni (LV) 167 F2
Neila (E) 64 C2
Nejdek (CZ) 89 E2
Nekla (PL) 187 F3
Nekromanteío Efýras (GR) 210 C3
Neksø (DK) 145 D3
Nelas (P) 62 C4
Nelidovo (RUS) 7 E2
Nellim (FIN) 125 F3
Nelson (GB) 33 D2
Nėlupji (LV) 163 D1
Nemaitonys (LT) 177 D2
Nemajūnai (LT) 176 C2
Nemakščiai (LT) 169 E3
Neman (RUS) 6 C2
Neméa (GR) 217 D1
Nemenčinė (LT) 177 F1
Nemenčinėlė (LT) 177 E1
Nemėžis (LT) 177 E2
Nemours (F) 43 D3
Nemunaitis (LT) 176 C2
Nemunėlio Radviliškis (LT) 165 E3

Nemyriv (UA) 13 E2
Nenagh / An tAonach (IRL) 24 C2
Nénita (GR) 220 C1
Nenzing (A) 93 D4
Neo Chorio (Akamas) (CY) 230 A3
Neo Chorio (Kythrea) (CY) 231 D2
Neochoráki (GR) 218 B1
Neochóri Árta (GR) 216 C2
Neochóri Etolía-Akarnanía (GR) 216 C1
Neochóri Évros (GR) 208 C1
Neochóri Éwoia (GR) 218 C1
Neochóri Fthiótida (GR) 211 F4
Neochóri Ilia (GR) 217 D3
Neochóri Kardítsa (GR) 211 F3
Neochóri Magnissía (GR) 212 B1
Neochóri Trikala (GR) 211 F2
Nepomuk (CZ) 90 A4
Nérac (F) 50 C2
Neráida (GR) 211 F3
Neratovice (CZ) 90 B2
Nerdvika (N) 130 C2
Neresheim (D) 93 E1
Nereta (LV) 165 E2
Nereto (I) 102 C3
Nerezi (MK) 122 B2
Nerežišća (HR) 120 A1
Nerimdaičiai (LT) 163 D4
Néris-les-Bains (F) 48 A4
Nerja (E) 76 B3
Néronde (F) 52 B1
Nérondes (F) 48 A3
Nerotriviá (GR) 212 C4
Nerpio (E) 77 D1
Nerva (E) 75 D1
Nervesa d. Battaglia (I) 98 B2
Nervi (I) 100 C2
Nes (N) 139 E2
Nes (NL) 82 C2
Nesbyen (N) 139 D2

Nesebăr (BG) 19 E1
Nesjahverfi (IS) 126 C2
Neskaupstaður (IS) 126 C2
Nesle (F) 39 D4
Nesna (N) 127 D4
Nesoddtangen (N) 139 E3
Nesseby (N) 125 F2
Nesselwang (D) 93 E3
Nestáni (GR) 217 E3
Nesteri (LV) 167 F1
Nestório (GR) 205 D4
Néstoros (Anáktora) (GR) 217 D4
Nesvik (N) 138 B3
Netičkampis (LT) 175 F2
Netolice (CZ) 90 B4
Netretić (HR) 99 F2
Nettetal (D) 87 D1
Nettuno (I) 105 D3
Neu Darchau (D) 84 B1
Neu-Isenburg (D) 45 F1
Neu Lübbenau (D) 85 E3
Neu Ulm (D) 93 D2
Neuastenberg (D) 88 A1
Neubeckum (D) 84 E4
Neubrandenburg (D) 80 C4
Neubukow (D) 79 E2
Neuburg a. d. Donau (D) 93 F1
Neuburg (D) 89 F3
Neuburg (D) 83 E1
Neuburg (D) 84 B2
Neuendorf b. Hiddensee (D) 80 C2
Neuenhaus (D) 83 D3
Neuenkirchen (D) 85 A2
Neuenstadt (D) 45 F2
Neuenstein (D) 88 B2
Neuerburg (D) 44 C1
Neuf-Brisach (F) 45 D4
Neufahrn (D) 94 A1
Neufchâteau (B) 39 F4
Neufchâteau (F) 44 B4
Neufchâtel-en-Bray (F) 38 B4
Neufchâtel-sur-Aisne (F) 39 E4

Neufelden (A) 94 C1
Neuffen (D) 45 F3
Neugersdorf (D) 90 B1
Neuhardenberg (D) 85 E2
Neuhaus (D) 89 D2
Neuhaus (D) 84 B1
Neuhaus (Oste) (D) 78 C4
Neuhaus i. Solling (D) 84 A4
Neuhaus-Schierschnitz (D) 89 D3
Neuhausen (CH) 92 C3
Neuhofen an der Krems (A) 94 C2
Neuillé-Pont-Pierre (F) 47 D2
Neuilly-en-Thelle (F) 43 D2
Neuilly-le-Réal (F) 48 B4
Neuilly-l'Évêque (F) 49 F2
Neuilly-St-Front (F) 43 E2
Neukalen (D) 79 F3
Neukirch Kreis Bautzen (D) 90 A1
Neukirchen (D) 78 B2
Neukirchen am Großvenediger (A) 94 A4
Neukloster (D) 79 E4
Neuleugbach (A) 95 D1
Neum (BIH) 120 C2
Neumarkt (A) 94 B2
Neumarkt i. d. Oberpfalz (D) 89 D4
Neumarkt in Steiermark (A) 95 D4
Neumarkt-St Veit (D) 94 A2
Neumünster (D) 78 C3
Neunagelberg (A) 95 D1
Neunburg v. Wald (D) 89 E4
Neundorf (D) 84 B2
Neung-sur-Beuvron (F) 47 D3
Neunkirchen (A) 95 E2
Neunkirchen (Saar) (D) 44 C2
Neunkirchen (D) 89 D2
Neupölla (D) 95 D1
Neuruppin (D) 80 B3
Neusiedl am See (A) 95 E2
Neuss (D) 87 E1
Neustadt (D) 90 A1
Neustadt (D) 85 D2
Neustadt (D) 89 D2
Neustadt Titisee- (D) 45 E4

Neustadt (Hessen) (D) 88 A2
Neustadt a. d. Aisch (D) 88 C4
Neustadt a. d. Donau (D) 93 F1
Neustadt a. d. Waldnaab (D) 89 E3
Neustadt a. d. Weinstraße (D) 45 E2
Neustadt a. Rübenberge (D) 84 A3
Neustadt b. Coburg (D) 89 D3
Neustadt-Glewe Kreis Ludwigslust (D) 79 E4
Neustadt i. Holstein (D) 79 D3
Neustrelitz (D) 80 C4
Neuves-Maisons (F) 44 C3
Neuvic (F) 51 F2
Neuvic (F) 50 C2
Neuville-aux-Bois (F) 43 D4
Neuville-de-Poitou (F) 47 D3
Neuville-sur-Saône (F) 52 C1
Neuvy-le-Roi (F) 42 B4
Neuvy-St-Sépulchre (F) 47 F3
Neuvy-sur-Barangeon (F) 48 A2
Neuwied (D) 87 F3
Névache (F) 53 E3
Nevarénai (LT) 163 D2
Neveja (LV) 157 D2
Nevejas Skola (LV) 157 D2
Nevel (RUS) 7 D2
Nevers (F) 48 B3
Neves (As) (E) 58 B4
Nevesinje (BIH) 117 E2
Nevėžis (LT) 171 D2
Nevieriai (LT) 171 F1
Nevlunghavn (N) 139 D2
Nevočlai (LT) 169 D2
New Abbey (GB) 31 D4
New Alresford (GB) 35 F3
New Cumnock (GB) 30 C3
New Deer (GB) 28 C3
New Galloway (GB) 30 C3
New Quay / Ceinewydd (GB) 32 A4
New Romney (GB) 36 C4

New Ross / Ros Mhic Thriúin (IRL)... 25 E 3
Newark-on-Trent (GB)....... 33 E 3
Newbiggin-by-the-Sea (GB)31 F 3
Newborough (GB)............ 32 A 3
Newbridge / An Droichead Nua (IRL) 25 E 1
Newburgh (D)............... 28 C 4
Newburgh (GB).............. 31 D 1
Newbury (GB)............... 35 F 2
Newcastle (GB)............. 23 F 3
Newcastle Emlyn / Castell Newydd Emlyn (GB).... 34 C 1
Newcastle-under-Lyme (GB).......... 32 C 3
Newcastle West / An Caisleán Nua (IRL)... 24 B 2
Newhaven (GB).............. 36 C 4
Newmarket (GB)............. 36 C 2
Newmarket (IRL)............ 24 B 3
Newmarket on Fergus (IRL)24 C 2
Newnham (GB).............. 35 E 1
Newport (GB)............... 34 B 1
Newport (GB)............... 32 C 4
Newport (GB)............... 35 F 3
Newport (IRL).............. 24 C 2
Newport / Baile Uí Fhiacháin (IRL) 22 B 3
Newport / Casnewydd (GB)35 D 2
Newport-on-Tay (GB)....... 31 D 1
Newport Pagnell (GB)....... 36 B 3
Newquay (GB).............. 34 B 3
Newry (GB)................. 23 E 3
Newton Abbot (GB)......... 35 D 3
Newton-Aycliffe (GB)....... 31 F 4
Newton Ferrers (GB)........ 34 C 4
Newton Stewart (GB)....... 30 C 4
Newtonmore (GB).......... 27 E 4
Newtown (GB)............. 35 E 1
Newtown / Drenewydd (GB).. 32 B 4
Newtown St Boswells (GB)31 E 1
Newtownabbey (GB)........ 23 F 2
Newtownards (GB)......... 23 F 2
Newtownbutler (GB)....... 23 D 3
Newtownhamilton (GB)..... 23 E 3
Newtownstewart (GB)...... 23 D 2
Nexon (F)................. 51 D 1
Neyland (GB).............. 34 B 1
Niáta (GR)................ 217 F 4
Niauduva (LT)............. 170 C 1
Nibe (DK)................. 142 B 3
Nīca (LV)................. 162 B 3
Nicastro (I).............. 109 E 2
Nice (F).................. 57 F 2
Nīcgale (LV).............. 166 C 4
Nīcgale (Neicgaļs) (LV)... 166 C 4
Nickelsdorf (A)........... 95 F 2
Nicolosi (I).............. 111 E 3
Nicosia (CY).............. 231 C 2
Nicosia (I)............... 111 D 2
Nicotera (I).............. 111 F 1
Nida (LV)................. 162 B 4
Nidderau (D).............. 88 A 3
Nideggen (D)............. 87 E 2
Nidzica (PL).............. 183 C 2
Niebla (E)................ 75 D 2
Nieborów (PL)............. 189 E 3
Niebüll (D)............... 78 B 2
Niebylec (PL)............. 202 D 2
Niechanowo (PL).......... 188 B 2
Niechlów (PL)............. 187 E 4
Niechmirów (PL)........... 194 C 2
Niechorze (PL)............ 180 C 2
Niederaltteich (D)......... 94 B 2
Niederaula (D)............ 88 B 2
Niederbronn-les-Bains (F). 45 E 3
Niederelsungen (D)....... 88 A 1
Niederjossa (D)........... 88 B 2
Niederkrüchten (D)....... 87 D 1
Niederstetten (D)......... 88 C 4
Niederstotzingen (D)...... 93 E 2
Niedras (LV).............. 162 C 2
Niedrzwica Duża (PL)..... 197 D 3
Niedzica (PL)............. 201 B 3
Niedźwiada (PL)........... 191 E 4
Niedźwiedź Małopolskie(PL). 201 A 3
Niedźwiedzia (Jaskinia) (PL). 193 E 4
Niegocin (Jezioro) (PL).. 184 C 2
Niegosławice Lubuskie(PL).. 187 D 4
Niegowa (PL)............. 195 E 3

Niegripp (D)............... 84 C 3
Nielisz (PL).............. 197 E 3
Niemce (PL)............... 197 D 1
Niemcza (PL).............. 193 E 3
Niemegk (D)............... 85 D 3
Niemisel (S).............. 128 B 4
Niemodlin (PL)............ 194 B 3
Nienadówka (PL).......... 197 D 4
Nienburg (D).............. 83 F 3
Nienburg (D).............. 84 C 4
Niepołomice (PL).......... 201 B 2
Nieporęt (PL)............. 190 B 2
Nierstein (D)............. 45 C 1
Niesky (D)................ 85 F 4
Niestronno (PL)........... 188 B 2
Nieszawa (PL)............. 189 D 1
Nieul (F)................. 51 D 1
Nieuweschans (NL)........ 83 D 2
Nieuwpoort-Bad (B)....... 37 B 4
Niforaiika (GR)........... 217 D 1
Nīgrande (LV)............. 163 D 2
Nigrita (GR).............. 206 C 2
Nigula (EST).............. 148 C 4
Niidu (EST)............... 153 C 3
Nilinsalo (FIN)........... 136 B 2
Nijar (E)................. 77 D 3
Nijkerk (NL).............. 82 B 4
Nijmegen (NL)............. 82 C 4
Nijverdal (NL)............ 82 C 3
Níkaia (GR)............... 212 B 2
Niki (GR)................. 205 E 2
Nikiá (GR)................ 225 F 2
Nikiföros (GR)............ 207 E 2
Nikisiani (GR)............ 207 E 2
Nikitari (CY)............. 230 B 3
Nikitas (CY).............. 230 B 3
Nikitas (GR).............. 207 D 4
Nikkaluokta (S)........... 128 A 2
Nikolaíika (GR)........... 217 E 1
Nikopol (BG).............. 13 D 4
Nikopói (GR).............. 211 D 3
Nikšić (MNE).............. 121 D 2
Nilivaara (S)............. 128 B 2
Nilsiä (FIN).............. 135 E 3
Nîmes (F)................. 56 B 1
Nímos (Nisí) (GR)......... 228 B 1
Nin (HR).................. 99 F 4
Nina (EST)................ 155 E 3
Ninove (B)................ 39 E 2
Niort (F)................. 46 C 4
Nípsa (GR)................ 208 C 2
Nirza (Nierza) (LV)....... 167 F 3
Niš (SRB)................. 119 E 3
Nisa (F).................. 68 C 2
Nisáki (GR)............... 210 B 1
Niscemi (I)............... 111 D 4
Niška Banja (SRB)......... 119 E 3
Nisko (PL)................ 197 D 4
Nissilä (FIN)............. 133 F 2
Nísyros (Nisí) (GR)....... 225 F 2
Nītaure (LV).............. 159 E 4
Niton (GB)................ 35 F 3
Nitra (SK)................ 12 A 3
Nitry (F)................. 43 F 4
Nittedal (N).............. 139 E 3
Nittenau (D).............. 89 E 4
Nittendorf (D)............ 94 A 1
Nivala (FIN).............. 133 E 2
Nivelles (B).............. 39 E 2
Niwiska Podkarpackie(PL).. 196 C 4
Nīzere (LV)............... 165 D 2
Niżyn (UA)................ 13 F 1
Nizza Monferrato (I)...... 100 C 2
Njasviž (BY).............. 7 D 4
Njivice (HR).............. 99 E 3
Njurundabommen (S)....... 132 A 4
Noailles (F).............. 43 D 1
Noáin (E)................. 54 A 3
Noblejas (E).............. 70 C 1
Nocera Inferiore (I)...... 105 F 3
Nocera Terinese (I)....... 109 E 2
Nocera Umbra (I).......... 102 B 3
Noceto (I)................ 97 F 4
Noci (I).................. 107 D 3
Nociūnai (LT)............. 170 C 3
Nodeland (N).............. 142 A 1
Nœux-les-Mines (F)........ 38 C 3
Nogale (LV)............... 157 E 3
Nogara (I)................ 98 A 4
Nogaro (F)................ 54 C 2
Nogent (F)................ 43 B 4
Nogent-le-Roi (F)......... 42 C 3
Nogent-le-Rotrou (F)...... 42 B 3
Nogent-sur-Seine (F)...... 43 E 3
Nõgiaru (EST)............. 155 D 4

Noginsk (RUS)............. 7 F 2
Nogueira de Ramuín (E)... 58 C 4
Noguera (E)............... 71 E 1
Nohfelden (D)............. 45 D 2
Noia (E).................. 58 A 3
Noirétable (F)............ 52 A 1
Noirmoutier-en-l'Ile (F).. 46 A 3
Noja (E).................. 60 D 3
Nokia (FIN)............... 136 C 2
Nola (I).................. 105 F 3
Nolay (F)................. 48 C 2
Noli (I).................. 100 C 2
Nomeny (F)................ 44 C 3
Nomexy (F)................ 44 C 3
Nómia (GR)................ 223 D 2
Nömmküla (EST)............ 153 A 2
Nonancourt (F)............ 42 C 2
Nonant-le-Pin (F)......... 42 B 2
Nonaspe (E)............... 66 A 3
None (I).................. 53
Nonio (I)................. 96 C 3
Nontron (F)............... 51 D 2
Nonza (F)................. 57 F 2
Nõo (EST)................. 154 C 4
Noordwijk aan Zee (NL)... 82 A 4
Noormarkku (FIN).......... 136 C 2
Nora (S).................. 140 B 4
Noragéliai (LT)........... 176 C 3
Noras (LV)................ 165 C 3
Norberg (S)............... 140 C 3
Norcia (I)................ 102 C 3
Nord Edewecht (D)......... 83 E 2
Nord-Lenangen (N)......... 124 C 2
Nordborg (DK)............. 142 B 4
Nordby (DK)............... 142 C 3
Nordby (DK)............... 142 A 4
Norddeich (D)............. 78 A 4
Nordeide (N).............. 138 C 1
Norden (D)................ 78 A 4
Nordenau (D).............. 88 A 1
Nordenham (D)............. 83 E 1
Norderney (D)............. 78 A 4
Norderstedt (D)........... 79 D 4
Nordfjordeid (N).......... 130 A 4
Nordfold (N).............. 127 E 2
Nordhalben (D)............ 89 D 2
Nordhausen (D)............ 84 B 4
Nordhorn (D).............. 83 D 3
Nordingrå (S)............. 132 B 3
Nordkjosbotn (N).......... 124 B 3
Nordli (N)................ 131 F 2
Nördlingen (D)............ 93 E 1
Nordmaling (S)............ 132 B 3
Nordmark (S).............. 140 B 3
Nordseter (N)............. 139 E 1
Norðurfjörður (IS)........ 126 A 1
Nore (N).................. 139 D 2
Noreikiai (LT)............ 164 C 1
Noreikiškés (LT).......... 176 C 1
Noreišiai (LT)............ 169 E 2
Noresund (N).............. 139 C 2
Norg (NL)................. 82 C 2
Norgélai Kauno(LT)........ 169 F 3
Norgélai Panevėžio(LT).... 164 C 3
Norgeliškés (LT).......... 176 C 3
Norheimsund (N)........... 138 C 2
Noriai (LT)............... 165 C 1
Noriūnai (LT)............. 171 E 1
Norkiškė (LT)............. 169 D 3
Norra Bergnäs (S)......... 127 E 3
Norra Råda (S)............ 140 A 3
Norråker (S).............. 132 A 4
Norrby (S)................ 132 B 1
Nørre Åby (DK)............ 142 B 4
Nørre Alslev (DK)......... 144 C 3
Nørre Nebel (DK).......... 142 A 4
Nørre Snede (DK).......... 142 B 3
Nørre Vorupør (DK)........ 142 A 2
Norrent-Fontes (F)........ 38 C 3
Norrköping (S)............ 143 F 1
Norrnäs (FIN)............. 132 C 4
Norrsunda (S)............. 141 D 3
Norrsundet (S)............ 140 C 2
Norrtälje (S)............. 141 D 3
Norrviken (S)............. 143 D 3
Norsjö (S)................ 132 B 1
Nor-sur-Erdre (F)......... 46 B 2
Nörten-Hardenberg (D)..... 84 A 4
North Berwick (GB)........ 31 E 1
North Walsham (GB)........ 37 D 1
Northallerton (GB)........ 33 C 2
Northam (GB).............. 34 C 2
Northampton (GB).......... 36 B 2
Northeim (D).............. 84 A 4
Northleach (GB)........... 35 F 1
Northwich (GB)............ 32 C 3
Norton (GB)............... 33 E 1

Nortorf (D)............... 78 C 3
Norwich (GB).............. 37 D 1
Nosénai (LT).............. 171 E 3
Nosivka (UA).............. 13 F 1
Nossebro (S).............. 143 D 1
Nossen (D)................ 89 F 1
Noteć (D)................. 188 B 2
Notecka (Puszcza) (PL)..187 D 1
Nótia (GR)................ 206 A 2
Noto (I).................. 111 E 4
Notodden (N).............. 139 D 3
Notre-Dame-de-Bellecombe (F)... 53 E 1
Nottingham (GB)........... 33 E 3
Nouan-le-Fuzelier (F)..... 47 F 2
Nõuni (EST)............... 154 A 2
Nousiainen (FIN).......... 136 B 3
Nouvion-en-Ponthieu (F)...38 B 3
Nouzonville (F)........... 39 F 4
Nõva Jõgeva(EST).......... 155 D 3
Nõva Lääne(EST)........... 148 C 3
Nova Breznica (MK)........ 122 A 3
Nová Bystřice (CZ)........ 90 C 4
Nova Crnja (SRB).......... 113 E 3
Nova Gorica (SLO)......... 98 C 2
Nova Gradiška (HR)........ 115 E 3
Nova Kachovka (UA)........ 13 F 2
Nova Levante / Welschnofen (I)... 98 A 1
Nová Paka (CZ)............ 90 C 2
Nova Pazova (SRB)......... 118 B 1
Nová Role (CZ)............ 89 E 2
Nova Siri Marina (I)...... 107 D 4
Nova Topola (BIH)......... 115 E 4
Nova Varoš (SRB).......... 118 B 3
Nova Vas (SLO)............ 99 D 2
Nova Zagora (BG).......... 19 D 1
Novaci (MK)............... 122 B 4
Novaci (SRB).............. 118 B 2
Novadnieki (LV)........... 163 E 2
Novafeltria (I)........... 102 A 2
Novales (E)............... 66 A 2
Novalija (HR)............. 99 E 4
Novara (I)................ 97 D 3
Novara di Sicilia (I)..... 111 E 2
Nové Město na Moravě (CZ)... 91 D 3
Nové Město nad Metují (CZ).. 91 D 2
Nové Město nad Váhom (SK)... 12 A 2
Nové Zámky (SK)........... 12 A 3
Novelda (E)............... 71 F 4
Novellara (I)............. 97 F 4
Noventa Vicentina (I)..... 98 A 3
Noves (F)................. 56 C 1
Novgorod (RUS)............ 7 F 4
Novhorod-Sivers'kyj (UA)..7 F 4
Novi Bečej (SRB).......... 113 E 4
Novi di Modena (I)........ 97 F 4
Novi Dojran (MK).......... 122 C 3
Novi Grad Brčko (BIH)..... 117 E 1
Novi Grad / Bosanski Novi (BIH)... 115 D 4
Novi Karlovci (SRB)....... 118 B 1
Novi Kneževac (SRB)....... 113 E 3
Novi Ligure (I)........... 100 C 1
Novi Marof (HR)........... 99 F 1
Novi Pazar (BG)........... 13 E 4
Novi Pazar (SRB).......... 118 C 4
Novi Sad (SRB)............ 113 E 4
Novi Šeher (BIH).......... 117 E 2
Novi Slankamen (SRB)...... 113 E 4
Novi Travnik (BIH)........ 117 E 3
Novi Vinodolski (HR)...... 99 E 3
Novigrad Poreč(HR)........ 98 C 3
Novigrad Zadar(HR)........ 116 B 3
Novigrad Podravski (HR).. 112 A 4
Novion-Porcien (F)........ 39 F 4
Novo Brdo (SRB)........... 119 D 4
Novo mesto (SLO).......... 99 E 2
Novo Miloševo (SRB)....... 113 E 3
Novo Selo (BIH)........... 115 E 4
Novo Zvečevo (HR)......... 115 E 4
Novohrad-Volyns'kyj (UA). 13 D 1
Novomyrhorod (UA)......... 13 F 2
Novoselycja (UA).......... 13 D 2
Novoukraïnka (UA)......... 13 F 2
Novovolyns'k (UA)......... 12 C 1
Novozybkov (RUS).......... 7 E 4
Novska (HR)............... 115 E 3
Nový Bor (CZ)............. 90 B 2
Nový Bydžov (CZ).......... 90 C 2
Nový Jičín (CZ)........... 91 F 3
Novyj Buh (UA)............ 13 F 2
Nowa Brzeźnica (PL)...... 195 D 2

Nowa Dęba (PL)............ 196 C 4
Nowa Huta (PL)............ 201 A 2
Nowa Karczma (PL)......... 182 C 2
Nowa Morawa (PL).......... 193 E 4
Nowa Pasłęka (PL)......... 183 C 1
Nowa Ruda (PL)............ 193 E 4
Nowa Sarzyna (PL)......... 197 D 4
Nowa Słupia (PL).......... 196 B 4
Nowa Sól (PL)............. 187 D 4
Nowa Sucha (PL)........... 189 F 3
Nowa Wieś Ełcka (PL)..... 185 D 3
Nowa Wieś Lęborska (PL)182 B 1
Nowa Wieś Wielka (PL).. 188 B 1
Nowe (PL)................. 182 C 3
Nowe Brzesko (PL)......... 201 B 1
Nowe Miasteczko (PL)...... 187 D 4
Nowe Miasto (PL).......... 189 F 2
Nowe Miasto Lubawskie (PL)... 183 E 4
Nowe Miasto nad Pilicą (PL)... 189 F 4
Nowe Miasto nad Wartą (PL)... 187 F 3
Nowe Ostrowy (PL)......... 189 D 3
Nowe Skalmierzyce (PL). 188 B 4
Nowe Warpno (PL).......... 180 B 3
Nowinka (PL).............. 185 E 2
Nowogard (PL)............. 180 C 3
Nowogród (PL)............. 184 C 3
Nowogród Bobrzański (PL)... 186 C 4
Nowogrodziec (PL)......... 192 C 2
Nowosolna (PL)............ 189 E 4
Nowy Bieruń (PL).......... 200 F 2
Nowy Duninów (PL)......... 189 E 3
Nowy Dwór Gdański (PL) 183 D 2
Nowy Dwór Mazowiecki (PL)... 189 F 2
Nowy Kawęczyn (PL)........ 189 F 4
Nowy Korczyn (PL)......... 196 B 4
Nowy Sącz (PL)............ 201 B 3
Nowy Staw (PL)............ 183 D 2
Nowy Targ (PL)............ 201 A 3
Nowy Tomyśl (PL).......... 187 D 3
Nowy Waliszów (PL)........ 193 E 4
Nowy Wiśnicz (PL)......... 201 B 2
Nowy Żmigród (PL)......... 202 D 3
Noyant (F)................ 47 D 2
Noyers (F)................ 43 F 4
Noyers-sur-Jabron (F)..... 53 D 4
Noyon (F)................. 39 D 4
Nozay (F)................. 41 F 4
Nozdrzec (PL)............. 202 E 2
Nueva (E)................. 59 F 2
Nueva Carteya (E)......... 76 A 1
Nuévalos (E).............. 65 E 3
Nuevo Baztán (E).......... 70 C 1
Nugariai (LT)............. 162 F 2
Nuijamaa (FIN)............ 137 F 3
Nuits-St-Georges (F)...... 49 D 2
Nukši (LV)................ 167 F 3
Nules (E)................. 72 A 2
Nulvi (I)................. 108 A 1
Numana (I)................ 102 C 2
Numancia (E).............. 65 D 2
Nummela (FIN)............. 136 C 4
Nummi (FIN)............... 136 C 4
Nummijärvi (FIN).......... 133 E 4
Numuri (LV)............... 159 F 1
Nuneaton (GB)............. 33 D 4
Nunnanen (FIN)............ 125 E 4
Nunspeet (NL)............. 82 C 3
Nuorgam (FIN)............. 125 E 2
Nuoro (I)................. 108 B 2
Nuoro (I)................. 108 B 2
Nuotekai (LT)............. 171 C 1
Nüpli (EST)............... 160 C 1
Nupronys (LT)............. 177 D 3
Nur (PL).................. 191 D 2
Nurallao (I).............. 108 B 3
Nürburg (D)............... 87 E 3
Núria (E)................. 55 F 3
Nurme (EST)............... 153 C 3
Nurmes (FIN).............. 135 F 2
Nurmijärvi (FIN).......... 135 F 2
Nurmijärvi (FIN).......... 137 D 3
Nurmiži (LV).............. 159 E 2
Nurmo (FIN)............... 133 D 3
Nürnberg (D).............. 89 D 4
Nürnberg (D).............. 89 D 4
Nursi (EST)............... 161 D 2
Nürtingen (D)............. 45 F 3
Nus (I)................... 53 F 1
Nusse (D)................. 79 D 4
Nuštar (HR)............... 117 F 1
Nuttlar (D)............... 88 A 1
Nuttupera (FIN)........... 133 F 2

Nuutajärvi (FIN).......... 136 C 3
Nyåker (S)................ 132 B 3
Nybergsund (N)............ 139 F 1
Nyborg (DK)............... 142 C 4
Nybro (S)................. 143 F 3
Nydri (GR)................ 211 D 4
Nyírbátor (H)............. 12 C 3
Nyíregyháza (H)........... 12 C 3
Nykarleby / Uusikaarlepyy (FIN)... 133 D 3
Nykøbing F (DK)........... 144 C 4
Nykøbing M (DK)........... 142 B 2
Nykøbing S (DK)........... 142 C 4
Nyköping (S).............. 140 C 4
Nykvarn (S)............... 141 D 4
Nymburk (CZ).............. 90 B 2
Nymfaía (GR).............. 208 B 2
Nymfaío (GR).............. 205 E 3
Nynäshamn (S)............. 141 D 4
Nyon (CH)................. 49 E 4
Nyons (F)................. 52 C 4
Nýřany (CZ)............... 89 F 3
Nýrsko (CZ)............... 89 F 4
Nyrud (N)................. 125 F 3
Nysa (PL)................. 193 F 4
Nysäter (S)............... 139 F 4
Nyseter (N)............... 130 C 4
Nyskie (Jezioro) (PL)... 193 F 4
Nysted (DK)............... 144 C 4
Nyvoll (N)................ 125 D 2

O

O Barco (E)............... 59 D 4
O Bolo (E)................ 58 C 4
O Cádabo (E).............. 58 C 3
O Grove (E)............... 58 A 3
Oadby (GB)................ 33 E 4
Oakham (GB)............... 33 E 4
Oandu (EST)............... 151 E 3
Oanes (N)................. 138 B 4
Oara (EST)................ 153 B 3
Óasi (GR)................. 217 E 2
Oban (GB)................. 30 B 1
Obbola (S)................ 132 C 3
Obdach (A)................ 95 D 4
Obejo (E)................. 70 A 4
Obeliai Panevėžio(LT)... 165 F 4
Obeliai Vilniaus(LT)...... 171 D 3
Oberammergau (D).......... 93 F 3
Oberau (D)................ 93 F 3
Oberaudorf (D)............ 94 A 3
Oberdrauburg (A).......... 98 B 1
Obereßfeld (D)............ 88 C 3
Obergrafendorf (A)........ 95 E 2
Obergünzburg (D).......... 93 E 3
Obergurgl (A)............. 97 F 1
Oberhaslach (F)........... 45 D 3
Oberhausen Kreis Oberhausen(D)...... 87 E 1
Oberhof Kreis Schmalkalden-Meiningen(D)... 88 C 2
Oberkirch Ortenaukreis(D) 45 E 3
Oberkirchen (D)........... 88 A 1
Oberkochen (D)............ 93 E 1
Obermarchtal (D).......... 93 D 2
Obernai (F)............... 45 D 3
Obernberg am Inn (A)...... 94 B 2
Obernburg (D)............. 45 F 1
Oberndorf a. Neckar Kreis Freiburg(D)... 45 F 4
Oberndorf bei Salzburg (A)94 B 3
Obernzell (D)............. 94 C 1
Oberölsbach (D)........... 89 D 4
Oberprechtal (D).......... 45 E 4
Oberpullendorf (A)........ 95 F 3
Obersontheim (D).......... 93 D 1
Oberstaufen Kreis Oberallgäu(D)... 93 E 4
Oberstdorf (D)............ 93 E 4
Obertauern (A)............ 94 C 4
Obertraun (A)............. 94 C 3
Oberursel (D)............. 88 A 3
Obervellach (A)........... 94 B 4
Oberwiehtach (D).......... 89 E 4
Oberwart (A).............. 95 F 3
Oberwesel (D)............. 45 D 1
Oberwiesenthal (D)........ 89 F 2
Oberwölz (A).............. 95 D 4
Óbidos (P)................ 68 A 4
Obing (D)................. 94 A 3
Obilić (SRB).............. 119 D 4
Obinitsa (EST)............ 161 E 2
Objat (F)................. 51 E 2
Obninsk (RUS)............. 7 F 2
Obón (E).................. 65 F 4
Oborniki (PL)............. 187 E 2

Oborniki Śląskie *(PL)*	193	F 2	Oinoússes (Nisí) *(GR)*	214	C 4	Ollepa *(EST)*	154	B 2	Opatowiec *(PL)*	196	B 4
Obornjača *(SRB)*	113	E 3	Oirschot *(NL)*	39	F 1	Ollerton *(GB)*	33	E 3	Opava *(CZ)*	91	F 2
Oborovo *(HR)*	99	F 2	Oisemont *(F)*	38	B 4	Olliergues *(F)*	52	A 1	Opava *(PL)*	200	D 2
Obrazów *(PL)*	196	C 3	Oisterwijk *(NL)*	39	F 1	Ollioules *(F)*	57	D 3	Opinogóra Górna *(PL)*	189	F 1
Obrenovac *(SRB)*	118	B 1	Oisu *(EST)*	154	B 2	Olmedillo de Roa *(E)*	64	B 2	Opladen *(D)*	87	E 2
Obrež *(SRB)*	118	B 1	Õisu *(EST)*	154	B 4	Olmedo *(E)*	64	A 3	Opočka *(RUS)*	7	D 2
Obrov *(SLO)*	99	C 4	Oiti *(GR)*	212	A 4	Olmedo *(I)*	108	A 2	Opoczno *(PL)*	195	F 2
Obrovac *(HR)*	99	F 4	Oitti *(FIN)*	137	D 3	Olmeto *(F)*	57	F 4	Opole *(PL)*	194	B 3
Obrovac Sinjski *(HR)*	117	D 4	Oitylo *(GR)*	222	C 2	Olocau del Rey *(E)*	66	A 4	Opole Lubelskie *(PL)*	196	C 2
Obrowo *(PL)*	189	D 1	Öja *(FIN)*	133	D 2	Olofström *(S)*	143	E 3	Oporów *(PL)*	189	D 2
Obršani *(MK)*	122	B 4	Ojaäärse *(EST)*	153	C 2	Olombrada *(E)*	64	B 3	Opovo *(SRB)*	118	B 1
Obrzycko *(PL)*	187	E 2	Ojaküla *(EST)*	151	E 3	Olomouc *(CZ)*	91	E 3	Oppach *(D)*	90	B 1
Obsteig *(A)*	93	F 4	Ojakylä *(FIN)*	133	E 1	Olonzac *(F)*	55	F 2	Oppdal *(N)*	130	C 4
Obsza *(PL)*	197	E 4	Ojasoo *(EST)*	149	E 3	Oloron-Ste-Marie *(F)*	54	B 3	Oppenau *(D)*	45	E 1
Obudavac *(BIH)*	117	E 1	Ojcowski Park			Olost *(E)*	67	D 2	Oppenheim *(D)*	45	E 1
Obzor *(BG)*	19	E 1	Narodowy *(PL)*	195	E 4	Olot *(E)*	55	F 4	Opphaug *(N)*	131	D 2
Očakiv *(UA)*	13	F 3	Öje *(S)*	140	B 2	Olovo *(BIH)*	117	E 3	Oppido Lucano *(I)*	106	C 3
Ocaña *(E)*	70	B 1	Öjebyn *(S)*	132	C 1	Olpe *(D)*	87	F 2	Oppido Mamertina *(I)*	111	F 1
Occhiobello *(I)*	98	A 4	Ojos Negros *(E)*	65	E 4	Olsberg *(D)*	88	A 1	Opuzen *(HR)*	120	B 2
Očevlja *(BIH)*	117	E 3	Ojrzeń *(PL)*	189	F 2	Olshammar *(S)*	140	B 4	Ora / Auer *(I)*	98	A 1
Ochagavía *(E)*	54	A 3	Ojuelos *(E)*	69	F 4	Olst *(NL)*	82	C 3	Oradea *(RO)*	113	F 1
Ochla *(PL)*	186	C 4	Öjung *(S)*	140	C 1	Ølstykke *(DK)*	143	D 4	Oradour-sur-Glane *(F)*	51	D 1
Ochsenfurt *(D)*	88	C 4	Okainiai *(LT)*	170	C 3	Olszanica			Oradour-sur-Vayres *(F)*	51	D 1
Ochsenhausen *(D)*	93	D 3	Okehampton *(GB)*	34	D 4	Podkarpackie *(PL)*	202	E 3	Orahovac *(SRB)*	121	F 2
Óchthia *(GR)*	211	E 4	Oker *Kreis Goslar* *(D)*	84	B 4	Olszanka			Oraío *(GR)*	207	F 1
Ochthoniá *(GR)*	213	E 4	Oknö *(S)*	143	F 3	Mazowieckie *(PL)*	191	D 3	Oraiókastro *(GR)*	206	B 3
Ochtrup *(D)*	83	D 4	Okonek *(PL)*	181	F 4	Olszana Opolskie *(PL)*	193	F 3	Oraison *(F)*	53	D 4
Ochyró *(GR)*	207	F 1	Oksa *(PL)*	195	E 4	Olszówka *(PL)*	189	D 3	Orajärvi *(FIN)*	128	C 2
Očikiai *(LT)*	169	E 3	Oksbøl *(DK)*	142	A 4	Olsztyn Śląskie *(PL)*	195	D 3	Orange *(F)*	52	C 4
Ockelbo *(S)*	140	C 2	Oksby *(DK)*	142	A 4	Olsztyn Warmińsko-			Orani *(I)*	108	B 2
Öckerö *(S)*	142	F 1	Øksfjord *(N)*	124	C 2	Mazurskie *(PL)*	183	F 3	Oranienbaum *(D)*	85	D 2
Ödåkra *(S)*	143	D 3	Okslindžiai *(LT)*	168	C 3	Olsztynek *(PL)*	183	F 3	Oranienburg *(D)*	85	D 2
Odda *(N)*	138	C 2	Ökskywie *(PL)*	182	C 1	Olszyna *(PL)*	192	C 2	Oranmore *(IRL)*	22	B 4
Odden Færgehavn *(DK)*	142	C 4	Okučani *(HR)*	115	E 3	Oltedal *(N)*	138	B 4	Orašac *(HR)*	120	C 2
Odder *(DK)*	142	B 3	Okulovka *(RUS)*	7	E 1	Olten *(CH)*	92	B 4	Orašac *(SRB)*	118	C 2
Odeceixe *(P)*	74	A 1	Ólafsfjörður *(IS)*	126	B 1	Olula del Río *(E)*	77	D 2	Orasi *(MNE)*	121	D 2
Odeleite *(P)*	74	B 1	Ólafsvík *(IS)*	126	A 2	Olustvere *(EST)*	154	B 3	Orašje *(BIH)*	117	E 1
Odelzhausen *(D)*	93	F 2	Olaine *(LV)*	164	C 1	Olüti *(LV)*	167	D 3	Orăştie *(RO)*	12	C 4
Odemira *(P)*	74	A 1	Olargues *(F)*	55	F 2	Ólvega *(E)*	65	E 2	Orava *(EST)*	161	E 2
Ödemiş *(TR)*	19	E 4	Oława *(PL)*	193	F 3	Olvera *(E)*	75	D 2	Oravais / Oravainen *(FIN)*	133	D 3
Odense *(DK)*	142	B 4	Olazti/Olazagutia *(E)*	61	D 4	Olympía *(GR)*	217	D 3	Oravikoski *(FIN)*	135	E 4
Odenthal *(D)*	87	E 2	Olbernhau *(D)*	89	F 2	Olympiáda *Halkidikí* *(GR)*	207	D 3	Oraviţa *(RO)*	12	C 4
Oderberg *(D)*	85	D 2	Olbia *(I)*	108	B 1	Olympiáda *Lárisa* *(GR)*	212	A 1	Orba *(E)*	72	A 4
Oderzo *(I)*	98	B 2	Oldcastle /			Ólympos *(GR)*	225	F 4	Ørbæk *(DK)*	142	C 4
Odesa *(UA)*	13	F 3	An Seanchaisleán *(IRL)*	23	D 4	Ólympos (Óros) *(GR)*	206	A 4	Orbassano *(I)*	53	F 2
Ödeshög *(S)*	143	E 1	Oldebroek *(NL)*	82	C 3	Ólynthos *(GR)*	206	A 4	Orbe *(CH)*	49	D 1
Odiste *(EST)*	154	C 3	Oldeide *(N)*	130	A 4	Olza *(PL)*	200	E 2	Orbec *(F)*	42	B 2
Odivelas *(P)*	68	B 4	Olden *(N)*	130	A 4	Omagh *(GB)*	23	D 2	Orbetello *(I)*	101	F 4
Odolanów *(PL)*	194	B 1	Oldenburg (Oldb) *Kr. Oldenburg*			Omali *(GR)*	205	F 2	Orbey *(F)*	45	D 4
Odolo *(I)*	97	F 3	*Oldb Stadt* *(D)*	83	E 2	Omalós *(GR)*	226	A 2	Orce *(E)*	77	D 1
Odorheiu Secuiesc *(RO)*	13	D 3	Oldenburg i. Holstein			Omarska *(BIH)*	115	E 4	Orcera *(E)*	70	C 4
Odra Wschodnia *(PL)*	180	F 1	*Kreis Ostholstein* *(D)*	79	D 3	Omedu *(EST)*	155	D 3	Orchies *(F)*	39	D 3
Odry *(CZ)*	91	F 3	Oldenzaal *(NL)*	83	D 3	Omegna *(I)*	96	C 3	Orchomenós *(GR)*	217	F 1
Odry *(PL)*	182	B 3	Olderdalen *(N)*	124	C 3	Omiš *(HR)*	117	D 4	Orchówek *(PL)*	191	F 4
Odrzykoń *(PL)*	202	D 2	Oldervik *(N)*	124	B 3	Omišalj *(HR)*	99	F 3	Orchowo *(PL)*	188	B 2
Odrzywół *(PL)*	195	F 1	Oldham *(GB)*	33	D 2	Ommen *(NL)*	82	C 3	Orcières *(F)*	53	D 3
Odžaci *(SRB)*	113	D 4	Oldmeldrum *(GB)*	28	B 2	Omodos *(CY)*	230	B 3	Orcival *(F)*	51	F 1
Odžak *(BIH)*	117	E 1	Oldsum *(D)*	78	B 2	Omoljica *(SRB)*	118	C 1	Ordes *(E)*	58	B 3
Odžak *(MNE)*	118	D 2	Olecko *(PL)*	185	D 2	Omorfochóri *(GR)*	212	A 1	Ordizia *(E)*	61	D 4
Odziena *(LV)*	165	F 2	Oleggio *(I)*	97	D 3	Ómossa *(FIN)*	132	C 4	Orduña *(E)*	60	C 3
Oebisfelde *(D)*	84	B 3	Oleiros *(E)*	58	B 2	Oña *(E)*	60	B 4	Ordžonikidze *(UA)*	13	F 2
Oederan *(D)*	89	F 1	Oleiros *(P)*	68	C 1	Oñati *(E)*	60	C 3	Ore *(S)*	140	B 2
Oeiras *(P)*	68	A 3	Oleksandrija *(UA)*	13	F 1	Ončiškiai *(LT)*	176	D 3	Orea *(E)*	65	E 3
Oelde *(D)*	83	E 4	Ølen *(N)*	138	B 3	Onda *(E)*	72	A 2	Orebić *(HR)*	120	B 2
Oelsnitz *(D)*	89	E 2	Olesa de Montserrat *(E)*	66	C 3	Ondara *(E)*	72	A 4	Örebro *(S)*	140	B 4
Oettingen *(D)*	93	E 1	Oleśnica			Ondarroa *(E)*	60	C 3	Öregrund *(S)*	141	D 2
Oetz *(A)*	93	F 4	*Dolnośląskie* *(PL)*	193	F 2	Oneglia *(I)*	57	F 1	Oreini *(GR)*	207	D 2
Offenbach *(D)*	88	A 3	Oleśnica			Onesse-et-Laharie *(F)*	50	B 4	Orellana de la Sierra *(E)*	69	F 3
Offenburg *(D)*	45	D 1	*Świętokrzyskie* *(PL)*	196	B 4	Oneşti *(RO)*	13	D 3	Orellana la Vieja *(E)*	69	F 3
Offida *(I)*	102	C 3	Olesno Opolskie *(PL)*	194	D 4	Onich *(GB)*	27	D 4	Oreoí *(GR)*	212	C 3
Offranville *(F)*	38	B 4	Oleszyce *(PL)*	197	E 4	Onkamo *(FIN)*	129	E 3	Orestiáda *(GR)*	209	D 1
Ofir *(P)*	62	B 4	Oletta *(F)*	57	F 4	Onkamo *(FIN)*	135	E 4	Orgáni *(GR)*	208	B 2
Oggiono *(I)*	97	D 3	Olette *(F)*	55	F 4	Ontaneda *(E)*	60	B 3	Organyà *(E)*	55	D 4
Oglaine *(LV)*	164	C 2	Olevs'k *(UA)*	13	D 1	Ontiñena *(E)*	66	A 3	Orgaz *(E)*	70	B 2
Ogliastro Cilento *(I)*	106	C 4	Olgina *(EST)*	151	F 2	Ontinyent *(E)*	71	F 4	Orgelet *(F)*	49	E 1
Ogonki *(PL)*	184	C 2	Ølgod *(DK)*	142	A 4	Ontur *(E)*	71	E 4	Orgères-en-Beauce *(F)*	42	C 3
Ogošte *(SRB)*	119	E 4	Olhão *(P)*	74	B 2	Onuškis *Panevėžio* *(LT)*	165	F 4	Orgita *(EST)*	149	D 4
Ogre *(LV)*	165	D 1	Olhava *(FIN)*	129	D 4	Onuškis *Vilniaus* *(LT)*	177	D 3	Orgiva *(E)*	76	B 3
Ogresgals *(LV)*	165	D 1	Oliana *(E)*	66	C 2	Onzain *(F)*	47	D 2	Orgon *(F)*	56	C 2
Ogrodniki *(PL)*	185	E 2	Olib *(HR)*	99	E 4	Oonurme *(EST)*	151	E 4	Orgosolo *(I)*	108	B 2
Ogrodzieniec *(PL)*	195	E 3	Olib (Otok) *(HR)*	99	E 4	Oost-Vlieland *(NL)*	82	B 2	Orhei *(MD)*	13	D 3
Ogulin *(HR)*	99	E 3	Oliena *(I)*	108	B 2	Oostburg *(NL)*	37	E 2	Oria *(E)*	77	D 2
Ohanes *(E)*	76	C 3	Oliete *(E)*	65	F 4	Oostende *(B)*	37	E 4	Oria *(I)*	107	E 3
Ohlstadt *(D)*	93	F 4	Oliva *(E)*	72	A 4	Oosterbeek *(NL)*	82	C 4	Oricáin *(E)*	54	A 4
Ohorn *(D)*	90	A 1	Oliva de la Frontera *(E)*	69	D 4	Oosterend *(NL)*	82	B 2	Origny-Ste-Benoite *(F)*	39	D 4
Ohrdruf *(D)*	88	C 2	Oliva de Mérida *(E)*	69	E 3	Oosterhout *(NL)*	39	F 1	Orihuela *(E)*	77	F 1
Ohrid *(MK)*	122	A 4	Olivares de Júcar *(E)*	71	D 2	Oostkamp *(B)*	37	F 4	Orihuela del Tremedal *(E)*	65	E 3
Öhringen *(D)*	93	D 1	Oliveira de Azeméis *(P)*	62	B 3	Oostmalle *(B)*	39	F 1	Orimattila *(FIN)*	137	D 3
Ohtu *(EST)*	149	D 3	Oliveira de Frades *(P)*	62	C 3	Öötla *(EST)*	149	F 4	Oriolo *(I)*	106	C 4
Oía *(GR)*	224	D 3	Oliveira do Bairro *(P)*	62	B 4	Ootmarsum *(NL)*	83	D 3	Oripää *(FIN)*	136	D 3
Oiartzun *(E)*	61	D 3	Oliveira do Douro *(P)*	62	C 3	Opalenica *(PL)*	187	E 2	Orissaare *(EST)*	152	C 2
Oidrema *(EST)*	153	B 3	Oliveira do Hospital *(P)*	62	C 1	Opatija *(HR)*	99	D 3	Oristano *(I)*	108	A 3
Oijärvi *(FIN)*	129	D 3	Olivenza *(E)*	69	D 3	Opatovac *(HR)*	117	E 1	Orivesi *(FIN)*	136	C 2
Oikarainen *(FIN)*	129	D 3	Olivet *(F)*	42	C 4	Opatów Śląskie *(PL)*	195	D 3	Orjahovo *(BG)*	13	D 4
Oinói *Ilia* *(GR)*	217	D 2	Olivone *(CH)*	97	D 1	Opatów			Ørje *(N)*	139	F 3
Oinói *Viotía* *(GR)*	218	B 1	Oliwa *(PL)*	182	C 1	*Świętokrzyskie* *(PL)*	196	B 4	Orkanger *(N)*	131	D 3
Oinoússes *(GR)*	214	C 4	Olkusz *(PL)*	195	E 4	Opatówek *(PL)*	188	C 4	Örkelljunga *(S)*	143	D 3
Orlane *(SRB)*	119	D 4	Osiek Kujawsko-		
Orlate *(SRB)*	122	A 2	Pomorskie *(PL)*	189	D 1
Orléans *(F)*	42	C 4	Osiek Pomorskie *(PL)*	182	C 3
Orlová *(CZ)*	91	F 2	Osiek Świętokrzyskie *(PL)*	196	C 4
Orlovat *(SRB)*	113	F 4	Osielsko *(PL)*	188	B 1
Orly *(F)*	43	D 2	Osijek *(HR)*	112	C 4
Orly *(PL)*	202	F 2	Osilo *(I)*	108	A 1
Orménio *(GR)*	208	C 1	Osimo *(I)*	102	C 2
Ormideia *(CY)*	231	D 3	Osinja *(BIH)*	115	F 4
Órmos *(GR)*	206	B 4	Ósios Loukás *(GR)*	217	F 1
Órmos Korthíou *(GR)*	219	E 2	Osipaonica *(SRB)*	118	C 1
Órmos Panagías *(GR)*	207	D 4	Osjaków *(PL)*	195	D 2
Órmos Prínou *(GR)*	207	E 3	Oškalni *(LV)*	159	D 3
Ormož *(SLO)*	99	F 1	Oskarshamn *(S)*	143	F 2
Ormsjö *(S)*	132	A 2	Oskarström *(S)*	143	D 3
Ormskirk *(GB)*	32	C 2	Oslo *(N)*	139	E 3
Ormýlia *(GR)*	207	D 4	Ösmo *(S)*	141	D 4
Ornans *(F)*	49	E 2	Osnabrück *(D)*	83	E 3
Ørnes *(N)*	138	C 1	Ośno Lubuskie *(PL)*	186	C 2
Ørnes *(N)*	127	D 3	Osoblaha *(CZ)*	91	E 2
Orneta *(PL)*	183	E 2	Osoppo *(I)*	98	C 1
Ornós *(GR)*	219	F 3	Osor *(HR)*	99	E 4
Örnsköldsvik *(S)*	132	B 3	Osorno la Mayor *(E)*	60	A 4
Or'ol *(RUS)*	7	F 3	Osøyro *(N)*	138	B 2
Orolik *(HR)*	117	F 1	Ospedaletti *(I)*	57	F 1
Orom *(SRB)*	113	D 3	Ospitaletto *(I)*	97	E 3
Oron-la-Ville *(CH)*	49	F 3	Oss *(NL)*	82	C 4
Orońsko *(PL)*	196	B 2	Óssa *(GR)*	206	C 3
Oropa *(I)*	53	F 1	Ossa de Montiel *(E)*	70	C 3
Oropesa *(E)*	69	F 1	Ossiach *(A)*	114	A 2
Oropesa del Mar *(E)*	72	A 1	Ossun *(F)*	54	C 3
Óros Ólimbos *(CY)*	230	B 3	Ostaškov *(RUS)*	7	E 2
Orosei *(I)*	108	C 2	Ostaszewo *(PL)*	183	D 2
Orosháza *(H)*	113	E 2	Østby *(N)*	139	F 1
Orounta *(CY)*	231	C 2	Oster *(UA)*	13	E 1
Orpesa /			Øster Vrå *(DK)*	142	C 2
Oropesa del Mar *(E)*	72	A 1	Osterburg *(D)*	84	C 2
Orpierre *(F)*	53	D 4	Osterburken *(D)*	45	F 2
Orpington *(GB)*	36	C 3	Osterby Havn *(DK)*	142	C 2
Orreaga /			Österbybruk *(S)*	141	D 3
Roncesvalles *(E)*	54	A 3	Österbymo *(S)*	143	F 2
Orrefors *(S)*	143	F 3	Österfärnebo *(S)*	140	C 3
Orša *(BY)*	7	F 3	Osterfeld		
Orsa *(S)*	140	B 2	*Burgenlandkreis* *(D)*	89	D 1
Orsay *(F)*	43	D 3	Osterhofen *(D)*	94	B 1
Orsières *(CH)*	49	F 4	Osterholz-Scharmbeck *Kreis*		
Orsogna *(I)*	103	D 4	*Osterholz* *(D)*	83	F 2
Orşova *(RO)*	119	E 1	Osteria del Gatto *(I)*	102	B 3
Ørsta *(N)*	130	B 4	Osterode a. Harz *Kreis*		
Örsundsbro *(S)*	141	D 3	*Braunschweig* *(D)*	84	A 4
Orta Nova *(I)*	106	B 2	Östersund *(S)*	131	F 3
Orta San Giulio *(I)*	96	C 3	Östersundom /		
Ortakioi *(CY)*	231	C 2	Itäsalmi *(FIN)*	137	D 4
Orte *(I)*	102	B 4	Östervåla *(S)*	141	D 3
Orth *(A)*	95	F 1	Osterwieck *(D)*	84	B 4
Orthez *(F)*	54	B 2	Östhammar *(S)*	141	D 3
Ortigueira *(E)*	58	C 2	Ostheim v. d. Rhön *Kreis*		
Ortisei / St Ulrich *(I)*	98	A 1	*Rhön-Grabfeld* *(D)*	88	C 2
Ortnevik *(N)*	138	C 1	Ostia Antica *(I)*	104	C 2
Orton *(GB)*	32	C 1	Ostiglia *(I)*	98	A 4
Ortona *(I)*	103	D 4	Östmark *(S)*	139	F 3
Ortrand *(D)*	85	E 4	Ostra *(I)*	102	B 2
Örträsk *(S)*	132	B 2	Ostrach *(D)*	93	D 3
Oru *(EST)*	149	E 3	Ostrava *(CZ)*	91	F 2
Õru *(EST)*	160	C 1	Oštrelj *(BIH)*	116	C 3
Orubica *(HR)*	115	E 4	Ostritz *(D)*	90	B 1
Orune *(I)*	108	B 2	Ostróda *(PL)*	183	E 2
Orusco de Tajuña *(E)*	70	C 1	Ostroh *(UA)*	13	D 1
Orvalho *(P)*	68	C 1	Ostrołęka *(PL)*	190	C 1
Orvieto *(I)*	102	A 4	Ostroróg *(PL)*	187	E 2
Orvinio *(I)*	105	D 1	Ostrov *(RO)*	13	E 4
Orzesze *(PL)*	200	E 1	Ostrov *(RUS)*	7	D 2
Orzinuovi *(I)*	97	E 3	Ostrov *Karlovarský kraj* *(CZ)*	89	F 2
Orzyc *(PL)*	183	F 4	Ostrów *(PL)*	202	D 1
Orzysz *(PL)*	184	C 3	Ostrów Lubelski *(PL)*	197	E 1
Os *(N)*	131	D 4	Ostrów Mazowiecka *(PL)*	190	C 1
Osa *(PL)*	183	D 4	Ostrów Wielkopolski *(PL)*	188	B 4
Osa de la Vega *(E)*	70	C 2	Ostrówek *Łódzkie* *(PL)*	194	C 2
Ošani *(LV)*	165	F 3	Ostrówek *Lubelskie* *(PL)*	191	D 4
Osby *(S)*	143	E 3	Ostrowice *(PL)*	181	D 3
Oschatz *(D)*	89	F 1	Ostrowiec		
Oschersleben *(D)*	84	B 4	Świętokrzyski *(PL)*	196	C 3
Oschiri *(I)*	108	B 1	Ostrowieckie		
Ościłowo *(PL)*	189	F 1	(Jezioro) *(PL)*	187	D 1
Osečina *(SRB)*	118	B 2	Ostrowite Kujawsko-		
Oseja de Sajambre *(E)*	59	F 3	Pomorskie *(PL)*	189	D 1
Osen *(N)*	131	D 2	Ostrowite		
Ošenieki *Jelgavas* *(LV)*	164	C 3	Wielkopolskie *(PL)*	188	B 3
Ošenieki *Saldus* *(LV)*	163	D 1	Ostrožac Bihać *(BIH)*	99	F 3
Osera *(E)*	65	F 3	Ostrožac Mostar *(BIH)*	117	E 4
Osie *(PL)*	182	C 3	Ostrzeszów *(PL)*	194	B 1
Osięciny *(PL)*	188	C 2	Ostuni *(I)*	107	E 3
Osiecza Pomorskie *(PL)*	182	C 3	Osula *(EST)*	161	C 2
Osieczna			Osuna *(E)*	75	D 2
Wielkopolskie *(PL)*	187	E 4	Ošupe *(LV)*	167	D 1
Osiecznica *(PL)*	192	C 2	Oswestry *(GB)*	32	C 3
			Oświęcim *(PL)*	200	F 2

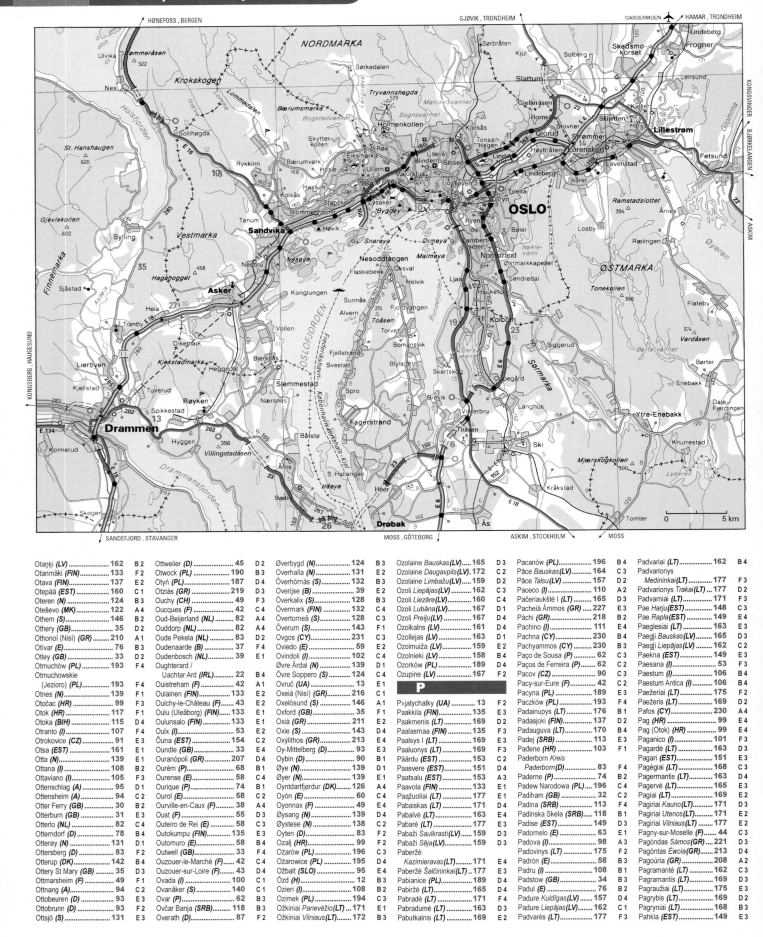

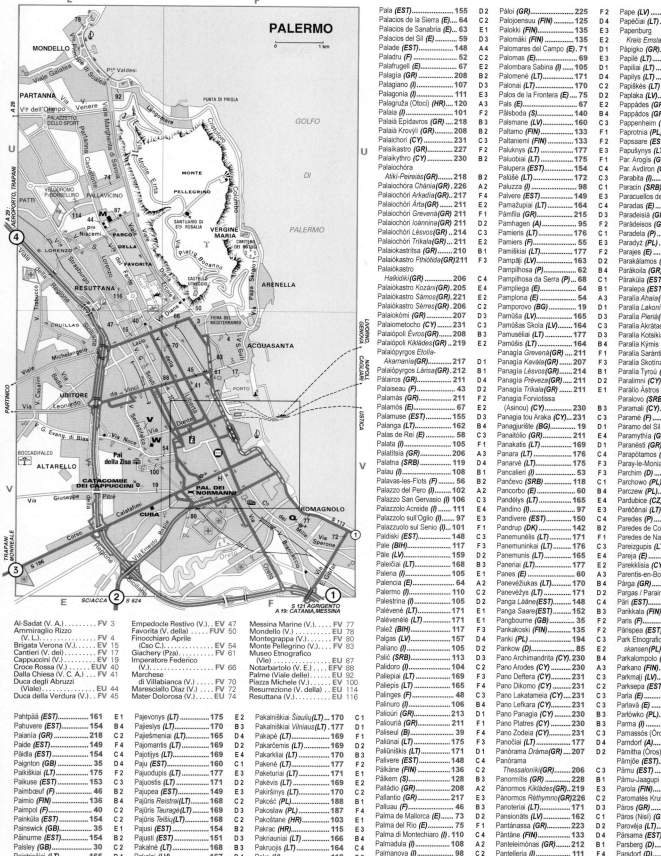

PALERMO

0 1 km

Pala (EST)....155 D2
Palacios de la Sierra (E).. 64 C2
Palacios de Sanabria (E).. 63 E1
Palacios del Sil (E)....59 D3
Palade (EST)....148 A4
Paladru (F)....52 C2
Palafrugell (E)....67 E2
Palagía (GR)....208 B2
Palagiano (I)....107 D3
Palagonia (I)....111 F3
Palagruža (Otoci) (HR)....120 A3
Palaía (I)....101 F1
Palaiá Epídavros (GR)....218 B3
Palaiá Krovýli (GR)....208 B2
Palaichóri (CY)....231 C3
Palaíkastro (GR)....227 C4
Palaíkythro (CY)....230 B2
Palaiochóra Atikí-Peireiás (GR)....218 B2
Palaiochóra Chánia (GR)..226 A2
Palaiochóri Arkadía (GR)..217 E4
Palaiochóri Árta (GR)....211 E4
Palaiochóri Grevená (GR) 211 F1
Palaiochóri Ioánnina (GR) 211 D2
Palaiochóri Lésvos (GR)....214 C3
Palaiochóri Tríkala (GR)....211 E2
Palaiokastrítsa (GR)....210 B1
Palaiókastro Fthiótida (GR)211 F3
Palaiókastro Halkidikí (GR)....206 C4
Palaiókastro Kozáni (GR)..205 E4
Palaiókastro Sámos (GR) 221 E2
Palaiókastro Sérres (GR) 206 C2
Palaiokómi (GR)....207 D3
Palaiometócho (CY)....231 C3
Palaiópoli Évros (GR)....208 B2
Palaiópoli Kikládes (GR)..219 E2
Palaiópyrgos Etolía-Akarnanía (GR)....217 D1
Palaiópyrgos Lárisa (GR) 212 B1
Pálairos (GR)....211 D4
Palaíseau (F)....43 D2
Palamás (GR)....211 F2
Palamós (E)....67 E2
Palamuse (EST)....155 D3
Palanga (LT)....162 B4
Palas de Rei (E)....58 C3
Palata (I)....105 F1
Palatna (SRB)....119 D4
Palau (I)....108 B1
Palavas-les-Flots (F)....56 B2
Palazzo del Pero (I)....102 A2
Palazzo San Gervasio (I) 106 C3
Palazzolo Acreide (I)....111 E4
Palazzolo sull'Oglio (I)....97 E2
Palazzuolo sul Senio (I)..101 F1
Paldiski (EST)....148 C3
Pale (BIH)....117 F3
Pāle (LV)....159 D2
Paleíčiai (LT)....168 B3
Palena (I)....105 E1
Palencia (E)....64 A2
Palermo (I)....110 C2
Palestrina (I)....105 D2
Palévenė (LT)....171 E1
Palévenėlė (LT)....171 E1
Palež (BIH)....117 F3
Palgas (LV)....157 D4
Paliano (I)....105 D2
Palić (SRB)....113 D3
Palidoro (I)....104 C2
Paliepiai (LT)....169 F3
Paliepis (LT)....165 F4
Palinges (F)....48 C3
Paliouri (GR)....213 D1
Paliouriá (GR)....211 F1
Paliseul (B)....39 F4
Paliūnai (LT)....175 F3
Paliūniškis (LT)....171 D1
Palivere (EST)....148 C4
Pälkäne (FIN)....136 C2
Pālkem (LV)....128 B3
Palládio (GR)....208 A2
Pallantio (GR)....217 E3
Palluau (F)....46 B3
Palma de Mallorca (E)....73 D2
Palma del Río (E)....75 F1
Palma di Montechiaro (I). 110 C4
Palmadula (I)....108 A3
Palmanova (I)....98 C3
Palmela (P)....68 A3
Palmi (I)....111 F1
Palmse (EST)....155 D2
Palnosai (LT)....163 E3
Palo del Colle (I)....107 D2

Palói (GR)....225 F2
Palojoensuu (FIN)....125 D4
Palokki (FIN)....135 E3
Palomäki (FIN)....135 E3
Palomares del Campo (E). 71 D1
Palomas (E)....69 E3
Palombara Sabina (I)....105 D1
Palomené (LT)....171 D4
Palonai (LT)....170 C2
Palos de la Frontera (E)....75 D2
Pålsboda (S)....140 B4
Palsmane (LV)....160 C3
Paltamo (FIN)....133 F2
Paltaniemi (FIN)....133 F2
Paluknys (LT)....177 E3
Paluobiai (LT)....175 F1
Palupera (EST)....154 C4
Palūšė (LT)....172 C3
Paluzza (I)....98 C1
Palvere (EST)....149 E3
Pamažupiai (LT)....164 C2
Pámfila (GR)....215 D3
Pamhagen (A)....95 F2
Pamieris (LT)....176 C1
Pamiers (F)....55 E3
Pamiškiai (LT)....177 F2
Pampáli (LV)....163 D2
Pampilhosa (P)....62 B4
Pampilhosa da Serra (P). 62 C1
Pampliega (E)....64 A2
Pamplona (E)....54 A3
Pamporovo (BG)....19 D1
Pamūša (LV)....165 D3
Pamūšas Skola (LV)....164 C3
Pamušėliai (LT)....177 D3
Pamūšis (LT)....164 B4
Panagía Grevená (GR)....211 F1
Panagía Kavála (GR)....207 D1
Panagía Lésvos (GR)....214 B3
Panagía Préveza (GR)....211 D2
Panagía Tríkala (GR)....211 E1
Panagia Forviotissa (Asinou) (CY)....230 B3
Panagia tou Araka (CY)....231 C3
Panagjurište (BG)....19 E1
Panaitólio (GR)....211 E4
Panakatis (LT)....169 D1
Panara (LT)....176 C2
Pancalieri (I)....53 F1
Pančevo (SRB)....118 C2
Pancorbo (E)....60 B4
Pandélys (LT)....165 E3
Pandino (I)....97 E2
Pandivere (LT)....150 C2
Pandrup (DK)....142 B2
Panemunélis (LT)....171 F1
Panemuninkai (LT)....176 C3
Panemunis (LT)....165 E4
Paneriai (LT)....177 E2
Panes (E)....60 A3
Panevėžiukas (LT)....170 C2
Panevėžys (LT)....171 D2
Panga Lääne (EST)....148 C2
Panga Saare (EST)....152 B3
Pangbourne (GB)....35 F2
Pankakoski (FIN)....135 F2
Panki (PL)....194 C3
Pankow (D)....85 E2
Pano Archimandrita (CY) 230 B4
Pano Arodes (CY)....230 A3
Pano Deftera (CY)....231 C3
Pano Dikomo (CY)....231 C2
Pano Lakatameia (CY)....231 C3
Pano Lefkara (CY)....231 C3
Pano Panagia (CY)....230 B3
Pano Platres (CY)....230 B3
Pano Zodeia (CY)....231 C3
Panočiai (LT)....177 D4
Panórama Dráma (GR)....207 D1
Panórama Thessaloníki (GR)....206 C2
Panormítis (GR)....228 B1
Pánormos Kikládes (GR)..219 E3
Pánormos Réthymno (GR)226 C2
Panoteriai (LT)....171 D3
Pansionāts (LV)....162 C1
Pantánassa (GR)....223 D2
Pänteri (FIN)....133 D4
Panteleímonas (GR)....212 B1
Pantelleria (I)....111 F4
Paobelys (LT)....171 D3
Paola (I)....109 E1
Pápa (H)....112 A1
Páparis (GR)....217 E4
Papasidero (I)....109 D1

Pape (LV)....162 B3
Papéčiai (LT)....176 B3
Papenburg Kreis Emsland (D)....83 D2
Pápigko (GR)....211 D1
Papilė (LT)....163 E3
Papiliai (LT)....171 E1
Papilys (LT)....165 E4
Papiškės (LT)....177 E3
Paplaka (LV)....162 C2
Pappádes (GR)....212 C3
Pappádos (GR)....215 D3
Pappenheim (D)....93 D1
Paprotnia (PL)....191 D3
Papsaare (EST)....153 C3
Papušynys (LT)....169 F2
Par. Arogís (GR)....207 F2
Par. Avdíron (GR)....207 F2
Parabita (I)....107 F4
Paracin (SRB)....119 D2
Paracuellos de Jiloca (E).. 65 E3
Paradas (E)....75 F2
Paradeisiá (GR)....217 E4
Parádeisos (GR)....207 F2
Paradela (I)....62 C2
Paradyż (PL)....195 F2
Parakálamos (GR)....210 C1
Parákoila (GR)....214 C3
Parákula (EST)....154 B3
Paralepa (EST)....148 B4
Paralía Ahaïa (GR)....217 D1
Paralía Lakonía (GR)....217 F4
Paralía Pieriá (GR)....206 B4
Paralía Akrátas (GR)....217 E1
Paralía Kotsikiás (GR)....212 C3
Paralía Kýmis (GR)....213 E4
Paralía Saránti (GR)....217 F1
Paralía Skotínas (GR)....212 B1
Paralía Tyroú (GR)....217 F4
Paralimni (CY)....231 E3
Parálio Ástros (GR)....217 F3
Paralovo (SRB)....122 A1
Paramali (CY)....230 B4
Paramé (F)....41 C2
Páramo del Sil (E)....59 D3
Paramythía (GR)....210 C2
Paranésti (GR)....207 E2
Parapótamos (GR)....210 C2
Paray-le-Monial (F)....48 C4
Parchim (D)....79 E4
Parchowo (PL)....182 B2
Parczew (PL)....191 E4
Pardubice (CZ)....90 C2
Pareččenai (LT)....176 B3
Paredes (P)....62 C2
Paredes de Coura (P)....62 B1
Paredes de Nava (E)....64 A1
Pareizgupis (LT)....169 E3
Pareja (E)....65 D2
Parekklisia (CY)....231 C4
Parentis-en-Born (F)....50 B4
Párga (GR)....210 C2
Pargas / Parainen (FIN) ..136 B4
Päri (EST)....154 B4
Párispea (EST)....149 F2
Paris (F)....43 D2
Park Etnograficzny skansen (PL)....183 F3
Parkalompolo (S)....128 B2
Parkano (FIN)....133 D4
Parkmaļi (LV)....159 E1
Parksepa (EST)....161 D1
Parla (E)....70 C1
Parlavà (E)....67 E2
Parłówko (PL)....180 C3
Parma (I)....97 F2
Parnassós (Óros) (GR) ...212 B4
Parndorf (A)....95 F2
Párnitha (Óros) (GR)....218 C1
Pärnjõe (EST)....154 A3
Pärnu (EST)....153 C3
Pärnu-Jaagupi (EST)....153 C3
Parola (FIN)....136 C3
Paromatės Krušonys (LT)171 D4
Páros (E)....219 E4
Páros (Nisí) (GR)....219 E4
Pärsama (EST)....152 C3
Parsberg (D)....89 E4
Parsdorf (D)....94 A2
Parsęta (PL)....181 E3
Pärsti (EST)....154 B3
Partakko (FIN)....125 D2
Partanna (I)....110 B3
Partenen (A)....97 E1

Al-Sadat (V. A.).........FV 3
Ammiraglio Rizzo (V. L.).........FV 4
Brigata Verona (V.).....EV 15
Cantieri (V. dei).........FV 17
Cappuccini (V.).........EUV 19
Croce Rossa (V.).....EUV 40
Dalla Chiesa (V. C. A.)...FV 41
Duca degli Abruzzi (Viale).........EU 44
Duca della Verdura (V.)..FV 45

Empedocle Restivo (V.)..EV 47
Favorita (V. della).....FUV 50
Finocchiaro Aprile (Cso C.).........EV 54
Giachery (Pza).........FV 61
Imperatore Federico (Vle).........FV 66
Marchese di Villabianca (V.)..FV 70
Maresciallo Diaz (V.)....FV 72
Mater Dolorosa (V.).....EU 74

Messina Marine (V.).....FV 77
Mondello (V.).........EU 78
Montegrappa (V.).........FV 80
Monte Pellegrino (V.)....FV 83
Museo Etnografico (Vle).........EU 87
Notarbartolo (V. E.).....EFV 88
Palme (Viale delle).....FV 92
Piazza Michele (V.).....EV 100
Resurrezione (V. della)..EU 114
Resuttana (V.).........EU 116

Pahtpää (EST)....161 E1
Pahuvere (EST)....154 B4
Paianía (GR)....218 C2
Paide (EST)....149 F4
Päidla (EST)....154 C4
Paignton (GB)....35 D4
Paikiškiai (LT)....175 F2
Paikuse (EST)....153 C3
Paimbœuf (F)....46 A2
Paímio (FIN)....136 B4
Paimpol (F)....40 C2
Painküla (EST)....154 C2
Painswick (GB)....35 E1
Päinurme (EST)....154 B2
Paisley (GB)....30 C1
Pajstriečiai (LT)....165 D4
Pajstrys (LT)....171 D1
Paistu (EST)....154 B4
Pajala (S)....128 B2
Pajęczno (PL)....195 D2

Pajevonys (LT)....175 E2
Pajieslys (LT)....170 B3
Pajiešmeniai (LT)....165 D4
Pajomantis (LT)....169 D2
Pajotijys (LT)....169 D2
Paju (EST)....160 C1
Pajuodupis (LT)....177 E3
Pajuostis (LT)....171 D2
Pajupea (EST)....149 E4
Pajūris Reistrai (LT)....168 C2
Pajūris Tauragé (LT)....169 D3
Pajūris Telšiū (LT)....168 C2
Pajusi (EST)....154 B2
Pajusti (EST)....151 D2
Pakalné (LT)....168 B2
Pakalni (LV)....167 D4
Pakalniai (LT)....171 E3
Pakalniškės (LT)....177 E3
Pakalniškiai Klaipėdos (LT)....162 C3

Pakalniškiai Šiauliū (LT)...170 C1
Pakalniškiai Vilniaus (LT)..177 D1
Pakapė (LT)....169 F1
Pakarčemis (LT)....169 D2
Pakarkliai (LT)....170 B3
Pakené (LT)....177 F2
Paketuriai (LT)....171 E1
Pakévis (LT)....170 C2
Pakiršinys (LT)....170 C2
Pakość (PL)....188 B1
Pakoslaw (PL)....187 F4
Pakoštane (HR)....103 E1
Pakrac (HR)....115 E3
Pakriauniai (LT)....166 B4
Pakruojis (LT)....164 C4
Paks (H)....112 C4
Pakšteliai (LT)....163 E4
Pakumulšiai (LT)....163 E4
Pakuonis (LT)....176 C2
Pal. Kavàla (GR)....207 E2

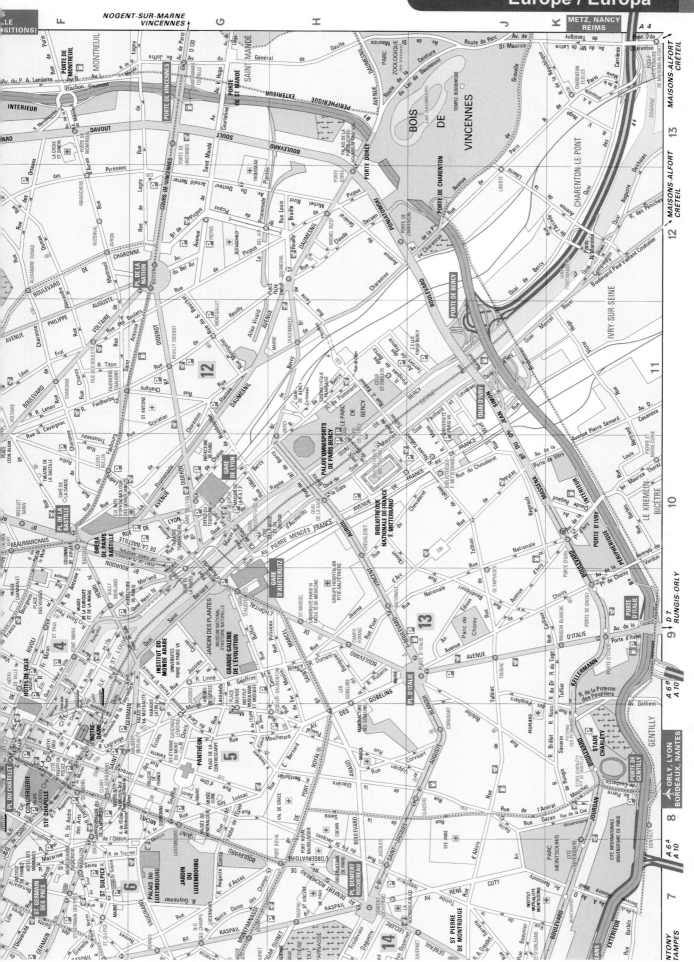

Parthenay (F) ...... 47 D 3
Parthéni (GR) ...... 221 D 4
Partille (S) ...... 143 D 1
Partinico (I) ...... 110 B 2
Partizani (SRB) ...... 118 C 2
Partizanske Vode (SRB) . 118 B 3
Partney (GB) ...... 33 F 3
Partsi (EST) ...... 161 E 1
Parudaminys (LT) ...... 177 E 3
Parupė (LT) ...... 165 D 3
Pārupe (LV) ...... 157 C 3
Parysów (PL) ...... 190 C 3
Pas-en-Artois (F) ...... 38 C 3
Pasá-Limáni (GR) ...... 220 D 1
Pasaia (E) ...... 61 D 3
Pašakiai (LT) ...... 170 C 2
Pašaltuonys III (LT) ...... 169 C 1
Pasás (Nisí) (GR) ...... 220 C 1
Pasavás (E) ...... 222 C 2
Paschalitsa (GR) ...... 211 F 2
Pašeimeniai (LT) ...... 175 E 2
Pašerkšnė (LT) ...... 163 D 3
Pašėtė (LT) ...... 170 C 2
Pasewalk (D) ...... 80 C 4
Pašiaušė (LT) ...... 169 F 2
Pasikovci (HR) ...... 115 E 3
Pašilė (LT) ...... 169 D 2
Pašiliai Utenos (LT) ...... 171 E 1
Pašiliai Vilniaus (LT) ...... 177 E 1
Pasłęk (PL) ...... 183 E 2
Pasłęka (PL) ...... 183 F 3
Pašlūžmis (LT) ...... 168 C 2
Pašman (HR) ...... 103 E 1
Pašman (Otok) (HR) ...... 103 E 1
Passais (F) ...... 41 F 3
Passau (D) ...... 94 B 1
Passignano
  sul Trasimeno (I) ...... 102 A 3
Pasta Mãja (LV) ...... 159 D 4
Pastrališki (LV) ...... 164 C 3
Pastavy (BY) ...... 7 D 3
Pastende (F) ...... 157 E 3
Pastrana (E) ...... 70 C 1
Pastrévys (LT) ...... 177 D 2
Pašuliene (LV) ...... 166 C 4
Pašušvys (LT) ...... 169 F 2
Pasvalys (LT) ...... 165 D 4
Pašventupys (LT) ...... 171 E 2
Pašvitinys (LT) ...... 164 C 4
Pasym (PL) ...... 183 F 3
Pašýšiai (LT) ...... 168 C 3
Pásztó (H) ...... 12 B 3
Patamošiupiai (LT) ...... 175 F 1
Patašinė (LT) ...... 175 F 2
Pataste (EST) ...... 155 D 3
Patay (F) ...... 42 C 4
Pateley Bridge (GB) ...... 33 D 1
Pateniemi (FIN) ...... 133 E 1
Paterna de Rivera (E) ...... 75 E 3
Paternion (A) ...... 114 A 2
Paternò (I) ...... 111 E 3
Paternopoli (I) ...... 106 A 3
Patersdorf (D) ...... 94 B 1
Patika (EST) ...... 149 E 3
Patilčiai (LT) ...... 175 E 3
Patiópoulo (GR) ...... 211 E 3
Patitíri (GR) ...... 213 D 3
Patküla (EST) ...... 160 E 1
Pátmos (GR) ...... 221 D 4
Pátmos (Nisí) (GR) ...... 221 D 4
Patnów Łódzkie (PL) ...... 194 C 3
Patnów Wielkopolskie (PL) 188 C 2
Pátra (GR) ...... 217 D 1
Patreksfjörður (IS) ...... 126 A 1
Patriki (CY) ...... 231 E 2
Patrington (GB) ...... 33 F 2
Pattada (I) ...... 108 B 2
Patterdale (GB) ...... 31 D 4
Patti (I) ...... 111 E 3
Pattijoki (FIN) ...... 133 E 1
Paturis (LT) ...... 177 D 4
Pau (F) ...... 54 E 3
Pauastvere (EST) ...... 154 C 3
Paugurciems (LV) ...... 157 B 2
Pauillac (F) ...... 50 B 2
Paúl (P) ...... 62 C 1
Paularo (I) ...... 98 A 2
Paulhaguet (F) ...... 52 A 2
Paullo (I) ...... 97 F 3
Paunküla (EST) ...... 149 F 3
Pavartyčiai (LT) ...... 170 B 1
Pavašuokiai II (LT) ...... 171 E 2
Paverpenis (LV) ...... 169 D 2
Pavia (I) ...... 97 D 4
Pavia (P) ...... 68 C 3
Pavia (Certosa di) (I) ...... 97 D 4
Paviliotė (LT) ...... 163 D 4

Pavilly (F) ...... 38 B 4
Pāvilosta (LV) ...... 156 B 4
Pavino Polje (MNE) ...... 118 B 4
Pavirčiuvė (LT) ...... 164 C 3
Pávliani (GR) ...... 212 A 4
Pavlica (SRB) ...... 118 C 3
Pávlos (GR) ...... 212 C 4
Pavullo nel Frignano (I) ...... 101 F 1
Pavydai (LT) ...... 169 F 2
Pawłów
  Świętokrzyskie (PL) ...... 196 B 2
Pawłowice Śląskie (PL) ...... 200 E 2
Pawłowiczki (PL) ...... 194 B 4
Pawłowo Warmińsko-
  Mazurskie (PL) ...... 183 F 4
Pawonków (PL) ...... 194 C 3
Paxoí (GR) ...... 210 C 3
Paxoí (Nisí) (GR) ...... 210 C 3
Payerne (CH) ...... 49 C 1
Paymogo (E) ...... 74 C 1
Payrac (F) ...... 51 E 3
Pazapsiai (LT) ...... 175 F 2
Pazardžik (BG) ...... 19 D 1
Pažagai (LT) ...... 165 D 4
Pažėžiai (LV) ...... 156 C 4
Pazin (HR) ...... 99 D 3
Pazlauga (LV) ...... 167 F 2
Pcim (PL) ...... 201 A 2
Peal de Becerro (E) ...... 76 C 1
Peć (SRB) ...... 121 F 1
Peč pod Sněžkou (CZ) ...... 90 F 3
Peccia (CH) ...... 97 D 2
Peccioli (I) ...... 101 F 2
Pečenjevce (SRB) ...... 119 F 3
Pećigrad (BIH) ...... 99 F 3
Pećinci (SRB) ...... 118 B 1
Pecka (SRB) ...... 118 B 1
Peckelsheim (D) ...... 88 A 1
Pęclaw (PL) ...... 187 E 4
Pécs (H) ...... 112 C 3
Pečurice (MNE) ...... 121 E 3
Pęczniew (PL) ...... 188 C 4
Pedaso (I) ...... 102 A 3
Pededze (LV) ...... 161 E 3
Pedersker (DK) ...... 145 E 3
Pedersöre /
  Pedersören Kunta (FIN) 133 D 3
Pédi (GR) ...... 228 B 1
Pediaios (CY) ...... 231 D 3
Pedoulas (CY) ...... 230 B 3
Pedrafita do Cebreiro (E) .. 59 D 3
Pedrajas
  de San Esteban (E) ...... 64 A 3
Pedralba (E) ...... 72 F 2
Pedralba de la Pradería (E) 63 E 1
Pedras Salgadas (P) ...... 63 D 2
Pedraza de la Sierra (E) ...... 64 B 3
Pedrera (E) ...... 75 F 2
Pedro Abad (E) ...... 76 A 1
Pedro Bernardo (E) ...... 70 A 1
Pedro Muñoz (E) ...... 70 C 2
Pedrógão (E) ...... 68 A 1
Pedrógão (P) ...... 68 C 4
Pedrógão Grande (P) ...... 68 B 3
Pedrola (E) ...... 65 F 2
Peebles (GB) ...... 31 B 3
Peel (GB) ...... 32 A 1
Peenemünde (D) ...... 80 C 3
Peetri Harju (EST) ...... 149 E 3
Peetri Järva (EST) ...... 149 F 4
Peetrimõisa (EST) ...... 154 B 4
Pefkári (GR) ...... 207 C 3
Pefkí (GR) ...... 212 C 3
Péfkos (GR) ...... 205 D 4
Pega (P) ...... 63 D 2
Pegalajar (E) ...... 76 B 1
Pegau (D) ...... 89 E 1
Pegeia (CY) ...... 230 D 4
Pegli (I) ...... 100 C 1
Pegnitz (D) ...... 89 D 3
Pego (E) ...... 72 A 4
Pegognaga (I) ...... 98 B 3
Pegolotte (I) ...... 98 B 3
Pęgów (PL) ...... 193 C 2
Peguera (E) ...... 73 D 2
Pehčevo (MK) ...... 122 C 2
Peine (D) ...... 84 C 1
Peio (I) ...... 97 F 1
Peïra-Cava (F) ...... 53 F 4
Peiraiás (GR) ...... 218 C 1
Peisiniíki (LV) ...... 166 B 1
Peißenberg (D) ...... 93 F 3
Peiting (D) ...... 93 F 3
Peitz (D) ...... 85 F 3
Pelagićevo (BIH) ...... 117 E 1
Pelaičiai (LT) ...... 168 B 2
Pelasgía (GR) ...... 212 B 3

Pelči (LV) ...... 157 D 4
Pełczyce (PL) ...... 186 C 1
Pelēči (LV) ...... 167 D 4
Pelekános (GR) ...... 205 E 4
Pélekas (GR) ...... 210 B 2
Pelekonys (LT) ...... 176 C 2
Pelendri (CY) ...... 230 B 3
Peletá (GR) ...... 217 C 4
Pelhřimov (CZ) ...... 90 C 3
Pelješac (Otok) (HR) ...... 120 B 2
Pelkelė (LT) ...... 163 E 2
Pelkės (LT) ...... 169 D 2
Pelkoseniemi (FIN) ...... 129 D 2
Pélla (GR) ...... 206 B 3
Pellegrino Parmense (I) ...... 97 E 4
Pellegrue (F) ...... 50 C 3
Pellesmäki (FIN) ...... 135 C 3
Pello (FIN) ...... 128 C 3
Pelplin (PL) ...... 182 C 3
Peltes (LT) ...... 159 F 4
Peltosalmi (FIN) ...... 133 F 2
Peltovuoma (FIN) ...... 125 D 4
Pelučiai (LT) ...... 169 F 4
Peluodžiai (LT) ...... 164 C 4
Pélussin (F) ...... 52 B 2
Pelutava (LT) ...... 170 B 3
Pembroke / Penfro (GB) ...... 34 B 1
Pembroke Dock /
  Doc Penfro (GB) ...... 34 B 1
Penacova (P) ...... 62 B 4
Peñafiel (E) ...... 64 B 2
Penafiel (P) ...... 62 C 2
Peñaflor (E) ...... 75 F 1
Penalva do Castelo (P) ...... 62 C 4
Penamacor (P) ...... 63 D 4
Peñaranda
  de Bracamonte (E) ...... 63 F 4
Peñaranda de Duero (E) ...... 64 C 2
Peñarroya-Pueblonuevo (E) 69 F 4
Penarth (GB) ...... 35 D 2
Peñas de San Pedro (E) ...... 71 D 4
Peñascosa (E) ...... 71 D 4
Peñausende (E) ...... 63 F 3
Pendine (GB) ...... 34 C 1
Penedono (P) ...... 63 D 3
Penela (P) ...... 68 B 1
Pénestin (F) ...... 41 B 4
Penhas da Saúde (P) ...... 62 C 4
Penhas Juntas (P) ...... 63 D 2
Peniche (P) ...... 68 A 1
Penicuik (GB) ...... 31 D 2
Penig (D) ...... 89 E 1
Peníscola / Peñíscola (E) .. 72 A 1
Penkule (LV) ...... 163 D 2
Penkun (D) ...... 81 D 4
Penmaenmawr (GB) ...... 32 B 3
Penna (Punta di) (I) ...... 103 A 2
Pennabilli (I) ...... 102 A 2
Penne (I) ...... 103 D 4
Penne-d'Agenais (F) ...... 51 A 1
Penrhyndeudraeth (GB) ...... 32 B 3
Penrith (GB) ...... 31 D 4
Penryn (GB) ...... 34 B 4
Pentageia (CY) ...... 230 B 3
Pentagioí (GR) ...... 211 F 4
Pentakomo (CY) ...... 231 C 4
Pentálofo (GR) ...... 216 C 1
Pentálofos (GR) ...... 205 E 4
Pénte Vrýses (GR) ...... 206 C 2
Pentéli (GR) ...... 218 C 2
Penteória (GR) ...... 217 E 1
Pentrofoelas (GB) ...... 32 B 3
Penuja (EST) ...... 159 F 1
Penzance (GB) ...... 34 A 4
Penzberg (D) ...... 93 F 3
Penzlin (D) ...... 80 C 4
Pępowo (PL) ...... 187 F 4
Pera (CY) ...... 231 C 3
Pera Chorio (CY) ...... 231 C 3
Perá-Posio (FIN) ...... 129 E 3
Perachóra (GR) ...... 217 F 2
Peraía Pélla (GR) ...... 205 D 2
Peraía Thessaloníki (GR) 206 C 2
Peraleda del Zaucejo (E).. 69 F 4
Peralejos
  de las Truchas (E) ...... 65 E 4
Perales de Tajuña (E) ...... 70 C 1
Perales del Alfambra (E) ...... 65 F 3
Perales del Puerto (E) ...... 69 D 1
Peralta (E) ...... 65 E 1
Peralta de Alcofea (E) ...... 66 A 2
Peralva (P) ...... 74 B 1
Pérama
  Atikí-Peireiás (GR) ...... 218 B 2
Pérama Ioánnina (GR) ...... 211 D 1

Pérama Kérkyra (GR) ...... 210 B 2
Pérama Lésvos (GR) ...... 215 D 3
Pérama Réthymno (GR) ... 226 C 2
Pérama spíleo (GR) ...... 211 D 1
Peranka (FIN) ...... 129 E 4
Peräseinäjoki (FIN) ...... 133 D 4
Pérasma (GR) ...... 207 C 1
Perast (MNE) ...... 121 D 2
Peratáta (GR) ...... 216 B 1
Percy (F) ...... 41 D 2
Pérdika Atikí-Peireiás (GR) 218 B 3
Pérdika Ioánnina (GR) ...... 211 D 2
Pérdika Thesprotía (GR) .. 210 C 4
Perdikáki (GR) ...... 211 E 3
Perdikas (GR) ...... 205 F 3
Perdíkkas (GR) ...... 205 F 3
Perejaslav-
  Chmel'nyc'kyj (UA) ...... 13 F 1
Pereruela (E) ...... 63 F 3
Pereslavl'-Zalesskij (RUS) .. 7 D 2
Perg (A) ...... 95 D 2
Pergine Valsugana (I) ...... 98 A 2
Pergola (I) ...... 102 E 3
Perho (FIN) ...... 133 E 3
Peri (EST) ...... 161 D 1
Periana (E) ...... 76 A 3
Périers (F) ...... 41 E 2
Périgueux (F) ...... 51 D 2
Períkleia (GR) ...... 206 B 1
Perila (EST) ...... 149 E 3
Perino (I) ...... 97 E 4
Perìškiai (LT) ...... 169 C 3
Períssa (GR) ...... 224 C 3
Perista (GR) ...... 211 F 4
Peristerá (GR) ...... 206 C 4
Peristéria (Tímvos) (GR) . 217 D 4
Peristerona (CY) ...... 231 C 3
Peristerona
  (Ammochostos) (CY) ... 230 B 2
Peristerona
  (Lefkosa) (CY) ...... 231 C 3
Peristerona (Pafos) (CY) . 230 A 3
Perithório (GR) ...... 207 D 1
Perívlepto (GR) ...... 212 D 1
Perivóli Fthiótida (GR) ...... 211 F 4
Perivóli Grevená (GR) ...... 211 D 1
Perivolia (GR) ...... 231 D 3
Perjasica (HR) ...... 99 F 3
Pérkonji (LV) ...... 159 F 4
Perković (HR) ...... 103 F 1
Perleberg (D) ...... 84 C 2
Perlez (SRB) ...... 113 E 4
Perloja (LT) ...... 177 D 4
Perly (PL) ...... 184 C 2
Përmet (AL) ...... 18 C 2
Pernå / Pernaja (FIN) ...... 137 D 3
Pernarava (LT) ...... 169 D 2
Pernarec (CZ) ...... 89 F 3
Pernes-les-Fontaines (F).. 52 C 4
Pernik (BG) ...... 18 C 1
Perniö (FIN) ...... 136 C 4
Pernitz (A) ...... 95 E 2
Péronne (F) ...... 39 D 4
Perosa Argentina (I) ...... 53 E 2
Pérouges (F) ...... 52 C 1
Perpignan (F) ...... 55 F 4
Perrero (I) ...... 53 E 2
Perreux (F) ...... 48 C 4
Perros-Guirec (F) ...... 40 C 2
Peršėkininkai (LT) ...... 176 B 3
Persenbeug (A) ...... 95 D 2
Pershore (GB) ...... 35 E 1
Persistéra (Nisí) (GR) ...... 213 D 3
Perstorp (S) ...... 143 E 2
Perth (GB) ...... 31 D 1
Pertisau (A) ...... 94 A 4
Pertočta (SLO) ...... 119 F 4
Pertoúli (GR) ...... 211 E 2
Pertteli (FIN) ...... 136 C 4
Pertuis (F) ...... 56 C 2
Pertunmaa (FIN) ...... 137 D 2
Pertusa (E) ...... 66 A 2
Perućac Vrelo (SRB) ...... 118 A 3
Perugia (I) ...... 102 B 3
Perūnai (LT) ...... 171 E 4
Peruščić (HR) ...... 99 F 4
Péruwelz (B) ...... 39 D 3
Pervenchères (F) ...... 42 B 3
Pervomajs'k (UA) ...... 13 F 2
Perzów (PL) ...... 194 B 2
Pesaro (I) ...... 102 B 1
Pescara (I) ...... 103 D 4
Pescasseroli (I) ...... 105 F 4
Peschici (I) ...... 103 F 4
Peschiera del Garda (I) ...... 97 F 4
Pescia (I) ...... 101 F 2
Pescina (I) ...... 105 D 1

Pescocostanzo (I) ...... 105 E 2
Pescolanciano (I) ...... 105 F 2
Pescopagano (I) ...... 106 B 3
Pescorocchiano (I) ...... 102 C 4
Peshkopi (AL) ...... 121 F 3
Pesiökylä (FIN) ...... 135 E 1
Peski (LV) ...... 172 C 1
Pesmes (F) ...... 49 D 2
Peso da Régua (P) ...... 62 C 3
Pesočani (MK) ...... 122 A 4
Pesoz (E) ...... 59 D 2
Pessáni (GR) ...... 208 C 2
Peštani (MK) ...... 122 A 4
Pestovo (RUS) ...... 7 F 1
Pešu Ciems (LV) ...... 162 B 3
Pešuríci (BIH) ...... 117 F 3
Petacinci (SRB) ...... 119 F 4
Petäjäskoski (FIN) ...... 128 C 3
Petäjävesi (FIN) ...... 133 E 4
Petalax (FIN) ...... 132 C 4
Petalídi (GR) ...... 217 D 2
Petalioí (Nisioí) (GR) ...... 219 D 2
Petaloúdes (GR) ...... 228 C 2
Pétange (L) ...... 44 C 2
Pétas (GR) ...... 211 D 3
Péteraičiai (LT) ...... 168 C 3
Peterborough (GB) ...... 33 E 4
Peterhead (GB) ...... 28 C 3
Pēterlauki (LV) ...... 164 C 2
Peterlee (GB) ...... 31 E 4
Pētermieki (LV) ...... 164 C 1
Petersfield (GB) ...... 35 F 3
Petershagen (D) ...... 83 F 3
Pēterupe (LV) ...... 159 D 3
Pethelinós (GR) ...... 207 D 2
Petilia Policastro (I) ...... 109 B 4
Petina (I) ...... 106 B 4
Petite-Rosselle (F) ...... 45 D 2
Petka (SRB) ...... 122 B 1
Petkalnis (LT) ...... 169 D 2
Petkula (FIN) ...... 129 D 2
Petkūnai (LT) ...... 170 C 3
Petlovača (SRB) ...... 117 F 1
Petoúsio (GR) ...... 211 D 2
Petra (CY) ...... 230 B 3
Petra (I) ...... 73 E 2
Pétra Lésvos (GR) ...... 206 A 4
Pétra Pieriá (GR) ...... 206 A 4
Petra tou Romiou (Aphrodite's
  birthplace) (CY) ...... 230 B 4
Petrália Sottana (I) ...... 111 D 3
Petrálona (GR) ...... 206 C 4
Petraná (GR) ...... 205 F 4
Petrašiūnai (LT) ...... 170 C 3
Petravičiai (LT) ...... 175 F 3
Petrčane (HR) ...... 103 E 1
Petreliai (LT) ...... 168 B 2
Petrer (E) ...... 71 F 4
Pétres (GR) ...... 205 F 3
Petreto-Bicchisano (F) ...... 57 F 3
Petrič (BG) ...... 19 D 1
Petrijevci (HR) ...... 112 C 4
Petrína (GR) ...... 217 C 4
Petrinja (HR) ...... 115 D 3
Petrochóri (GR) ...... 211 E 4
Petrodvorec (RUS) ...... 7 D 1
Pétrola (E) ...... 71 E 4
Petróna (GR) ...... 211 E 3
Petroşani (RO) ...... 12 C 4
Petroškai (LT) ...... 175 F 4
Petrotá (GR) ...... 208 C 2
Petrothálassa (GR) ...... 218 B 4
Petrotó (GR) ...... 211 E 2
Petroússa (GR) ...... 207 D 2
Petrovac (MK) ...... 122 B 2
Petrovac Bar (MNE) ...... 121 D 3
Petrovac Požarevac (SRB) 119 D 1
Petrovaradin (SRB) ...... 113 D 4
Petrovčić (SRB) ...... 118 B 1
Petrovice Příbram (CZ) ...... 90 B 3
Petrovka (LV) ...... 167 D 2
Petrovo / Bosansko Petrovo
  Selo (BIH) ...... 117 E 2
Petručai (LT) ...... 177 E 3
Pettenbach (A) ...... 94 C 2
Pettigoe (IRL) ...... 23 D 2
Petworth (GB) ...... 36 B 4
Peuerbach (A) ...... 94 C 2
Peura (FIN) ...... 128 C 2
Pewsey (GB) ...... 35 F 2
Peyrat-le-Château (F) ...... 51 E 1
Peyrehorade (F) ...... 54 A 2
Peyriac-Minervois (F) ...... 55 E 1
Peyrolles-en-Provence (F) 57 D 2
Peyruis (F) ...... 53 D 2
Pézenas (F) ...... 56 A 2
Pezinok (SK) ...... 12 A 3

Pezoúla (GR) ...... 207 F 2
Pfaffenhofen a. d. Ilm (D) .. 93 F 2
Pfäffikon (CH) ...... 92 C 4
Pfalzgrafenweiler (D) ...... 45 F 3
Pfarrkirchen (D) ...... 94 B 2
Pfeffenhausen (D) ...... 94 A 1
Pforzheim (D) ...... 45 F 3
Pfreimd (D) ...... 89 E 4
Pfronten (D) ...... 93 E 3
Pfullendorf (D) ...... 45 F 4
Pfullingen (D) ...... 45 F 4
Pfunds (A) ...... 93 E 4
Pfungstadt (D) ...... 45 E 1
Phalsbourg (F) ...... 45 D 3
Philippeville (B) ...... 39 E 3
Philippsreut (D) ...... 94 B 1
Piacenza (I) ...... 97 E 4
Piadena (I) ...... 97 F 4
Pian del Voglio (I) ...... 101 F 1
Piana (F) ...... 57 E 3
Piana degli Albanesi (I) ...... 110 B 2
Piancastagnaio (I) ...... 102 A 4
Piancavallo (I) ...... 98 B 2
Piandelagotti (I) ...... 101 E 1
Pianella (I) ...... 103 D 4
Pianello (I) ...... 102 B 2
Piano del Cansiglio (I) ...... 98 B 2
Pianoro (I) ...... 101 F 1
Piansano (I) ...... 102 A 4
Piaseczno
  Mazowieckie (PL) ...... 190 B 3
Piaski Lubelskie (PL) ...... 197 E 2
Piaski Pomorskie (PL) ...... 183 E 1
Piaski Warmińsko-
  Mazurskie (PL) ...... 184 C 3
Piaski Wielkopolskie (PL). 187 F 4
Piastów (PL) ...... 190 B 3
Piątek (PL) ...... 189 E 3
Piątkowisko (PL) ...... 189 D 4
Piątnica
  Poduchowna (PL) ...... 184 C 3
Piatra-Neamţ (RO) ...... 13 D 3
Piazza al Serchio (I) ...... 101 E 1
Piazza Armerina (I) ...... 111 D 3
Piazza Brembana (I) ...... 97 E 2
Piazzola sul Brenta (I) ...... 98 A 3
Piber (A) ...... 95 E 4
Pićan (HR) ...... 99 D 3
Picassent (E) ...... 71 F 3
Picerno (I) ...... 106 B 3
Pickering (GB) ...... 33 E 1
Pico (I) ...... 105 E 2
Picquigny (F) ...... 38 C 4
Piebalgas (LV) ...... 165 D 2
Piechowice (PL) ...... 193 D 3
Piecki (PL) ...... 184 B 3
Piedicavallo (I) ...... 53 F 1
Piedicroce (F) ...... 57 F 3
Piediluco (I) ...... 102 B 4
Piedimonte Matese (I) ...... 105 F 2
Piedra (Monasterio de) (E) 65 F 3
Piedrabuena (E) ...... 70 A 3
Piedrafita de Babia (E) ...... 59 E 3
Piedrahita (E) ...... 63 F 4
Piedralaves (E) ...... 70 A 1
Piedras Albas (E) ...... 69 D 1
Piedratajada (E) ...... 54 B 4
Piedruja (LV) ...... 173 E 1
Piekary Śląskie (PL) ...... 195 D 4
Piekoszów (PL) ...... 195 F 3
Pieksämäki (FIN) ...... 133 F 4
Pielavesi (FIN) ...... 133 F 3
Pielgrzymka
  Dolnośląskie (PL) ...... 193 D 2
Pielgrzymka
  Podkarpackie (PL) ...... 202 D 3
Pienava (LV) ...... 163 F 1
Pieniężno (PL) ...... 183 E 2
Pieniņi (Pīneņi) (LV) ...... 167 B 3
Pieniny (PL) ...... 201 B 3
Pienionys (LT) ...... 171 E 3
Piennes (F) ...... 44 D 2
Pieńsk (PL) ...... 192 C 2
Pienza (I) ...... 102 A 3
Piepaliai Kauno (LT) ...... 170 E 4
Piepaliai Panevėžio (LT) ... 165 F 4
Pierowall (GB) ...... 29 D 3
Pierre-Buffière (F) ...... 51 E 1
Pierre-de-Bresse (F) ...... 49 D 3
Pierrefitte-Nestalas (F) ...... 54 C 3
Pierrefitte-sur-Aire (F) ...... 44 B 1
Pierrefonds (F) ...... 43 F 3
Pierrefontaine-
  les-Varans (F) ...... 49 E 2
Pierrefort (F) ...... 51 F 3
Pierrelatte (F) ...... 52 B 4

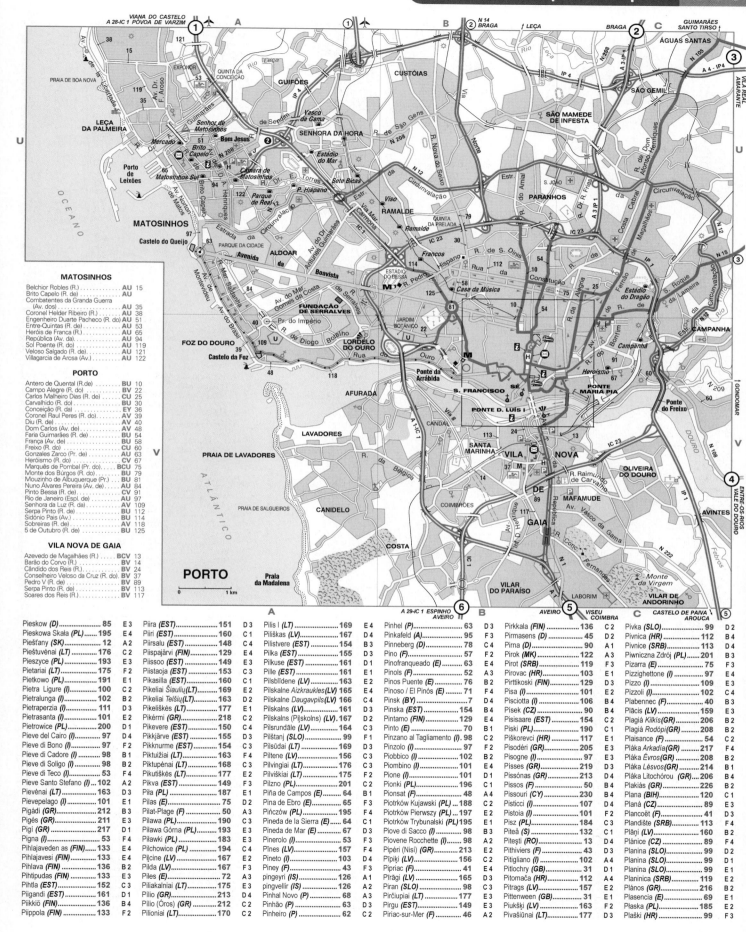

MATOSINHOS

Belchior Robles (R.) . . . . **AU** 15
Brito Capelo (R. de) . . . . **AU**
Combatentes da Granda Guerra
  (Av. dos) . . . . **AU** 35
Coronel Helder Ribeiro (R.) . . . . . . **AU** 38
Engenheiro Duarte Pacheco (R. do) **AU** 51
Entre-Quintas (R. de) . . . . **AU** 53
Heróis de Franca (R.) . . . . **AU** 65
República (Av. da) . . . . **AU** 94
Sol Poente (R. do) . . . . **AU** 119
Veloso Salgado (R. de) . . . . **AU** 121
Villagarcia de Arosa (Av.) . . . . **AU** 122

PORTO

Antero de Quental (R.de) . . . . **BU** 10
Campo Alegre (R. do) . . . . **BV** 22
Carlos Malheiro Dias (R. de) . . . . . **CU** 25
Carvalhido (R. do) . . . . **BU** 30
Conceição (R. da) . . . . **EY** 36
Coronel Raul Peres (R. do) . . . . . . **AV** 39
Diu (R. de) . . . . **AV** 40
Dom Carlos (Av. de) . . . . **AV** 48
Faria Guimarães (R. de) . . . . **BU** 54
França (Av. de) . . . . **BU** 58
Freixo (R. do) . . . . **CU** 60
Gonzales Zarco (Pr. de) . . . . **AU** 63
Heróismo (R. do) . . . . **CV** 67
Marquês de Pombal (Pr. do) . . . . . **BCU** 75
Monte dos Búrgos (R. do) . . . . **BU** 79
Mouzinho de Albuquerque (Pr.) . . . **BU** 81
Nuno Álvares Pereira (Av. de) . . . . **AU** 84
Pinto Bessa (R. de) . . . . **CV** 91
Rio de Janeiro (Espl. de) . . . . **AU** 97
Senhora da Luz (R. da) . . . . **AV** 109
Serpa Pinto (R. de) . . . . **BU** 112
Sidónio Pais (Av.) . . . . **BU** 114
Sobreiras (R. de) . . . . **AV** 118
5 de Outubro (R. de) . . . . **BU** 125

VILA NOVA DE GAIA

Azevedo de Magalhães (R.) . . . . . **BCV** 13
Barão do Corvo (R.) . . . . **BV** 14
Cândido dos Reis (R.) . . . . **BV** 24
Conselheiro Veloso da Cruz (R. do). **BV** 37
Pedro V (R. de) . . . . **BV** 89
Serpa Pinto (R.) . . . . **BV** 113
Soares dos Reis (R.) . . . . **BV** 117

PORTO

Pieskow (D) . . . . . 85 E 3
Pieskowa Skała (PL) . . 195 E 4
Piešťany (SK) . . . 12 A 2
Pieštuvénai (LT) . 176 C 2
Pieszyce (PL) . . . 193 E 3
Pietariai (LT) . . . 175 F 2
Pietkowo (PL) . . . 191 E 1
Pietra Ligure (I) . . 100 C 2
Pietralunga (I) . . . 102 D 3
Pietraperzia (I) . . . 111 D 3
Pietrasanta (I) . . . 101 E 2
Pietrowice (PL) . . . 200 D 1
Pieve del Cairo (I) . . 97 D 4
Pieve di Bono (I) . . 97 F 2
Pieve di Cadore (I) . 98 B 1
Pieve di Soligo (I) . 98 B 1
Pieve di Teco (I) . . 53 F 4
Pieve Santo Stefano (I) . 102 D 3
Pievénai (LT) . . . 163 D 3
Pievepelago (I) . . . 101 E 1
Pigádi (GR) . . . . . 212 B 3
Pigés (GR) . . . . . 211 D 1
Pigi (GR) . . . . . . 217 D 1
Pigna (I) . . . . . . 53 F 4
Pihlajaveden as (FIN) 133 F 2
Pihlajavesi (FIN) . . 133 E 4
Pihlava (FIN) . . . . 136 B 3
Pihtipudas (FIN) . . 133 E 3
Pihtla (EST) . . . . 152 C 3
Piigandi (EST) . . . 161 D 4
Piikkiö (FIN) . . . . 136 B 4
Piippola (FIN) . . . 133 F 2

Piira (EST) . . . . . 151 D 3
Piiri (EST) . . . . . 160 C 1
Piirsalu (EST) . . . 148 C 4
Piispajärvi (FIN) . . 129 E 4
Piissoo (EST) . . . 149 E 3
Piistaoja (EST) . . . 153 C 3
Pikasilla (EST) . . . 160 C 1
Pikeliai Šiaulių(LT) . 169 E 2
Pikeliai Telšių(LT) . 163 D 2
Pikeliškés (LT) . . . 177 E 1
Pikérmi (GR) . . . . 218 C 2
Pikevere (EST) . . . 154 C 4
Pikkjärve (EST) . . . 155 D 3
Pikknurme (EST) . . 154 C 2
Piktuižiai (LT) . . . 163 F 4
Piktupénai (LT) . . . 168 C 3
Pikutiškés (LT) . . . 177 E 2
Pikva (EST) . . . . 149 F 3
Piła (PL) . . . . . . 187 E 1
Pilas (E) . . . . . . 75 D 2
Pilat-Plage (F) . . . 50 A 3
Pilawa (PL) . . . . 190 E 2
Pilawa Górna (PL) . 193 E 3
Piławki (PL) . . . . 183 E 3
Pilchowice (PL) . . . 194 C 4
Pilcine (LV) . . . . 167 E 4
Pilda (LV) . . . . . 167 F 3
Piles (E) . . . . . . 72 A 3
Piliakalniai (LT) . . . 175 E 3
Pilio (Óros) (GR) . . 213 D 4
Pilioniai (LT) . . . . 170 C 2

Pilis I (LT) . . . . . 169 E 4
Piliškas (LV) . . . . 167 D 4
Pilistvere (EST) . . . 154 B 3
Pilka (EST) . . . . . 155 D 3
Pilkuse (EST) . . . . 161 D 1
Pille (EST) . . . . . 161 E 1
Pilsblīdene (LV) . . 163 E 2
Pilskalne Aizkraukles(LV) 165 E 4
Pilskalne Daugavpils(LV) 160 C 4
Pilskalns (LV) . . . . 161 D 2
Pilskalns (Pilskolns) (LV).167 D 2
Pilštanj (SLO) . . . . 99 F 1
Pilsūdai (LT) . . . . 169 D 3
Piltene (LV) . . . . 156 C 3
Pilvingiai (LT) . . . . 176 F 2
Pilviškiai (LT) . . . . 175 F 2
Piña de Campos (E) . 64 B 1
Pina de Ebro (E) . . 65 F 3
Piñc%ów (PL) . . . . 195 F 4
Pineda de la Sierra (E) 64 C 2
Pineda de Mar (E) . 67 D 3
Pinerolo (I) . . . . . 53 F 3
Pīnes (LV) . . . . . 157 D 4
Pineto (I) . . . . . . 103 D 4
Piniec (LV) . . . . . 167 F 3
pingeyri (IS) . . . . 126 A 1
pingvellir (IS) . . . 126 A 2
Pinhal Novo (P) . . 68 A 3
Pinhão (P) . . . . . 63 D 4
Pinheiro (P) . . . . 62 C 2

Pinhel (P) . . . . . 63 D 3
Pinkafeld (A) . . . . 95 F 3
Pinneberg (D) . . . 78 C 2
Pino (F) . . . . . . 57 F 2
Pinofranqueado (E) . 63 E 4
Pinols (E) . . . . . 52 A 3
Pinos Puente (E) . . 76 B 2
Pinoso / El Pinós (E) . 71 F 4
Pinsk (BY) 7
Pinska (EST) . . . . 154 B 4
Pintamo (FIN) . . . 129 E 4
Pinto (E) . . . . . . 70 B 1
Pinzano al Tagliamento (I). 98 C 2
Pinzolo (I) . . . . . 97 F 2
Piobbico (I) . . . . 102 D 3
Piombino (I) . . . . 101 E 4
Pione (I) . . . . . . 101 D 1
Pionki (PL) . . . . . 196 E 1
Pionsat (F) . . . . . 48 A 4
Piotrków Kujawski (PL) . 188 C 2
Piotrków Pierwszy (PL) . 197 F 4
Piotrków Trybunalski (PL)195 E 1
Piove di Sacco (I) . 98 B 3
Piovene Rocchette (I). 98 A 2
Pipéri (Nisí) (GR) . . 213 E 2
Pīpiķi (LV) . . . . . 156 C 2
Pipriac (F) . . . . . 41 D 1
Pīrāģi (LV) . . . . . 165 D 3
Piran (SLO) . . . . 98 C 3
Pirčiupiai (LT) . . . 177 E 3
Pirgu (EST) . . . . 149 E 3
Piriac-sur-Mer (F) . 46 A 2

Pirkkala (FIN) . . . 136 C 2
Pirmasens (D) . . . 45 D 2
Pirna (D) . . . . . . 90 A 1
Pirok (MK) . . . . . 122 A 3
Pirovac (HR) . . . . 103 E 1
Pirttikoski (FIN) . . 129 D 3
Pirttikoski (FIN) . . 129 D 3
Pirot (SRB) . . . . 119 F 3
Pisa (I) . . . . . . 101 E 2
Pisciotta (I) . . . . 106 B 4
Písek (CZ) . . . . . 90 B 4
Pisisaare (EST) . . 154 C 2
Piski (LT) . . . . . 190 C 1
Piškorevci (HR) . . 117 E 1
Pisodéri (GR) . . . 205 E 3
Pisogne (I) . . . . 97 E 3
Pisses (GR) . . . . 219 D 3
Pissónas (GR) . . . 213 D 4
Pissos (F) . . . . . 50 B 4
Pissouri (CY) . . . 230 B 4
Pisticci (I) . . . . . 107 D 4
Pistoia (I) . . . . . 101 F 2
Pisz (PL) . . . . . 184 C 3
Piteå (S) . . . . . 132 C 1
Pitești (RO) . . . . 13 D 4
Pithiviers (F) . . . 43 F 3
Pitigliano (I) . . . . 102 A 4
Pitlochry (GB) . . . 31 D 1
Pitomača (HR) . . . 112 A 4
Pitrags (LV) . . . . 157 D 2
Pittenween (GB) . . 31 E 1
Piukšķi (LV) . . . . 163 E 3
Pivašiūnai (LT) . . 177 D 3

Pivka (SLO) . . . . 99 D 2
Pivnica (HR) . . . . 112 B 4
Pivnice (SRB) . . . 113 D 4
Piwniczna Zdrój (PL) . 201 B 3
Pizarra (E) . . . . . 75 F 3
Pizzighettone (I) . . 97 E 4
Pizzo (I) . . . . . . 109 E 3
Pizzoli (I) . . . . . 102 C 4
Plabennec (F) . . . 40 B 3
Plācis (LV) . . . . 159 E 3
Plagiá Kilkis(GR) . . 206 B 2
Plagiá Rodópi(GR) . 208 B 2
Plaisance (F) . . . 54 C 2
Pláka Arkadía(GR) . 217 F 4
Pláka Évros(GR) . . 208 B 2
Pláka Lésvos(GR) . 214 B 1
Pláka Litochórou (GR). 206 B 2
Plakiás (GR) . . . . 226 B 2
Plana (BIH) . . . . 120 C 1
Planá (CZ) . . . . . 89 E 3
Plancoët (F) . . . . 41 D 3
Plandište (SRB) . . 113 E 4
Plāņi (LV) . . . . . 160 B 2
Plánice (CZ) . . . . 89 F 4
Planina (SLO) . . . 99 D 2
Planina (SLO) . . . 99 D 1
Planina (SLO) . . . 99 E 1
Planinica (SRB) . . 119 E 2
Plános (GR) . . . . 216 B 2
Plasencia (E) . . . 63 E 1
Plaska (PL) . . . . 185 E 2
Plaški (HR) . . . . 99 F 3

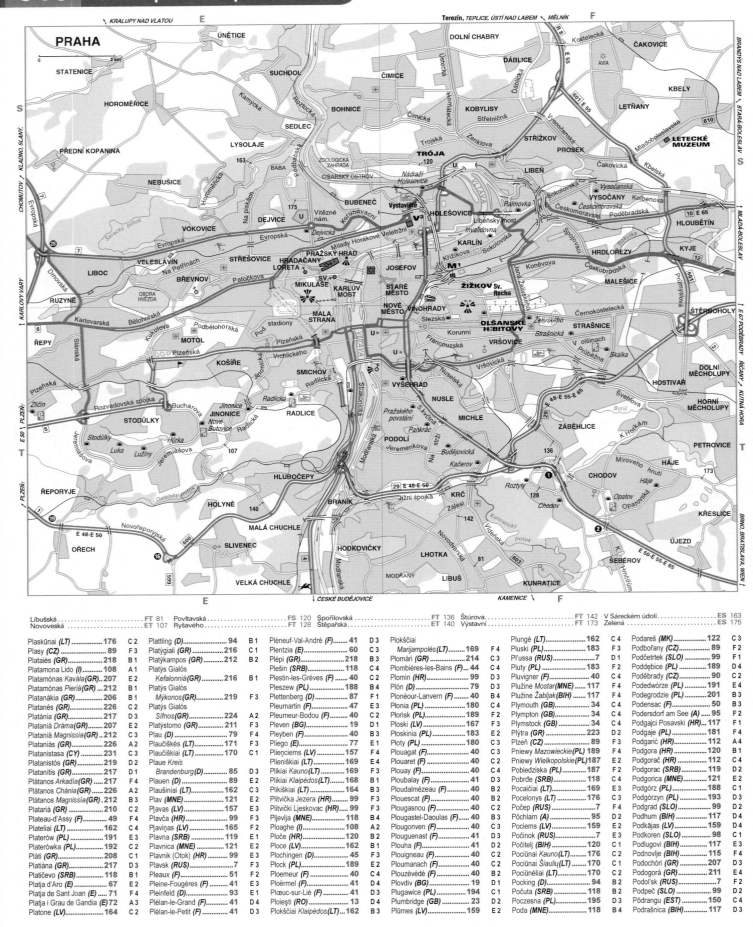

PRAHA

Líbušská .... FT 81 | Povltavská .... FS 120 | Spořilovská .... FT 136 | Štúrova .... FT 142 | V Sáreckém údolí .... ES 163
Novoveská .... ET 107 | Ryšavého .... FT 128 | Štěpařská .... ET 140 | Výstavní .... FT 173 | Zelená .... ES 175

Plaskūnai (LT) .... 176 C 2
Plasy (CZ) .... 89 F 3
Plataiés (GR) .... 218 B 1
Platamona Lido (I) .... 108 A 1
Platamónas Kavála(GR)..207 E 2
Platamónas Pieriá(GR) .. 212 B 1
Platanákia (GR) .... 206 B 1
Platanés (GR) .... 226 C 2
Platánia (GR) .... 217 D 3
Platanía Dráma(GR) .... 207 E 2
Platania Magníssia(GR).. 212 C 3
Plataniás (GR) .... 226 A 2
Platanistasa (CY) .... 231 C 3
Platanistós (GR) .... 219 D 2
Platanítis (GR) .... 217 D 1
Plátanos Arkadía(GR) .... 217 F 4
Plátanos Chánia(GR) .... 226 A 2
Plátanos Magníssia(GR) .212 B 3
Plataniá (GR) .... 210 C 2
Plateau-d'Assy (F) .... 49 F 4
Platelíai (LT) .... 162 C 4
Platerów (PL) .... 191 E 3
Platerówka (PL) .... 192 C 2
Pláti (GR) .... 208 C 1
Platiána (GR) .... 217 D 3
Platičevo (SRB) .... 118 B 1
Platja d'Aro (E) .... 67 F 4
Platja de Sant Joan (E) ..... 71 F 4
Platja i Grau de Gandia (E)72 A 3
Platone (LV) .... 164 C 2

Plattling (D) .... 94 B 1
Platýgiali (GR) .... 216 C 1
Platýkampos (GR) .... 212 B 2
Platýs Gialós
  Kefalonniá(GR) .... 216 B 1
Platýs Gialós
  Mýkonos(GR) .... 219 F 3
Platýs Gialós
  Sífnos(GR) .... 224 A 2
Platýstomo (GR) .... 211 F 3
Plau (D) .... 79 F 4
Plaučiškes (LT) .... 171 F 3
Plaučiūkiai (LT) .... 170 C 1
Plaue Kreis
  Brandenburg(D) .... 85 D 3
Plauen (D) .... 89 E 2
Plaušiniai (LT) .... 162 C 3
Plav (MNE) .... 121 E 3
Plavas (LV) .... 157 E 3
Plavča (HR) .... 99 F 3
Plaviņas (LV) .... 165 F 2
Plavna (SRB) .... 119 E 1
Plavnica (MNE) .... 121 E 2
Plavnik (Otok) (HR) .... 99 E 3
Plavsk (RUS) .... 7 F 1
Pleaux (F) .... 51 F 2
Pleine-Fougères (F) .... 41 E 1
Pleinfeld (D) .... 93 E 1
Plélan-le-Grand (F) .... 41 D 4
Plélan-le-Petit (F) .... 41 D 3

Pléneuf-Val-André (F) .... 41 D 3
Plentzia (E) .... 60 C 3
Plépi (GR) .... 218 D 2
Plešin (SRB) .... 118 C 4
Plestin-les-Grèves (F) .... 40 C 2
Pleszew (PL) .... 188 B 4
Plettenberg (D) .... 87 F 1
Pleumartin (F) .... 47 E 3
Pleumeur-Bodou (F) .... 40 C 2
Pleven (BG) .... 19 D 1
Pleyben (F) .... 40 B 3
Pliego (E) .... 77 E 1
Plienciems (LV) .... 157 F 4
Plieniškiai (LT) .... 169 E 4
Plikiai Kauno(LT) .... 169 F 3
Plikiai Klaipédos(LT) .... 168 B 1
Plikiškiai (LT) .... 164 B 3
Plitvica Jezera (HR) .... 99 F 3
Plitvički Ljeskovac (HR) .... 99 F 3
Pljevlja (MNE) .... 118 B 4
Ploče (HR) .... 120 B 2
Ploče (LV) .... 162 B 1
Plochingen (D) .... 92 E 3
Płock (PL) .... 189 E 2
Ploemeur (F) .... 40 C 4
Ploërmel (F) .... 41 D 4
Plœuc-sur-Lié (F) .... 41 D 3
Ploiești (RO) .... 13 D 4
Plokščiai Klaipédos(LT) 162 B 3

Plokščiai
  Marijampolés(LT) .... 169 F 4
Plomári (GR) .... 214 C 2
Plombières-les-Bains (F)... 44 C 1
Plomin (HR) .... 99 D 3
Plön (D) .... 79 D 1
Plonéour-Lanvern (F) .... 40 B 4
Płońsk (PL) .... 189 F 2
Ploski (LV) .... 167 F 3
Płoskinia (PL) .... 183 E 2
Ploty (PL) .... 180 C 3
Plouagat (F) .... 40 C 3
Plouaret (F) .... 40 C 2
Plouay (F) .... 40 C 4
Ploubalay (F) .... 41 D 3
Ploudalmézeau (F) .... 40 B 2
Plouescat (F) .... 40 B 2
Plougasnou (F) .... 40 C 2
Plougastel-Daoulas (F) .... 40 B 3
Plougonven (F) .... 40 C 3
Plouguenast (F) .... 41 D 3
Plouha (F) .... 41 D 3
Plouigneau (F) .... 40 C 2
Ploumanach (F) .... 40 C 2
Plouézévédé (F) .... 40 B 2
Plovdiv (BG) .... 19 D 1
Plugawice (PL) .... 194 C 1
Plumbridge (GB) .... 23 C 4
Plūmes (LV) .... 159 E 2

Plungé (LT) .... 162 C 4
Pluski (PL) .... 183 F 3
Pl'ussa (RUS) .... 7 F 1
Pluty (PL) .... 183 F 2
Pluvigner (F) .... 40 C 4
Plužine Mostar(MNE) .... 117 F 4
Plužine Žabljak(BIH) .... 117 F 4
Plymouth (GB) .... 34 C 4
Plympton (GB) .... 34 C 4
Plymstock (GB) .... 34 C 4
Płytra (GR) .... 223 D 2
Plzeň (CZ) .... 89 F 3
Pniewy Mazowieckie(PL) 189 E 2
Pniewy Wielkopolskie(PL)187 E 2
Pobiedziska (PL) .... 187 F 2
Pobrde (SRB) .... 118 C 4
Pocaičiai (LT) .... 169 D 3
Pocelonys (LT) .... 176 C 3
Počep (RUS) .... 7 F 4
Pöchlarn (A) .... 95 D 2
Pociems (LV) .... 159 D 2
Pocinok (RUS) .... 7 F 2
Počitelj (BIH) .... 120 C 1
Pociūnai Kauno(LT) .... 176 D 2
Pociūnai Šiauliu(LT) .... 170 C 1
Pociūnéliai (LT) .... 170 C 2
Pocking (D) .... 94 B 2
Počuta (SRB) .... 118 B 2
Poczesna (PL) .... 195 D 3
Poda (MNE) .... 118 B 4

Podareš (MK) .... 122 C 3
Podbořany (CZ) .... 89 E 3
Podčetrtek (SLO) .... 99 F 1
Poddębice (PL) .... 189 D 4
Poděbrady (CZ) .... 90 C 2
Podedwórze (PL) .... 191 E 4
Podegrodzie (PL) .... 201 B 3
Podensac (F) .... 50 B 3
Podersdorf am See (A) .... 95 C 3
Podgajci Posavski (HR)... 117 F 1
Podgaje (PL) .... 181 F 4
Podgarić (HR) .... 112 A 4
Podgora (HR) .... 120 B 1
Podgorač (HR) .... 112 C 4
Podgorac (SRB) .... 119 D 2
Podgorica (MNE) .... 121 E 2
Podgórz (PL) .... 188 C 1
Podgórzyn (PL) .... 193 D 3
Podgrad (SLO) .... 99 D 2
Podhum (BIH) .... 117 D 4
Podkájas (LV) .... 159 D 4
Podkoren (SLO) .... 98 C 1
Podlugov (BIH) .... 117 E 4
Podnovlje (BIH) .... 115 F 4
Podochóri (GR) .... 207 D 3
Podogorá (GR) .... 211 E 4
Podol'sk (RUS) .... 7 F 1
Podpeč (SLO) .... 99 D 2
Põdrangu (EST) .... 150 C 4
Podrašnica (BIH) .... 117 D 3

Place	Page	Grid
Podravski Kloštar (HR)	112	A 4
Podromanija (BIH)	117	F 3
Põdruse (EST)	151	D 3
Podsreda (SLO)	99	F 1
Podsused (HR)	99	F 2
Podturen (HR)	95	F 4
Podujevo (SRB)	119	D 2
Podunavci (SRB)	118	C 3
Podzěni (LV)	159	E 3
Poggibonsi (I)	101	F 3
Poggio Imperiale (I)	106	B 1
Poggio Mirteto (I)	102	B 4
Poggio Renatico (I)	98	A 4
Poggio Rusco (I)	98	A 4
Pöggstall (A)	95	D 1
Pogonianí (GR)	210	B 2
Pogorzel (PL)	185	D 2
Pogorzela (PL)	187	F 4
Pogradec (AL)	122	A 4
Pogwizdów (PL)	200	E 2
Põhara (EST)	153	B 3
Pohja / Pojo (FIN)	136	C 4
Pohja-Lankila (FIN)	137	F 2
Põhjaka (EST)	154	B 3
Pohjaslahti (FIN)	133	F 2
Pohjaslahti (FIN)	129	D 3
Pohořelice (CZ)	91	D 4
Poiana Brașov (RO)	13	B 3
Põikva (EST)	154	A 2
Poio (E)	58	B 4
Poirino (I)	53	F 2
Poissons (F)	44	B 4
Poitiers (F)	47	D 3
Poix-de-Picardie (F)	38	C 2
Poix-Terron (F)	39	F 4
Pojate (SRB)	119	D 3
Poki (LV)	164	C 2
Pokka (FIN)	125	E 4
Poklečani (BIH)	117	D 4
Pokój (PL)	194	B 3
Pokrówka (PL)	197	F 2
Pokupsko (HR)	99	F 2
Pola de Allande (E)	59	D 2
Pola de Laviana (E)	59	F 3
Pola de Lena (E)	59	E 3
Pola de Siero (E)	59	E 3
Polače (HR)	120	B 2
Polack (BY)	7	D 2
Połajewo (PL)	187	E 1
Połajkas (E)	166	C 3
Polán (E)	70	C 1
Polana Śląskie (PL)	200	E 3
Polanica-Zdrój (PL)	193	E 2
Połaniec (PL)	196	C 4
Polanów (PL)	181	E 2
Polany (PL)	201	E 3
Polbrenči (LV)	159	F 1
Polčane (SLO)	99	F 1
Polcenigo (I)	98	B 2
Połczyn Zdrój (PL)	181	D 1
Põlde (EST)	154	A 4
Põldeotsa (EST)	153	B 3
Polegate (GB)	36	C 4
Polekělė (LT)	169	F 1
Polemi (CY)	230	A 3
Põlendmaa (EST)	153	C 3
Polesella (I)	98	A 4
Poleski Park Narodowy (PL)	197	E 1
Polessk (RUS)	6	B 4
Põlgaste (EST)	161	D 1
Polhov Gradec (SLO)	99	E 1
Policastro Bussentino (I)	106	B 4
Police (PL)	180	B 3
Polichnítos (GR)	214	C 3
Polička (CZ)	91	D 3
Poličnik (HR)	103	E 3
Policoro (I)	107	D 4
Policzna (PL)	196	C 1
Polignano a Mare (I)	107	D 2
Poligny (F)	49	E 1
Políochni (GR)	214	B 1
Polis (CY)	230	A 3
Polistena (I)	111	E 4
Politiká (GR)	212	C 4
Poljana (SLO)	99	E 1
Poljana (SRB)	118	C 1
Poljana Pakračka (HR)	115	E 3
Polje (BIH)	115	F 4
Poljica (HR)	120	A 2
Poljice (BIH)	117	E 3
Polkorona (LV)	167	D 3
Polkowice (PL)	193	D 1
Polla (I)	106	B 4
Pölläkkä (FIN)	135	F 4
Pöllau (A)	95	E 3
Polle (D)	84	A 4
Pollença (E)	73	E 2
Pollfoss (N)	130	B 4
Polli (EST)	154	B 4
Pollos (E)	64	A 3
Polmak (N)	125	E 2
Polonne (UA)	13	D 1
Polperro (GB)	34	C 4
Polska Cerekiew (PL)	194	C 4
Poltava (UA)	13	F 1
Põltsamaa (EST)	154	C 3
Põlva (EST)	161	D 1
Polvijärvi (FIN)	135	F 3
Polydéndri (GR)	218	C 1
Polýdrosos (GR)	212	B 4
Polýegos (Nisí) (GR)	224	A 2
Polýgyros (GR)	206	C 4
Polykárpi (GR)	205	F 2
Polykástano (GR)	205	E 2
Polýkastro (GR)	206	B 2
Polýmylos (GR)	205	F 4
Polynéri Grevená (GR)	205	E 2
Polynéri Tríkala (GR)	211	E 2
Polypótamo (GR)	205	E 3
Polypótamos (GR)	219	D 1
Polýrracho (GR)	205	F 4
Polyrrínia (GR)	226	A 2
Polýsito (GR)	207	F 2
Polythéa (GR)	211	E 2
Polzela (SLO)	99	E 1
Pomar (E)	66	A 2
Pomarance (I)	101	F 3
Pomarkku (FIN)	136	B 2
Pombal (P)	68	B 1
Pomellen (D)	81	D 4
Pomezí (CZ)	91	D 3
Pomezia (I)	104	C 2
Pomiechówek (PL)	189	F 1
Pomieczyno (PL)	182	C 1
Pomigliano d'Arco (I)	105	F 3
Pommersfelden (D)	88	C 4
Pomorie (BG)	19	E 1
Pomorska (Zatoka) (PL)	180	B 2
Pomos (CY)	230	A 3
Pompei (I)	105	F 3
Pómpia (GR)	226	C 3
Pomposa (Abbazia di) (I)	98	B 4
Poncin (F)	49	D 4
Ponferrada (E)	59	D 4
Poniatowa (PL)	197	D 2
Poniec (PL)	187	E 1
Ponikovica (SRB)	118	B 3
Ponikškiai (LT)	175	F 3
Pons (F)	50	B 2
Ponsacco (I)	101	E 2
Ponte da Barca (P)	62	C 1
Ponte de Lima (P)	62	B 1
Ponte de Sor (P)	68	C 2
Ponte di Legno (I)	97	F 2
Ponte di Piave (I)	98	B 2
Ponte-Leccia (F)	57	F 3
Ponte nelle Alpi (I)	98	B 2
Ponte San Pietro (I)	97	E 3
Ponteareas (E)	58	B 4
Pontebba (I)	98	C 1
Pontecagnano (I)	106	A 4
Ponteceno (I)	101	D 1
Ponteceso (E)	58	A 2
Pontecorvo (I)	105	E 2
Pontedecimo (I)	100	C 1
Pontedera (I)	101	E 2
Pontedeume (E)	58	B 2
Pontefract (GB)	33	D 2
Pontelandolfo (I)	105	F 3
Pontes de García Rodríguez (As) (E)	58	C 2
Pontevedra (E)	58	B 4
Pontevico (I)	97	E 3
Pontfaverger-Moronvilliers (F)	43	F 1
Pontgibaud (F)	51	F 1
Pontigny (F)	43	E 4
Pontinia (I)	105	D 3
Pontinvrea (I)	100	C 1
Pontivy (F)	40	C 3
Pontlevoy (F)	47	F 3
Pontoïrákleia (GR)	206	B 2
Pontoise (F)	43	D 2
Pontokómi (GR)	205	E 2
Pontorson (F)	41	E 3
Pontremoli (I)	101	D 1
Pontresina (CH)	97	E 1
Pontrieux (F)	40	C 3
Pontrilas (GB)	35	D 1
Ponts Lleida (E)	66	B 2
Pontvallain (F)	42	A 4
Pontypool / Pontypŵl (GB)	35	D 1
Pontypridd (GB)	35	D 1
Poole (GB)	35	E 3
Pootsi (EST)	153	B 4
Popadić (SRB)	118	A 3
Pope (LV)	157	D 3
Poperinge (B)	37	E 4
Popielów (PL)	194	B 3
Popinci (SRB)	118	B 1
Popoli (I)	103	E 2
Popov Most (BIH)	117	F 4
Popovac (SRB)	119	D 2
Popovača (HR)	115	D 3
Popovo (BG)	13	E 4
Poppenhausen (D)	88	C 3
Poppi (I)	102	A 2
Poprad (PL)	201	B 3
Poprad (SK)	12	B 2
Poraj (PL)	195	D 2
Porcari (I)	101	E 2
Porcuna (E)	76	A 1
Pordenone (I)	98	B 2
Poręba (PL)	195	D 4
Poreč (HR)	99	D 3
Porečje (Pareči) (LV)	167	F 4
Pori (Björneborg) (FIN)	136	B 2
Porijai (EST)	165	D 4
Porjus (S)	128	A 3
Porkuni (EST)	150	C 3
Porlock (GB)	35	D 1
Pornainen (FIN)	137	D 3
Pörnbach (D)	93	F 1
Pornic (F)	46	A 2
Pornichet (F)	46	A 2
Porrentruy (CH)	49	E 1
Porretta Terme (I)	101	F 1
Porriño (E)	58	B 4
Porsgrunn (N)	139	B 2
Port Askaig (GB)	30	A 2
Port-Barcarès (F)	55	F 1
Port Charlotte (GB)	30	A 2
Port d'Alcúdia (E)	73	E 2
Port d'Andratx (E)	73	E 2
Port-de-Bouc (F)	56	C 2
Port de Pollença (E)	73	E 2
Port de Sóller / Puerto de Sóller (E)	73	D 2
Port Ellen (GB)	30	A 2
Port-en-Bessin (F)	41	F 1
Port Erin (GB)	32	A 1
Port-Eynon (GB)	34	C 1
Port Glasgow (GB)	30	C 2
Port-Joinville (F)	46	A 3
Port-la-Nouvelle (F)	55	F 3
Port-Leucate (F)	67	F 1
Port-Louis (F)	40	C 4
Port-Manech (F)	40	B 4
Port-Navalo (F)	40	C 4
Port of Ness (GB)	27	D 1
Port-St-Louis-du-Rhône (F)	56	C 2
Port St Mary (GB)	32	A 1
Port-Ste-Marie (F)	50	C 4
Port-sur-Saône (F)	49	E 1
Port Talbot (GB)	34	C 1
Port-Vendres (F)	56	A 4
Port William (GB)	30	C 4
Porta Westfalica (D)	83	F 3
Portadown (GB)	23	E 2
Portaferry (GB)	23	F 2
Portalegre (P)	68	C 2
Portalrubio (E)	65	F 4
Portariá (GR)	212	B 2
Portarlington / Cúil an tSúdaire (IRL)	25	D 1
Portavogie (GB)	23	F 3
Portbail (F)	41	E 1
Portbou (F)	56	A 4
Portel (P)	68	C 4
Portelo (P)	63	E 1
Pórtes (GR)	218	C 2
Portezuelo (E)	69	E 1
Portglenone (GB)	23	E 2
Porthcawl (GB)	35	D 1
Porthmadog (GB)	32	B 3
Portici (I)	105	F 3
Portilla de la Reina (E)	59	F 3
Portillo (E)	64	A 3
Portimão (P)	74	A 2
Portimo (FIN)	129	D 1
Portinho da Arrábida (P)	68	A 3
Portishead (GB)	35	E 2
Portlaoise / Port Laoise (IRL)	25	D 2
Portman (E)	77	F 2
Portmarnock (IRL)	23	E 4
Portnacroish (GB)	30	B 1
Portnaguran (GB)	27	D 2
Portnahaven (GB)	30	A 2
Porto (F)	57	E 3
Porto (P)	62	B 3
Porto Alto (P)	68	A 2
Porto Azzurro (I)	101	E 4
Porto Boúfalo (I)	218	C 1
Porto Ceresio (I)	97	D 3
Porto Cervo (I)	108	B 2
Porto Cesareo (I)	107	E 3
Porto Cristo (E)	73	E 2
Porto Empedocle (I)	110	C 3
Porto Ercole (I)	101	F 4
Porto Garibaldi (I)	98	B 4
Portó Germenó (GR)	218	B 1
Pórto Kágio (GR)	222	C 3
Porto Pino (I)	108	B 4
Pórto Ráfti (GR)	218	C 2
Porto Recanati (I)	102	C 2
Porto Rotondo (I)	108	B 1
Porto San Elpidio (I)	102	C 2
Porto San Giorgio (I)	102	C 3
Porto Santo Stefano (I)	101	F 4
Porto Tolle (I)	98	B 4
Porto Torres (I)	108	A 1
Porto-Vecchio (I)	57	F 4
Portochéli (GR)	218	B 4
Portoferraio (I)	101	E 4
Portofino (I)	101	D 1
Portogruaro (I)	98	B 2
Pörtom (FIN)	133	D 4
Portomaggiore (I)	98	A 4
Portomarín (E)	58	C 3
Portomouro (E)	58	B 3
Portonovo (E)	58	B 4
Portopetro (E)	73	E 3
Portoroz (SLO)	98	C 3
Portoscuso (I)	108	A 4
Portovenere (I)	101	D 2
Portpatrick (GB)	23	F 2
Portree (GB)	26	C 3
Portrush (GB)	23	E 1
Portsalon (IRL)	23	D 1
Pörtschach (A)	99	D 1
Portsmouth (GB)	35	F 3
Portstewart (GB)	23	E 1
Portugalete (E)	60	C 3
Portumna / Port Omna (IRL)	24	C 1
Poruba (CZ)	91	F 2
Porvoo / Borgå (FIN)	137	D 3
Porzuna (E)	70	B 3
Posada (I)	108	C 2
Posadas (E)	75	F 1
Poschiavo (CH)	97	E 2
Posedarje (HR)	99	F 4
Poseidi (GR)	212	C 1
Poseidonía (GR)	219	E 3
Posio (FIN)	129	E 3
Positano (I)	105	F 4
Poškakaimis (LT)	169	E 2
Poškonys (LT)	177	F 3
Posta (I)	102	C 4
Postira (HR)	117	D 4
Postojna (SLO)	99	D 2
Postomino (PL)	181	E 1
Pošupės (LT)	164	B 3
Posušje (BIH)	117	D 4
Poświętne Łodzkie (PL)	195	F 1
Poświętne Mazowieckie (PL)	190	C 3
Poświętne Podlaskie (PL)	191	E 1
Potamí (GR)	207	E 1
Potamia (CY)	231	D 3
Potamiá (GR)	217	E 4
Potamiés (GR)	227	D 2
Potamós Antikýthira (GR)	223	E 4
Potamós Kythíra (GR)	223	D 3
Potamoúla (GR)	211	E 4
Potęgowo (PL)	181	F 1
Potenza (I)	106	C 3
Potenza Picena (I)	102	C 2
Potes (E)	60	A 3
Potigny (F)	42	A 2
Potoci (BIH)	117	E 4
Potok (HR)	115	D 3
Potorova (LV)	167	F 3
Potós (GR)	207	E 3
Potsdam (D)	85	D 3
Pottenstein (A)	95	E 2
Potters Bar (GB)	36	B 3
Pöttmes (D)	93	F 2
Potton (GB)	36	B 3
Potworów (PL)	195	F 1
Pouancé (F)	41	E 4
Pougues-les-Eaux (F)	48	B 3
Pouilly-en-Auxois (F)	48	C 2
Pouilly-sous-Charlieu (F)	48	C 4
Pouilly-sur-Loire (F)	48	A 2
Poúlithra (GR)	217	E 4
Poúnta (GR)	219	E 4
Pournári (GR)	212	A 3
Poussu (FIN)	129	E 3
Pouyastruc (F)	54	C 2
Pouzauges (F)	46	C 3
Považská Bystrica (SK)	12	A 2
Poveda de la Sierra (E)	65	D 4
Povilai (LT)	168	B 2
Povlja (HR)	117	D 4
Povljana (HR)	99	F 4
Póvoa de Lanhoso (P)	62	C 2
Póvoa de Varzim (P)	62	B 2
Powidz (PL)	188	B 2
Powodowo (PL)	187	D 3
Powroźnik (PL)	201	C 3
Poysdorf (A)	95	F 1
Pöytyä (FIN)	136	B 3
Poza de la Sal (E)	60	B 4
Pozaldez (E)	64	A 3
Pozo Alcón (E)	76	C 1
Pozo Cañada (E)	71	E 4
Pozo de Guadalajara (E)	64	C 4
Pozo Higuera (E)	77	E 3
Pozoblanco (E)	69	F 4
Pozohondo (E)	71	E 4
Pozondón (E)	65	D 4
Pozuelo (E)	71	D 4
Pozuelo de Calatrava (E)	70	B 3
Pozuelo de Zarzón (E)	69	E 1
Pozzallo (I)	111	E 4
Pozzomaggiore (I)	108	A 2
Pozzomaggiore (I)	108	A 2
Pozzuoli (I)	105	F 3
Pozzuolo del Friuli (I)	98	C 2
Pra-Loup (F)	53	E 4
Prabaščiškės (LT)	177	F 4
Prabuty (PL)	183	D 3
Prača (BIH)	117	F 3
Prachatice (CZ)	90	B 4
Pradelles (F)	52	A 3
Prádena (E)	64	B 3
Prades (F)	55	F 4
Pradła (PL)	195	E 4
Prado del Rey (E)	75	E 3
Pradoluengo (E)	64	C 1
Præstø (DK)	144	C 3
Pragarélė (LT)	171	D 1
Prägraten (A)	94	A 4
Praha (CZ)	90	B 2
Prahecq (F)	47	D 4
Praia a Mare (I)	109	D 1
Praia da Barra (P)	62	B 3
Praia da Rocha (P)	74	A 2
Praia da Tocha (P)	62	B 4
Praia da Vieira (P)	68	A 1
Praia de Mira (P)	62	B 4
Praia de Santa Cruz (P)	68	A 2
Prali (Ammochostos) (CY)	231	D 3
Prastio (Morfou) (CY)	230	B 3
Prat del Comte (E)	66	A 4
Pratella (I)	105	F 2
Prati di Tivo (I)	102	C 4
Prato (I)	101	F 2
Prato (I)	102	B 4
Prats de Lluçanès (E)	67	D 2
Prats-de-Mollo-la-Preste (F)	55	F 4
Prauliai (LT)	170	C 4
Prauliena (LV)	166	C 1
Prauthoy (F)	49	D 1
Pravdinsk (RUS)	6	
Pravia (E)	59	E 2
Pravieniškės I (LT)	176	C 1
Pravieniškės II (LT)	170	C 4
Prebold (SLO)	99	E 1
Précy-sous-Thil (F)	48	C 2
Predappio (I)	102	A 1
Predazzo (I)	98	A 1
Preddvor (SLO)	99	D 1
Predeal (RO)	13	B 3
Predejane (SRB)	119	E 4
Predel (SLO)	98	C 1
Predoi / Prettau (I)	94	A 4
Predošćica (HR)	99	D 3
Preetz (D)	79	D 3
Pregarten (A)	95	D 2
Preiļi (LV)	167	D 3
Prekaja (BIH)	116	C 3
Preko (HR)	103	E 1
Preljina (SRB)	118	C 3
Prelog (SLO)	112	A 3
Preloščica (HR)	115	D 3
Přelouč (CZ)	90	C 2
Premantura (HR)	99	D 4
Prémery (F)	48	B 2
Premià de Mar (E)	67	D 3
Premilcuore (I)	102	A 2
Premnitz (D)	84	C 3
Premuda (HR)	99	E 4
Premuda (Otok) (HR)	99	E 4
Prenzlau (D)	80	C 4
Přerov (CZ)	91	E 3
Prerow (D)	79	F 2
Preševo (SRB)	122	B 2
Presjeka (MNE)	121	D 2
Prešov (SK)	12	B 2
Préspa (GR)	205	D 3
Pressath (D)	89	E 3

Pressbaum (A) .... 95 E 2
Prestatyn (GB) .... 32 B 2
Presteigne (GB) .... 32 C 4
Prestfoss (N) .... 139 D 3
Přeštice (CZ) .... 89 F 4
Preston (GB) .... 32 C 2
Prestonpans (GB) .... 31 D 2
Prestwick (GB) .... 30 C 3
Pretoro (I) .... 103 D 4
Prettin (D) .... 85 D 4
Pretzsch (D) .... 85 D 4
Preuilly-sur-Claise (F) .... 47 E 3
Préveza (GR) .... 211 D 3
Prevršac (HR) .... 115 D 4
Prezid (HR) .... 99 E 2
Prezma (LV) .... 167 E 3
Prialgava (LT) .... 162 C 3
Pribini (BIH) .... 117 D 2
Priboj (BIH) .... 117 F 2
Priboj (SRB) .... 118 B 3
Příbor (CZ) .... 91 F 3
Příbram (CZ) .... 90 A 3
Priedaine (LV) .... 157 D 4
Priedāji (LV) .... 159 E 1
Priedes Dobeles(LV) .... 163 E 2
Priedes Limbažu(LV) .... 159 E 2
Priedes Talsu(LV) .... 157 E 4
Priedes Valmieras(LV) .... 159 F 2
Priednieki (LV) .... 165 F 2
Priedula (LV) .... 163 E 3
Priego (E) .... 71 D 1
Priego de Córdoba (E) .... 76 A 2
Priekule (LT) .... 168 C 2
Priekule (LV) .... 162 C 2
Priekuļi (LV) .... 159 F 3
Prien (D) .... 94 A 3
Prienai Kauno(LT) .... 176 C 2
Prienai Vilniaus(LT) .... 177 F 1
Prievidza (SK) .... 12 B 2
Priežmale (LV) .... 167 E 4
Priežu Sils (LV) .... 167 D 4
Prigradica (HR) .... 120 A 2
Prijeboj (HR) .... 99 F 3
Prijedor (BIH) .... 115 E 4
Prijepolje (SRB) .... 118 B 4
Prīkuļi (LV) .... 167 D 3
Prilep (MK) .... 122 B 3
Prilike (BIH) .... 118 B 3
Prillimäe (EST) .... 149 E 3
Priluka (BIH) .... 117 D 4
Primel-Trégastel (F) .... 40 C 2
Primišlje (HR) .... 99 F 3
Primolano (I) .... 98 A 2
Primošten (HR) .... 103 F 1
Primstal (D) .... 45 D 2
Princetown (GB) .... 34 C 3
Principauté
de Monaco (MC) .... 57 F 1
Prinés (GR) .... 226 B 2
Pringi (EST) .... 149 E 2
Prinkas (LV) .... 159 D 3
Prínos (GR) .... 207 E 3
Prisad (MK) .... 122 B 3
Prisoje (BIH) .... 117 D 4
Priština (SRB) .... 119 D 4
Pritzerbe (D) .... 85 D 3
Pritzier (D) .... 79 E 4
Pritzwalk (D) .... 84 C 1
Privas (F) .... 52 B 3
Priverno (I) .... 105 D 2
Privlaka Vukovar(HR) .... 99 F 4
Privlaka Zadar(HR) .... 117 F 1
Prizren (SRB) .... 122 A 2
Prizzi (I) .... 110 C 3
Prnjavor (BIH) .... 115 F 4
Prnjavor (SRB) .... 117 F 1
Proaza (E) .... 59 E 3
Probište (MK) .... 122 C 2
Probstzella (D) .... 89 D 2
Próchoma (GR) .... 206 B 2
Prochowice (PL) .... 193 E 2
Procida (I) .... 105 F 3
Pročiūnai I (LT) .... 164 B 3
Prodromos (CY) .... 230 B 3
Pródromos (GR) .... 217 F 1
Proença-a-Nova (P) .... 68 C 2
Proevska Banja (MK) .... 122 B 2
Profitis Ilias (GR) .... 228 C 2
Profondeville (B) .... 39 F 2
Prokópi (GR) .... 212 C 4
Prokuplje (SRB) .... 119 D 3
Prolom (SRB) .... 119 D 4
Prómachoi (GR) .... 205 F 2
Promachónas (GR) .... 206 C 1
Promna (PL) .... 190 B 4
Promýri (GR) .... 212 C 3
Pronsfeld (D) .... 44 C 1

Propriano (F) .... 57 F 4
Prosílio (GR) .... 207 F 2
Prosity (PL) .... 183 F 2
Proskynás (GR) .... 212 C 4
Prosotsáni (GR) .... 207 D 2
Prossedi (I) .... 105 D 2
Prostějov (CZ) .... 91 E 3
Prostki (PL) .... 185 D 3
Prószków (PL) .... 194 B 4
Proszowice (PL) .... 195 F 4
Próti (GR) .... 207 D 2
Próti (Nisí) (GR) .... 217 D 4
Protokklisi (GR) .... 208 C 1
Prötzel (D) .... 85 E 2
Prousós (GR) .... 211 E 4
Provatónas (GR) .... 208 C 2
Provenchères-sur-Fave(F) .... 45 E 2
Provins (F) .... 43 E 3
Prozor (BIH) .... 117 E 3
Pruchnik (PL) .... 202 F 2
Prudhoe (GB) .... 31 E 4
Prudnik (PL) .... 194 B 4
Prüm (D) .... 87 E 3
Pruna (E) .... 75 F 2
Prunetta (I) .... 101 F 2
Prūsaliai (LT) .... 162 C 4
Prūseliai
Marijampolés(LT) .... 169 E 4
Prūseliai Panevėžio(LT) .... 171 D 1
Prusice (PL) .... 193 F 2
Pruszcz (PL) .... 182 C 2
Pruszcz Gdański (PL) .... 182 C 2
Pruszków (PL) .... 189 F 3
Pružany (BY) 6
Prvić (Otok) (HR) .... 99 E 3
Pryluky (UA) .... 13 F 1
Przasnysz (PL) .... 190 B 1
Przechlewo (PL) .... 181 F 2
Przeciszów (PL) .... 200 F 2
Przedbórz Łódzkie(PL) .... 195 E 4
Przedecz (PL) .... 189 D 3
Przelewice (PL) .... 186 C 1
Przemków (PL) .... 193 D 2
Przemyśl (PL) .... 202 F 2
Przerośl (PL) .... 185 D 2
Przesmyki (PL) .... 191 F 3
Przeworno (PL) .... 193 F 3
Przeworsk (PL) .... 202 E 1
Przewóz (PL) .... 192 C 1
Przezmark (PL) .... 183 D 3
Przodkowo (PL) .... 182 C 2
Przybiernów (PL) .... 180 C 3
Przygodzice (PL) .... 194 B 1
Przykona (PL) .... 188 C 4
Przyłęk Mazowieckie(PL) .... 196 E 3
Przyrów (PL) .... 195 E 3
Przystajń (PL) .... 194 C 3
Przysucha (PL) .... 195 E 4
Przytoczna (PL) .... 187 D 2
Przytuły (PL) .... 185 D 4
Przytyk (PL) .... 196 B 1
Przywidz (PL) .... 182 C 2
Przywory (PL) .... 194 B 4
Psača (MK) .... 122 C 2
Psachná (GR) .... 213 D 4
Psáka (GR) .... 210 C 2
Psará (GR) .... 214 B 3
Psará (Nisí) (GR) .... 214 B 4
Psarádes (GR) .... 205 D 2
Psári Korinthía(GR) .... 217 F 2
Psári Messinía(GR) .... 217 D 3
Psáthi (GR) .... 224 C 1
Psathópyrgos (GR) .... 217 D 1
Psathotópi (GR) .... 211 D 3
Psérimos (Nisí) (GR) .... 221 E 4
Psie Pole (PL) .... 193 F 2
Psimolofou (CY) .... 231 C 3
Psínthos (GR) .... 228 C 2
Pskov (RUS) .... 7 D 2
Psychikó (GR) .... 212 A 2
Psyró (GR) .... 227 F 3
Pszczółki (PL) .... 182 C 2
Pszczyna (PL) .... 200 F 2
Pszów (PL) .... 200 E 2
Pteléa (GR) .... 207 E 2
Ptolemaḯda (GR) .... 205 F 3
Ptuj (SLO) .... 99 E 1
Puchaczów (PL) .... 197 E 1
Puchberg
am Schneeberg (A) .... 95 E 2
Pučišća (HR) .... 117 D 4
Puck (PL) .... 182 C 1
Pūčkoriai (LT) .... 162 C 4
Puçol (E) .... 72 A 2
Pudasjärvi /
Kurenalus (FIN) .... 129 D 4

Pūdinova (LV) .... 167 F 2
Pūdukolni (LV) .... 167 F 2
Puebla de Alcocer (E) .... 69 F 3
Puebla de Almenara (E) .... 70 C 2
Puebla de Beleña (E) .... 64 C 4
Puebla de Don Fadrique (E) 77 D 1
Puebla de Don Rodrigo (E) 70 A 3
Puebla de Guzmán (E) .... 74 C 1
Puebla de la Calzada (E) .. 69 D 3
Puebla de la Reina (E) 69
Puebla de Lillo (E) .... 59 F 3
Puebla de Obando (E) .... 69 D 2
Puebla de Sanabria (E) .... 63 E 1
Puebla de Trives (E) .... 58 C 4
Pueblica de Valverde (E) ... 63 F 2
Puente de
Domingo Flórez (E) .... 59 D 4
Puente de Génave (E) .... 70 C 4
Puente de los Fierros (E) .. 59 E 2
Puente de Montañana (E). 55 D 4
Puente Genil (E) .... 75 F 2
Puente la Reina (E) .... 61 D 4
Puente
la Reina de Jaca (E) .... 54 B 3
Puente Viesgo (E) .... 60 A 3
Puentenansa (E) .... 60 A 3
Puerto Castilla (E) .... 69 F 1
Puerto de la Encina (E) .... 75 E 2
Puerto de Mazarrón (E) .... 77 E 2
Puerto de San Vicente (E). 69 F 2
Puerto Lápice (E) .... 70 B 2
Puerto Lumbreras (E) .... 77 D 2
Puerto Real (E) .... 75 D 4
Puerto Serrano (E) .... 75 E 2
Puertollano (E) .... 70 A 4
Puget-Théniers (F) .... 53 E 2
Pūha (EST) .... 152 C 3
Pūhajärve (EST) .... 160 C 1
Pūhajõe (EST) .... 151 C 3
Puhja (EST) .... 154 E 4
Puhos (FIN) .... 135 C 2
Puhos (FIN) .... 129 B 4
Puiatu (EST) .... 154 C 2
Puig-reig (E) .... 66 C 2
Puiga (EST) .... 161 D 2
Puigcerdà (E) .... 55 E 4
Puikule (LV) .... 159 E 2
Puiseaux (F) .... 43 D 3
Puisserguier (F) .... 55 C 3
Pujols (F) .... 50 D 4
Puka (EST) .... 160 C 1
Pukë (AL) .... 121 F 3
Pukenieki (LV) .... 162 B 1
Pukiš (BIH) .... 117 D 3
Pukkila (FIN) .... 137 C 3
Puksti (LV) .... 160 C 3
Pula (HR) .... 99 E 3
Pula (I) .... 108 B 4
Puławy (PL) .... 196 C 1
Pulborough (GB) .... 36 E 1
Pulkau (A) .... 95 E 1
Pulkkila (FIN) .... 133 E 2
Pullans (EST) .... 161 C 3
Pulli (EST) .... 153 C 1
Pulpí (E) .... 77 D 2
Pulsnitz (D) .... 90 A 1
Pulstakai (LT) .... 177 E 3
Pułtusk (PL) .... 190 B 4
Pumpėnai (LT) .... 165 D 4
Pumpuri (LV) .... 163 D 2
Punaküla (EST) .... 154 A 4
Pūņas (EST) .... 157 D 2
Punat (HR) .... 99 E 3
Punduri (LV) .... 167 F 4
Punia (LT) .... 176 C 2
Punkaharju (FIN) .... 135 F 4
Punkalaidun (FIN) .... 136 C 3
Punta Ala (I) .... 101 E 4
Punta Križa (HR) .... 99 E 4
Punta Umbría (E) .... 74 C 2
Puntuži (LV) .... 167 C 2
Puodkaliai (LT) .... 162 C 3
Puodžiai (LT) .... 164 C 3
Puodžiūnai Kyburiai(LT). 164 C 3
Puodžiūnai Pasvalys(LT). 171 D 1
Puoké (LT) .... 162 C 3
Puokio (FIN) .... 133 F 1
Puolanka (FIN) .... 133 F 1
Puoriai (LT) .... 171 E 4
Pupiškė (LT) .... 172 B 3
Pūpoli (LV) .... 159 F 2
Puponys (LT) .... 171 E 1
Purbach
am Neusiedler See (A). 95 F 2
Purchena (E) .... 72 A 2
Purda (PL) .... 183 F 2
Pūre (LV) .... 157 E 4

Purgstall (A) .... 95 D 2
Purila (EST) .... 149 E 4
Purkersdorf (A) .... 95 E 1
Pürksi (EST) .... 148 B 4
Purku (EST) .... 149 E 4
Purmaļi (LV) .... 162 C 2
Purmerend (NL) .... 82 B 3
Purmsāti (LV) .... 162 C 2
Purtse (EST) .... 151 E 3
Purullena (E) .... 76 C 2
Purvėnai (LT) .... 163 E 3
Purviņi (LV) .... 164 C 2
Purviniškė (LT) .... 175 F 2
Purviškiai (LT) .... 169 F 4
Purvynė (LT) .... 172 B 2
Puša (LV) .... 167 E 3
Pušalotas (LT) .... 164 C 4
Pūšiliai (LT) .... 163 E 4
Puškin (RUS) .... 7 D 1
Puškoniai (LT) .... 165 D 4
Pušmucova (LV) .... 167 F 2
Pusne (LT) .... 171 E 4
Püspökladány (H) .... 12 B 3
Püssi (EST) .... 151 E 3
Pusta Kuznica (PL) .... 194 C 4
Pustinka (LV) .... 167 D 3
Pustoška (RUS) .... 7 D 1
Pusula (FIN) .... 136 C 3
Puszcza Mariańska (PL) . 189 F 3
Puszczykowo (PL) .... 187 E 3
Putanges-Pont-Écrepin (F) 41 F 2
Putbus (D) .... 80 C 2
Putgarten (D) .... 80 C 2
Putignano (I) .... 107 D 3
Putkaste (EST) .... 148 A 4
Putlitz (D) .... 84 C 1
Putni (LV) .... 165 D 3
Puttelange-aux-Lacs (F) .. 45 D 2
Putten (NL) .... 82 C 4
Puttgarden (D) .... 79 D 2
Putyv'l (UA) .... 7 F 4
Puumala (FIN) .... 137 E 2
Pūünsi (EST) .... 149 E 2
Puuri (EST) .... 161 D 1
Puurmani (EST) .... 154 C 3
Puusepa (EST) .... 161 D 1
Puy-Guillaume (F) .... 48 B 4
Puy-l'Évêque (F) .... 51 D 4
Puylaurens (F) .... 55 E 2
Puymirol (F) .... 51 D 4
Pūžai (LT) .... 169 D 3
Puze (LV) .... 157 D 3
Pwllheli (GB) .... 32 A 3
Pyhäjärvi (FIN) .... 133 F 2
Pyhäjoki (FIN) .... 136 B 3
Pyhäjoki (FIN) .... 133 E 2
Pyhältö (FIN) .... 137 E 3
Pyhäntä (FIN) .... 133 F 2
Pyhäntä (FIN) .... 135 E 1
Pyhäranta (FIN) .... 136 B 3
Pyhäsalmi (FIN) .... 133 E 1
Pyhäselkä (FIN) .... 135 F 2
Pyhtää / Pyttis (FIN) .... 137 E 3
Pyktiškė (LT) .... 168 C 1
Pyla (CY) .... 231 D 3
Pyla (Cape) (CY) .... 231 D 3
Pyla-sur-Mer (F) .... 50 A 3
Pylaia (GR) .... 208 C 2
Pylés (GR) .... 228 A 4
Pýli Flórina(GR) .... 205 D 3
Pýli Trikala(GR) .... 211 E 2
Pýli Viotía(GR) .... 218 B 1
Pylío (GR) .... 225 F 2
Pylkönmäki (FIN) .... 133 E 4
Pyloroí (GR) .... 205 E 4
Pýlos (GR) .... 222 B 2
Pylpiai (LT) .... 171 D 4
Pyrga (CY) .... 231 C 3
Pyrgadíkia (GR) .... 207 D 4
Pyrgetós (GR) .... 212 B 1
Pyrgí Chíos(GR) .... 220 C 1
Pyrgí Kérkyra(GR) .... 210 B 1
Pýrgoi Dráma(GR) .... 207 D 2
Pýrgoi Kozáni(GR) .... 205 F 3
Pyrgos (CY) .... 230 B 3
Pyrgos (CY) .... 231 C 4
Pýrgos Ilía(GR) .... 216 C 3
Pyrgos Irákleio(GR) .... 227 F 3
Pýrgos Sámos(GR) .... 221 D 2
Pýrgos Viotía(GR) .... 218 A 1
Pýrgos Diroú (GR) .... 222 C 2
Pyrjatyn (UA) .... 13 F 1
Pyrsógianni (GR) .... 205 D 4
Pyry (PL) .... 190 B 3
Pyrzyce (PL) .... 186 C 1
Pyskowice (PL) .... 194 C 4
Pythagóreio (GR) .... 221 E 3

Q

Quakenbrück (D) .... 83 E 3
Quarré-les-Tombes (F) .... 48 C 2
Quarteira (P) .... 74 B 2
Quarto d'Altino (I) .... 98 B 3
Quartu San Elena (I) .... 108 B 4
Quatretonda (E) .... 71 F 3
Quedlinburg (D) .... 84 B 4
Queenborough (GB) .... 36 C 3
Queensferry (GB) .... 32 C 3
Queluz (P) .... 68 A 3
Queralbs (E) .... 55 E 4
Querfurt (D) .... 89 D 1
Quérigut (F) .... 55 E 4
Quero (E) .... 70 C 2
Quesada (Estación de) (E) 76 C 1
Questembert (F) .... 41 D 4
Quettehou (F) .... 41 E 1
Quiberon (F) .... 40 C 4
Quickborn (D) .... 78 C 4
Quiévrain (B) .... 39 E 3
Quigley's Point (IRL) .... 23 D 1
Quillan (F) .... 55 E 3
Quilleboeuf-sur-Seine (F) . 38 A 4
Quimper (F) .... 40 B 3
Quimperlé (F) .... 40 C 4
Quincinetto (I) .... 53 F 1
Quincoces de Yuso (E) .... 60 B 3
Quingey (F) .... 49 E 2
Quinta de la Serena (E). 69 D 2
Quintana del Puente (E). 64 B 2
Quintana-Martín
Galíndez (E) .... 60 B 4
Quintana Redonda (E) .... 65 D 2
Quintanar de la Orden (E). 70 C 2
Quintanar de la Sierra (E). 64 C 2
Quintanar del Rey (E) .... 71 D 3
Quintanilha (P) .... 63 E 2
Quintanilla de Onésimo (E)64 B 2
Quintin (F) .... 41 D 3
Quinto (E) .... 65 F 3
Quinzano d'Oglio (I) .... 97 E 2
Quiroga (E) .... 58 C 4
Quissac (F) .... 56 B 1

R

Raab (A) .... 94 C 2
Rääbise (EST) .... 155 D 2
Raabs an der Thaya (A). 90 C 4
Raadama (EST) .... 155 E 4
Raahe (FIN) .... 133 E 1
Raajärvi (FIN) .... 129 D 3
Rääkkylä (FIN) .... 135 F 4
Raalte (NL) .... 82 C 3
Raanujärvi (FIN) .... 128 C 3
Raasiku (EST) .... 149 E 3
Raate (FIN) .... 135 E 1
Raattama (FIN) .... 125 D 4
Raba (HR) .... 99 E 4
Rab (Otok) (HR) .... 99 E 4
Raba Wyżna (PL) .... 201 A 3
Rabac (HR) .... 99 D 3
Rábade (E) .... 58 C 3
Rabastens (F) .... 55 E 2
Rabastens-de-Bigorre (F).. 54 C 2
Rabat (M) .... 110 A 4
Rabe (M) .... 202 E 3
Rabe (SRB) .... 113 E 3
Rábida
(Monasterio de la) (E) .... 75 D 2
Rabikiai (LT) .... 170 C 1
Rabino (PL) .... 181 D 3
Rabivere (EST) .... 149 D 3
Rabka-Zdrój (PL) .... 201 A 3
Rabrovo (MK) .... 122 C 3
Rabrovo (SRB) .... 119 D 1
Rača Kragujevac(SRB) .... 118 C 2
Rača Priština(SRB) .... 119 D 4
Rača /
Bosanska Rača (BIH).. 117 F 1
Racconigi (I) .... 53 F 3
Rače (SLO) .... 99 F 1
Račeva (LV) .... 167 E 4
Rachanie (PL) .... 197 F 3
Răches (GR) .... 212 B 4
Rachiv (UA) .... 12 C 1
Rachóni (GR) .... 207 F 3
Raciąż Kujawsko-
Pomorskie(PL) .... 182 B 3
Raciąż Mazowieckie(PL). 189 E 1
Raciborowice (PL) .... 197 C 1
Racibórz (PL) .... 200 D 2
Raciechowice (PL) .... 201 A 2

Račinovci (HR) .... 117 F 1
Račišće (HR) .... 120 B 2
Racławice (PL) .... 195 F 4
Racłova (LV) .... 167 E 4
Raczki (PL) .... 185 D 2
Radailiai (LT) .... 168 B 1
Radalj (SRB) .... 117 F 2
Rădăuți (RO) .... 13 D 2
Rade (D) .... 84 A 1
Råde (N) .... 139 E 4
Radeberg (D) .... 89 F 1
Radebeul (D) .... 89 F 1
Radeburg (D) .... 89 F 1
Radeče (SLO) .... 99 E 1
Radechiv (UA) .... 12 C 1
Radecznica (PL) .... 197 E 3
Radegunda (SLO) .... 99 E 1
Radeikiai (LT) .... 171 E 2
Radenci (SLO) .... 95 F 4
Radenthein (A) .... 94 C 4
Radevormwald (D) .... 87 F 1
Radicondoli (I) .... 101 F 3
Radimlja (BIH) .... 120 C 1
Radiovce (MK) .... 122 A 3
Radków Dolnośląskie(PL)193 E 4
Radlin (PL) .... 196 B 3
Radlje ob Dravi (SLO) .... 95 E 4
Radljevo (SRB) .... 118 B 2
Radłów Małopolskie(PL) . 201 C 1
Radłów Opolskie(PL) .... 194 C 3
Radnice (CZ) .... 89 F 3
Radolevo (SRB) .... 113 F 3
Radolfzell (D) .... 92 C 3
Radom (PL) .... 196 B 1
Radomice (PL) .... 189 D 1
Radomin (PL) .... 189 D 1
Radomsko (PL) .... 195 E 2
Radomyšľ (UA) .... 13 E 1
Radomyśl Wielki (PL) .... 196 C 4
Radopole (LV) .... 167 D 2
Radostowice (PL) .... 200 E 2
Radoszyce (PL) .... 195 F 2
Radotín (CZ) .... 90 B 3
Radovče (MNE) .... 121 E 2
Radovići (MNE) .... 121 D 2
Radoviš (MK) .... 122 C 3
Radovljica (SLO) .... 99 D 1
Radovnica (SRB) .... 122 B 1
Radruż (PL) .... 197 F 4
Radstädt (A) .... 94 C 3
Radstock (GB) .... 35 E 2
Raduša (MK) .... 122 A 2
Radviliškis (LT) .... 169 F 1
Radvilonys (LT) .... 175 F 4
Radwanice
Dolnośląskie(PL) .... 193 D 1
Radymno (PL) .... 202 F 2
Radzanów
Mazowieckie(PL) .... 196 B 1
Radziejów (PL) .... 188 C 2
Radziejowa (PL) .... 201 B 3
Radziejowice (PL) .... 189 F 3
Radziłów (PL) .... 185 D 4
Radziwie (PL) .... 189 E 2
Radzymin (PL) .... 190 B 2
Radzyń Chełmiński (PL).. 183 D 1
Radzyń Podlaski (PL) .... 191 D 4
Rae (EST) .... 149 E 3
Raesfeld (D) .... 83 E 4
Raffadali (I) .... 110 C 3
Rafina (GR) .... 218 C 2
Ragaciems (LV) .... 158 B 4
Rāgama (E) .... 64 A 3
Ragana (LV) .... 159 D 4
Ragaz, Bad (CH) .... 97 D 1
Rageliai (LT) .... 171 F 1
Raglan (GB) .... 35 D 1
Ragožiai (LT) .... 170 C 4
Raguhn (D) .... 85 D 4
Ragūnai (LT) .... 171 D 2
Ragunda (S) .... 132 A 3
Ragusa (I) .... 111 E 4
Raguva (LT) .... 171 D 2
Raguvėlė (LT) .... 171 D 2
Raguviškiai (LT) .... 162 B 4
Rahačoŭ (BY) 7
Rahden (D) .... 83 F 3
Rahinge (EST) .... 155 D 4
Rahkla (EST) .... 151 D 4
Rahlstedt (D) .... 79 D 4
Rahumäe (EST) .... 161 D 2
Raibamuiža (LV) .... 162 C 4
Raigaste (EST) .... 154 C 4
Raigla (EST) .... 155 E 4
Raikküla (EST) .... 149 D 4
Rain a. Lech (D) .... 93 E 1
Räisälä (FIN) .... 129 E 3

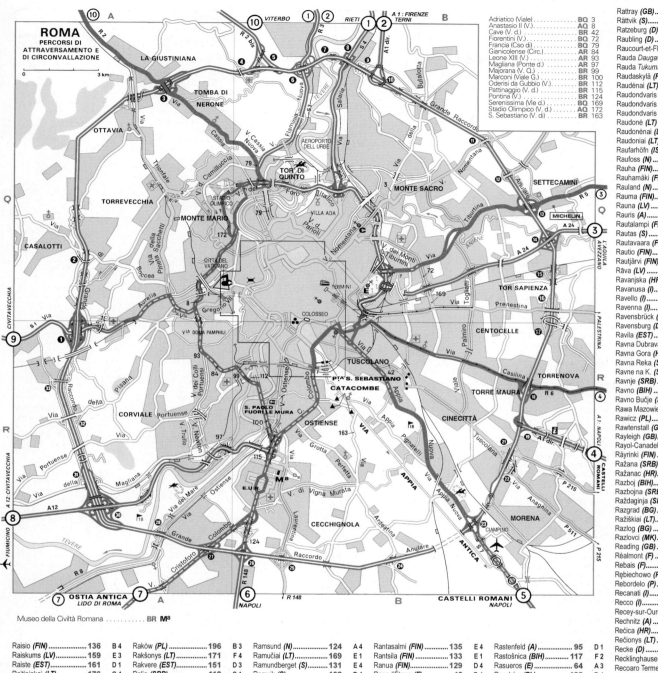

ROMA
PERCORSI DI
ATTRAVERSAMENTO E
DI CIRCONVALLAZIONE

0   3 km

Museo della Civiltà Romana . . . . BR **M8**

Adriatico (Viale) . . . . BQ	3	
Anastasio II (V.) . . . . AQ	8	
Cave (V. d.) . . . . BR	42	
Fiorentini (V.) . . . . BR	72	
Francia (Cso di) . . . . BQ	79	
Gianicolense (Circ.) . . . . AR	84	
Leone XIII (V.) . . . . AR	93	
Magliana (Ponte d.) . . . . AR	97	
Majorana (V. Q.) . . . . AR	99	
Marconi (Viale G.) . . . . BR	100	
Oderisi da Gubbio (V.) . . . . BR	112	
Pattinaggio (V. d.) . . . . BR	115	
Pontina (V.) . . . . BR	124	
Serenissima (Vle d.) . . . . BQ	169	
Stadio Olimpico (V. d.) . . . . AQ	172	
S. Sebastiano (V. di) . . . . BR	163	

Rattray (GB)	31	D 1				
Rättvik (S)	140	B 2				
Ratzeburg (D)	79	D 4				
Raubling (D)	94	A 3				
Raucourt-et-Flaba (F)	39	F 4				
Rauda Daugavpils (LV)	172	C 1				
Rauda Tukuma (LV)	157	F 4				
Raudaskylä (FIN)	133	E 2				
Raudénai (LT)	163	E 4				
Raudondvaris Kauno (LT)	170	B 4				
Raudondvaris Šiaulių (LT)	170	C 1				
Raudondvaris Vilniaus (LT)	177	E 1				
Raudoné (LT)	169	E 4				
Raudonénai (LT)	169	E 4				
Raudoniai (LT)	162	C 3				
Raufarhöfn (IS)	126	C 1				
Raufoss (N)	139	E 2				
Rauha (FIN)	137	F 2				
Rauhamäki (FIN)	137	D 2				
Rauland (N)	139	D 3				
Rauma (FIN)	136	B 3				
Rauna (LV)	159	F 3				
Rauris (A)	94	B 4				
Rautalampi (FIN)	133	F 4				
Rautas (S)	128	A 2				
Rautavaara (FIN)	135	E 2				
Rautio (FIN)	133	E 2				
Rautjärvi (FIN)	137	F 2				
Rāva (LV)	162	C 2				
Ravanjska (HR)	99	F 4				
Ravanusa (I)	111	D 3				
Ravello (I)	105	F 4				
Ravenna (I)	102	A 1				
Ravensbrück (D)	85	D 1				
Ravensburg (D)	93	D 3				
Ravila (EST)	149	E 3				
Ravna Dubrava (SRB)	119	E 3				
Ravna Gora (HR)	99	E 3				
Ravna Reka (SRB)	119	D 2				
Ravne na K. (SLO)	99	E 1				
Ravnje (SRB)	117	C 1				
Ravno (BIH)	120	C 2				
Ravno Bučje (SRB)	119	E 3				
Rawa Mazowiecka (PL)	189	F 4				
Rawicz (PL)	187	E 4				
Rawtenstall (GB)	32	C 2				
Rayleigh (GB)	36	C 3				
Rayol-Canadel-sur-Mer (F)	57	E 3				
Räyrinki (FIN)	133	E 3				
Ražana (SRB)	118	B 2				
Ražanac (HR)	99	F 4				
Razboj (BIH)	115	E 4				
Razbojna (SRB)	119	D 3				
Raždaginja (SRB)	118	B 4				
Razgrad (BG)	13	E 4				
Ražiškiai (LT)	176	C 1				
Razlog (BG)	19	D 1				
Razlovci (MK)	122	C 2				
Reading (GB)	35	F 2				
Réalmont (F)	55	E 2				
Rebais (F)	43	E 2				
Rębiechowo (PL)	182	C 2				
Rebordelo (P)	63	D 2				
Recanati (I)	102	C 2				
Recco (I)	101	D 1				
Recey-sur-Ource (F)	49	D 1				
Rechnitz (A)	95	F 3				
Rečica (HR)	99	F 2				
Rečionys (LT)	171	D 3				
Recke (D)	83	E 3				
Recklinghausen (D)	87	E 1				
Recoaro Terme (I)	98	A 3				
Recuerda (E)	64	C 3				
Rečyca (BY)	7	E 4				
Recz (PL)	181	D 4				
Ręczno (PL)	195	E 2				
Reda (PL)	182	C 1				
Redalen (N)	139	E 2				
Redange (L)	44	F 3				
Redcar (GB)	31	F 4				
Redditch (GB)	33	D 4				
Redhill (GB)	36	B 4				
Redon (F)	41	D 4				
Redondela (E)	58	B 4				
Redondo (E)	68	C 3				
Redruth (GB)	34	B 4				
Rędziny (PL)	195	D 3				
Rēdznieciems (LV)	156	C 3				
Reegoldi (EST)	154	B 3				
Rees (D)	82	C 2				
Reeth (GB)	33	D 1				
Refsnes (N)	124	A 4				
Reftele (S)	143	E 2				
Rega (PL)	181	D 2				
Regalbuto (I)	111	D 3				
Regen (D)	94	B 1				
Regensburg (D)	94	A 1				

Raisio (FIN)	136	B 4	Raków (PL)	196	B 3	Ramsund (N)	124	A 4	Rantasalmi (FIN)	135	E 4
Raiskums (LV)	159	E 3	Rakšonys (LT)	171	F 4	Ramučiai (LT)	169	E 1	Rantsila (FIN)	133	E 1
Raiste (EST)	161	D 1	Rakvere (EST)	151	D 3	Ramundberget (S)	131	B 4	Ranua (FIN)	129	D 4
Raitininkai (LT)	176	C 4	Ralja (SRB)	118	C 1	Ramvik (S)	132	B 3	Raon-l'Étape (F)	45	D 4
Raittijärvi (FIN)	124	C 3	Ram (SRB)	118	C 1	Ramygala (LT)	170	C 2	Rapallo (I)	101	D 1
Raj (Jaskinia) (PL)	195	F 3	Ramacca (I)	111	D 3	Ranalt (A)	93	F 4	Rapice (PL)	186	B 3
Raja (EST)	155	D 2	Ramales de la Victoria (E)	60	B 3	Randaberg (N)	138	B 3	Räpina (EST)	155	E 4
Raja Jooseppi (FIN)	125	F 4	Ramallosa (E)	58	A 4	Randalstown (GB)	23	E 2	Rapla (EST)	149	E 4
Rajac (SRB)	119	E 2	Ramanava (LT)	177	D 3	Randan (F)	48	B 4	Rapolano Terme (I)	102	A 3
Rajadell (E)	66	C 3	Ramata (LV)	159	E 1	Randanne (F)	51	F 1	Rapolla (I)	106	B 3
Rajamäki (FIN)	137	D 3	Rāmava (LV)	164	C 3	Randazzo (I)	111	E 2	Rapperswil (CH)	92	C 4
Rajgród (PL)	185	D 2	Ramberg (N)	127	D 1	Randers (DK)	142	B 3	Rapsáni (GR)	212	B 1
Rajince (SRB)	122	B 2	Rambervillers (F)	44	C 4	Randvere (EST)	149	E 2	Raptópoulo (GR)	217	D 4
Rājumi (LV)	164	C 2	Rambouillet (F)	42	C 1	Råneå (S)	128	B 4	Raša (HR)	99	D 3
Raka (SLO)	99	E 1	Rambucourt (F)	44	B 3	Rangsdorf (D)	85	E 3	Räsälä (FIN)	135	E 3
Rakai (LT)	177	D 4	Ramnoús (GR)	218	C 1	Rangu (EST)	149	E 3	Rasbo (S)	141	D 3
Rakalj (HR)	99	D 3	Ramoniškiai (LT)	175	F 2	Räni (EST)	155	D 4	Rascafría (E)	64	B 4
Rakitna (SLO)	99	E 1	Ramsau am Dachstein (A)	94	C 3	Raniżów (PL)	197	D 3	Raščiúnai (LT)	173	D 3
Rakitnika (HR)	112	A 4	Ramsau b. Berchtesgaden (D)	94	B 3	Ranka (LV)	160	C 3	Rasdorf (D)	88	B 2
Rakke (EST)	150	C 4	Ramsele (S)	132	A 3	Raņķi (LV)	163	D 1	Raseiniai (LT)	169	F 3
Rakkestad (N)	139	E 3	Ramsey (GB)	32	A 1	Rankweil (A)	93	D 4	Rasina (EST)	155	E 4
Rakoniewice (PL)	187	E 3	Ramsey (GB)	33	F 4	Rannaküla (EST)	148	C 3	Raška (SRB)	118	C 4
Rakonys (LT)	177	F 3	Ramsgate (GB)	37	D 3	Rannametsa (EST)	153	D 2	Rasno (BIH)	117	A 4
Rakoszyce (PL)	193	E 2	Ramsi (EST)	154	B 4	Rannamõisa (EST)	149	D 2	Rasnupļi (LV)	167	D 4
Rakova Bara (SRB)	119	D 1	Rannapungerja (EST)	151	E 4	Rasquera (E)	66	B 4			
Rakovac (BIH)	115	F 4	Rannu Ida-Viru (EST)	151	D 3	Rastatt (D)	45	D 2			
Rakovica (HR)	99	F 3	Ramsjö (S)	131	F 4	Rannu Tartu (EST)	154	D 4	Rastede (D)	83	E 2
Rakovník (CZ)	90	A 3	Ramstein-Miesenbach (D)	45	D 2	Ranovac (SRB)	119	D 1	Rastenberg (D)	89	D 1
									Rantasalmi		
Rastenfeld (A)	95	D 1									
Rastošnica (BIH)	117	F 2									
Rasueros (E)	64	A 3									
Raszków (PL)	188	B 4									
Raszyn (PL)	190	B 3									
Rätan (S)	131	F 4									
Rateče (SLO)	98	C 1									
Ratekau (D)	79	D 4									
Rates (P)	62	B 2									
Rathdowney (IRL)	25	D 2									
Rathdrum / Ráth Droma (IRL)	25	E 2									
Rathenow (D)	84	C 2									
Rathfriland (GB)	23	E 3									
Rathkeale / Ráth Caola (IRL)	24	C 2									
Rathmelton (IRL)	23	D 1									
Rathmore (IRL)	24	B 3									
Rathmullan (IRL)	23	D 1									
Rathnew (IRL)	25	E 2									
Ratingen (D)	87	E 1									
Ratković (SRB)	121	F 2									
Ratkovo (SRB)	113	D 4									
Ratnieki Cēsu (LV)	159	E 4									
Ratnieki Talsu (LV)	157	E 4									
Ratnīki (LV)	167	E 4									
Rätsepa (EST)	154	A 3									
Ratten (A)	95	E 2									
Rattenberg (A)	94	A 4									
Rattersdorf-Liebing (A)	95	F 3									

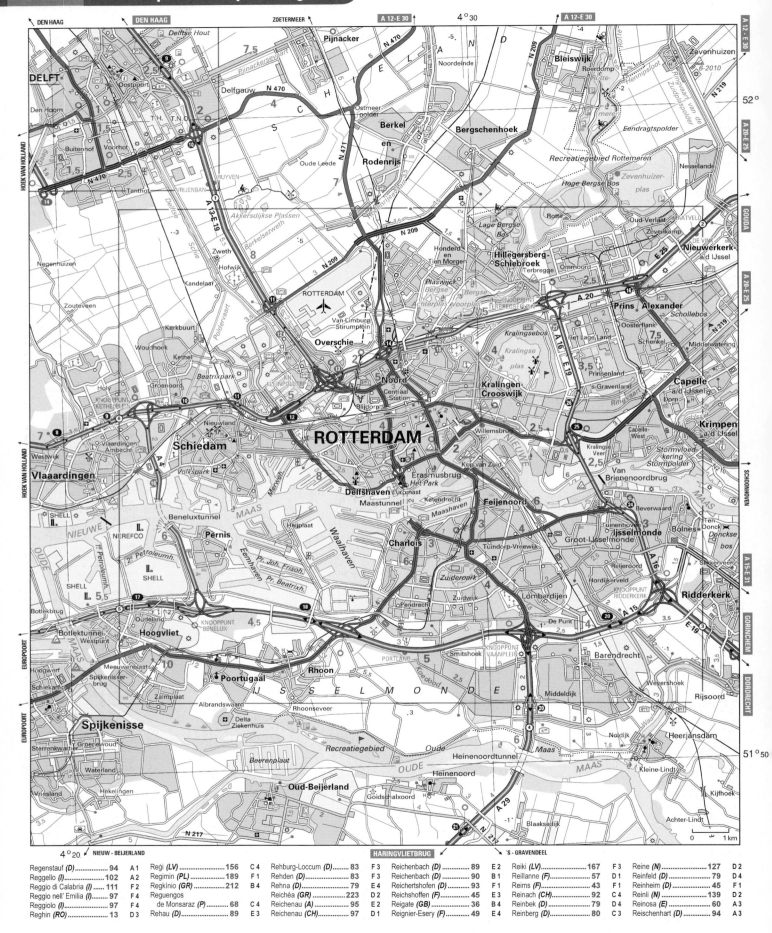

Regenstauf (D)	94	A1	Regi (LV)	156	C4	Rehburg-Loccum (D)	83	F3
Reggello (I)	102	A2	Regimin (PL)	189	F1	Rehden (D)	83	F3
Reggio di Calabria (I)	111	F2	Regkínio (GR)	212	B4	Rehna (D)	79	E4
Reggio nell' Emilia (I)	97	F4	Reguengos			Reichéa (GR)	223	D2
Reggiolo (I)	97	F4	de Monsaraz (P)	68	C4	Reichenau (A)	95	D1
Reghin (RO)	13	D3	Rehau (D)	89	E3	Reichenau (CH)	97	D1

Reichenbach (D)	89	E2	Reiki (LV)	167	F3	Reine (N)	127	D2
Reichenbach (D)	90	B1	Reillanne (F)	57	D1	Reinfeld (D)	79	D4
Reichertshofen (D)	93	F1	Reims (F)	43	F1	Reinheim (D)	45	F1
Reichshoffen (F)	45	E3	Reinach (CH)	92	C4	Reinli (N)	139	D2
Reigate (GB)	36	B4	Reinbek (D)	79	D4	Reinosa (E)	60	A3
Reignier-Esery (F)	49	E4	Reinberg (D)	80	C3	Reischenhart (D)	94	A3

Reisjärvi (FIN) .... 133 E 3
Reiss (GB) .... 27 F 1
Reistrai (LT) .... 168 C 2
Reit i. Winkl (D) .... 94 A 3
Reitzenhain (D) .... 89 F 2
Reiu (EST) .... 153 C 4
Reizgiai (LT) .... 168 C 3
Rejowiec (PL) .... 197 E 2
Rejowiec Fabryczny (PL) 197 E 2
Rekava (LV) .... 161 E 4
Rekovac (SRB) .... 118 C 2
Rėkučiai (LT) .... 172 C 3
Rėkyva (LT) .... 169 F 1
Remagen (D) .... 87 F 2
Rémalard (F) .... 42 B 3
Rembate (LV) .... 165 E 2
Remeskylä (FIN) .... 133 F 2
Remich (L) .... 44 C 2
Remiremont (F) .... 44 C 4
Remolinos (E) .... 65 F 2
Remoulins (F) .... 56 B 1
Rempstone (GB) .... 33 E 4
Remscheid (D) .... 87 E 1
Remte (LV) .... 163 E 1
Rémuzat (F) .... 52 C 4
Rena (N) .... 139 F 1
Renavas (LT) .... 163 D 3
Renazé (F) .... 41 F 4
Rencēni (LV) .... 159 F 2
Renchen (D) .... 45 E 3
Renda (LV) .... 157 D 4
Rende (I) .... 109 E 1
Rendsburg (D) .... 78 C 3
Rengsdorf (D) .... 87 F 3
Reni (UA) .... 13 E 4
Renko (FIN) .... 136 C 3
Renkum (NL) .... 82 C 4
Rennebu (N) .... 131 D 3
Rennerod (D) .... 87 F 2
Rennes (F) .... 41 E 3
Rennes-les-Bains (F) .. 55 F 4
Rennweg (A) .... 94 C 4
Rensjön (S) .... 128 A 1
Reńska Wieś (PL) ...... 194 C 4
Rentína Karditsa(GR) .. 211 F 3
Rentína
  Thessaloniki(GR) .... 207 D 3
Renwez (F) .... 39 F 4
Reola (EST) .... 155 D 4
Reopalu (EST) .... 149 F 4
Repki (PL) .... 191 D 2
Replot (FIN) .... 132 C 3
Repojoki (FIN) .... 125 E 4
Reposaari (FIN) .... 136 B 2
Repubblica
  di San Marino (RSM) .. 102 B 1
Repvåg (N) .... 125 D 1
Requena (E) .... 71 F 4
Réquista (F) .... 51 F 4
Rerik (D) .... 79 E 3
Resanovci (BIH) .... 116 C 3
Resavica (SRB) .... 119 D 2
Resen (MK) .... 122 A 4
Resende (P) .... 62 C 3
Reşiţa (RO) .... 12 C 4
Resko (PL) .... 181 D 3
Reškutėnai (LT) .... 172 C 4
Resmo (S) .... 143 F 3
Resna (MNE) .... 121 D 2
Resnik (SRB) .... 118 B 1
Restelica (SRB) .... 122 A 3
Restu (EST) .... 160 C 1
Resuttano (I) .... 111 D 4
Reszel (PL) .... 184 B 2
Retford (GB) .... 33 E 3
Rethel (F) .... 39 F 2
Rethem (D) .... 83 F 2
Rethen (Leine) (D) ..... 84 A 3
Réthymno (GR) .... 226 C 2
Retiers (F) .... 41 E 4
Retla (EST) .... 149 B 2
Retortillo de Soria (E) .. 64 C 3
Retournac (F) .... 52 B 2
Retuerta del Bullaque (E).. 70 A 2
Retz (A) .... 95 E 1
Reuilly (F) .... 47 F 3
Reus (E) .... 66 B 4
Reusel (NL) .... 39 F 1
Reutlingen (D) .... 45 F 3
Reutte (A) .... 93 E 4
Revel (F) .... 55 F 2
Rēveļi (LV) .... 160 C 4
Revigny-sur-Ornain (F).. 44 B 3
Revin (F) .... 39 F 4
Řevničov (CZ) .... 90 A 2
Revonlahti (FIN) .... 133 E 1
Rewa (PL) .... 182 C 1

Rewal (PL) .... 180 C 2
Reyðarfjörður (IS) ..... 126 C 2
Reykhólar (IS) .... 126 A 1
Reykholt (IS) .... 126 A 2
Reykjahlíð (IS) .... 126 B 1
Reykjavík (IS) .... 126 A 2
Rēzekne (LV) .... 167 E 3
Rēžgaliai (LT) .... 169 E 4
Rēžiai (LT) .... 177 E 4
Rezzato (I) .... 97 F 3
Rezzoaglio (I) .... 101 D 1
Rgotina (SRB) .... 119 E 2
Rhade (D) .... 83 F 1
Rhayader / Rhaeadr (GB) . 32 B 4
Rheda (D) .... 83 E 4
Rhede (D) .... 83 D 4
Rhede (D) .... 83 D 4
Rheinbach (D) .... 87 E 2
Rheinberg (D) .... 87 E 1
Rheinböllen (D) .... 45 D 1
Rheine (D) .... 83 E 3
Rheinfelden (CH) ...... 92 B 4
Rheinfelden (D) .... 92 B 4
Rheinhausen (D) .... 87 E 1
Rheinsberg (D) .... 79 D 1
Rhêmes-Notre Dame (I).. 53 D 1
Rhenen (NL) .... 82 C 4
Rheydt (D) .... 87 E 1
Rhinau (F) .... 45 C 4
Rhinow (D) .... 84 C 2
Rho (I) .... 97 D 3
Rhondda (GB) .... 35 A 3
Rhosneigr (GB) .... 32 E 1
Rhossili (GB) .... 34 A 4
Rhüden (D) .... 84 A 4
Rhyl (GB) .... 32 B 2
Rhynern (D) .... 87 C 4
Rhynie (GB) .... 28 B 3
Riaillé (F) .... 46 C 2
Rial (E) .... 58 E 3
Riaño (E) .... 59 F 3
Rians (F) .... 57 D 2
Rianxo (E) .... 58 A 3
Riaza (E) .... 64 C 3
Riba de Saelices (E) ... 65 D 4
Riba de Santiuste (E) .. 65 D 3
Ribadavia (E) .... 58 B 4
Ribadelago (E) .... 59 B 4
Ribadeo (E) .... 59 D 2
Ribadesella (E) .... 59 F 2
Ribarci (SRB) .... 119 D 3
Ribarić (SRB) .... 118 C 4
Ribarska Banja (SRB) .. 119 D 3
Ribčev Laz (SLO) ...... 99 B 1
Ribe (DK) .... 142 A 4
Ribeauvillé (F) .... 45 D 4
Ribécourt (F) .... 39 D 4
Ribeira de Pena (P) .... 62 C 2
Ribemont (F) .... 39 D 4
Ribera (E) .... 110 C 3
Ribera de Cardós (E) .. 55 D 4
Ribera del Fresno (E) .. 69 E 3
Ribérac (F) .... 50 B 2
Ribes de Freser (E) .... 55 E 2
Ribiers (F) .... 53 E 2
Ribnica (BIH) .... 117 E 2
Ribnica (SLO) .... 99 D 2
Ribnica (SLO) .... 99 D 2
Ribnica na P. (SLO) .... 114 C 2
Ribnik (HR) .... 99 E 2
Ribnița (MD) .... 13 B 2
Ribnitz-Damgarten (D) . 79 F 3
Ribolla (I) .... 101 F 3
Ričany
  Středočeský kraj(CZ) . 90 B 3
Riccia (I) .... 105 F 2
Riccione (I) .... 102 B 1
Richelieu (F) .... 47 C 2
Richmond (GB) .... 33 D 1
Richmond-
  upon-Thames (GB) ... 36 B 3
Richtenberg (D) .... 79 F 3
Rickliai (LT) .... 176 C 4
Rickling (D) .... 79 E 1
Ricla (E) .... 65 E 3
Ridaküla (EST) .... 150 C 3
Ridalepa (EST) .... 153 D 3
Ridica (SRB) .... 113 D 3
Ridzene (LV) .... 159 F 3
Riebiņi (LV) .... 167 C 4
Riec-sur-Belon (F) .... 40 C 4
Ried im Innkreis (A) ... 94 B 3
Ried im Oberinntal (A) . 93 B 2
Riedenburg (D) .... 93 F 1
Riedlingen (D) .... 93 D 3
Riegel (D) .... 45 E 4

Riegersburg (A) .... 95 E 4
Riego de la Vega (E) ... 59 E 4
Riesa (D) .... 89 F 1
Riešė (LT) .... 177 D 3
Riesi (I) .... 111 D 3
Riestapurvs (LV) ...... 161 E 3
Riestedt (D) .... 84 A 4
Rietavas (LT) .... 168 C 1
Rietberg (D) .... 83 F 4
Rieti (I) .... 102 B 4
Rieumes (F) .... 55 D 2
Rieupeyroux (F) .... 51 F 4
Rieux (F) .... 55 D 3
Riez (F) .... 57 D 1
Riezlern (A) .... 93 E 4
Rigaio (GR) .... 212 B 2
Rigáni (GR) .... 217 D 1
Rignac (F) .... 51 F 4
Rignano Flaminio (I) ... 104 C 1
Riguldi/Rickul (EST) ... 148 C 3
Riidaja (EST) .... 154 D 3
Riihimäki (FIN) .... 137 D 3
Riisipere (EST) .... 149 D 3
Riistavesi (FIN) .... 135 E 3
Riječa (BIH) .... 117 F 3
Rijeka (HR) .... 99 D 3
Rijeka Crnojevica (MNE) 121 D 2
Rijssen (NL) .... 83 D 2
Rikava (Rikova) (LV) ... 167 D 2
Riksgränsen (S) .... 124 B 4
Rillo (E) .... 65 F 4
Rillo de Gallo (E) ...... 65 E 4
Rimavská Sobota (SK) . 12 B 2
Rimbo (S) .... 141 D 3
Rimeikēni (LV) .... 166 C 4
Riménai (LT) .... 176 C 3
Rimini (I) .... 102 B 1
Rimkai (LT) .... 170 C 4
Rimkūnai (LT) .... 164 C 4
Rimmi (EST) .... 161 D 2
Rîmnicu Sărat (RO) .... 13 E 4
Rîmnicu Vîlcea (RO) ... 13 D 4
Rimšė (LT) .... 172 C 2
Rimšėnai (LT) .... 172 C 4
Rimske Toplice (SLO) .. 99 E 1
Rimstavas (LV) .... 161 D 4
Rincón de la Victoria (E) 76 D 2
Rincón de Soto (E) .... 65 E 1
Rindal (N) .... 130 C 3
Ríneia (Nisí) (GR) ..... 219 F 3
Ringaskiddy (IRL) ..... 24 C 4
Ringaudai (LT) .... 176 B 1
Ringe (DK) .... 142 B 4
Ringebu (N) .... 139 E 1
Ringford (GB) .... 30 C 4
Ringkøbing (DK) .... 142 A 3
Ringsaker (N) .... 139 E 2
Ringstad (N) .... 138 B 1
Ringsted (DK) .... 142 C 4
Ringwood (GB) .... 35 E 3
Rinkaby (S) .... 143 E 4
Rinkšeliai (LT) .... 169 F 2
Rinkūnai (LT) .... 165 D 4
Rinkuškiai (LT) .... 165 D 3
Rinteln (D) .... 83 F 4
Río (GR) .... 217 D 1
Rio Maior (P) .... 68 A 2
Rio Marina (I) .... 101 A 4
Riocavado de la Sierra (E) 64 C 2
Riogordo (E) .... 76 A 3
Riola Sardo (I) .... 108 A 3
Riolo Terme (I) .... 102 A 1
Riom (F) .... 52 A 1
Riom-ès-Montagnes (F) . 51 F 2
Riomaggiore (I) .... 101 D 2
Rionero in Vulture (I) .. 106 B 3
Rioseco de Tapia (E) .. 59 E 1
Rioveggio (I) .... 101 F 1
Rioz (F) .... 49 E 2
Ripač (BIH) .... 99 F 3
Ripanj (SRB) .... 118 B 1
Riparbella (I) .... 101 E 3
Ripatransone (I) .... 102 C 3
Ripley (GB) .... 33 D 3
Ripoll (E) .... 55 E 4
Ripollet (E) .... 67 D 2
Ripon (GB) .... 33 D 1
Riquewihr (F) .... 45 D 4
Risan (MNE) .... 121 D 2
Risbäck (S) .... 131 F 1
Risca (GB) .... 35 D 1
Riscle (F) .... 54 C 2
Risnes (N) .... 138 C 4
Risør (N) .... 139 D 4
Risøyhamn (N) .... 124 A 3
Rissa (N) .... 131 D 2

Risti (EST) .... 148 C 4
Ristiina (FIN) .... 137 E 2
Ristijärvi (FIN) .... 135 E 1
Ristiküla (EST) .... 153 C 4
Ristilampi (FIN) .... 129 D 3
Ristipalo (EST) .... 161 E 1
Ristovac (SRB) .... 122 B 1
Risum-Lindholm (D) ... 78 A 4
Rīteri (LV) .... 165 F 2
Rītíni (GR) .... 206 A 4
Ritiniai (LT) .... 169 E 4
Ritoniemi (FIN) .... 135 E 3
Ritsóna (GR) .... 218 B 1
Rittmannshausen (D) .. 88 B 4
Riva (I) .... 156 C 4
Riva del Garda (I) ..... 97 D 4
Rivarolo Canavese (I) .. 53 F 2
Rive-de-Gier (F) ...... 52 B 2
Rives (F) .... 52 C 2
Rivesaltes (F) .... 55 F 3
Rívio (GR) .... 211 E 4
Rivisondoli (I) .... 105 D 3
Rivne (UA) .... 13 D 1
Rivoli (I) .... 53 F 2
Rivolta d'Adda (I) ..... 97 F 3
Ríza (GR) .... 217 D 1
Rizário (GR) .... 205 D 2
Rízia (GR) .... 208 C 1
Rizokarpaso (CY) ...... 231 F 1
Rizóma (GR) .... 211 F 2
Rizómylos (GR) .... 212 B 2
Rizovoúni (GR) .... 211 F 2
Rjånes (N) .... 130 A 4
Rjukan (N) .... 139 D 3
Röa (EST) .... 149 F 4
Roa de Duero (E) ..... 64 B 2
Roadside (GB) .... 27 B 4
Roan (N) .... 131 D 2
Robbio (I) .... 97 A 1
Röbel (D) .... 79 D 3
Robertsfors (S) .... 132 B 2
Robertville (B) .... 87 D 3
Robežnieki (LV) .... 167 B 2
Robežnieki (Pustiņa) (LV)167 F 4
Robežsils (LV) .... 161 D 4
Robič (SLO) .... 98 C 1
Robledillo de Gata (E) . 63 E 4
Robledo (E) .... 71 E 4
Robledo de Chavela (E) . 64 B 4
Robres (E) .... 65 F 2
Rocamadour (F) .... 51 E 3
Rocca di Mezzo (I) .... 102 C 4
Rocca di Papa (I) ...... 105 C 4
Rocca San Casciano (I) . 102 A 1
Rocca Sinibalda (I) .... 102 A 1
Roccadaspide (I) ...... 106 B 4
Roccalbegna (I) .... 102 A 4
Roccalumera (I) .... 111 E 2
Roccamonfina (I) ...... 105 E 2
Roccapalumba (I) ..... 110 C 3
Roccaraso (I) .... 105 C 4
Roccastrada (I) .... 101 A 1
Roccella Ionica (I) .... 111 F 1
Rocchetta San Antonio (I)106 B 3
Roceji (LV) .... 157 C 2
Rochdale (GB) .... 33 D 1
Rochechouart (F) ..... 51 D 1
Rochefort (B) .... 39 B 1
Rochefort (F) .... 46 C 4
Rochefort-en-Terre (F) . 41 C 4
Rochefort-Montagne (F) . 51 C 4
Rochefort-sur-Nenon (F) . 49 D 2
Rochehaut (B) .... 39 F 4
Rochemaure (F) .... 52 B 3
Rocheservière (F) ..... 46 B 3
Rochester (GB) .... 36 C 3
Rochlitz (D) .... 89 E 2
Rociana del Condado (E)..75 D 2
Rociñas (E) .... 163 C 3
Ročiškiai (LT) .... 169 D 3
Rockenhausen (D) ..... 45 E 3
Rocroi (F) .... 39 F 2
Róda (GR) .... 210 B 1
Roda de Isábena (E) .. 54 C 4
Rodacherbrunn (D) .... 89 D 2
Rodavgí (GR) .... 211 D 2
Rødberg (N) .... 139 D 4
Rødby (DK) .... 144 B 4
Rødbyhavn (DK) ...... 144 B 4
Rødding (DK) .... 142 B 3
Rødding (DK) .... 142 B 4
Rödeby (S) .... 143 F 3
Rødekro (DK) .... 142 B 4
Rodel (GB) .... 26 A 4

Rodellar (E) .... 54 C 4
Roden (NL) .... 82 C 2
Ródenas (E) .... 65 E 4
Rödermark (D) .... 45 F 1
Rodewisch (D) .... 89 E 2
Rodez (F) .... 51 F 4
Rodi Garganico (I) ..... 103 F 4
Rodiezmo (E) .... 59 E 3
Roding (D) .... 89 F 2
Roditis (GR) .... 208 B 2
Rodochóri (GR) .... 205 F 4
Rododáfni (GR) .... 217 E 1
Rodolívos (GR) .... 207 D 2
Rödön (S) .... 131 F 2
Rodópoli (GR) .... 206 C 2
Rodopós (GR) .... 226 A 1
Ródos (GR) .... 228 C 2
Ródos (Nisí) (GR) ..... 228 C 2
Rodováni (GR) .... 226 A 2
Rodvattnet (S) .... 132 B 3
Rødven (N) .... 130 B 3
Rødvig (DK) .... 143 C 4
Rodžia (LT) .... 176 C 3
Roela (EST) .... 151 D 4
Roermond (NL) .... 87 D 1
Roeselare (B) .... 37 F 4
Rogač (HR) .... 103 F 2
Rogača (SRB) .... 118 C 2
Rogačica Užice(SRB) .. 119 E 4
Rogačica Vranje(SRB) .. 118 B 3
Rogalin (PL) .... 187 D 4
Rogas Kuldīgas(LV) .... 157 D 2
Rogas Saldus(LV) ...... 163 D 2
Rogaška Slatina (SLO) . 99 F 1
Rogatec (SLO) .... 99 F 1
Rogatica (BIH) .... 117 F 3
Rogätz (D) .... 84 C 2
Roggendorf (D) .... 79 E 4
Roggiano Gravina (I) .. 109 E 1
Roggosen (D) .... 85 F 2
Rogliano (F) .... 57 F 2
Rogliano (I) .... 109 E 2
Rogoviki (LV) .... 167 D 3
Rogovka (LV) .... 167 E 2
Rogów (PL) .... 189 F 4
Rogowo Rypin(PL) .... 189 D 1
Rogowo Żnin(PL) ..... 188 B 2
Rogoznica (HR) .... 103 E 4
Rogoźnica (PL) .... 193 E 2
Rogoźno (PL) .... 187 F 2
Rogózno Kujawsko-
  Pomorskie(PL) .... 183 D 4
Roguszyn (PL) .... 190 C 2
Rohan (F) .... 41 D 3
Rohatyn (UA) .... 12 C 2
Rohr (D) .... 88 C 2
Rohrbach
  im Oberösterreich (A) .. 94 C 1
Rohrbach-lès-Bitche (F) . 45 D 2
Rohrbrunn (D) .... 45 F 1
Rõhu (EST) .... 154 C 4
Rohukūla (EST) .... 148 C 4
Rohuneeme (EST) ..... 149 E 2
Roisel (F) .... 39 D 4
Roissy-en-France (F) .. 43 D 4
Roiu (EST) .... 155 D 4
Roja (LV) .... 157 E 2
Rojales (E) .... 77 E 2
Rojewo (PL) .... 188 C 1
Rokaiži (LV) .... 162 C 1
Rokasbirze (LV) .... 162 C 1
Rokiciny (PL) .... 189 E 4
Rokietnica
  Podkarpackie(PL) .... 202 E 2
Rokietnica
  Wielkopolskie(PL) ... 187 E 2
Rokiškis (LT) .... 165 E 3
Rokitno Lubelskie(PL) . 191 E 3
Rokland (N) .... 127 E 3
Rokovci (HR) .... 117 F 3
Rokycany (CZ) .... 89 F 3
Røldal (N) .... 138 C 3
Rolfstorp (S) .... 143 D 2
Rolle (CH) .... 49 E 1
Roma (I) .... 104 C 2
Romagnano Sesia (I) .. 96 D 1
Roman (RO) .... 13 D 3
Romana (I) .... 108 A 2
Romangordo (E) ...... 69 F 3
Romanija (BIH) .... 117 F 3
Romans-sur-Isère (F) .. 52 C 3
Romanshorn (CH) ..... 93 C 2
Rombas (F) .... 44 C 2
Römhild (D) .... 88 C 2
Romilly-sur-Seine (F) .. 43 D 4

Romont (CH) .... 49 F 3
Romorantin-Lanthenay (F) 47 F 2
Romsey (GB) .... 35 F 3
Romučiai (LT) .... 163 E 4
Roncade (I) .... 98 C 3
Roncal/Erronkari (E) .. 54 B 3
Ronce-les-Bains (F) ... 50 B 1
Roncegno (I) .... 98 A 2
Ronchamp (F) .... 49 F 1
Ronchi dei Legionari (I) . 98 C 2
Ronciglione (I) .... 102 B 4
Roncobilaccio (I) ...... 101 F 1
Ronda (E) .... 75 F 3
Rønde (DK) .... 142 C 3
Rondissone (I) .... 53 F 2
Rõngu (EST) .... 154 C 2
Rönnäng (S) .... 142 C 1
Rønne (DK) .... 145 E 3
Ronneburg (D) .... 89 E 1
Ronneby (S) .... 143 F 3
Rønnede (DK) .... 142 C 4
Rönnöfors (S) .... 131 F 3
Ronse (B) .... 39 D 2
Roosendaal (NL) ...... 39 E 1
Roosna (EST) .... 150 C 4
Roosna-Alliku (EST) ... 149 E 4
Rootsiküla (EST) ...... 153 B 4
Ropaži (LV) .... 159 D 4
Ropczyce (PL) .... 202 D 2
Roperuelos del Páramo (E)59 E 4
Ropinsalmi (FIN) ...... 124 C 4
Ropotovo (MK) .... 122 B 3
Roquebilière (F) ...... 53 F 4
Roquebrun (F) .... 55 F 2
Roquebrune-Cap-Martin (F)57 F 1
Roquecourbe (F) ..... 55 F 2
Roquefort (F) .... 50 B 4
Roquefort-sur-Soulzon (F). 51 F 4
Roquemaure (F) ...... 52 C 4
Roquesteron (F) ...... 53 E 4
Roquetas de Mar (E) .. 76 C 3
Roquevaire (F) .... 57 D 2
Rore (BIH) .... 116 C 3
Røros (N) .... 131 D 4
Rørøy (N) .... 126 C 4
Rørvig (DK) .... 142 C 4
Rørvik (N) .... 131 D 1
Rørvik (N) .... 131 D 1
Roś (Jezioro) (PL) .... 184 C 3
Rosà (I) .... 98 A 2
Rosal de la Frontera (E) . 68 C 4
Rosans (F) .... 52 C 4
Rosarno (I) .... 111 F 1
Rościszewo (PL) ...... 189 E 1
Roscoff (F) .... 40 B 2
Roscommon /
  Ros Comáin (IRL) .... 22 C 4
Roscrea / Ros Cré (IRL) . 25 D 2
Rose (I) .... 109 E 1
Rose (MNE) .... 121 D 2
Rosegg (A) .... 99 D 1
Rosendal (N) .... 138 B 2
Rosenheim (D) .... 94 A 3
Rosenthal (D) .... 90 A 1
Roses / Rosas (E) ..... 56 A 4
Roseto degli Abruzzi (I) . 103 D 3
Rosheim (F) .... 45 D 3
Rosice (CZ) .... 90 B 4
Rosières-en-Santerre (F). 38 C 4
Rosignano Marittimo (I) . 101 E 3
Rosignano Solvay (I) .. 101 E 3
Roşiori de Vede (RO) .. 13 D 4
Roskilde (DK) .... 143 D 4
Rosko (PL) .... 187 E 3
Roslavl' (RUS) .... 7 E 3
Rosma (EST) .... 161 D 1
Rosmaninhal (P) ...... 69 D 1
Rosme (LV) .... 164 C 3
Rosolina Mare (I) ..... 98 B 3
Rosolini (I) .... 111 E 4
Rosoman (MK) .... 122 B 3
Rosporden (F) .... 40 B 4
Ross-on-Wye (GB) .... 35 E 1
Rossano (I) .... 109 E 1
Roßberg (A) .... 94 C 1
Rosscarbery (IRL) .... 24 B 4
Roßdorf (D) .... 45 F 1
Rossell (E) .... 66 A 4
Rosses Point (IRL) .... 22 C 2
Rossio ao Sul do Tejo (P). 68 B 2
Rosslare / Ros Láir (IRL) . 25 E 3
Rosslare Harbour /
  Calafort Ros Láir (IRL) . 25 E 3
Roßlau (D) .... 85 D 4
Rosslea (GB) .... 23 D 3

Rossön (S) ....132 A 2
Rossosz (PL) ....191 E 4
Roßwein (D) ....89 F 1
Rosthwaite (GB) ......31 D 4
Røstlandet (N) ....127 D 2
Rostock (D) ....79 F 3
Rostov (RUS) ....7 F 1
Rostrenen (F) ....40 C 3
Rostrevor (GB) ....23 E 3
Røsvik (N) ....127 E 2
Rosvik (S) ....132 C 1
Rota (E) ....75 D 3
Rotenburg (D) ....88 B 2
Rotenburg (D) ....83 F 2
Roth (D) ....89 D 4
Rötha (D) ....89 E 1
Rothbury (GB) ....31 E 3
Röthenbach
  a. d. Pegnitz (D) ...89 D 4
Rothenburg (D) ....85 F 4
Rothenburg
  o. d. Tauber (D) ....88 C 4
Rothéneuf (F) ....41 E 2
Rotherham (GB) ....33 D 2
Rothes (GB) ....27 F 3
Rothesay (GB) ....30 B 2
Rothwell (GB) ....33 E 4
Rotinénai (LT) ....163 D 4
Rotonda (I) ....106 C 4
Rotondella (I) ....107 D 4
Rott (D) ....93 F 3
Rott a. Inn (D) ......94 A 3
Rottach-Egern (D) ....94 A 3
Rottenbach (D) ....88 C 2
Rottenburg a. d. Laaber (D) 94 A 1
Rottenburg a. Neckar (D) .. 45 F 3
Rottenmann (A) ....95 D 3
Rotterdam (NL) ....82 A 4
Rotterdam (NL) ....82 A 4
Rottne (S) ....143 E 2
Rottneros (S) ....139 F 3
Rottweil (D) ....45 F 4
Rötz (D) ....89 E 4
Roubaix (F) ....39 D 2
Rõude (EST) ....153 B 2
Roudnice nad Labem (CZ) 90 B 2
Rouen (F) ....38 B 4
Rouffach (F) ....45 D 4
Rõuge (EST) ....161 D 2
Rougé (F) ....41 E 4
Rougemont (F) ....49 E 2
Rougemont-le-Château (F) 49 F 1
Rouillac (F) ....50 C 1
Roujan (F) ....56 A 2
Roulans (F) ....49 E 2
Roundstone (IRL) .....22 A 4
Roússa (GR) ....208 C 1
Rovaniemi (FIN) ......129 D 3
Rovato (I) ....97 E 3
Rovereto (I) ....97 F 2
Roverud (N) ....139 F 3
Roves (LV) ....165 D 1
Roviés (GR) ....212 C 4
Rovigo (I) ....98 A 4
Roviśće (HR) ....112 A 4
Równia (PL) ....202 E 3
Rowy (PL) ....181 F 1
Royal
  Leamington Spa (GB) .33 D 4
Royal
  Tunbridge Wells (GB) .36 C 4
Royan (F) ....50 B 1
Royat (F) ....51 F 1
Roybon (F) ....52 C 2
Roye (F) ....39 D 4
Royère-de-Vassivière (F) .51 E 1
Røyrvik (N) ....131 F 2
Royston (GB) ....36 B 2
Röyttä (FIN) ....128 C 4
Rožaje (MNE) ....118 C 4
Rozalimas (LT) ....170 C 1
Różan (PL) ....190 B 1
Rožanstvo (SRB) ......118 B 3
Rozay-en-Brie (F) ....43 E 3
Rozēni (LV) ....159 D 1
Rozentova (LV) ....167 D 4
Rozes (LV) ....159 F 3
Rozītes (LV) ....165 D 2
Rožkalni (LV) ....165 E 1
Rožmitál
  pod Třemšínem (CZ) ..90 A 3
Rožňava (SK) ....12 B 2
Rožnov
  pod Radhoštěm (CZ) ..91 F 3
Rożnowskie
  (Jezioro) (PL) ......201 B 2

Rozogi (PL) ....184 B 4
Rozoy-sur-Serre (F) ..39 E 4
Rozprza (PL) ....195 E 2
Roztoczanski Park
  Narodowy (PL) ....197 E 3
Roztocze (PL) ....197 E 3
Roztoka (PL) ....193 D 3
Roztoky Praha-západ (CZ) 90 E 4
Rozula (LV) ....159 E 3
Rozupe (LV) ....166 C 3
Rozvadov (CZ) ....89 D 3
Rozwadów (PL) ....197 D 3
Roźwienica (PL) ......202 E 2
Rrogozhinë (AL) ......121 D 2
Rtanj (SRB) ....119 D 2
Ruabon (GB) ....32 C 3
Ruba (LV) ....163 E 3
Rubbestadneset (N) ...138 B 3
Rubeļņinkai (LT) .....172 C 3
Rubena (LV) ....60 B 1
Rubene (LV) ....159 E 3
Rubeņi (LV) ....166 B 4
Rubí (E) ....67 A 3
Rubí de Bracamonte (E) .64 A 3
Rubiães (P) ....62 B 1
Rubielos de Mora (E) .71 F 4
Rubiera (I) ....97 F 4
Rubikai (LT) ....163 D 3
Rubuļi (LT) ....167 D 4
Rubuliai (LT) ....162 B 4
Rucava (LV) ....162 B 3
Ruciane-Nida (PL) ....184 C 3
Ručiūnai (LT) ....170 C 4
Rūda Alytaus (LT) ....175 F 4
Rūda Marijampolés (LT) .175 F 2
Ruda Maleniecka (PL) .195 F 2
Ruda Śląska (PL) .....195 D 4
Rūdaičiai (LT) ....162 B 4
Rudaičiai (LT) ....168 B 1
Rudamina Alytaus (LT) .175 F 3
Rudamina Vilniaus (LT) .177 E 3
Rudare (LV) ....119 D 4
Rūdava (LV) ....167 D 2
Rudbārži (LV) ....163 D 2
Rude Liepājas (LV) ...162 B 2
Rude Talsu (LV) ......157 F 4
Rüdersdorf (D) ....85 E 2
Rüdesheim a. Rhein (D) .45 E 1
Rūdiškės (LT) ....177 D 3
Rudiškiai (LT) ....163 F 4
Rudka (PL) ....191 D 1
Rudkøbing (DK) ....144 C 4
Rudn'a (RUS) ....7 E 3
Rudna Dolnośląskie (PL) .193 E 1
Rudna Glava (SRB) ....119 D 4
Rudnia Alytaus (LT) ..177 D 4
Rudnia Vilniaus (LT) .177 F 4
Rudnica Novi Pazar (SRB) 118 C 3
Rudnica Pljevlja (MNE) 118 B 4
Rudnik Kragujevac (SRB) 118 C 2
Rudnik Peć (SRB) .....118 C 4
Rudnik n. Sanem
  Podkarpackie (PL) ...197 D 4
Rudniki Opolskie (PL) .194 C 2
Rūdninkai (LT) ....177 E 3
Rudno Pomorskie (PL) .182 C 3
Rudolphstein (D) .....89 D 2
Rudolstadt (D) ....89 D 2
Ruduśi (LV) ....167 F 2
Rudzāti (LV) ....166 C 3
Rudžiai (LT) ....170 C 3
Rudzica (PL) ....200 B 2
Rudziniec (PL) ....194 C 4
Rue (F) ....38 B 3
Rueda (E) ....64 D 4
Rueda de Jalón (E) ...65 E 3
Ruelle-sur-Touvre (F) .50 C 1
Ruffec (F) ....47 D 1
Ruffieux (F) ....53 D 1
Rugāji (LV) ....161 E 4
Rugby (GB) ....33 D 4
Rugeley (GB) ....33 D 4
Rügen (D) ....80 C 2
Rugles (F) ....42 C 4
Ruhla (D) ....88 C 2
Ruhland (D) ....85 E 4
Ruhnu (EST) ....157 F 1
Ruhpolding (D) ....94 B 3
Ruidera (E) ....70 C 3
Ruidoms (E) ....66 B 2
Rūjiena (LV) ....159 F 1
Ruka (FIN) ....129 E 3
Rukainiai (LT) ....177 F 2
Rūķi (LV) ....163 F 2
Rukiškis (LT) ....171 D 2
Rukla (LT) ....171 D 4

Ruma (SRB) ....118 B 1
Rumboci (BIH) ....117 D 3
Rumburk (CZ) ....90 B 1
Rūmene (LV) ....157 F 4
Rumengol (F) ....40 B 3
Rumenka (SRB) ....113 E 4
Rumia (PL) ....182 C 1
Rumigny (F) ....39 E 4
Rumilly (F) ....53 D 1
Rummu (EST) ....149 B 1
Rumšiškés (LT) ....176 C 1
Runcorn (GB) ....32 C 3
Rundāni (LV) ....167 F 3
Runde (N) ....130 A 4
Rundvik (S) ....132 B 3
Runni (FIN) ....133 F 2
Runtuna (S) ....140 C 4
Ruokojärvi (FIN) .....135 F 4
Ruokolahti (FIN) .....137 F 2
Ruokto (S) ....128 A 2
Ruoms (F) ....52 B 4
Ruotsinpyhtää /
  Strömfors (FIN) .....137 E 3
Ruovesi (FIN) ....133 C 4
Rupa (HR) ....99 D 2
Rūpnieki (LV) ....159 F 2
Ruponiai (LT) ....164 C 4
Rupt-sur-Moselle (F) .45 D 4
Rusakalnis (LT) ......177 D 2
Ruse (BG) ....13 D 4
Ruše (SLO) ....114 C 2
Ruševo (HR) ....115 F 3
Rush / An Ros (IRL) ..23 E 4
Rushden (GB) ....33 E 4
Rusiec (PL) ....195 D 2
Rusinów (PL) ....195 F 1
Rusiu Ragas (LT) .....171 D 4
Rusko (PL) ....136 B 3
Rusko Selo (SRB) .....113 E 3
Ruskele (S) ....132 B 1
Ruskulova (LV) ....167 E 1
Rusné (LT) ....168 B 3
Rušona (LV) ....167 D 4
Rusonys (LT) ....176 C 1
Rüsselsheim (D) ......45 E 1
Russi (I) ....102 A 1
Russenes (N) ....125 D 2
Russów (PL) ....188 B 4
Rust (A) ....95 F 2
Rustefjelbma (N) .....125 E 1
Ruswil (CH) ....96 C 1
Rute (E) ....76 A 2
Rūteliai (LT) ....169 D 2
Rüthen (D) ....88 A 1
Ruthin / Rhuthun (GB) .32 B 3
Rūti (LT) ....92 C 4
Rutigliano (I) ....107 D 2
Rutka-Tartak (PL) ....185 D 1
Rutki-Kossaki (PL) ...191 E 1
Rutkiškiai (LT) ......169 E 3
Rutledal (N) ....138 B 1
Ruukki (FIN) ....133 E 1
Ruuponsaari (FIN) ....133 F 3
Ruurlo (NL) ....82 C 4
Ruusa (EST) ....161 E 1
Ruusmäe (EST) ....161 D 2
Ruvo di Puglia (I) ...106 C 2
Ruwer (D) ....44 C 2
Ruynes-en-Margeride (F) .52 A 3
Ružomberok (SK) ......12 B 2
Ry (DK) ....142 B 3
Ryákia (GR) ....206 A 4
Rybczewice Drugie (PL) 197 E 2
Rybinsk (RUS) ....7 E 2
Rybnik (PL) ....200 E 3
Rybno Mazowieckie (PL) 189 E 4
Rybno Warmińsko-
  Mazurskie (PL) ......183 E 4
Rychliki (PL) ....183 D 2
Rychnov
  nad Kněžnou (CZ) ....91 D 2
Rychtal (PL) ....194 B 2
Rychwał (PL) ....188 C 3
Rychwał-Królewski (PL) 183 F 1
Ryczywół
  Wielkopolskie (PL) ..187 E 3
Ryd (S) ....143 E 3
Ryde (GB) ....35 F 3
Rydułtowy (PL) ....200 E 4
Rydzyna (PL) ....187 E 2
Rye (GB) ....36 C 4
Rygge (N) ....139 D 4
Ryglice (PL) ....201 C 2
Rykene (N) ....139 D 4
Ryki (PL) ....190 C 4
Ryl'sk (RUS) ....7 F 4

Rymań (PL) ....181 D 3
Rymanów (PL) ....202 D 3
Rýmařov (CZ) ....91 E 2
Rymättylä (FIN) ......136 B 4
Rýmnio (GR) ....205 F 4
Ryn (PL) ....184 C 3
Rynia (PL) ....190 B 2
Rypefjord (N) ....125 D 1
Rypin (PL) ....189 D 1
Rysjedalsvika (N) ....138 B 1
Rysy (PL) ....201 A 4
Ryttyla (FIN) ....137 D 3
Rytwiany (PL) ....196 B 4
Rząśnia (PL) ....195 D 2
Rzeczenica (PL) ......181 F 3
Rzeczniów (PL) ....196 C 2
Rzeczyca Łodzkie (PL) 189 F 4
Rzekuń (PL) ....190 C 1
Rzemień (PL) ....196 C 4
Rzepedź (PL) ....202 E 3
Rzepiennik
  Strzyżewski (PL) ....201 C 2
Rzepin (PL) ....186 C 3
Rzepińska (Puszcza) (PL) 186 C 2
Rzeszów (PL) ....202 D 2
Ržev (RUS) ....7 F 2
Rzezawa (PL) ....201 B 2
Rzgów Łodzkie (PL) ...189 E 4
Rzgów Wielkopolskie (PL) 188 B 3

S

's-Gravendeel (NL) ...82 B 4
's-Heerenberg (NL) ...82 C 4
's-Hertogenbosch (NL) 86 C 1
S. Karlovci (SRB) ....113 E 4
Sa Calobra (E) ....73 E 2
Sa Pobla (E) ....73 E 2
Saadjärve (EST) ......155 D 3
Sääksjärvi (FIN) .....133 E 3
Saal a. d. Donau (D) .94 A 1
Saalbach (A) ....94 B 4
Saales (F) ....45 D 4
Saalfeld (D) ....89 D 2
Saalfelden (A) ....94 B 3
Saanen (CH) ....96 C 1
Saarbrücken (D) ......45 D 2
Saarburg (D) ....44 C 2
Saarde (EST) ....154 A 4
Sääre Pärnu (EST) ....153 B 4
Sääre Saare (EST) ....157 D 1
Saarenkylä (FIN) .....129 D 3
Saarepeedi (EST) .....154 C 4
Saari (FIN) ....135 F 4
Saariharju (FIN) .....129 D 4
Saarijärvi (FIN) .....133 E 4
Saarikoski (FIN) .....124 C 4
Saariselkä (FIN) .....125 F 4
Saarlouis (D) ....44 C 2
Saas Fee (CH) ....96 C 2
Sääse (EST) ....150 C 4
Saatse (EST) ....161 F 1
Šabac (SRB) ....118 A 1
Sabadell (E) ....67 D 3
Sabaudia (I) ....105 D 3
Sabbioneta (I) ....97 F 4
Sabero (E) ....59 F 3
Sabile (LV) ....157 E 4
Sabiñánigo (E) ....54 B 2
Sabiote (E) ....76 B 1
Sablé-sur-Sarthe (F) .41 F 4
Sables-d'Or-les-Pins (F) 41 D 2
Sabnie (PL) ....191 D 2
Sabóia (P) ....74 B 1
Sabres (F) ....50 B 4
Sabrosa (P) ....63 D 3
Sabugal (P) ....63 D 4
Sacavém (P) ....68 A 3
Sacedón (E) ....71 D 1
Saceruela (E) ....70 A 3
Sacile (I) ....98 B 2
Sacramenia (E) ....64 B 3
Sada (E) ....58 B 2
Sádaba (E) ....54 A 4
Sadala (EST) ....155 D 2
Sadki (PL) ....187 F 1
Sadlowo (PL) ....189 E 1
Sadowie (PL) ....196 C 3
Sadowne (PL) ....190 C 2
Sadukūla (EST) ....154 C 4
Sadūnai (LT) ....172 B 2
Sadurki (PL) ....197 D 2
Šadžiūnai (LT) ....176 B 4
Sæby (N) ....139 D 1
Sæby (DK) ....142 C 1
Saelices (E) ....70 C 1
Sælvig (DK) ....142 C 3
Sævråsvåg (N) ....138 B 1

Safara (P) ....68 C 4
Säffle (S) ....139 F 4
Saffron Walden (GB) ..36 C 2
Safonovo (RUS) ....7 E 2
Sagaïka (GR) ....217 D 1
Sagard (D) ....80 C 2
S'Agaró (E) ....67 E 2
Sagiáda (GR) ....210 C 2
Sagres (P) ....74 A 2
Sagunt / Sagunto (E) .72 A 2
Sagunto / Sagunt (E) .72 A 2
Sagvåg (N) ....138 B 3
Saha (EST) ....149 B 4
Sahagún (E) ....59 F 4
Sahalahti (FIN) ......136 C 2
Šahinovići (BIH) .....117 C 2
Sahl (DK) ....142 B 3
Sahloinen (FIN) ......133 E 4
Saignelégier (CH) ....49 F 2
Saija (FIN) ....129 E 2
Saillagouse (F) ......55 C 4
Saillans (F) ....52 C 3
Saint-Étienne-
  Cantalès Barrage de (F) 51 F 3
Saint-Affrique (F) ...55 F 1
Saint-Agnant (F) .....50 B 1
Saint-Agrève (F) .....52 B 3
Saint-Aignan (F) .....47 F 2
Saint-Aignan-sur-Roë (F) 41 E 4
Saint-Alban-
  sur-Limagnole (F) ...52 A 3
Saint Albans (GB) ....36 B 3
Saint-Amand-
  en-Puisaye (F) ......48 A 2
Saint-Amand-les-Eaux (F) 39 D 3
Saint-Amand-Longpré (F) 42 A 3
Saint-Amand-Montrond (F) 48 A 3
Saint-Amans-des-Cots (F) 51 F 3
Saint-Amans-Soult (F) 55 F 2
Saint-Amant-
  Roche-Savine (F) ....52 A 2
Saint-Amant-Tallende (F) 52 A 1
Saint-Amarin (F) .....49 F 1
Saint-Ambroix (F) ....52 B 4
Saint-Amé (F) ....45 D 4
Saint-André-de-Cubzac (F) 50 B 3
Saint-André-de-l'Eure (F) 42 C 2
Saint-André-
  de-Valborgne (F) ....52 A 4
Saint-André-les-Alpes (F) 53 E 4
Saint Andrews (GB) ...31 E 1
Saint-Anthème (F) ....52 A 2
Saint-Antonin-Noble-Val (F) 51 E 4
Saint-Arnoult-
  en-Yvelines (F) .....42 C 3
Saint Asaph (GB) .....32 B 3
Saint-Astier (F) .....51 D 2
Saint-Auban (F) ......57 E 1
Saint-Aubin-d'Aubigné (F) 41 E 3
Saint-Aubin-du-Cormier (F) 41 E 3
Saint-Aubin-sur-Mer (F) 41 F 1
Saint-Aulaye (F) .....50 C 2
Saint Austell (GB) ...34 B 4
Saint-Avold (F) ......44 C 2
Saint-Ayguif (F) .....57 E 2
Saint-Béat (F) ....55 D 3
Saint-Beauzély (F) ...51 F 4
Saint-Benin-d'Azy (F) 48 B 3
Saint-Benoît-du-Sault (F) 47 D 4
Saint-Benoît-sur-Loire (F) 43 D 4
Saint-Bertrand-
  de-Comminges (F) ....54 C 3
Saint-Blin (F) ....44 B 4
Saint-Bonnet-de-Joux (F) 48 C 4
Saint-Bonnet-
  en-Champsaur (F) ....53 D 3
Saint-Bonnet-
  le-Château (F) ......52 B 2
Saint-Brevin-les-Pins (F) 46 B 1
Saint-Briac-sur-Mer (F) 41 D 3
Saint-Brice-en-Coglès (F) 41 E 3
Saint-Brieuc (F) .....41 D 3
Saint-Calais (F) .....42 B 4
Saint-CaSaint-le-Guildo (F) 41 D 2
Saint-Céré (F) ....51 E 3
Saint-Cergue (CH) ....49 E 4
Saint-Cernin (F) .....51 F 2
Saint-Chamas (F) .....56 C 2
Saint-Chamond (F) ....52 B 2
Saint-Chély-d'Apcher (F) 52 A 3
Saint-Chély-d'Aubrac (F) 51 F 3
Saint-Chinian (F) ....55 F 2
Saint-Ciers-sur-Gironde (F) 50 B 3
Saint-Cirq-Lapopie (F) 51 E 4

Saint-Clair-sur-l'Elle (F) 41 F 2
Saint-Clar (F) ....55 D 1
Saint-Claud (F) ......50 C 1
Saint-Claude (F) .....49 E 4
Saint Clears / Sanclêr (GB) 34 C 1
Saint-Cyprien (F) ....51 D 3
Saint-Cyprien-Plage (F) 55 F 4
Saint David's /
  Tyddewi (GB) ....25 F 1
Saint-Denis (F) ......43 D 2
Saint-Denis-d'Oléron (F) 46 B 4
Saint-Denis-d'Orques (F) 41 F 4
Saint-Didier-en-Velay (F) 52 B 2
Saint-Dié-des-Vosges (F) 45 D 4
Saint-Dier-d'Auvergne (F) 52 A 1
Saint-Dizier (F) .....44 B 3
Saint-Donat-
  sur-l'Herbasse (F) ..52 C 2
Saint-Éloy-les-Mines (F) 48 A 4
Saint-Émilion (F) ....50 C 3
Saint-Étienne (F) ....52 B 2
Saint-Étienne-
  de-Baïgorry (F) .....54 A 3
Saint-Étienne-
  de-Lugdarès (F) .....52 B 3
Saint-Étienne-
  de-Montluc (F) ......46 B 2
Saint-Étienne-
  de-Saint-Geoirs (F) .52 C 2
Saint-Étienne-de-Tinée (F) 53 E 4
Saint-Étienne-
  en-Dévoluy (F) ......53 D 3
Saint-Étienne-
  les-Orgues (F) ......53 D 4
Saint-Fargeau (F) ....43 E 4
Saint-Félicien (F) ...52 B 2
Saint-Firmin (F) .....53 D 3
Saint-Florent (F) ....57 F 3
Saint-Florent-le-Vieil (F) 46 C 2
Saint-Florent-sur-Cher (F) 48 A 3
Saint-Florentin (F) ..43 E 4
Saint-Flour (F) ......52 A 3
Saint-François-
  Longchamp (F) ....53 D 2
Saint-Fulgent (F) ....46 C 3
Saint-Galmier (F) ....52 B 2
Saint-Gaudens (F) ....55 D 3
Saint-Gaultier (F) ...47 F 3
Saint-Genest-Malifaux (F) 52 B 2
Saint-Gengoux-
  le-National (F) .....48 C 3
Saint-Geniez-d'Olt (F) 51 F 4
Saint-Genis-
  de-Saintonge (F) ....50 B 2
Saint-Genis-Laval (F) 52 B 1
Saint-Genix-sur-Guiers (F) 52 C 2
Saint-Geoire-
  en-Valdaine (F) .....52 C 2
Saint-Georges-
  de-Didonne (F) ......50 B 2
Saint-Georges-
  en-Couzan (F) ....52 A 1
Saint-Georges-
  sur-Loire (F) ....46 C 2
Saint-Germain-
  de-Calberte (F) .....52 A 4
Saint-Germain-
  des-Fossés (F) ......48 B 4
Saint-Germain-du-Bois (F) 49 D 3
Saint-Germain-du-Plain (F) 49 D 3
Saint-Germain-du-Teil (F) 52 A 4
Saint-Germain-en-Laye (F) 43 D 3
Saint-Germain-Laval (F) 52 B 1
Saint-Germain-Lembron (F) 52 A 2
Saint-Germain-
  les-Belles (F) ......51 E 2
Saint-Germain-l'Herm (F) 52 A 2
Saint-Gervais-
  d'Auvergne (F) ......48 A 4
Saint-Gervais-les-Bains (F) 49 F 4
Saint-Gervais-
  les-Trois-Clochers (F) 47 E 3
Saint-Gervais-sur-Mare (F) 55 F 2
Saint-Géry (F) ....51 E 4
Saint-Gildas-de-Rhuys (F) 40 D 4
Saint-Gildas-des-Bois (F) 41 D 4
Saint-Gilles-
  Croix-de-Vie (F) ....46 B 3
Saint-Gingolph (F) ...49 F 4
Saint-Girons (F) .....55 D 3
Saint-Girons-Plage (F) 50 A 4
Saint-Gobain (F) .....39 D 4
Saint-Guénolé (F) ....40 B 4
Saint-Guilhem-le-Désert (F) 56 A 2

Saint-Haon-le-Châtel (F) ... 48 C 4
Saint-Helens (GB) ... 32 C 2
Saint-Herblain (F) ... 46 B 2
Saint-Hilaire (F) ... 55 F 3
Saint-Hilaire-de-Riez (F).. 46 B 3
Saint-Hilaire-de-Villefranche (F) ... 50 B 1
Saint-Hilaire-des-Loges (F) 46 C 4
Saint-Hilaire-du-Harcouët (F) ... 41 F 3
Saint-Hippolyte (F) ... 49 F 2
Saint-Hippolyte-du-Fort (F) 52 B 3
Saint-Honoré-les-Bains (F) 48 B 3
Saint Hubert (B) ... 39 F 3
Saint-Imier (CH) ... 49 F 2
Saint-Ives (GB) ... 34 A 4
Saint-Ives (GB) ... 33 F 4
Saint-Jacques-de-la-Lande (F) ... 41 E 4
Saint-Jacut-de-la-Mer (F).. 41 D 3
Saint-James (F) ... 41 E 3
Saint-Jean-Brévelay (F) ... 41 D 4
Saint-Jean-Cap-Ferrat (F).57 F 2
Saint-Jean-d'Angély (F).. 46 C 4
Saint-Jean-de-Bournay (F)52 C 2
Saint-Jean-de-Daye (F).. 41 F 1
Saint-Jean-de-Losne (F).. 49 D 2
Saint-Jean-de-Luz (F) ... 54 A 2
Saint-Jean-de-Maurienne (F) ... 53 D 2
Saint-Jean-de-Monts (F).. 46 B 3
Saint-Jean-du-Bruel (F) .. 52 A 4
Saint-Jean-du-Gard (F).. 52 A 4
Saint-Jean-en-Royans (F).52 C 3
Saint-Jean-Pied-de-Port (F)54 A 3
Saint-Jeoire (F) ... 49 E 4
Saint-Jouin-de-Marnes (F) 47 D 3
Saint-Juéry (F) ... 55 E 1
Saint-Julien (F) ... 49 D 4
Saint-Julien-Chapteuil (F).. 52 B 3
Saint-Julien-de-Vouvantes (F) ... 41 E 4
Saint-Julien-du-Sault (F) ... 43 E 4
Saint-Julien-en-Genevois (F) ... 49 E 4
Saint-Julien-l'Ars (F) ... 47 E 3
Saint-Junien (F) ... 51 D 1
Saint-Just-en-Chaussée (F)38 C 4
Saint-Just-en-Chevalet (F) 52 A 1
Saint-Just (GB) ... 34 A 4
Saint-Justin (F) ... 50 C 4
Saint-Keverne (GB) ... 34 B 4
Saint-Lary-Soulan (F) ... 54 C 3
Saint-Laurent-de-Chamousset (F) .. 52 B 1
Saint-Laurent-de-la-Salanque (F) ... 55 F 3
Saint-Laurent-du-Pont (F).53 D 2
Saint-Laurent-en-Grandvaux (F) ... 49 E 3
Saint-Laurent-les-Bains (F)52 B 3
Saint-Laurent-Médoc (F).. 50 B 2
Saint-Laurent-sur-Gorre (F)51 D 1
Saint-Laurent-sur-Mer (F).. 41 F 1
Saint-Laurent-sur-Sèvre (F)46 C 3
Saint-Léger-sous-Beuvray (F) ... 48 C 3
Saint-Léonard-de-Noblat (F) ... 51 E 1
Saint-Lô (F) ... 41 F 2
Saint-Louis (F) ... 92 B 4
Saint-Loup-Lamairé (F) ... 47 D 3
Saint-Loup-sur-Semouse (F) ... 49 E 4
Saint-Luc (CH) ... 96 B 2
Saint-Lunaire (F) ... 41 D 2
Saint-Lys (F) ... 55 D 2
Saint-Macaire (F) ... 50 C 3
Saint-Maixent-l'École (F)... 47 D 4
Saint-Malo (F) ... 41 E 2
Saint-Malo-de-la-Lande (F)41 E 2
Saint-Mamet-la-Salvetat (F)51 F 3
Saint-Mandrier-sur-Mer (F) 57 D 3
Saint-Marcellin (F) ... 52 C 2
Saint Margaret's Hope (GB) ... 28 B 1
Saint-Mars-la-Jaille (F) ... 46 C 2
Saint-Martin-d'Auxigny (F) 48 A 2
Saint-Martin-de-Belleville (F) ... 53 E 2
Saint-Martin-de-Crau (F).. 56 C 2
Saint-Martin-de-Londres (F)56 A 2
Saint-Martin-de-Ré (F) ... 46 B 4
Saint-Martin-de-Seignanx (F) ... 54 A 2
Saint-Martin-de-Valamas (F) ... 52 B 3

Saint-Martin-en-Bresse (F) 49 D 3
Saint-Martin-Vésubie (F) .. 53 F 4
Saint-Martory (F) ... 55 D 3
Saint-Mathieu (F) ... 51 D 1
Saint-Maurice (CH) ... 49 F 4
Saint-Mawes (GB) ... 34 B 4
Saint-Maximin-la-Sainte-Baume (F) ... 57 D 2
Saint-Médard-en-Jalles (F) 50 B 3
Saint-Méen-le-Grand (F) .. 41 D 3
Saint-Michel (F) ... 39 E 4
Saint-Michel-de-Maurienne (F) ... 53 E 2
Saint-Michel-en-Grève (F). 40 C 2
Saint-Michel-en-l'Herm (F) 46 C 4
Saint-Michel-Mont-Mercure (F)... 46 C 3
Saint-Mihiel (F) ... 44 B 3
Saint-Monans (GB) ... 31 E 1
Saint-Nazaire (F) ... 46 B 2
Saint-Nectaire (F) ... 51 F 2
Saint-Neots (GB) ... 36 A 4
Saint-Nicolas-d'Aliermont (F) ... 38 B 4
Saint-Nicolas-de-la-Grave (F) ... 51 D 4
Saint-Nicolas-de-Port (F).. 44 C 3
Saint-Nicolas-du-Pélem (F)40 C 3
Saint-Omer (F) ... 38 C 2
Saint-Pair-sur-Mer (F) ... 41 E 2
Saint-Palais (F) ... 54 B 2
Saint-Palais-sur-Mer (F) .. 50 B 1
Saint-Pardoux-la-Rivière (F)51 D 2
Saint-Paul (F) ... 57 E 2
Saint-Paul-Cap-de-Joux (F)55 E 2
Saint-Paul-de-Fenouillet (F)55 F 3
Saint-Paul-sur-Ubaye (F).. 53 E 2
Saint-Paul-Trois-Châteaux (F) ... 52 C 4
Saint-Paulien (F) ... 52 A 2
Saint-Pé-de-Bigorre (F) ... 54 C 3
Saint-Pée-sur-Nivelle (F).. 54 A 2
Saint-Péray (F) ... 52 C 3
Saint-Père-en-Retz (F) ... 46 B 2
Saint-Philbert-de-Grand-Lieu (F) ... 46 B 2
Saint-Pierre-d'Albigny (F).. 53 D 2
Saint-Pierre-de-Chartreuse (F) ... 53 D 2
Saint-Pierre-de-Chignac (F)51 D 2
Saint-Pierre-d'Oléron (F).. 46 B 4
Saint-Pierre-Église (F) ... 41 E 1
Saint-Pierre-le-Moûtier (F). 48 B 3
Saint-Pierre-Quiberon (F)..40 C 4
Saint-Pierre-sur-Dives (F).. 42 A 2
Saint-Pois (F) ... 41 F 2
Saint-Pol-de-Léon (F) ... 40 B 2
Saint-Pol-sur-Ternoise (F).38 C 3
Saint-Pons-de-Thomières (F) ... 55 F 2
Saint-Porchaire (F) ... 50 B 1
Saint-Pourçain-sur-Sioule (F) ... 48 B 4
Saint-Privat (F) ... 51 E 2
Saint-Quay-Portrieux (F).. 41 D 2
Saint-Quentin (F) ... 39 D 4
Saint-Rambert-d'Albon (F) 52 C 2
Saint-Rambert-en-Bugey (F)49 D 4
Saint-Raphaël (F) ... 57 E 2
Saint-Rémy-de-Provence (F) ... 56 C 2
Saint-Rémy-sur-Durolle (F)52 A 1
Saint-Renan (F) ... 40 B 3
Saint-Riquier (F) ... 38 C 3
Saint-Romain-de-Colbosc (F) ... 38 A 4
Saint-Rome-de-Tarn (F) ... 51 F 4
Saint-Satur (F) ... 48 A 2
Saint-Saulge (F) ... 48 B 2
Saint-Sauveur-en-Puisaye (F) ... 43 E 2
Saint-Sauveur-le-Vicomte (F) ... 41 E 1
Saint-Sauveur-Lendelin (F)41 E 2
Saint-Sauveur-sur-Tinée (F) ... 53 E 4
Saint-Savin (F) ... 50 B 2
Saint-Savin (F) ... 47 E 3
Saint-Savinien (F) ... 50 B 1
Saint-Seine-l'Abbaye (F).. 48 C 2
Saint-Sernin-sur-Rance (F)55 F 2
Saint-Servan-sur-Mer (F).. 41 E 2
Saint-Sever (F) ... 54 B 2
Saint-Sever-Calvados (F).. 41 F 2
Saint-Sulpice-les-Feuilles (F) ... 47 F 4

Saint-Symphorien (F) ... 50 B 4
Saint-Symphorien-de-Lay (F) ... 48 C 4
Saint-Symphorien-d'Ozon (F) ... 52 C 2
Saint-Symphorien-sur-Coise (F) ... 52 B 2
Saint-Thégonnec (F) ... 40 B 3
Saint-Trivier-de-Courtes (F)49 D 4
Saint-Trivier-sur-Moignans (F) ... 49 D 4
Saint-Trojan-les-Bains (F). 50 B 1
Saint-Tropez (F) ... 57 E 2
Saint-Vaast-la-Hougue (F). 41 E 1
Saint-Valery-en-Caux (F).. 38 A 4
Saint-Valery-sur-Somme (F) ... 38 B 3
Saint-Vallier (F) ... 52 C 2
Saint-Vallier-de-Thiey (F).. 57 E 2
Saint-Varent (F) ... 47 D 3
Saint-Vaury (F) ... 47 F 4
Saint-Véran (F) ... 53 E 2
Saint Vincent (I) ... 53 F 1
Saint-Vincent-de-Tyrosse (F) ... 54 A 2
Saint-Vivien-de-Médoc (F) 50 B 2
Saint-Wandrille-Rançon (F)38 A 4
Saint-Yorre (F) ... 48 B 4
Saint-Yrieix-la-Perche (F).. 51 D 2
Sainte-Adresse (F) ... 38 A 4
Sainte-Anne-d'Auray (F) .. 40 C 4
Sainte-Croix (CH) ... 49 E 3
Sainte-Croix-du-Mont (F).. 50 B 3
Sainte-Croix-Volvestre (F). 55 D 3
Sainte-Enimie (F) ... 52 A 4
Sainte-Foy-la-Grande (F).. 50 C 3
Sainte-Foy-l'Argentière (F) 52 B 1
Sainte-Geneviève-sur-Argence (F) ... 51 F 3
Sainte-Hélène (F) ... 50 B 3

Sainte-Hermine (F) ... 46 C 3
Sainte-Livrade-sur-Lot (F). 51 D 4
Sainte-Lucie-de-Tallano (F)57 F 4
Sainte-Marie-aux-Mines (F)45 D 4
Sainte-Marie-Sicché (F) .. 57 F 4
Sainte-Maure-de-Touraine (F) ... 47 E 2
Sainte-Maxime (F) ... 57 E 2
Sainte-Menéhould (F) ... 44 A 3
Sainte-Mère-Église (F) ... 41 E 1
Sainte-Sévère-sur-Indre (F)47 F 4
Sainte-Suzanne (F) ... 41 F 4
Sainte-Tulle (F) ... 57 D 2
Saintes (F) ... 50 B 1
Saintes-Maries-de-la-Mer (F) ... 56 B 2
Saintfield (GB) ... 23 F 2
Saissac (F) ... 55 E 2
Šajkaš (SRB) ... 113 E 4
Saka (EST) ... 151 E 3
Saka (F) ... 156 B 4
Sakaliné (LT) ... 169 D 3
Šakarnai (LT) ... 165 D 3
Šakiai (LT) ... 175 E 2
Šakiai Kauno (LT) ... 170 C 4
Šakiai Miestas (LT) ... 169 E 4
Šakiai Utenos (LT) ... 171 F 3
Sakla (EST) ... 152 C 3
Sakskøbing (DK) ... 144 C 4
Sakstagals (Sakstagols) (LV) ... 167 E 2
Sakula (SRB) ... 113 F 4
Säkylä (FIN) ... 136 B 3
Šakyna (LT) ... 163 F 3
Sala (HR) ... 103 F 3
Sala (LV) ... 165 F 2
Sala (S) ... 140 C 3
Sala Consilina (I) ... 106 B 4
Salacgrīva (LV) ... 159 D 2
Salakas (LT) ... 172 C 2

Salamajärvi (FIN) ... 133 E 3
Salamanca (E) ... 63 F 3
Salamiestis (LT) ... 165 E 4
Salamína (GR) ... 218 B 3
Salamína (Nisi) (GR) ... 218 B 3
Salamiou (CY) ... 230 B 3
Salamis (CY) ... 231 E 2
Salantai (LT) ... 162 C 4
Salánti (GR) ... 218 B 3
Salar (E) ... 76 A 2
Salardú (E) ... 55 D 3
Salas (E) ... 59 E 2
Salaš (SRB) ... 119 E 2
Salas de los Infantes (E).. 64 C 3
Salaspils (LV) ... 165 D 1
Salbohed (S) ... 140 C 3
Salbris (F) ... 47 E 3
Šalčininkai (LT) ... 177 E 3
Salcombe (GB) ... 34 C 4
Salda (EST) ... 150 D 2
Saldaña (E) ... 59 F 4
Saldus (LV) ... 163 E 2
Saldutiškis (LT) ... 171 F 4
Sale (I) ... 97 D 4
Salem (D) ... 45 F 4
Salemi (I) ... 110 B 3
Salen (D) ... 27 D 4
Sälen (S) ... 140 A 2
Salen Argyll and Bute (GB) 30 D 2
Salernes (F) ... 57 D 2
Salerno (I) ... 106 A 4
Salers (F) ... 51 F 2
Salgótarján (H) ... 12 B 3
Salgueiro do Campo (P).. 68 C 1
Sali (HR) ... 103 F 3
Salice Terme (I) ... 97 D 4
Saliena (Salonāja) (LV) .. 173 D 1
Salies-de-Béarn (F) ... 54 A 3
Salies-du-Salat (F) ... 55 D 3
Salignac-Eyvigues (F) ... 51 D 3

Salihli (TR) ... 19 F 3
Salihorsk (BY) ... 7 D 4
Salinas (E) ... 59 E 2
Salindres (F) ... 52 B 4
Salins-les-Bains (F) ... 49 E 3
Salisbury (GB) ... 35 E 3
Salkininkai (LT) ... 177 D 2
Salla (EST) ... 151 D 4
Salla (FIN) ... 129 E 2
Sallanches (F) ... 49 F 4
Sallent (E) ... 66 C 2
Sallent de Gállego (E) ... 54 B 3
Salles-Curan (F) ... 51 F 4
Salles-d'Aude (F) ... 56 A 3
Salme (EST) ... 152 B 4
Salmerón (E) ... 65 D 4
Salmiņi (LV) ... 157 D 4
Salmoral (E) ... 63 F 4
Salmünster (D) ... 88 B 3
Salnava (Saļnova) (LV) ... 167 E 1
Salo (FIN) ... 136 C 4
Salò (I) ... 97 F 3
Salobreña (E) ... 76 B 3
Saločiai (LT) ... 165 D 3
Salomenka (LT) ... 172 C 4
Salon-de-Provence (F) ... 56 C 2
Salonta (RO) ... 113 D 2
Salorino (E) ... 69 D 2
Salos Alytaus (LT) ... 175 F 3
Salos Panevėžio (LT) ... 171 F 1
Salou (E) ... 66 B 4
Salsbruket (N) ... 131 E 1
Salses-le-Château (F) ... 55 F 3
Salsomaggiore Terme (I) .. 97 E 4
Salsta (S) ... 141 D 3
Saltash (GB) ... 34 C 3
Saltburn-by-the-Sea (GB).31 F 4
Saltcoats (GB) ... 30 C 2
Salto (P) ... 62 C 2

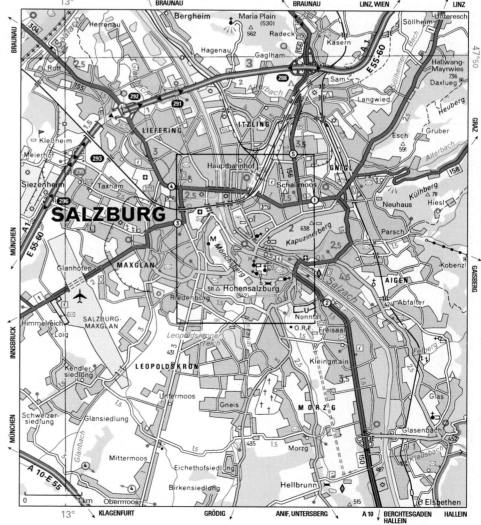

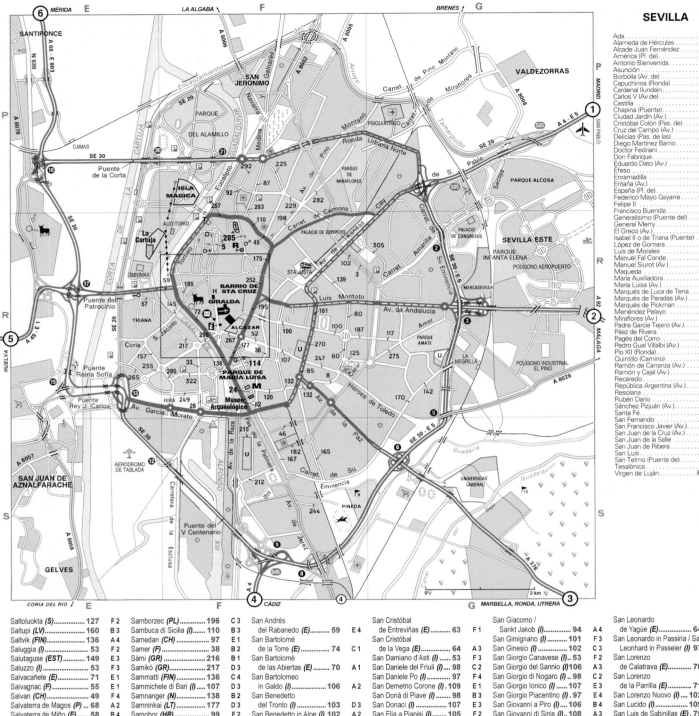

SEVILLA

Ada . . . . **FR** 3
Alameda de Hércules . . . . **FR** 5
Alcade Juan Fernández . . . . . . **FR** 8
América (Pl. de) . . . . **FR** 24
Antonio Bienvenida . . . . **FR** 28
Asunción . . . . **FR** 33
Borbolla (Av. de) . . . . **FR** 38
Capuchinos (Ronda) . . . . **FR** 45
Cardenal Ilundain . . . . **FS** 46
Carlos V (Av.de) . . . . **FR** 52
Castilla . . . . **ER** 57
Chapina (Puente) . . . . **FR** 59
Ciudad Jardín (Av.) . . . . **FR** 60
Cristóbal Colón (Pas. de) . . . . **FR** 72
Cruz del Campo (Av.) . . . . **FR** 80
Delicias (Pas. de las) . . . . **FR** 82
Diego Martínez Barrio . . . . . . **FP** 85
Doctor Fedriani . . . . **FP** 87
Don Fabrique . . . . **FP** 92
Eduardo Dato (Av.) . . . . **FR** 100
Éfeso . . . . **FR** 102
Enramadilla . . . . **FR** 107
Eritaña (Av.) . . . . **FR** 110
España (Pl. de) . . . . **FR** 114
Federico Mayo Gayarre . . . . . **GR** 117
Felipe II . . . . **FR** 120
Francisco Buendía . . . . **FR** 125
Generalísimo (Puente del) . . . **FR** 136
General Merry . . . . **FR** 132
El Greco (Av.) . . . . **FR** 139
Isabel II o de Triana (Puente) . **FR** 157
López de Gomara . . . . **ER** 157
Luis de Morales . . . . **FR** 161
Manuel Fal Conde . . . . **FS** 165
Manuel Siurot (Av.) . . . . **FS** 167
Maqueda . . . . **GR** 170
María Auxiliadora . . . . **FR** 175
María Luisa (Av.) . . . . **FR** 177
Marqués de Luca de Tena . . . . **FS** 182
Marqués de Paradas (Av.) . . . . **FR** 185
Marqués de Pickman . . . . **FR** 187
Menéndez Pelayo . . . . **FR** 195
Miraflores (Av.) . . . . **FR** 198
Padre García Tejero (Av.) . . . . **FS** 212
Páez de Rivera . . . . **FS** 215
Pagés del Corro . . . . **FP** 225
Pedro Gual Villalbi (Av.) . . . . . **FR** 217
Pío XII (Ronda) . . . . **GR** 229
Quintillo (Camino) . . . . **FS** 244
Ramón de Carranza (Av.) . . . . **FR** 247
Ramón y Cajal (Av.) . . . . **FR** 247
Recaredo . . . . **FR** 252
República Argentina (Av.) . . . . **ER** 255
Resolana . . . . **FR** 257
Rubén Darío . . . . **ER** 265
Sánchez Pizjuán (Av.) . . . . **FR** 292
Santa Fé . . . . **FR** 295
San Fernando . . . . **FR** 267
San Francisco Javier (Av.) . . . . **FR** 270
San Juan de la Cruz (Av.) . . . . **FR** 275
San Juan de la Salle . . . . **FP** 282
San Juan de Ribera . . . . **FP** 283
San Luis . . . . **FR** 285
San Telmo (Puente de) . . . . . . **FR** 290
Tesalónica . . . . **GR** 305
Virgen de Luján . . . . **FPR** 322

Saltoluokta *(S)* . . . . **127** F 2
Saltupi *(LV)* . . . . **160** B 3
Saltvik *(FIN)* . . . . **136** A 4
Saluggia *(I)* . . . . **53** F 2
Salutaguse *(EST)* . . . . **149** E 3
Saluzzo *(I)* . . . . **53** F 3
Salvacañete *(E)* . . . . **71** E 1
Salvagnac *(F)* . . . . **55** F 4
Salvan *(CH)* . . . . **49** F 4
Salvaterra de Magos *(P)* . . . **68** A 2
Salvaterra de Miño *(E)* . . . . **58** B 4
Salvatierra / Agurain *(E)* . . . **60** C 4
Salvatierra
  de los Barros *(E)* . . . . **69** D 4
Salviac *(F)* . . . . **51** D 3
Salzburg *(A)* . . . . **94** B 3
Salzgitter-Bad *(D)* . . . . **84** B 3
Salzhausen *(D)* . . . . **84** A 2
Salzkotten *(D)* . . . . **83** F 4
Salzwedel *(D)* . . . . **84** B 2
Sama de Langreo *(E)* . . . . . . **59** E 3
Šamac /
  Bosanski Šamac *(BIH)* **117** E 1
Samaniai *(LT)* . . . . **172** C 1
Samariás
  (Farángi) *(GR)* . . . . **226** D 4
Samarína *(GR)* . . . . **205** D 4
Samatan *(F)* . . . . **55** D 2
Sambiase *(I)* . . . . **109** E 4
Sambir *(UA)* . . . . **12** C 2
Samboal *(E)* . . . . **64** A 3

Samborzec *(PL)* . . . . **196** C 3
Sambuca di Sicilia *(I)* . . . . . **110** B 3
Samedan *(CH)* . . . . **97** E 1
Samer *(F)* . . . . **38** B 2
Sámi *(GR)* . . . . **216** B 1
Samikó *(GR)* . . . . **217** B 1
Sammatti *(FIN)* . . . . **136** C 4
Sammichele di Bari *(I)* . . . . **107** D 3
Samnanger *(N)* . . . . **138** C 2
Samninkai *(LT)* . . . . **177** D 3
Samobor *(HR)* . . . . **99** F 2
Samodreža *(SRB)* . . . . **119** D 4
Samoëns *(F)* . . . . **49** F 4
Samoklęski Małe *(PL)* . . . . **188** B 1
Samokov *(BG)* . . . . **19** D 1
Samos *(E)* . . . . **58** C 3
Sámos *(GR)* . . . . **221** E 2
Samoš *(SRB)* . . . . **113** C 4
Samothráki *(I)* . . . . **208** B 3
Samothráki (Nisí) *(GR)* . . . . **208** B 3
Sampatikí *(GR)* . . . . **217** F 4
Samper de Calanda *(E)* . . . . **65** F 3
Sampeyre *(I)* . . . . **53** E 3
Samtens *(D)* . . . . **80** C 2
Samugheo *(I)* . . . . **108** B 3
San *(PL)* . . . . **202** E 3
San Adrián *(E)* . . . . **65** E 1
San Agustín
  del Guadalix *(E)* . . . . **64** C 2
San Amaro *(E)* . . . . **58** B 4

San Andrés
  del Rabanedo *(E)* . . . . **59** E 4
San Bartolomé
  de la Torre *(E)* . . . . **74** C 1
San Bartolomé
  de las Abiertas *(E)* . . . . . . **70** A 1
San Bartolomeo
  in Galdo *(I)* . . . . **106** A 2
San Benedetto
  del Tronto *(I)* . . . . **103** D 3
San Benedetto in Alpe *(I)* **102** C 3
San Benedetto Po *(I)* . . . . . . **97** F 4
San Bernardino *(CH)* . . . . . . **97** D 1
San Bernardino
  (Passo del) *(CH)* . . . . **97** D 1
San Biagio Platani *(I)* . . . . . **110** C 3
San Bonifacio *(I)* . . . . **98** A 3
San Candido /
  Innichen *(I)* . . . . **98** B 1
San Carlos del Valle *(E)* . . . . **70** C 3
San Casciano
  in Val di Pesa *(I)* . . . . **101** F 2
San Cataldo *(I)* . . . . **107** F 3
San Cataldo *(I)* . . . . **110** C 3
San Cipirello *(I)* . . . . **110** B 2
San Clemente *(E)* . . . . **71** D 2
San Clemente a Casauria
  (Abbazia) *(I)* . . . . **103** D 4
San Colombano
  al Lambro *(I)* . . . . **97** E 4
San Cosme *(E)* . . . . **59** D 2

San Cristóbal
  de Entreviñas *(E)* . . . . **63** F 1
San Cristóbal
  de la Vega *(E)* . . . . **64** A 3
San Damiano d'Asti *(I)* . . . . **53** F 3
San Daniele del Friuli *(I)* . . . **98** C 2
San Daniele Po *(I)* . . . . **97** F 4
San Demetrio Corone *(I)* . . **109** E 3
San Donà di Piave *(I)* . . . . . . **98** B 3
San Donaci *(I)* . . . . **107** E 3
San Elia a Pianisi *(I)* . . . . . . **105** F 2
San Elpidio a Mare *(I)* . . . . . **102** C 3
San Emiliano *(E)* . . . . **59** E 3
San Esteban *(E)* . . . . **59** E 2
San Esteban
  de Gormaz *(E)* . . . . **64** C 3
San Esteban del Molar *(E)* . . **63** F 2
San Esteban del Valle *(E)* . . . **70** A 1
San Eufemia Lamezia *(I)* . . **109** E 2
San Fele *(I)* . . . . **106** B 3
San Felice a Cancello *(I)* . . **105** F 3
San Felice Circeo *(I)* . . . . . . **105** D 3
San Felice sul Panaro *(I)* . . . **98** A 4
San Felices
  de los Gallegos *(E)* . . . . . **63** E 3
San Ferdinando
  di Puglia *(I)* . . . . **106** C 2
San Fernando *(E)* . . . . **75** D 3
San Fratello *(I)* . . . . **111** D 2
San Gavino Monreale *(I)* . . **108** B 4
San Gemini *(I)* . . . . **102** B 4

San Giacomo /
  Sankt Jakob *(I)* . . . . **94** A 4
San Gimignano *(I)* . . . . **101** F 3
San Ginesio *(I)* . . . . **102** C 3
San Giorgio Canavese *(I)* . . **53** F 2
San Giorgio del Sannio *(I)* **106** F 3
San Giorgio di Nogaro *(I)* . . **98** C 2
San Giorgio Ionico *(I)* . . . . **107** E 3
San Giorgio Piacentino *(I)* . **97** F 4
San Giovanni a Piro *(I)* . . . . **106** B 4
San Giovanni di Sinis *(I)* . . **108** A 3
San Giovanni in Fiore *(I)* . . **109** E 1
San Giovanni
  in Persiceto *(I)* . . . . **98** A 4
San Giovanni Lupatoto *(I)* . . **97** F 2
San Giovanni Rotondo *(I)* . **106** B 1
San Giovanni Suergiu *(I)* . . **108** A 4
San Giovanni Valdarno *(I)* **102** A 2
San Giuliano Terme *(I)* . . . . **101** E 2
San Giustino *(I)* . . . . **102** A 2
San Ildefonso
  o la Granja *(E)* . . . . **64** B 4
San Isidro *(E)* . . . . **77** D 3
San Javier *(E)* . . . . **77** F 1
San José *(E)* . . . . **77** D 3
San Juan
  de los Terreros *(E)* . . . . . . **77** E 2
San Juan del Olmo *(E)* . . . . . **64** A 4
San Juan del Puerto *(E)* . . . . **75** D 2
San Lazzaro di Savena *(I)* . **101** F 4
San Leo *(I)* . . . . **102** A 2

San Leonardo
  de Yagüe *(E)* . . . . **64** C 2
San Leonardo in Passiria / Sankt
  Leonhard in Passeier *(I)* **97** F 1
San Lorenzo
  de Calatrava *(E)* . . . . **70** B 4
San Lorenzo
  de la Parrilla *(E)* . . . . **71** D 2
San Lorenzo Nuovo *(I)* . . . . **102** A 4
San Lucido *(I)* . . . . **109** E 2
San Luis de Sabinillas *(E)* . . **75** D 3
San Marcello *(I)* . . . . **102** C 2
San Marcello Pistoiese *(I)* **101** F 2
San Marco Argentano *(I)* . . **109** E 1
San Marco dei Cavoti *(I)* . . **105** F 2
San Marco in Lamis *(I)* . . . . **106** B 2
San Martín
  de Castañeda *(E)* . . . . **59** D 4
San Martín de la Vega *(E)* . . **70** B 1
San Martín
  de Mondoñedo *(E)* . . . . . **58** C 2
San Martín
  de Montalbán *(E)* . . . . **70** A 2
San Martín
  de Valdeiglesias *(E)* . . . . . **70** A 1
San Martino
  di Castrozza *(I)* . . . . **98** A 2
San Mateo de Gállego *(E)* . . **65** F 2
San Mauro Forte *(I)* . . . . . . **106** C 4
San Michele all'Adige *(I)* . . . **97** F 1
San Miguel de Escalada *(E)* **59** F 4

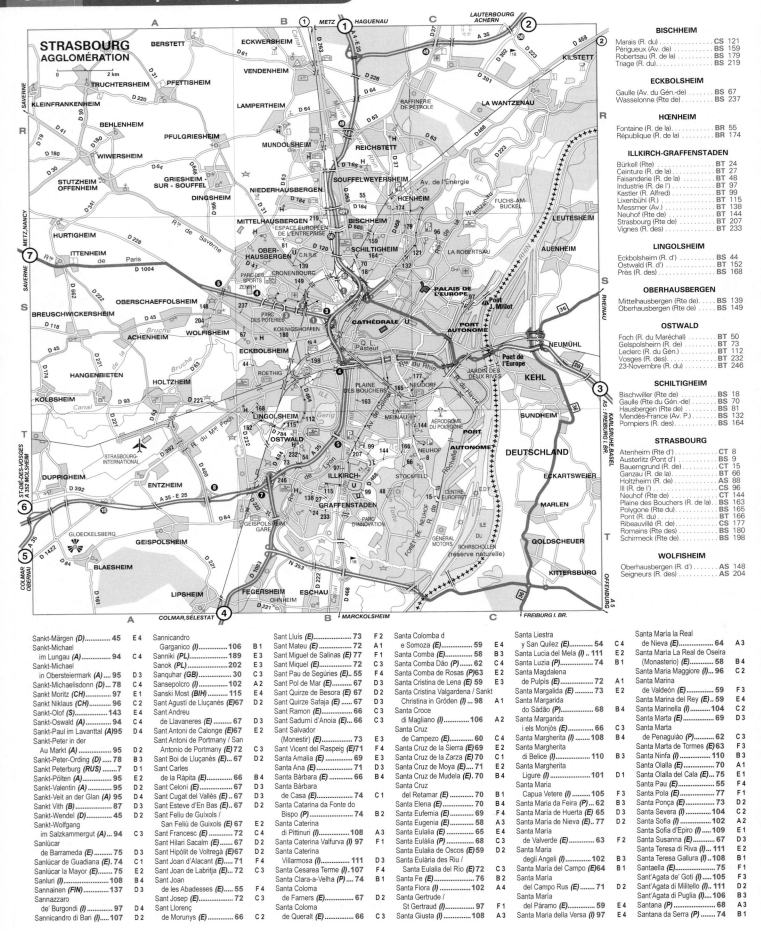

STRASBOURG AGGLOMÉRATION

BISCHHEIM
Marais (R. du) . . . . **CS** 121
Périgueux (Av. de) . . . . **BS** 159
Robertsau (R. de la) . . . . **BS** 179
Triage (R. du) . . . . **BS** 219

ECKBOLSHEIM
Gaulle (Av. du Gén.-de) . . . . . . **BS** 67
Wasselonne (Rte de) . . . . **BS** 237

HŒNHEIM
Fontaine (R. de la) . . . . **BR** 55
République (R. de la) . . . . **BR** 174

ILLKIRCH-GRAFFENSTADEN
Bürkell (Rte) . . . . **BT** 24
Ceinture (R. de la) . . . . **BT** 27
Faisanderie (R. de la) . . . . **BT** 48
Industrie (R. de l') . . . . **BT** 97
Kastler (R. Alfred) . . . . **BT** 99
Lixenbühl (R.) . . . . **BT** 115
Messmer (Av.) . . . . **BT** 138
Neuhof (Rte de) . . . . **BT** 144
Strasbourg (Rte de) . . . . **BT** 207
Vignes (R. des) . . . . **BT** 233

LINGOLSHEIM
Eckbolsheim (R. d') . . . . **BS** 44
Ostwald (R. d') . . . . **BT** 152
Près (R. des) . . . . **BS** 168

OBERHAUSBERGEN
Mittelhausbergen (Rte de) . . . . . **BS** 139
Oberhausbergen (Rte de) . . . . . **BS** 149

OSTWALD
Foch (R. du Maréchal) . . . . **BT** 50
Gelspolsheim (R. de) . . . . **BT** 73
Leclerc (R. du Gén.) . . . . **BT** 112
Vosges (R. des) . . . . **BT** 232
23-Novembre (R. du) . . . . **BT** 246

SCHILTIGHEIM
Bischwiller (Rte de) . . . . **BS** 18
Gaulle (Rte du Gén.-de) . . . . . . **BS** 70
Hausbergen (Rte de) . . . . **BS** 81
Mendès-France (Av. P.) . . . . **BS** 132
Pompiers (R. des) . . . . **BS** 164

STRASBOURG
Atenheim (Rte d') . . . . **CT** 8
Austerlitz (Pont d') . . . . **BS** 9
Bauerngrund (R. de) . . . . **CT** 15
Ganzau (R. de la) . . . . **BT** 66
Holtzheim (R. de) . . . . **AS** 88
Ill (R. de l') . . . . **CS** 96
Neuhof (Rte de) . . . . **CT** 144
Plaine des Bouchers (R. de la) . . **BS** 163
Polygone (Rte du) . . . . **BS** 165
Pont (R. du) . . . . **BT** 166
Ribeauvillé (R. de) . . . . **CS** 177
Romains (Rte des) . . . . **BS** 180
Schirmeck (Rte de) . . . . **BS** 198

WOLFISHEIM
Oberhausbergen (R. d') . . . . **AS** 148
Seigneurs (R. des) . . . . **AS** 204

Sankt-Märgen *(D)* . . . . **45** E 4
Sankt-Michael
  im Lungau *(A)* . . . . **94** C 4
Sankt-Michael
  in Obersteiermark *(A)* . . **95** D 3
Sankt-Michaelisdonn *(D)* . . **78** C 4
Sankt Moritz *(CH)* . . . . **97** E 1
Sankt Niklaus *(CH)* . . . . . . **96** C 2
Sankt-Olof *(S)* . . . . **143** E 4
Sankt-Oswald *(A)* . . . . **94** C 4
Sankt-Paul im Lavanttal *(A)* **95** D 4
Sankt-Peter in der
  Au Markt *(A)* . . . . **95** D 2
Sankt-Peter-Ording *(D)* . . . **78** B 3
Sankt Peterburg *(RUS)* . . . . **7** D 1
Sankt-Pölten *(A)* . . . . **95** E 2
Sankt-Valentin *(A)* . . . . **95** D 2
Sankt-Veit an der Glan *(A)* **95** D 4
Sankt Vith *(B)* . . . . **87** D 3
Sankt-Wendel *(D)* . . . . **45** D 2
Sankt-Wolfgang
  im Salzkammergut *(A)* . . **94** C 3
Sanlúcar
  de Barrameda *(E)* . . . . . **75** D 3
Sanlúcar de Guadiana *(E)* . **74** C 1
Sanlúcar la Mayor *(E)* . . . . **75** E 2
Sanluri *(I)* . . . . **108** A 2
Sannainen *(FIN)* . . . . **137** D 3
Sannazzaro
  de' Burgondi *(I)* . . . . **97** D 4
Sannicandro di Bari *(I)* . . **107** D 2

Sannicandro
  Garganico *(I)* . . . . **106** B 1
Sanniki *(PL)* . . . . **189** E 3
Sanok *(PL)* . . . . **202** E 3
Sanquhar *(GB)* . . . . **30** C 3
Sansepolcro *(I)* . . . . **102** A 2
Sanski Most *(BIH)* . . . . . . **115** E 4
Sant Agustí de Lluçanès *(E)* 67 D 2
Sant Andreu
  de Llavaneres *(E)* . . . . . **67** D 3
Sant Antoni de Calonge *(E)* 67 E 2
Sant Antoni de Portmany / San
  Antonio de Portmany *(E)* 72 C 3
Sant Boi de Lluçanès *(E)* . . **67** D 2
Sant Carles
  de la Ràpita *(E)* . . . . . . **66** B 4
Sant Celoni *(E)* . . . . **67** D 3
Sant Cugat del Vallès *(E)* . **67** D 3
Sant Esteve d'En Bas *(E)* . **67** D 2
Sant Feliu de Guíxols /
  San Feliú de Guixols *(E)* **67** E 2
Sant Francesc *(E)* . . . . **72** C 4
Sant Hilari Sacalm *(E)* . . . . **67** D 2
Sant Hipòlit de Voltregà *(E)* 67 D 2
Sant Joan d'Alacant *(E)* . . **71** F 4
Sant Joan de Labritja *(E)* . **72** C 3
Sant Joan
  de les Abadesses *(E)* . . **55** F 4
Sant Josep *(E)* . . . . **72** C 4
Sant Llorenç
  de Morunys *(E)* . . . . . . **66** C 2

Sant Lluís *(E)* . . . . **73** F 2
Sant Mateu *(E)* . . . . **72** A 1
Sant Miguel de Salinas *(E)* 77 F 1
Sant Miquel *(E)* . . . . **72** C 3
Sant Pau de Segúries *(E)* . **55** F 4
Sant Pol de Mar *(E)* . . . . . **67** D 3
Sant Quirze de Besora *(E)* **67** D 2
Sant Quirze Safaja *(E)* . . . **67** D 3
Sant Ramon *(E)* . . . . **66** C 2
Sant Sadurní d'Anoia *(E)* . **66** C 3
Sant Salvador
  (Monestir) *(E)* . . . . **73** E 3
Sant Vicent del Raspeig *(E)* 71 F 4
Santa Amalia *(E)* . . . . **69** E 3
Santa Ana *(E)* . . . . **71** F 1
Santa Bárbara *(E)* . . . . **66** B 4
Santa Bárbara
  de Casa *(E)* . . . . **74** C 1
Santa Catarina da Fonte do
  Bispo *(P)* . . . . **74** B 2
Santa Caterina
  di Pittinuri *(I)* . . . . **108** A 3
Santa Caterina Valfurva *(I)* 97 F 1
Santa Caterina
  Villarmosa *(I)* . . . . **111** D 3
Santa Cesarea Terme *(I)* . **107** F 4
Santa Clara-a-Velha *(P)* . . . **74** B 1
Santa Coloma
  de Farners *(E)* . . . . **67** D 2
Santa Coloma
  de Queralt *(E)* . . . . **66** C 3

Santa Colomba d
  e Somoza *(E)* . . . . **59** E 4
Santa Comba *(E)* . . . . **58** B 3
Santa Comba Dão *(P)* . . . . **62** C 4
Santa Comba de Rosas *(P)* 63 E 4
Santa Cristina de Lena *(E)* **59** E 3
Santa Cristina Valgardena / Sankt
  Christina in Gröden *(I)* . . **98** A 1
Santa Croce
  di Magliano *(I)* . . . . . . **106** A 2
Santa Cruz
  de Campezo *(E)* . . . . . . **60** C 4
Santa Cruz de la Sierra *(E)* 69 E 2
Santa Cruz de la Zarza *(E)* **70** C 1
Santa Cruz de Moya *(E)* . . **71** D 2
Santa Cruz de Mudela *(E)* . **70** B 4
Santa Cruz
  del Retamar *(E)* . . . . . . **70** B 1
Santa Elena *(E)* . . . . **70** B 4
Santa Eufemia *(E)* . . . . **69** F 4
Santa Eugenia *(E)* . . . . **58** A 3
Santa Eulalia *(E)* . . . . **65** E 4
Santa Eulàlia *(E)* . . . . **68** C 3
Santa Eulalia de Oscos *(E)* 59 D 2
Santa Eulària des Riu /
  Santa Eulalia del Río *(E)* 72 C 4
Santa Fe *(E)* . . . . **76** B 2
Santa Fiora *(I)* . . . . **102** A 4
Santa Gertrude /
  St Gertraud *(I)* . . . . **97** F 1
Santa Giusta *(I)* . . . . **108** A 3

Santa Liestra
  y San Quílez *(E)* . . . . . . **54** C 4
Santa Lucia del Mela *(I)* . . **111** E 2
Santa Luzia *(P)* . . . . **74** B 1
Santa Magdalena
  de Pulpís *(E)* . . . . **72** A 1
Santa Margalida *(E)* . . . . . . **73** E 2
Santa Margarida
  do Sàdão *(P)* . . . . **68** B 4
Santa Margarida
  i els Monjòs *(E)* . . . . . . **66** C 3
Santa Margherita *(I)* . . . . **108** B 4
Santa Margherita
  di Belice *(I)* . . . . **110** B 3
Santa Margherita
  Ligure *(I)* . . . . **101** D 1
Santa Maria
  Capua Vetere *(I)* . . . . . **105** F 3
Santa Maria da Feira *(P)* . . **62** B 3
Santa María de Huerta *(E)* **65** D 2
Santa María de Nieva *(E)* . **77** D 2
Santa María
  de Valverde *(E)* . . . . **63** F 1
Santa María
  degli Angeli *(I)* . . . . . . **102** B 3
Santa María del Campo *(E)* 64 B 1
Santa María
  del Campo Rus *(E)* . . . . **71** D 2
Santa Maria
  del Páramo *(E)* . . . . **59** E 4
Santa Maria della Versa *(I)* 97 E 4

Santa María la Real
  de Nieva *(E)* . . . . **64** A 3
Santa María La Real de Oseira
  (Monasterio) *(E)* . . . . . . **58** B 4
Santa Maria Maggiore *(I)* . **96** C 2
Santa Marina
  de Valdeón *(E)* . . . . **59** F 3
Santa Marina del Rey *(E)* . **59** E 4
Santa Marinella *(I)* . . . . . . **104** C 2
Santa Marta *(E)* . . . . **69** D 3
Santa Marta
  de Penaguião *(P)* . . . . . **62** C 3
Santa Marta de Tormes *(E)* **63** F 3
Santa Ninfa *(I)* . . . . **110** B 3
Santa Olalla *(E)* . . . . **70** A 1
Santa Olalla del Cala *(E)* . . **75** E 1
Santa Pau *(E)* . . . . **55** F 4
Santa Pola *(E)* . . . . **77** F 1
Santa Ponça *(E)* . . . . **73** D 2
Santa Severa *(I)* . . . . **104** C 2
Santa Sofia *(I)* . . . . **102** A 2
Santa Sofia d'Epiro *(I)* . . . **109** E 1
Santa Susanna *(E)* . . . . **67** E 2
Santa Teresa di Riva *(I)* . . **111** E 2
Santa Teresa Gallura *(I)* . . **108** B 1
Santaella *(E)* . . . . **75** F 1
Sant'Agata de' Goti *(I)* . . . **105** F 3
Sant'Agata di Militello *(I)* . **111** D 2
Sant'Agata di Puglia *(I)* . . **106** B 1
Santana *(P)* . . . . **68** A 3
Santana da Serra *(P)* . . . . . **74** B 1

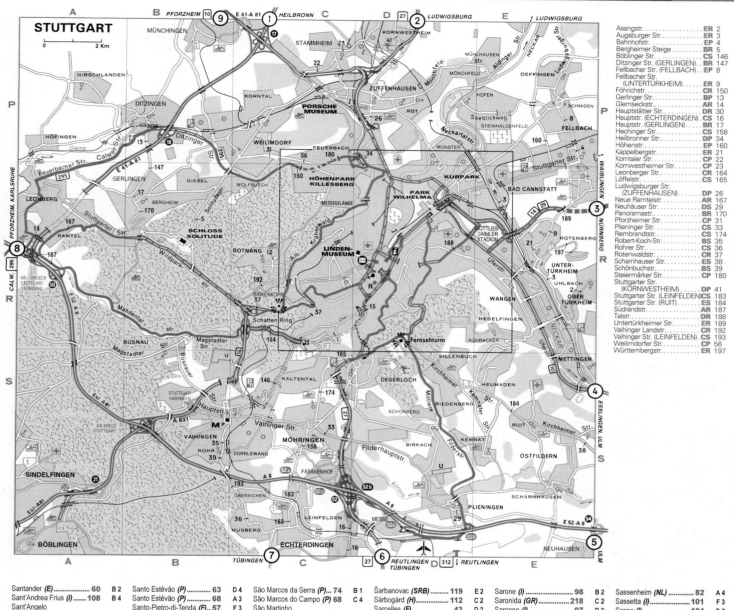

STUTTGART

0 — 2 Km

Asangstr.	ER	2
Augsburger Str.	ER	3
Bahnhofstr.	EP	4
Bergheimer Steige	BR	5
Böblinger Str.	CS	146
Ditzinger Str. (GERLINGEN)	BR	147
Fellbacher Str. (FELLBACH)	EP	8
Fellbacher Str. (UNTERTÜRKHEIM)	ER	9
Föhrichstr.	CR	150
Gerlinger Str.	BP	13
Glemseckstr.	AR	14
Hauptstätter Str.	DR	30
Hauptstr. (ECHTERDINGEN)	CS	16
Hauptstr. (GERLINGEN)	BR	17
Hechinger Str.	CS	158
Heilbronner Str.	DP	34
Höhenstr.	ER	160
Kappelbergstr.	ER	21
Korntaler Str.	CP	22
Kornwestheimer Str.	CP	23
Leonberger Str.	CR	164
Löffelstr.	CS	165
Ludwigsburger Str. (ZUFFENHAUSEN)	DP	26
Neue Ramtelstr.	AR	167
Neuhäuser Str.	DS	29
Panoramastr.	BR	170
Pforzheimer Str.	CP	31
Plieninger Str.	CS	33
Rembrandtstr.	CS	174
Robert-Koch-Str.	BS	35
Rohrer Str.	CS	36
Rotenwaldstr.	CR	37
Scharnhauser Str.	ES	38
Schönbuchstr.	BS	39
Steiermärker Str.	CP	180
Stuttgarter Str. (KORNWESTHEIM)	DP	41
Stuttgarter Str. (LEINFELDEN)	CS	183
Stuttgarter Str. (RUIT)	ES	184
Südrandstr.	AR	187
Talstr.	DR	188
Untertürkheimer Str.	ER	189
Vaihinger Landstr.	CS	192
Vaihinger Str. (LEINFELDEN)	CS	193
Weilimdorfer Str.	CP	56
Württembergstr.	ER	197

Santander (E)	60	B 2
Sant'Andrea Frius (I)	108	B 4
Sant'Angelo dei Lombardi (I)	106	B 3
Sant'Angelo in Vado (I)	102	B 2
Sant'Angelo Lodigiano (I)	97	D 1
Sant'Antioco (I)	108	A 4
Sant'Antonio di Gallura (I)	108	B 1
Santanyí (E)	73	E 3
Sant'Apollinare in Classe (I)	102	A 1
Santarcangelo di Romagna (I)	102	B 1
Santarém (P)	68	B 2
Santas Martas (E)	59	F 4
Santeramo in Colle (I)	107	D 3
Santhià (I)	53	F 2
Santiago de Alcántara (E)	69	D 1
Santiago de Compostela (E)	58	B 3
Santiago de la Espada (E)	76	C 1
Santiago de la Ribera (E)	77	F 1
Santiago do Cacém (P)	68	A 4
Santiago do Escorial (P)	68	B 3
Santibáñez de Béjar (E)	63	E 4
Santibáñez de la Peña (E)	59	F 4
Santibáñez de la Sierra (E)	63	E 4
Santibáñez de Vidriales (E)	63	F 1
Santillana del Mar (E)	60	A 3
Santiponce (E)	75	E 1
Santisteban del Puerto (E)	70	C 4
Santo Domingo de la Calzada (E)	60	C 4
Santo Domingo de Silos (E)	64	C 2
Santo Estêvão (P)	63	D 4
Santo Estêvão (P)	68	A 3
Santo-Pietro-di-Tenda (F)	57	F 3
Santo Stefano d'Aveto (I)	101	D 1
Santo Stefano di Cadore (I)	98	B 1
Santo Stefano di Camastra (I)	111	D 2
Santo Stefano Quisquina (E)	110	D 3
Santo Stino di Livenza (I)	98	B 2
Santo Tirso (P)	62	B 2
Santo Tomé (E)	76	C 1
Santok (PL)	186	C 2
Santoméri (GR)	217	D 2
Santoña (E)	60	B 3
Sant'Onofrio (I)	109	E 3
Santu Lussurgiu (I)	108	A 3
Santurtzi (E)	60	C 3
Sanxenxo / Sangenjo (E)	58	A 4
Sanza (I)	106	B 4
São Bartolomeu de Messines (P)	74	B 1
São Brás de Alportel (P)	74	B 2
São Cristóvão (P)	68	B 3
São Domingos (P)	68	B 4
São Gregório (P)	58	B 4
São Jacinto (P)	62	B 3
São João da Madeira (P)	62	B 3
São João da Pesqueira (P)	63	D 3
São João de Tarouca (P)	62	C 3
São João dos Caldeireiros (P)	74	B 1
São José da Lamarosa (P)	68	B 2
São Leonardo (P)	68	C 4
São Manços (P)	68	C 3
São Marcos da Serra (P)	74	B 1
São Marcos do Campo (P)	68	C 4
São Martinho das Amoreiras (P)	74	B 1
São Martinho do Porto (P)	68	A 1
São Matias (P)	68	B 4
São Miguel de Machede (P)	68	C 3
São Pedro da Torre (P)	58	A 4
São Pedro de Moel (P)	68	A 1
São Pedro do Sul (P)	62	C 3
São Romão (P)	62	C 4
São Teotónio (P)	74	A 1
São Vicente da Beira (P)	68	C 1
Saorge (F)	53	F 4
Sapanca (TR)	19	F 1
Sapataria (P)	68	A 2
Sápes (GR)	208	B 2
Sapiéntza (Nísi) (GR)	222	B 4
Sappada (I)	98	B 1
Sappee (FIN)	136	C 3
Sapri (I)	106	B 4
Saraiķi (LV)	162	B 1
Säräisniemi (FIN)	133	F 1
Sarajärvi (FIN)	129	D 4
Sarajevo (BIH)	117	D 4
Sarakini (GR)	205	F 2
Sarakíniko (GR)	213	F 3
Saramon (F)	55	D 2
Sarandë (AL)	78	A 4
Sarantáporo (GR)	205	D 2
Sarapiniškės (LT)	177	D 3
Saraváli (GR)	217	D 1
Saray (TR)	19	E 1
Sarayköy (TR)	19	F 3
Šarbanovac (SRB)	119	E 2
Sárbogárd (H)	112	C 2
Sarcelles (F)	43	D 2
Sardara (I)	108	B 3
Sardínia (GR)	211	E 4
Sardoal (P)	68	B 1
S'Arenal (E)	73	D 2
Šarengrad (HR)	117	F 1
Sarentino / Sarntal (I)	98	A 1
Sărevere (EST)	154	D 2
Sargans (CH)	93	D 4
Sargvere (EST)	149	F 4
Sari-d'Orcino (F)	57	F 4
Sariá (Nísi) (GR)	225	F 4
Sariai (LT)	172	C 4
Sariñena (E)	66	A 2
Šarkaičiai (LT)	177	F 4
Sarkaņi Cēsu (LV)	159	F 3
Sarkaņi Madonas (LV)	166	F 4
Särkisalmi (FIN)	135	F 4
Särkisalo / Finby (FIN)	136	C 4
Sarlat-la-Canéda (F)	51	D 3
Sarma (LV)	165	D 2
Särna (S)	140	A 1
Sarnaki (PL)	191	D 2
Sarnano (I)	102	C 3
Sarnen (CH)	96	C 1
Sarnico (I)	97	E 3
Sarno (I)	105	F 3
Sárnow (PL)	122	D 4
Sarnów Mazowieckie (PL)	195	F 4
Sarnówka (PL)	187	F 4
Sarny (UA)	13	D 1
Sarón (E)	60	B 3
Sarone (I)	98	B 2
Saronída (GR)	218	C 2
Saronno (I)	97	D 3
Sárospatak (H)	12	B 3
Sarpsborg (N)	139	E 4
Sarracín (E)	64	C 1
Sarral (E)	66	C 3
Sarralbe (F)	45	D 3
Sarre-Union (F)	45	D 3
Sarrebourg (F)	45	D 3
Sarreguemines (F)	45	D 3
Sarria (E)	58	C 3
Sarrión (E)	71	F 1
Sarroch (I)	108	A 4
Sars-Poteries (F)	39	E 3
Sarsina (I)	102	A 2
Sarstedt (D)	84	A 1
Sarteano (I)	102	A 3
Sartène (F)	57	F 4
Sárti (GR)	207	F 1
Sartilly (F)	41	E 2
Sartininkai (LT)	168	C 3
Saru (EST)	161	D 2
Sarule (I)	108	B 2
Sárvár (H)	112	A 2
Sarvsjö (S)	131	E 2
Sarzana (I)	101	E 2
Sarzeau (F)	41	D 4
Sarzedas (P)	68	C 1
Sasa (MK)	122	C 4
Sasnava (LT)	175	F 2
Sassari (I)	108	A 2
Sassello (I)	100	C 1
Sassenage (F)	53	D 2
Sassenberg (D)	83	E 4
Sassenheim (NL)	82	A 4
Sassetta (I)	101	F 3
Sasso (I)	104	C 2
Sasso Marconi (I)	101	F 1
Sassoferrato (I)	102	B 2
Sassoleone (I)	101	F 1
Sassuolo (I)	101	F 1
Sástago (E)	66	A 3
Sátão (P)	62	C 3
Šateikiai (LT)	162	C 4
Säter (S)	140	C 3
Šatės (LT)	162	C 3
Sāti (LV)	157	F 4
Satiķi (LV)	163	E 1
Satillieu (F)	52	B 2
Sátiņi (LV)	157	D 4
Satkūnai Kauno (LT)	171	D 4
Satkūnai Panevėžio (LT)	165	E 4
Satolas-et-Bonce (F)	52	C 1
Sątopy (PL)	184	C 2
Sátoraljaújhely (H)	12	B 3
Šatov (CZ)	91	D 4
Satow (D)	79	E 3
Sátres (GR)	207	F 2
Satrup (D)	78	C 2
Sattel (CH)	92	C 4
Sattledt (A)	94	C 2
Satu Mare (RO)	12	C 3
Sauca (E)	65	D 4
Sauda (N)	138	C 3
Sauðárkrókur (IS)	126	B 1
Saue (EST)	149	D 3
Sauerlach (D)	93	F 3
Sauga (EST)	153	C 3
Saugailiai (LT)	169	F 3

Saugos (LT)............168 B 2
Saugues (F)..............52 A 3
Saujon (F)...............50 B 1
Sauka (LV)..............165 F 3
Šaukėnai (LT)...........169 E 1
Šaukliai (LT)............162 C 3
Šaukliškiai (LT).........171 D 1
Šaukotas (LT)...........169 F 2
Saula (EST)............149 E 3
Saulaine Bauskas(LV)..164 C 3
Saulaine Liepājas(LV)..162 C 2
Sauland (N).............139 D 3
Sauleskalns (LV).......166 C 1
Saulėtekiai (LT)........169 F 4
Šauliai (LT).............177 E 3
Saulieu (F)...............48 C 2
Saulkrasti (LV).........159 D 3
Sault (F)................52 C 4
Saulx (F)................49 E 1
Saulxures-
  sur-Moselotte (F).....45 D 4
Saumur (F)..............47 D 2
Saundersfoot (GB).......34 C 1
Sauris (I)...............98 B 1
Sausgalviai (LT).......168 B 3
Sausininkai (LT).......175 E 2
Sausnėja (LV)..........165 F 1
Sauve (F)...............56 B 1
Sauvere (EST).........152 B 3
Sauveterre-de-Béarn (F)..54 B 2
Sauveterre-de-Guyenne(F)50 C 3
Sauveterre-
  de-Rouergue (F).......51 F 4
Sauvo (FIN)............136 B 4
Sauxillanges (F)........52 A 2
Sauze d'Oulx (I)........53 E 2
Sauzé-Vaussais (F)......46 D 4
Sauzon (F)..............40 C 4
Sava (I)...............107 E 3
Sävainį (LT)...........163 F 2
Savala (EST)..........151 E 3
Savália (GR)...........216 C 2
Sävar (S)..............132 C 2
Saveikiai (LT).........163 F 4
Savelli (I)............109 E 1
Savenay (F).............46 B 2
Saverdun (F)............55 E 3
Saverna (EST).........161 D 1
Saverne (F).............45 D 3
Sāviena (LV)..........166 C 2
Savigliano (I)..........53 F 3
Savignac-les-Églises (F)..51 D 2
Savignano Irpino (I)....106 B 2
Savignano
  sul Rubicone (I)......102 A 1
Savigny-sur-Braye (F)...42 B 4
Savikoti (EST).........154 B 3
Saviñán (E).............65 E 3
Savines-le-Lac (F)......53 D 3
Savino Selo (SRB)......113 D 4
Savitaipale (FIN)......137 E 2
Sävja (S)..............141 D 3
Šavnik (MNE)..........121 D 1
Savognin (CH)..........97 E 1
Savona (I).............100 C 1
Savonlinna (FIN)......135 F 4
Savonranta (FIN)......135 F 4
Sävsjö (S).............143 E 2
Savudrija (HR)..........98 C 3
Savukoski (FIN).......129 E 2
Sawbridgeworth (GB)....36 C 3
Sawin (PL)............197 F 2
Sax (E).................71 F 4
Saxmundham (GB).......37 D 2
Saxnäs (S)............131 F 1
Sayatón (E)............70 C 1
Säynätsalo (FIN)......133 F 4
Säyneinen (FIN).......135 E 3
Scaër (F)...............40 C 3
Scafa (I)..............103 D 4
Scafati (I)............105 F 3
Scalasaig (GB)..........30 A 1
Scalby (GB)............33 E 1
Scalea (I).............109 D 1
Scalloway (GB)..........29 F 2
Scandiano (I)..........101 E 1
Scanno (I).............105 E 2
Scansano (I)...........104 B 1
Scanzano Ionico (I)....107 D 4
Scarborough (GB).......33 E 1
Scardovari (I)..........98 B 4
Scarinish (GB)..........30 A 1
Scarriff / An Scairbh (IRL)..24 C 3
Šćedro (Otok) (HR)....120 A 2
Ščekino (RUS)...........7 F 3
Šćepan (MNE)..........117 F 4
Scey-sur-Saône-

et-St-Albin (F).........49 E 1
Schachendorf (A).......95 F 3
Schaffhausen (CH)......92 C 3
Schafstädt (D)..........89 D 1
Schagen (NL)...........82 B 3
Schaprode (D)..........79 F 2
Scharbeutz (D).........79 D 3
Schärding (A)..........94 B 2
Scharnitz (A)..........93 F 4
Scheeßel (D)...........83 F 2
Scheggia (I)..........102 D 2
Scheibbs (A)...........95 D 2
Scheifling (A).........95 D 1
Scheinfeld (D).........88 C 4
Schenefeld (D).........78 A 1
Schenefeld (D).........78 C 4
Scherfede (D)..........88 A 1
Schermbeck (D).........87 E 1
Scheßlitz (D)..........89 D 3
Scheveningen (NL).....82 A 4
Schieder (D)...........83 F 4
Schierling (D).........94 A 1
Schiermonnikoog (NL)..82 C 1
Schiers (CH)...........97 E 1
Schifferstadt (D)......45 E 2
Schildau (D)...........85 D 4
Schilpario (I).........97 E 3
Schiltach (D)..........45 E 4
Schinias (GR).........218 C 1
Schínos (GR)..........211 E 4
Schinoússa (Nisí) (GR)..224 C 2
Schio (I)..............98 A 3
Schirmeck (F)..........45 D 3
Schirnding (D).........89 E 3
Schizá (Nisí) (GR)....222 A 3
Schkeuditz (D).........85 D 4
Schkölen (D)...........89 D 1
Schladming (A).........94 C 3
Schlagbrügge (D).......79 D 4
Schlangenbad (D).......45 E 1
Schleching (D).........94 A 3
Schleiden (D)..........87 E 3
Schleiz (D)............89 D 2
Schleswig (D)..........78 C 2
Schleusingen (D).......88 C 2
Schlieben (D)..........85 E 4
Schliersee (D).........94 A 3
Schlitz (D)............88 B 2
Schlotheim (D).........88 C 1
Schluchsee (D).........92 C 3
Schlüchtern (D)........88 B 3
Schlüsselfeld (D)......88 C 4
Schlutup (D)...........79 D 4
Schmalkalden (D).......88 C 2
Schmallenberg (D)......88 A 1
Schmidmühlen (D)......89 E 4
Schmilka (D)...........90 A 1
Schmölln (D)...........81 D 4
Schmölln (D)...........89 D 1
Schnackenburg (D)......84 C 2
Schnaittenbach (D).....89 E 4
Schneeberg (D).........89 E 3
Schneverdingen (D).....84 A 2
Schoinás (GR).........206 A 3
Scholári (GR).........206 C 3
Schönau (A)............95 B 3
Schönberg (D)..........92 B 1
Schönberg (D)..........94 B 1
Schönberg (D)..........79 E 2
Schönberg (D)..........89 E 2
Schönberg im Stubaital (A)93 F 1
Schönbrunn (A).........95 C 4
Schönebeck (D).........84 C 4
Schöneck (D)...........89 E 2
Schönecken (D).........44 C 1
Schönewalde (D)........85 E 4
Schongau (D)...........93 F 3
Schöningen (D).........84 B 3
Schönmünzach (D).......45 E 3
Schönsee (D)...........89 E 4
Schönthal (D)..........89 E 4
Schönwald
  i. Schwarzwald (D)...45 E 4
Schönwalde (D).........79 D 3
Schoonhoven (NL)......82 B 4
Schopfheim (D).........92 B 3
Schöppenstedt (D).....84 B 3
Schoppernau (A)........93 E 4
Schorndorf (D).........93 D 1
Schortens (D)..........83 F 1
Schotten (D)...........88 B 2
Schramberg (D).........45 E 4
Schrems (A)............95 D 1
Schrobenhausen (D)....89 F 2
Schröcken (A)..........93 E 4
Schrozberg (D).........88 C 4
Schruns (A)............93 E 4
Schüttorf (D)..........83 D 3

Schwaan (D)............79 F 3
Schwabach (D)..........89 D 4
Schwäbisch-Gmünd (D)..93 D 1
Schwäbisch-Hall (D)....93 D 1
Schwabmünchen (D)....93 E 2
Schwaigern (D).........45 F 2
Schwalenberg (D)......83 F 4
Schwalmstadt-Treysa (D)..88 B 2
Schwalstadt-Ziegenhain (D)88 B 2
Schwandorf (D).........89 E 4
Schwanebeck (D).......84 B 4
Schwanenstadt (A).....94 C 2
Schwanewede (D).......83 F 2
Schwarmstedt (D)......84 A 3
Schwarza (D)...........89 D 2
Schwarzach im Pongau (A)94 B 3
Schwarzenbach
  a. d. Saale (D).......89 E 3
Schwarzenbek (D)......79 D 4
Schwarzenberg (D).....89 E 2
Schwarzenburg (CH)....49 F 3
Schwarzenfeld (D).....89 E 4
Schwarzheide (D)......85 E 4
Schwarzsee (CH).......49 F 3
Schwaz (A).............94 A 4
Schwechat (A)..........95 F 2
Schwedt (D)............85 E 1
Schweich (D)...........44 C 1
Schweinfurt (D)........88 C 3
Schweinitz (D).........85 D 4
Schweitz (D)...........87 F 1
Schwendi (D)...........93 D 2
Schwenningen Villingen- (D)45 F 4
Schwerin (D)...........79 E 4
Schwerte (D)...........87 F 1
Schwetzingen (D)......45 E 2
Schwyz (CH)............97 D 1
Sciacca (I)...........110 B 3
Scicli (I).............111 E 4
Scilla (I).............111 E 1
Ścinawa (PL)..........193 E 1
Ścinawka Średnia (PL)..193 E 4
Scole (GB).............37 D 2
Sconser (GB)...........26 C 3
Scopello (I)...........53 F 1
Scordia (I)...........111 E 3
Ščors (UA)..............7 E 4
Scorzè (I).............98 B 3
Scourie (GB)...........27 E 1
Scrabster (GB).........27 F 1
Ščučyn (BY).............6 C 4
Scunthorpe (GB)........33 E 2
Scuol / Schuls (CH)....97 E 1
Seaford (GB)...........36 C 4
Seaham (GB)............31 F 4
Seaton (GB)............35 D 3
Seaton Delaval (GB)....31 E 4
Sebecevo (SRB)........118 C 4
Sebeş (RO).............12 C 4
Sebež (RUS)............7 E 2
Sebnitz (D)............90 A 1
Sečanj (SRB)..........113 F 4
Sece (LV).............165 F 2
Secemin (PL)..........195 E 3
Seckau (A).............95 D 3
Seclin (F).............39 E 2
Secondigny (F).........47 D 3
Seda (LT).............163 D 3
Seda (LV).............159 F 2
Sedan (F)..............39 F 4
Sedano (E).............60 B 4
Sedbergh (GB)..........32 C 1
Šēdere (LV)...........172 C 1
Séderon (F)............52 C 4
Sedgefield (GB)........31 F 4
Sedico (I).............98 B 2
Sedilo (I)............108 B 2
Sedini (I)............108 B 1
Sedlare (SRB).........122 A 2
Sedlčany (CZ)..........90 A 2
Sedlec-Prčice (CZ).....90 B 3
Šeduva (LT)...........170 B 1
Seebenau (D)...........84 B 2
Seeboden (A)...........94 C 4
Seebruck (D)...........94 A 3
Seefeld in Tirol (A)...93 F 4
Seehaus (A)............94 C 3
Seehausen (D)..........84 B 3
Seeheim-Jugenheim (D)..45 E 2
Seelisberg (CH)........96 C 1
Seelow (D).............85 F 2
Seelze (D).............84 A 3
Sées (F)...............42 A 3
Seesen (D).............84 A 4

Seevetal (D)...........84 A 1
Seewalchen (A).........94 C 2
Seewiesen (A)..........95 E 3
Sefkerin (SRB)........118 B 1
Segesta (I)...........110 B 2
Segni (I).............105 D 1
Segonzac (F)...........50 C 2
Segorbe (E)............71 C 4
Segovia (E)............64 B 4
Segré (F)..............41 F 4
Segura (P).............69 D 1
Segura de la Sierra (E)..70 C 4
Segura de Léon (E).....69 D 4
Segura de los Baños (E)..65 A 3
Sehnde (D).............84 A 3
Seia (P)...............62 C 4
Seiches-sur-le-Loir (F)..41 F 4
Seierstad (N).........131 D 1
Seifhennersdorf (D)....90 B 1
Seignelay (F)..........43 E 2
Seilhac (F)............51 E 2
Seimeniškiai (LT).....175 F 3
Šeimyniškiai (LT).....171 E 4
Seinäjoki (FIN).......133 D 4
Seira (EST)...........153 D 2
Seirijai (LT).........176 B 3
Seissan (F)............55 D 2
Seitenstetten Markt (A)..95 D 2
Seixal (E).............68 A 3
Sēja (LV).............159 D 4
Sėjas (LV)............163 F 2
Sejny (PL)............185 D 1
Sėkoulas (GR).........217 D 3
Sękowa (PL)...........201 C 3
Selargius (I).........108 B 4
Selb (D)...............89 E 3
Selbekken (N).........131 D 3
Selbu (N).............131 D 3
Selby (GB).............33 E 2
Selce (HR).............99 E 3
Selçuk (TR)............19 E 4
Sėlė (LT).............171 F 3
Selema (LT)...........175 F 2
Sēleniai (LT).........162 C 2
Sélero (GR)...........207 F 2
Sėlestat (F)...........45 D 4
Selevac (SRB).........118 C 1
Selfoss (IS)..........126 A 2
Séli (GR).............205 F 3
Selia (EST)...........153 C 3
Seljametsa (EST).....153 C 2
Selje (N).............130 A 4
Seljord (N)...........139 D 3
Selkirk (GB)...........31 E 4
Sella Nevea (I)........98 C 1
Sellasía (GR).........217 E 4
Selles-sur-Cher (F)....47 F 2
Selli (GR)............226 C 2
Sellia (GR)...........226 B 2
Sellières (F)..........49 D 3
Sellin (D).............80 C 2
Selm (D)...............83 E 4
Selmsdorf (D).........79 D 4
Selna (HR)............115 F 3
Selommes (F)...........42 C 4
Selongey (F)...........49 D 3
Seløy (N).............127 D 4
Sėlpils (LV)..........165 F 2
Selsey (GB)............36 B 4
Selters (D)............88 A 3
Seltz (F)..............45 E 3
Selva (I).............107 D 3
Selva di Val Gardena /
  Wölkenstein in Gröden (I)98 A 1
Selvino (I)............97 E 3
Semanova (LV)........161 F 4
Sēme (LV)............157 F 4
Semeliškės (LT)......177 D 1
Semeljci (HR).........117 E 1
Semič (SLO)............99 C 5
Semily (CZ)............90 B 1
Seminara (I)..........111 F 1
Semizovac (BIH)......117 C 3
Semmering Kurort (A)..95 E 3
Semproniano (I).......102 A 4
Semur-en-Auxois (F)....48 C 2
Semur-en-Brionnais (F)..48 C 4
Sena (E)...............66 A 3
Sénas (F)..............56 C 2

Senasis Tarpupis (LT)..177 E 2
Senden (D).............93 E 2
Sendim (P).............63 E 2
Senez (F)..............53 E 4
Senftenberg (D)........85 E 4
Senieji Trakai (LT)...177 E 2
Senise (I)............106 C 4
Senj (HR)..............99 E 3
Senje (SRB)...........119 D 2
Senlis (F).............43 D 3
Sennecey-le-Grand (F)..49 C 4
Sennen (E).............34 E 4
Sennestadt (D).........83 F 4
Sennori (I)...........108 A 1
Sennybridge (GB).......35 D 1
Senoji Radiškė (LT)...175 F 3
Senonches (F)..........42 B 3
Senones (F)............45 D 4
Senorbì (I)...........108 B 4
Senožeče (SLO).........99 D 2
Šentjernej (SLO).......99 E 2
Šentilj (SLO)..........95 E 4
Šentjur (SLO)..........99 E 1
Sepeaux (F)............43 E 4
Šepeta (LT)...........171 E 4
Šepetivka (UA).........13 D 1
Sepino (I)............105 F 2
Sępólno Krajeńskie (PL)182 B 2
Sępopol (PL)..........184 B 2
Sepúlveda (E)..........64 B 3
Sequeros (E)...........63 E 2
Seraing (B)............39 F 2
Serapiniškė (LT)......172 C 3
Seravezza (I).........101 E 2
Serdokai (LT).........175 E 2
Seredžius (LT)........169 F 4
Seregno (I)............97 D 3
Sereikiai (LT)........163 E 4
Serene (LV)...........165 E 2
Serfaus (A)............93 E 1
Serfopoúla (Nisí) (GR)..219 D 4
Sergijev Posad (RUS)...7 F 2
Seriate (I)............97 E 3
Šerići (BIH)..........117 C 2
Sérifos (GR)..........219 D 4
Sérifos (Nisí) (GR)...219 D 4
Šėrikai (LT)..........169 D 2
Šerkšnėnai (LT).......163 D 3
Sermaize-les-Bains (F)..44 A 3
Sermide (I)............98 A 4
Se, mite (LV).........162 C 1
Sermoneta (I).........105 B 2
Sėrmūkši (LV).........159 F 4
Sernancelhe (P)........63 E 2
Serniki (PL)..........197 D 1
Serock Mazowieckie (PL)190 B 2
Serokomla (PL)........191 C 2
Serón (E)..............76 D 3
Serón de Nágima (E)....65 D 3
Serós (E)..............66 B 3
Serpa (P)..............68 C 4
Serpuchov (RUS)........7 F 2
Serra (I).............71 C 2
Serra de Outes (E).....58 A 3
Serra San Bruno (I)...111 F 1
Serracapriola (I).....106 A 1
Serrada (E)............64 A 3
Serradifalco (I)......110 C 3
Serradilla (E).........69 C 1
Serramanna (I)........108 B 4
Serravalle Scrivia (I)..100 C 1
Serrières (F)..........52 B 2
Sersale (I)...........109 E 1
Sertã (P)..............68 C 1
Sérvia (GR)...........205 F 4
Servian (F)............56 A 2
Servigliano (I).......102 A 2
Sesa (E)...............66 A 2
Sesava (LV)...........164 C 3
Seseña (E).............70 B 1
Sesimbra (P)...........68 A 3
Sesklió (Nisí) (GR)...228 D 1
Sesma (E)..............61 D 4
Sessa Aurunca (I).....105 E 3
Sesta Godano (I)......101 D 1
Seštanovac (HR).......117 C 4
Sestino (I)...........102 A 2
Sesto / Sexten (I).....98 B 1
Sesto Calende (I)......97 D 3
Sesto Fiorentino (I)...101 F 2
Sesto San Giovanni (I)..97 D 3
Šeštokai (LT).........175 F 3

Sestola (I)...........101 F 1
Sestri Levante (I)....101 D 1
Sestriere (I)..........53 E 3
Sestrunj (HR).........103 E 1
Sestrunj (Otok) (HR)..103 E 1
Sestu (I).............108 B 4
Šešuolėliai I (LT)....171 E 4
Šešuolėliai II (LT)...171 E 4
Šešuoliai (LT)........171 E 4
Sesvete (HR)...........99 F 2
Séta (GR).............213 D 4
Šėta (LT).............170 C 3
Setcases (E)...........55 F 4
Sète (F)...............56 A 2
Setenil de las Bodegas (E)75 F 3
Setermoen / Bardu (N)..124 B 4
Setrachos (CY)........230 B 3
Settebagni (I)........104 C 2
Settimo Torinese (I)...53 F 2
Settle (GB)............33 D 1
Setúbal (P)............68 A 3
Seui (I)..............108 B 3
Seulo (I).............108 B 3
Seurre (F).............49 D 3
Sevastianá (GR).......205 F 3
Sevenoaks (GB).........36 C 4
Sever do Vouga (P).....62 B 3
Sévérac-le-Château (F)..55 F 1
Severėnai (LT)........169 D 2
Seveso (I).............97 D 3
Sevettijärvi (FIN)....125 F 2
Sevilla (E)............75 E 2
Sevilleja de la Jara (E)..70 A 2
Sevlievo (BG)..........19 D 1
Sevnica (SLO)..........99 E 1
Sevojno (SRB).........118 B 3
Sevsk (RUS)............7 F 4
Seyches (F)............50 C 3
Seyda (D)..............85 D 4
Seyðisfjörður (IS)....126 C 1
Seyne (F)..............53 D 4
Seyssel (F)............49 E 4
Seyssel (F)............49 E 4
Sežana (SLO)...........99 D 2
Sézanne (F)............43 E 2
Sezimovo Ústí (CZ).....90 B 4
Sezze (I).............105 D 2
Sfáka (GR)............227 E 2
Sfakiá (GR)...........226 B 2
Sfaktiría (Nisí) (GR)..217 D 4
Sferracavallo (I).....110 B 2
Sfîntu Gheorghe (RO)...13 D 4
Sforzacosta (I).......102 C 3
Shaftesbury (GB).......35 E 3
Shanklin (GB)..........35 F 3
Shap (GB).............31 D 4
Sheerness (GB).........36 C 3
Sheffield (GB).........33 D 3
Shefford (GB)..........36 B 2
Shëngjin (AL).........121 E 4
Shepshed (GB)..........33 D 4
Shepton Mallet (GB)....35 E 2
Sherborne (GB).........35 E 3
Shercock (IRL).........23 E 3
Sheringham (GB)........37 D 1
Shiel Bridge (GB)......27 D 3
Shieldaig (GB).........27 D 3
Shijak (AL)...........121 E 4
Shipston-on-Stour (GB)..35 F 1
Shkodër (AL)..........121 E 3
Shoreham (GB)..........36 B 4
Shrewsbury (GB)........32 C 4
Shrewton (GB)..........35 E 2
Sianów (PL)...........181 E 2
Siátista (GR).........205 E 4
Šiaudėnai I (LT)......168 C 2
Šiaudinė
  Marijampolės (LT)...169 E 4
Šiaudinė Šiaulių (LT)..163 E 4
Šiaudinė Vilniaus(LT)..177 E 2
Šiaudiniškis (LT).....175 E 2
Šiauduva (LT).........169 D 2
Šiaulėnai (LT)........169 F 2
Šiauliai Antanaičiai(LT)171 D 4
Šiauliai Bagaslaviškis(LT)171 D 4
Šiauliai Šiaulių(LT)..163 F 4
Šiauliai (LT).........176 E 2
Sibari (I)............109 E 1
Sibbhult (S)..........143 E 3
Šibenik (HR)..........115 F 3
Sibiņ (HR)............115 F 3
Sibiu (RO).............13 D 4
Sićevo (SRB)..........119 E 3
Sicienko (PL).........182 B 4
Sicignano degli Alburni (I)106 B 4
Sick (D)...............83 D 2
Sićuraj (HR)..........120 B 2

Name	Pg.	Grid
Šid (SRB)	117	F 1
Sidabravas (LT)	170	C 2
Sidabrinės (LT)	171	F 3
Sidári (GR)	210	B 1
Sideby (FIN)	136	B 2
Sidensjö (S)	132	B 3
Siderno (I)	111	F 1
Sidgunda (LV)	159	E 4
Sidiró (GR)	208	C 1
Sidirókastro (GR)	206	C 2
Sidirónero (GR)	207	E 1
Sidmouth (GB)	35	D 3
Sidrabiņi (LV)	165	F 1
Sidrabnieki (LV)	164	B 3
Siebenlehn (D)	89	F 1
Sieciechów (PL)	196	C 1
Siecino (Jezioro) (PL)	181	D 3
Siedlce (PL)	191	D 3
Siedlec Wielkopolskie (PL)	187	D 3
Siedlisko Lubuskie (PL)	187	D 4
Siedliszcze Lubelskie (PL)	197	E 2
Siegburg (D)	87	F 2
Siegen (D)	87	F 2
Siegsdorf (D)	94	B 3
Siekierczyn (PL)	192	C 2
Sieksāte (Kalnmuiža) (LV)	163	D 1
Siemianowice Śląskie (PL)	195	D 4
Siemianowskie (Jezioro) (PL)	191	F 1
Siemiatycze (PL)	191	E 2
Siemień (PL)	191	E 4
Siemkowice (PL)	195	D 2
Siemyśl (PL)	181	D 2
Siena (I)	101	F 3
Sieniawa (PL)	197	E 2
Šienlaukis (LT)	169	E 2
Siennica (PL)	190	C 3
Siennica Różana (PL)	197	F 2
Sienno (PL)	196	C 1
Sieppijärvi (FIN)	128	C 2
Sieradz (PL)	194	C 1
Sieraków (PL)	187	D 2
Sierakowice Pomorskie (PL)	182	B 2
Sierck-les-Bains (F)	44	C 2
Sierentz (F)	49	F 1
Sierninghofen (A)	94	C 2
Sieroszewice (PL)	188	B 4
Sierpc (PL)	189	E 1
Sierpowo (PL)	181	F 3
Sierra de Fuentes (E)	69	F 2
Sierra de Yeguas (E)	75	F 2
Sierra Nevada (E)	76	B 2
Sierre (CH)	96	B 2
Siersza (PL)	200	F 1
Siesikai (LT)	171	D 3
Siestrzeń (PL)	189	E 2
Sievi (FIN)	133	E 2
Sievin as (FIN)	133	E 2
Siewierz (PL)	195	D 4
Sífnos (Nísí) (GR)	219	E 4
Sigaste (EST)	153	C 4
Sigean (F)	55	F 3
Sigerfjord (N)	124	A 4
Siggjarvág (N)	138	B 3
Sighetu Marmației (RO)	12	C 1
Sighişoara (RO)	13	D 3
Siglufjörður (IS)	126	B 1
Sigmaringen (D)	45	E 4
Signy-l'Abbaye (F)	39	E 4
Sigri (GR)	214	B 3
Sigtuna (S)	141	D 3
Sigüenza (E)	65	D 3
Sigulda (LV)	159	E 4
Sihva (EST)	160	C 1
Siikainen (FIN)	136	B 2
Siikajoki (FIN)	133	E 4
Siilinjärvi (FIN)	135	E 3
Siimusti (EST)	154	C 2
Sijarinska Banja (SRB)	119	E 4
Sikås (S)	131	F 2
Síkinos (GR)	224	B 2
Síkinos (GR)	224	B 2
Síkovuono (FIN)	125	E 3
Sīkrags (LV)	157	D 2
Sikšņi (LV)	162	B 3
Šikšniai (LT)	175	E 2
Sikyóna (GR)	217	F 2
Šilai Kauno (LT)	170	C 4
Šilai Panevėžio (LT)	171	E 3
Šilai Tauragės (LT)	169	D 2
Silajāņi (LV)	167	E 3
Silaktis (LT)	161	D 3
Šilalė (LT)	169	D 2
Silandro / Schlanders (I)	97	F 1
Šilavotas (LT)	176	C 2
Silba (HR)	99	E 4
Silba (Otok) (HR)	99	E 4
Silbaš (SRB)	113	D 4
Šile (TR)	19	F 1
Šileikoniai (LT)	170	C 1
Šilėnai Kuršėnai (LT)	163	E 4
Šilėnai Šiauliai (LT)	169	F 1
Silene (LV)	173	D 2
Siles (E)	70	C 4
Šilgaliai Šakiai (LT)	169	E 4
Šilgaliai Slavikai (LT)	169	E 4
Sīļi Alūksnes (LV)	161	E 3
Sīļi Liepājas (LV)	162	F 1
Siliņi Alūksnes (LV)	161	D 3
Siliņi Ventspils (LV)	156	C 4
Siliqua (I)	108	A 3
Silistra (BG)	13	E 4
Silivri (TR)	19	E 1
Siljan (N)	139	D 4
Siljansnäs (S)	140	B 2
Silkeborg (DK)	142	B 3
Silla (E)	71	F 3
Silla (EST)	153	C 4
Sillamäe (EST)	151	F 3
Sillé-le-Guillaume (F)	42	A 2
Silleda (E)	58	B 3
Sillian (A)	98	B 1
Silloth (GB)	31	D 4
Silmači (LV)	160	C 4
Silmala (LV)	167	E 3
Silnowo (PL)	181	E 3
Šilo (HR)	99	E 3
Sils (E)	67	D 2
Sils Maria / Segl Maria (CH)	97	E 1
Silvalen (N)	127	D 4
Silvaplana (CH)	97	E 1
Silvares (P)	62	C 4
Silves (P)	74	B 1
Silvi Marina (I)	103	E 3
Silz (A)	93	F 4
Simancas (E)	64	A 2
Šimanovci (SRB)	118	B 1
Símantra (GR)	206	C 4
Simav (TR)	19	F 2
Simaxis (I)	108	A 3
Simbach (D)	94	B 1
Simbach a. Inn (D)	94	B 2
Šimići (BIH)	115	E 4
Šimkaičiai (LT)	169	E 3
Simlångsdalen (S)	143	D 3
Simmerath (D)	87	E 2
Simmern (Hunsrück) (D)	45	D 1
Simnas (LT)	175	F 3
Simo (FIN)	128	C 4
Simola (FIN)	137	E 3
Simonsbath (GB)	34	C 2
Simonswald (D)	45	E 4
Šimonys (LT)	171	E 2
Símópoulo (GR)	217	D 2
Simrishamn (S)	143	E 4
Simuna (EST)	151	D 4
Sinaia (RO)	13	D 4
Sinalunga (I)	102	A 3
Sinarádes (GR)	210	B 2
Sinarcas (E)	71	E 2
Sindelfingen (D)	45	F 3
Sindi (EST)	153	C 3
Šíndrgi (TR)	19	F 2
Síndos (GR)	206	B 3
Sinettä (FIN)	128	C 3
Sineu (E)	73	D 2
Singen (Hohentwiel) (D)	92	C 3
Sinikūla (LT)	177	E 2
Sinimäe (EST)	151	F 3
Siniscola (I)	108	C 2
Sinj (HR)	116	C 4
Sînnicolau Mare (RO)	113	D 3
Sinole (LV)	160	C 3
Sinopoli (I)	111	F 1
Sinsheim (D)	45	F 2
Sint-Niklaas (B)	39	E 1
Sint-Oedenrode (NL)	39	F 1
Sint-Truiden (B)	39	F 2
Sintautai (LT)	170	A 4
Sintra (P)	68	A 2
Sinzig (D)	87	F 3
Siófok (H)	112	B 2
Sion (CH)	96	B 2
Sipa (EST)	149	D 4
Šipan (Otok) (HR)	120	C 2
Šipanska Luka (HR)	120	C 2
Stpoli (LV)	159	E 2
Sipoo / Sibbo (FIN)	137	D 3
Šipovo (BIH)	117	D 3
Sippola (FIN)	137	E 3
Siprage (BIH)	117	D 2
Sira (N)	138	C 2
Siracusa (I)	111	E 3
Siret (RO)	13	D 2
Sirevåg (N)	138	B 1
Sirig (SRB)	113	E 4
Širitovci (HR)	103	F 1
Sirkka (N)	128	C 2
Sirma (N)	125	E 2
Simione (I)	97	F 3
Široki Brijeg (BIH)	117	C 4
Široko Polje (HR)	112	C 4
Sirolo (I)	102	C 2
Siručiai (LT)	169	F 3
Siruela (E)	69	F 3
Siruténai (LT)	171	F 2
Sirutiškis (LT)	170	E 4
Širvintos (LT)	171	E 4
Sisak (HR)	115	D 3
Šišan (HR)	99	D 4
Sisante (E)	71	D 2
Sissa (I)	97	F 4
Sissach (CH)	92	A 4
Sissonne (F)	39	E 4
Sisteron (F)	53	D 4
Sistiana (I)	98	C 3
Sistranda (N)	130	C 2
Siteia (GR)	227	F 2
Sitges (E)	66	C 4
Sithonía (GR)	207	D 4
Sitkúnai (LT)	170	B 4
Sitno Kujawsko-Pomorskie (PL)	189	D 1
Sittard (NL)	87	E 2
Sittensen (D)	83	F 2
Sittingbourne (GB)	36	C 3
Šiūlėnai (LT)	172	C 3
Šiuliai (LT)	169	F 4
Siuntio / Sjundeå (FIN)	136	C 4
Šiupyliai (LT)	163	F 4
Siuro (FIN)	136	C 2
Siusi / Seis (I)	98	A 1
Sivac (SRB)	113	D 4
Sivaslı (TR)	19	F 3
Siviri (GR)	212	C 1
Six-Fours-les-Plages (F)	57	D 3
Siziano (I)	97	D 2
Sizun (F)	40	B 3
Sjenica (SRB)	118	B 4
Sjenićak Lasinjski (HR)	99	D 2
Sjøåsen (N)	131	D 2
Sjöbo (S)	143	E 4
Sjøholt (N)	130	B 4
Sjötorp (S)	140	B 4
Sjoutnäset (S)	131	F 1
Sjøvegan / Salangen (N)	124	B 4
Sjulsmark (S)	132	C 2
Sjusjøen (N)	139	E 1
Skaborai (LT)	169	D 2
Skåbu (N)	139	D 1
Skačiai (LT)	163	E 4
Skadovs'k (UA)	13	F 3
Skælskør (DK)	142	C 4
Skærbæk (DK)	142	A 4
Skaftafell (IS)	126	B 1
Skagaströnd (IS)	126	B 1
Skage (N)	131	D 2
Skagen (DK)	142	C 1
Skaidiškės (LT)	177	E 2
Skaill (GB)	28	B 1
Skaista (Geibi) (LV)	167	E 4
Skaistgirial (LT)	170	B 3
Skaistgirys (LT)	163	F 3
Skaistkalne (LV)	165	D 3
Skakai (LT)	164	C 3
Skała (PL)	200	F 1
Skála Dodekánissa (GR)	221	D 3
Skála Fthiótida (GR)	212	C 4
Skála Kefaloniniá (GR)	216	B 2
Skála Lakonía (GR)	223	D 2
Skála Lésvos (GR)	214	C 3
Skála Eresoú (GR)	214	C 3
Skála Kalliráchis (GR)	207	E 3
Skála Oropoú (GR)	218	C 1
Skála Rachoníou (GR)	207	E 3
Skála Volissoú (GR)	220	C 1
Skaland / Berg (N)	124	A 3
Skalavik (DK)	126	A 4
Skalbes (LV)	159	D 2
Skalbmierz (PL)	195	E 4
Skalevik (N)	142	A 1
Skalochóri Kozáni (GR)	205	E 4
Skalochóri Lésvos (GR)	214	C 3
Skaloti (GR)	207	E 1
Skalupes (LV)	159	E 3
Skamnélli (GR)	211	D 2
Skandáli (GR)	214	B 1
Skanderborg (DK)	142	B 3
Skånevik (N)	138	B 3
Skangaļi (LV)	159	F 3
Skåningsbukt (N)	124	B 2
Skaņkalne (LV)	159	E 1
Skänninge (S)	143	F 1
Skanör-Falsterbo (S)	143	D 4
Skantzoúra (Nísí) (GR)	213	E 3
Skåpe (N)	186	C 3
Skapiškis (LT)	171	E 1
Skara (S)	143	E 1
Skaramagkás (GR)	218	B 2
Skarberget (N)	124	A 4
Skårda (Otok) (HR)	116	A 4
Skåre (N)	140	A 4
Skárfeia (GR)	212	B 4
Skärhamn (S)	142	C 1
Skarnes (N)	139	F 3
Skarplinge (S)	141	D 2
Skarsvåg (N)	125	D 1
Skarszewy (PL)	182	C 2
Skärvången (S)	131	F 2
Skaržysko-Kamienna (PL)	196	B 2
Skattungbyn (S)	140	B 2
Skatval (N)	131	D 3
Skaudvilė (LT)	169	D 3
Skaulo (N)	128	A 2
Skaun (N)	131	D 3
Skaune (N)	167	F 4
Skawina (PL)	201	B 2
Škėde Liepājas (LV)	162	D 1
Škėde Saldus (LV)	163	D 1
Skee (S)	139	F 3
Skegness (GB)	33	F 3
Skei (N)	138	C 1
Skei (N)	130	C 3
Skela (SRB)	118	B 1
Skellefteå (S)	132	C 1
Skelleftehamn (S)	132	C 1
Skelmersdale (GB)	32	C 2
Skepastó (GR)	206	C 3
Skępe (PL)	189	E 4
Skerries / Na Sceiri (IRL)	23	E 4
Skersabaliai (LT)	177	F 1
Ski (N)	139	E 4
Skíathos (GR)	212	C 3
Skíathos (Nísí) (GR)	212	C 3
Skibbereen / An Sciobairín (IRL)	24	B 4
Skibby (DK)	142	C 4
Škibe (LT)	163	F 2
Skibotn (N)	124	C 1
Skiemonys (LT)	171	E 3
Skierbieszów (PL)	197	F 4
Skierniewice (PL)	189	F 4
Šķilbani (LV)	161	C 3
Skillingaryd (S)	143	E 2
Skilvioniai (LT)	164	B 3
Skindzierz (PL)	185	D 3
Skiniás (GR)	227	D 3
Skinnarbu (N)	139	D 3
Skinnskatteberg (S)	140	C 2
Skipagurra (N)	125	F 2
Skipton (GB)	33	D 1
Skirmantiškė (LT)	169	F 4
Skíti (GR)	212	B 2
Skive (DK)	142	B 3
Skivjane (SRB)	121	E 2
Skjeberg (N)	139	E 4
Skjelvik (N)	127	E 3
Skjern (DK)	142	A 3
Skjersholmane (N)	138	B 3
Skjerstad (N)	127	E 2
Skjervøy (N)	124	C 1
Skjønhaug (N)	139	E 2
Sklavopoúla (GR)	226	A 2
Šklėriai (LT)	177	F 2
Sklíthro (GR)	212	B 2
Škloù (BY)	7	E 3
Škočivir (MK)	122	B 4
Skoczów (PL)	200	E 2
Skodje (N)	130	B 3
Škofja Loka (SLO)	99	D 1
Škofljica (SLO)	99	D 2
Skog (S)	140	C 2
Skog (S)	132	B 4
Skogar (IS)	126	B 3
Skoghall (S)	140	A 4
Skogstorp (S)	140	C 4
Skoki (PL)	187	F 2
Skokloster (S)	141	D 3
Skollenborg (N)	139	D 3
Skołyszyn (PL)	201	C 2
Skomlin (PL)	194	C 2
Skópelos Lésvos (GR)	215	D 3
Skópelos Magníssía (GR)	213	D 3
Skópelos (Nísí) (GR)	213	D 3
Skopiá (GR)	212	B 3
Skopje (MK)	122	B 2
Skopós (GR)	205	F 2
Skopun (DK)	126	A 4
Skórcz (PL)	182	C 3
Skorenovac (SRB)	118	C 1
Skoroszyce (PL)	193	F 4
Skorovatn (N)	131	E 1
Skorped (S)	132	B 3
Skórzec (PL)	191	D 3
Skorzęcin (PL)	188	B 2
Skotína (GR)	212	B 1
Skotterud (N)	139	F 3
Skoulikariá (GR)	211	E 3
Skoúra (GR)	217	E 4
Skoúrta (GR)	218	B 1
Skoutári (GR)	206	C 2
Skoútari (GR)	222	C 2
Skoutáros (GR)	214	C 3
Skövde (S)	143	E 1
Skrá (GR)	206	A 2
Skrad (HR)	99	E 2
Skradin (HR)	103	F 1
Skraičionys (LT)	176	C 3
Skreia (N)	139	E 2
Skrīveri (LV)	165	E 2
Skroblis (LT)	168	C 1
Skroderi (LV)	162	C 1
Skrolsvik (N)	124	A 3
Skrunda (LV)	163	D 2
Skrydstrup (DK)	142	B 4
Skrynupis (LT)	176	B 2
Skrzyczne (PL)	200	F 3
Skrzyszów (PL)	201	B 2
Skudeneshavn (N)	138	B 3
Skudutiškis (LT)	171	F 3
Skuigė (LT)	176	B 2
Skujaine (LV)	163	F 2
Skujene (LV)	159	F 4
Skujenieki (LV)	161	D 4
Skujetnīki (LV)	167	E 1
Skujiņas (LV)	172	C 1
Skuķi (LV)	165	F 1
Skuki (LV)	173	E 1
Skuķīši (LV)	159	D 4
Skulsk (PL)	188	C 2
Skulte (LV)	164	C 1
Skultuna (S)	140	C 3
Skuodas (LT)	162	C 3
Skuoliai (LT)	171	D 4
Skuteč (CZ)	91	D 3
Skutskär (S)	141	D 2
Skutvik (N)	127	E 1
Skvyra (UA)	13	E 1
Skwierzyna (PL)	187	D 3
Skýdra (GR)	205	F 3
Skylloura (CY)	223	C 2
Skynimai Merkinė (LT)	177	F 2
Skynimai Mostiškės (LT)	177	F 2
Skýros (GR)	213	E 4
Skýros (Nísí) (GR)	213	E 4
Slabadai (LT)	175	C 2
Slagelse (DK)	142	C 4
Slagnäs (S)	127	F 4
Slakovac (SRB)	118	C 1
Slampe (LV)	163	F 1
Slănčev Brjag (BG)	19	E 1
Slancy (RUS)	7	D 1
Slane (IRL)	23	E 1
Slangerup (DK)	143	D 4
Slano (HR)	120	C 2
Slaný (CZ)	90	A 2
Šlapaberžė (LT)	170	C 3
Šlapaki (LV)	173	D 1
Šlapanice (CZ)	91	E 4
Slapy (CZ)	90	B 3
Śląskie-Zdrój (PL)	193	D 3
Slate (LT)	166	C 4
Slatina (BIH)	115	E 4
Slatina (HR)	112	B 4
Slatina (RO)	13	D 4
Slatina Bor (SRB)	119	E 2
Slatina Čačak (SRB)	118	C 3
Slatine (HR)	103	F 1
Slatinski Drenovac (HR)	112	B 4
Slaŭharad (BY)	7	E 4
Slav. Šamac (HR)	117	E 1
Slavēkas (LV)	159	E 4
Slavičín (CZ)	91	E 4
Slavikai (LT)	169	E 4
Slavinčiškis (LT)	171	E 1
Slavija (HR)	119	F 3
Slavkov u Brna (CZ)	91	E 4
Slavkovica (SRB)	118	B 2
Slavonice (CZ)	90	C 4
Slavonski Brod (HR)	115	F 3
Slavonski Kobaš (HR)	115	F 4
Slavuta (UA)	13	D 1
Sława Lubuskie (PL)	187	D 4
Sławatycze (PL)	191	F 4
Sławęcice (PL)	194	C 4
Sławków (PL)	195	D 4
Sławno Łódzkie (PL)	195	F 1
Sławno Zachodnio-pomorskie (PL)	181	E 2
Sławoborze (PL)	181	D 3
Šlažai (LT)	168	B 3
Sleaford (GB)	33	E 3
Šlečkai (LT)	162	C 4
Šlengiai (LT)	168	B 2
Šlepečiai (LT)	172	B 2
Šlesin Kujawsko-Pomorskie (PL)	188	B 1
Šlesin Wielkopolskie (PL)	188	C 3
Sliedrecht (NL)	82	B 4
Sliema (M)	110	A 4
Šlienava (LT)	176	C 1
Sligachan (Loch) (GB)	26	C 3
Sligo / Sligeach (IRL)	22	C 2
Slikiai (LT)	170	C 3
Šliktinė (LT)	162	C 1
Slipinčiems (LV)	157	D 4
Slišane (SRB)	119	D 4
Slite (S)	146	B 2
Sliven (BG)	19	E 1
Śliwice (PL)	182	C 3
Sližiūnai (LT)	177	E 3
Šljivovica (SRB)	118	B 3
Slobozia (RO)	13	E 4
Słomniki (PL)	195	F 4
Slonim (BY)	6	
Słońsk (PL)	186	C 2
Sloten (NL)	82	C 2
Slough (GB)	36	B 3
Sloup (CZ)	91	E 3
Slovac (SRB)	118	B 2
Slovenj Gradec (SLO)	99	E 1
Slovenska Bistrica (SLO)	99	E 1
Slovenske Konjice (SLO)	99	E 1
Slovinci (HR)	115	E 4
Słowiński Park Narodowy (PL)	181	F 1
Słubice Lubuskie (PL)	186	B 2
Słubice Mazowieckie (PL)	189	E 3
Sluck (UA)	13	D 4
Sluderno / Schluderns (I)	97	F 4
Sluis (NL)	37	F 4
Šluknov (CZ)	90	B 1
Slunj (HR)	99	F 3
Słup (PL)	193	D 2
Słupca (PL)	188	B 3
Słupia Łódzkie (PL)	189	E 4
Słupia Świętokrzyskie (PL)	195	E 3
Słupno (PL)	189	E 2
Słupsk (PL)	181	F 1
Smålands-stenar (S)	143	D 2
Smalininkai (LT)	169	D 4
Smalvos (LT)	172	C 2
Smaljavičy (BY)	7	D 4
Smarhon' (BY)	6	C 3
Šmarje (SLO)	99	D 3
Šmarješke Toplice (SLO)	99	D 2
Šmarliūnai (LT)	176	B 4
Šmartno (SLO)	99	E 1
Smed. Palanka (SRB)	118	C 2
Smedby (S)	143	F 3
Smědeč (CZ)	94	C 1
Smederevo (SRB)	118	C 1
Smedjebacken (S)	140	C 3

Smeļteri (LV).....167 D3
Smėlynė (LT).....171 E2
Smętowo Graniczne (PL) 182 C3
Smigáda (GR).....208 B1
Śmigiel (PL).....187 E3
Smila (UA).....13 F1
Smilčić (HR).....103 E1
Smilde (NL).....82 C2
Smilgiai Daujénai(LT) 165 D4
Smilgiai Sujetai(LT).....170 C1
Smilgudruvas (LV).....166 C3
Smiltiņi (LV).....157 E3
Smiltene (LV).....160 B3
Smojmírovo (MK).....122 C2
Smokovljani (HR).....120 C2
Smolensk (RUS).....7 E3
Smoljan (BG).....19 D1
Smolnica (PL).....186 B1
Smolnik (PL).....202 F4
Smørhamn (N).....130 A4
Šmotiškiai (LT).....170 B3
Smygehamn (S).....143 D4
Smyków (PL).....195 F2
Snaigupė (LT).....176 C4
Snaith (GB).....33 E2
Snåsa (N).....131 E2
Sneek (NL).....82 C2
Sneem (IRL).....24 A3
Sněpele (LV).....163 D1
Śniadowo (PL).....190 C1
Śniardwy (Jezioro) (PL)..184 C3
Śnieżka (PL).....193 D3
Snihurivka (UA).....13 F2
Sniķere (LV).....163 F3
Snillfjord (N).....130 C3
Śniukščiai (LT).....165 D4
Šniukštai (LT).....172 B1
Šniūraičiai (LT).....169 F1
Šnjegotina Velika (BIH)..115 F4
Snotiuļi (LV).....167 F2
Soave (I).....98 A3
Soběslav (CZ).....90 B4
Sobienie-Jeziory (PL)..190 B4
Sobieszewo (PL).....182 C2
Sobieszów (PL).....193 D3
Sobolew (PL).....190 C4
Sobotka (CZ).....90 C2
Sobótka Dolnośląskie(PL)193 E3
Sobra (HR).....120 C2
Sobrado dos Monxes (E)..58 C3
Sobral da Adiça (P).....68 C4
Sobral de Monte
  Agraço (P).....68 A2
Sobreira Formosa (P).....68 C1
Søby (DK).....144 B3
Sočanica (SRB).....118 C4
Soccia (F).....57 F3
Sochaczew (PL).....189 F3
Sochaux (F).....49 F2
Sochocin (PL).....189 F2
Sochós (GR).....206 C3
Socka (SLO).....98 C1
Socovos (E).....71 C4
Socuéllamos (E).....70 C3
Sodankylä (FIN).....129 D2
Sodeliai Juodupė(LT)..165 F4
Sodeliai Prūseliai(LT)..171 D1
Sodeliškiai (LT).....165 D3
Söderåkra (S).....143 F3
Söderbärke (S).....140 C3
Söderfors (S).....141 D3
Söderhamn (S).....140 C1
Söderköping (S).....143 F1
Södertälje (S).....141 D4
Sodražica (SLO).....99 C2
Sodupe (E).....60 C3
Soe (EST).....154 B4
Soest (D).....87 F1
Soest (NL).....82 B4
Soestdijk (NL).....82 B4
Soeva (EST).....153 B3
Sofádes (GR).....211 F2
Sofia (BG).....18 C1
Sofiero (S).....143 D3
Sofikó (GR).....218 A2
Sofó (GR).....212 B2
Sögel (D).....87 E1
Sogliano al Rubicone (I)..102 A1
Soglio (CH).....97 C1
Søgne (N).....142 A4
Soham (GB).....33 F4
Soignies (B).....39 E2
Soini (FIN).....133 E3
Soinlahti (FIN).....133 F2
Soissons (F).....43 E1
Sojamaa (EST).....155 D3
Söke (TR).....19 E3

Sokna (N).....139 E2
Sokobanja (SRB).....119 D1
Sokolac (BIH).....117 F3
Sokolany (PL).....185 E4
Sokółka (PL).....185 E4
Sokolniki (PL).....194 C2
Sokolov (CZ).....89 E3
Sokołów Małopolski (PL).197 D2
Sokołów Podlaski (PL).....191 D1
Sokoły (PL).....191 D1
Sola (N).....138 A3
Solana de los Barros (E)..69 D3
Solana del Pino (E).....70 B3
Solares (E).....60 B3
Solberg (S).....132 A3
Solčava (SLO).....99 D1
Sol'cy (RUS).....7 D1
Solda / Sulden (I).....97 F1
Sölden (A).....93 F4
Solec Kujawski (PL).....188 C1
Solec n. Wisła (PL).....196 C2
Solenzara (F).....57 F4
Solesmes (F).....39 D3
Solesmes (F).....41 F4
Solevågen (N).....130 B4
Solf (FIN).....133 D1
Solferino (I).....97 F3
Solholmen (N).....130 B3
Solignac (F).....51 D1
Solignac-sur-Loire (F).....52 A3
Solihull (GB).....33 D4
Solin (HR).....116 C4
Solina (PL).....202 E3
Soline (HR).....103 D1
Solingen (D).....87 E1
Solinske (Jezioro) (PL)..202 E3
Soliškės (LT).....177 D2
Sollana (E).....71 F3
Solleftteå (S).....132 A3
Sollenau (A).....95 D4
Sollentuna (S).....141 D4
Sóller (E).....73 D2
Sollerön (S).....140 C3
Søllested (DK).....144 C4
Solliès-Pont (F).....57 D3
Solnečnogorsk (RUS).....7 F2
Solofra (I).....106 A3
Soloi (CY).....230 B3
Solosancho (E).....64 C3
Solothurn (CH).....92 B4
Solre-le-Château (F).....39 E3
Solrød (DK).....143 D2
Solska (Puszcza) (PL)..197 E4
Solsona (E).....66 C2
Šolta (Otok) (HR).....103 F2
Soltau (D).....84 A2
Sölvesborg (S).....143 E4
Solvorn (N).....138 C1
Soma (TR).....19 E2
Sombernon (F).....48 C2
Sombor (SRB).....113 D4
Someren (NL).....87 D1
Somero (FIN).....136 C3
Sőmerpalu (EST).....161 D1
Sőmeru (EST).....151 D3
Somianka (PL).....190 B3
Sommatino (I).....111 D3
Sömmerda (D).....89 D1
Sommarøy (N).....124 B3
Sommesous (F).....43 F2
Sommières (F).....56 B2
Somolinos (E).....64 C3
Somonino (PL).....182 C2
Sompa (EST).....151 E3
Sompolno (PL).....188 C2
Son Servera (E).....73 E2
Soncillo (E).....60 B3
Soncino (I).....97 D2
Sonda (EST).....151 D3
Søndeled (N).....139 D4
Sønder Felding (DK).....142 B3
Sønderborg (DK).....144 B3
Sønderby (DK).....144 B3
Sondershausen (D).....88 C1
Søndersø (DK).....142 B4
Sondrio (I).....97 E2
Songeons (F).....38 C2
Sonkajärvi (FIN).....133 F2
Sonneberg (D).....89 D2
Sonnewalde (D).....85 E2
Sonogno (CH).....97 D2
Sonsbeck (D).....87 E1
Sonseca (E).....70 B2
Sonta (SRB).....113 D4
Sonthofen (D).....93 E4

Sontra (D).....88 B1
Soodoma (EST).....161 D1
Soometsa (EST).....153 C4
Soomevere (EST).....154 B3
Soonurme (EST).....151 E3
Sooru (EST).....160 C1
Sopeira (E).....55 D4
Sopilja (BIH).....117 E4
Sopište (MK).....122 B2
Sopot (PL).....182 C1
Sopot (SRB).....118 C1
Sopotnica (MK).....122 B4
Sopron (H).....95 F2
Sør-Flatanger (N).....131 D2
Sora (I).....105 E2
Soragna (I).....97 F4
Söråker (S).....132 A4
Sőrandu (EST).....149 F4
Sørarnøy (N).....127 D2
Sorbas (E).....77 D2
Sore (F).....50 B4
Soresina (I).....97 E3
Söreste (EST).....161 D1
Sorga (I).....88 B2
Sorgono (I).....108 B3
Sorgues (F).....52 C4
Sørgutvik (N).....131 E1
Soria (E).....65 D2
Soriano nel Cimino (I)..102 B4
Sørkjosen (N).....124 C2
Sorkwity (PL).....184 B3
Sorø (DK).....142 C4
Soroca (MD).....13 E1
Soroní (GR).....228 C2
Sorrento (I).....105 F4
Sørreisa (N).....124 B3
Sørrollnes (N).....124 A4
Sorsakoski (FIN).....135 E4
Sorsele (S).....127 F4
Sorso (I).....108 A1
Sort (E).....55 D4
Sortino (I).....111 E4
Sortland (N).....124 A4
Sõru (EST).....152 B2
Sorunda (S).....141 D4
Sørvær (N).....124 C1
Sørværøy (N).....127 D2
Sørvågen (N).....127 D2
Sørvagur (DK).....126 A4
Sørvattnet (N).....131 E4
Sørvik (N).....124 A4
Sos del Rey Católico (E)..54 A4
Sosdvaris (LT).....164 C1
Soses (E).....66 B3
Sośnicowice (PL).....194 C2
Sośno (PL).....182 B2
Sosnovyj Bor (RUS).....7 D1
Sosnowica (PL).....191 E4
Sosnowiec (PL).....195 D3
Sospel (F).....53 F4
Šoštanj (SLO).....99 E1
Šóstis (GR).....208 A2
Šostka (UA).....7 F4
Sota Seter (N).....130 B4
Sotillo de la Adrada (E)..70 A1
Sotira (CY).....231 E3
Sotíra (GR).....205 F2
Sotkalnis (LT).....169 E2
Sotkamo (FIN).....135 E2
Soto de los Infantes (E)..59 E2
Soto de Luiña (E).....59 E2
Soto de Sajambre (E)..59 F3
Soto del Barco (E).....59 E2
Sotogrande (E).....75 F4
Sotopalacios (E).....60 B3
Sotrondio (E).....59 F3
Sottomarina (I).....98 B3
Sottrum (D).....83 F2
Sottunga (FIN).....136 A3
Sotuélamos (E).....71 D3
Soúda (GR).....226 B2
Souesmes (F).....47 D2
Soufflenheim (F).....45 E3
Souflí (GR).....208 C2
Soúgia (GR).....226 A2
Sougné-
  Remouchamps (B).....87 D3
Souillac (F).....51 D2
Souilly (F).....44 B3
Soulac-sur-Mer (F).....50 B2
Soulaines-Dhuys (F).....44 A2
Soulinári (GR).....217 D4
Soulópoulo (GR).....211 D1
Soultz-Haut-Rhin (F).....45 E4
Soultz-sous-Forêts (F).....45 E3

Soúnio (GR).....218 C3
Soúnio (Akr.) (GR).....218 C3
Souni-Zanakia (CY).....230 B4
Souppes-sur-Loing (F)..43 D3
Sourdeval (F).....41 F2
Soure (P).....62 B4
Sournia (F).....55 F3
Souroti (GR).....206 C4
Springe (D).....84 A3
Soúrpi (GR).....212 B3
Sousceyrac (F).....51 E3
Sousel (P).....68 C2
Soustons (F).....54 A2
Soutelo (P).....58 B3
South Molton (GB).....34 C4
South Queensferry (GB)..31 D2
South Shields (GB).....31 F4
Southam (GB).....36 A4
Southampton (GB).....35 F3
Southborough (GB).....36 C4
Southend (GB).....23 D2
Southend-on-Sea (GB)..36 C3
Southport (GB).....32 C2
Southsea (GB).....35 F4
Southwell (GB).....33 E3
Southwold (GB).....37 D2
Souvála (GR).....218 C3
Souvigny (F).....48 B3
Sovata (RO).....13 D3
Sövdeborg (S).....143 E4
Soverato (I).....109 E3
Soveria Mannelli (I).....109 E2
Søvik (N).....130 B3
Sozopol (BG).....19 E1
Sp. Brnik (SLO).....99 D1
Spa (B).....87 D2
Spaichingen (D).....45 F4
Spaigiai (LT).....163 E3
Spakenburg (NL).....82 B4
Spalding (GB).....33 F4
Spalviškiai (LT).....165 F2
Spandau (D).....85 D2
Spanénai (LT).....170 C4
Spangenberg (D).....88 B1
Spāre Cēsu(LV).....159 E4
Spāre Talsu(LV).....157 D3
Sparlösa (S).....143 D1
Spárta (GR).....218 C2
Spárti (GR).....217 E4
Spárto (GR).....211 D3
Spas-Demensk (RUS).....7 F3
Spáta (GR).....218 C2
Spathapaioí (GR).....221 D3
Spean Bridge (GB).....27 F4
Spello (I).....102 B3
Spennymoor (GB).....31 F4
Sperchiáda (GR).....211 F2
Sperlonga (I).....105 E3
Spernia (LT).....175 F3
Spetsai (GR).....218 B3
Spétses (Nisí) (GR).....218 B3
Spetsopoúla (Nisí) (GR)..218 B3
Speyer (D).....45 E2
Spezzano Albanese
  Terme (I).....109 E1
Spezzano della Sila (I)..109 E1
Spičiai (LT).....169 F2
Spiczyn (PL).....197 E3
Spiddal / An Spidéal (IRL)..22 B4
Spidolas (LV).....173 D1
Spiekeroog (D).....78 A4
Spielfeld (A).....95 E4
Spiez (CH).....92 B1
Spijkenisse (NL).....82 A4
Spili (GR).....226 C2
Spília (CY).....230 B3
Spiliá (GR).....212 B1
Spilimbergo (I).....98 B2
Spilsby (GB).....33 F3
Spinalógka
  (Chersónisos) (GR).....227 E2
Spinazzola (I).....106 C3
Spincourt (F).....44 B2
Špindlerův Mlýn (CZ).....90 C1
Spinpi (GR).....157 D2
Spionica Donja (BIH).....117 E3
Špišić Bukovica (HR).....112 B4
Spišská Nová Ves (SK)..12 B2
Spital am Pyhrn (A).....95 D3
Spithami/Spithamn (EST)..148 B3
Spittal an der Drau (A)..94 C4
Spitz (A).....95 E1
Spjelkavik (N).....130 B3
Split (HR).....103 F1
Splügen (CH).....97 D1
Spodsbjerg (DK).....144 C4
Špoģi (Špogi) (LV).....167 D4
Špola (UA).....13 F1

Spoleto (I).....102 B4
Sportnitz (D).....79 E4
Spotorno (I).....100 C2
Spremberg (D).....85 F2
Spresiano (I).....98 B2
Sprīdīšti (LV).....159 F2
Sprikutova (LV).....167 F3
Sproģi (Oškalns) (LV)..165 E3
Sprungas (LV).....163 F1
Spunciems (LV).....158 C4
Spungēni (LV).....165 F2
Spuž (MNE).....121 D4
Spytkowice
  Małopolskie(PL).....200 F2
Staporków (PL).....195 F2
Squillace (I).....109 E3
Squinzano (I).....107 E3
Srb (HR).....116 C3
Srbac (BIH).....115 F4
Srbica (SRB).....119 D4
Srbinje / Foca (BIH).....117 F4
Srbobran (SRB).....113 E4
Srđevići (BIH).....117 D4
Srebrenica (BIH).....117 F3
Srebrenik (BIH).....117 E3
Središče ob Dravi (SLO)..115 F3
Srednje (BIH).....117 E3
Sredska (SRB).....122 C4
Šrem (PL).....187 F3
Srem. Kamenica (SRB)..113 E4
Sremska Mitrovica (SRB)..118 C3
Sremska Rača (SRB).....117 F1
Šriubiškės (LT).....171 E4
Srnetica (BIH).....116 C3
Srnice Donje (BIH).....117 E3
Srokowo (PL).....184 B2
Srpska Crnja (SRB).....113 F3
Srpska Kostajnica / Bosanska
  Kostajnica (BIH).....115 D4
Srpski Brod /
  Bosanski Brod (BIH)..115 F3
Srpski Itebej (SRB).....113 F4
Srpski Miletić (SRB).....113 D4
Srpsko Sarajevo (BIH)..117 E3
Stabaunyčius (LT).....170 B4
Stabintiškės (LT).....177 D1
Stabulnieki
  (Stabuļnīki) (LV).....167 D3
Stacija Ventspils-2 (LV)..156 C3
Stačiūnai Panevėžio(LT)..164 C4
Stačiūnai Šiauliu(LT).....164 B4
Stade (D).....78 C4
Stádio (GR).....217 E4
Stadskanaal (NL).....83 D2
Stadt Wehlen (D).....90 A1
Stadthagen (D).....83 F3
Stadtilm (D).....89 D2
Stadtkyll (D).....87 E3
Stadtlohn (D).....83 D4
Stadtoldendorf (D).....84 A4
Stadtroda (D).....89 D2
Stadtsteinach (D).....89 D3
Staffanstorp (S).....143 D4
Staffelstein (D).....89 D3
Staffin (GB).....26 B3
Stafford (GB).....33 D3
Stágira (GR).....207 D3
Stahle (D).....84 A4
Stahovica (SLO).....99 D1
Staicele (LV).....159 E4
Staines (GB).....36 B3
Stainz (A).....95 E4
Stakai (GR).....177 E4
Staklišķes (LT).....176 C2
Stalać (SRB).....119 D3
Stalbe (LV).....159 E3
Štalcerji (SLO).....99 D1
Staldzene (LV).....156 C2
Stalģene (LV).....164 C2
Stalida (GR).....227 D2
Stalidzāni (LV).....167 D3
Stall (A).....94 B4
Stalowa Wola (PL).....197 D3
Stămeriena (LV).....161 D4
Stamford (GB).....33 E4
Stamnes (N).....138 B2
Stams (A).....93 F4
Stamsund (N).....127 D1
Stančaliai (LT).....162 C2
Stange (N).....139 E2
Stanin (PL).....191 D4
Stanišić (SRB).....113 D4

Stanišinci (SRB).....118 C3
Stanisławów (PL).....190 C3
Štanjel (SLO).....99 D2
Stankiškiai (LT).....168 B3
Staňkov (CZ).....89 F4
Stankovci (HR).....103 E1
Stanley (GB).....31 E4
Stanós (GR).....207 D3
Stános (GR).....211 E4
Stans (A).....96 C1
Stansstad (CH).....96 C1
Stansted
  Mountfitchet (GB).....36 C2
Stapar (SRB).....113 D4
Staporków (PL).....195 F2
Stara Błotnica (PL).....196 B3
Stará Boleslav (CZ).....90 B2
Stara Kamienica (PL)..192 C3
Stara Kiszewa (PL).....182 C3
Stara Kornica (PL).....191 E3
Stara Moravica (SRB)..113 D3
Stara Novalija (HR).....99 E4
Stara Pazova (SRB).....118 B1
Stara Wieś
  Mazowieckie(PL).....190 C2
Stara Zagora (BG).....19 D1
Starachowice (PL).....196 B3
Staraja Russa (RUS).....7 D1
Staravina (MK).....122 B4
Starcza (PL).....195 D3
Stare Babice (PL).....190 B3
Stare Bogaczowice (PL)..193 D3
Stare Czarnowo (PL).....180 C4
Stare Iganie (PL).....191 D3
Stare Jabłonki (PL).....183 E3
Stare Kurowo (PL).....187 D1
Stare Pole (PL).....183 D2
Stare Sady (PL).....184 C3
Stargard Szczeciński (PL)180 C4
Stårheim (N).....130 A4
Stari (LV).....161 D4
Stari Bar (MNE).....121 E3
Stari Dojran (MK).....122 C3
Stari Gradac (HR).....112 B4
Stari Jankovci (HR).....117 F1
Stari Log (SLO).....99 D2
Stari Majdan (BIH).....115 E4
Stari Mikanovci (HR).....117 E1
Starica (RUS).....7 F2
Starigrad Hvar Otok(HR)..99 E4
Starigrad Senj(HR).....120 A2
Starigrad Paklenica (HR)..99 F4
Starnberg (D).....93 F3
Staro Petrovo Selo (HR)..115 F3
Staro Slano (BG).....120 C2
Starodub (RUS).....7 F4
Starogard Gdański (PL)..182 C3
Starokostjantyniv (UA)..13 D1
Starozreby (PL).....189 E2
Stary Brus (PL).....197 E1
Stary Dzierzgoń (PL).....183 D3
Stary Dzikowiec (PL).....196 C4
Stary Gózd (PL).....190 B4
Stary Jarosław (PL).....181 E1
Stary Lubotyń (PL).....190 C1
Stary Sącz (PL).....201 B2
Starý Smokovec (SK).....12 B2
Stary Targ (PL).....183 D3
Stary Zamość (PL).....197 E3
Staškūniškis (LT).....171 E3
Staßfurt (D).....84 C4
Stasylos (LT).....177 E3
Staszów (PL).....196 B3
Stathm. Angistis (GR)..207 D2
Statland (N).....138 B2
Statos-Agios Fotios (CY).230 B3
Stavanger (N).....138 B4
Staveley (GB).....33 D3
Stavelot (B).....87 D3
Stavenhagen
  Reuterstadt (D).....79 F4
Stavenisse (NL).....39 E1
Stavern (N).....139 E4
Stavoren (N).....82 B3
Stavrochóri (GR).....227 E3
Stavrodrómi (GR).....217 D2
Stavrós Chánia(GR).....226 B1
Stavrós Éwoia(GR).....213 D4
Stavrós Imathía(GR).....206 A3
Stavrós Kefalonniá(GR)..216 B1
Stavrós Lárisa(GR).....212 A2
Stavrós Thessaloníki(GR)207 D3
Stavroúpoli (GR).....207 E2
Stavrovouni (CY).....231 C3
Stavsjo (N).....139 E2
Stawiguda (PL).....183 F3
Stawiski (PL).....184 C4

Stawiszyn *(PL)* .... 188 C 4
Stebuliai *(LT)* .... 175 F 3
Štěchovice *(CZ)* .... 90 B 3
Steckborn *(CH)* .... 92 C 3
Steeg *(A)* .... 93 E 4
Steenbergen *(NL)* .... 39 E 1
Steenvoorde *(F)* .... 37 E 4
Steenwijk *(NL)* .... 82 C 4
Stefáni *Préveza(GR)* ... 211 D 3
Stefáni *Viotía(GR)* ...... 218 B 1
Stefaniná *(GR)* .... 207 D 3
Stefanodíkeio *(GR)* ...... 212 B 2
Stege *(D)* .... 145 D 3
Stegersbach *(A)* .... 95 E 4
Stegna *(PL)* .... 183 D 2
Steibis *(D)* .... 93 E 4
Steigen *(N)* .... 127 C 3
Steigviliai *(LT)* .... 164 C 3
Stein *(A)* .... 95 E 1
Stein *(D)* .... 89 D 4
Stein *(N)* .... 139 E 2
Stein am Rhein *(CH)* ... 92 C 3
Steinach *(A)* .... 93 E 4
Steinach *(D)* .... 89 D 2
Šteinalti *(LV)* .... 165 E 2
Steinau a. d. Straße *(D)* .. 88 B 3
Steinbach-Hallenberg *(D)*.. 88 C 2
Steine *(N)* .... 138 B 1
Steinfeld *(A)* .... 98 C 4
Steinfeld (Oldenburg) *(D)* .. 83 E 3
Steinfurt *(D)* .... 83 D 4
Steingaden *(D)* .... 93 E 4
Steinhausen *(D)* .... 93 D 3
Steinheim *(D)* .... 93 E 3
Steinheim *(D)* .... 83 F 4
Steinkjer *(N)* .... 131 D 2
Steinshamn *(N)* .... 130 B 3
Steinsland *(N)* .... 138 B 2
Stekene *(B)* .... 39 E 1
Stelmužė *(LT)* .... 172 C 1
Stelpe *(LV)* .... 165 C 2
Stemnitsa *(GR)* .... 217 E 3
Stenay *(F)* .... 39 F 4
Stendal *(D)* .... 84 C 2
Stende *(LV)* .... 157 E 4
Steni *(GR)* .... 213 D 3
Stenlille *(DK)* .... 142 C 4
Stenløse *(DK)* .... 143 D 4
Stenness *(GB)* .... 29 D 4
Stenó *(GR)* .... 217 E 3
Sténoma *(GR)* .... 211 F 3
Stenudden *(S)* .... 127 E 4
Stenungsund *(S)* .... 143 D 1
Stepanci *(MK)* .... 122 B 4
Stepi *(LV)* .... 160 C 2
Stepnica *(PL)* .... 180 B 3
Stepojevac *(SRB)* .... 118 E 2
Steponkaimis *(LT)* .... 169 F 3
Sterdyń-Osada *(PL)* ... 191 D 2
Sterkrade *(D)* .... 87 E 1
Stérna *Argolída(GR)* .. 217 F 3
Stérna *Dráma(GR)* ..... 207 E 2
Stérna *Évros(GR)* ..... 208 C 1
Sternberg *(D)* .... 79 E 4
Šternberk *(CZ)* .... 91 E 3
Stérnes *(GR)* .... 226 B 2
Sterup *(D)* .... 78 C 2
Stęszew *(PL)* .... 187 E 3
Stevenage *(GB)* .... 36 E 3
Stewarton *(GB)* .... 30 C 2
Steyr *(A)* .... 95 D 2
Steyrermühl *(A)* .... 94 C 2
Stężyca *Lubelskie(PL)* ... 190 C 4
Stężyca *Pomorskie(PL)* .. 182 B 2
Stia *(I)* .... 102 A 2
Stigliano *(I)* .... 106 C 4
Stigtomta *(S)* .... 140 C 4
Stiklestad *(N)* .... 131 E 2
Stikli *(LV)* .... 157 E 4
Štikoni *(LV)* .... 167 D 3
Stilo *(I)* .... 109 E 3
Štimlje *(SRB)* .... 122 A 2
Stintino *(I)* .... 108 A 1
Štip *(MK)* .... 122 B 4
Stīpnieki *(LV)* .... 164 C 2
Stirling *(GB)* .... 30 C 2
Stirniene *(LV)* .... 167 C 2
Stirniškiai *(LT)* .... 175 E 2
Štirovača *(HR)* .... 99 E 4
Štitar *(SRB)* .... 118 A 1
Štivan *(HR)* .... 99 E 4
Stīveri *(LV)* .... 159 E 4
Stjärnhov *(S)* .... 140 C 4
Stjärnsund *(S)* .... 140 B 4
Stjørdal *(N)* .... 131 D 3
Stockach *(D)* .... 45 F 4
Stockbridge *(GB)* .... 35 F 2

Stockelsdorf *(D)* .... 79 D 4
Stockerau *(A)* .... 95 E 1
Stockholm *(S)* .... 141 D 4
Stockport *(GB)* .... 33 D 2
Stocksbridge *(GB)* .... 33 D 2
Stockton-on-Tees *(GB)* ..... 31 F 4
Stoczek Łukowski *(PL)*.. 190 C 3
Stod *(CZ)* .... 89 F 3
Stöde *(S)* .... 132 A 4
Stoke-on-Trent *(GB)* ...... 33 D 2
Stokke *(N)* .... 139 E 3
Stokmarknes *(N)* .... 127 E 1
Stolac *(BIH)* .... 120 C 1
Stolberg *(D)* .... 87 D 2
Stolberg *(D)* .... 84 B 4
Stojerova *(LV)* .... 167 E 4
Stolice *(SRB)* .... 117 F 2
Stolin *(BY)* .... 13 D 1
Stollberg *(D)* .... 89 E 2
Stöllet *(S)* .... 140 A 2
Stolno *(PL)* .... 182 C 4
Stolpen *(D)* .... 90 A 1
Stolzenau *(D)* .... 83 F 3
Stómio *(GR)* .... 212 B 1
Ston *(HR)* .... 120 C 2
Stone *(GB)* .... 33 D 3
Stonehaven *(GB)* .... 28 B 4
Stonglandet *(N)* .... 124 B 1
Stoniava *(LT)* .... 177 D 1
Stopanja *(SRB)* .... 119 D 3
Stopnica *(PL)* .... 196 B 4
Storå *(S)* .... 140 B 3
Stora Blåsjön *(S)* .... 131 F 1
Stora Skedvi *(S)* .... 140 C 3
Storby *(FIN)* .... 136 A 4
Stordal *(N)* .... 130 B 4
Store Heddinge *(DK)* ..... 143 D 4
Store Molvik *(N)* .... 125 F 1
Storebø *(N)* .... 138 B 2
Storebro *(S)* .... 143 F 2
Støren *(N)* .... 131 D 3
Storfors *(S)* .... 140 B 3
Storforshei *(N)* .... 127 E 4
Storkow *(D)* .... 85 E 3
Stormi *(FIN)* .... 136 C 2
Stornoway *(GB)* .... 26 C 2
Storo *(I)* .... 97 F 2
Storožynec' *(UA)* .... 13 D 4
Storsjö *(S)* .... 131 E 4
Storslett / Nordreisa *(N)*... 124 C 3
Storsteinen *(N)* .... 124 C 3
Storsteinnes *(N)* .... 124 B 3
Strömsbruk *(S)* .... 141 D 1
Strömsnasbruk *(S)* .... 143 E 4
Strömstad *(S)* .... 139 E 4
Strömsund *(S)* .... 131 F 2
Strongoli *(I)* .... 109 E 4
Stronie Śląskie *(PL)* ...... 193 E 4
Strontian *(GB)* .... 27 D 1
Stroud *(GB)* .... 35 E 1
Stroumpi *(CY)* .... 230 A 4
Strovlés *(GR)* .... 226 A 2
Strovolos *(CY)* .... 231 C 3
Struer *(DK)* .... 142 B 2
Struga *(MK)* .... 122 A 4
Struga *(PL)* .... 190 B 2
Struge *(SLO)* .... 99 E 2
Strumica *(MK)* .... 122 B 4
Strumień *(PL)* .... 200 E 2
Strūna *(LT)* .... 172 C 4
Strūnķi *(LV)* .... 161 D 4
Strupli *(LV)* .... 167 D 2
Strūžāni *(LV)* .... 167 C 2
Stryj *(UA)* .... 12 C 2
Stryjów *(PL)* .... 197 E 3
Stryków *(PL)* .... 189 E 4
Strykowo *(PL)* .... 187 E 3
Strymonikó *(GR)* .... 206 C 2
Stryn *(N)* .... 130 B 4
Strzałkowo *(PL)* .... 188 B 4
Strzegom *(PL)* .... 193 E 3
Strzegów *Opolskie(PL)* ... 193 F 1
Strzegowo *(PL)* .... 189 F 1
Strzelce *Łódzkie(PL)* ...... 189 D 3
Strzelce Krajeńskie *(PL)*.. 187 F 3
Strzelce Opolskie *(PL)* ... 194 C 4
Strzelce Wielkie *(PL)* ..... 195 D 2
Strzeleczki *(PL)* .... 194 B 4
Strzelin *(PL)* .... 193 F 3
Strzelno *(PL)* .... 188 C 2
Strzybnica *(PL)* .... 195 D 2
Strzyżewice *(PL)* .... 197 D 2
Strzyżów
  Podkarpackie(PL) ..... 202 D 2
Stubbekøbing *(DK)* .... 144 C 4
Stubičke Toplice *(HR)* ... 99 F 1
Ștubik *(SRB)* .... 119 E 1

Stratóni *(GR)* .... 207 D 3
Stratoníki *(GR)* .... 207 D 3
Strátos *(GR)* .... 211 E 4
Stratton *(GB)* .... 34 C 3
Straubing *(D)* .... 94 A 1
Straumen *(N)* .... 127 E 2
Straumen *(N)* .... 131 D 2
Straumen *(N)* .... 127 E 2
Straumsjøen *(N)* .... 127 E 1
Straumsnes *(N)* .... 127 E 2
Straupe *(LV)* .... 159 E 3
Straupitz *(D)* .... 85 E 3
Strausberg *(D)* .... 85 E 2
Straußfurt *(D)* .... 88 C 1
Strauti *(LV)* .... 162 B 2
Strautiņi *(LV)* .... 161 D 3
Strautmaļi *(LV)* .... 159 F 3
Strawczyn *(PL)* .... 195 F 3
Straža *(SLO)* .... 99 E 2
Straža *(SRB)* .... 113 F 4
Strazde *(LV)* .... 157 E 4
Strážnice *(CZ)* .... 91 E 4
Strážný *(CZ)* .... 94 C 1
Streatley *(GB)* .... 35 F 2
Street *(GB)* .... 35 E 2
Strehaia *(RO)* .... 12 C 4
Strehla *(D)* .... 85 E 4
Streitberg *(D)* .... 89 D 3
Strēlnieki Aizkraukles(LV) 165 F 2
Strēlnieki Bauskas(LV) ... 164 C 2
Strenči *(LV)* .... 159 F 2
Strengberg *(A)* .... 95 D 2
Stresa *(I)* .... 97 D 3
Strezimirovci *(SRB)* ...... 119 E 4
Strezovce *(SRB)* .... 119 D 4
Stříbro *(CZ)* .... 89 F 3
Strīķi *(LV)* .... 162 B 2
Striķi *(LV)* .... 163 E 2
Strmac *(HR)* .... 115 E 3
Strmica *(HR)* .... 116 C 3
Strmosten *(SRB)* .... 119 D 2
Strobl *(A)* .... 94 C 3
Strofádes (Nisiá) *(GR)* .. 216 C 4
Strofyliá *(GR)* .... 212 C 4
Strojkovce *(SRB)* .... 119 E 4
Strokestown *(IRL)* .... 22 C 3
Stromberg *(D)* .... 45 D 2
Stromeferry *(GB)* .... 27 D 3
Strömfors *(S)* .... 128 B 2

Stubline *(SRB)* .... 118 B 1
Stubno *(PL)* .... 202 F 2
Stuburai *(LT)* .... 171 E 3
Studena *(SRB)* .... 119 F 3
Studenci *(HR)* .... 117 D 4
Studenica *(SRB)* .... 118 A 2
Studénka *(CZ)* .... 91 F 2
Studzienna *(PL)* .... 200 D 2
Stügliai *(LT)* .... 171 F 3
Stugun *(S)* .... 131 F 3
Stühlingen *(D)* .... 92 C 3
Stuhr *(D)* .... 83 F 4
Stukmaņi *(LV)* .... 165 F 2
Stulgiai *(LT)* .... 169 E 2
Sultanhisar *(TR)* .... 19 C 2
Stultiškiai *(LT)* .... 170 C 2
Stumbrės *(LT)* .... 168 C 2
Stumbriškis Pažąsai(LT).. 164 C 2
Stumbriškis Sodeliai(LT). 171 D 1
Stupari *(BIH)* .... 117 E 2
Stupnik *(HR)* .... 99 F 2
Stupsk *(PL)* .... 189 F 1
Stupurai *(LT)* .... 164 B 4
Sturehov *(S)* .... 141 D 4
Sturminster Newton *(GB)*.. 35 E 3
Stuttgart *(D)* .... 45 E 3
Stykkishólmur *(IS)* ...... 126 A 2
Stylida *(GR)* .... 212 B 3
Šumperk *(CZ)* .... 91 F 2
Stylloi *(CY)* .... 231 D 1
Stymfalía (Limni) *(GR)* .. 217 E 2
Stýpsi *(GR)* .... 214 C 3
Stýra *(GR)* .... 219 D 1
Su *(E)* .... 60 E 4
Subačiškės *(LT)* .... 175 F 3
Subačius *(LT)* .... 171 D 2
Subate *(LV)* .... 166 B 4
Subbiano *(I)* .... 102 A 2
Subiaco *(I)* .... 105 D 2
Subijana *(E)* .... 60 C 4
Subkowy *(PL)* .... 182 C 2
Subotica *(SRB)* .... 113 D 3
Subotište *(SRB)* .... 118 B 1
Suceava *(RO)* .... 13 D 3
Suceviţa *(RO)* .... 13 D 3
Sucha Beskidzka *(PL)* ... 201 C 3
Suchacz *(PL)* .... 183 D 2
Suchań *(PL)* .... 180 C 4
Suchedniów *(PL)* .... 196 B 2
Suchiniči *(RUS)* .... 7 F 3
Suchowola Podlaskie(PL)185 E 3
Suchożebry *(PL)* .... 191 D 3
Süchteln *(D)* .... 87 E 1
Suchy Las *(PL)* .... 187 F 2
Sucina *(E)* .... 77 F 1
Sudarbe *(LV)* .... 161 E 4
Sudargas *(LT)* .... 169 E 4
Sudbury *(GB)* .... 33 D 4
Sudbury *(GB)* .... 36 C 2
Suddesjaur *(S)* .... 128 A 4
Sudeikiai *(LT)* .... 171 F 2
Sūdėnai *(LT)* .... 162 B 3
Süderbrarup *(D)* .... 78 C 2
Sudervė *(LT)* .... 177 E 2
Sudiste *(EST)* .... 154 B 4
Sudoł *(PL)* .... 196 C 2
Sudrabkalns *(LV)* .... 166 C 3
Sudža *(RUS)* .... 7 F 4
Sueca *(E)* .... 71 F 3
Sueros de Cepeda *(E)*.... 59 F 4
Suginčiai *(LT)* .... 171 F 3
Suhl *(D)* .... 88 C 2
Suho Polje *(BIH)* .... 117 F 2
Suhopolje *(HR)* .... 112 B 4
Šuica *(BIH)* .... 117 D 4
Suigu *(EST)* .... 153 C 2
Suinula *(FIN)* .... 136 C 2
Suippes *(F)* .... 43 F 2
Suislepa *(EST)* .... 154 C 4
Sujainiai *(LT)* .... 169 E 3
Sujetai *(LT)* .... 170 C 1
Šuké *(LT)* .... 162 B 4
Sukeva *(FIN)* .... 135 D 1
Šukioniai *(LT)* .... 164 D 4
Šukionys *(LT)* .... 165 E 3
Sukobin *(MNE)* .... 121 E 3
Sukošan *(HR)* .... 103 E 1
Sukovo *(SRB)* .... 119 F 3
Sūkuriai *(LT)* .... 176 B 4
Šula *(MNE)* .... 117 F 4
Sulbi *(EST)* .... 154 A 4
Sulechów *(PL)* .... 187 D 1
Sulęcin *(PL)* .... 186 C 2
Sulęczyno *(PL)* .... 182 B 2
Sulejów *(PL)* .... 195 D 4
Sulejówek *(PL)* .... 190 B 3
Sulejowski (Jezioro) *(PL)* 195 E 1

Sulików *(PL)* .... 192 C 2
Sulina *(RO)* .... 13 E 4
Sulingen *(D)* .... 83 F 3
Sulitjelma *(N)* .... 127 E 3
Sulkava *(FIN)* .... 135 D 4
Sułkowice *(PL)* .... 201 A 2
Sully-sur-Loire *(F)* ...... 43 D 4
Sulmierzyce Łódzkie(PL) 195 D 2
Sulmierzyce
  Wielkopolskie(PL) ..... 187 F 4
Sulmona *(I)* .... 105 A 1
Sułoszowa *(PL)* .... 195 E 4
Sułów Lubelskie(PL) ...... 197 E 3
Sultanhisar *(TR)* .... 19 E 2
Sultsi *(EST)* .... 154 B 4
Sulustvere *(EST)* .... 154 C 2
Sulz a. Neckar *(D)* ...... 45 F 4
Sulz a. d. Murr *(D)* ..... 93 D 1
Sulzbach (Saar) *(D)* ...... 45 D 2
Sulzbach a. d. Murr *(D)* .... 93 D 1
Sulzbach-Rosenberg *(D)*.. 89 E 4
Sulzemoos *(D)* .... 93 F 2
Sumartin *(HR)* .... 120 A 1
Sumba *(DK)* .... 126 A 4
Sumburgh *(GB)* .... 29 F 2
Sümeg *(H)* .... 112 A 2
Šumen *(BG)* .... 19 E 1
Sumiainen *(FIN)* .... 133 F 4
Sumiswald *(CH)* .... 96 B 1
Šumkas *(LT)* .... 177 F 2
Sumy *(UA)* .... 7 F 4
Šunakojai *(LT)* .... 171 E 3
Sunākste *(LV)* .... 165 F 3
Sünciems *(LV)* .... 162 B 3
Sund *(FIN)* .... 136 A 4
Sundakai *(LT)* .... 176 C 2
Sunde *(N)* .... 130 C 3
Sunde *(N)* .... 138 B 3
Sunderland *(GB)* .... 31 F 4
Sundern (Sauerland) *(D)*.. 87 F 1
Sundom *(FIN)* .... 132 C 3
Sundsvall *(S)* .... 132 A 4
Suni *(I)* .... 108 A 2
Sunīši *(LV)* .... 159 D 4
Sunja *(HR)* .... 115 D 3
Sunnansjö *(S)* .... 140 B 3
Sunndalsøra *(N)* .... 130 C 3
Sunne *(S)* .... 139 F 3
Sunne *(S)* .... 131 F 3
Sunnemo *(S)* .... 140 B 3
Šunskai *(LT)* .... 175 F 2
Suntaži *(LV)* .... 165 E 1
Suodenniemi *(FIN)* .... 136 B 2
Suolahti *(FIN)* .... 133 F 4
Suolijoki *(FIN)* .... 129 D 3
Suomenlinna *(FIN)* .... 137 D 4
Suomenniemi *(FIN)* .... 137 E 2
Suomusjärvi *(FIN)* .... 136 C 4
Suomussalmi *(FIN)* .... 135 E 1
Suonenjoki *(FIN)* .... 133 F 4
Suopelto *(FIN)* .... 133 F 3
Suostas *(LT)* .... 165 D 3
Super-Besse *(F)* .... 51 F 2
Super Molina *(E)* .... 55 E 4
Supetar *(HR)* .... 116 A 4
Supetarska Draga *(HR)*.. 99 E 4
Supino *(I)* .... 105 D 2
Supraśl *(PL)* .... 185 D 4
Supsi *(EST)* .... 154 A 4
Surahammar *(S)* .... 140 C 3
Suraż *(PL)* .... 191 E 1
Suraż *(RUS)* .... 7 E 4
Surbo *(I)* .... 107 F 3
Surčin *(SRB)* .... 118 B 1
Surdegis *(LT)* .... 171 D 2
Surdulica *(SRB)* .... 119 E 4
Surenenpass *(CH)* .... 96 C 1
Sürgavere *(EST)* .... 154 B 3
Surgères *(F)* .... 46 C 4
Súria *(E)* .... 66 C 4
Surju *(EST)* .... 153 C 1
Surnadalsøra *(N)* .... 130 C 3
Sursee *(CH)* .... 92 C 4
Surviliškis *(LT)* .... 170 C 3
Survilliers *(F)* .... 43 D 2
Susa *(I)* .... 53 C 4
Sušac (Otok) *(HR)* ...... 120 A 2
Sušak *(HR)* .... 99 D 4
Sušara *(SRB)* .... 118 C 3
Susch *(CH)* .... 97 E 1
Susek *(SRB)* .... 118 F 1
Sušice *(CZ)* .... 89 F 4
Susiec *(PL)* .... 197 F 3
Suškova *(LV)* .... 167 E 4
Suslejka *(RUS)* .... 93 D 2
Susrēni *(LV)* .... 166 B 1
Susurluk *(TR)* .... 19 F 2

Susz *(PL)* .... 183 D 3
Suszec *(PL)* .... 200 E 2
Šutai *(LT)* .... 172 C 4
Sutinjske Toplice *(HR)*.. 99 F 1
Sutjeska *(BIH)* .... 117 E 3
Sutjeska *(SRB)* .... 113 F 4
Sutkiai *(LT)* .... 169 E 4
Sutlema *(EST)* .... 149 D 3
Sutlepa *(EST)* .... 148 C 4
Sutomore *(MNE)* .... 121 D 3
Sutri *(I)* .... 102 B 4
Sutri *(LV)* .... 166 C 3
Sutterton *(GB)* .... 33 F 3
Sutton *(GB)* .... 36 B 3
Sutton Coldfield *(GB)* ... 33 D 4
Sutton-in-Ashfield *(GB)* .. 33 D 3
Sutvan *(HR)* .... 116 C 4
Suure-Jaani *(EST)* .... 154 B 3
Suurejõe *(EST)* .... 154 A 3
Suuremõisa *(EST)* .... 148 A 4
Suurküla *(EST)* .... 161 D 1
Suurpea *(EST)* .... 149 F 2
Suur-Rahula *(LV)* .... 152 C 3
Suva Reka *(SRB)* .... 122 A 2
Suvainiškis *(LT)* .... 165 E 4
Suvénai *(LT)* .... 172 C 1
Suvereto *(I)* .... 101 F 3
Suviekas *(LT)* .... 172 C 1
Suvodanja *(SRB)* .... 118 B 2
Suvodol *(MK)* .... 122 B 3
Suwałki *(PL)* .... 185 D 2
Suži *(LV)* .... 159 D 4
Sužionys *(LT)* .... 171 F 4
Suzzara *(I)* .... 97 F 4
Svaljava *(UA)* .... 12 C 2
Svalöv *(S)* .... 143 D 4
Svaneke *(DK)* .... 145 E 3
Svanvik *(N)* .... 125 F 2
Svappavaara *(S)* .... 128 A 2
Svärdsjö *(S)* .... 140 C 2
Sväriņi (Svarinci) *(LV)*... 167 F 4
Svarstad *(N)* .... 139 E 3
Svartå *(S)* .... 140 B 4
Svartevatn *(N)* .... 138 C 4
Svedala *(S)* .... 143 D 4
Švėdasai *(LT)* .... 171 F 2
Švedriškė *(LT)* .... 172 C 3
Sveg *(S)* .... 140 B 1
Švėkšna *(LT)* .... 168 C 2
Svelbergis *(LV)* .... 161 D 4
Svelgen *(N)* .... 130 A 4
Svelvik *(N)* .... 139 E 3
Švenčionėliai *(LT)* .... 172 B 4
Švenčionys *(LT)* .... 172 C 4
Svendborg *(DK)* .... 144 C 3
Švendriai *(LT)* .... 163 E 4
Svenljunga *(S)* .... 143 D 2
Svensby *(N)* .... 124 B 3
Svenstavik *(S)* .... 131 F 4
Svente *(LV)* .... 172 C 1
Sventes *(LV)* .... 172 C 1
Šventežeris *(LT)* .... 175 F 3
Šventininkai Kauno(LT) ... 176 C 2
Šventininkai Vilniaus(LT). 177 F 2
Šventragis *(LT)* .... 175 F 2
Šventupė *(LT)* .... 171 E 3
Šventybrastis *(LT)* .... 170 C 3
Svetac (Otok) *(HR)* ...... 103 F 2
Sveti Dorde
  (Manastir) *(MK)* .... 122 B 2
Sveti Filip-Jakov *(HR)*.. 103 E 1
Sveti Ivan Žabno *(HR)* ... 112 A 4
Sveti Ivan Zelina *(HR)* ... 99 F 1
Sveti Jovan Bigorski *(MK)*122 A 3
Sveti Juraj *(HR)* .... 99 E 3
Sveti Naum *(MK)* .... 122 A 4
Sveti Nikola *(MNE)* ...... 121 E 3
Sveti Nikole *(MK)* .... 122 B 2
Sveti Petar na moru *(HR)*103 E 1
Sveti Rok *(HR)* .... 99 F 4
Sveti Stefan *(MNE)* ...... 121 D 3
Svetlahorsk *(BY)* .... 7 F 4
Svetlogorsk *(RUS)* .... 6 B 4
Svetozar Miletić *(SRB)*.. 113 D 4
Sviby *(EST)* .... 148 B 3
Svidník *(SK)* .... 12 B 2
Svidžiai *(LT)* .... 165 D 3
Sviesta Gārša *(LV)* ...... 161 C 2
Švihov *(CZ)* .... 89 F 4
Svilajnac *(SRB)* .... 118 C 2
Svilengrad *(BG)* .... 19 E 1
Sviliai Kauno(LT) .... 170 B 3
Sviliai Panevėžio(LT) ...... 165 E 4
Svingvoll *(N)* .... 139 E 1

TORINO

Aeroporto (Strada dell')	GT 2	De Sanctis (V. F.)	FT 30	Sestriere (V.)	GU 74
Agnelli (Cso G.)	FU 3	Garibaldi (Cso)	GT 36	Stampini (V. E.)	GT 78
Agudio (V. T.)	HT 5	Grosseto (Cso)	GT 39	Stradella (V.)	GT 79
Bogino (V.)	GT 8	Lazio (Lungo Stura)	HT 41	S. M. Mazzarello (V.)	FT 68
Borgaro (V.)	GT 9	Maroncelli (Cso P.)	GU 43	Thovez (Viale E.)	GHT 80
Cebrosa (Str. d.)	HT 22	Potenza (Cso)	GT 58	Torino (Strada)	GU 81
Cosenza (Cso)	FGU 29	Rebaudengo (P. Conti)	GT 59	Torino (Viale)	FU 82
		Regio Parco (Cso)	HT 61	Unità d'Italia (Cso)	GU 86
		Sansovino (V. A.)	FGT 71	Vercelli (Cso)	HT 89
		Savona (Cso)	GU 72	Voghera (Lungo Dora)	HT 92

Museo dell' Automobile Carlo Biscaretti di Ruffia .... GU M5

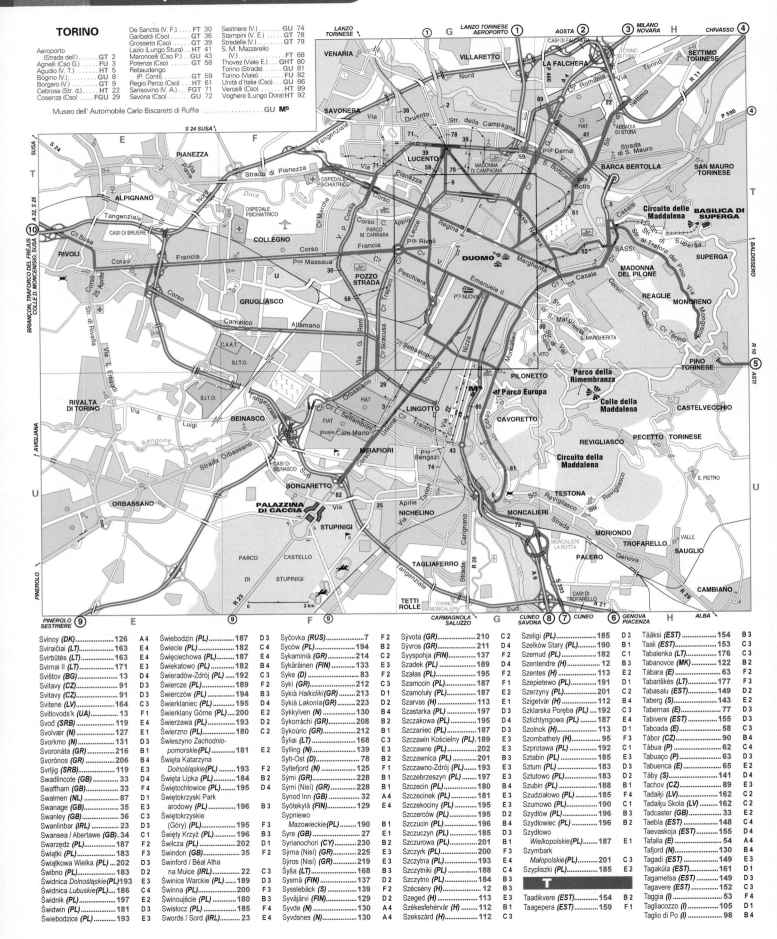

Svinoy (DK) 126 A4
Sviraičiai (LT) 163 E4
Svirbūtės (LT) 163 E4
Svirnai II (LT) 171 E3
Svištov (BG) 13 D4
Svitavy (CZ) 91 D3
Svitavy (CZ) 91 D3
Svitene (LV) 164 C3
Svitlovods'k (UA) 13 F1
Svod (SRB) 119 E4
Svolvær (N) 127 E1
Svorkmo (N) 131 D3
Svoronáta (GR) 216 B1
Svorónos (GR) 206 B4
Svrljig (SRB) 119 E3
Swadlincote (GB) 33 D4
Swaffham (GB) 33 F4
Swalmen (NL) 87 D1
Swanage (GB) 35 E4
Swanley (GB) 36 C3
Swanlinbar (IRL) 23 D3
Swansea / Abertawe (GB) 34 C1
Swarzędz (PL) 187 F2
Świątki (PL) 183 F3
Świątkowa Wielka (PL) 202 D1
Świbno (PL) 183 D2
Świdnica Dolnośląskie (PL) 193 E3
Świdnica Lubuskie (PL) 186 C4
Świdnik (PL) 197 D3
Świdwin (PL) 181 D3
Świebodzice (PL) 193 E3

Świebodzin (PL) 187 D3
Świecie (PL) 182 C4
Święciechowa (PL) 187 E4
Świekatowo (PL) 182 B4
Świeradów-Zdrój (PL) 192 C3
Świercze (PL) 189 F2
Świerczów (PL) 194 B3
Świerklaniec (PL) 195 D1
Świerklany Górne (PL) 200 E2
Świerzawa (PL) 193 D2
Świerzno (PL) 180 C2
Świeszyno Zachodnio- pomorskie (PL) 181 D3
Święta Katarzyna Dolnośląskie (PL) 193 F2
Święta Lipka (PL) 184 B2
Świętochłowice (PL) 195 D4
Świętokrzyski Park Narodowy (PL) 196 B3
Świętokrzyskie (Góry) (PL) 195 F3
Święty Krzyż (PL) 196 B3
Świlcza (PL) 202 D1
Swinford / Béal Atha na Muice (IRL) 22 C3
Świnice Warckie (PL) 189 D3
Świnna (PL) 200 F3
Świnoujście (PL) 180 B3
Swinton (GB) 35 F2
Swisłocz (PL) 185 F4
Swords / Sord (IRL) 23 E4

Syčovka (RUS) 7 F2
Syców (PL) 194 B2
Sykaminiá (GR) 214 C2
Sykäräinen (FIN) 133 E3
Syki (GR) 212 C3
Sykiá Halkidikí (GR) 213 D1
Sykiá Lakonía (GR) 223 D2
Sykkylven (N) 130 B4
Sykorráchi (GR) 208 B2
Sykoúrio (GR) 212 B1
Šyliai (LT) 168 C3
Sylling (N) 139 E3
Sylt-Ost (D) 78 A1
Syltefjord (N) 125 F1
Sými (Nisí) (GR) 228 B1
Sými (Nisí) (GR) 228 B1
Synod Inn (GB) 32 A4
Synpniewo Mazowieckie (PL) 190 B1
Syre (GB) 27 E1
Syrianochori (CY) 230 B3
Sýrna (Nisí) (GR) 225 E3
Sýros (Nisí) (GR) 219 D3
Šyša (LT) 168 B3
Sysmä (FIN) 137 D2
Syssleback (S) 139 E1
Syötekylä (FIN) 129 E4
Sypniewo Wielkopolskie (PL) 190 B1
Syre (GB) 27 E1
Syväjärvi (FIN) 129 D2
Syvde (N) 130 A4
Syvdsnes (N) 130 A4

Sývota (GR) 210 C2
Sývros (GR) 211 D4
Syyspohja (FIN) 137 F2
Szadek (PL) 189 D4
Szałas (PL) 195 F2
Szamocin (PL) 187 F1
Szamotuły (PL) 187 E2
Szarvas (H) 113 E1
Szastarka (PL) 197 D3
Szczakowa (PL) 195 D4
Szczaniec (PL) 187 D3
Szczawin Kościelny (PL) 189 E3
Szczawne (PL) 202 B3
Szczawnica (PL) 201 B3
Szczawno-Zdrój (PL) 193 E3
Szczebrzeszyn (PL) 197 E3
Szczecin (PL) 180 B4
Szczecinek (PL) 181 E3
Szczekociny (PL) 195 D2
Szczerców (PL) 195 D2
Szczucin (PL) 196 B4
Szczuczyn (PL) 185 D3
Szczurowa (PL) 201 B1
Szczyrk (PL) 200 E4
Szczytna (PL) 193 E4
Szczytniki (PL) 194 C4
Szczytno (PL) 184 B3
Szécsény (H) 112 B1
Szeged (H) 113 E3
Székesfehérvár (H) 112 B1
Szekszárd (H) 112 C3

Szeligi (PL) 185 D3
Szelków Stary (PL) 190 B1
Szemud (PL) 182 C1
Szentendre (H) 12 B2
Szepietowo (PL) 191 D1
Szerzyny (PL) 201 C3
Szigetvár (H) 112 B4
Szklarska Poręba (PL) 192 C3
Szlichtyngowa (PL) 187 E3
Szolnok (H) 113 D1
Szombathely (H) 95 F3
Szprotawa (PL) 192 C1
Sztabin (PL) 185 E2
Sztum (PL) 183 D3
Sztutowo (PL) 183 D2
Szubin (PL) 188 B1
Szudziałowo (PL) 185 E3
Szumowo (PL) 190 C1
Szydłów (PL) 196 B3
Szydłowiec (PL) 196 B2
Szydłowo Wielkopolskie (PL) 187 E1
Szymbark Małopolskie (PL) 201 C3
Szypliszki (PL) 185 E2

T

Taadikvere (EST) 154 B2
Taagepera (EST) 159 F1

Tääksi (EST) 154 B3
Taali (EST) 153 C3
Tabalenka (LT) 176 C3
Tabanovce (MK) 122 B2
Tábara (E) 63 F2
Tabariškės (LT) 177 F3
Tabasalu (EST) 149 D3
Taberg (S) 143 E2
Tabernas (E) 77 D3
Tabivere (EST) 155 D3
Taboada (E) 58 C3
Tábor (CZ) 90 B4
Tábua (P) 62 C4
Tabuaço (P) 63 D3
Tabuenca (E) 65 E2
Täby (S) 141 D4
Tachov (CZ) 89 E3
Tadaiki (LV) 162 C2
Tadaiķu Skola (LV) 162 C2
Tadcaster (GB) 33 E2
Taebla (EST) 148 C4
Taevaskoja (EST) 155 D4
Tafalla (E) 54 A4
Tafjord (N) 130 B4
Tagadi (EST) 149 E3
Tagaküla (EST) 161 D1
Tagametsa (EST) 149 D3
Tagavere (EST) 152 C3
Taggia (I) 53 F4
Tagliacozzo (I) 105 D1
Taglio di Po (I) 98 B4

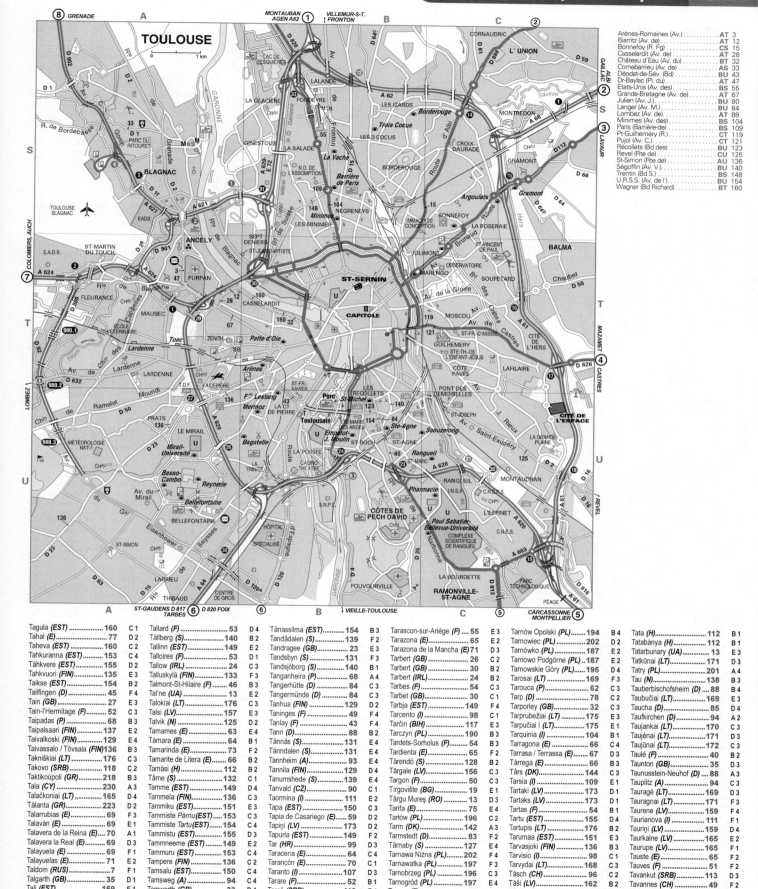

TOULOUSE

Arènes-Romaines (Av.)	AT	3	
Biarritz (Av. de)	AT	12	
Bonnefoy (R. Fg)	CS	15	
Casselardit (Av. de)	AT	28	
Château d'Eau (Av. du)	BT	32	
Cornebarrieu (Av. de)	AS	33	
Déodat-de-Sév. (Bd)	BU	43	
Dr-Baylac (Pl. du)	AT	47	
Etats-Unis (Av. des)	BS	55	
Grande-Bretagne (Av. de)	AT	67	
Julien (Av. J.)	BU	80	
Langer (Av. M.)	BU	84	
Lombez (Av. de)	AT	88	
Minimes (Av. des)	BS	104	
Paris (Barrière-de)	BS	109	
Pt-Guilhemery (R.)	CT	119	
Pujol (Av. C.)	CT	121	
Récollets (Bd des)	BU	123	
Revel (Rte de)	CU	125	
St-Simon (Rte de)	AU	136	
Ségoffin (Av. V.)	BU	140	
Trentin (Bd S.)	BS	148	
U.R.S.S. (Av. de l')	BU	154	
Wagner (Bd Richard)	BT	160	

Name	No.	Grid		Name	No.	Grid		Name	No.	Grid		Name	No.	Grid		Name	No.	Grid		Name	No.	Grid
Tagula (EST)	160	C 1		Tallard (F)	53	D 4		Tänassilma (EST)	154	B 3		Tarascon-sur-Ariège (F)	55	E 3		Tarnów Opolski (PL)	194	B 4		Tata (H)	112	B 1
Tahal (E)	77	D 2		Tällberg (S)	140	B 2		Tandådalen (S)	139	F 2		Tarazona (E)	65	E 2		Tarnowiec (PL)	202	D 2		Tatabánya (H)	112	B 1
Taheva (EST)	160	C 2		Tallinn (EST)	149	E 2		Tandragee (GB)	23	E 2		Tarazona de la Mancha (E)	71	D 3		Tarnówko (PL)	187	E 2		Tatarbunary (UA)	13	E 3
Tahkuranna (EST)	153	C 4		Talloires (F)	53	D 1		Tandsbyn (S)	131	F 3		Tarbert (E)	26	C 2		Tarnowo Podgórne (PL)	187	D 4		Tatkūnai (LT)	171	D 3
Tähkvere (EST)	155	D 2		Tallow (IRL)	24	C 3		Tandsjöborg (S)	140	B 1		Tarbert (GB)	30	B 2		Tarnowskie Góry (PL)	195	D 4		Tatry (PL)	201	A 4
Tahkvuori (FIN)	135	E 3		Talluskylä (FIN)	133	F 3		Tanganheira (P)	68	A 4		Tarbert (IRL)	24	B 2		Tarosai (F)	169	F 3		Tau (N)	138	B 3
Taikse (EST)	154	B 2		Talmont-St-Hilaire (F)	46	B 3		Tangerhütte (D)	84	C 3		Tarbes (F)	54	C 3		Tarouca (P)	62	D 1		Tauberbischofsheim (D)	88	B 4
Tailfingen (D)	45	F 4		Tal'ne (UA)	13	E 2		Tangermünde (D)	84	C 3		Tarbet (GB)	30	C 1		Tarp (D)	78	C 2		Taubučiai (LT)	169	E 3
Tain (GB)	27	E 3		Talokiai (LT)	176	D 3		Tanhua (FIN)	129	D 2		Tarbja (EST)	149	F 4		Tarporley (GB)	32	C 3		Taucha (D)	85	D 4
Tain-l'Hermitage (F)	52	C 3		Talsi (LV)	157	E 3		Taninges (F)	49	F 4		Tarcento (I)	98	C 1		Tarprubežiai (LT)	175	E 1		Taufkirchen (D)	94	A 2
Taipadas (P)	68	B 3		Talvik (N)	125	D 2		Tanlay (F)	43	F 4		Tarčin (BIH)	117	E 3		Tarpučiai I (LT)	175	E 1		Taujankai (LT)	170	C 3
Taipalsaari (FIN)	137	E 2		Tamames (E)	63	E 4		Tann (D)	88	B 2		Tarczyn (PL)	190	B 3		Tarquinia (I)	104	B 1		Taujėnai (LT)	171	D 3
Taivalkoski (FIN)	129	E 4		Támara (E)	64	B 1		Tännäs (S)	131	E 4		Tardets-Sorholus (F)	54	B 3		Tarragona (E)	66	C 3		Taujūnai (LT)	172	C 3
Taivassalo / Tövsala (FIN)	136	B 3		Tamarinda (E)	73	F 2		Tänndalen (S)	131	E 4		Tardienta (E)	65	F 2		Tarrasa / Terrassa (E)	67	D 3		Taulé (F)	40	B 2
Taknišķiai (LT)	176	C 3		Tamarite de Litera (E)	66	C 2		Tannheim (A)	93	E 4		Tärendö (S)	128	B 2		Tàrrega (E)	66	B 3		Taunton (GB)	35	D 3
Takovo (SRB)	118	C 2		Tamási (H)	112	B 2		Tannila (FIN)	129	D 4		Targon (F)	50	A 4		Tårs (DK)	144	C 3		Taunusstein-Neuhof (D)	88	A 3
Taktikoúpoli (GR)	218	B 3		Tâme (S)	132	C 1		Tanumshede (S)	139	E 3		Tirgoviște (BG)	19	E 1		Tarsia (I)	109	E 1		Tauplitz (A)	94	C 3
Tala (CY)	230	A 3		Tamme (EST)	149	E 3		Tanvald (CZ)	90	C 1		Târgu Mureş (RO)	13	D 3		Tartaki (LV)	173	D 1		Tauragė (LT)	169	D 3
Talačkoniai (LT)	165	D 4		Tammela (FIN)	136	C 3		Taormina (I)	111	E 2		Tapa (EST)	150	C 3		Tartaks (LV)	173	D 1		Tauragnai (LT)	171	F 3
Tálanta (GR)	223	F 2		Tammiku (EST)	151	E 3		Tapia de Casariego (E)	59	D 2		Tarifa (E)	75	E 4		Tartas (F)	54	B 1		Taurene (LV)	159	F 4
Talarrubias (E)	69	F 3		Tammiste Pärnu (EST)	153	C 4		Tapiņi (LV)	173	D 2		Tarłów (PL)	196	C 2		Tartu (EST)	155	D 2		Taurianova (I)	111	F 1
Talaván (E)	69	E 1		Tammiste Tartu (EST)	154	C 4		Tapiņi (LV)	173	D 2		Tarm (DK)	142	A 3		Tartupis (LT)	176	E 1		Tauriņi (LV)	159	D 4
Talavera de la Reina (E)	70	A 1		Tamminstu (EST)	155	D 3		Tapurla (EST)	149	F 2		Tarmstedt (D)	83	F 2		Tarumaa (EST)	151	E 3		Taurkalne (LV)	165	E 2
Talavera la Real (E)	69	D 3		Tammneeme (EST)	149	E 2		Tar (HR)	99	D 3		Tärnaby (S)	127	E 4		Tarvasjoki (FIN)	136	B 3		Taurupe (LV)	165	F 1
Talayuela (E)	69	F 1		Tammuru (EST)	153	C 4		Taracena (E)	64	C 4		Tarnawa Niżna (PL)	202	F 4		Tarvisio (I)	98	C 1		Tauste (E)	65	F 2
Talayuelas (E)	71	E 2		Tampere (FIN)	136	C 2		Tarancón (E)	70	C 1		Tarnawatka (PL)	197	D 3		Tarvydai (LT)	168	C 3		Tauves (F)	51	F 2
Taldom (RUS)	7	F 1		Tamsalu (EST)	150	D 3		Taranto (I)	107	D 3		Tarnobrzeg (PL)	196	C 2		Täsch (CH)	96	C 2		Tavankut (SRB)	113	C 3
Talgarth (GB)	35	D 1		Tamsweg (A)	94	C 4		Tarare (F)	52	B 1		Tarnogród (PL)	197	D 3		Tăşi (LV)	162	B 2		Tavannes (CH)	49	F 2
Tali (EST)	159	C 4		Tamworth (GB)	33	D 4		Taraš (SRB)	113	C 4		Tarnos (F)	54	A 2		Tåsjö (S)	132	A 2		Tavarnelle Val di Pesa (I)	101	F 2
Talla (I)	102	A 2		Tana (N)	125	F 2		Tarašča (UA)	13	E 1		Tarnów Lubuskie (PL)	186	C 1		Tassin-la-Demi-Lune (F)	52	B 1		Tavastila (FIN)	137	E 3
Tallante (E)	77	E 2		Tanágra (GR)	218	B 1		Tarascon (F)	56	B 2		Tarnów Małopolskie (PL)	201	C 2		Tåstrup (DK)	143	D 4		Tavaux (F)	49	D 3

Taverna (I) 109 E2
Tavernelle (I) 102 A3
Tavernes (F) 57 D2
Tavernes de la Valldigna (E) 72 A3
Tavira (P) 74 C2
Tavistock (GB) 34 C3
Tavşanlı (TR) 19 F2
Taxenbach (A) 94 B4
Taxiárchis (GR) 206 C4
Tayinloan (GB) 30 B2
Taynuilt (GB) 30 B1
Tayport (GB) 31 D1
Tazones (E) 59 F2
Tczew (PL) 182 C2
Tczów (PL) 196 C2
Teano (I) 105 E3
Teba (E) 75 F2
Tebay (GB) 32 C1
Tēcēni (LV) 159 F1
Techendorf (A) 98 C1
Tecklenburg (D) 83 E4
Tecuci (RO) 13 E3
Teedla (EST) 154 C4
Teenuse (EST) 149 D4
Teeriranta (FIN) 129 E4
Teféli (GR) 227 D3
Tegéa (GR) 217 E3
Tegelen (NL) 87 D1
Tegernsee (D) 94 A3
Teggiano (I) 106 B4
Teiberiai (LT) 175 E2
Teignmouth (GB) 35 D3
Teijo (FIN) 136 C4
Teisendorf (D) 94 B3
Teisko (FIN) 136 C2
Teixeiro (E) 58 C2
Teixoso (P) 62 C4
Teizai (LT) 175 F3
Teizininkai (LT) 175 F3
Tekeriš (SRB) 118 A2
Tekija (SRB) 119 E1
Tekirdağ (TR) 19 E1
Teļakolni (LV) 167 F2
Telatyn (PL) 197 F3
Telavåg (N) 138 B2
Telč (CZ) 90 A1
Télendos (Nisí) (GR) 221 E4
Telese (I) 105 F3
Telford (GB) 32 C4
Telfs (A) 93 F4
Telgte (D) 83 E4
Tellingstedt (D) 78 C2
Telšiai (LT) 163 D4
Telti (I) 108 B1
Teltow (D) 85 D3
Tembleque (E) 70 B2
Temerin (SRB) 113 E4
Temmes (FIN) 133 E1
Témpi (GR) 212 B1
Tempio Pausania (I) 108 B1
Templemore / An Teampall Mór (IRL) 25 D2
Templin (D) 85 E1
Temse (B) 39 E1
Temska (SRB) 119 E3
Temvria (CY) 230 B3
Tenala / Tenhola (FIN) 136 C4
Tenbury Wells (GB) 32 C4
Tenby / Dinbych-y-pysgod (GB) 34 C1
Tence (F) 52 B2
Tende (F) 53 F4
Tendilla (E) 64 C2
Teneniai (LT) 168 C2
Tenja (HR) 112 C4
Tennes (N) 124 B3
Tensta (S) 141 D3
Tenterden (GB) 36 C4
Teolo (I) 98 A3
Teovo (MK) 122 B3
Tepasto (FIN) 125 D4
Tepelenë (AL) 18 E2
Teplá (CZ) 89 F3
Teplice (CZ) 89 F2
Teplice (CZ) 89 F2
Tepsa (FIN) 128 C2
Ter Apel (NL) 83 D2
Teramo (I) 102 C4
Terebovlja (UA) 13 D2
Terena (P) 68 C3
Teresin (PL) 189 F3
Terespol (PL) 191 F3
Tereszpol-Zaorenda (PL) 197 E3
Terezino Polje (HR) 112 C4
Tergnier (F) 39 D4
Terjärv (FIN) 133 D3
Terlizzi (I) 106 C2

Termas de Monfortinho (P) 69 D1
Terme Luigiane (I) 109 D1
Termini Imerese (I) 110 C2
Terminillo (I) 102 C4
Termoli (I) 103 E4
Terneuzen (NL) 39 E1
Terni (I) 102 B4
Ternitz (A) 95 E2
Ternopil' (UA) 13 D2
Térovo (GR) 211 D2
Terpní (GR) 206 C2
Terpsithéa (GR) 211 D2
Térpyllos (GR) 206 B2
Terracina (I) 105 D3
Terråk (N) 131 E1
Terralba (I) 108 A3
Terranova di Pollino (I) 106 C4
Terranuova Bracciolini (I) 102 A2
Terras de Bouro (P) 62 C2
Terrassa / Tarrasa (E) 67 D3
Terrasson-Lavilledieu (F) 51 D2
Terrenoire (F) 52 B2
Terriente (E) 71 E1
Teruel (E) 71 E1
Tervakoski (FIN) 136 C3
Tervete (LV) 163 F2
Tervo (FIN) 133 F3
Tervola (FIN) 128 C4
Tervuren (B) 39 E2
Terzaga (E) 65 E4
Tešani (BIH) 115 F4
Teslić (BIH) 115 F4
Tessin (D) 79 F3
Tessy-sur-Vire (F) 41 F2
Tetbury (GB) 35 E1
Tetele (LV) 164 C2
Teténai (LT) 177 E3
Teterow (D) 79 F4
Tetiïv (UA) 13 E1
Tetovo (MK) 122 A2
Tetrákomo (GR) 211 E2
Tettnang (D) 93 D3
Teuchern (D) 89 D1
Teufen (CH) 93 D4
Teulada (I) 108 B4
Teupitz (D) 85 E3
Teuva (FIN) 133 D4
Tewkesbury (GB) 35 E1
Tezze (I) 98 B2
Thale (D) 84 B4
Thalfang (D) 45 D1
Thalgau (A) 94 B3
Thalheim (D) 89 E2
Thalmässing (D) 93 F1
Thalwil (CH) 92 C4
Thame (GB) 35 F1
Thann (F) 49 F1
Thannhausen (D) 93 E4
Thaon-les-Vosges (F) 44 C4
Tharandt (D) 89 F1
Tharsis (E) 74 C1
Thásos (GR) 207 F3
Thásos (Nisí) (GR) 207 F3
The Mumbles (GB) 34 C1
Themar (D) 88 C2
Thénezay (F) 47 D3
Thenon (F) 51 D2
Theológos Fthiótida (GR) 212 C4
Theológos Kavála (GR) 207 F3
Théoule-sur-Mer (F) 57 E2
Thermá (GR) 207 D2
Thérma Évros (GR) 208 B3
Thérma Sámos (GR) 220 C3
Thérma Lefkádas (GR) 220 C3
Thermí (GR) 215 D3
Thérmi (GR) 206 C3
Thermisía (GR) 218 B3
Thérmo (GR) 211 E2
Thermopýles (GR) 212 B4
Thérouanne (F) 38 C2
Thespiés (GR) 218 B1
Thesprotikó (GR) 211 D3
Thessaloníki (GR) 206 B3
Thetford (GB) 33 F4
Theux (B) 87 D3
Thèze (F) 54 B2
Thiaucourt-Regniéville (F) 44 C3
Thiberville (F) 42 B3
Thiéblemont-Farémont (F) 44 A3
Thiendorf (D) 85 E4
Thiene (I) 98 A3
Thiers (F) 52 A1
Thiesi (I) 108 A2
Thiessow (D) 80 A2
Thionville (F) 44 C2
Thíra (GR) 224 C3
Thíra (Nisí) (GR) 224 C3

Thirasía (Nisí) (GR) 224 C3
Thirsk (GB) 33 D1
Thisted (DK) 142 B2
Thíva (GR) 218 B1
Thiviers (F) 51 D2
Thizy (F) 48 C4
Thoissey (F) 49 D4
Tholey (D) 45 D2
Thollon-les-Mémises (F) 49 F4
Tholó (GR) 217 D2
Tholopotámi (GR) 220 C1
Tholós (GR) 207 D2
Thomastown / Baile Mhic Andáin (IRL) 25 D3
Thônes (F) 53 D1
Thonon-les-Bains (F) 49 E4
Thorens-Glières (F) 49 E4
Thorikó (GR) 218 C2
Thorne (GB) 33 E2
Thornhill (GB) 30 C3
Thouarcé (F) 46 C2
Thouars (F) 47 D3
Thouría (GR) 217 E4
Thoúrio (GR) 209 D1
Thrapston (GB) 33 E4
Threshfield (GB) 33 D1
Thueyts (F) 52 B3
Thuin (B) 39 E3
Thuir (F) 55 F4
Thum (D) 89 F2
Thun (CH) 96 B1
Thüringen (A) 93 D4
Thurles / Durlas (IRL) 25 D2
Thursby (GB) 31 D4
Thurso (GB) 27 F1
Thury-Harcourt (F) 41 F2
Thusis (CH) 97 D1
Thyborøn (DK) 142 A2
Thýmaina (GR) 221 D3
Thýmaina (Nisí) (GR) 221 D3
Thymariá (GR) 208 C2
Tibro (S) 143 E1
Tidö (S) 140 C4
Tiefenbronn (D) 45 F3
Tiefencastel (CH) 97 E1
Tiefensee (D) 85 E2
Tiegaži (LV) 159 D2
Tiel (NL) 82 B4
Tielt (B) 39 D2
Tienen (B) 39 E2
Tiengen (D) 92 C4
Tiercé (F) 41 F4
Tierga (E) 65 E3
Tierp (S) 141 D3
Tigharry (GB) 26 B3
Tighnabruaich (GB) 30 B2
Tigkáki (GR) 225 F2
Tignes (F) 53 E2
Tiheda (EST) 155 D2
Tihemetsa (EST) 154 A4
Tiidu (EST) 160 C1
Tiistenjoki (FIN) 133 D3
Tíjola (E) 77 D2
Tikaiņi (LV) 167 D1
Tikkakoski (FIN) 133 F4
Tikkala (FIN) 135 F4
Tilburg (NL) 39 F1
Tilbury (GB) 36 C3
Tilga (EST) 154 C3
Tillberga (S) 140 C3
Tillières-sur-Avre (F) 42 B2
Tilly-sur-Seulles (F) 41 F2
Tílos (Nisí) (GR) 228 A2
Tilsi (EST) 161 D1
Tilsit (RUS) 6 B3
Tiltai (LT) 177 D2
Tilvikai (LT) 168 C1
Tilža (Tilža) (LV) 167 E1
Tilžė Šiaulių (LT) 163 E4
Tilžė Utenos (LT) 173 D2
Timi (CY) 230 A4
Timişoara (RO) 113 D3
Timmendorfer Strand (D) 79 D3
Timoleague (IRL) 24 C4
Timrå (S) 132 A2
Tinahely (IRL) 25 E2
Tinchebray (F) 41 F2
Tineo (E) 59 D2
Tíngere (LV) 157 E3
Tinglev (DK) 144 B3
Tingsryd (S) 143 E3
Tingvoll (N) 130 C3
Tinnikuru (EST) 154 B4
Tinnoset (N) 139 D1
Tinos (GR) 219 E3
Tínos (Nisí) (GR) 219 E3
Tiñosillos (E) 64 A4

Tintagel (GB) 34 B3
Tinténiac (F) 41 E3
Tiņūži (LV) 165 D1
Tione di Trento (I) 97 F2
Tipasoja (FIN) 135 E2
Tipperary / Tiobraid Árann (IRL) 24 C2
Tipu (EST) 154 A4
Tiranë (AL) 121 F4
Tirano (I) 97 E2
Tiraspol (MD) 13 E3
Tire (TR) 19 F3
Tireļi (LV) 164 B1
Tîrgovişte (RO) 13 D4
Tirgu Frumos (RO) 13 D3
Tirgu-Neamţ (RO) 13 D3
Tirgu Secuiesc (RO) 13 D3
Tirig (E) 72 A1
Tiriolo (I) 109 E2
Tirkšliai (LT) 163 D3
Tírnavos (GR) 212 A1
Tirrenia (I) 101 E2
Tirschenreuth (D) 89 E3
Tirstrup (DK) 142 C3
Tirumi (LV) 157 D2
Tíryntha (GR) 217 F3
Tirza (LV) 160 C4
Tįsaičiai (LT) 167 E2
Tiskadi (Ciskodi) (LV) 167 D3
Tiškai (LT) 163 D3
Tiskre (EST) 149 D2
Tisno (HR) 103 E1
Tišnov (CZ) 91 D3
Tisvildeleje (DK) 143 D3
Tiszaföldvár (H) 12 B3
Tiszavasvári (H) 12 B3
Titaguas (E) 71 F2
Titel (SRB) 113 E4
Titisee (D) 45 E4
Titkoniai (LT) 165 D4
Tito (I) 106 B3
Titoniai (LT) 164 C4
Titran (N) 130 C2
Tittmoning (D) 94 B2
Tivat (MNE) 121 D2
Tivenys (E) 66 B4
Tiverton (GB) 35 D3
Tivissa (E) 66 B4
Tivoli (I) 105 D2
Tjällmo (S) 140 B4
Tjeldstø (N) 138 B2
Tjentište (BIH) 117 F4
Tjøme (N) 139 E4
Tjong (N) 127 D3
Tjørnuvik (DK) 126 A4
Tjøtta (N) 127 D4
Tkon (HR) 103 E1
Tługowo (PL) 189 D2
Tłumaczów (PL) 193 E4
Tłuszcz (PL) 190 C2
Tobarra (E) 71 E4
Tobermore (GB) 23 E2
Tobermory (GB) 26 C4
Toberonochy (GB) 30 B1
Tocha (P) 62 B4
Tochni (CY) 231 C4
Tocina (E) 75 E1
Todi (I) 102 B4
Todmorden (GB) 33 D2
Todoriči (BIH) 117 D3
Todtmoos (D) 92 B3
Todtnau (D) 92 B3
Tõdva (EST) 149 E3
Toft (GB) 29 F1
Tofte (N) 139 E3
Toftir (DK) 126 A4
Toftlund (DK) 142 B4
Tohmajärvi (FIN) 135 F3
Toholampi (FIN) 133 E2
Tohvri (EST) 154 B4
Toichío (GR) 205 F3
Toijala (FIN) 136 C3
Toila (EST) 151 D2
Toivakka (FIN) 133 F4
Toivala (FIN) 135 E3
Tojšici (BIH) 117 F2
Tokaj (H) 12 B3
Tokamia Świętokrzyskie (PL) 195 F4
Toledo (E) 70 B1
Tolentino (I) 102 C3
Tolfa (I) 104 C1
Tolg (S) 143 E2
Tolga (N) 131 D4
Tolkmicko (PL) 183 D2
Tõlla (EST) 154 A4
Tollarp (S) 143 E4

Tõlliste (EST) 160 C1
Tølløse (DK) 142 C4
Tolmezzo (I) 98 C1
Tolmin (SLO) 98 C1
Toló (GR) 217 F3
Tolosa (E) 61 D3
Tolosa (P) 68 C2
Tolox (E) 75 F3
Tolva (FIN) 129 E3
Tolve (I) 106 C3
Tomakaimis (LT) 171 D1
Tomar (P) 68 B1
Tomaševac (SRB) 113 E4
Tomašica (BIH) 115 E4
Tomaszów Lubelski (PL) 197 F4
Tomaszów Mazowiecki (PL) 195 E1
Tomaszowice (PL) 197 D2
Tombebœuf (F) 50 C4
Tome (LV) 165 D2
Tomelilla (E) 143 E4
Tomelloso (E) 70 C3
Tomice (PL) 200 F2
Tomiño (E) 58 A4
Tomintoul (GB) 27 F4
Tomislavgrad (BIH) 117 D4
Tømmervåg (N) 130 B3
Tomra (N) 130 B3
Tona (E) 67 D2
Tonara (I) 108 B3
Tonbridge (GB) 36 C4
Tondela (P) 62 C4
Tønder (DK) 144 C2
Tongeren (B) 39 F2
Tongue (GB) 27 E1
Tonnay-Boutonne (F) 46 C4
Tonnay-Charente (F) 46 C4
Tonneins (F) 50 C4
Tonnerre (F) 43 D4
Tönning (D) 78 B3
Tønsberg (N) 139 E4
Tonstad (N) 138 C2
Toomja (EST) 149 E4
Tooste (EST) 155 E4
Tootsi (EST) 153 C4
Töpen (D) 89 D2
Topeno (FIN) 136 C3
Topla (SLO) 99 E1
Topli Dol (SRB) 119 F3
Topliţa (RO) 13 D3
T'oplou (RUS) 7 F3
Topola (SRB) 118 C2
Topólka (PL) 188 C2
Topolčani (MK) 122 B4
Topolčany (SK) 12 A2
Topólia (GR) 226 B2
Topolovnik (SRB) 119 D1
Topusko (HR) 99 F2
Torà (E) 66 C2
Torano Castello (I) 109 E1
Töravere (EST) 154 C4
Torbole (I) 97 F2
Torcello (I) 98 B3
Torchiarolo (I) 107 E3
Torcy (F) 43 D2
Tordera (E) 67 D3
Tordesillas (E) 64 A2
Tordesilos (E) 65 E4
Tore (GB) 27 E3
Töre (S) 128 B4
Töreboda (S) 140 B4
Toreno (E) 59 D3
Torgau (D) 85 D4
Torgelow (D) 80 C2
Torhout (B) 37 F4
Tori (EST) 153 C4
Torigni-sur-Vire (F) 41 F2
Torija (E) 64 C2
Torino (I) 53 F2
Torla (E) 54 C4
Torma (EST) 155 D2
Törma (EST) 151 D3

Torpoint (GB) 34 C4
Torpshammar (S) 132 A4
Torquay (GB) 35 D3
Torquemada (E) 64 C1
Torralba de Calatrava (E) 70 B3
Torrão (P) 68 B4
Torre Annunziata (I) 105 F3
Torre Beretti e Castellaro (I) 97 D4
Torre Canne (I) 107 E3
Torre de Dom Chama (P) 63 D2
Torre de Juan Abad (E) 70 C4
Torre de la Higuera (E) 75 D2
Torre de Moncorvo (P) 63 D3
Torre de' Passeri (I) 103 D4
Torre del Bierzo (E) 59 D4
Torre del Campo (E) 76 B1
Torre del Greco (I) 105 F3
Torre del Mar (E) 76 A3
Torre dell'Impiso (I) 110 B2
Torre Faro (I) 111 E1
Torre la Cárcel (E) 65 E4
Torre Orsaia (I) 106 B4
Torre Pacheco (E) 77 F2
Torre Pellice (I) 53 E3
Torrebaja (E) 71 E1
Torreblanca (E) 72 A1
Torrecaballeros (E) 64 B3
Torrecampo (E) 70 A4
Torrecilla en Cameros (E) 65 D1
Torrecillas de la Tiesa (E) 69 F2
Torredembarra (E) 66 C4
Torredonjimeno (E) 76 B1
Torregrossa (E) 66 B3
Torreira (P) 62 B3
Torrejón de Ardoz (E) 64 B3
Torrejón de la Calzada (E) 70 B1
Torrejón el Rubio (E) 69 E1
Torrejoncillo (E) 69 E1
Torrejoncillo del Rey (E) 71 D1
Torrelaguna (E) 64 C4
Torrelapaja (E) 65 E3
Torrelavega (E) 60 A3
Torrellano (E) 71 F4
Torrelobatón (E) 64 A2
Torrelodones (E) 64 B4
Torremaggiore (I) 106 B2
Torremegía (E) 69 E3
Torremocha (E) 69 E2
Torremolinos (E) 76 A3
Torrent (E) 71 F3
Torrente de Cinca (E) 66 A3
Torrenueva (E) 70 B4
Torreperogil (E) 76 B1
Torres del Río (E) 60 C4
Torres Novas (P) 68 B1
Torres Vedras (P) 68 A2
Torrevieja (E) 77 F1
Torri del Benaco (I) 97 F3
Torridon (GB) 27 D3
Torriglia (I) 101 D2
Torrijas (E) 71 F1
Torrijo (E) 65 E3
Torrijos (E) 70 A1
Tørring (DK) 142 B4
Torrita di Siena (I) 102 A3
Torroella de Montgrí (E) 67 E2
Torrox (E) 76 A3
Torsås (S) 143 F3
Torsby (S) 139 E1
Torshälla (S) 140 C4
Torshavn (DK) 126 A4
Torsminde (DK) 142 B2
Tórtoles de Esgueva (E) 64 B2
Tortoli (I) 108 C3
Tortona (I) 97 D4
Tortorici (I) 111 D2
Tortosa (E) 66 B4
Tortosendo (P) 62 B4
Toruń (PL) 188 C1
Torup (S) 143 D2
Tõrva (EST) 160 B1
Tõrvandi (EST) 155 D4
Tørvikbygd (N) 138 C2
Toržok (RUS) 7 F1
Torzym (PL) 186 C3
Tosbotn (N) 131 E1
Toscolano-Maderno (I) 97 F3
Tosno (RUS) 7 D1
Tossa de Mar (E) 67 D3
Tõstamaa (EST) 153 B4
Tostedt (D) 84 A2
Toszek (PL) 194 C2
Totana (E) 77 E1
Tôtes (F) 38 B4
Tøtlandsvik (N) 138 B3

Totnes *(GB)* 34 C 4
Toucy *(F)* 43 E 4
Toul *(F)* 44 C 3
Toulon *(F)* 57 D 3
Toulon-sur-Arroux *(F)* 48 C 3
Toulouse *(F)* 55 E 2
Toumpítsi *(GR)* 217 D 3
Tourcoing *(F)* 39 D 2
Tourlida *(GR)* 216 C 1
Tournai *(B)* 39 D 2
Tournan-en-Brie *(F)* 43 D 2
Tournay *(F)* 54 C 3
Tournon-d'Agenais *(F)* 51 D 4
Tournon-St-Martin *(F)* 47 E 3
Tournon-sur-Rhône *(F)* 52 C 3
Tournus *(F)* 49 D 3
Tourouvre *(F)* 42 B 3
Tours *(F)* 47 E 2
Toury *(F)* 42 C 3
Tõusi *(EST)* 153 B 3
Toužim *(CZ)* 89 F 3
Tovariševo *(SRB)* 113 D 4
Tovarnik *(HR)* 117 F 1
Towcester *(GB)* 35 F 1
Töysä *(FIN)* 133 E 4
Tožas *(LV)* 159 F 2
Trabanca *(E)* 63 E 3
Trabazos *(E)* 63 E 2
Traben-Trarbach *(D)* 45 D 1
Trabia *(I)* 110 C 2
Trąbki *(PL)* 201 A 2
Trąbki Wielkie *(PL)* 182 C 2
Trabotivište *(MK)* 122 C 2
Tracheiá *(GR)* 218 B 3
Trachíli *(GR)* 218 C 1
Trachonas *(CY)* 231 C 2
Trachoni *(CY)* 230 B 2
Tracino *(I)* 111 F 4
Trafaria *(P)* 68 A 3
Trafoi *(I)* 97 F 1
Tragacete *(E)* 71 E 1
Traiguera *(E)* 72 A 1
Traisen *(A)* 95 E 2
Traiskirchen *(A)* 95 F 2
Traismauer *(A)* 95 E 1
Trakai *(LT)* 177 E 2
Trakiškiai *Kalvarija(LT)* 175 F 3
Trakiškiai
Marijambolė(LT) 175 F 2
Trakiškis *(LT)* 171 D 2
Trakošćan *(HR)* 99 F 1
Traksėdis *(LT)* 169 D 2
Tralee / Trá Lí *(IRL)* 24 B 3
Tramagal *(P)* 68 B 2
Tramariglio *(I)* 108 A 2
Tramatza *(I)* 108 A 3
Tramonti di Sopra *(I)* 98 B 1
Tramore / Trá Mhór *(IRL)* 25 D 3
Trăn *(BG)* 18 C 1
Tranås *(S)* 143 E 1
Trancoso *(P)* 63 D 3
Tranebjerg *(DK)* 142 C 4
Tranemo *(S)* 143 D 2
Tranent *(GB)* 31 D 2
Trani *(I)* 106 C 2
Tranóvalto *(GR)* 205 F 4
Transtrand *(S)* 140 A 2
Trapani *(I)* 110 A 2
Trapene *(LV)* 161 D 3
Trápeza *(GR)* 217 E 1
Trappstadt *(D)* 88 C 3
Trasacco *(I)* 105 E 1
Trassem *(D)* 44 C 2
Traun *(A)* 94 C 2
Traunkirchen *(A)* 94 C 3
Traunreut *(D)* 94 A 3
Traunstein *(D)* 94 B 3
Traupis *(LT)* 171 D 2
Travemünde *(D)* 79 D 3
Travnik *(BIH)* 117 E 3
Trawniki *(PL)* 197 E 2
Trbovlje *(SLO)* 99 E 1
Trbuk *(BIH)* 115 F 4
Trbušani *(SRB)* 118 C 3
Trebbin *(D)* 85 D 3
Trébeurden *(F)* 40 C 2
Třebíč *(CZ)* 91 D 4
Trebinje *(BIH)* 120 C 2
Trebisacce *(I)* 107 D 4
Trebišnjica *(BIH)* 120 C 2
Trebišov *(SK)* 12 C 2
Trebnje *(SLO)* 99 E 2
Třeboň *(CZ)* 90 B 4
Tréboul *(F)* 40 B 3
Trebsen *(D)* 89 E 1
Trebujena *(E)* 75 E 2
Trecastagni *(I)* 111 E 3
Trecate *(I)* 97 D 3
Tredegar *(GB)* 35 D 1
Tredozio *(I)* 102 A 1
Treffort *(F)* 49 D 4
Treffurt *(D)* 88 C 1
Tregaron *(GB)* 32 B 4
Trégastel *(F)* 40 C 2
Tregnago *(I)* 98 A 3
Tregony *(GB)* 34 B 4
Tréguier *(F)* 40 C 2
Trehörningsjö *(S)* 132 B 3
Treia *(D)* 78 C 3
Treia *(I)* 102 C 2
Treignac *(F)* 51 E 2
Treimani *(EST)* 159 D 1
Treis Ekklisíes *(GR)* 227 D 3
Trekaiņi *(LV)* 165 F 2
Trelleborg *(DK)* 142 C 4
Trelleborg *(S)* 143 D 4
Trélon *(F)* 39 E 3
Tremestieri *(I)* 111 E 2
Tremetousia *(CY)* 231 D 3
Tremezzo *(I)* 97 D 2
Tremithos *(CY)* 231 D 3
Tremp *(E)* 55 D 4
Trenčín *(SK)* 12 A 2
Trendelburg *(D)* 88 B 1
Trenta *(SLO)* 98 C 1
Trento *(I)* 97 F 2
Trepča *Berane(MNE)* 121 E 1
Trepča *Kosovska*
Mitrovica(SRB) 119 D 4
Trepuzzi *(I)* 107 E 3
Trescore Balneario *(I)* 97 E 3
Tresenda *(I)* 97 E 2
Tresfjord *(N)* 130 B 4
Tresjuncos *(E)* 70 C 2
Treski *(EST)* 161 E 1
Trešnjevica *(SRB)* 119 D 2
Trespaderne *(E)* 60 B 4
Třešť *(CZ)* 90 C 4
Trets *(F)* 57 D 2
Tretten *(N)* 139 E 1
Treuchtlingen *(D)* 93 E 1
Treuen *(D)* 89 E 2
Treuenbrietzen *(D)* 85 D 3
Treungen *(N)* 139 D 4
Trevélez *(E)* 76 B 3
Trèves *(F)* 43 A 4
Trevi *(I)* 102 B 3
Trévières *(F)* 41 F 1
Treviglio *(I)* 97 E 3
Trevignano Romano *(I)* 104 C 1
Treviño *(E)* 60 C 4
Treviso *(I)* 98 B 3
Trévoux *(F)* 49 D 4
Trezzo sull'Adda *(I)* 97 E 3
Trgovište *(SRB)* 122 B 1
Trhové Sviny *(CZ)* 95 D 1
Tría Nisiá *(GR)* 225 E 3
Triánta *(GR)* 228 C 2
Triaucourt-en-Argonne *(F)* 44 B 3
Tribanj Krušćica *(HR)* 99 F 4
Triberg *(D)* 45 E 4
Tribsees *(D)* 79 F 3
Tricarico *(I)* 106 C 3
Tricase *(I)* 107 F 4
Tricesimo *(I)* 98 C 2
Trichiana *(I)* 98 B 2
Trie-sur-Baïse *(F)* 54 C 3
Trieben *(A)* 95 D 3
Trier *(D)* 44 C 1
Trieste *(I)* 99 D 2
Trifýlli *(GR)* 208 C 2
Trigueros *(E)* 75 D 1
Triigi *Lääne-Viru(EST)* 151 D 4
Triigi *Saare(EST)* 152 C 2
Trijueque *(E)* 64 C 4
Trikala *Imathía(GR)* 206 B 3
Trikala *Korinthía(GR)* 217 E 4
Trikala *Trikala(GR)* 211 F 2
Trikāta *(LV)* 159 F 2
Trikeri *(GR)* 212 C 3
Trikomo *(CY)* 231 E 2
Trilj *(HR)* 117 D 4
Trillevallen *(S)* 131 E 3
Trillo *(E)* 65 E 4
Trilofo *(GR)* 211 F 3
Trim / Baile Átha
Troim *(IRL)* 23 E 4
Trindade *(P)* 63 D 2
Třinec *(CZ)* 91 F 2
Tring *(GB)* 36 B 3
Trinità d'Agultu
e Vignola *(I)* 108 B 1
Trinitapoli *(I)* 106 C 2
Trino *(I)* 96 C 4
Triobiškiai *(LT)* 175 F 2
Triora *(I)* 53 F 4
Trípoli *(GR)* 217 E 3
Triponzo *(I)* 102 B 3
Tripótama *(GR)* 217 D 2
Triptis *(D)* 89 D 2
Triškoniai *(LT)* 164 C 4
Trittau *(D)* 79 D 4
Trittenheim *(D)* 45 D 1
Trivento *(I)* 105 F 2
Trnava *(SK)* 12 A 3
Trnova Poljana *(BIH)* 117 D 4
Trnovo *(BIH)* 117 F 4
Trnovo *(SLO)* 98 C 1
Troarn *(F)* 42 A 2
Trofa *perto de*
Felgueiras(P) 62 C 2
Trofa *perto de*
Santo Tirso(P) 62 B 2
Trofaiach *(A)* 95 D 3
Trofors *(N)* 127 D 4
Trogir *(HR)* 103 F 1
Troia *(I)* 106 B 2
Troina *(I)* 111 D 2
Trois-Ponts *(B)* 87 D 3
Troisdorf *(D)* 87 E 2
Troizina *(GR)* 218 B 3
Trojan *(BG)* 19 D 1
Trojane *(SLO)* 99 E 1
Trojanów *(PL)* 190 C 4
Trollhättan *(S)* 143 D 1
Tromsdalen *(N)* 124 B 3
Tromsø *(N)* 124 B 3
Trondheim *(N)* 131 D 3
Tronö *(S)* 140 C 1
Troo *(F)* 42 B 4
Trooditissa *(CY)* 230 B 3
Troon *(GB)* 30 C 3
Trópaia *(GR)* 217 D 2
Tropea *(I)* 111 F 1
Tropy Sztumskie *(PL)* 183 D 3
Trosa *(S)* 141 D 4
Troškas *(LV)* 166 C 2
Troškūnai *(LT)* 171 E 2
Trostberg *(D)* 94 A 2
Troulloi *(CY)* 231 D 3
Trouville-sur-Mer *(F)* 42 A 1
Trowbridge *(GB)* 35 E 2
Troyes *(F)* 43 F 3
Trpanj *(HR)* 120 B 3
Trpezi *(MNE)* 118 C 4
Trpinja *(HR)* 113 D 4
Trsa *(MNE)* 117 F 4
Tršić *(SRB)* 117 F 2
Trstenik *(HR)* 120 B 2
Trstenik *Kruševac(SRB)* 121 F 1
Trstenik *Priština(SRB)* 118 C 3
Trsteno *(HR)* 120 C 2
Trubčevsk *(RUS)* 7 F 4
Trubia *(E)* 59 E 2
Trubjela *(MNE)* 121 D 2
Truchas *(E)* 59 D 4
Truchtersheim *(F)* 45 D 3
Trūdai *(LT)* 172 C 4
Truikinai *(LT)* 162 C 3
Trujillo *(E)* 69 E 2
Trun *(F)* 42 A 2
Truro *(GB)* 34 B 4
Truskava *(LT)* 170 C 3
Trutnov *(CZ)* 90 C 1
Truva *(TR)* 19 E 2
Trybsz *(PL)* 201 A 3
Tryde *(S)* 143 E 4
Trygóna *(GR)* 211 E 1
Tryńcza *(PL)* 197 E 4
Trýpi *(GR)* 217 E 4
Trypití *Halkidikí(GR)* 207 D 4
Trypití *Irákleio(GR)* 227 D 3
Tryškiai *(LT)* 163 E 4
Tržac *(BIH)* 99 F 3
Trzcianka
Wielkopolskie(PL) 187 E 1
Trzcianne *(PL)* 185 D 4
Trzciel *(PL)* 187 D 3
Trzcinica *(PL)* 194 B 2
Trzcińsko-Zdrój *(PL)* 186 B 1
Trzebiatów *(PL)* 180 C 2
Trzebiechów
Lubuskie(PL) 187 D 3
Trzebiel *(PL)* 186 B 4
Trzebielino *(PL)* 181 F 2
Trzebieszów *(PL)* 191 D 3
Trzebieszowice *(PL)* 193 E 4
Trzebież *(PL)* 180 B 3
Trzebinia *(PL)* 200 F 1
Trzebnica *(PL)* 193 F 2
Trzebownisko *(PL)* 202 D 1
Trzemeśnia *(PL)* 201 A 2
Trzemeszno *(PL)* 188 B 2
Trześń
wiełokrzyskie(PL) 196 C 3
Tržič *(SLO)* 99 D 1
Trzyciąż *(PL)* 195 E 4
Trzydnik Duży *(PL)* 197 D 3
Tsada *(CY)* 230 A 3
Tsagkaráda *(GR)* 212 C 2
Tsakaíoi *(GR)* 219 D 1
Tsamantás *(GR)* 210 C 1
Tsangário *(GR)* 211 D 2
Tsarítsani *(GR)* 212 A 1
Tsarkasiános *(GR)* 216 B 1
Tseri *(CY)* 231 C 3
Tsirguliina *(EST)* 160 C 1
Tsolgo *(EST)* 161 E 1
Tsooru *(EST)* 161 D 2
Tsotíli *(GR)* 205 E 4
Tsoukaládes *(GR)* 211 D 4
Tsoútsouros *(GR)* 227 D 3
Tuam / Tuaim *(IRL)* 22 C 4
Tubbercurry /
Tobar an Choire *(IRL)* 22 C 3
Tubilla del Agua *(E)* 60 B 4
Tūbinės I *(LT)* 169 D 2
Tübingen *(D)* 45 F 3
Tubre / Taufers
im Münstertal *(I)* 97 F 1
Tučepi *(HR)* 120 B 1
Tuchan *(F)* 55 F 3
Tuchola *(PL)* 182 B 4
Tucholski Park
Narodowy *(PL)* 182 B 3
Tuchomie *(PL)* 181 F 2
Tuchów *(PL)* 201 C 2
Tuczno *Zachodnio-*
pomorskie(PL) 181 E 4
Tudela *(E)* 65 E 2
Tudela de Duero *(E)* 64 A 2
Tudu *(EST)* 151 D 4
Tudulinna *(EST)* 151 E 4
Tuffé *(F)* 42 B 4
Tuhalaane *(EST)* 154 B 4
Tuheljske Toplice *(HR)* 99 F 1
Tuhkakylä *(FIN)* 135 E 2
Tui *(E)* 58 B 4
Tūja *(LV)* 159 D 3
Tūjasmuiža *(LV)* 159 D 3
Tüki *(EST)* 155 D 3
Tukums *(LV)* 157 F 4
Tula *(RUS)* 7 F 3
Tulare *(SRB)* 119 D 4
Tulcea *(RO)* 13 E 4
Tul'čyn *(UA)* 13 E 2
Tuliszków *(PL)* 188 C 3
Tulla *(IRL)* 24 C 2
Tullamore /
Tulach Mhór *(IRL)* 23 D 4
Tulle *(F)* 51 E 2
Tullgarn *(S)* 141 D 4
Tullins *(F)* 52 C 2
Tulln *(A)* 95 E 1
Tullow / An Tulach *(IRL)* 25 E 2
Tulnikiai *(LT)* 163 D 3
Tułowice
Mazowieckie(PL) 189 F 3
Tułowice *Opolskie(PL)* 194 B 4
Tulpes *(LV)* 164 C 1
Tulpiakiemis *(LT)* 171 D 3
Tulppio *(FIN)* 125 F 4
Tulsk *(IRL)* 22 C 3
Tumba *(S)* 141 D 4
Tume *(LV)* 157 F 4
Tumšupe *(LV)* 159 D 4
Tuohikotti *(FIN)* 137 E 3
Tuoro sul Trasimeno *(I)* 102 A 3
Tupadły *(PL)* 188 C 2
Tuplice *(PL)* 186 B 4
Turaida *(LV)* 159 E 4
Turalići *(BIH)* 117 F 2
Turawa *(PL)* 194 B 3
Turawskie (Jezioro) *(PL)* 194 C 3
Turba *(EST)* 149 D 4
Turbe *(BIH)* 117 D 3
Turbinava *(LT)* 169 F 3
Turckheim *(F)* 45 D 4
Turda *(RO)* 12 C 3
Turégano *(E)* 64 B 3
Turek *(PL)* 188 C 3
Turenki *(FIN)* 136 C 3
Turgeliai *(LT)* 177 F 3
Turgutlu *(TR)* 19 F 3
Türi *(EST)* 154 B 2
Turi *(I)* 107 D 3
Türi-Alliku *(EST)* 154 B 2
Turija *(BIH)* 117 E 2
Turija *(SRB)* 113 E 4
Turinge *(S)* 141 D 4
Turís *(E)* 71 F 3
Türisalu *(EST)* 149 D 2
Turja *(SRB)* 119 D 1
Turjak *(SLO)* 99 E 2
Türkheim *(D)* 93 E 3
Turki *(LV)* 166 C 3
Turku / Åbo *(FIN)* 136 B 4
Turlava (Lipaiķi) *(LV)* 162 C 1
Turmantas *(LT)* 172 C 2
Turmiel *(E)* 65 D 4
Turnberry *(GB)* 30 B 3
Turnhout *(B)* 39 F 1
Türnitz *(A)* 95 E 2
Turnov *(CZ)* 90 B 1
Turnov *(CZ)* 90 B 1
Turnu Măgurele *(RO)* 13 D 4
Turobin *(PL)* 197 E 3
Turośl *Podlaskie(PL)* 184 C 4
Turowo *Warmińsko-*
Mazurskie(PL) 185 D 2
Turre *(E)* 77 D 2
Turriers *(F)* 53 D 4
Turriff *(GB)* 28 B 3
Tursi *(I)* 106 C 4
Tursučiai *(LT)* 175 F 2
Turtola *(FIN)* 128 C 3
Turzańsk *(PL)* 202 E 3
Turženai *(LT)* 170 C 4
Tuscania *(I)* 102 A 4
Tuse *(DK)* 142 C 4
Tušilović *(HR)* 99 F 2
Tusti *(EST)* 154 B 3
Tuszów Narodowy *(PL)* 196 C 4
Tuszyn *(PL)* 189 E 4
Tutajev *(RUS)* 7 F 1
Tutini *(LV)* 167 F 2
Tutrakan *(BG)* 13 E 4
Tuttlingen *(D)* 45 F 4
Tuturano *(I)* 107 E 3
Tutzing *(D)* 93 F 3
Tuudi *(EST)* 153 A 2
Tuula *(EST)* 149 D 3
Tuulos *(FIN)* 137 D 3
Tuupovaara *(FIN)* 135 F 3
Tuusniemi *(FIN)* 135 E 3
Tuusula *(FIN)* 137 D 3
Tuxford *(GB)* 32 C 2
Tuzi *(MNE)* 121 E 2
Tuzla *(BIH)* 117 E 2
Tvedestrand *(N)* 139 D 4
Tver' *(RUS)* 7 E 2
Tverai *(LT)* 169 D 1
Tverečius *(LT)* 173 D 3
Tvøroyri *(DK)* 126 A 4
Twardogóra *(PL)* 193 F 2
Twimberg *(A)* 95 D 4
Twist *(D)* 83 D 3
Twistringen *(D)* 83 D 2
Tworóg *(PL)* 194 C 4
Tycheró *(GR)* 208 C 2
Tychowo *Białogard(PL)* 181 E 3
Tychowo *Sławno(PL)* 181 E 2
Tychy *(PL)* 200 F 1
Tyczyn *(PL)* 202 D 2
Tydal *(N)* 131 D 3
Tyin *(N)* 139 D 1
Tykocin *(PL)* 185 D 4
Tyława *(PL)* 202 D 3
Tylicz *(PL)* 201 C 3
Tylisos *(GR)* 227 D 2
Tymbark *(PL)* 201 B 2
Tymfristós *(GR)* 211 F 4
Tympáki *(GR)* 226 C 3
Týmpano *(GR)* 207 F 2
Tymvou *(CY)* 231 E 3
Tyń *(PL)* 181 E 1
Týn nad Vltavou *(CZ)* 90 B 4
Tyndaris *(I)* 111 E 2
Tyndrum *(GB)* 30 C 1
Tynemouth *(GB)* 31 F 4
Tyniec *(PL)* 201 A 2
Tynkä *(FIN)* 133 E 2
Tynset *(N)* 131 D 4
Tyrawa Wołoska *(PL)* 202 E 3
Tyresö *(S)* 141 D 4
Tyringe *(S)* 143 E 3
Tyristrand *(N)* 139 E 3
Tyrnävä *(FIN)* 133 E 1
Tyrós *(GR)* 217 F 4
Tyruliai *(LT)* 169 F 1
Tysse *(N)* 138 B 2
Tyssebotn *(N)* 138 B 2
Tyssedal *(N)* 138 C 2
Tyszowce *(PL)* 197 F 3
Tytuvėnai *(LT)* 169 F 2
Tywa *(PL)* 180 B 4
Tywyn *(GB)* 32 B 4
Tzermiádo *(GR)* 227 E 2

U

Ub *(SRB)* 118 B 2
Úbeda *(E)* 76 B 1
Überlingen *(D)* 93 D 3
Ubiškė *(LT)* 163 D 4
Ubiškės *(LT)* 177 D 2
Ubja *(EST)* 151 D 3
Ubľa *(SK)* 12 C 2
Ubli *(HR)* 120 B 2
Ubli *(MNE)* 121 D 2
Ubrique *(E)* 75 E 3
Uchanie *(PL)* 197 F 2
Uchte *(D)* 83 F 3
Uckange *(F)* 44 C 2
Uckfield *(GB)* 36 C 4
Uclés *(E)* 70 C 1
Udbina *(HR)* 99 F 4
Udbyhøj *(DK)* 142 C 3
Uddevalla *(S)* 143 D 1
Uddheden *(S)* 139 F 3
Uden *(NL)* 87 D 1
Uderna *(EST)* 154 C 4
Udine *(I)* 98 C 2
Udovo *(MK)* 122 C 3
Ūdrija *(LT)* 176 C 3
Udriku *(EST)* 150 C 3
Ūdriņas *(LV)* 159 F 2
Ūdruma *(EST)* 148 C 4
Ūdrupe *(LV)* 160 C 3
Udvar *(H)* 112 C 4
Uebigau *(D)* 85 E 4
Ueckermünde *(D)* 80 C 3
Uelzen *(D)* 84 B 2
Uetersen *(D)* 78 C 4
Uetze *(D)* 84 A 3
Uffenheim *(D)* 88 C 4
Ugāle *(LV)* 157 D 3
Ugao *(SRB)* 118 C 4
Ugento *(I)* 107 F 4
Ugíjar *(E)* 76 C 3
Ugine *(F)* 53 D 1
Uglič *(RUS)* 7 F 1
Ugljan *(HR)* 103 E 1
Ugljan (Otok) *(HR)* 103 E 1
Ugljane *(HR)* 117 D 4
Ugljevik *(BIH)* 117 F 2
Ugrinovci *(SRB)* 118 C 2
Ugunciems *(LV)* 157 F 3
Uherské Hradiště *(CZ)* 91 E 4
Uherský Brod *(CZ)* 91 F 4
Uhingen *(D)* 93 D 2
Uhlířské Janovice *(CZ)* 90 C 3
Uhrsleben *(D)* 84 B 3
Uhti *(EST)* 155 D 4
Uhtna *(EST)* 151 D 3
Uig *(GB)* 26 C 3
Uimaharju *(FIN)* 135 F 3
Uithoorn *(NL)* 82 B 4
Uithuizen *(NL)* 83 D 2
Ujazd *Łodzkie(PL)* 189 E 4
Ujazd *Opolskie(PL)* 194 C 4
Ujejsce *(PL)* 195 D 4
Ujście *(PL)* 187 E 1
Ukkola *(FIN)* 135 F 3
Ukmergė *(LT)* 171 D 3
Ukri *(LV)* 163 F 3
Ulan-Majorat *(PL)* 191 D 4
Ulanów *(PL)* 197 D 4
Ulcinj *(MNE)* 121 E 3
Ülde *(EST)* 154 B 3
Ulefoss *(N)* 139 D 4
Uleila del Campo *(E)* 77 D 2
Ülejõe *(EST)* 149 F 3
Ülensi *(EST)* 154 B 4
Ülenurme *(EST)* 155 D 4
Ulfborg *(DK)* 142 A 3
Ulila *(EST)* 154 C 4
Uljanik *(HR)* 115 E 3
Uljanova *(LT)* 167 D 2
Ul'janovka *(UA)* 13 E 2
Uljma *(SRB)* 113 F 4
Ullånger *(S)* 132 B 3
Ullapool *(GB)* 27 D 2
Ullared *(S)* 143 D 2
Ullava *(FIN)* 133 E 2
Ulldecona *(E)* 66 B 4
Ulm (Donau) *(D)* 93 D 2
Ulmen *(D)* 87 E 3
Ulog *(BIH)* 117 F 4
Ulricehamn *(S)* 143 E 1
Ulrichsberg *(A)* 94 C 1
Ulsberg *(N)* 131 D 3
Ulsta *(GB)* 29 F

VALÈNCIA

Alcade Reig . . . . **BV** 2
Ángel Guimerá . . . . **AU** 7
Burjassot (Av. de) . . . . **AU** 9
Campanar (Av.) . . . . **AU** 14
Cavanilles . . . . **BU** 15
Constitución (Av. de la) . . . . **BU** 15
Doctor Peset Aleixandre (Av.) **BU** 20
Doctor Tomás Sala (Av. del) . **AV** 21
Fernando el Católico (G. Vía) **AU** 26
Filipinas . . . . **BV** 29
Gaspar Aguilar (Av. del) . . . . **AV** 31
General Avilés (Av.) . . . . **AU** 32
General Urrutia . . . . **BV** 36
Giorgeta (Av.) . . . . **AV** 37
Guadalaviar . . . . **BU** 38
Hermanos Maristas (Av. del) **BV** 42
Ingeniero Manuel Soto (Av.) . **CV** 43
José Soto Mico . . . . **AV** 46
Junta de Murs y Valls . . . . . . **BV** 44
Llano de la Zaidia . . . . **AU** 51
Maestro Rodrigo (Av.) . . . . . . **AU** 51
Mandingora (Av. de) . . . . **AV** 52
Manuel de Falla (Av.) . . . . . . **AU** 53
Menéndez Pidal (Av.) . . . . . . **AU** 58
Morenas (Camino) . . . . **CV** 60
Pechina (Paseo) . . . . **AU** 68
Pérez Galdós (Av. de) . . . . . . **AU** 69
Peris y Valero (Av.) . . . . **BV** 71
Pianista Martínez Carrasco
(Av. del) . . . . **BV** 72
Plata (Av. de la) . . . . **BV** 76
Primado Reig (Av.) . . . . **BU** 78
San José de Calasanz . . . . . . **AU** 82
San Vicente Mártir (Av.) . . . . **AV** 84
Tirso de Molina (Av.) . . . . **AU** 92
9 de Octubre . . . . **AU** 99

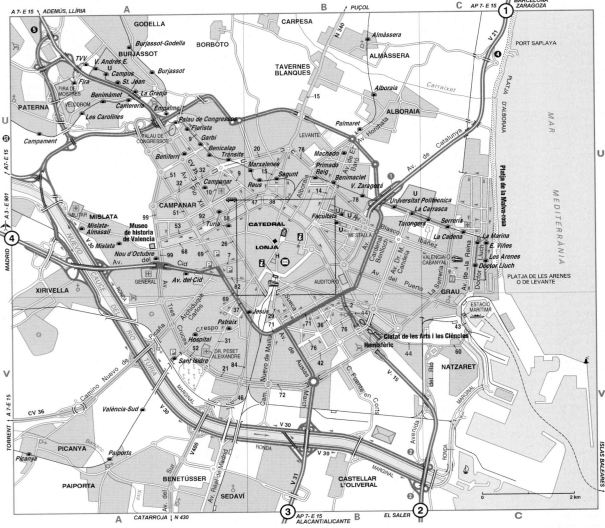

Ulsteinvik *(N)*	130	A 4	Unnaryd *(S)*	143	E 2	Urdziņas *(LV)*	165	D 1	Ussel *(F)*	51	F 2
Ulverston *(GB)*	32	C 1	Unquera *(E)*	60	A 3	Urepel *(F)*	54	A 3	Usseln *(D)*	88	A 1
Ulvi *Ida-Viru(EST)*	151	D 4	Unterach *(A)*	94	C 3	Urfahr *(A)*	94	C 2	Ussimäe *(EST)*	151	D 3
Ulvi *Lääne-Viru(EST)*	151	D 3	Unterhaching *(D)*	93	F 2	Urfeld *(D)*	93	F 2	Ustaoset *(N)*	139	D 2
Ulvik *(N)*	138	C 2	Unterschleißheim *(D)*	93	D 4	Urga *(LV)*	159	E 2	Ustaritz *(F)*	54	A 2
Ulvila *(FIN)*	136	B 2	Unterwasser *(CH)*	93	D 4	Urge *(EST)*	153	C 3	Uster *(CH)*	92	C 4
Ulvsjö *(S)*	140	B 1	Unterweißenbach *(A)*	95	D 1	Uri *(I)*	108	A 2	Usna *(EST)*	154	B 3
Umag *(HR)*	98	C 3	Uoginiai *(LT)*	171	D 1	Uriage-les-Bains *(F)*	53	D 2	Uvac *(SRB)*	118	B 3
Uman' *(UA)*	13	E 2	Uosininkai I *(LT)*	177	F 2	Urissaare *(EST)*	159	D 1	Uvdal *(N)*	139	D 2
Umbertide *(I)*	102	B 3	Uosininkai II *(LT)*	177	F 2	Urjala *(FIN)*	136	C 3	Užava *(LV)*	156	C 3
Umbukta *(N)*	127	E 4	Uostavaris *(LT)*	168	B 3	Urk *(NL)*	82	C 3	Uzdin *(SRB)*	113	F 4
Umbusi *(EST)*	154	C 3	Upa *(EST)*	152	B 4	Urla *(TR)*	19	E 3	Uzdowo *(PL)*	183	D 3
Umčari *(SRB)*	118	C 2	Upavon *(GB)*	35	F 2	Urlingford *(IRL)*	25	D 2	Uzel *(F)*	41	D 3
Umeå *(S)*	132	C 2	Upenieki *Dobeles(LV)*	163	D 1	Urnäsch *(CH)*	93	D 4	Uzès *(F)*	52	B 4
Umhausen *(A)*	93	F 4	Upenieki *Kuldīgas(LV)*	163	D 1	Urnėžiai *(LT)*	170	C 4	Užģirėlis *(LT)*	176	C 2
Umin Dol *(MK)*	122	B 4	Upenieki *Liepājas(LV)*	162	C 2	Uroševac *(SRB)*	122	A 2	Ustronie Morskie *(PL)*	181	D 2
Umka *(SRB)*	118	B 1	Upenieki *Preiļu(LV)*	166	C 3	Urovica *(SRB)*	119	E 1	Ustrzyki Dolne *(PL)*	202	F 4
Umljanović *(HR)*	103	F 1	Upesgrīva *(LV)*	157	F 3	Urshult *(S)*	143	E 3	Ustrzyki Górne *(PL)*	202	F 4
Umurga *(LV)*	159	D 4	Úpice *(CZ)*	90	C 1	Uršna *(EST)*	154	B 4	Ust'-uźna *(RUS)*	7	F 1
Unametsa *(EST)*	154	B 4	Upinniemi *(FIN)*	136	C 4	Urvaste *(EST)*	161	D 1	Ūta *(LT)*	177	F 2
Unari *(FIN)*	128	C 2	Upīte *(LV)*	161	F 4	Urvikiai *(LT)*	163	D 3	Utajärvi *(FIN)*	133	F 1
Uncastillo *(E)*	54	A 4	Upītes *(LV)*	157	E 3	Ury *(F)*	43	D 3	Utåker *(N)*	138	B 3
Undersåker *(S)*	131	E 3	Upmala *(LV)*	166	C 3	Urzędów *(PL)*	197	D 2	Utbjoa *(N)*	138	B 3
Undredal *(N)*	138	C 1	Upmalas *Carnikava(LV)*	159	D 4	Urziceni *(RO)*	13	E 4	Utebo *(E)*	65	F 2
Uneča *(RUS)*	7	F 4	Upmalas *Sidgunda(LV)*	159	E 4	Usagre *(E)*	69	E 4	Utelle *(F)*	53	F 4
Unešić *(HR)*	103	F 1	Upninkai *(LT)*	171	D 1	Ušča *(SRB)*	118	C 3	Utena *(LT)*	171	F 2
Úněšov *(CZ)*	89	F 3	Uppingham *(GB)*	33	E 4	Usedom *(D)*	80	C 3	Utiel *(E)*	71	E 2
Ungheni *(MD)*	13	E 1	Upplands-Väsby *(S)*	141	D 4	Ušėnai *(LT)*	168	C 3	Utne *(N)*	138	C 2
Ungilde *(E)*	63	E 1	Uppsala *(S)*	141	D 3	Utrecht *(NL)*	82	B 4	Utrecht *(NL)*	82	B 4
Ungurpils *(LV)*	159	E 2	Upton-upon-Severn *(GB)*	35	E 1	Usk / Brynbuga *(GB)*	35	E 1	Utrera *(E)*	75	D 2
Unhais da Serra *(P)*	62	C 1	Upyna *(LT)*	169	D 2	Usingen *(D)*	88	A 3	Utrillas *(E)*	65	F 2
Unhošť *(CZ)*	90	B 3	Upytė *(LT)*	170	C 1	Usk / Brynbuga *(GB)*	35	D 1	Utsjoki *(FIN)*	125	E 2
Uničov *(CZ)*	91	E 3	Uras *(I)*	108	B 3	Uskoplje *(BIH)*	120	C 2	Uttendorf *(A)*	94	B 2
Uniejów *(PL)*	189	D 4	Urbania *(I)*	102	B 3	Üsküdar *(TR)*	19	F 1	Uttendorf *(A)*	94	B 2
Unije *(HR)*	99	D 4	Urbe *(I)*	100	C 1	Uslar *(D)*	84	A 4	Utting *(D)*	93	F 3
Unikūla *Ida-Viru(EST)*	151	E 3	Urbino *(I)*	102	B 3	Usma *(LV)*	157	D 3	Uttoxeter *(GB)*	33	D 3
Unikūla *Tartu(EST)*	155	F 3	Urda *(E)*	70	C 2	Ussat *(F)*	55	E 3	Uudeküla *(EST)*	150	C 4
Unisław *(PL)*	182	C 4	Urdos *(F)*	54	B 3	Ussé *(F)*	47	D 2	Uue-Antsla *(EST)*	161	D 1
Universitāte *(LV)*	159	D 3	Urdzenieki *(LV)*	156	B 4	Usseglio *(I)*	53	E 2	Uuemõisa *(EST)*	148	C 4
Unna *(D)*	87	F 1							Uulu *(EST)*	153	C 4

Uurainen *(FIN)*	133	F 4			
Uuri *(EST)*	149	F 2			
Uusikaupunki *(FIN)*	136	B 3			
Uuskūla *Harju(EST)*	149	E 4			
Uuskūla *Rapla(EST)*	149	E 4			
Uva *(I)*	108	A 2			

V

V. Jablanica *(SRB)*	121	F 1
V. Prolog *(HR)*	120	B 1
Vä *(S)*	143	E 4
Vaabina *(EST)*	161	D 1
Vaajakoski *(FIN)*	133	F 4
Vääkiö *(FIN)*	129	E 4
Vaala *(FIN)*	133	F 1
Vaalbaliai *(LT)*	175	E 2
Vaalajärvi *(FIN)*	129	D 2
Vaalimaa *(FIN)*	137	E 3
Vaals *(NL)*	87	D 2
Väänä *(EST)*	149	D 2
Väänä-Jõesuu *(EST)*	149	D 2
Vaaraslahti *(FIN)*	133	F 3
Vaasa / Vasa *(FIN)*	132	C 3
Vaassen *(NL)*	82	C 4
Väätsa *(EST)*	149	F 4
Vabaliai *(LT)*	170	C 2
Vabalninkas *(LT)*	165	D 4
Vabole (Vabale) *(LV)*	166	C 4
Vabre *(F)*	55	F 2
Vác *(H)*	12	B 3
Vacha *(D)*	88	B 2
Vācpēteri *(LV)*	163	F 2
Vacpils *(LV)*	167	E 1
Vadakste *(LT)*	163	E 3
Vadaktai *(LT)*	170	C 2
Vadaktėliai *(LT)*	170	C 2
Väddö *(S)*	141	D 3
Vadheim *(N)*	138	C 1
Vado Ligure *(I)*	100	C 1
Vadokliai *(LT)*	171	D 2
Vadsø *(N)*	125	F 2
Vadstena *(S)*	143	E 1
Vaduz *(FL)*	93	D 4
Vadžgirys *(LT)*	169	E 3
Væggerløse *(DK)*	144	C 4
Vaeküla *(EST)*	151	D 3
Vafaïika *(GR)*	207	F 2

Vafiochóri *(GR)* 206   B 2
Vågaholmen *(N)* 127   D 3
Vågåmo *(N)* 130   C 4
Vågan *(N)* 127   E 2
Vägari *(EST)* 154   C 2
Våge *(N)* 138   B 2
Vågeva *(EST)* 150   C 4
Vaggeryd *(S)* 143   E 2
Vágia *(GR)* 218   B 1
Vagioniá *(GR)* 227   D 3
Vagnhärad *(S)* 141   E 2
Vagos *(P)* 62   B 4
Vagula *(EST)* 161   D 1
Vagur *(DK)* 126   A 4
Vahakulmu *(EST)* 150   C 3
Vähäkyrö *(FIN)* 133   D 3
Vahastu *(EST)* 149   D 3
Vahenurme *(EST)* 153   C 3
Vahi *(EST)* 155   D 3
Vahto *(FIN)* 136   B 3
Vahuküla *(EST)* 150   C 4
Väi *(GR)* 227   F 2
Vaiano *(I)* 101   E 4
Vaiatu *(EST)* 155   D 2
Vaičiai *(LT)* 169   D 2
Vaičlaukis *(LT)* 175   E 2
Vaiculeva *(LV)* 173   E 1
Vaida *(EST)* 149   E 3
Vaidasoo *(EST)* 149   E 3
Vaidava *(LV)* 159   F 3
Vaidlonys *(LT)* 171   E 2
Vaiges *(F)* 41   F 4
Vaiguva *(LT)* 169   E 2
Vaihingen a. d. Enz *(D)* 45   F 3
Väike-Kamari *(EST)* 154   C 3
Väike-Maarja *(EST)* 150   C 4
Väike-Rakke *(EST)* 154   C 4
Vailainiai *(LT)* 170   B 2
Vailly-sur-Aisne *(F)* 39   D 4
Vailly-sur-Sauldre *(F)* 48   A 2
Vaimastvere *(EST)* 154   C 2
Väimela *(EST)* 161   D 1
Vainikai *(LT)* 170   C 3
Vainikkala *(FIN)* 137   E 3
Vainiūnai *(LT)* 170   C 2
Vainiūniškis *(LT)* 165   E 4
Vainode *(LV)* 162   C 2
Vainodes Muiža *(LV)* 162   C 2
Vainotiškiai *(LT)* 170   C 3
Vainova *(LV)* 167   E 3
Vainupea *(EST)* 150   C 2
Vainutas *(LT)* 168   C 3
Vaisaluokta *(S)* 127   F 2
Vaišniūnai *(LT)* 172   B 2
Vaison-la-Romaine *(F)* 52   C 4
Vaiste *(EST)* 153   B 3
Vaišvilčiai I *(LT)* 170   C 2
Vaišvydava *(LT)* 176   C 1
Vaitiekūnai *(LT)* 170   B 2
Vaitkūnai *(LT)* 171   F 2
Vaivadai *(LT)* 171   D 2
Vaivadi *(LV)* 164   C 2
Vaivadiškiai *(LT)* 171   D 3
Vaivara *(EST)* 151   F 3
Vaižgai *(LT)* 170   C 2
Vaizgučiai *(LT)* 164   B 4
Vajangu *(EST)* 150   C 4
Vajasiškis *(LT)* 172   B 2
Vaki *(EST)* 154   A 3
Val-de-Reuil *(F)* 42   C 1
Val-d'Isère *(F)* 53   E 2
Val-Thorens *(F)* 53   E 2
Vålådalen *(S)* 131   E 3
Valadares *(P)* 62   B 3
Valai *(LT)* 171   F 4
Valakėliai *(LT)* 165   D 4
Valalta *(HR)* 99   D 3
Valamen *(FIN)* 135   E 3
Valandovo *(MK)* 122   C 3
Valareña *(E)* 54   A 4
Valašské Meziříčí *(CZ)* 91   F 3
Valasti *(EST)* 149   F 4
Valāta *(LV)* 162   C 1
Valatkoniai *(LT)* 170   C 2
Valavičiai *(LT)* 175   F 2
Valax *(FIN)* 137   D 4
Valbella *(CH)* 97   E 1
Valberg *(F)* 53   E 4
Vålberg *(S)* 139   F 4
Valbiska *(HR)* 99   E 3
Valbo *(S)* 140   C 2
Valbondione *(I)* 97   E 2
Valbonnais *(F)* 53   D 3
Valčiūnai *(LT)* 177   E 2
Valdagno *(I)* 98   A 3
Valdahon *(F)* 49   E 2

Valdaj *(RUS)* 7   E 1
Valdaora / Olang *(I)* 98   A 1
Valdecaballeros *(E)* 69   F 2
Valdecabras *(E)* 71   D 1
Valdecarros *(E)* 63   F 4
Valdedios *(E)* 59   F 2
Valdefuentes *(E)* 69   E 2
Valdeganga *(E)* 71   E 3
Valdelacasa de Tajo *(E)* 69   F 1
Valdelinares *(E)* 71   F 1
Valdemārpils *(LV)* 157   E 3
Valdemarsvik *(S)* 143   F 1
Valdemeca *(E)* 71   E 1
Valdemorillo *(E)* 64   B 4
Valdemoro *(E)* 70   B 3
Valdenoceda *(E)* 60   B 4
Valdepeñas *(E)* 70   B 3
Valdepeñas de Jaén *(E)* 76   B 3
Valderas *(E)* 63   F 1
Valderiès *(F)* 51   F 4
Valderrobres *(E)* 66   A 4
Valdestillas *(E)* 64   A 3
Valdeverdeja *(E)* 69   F 1
Valdevimbre *(E)* 59   E 4
Valdezcaray *(E)* 64   C 1
Valdgale *(LV)* 157   E 3
Valdieri *(I)* 53   F 4
Valdobbiadene *(I)* 98   A 2
Vale de Açor *(P)* 74   B 1

Vale de Cambra *(P)* 62   B 3
Vale de Estrela *(P)* 63   D 4
Vale de Prazeres *(P)* 68   C 1
Valeggio sul Mincio *(I)* 97   F 3
Valença do Minho *(P)* 58   B 4
Valençay *(F)* 47   F 2
Valence *(F)* 52   C 3
Valence-d'Agen *(F)* 51   D 4
Valence-d'Albigeois *(F)* 51   F 4
Valence-sur-Baïse *(F)* 54   C 1
València *(E)* 71   F 2
Valencia de Alcántara *(E)* 69   D 2
Valencia de Don Juan *(E)* 59   E 4
Valencia de las Torres *(E)* 69   E 4
Valencia del Ventoso *(E)* 69   D 4
Valenciennes *(F)* 70   D 3
Valenčiūnai *(LT)* 169   E 4
Valensole *(F)* 57   D 1
Valentano *(I)* 102   A 4
Valentigney *(F)* 49   F 2
Valenza *(I)* 97   D 4
Valeria *(E)* 71   D 2
Valevåg *(N)* 138   B 3
Valfabbrica *(I)* 102   B 3
Valga *(EST)* 160   C 2
Valgalciems *(LV)* 157   F 3
Valgale *(LV)* 157   E 4
Välgita *(EST)* 154   B 3

Valgjärve *(EST)* 161   D 1
Valgorge *(F)* 52   B 3
Valgrisenche *(I)* 53   E 1
Valgu *(EST)* 149   D 4
Valguarnera *(I)* 111   D 3
Valgunde *(LV)* 164   C 1
Valguta *(EST)* 154   C 4
Valhelhas *(P)* 63   D 4
Valimítika *(GR)* 217   E 1
Valingu *(EST)* 149   D 4
Valjala *(EST)* 152   C 3
Valjevo *(SRB)* 118   B 2
Valjok *(N)* 125   E 2
Valjunquera *(E)* 66   A 4
Valka *(LV)* 160   C 2
Valkeakoski *(FIN)* 136   C 3
Valkeala *(FIN)* 137   E 3
Valkenburg
  aan de Geul *(NL)* 87   D 2
Valkenswaard *(NL)* 39   F 1
Valkininkai *(LT)* 177   D 3
Valko *(FIN)* 137   D 3
Vall d'Alba *(E)* 72   A 1
Valladolid *(E)* 64   A 2
Vallata *(I)* 106   B 3
Vallbo *(S)* 131   E 3
Valldal *(N)* 130   B 2
Valldemossa *(E)* 73   D 2
Valle *(LV)* 165   D 2

Valle *(N)* 138   C 3
Valle Castellana *(I)* 102   A 3
Valle de Abdalajís *(E)* 75   F 3
Valle de la Serena *(E)* 69   E 3
Valle de los Caídos *(E)* 64   B 4
Valle de Matamoros *(E)* 69   D 4
Valle Mosso *(I)* 53   F 1
Valleberga *(S)* 143   E 4
Vallejera de Riofrío *(E)* 63   F 4
Vallentuna *(S)* 141   D 4
Valleraugue *(F)* 52   A 4
Vallet *(F)* 46   C 2
Valletta *(M)* 110   A 4
Vallgrund *(FIN)* 132   C 3
Vallø *(DK)* 143   D 4
Vallo della Lucania *(I)* 106   C 4
Valloire *(F)* 53   D 2
Vallombrosa *(I)* 102   A 2
Vallon-en-Sully *(F)* 48   A 3
Vallon-Pont-d'Arc *(F)* 52   B 4
Vallorbe *(CH)* 49   E 3
Vallorcine *(F)* 49   E 4
Vallouise *(F)* 53   E 3
Valls *(E)* 66   C 3
Vallsta *(S)* 140   C 1
Valma *(EST)* 154   C 4
Valmantiškiai *(LT)* 169   F 4
Valmiera *(LV)* 159   F 2
Valmojado *(E)* 70   B 1
Valmont *(F)* 38   A 4

Valmontone *(I)* 105   D 2
Valmorel *(F)* 53   D 2
Välodzes *(LV)* 157   D 4
Välodzītes *(LV)* 161   F 4
Valognes *(F)* 41   E 1
Valongo *(P)* 62   B 2
Valoria la Buena *(E)* 64   A 2
Valøya *(N)* 131   D 1
Valožyn *(BY)* 7   D 4
Valpaços *(P)* 63   D 2
Valpainiai *(LT)* 169   E 4
Valpalmas *(E)* 54   B 4
Valpovo *(HR)* 112   C 4
Valprato Soana *(I)* 53   F 2
Valras-Plage *(F)* 56   A 3
Valréas *(F)* 52   C 4
Vals-les-Bains *(F)* 52   B 3
Valsamónero *(GR)* 226   C 2
Valsavarenche *(I)* 53   E 1
Valset *(N)* 131   F 2
Valsjöbyn *(S)* 131   F 2
Valtaiķi *(LV)* 162   C 1
Valtessiníko *(GR)* 217   E 3
Valtierra *(E)* 54   A 4
Valtimo *(FIN)* 135   E 2
Váltos *(GR)* 208   C 1
Valtotópi *(GR)* 207   D 2
Valtournenche *(I)* 53   F 1
Valtu *(EST)* 149   E 4
Valun *(HR)* 99   D 3

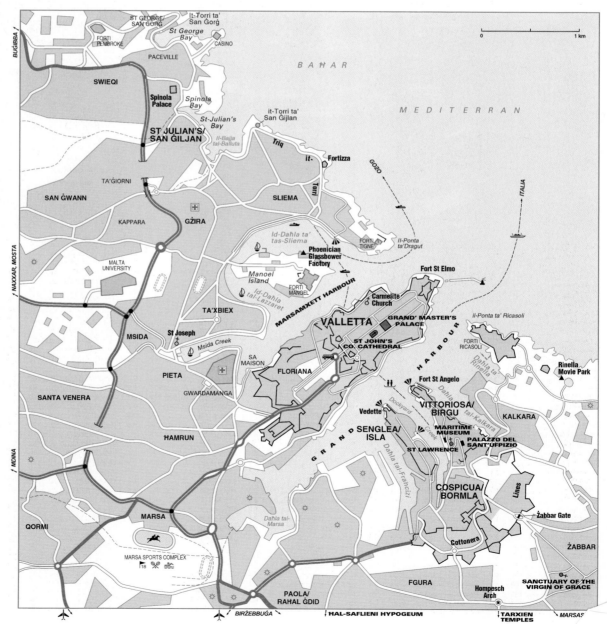

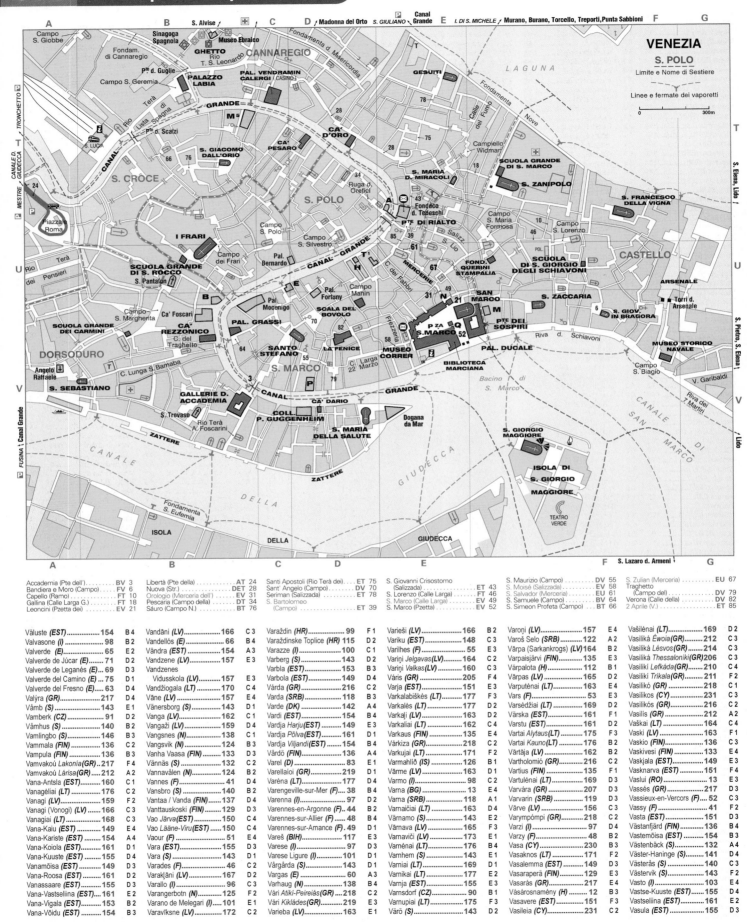

Vašuokėnai (LT) 171 E 2
Vasyl'kiv (UA) 13 E 1
Vatan (F) 47 F 3
Väte (S) 146 B 2
Vaterá (GR) 214 C 3
Vateró (GR) 205 F 4
Vátheia (GR) 222 C 3
Vathý Dodekánissa(GR) 225 E 2
Vathý Éwoia(GR) 218 B 1
Vathý Kilkís(GR) 206 B 2
Vathý Lefkáda(GR) 211 D 4
Vathýlakkos Dráma(GR) 207 E 2
Vathýlakkos Kozáni(GR) 205 F 4
Vathýlakkos Thessaloníki(GR) 206 B 3
Vathypetro (GR) 227 D 2
Vathýs (GR) 221 E 4
Vatili (CY) 231 D 3
Vatin (SRB) 113 F 4
Vatla (EST) 153 A 3
Vatne (N) 130 B 3
Vatólakkos (GR) 205 E 4
Vatra Dornei (RO) 13 D 3
Vattholma (S) 141 D 3
Vaucouleurs (F) 44 B 3
Vaŭkavysk (BY) 6 C 4
Vauvert (F) 56 B 2
Vauvillers (F) 49 E 1
Vávdos (GR) 206 C 4
Växjö (S) 143 E 3
Våxtorp (S) 143 D 3
Vayrac (F) 51 E 3
V'az'ma (RUS) 7 F 2
Veberöd (S) 143 D 4
Vecate (LV) 159 E 2
Vecauce (LV) 163 E 2
Vecbebri (LV) 165 F 2
Vecgaiķi (LV) 163 E 1
Vechta (D) 83 E 3
Vecinos (E) 63 F 4
Veckrape (LV) 165 E 2
Vecmiķeļi (LV) 163 F 2
Vecmuiža (LV) 159 D 4
Vecpiebalga (LV) 159 F 4
Vecpils (Dižlāņi) (LV) 162 C 2
Vecružina (Vacružina) (LV) 167 E 3
Vecsaikava (LV) 166 C 2
Vecsalaca (LV) 159 D 2
Vecsaule (LV) 165 D 3
Vecsiķeļi (LV) 173 D 1
Vecsīpoli (LV) 162 B 3
Vecslabada (Vacsloboda) (LV) 167 F 3
Vecstāmeriena (LV) 161 D 4
Vecstārasti (LV) 159 E 3
Vecstropi (LV) 173 D 1
Vecstrūžāni (Strūžāni) (LV) 167 E 2
Vecsvirlauka (LV) 164 C 2
Vectilža (Vactiļža) (LV) 167 E 1
Vecumi (Vacumi) (LV) 161 F 4
Vecumnieki (LV) 165 D 2
Veczosna (Vaczosna) (LV) 167 E 3
Vēde (LV) 157 D 2
Vedelago (I) 98 B 3
Vedu (EST) 155 D 3
Veelikse Pärnu(EST) 159 E 1
Veelikse Viljandi(EST) 154 A 4
Veendam (NL) 83 D 2
Veenendaal (NL) 82 C 4
Veere (NL) 37 F 3
Vef Ozoli (LV) 159 D 4
Vef-Pabaži (LV) 159 D 3
Vega de Espinareda (E) 59 D 3
Vega de Valcarce (E) 59 D 3
Vegadeo (E) 59 D 2
Vegarienza (E) 59 E 3
Vegårshei (N) 139 D 4
Vēgas (LV) 157 D 4
Vegas del Condado (E) 59 F 4
Vegesack (D) 83 F 2
Veghel (NL) 39 F 1
Veģi (LV) 157 E 4
Veguellina de Órbigo (E) 59 E 4
Vehkalahti (FIN) 137 E 3
Vehmaa (FIN) 136 B 3
Vehmersalmi (FIN) 135 E 3
Veidnesklubben (N) 125 E 1
Veikkola (FIN) 136 C 4
Veinge (S) 143 D 3
Veiros (P) 68 C 3
Veisiejai (LT) 175 F 4
Veiveriai (LT) 176 B 2
Veivirženai (LT) 168 C 2
Vejen (DK) 142 B 4
Vejer de la Frontera (E) 75 E 4
Vejle (DK) 142 B 4
Vejos (LT) 169 D 2
Vel.-Kopanica (HR) 117 E 1
Vel. Lašče (SLO) 99 E 2
Vel. Trnovac (SRB) 122 B 1
Vela Luka (HR) 120 A 2
Velada (E) 70 A 1
Velagići (BIH) 116 C 2
Velanídia (GR) 223 D 3
Velayos (E) 64 A 4
Velbert (D) 87 E 1
Velburg (D) 89 D 4
Velde (N) 131 D 2
Velden (A) 99 D 1
Velden (D) 94 A 2
Velden (D) 89 D 4
Veldhoven (NL) 39 F 1
Veldres (LV) 164 B 2
Veldze (Rumbenieki) (LV) 157 D 4
Velēna (LV) 160 C 4
Velenje (SLO) 99 E 4
Veles (MK) 122 B 3
Veleška (MK) 122 A 4
Velestíno (GR) 212 B 2
Vélez Blanco (E) 77 D 1
Vélez de Benaudalla (E) 76 B 3
Vélez Málaga (E) 76 A 3
Vélez Rubio (E) 77 D 2
Veli Iz (HR) 103 E 1
Veli Lošinj (HR) 99 E 4
Veličani (BIH) 120 C 2
Veliés (GR) 223 D 2
Velika (HR) 115 F 3
Velika Drenova (SRB) 119 D 3
Velika Gorica (HR) 99 F 2
Velika Jamnička (HR) 99 F 2
Velika Kladuša (BIH) 99 F 3
Velika Kruša (SRB) 121 F 2
Velika Mučna (HR) 112 A 4
Velika Plana Jagodina(SRB) 118 C 2
Velika Plana Prokuplje(SRB) 119 D 3
Veliki Bastaji (HR) 112 B 4
Veliki Gaj (SRB) 113 F 4
Veliki Grđevac (HR) 112 A 4
Veliki Izvor (SRB) 119 E 2
Veliki Popović (SRB) 119 D 2
Veliki Preslav (BG) 19 E 1
Veliki Radinci (SRB) 118 A 1
Veliki Raven (HR) 112 A 4
Veliki Zdenci (HR) 112 A 4
Velikije Luki (RUS) 7 D 2
Veliko Gradište (SRB) 119 D 1
Veliko Orašje (SRB) 118 C 2
Veliko Tărnovo (BG) 19 D 1
Velilla del Río Carrión (E) 59 F 3
Velimlje (MNE) 121 D 2
Vélines (F) 50 C 3
Velingrad (BG) 19 D 1
Vėliučionys (LT) 177 F 4
Veliuona (LT) 169 F 4
Velíž (RUS) 7 E 3
Veljun (HR) 99 F 3
Velká Bíteš (CZ) 91 D 4
Velká Bystřice (CZ) 91 E 3
Velká nad Veličkou (CZ) 91 F 4
Velké Meziříčí (CZ) 91 D 3
Velkua (FIN) 136 B 4
Vellahn (D) 79 E 4
Velletri (I) 105 D 2
Vellinge (S) 143 D 4
Velopoúla (Nisí) (GR) 223 E 2
Vélos (GR) 218 C 1
Velpke (D) 84 B 3
Velten (D) 85 D 2
Veltsi (EST) 150 C 3
Velventós (GR) 205 F 4
Velyka Lepetycha (UA) 13 F 2
Velžys (LT) 171 D 2
Vembūtai (LT) 163 D 4
Vemdalen (S) 131 F 4
Vemdalsskalet (S) 131 F 4
Vemhån (S) 131 F 4
Venaco (F) 57 F 3
Venafro (I) 105 E 2
Venarey-les-Laumes (F) 48 C 2
Venaria Reale (I) 53 F 2
Vence (F) 57 E 2
Venciūnai (LT) 176 C 3
Venckai (LT) 168 B 2
Venda Nova (P) 62 C 2
Vendas Novas (P) 68 B 3
Vendeuvre-sur-Barse (F) 43 E 4
Vendôme (F) 42 B 4
Veneheitto (FIN) 133 F 1
Venevere (EST) 151 D 4
Venezia (I) 98 B 3
Vengjaneset (N) 138 B 2
Venialbo (E) 63 F 3
Venjan (S) 140 B 2
Venlo (NL) 87 D 1
Vénna (GR) 208 B 2
Vennesla (N) 142 A 1
Vennesund (N) 131 E 1
Venosa (I) 106 B 3
Venray (NL) 87 D 1
Venta (LT) 163 E 3
Venta (LV) 157 D 4
Venta Nueva (E) 59 D 3
Ventas con Peña Aguilera (E) 70 A 2
Ventas de Huelma (E) 76 B 2
Ventava (LV) 156 C 3
Ventė (LT) 168 B 3
Ventimiglia (I) 57 F 1
Ventnor (GB) 35 F 3
Ventspils (LV) 156 C 3
Venturina (I) 101 F 3
Vepriai (LT) 171 D 4
Vera (E) 77 D 2
Vera (N) 131 E 2
Verbania (I) 97 D 3
Verberie (F) 43 D 1
Verbicaro (I) 109 D 1
Verbier (CH) 49 F 4
Verbūnai (LT) 163 F 4
Verbuškės (LT) 177 F 2
Verčane (SRB) 118 C 2
Vercel-Villedieu-le-Camp (F) 49 E 2
Vercelli (I) 96 C 4
Verchnjadzvinsk (BY) 7 D 3
Verchn'odniprovs'k (UA) 13 F 1
Verdalsøra (N) 131 D 2
Verde Col de(F) 57 F 4
Verden (D) 83 F 2
Verdikoússa (GR) 211 F 1
Vērdiņi (LV) 165 D 3
Verdun (F) 44 B 2
Verdun-sur-Garonne (F) 55 D 1
Verdun-sur-le-Doubs (F) 49 D 3
Verebiejai (LT) 175 F 3
Verėduva (LT) 169 F 3
Vērgale (LV) 162 B 1
Vergato (I) 101 F 1
Vergi (EST) 150 C 2
Vérgi (GR) 206 C 2
Vergiate (I) 97 D 3
Vergio Col de(F) 57 F 3
Vergt (F) 51 D 3
Verijärve (EST) 161 D 2
Verilaske (EST) 154 B 4
Verín (E) 63 D 1
Veriora (EST) 161 E 1
Verioramõisa (EST) 161 E 1
Veriškės (LT) 177 F 1
Vėriškiai (LT) 170 B 2
Verksnionys (LT) 171 F 1
Verl (D) 83 F 4
Vermand (F) 39 D 4
Vermenton (F) 43 E 4
Vernet-les-Bains (F) 55 F 4
Verneuil-sur-Avre (F) 42 B 2
Vernon (F) 42 C 2
Vernoux-en-Vivarais (F) 52 B 3
Verny (F) 44 C 3
Véroia (GR) 206 A 3
Veroli (I) 105 E 2
Verona (I) 97 F 3
Vērpeļi (LV) 157 E 4
Verpena (LT) 169 E 2
Verpuļeva (LV) 161 E 4
Verran (N) 131 D 2
Verrès (I) 53 F 1
Versailles (F) 43 D 2
Versmold (D) 83 E 4
Verstaminai (LT) 175 F 3
Verteillac (F) 50 C 2
Vertimai (LT) 169 E 3
Vertus (F) 43 F 2
Verucchio (I) 102 B 1
Verviers (B) 87 D 3
Vervins (F) 39 E 4
Verzuolo (I) 53 F 3
Verzy (F) 43 F 2
Vesanto (FIN) 133 F 3
Vescovato (F) 57 F 3
Veselava (LV) 159 F 3
Veselí nad Lužnicí (CZ) 90 B 4
Veselí nad Moravou (CZ) 91 E 4
Veselība (LV) 166 C 3
Vesilahti (FIN) 136 C 2
Vesivehmaa (FIN) 137 D 3
Vesjegonsk (RUS) 7 F 1
Veskimäe (EST) 154 A 4
Veskoniemi (FIN) 125 F 3
Vesna (LV) 167 D 4
Vesneri (EST) 155 D 3
Vesoul (F) 49 E 1
Véssa (GR) 220 C 1
Vestby (N) 139 E 3
Vestbygda (N) 142 A 1
Vesterø Havn (DK) 142 C 2
Vestertana (N) 125 E 1
Vestiena (LV) 166 B 1
Vestmanna (DK) 126 A 4
Vestnes (N) 130 B 3
Vestone (I) 97 F 3
Vestre jakobselv (N) 125 F 2
Veszprém (H) 112 B 2
Veteli (FIN) 133 E 3
Vetiku (EST) 151 D 3
Vetlanda (S) 143 F 2
Vetralla (I) 102 A 4
Vetriolo Terme (I) 98 A 2
Vetschau (D) 85 E 4
Veules-les-Roses (F) 38 A 4
Veulettes-sur-Mer (F) 38 A 4
Veurne (B) 37 E 4
Vevey (CH) 49 F 3
Vévi (GR) 205 E 3
Veynes (F) 53 D 3
Veyre-Monton (F) 52 A 1
Veyrier-du-Lac (F) 53 D 1
Vėžaičiai (LT) 168 B 1
Vezdemarbán (E) 63 F 2
Vézelay (F) 48 B 2
Vézelise (F) 44 C 4
Vézénobres (F) 52 B 4
Vézins-de-Lévézou (F) 51 F 4
Vėžionys (LT) 176 C 2
Vezzani (F) 57 F 3
Vezzano (I) 97 F 2
Viadana (I) 97 F 4
Viana (E) 60 C 4
Viana do Alentejo (P) 68 B 4
Viana do Bolo (E) 58 C 4
Viana do Castelo (P) 62 B 2
Vianden (L) 44 C 1
Vianen (NL) 82 B 4
Viareggio (I) 101 E 2
Vias (F) 56 A 2
Vībiņi (LV) 162 C 2
Vibo Valentia (I) 109 E 3
Viborg (DK) 142 B 3
Vibraye (F) 42 B 4
Vic (E) 67 D 2
Vič (SLO) 114 B 2
Vic-en-Bigorre (F) 54 C 2
Vic-Fezensac (F) 54 C 2
Vic-le-Comte (F) 52 A 1
Vic-sur-Aisne (F) 43 E 1
Vic-sur-Cère (F) 51 F 3
Vicdessos (F) 55 E 3
Vicebsk (BY) 7 E 3
Vicenza (I) 98 A 3
Vichy (F) 48 B 4
Vico (F) 57 F 3
Vico del Gargano (I) 103 F 4
Vico Equense (I) 105 F 4
Victoria (M) 110 A 4
Vidaga (LV) 160 C 3
Vidago (P) 63 D 2
Vīdale (LV) 157 E 2
Vidareidi (DK) 126 A 4
Vidauban (F) 57 E 2
Viddal (N) 130 B 4
Videbæk (DK) 142 A 3
Videm (SLO) 99 E 2
Videniškiai (LT) 171 E 3
Vidiáki (GR) 217 D 2
Vidigueira (P) 68 C 4
Vidin (BG) 12 C 4
Vidiškės (LT) 172 C 3
Vidiškiai (LT) 171 E 3
Vidnava (CZ) 91 E 1
Vidreres (E) 67 D 2
Vidriži (LV) 159 D 3
Vidrovan (MNE) 121 D 2
Vidsala (LV) 166 B 3
Vidsel (S) 128 A 4
Vidukle (LT) 169 E 3
Vidutinė (LT) 172 C 4
Vidzeme (LV) 160 B 3
Vidzgailai (LT) 175 F 3
Viechtach (D) 89 F 4
Viechtwang (A) 94 C 2
Vieira de Leiria (P) 68 A 1
Vieira do Minho (P) 62 C 2
Viekšniai (LT) 163 E 3
Vielha (E) 55 D 3
Vielle-Aure (F) 54 C 3
Vielmur-sur-Agout (F) 55 E 2
Vielsalm (B) 87 D 3
Vienenburg (D) 84 B 4
Vienība (LV) 163 F 1
Vienne (F) 52 C 2
Vieremä (FIN) 133 F 2
Viernheim (D) 45 E 1
Vierraden (D) 85 E 1
Viersen (D) 87 E 1
Viertiukšne (LV) 167 E 3
Vierumäki (FIN) 137 D 3
Vierzon (F) 47 F 2
Viesatas (Viesati) (LV) 163 E 1
Viešintėlės (LT) 171 E 2
Viešintos (LT) 171 E 2
Viesīte (LV) 165 F 3
Vieste (I) 106 C 1
Viesturi Bauskas(LV) 164 C 2
Viesturi Jelgavas(LV) 164 B 2
Viešvėnai l (LT) 163 D 4
Viešvilė Šiaulių(LT) 170 C 2
Viešvilė Tauragės(LT) 169 D 4
Vietalva (LV) 165 F 2
Vietas (S) 127 F 2
Vietri di Potenza (I) 106 B 3
Vietri sul Mare (I) 105 F 4
Vieux-Boucau-les-Bains (F) 54 A 1
Vievis (LT) 177 D 2
Vif (F) 53 D 2
Vig (DK) 142 C 4
Vīgante (LV) 165 F 2
Vīganti (Lukna) (LV) 167 D 4
Vigeland (N) 142 A 1
Vigeois (F) 51 E 2
Vigevano (I) 97 D 4
Viggiano (I) 106 C 4
Vígla (GR) 211 D 3
Vignale Monferrato (I) 96 C 4
Vignanello (I) 102 B 4
Vigneulles-lès-Hattonchâtel (F) 44 B 3
Vignola (I) 101 F 1
Vignole Borbera (I) 100 C 1
Vignory (F) 44 B 4
Vigo (E) 58 A 4
Vigo di Fassa (I) 98 A 1
Vigone (I) 53 F 3
Vigonza (I) 98 B 3
Vigori (LV) 167 E 4
Vihanti (FIN) 133 E 1
Vihasoo (EST) 149 F 2
Vihiers (F) 46 C 2
Vihtavuori (FIN) 133 F 4
Vihteljärvi (FIN) 136 B 2
Vihti (FIN) 136 C 4
Vihtra (EST) 154 A 3
Vihula (EST) 150 C 2
Viiala (FIN) 136 C 3
Viiksimo (FIN) 135 F 1
Viimsi (EST) 149 E 2
Viinijärvi (FIN) 135 F 3
Viinistu (EST) 149 F 2
Viiratsi (EST) 154 B 4
Viisu (EST) 149 F 4
Viitasaari (FIN) 133 F 3
Viitina (EST) 161 E 2
Viitka (EST) 161 E 2
Viitna (EST) 150 C 3
Vijciems (LV) 160 B 2
Vijeikiai (LT) 171 F 3
Vik (IS) 126 B 3
Vik (N) 142 B 1
Vik (N) 131 E 1
Vik (N) 138 C 1
Vika (S) 140 C 2
Vikaičiai (LT) 170 C 2
Vikajärvi (FIN) 129 D 3
Vikedal (N) 138 B 3
Vikersund (N) 139 C 3
Vikeså (N) 138 B 4
Vikevåg (N) 138 B 3
Vīķi (LV) 159 E 1
Vikingstad (S) 143 E 1
Vikoč (BIH) 117 F 4
Vikran (N) 124 B 3
Viksdalen (N) 138 C 1
Viksjö (S) 132 A 4
Vīksna (Viksna) (LV) 161 E 4
Viktarinas (LT) 176 B 4
Vila Boim (P) 68 C 3
Vila de Cruces (E) 58 B 3
Vila de Rei (P) 68 B 1
Vila do Bispo (P) 74 A 2
Vila do Conde (P) 62 B 2
Vila Fernando (P) 68 C 3
Vila Flor (P) 63 D 3
Vila Franca das Naves (P) 63 D 4
Vila Franca de Xira (P) 68 A 2
Vila Fresca de Azeitão (P) 68 A 3
Vila Nova da Barquinha (P) 68 B 2
Vila Nova de Cerveira (P) 58 A 4
Vila Nova de Famalicão (P) 62 B 2
Vila Nova de Foz Côa (P) 63 D 3
Vila Nova de Gaia (P) 62 B 3
Vila Nova de Milfontes (P) 68 A 4
Vila Nova de Paiva (P) 62 C 3
Vila Nova de Poiares (P) 62 B 4
Vila Nova de Santo André (P) 68 A 4
Vila Nova de São Bento (P) 68 C 4
Vila Pouca de Aguiar (P) 62 C 2
Vila Praia de Âncora (P) 62 B 1
Vila-real (E) 72 A 2
Vila Real (P) 62 C 2
Vila Real de Santo António (P) 74 C 2
Vila-rodona (E) 66 C 3
Vila-seca (E) 66 B 4
Vila Velha de Ródão (P) 68 C 1
Vila Verde (P) 62 C 2
Vila Verde da Raia (P) 63 D 2
Vila Verde de Ficalho (P) 68 C 4
Vila Viçosa (P) 68 C 3
Vilada (E) 66 C 2
Viladamat (E) 67 E 2
Viladrau (E) 67 D 2
Vilafamés (E) 72 A 1
Vilafranca del Penedès (E) 66 C 3
Vilagarcía de Arousa (E) 58 A 3
Viļaka (LV) 161 F 4
Vilalba / Villalba (E) 58 C 2
Vilaller (E) 55 D 4
Vilallonga (E) 72 A 3
Vilamarxant (E) 71 F 2
Viļāni (LV) 167 D 2
Vilanova (E) 58 C 2
Vilanova d'Alcolea (E) 72 A 1
Vilanova de Arosa (E) 58 A 3
Vilanova de Sau (E) 67 D 2
Vilanova i la Geltrú / Villanueva y Geltrú (E) 66 C 3
Vilar de Barrio (E) 58 C 4
Vilar Formoso (P) 63 D 4
Vilcāni (LV) 167 D 3
Vilce (LV) 164 B 3
Vilches (E) 70 B 4
Vildūnai (LT) 164 C 4
Vileikiai Klaipėdos(LT) 168 B 3
Vileikiai Vilniaus(LT) 171 D 4
Vileikiškiai (LT) 171 E 4
Vilejka (BY) 7 D 3
Vilgāle (Saldenieki) (LV) 156 C 4
Vilhelmina (S) 132 A 2
Vília (GR) 218 B 1
Vilina Vlas (BIH) 118 A 3
Viliotės Užpelkis (LT) 162 C 3
Viljakkala (FIN) 136 C 2
Viljandi (EST) 154 B 4
Viljete (LV) 157 E 4
Vilkakrūgs (LV) 167 E 3
Vilkaviškis (LT) 175 E 2
Vilkėnas I (LT) 168 C 2
Viļķene (LV) 159 D 2
Vilkija (LT) 169 F 4
Vilkiškiai Kauno(LT) 169 F 2
Vilkiškiai Panevėžio(LT) 171 D 1
Vilkupiai (LT) 175 E 2
Vilkyškiai (LT) 169 D 4
Villa (EST) 154 B 4
Villa Adriana (I) 105 D 2
Villa Bartolomea (I) 98 A 4
Villa de Don Fadrique (La) (E) 70 C 2
Villa del Prado (E) 70 A 1
Villa del Río (E) 76 A 1
Villa Literno (I) 105 F 3
Villa Minozzo (I) 101 E 1
Villa Opicina (I) 99 D 2
Villa Potenza (I) 102 C 2
Villa San Giovanni (I) 111 E 1
Villa Santa Maria (I) 105 F 1
Villa Santina (I) 98 B 1
Villa Vomano (I) 102 C 4
Villabassa / Niederdorf (I) 98 B 1
Villablanca (E) 74 C 1
Villablino (E) 59 E 3
Villabona (E) 61 D 3
Villabrágima (E) 64 A 2
Villabuena del Puente (E) 63 F 3
Villacañas (E) 70 C 2
Villacarriedo (E) 60 B 2

Name	Page	Ref
Villacarrillo (E)	76	C 1
Villacastín (E)	64	A 4
Villach (A)	98	C 1
Villacidro (I)	108	B 4
Villada (E)	59	F 4
Villadiego (E)	60	A 4
Villadossola (I)	96	C 2
Villaescusa de Haro (E)	70	C 2
Villafáfila (E)	63	F 2
Villaflores (E)	63	F 3
Villafranca (E)	54	A 4
Villafranca de los Barros (E)	69	E 3
Villafranca de los Caballeros (E)	70	C 2
Villafranca del Bierzo (E)	59	D 4
Villafranca del Cid / Vilafranca (E)	72	A 1
Villafranca di Verona (I)	97	F 3
Villafranca in Lunigiana (I)	101	E 1
Villafranca-Montes de Oca (E)	60	B 4
Villafranca Piemonte (I)	53	F 3
Villafranca Tirrena (I)	111	E 1
Villafranco del Guadalquivir (E)	75	E 2
Villafrati (I)	110	C 2
Villafrechós (E)	64	A 4
Villafruela (E)	64	B 2
Villafuerte (E)	64	B 2
Villager de Laciana (E)	59	E 4
Villaggio Mancuso (I)	109	E 2
Villaharta (E)	69	F 4
Villahermosa (E)	70	C 4
Villahoz (E)	64	B 2
Villaines-la-Juhel (F)	41	F 3
Villala (FIN)	135	F 4
Villalba de la Sierra (E)	71	D 1
Villalba de los Barros (E)	69	D 3
Villalba del Rey (E)	71	D 1
Villalcázar de Sirga (E)	60	A 4
Villalgordo del Marquesado (E)	71	D 2
Villalón de Campos (E)	64	A 1
Villalpando (E)	63	F 2
Villalpardo (E)	71	E 2
Villaluenga (E)	65	E 3
Villamañan (E)	59	E 4
Villamanrique (E)	70	C 4
Villamanrique de la Condesa (E)	75	D 2
Villamartín (E)	75	E 3
Villamartín de Campos (E)	64	A 2
Villamassargia (I)	108	B 4
Villamayor (E)	65	E 3
Villamayor de Campos (E)	63	F 2
Villamayor de Santiago (E)	70	C 2
Villandraut (F)	50	B 4
Villandry (F)	47	E 2
Villanova Monteleone (I)	108	A 2
Villanubla (E)	64	A 2
Villanueva de Alcardete (E)	70	C 2
Villanueva de Alcorón (E)	65	D 4
Villanueva de Algaidas (E)	76	A 2
Villanueva de Argaño (E)	60	A 4
Villanueva de Bogas (E)	70	C 2
Villanueva de Cameros (E)	65	D 2
Villanueva de Córdoba (E)	70	A 4
Villanueva de Franco (E)	70	B 3
Villanueva de Gállego (E)	65	F 2
Villanueva de la Concepción (E)	76	A 3
Villanueva de la Fuente (E)	70	C 4
Villanueva de la Jara (E)	71	D 2
Villanueva de la Reina (E)	76	A 1
Villanueva de la Serena (E)	69	E 3
Villanueva de la Sierra (E)	69	E 1
Villanueva de la Vera (E)	69	F 1
Villanueva de las Torres (E)	76	C 2
Villanueva de los Castillejos (E)	74	C 1
Villanueva de los Infantes (E)	70	C 4
Villanueva de San Carlos (E)	70	B 4
Villanueva del Arzobispo (E)	76	C 1
Villanueva del Campo (E)	63	F 2
Villanueva del Duque (E)	69	F 4
Villanueva del Fresno (E)	68	C 4
Villanueva del Huerva (E)	65	F 3
Villanueva del Rey (E)	69	F 4
Villanueva del Río y Minas (E)	75	E 1
Villanueva del Trabuco (E)	76	A 2
Villaquejida (E)	63	F 1
Villaquilambre (E)	59	E 4
Villar de Cañas (E)	71	D 2
Villar de Domingo García (E)	71	D 1
Villar de Peralonso (E)	63	E 3
Villar del Arzobispo (E)	71	F 2
Villar del Rey (E)	69	D 2
Villarcayo (E)	60	B 3
Villard-de-Lans (F)	52	C 2
Villardeciervos (E)	63	F 2
Villardefrades (E)	63	F 2
Villarejo de Fuentes (E)	70	C 2
Villarejo de Salvanés (E)	70	C 1
Villarente (E)	59	F 4
Villares de la Reina (E)	63	F 3
Villares del Saz (E)	71	D 2
Villargarcía del Llano (E)	71	E 3
Villargordo del Cabriel (E)	71	E 2
Villaricos (E)	77	D 2
Villarino (E)	63	E 3
Villaroya de los Pinares (E)	71	E 1
Villarquemado (E)	71	E 1
Villarramiel (E)	64	A 2
Villarrín de Campos (E)	63	F 2
Villarrobledo (E)	71	D 3
Villarroya (E)	65	E 2
Villarroya de la Sierra (E)	65	E 2
Villarrubia de los Ojos (E)	70	B 3
Villarrubia de Santiago (E)	70	C 1
Villarrubio (E)	70	C 1
Villars-les-Dombes (F)	49	D 4
Villars-sur-Ollon (CH)	49	F 4
Villarta de San Juan (E)	70	B 3
Villasalto (I)	108	B 4
Villasana de Mena (E)	60	B 3
Villasandino (E)	60	A 4
Villasante de Montija (E)	60	B 3
Villasarracino (E)	60	A 4
Villaseco de los Reyes (E)	63	E 3
Villasequilla (E)	70	B 1
Villasimius (I)	108	C 4
Villasor (I)	108	B 4
Villatobas (E)	70	C 1
Villatoya (E)	71	E 3
Villava (E)	54	A 3
Villaverde del Río (E)	75	E 1
Villaviciosa (E)	59	F 2
Villaviciosa de Córdoba (E)	69	F 4
Villaviciosa de Odón (E)	70	B 1
Villavieja de Yeltes (E)	63	E 3
Villé (F)	45	F 2
Ville-en-Tardenois (F)	43	F 2
Ville-sur-Tourbe (F)	44	A 2
Villebois-Lavalette (F)	50	C 2
Villedieu-les-Poêles (F)	41	E 2
Villefagnan (F)	47	D 4
Villefort (F)	52	B 4
Villefranche-d'Albigeois (F)	55	F 1
Villefranche-de-Lauragais (F)	55	E 2
Villefranche-de-Lonchat (F)	50	C 3
Villefranche-de-Rouergue (F)	51	E 4
Villefranche-du-Périgord (F)	51	D 3
Villefranche-sur-Cher (F)	47	F 2
Villefranche-sur-Mer (F)	57	F 2
Villefranche-sur-Saône (F)	48	C 4
Villel (E)	71	E 1
Villemur-sur-Tarn (F)	55	E 1
Villena (E)	71	F 4
Villenauxe-la-Grande (F)	43	E 3
Villeneuve (F)	51	E 4
Villeneuve-d'Ascq (F)	39	D 2
Villeneuve-de-Berg (F)	52	B 3
Villeneuve-de-Marsan (F)	54	B 3
Villeneuve-l'Archevêque (F)	43	E 3
Villeneuve-lès-Avignon (F)	52	C 4
Villeneuve-sur-Lot (F)	51	D 4
Villeneuve-sur-Yonne (F)	43	E 4
Villeréal (F)	51	D 3
Villers-Bocage (F)	41	F 2
Villers-Bocage (F)	38	C 3
Villers-Bretonneux (F)	38	C 4
Villers-Cotterêts (F)	43	E 2
Villers-devant-Orval (B)	39	F 4
Villers-Farlay (F)	49	E 3
Villers-la-Ville (B)	39	E 2
Villers-le-Lac (F)	49	F 2
Villers-sur-Mer (F)	42	A 1
Villersexel (F)	49	E 2
Villerupt (F)	44	C 2
Villerville (F)	38	A 4
Villetta Barrea (I)	105	D 2
Villevere (EST)	154	B 3
Villiers-St-Georges (F)	43	E 3
Villingen (D)	45	F 4
Villoldo (E)	64	A 1
Villoria (E)	63	F 3
Villotta (I)	98	B 2
Vilnius (LT)	177	E 2
Vil'nohirs'k (UA)	13	F 1
Vilppula (FIN)	133	E 4
Vilpulka (LV)	159	E 1
Vilsbiburg (D)	94	A 3
Vilseck (D)	89	E 4
Vilshofen (D)	94	B 1
Vilučiai (LT)	171	F 2
Viļumi (LV)	164	C 2
Vilūnaičiai (LT)	164	C 4
Vilusi (MNE)	121	F 4
Viluste (EST)	161	E 1
Vilvoorde (B)	39	E 2
Vilzēni (LV)	159	E 2
Vimbas (LV)	163	E 3
Vimercate (I)	97	E 3
Vimianzo (E)	58	A 2
Vimieiro (P)	68	C 3
Vimioso (P)	63	E 2
Vimmerby (S)	143	F 2
Vimoutiers (F)	42	A 3
Vimpeli / Vindala (FIN)	133	E 3
Vimperk (CZ)	90	A 3
Vinac (BIH)	117	D 3
Vinadio (I)	53	E 4
Vinaixa (E)	66	B 3
Vinarós (E)	72	B 1
Vinay (F)	52	C 2
Vinça (F)	55	F 4
Vinča (SRB)	118	C 1
Vinchiaturo (I)	105	F 2
Vinci (I)	101	F 2
Vindeikiai (LT)	162	C 3
Vindeln (S)	132	C 2
Vinderup (DK)	142	B 3
Vindsvik (N)	138	B 3
Vingåker (S)	140	C 4
Vingelen (N)	131	D 2
Vingininkai (LT)	169	D 2
Vinhais (P)	63	D 2
Vinica (MK)	122	C 2
Vinica (SLO)	99	E 2
Viničani (MK)	122	B 3
Vinje (N)	138	C 3
Vinkovci (HR)	117	E 2
Vinkšnėnai Panevėžio (LT)	170	C 2
Vinkšnėnai Šiaulių (LT)	163	F 4
Vinkšnininiai (LT)	165	E 2
Vinni (EST)	151	D 3
Vinnycja (UA)	13	A 2
Vinsternes (N)	130	C 3
Vinstra (N)	139	E 1
Viñuelas (E)	64	C 4
Vinuesa (E)	65	D 2
Vipava (SLO)	99	D 2
Vīpe (LV)	166	C 2
Vipiteno / Sterzing (I)	93	F 4
Vir (BIH)	117	D 4
Vir (HR)	99	E 4
Vir (Otok) (HR)	99	E 4
Vira (N)	120	A 2
Virbalai (LT)	162	C 3
Virbalis (LT)	175	E 2
Virbališkiai (LT)	165	E 4
Vircava (LV)	164	C 2
Vire (F)	41	F 2
Vireši (LV)	160	C 3
Vireux-Wallerand (F)	39	E 4
Virga (LV)	162	C 2
Virgen de la Cabeza (Santuario) (E)	70	B 4
Virginia (IRL)	23	D 3
Virieu (F)	52	C 1
Virieu-le-Grand (F)	52	C 1
Virkkala / Virkby (FIN)	136	F 1
Virkkula (FIN)	129	D 3
Virkliai (LT)	162	C 2
Virkščiai (LT)	171	C 3
Virmutjoki (FIN)	137	F 2
Virolahti (FIN)	137	F 2
Virovitica (HR)	112	B 4
Virpazar (MNE)	121	E 3
Virrat (FIN)	133	E 3
Virsbo (S)	140	C 3
Virserum (S)	143	F 2
Virtasalmi (FIN)	135	E 2
Virton (B)	44	B 2
Virtsu (EST)	153	A 3
Viru-Jaagupi (EST)	151	D 3
Viru-Kabala (EST)	151	D 3
Viru-Nigula (EST)	151	D 3
Vis (HR)	103	F 2
Vis (Otok) (HR)	103	F 2
Visaginas (LT)	172	C 2
Višakio Rūda (LT)	175	F 1
Visby (S)	146	B 2
Visé (B)	87	D 2
Višegrad (BIH)	118	A 3
Visela (EST)	160	C 1
Viserba (I)	102	B 1
Viseu (P)	62	C 4
Viški (Viški) (LV)	167	D 4
Viskla (EST)	149	E 3
Višnjagora (SLO)	99	E 2
Višnjica (SRB)	118	B 1
Viso del Marqués (E)	70	B 4
Visoko (BIH)	117	E 3
Visp (CH)	96	C 2
Vissani (GR)	210	C 1
Visselhövede (D)	84	A 2
Vissenbjerg (DK)	142	B 4
Vissiniá (GR)	205	E 3
Visso (I)	102	C 3
Vistabella del Maestrazgo (E)	72	A 1
Vistheden (S)	128	A 4
Vištyčio Laukas I (LT)	175	E 2
Vištytis (LT)	175	E 3
Visusti (EST)	154	C 3
Visuvesi (FIN)	133	E 4
Vitaby (S)	143	E 4
Vitala (GR)	213	D 4
Vitanovac (SRB)	118	C 3
Viténai (LT)	170	C 3
Viterbo (I)	102	A 4
Vitez (BIH)	117	E 3
Viti (GR)	211	F 3
Vitigudino (E)	63	E 3
Vitina (BIH)	117	E 4
Vitina (SRB)	122	A 2
Vitiņi (LV)	163	E 2
Vitkov (CZ)	91	E 2
Vitkuški (LV)	166	C 4
Vitoli (GR)	211	F 3
Vitoliņi (LV)	164	C 2
Vitolište (MK)	122	B 4
Vitomirica (SRB)	121	F 1
Vitoria-Gasteiz (E)	60	C 4
Vitovlje (BIH)	117	D 3
Vitré (F)	41	E 3
Vitrey-sur-Mance (F)	49	E 1
Vitriola (I)	101	E 1
Vitrupe (LV)	159	D 2
Vitry-en-Artois (F)	39	D 3
Vitry-le-François (F)	43	F 2
Vitsa (GR)	211	D 1
Vitsand (S)	139	E 1
Vittangi (S)	128	B 2
Vitteaux (F)	48	C 2
Vittel (F)	44	C 4
Vittoria (I)	111	D 4
Vittorio Veneto (I)	98	B 2
Vittoriosa (M)	110	A 4
Vittsjö (S)	143	E 3
Vitznau (CH)	96	C 1
Viù (I)	53	F 2
Vivaro (I)	98	B 2
Viveiro (E)	58	C 2
Vivel del Río Martín (E)	65	F 3
Viver (E)	71	F 2
Viverols (F)	52	A 2
Viveros (E)	71	D 3
Viviers (F)	52	B 4
Vivonne (F)	47	D 4
Vizille (F)	53	D 2
Vižinada (HR)	99	D 3
Vizovice (CZ)	91	F 3
Vizzavona (F)	57	F 3
Vizzavona Col de (F)	57	F 3
Vizzini (I)	111	E 3
Vlaardingen (NL)	82	A 4
Vlacháva (GR)	211	E 1
Vlachérna Arkadía (GR)	217	E 2
Vlachérna Árta (GR)	211	D 2
Vlachiótis (GR)	223	E 3
Vlachokerasiá (GR)	217	E 3
Vlachomándra (GR)	217	D 1
Vlachópoulo (GR)	217	D 4
Vladičin Han (SRB)	119	E 4
Vladievci (MK)	122	C 2
Vladimirci (SRB)	118	B 2
Vladimirovac (SRB)	113	F 4
Vladimirovo (MK)	122	C 2
Vlagtwedde (NL)	83	D 2
Vlasenica (BIH)	117	F 2
Vlašim (CZ)	90	B 1
Vlasina Okruglica (SRB)	119	E 4
Vlásio (GR)	211	E 3
Vlasotince (SRB)	119	E 4
Vlásti (GR)	205	E 3
Vlissingen (NL)	37	F 3
Vlorë (AL)	18	B 2
Vlotho (D)	83	F 4
Vlychó (GR)	211	D 2
Vobbia (I)	100	C 1
Voćin (HR)	112	B 4
Vöcklabruck (A)	94	C 2
Vodice (HR)	99	D 3
Vodice (HR)	103	F 1
Vodňany (CZ)	90	A 1
Vodnjan (HR)	99	D 3
Võduvere (EST)	154	C 2
Voe (GB)	29	F 1
Vogatsikó (GR)	205	E 2
Vogelsdorf (D)	85	E 2
Voghera (I)	97	D 4
Vogošća (BIH)	117	E 4
Vohenstrauß (D)	89	E 4
Vöhma Saare (EST)	152	B 3
Vöhma Viljandi (EST)	154	C 3
Vöhmanõmme (EST)	154	C 3
Vohnja (EST)	150	C 2
Vöhringen (D)	93	E 2
Võibla (EST)	155	D 3
Void (F)	44	B 3
Võidu (EST)	153	C 4
Voika (EST)	154	C 4
Voikka (FIN)	137	E 2
Voikoski (FIN)	137	E 2
Voinić (HR)	99	F 2
Voiron (F)	52	C 2
Võisiku (EST)	154	B 3
Võiste (EST)	153	C 4
Võistre (EST)	154	B 3
Voiteur (F)	49	D 3
Voitsberg (A)	95	E 4
Võivaku (EST)	154	B 3
Vojakkala (FIN)	128	C 4
Vojens (DK)	142	B 4
Vojka (SRB)	118	B 1
Vojnik (SLO)	99	E 1
Vojska (SRB)	119	D 2
Vojtanov (CZ)	89	E 2
Voka (EST)	151	F 3
Vólakas (GR)	207	D 1
Volary (CZ)	94	B 1
Volda (N)	130	A 4
Volders (A)	93	F 4
Voldi (EST)	155	D 3
Volendam (NL)	82	B 3
Volímes (GR)	216	B 2
Volissós (GR)	220	C 1
Volkach (D)	88	C 3
Völkermarkt (A)	95	D 4
Völklingen (D)	45	E 2
Volkmarsen (D)	88	A 1
Volkovija (MK)	122	A 3
Volmunster (F)	45	E 2
Voločys'k (UA)	13	D 2
Volodymyr-Volyns'kyj (UA)	12	C 1
Volokolamsk (RUS)	7	D 1
Volonne (F)	53	D 4
Vólos (GR)	212	B 2
Volpiano (I)	53	E 2
Volta Mantovana (I)	97	F 3
Volterra (I)	101	F 3
Voltri (I)	100	C 1
Volturara Appula (I)	106	A 2
Volvic (F)	51	F 1
Volx (F)	57	B 4
Volyně (CZ)	90	A 4
Vónitsa (GR)	211	D 2
Vonnas (F)	49	D 4
Võnnu (EST)	155	E 4
Vööpste (EST)	155	D 3
Võõpsu (EST)	161	E 1
Voore (EST)	155	D 2
Voorschoten (NL)	82	A 4
Voorst (NL)	82	C 4
Voorthuizen (NL)	82	B 4
Vooru (EST)	154	B 4
Voose (EST)	149	F 3
Vopnafjörður (IS)	126	C 1
Võra / Vöyri (FIN)	133	D 3
Vorau (A)	95	E 3
Vorbuse (EST)	155	D 3
Vorchdorf (A)	94	C 2
Vorden (NL)	82	C 4
Vordernberg (A)	95	D 3
Vorderriß (D)	93	F 3
Vordingborg (DK)	144	C 4
Voreppe (F)	52	C 2
Vorey (F)	52	A 2
Voriškés (LT)	177	D 3
Vorna (FIN)	133	F 2
Vóroi (GR)	226	C 2
Voroklíni (CY)	231	D 3
Voroneţ (RO)	13	D 3
Vorsfelde (D)	84	B 3
Võru (EST)	161	D 1
Võrumõisa (EST)	161	D 1
Vosbutai (LT)	169	F 3
Vosgéliai (LT)	171	F 2
Vosiliškis (LT)	169	F 2
Vošiškės (LT)	176	C 2
Vosišķiai (LT)	170	B 4
Vosiūnai (LT)	173	D 3
Voskoniai (LT)	169	F 1
Voss (N)	138	C 2
Võsupere (EST)	150	C 2
Vothylakas (CY)	231	E 2
Votice (CZ)	90	B 3
Võtikvere (EST)	155	D 2
Votonósi (GR)	211	D 1
Vouchorína (GR)	205	E 4
Voúdia (GR)	224	A 2
Vouillé (F)	47	D 3
Voukoliés (GR)	226	A 2
Voúla (GR)	218	C 2
Vouliagméni (GR)	218	C 2
Voúlpi (GR)	211	E 3
Vouni (CY)	230	B 3
Vouraïkós (GR)	217	E 1
Vourgaréli (GR)	211	E 2
Vourkári (GR)	219	D 3
Vourliótes (GR)	221	D 2
Voúrvoura (GR)	217	E 3
Vourvourou (GR)	207	D 4
Võsu (EST)	150	C 2
Voutás (GR)	212	C 4
Vouvant (F)	46	C 3
Vouvray (F)	47	E 2
Vouzéla (GR)	62	C 3
Vouziers (F)	39	F 4
Voves (F)	42	C 3
Vovoúsa (GR)	211	D 1
Voz (HR)	99	E 3
Vozarci (MK)	122	B 3
Voznesens'k (UA)	13	F 2
Vrå (DK)	142	B 2
Vraca (BG)	19	D 1
Vračev Gaj (SRB)	118	C 1
Vračevšnica (SRB)	118	C 2
Vracháti (GR)	217	F 2
Vrachnaíika (GR)	217	D 1
Vrådal (N)	139	D 3
Vrams-Gunnarstorp (S)	143	D 3
Vrana (HR)	99	E 4
Vranduk (BIH)	117	E 3
Vranja (HR)	99	D 3
Vranje (SRB)	119	E 4
Vranjska Banja (SRB)	119	E 4
Vransko (SLO)	99	E 1
Vranštica (MNE)	118	B 4
Vrasná (GR)	207	D 3
Vrástama (GR)	206	C 4
Vratarnica (SRB)	119	E 2
Vratnica (MK)	122	A 2
Vravróna (GR)	218	C 2
Vražogrnac (SRB)	119	E 2
Vrbanja (HR)	117	F 1
Vrbas (BIH)	117	E 3
Vrbas (SRB)	113	D 4
Vrbaška (BIH)	115	E 4
Vrbljani (BIH)	116	C 3
Vrbnica (SRB)	121	F 1
Vrbnik (HR)	99	E 3
Vrbno pod Pradědem (CZ)	91	E 2
Vrboska (HR)	120	A 2
Vrbovec (HR)	112	A 4
Vrbovsko (HR)	99	E 3
Vrchlabí (CZ)	90	C 1
Vrčin (SRB)	118	C 1
Vrdnik (SRB)	118	A 1
Vrela (SRB)	121	F 2
Vrelo (HR)	99	F 3
Vreoci (SRB)	118	B 2
Vreden (D)	83	D 4
Vresse-sur-Semois (B)	39	F 4
Vrésthena (GR)	217	E 4
Vreta Kloster (S)	143	E 1
Vrgorac (HR)	120	B 1
Vría (GR)	206	A 4
Vríses (GR)	214	C 3
Vrlika (HR)	103	F 3
Vrnjačka Banja (SRB)	118	C 3
Vrpolje (BIH)	99	D 1
Vrontádos (GR)	220	C 1
Vrontamás (GR)	217	F 4
Vronteró (GR)	205	D 3
Vrontisí (GR)	226	C 2

Vrontoú *(GR)* 206	A 4	
Vrosína *(GR)* 210	C 2	
Vrouchás *(GR)* 227	E 2	
Vrpolje Šibenik *(HR)* ... 103	F 1	
Vrpolje		
Slavonski Brod *(HR)* 117	E 1	
Vršac *(SRB)* 113	D 3	
Vršani *(BIH)* 117	F 1	
Vrsar *(HR)* 99	D 3	
Vrsi *(HR)* 99	F 1	
Vrtoče *(BIH)* 116	C 2	
Vrutok *(MK)* 122	A 3	
Vrýses *(GR)* 226	A 3	
Vrysiá *(GR)* 212	A 3	
Vrysoúla *(GR)* 211	D 3	
Vrývaina *(GR)* 212	A 3	
Vsetín *(CZ)* 91	F 3	
Vučitrn *(SRB)* 119	D 4	
Vučkovica *(SRB)* 118	C 2	
Vukosavlje *(BIH)* 115	F 4	
Vukovar *(HR)* 113	D 4	
Vuohijärvi *(FIN)* 137	F 3	
Vuokatti *(FIN)* 135	E 2	
Vuolijoki *(FIN)* 133	F 2	
Vuollerim *(S)* 128	A 3	
Vuonislahti *(FIN)* 135	F 3	

Vuoskojaure *(S)* 124	C 4	
Vuostimo *(FIN)* 129	D 2	
Vuotso *(FIN)* 125	E 4	
Vydeikiai *(LT)* 162	C 4	
Vydmantai *(LT)* 162	B 4	
Vygreliai *(LT)* 175	E 3	
Vylkove *(UA)* 13	C 1	
Vyróneia *(GR)* 206	C 2	
Vyškov *(CZ)* 91	E 3	
Vyšnij Voločok *(RUS)* 7	E 1	
Vyšniūnai *(LT)* 176	C 2	
Vysoké Mýto *(CZ)* 91	D 2	
Vyšší Brod *(CZ)* 94	C 1	
Vytína *(GR)* 217	E 3	
Vytogala *(LT)* 169	D 2	
Vyzítsa *(GR)* 212	C 2	
Vyžuonos *(LT)* 171	F 2	

W

Waalwijk *(NL)* 86	C 1	
Waasmunster *(B)* 39	E 1	
Wabern *(D)* 88	B 1	
Wąbrzeźno *(PL)* 183	D 4	
Wąchock *(PL)* 196	B 2	
Wachow *(D)* 85	D 2	
Wächtersbach *(D)* 88	B 3	

Wadebridge *(GB)* 34	B 3	
Wädenswil *(CH)* 92	C 4	
Wadlew *(PL)* 195	D 1	
Wadowice *(PL)* 200	F 2	
Waganiec *(PL)* 189	D 1	
Wagenfeld *(D)* 83	F 3	
Wageningen *(NL)* 82	C 4	
Waging a. See *(D)* 94	B 4	
Wagrain *(A)* 94	B 4	
Wągrowiec *(PL)* 187	F 1	
Wahlstedt *(D)* 79	D 1	
Waiblingen *(D)* 45	F 3	
Waidhaus *(D)* 89	E 4	
Waidhofen		
an der Thaya *(A)* 95	D 1	
Waidhofen		
an der Ybbs *(A)* 95	D 2	
Waidring *(A)* 94	B 3	
Waischenfeld *(D)* 89	D 3	
Waizenkirchen *(A)* 94	C 4	
Wakefield *(GB)* 33	D 2	
Wałbrzych *(PL)* 193	E 3	
Walce *(PL)* 194	B 3	
Walchensee *(D)* 93	F 3	
Walchsee *(A)* 94	A 3	
Wałcz *(PL)* 181	E 4	

Wald *(CH)* 92	C 4	
Wald-Michelbach *(D)* 45	F 1	
Waldbröl *(D)* 87	F 2	
Waldeck *(D)* 88	A 1	
Waldenbuch *(D)* 45	F 3	
Waldenburg *(D)* 89	E 1	
Waldfischbach-		
Burgalben *(D)* 45	D 2	
Waldheim *(D)* 89	F 1	
Waldkappel *(D)* 88	B 1	
Waldkirch *(D)* 45	C 4	
Waldkirchen *(D)* 94	B 1	
Waldkraiburg *(D)* 94	A 3	
Waldmünchen *(D)* 89	F 4	
Waldsassen *(D)* 89	E 3	
Waldshut *(D)* 92	C 4	
Walenstadt *(CH)* 93	D 4	
Walim *(PL)* 193	E 3	
Wallasey *(GB)* 32	C 2	
Walldorf *(D)* 45	E 1	
Walldürn *(D)* 45	F 1	
Wallenfels *(D)* 89	D 3	
Wallersdorf *(D)* 94	A 1	
Wallerstein *(D)* 93	E 1	
Wallingford *(GB)* 35	F 2	
Walls *(GB)* 29	F 2	

Walsall *(GB)* 33	D 4	
Walsrode *(D)* 84	A 2	
Walsum *(D)* 87	E 1	
Waltershausen *(D)* 88	C 2	
Walton-on-the-Naze *(GB)*.. 37	D 3	
Waltrop *(D)* 87	F 1	
Wambierzyce *(PL)* 193	E 4	
Wanderup *(D)* 78	C 2	
Wandlitz *(D)* 85	E 2	
Wandowo *(PL)* 183	D 3	
Wanfried *(D)* 88	C 1	
Wangen i. Allgäu *(D)* 93	D 3	
Wangenbourg *(F)* 45	D 3	
Wangerland-Hooksiel *(D)*.. 78	B 4	
Wangerooge *(D)* 78	A 4	
Wängi *(CH)* 92	C 4	
Wanna *(D)* 78	B 4	
Wanne-Eickel *(D)* 87	E 1	
Wantage *(GB)* 35	F 2	
Wanzleben *(D)* 84	C 3	
Warburg *(D)* 88	A 1	
Wardenburg *(D)* 83	E 2	
Ware *(GB)* 36	B 3	
Waregem *(B)* 37	F 4	
Wareham *(GB)* 35	E 3	
Waremme *(B)* 39	F 2	

Waren *(D)* 79	F 4	
Warendorf *(D)* 83	E 4	
Warin *(D)* 79	E 4	
Warka *(PL)* 190	B 4	
Warkworth *(GB)* 31	F 3	
Warlubie *(PL)* 182	C 4	
Warmensteinach *(D)* 89	D 3	
Warminster *(GB)* 35	E 2	
Warnemünde *(D)* 79	F 3	
Warnice Zachodnio-		
pomorskie *(PL)* 186	B 1	
Warpuny *(PL)* 184	B 3	
Warrenpoint *(GB)* 23	E 3	
Warrington *(GB)* 32	C 2	
Warstein *(D)* 88	A 1	
Warszawa *(PL)* 190	B 3	
Warta *(PL)* 188	C 2	
Warta Bolesławiecka *(PL)*193	D 2	
Warth *(A)* 93	E 4	
Wartha *(D)* 88	C 1	
Wartkowice *(PL)* 189	D 4	
Warwick *(GB)* 33	D 4	
Washington *(GB)* 31	F 3	
Wasilków *(PL)* 185	E 4	
Waśniów *(PL)* 196	B 3	
Wąsosz Dolnośląskie *(PL)*193	E 1	

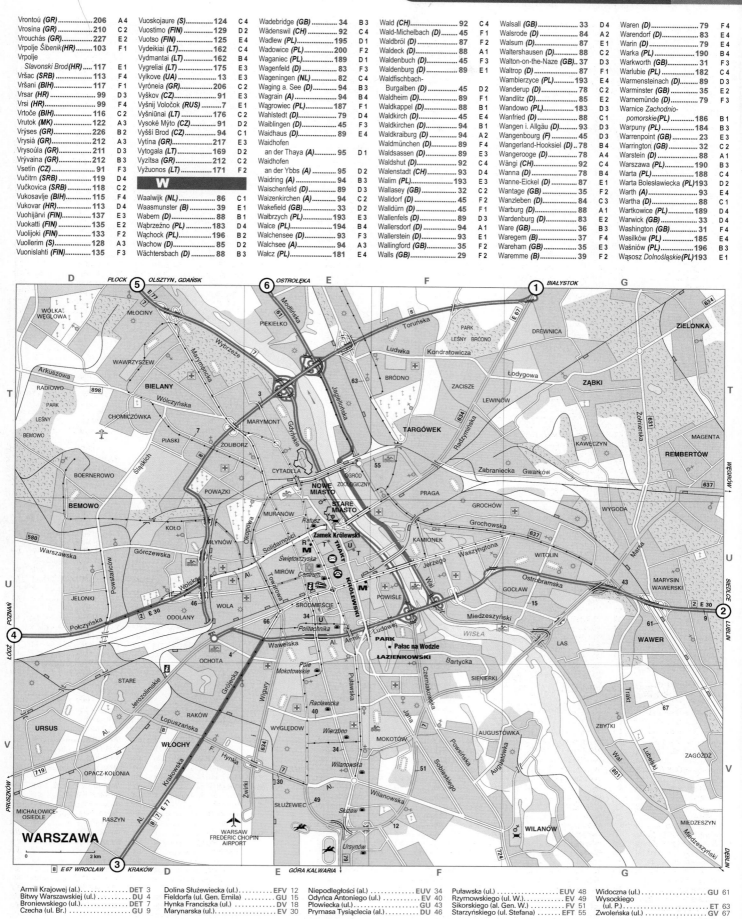

Armii Krajowej (al.) .... DET 3	Dolina Służewiecka (ul.) .... EFV 12	Niepodległości (al.) .... EUV 34	Puławska (ul.) .... EUV 48	Widoczna (ul.) .... GU 61
Bitwy Warszawskiej (ul.) .... DU 4	Fieldorfa (ul. Gen. Emila) ...... GU 15	Odyńca Antoniego (ul.) .... EV 40	Rzymowskiego (ul. W.) ...... EV 49	Wysockiego
Broniewskiego (ul.) .... DET 7	Hynka Franciszka (ul.) .... DV 18	Płowiecka (ul.) .... DU 43	Sikorskiego (al. Gen. W.) ... FV 51	(ul. P.) .... ET 63
Czecha (ul. Br.) .... GU 9	Marynarska (ul.) .... EV 30	Prymasa Tysiąclecia (al.) ...... DU 46	Starzyńskiego (ul. Stefana) ... EFT 55	Zwoleńska (ul.) .... GV 67

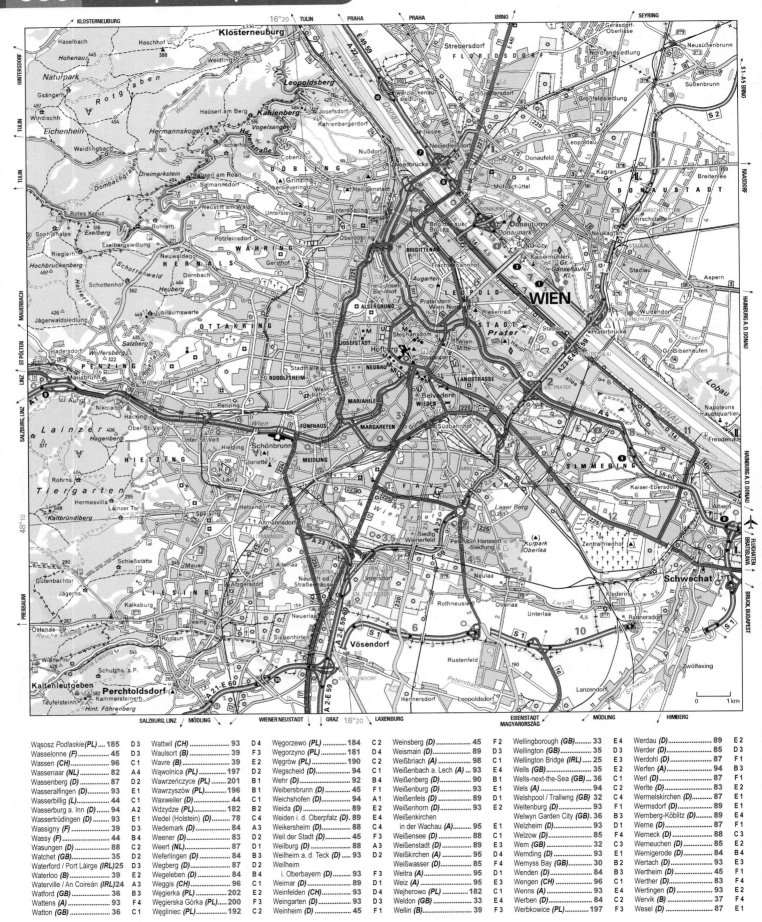

Wąsosz *Podlaskie*(*PL*).... 185	D 3	Wattwil (*CH*) 93	D 4	Węgorzewo (*PL*) 184	C 2
Wasselonne (*F*) 45	D 3	Waulsort (*B*) 39	F 3	Węgorzyno (*PL*) 181	D 4
Wassen (*CH*) 96	C 1	Wavre (*B*) 39	E 2	Węgrów (*PL*) 190	C 2
Wassenaar (*NL*) 82	A 4	Wąwolnica (*PL*) 197	D 2	Wegscheid (*D*) 94	C 1
Wassenberg (*D*) 87	D 2	Wawrzeńczyce (*PL*) 201	B 1	Wehr (*D*) 92	B 4
Wasseralfingen (*D*) 93	E 1	Wawrzyszów (*PL*) 196	B 1	Weiberbrunn (*D*) 45	E 1
Wasserbillig (*L*) 44	C 1	Waxweiler (*D*) 44	C 1	Weichshofen (*D*) 94	A 1
Wasserburg a. Inn (*D*) 94	A 2	Wdzydze (*PL*) 182	B 2	Weida (*D*) 89	E 2
Wassertrüdingen (*D*) 93	E 1	Wedel (Holstein) (*D*) 78	C 4	Weiden i. d. Oberpfalz (*D*). 89	E 4
Wassigny (*F*) 39	D 3	Wedemark (*D*) 84	A 3	Weikersheim (*D*) 88	C 4
Wassy (*F*) 44	B 4	Weener (*D*) 83	D 2	Weil der Stadt (*D*) 45	E 1
Wasungen (*D*) 88	C 2	Weert (*NL*) 87	D 1	Weilburg (*D*) 88	A 3
Watchet (*GB*) 35	D 2	Weferlingen (*D*) 84	B 3	Weilheim a. d. Teck (*D*) ... 93	D 2
Waterford / Port Láirge (*IRL*)25	D 3	Wegberg (*D*) 87	D 2	Weilheim	
Waterloo (*B*) 39	E 2	Wegeleben (*D*) 84	B 4	i. Oberbayern (*D*) 93	F 3
Waterville / An Coireán (*IRL*)24	A 3	Weggis (*CH*) 96	C 1	Weimar (*D*) 89	D 1
Watford (*GB*) 36	C 4	Węgierka (*PL*) 202	E 2	Weinfelden (*CH*) 93	D 2
Wattens (*A*) 93	F 4	Węgierska Górka (*PL*) 200	F 3	Weingarten (*D*) 93	D 3
Watton (*GB*) 36	C 1	Węgliniec (*PL*) 192	C 2	Weinheim (*D*) 45	F 1

Weinsberg (*D*) 45	F 2	Wellingborough (*GB*) 33	E 4	Werdau (*D*) 89	E 2
Weismain (*D*) 89	D 3	Wellington (*GB*) 35	E 3	Werder (*D*) 85	D 3
Weißbriach (*A*) 98	C 1	Wellington Bridge (*IRL*) ... 25	E 3	Werdohl (*D*) 87	F 1
Weißenbach a. Lech (*A*) ... 93	E 4	Wells (*GB*) 35	E 2	Werfen (*A*) 94	B 3
Weißenberg (*D*) 90	B 1	Wells-next-the-Sea (*GB*) .. 36	C 1	Werl (*D*) 87	F 1
Weißenburg (*D*) 93	E 1	Wels (*A*) 94	C 2	Werlte (*D*) 83	E 2
Weißenfels (*D*) 89	D 1	Welshpool / Trallwng (*GB*) 32	C 4	Wermelskirchen (*D*) 87	E 1
Weißenhorn (*D*) 93	E 2	Weltenburg (*D*) 93	F 1	Wermsdorf (*D*) 89	E 1
Weißenkirchen		Welwyn Garden City (*GB*). 36	B 3	Wernberg-Köblitz (*D*) 89	E 4
in der Wachau (*A*) 95	E 1	Welzheim (*D*) 93	D 1	Werne (*D*) 87	F 1
Weißensee (*D*) 88	C 4	Welzow (*D*) 85	F 4	Werneck (*D*) 88	C 3
Weißenstadt (*D*) 89	E 3	Wem (*GB*) 32	C 3	Werneuchen (*D*) 85	E 2
Weißkirchen (*A*) 95	D 4	Wemding (*D*) 93	E 1	Wernigerode (*D*) 84	B 4
Weißwasser (*D*) 85	F 4	Wemyss Bay (*GB*) 30	B 2	Wertach (*D*) 93	E 3
Weitra (*A*) 95	D 1	Wenden (*D*) 84	B 3	Wertheim (*D*) 45	F 1
Weiz (*A*) 95	E 2	Wengen (*CH*) 93	C 1	Werther (*D*) 83	F 4
Wejherowo (*PL*) 182	C 1	Wenns (*A*) 93	E 4	Wertingen (*D*) 93	E 2
Weldon (*GB*) 33	E 4	Werben (*D*) 84	C 2	Wervik (*B*) 37	F 4
Wellin (*B*) 39	F 3	Werbkowice (*PL*) 197	F 3	Wesel (*D*) 87	E 1

Wesenberg *(D)* 80	B 4
Wesendorf *(D)* 84	B 3
Wesoła *Mazowieckie(PL)* 190	B 3
Wesselburen *(D)* 78	A 3
Wessobrunn *(D)* 93	F 3
West Auckland *(GB)* 31	E 4
West Bridgford *(GB)* 33	E 3
West Kilbride *(GB)* 30	B 2
West Linton *(GB)* 31	D 2
West Looe *(GB)* 34	C 4
West Mersea *(GB)* 36	C 3
West-Terschelling *(NL)* ... 82	
Westbury *(GB)* 35	E 2
Westendorf *(A)* 94	A 4
Westenholz *(D)* 84	A 2
Westerburg *(D)* 87	F 2
Westerholt *(D)* 78	A 4
Westerland *(D)* 78	A 2
Westerlo *(B)* 39	F 1
Westernbödefeld *(D)* 88	A 1
Westerstede *(D)* 83	A 2
Westhofen *(D)* 45	E 1
Weston-super-Mare *(GB)*.. 35	D 2
Westport /	
Cathair na Mart *(IRL)* 22	B 3

Wetherby *(GB)* 33	D 2
Wetlina *(PL)* 202	E 4
Wetter (Ruhr) *(D)* 87	F 1
Wetteren *(B)* 39	E 2
Wettin *(D)* 84	C 4
Wettringen *(D)* 83	D 4
Wetwang *(GB)* 33	E 1
Wetzikon *(CH)* 92	C 4
Wetzlar *(D)* 88	A 2
Wexford /	
Loch Garman *(IRL)* .. 25	E 3
Weyer Markt *(A)* 95	D 2
Weyhausen *(D)* 84	A 2
Weyhill *(GB)* 35	F 2
Weymouth *(GB)* 35	E 3
Weyregg a. Attersee *(A)*... 94	C 2
Whaley Bridge *(GB)* 33	D 3
Whitburn *(GB)* 31	D 2
Whitby *(GB)* 33	E 1
Whitchurch *(GB)* 32	C 3
Whitebridge *(GB)* 30	
Whitehaven *(GB)* 31	D 4
Whitehead *(GB)* 23	F 2
Whiteness *(GB)* 29	F 2
Whithorn *(GB)* 30	

Whitland *(GB)* 34	C 1
Whitley Bay *(GB)* 31	F 4
Whitstable *(GB)* 37	D 3
Whittlesey *(GB)* 33	F 4
Wiązów *(PL)* 193	F 3
Wiązowna *(PL)* 190	B 3
Wiązownica *(PL)* 202	E 1
Wick *(GB)* 27	F 1
Wickford *(GB)* 36	C 3
Wicklow /	
Cill Mhantáin *(IRL)* ... 25	F 2
Wicko *(PL)* 182	B 1
Widawa *(PL)* 195	A 2
Widnes *(GB)* 32	C 2
Widuchowa *(PL)* 186	B 1
Więcbork *(PL)* 181	C 4
Więckowice *(PL)* 187	E 2
Wiedenbrück *(D)* 83	E 4
Wiefelstede *(D)* 83	D 1
Wiehe *(D)* 89	D 1
Wiehl *(D)* 80	D 2
Większyce *(PL)* 194	B 4
Wielbark *(PL)* 184	B 4
Wiele *(PL)* 182	B 3
Wieleń *(PL)* 187	E 1

Wielgie *Kujawsko-*	
Pomorskie(PL) 189	D 2
Wielgowo *(PL)* 180	C 4
Wielichowo *(PL)* 187	E 3
Wieliczka *(PL)* 201	A 2
Wieliczki *(PL)* 185	C 2
Wielka Nieszawka *(PL)*... 188	C 1
Wielka Sowa *(PL)* 193	E 3
Wielka Wieś *(PL)* 201	A 1
Wielki Wełcz *(PL)* 182	A 4
Wielkopolski Park	
Etnograficzny *(PL)*..... 187	F 2
Wielkopolski Park	
Narodowy *(PL)* 187	E 3
Wielopole Skrzyńskie *(PL)*202	D 2
Wielowieś *Śląskie (PL)*.... 194	C 4
Wielowieś	
Świętokrzyskie(PL) .. 196	C 2
Wieluń *(PL)* 194	C 2
Wien *(A)* 95	F 1
Wiener Neudorf *(A)* 95	F 2
Wiener Neustadt *(A)*..... 95	F 2
Wieniawa *(PL)* 196	B 2
Wieprz *Małopolskie(PL)*.. 200	F 2
Wieprza *(PL)* 181	F 2

Wieruszów *(PL)* 194	C 2
Wierzbica *Chełm(PL)* 197	F 2
Wierzbica *Lublin(PL)* 197	D 2
Wierzbica	
Mazowieckie(PL) 196	B 2
Wierzbica Górna *(PL)* 194	B 2
Wierzbięcin *(PL)* 180	C 3
Wierzbinek *(PL)* 188	C 2
Wierzchlas *(PL)* 194	C 2
Wierzchosławice *(PL)*.... 201	A 2
Wierzchowo *Zachodnio-*	
pomorskie(PL) 181	D 4
Wiesau *(D)* 89	E 3
Wiesbaden *(D)* 45	E 1
Wieselburg *(A)* 95	D 2
Wiesenburg *(D)* 85	D 3
Wiesensteig *(D)* 93	D 2
Wiesentheid *(D)* 88	C 4
Wiesenttal *(D)* 89	D 3
Wiesing *(A)* 94	A 4
Wiesloch *(D)* 45	F 2
Wiesmath *(A)* 95	F 2
Wiesmoor *(D)* 83	E 1
Wietrzychowice *(PL)* 196	B 4

Wigan *(GB)* 32	C 2
Wigierski Park	
Narodowy *(PL)* 185	E 2
Wigry (Jezioro) *(PL)* 185	E 2
Wigton *(GB)* 31	D 4
Wigtown *(GB)* 30	C 4
Wijewo *(PL)* 187	D 4
Wijhe *(NL)* 82	C 3
Wil *(CH)* 93	D 4
Wilamowice *(PL)* 200	E 2
Wilczęta *(PL)* 183	E 2
Wilczy Szaniec *(PL)* 184	B 2
Wilczyce *(PL)* 196	C 3
Wilczyn *(PL)* 188	C 2
Wildalpen *(A)* 95	D 3
Wildbad	
i. Schwarzwald *(D)*.... 45	F 3
Wildeck *(D)* 88	B 2
Wildeck *(D)* 88	B 2
Wildeshausen *(D)* 83	E 2
Wildon *(A)* 95	E 4
Wilfersdorf *(A)* 95	F 1
Wilga *(PL)* 190	C 4
Wilhelmsburg *(A)* 95	E 2
Wilhelmshaven *(D)* 83	E 1

Augusta Šenoe........	BCZ	19
Bakačeva	BY	17
Ćirilometodska	AY	5
Felbingerove stube ...	BY	8
Frane Petrića	BY	14
Freudenreichova......	AY	6
Habdelićeva..........	BY	13
Kapucinske stube	AY	3
Male stube	BY	10
Mletačka	AY	7
Mlinarske stube	BY	9
Perkovčeva	AZ	16
Runjaninova	AZ	18
Skalinska	BY	12
Vranicanijeva.........	AZ	4
Vukotinovićeva.......	AZ	15

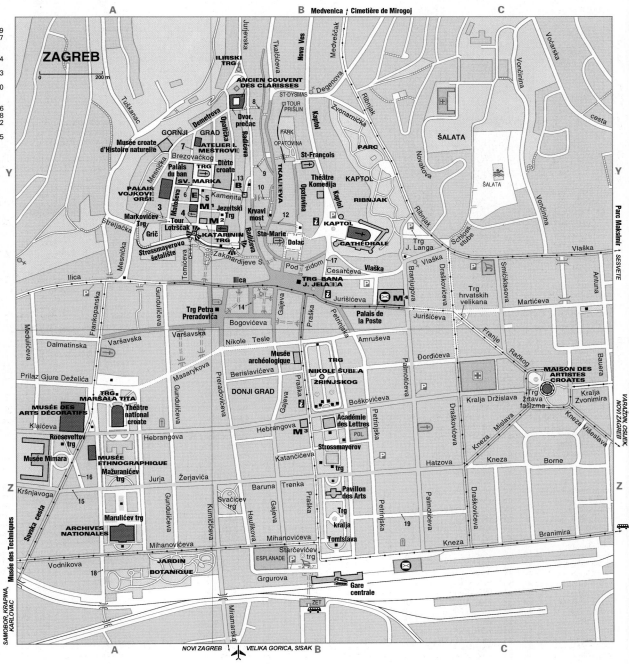

ZAGREB

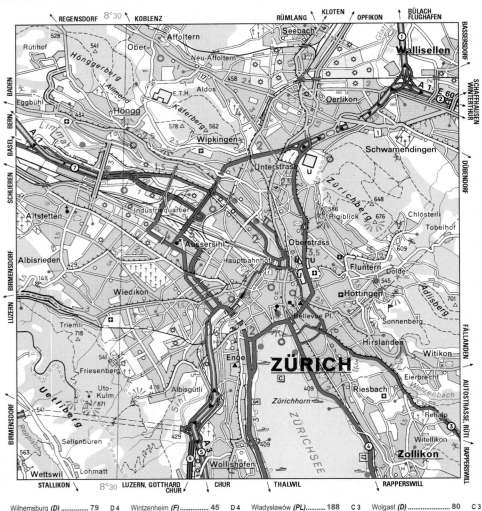

Woźniki (PL)	195	D 4	
Wragby (GB)	33	E 3	
Wręczyca Wielka (PL)	195	D 3	
Wrexham / Wrecsam (GB)	32	E 2	
Wriezen (D)	85	E 2	
Wróblew (PL)	188	C 4	
Wrocław (PL)	193	F 2	
Wronki Warmińsko-Mazurskie(PL)	184	C 2	
Wronki Wielkopolskie(PL)	187	E 2	
Wroughton (GB)	35	F 2	
Września (PL)	188	B 3	
Wschowa (PL)	187	E 4	
Wsi Lubelskiej (PL)	197	D 2	
Wsi Radomskiej (PL)	196	B 1	
Wulfen (D)	83	F 3	
Wullowitz (A)	94	C 1	
Wünnenberg (D)	88	A 1	
Wünsdorf (D)	85	E 3	
Wunsiedel (D)	89	E 3	
Wunstorf (D)	84	A 3	
Wuppertal (D)	87	F 3	
Würzburg (D)	88	B 4	
Wurzen (D)	85	D 4	
Wusterhausen (D)	85	D 2	
Wustrow (D)	79	E 3	
Wustrow Kreis Nordvorpommern(D)	79	F 3	
Wuustwezel (B)	39	E 1	
Wyczerpy Górne (PL)	195	D 3	
Wydminy (PL)	184	C 2	
Wyk a. Föhr (D)	78	B 2	
Wymondham (GB)	37	D 1	
Wyry (PL)	200	E 2	
Wyryki-Połód (PL)	191	F 4	
Wyrzysk (PL)	187	E 2	
Wyśmierzyce (PL)	190	B 4	
Wysoka Wielkopolskie(PL)	187	F 1	
Wysoka Kamieńska (PL)	180	C 3	
Wysokie Lubelskie(PL)	197	E 3	
Wysokie Mazowieckie (PL)	191	D 1	
Wysowa (PL)	201	C 3	
Wyszków Mazowieckie(PL)	190	C 2	
Wyszogród (PL)	189	F 2	

Ylämylly (FIN)	135	F 3	
Yläne (FIN)	136	B 3	
Yli-Ii (FIN)	129	D 4	
Yli-Kärppä (FIN)	129	D 4	
Yli-Muonio (FIN)	125	D 4	
Yli Nampa (FIN)	129	D 3	
Yli-Olhava (FIN)	129	D 4	
Ylihärmä (FIN)	133	D 3	
Yliki (GR)	218	B 1	
Ylikiiminki (FIN)	133	F 1	
Ylistaro (FIN)	133	D 3	
Ylitornio (FIN)	128	C 3	
Ylivieska (FIN)	133	F 4	
Ylläsjärvi (FIN)	128	C 2	
Ylöjärvi (FIN)	136	C 2	
Ymittós (GR)	218	C 2	
York (GB)	33	E 1	
Youghal / Eochaill (IRL)	25	D 3	
Yoxford (GB)	37	D 2	
Ypäjä (FIN)	136	C 3	
Ypáti (GR)	212	A 1	
Ypéreia (GR)	212	A 2	
Yport (F)	38	A 4	
Yppäri (FIN)	133	C 2	
Ypsili Ráchi (GR)	207	E 2	
Ypsonas (CY)	230	B 4	
Ýpsos (GR)	210	B 1	
Yssingeaux (F)	52	E 4	
Ystad (S)	143	E 4	
Ytterhogdal (S)	131	F 4	
Yttermalung (S)	140	B 2	
Yuncos (E)	70	B 1	
Yunquera (E)	75	F 3	
Yunquera de Henares (E)	64	C 4	
Yuste (Monasterio de) (E)	69	F 1	
Yverdon-les-Bains (CH)	49	F 3	
Yvetot (F)	38	A 4	
Yvoir (B)	39	F 3	
Yvoire (F)	49	E 4	
Yzeure (F)	48	B 3	

Z

Zaandam (NL)	82	B 3	
Zabaka (LT)	177	D 2	
Zabalj (SRB)	113	E 4	
Žabari (SRB)	118	C 2	
Žabia Wola Mazowieckie(PL)	189	F 3	
Zabičiūnai (LT)	171	F 2	
Zabierzów (PL)	201	A 1	
Ząbki (PL)	190	B 3	
Ząbkowice Śląskie (PL)	193	D 4	
Zablace (HR)	103	F 1	
Žabljak Pljevlja(MNE)	118	A 4	
Žabljak Podgorica(MNE)	121	E 2	
Zabłudów (PL)	191	E 1	
Żabno (PL)	201	C 1	
Zabok (HR)	99	F 3	
Zabór (PL)	187	D 4	
Zaborowo (PL)	187	E 4	
Zábrdě (BIH)	117	F 2	
Zábřeh (CZ)	91	E 2	
Ząbrowo (PL)	181	D 2	
Zabrze (PL)	195	D 4	
Zabrzeg (PL)	200	F 2	
Zacháro (GR)	217	D 3	
Zadar (HR)	103	E 1	
Žadeikiai (LT)	169	D 2	
Žadeikoniai (LT)	165	D 4	
Žaduvénai (LT)	169	D 1	
Zadvarje (HR)	117	D 4	
Zádzene (LV)	165	E 1	
Zadzim (PL)	189	D 4	
Žadžiūnai (LT)	163	F 4	
Zafarraya (E)	76	A 3	
Zafóra (Nisoí) (GR)	225	D 1	
Zafra (E)	69	D 4	
Żagań (PL)	186	C 4	
Żagarė (LT)	163	F 3	
Žagariai (LT)	176	C 3	
Žagarinė (LT)	177	E 3	
Žagariškiai (LT)	163	F 3	
Zagklivéri (GR)	206	C 3	
Zaglavak (SRB)	118	A 3	
Zagnańsk (PL)	195	F 2	
Zagora (GR)	212	C 2	
Zagorje (SLO)	99	F 3	
Zagórów (PL)	188	B 3	
Zagórz (PL)	202	C 2	
Zagorzyce (PL)	202	D 2	
Zagreb (HR)	99	F 2	
Zagrodno (PL)	193	D 2	
Žagubica (SRB)	119	D 2	
Zagvozd (HR)	117	D 4	
Zahara de los Atunes (E)	75	D 4	
Zahinos (E)	69	D 4	

X

Xàbia / Jávea (E)	72	A 4	
Xanten (D)	87	E 1	
Xánthi (GR)	207	A 4	
Xàtiva (E)	71	F 3	
Xeresa (E)	72	A 3	
Xeros (CY)	230	B 3	
Xeros Potamos (CY)	230	B 3	
Xert (E)	72	A 1	
Xerta (E)	66	B 3	
Xertigny (F)	44	C 4	
Xifiani (GR)	205	F 2	
Xinó Neró (GR)	205	F 4	
Xinzo de Limia (E)	58	C 4	
Xirokámpi (GR)	217	E 4	
Xirókampos (GR)	221	F 4	
Xirolimni (GR)	205	F 4	
Xiropótamos (GR)	206	C 3	
Xixona (E)	71	F 4	
Xubia (E)	58	B 2	
Xunqueira de Ambía (E)	58	C 4	
Xylaganí (GR)	208	A 2	
Xylikó (GR)	212	B 4	
Xylofagou (CY)	231	D 3	
Xylókastro (GR)	217	E 3	
Xylopároiko (GR)	211	E 2	
Xylópoli (GR)	206	C 2	
Xylóskalo (GR)	226	A 2	
Xylotymvou (CY)	231	D 3	
Xyniáda (GR)	212	A 3	

Y

Yalova (TR)	19	F 1	
Yanguas (E)	65	D 2	
Yarmouth (GB)	35	F 3	
Ybbs an der Donau (A)	95	D 2	
Ydra (GR)	218	B 3	
Ýdra (Nisí) (GR)	218	B 3	
Yebra (E)	70	C 1	
Yecla (E)	71	E 4	
Yenne (F)	53	D 1	
Yeovil (GB)	35	E 3	
Yepes (E)	70	B 1	
Yerville (F)	38	B 4	
Yesa (E)	65	A 4	
Yeşilova (TR)	19	F 3	
Yeste (E)	71	D 4	
Ylakiai (LT)	162	C 3	
Ylämaa (FIN)	137	E 3	

Wilhemsburg (D)	79	D 4	
Wilhering (A)	94	C 2	
Wilkasy (PL)	184	C 2	
Wilkau-Haßlau (D)	89	E 2	
Wilkołaz Pierwszy (PL)	197	D 2	
Wilków Opolskie(PL)	194	B 2	
Wilkowice (PL)	200	F 2	
Willebroek (B)	39	E 2	
Willemstad (NL)	86	B 1	
Willingen (D)	88	A 1	
Williton (GB)	35	D 2	
Wilmslow (GB)	33	D 3	
Wilnsdorf (D)	87	F 2	
Wilsdruff (D)	89	F 1	
Wilster (D)	78	C 4	
Wilton (GB)	35	E 2	
Wiltz (L)	44	C 1	
Wimborne Minster (GB)	35	E 3	
Wimereux (F)	37	D 4	
Wincanton (GB)	35	E 2	
Winchcombe (GB)	35	E 1	
Winchelsea (GB)	36	C 4	
Winchester (GB)	35	F 3	
Windeck (D)	87	F 2	
Windermere (GB)	32	C 1	
Windischeschenbach (D)	89	E 3	
Windischgarsten (A)	94	C 3	
Windsbach (D)	89	D 2	
Windsor (GB)	36	B 3	
Winkleigh (GB)	34	C 3	
Winklern (A)	94	B 4	
Winnenden (D)	45	F 3	
Winnica (PL)	190	B 2	
Winnigstedt (D)	84	B 4	
Winnweiler (D)	45	E 1	
Winschoten (NL)	83	D 2	
Winsen (D)	84	A 1	
Winsen (Aller) (D)	84	A 3	
Winsford (GB)	32	C 3	
Wińsko (PL)	193	D 1	
Winsum (NL)	82	C 2	
Winterberg (D)	88	A 1	
Winterswijk (NL)	83	D 4	
Winterthur (CH)	92	C 4	

Wintzenheim (F)	45	D 4	
Wipperfürth (D)	87	F 2	
Wisbech (GB)	33	F 4	
Wischhafen (D)	78	C 4	
Wishaw (GB)	30	C 2	
Wiskitki (PL)	189	F 3	
Wisła (PL)	200	F 2	
Wiślana (Mierzeja) (PL)	183	D 2	
Wiślane (Żuławy) (PL)	183	D 2	
Wiślany (Zalew) (PL)	183	D 2	
Wiślica (PL)	195	F 4	
Wismar (D)	79	E 3	
Wiśniew (PL)	191	D 3	
Wiśniewo (PL)	189	F 1	
Wiśniowa Małopolskie(PL)	201	A 2	
Wiśniowa Podkarpackie(PL)	202	D 2	
Wissant (F)	37	D 4	
Wissembourg (F)	45	D 2	
Wissen (D)	87	F 2	
Wisznia Mała (PL)	193	D 2	
Wisznice (PL)	191	E 4	
Witham (GB)	36	C 3	
Withernsea (GB)	33	F 2	
Witkowo Wielkopolskie(PL)	188	B 2	
Witkowo Zachodniopomorskie(PL)	180	C 4	
Witney (GB)	35	F 1	
Witnica Lubuskie(PL)	186	C 2	
Witonia (PL)	189	D 3	
Wittdün (D)	78	B 3	
Witten (D)	87	F 1	
Wittenberg (D)	85	D 4	
Wittenberge (D)	84	C 2	
Wittichenau (D)	85	F 4	
Wittingen (D)	84	B 2	
Wittlich (D)	45	D 1	
Wittmund (D)	78	A 4	
Wittstock (D)	84	C 1	
Witzenhausen (D)	88	B 1	
Wiżajny (PL)	185	D 1	
Wizna (PL)	185	D 4	

Władysławów (PL)	188	C 3	
Władysławowo Pomorskie(PL)	182	C 1	
Wleń (PL)	193	D 2	
Włocławek (PL)	189	D 2	
Włodawa (PL)	191	F 4	
Włodowice (PL)	195	E 4	
Włoszakowice (PL)	187	E 4	
Włoszczowa (PL)	195	E 3	
Wöbbelin (D)	79	E 2	
Woburn (GB)	36	B 2	
Wodynie (PL)	190	C 3	
Wodzisław (PL)	195	E 4	
Wodzisław Śląski (PL)	200	E 2	
Woensdrecht (NL)	39	E 1	
Woerden (NL)	82	B 4	
Wœrth (F)	45	D 2	
Wohlen (CH)	92	C 4	
Woippy (F)	44	C 2	
Wojaszówka (PL)	202	D 2	
Wojciechów (PL)	197	D 2	
Wojcieszków (PL)	191	D 4	
Wojcieszów (PL)	193	D 3	
Wojnicz (PL)	201	C 2	
Wojsławice (PL)	197	F 2	
Woking (GB)	36	B 3	
Wokingham (GB)	36	B 3	
Wola (PL)	200	F 2	
Wola Jedlińska (PL)	195	E 3	
Wola Krzysztoporska (PL)	195	E 2	
Wola Prażmowska (PL)	190	B 4	
Wola Uhruska (PL)	197	F 1	
Wolanów (PL)	196	B 1	
Wolbrom (PL)	195	E 4	
Wołczyn (PL)	194	B 1	
Woldegk (D)	80	C 4	
Wolfach (D)	45	E 3	
Wolfegg (D)	93	D 2	
Wolfen (D)	85	D 4	
Wolfenbüttel (D)	84	B 4	
Wolfhagen (D)	88	A 1	
Wolfratshausen (D)	93	F 3	
Wolfsberg (D)	95	D 2	
Wolfsburg (D)	84	B 3	

Wolgast (D)	80	C 3	
Wolibórz (PL)	193	E 4	
Wolin (PL)	180	B 3	
Woliński Park Narodowy(PL)	180	B 3	
Wólka Lubelskie(PL)	197	D 2	
Wólka Mlądzka (PL)	190	B 4	
Wolkersdorf (A)	95	F 1	
Wöllersdorf (A)	95	F 1	
Wollersheim (D)	87	E 2	
Wollin (D)	85	D 3	
Wolmirstedt (D)	84	C 3	
Wolnzach (D)	93	F 1	
Wołomin (PL)	190	B 3	
Wołosate (PL)	202	F 4	
Wołów (PL)	193	D 2	
Wolsingham (GB)	33	E 4	
Wolsztyn (PL)	187	D 3	
Wolvega (NL)	82	C 3	
Wolverhampton (GB)	33	D 4	
Wolverton (GB)	36	B 2	
Wonieść (Jezioro) (PL)	187	E 4	
Woodbridge (GB)	37	D 2	
Woodhall Spa (GB)	33	F 3	
Woodstock (GB)	35	F 1	
Wooler (GB)	31	E 3	
Worb (CH)	96	B 1	
Worbis (D)	88	C 1	
Worcester (GB)	35	E 1	
Wörgl (A)	94	A 3	
Workington (GB)	31	D 4	
Worksop (GB)	33	E 3	
Workum (NL)	82	B 2	
Wormerveer (NL)	82	B 3	
Wormhout (F)	37	E 4	
Worms (D)	45	E 1	
Wörrstadt (D)	45	E 1	
Wörth a. d. Donau (D)	94	A 1	
Wörth a. Main (D)	45	F 1	
Wörth a. Rhein (D)	45	E 2	
Worthing (GB)	36	B 4	
Woszczyce (PL)	200	E 2	
Wozławki (PL)	183	F 2	

Zahna (D).....85 D 4
Záhony (H).....12 B 3
Zaiceva (LV).....161 E 3
Zaidín (E).....66 A 3
Žaiginys (LT).....169 F 2
Žaizdriai (LT).....177 E 2
Zajas (MK).....122 A 3
Zaječar (SRB).....119 E 2
Žakainiai (LT).....168 C 2
Zakliczyn (PL).....201 C 2
Zaklików (PL).....197 D 3
Zakopane (PL).....201 A 4
Zakroczym (PL).....189 F 2
Zákros (GR).....227 F 2
Zakrzew Mazowieckie(PL).....196 B 1
Zakrzewo Kujawsko-Pomorskie(PL).....188 C 2
Zakrzewo Wielkopolskie(PL).....181 F 4
Zakrzówek-Osada (PL).....197 D 2
Zakumuiža (LV).....159 D 4
Zákynthos (GR).....216 B 2
Zákynthos (Nisi) (GR).....216 B 2
Zalaegerszeg (H).....112 A 2
Zālāji (LV).....161 D 3
Zalamea de la Serena (E).69 F 3
Zalamea la Real (E).....75 D 1
Zalasowa (PL).....201 C 2
Zalău (RO).....12 C 3
Zalavas (LT).....172 B 4
Žalec (SLO).....99 E 1
Zaļenieki (LV).....163 F 2
Zalesie Lubelskie(PL).....191 E 3
Zalesie Śląskie (PL).....194 C 4
Zalęsie (LV).....167 F 3
Zaleszany (PL).....196 C 3
Zalewo (PL).....183 A 3
Žalgiriai (LT).....162 C 3
Zališčyky (UA).....13 D 2
Zālīte (LV).....164 C 2
Zalla (E).....60 B 3
Zálongo (GR).....211 D 3
Žalpiai Klaipėdos(LT).....168 C 4
Žalpiai Šiaulių(LT).....169 E 2
Zaltbommel (NL).....82 B 4
Zaltriškiai (LT).....169 D 3
Zaļumi (LV).....167 D 4
Załuski (PL).....189 F 2
Zalužnica (HR).....99 F 3
Žalvariai (LT).....171 E 4
Zalve (LV).....165 E 3
Žamberk (CZ).....91 D 2
Zambrana (E).....60 C 4
Zambrów (PL).....191 D 1
Zamora (E).....63 F 2
Zamość (PL).....197 E 3
Zandvoort (NL).....82 A 3
Zaniemyśl (PL).....187 F 3
Zante (LV).....163 E 1
Zaorejas (E).....65 D 4
Zaostrog (HR).....120 B 1
Zaovine Vežanja (SRB)...118 A 3
Zapadnaja Dvina (RUS).....7 E 2
Zapāni (LV).....167 F 3
Záppeio (GR).....212 A 2
Zapponeta (I).....106 B 2
Zaprešić (HR).....99 F 1
Zapyškis (LT).....169 F 4
Zaragoza (E).....65 F 3
Zárakes (GR).....219 D 1
Zarasai (LT).....172 C 2
Zaratán (E).....64 A 2
Zarautz (E).....61 D 3
Zarcilla de Ramos (E).....77 D 1
Žarėnai Šiaulių(LT).....163 F 3
Žarėnai Telšių(LT).....169 D 1
Žarijos (LT).....176 C 2
Żarki Śląskie(PL).....195 D 3
Zárkos (GR).....211 F 2
Żarnów (PL).....195 F 2
Zarós (GR).....226 C 2
Zaroúchla (GR).....217 E 2
Żarów (PL).....193 E 3
Zarrentin (D).....79 D 4
Zarszyn (PL).....202 D 3
Żary (PL).....186 C 4
Zarza la Mayor (E).....69 D 1
Zasa (LV).....166 B 3
Žaškiv (UA).....13 E 1
Žasliai (LT).....177 D 1
Žatec (CZ).....89 F 2
Zatišje (LV).....161 F 4
Zaton (HR).....120 C 2
Zator (PL).....200 F 2
Zaube (LV).....159 E 4
Žaunieriškiai (LT).....176 C 3

Zavala (BIH).....120 C 2
Zavattarello (I).....97 E 4
Zavidovići (BIH).....117 E 2
Zavlaka (SRB).....118 A 2
Zavodnje (SLO).....99 E 1
Zawady (PL).....185 D 3
Zawady Podlaskie(PL).....185 D 4
Zawady Śląskie(PL).....195 D 2
Zawadzkie (PL).....194 C 4
Zawichost (PL).....196 C 3
Zawidów (PL).....192 C 2
Zawidz Kościelny (PL)...189 E 1
Zawiercie (PL).....195 E 4
Zawoja (PL).....201 A 3
Zawonia (PL).....193 F 2
Zawroty (PL).....183 E 3
Žažina (HR).....115 D 3
Zbaraž (UA).....13 D 2
Zbąszyń (PL).....187 D 3
Zbąszynek (PL).....187 D 3
Zbiersk (PL).....188 C 4
Zblewo (PL).....182 C 4
Zbludowice (PL).....196 B 4
Zbójna (PL).....184 C 4
Zbójno (PL).....189 C 4
Zbraslav Praha(CZ).....90 B 3
Zbraslavice (CZ).....90 C 3
Zbrosławice (PL).....194 C 4
Zbuczyn-Poduchowny (PL).....191 D 3
Žďár nad Sázavou (CZ)...91 D 3
Zdenac (HR).....99 F 3
Zdice (CZ).....90 A 3
Ždírec nad Doubravou (CZ).....90 C 3
Ždrelac (HR).....103 E 1
Ždrelo (SRB).....119 D 2
Zdunje (MK).....122 A 3
Zduńska Wola (PL).....195 D 1
Zduny Łódzkie(PL).....189 F 4
Zduny Wielkopolskie(PL).187 F 4
Zdziesowice (PL).....194 C 4
Žeberiai Šiaulių(LT).....169 E 1
Žeberiai Telšių(LT).....169 D 2
Žebertonys (LT).....177 D 2
Zebreira (P).....69 D 1
Zebrene (LV).....163 E 2
Zebrzydowice (PL).....200 F 3
Žednik (SRB).....113 D 3
Zeebrugge (B).....37 F 3
Zefyría (GR).....224 A 2
Żegocina (PL).....201 B 2
Žegra (SRB).....122 B 2
Žegulja (BIH).....120 C 1
Zehdenick (D).....85 D 2
Žeimiai Alytaus(LT).....176 C 4
Žeimiai Kauno(LT).....170 C 4
Žeimiai Šiaulių(LT).....169 F 2
Zeist (NL).....82 B 4
Zeitz (D).....89 E 1
Zejtun (M).....110 A 4
Żelazków (PL).....188 C 4
Żelazno (PL).....193 E 4
Żelazowa Wola (PL).....189 F 3
Žele (B).....39 E 2
Żelechów (PL).....190 C 4
Zelengora (BIH).....117 E 4
Zelenika (MNE).....121 D 2
Železná Ruda (CZ).....89 F 4
Železniki (SLO).....99 D 1
Železnjik (SRB).....118 B 1
Železnogorsk (RUS).....7 F 4
Zelgauska (LV).....166 C 1
Zélio (GR).....212 B 4
Željezno Polje (BIH).....117 E 2
Želkūnai (LT).....176 C 2
Zell (Mosel) (D).....45 C 2
Zell am See (A).....94 B 4
Zell am Ziller (A).....94 A 4
Zell an der Pram (A).....94 C 2
Zella-Mehlis (D).....88 C 2
Zelmeņi Daugavpils(LV)..172 C 1
Zelmeņi Dobeles(LV).....163 F 2
Zelów (PL).....195 D 1
Zeltiņi Alūksnes(LV).....161 D 3
Zeltiņi Kuldīgas(LV).....157 D 4
Zeltweg (A).....95 D 4
Zelva (LT).....171 E 3
Zelzate (B).....39 E 1
Žemaičių Kalvarija (LT)...163 D 4
Žemaičių Naumiestis (LT)168 C 4
Žemaitėliai (LT).....177 F 2
Žemaitkiemis Alytaus(LT) 175 F 3
Žemaitkiemis Klaipėdos(LT).....168 C 3

Žemaitkiemis Matiešionys(LT).....176 C 2
Žemaitkiemis Tartupis(LT)176 B 2
Žemaitkiemis Vilniaus(LT)171 B 3
Žemalė (LT).....163 D 3
Zembrzyce (PL).....201 A 2
Zemgale Demene(LV).....172 C 2
Zemgale Ilūkste(LV).....166 C 4
Zemgale Jelgavas(LV).....164 B 2
Zemīte (LV).....157 E 4
Zemītes (LV).....160 C 4
Zemkopības Institūts (LV)165 C 4
Zemnieki (LV).....164 C 3
Žemoji Panemunė (LT)...169 F 4
Zenica (BIH).....117 E 3
Zentene (LV).....157 F 4
Žepče (BIH).....117 E 2
Zerbst (D).....84 C 2
Zerf (D).....44 C 2
Zeri (I).....101 D 1
Žerków (PL).....188 C 3
Zermatt (CH).....96 C 2
Zernez (CH).....97 E 1
Zerqan (AL).....121 F 3
Zestoa (E).....60 C 3
Zetel (D).....83 E 1
Zeulenroda (D).....89 E 2
Zeven (D).....83 F 2
Zevenaar (NL).....82 C 4
Zevgaráki (GR).....211 E 2
Zevgari (Cape) (CY).....230 B 4
Zevgolateió (GR).....217 D 4
Zevio (I).....98 A 3
Zg. Jezersko (SLO).....99 D 1
Zgierz (PL).....189 D 4
Zgorzelec (PL).....192 C 2
Žibalai (LT).....171 E 4
Žibavičiai (LT).....177 D 1
Žibininkai (LT).....162 B 4
Žiča (SRB).....118 C 3
Zicavo (F).....57 F 4
Zicavo (F).....57 F 4
Židikai (LT).....163 D 3
Židlochovice (CZ).....91 D 4
Ziedkalne (LV).....163 F 3
Ziedonis (LV).....163 E 2
Ziedugravas (LV).....165 D 2
Ziegenrück (D).....89 D 2
Žiegždriai (LT).....176 C 1
Zieleniec Dolnośląskie(PL).....193 E 4
Zieleniewo (PL).....187 D 1
Zielona Góra (PL).....186 C 3
Zielonka (PL).....190 B 3
Zielonki (PL).....201 A 1
Ziemeļblāzma (LV).....159 D 3
Ziemeļi (LV).....164 C 2
Ziemeļnieki (LV).....157 D 2
Ziemupe (LV).....162 B 1
Zierikzee (NL).....39 E 1
Ziersdorf (D).....95 E 1
Zierzow (D).....84 C 1
Ziesar (D).....84 C 3
Žiežmariai (LT).....177 D 1
Žīguri (LV).....161 F 3
Zijemlje (BIH).....117 E 4
Zilaiskalns (LV).....159 E 2
Zīles Dobeles(LV).....163 F 2
Zīles Jelgavas(LV).....164 C 3
Žilina (SK).....12 B 1
Žilinai (LT).....177 D 3
Žilpamūšis (LT).....165 D 4
Zilupe (LV).....167 F 3
Zimnicea (RO).....13 D 4
Zinal (CH).....96 C 2
Žindaičiai (LT).....169 E 3
Zingst (D).....79 F 2
Zin'kiv (UA).....13 F 1
Zinnowitz (D).....80 C 3
Zinnwald (D).....89 D 2
Žiobiškis (LT).....165 F 4
Ziorraga (E).....60 C 3
Ziras (LV).....156 C 2
Žirje (Otok) (HR).....103 E 3
Zirchow (D).....81 D 3
Žiri (SLO).....99 D 2
Žirje (Otok) (HR).....103 F 4
Zirl (A).....93 F 4
Zirndorf (D).....89 D 4
Zirņi (LT).....163 D 2
Žíros (GR).....227 F 3
Zistersdorf (A).....95 F 1
Žitište (SRB).....113 E 4
Žitkovac (SRB).....119 D 3
Zitomislići (BIH).....117 E 4

Žitorada (SRB).....119 D 3
Zitsa (GR).....211 D 1
Zittau (D).....90 B 1
Žiūronys (LT).....176 B 3
Živinice (BIH).....117 F 2
Živogošće (HR).....120 B 1
Žizdra (RUS).....7 F 3
Zizonys (LT).....165 E 4
Zjum (SRB).....121 F 2
Zlarin (HR).....103 F 1
Zlarin (Otok) (HR).....103 F 1
Zlata (SRB).....119 D 4
Zlatar Bistrica (HR).....99 F 1
Zlatari (SRB).....119 D 3
Zlaté Hory (CZ).....91 E 3
Zlatica (BG).....19 D 1
Zlatni Pjasăci (BG).....13 E 4
Zlatni rat (HR).....120 A 1
Zlatokop (SRB).....119 E 4
Zławieś Wielka (PL).....188 C 1
Žlebovi (BIH).....117 F 3
Zlēkas (LV).....157 D 4
Zletovo (MK).....122 C 2
Žlibinai (LT).....163 D 4
Zlín (CZ).....91 F 3
Žlobin (BY).....7 E 4
Złocieniec (PL).....181 D 4
Złoczew (PL).....194 C 1
Zlot (SRB).....119 D 2
Złotniki Kujawskie(PL)...188 C 1
Złotoria Podlaskie(PL)...185 E 4
Złotoryja (PL).....193 D 2
Złotów (PL).....181 F 4
Złoty Stok (PL).....193 E 4
Žlutice (CZ).....89 F 3
Zmajevo (SRB).....113 D 4
Žman (HR).....103 E 1
Žmerynka (UA).....13 E 2
Żmigród (PL).....193 F 1
Žminj (HR).....99 D 3
Žmudź (PL).....197 F 2
Znam»janka (UA).....13 F 1
Žnin (PL).....188 B 1
Znojmo (CZ).....91 D 4
Znojmo (CZ).....91 D 4
Zöblitz (D).....89 F 2
Zoetermeer (NL).....82 A 4
Żółkiewka (PL).....197 E 2
Zollikofen (CH).....96 B 1
Zoločiv (UA).....12 C 2
Zolotonoša (UA).....13 F 1
Żołynia (PL).....197 D 4
Zóni (GR).....208 C 1
Zonianá (GR).....226 C 2
Zonza (F).....57 F 4
Zoodóchos Pigí Atikí-Peireiás(GR).....218 B 3
Zoodóchos Pigí Kozáni(GR).....205 F 4
Žórawina (PL).....193 F 3
Zörbig (D).....84 C 4
Žorgi (LV).....164 C 2
Zorita (E).....69 F 2
Żory (PL).....200 F 3
Zoseni Cēsu(LV).....160 B 4
Zoseni Preiļu(LV).....166 C 4
Zosna (LV).....167 E 4
Zossen (D).....85 E 3
Žostautai (LT).....177 D 2
Zosuļi (LV).....159 E 4
Zoutkamp (NL).....82 C 2
Zoutleeuw (B).....39 F 2
Zoúzouli (GR).....205 D 4
Žovkva (LV).....12 C 1
Žovti Vody (UA).....13 F 2
Zrenjanin (SRB).....113 E 4
Zrin (HR).....115 D 4
Zrmanja (HR).....116 C 3
Zrnovnica (HR).....116 C 4
Zrze (SRB).....121 F 2
Zschopau (D).....89 F 2
Zubcov (RUS).....7 F 2
Zubin Potoku (SRB).....118 C 4
Zūbišķes (LT).....171 D 4
Zubrzyca Górna (PL).....201 A 3
Žuč (SRB).....119 D 4
Zucaina (E).....71 F 1
Zudar (D).....80 C 3
Zuera (E).....65 F 2
Zufre (E).....75 D 1
Zug (CH).....92 C 4
Zuidlaren (NL).....82 D 2
Zújar (E).....76 C 2
Zujūnai (LT).....177 E 2
Žukai (LT).....169 D 4
Žukaičiai (LT).....169 E 3
Žukovka (RUS).....7 F 3

Žuków Zachodnio-pomorskie(PL).....180 C 4
Żukowice (PL).....187 D 4
Żukowo (PL).....182 C 2
Zukuli (LV).....167 D 4
Žuljana (HR).....120 B 2
Zülpich (D).....87 E 2
Zumaia (E).....61 D 3
Zumarraga (E).....60 C 3
Zundert (NL).....39 F 1
Zuoz (CH).....97 E 1
Županja (HR).....117 E 1
Žur (SRB).....121 F 2
Žūras (LV).....156 C 3
Žuravica (PL).....202 F 2
Zürich (CH).....92 C 4
Žuromin (PL).....189 E 1
Zurrieq (M).....110 A 4
Zürs (A).....93 E 4
Zusmarshausen (D).....93 E 2
Žut (Otok) (HR).....103 E 1
Žuta Lokva (HR).....99 E 3
Zutphen (NL).....82 C 4
Zuvintai (LT).....175 F 3
Žužemberk (SLO).....99 E 2
Zvaigzne (LV).....165 D 3
Zvečan (SRB).....119 D 4
Zvejniekciems (LV).....159 D 3
Zvejnieki (LV).....163 E 2
Zvenyhorodka (UA).....13 E 1
Žvilgūri (LV).....159 F 3
Žvingiai (LT).....168 C 3
Žvirblaičiai (LT).....162 C 4
Žvirgždaičiai (LT).....175 E 1
Žvirgždėnai (LT).....176 C 3
Zvirgzdene (Zviergzdine) (LV).....167 F 2
Zvolen (SK).....12 B 2
Zvonce (SRB).....119 F 4
Zvornik (BIH).....117 F 4
Žvyriai (LT).....169 E 4
Zwardoń (PL).....200 F 3
Zweibrücken (D).....45 D 2
Zweisimmen (CH).....49 F 3
Zwenkau (D).....89 E 1
Zwettl (A).....95 D 1
Zwettl an der Rodl (A).....94 C 1
Zwickau (D).....89 E 2
Zwiefalten (D).....93 D 2
Zwierzyn (PL).....187 D 1
Zwierzyniec (PL).....197 E 3
Zwiesel (D).....94 B 1
Zwijndrecht (NL).....82 B 4
Zwoleń (PL).....196 C 1
Zwolle (NL).....82 C 3
Żychlin (PL).....189 E 3
Žygaičiai (LT).....168 C 3
Žygėnai (LT).....169 E 4
Zygi (CY).....231 C 4
Żyglin (PL).....195 D 4
Żyrardów (PL).....189 F 3
Žytkavičy (BY).....7 D 1
Żytno (PL).....195 E 3
Žytomyr (UA).....13 E 1
Żywiec (PL).....200 F 3

Légende — Key

Routes — Roads

Légende	Key
Autoroute	Motorway
Échangeurs : complet, partiels, sans précision	Interchanges : complete, limited, not specified
Numéros d'échangeurs	Interchange numbers
Double chaussée de type autoroutier	Dual carriageway with motorway characteristics
Route de liaison internationale ou nationale	International and national road network
Route de liaison interrégionale ou de dégagement	Interregional and less congested road
Autre route	Other road
Autoroute , route en construction (le cas échéant : date de mise en service prévue)	Motorway, road under construction (when available: with scheduled opening date)

Largeur des routes — Road widths

Légende	Key
Chaussées séparées	Dual carriageway
4 voies	4 lanes
3 voies	3 lanes
2 voies larges	2 wide lanes
2 voies	2 lanes
1 voie	1 lane

Distances (totalisées et partielles) — Distances (total and intermediate)

Légende	Key
section à péage sur autoroute	toll roads on motorway
section libre sur autoroute	toll-free section on motorway
GB / IRL 39 en kilomètres, 24 en miles	GB , IRL 39 in kilometres, 24 in miles

Numérotation - Signalisation — Numbering - Signs

Légende	Key
Autoroute, route européenne, autre route A 6 E 10 N 51	Motorway, european route, other road
Ville signalisée par un panneau vert sur les grandes liaisons routières YORK Wells	Town name is shown on a green sign on major routes

Obstacles — Obstacles

Légende	Key
Forte déclivité (flèches dans le sens de la montée)	Steep hill (ascent in direction of the arrow)
Barrière de péage	Toll barrier

Transports — Transportation

Légende	Key
Voie ferrée, auto/train - Bac pour autos	Railway, motorail - Car Ferry
Liaison maritime : permanente - saisonnière	Ferry lines : year-round - seasonal
Aéroport	Airport

Hébergement - Administration — Accommodation - Administration

Légende	Key
Localité ayant des ressources hôtelières	Place with at least one hotel
Refuge de montagne - Camping	Mountain refuge hut - Camping site
Capitale de division administrative	Administrative district seat
Frontiere : Douane principale - Douane avec restriction	National boundary : Principal customs post - Secondary customs post

Curiosités — Sights

Légende	Key
Édifice religieux - Château	Religious building - Historic house, castle
Église en bois debout	Stave church
Monastère - Ruines	Monastery - Ruins
Gravure rupestre - Site antique	Rock carving - Antiquities
Pierre runique - Autre curiosité	Rune stone - Other place of interest
Monument mégalithique - Grotte	Prehistoric monument - Cave
Parcours pittoresque - Parc national	Scenic route - National park

Zeichenererklärung | Verklaring van de tekens

Straßen | Wegen

Autobahn	Autosnelweg
Anschlussstellen : Voll - bzw. Teilanschluss, ohne Angabe	Aansluitingen : volledig, gedeeltelijk, zonder aanduiding
Anschlussstellennummern	Afritnummers
Schnellstraße mit getrennten Fahrbahnen	Gescheiden rijbanen van het type autosnelweg
Internationale bzw. nationale Hauptverkehrsstraße	Internationale of nationale verbindingsweg
Überregionale Verbindungsstraße oder Umleitungsstrecke	Interregionale verbindingsweg
Sonstige Straße	Andere weg
Autobahn, Straße im Bau (ggf. voraussichtliches Datum der Verkehrsfreigabe)	Autosnelweg, weg in aanleg (indien bekend : datum openstelling)

Straßenbreiten | Breedte van de wegen

Getrennte Fahrbahnen	Gescheiden rijbanen
4 Fahrspuren	4 rijstroken
3 Fahrspuren	3 rijstroken
2 breite Fahrspuren	2 brede rijstroken
2 Fahrspuren	2 rijstroken
1 Fahrspur	1 rijstrook

Straßenentfernungen (Gesamt - und Teilentfernungen) | Afstanden (totaal en gedeeltelijk)

Mautstrecke auf der Autobahn	gedeelte met tol op autosnelwegen
Mautfreie Strecke auf der Autobahn	tolvrij gedeelte op autosnelwegen
GB, IRL 39 in Kilometern, 24 in Meilen	GB, IRL 39 in kilometers, 24 in mijlen

Nummerierung - Wegweisung | Wegnummers - Bewegwijzering

Autobahn, Europastraße, sonstige Straße	Autosnelweg, europaweg, andere weg
	A 6 E 10 N 51
Grün beschilderte Ortsdurchfahrt an Fernverkehrsstrecken	Stad aangegeven met een groen bord op de grote verbindingswegen
	YORK Wells

Verkehrshindernisse | Hindernissen

Starke Steigung (Steigung in Pfeilrichtung)	Steile helling (pijlen in de richting van de helling)
Mautstelle	Tol

Verkehrsmittel | Vervoer

Bahnlinie - Autoreisezug - Autofähre	Spoorweg - Autotrein - Veerpont voor auto's
Schiffsverbindung : ganzjährig - saisonbedingte Verbindung	Ferry : het hele jaar - tijdens het seizoen
Flughafen	Luchthaven

Unterkunft - Verwaltung | Verblijf - Administratie

Ort mit Übernachtungsmöglichkeiten	Plaats met hotel
Schutzhütte - Campingplatz	Berghut - Kampeerterrein
Verwaltungshauptstadt	Hoofdplaats van administratief gebied
Staatsgrenze : Hauptzollamt - Zollstation mit Einschränkungen	Staatsgrens : Hoofddouanekantoor - Douanekantoor met beperkte bevoegdheden

Sehenswürdigkeiten | Bezienswaardigheden

Sakral-Bau - Schloss, Burg	Kerkelijk gebouw - Kasteel
Strabkirche	Stavkirke (houten kerk)
Kloster - Ruine	Klooster - Ruïne
Felsbilder - Antike Fundstätte	Rotstekening - Overblijfsel uit de Oudheid
Runenstein - Sonstige Sehenswürdigkeit	Runensteen - Andere bezienswaardigheid
Vorgeschichtliches Steindenkmal - Höhle	Megaliet - Grot
Landschaftlich schöne Strecke - Nationalpark	Schilderachtig traject - Nationaal park

Légende / Legenda

Routes — Strade

Autoroute	Autostrada
Échangeurs : complet, partiels, sans précision	Svincoli : completo, parziale, imprecisato
Numéros d'échangeurs	Svincoli numerati
Double chaussée de type autoroutier	Doppia carreggiata di tipo autostradale
Route de liaison internationale ou nationale	Strada di collegamento internazionale o nazionale
Route de liaison interrégionale ou de dégagement	Strada di collegamento interregionale o di disimpegno
Autre route	Altra strada
Autoroute , route en construction (le cas échéant : date de mise en service prévue)	Autostrada, strada in costruzione (data di apertura prevista)

Largeur des routes — Larghezza delle strade

Chaussées séparées	Carreggiate separate
4 voies	4 corsie
3 voies	3 corsie
2 voies larges	2 corsie larghe
2 voies	2 corsie
1 voie	1 corsia

Distances (totalisées et partielles) — Distanze (totali e parziali)

section à péage sur autoroute	tratto a pedaggio su autostrada
section libre sur autoroute	tratto esente da pedaggio su autostrada
GB / IRL 39 en kilomètres, 24 en miles	GB , IRL 39 in chilometri, 24 in miglia

Numérotation - Signalisation — Numerazione - Segnaletica

Autoroute, route européenne, autre route	Autostrada, strada europea, altra strada
A 6 E 10 N 51	
Ville signalée par un panneau vert sur les grandes liaisons routières	Città segnalata con cartello verde lungo importanti collegamenti stradali
YORK Wells	

Obstacles — Ostacoli

Forte déclivité (flèches dans le sens de la montée)	Forte pendenza (salita nel senso della freccia)
Barrière de péage	Casello

Transports — Trasporti

Voie ferrée, auto/train - Bac pour autos	Ferrovia - Auto/treno - Trasporto auto su chiatta
Liaison maritime : permanente - saisonnière	Trasporto marittimo : trasporto marittimo - stagionale
Aéroport	Aeroporto

Hébergement - Administration — Risorse alberghiere - Amministrazione

Localité ayant des ressources hôtelières	Località con risorse alberghiere
Refuge de montagne - Camping	Rifugio - Campeggio
Capitale de division administrative	Capoluogo amministrativo
Frontiere : Douane principale - Douane avec restriction	Frontiera: Dogana principale - Dogana con limitazioni

Curiosités — Mete e luoghi d'interesse

Édifice religieux - Château	Edificio religioso - Castello
Église en bois debout	Chiesa in legno di testa
Monastère - Ruines	Monastero - Rovine
Gravure rupestre - Site antique	Incisione rupestre - Sito antico
Pierre runique - Autre curiosité	Pietra runica - Altri luoghi d'interesse
Monument mégalithique - Grotte	Monumento megalitico - Grotta
Parcours pittoresque - Parc national	Percorso pittoresco - Parco nazionale

Signos convencionales | Legenda

Carreteras | Estradas

Signos convencionales		Legenda
Autopista		Auto-estrada
Accesos: completo, parcial, sin precisar		Nós : completo - parciais - sem precisão
Números de los accesos		Número de nós
Autovía		Estrada com 2 faixas de rodagem do tipo auto-estrada
Carretera de comunicación internacional o nacional		Estrada de ligação internacional o nacional
Carretera de comunicación interregional o alternativo		Estrada de ligação interregional ou alternativo
Otra carretera		Outra estrada
Autopista, carretera en construcción (en su caso : fecha prevista de entrada en servicio)		Auto-estrada, estrada em construção (eventualmente : data prevista estrada transitável)

Ancho de las carreteras | Largura das estradas

Calzadas separadas		Faixas de rodagem separadas
Cuatro carriles		com 4 vias
Tres carriles		com 3 vias
Dos carriles anchos		com 2 vias largas
Dos carriles		com 2 vias
Un carril		com 1 via

Distancias (totales y parciales) | Distâncias (totais e parciais)

Tramo de peaje en autopista	12	Em secção com portagem em auto-estrada
	5 / 7 12	
Tramo libre en autopista	5 / 7	Em secção sem portagem em auto-estrada
GB / IRL 39 en kilómetros, 24 en millas	39 24 / 19 12	GB , IRL 39 em quilómetros, 24 em milhas
	5 / 7	

Numeración - Señalización | Numeração - Sinalização

Autopista, carretera europea, otra carretera	A 6 E 10 N 51	Auto-estrada, estrada Europeia, outra estrada
Ciudad anunciada con un cartel verde en las carreteras principales	YORK Wells	Cidade sinalizada a verde nas estradas principais

Obstáculos | Obstáculos

Pendiente Pronunciada (las flechas indican el sentido del ascenso)	→	Forte declive (flechas no sentido da subida)
Barrera de peaje		Portagem

Transportes | Transportes

Línea férrea - Auto-tren - Barcaza para el paso de coches		Via férrea - Auto/trem - Barcaça para automóveis
Líneas maritimas : todo el año - de temporada		Ligação marítima : permanente - temporal
Aeropuerto		Aeroporto

Alojamiento - Administración | Alojamento - Administração

Localidad con recursos hoteleros	⊙ ♣	Localidade com recursos hoteleiros
Refugio de montaña - Camping	▲ △	Refúgio de montanha - Campismo
Capital de división administrativa	A L P	Capital de divisão administrativa
Frontera: Aduana principal - Aduana con restricciones	+++++++++	Fronteira : Alfândega principal - Alfândega com restrições

Curiosidades | Curiosidades

Edificio religioso - Castillo	♦ ✕	Edifício religioso - Castelo
Iglesia de madera	✸	Igreja de madeira
Monasterio - Ruinas	♨ ∴	Mosteiro - Ruínas
Grabado rupestre - Zona de vestigios antiguos	� ⊓	Gravura rupestre - Zona de vestígios antigos
Piedra rúnica - Otra curiosidad	⌺ ▲	Pedra rúnica - Outra curiosidade
Monumento megalítico - Cueva	⊓ ∩	Monumento megalítico - Gruta
Recorrido pintoresco - Parque nacional		Percuso pitoresco - Parque nacional

Merkkien selite		УСЛОВНЫЕ ОБОЗНАЧЕНИЯ
Tiet		**Дороги**
Moottoritie		Автострады
Liittymät: täydelliset, osittaiset, määrittelemättömät		Развязки: полные, частичные, не указано
Liittymänumerot		Номер развязки
Kaksiajoratainen tie, jolla on moottoritien tunnusmerkit		Дороги с двусторонним движением по типу автострад
Kansainvälinen tai kansallinen yhdystie		Автомобильные дороги государственного или международного значения
Alueellinen yhdys- tai ohitustie		Автомобильные дороги регионального значения, объездные
Muu tie		Прочие дороги
Moottoritie , rakenteilla oleva tie (mahdollisesti : arvioitu käyttöönottoajankohta)		МАвтострады, Строящиеся дороги
		(при необходимости: планируемая дата ввода в эксплуатацию)
Teiden leveys		**Ширина дорог**
Kaksiajoratainen tie		Автомобильные дороги с разделительной полосой
4 ajokaistaa		4 полосы
3 ajokaistaa		3 полосы
2 leveää ajokaistaa		2 широкие полосы
2 ajokaistaa		2 полосы
1 ajokaista		1 полоса
Välimatkat (kokonais - ja osittaisvälimatkat)		**Протяженность (полная и частичная)**
Tietulliosuus moottoritiellä	12 / 5 7	Платный участок по автостраде
Ilmainen osuus moottoritiellä	12 / 5 7	Бесплатный участок по автостраде
GB / IRL 39 kilometreinä, 24 maileina	39/24 19/12 / 5 7	GB , IRL 39 в километрах, 24 в милях
Numerointi - Opastemerkinnät		**Нумерация - Обозначения**
Moottoritie, Eurooppalainen tie, Muu tie	A 6 E 10 N 51	Автострада, Европейская дорога, Прочие дороги
Kaupunki, joka on merkitty tärkeisiin tieliittymiin vihreällä opasteella	YORK Wells	На крупных дорожных развязках город отмечается зеленой табличкой
Esteet		**Препятствия**
Jyrkkä nousu (nuolet nousun suuntaan)		Крутой уклон (стрелка в направлении подъема)
Tullipuomi		Шлагбаум платной дороги
Kulkuyhteydet		**Транспорт**
Rautatie, Auto/Juna - Autolautta		Поезд с перевозкой автомобилей? Автомобиль/Поезд - Паром для автомобилей
Meriyhteys : ympärivuotinen - kausiluonteinen		Морская переправа : постоянная - сезонная
Lentokenttä		Аэропорт
Majoitus - Hallinto		**Гостиничные услуги - Администрация**
Paikkakunta, jossa on hotellimajoitusmahdollisuudet		В населенном пункте есть гостиницы
Vuoristomajatalo - Leirintäalue		Горный домик - Кемпинг
Hallintoalueen pääkaupunki	A L P	Центр административного деления
Raja-alue : Rajoitettu tulli - Tullilaitos		Граница : Таможня с ограничениями - Главная таможня
Nähtävyydet		**Достопримечательности**
Kirkko - Linna		Религиозное здание - Замок
Sauvakirkko		Деревянный храм
Luostari - Rauniot		Монастырь - Руины
Kalliokaiverrus - Muinaisnähtävyys		Наскальные гравюры - Древние территории
Riimukivi - Muu nähtävyys		Рунические камни - Прочие достопримечательности
Megaliittiajan nähtävyys - Luola		Мегалитический памятник - Пещера
Maisemareitti - Kansallispuisto		Живописные маршруты - Национальный парк

Edition 2010 by Manufacture Française des Pneumatiques Michelin
Société en commandite par actions au capital de 304 000 000 EUR
Place des Carmes-Déchaux - 63 Clermont-Ferrand (France)
R.C.S. Clermont-Fd B 855 200 507
© 2009 Michelin, Propriétaires-Éditeurs

CARTE STRADALI E TURISTICHE PUBBLICAZIONE PERIODICA
Reg. Trib. Di Milano N° 80 del 24/02/1997 Dir. Resp. FERRUCCIO ALONZI

In spite of the care taken in the production of this book, it is possible that a defective copy
may have escaped our attention. If this is so, please return it to your bookseller,
who will exchange it for you, or contact :
Michelin
Cartes et Guides
46, av. de Breteuil
75324 PARIS CEDEX 07
www.cartesetguides.michelin.fr
www.ViaMichelin.com

Dépôt légal Janvier 2010
Imprimé en Italie en 11-09
Impression : CANALE - Borgaro Torinese (Italie)